Why Do You Need This New Edition?

If you are wondering why you should buy this eleventh edition of *An Introduction to Fiction*, here are six good reasons!

1. Interested in an insider's look into the importance of reading fiction? You'll find an exclusive conversation between Dana Gioia and celebrated fiction writer Amy Tan.

2. Fascinated by Latin American culture? Discover the enduring influences of "El Boom" found in the new chapter "Latin American Fiction."

3. Looking to meet some interesting people? *Fiction*'s 10 new stories introduce a host of memorable characters including a man who travels through his neighborhood swimming pool by swimming pool ("The Swimmer"); a family member who leaves home and moves to the post office ("Why I Live at the P.O."); and an angel who crash-lands in a backyard ("A Very Old Man with Enormous Wings").

4. Looking for a writing topic? The new casebook on Nathaniel Hawthorne's "Young Goodman Brown" provides helpful critical insights.

5. Find sample student papers helpful? You'll find a new section on writing a response paper and a new sample student essay for this popular type of writing assignment.

6. Need all the help you can get to format your papers correctly? The new 2009 MLA documentation guidelines, found only in the eleventh edition of *Fiction*, show you how to correctly cite your sources in the format your instructors will expect.

PEARSON

ABOUT THE AUTHORS

X. J. KENNEDY after graduation from Seton Hall and Columbia, became a journalist second class in the Navy ("Actually, I was pretty eighth class"). His poems, some published in the *New Yorker*, were first collected in *Nude Descending a Staircase* (1961). Since then he has published seven more collections, including a volume of new and selected poems in 2007, several widely adopted literature and writing textbooks, and seventeen books for children, including two novels. He has taught at Michigan, North Carolina (Greensboro), California (Irvine), Wellesley, Tufts, and Leeds. Cited in *Bartlett's Familiar Quotations* and reprinted in some 200 anthologies, his verse has brought him a Guggenheim fellowship, a Lamont Award, a *Los Angeles Times* Book Prize, an award from the American Academy and Institute of Arts and Letters, an Aiken-Taylor prize, and the Award for Poetry for Children from the National Council of Teachers of English. He now lives in Lexington, Massachusetts, where he and his wife Dorothy have collaborated on five books and five children.

DANA GIOIA is a poet, critic, and teacher. Born in Los Angeles of Italian and Mexican ancestry, he attended Stanford and Harvard before taking a detour into business. ("Not many poets have a Stanford M.B.A., thank goodness!") After years of writing and reading late in the evenings after work, he quit a vice presidency to write and teach. He has published three collections of poetry, *Daily Horoscope* (1986), *The Gods of Winter* (1991), and *Interrogations at Noon* (2001), which won the American Book Award; and three critical volumes, including *Can Poetry Matter?* (1992), an influential study of poetry's place in contemporary America. Gioia has taught at Johns Hopkins, Sarah Lawrence, Wesleyan (Connecticut), Mercer, and Colorado College. He is also the co-founder of the summer poetry conference at West Chester University in Pennsylvania. From 2003 to 2009 he served as Chairman of the National Endowment for the Arts. At the NEA he created the largest literary programs in federal history, including Shakespeare in American Communities and Poetry Out Loud, the national high school poetry recitation contest. He also led the campaign to restore active and engaged literary reading by creating The Big Read, which has helped reverse a quarter century of decline in U.S. reading. He currently divides his time between Washington, D.C. and Santa Rosa, California, living with his wife Mary, their two sons, and two uncontrollable cats.

(The surname Gioia is pronounced JOY-A. As some of you may have already guessed, Gioia is the Italian word for joy.)

An Introduction to

FICTION

ELEVENTH EDITION

X. J. Kennedy
Dana Gioia

Longman

Boston Columbus Indianapolis New York San Francisco Upper Saddle River Amsterdam
Cape Town Dubai London Madrid Milan Munich Paris Montreal Toronto
Delhi Mexico City São Paulo Sydney Hong Kong Seoul Singapore Taipei Tokyo

Vice President and Editor in Chief: Joe Terry
Development Editor: Katharine Glynn
Executive Marketing Manager: Joyce Nilsen
Senior Supplements Editor: Donna Campion
Production Manager: Savoula Amanatidis
Project Coordination, Text Design, and Electronic Page Makeup: Nesbitt Graphics, Inc.
Cover Design Manager: John Callahan
Cover Image: Edward Hopper/Corbis Art/Corbis
Photo Researcher: Pearson Image Resource Center/Teri Stratford
Senior Manufacturing Buyer: Roy L. Pickering, Jr.
Printer and Binder: QuadGraphics–Taunton
Cover Printer: Lehigh-Phoenix Color Corporation

For permission to use copyrighted material, grateful acknowledgment is made to the copyright holders on pp. 728–731, which are hereby made part of this copyright page.

Library of Congress Cataloging-in-Publication Data

Kennedy, X. J.
    An introduction to fiction / X. J. Kennedy, Dana Gioia.—11th ed.
        p. cm.
    Includes index.
    ISBN 978-0-205-68788-6
 1. Fiction—Collections.   I. Gioia, Dana. II. Title.
PN6120.2.I5 2010
808.3—dc22

                                        2009029675

3 4 5 6 7 8 9 10—QGT—14 13 12 11

Longman
is an imprint of

ISBN-13: 978–0–205–68788–6
ISBN-10: 0-205-68788-1

www.pearsonhighered.com

CONTENTS

FICTION

TALKING WITH *Amy Tan*   2

1   READING A STORY   5

2   POINT OF VIEW   25

3   CHARACTER   77

4 SETTING   107

5 TONE AND STYLE   148

6 THEME   183

8 READING LONG STORIES AND NOVELS 259

9 LATIN AMERICAN FICTION 341

10 CRITICAL CASEBOOK
Flannery O'Connor   368

■ WRITING *effectively*

11 CRITICAL CASEBOOK
Three Stories in Depth 419

WRITING

15 CRITICAL APPROACHES TO LITERATURE 678

PREFACE

Storytelling is a basic human activity. The urge to tell stories and the desire to hear them is so primal that it is difficult to imagine a time in human existence without them. The gift of narrative—whether in myth, parable, epic, film, or short story—is so deep and universal that it seems one of the attributes that most clearly separates humanity from other species. Dolphins may have a vocabulary, but they do not create novels or short stories.

Why humans tell stories may differ from case to case, but whether the narrator speaks around a tribal fire or through the printed letters of a book, certain general impulses usually apply. Stories exist to delight, instruct, or console us. Some stories warn; others enlighten. At the root of the narrative urge, however, is the conviction that there are some truths we can only tell one another as stories. Conveyed in any other form, these insights evaporate into airy and intangible abstractions.

Storytelling also affects us differently from other modes of language. We hear or read a story with the fullness of our humanity—not merely with our intellects but also our emotions, intuition, and physical senses. A strong story has the ability to reach us in ways that logic alone cannot match. "A book," wrote Franz Kafka, "must be the axe for the frozen sea inside us." Religious leaders and philosophers have long understood the deep power of narrative. Jesus instructed his followers with parables. The Taoist Chuang Tzu embodied his philosophy in moral fables. The right story encountered at the right moment should be able to change your life perhaps only in a small way or sometimes perhaps in a larger sense. We hope that sort of story is waiting for you somewhere in this book.

In this volume we have tried to offer a broad range of fine short fiction of many kinds. Although we cannot help having a few convictions about the meanings of stories, we have tried to step back and give you room to make up your own mind. Here and there, in the wording of a question, our opinions may occasionally stick out. If you should notice any, please feel free to ignore them. Be assured that no one interpretation, laid down by authority, is the only right one for any work of literature. Trust your own interpretation—provided that in making it you have looked clearly and carefully at the evidence.

Reading literature often will provide you with reason to write. At the back of the book, there are several chapters that give the student writer some practical advice. It will guide you step by step, in finding a topic, planning an essay, writing, revising, and putting your paper into finished form. There are also short features at the end of every chapter that provide help and perspective on writing about literature.

A WORD ABOUT CAREERS

Most students agree that to read celebrated writers such as William Faulkner or Willa Cather is probably good for the spirit. Most students even take some pleasure in the experience. But many, not planning to teach English and impatient to begin some other career, wonder if the study of literature, however enjoyable, isn't a waste of time—or at least, an annoying obstacle.

This objection may seem reasonable at first glance, but it rests on a shaky assumption. It can be convincingly argued that success in a career is not merely a matter of learning the specialized information and skills required to join a profession. In most careers, according to one senior business executive, people often fail not because they don't understand their jobs, but because they don't understand the people they work with, or their clients or customers. They don't ever see the world from another person's point of view. Their problem is a failure of imagination.

To leap over the wall of self, to look through another's eyes—this is valuable experience, which literature offers. If you are lucky, you may never meet (or have to do business with) anyone *exactly* like Mrs. Turpin in the story "Revelation," and yet you will learn much about the kind of person she is from Flannery O'Connor's fictional portrait of her.

What is it like to be black, a white may wonder? James Baldwin, Zora Neale Hurston, Alice Walker, and Jamaica Kincaid have knowledge to impart. What is it like to be a woman? If a man would learn, let him read (for a start) Sandra Cisneros, Kate Chopin, Alice Munro, Katherine Anne Porter, Flannery O'Connor, Tillie Olsen, and Amy Tan, and perhaps, too, John Steinbeck's "The Chrysanthemums."

Plodding single-mindedly toward careers, some people are like horses wearing blinders. For many, the goals looked fixed and predictable. Competent nurses, accountants, and dental technicians seem always in demand. Others may find that in our society some careers, like waves in the sea, will rise or fall unexpectedly. Think of how many professions we now take for granted, which a few years ago didn't even exist: genetic engineering, energy conservation, digital editing, and Web site design. Others that once looked like lifetime meal tickets have been cut back and nearly ruined: shoe repairing, commercial fishing, railroading.

In a perpetually changing society, it may be risky to lock yourself on one track to a career, refusing to consider any other. "We are moving," writes John Naisbitt in *Megatrends,* a study of our changing society, "from the specialist, soon obsolete, to the generalist who can adapt." Perhaps the greatest opportunity in your whole life lies in a career that has yet to be invented. If you do change your career as you go along, you will be like most people. According to a U.S. Bureau of Labor Statistics survey conducted in April 2000, the average person holds over nine jobs between the ages of 18 and 34—often completely changing his or her basic occupation. When for some unforeseen reason you have to make such a change, basic skills—and a knowledge of humanity—may be your most valuable credentials.

Literature has much practical knowledge to offer you. An art of words, it can help you become more sensitive to language—both your own and other people's. It can make you aware of the difference between the word that is exactly right and the word that is merely good enough—Mark Twain calls it "the difference between the lightning and the lightning-bug." Read a fine work of literature alertly, and some of its writer's sensitivity to words may grow on you. A Supreme Court Justice, John Paul Stevens, once remarked that the best preparation for law school is to study poetry. Why? George D. Gopen, an English professor with a law degree, says it may be because "no other discipline so closely replicates the central question asked in the study of legal thinking: Here is a text; in how many ways can it have meaning?"

Many careers today, besides law, call for close reading and clear writing—as well as careful listening and thoughtful speech. Lately, college placement directors have reported more demand for graduates who are good readers and writers. The reason is evident: employers need people who can handle words. In a survey conducted by Cornell University, business executives were asked to rank in importance the traits they look for when hiring. Leadership was first, but skill in writing and speaking came in fourth, ahead of both managerial and analytical skills. Times change, but to think cogently and to express yourself well will always be the abilities the world needs.

KEY LITERARY TERMS

Every discipline has its own terminology. This book introduces a large range of critical terms that may help you in both your reading and writing. When these important words and phrases are first defined, they are printed in **boldface.** If you meet a critical term anywhere in this book you don't know or don't recall—what is an *interior monologue* or an *initiation story?*—just check the "Index of Literary Terms" in the back of the book, and you'll see the page where the term is discussed; or, look it up in the "Glossary of Literary Terms," also in the back of the book.

TEXTS AND DATES

Every effort has been made to supply each selection in its most accurate text and (where necessary) in a lively, faithful translation. For the reader who wishes to know when a work was written, at the right of each title appears the date of its first publication in book form. Parentheses around a date indicate the work's date of composition or first magazine publication, given when it was composed much earlier than when it was first published in book form.

But enough housekeeping, let's have fun and read some stories.

X. J. K. AND D. G.

TO THE INSTRUCTOR

*A*n *Introduction to Fiction* is a book with two major goals. First, it introduces college students to the appreciation and experience of short fiction. Second, the book tries to develop the student's ability to think critically and communicate effectively through writing.

Both editors of this volume are writers. We believe that textbooks should be not only informative and accurate but also lively, accessible, and engaging. In education, it never hurts to have a little fun. Our intent has always been to write a book that students will read eagerly and enjoy.

WHAT'S NEW TO THIS EDITION?

- **Exclusive conversation between Dana Gioia and celebrated fiction writer Amy Tan**—offers students an insider's look into the importance of literature and reading in the life of a modern master.
- **New stories and critical prose**—offer traditional favorites with exciting and sometimes surprising contemporary selections.
  - **64 stories, 10 new selections**—with new stories by Egyptian Nobel Prize-winner Naguib Mahfouz, Virginia Woolf, John Cheever, Eudora Welty, Sherman Alexie, Franz Kafka, and Lorrie Moore.
  - **54 critical prose pieces, 10 new selections**—help students think about different approaches to interpreting literature.
- **New "Latin American Fiction" chapter**—presents some of the finest authors of the region, including Jorge Luis Borges, Octavio Paz, Gabriel García Márquez, and Inés Arredondo.
- **New casebook on Nathaniel Hawthorne's "Young Goodman Brown"**—provides students critical insight into this ever-popular and fascinating story.
- **New "Terms for Review" feature at the end of every major chapter**—provides students a simple study guide to go over key concepts and terms in each chapter.
- **New 2009 MLA guidelines**—provide students the updated source citation requirements from the new 7th edition of the *MLA Handbook* and incorporates them in all sample student papers.
- **New section on writing a response paper**—provides instructions and a sample student essay for this popular type of writing assignment.
- **Updated, revised format to increase accessibility and ease of use**—newly added section titles and subtitles will help Web-oriented students navigate easily from topic to topic in every chapter. Additionally, all chapters have been reviewed and updated to include relevant cultural references.

Overall, we have tried to create a book to help readers develop sensitivity to language, culture, and identity, to lead them beyond the boundaries of their own selves, and to see the world through the eyes of others. This book is built on the assumption that great literature can enrich and enlarge the lives it touches.

KEY FEATURES

We have revised this edition of *An Introduction to Fiction* with the simple aim of introducing useful new features and selections without losing the best-liked material. We have been guided in this effort by scores of instructors and students who use the book in their classrooms. Teaching is a kind of conversation between instructor and student and between reader and text. By revising *Fiction*, we try to help keep this conversation fresh by mixing the classic with the new and the familiar with the surprising.

Casebooks on a Major Author and Three Literary Masterpieces

There are four casebooks: one on Flannery O'Connor and three on popular stories frequently used by students for critical analyses or research papers (Nathaniel Hawthorne's "Young Goodman Brown," Charlotte Perkins Gilman's "The Yellow Wallpaper," and Alice Walker's "Everyday Use"). These special chapters present a variety of material—biographies, photographs, critical commentaries, and statements by the authors. Our aim has been to provide everything a student might need to begin an in-depth study of an author or work.

Updated Writing Material

Because today's students need a more concise, visual, and schematic approach than did the previous generation, we continue to refine and edit our extensive writing coverage so that students can easily find useful and accessible information—in outline form wherever possible.

Every major chapter includes a **Writing Effectively** section that has four elements: **Writers on Writing**, which personalizes the composition process; **Thinking About . . .** , which discusses the specific topic of the chapter; a **Checklist**, which provides a step-by-step approach to composition and critical thinking; and a **Writing Assignment** plus **More Topics for Writing**, which provide a rich source of ideas for writing a paper. These features are designed to make the writing process easier, clearer, and less intimidating.

We have two full writing chapters at the end of *An Introduction to Fiction* to provide comprehensive coverage of the composition and research process. All chapters have been edited for clarity and accessibility. We strive to simplify the text but not to dumb it down. Clarity and concision are never out of place in a textbook, but condescension is fatal. One of our chief aims is to make the information and structure of the writing chapters more visual for today's Internet-oriented students. Instructors will note how information that appeared in prose paragraphs in earlier editions now appears in outline or checklist form.

Six Student Papers Plus Work-in-Progress Samples

We have six annotated student papers to provide models for critical writing, including a research paper. (There is also a card report.) Four of the papers are found in the final writing chapters, where they illustrate different approaches to critical writing—explication, analysis, comparison and contrast, and personal response. Each paper focuses on a story or author in the book and often provides a close reading of the literary work that emphasizes specific elements of its structure and meaning. All papers reflect the newly updated 2009 MLA guidelines.

We also show many samples of student work-in-progress as a way of illustrating the writing process. We include, for example, a step-by-step presentation of how students can develop topics, generate ideas, and formulate a strong thesis. We include sample brainstorming notes and other prewriting techniques, among many other items, to provide students with a more helpful and systematic account of the writing process.

Critical Approaches to Literature

Chapter 15, "Critical Approaches to Literature," is an ever-popular feature of *An Introduction to Fiction*. There are two selections for every major critical school—20 selections in all. The critical excerpts have been carefully chosen both to illustrate the major theoretical approaches and to be accessible to beginning students. The selections focus on literary works found in the present edition. Taken together with the many commentaries in the casebooks and Writers on Writing, *An Introduction to Fiction* now includes a total of 54 critical excerpts. This coverage gives *Fiction* both more depth and flexibility for instructors who prefer to incorporate literary theory and criticism into their introductory courses.

Glossary of Literary Terms

The comprehensive Glossary of Literary Terms at the end of this book includes every term highlighted in boldface throughout the text as well as other important terms— over 150 entries in all—providing a clear and accurate definition, usually with cross references to related terms. The purpose of the glossary is to provide students with a single, accessible reference of all key literary terms.

OTHER EDITIONS AVAILABLE

Poetry

An Introduction to Poetry, Thirteenth Edition, contains over 460 poems, mixing classic favorites with exciting contemporary work, plus complete coverage of the writing process.

Literature: An Introduction to Fiction, Poetry, Drama, and Writing

Instructors who wish to cover the other major forms of literature may want to know about *Literature: An Introduction to Fiction, Poetry, Drama, and Writing*, Eleventh Edition. This comprehensive book includes the complete contents of *An Introduction to Fiction*, along with full coverage of poetry (including over 460 poems) and drama (with 16 plays), and expanded writing coverage appropriate for all three genres.

Literature, Portable Edition

This edition provides all the content of the hardcover text in four lightweight paperback volumes—*Fiction*, *Poetry*, *Drama*, and *Writing*—packed in a slipcase.

Literature, Compact Edition

There is also the Sixth Compact Edition of *Literature: An Introduction to Fiction, Poetry, Drama, and Writing* in paperback, for instructors who find the full edition "too much book." Although this compact version offers a slightly abridged table of contents, it still covers the complete range of topics presented in the full edition. Both the full text and the compact edition are available in interactive editions.

Literature, Backpack Edition

There is an even more compact edition of this book, which we have titled *Backpack Literature*, Third Edition, in honor of the heavy textbook loads many students must carry from class to class. This much briefer anthology contains only the most essential selections and writing apparatus, and it is published in a smaller format to create a more travel-friendly book.

Literature, Interactive Editions

Both *Compact*, Sixth Edition and *Literature*, Eleventh Edition are published as interactive editions and come with access to *MyLiteratureLab.com* (as described below) for instructors who want to incorporate media into their class.

RESOURCES FOR STUDENTS AND INSTRUCTORS

For Students

MyLiteratureLab.com

MyLiteratureLab.com is a Web-based state-of-the-art interactive learning system designed to accompany *Literature* and help students in their literature course. It adds a new dimension to the study of literature with Longman Lectures—evocative, richly illustrated audio readings along with advice on how to read, interpret, and write about literary works from our roster of Longman authors (including X. J. Kennedy). This powerful program also features Diagnostic Tests, Interactive Readings with clickable prompts, film clips of selections in *Literature*, Writers on Writing (which consists of video interviews with distinguished authors that inspire students to explore their creativity), sample student papers, Literature Timelines, and Avoiding Plagiarism. *MyLiteratureLab.com* can be delivered within Course Compass, Web CT, or Blackboard course management systems, enabling instructors to administer their entire course online.

Handbook of Literary Terms

Handbook of Literary Terms by X. J. Kennedy, Dana Gioia, and Mark Bauerlein is a user-friendly primer of over 350 critical terms brought to life with literary examples, pronunciation guides, and scholarly yet accessible explanations. Aimed at undergraduates getting their first taste of serious literary study, the volume will help students engage with the humanities canon and become critical readers and writers ready to experience the insights and joys of great fiction, poetry, and drama.

Responding to Literature: A Writer's Journal

This journal provides students with their own personal space for writing and is available at no additional cost when packaged with this anthology. Helpful writing prompts for responding to fiction, poetry, and drama are also included.

For Instructors

Instructor's Manual

A separate *Instructor's Manual* is available to instructors. If you have never seen our *Instructor's Manual* before, don't prejudge it. We actually write the manual ourselves, and we work hard to make it as interesting, lively, and informed as is the parent text. It offers commentary and teaching ideas for every selection in the book. It also contains additional commentary, debate, qualifications and information—including scores of classroom ideas—from over 100 teachers and authors. As you will see, our *Instructor's Manual* is no ordinary supplement.

Penguin Discount Novel Program

In cooperation with Penguin Group USA, Pearson is proud to offer a variety of Penguin paperbacks at a significant discount—almost sixty percent off the retail price—when packaged with any Pearson title. To review the list of titles available, visit the Pearson Penguin Web site at *www.pearsonhighered.com/penguin*.

Video Program

For qualified adopters, an impressive selection of videotapes is available to enrich students' experience of literature. The videos include selections from William Shakespeare, Sylvia Plath, Ezra Pound, and Alice Walker. Contact your Pearson Longman sales representative to see if you qualify.

Contact Us

For examination copies of any of these books, CDs, videos, and programs, contact your Pearson Longman sales representative, or write to Literature Marketing Manager, Pearson Longman, 51 Madison Avenue, New York, NY 10010. For examination copies only, call (800) 922-0579.

To order an examination copy online, go to: *http://www.pearsonhighered.com* or send an e-mail to: *exam.copies@pearsonhighered.com*.

THANKS

The collaboration necessary to create this new edition goes far beyond the partnership of its two editors. *An Introduction to Fiction* has once again been revised, corrected, and shaped by wisdom and advice from instructors who actually put it to the test—and also from a number who, in teaching literature, preferred other textbooks to it, but who generously criticized this book anyway and made suggestions for it. (Some responded to the book in part, focusing their comments on the previous editions of *Literature: An Introduction to Fiction, Poetry, Drama, and Writing*.) Deep thanks to:

Alvaro Aleman, University of Florida
Jonathan Alexander, University of Southern Colorado
Ann P. Allen, Salisbury State University
Karla Alwes, SUNY Cortland
Brian Anderson, Central Piedmont Community College
Kimberly Green Angel, Georgia State University
Carmela A. Arnoldt, Glendale Community College
Herman Asarnow, University of Portland
Beverly Bailey, Seminole Community College
Carolyn Baker, San Antonio College
Rosemary Baker, SUNY Morrisville
Lee Barnes, Community College of Southern Nevada, Las Vegas
Sandra Barnhill, South Plains College

Bob Baron, Mesa Community College
Melinda Barth, El Camino Community College
Robin Barrow, University of Iowa
Joseph Bathanti, Mitchell Community College
Judith Baumel, Adelphi University
Anis Bawarski, University of Kansas
Bruce Beckum, Colorado Mountain College
Elaine Bender, El Camino Community College
Pamela Benson, Tarrant County Junior College
Jennifer Black, McLennan Community College
Brian Blackley, North Carolina State University
Debbie Borchers, Pueblo Community College
Alan Braden, Tacoma Community College
Glenda Bryant, South Plains College
Paul Buchanan, Biola University

Andrew Burke, University of Georgia

Jolayne Call, Utah Valley State College

Stasia Callan, Monroe Community College

Uzzie T. Cannon, University of North Carolina at Greensboro

Al Capovilla, Folsom Lake Community College

Eleanor Carducci, Sussex County Community College

Thomas Carper, University of Southern Maine

Jean W. Cash, James Madison University

Michael Cass, Mercer University

Patricia Cearley, South Plains College

Fred Chancey, Chemeketa Community College

Kitty Chen, Nassau Community College

Edward M. Cifelli, County College of Morris

Marc Cirigliano, Empire State College

Bruce Clary, McPherson College

Maria Clayton, Middle Tennessee State University

Cheryl Clements, Blinn College

Jerry Coats, Tarrant County Community College

Peggy Cole, Arapahoe Community College

Doris Colter, Henry Ford Community College

Dean Cooledge, University of Maryland Eastern Shore

Patricia Connors, University of Memphis

Steve Cooper, California State University, Long Beach

Cynthia Cornell, DePauw University

Ruth Corson, Norwalk Community Technical College, Norwalk

James Finn Cotter, Mount St. Mary College

Dessa Crawford, Delaware Community College

Janis Adams Crowe, Furman University

Allison M. Cummings, University of Wisconsin, Madison

Elizabeth Curtin, Salisbury State University

Robert Darling, Keuka College

Denise David, Niagara County Community College

Alan Davis, Moorhead State University

Michael Degen, Jesuit College Preparatory School, Dallas

Kathleen De Grave, Pittsburg State University

Apryl Denny, Viterbo University

Fred Dings, University of South Carolina

Leo Doobad, Stetson University

Stephanie Dowdle, Salt Lake Community College

Dennis Driewald, Laredo Community College

David Driscoll, Benedictine College

John Drury, University of Cincinnati

Tony D'Souza, Shasta College

Victoria Duckworth, Santa Rosa Junior College

Ellen Dugan-Barrette, Brescia University

Dixie Durman, Chapman University

Bill Dynes, University of Indianapolis

Janet Eber, County College of Morris

Terry Ehret, Santa Rosa Junior College

George Ellenbogen, Bentley College

Peggy Ellsberg, Barnard College

Toni Empringham, El Camino Community College

Lin Enger, Moorhead State University

Alexina Fagan, Virginia Commonwealth University

Lynn Fauth, Oxnard College

Annie Finch, University of Southern Maine

Katie Fischer, Clarke College

Susan Fitzgerald, University of Memphis

Juliann Fleenor, Harper College

Richard Flynn, Georgia Southern University

Billy Fontenot, Louisiana State University at Eunice

Deborah Ford, University of Southern Mississippi

Doug Ford, Manatee Community College

James E. Ford, University of Nebraska, Lincoln

Peter Fortunato, Ithaca College

Ray Foster, Scottsdale Community College

Maryanne Garbowsky, County College of Morris

John Gery, University of New Orleans

Mary Frances Gibbons, Richland College

Maggie Gordon, University of Mississippi

Joseph Green, Lower Columbia College

William E. Gruber, Emory University

Huey Guagliardo, Louisiana State University

R. S. Gwynn, Lamar University

Steven K. Hale, DeKalb College

Renée Harlow, Southern Connecticut State University

David Harper, Chesapeake College

John Harper, Seminole Community College

Iris Rose Hart, Santa Fe Community College

Karen Hatch, California State University, Chico

Jim Hauser, William Patterson College

Kevin Hayes, Essex County College

Jennifer Heller, Johnson County Community College

Hal Hellwig, Idaho State University

Gillian Hettinger, William Paterson University

Mary Piering Hiltbrand, University of Southern Colorado

Martha Hixon, Middle Tennessee State University

Jan Hodge, Morningside College

David E. Hoffman, Averett University

Mary Huffer, Lake-Sumter Community College

Patricia Hymson, Delaware County Community College

Carol Ireland, Joliet Junior College

Alan Jacobs, Wheaton College

Ann Jagoe, North Central Texas College

Kimberlie Johnson, Seminole Community College

Peter Johnson, Providence College

Ted E. Johnston, El Paso Community College

Cris Karmas, Graceland University

Howard Kerner, Polk Community College

Lynn Kerr, Baltimore City Community College

D. S. Koelling, Northwest College

Dennis Kriewald, Laredo Community College

Paul Lake, Arkansas Technical University

Susan Lang, Southern Illinois University

Greg LaPointe, Elmira College

Tracy Lassiter, Eastern Arizona College

Sherry Little, San Diego State University

Alfred Guy Litton, Texas Woman's University

Heather Lobban-Viravong, Grinnell College

Karen Locke, Lane Community College

Eric Loring, Scottsdale Community College

Gerald Luboff, County College of Morris

Susan Popkin Mach, UCLA

Samuel Maio, California State University, San Jose

Paul Marx, University of New Haven

David Mason, Colorado College

Mike Matthews, Tarrant County Junior College

Beth Maxfield, Henderson State University

Janet McCann, Texas A&M University

Susan McClure, Indiana University of Pennsylvania

Kim McCollum-Clark, Millersville University

David McCracken, Texas A&M University

Nellie McCrory, Gaston College

William McGee, Jr., Joliet Junior College

Kerri McKeand, Joliet Junior College

Robert McPhillips, Iona College

Jim McWilliams, Dickinson State University

Elizabeth Meador, Wayne Community College

Bruce Meyer, Laurentian University

Tom Miller, University of Arizona

Joseph Mills, University of California at Davis

Cindy Milwe, Santa Monica High School

Dorothy Minor, Tulsa Community College

Mary Alice Morgan, Mercer University

Samantha Morgan, University of Tennessee

Bernard Morris, Modesto Junior College

Brian T. Murphy, Burlington Community College

William Myers, University of Colorado at Colorado Springs

Madeleine Mysko, Johns Hopkins University

Kevin Nebergall, Kirkwood Community College

Eric Nelson, Georgia Southern University

Jeff Newberry, University of West Florida

Marsha Nourse, Dean College

Hillary Nunn, University of Akron

James Obertino, Central Missouri State University

Julia O'Brien, Meredith College

Sally O'Friel, John Carroll University

Elizabeth Oness, Viterbo College

Regina B. Oost, Wesleyan College

Mike Osborne, Central Piedmont Community College

Jim Owen, Columbus State University

Jeannette Palmer, Motlow State Community College

Mark Palmer, Tacoma Community College

Dianne Peich, Delaware County Community College

Betty Jo Peters, Morehead State University

Timothy Peters, Boston University

Norm Peterson, County College of Morris

Susan Petit, College of San Mateo

Louis Phillips, School of Visual Arts

Robert Phillips, University of Houston

Jason Pickavance, Salt Lake Community College

Teresa Point, Emory University

Deborah Prickett, Jacksonville State University

William Provost, University of Georgia

Wyatt Prunty, University of the South, Sewanee

Allen Ramsey, Central Missouri State University

Ron Rash, Tri-County Technical College

Michael W. Raymond, Stetson University

Mary Anne Reiss, Elizabethtown Community College

Barbara Rhodes, Central Missouri State University

Diane Richard-Alludya, Lynn University

Gary Richardson, Mercer University

Fred Robbins, Southern Illinois University

Doulgas Robillard Jr., University of Arkansas at Pine Bluff

Daniel Robinson, Colorado State University

Dawn Rodrigues, University of Texas, Brownsville

Linda C. Rollins, Motlow State Community College

Mark Rollins, Ohio University

Laura Ross, Seminole Community College

Jude Roy, Madisonville Community College

M. Runyon, Saddleback College

Mark Sanders, College of the Mainland

Kay Satre, Carroll College

Ben Sattersfield, Mercer University

SueAnn Schatz, University of New Mexico

Roy Scheele, Doane College

Bill Schmidt, Seminole Community College

Beverly Schneller, Millersville University

Meg Schoerke, San Francisco State University

Janet Schwarzkopf, Western Kentucky University

William Scurrah, Pima Community College

Susan Semrow, Northeastern State University

Tom Sexton, University of Alaska, Anchorage

Chenliang Sheng, Northern Kentucky University

Roger Silver, University of Maryland–Asian Division

Phillip Skaar, Texas A&M University

Michael Slaughter, Illinois Central College

Martha K. Smith, University of Southern Indiana

Richard Spiese, California State, Long Beach

Lisa S. Starks, Texas A&M University

John R. Stephenson, Lake Superior State University

Jack Stewart, East Georgia College

Dabney Stuart, Washington and Lee University

David Sudol, Arizona State University

Stan Sulkes, Raymond Walters College
Gerald Sullivan, Savio Preparatory School
Henry Taylor, American University
Jean Tobin, University of Wisconsin Center,
Sheboygan County
Linda Travers, University of Massachusetts,
Amherst
Tom Treffinger, Greenville Technical College
Peter Ulisse, Housatonia Community College
Lee Upton, Lafayette College
Rex Veeder, St. Cloud University
Deborah Viles, University of Colorado,
Boulder

Joyce Walker, Southern Illinois
University–Carbondale
Sue Walker, University of South Alabama
Irene Ward, Kansas State University
Penelope Warren, Laredo Community College
Barbara Wenner, University of Cincinnati
Terry Witek, Stetson University
Sallie Wolf, Arapahoe Community College
Beth Rapp Young, University of Alabama
William Zander, Fairleigh Dickinson University
Tom Zaniello, Northern Kentucky University
Guanping Zeng, Pensacola Junior College
John Zheng, Mississippi Valley State University

Special thanks go to Michael Palma, who scrupulously examined and updated every chapter from the previous edition. His deep knowledge of literature, crisp sense of style, and sense of humor kept the new edition fresh, informed, and accessible. Ongoing thanks also go to Susan Balée, who contributed to the chapter on writing a research paper; April Lindner of Saint Joseph's University in Philadelphia, Pennsylvania, who served as associate editor for the writing sections in the previous edition; Mark Bernier of Blinn College in Brenham, Texas, who helped improve the writing material of earlier editions; Joseph Aimone of Santa Clara University, who helped integrate Web-based materials and research techniques into an earlier edition; and John Swensson of De Anza College, who provided excellent practical suggestions from the classroom.

On the publisher's staff, Joseph Terry, Katharine Glynn, and Joyce Nilsen made many contributions to the development and revision of the new edition. Savoula Amanatidis and Lois Lombardo directed the complex job of managing the production of the book from the manuscript to the final printed form. Beth Keister handled the difficult job of permissions. Rona Tuccillo and Teri Stratford supervised the expansion of photographs in the new edition.

Mary Gioia was involved in every stage of planning, editing, and execution. Not only could the book not have been done without her capable hand and careful eye, but her expert guidance made every chapter better.

Past debts that will never be repaid are outstanding to hundreds of instructors named in prefaces past and to Dorothy M. Kennedy.

X. J. K. AND D. G.

Amy Tan in Chinatown, San Francisco, 1989.

FICTION

TALKING WITH *Amy Tan*

"Life Is Larger Than We Think"
Dana Gioia Interviews Amy Tan

Q: You were born in Oakland in a family where both parents had come from China. Were you raised bilingually?

AMY TAN: Until the age of five, my parents spoke to me in Chinese or a combination of Chinese and English, but they didn't force me to speak Mandarin. In retrospect, this was sad, because they believed that my chance of doing well in America hinged on my fluency in English. Later, as an adult, I wanted to learn Chinese. Now I make an effort when I am with my sisters, who don't speak English well.

Amy Tan with her mother.

Q: What books do you remember reading early in your childhood?

AMY TAN: I read every fairy tale I could lay my hands on at the public library. It was a wonderful world to escape to. I say "escape" deliberately, because I look back and I feel that my childhood was filled with a lot of tensions in the house, and I was able to go to another place. These stories were also filled with their own kinds of dangers and tensions, but they weren't mine. And they were usually solved in the end. This was something satisfying. You could go through these things and then suddenly, you would have some kind of ending. I think that every lonely kid loves to escape through stories. And what kids never thought that they were lonely at some point in their life?

Q: Your mother—to put it mildly—did not approve of your ambition to be a writer.

AMY TAN: My mother and father were immigrants and they were practical people. They wanted us to do well in the new country. They didn't want us to be starving artists. Going into the arts was considered a luxury—that was something you did if you were born to wealth. When my mother found out that I had switched from pre-med to English literature, she imagined that I would lead this life of poverty, that this was a dream that couldn't possibly lead to anything. I didn't know what it would lead to. It just occurred to me I could finally make a choice when I was in college. I didn't have to follow what my parents had set out for me from the age of six—to become a doctor.

Q: What did your mother think of *The Joy Luck Club*?

AMY TAN: Well, by the time I wrote *The Joy Luck Club*, she had changed her opinion. I was making a very good living as a business writer, enough to buy a house for her to live in. When you can do that for your parents they think you're doing fairly well. That was the goal, to become a doctor and be able to make enough money to take care of my mother in her old age. Because I was able to do that as a business writer, she thought it was great. When I decided to write fiction and I said I needed to interview her for stories from her past, she thought that was even better. Then when I got published, and it became a success, she said, "I always knew she was going to be a writer, because she had a wild imagination."

Q: *The Joy Luck Club* is a book of enormous importance, because it brought the complex history of Chinese immigration into the mainstream of American literature. Writing this book, did you have any sense that you were opening up a whole new territory?

AMY TAN: No, I had no idea this was going to be anything but weird stories about a weird family that was unique to us. To think that they would apply to other people who would find similarities to their own families or conflicts was beyond my imagination, and I have a very good imagination.

I wanted to write this book for very personal reasons. One of them, of course, was to learn the craft of writing. The other reason was to understand myself, to figure out who I was. A lot of writers use writing as a way of finding their own personal meaning. I wrote out of total chaos and personal history, which did not seem like something that would ever be used by other people as a way of understanding their lives.

Q: Did you have any literary models in writing your short stories or putting them together as a book? Or did you just do it on intuition?

AMY TAN: I look back, and there were unconscious models—fairy tales, the Bible, especially the cadence of the Bible. There was a book called *Little House in the Big Woods*, by Laura Ingalls Wilder. Wilder wrote this fictional story based on her life as a lonely little girl, moving from place to place. She lived 100 years ago, but that was my life.

The other major influence was my parents. My father wrote sermons and he read them aloud to me, as his test audience. They were not the kind of hell and brimstone sermons. They were stories about himself and his doubts, what he wanted and how he tried to do it.

Then, of course, there was my mother, who told stories as though they were happening right in front of her. She would remember what happened to her in life and act them out in front of me. That's oral storytelling at its best.

Q: Is there anything else that you'd like to say?

AMY TAN: I think reading is really important. It provided for me a refuge, especially during difficult times. It provided me with the notion that I could find an ending that was different from what was happening to me at the time. When you read about the lives of other people, people of different circumstances or similar circumstances, you are part of their lives for that moment. You inhabit their lives and you feel what they're feeling and that is compassion.

Life is larger than we think it is. Certain events can happen that we don't understand. We can take it as faith or as superstition, or as a fairy tale. The possibilities are wide open as to how we look at them.

It's a wonderful part of life to come to a situation and think that it can offer all kinds of possibilities and you get to choose them. I look at what's happened to me as a published writer, and sometimes I think it's a fairy tale.

H ere is a story, one of the shortest ever written and one of the most difficult to forget:

> A woman is sitting in her old, shuttered house. She knows that she is alone in the whole world; every other thing is dead.
> The doorbell rings.

In a brief space this small tale of terror, credited to Thomas Bailey Aldrich, makes itself memorable. It sets a promising scene—is this a haunted house?—introduces a character, and places her in a strange and intriguing situation. Although in reading a story that is over so quickly we don't come to know the character well, for a moment we enter her thoughts and begin to share her feelings. Then something amazing happens. The story leaves us to wonder: who or what rang that bell?

Like many richer, longer, more complicated stories, this one, in its few words, engages the imagination. Evidently, how much a story contains and suggests doesn't depend on its size. In the opening chapter of this book, we will look first at other brief stories—examples of three ancient kinds of fiction, a fable, a parable, and a tale— then at a contemporary short story. We will consider the elements of fiction one after another. By seeing a few short stories broken into their parts, you will come to a keener sense of how a story is put together. Not all stories are short, of course; later in the book, you will find a chapter on reading long stories and novels.

All in all, here are sixty-four stories. Among them, may you find at least a few you'll enjoy and care to remember.

1 READING A STORY

When I read a good book . . . I wish that life were
three thousand years long.

—RALPH WALDO EMERSON

After the shipwreck that marooned him on his desert island, Robinson Crusoe, in the novel by Daniel Defoe, stood gazing over the water where pieces of cargo from his ship were floating by. Along came "two shoes, not mates." It is the qualification *not mates* that makes the detail memorable. We could well believe that a thing so striking and odd must have been seen, and not invented. But in truth Defoe, like other masters of the art of fiction, had the power to make us believe his imaginings. Borne along by the art of the storyteller, we trust what we are told, even though the story may be sheer fantasy.

THE ART OF FICTION

Fiction (from the Latin *fictio*, "a shaping, a counterfeiting") is a name for stories not entirely factual, but at least partially shaped, made up, imagined. It is true that in some fiction, such as a historical novel, a writer draws on factual information in presenting scenes, events, and characters. But the factual information in a historical novel, unlike that in a history book, is of secondary importance.

Many firsthand accounts of the American Civil War were written by men who had fought in it, but few eyewitnesses give us so keen a sense of actual life on the battlefront as the author of *The Red Badge of Courage*, Stephen Crane, who was born after the war was over. In fiction, the "facts" may or may not be true, and a story is none the worse for their being entirely imaginary. We expect from fiction a sense of how people act, not an authentic chronicle of how, at some past time, a few people acted.

Human beings love stories. We put them everywhere—not only in books, films, and plays, but also in songs, news articles, cartoons, and videogames. There seems to be a general human curiosity about how other lives, both real and imaginary, take shape and unfold. Some stories provide simple and predictable pleasures according to a conventional plan. Each episode of *Law and Order* or *The Simpsons*, for instance, follows a roughly similar structure, so that regular viewers feel comfortably engaged and entertained. But other stories may seek to challenge rather than comfort us, by finding new and exciting ways to tell a tale, or delving deeper into the mysteries of human nature, or both.

Literary Fiction

Literary fiction calls for close attention. Reading a short story by Ernest Hemingway instead of watching an episode of *Grey's Anatomy* is a little like playing chess rather than checkers. It isn't that Hemingway isn't entertaining. Great literature provides deep and genuine pleasures. But it also requires great attention and skilled engagement from the reader. We are not necessarily led on by the promise of thrills; we do not keep reading mainly to find out what happens next. Indeed, a literary story might even disclose in its opening lines everything that happened, then spend the rest of its length revealing what that happening meant.

Reading literary fiction is no merely passive activity, but is one that demands both attention and insight-lending participation. In return, it offers rewards. In some works of literary fiction, such as Stephen Crane's "The Open Boat" and Flannery O'Connor's "Revelation," we see more deeply into the minds and hearts of the characters than we ever see into those of our families, our close friends, our lovers—or even ourselves.

TYPES OF SHORT FICTION

Modern literary fiction in English has been dominated by two forms: the novel and the short story. The two have many elements in common. Perhaps we will be able to define the short story more meaningfully—for it has traits more essential than just a particular length—if first, for comparison, we consider some related varieties of fiction: the fable, the parable, and the tale. Ancient forms whose origins date back to the time of word-of-mouth storytelling, the fable and the tale are relatively simple in structure; in them we can plainly see elements also found in the short story (and in the novel).

Fable

The **fable** is a brief, often humorous narrative told to illustrate a moral. The characters in a fable are often animals who represent specific human qualities. An ant, for example, may represent a hard-working type of person, or a lion nobility. But fables can also present human characters. To begin, here is a fable by W. Somerset Maugham (1874–1965), an English novelist and playwright, that retells an Arabian folk story. The narrator of the story is Death. (Samarra, by the way, is a city sixty miles from Baghdad.)

W. Somerset Maugham

The Appointment in Samarra   1933

Death speaks: There was a merchant in Baghdad who sent his servant to market to buy provisions and in a little while the servant came back, white and trembling, and said, Master, just now when I was in the marketplace I was jostled by a woman in the crowd and when I turned I saw it was Death that jostled me. She looked at me and made a threatening gesture; now, lend me your horse, and I will ride away from this city and avoid my fate. I will go to Samarra and there Death will not find me. The merchant lent him his horse, and the servant mounted it, and he dug his spurs in its flanks and as fast as the horse could gallop he went. Then the merchant went down to the marketplace and he saw me standing in the crowd and he came to me and said, Why did you make a threatening gesture to my servant when you saw him this morning? That was not a threatening gesture, I said, it was only a start of surprise. I was astonished to see him in Baghdad, for I had an appointment with him tonight in Samarra.

Elements of Fable

This brief story seems practically all skin and bones; that is, it contains little decoration. For in a fable everything leads directly to the **moral**, or message, sometimes stated at the end (moral: "Haste makes waste"). In "The Appointment in Samarra" the moral isn't stated outright, it is merely implied. How would you state it in your own words?

You are probably acquainted with some of the fables credited to the Greek slave Aesop (about 620–560 B.C.), whose stories seem designed to teach lessons about human life. Such is the fable of "The Goose That Laid the Golden Eggs," in which the owner of this marvelous creature slaughters her to get at the great treasure that he thinks is inside her, but finds nothing (implied moral: "Be content with what you have"). Another is the fable of "The Tortoise and the Hare" (implied moral: "Slow, steady plodding wins the race"). The characters in a fable may be talking animals (as in many of Aesop's fables), inanimate objects, or people and supernatural beings (as in "The Appointment in Samarra"). Whoever they may be, these characters are merely sketched, not greatly developed. Evidently, it would not have helped Maugham's fable to make its point if he had portrayed the merchant, the servant, and Death in fuller detail. A more elaborate description of the marketplace would not have improved the story. Probably, such a description would strike us as unnecessary and distracting. By its very bareness and simplicity, a fable fixes itself—and its message—in memory.

Aesop

The North Wind and the Sun   6th century B.C.

Translated by V. S. Vernon Jones

Very little is known with certainty about the man called Aesop, but several accounts and many traditions survive from antiquity. According to the Greek historian Herodotus, Aesop was a slave on the island of Samos. He gained great fame from his fables, but he somehow met his death at the hands of the people of Delphi. According to one tradition, Aesop was an ugly and misshapen man who charmed and amused people with his stories. No one knows if Aesop himself wrote down any of his fables, but they circulated widely in ancient Greece and were praised by Plato, Aristotle, and many other authors. His short and witty tales with their incisive morals have remained constantly popular and influenced innumerable later writers.

A dispute arose between the North Wind and the Sun, each claiming that he was stronger than the other. At last they agreed to try their powers upon a traveler, to see which could soonest strip him of his cloak. The North Wind had the first try; and, gathering up all his force for the attack, he came whirling furiously down upon the man, and caught up his cloak as though he would wrest it from him by one single effort: but the harder he blew, the more closely the man wrapped it round himself. Then came the turn of the Sun. At first he beamed gently upon the traveler, who soon unclasped his cloak and walked on with it hanging loosely about his shoulders:

then he shone forth in his full strength, and the man, before he had gone many steps, was glad to throw his cloak right off and complete his journey more lightly clad.

Moral: Persuasion is better than force.

Questions

1. Describe the different personalities of the North Wind and the Sun.
2. What was ineffective about the North Wind's method of attempting to strip the man of his cloak?
3. Why was the Sun successful in his attempts? What did he do differently than the North Wind?
4. What purpose does the human serve in this dispute?
5. Explain the closing moral in terms of the fable.

We are so accustomed to the phrase *Aesop's fables* that we might almost start to think the two words inseparable, but in fact there have been fabulists (creators or writers of fables) in virtually every culture throughout recorded history. Here is another fable from many centuries ago, this time from India.

Bidpai

The Tortoise and the Geese   c. 4th century

Retold in English by Maude Barrows Dutton

The Panchatantra *(Pañca-tantra), a collection of beast fables from India, is attributed to its narrator, a sage named Bidpai, a legendary figure about whom almost nothing is known for certain. The* Panchatantra, *which means the "The Five Chapters" in Sanskrit, is based on*

Illustration for "The Tortoise and the Geese" by E. Boyd Smith (1908).

earlier oral folklore. The collection was composed some time between 100 B.C. and 500 A.D. in a Sanskrit original now lost, and is primarily known through an Arabic version of the eighth century and a twelfth-century Hebrew translation. The stories are didactic, teaching niti, *the wise conduct of life, and* artha, *practical wisdom that stresses cleverness and self-reliance above more altruistic virtues.*

A Tortoise and two Geese lived together in a pond for many years. At last there came a drought and dried up the pond. Then the Geese said to one another, "We must seek a new home quickly, for we cannot live without water. Let us say farewell to the Tortoise and start at once."

When the Tortoise heard that they were going, he trembled with fear, and besought them by their friendship not to desert him.

"Alas," the Geese replied, "there is no help for it. If we stay here, we shall all three die, and we cannot take you with us, for you cannot fly."

Still the Tortoise begged so hard not to be left behind that the Geese finally said, "Dear Friend, if you will promise not to speak a word on the journey, we will take you with us. But know beforehand, that if you open your mouth to say one single word, you will be in instant danger of losing your life."

"Have no fear," replied the Tortoise, "but that I will be silent until you give me   5 leave to speak again. I would rather never open my mouth again than be left to die alone here in the dried-up pond."

So the Geese brought a stout stick and bade the Tortoise grasp it firmly in the middle by his mouth. Then they took hold of either end and flew off with him. They had gone several miles in safety, when their course lay over a village. As the country people saw this curious sight of a Tortoise being carried by two Geese, they began to laugh and cry out, "Oh, did you ever see such a funny sight in all your life!" And they laughed loud and long.

The Tortoise grew more and more indignant. At last he could stand their jeering no longer. "You stupid . . ." he snapped, but before he could say more he had fallen to the ground and was dashed to pieces.

Questions

1. Under what condition do the Geese agree to transport the Tortoise?
2. What motivates the Tortoise to break his agreement?
3. How would you summarize the moral of the fable?

Parable

Another traditional form of storytelling is the **parable**. Like the fable, a parable is a brief narrative that teaches a moral, but unlike the fable, its plot is plausibly realistic, and the main characters are human rather than anthropomorphized animals or natural forces. The other key difference is that parables usually possess a more mysterious and suggestive tone. A fable customarily ends by explicitly stating its moral, but parables often present their morals implicitly, and their meanings can be open to several interpretations.

In the Western tradition, the literary conventions of the parable are largely based on the brief stories told by Jesus in his preaching. The forty-three parables recounted in the four Gospels reveal how frequently he used the form to teach. Jesus designed his parables to have two levels of meaning—a literal story that could immediately be understood by the crowds he addressed and a deeper meaning fully comprehended only by his disciples, an inner circle who understood the nature of his ministry. (You can see the richness of interpretations suggested by Jesus's parables by reading and analyzing "The Parable of the Prodigal Son" from St. Luke's Gospel, which appears in Chapter 6.) The parable was also widely used by Eastern philosophers. The Taoist sage Chuang Tzu often portrayed the principles of Tao—which he called the "Way of Nature"—in witty parables such as the following one, traditionally titled "Independence."

Chuang Tzu

Independence   Chou Dynasty (4th century B.C.)
Translated by Herbert Giles

Chuang Chou, usually known as Chuang Tzu (approximately 390–365 B.C.), was one of the great philosophers of the Chou period in China. He was born in the Sung feudal state and received an excellent education. Unlike most educated men, however, Chuang Tzu did not seek public office or political power. Influenced by Taoist philosophy, he believed that individuals should transcend their desire for success and wealth, as well as their fear of failure and poverty. True freedom, he maintained, came from escaping the distractions of worldly affairs. Chuang Tzu's writings have been particularly praised for their combination of humor and wisdom. His parables and stories are classics of Chinese literature.

Chuang Tzu was one day fishing, when the Prince of Ch'u sent two high officials to interview him, saying that his Highness would be glad of Chuang Tzu's assistance in the administration of his government. The latter quietly fished on, and without looking round, replied, "I have heard that in the State of Ch'u there is a sacred tortoise, which has been dead three thousand years, and which the prince keeps packed up in a box on the altar in his ancestral shrine. Now do you think that tortoise would rather be dead and have its remains thus honoured, or be alive and wagging its tail in the mud?" The two officials answered that no doubt it would rather be alive and wagging its tail in the mud; whereupon Chuang Tzu cried out "Begone! I too elect to remain wagging my tail in the mud."

Questions

1. What part of this story is the exposition? How many sentences does Chuang Tzu use to set up the dramatic situation?
2. Why does the protagonist change the subject and mention the sacred tortoise? Why doesn't he answer the request directly and immediately? Does it serve any purpose that Chuang Tzu makes the officials answer a question to which he knows the answer?
3. What does this story tell us about the protagonist Chuang Tzu's personality?

Tale

The name *tale* (from the Old English *talu,* "speech") is sometimes applied to any story, whether short or long, true or fictitious. *Tale* being a more evocative name than *story,* writers sometimes call their stories "tales" as if to imply something handed down from the past. But defined in a more limited sense, a **tale** is a story, usually short, that sets forth strange and wonderful events in more or less bare summary, without detailed character-drawing. "Tale" is pretty much synonymous with "yarn," for it implies a story in which the goal is revelation of the marvelous rather than revelation of character. In the English folktale "Jack and the Beanstalk," we take away a more vivid impression of the miraculous beanstalk and the giant who dwells at its top than of Jack's mind or personality. Because such venerable stories were told aloud before someone set them down in writing, the storytellers had to limit themselves to brief descriptions. Probably spoken around a fire or hearth, such a tale tends to be less complicated and less closely detailed than a story written for the printed page, whose reader can linger over it. Still, such tales *can* be complicated. It is not merely greater length that makes a short story different from a tale or a fable: one mark of a short story is a fully delineated character.

Types of Tales

Even modern tales favor supernatural or fantastic events: for instance, the **tall tale**, a variety of folk story that recounts the deeds of a superhero (Paul Bunyan, John Henry, Sally Ann Thunder) or of the storyteller. If the storyteller is describing his or her own imaginary experience, the bragging yarn is usually told with a straight face to listeners who take pleasure in scoffing at it. Although the **fairy tale**, set in a world of magic and enchantment, is sometimes the work of a modern author (notably Hans Christian Andersen), well-known examples are those German folktales that probably originated in the Middle Ages, collected by the Brothers Grimm. The label *fairy tale* is something of an English misnomer, for in the Grimm stories, though witches and goblins abound, fairies are a minority.

Jakob and Wilhelm Grimm

Godfather Death

1812 (from oral tradition)

Translated by Dana Gioia

Jakob Grimm (1785–1863) and Wilhelm Grimm (1786–1859), brothers and scholars, were born near Frankfurt am Main, Germany. For most of their lives they worked together—lived together, too, even when in 1825 Wilhelm married. In 1838, as librarians, they began toiling on their Deutsch Wörterbuch, *or German dictionary, a vast project that was to outlive them by a century. (It was completed only in 1960.) In 1840 King Friedrich Wilhelm IV appointed both brothers to the Royal Academy of Sciences, and both taught at the University of Berlin for the rest of their days.*

Jakob and Wilhelm Grimm

The name Grimm is best known to us for that splendid collection of ancient German folk stories we call Grimm's Fairy Tales—in German, Kinder- und Hausmärchen *("Childhood and Household Tales," 1812–15). This classic work spread German children's stories around the world. Many tales we hear early in life were collected by the Grimms: "Hansel and Gretel," "Snow White and the Seven Dwarfs," "Rapunzel," "Tom Thumb," "Little Red Riding Hood," "Rumpelstiltskin." Versions of some of these tales had been written down as early as the sixteenth century, but mainly the brothers relied on the memories of Hessian peasants who recited the stories aloud for them.*

A poor man had twelve children and had to work day and night just to give them bread. Now when the thirteenth came into the world, he did not know what to do, so he ran out onto the main highway intending to ask the first one he met to be the child's godfather.

The first person he met was the good Lord God, who knew very well what was weighing on the man's heart. And He said to him, "Poor man, I am sorry for you. I will hold your child at the baptismal font. I will take care of him and fill his days with happiness."

The man asked, "Who are you?"

"I am the good Lord."

"Then I don't want you as godfather. You give to the rich and let the poor starve."   5

The man spoke thus because he did not know how wisely God portions out wealth and poverty. So he turned away from the Lord and went on.

Then the Devil came up to him and said, "What are you looking for? If you take me as your child's sponsor, I will give him gold heaped high and wide and all the joys of this world."

The man asked, "Who are you?"

"I am the Devil."

"Then I don't want you as godfather," said the man. "You trick men and lead   10
them astray."

He went on, and bone-thin Death strode up to him and said, "Choose me as godfather."

The man asked, "Who are you?"

"I am Death, who makes all men equal."

Then the man said, "You are the right one. You take the rich and the poor without distinction. You will be the godfather."

Death answered, "I will make your child rich and famous. Whoever has me as a   15
friend shall lack for nothing."

The man said, "The baptism is next Sunday. Be there on time."

Death appeared just as he had promised and stood there as a proper godfather.

When the boy had grown up, his godfather walked in one day and said to come along with him. Death led him out into the woods, showed him an herb, and said, "Now you are going to get your christening present. I am making you a famous doctor. When you are called to a patient, I will always appear to you. If I stand next to the sick person's head, you may speak boldly that you will make him healthy again. Give him some of this herb, and he will recover. But if you see me standing by the sick person's feet, then he is mine. You must say that nothing can be done and that no doctor in the world can save him. But beware of using the herb against my will, or it will turn out badly for you."

It was not long before the young man was the most famous doctor in the whole world. "He needs only to look at the sick person," everyone said, "and then he knows how things stand—whether the patient will get well again or whether he must die." People came from far and wide to bring their sick and gave him so much gold that he quickly became quite rich.

Now it soon happened that the king grew ill, and the doctor was summoned to say   20
whether a recovery was possible. But when he came to the bed, Death was standing at the sick man's feet, and now no herb grown could save him.

"If I cheat Death this one time," thought the doctor, "he will be angry, but since I am his godson, he will turn a blind eye, so I will risk it." He took up the sick man and turned him around so that his head was now where Death stood. Then he gave the king some of the herb. The king recovered and grew healthy again.

But Death then came to the doctor with a dark and angry face and threatened him with his finger. "You have hoodwinked me this time," he said. "And I will forgive you once because you are my godson. But if you try such a thing again, it will be your neck, and I will take you away with me."

Not long after, the king's daughter fell into a serious illness. She was his only child, and he wept day and night until his eyes went blind. He let it be known that whoever saved her from death would become her husband and inherit the crown.

When the doctor came to the sick girl's bed, he saw Death standing at her feet. He should have remembered his godfather's warning, but the princess's great beauty and the happy prospect of becoming her husband so infatuated him that he flung all caution to the wind. He didn't notice that Death stared at him angrily or that he raised his hand and shook his bony fist. The doctor picked up the sick girl and turned her around to place her head where her feet had been. He gave her the herb, and right away her cheeks grew rosy and she stirred again with life.

When Death saw that he had been cheated out of his property a second time, he 25 strode with long steps up to the doctor and said, "It is all over for you. Now it's your turn." Death seized him so firmly with his ice-cold hand that the doctor could not resist. He led him into an underground cavern. There the doctor saw thousands and thousands of candles burning in endless rows. Some were tall, others medium-sized, and others quite small. Every moment some went out and others lit up, so that the tiny flames seemed to jump to and fro in perpetual motion.

"Look," said Death, "these are the life lights of mankind. The tall ones belong to children, the middle-size ones to married people in the prime of life, and the short ones to the very old. But sometimes even children and young people have only a short candle."

"Show me my life light," said the doctor, assuming it would be very tall.

Death pointed to a small stub that seemed about to flicker out.

"Oh, dear godfather!" cried the terrified doctor. "Light a new candle for me. If you love me, do it, so that I may enjoy my life, become king, and marry the beautiful princess."

"That I cannot do," Death replied. "One candle must first go out before a new 30 one is lighted."

"Then put my old one on top of a new candle that will keep burning when the old one goes out," begged the doctor.

Death acted as if he were going to grant the wish and picked up a tall new candle. But because he wanted revenge, he deliberately fumbled in placing the new candle, and the stub toppled over and went out. The doctor immediately dropped to the ground and fell into the hands of Death.

PLOT

Like a fable, the Grimm brothers' tale seems stark in its lack of detail and in the swiftness of its telling. Compared with the fully portrayed characters of many modern stories, the characters of father, son, king, princess, and even Death himself seem hardly more than stick figures. It may have been that to draw ample characters would not have contributed to the storytellers' design; that, indeed, to have done so would have been inartistic. Yet "Godfather Death" is a compelling story. By what methods does it arouse and sustain our interest?

Elements of Plot

Plot sometimes refers simply to the events in a story. In this book, though, **plot** will mean the artistic arrangement of those events. From the opening sentence of "Godfather Death," we watch the unfolding of a **dramatic situation**: a person is involved in some **conflict**. First, this character is a poor man with children to feed, in conflict with the world; very soon, we find him in conflict with God and with the Devil besides. Drama in fiction occurs in any clash of wills, desires, or powers—whether it be a conflict of character against character, character against society, character against some natural force, or, as in "Godfather Death," character against some supernatural entity.

Like any shapely tale, "Godfather Death" has a beginning, a middle, and an end. In fact, it is unusual to find a story so clearly displaying the elements of structure that critics have found in many classic works of fiction and drama. The tale begins with an **exposition**: the opening portion that sets the scene (if any), introduces the main characters, tells us what happened before the story opened, and provides any other background information that we need in order to understand and care about the events to follow. In "Godfather Death," the exposition is brief—all in the opening paragraph. The middle section of the story begins with Death's giving the herb to the boy and his warning not to defy him. This moment introduces a new conflict (a **complication**), and by this time it is clear that the son and not the father is to be the central human character of the story.

Protagonist Versus Antagonist

Death's godson is the principal person who strives: the **protagonist** (a better term than **hero**, for it may apply equally well to a central character who is not especially brave or virtuous). The **suspense**, the pleasurable anxiety we feel that heightens our attention to the story, resides in our wondering how it will all turn out. Will the doctor triumph over Death? Even though we suspect, early in the story, that the doctor stands no chance against such a superhuman **antagonist**, we want to see for ourselves the outcome of his defiance.

Crisis and Climax

When the doctor defies his godfather for the first time—when he saves the king—we have a **crisis**, a moment of high tension. The tension is momentarily resolved when Death lets him off. Then an even greater crisis—the turning point in the action—occurs with the doctor's second defiance in restoring the princess to life. In the last section of the story, with the doctor in the underworld, events come to a **climax**, the moment of greatest tension at which the outcome is to be decided, when the terrified doctor begs for a new candle. Will Death grant him one? Will he live, become king, and marry the princess? The outcome or **conclusion**—also called the **resolution** or **dénouement** (French for "the untying of the knot")—quickly follows as Death allows the little candle to go out.

Narrative Techniques

The treatment of plot is one aspect of an author's artistry. Different arrangements of the same material are possible. A writer might decide to tell of the events in chronological order, beginning with the earliest; or he or she might open the story with the last event, then tell what led up to it. Sometimes a writer chooses to skip rapidly over the exposition and begin *in medias res* (Latin for "in the midst of things"), first presenting some exciting or significant moment, then filling in what happened earlier. This method is by no means a modern invention: Homer begins the *Odyssey* with his hero mysteriously late in returning from war and his son searching for him; John Milton's *Paradise Lost* opens with Satan already defeated in his revolt against the Lord. A device useful to writers for filling in what happened earlier is the **flashback** (or **retrospect**), a scene relived in a character's memory. Alternatively, a storyteller can try to incite our anticipation by giving us some **foreshadowing** or indication of events to come. In "Godfather Death" the foreshadowings are apparent in Death's warnings ("But if you try such a thing again, it will be your neck").

THE SHORT STORY

The teller of tales relies heavily on the method of **summary**: terse, general narration. In a **short story**, a form more realistic than the tale and of modern origin, the writer usually presents the main events in greater fullness. Fine writers of short stories, although they may use summary at times (often to give some portion of a story less emphasis), are skilled in rendering a **scene**: a vivid or dramatic moment described in enough detail to create the illusion that the reader is practically there. Avoiding long summary, they try to *show* rather than simply to *tell*, as if following Mark Twain's advice to authors: "Don't say, 'The old lady screamed.' Bring her on and let her scream."

A short story is more than just a sequence of happenings. A finely wrought short story has the richness and conciseness of an excellent lyric poem. Spontaneous and natural as the finished story may seem, the writer has crafted it so artfully that there is meaning in even seemingly casual speeches and apparently trivial details. If we skim it hastily, skipping the descriptive passages, we miss significant parts.

Some literary short stories, unlike commercial fiction in which the main interest is in physical action or conflict, tell of an **epiphany**: some moment of insight, discovery, or revelation by which a character's life, or view of life, is greatly altered. The term, which means "showing forth" in Greek, was first used in Christian theology to signify the manifestation of God's presence in the world. This theological idea was adapted by James Joyce to refer to a heightened moment of secular revelation. (For such moments in fiction, see the stories in this book by Joyce, John Steinbeck, and Joyce Carol Oates.) Other short stories tell of a character initiated into experience or maturity: one such **story of initiation** is William Faulkner's "Barn Burning" (Chapter 5), in which a boy finds it necessary to defy his father and suddenly to grow into manhood. Less obviously dramatic, perhaps, than "Godfather Death," such a story may be no less powerful.

The fable and the tale are ancient forms; the short story is of more recent origin. In the nineteenth century, writers of fiction were encouraged by a large, literate audience of middle-class readers who wanted to see their lives reflected in faithful mirrors. Skillfully representing ordinary life, many writers perfected the art of the short story: in Russia, Anton Chekhov; in France, Honoré de Balzac and Guy de Maupassant; and in America, Nathaniel Hawthorne and Edgar Allan Poe (although the Americans seem less fond of everyday life than of dream and fantasy). It would be false to claim that, in passing from the fable and the tale to the short story, fiction has made a triumphant progress; or to claim that, because short stories are modern, they are superior to fables and tales. Fable, tale, and short story are distinct forms, each achieving its own effects. Far from being extinct, fable and tale have enjoyed a resurgence in recent years. Jorge Luis Borges, Italo Calvino, and Gabriel García Márquez have all used fable and folktale to create memorable and very modern fiction. All forms of fiction are powerful in the right authorial hands.

Let's begin with a contemporary short story whose protagonist undergoes an initiation into maturity. To notice the difference between a short story and a tale, you may find it helpful to compare John Updike's "A & P" with "Godfather Death." Although Updike's short story is centuries distant from the Grimm tale in its method of telling and in its setting, you may be reminded of "Godfather Death" in the main character's dramatic situation. To defend a young woman, a young man has to defy his mentor—here, the boss of a supermarket! In so doing, he places himself in jeopardy. Updike has the protagonist tell his own story, amply and with humor. How does it differ from a tale?

John Updike

A & P   1961

John Updike (1932–2009), was born in Pennsylvania, received his B.A. from Harvard, then went to Oxford to study drawing and fine art. In the mid-1950s he worked on the staff of the New Yorker, *at times doing errands for the aged James Thurber. Although he left the magazine to become a full-time writer, Updike continued to supply it with memorable stories, witty light verse, and searching reviews. A famously prolific writer, he published more than fifty books. Updike is best known as a hardworking, versatile, highly productive writer of fiction. For his novel* The Centaur *(1963) he received a National Book Award, and for* Rabbit Is Rich *(1982) a Pulitzer Prize and an American Book Award. The fourth and last Rabbit Angstrom novel,* Rabbit at Rest *(1990), won him a second Pulitzer. Updike is one of the few Americans ever to be awarded both the National Medal of Arts (1989) and the National Humanities Medal (2003)—the nation's highest honors in each respective field. His many other books include* The Witches of Eastwick *(1984), made into a successful film starring Jack Nicholson,* Terrorist *(2006), and his final novel,* The Widows of Eastwick *(2008).*

Almost uniquely among contemporary American writers, Updike moved back and forth successfully among a variety of literary genres: light verse, serious poetry, drama, criticism, children's books, novels, and short stories. But it is perhaps in short fiction that he did his finest work. Some critics, such as Washington Post writer Jonathan Yardley, believe that "It is in his short stories that we find Updike's most assured work, and no doubt it is upon the best of them that his reputation ultimately will rest."

In walks three girls in nothing but bathing suits. I'm in the third check-out slot, with my back to the door, so I don't see them until they're over by the bread. The one that caught my eye first was the one in the plaid green two-piece. She was a chunky kid, with a good tan and a sweet broad soft-looking can with those two crescents of white just under it, where the sun never seems to hit, at the top of the backs of her legs. I stood there with my hand on a box of HiHo crackers trying to remember if I rang it up or not. I ring it up again and the customer starts giving me hell. She's one of these cash-register-watchers, a witch about fifty with rouge on her cheekbones and no eyebrows, and I know it made her day to trip me up. She'd been watching cash registers for fifty years and probably never seen a mistake before.

By the time I got her feathers smoothed and her goodies into a bag—she gives me a little snort in passing, if she'd been born at the right time they would have burned her over in Salem—by the time I get her on her way the girls had circled around the bread and were coming back, without a pushcart, back my way along the counters, in the aisle between the check-outs and the Special bins. They didn't even have shoes on. There was this chunky one, with the two-piece—it was bright green and the seams on the bra were still sharp and her belly was still pretty pale so I guessed she just got it (the suit)—there was this one, with one of those chubby berry-faces, the lips all bunched together under her nose, this one, and a tall one, with black hair that hadn't quite frizzed right, and one of these sunburns right across under the eyes, and a chin that was too long—you know, the kind of girl other girls think is very "striking" and "attractive" but never quite makes it, as they very well know, which is why they like her so much—and then the third one, that wasn't quite so tall. She was the queen. She kind of led them, the other two peeking around and making their shoulders round. She didn't look around, not this queen, she just walked straight on slowly, on these long white prima-donna legs. She came down a little hard on her heels, as if she didn't walk in her bare feet that much, putting down her heels and then letting the weight move along to her toes as if she was testing the floor with every step, putting a little deliberate extra action into it. You never know for sure how girls' minds work (do you really think it's a mind in there or just a little buzz like a bee in a glass jar?) but you got the idea she had talked the other two into coming in here with her, and now she was showing them how to do it, walk slow and hold yourself straight.

She had on a kind of dirty-pink—beige maybe, I don't know—bathing suit with a little nubble all over it and, what got me, the straps were down. They were off her shoulders looped loose around the cool tops of her arms, and I guess as a result the suit had slipped a little on her, so all around the top of the cloth there was this shining rim. If it hadn't been there you wouldn't have known there could have been anything whiter than those shoulders. With the straps pushed off, there was nothing between the top of the suit and the top of her head except just *her*, this clean bare plane of the top of her chest down from the shoulder bones like a dented sheet of metal tilted in the light. I mean, it was more than pretty.

She had sort of oaky hair that the sun and salt had bleached, done up in a bun that was unraveling, and a kind of prim face. Walking into the A & P with your straps down, I suppose it's the only kind of face you *can* have. She held her head so high her neck, coming up out of those white shoulders, looked kind of stretched, but I didn't mind. The longer her neck was, the more of her there was.

She must have felt in the corner of her eye me and over my shoulder Stokesie in the second slot watching, but she didn't tip. Not this queen. She kept her eyes moving across the racks, and stopped, and turned so slow it made my stomach rub the inside of my apron, and buzzed to the other two, who kind of huddled against her for relief, and they all three of them went up the cat-and-dog-food-breakfast-cereal-macaroni-rice-raisins-seasonings-spreads-spaghetti-soft-drinks-crackers-and-cookies aisle. From the third slot I look straight up this aisle to the meat counter, and I watched them all the way. The fat one with the tan sort of fumbled with the cookies, but on second thought she put the packages back. The sheep pushing their carts down the aisle—the girls were walking against the usual traffic (not that we have one-way signs or anything)—were pretty hilarious. You could see them, when Queenie's white shoulders dawned on them, kind of jerk, or hop, or hiccup, but their eyes snapped back to

5

their own baskets and on they pushed. I bet you could set off dynamite in an A & P and the people would by and large keep reaching and checking oatmeal off their lists and muttering "Let me see, there was a third thing, began with A, asparagus, no, ah, yes, applesauce!" or whatever it is they do mutter. But there was no doubt, this jiggled them. A few houseslaves in pin curlers even looked around after pushing their carts past to make sure what they had seen was correct.

You know, it's one thing to have a girl in a bathing suit down on the beach, where what with the glare nobody can look at each other much anyway, and another thing in the cool of the A & P, under the fluorescent lights, against all those stacked packages, with her feet padding along naked over our checkerboard green-and-cream rubber-tile floor.

"Oh Daddy," Stokesie said beside me. "I feel so faint."

"Darling," I said. "Hold me tight." Stokesie's married, with two babies chalked up on his fuselage already, but as far as I can tell that's the only difference. He's twenty-two, and I was nineteen this April.

"Is it done?" he asks, the responsible married man finding his voice. I forgot to say he thinks he's going to be manager some sunny day, maybe in 1990 when it's called the Great Alexandrov and Petrooshki Tea Company or something.

What he meant was, our town is five miles from a beach, with a big summer colony out on the Point, but we're right in the middle of town, and the women generally put on a shirt or shorts or something before they get out of the car into the street. And anyway these are usually women with six children and varicose veins mapping their legs and nobody, including them, could care less. As I say, we're right in the middle of town, and if you stand at our front doors you can see two banks and the Congregational church and the newspaper store and three real-estate offices and about twenty-seven old freeloaders tearing up Central Street because the sewer broke again. It's not as if we're on the Cape; we're north of Boston and there's people in this town haven't seen the ocean for twenty years. The girls had reached the meat counter and were asking McMahon something. He pointed, they pointed, and they shuffled out of sight behind a pyramid of Diet Delight peaches. All that was left for us to see was old McMahon patting his mouth and looking after them sizing up their joints. Poor kids, I began to feel sorry for them, they couldn't help it.

Now here comes the sad part of the story, at least my family says it's sad but I don't think it's sad myself. The store's pretty empty, it being Thursday afternoon, so there was nothing much to do except lean on the register and wait for the girls to show up again. The whole store was like a pinball machine and I didn't know which tunnel they'd come out of. After a while they come around out of the far aisle, around the light bulbs, records at discount of the Caribbean Six or Tony Martin Sings or some such gunk you wonder they waste the wax on, six-packs of candy bars, and plastic toys done up in cellophane that fall apart when a kid looks at them anyway. Around they come, Queenie still leading the way, and holding a little gray jar in her hand. Slots Three through Seven are unmanned and I could see her wondering between Stokes and me, but Stokesie with his usual luck draws an old party in baggy gray pants who stumbles up with four giant cans of pineapple juice (what do these bums *do* with all that pineapple juice? I've often asked myself) so the girls come to me. Queenie puts down the jar and I take it into my fingers icy cold. Kingfish Fancy Herring Snacks in Pure Sour Cream: 49¢. Now her hands are empty, not a ring or a bracelet, bare as God

10

made them, and I wonder where the money's coming from. Still with that prim look she lifts a folded dollar bill out of the hollow at the center of her nubbled pink top. The jar went heavy in my hand. Really, I thought that was so cute.

Then everybody's luck begins to run out. Lengel comes in from haggling with a truck full of cabbages on the lot and is about to scuttle into that door marked MANAGER behind which he hides all day when the girls touch his eye. Lengel's pretty dreary, teaches Sunday school and the rest, but he doesn't miss that much. He comes over and says, "Girls, this isn't the beach."

Queenie blushes, though maybe it's just a brush of sunburn I was noticing for the first time, now that she was so close. "My mother asked me to pick up a jar of herring snacks." Her voice kind of startled me, the way voices do when you see the people first, coming out so flat and dumb yet kind of tony, too, the way it ticked over "pick up" and "snacks." All of a sudden I slid right down her voice into her living room. Her father and the other men were standing around in ice-cream coats and bow ties and the women were in sandals picking up herring snacks on toothpicks off a big plate and they were all holding drinks the color of water with olives and sprigs of mint in them. When my parents have somebody over they get lemonade and if it's a real racy affair Schlitz in tall glasses with "They'll Do It Every Time" cartoons stencilled on.

"That's all right," Lengel said. "But this isn't the beach." His repeating this struck me as funny, as if it had just occurred to him, and he had been thinking all these years the A & P was a great big dune and he was the head lifeguard. He didn't like my smiling—as I say he doesn't miss much—but he concentrates on giving the girls that sad Sunday-school-superintendent stare.

Queenie's blush is no sunburn now, and the plump one in plaid, that I liked bet- [15] ter from the back—a really sweet can—pipes up, "We weren't doing any shopping. We just came in for the one thing."

"That makes no difference," Lengel tells her, and I could see from the way his eyes went that he hadn't noticed she was wearing a two-piece before. "We want you decently dressed when you come in here."

"We *are* decent," Queenie says suddenly, her lower lip pushing, getting sore now that she remembers her place, a place from which the crowd that runs the A & P must look pretty crummy. Fancy Herring Snacks flashed in her very blue eyes.

"Girls, I don't want to argue with you. After this come in here with your shoulders covered. It's our policy." He turns his back. That's policy for you. Policy is what the kingpins want. What the others want is juvenile delinquency.

All this while, the customers had been showing up with their carts but, you know, sheep, seeing a scene, they had all bunched up on Stokesie, who shook open a paper bag as gently as peeling a peach, not wanting to miss a word. I could feel in the silence everybody getting nervous, most of all Lengel, who asks me, "Sammy, have you rung up this purchase?"

I thought and said "No" but it wasn't about that I was thinking. I go through the [20] punches, 4, 9, GROC, TOT—it's more complicated than you think, and after you do it often enough, it begins to make a little song, that you hear words to, in my case "Hello (*bing*) there, you (*gung*) hap-py *pee*-pul (*splat*)!"—the *splat* being the drawer flying out. I uncrease the bill, tenderly as you may imagine, it just having come from between the two smoothest scoops of vanilla I had ever known were there, and pass a half and a penny into her narrow pink palm, and nestle the herrings in a bag and twist its neck and hand it over, all the time thinking.

The girls, and who'd blame them, are in a hurry to get out, so I say "I quit" to Lengel quick enough for them to hear, hoping they'll stop and watch me, their unsuspected hero. They keep right on going, into the electric eye; the door flies open and they flicker across the lot to their car, Queenie and Plaid and Big Tall Goony-Goony (not that as raw material she was so bad), leaving me with Lengel and a kink in his eyebrow.

"Did you say something, Sammy?"

"I said I quit."

"I thought you did."

"You didn't have to embarrass them."   25

"It was they who were embarrassing us."

I started to say something that came out "Fiddle-de-doo." It's a saying of my grandmother's, and I know she would have been pleased.

"I don't think you know what you're saying," Lengel said.

"I know you don't," I said. "But I do." I pull the bow at the back of my apron and start shrugging it off my shoulders. A couple customers that had been heading for my slot begin to knock against each other, like scared pigs in a chute.

Lengel sighs and begins to look very patient and old and gray. He's been a friend   30
of my parents for years. "Sammy, you don't want to do this to your Mom and Dad," he tells me. It's true, I don't. But it seems to me that once you begin a gesture it's fatal not to go through with it. I fold the apron, "Sammy" stitched in red on the pocket, and put it on the counter, and drop the bow tie on top of it. The bow tie is theirs, if you've ever wondered. "You'll feel this for the rest of your life," Lengel says, and I know that's true, too, but remembering how he made that pretty girl blush makes me so scrunchy inside I punch the No Sale tab and the machine whirs "peepul" and the drawer splats out. One advantage to this scene taking place in summer, I can follow this up with a clean exit, there's no fumbling around getting your coat and galoshes, I just saunter into the electric eye in my white shirt that my mother ironed the night before, and the door heaves itself open, and outside the sunshine is skating around on the asphalt.

I look around for my girls, but they're gone, of course. There wasn't anybody but some young married screaming with her children about some candy they didn't get by the door of a powder-blue Falcon station wagon. Looking back in the big windows, over the bags of peat moss and aluminum lawn furniture stacked on the pavement, I could see Lengel in my place in the slot, checking the sheep through. His face was dark gray and his back stiff, as if he'd just had an injection of iron, and my stomach kind of fell as I felt how hard the world was going to be to me hereafter.

Questions

1. Notice how artfully Updike arranges details to set the story in a perfectly ordinary super-market. What details stand out for you as particularly true to life? What does this close attention to detail contribute to the story?

2. How fully does Updike draw the character of Sammy? What traits (admirable or otherwise) does Sammy show? Is he any less a hero for wanting the girls to notice his heroism? To what extent is he more thoroughly and fully portrayed than the doctor in "Godfather Death"?

3. What part of the story seems to be the exposition? (See the definition of *exposition* in the discussion of plot earlier in the chapter.) Of what value to the story is the carefully detailed portrait of Queenie, the leader of the three girls?

4. As the story develops, do you detect any change in Sammy's feelings toward the girls?

5. Where in "A & P" does the dramatic conflict become apparent? What moment in the story brings the crisis? What is the climax of the story?

6. Why, exactly, does Sammy quit his job?
7. Does anything lead you to *expect* Sammy to make some gesture of sympathy for the three girls? What incident earlier in the story (before Sammy quits) seems a foreshadowing?
8. What do you understand from the conclusion of the story? What does Sammy mean when he acknowledges "how hard the world was going to be . . . hereafter"?
9. What comment does Updike—through Sammy—make on supermarket society?

■ WRITING *effectively*

John Updike on Writing

Why Write? 1975

Most people sensibly assume that writing is propaganda. Of course, they admit, there is bad propaganda, like the boy-meets-tractor novels of socialist realism, and old-fashioned propaganda, like Christian melodrama and the capitalist success stories of Horatio Alger or Samuel Smiles. But that some message is intended, wrapped in the story like a piece of crystal carefully mailed in cardboard and excelsior, is not doubted. Scarcely a day passes in my native land that I don't receive some letter from a student or teacher asking me *what I meant to say* in such a book, asking me to elaborate more fully on some sentence

John Updike

I deliberately whittled into minimal shape, or inviting me to speak on some topic, usually theological or sexual, on which it is pleasantly assumed I am an expert. The writer as hero, as Hemingway or Saint-Exupéry or D'Annunzio, a tradition of which Camus was perhaps the last example, has been replaced in America by the writer as educationist. Most writers teach, a great many teach writing; writing is furiously taught in the colleges even as the death knell of the book and the written word is monotonously tolled; any writer, it is assumed, can give a lecture, and the purer products of his academic mind, the "writings" themselves, are sifted and, if found of sufficient quality, installed in their places on the assembly belt of study, as objects of educational contemplation.

How dare one confess, to the politely but firmly inquiring letter-writer who takes for granted that as a remote but functioning element of his education you are duty-bound to provide the information and elucidating essay that will enable him to complete his term paper, or his Ph.D. thesis, or his critical *opus*—how dare one confess that the absence of a swiftly expressible message is, often, *the* message; that reticence is as important a tool to the writer as expression; that the hasty filling out of a questionnaire is not merely irrelevant but *inimical* to the writer's proper activity; that this activity is rather curiously private and finicking, a matter of exorcism and manufacture rather than of toplofty proclamation; that what he makes is ideally as ambiguous and opaque as life itself.

From "Why Write?"

THINKING ABOUT PLOT

A day without conflict is pleasant, but a story without conflict is boring. The plot of every short story, novel, or movie derives its energy from conflict. A character desperately wants something he or she can't have, or is frantic to avoid an unpleasant (or deadly) event. In most stories, conflict is established and tension builds, leading to a crisis and, finally, a resolution of some sort. When analyzing a story, be sure to remember these points:

- **Plotting isn't superficial.** Although plot might seem like the most obvious and superficial part of a story, it is an important expressive device. Plot combines with the other elements of fiction—imagery, style, and symbolism, for example—to create an emotional response in the reader: suspense, humor, sadness, excitement, terror.

- **Small events can have large consequences.** In most short stories, plot depends less on large external events than on small occurrences that set off large internal changes in the main character.

- **Action reveals character.** Good stories are a lot like life: the protagonist's true nature is usually revealed not just by what he or she says but also by what he or she does. Stories often show how the protagonist comes to a personal turning point, or how his or her character is tested or revealed by events.

- **Plot is about cause and effect.** Plot is more than just a sequence of events ("First A happens, and then B, and then C . . . "). The actions, events, and situations described in most stories are related to each other by more than just accident ("First A happens, which causes B to happen, which makes C all the more surprising, or inevitable, or ironic . . . ").

CHECKLIST: Writing About Plot

- ☐ What is the story's central conflict?
- ☐ Who is the protagonist? What does he or she want?
- ☐ What is at stake for the protagonist in the conflict?
- ☐ What stands in the way of the protagonist's easily achieving his or her goal?
- ☐ What are the main events that take place in the story? How does each event relate to the protagonist's struggle?
- ☐ Where do you find the story's climax, or crisis?
- ☐ How is the conflict resolved?
- ☐ Does the protagonist succeed in achieving his or her goals?
- ☐ What is the impact of success, failure, or a surprising outcome on the protagonist?

WRITING ASSIGNMENT ON PLOT

Choose and read a story from this collection, and write a brief description of its plot and main characters. Then write at length about how the protagonist is changed or tested by the story's events. What do the main character's actions reveal about his or her personality?

Some possible story choices are Updike's "A & P," Alice Walker's "Everyday Use," Alice Munro's "How I Met My Husband," and T. C. Boyle's "Greasy Lake."

MORE TOPICS FOR WRITING

1. Briefly list the events described in "A & P." Now write several paragraphs about the ways in which the story adds up to more than the sum of its events. Why should the reader care about Sammy's thoughts and decisions?

2. How do Sammy's actions in "A & P" reveal his character? In what ways are his thoughts and actions at odds with each other?

3. Write a brief fable modeled on either "The Appointment in Samarra," "The North Wind and the Sun," or "The Tortoise and the Geese." Begin with a familiar proverb—"A penny saved is a penny earned" or "Too many cooks spoil the broth"—and invent a story to make the moral convincing.

4. With "Godfather Death" in mind, write a fairy tale set in the present, in a town or city much like your own. After you've completed your fairy tale, write a paragraph explaining what aspects of the fairy tale by the Brothers Grimm you hoped to capture in your story.

5. The Brothers Grimm collected and wrote down many of our best-known fairy tales—"Cinderella," "Snow White and the Seven Dwarfs," and "Little Red Riding Hood," for example. If you have strong childhood recollections of one of these stories—perhaps based on picture books or on the animated Disney versions—find and read the Brothers Grimm version. Are you surprised by the differences? Write a brief essay contrasting the original with your remembered version. What does the original offer that the adaptation does not?

▶ TERMS FOR *review*

Types of Short Fiction

Fable ▶ A brief, often humorous narrative told to illustrate a moral. The characters in fables are traditionally animals whose personality traits symbolize human traits.

Parable ▶ A brief, usually allegorical narrative that teaches a moral. In parables, unlike fables (where the moral is explicitly stated within the narrative), the moral themes are implicit and can often be interpreted in several ways.

Tale ▶ A short narrative without a complex plot. Tales are an ancient form of narrative found in folklore, and traditional tales often contain supernatural elements. A tale differs from a short story by its tendency toward lesser-developed characters and linear plotting.

Tall tale ▶ A humorous short narrative that provides a wildly exaggerated version of events. Originally an oral form, the tall tale usually assumes that its audience knows the narrator is distorting the events. The form is often associated with the American frontier.

Fairy tale, folktale ▶ A traditional form of short narrative folklore, originally transmitted orally, which features supernatural characters such as witches, giants, fairies, or animals with human personality traits. Fairy tales often feature a hero or heroine who strives to achieve some desirable fate—such as marrying royalty or finding great wealth.

Short story ▶ A prose narrative too brief to be published in a separate volume—as novellas and novels frequently are. The short story is usually a focused narrative that presents one or two characters involved in a single compelling action.

Initiation story ▶ (also called **coming-of-age story**) A narrative in which the main character, usually a child or adolescent, undergoes an important experience (or "rite of passage") that prepares him or her for adulthood.

Elements of Plot

Protagonist ▶ The main or central character in a narrative. The protagonist usually initiates the main action of the story, often in conflict with the antagonist.

Antagonist ▶ The most significant character or force that opposes the protagonist in a narrative. The antagonist may be another character, society itself, a force of nature, or even—in modern literature—conflicting impulses within the protagonist.

Exposition ▶ The opening portion of a narrative. In the exposition, the scene is set, the protagonist is introduced, and the author discloses any other background information necessary for the reader to understand the events that follow.

Conflict ▶ The central struggle between two or more forces in a story. Conflict generally occurs when some person or thing prevents the protagonist from achieving his or her goal. Conflict is the basic material out of which most plots are made.

Complication ▶ The introduction of a significant development in the central conflict between characters (or between a character and his or her situation). Complications may be *external* (an outside problem that the characters cannot avoid) or *internal* (a complication that originates in some important aspect of a character's values or personality).

Crisis ▶ The point in a narrative when the crucial action, decision, or realization must take place. From the Greek word *krisis*, meaning "decision."

Climax ▶ The moment of greatest intensity in a story, which almost inevitably occurs toward the end of the work. The climax often takes the form of a decisive confrontation between the protagonist and antagonist.

Conclusion ▶ In plotting, the logical end or outcome of a unified plot, shortly following the climax. Also called **resolution** or **dénouement** ("the untying of the knot"), as in resolving—or untying the knots created by—plot complications earlier in the narrative.

Narrative Techniques

Foreshadowing ▶ An indication of events to come in a narrative. The author may introduce specific words, images, or actions in order to suggest significant later events.

Flashback ▶ A scene relived in a character's memory. Flashbacks may be related by the narrator in a summary, or they may be experienced by the characters themselves. Flashbacks allow the author to include significant events that occurred before the opening of the story.

Epiphany ▶ A moment of profound insight or revelation by which a character's life is greatly altered.

In medias res ▶ A Latin phrase meaning "in the midst of things"; refers to the narrative device of beginning a story midway in the events it depicts (usually at an exciting or significant moment) before explaining the context or preceding actions.

2

POINT OF VIEW

An author in his book must be like God in his universe,
present everywhere and visible nowhere.

—GUSTAVE FLAUBERT

In the opening lines of *The Adventures of Huckleberry Finn*, Mark Twain takes care to separate himself from the leading character, who is to tell his own story:

> You don't know about me, without you have read a book by the name of *The Adventures of Tom Sawyer*, but that ain't no matter. That book was made by Mr. Mark Twain, and he told the truth, mainly.

Twain wrote the novel, but the **narrator** or speaker is Huck Finn, a fictional character who supposedly tells the story. Obviously, in *Huckleberry Finn*, the narrator of the story is not the same person as the "real-life" author. In employing Huck as his narrator, Twain selects a special angle of vision: not his own, exactly, but that of a resourceful boy moving through the thick of events, with a mind at times shrewd, at other times innocent. Through Huck's eyes, Twain takes in certain scenes, actions, and characters and—as only Huck's angle of vision could have enabled Twain to do so well— records them memorably.

Not every narrator in fiction is, like Huck Finn, a main character, one in the thick of events. Some narrators play only minor parts in the stories they tell; others take no active part at all. In the tale of "Godfather Death," we have a narrator who does not participate in the events he recounts. He is not a character in the story but is someone not even named, who stands at some distance from the action recording what the main characters say and do; recording also, at times, what they think, feel, or desire. He seems to have unlimited knowledge: he even knows the mind of Death, who "because he wanted revenge" let the doctor's candle go out.

More humanly restricted in their knowledge, other narrators can see into the mind of only one character. They may be less willing to express opinions than the narrator of "Godfather Death" ("He ought to have remembered his godfather's warning"). A story may even be told by a narrator who seems so impartial and aloof that he limits himself to reporting only overheard conversation and to describing, without comment or opinion, the appearances of things.

IDENTIFYING POINT OF VIEW

Narrators come in many forms; however, because stories usually are told by some-one, almost every story has some kind of narrator. Some theorists reserve the term *narrator* for a character who tells a story in the first person. We use it in a wider sense, to mean a recording consciousness that an author creates, who may or may not be a participant in the events of the story. It is rare in modern fiction for the "real-life" author to try to step out from behind the typewriter and tell the story. Real persons can tell stories, but when such a story is *written,* the result is usually *nonfiction:* a memoir, an account of travels, an autobiography.

To identify a story's **point of view**, describe the role the narrator plays in the events and any limits placed on his or her knowledge of the events. In a short story, it is usual for the writer to maintain one point of view from beginning to end, but there is nothing to stop him or her from introducing other points of view as well. In his long, panoramic novel *War and Peace,* encompassing the vast drama of Napoleon's invasion of Russia, Leo Tolstoy freely shifts the point of view in and out of the minds of many characters, among them Napoleon himself.

TYPES OF NARRATORS

Theoretically, a great many points of view are possible. A narrator's knowledge might vary in gradations from total omniscience to almost total ignorance. But in reading fiction, again and again we encounter familiar and recognizable points of view. Here is a list of them—admittedly just a rough abstraction—that may provide a few terms with which to discuss the stories that you read and to describe their points of view:

Participant Narrator
- Writes in the first person ("I")
- Can be either a major or minor character

Nonparticipant Narrator
- Writes in the third person ("he," "she")
- Can possess different levels of knowledge about characters
  - **All-knowing** or **omniscient** (sees into any or all of the characters)
  - **Limited omniscience** (sees into one character)
  - **Objective** (does not see into any characters, reports events from outside)

When the narrator is cast as a **participant** in the events of the story, he or she is a dramatized character who says "I." Such a narrator may be the protagonist (Huck Finn) or may be an **observer**, a minor character standing a little to one side, watching a story unfold that mainly involves someone else. A famous example of a partici-pant narrator occurs in F. Scott Fitzgerald's *The Great Gatsby.* The novel's narrator is not Jay Gatsby, but his friend Nick Carraway, who knows only portions of Gatsby's mysterious life.

A narrator who remains a **nonparticipant** does not appear in the story as a charac-ter. Viewing the characters, perhaps seeing into the minds of one or more of them, such a narrator refers to them as "he," "she," or "they."

How Much Does a Narrator Know?

The **all-knowing** (or **omniscient**) narrator sees into the minds of all (or some) characters, moving when necessary from one to another. This is the point of view in "Godfather Death," in which the narrator knows the feelings and motives of the father, of the doctor, and even of Death himself. Since he adds an occasional comment or opinion, this narrator may be said also to show **editorial omniscience** (as we can tell from his disapproving remark that the doctor "should have remembered" and his observation that the father did not understand "how wisely God shares out wealth and poverty"). A narrator who shows **impartial omniscience** presents the thoughts and actions of the characters, but does not judge them or comment on them.

When a nonparticipating narrator sees events through the eyes of a single character, whether a major character or a minor one, the resulting point of view is sometimes called **limited omniscience** or **selective omniscience**. The author, of course, selects which character to see through; the omniscience is his and not the narrator's. In William Faulkner's "Barn Burning" (Chapter 5), the narrator is almost entirely confined to knowing the thoughts and perceptions of a boy, the central character.

In the **objective point of view**, the narrator does not enter the mind of any character but describes events from the outside. Telling us what people say and how their faces look, he or she leaves us to infer their thoughts and feelings. So inconspicuous is the narrator that this point of view has been called "the fly on the wall." This metaphor assumes the existence of a fly with a highly discriminating gaze, who knows which details to look for to communicate the deepest meaning. Some critics would say that in the objective point of view, the narrator disappears altogether. Consider this passage by a writer famous for remaining objective, Dashiell Hammett, in his mystery novel *The Maltese Falcon*, describing his private detective Sam Spade:

> Spade's thick fingers made a cigarette with deliberate care, sifting a measured quantity of tan flakes down into curved paper, spreading the flakes so that they lay equal at the ends with a slight depression in the middle, thumbs rolling the paper's inner edge down and up under the outer edge as forefingers pressed it over, thumb and fingers sliding to the paper cylinder's ends to hold it even while tongue licked the flap, left forefinger and thumb pinching their ends while right forefinger and thumb smoothed the damp seam, right forefinger and thumb twisting their end and lifting the other to Spade's mouth.

In Hammett's novel, this sentence comes at a moment of crisis: just after Spade has been roused from bed in the middle of the night by a phone call telling him that his partner has been murdered. Even in times of stress (we infer) Spade is deliberate, cool, efficient, and painstaking. Hammett refrains from applying all those adjectives to Spade; to do so would be to exercise editorial omniscience and to destroy the objective point of view.

Other Narrative Points of View

Besides the common points of view just listed, uncommon points of view are possible. In *Flush*, a fictional biography of Elizabeth Barrett Browning, Virginia Woolf employs an unusual observer as narrator: the poet's pet cocker spaniel. In "The Circular Valley," a short story by Paul Bowles, a man and a woman are watched by a sinister spirit trying to take possession of them, and we see the human characters through the spirit's vague consciousness.

Also possible, but unusual, is a story written in the second person, *you*. This point of view results in an attention-getting directness, as in Jay McInerney's novel *Bright Lights, Big City* (1985), which begins:

> You are not the kind of guy who would be at a place like this at this time of the morning. But here you are, and you cannot say that the terrain is entirely unfamiliar, although the details are *fuzzy*. You are at a nightclub talking to a girl with a shaved head.

The attitudes and opinions of a narrator aren't necessarily those of the author; in fact, we may notice a lively conflict between what we are told and what, apparently, we are meant to believe. A story may be told by an **innocent narrator** or a **naive narrator**, a character who fails to understand all the implications of the story. One such innocent narrator (despite his sometimes shrewd perceptions) is Huckleberry Finn. Because Huck accepts without question the morality and lawfulness of slavery, he feels guilty about helping Jim, a runaway slave. But, far from condemning Huck for his defiance of the law—"All right, then, I'll *go* to hell," Huck tells himself, deciding against returning Jim to captivity—the author, and the reader along with him, silently applaud.

Naive in the extreme is the narrator of one part of William Faulkner's novel *The Sound and the Fury*, the idiot Benjy, a grown man with the intellect of a child. In a story told by an **unreliable narrator**, the point of view is that of a person who, we perceive, is deceptive, self-deceptive, deluded, or deranged. As though seeking ways to be faithful to uncertainty, contemporary writers have been particularly fond of unreliable narrators.

STREAM OF CONSCIOUSNESS

Virginia Woolf compared life to "a luminous halo, a semi-transparent envelope surrounding us from the beginning of consciousness to the end." To capture such a reality, modern writers of fiction have employed many strategies. One is the method of writing called **stream of consciousness**, from a phrase coined by psychologist William James to describe the procession of thoughts passing through the mind. In fiction, the stream of consciousness is a kind of selective omniscience: the presentation of thoughts and sense impressions in a lifelike fashion—not in a sequence arranged by logic, but mingled randomly. When in his novel *Ulysses* James Joyce takes us into the mind of Leopold Bloom, an ordinary Dublin mind well-stocked with trivia and fragments of odd learning, the reader may have an impression not of a smoothly flowing stream but of an ocean of miscellaneous things, all crowded and jostling.

> As he set foot on O'Connell bridge a puffball of smoke plumed up from the parapet. Brewery barge with export stout. England. Sea air sours it, I heard. Be interesting some day to get a pass through Hancock to see the brewery. Regular world in itself. Vats of porter, wonderful. Rats get in too. Drink themselves bloated as big as a collie floating.

Perceptions—such as the smoke from the brewery barge—trigger Bloom's reflections. A moment later, as he casts a crumpled paper ball off the bridge, he recalls a bit of science he learned in school, the rate of speed of a falling body: "thirty-two feet per sec."

Stream-of-consciousness writing usually occurs in relatively short passages, but in *Ulysses* Joyce employs it extensively. Similar in method, an **interior monologue** is an extended presentation of a character's thoughts, not in the seemingly helter-skelter order of a stream of consciousness, but in an arrangement as if the character were speaking out loud to himself, for us to overhear.

Every point of view has limitations. Even **total omniscience**, a knowledge of the minds of all the characters, has its disadvantages. Such a point of view requires high skill to manage, without the storyteller's losing his or her way in a multitude of perspectives. In fact, there are evident advantages in having a narrator not know everything. We are accustomed to seeing the world through one pair of eyes, to having truths gradually occur to us. Henry James, whose theory and practice of fiction have been influential, held that an excellent way to tell a story was through the fine but bewildered mind of an observer. "It seems probable," James wrote, "that if we were never bewildered there would never be a story to tell about us; we should partake of the superior nature of the all-knowing immortals whose annals are dreadfully dull so long as flurried humans are not, for the positive relief of bored Olympians, mixed up with them."

By using a particular point of view, an author may artfully withhold information, if need be, rather than immediately present it to us. If, for instance, the suspense in a story depends on our not knowing until the end that the protagonist is a spy, the author would be ill advised to tell the story from the protagonist's point of view. Clearly, the author makes a fundamental decision in selecting, from many possibilities, a story's point of view.

Here is a short story memorable for many reasons, among them its point of view.

William Faulkner

A Rose for Emily   1931

William Faulkner (1897–1962) spent most of his days in Oxford, Mississippi, where he attended the University of Mississippi and where he served as postmaster until angry townspeople ejected him because they had failed to receive mail. During World War I he served with the Royal Canadian Air Force and afterward worked as a feature writer for the New Orleans Times-Picayune. *Faulkner's private life was a long struggle to stay solvent: even after fame came to him, he had to write Hollywood scripts and teach at the University of Virginia to support himself. His violent comic novel* Sanctuary *(1931) caused a stir and turned a profit, but critics tend most to admire* The Sound and the Fury *(1929), a tale partially told through the eyes of an idiot;* As I Lay Dying *(1930);* Light in August *(1932);* Absalom, Absalom *(1936); and* The Hamlet *(1940). Beginning with* Sartoris *(1929), Faulkner in*

William Faulkner

his fiction imagines a Mississippi county named Yoknapatawpha and traces the fortunes of several of its families, including the aristocratic Compsons and Sartorises and the white-trash, dollar-grabbing Snopeses, from the Civil War to modern times. His influence on his fellow Southern writers (and others) has been profound. In 1950 he received the Nobel Prize in Literature. Although we think of Faulkner primarily as a novelist, he wrote nearly a hundred short stories. Forty-two of the best are available in his Collected Stories *(1950; 1995).*

I

When Miss Emily Grierson died, our whole town went to her funeral: the men through a sort of respectful affection for a fallen monument, the women mostly out of curiosity to see the inside of her house, which no one save an old manservant—a combined gardener and cook—had seen in at least ten years.

It was a big, squarish frame house that had once been white, decorated with cupolas and spires and scrolled balconies in the heavily lightsome style of the seventies, set on what had once been our most select street. But garages and cotton gins had encroached and obliterated even the august names of that neighborhood; only Miss Emily's house was left, lifting its stubborn and coquettish decay above the cotton wagons and the gasoline pumps—an eyesore among eyesores. And now Miss Emily had gone to join the representatives of those august names where they lay in the cedar-bemused cemetery among the ranked and anonymous graves of Union and Confederate soldiers who fell at the battle of Jefferson.

Alive, Miss Emily had been a tradition, a duty, and a care; a sort of hereditary obligation upon the town, dating from that day in 1894 when Colonel Sartoris, the mayor—he who fathered the edict that no Negro woman should appear on the streets without an apron—remitted her taxes, the dispensation dating from the death of her father on into perpetuity. Not that Miss Emily would have accepted charity. Colonel Sartoris invented an involved tale to the effect that Miss Emily's father had loaned money to the town, which the town, as a matter of business, preferred this way of re-paying. Only a man of Colonel Sartoris' generation and thought could have invented it, and only a woman could have believed it.

When the next generation, with its more modern ideas, became mayors and aldermen, this arrangement created some little dissatisfaction. On the first of the year they mailed her a tax notice. February came, and there was no reply. They wrote her a formal letter, asking her to call at the sheriff's office at her convenience. A week later the mayor wrote her himself, offering to call or to send his car for her, and received in reply a note on paper of an archaic shape, in a thin, flowing calligraphy in faded ink, to the effect that she no longer went out at all. The tax notice was also enclosed, without comment.

They called a special meeting of the Board of Aldermen. A deputation waited ⁵ upon her, knocked at the door through which no visitor had passed since she ceased giving china-painting lessons eight or ten years earlier. They were admitted by the old Negro into a dim hall from which a stairway mounted into still more shadow. It smelled of dust and disuse—a close, dank smell. The Negro led them into the parlor. It was furnished in heavy, leather-covered furniture. When the Negro opened the blinds of one window, they could see that the leather was cracked; and when they sat down, a faint dust rose sluggishly about their thighs, spinning with slow motes in the single sun-ray. On a tarnished gilt easel before the fireplace stood a crayon portrait of Miss Emily's father.

They rose when she entered—a small, fat woman in black, with a thin gold chain descending to her waist and vanishing into her belt, leaning on an ebony cane with a tarnished gold head. Her skeleton was small and spare; perhaps that was why what would have been merely plumpness in another was obesity in her. She looked bloated, like a body long submerged in motionless water, and of that pallid hue. Her eyes, lost in the fatty ridges of her face, looked like two small pieces of coal pressed into a lump of dough as they moved from one face to another while the visitors stated their errand.

She did not ask them to sit. She just stood in the door and listened quietly until the spokesman came to a stumbling halt. Then they could hear the invisible watch ticking at the end of the gold chain.

Her voice was dry and cold. "I have no taxes in Jefferson. Colonel Sartoris explained it to me. Perhaps one of you can gain access to the city records and satisfy yourselves."

"But we have. We are the city authorities, Miss Emily. Didn't you get a notice from the sheriff, signed by him?"

"I received a paper, yes," Miss Emily said. "Perhaps he considers himself the sheriff . . . I have no taxes in Jefferson."   10

"But there is nothing on the books to show that, you see. We must go by the—"

"See Colonel Sartoris. I have no taxes in Jefferson."

"But, Miss Emily—"

"See Colonel Sartoris." (Colonel Sartoris had been dead almost ten years.) "I have no taxes in Jefferson. Tobe!" The Negro appeared. "Show these gentlemen out."

II

So she vanquished them, horse and foot, just as she had vanquished their fathers   15
thirty years before about the smell. That was two years after her father's death and a short time after her sweetheart—the one we believed would marry her—had deserted her. After her father's death she went out very little; after her sweetheart went away, people hardly saw her at all. A few of the ladies had the temerity to call, but were not received, and the only sign of life about the place was the Negro man—a young man then—going in and out with a market basket.

"Just as if a man—any man—could keep a kitchen properly," the ladies said; so they were not surprised when the smell developed. It was another link between the gross, teeming world and the high and mighty Griersons.

A neighbor, a woman, complained to the mayor, Judge Stevens, eighty years old.

"But what will you have me do about it, madam?" he said.

"Why, send her word to stop it," the woman said. "Isn't there a law?"

"I'm sure that won't be necessary," Judge Stevens said. "It's probably just a snake   20
or a rat that nigger of hers killed in the yard. I'll speak to him about it."

The next day he received two more complaints, one from a man who came in diffident deprecation. "We really must do something about it, Judge. I'd be the last one in the world to bother Miss Emily, but we've got to do something." That night the Board of Aldermen met—three graybeards and one younger man, a member of the rising generation.

"It's simple enough," he said. "Send her word to have her place cleaned up. Give her a certain time to do it in, and if she don't . . ."

"Dammit, sir," Judge Stevens said, "will you accuse a lady to her face of smelling bad?"

So the next night, after midnight, four men crossed Miss Emily's lawn and slunk about the house like burglars, sniffing along the base of the brickwork and at the cellar openings while one of them performed a regular sowing motion with his hand out of a sack slung from his shoulder. They broke open the cellar door and sprinkled lime there, and in all the outbuildings. As they recrossed the lawn, a window that had been dark was lighted and Miss Emily sat in it, the light behind her, and her upright torso motionless as that of an idol. They crept quietly across the lawn and into the shadow of the locusts that lined the street. After a week or two the smell went away.

That was when people had begun to feel really sorry for her. People in our town, remembering how old lady Wyatt, her great-aunt, had gone completely crazy at last, believed that the Griersons held themselves a little too high for what they really were. None of the young men were quite good enough for Miss Emily and such. We had long thought of them as a tableau, Miss Emily a slender figure in white in the background, her father a spraddled silhouette in the foreground, his back to her and clutching a horsewhip, the two of them framed by the back-flung front door. So when she got to be thirty and was still single, we were not pleased exactly, but vindicated; even with insanity in the family she wouldn't have turned down all of her chances if they had really materialized.

When her father died, it got about that the house was all that was left to her; and in a way, people were glad. At last they could pity Miss Emily. Being left alone, and a pauper, she had become humanized. Now she too would know the old thrill and the old despair of a penny more or less.

The day after his death all the ladies prepared to call at the house and offer condolence and aid, as is our custom. Miss Emily met them at the door, dressed as usual and with no trace of grief on her face. She told them that her father was not dead. She did that for three days, with the ministers calling on her, and the doctors, trying to persuade her to let them dispose of the body. Just as they were about to resort to law and force, she broke down, and they buried her father quickly.

We did not say she was crazy then. We believed she had to do that. We remembered all the young men her father had driven away, and we knew that with nothing left, she would have to cling to that which had robbed her, as people will.

III

She was sick for a long time. When we saw her again, her hair was cut short, making her look like a girl, with a vague resemblance to those angels in colored church windows—sort of tragic and serene.

The town had just let the contracts for paving the sidewalks, and in the summer after her father's death they began the work. The construction company came with niggers and mules and machinery, and a foreman named Homer Barron, a Yankee—a big, dark, ready man, with a big voice and eyes lighter than his face. The little boys would follow in groups to hear him cuss the niggers, and the niggers singing in time to the rise and fall of picks. Pretty soon he knew everybody in town. Whenever you heard a lot of laughing anywhere about the square, Homer Barron would be in the center of the group. Presently we began to see him and Miss Emily on Sunday afternoons driving in the yellow-wheeled buggy and the matched team of bays from the livery stable.

At first we were glad that Miss Emily would have an interest, because the ladies all said, "Of course a Grierson would not think seriously of a Northerner, a day laborer." But there were still others, older people, who said that even grief could not cause a real lady to forget *noblesse oblige*°—without calling it *noblesse oblige*. They just said, "Poor Emily. Her kinsfolk should come to her." She had some kin in Alabama; but years ago her father had fallen out with them over the estate of old lady Wyatt,

noblesse oblige: the obligation of a member of the nobility to behave with honor and dignity.

the crazy woman, and there was no communication between the two families. They had not even been represented at the funeral.

And as soon as the old people said, "Poor Emily," the whispering began. "Do you suppose it's really so?" they said to one another. "Of course it is. What else could . . ." This behind their hands; rustling of craned silk and satin behind jalousies closed upon the sun of Sunday afternoon as the thin, swift clop-clop-clop of the matched team passed: "Poor Emily."

She carried her head high enough—even when we believed that she was fallen. It was as if she demanded more than ever the recognition of her dignity as the last Grierson; as if it had wanted that touch of earthiness to reaffirm her imperviousness. Like when she bought the rat poison, the arsenic. That was over a year after they had begun to say "Poor Emily," and while the two female cousins were visiting her.

"I want some poison," she said to the druggist. She was over thirty then, still a slight woman, though thinner than usual, with cold, haughty black eyes in a face the flesh of which was strained across the temples and about the eye-sockets as you imagine a lighthouse-keeper's face ought to look. "I want some poison," she said.

"Yes, Miss Emily. What kind? For rats and such? I'd recom—" 35

"I want the best you have. I don't care what kind."

The druggist named several. "They'll kill anything up to an elephant. But what you want is—"

"Arsenic," Miss Emily said. "Is that a good one?"

"Is . . . arsenic? Yes, ma'am. But what you want—"

"I want arsenic." 40

The druggist looked down at her. She looked back at him, erect, her face like a strained flag. "Why, of course," the druggist said. "If that's what you want. But the law requires you to tell what you are going to use it for."

Miss Emily just stared at him, her head tilted back in order to look him eye for eye, until he looked away and went and got the arsenic and wrapped it up. The Negro delivery boy brought her the package; the druggist didn't come back. When she opened the package at home there was written on the box, under the skull and bones: "For rats."

IV

So the next day we all said, "She will kill herself"; and we said it would be the best thing. When she had first begun to be seen with Homer Barron, we had said, "She will marry him." Then we said, "She will persuade him yet," because Homer himself had remarked—he liked men, and it was known that he drank with the younger men in the Elks' Club—that he was not a marrying man. Later we said, "Poor Emily," behind the jalousies as they passed on Sunday afternoon in the glittering buggy, Miss Emily with her head high and Homer Barron with his hat cocked and a cigar in his teeth, reins and whip in a yellow glove.

Then some of the ladies began to say that it was a disgrace to the town and a bad example to the young people. The men did not want to interfere, but at last the ladies forced the Baptist minister—Miss Emily's people were Episcopal—to call upon her. He would never divulge what happened during that interview, but he refused to go back again. The next Sunday they again drove about the streets, and the following day the minister's wife wrote to Miss Emily's relations in Alabama.

So she had blood-kin under her roof again and we sat back to watch develop- 45 ments. At first nothing happened. Then we were sure that they were to be married.

We learned that Miss Emily had been to the jeweler's and ordered a man's toilet set in silver, with the letters H.B. on each piece. Two days later we learned that she had bought a complete outfit of men's clothing, including a nightshirt, and we said, "They are married." We were really glad. We were glad because the two female cousins were even more Grierson than Miss Emily had ever been.

So we were not surprised when Homer Barron—the streets had been finished some time since—was gone. We were a little disappointed that there was not a public blowing-off, but we believed that he had gone on to prepare for Miss Emily's coming, or to give her a chance to get rid of the cousins. (By that time it was a cabal, and we were all Miss Emily's allies to help circumvent the cousins.) Sure enough, after another week they departed. And, as we had expected all along, within three days Homer Barron was back in town. A neighbor saw the Negro man admit him at the kitchen door at dusk one evening.

And that was the last we saw of Homer Barron. And of Miss Emily for some time. The Negro man went in and out with the market basket, but the front door remained closed. Now and then we would see her at a window for a moment, as the men did that night when they sprinkled the lime, but for almost six months she did not appear on the streets. Then we knew that this was to be expected too; as if that quality of her father which had thwarted her woman's life so many times had been too virulent and too furious to die.

When we next saw Miss Emily, she had grown fat and her hair was turning gray. During the next few years it grew grayer and grayer until it attained an even pepper-and-salt iron-gray, when it ceased turning. Up to the day of her death at seventy-four it was still that vigorous iron-gray, like the hair of an active man.

From that time on her front door remained closed, save for a period of six or seven years, when she was about forty, during which she gave lessons in china-painting. She fitted up a studio in one of the downstairs rooms, where the daughters and granddaughters of Colonel Sartoris' contemporaries were sent to her with the same regularity and in the same spirit that they were sent to church on Sundays with a twenty-five-cent piece for the collection plate. Meanwhile her taxes had been remitted.

Then the newer generation became the backbone and the spirit of the town, and the painting pupils grew up and fell away and did not send their children to her with boxes of color and tedious brushes and pictures cut from the ladies' magazines. The front door closed upon the last one and remained closed for good. When the town got free postal delivery, Miss Emily alone refused to let them fasten the metal numbers above her door and attach a mailbox to it. She would not listen to them.

Daily, monthly, yearly we watched the Negro grow grayer and more stooped, going in and out with the market basket. Each December we sent her a tax notice, which would be returned by the post office a week later, unclaimed. Now and then we would see her in one of the downstairs windows—she had evidently shut up the top floor of the house—like the carven torso of an idol in a niche, looking or not looking at us, we could never tell which. Thus she passed from generation to generation—dear, inescapable, impervious, tranquil, and perverse.

And so she died. Fell ill in the house filled with dust and shadows, with only a doddering Negro man to wait on her. We did not even know she was sick; we had long since given up trying to get any information from the Negro. He talked to no one, probably not even to her, for his voice had grown harsh and rusty, as if from disuse.

50

She died in one of the downstairs rooms, in a heavy walnut bed with a curtain, her gray head propped on a pillow yellow and moldy with age and lack of sunlight.

V

The Negro met the first of the ladies at the front door and let them in, with their hushed, sibilant voices and their quick, curious glances, and then he disappeared. He walked right through the house and out the back and was not seen again.

The two female cousins came at once. They held the funeral on the second day, with the town coming to look at Miss Emily beneath a mass of bought flowers, with the crayon face of her father musing profoundly above the bier and the ladies sibilant and macabre; and the very old men—some in their brushed Confederate uniforms—on the porch and the lawn, talking of Miss Emily as if she had been a contemporary of theirs, believing that they had danced with her and courted her perhaps, confusing time with its mathematical progression, as the old do, to whom all the past is not a diminishing road but, instead, a huge meadow which no winter ever quite touches, divided from them now by the narrow bottleneck of the most recent decade of years.

Already we knew that there was one room in that region above stairs which no one had seen in forty years, and which would have to be forced. They waited until Miss Emily was decently in the ground before they opened it.

The violence of breaking down the door seemed to fill this room with pervading dust. A thin, acrid pall as of the tomb seemed to lie everywhere upon this room decked and furnished as for a bridal: upon the valance curtains of faded rose color, upon the rose-shaded lights, upon the dressing table, upon the delicate array of crystal and the man's toilet things backed with tarnished silver, silver so tarnished that the monogram was obscured. Among them lay collar and tie, as if they had just been removed, which, lifted, left upon the surface a pale crescent in the dust. Upon a chair hung the suit, carefully folded; beneath it the two mute shoes and the discarded socks.

The man himself lay in the bed.

For a long while we just stood there, looking down at the profound and fleshless grin. The body had apparently once lain in the attitude of an embrace, but now the long sleep that outlasts love, that conquers even the grimace of love, had cuckolded him. What was left of him, rotted beneath what was left of the nightshirt, had become inextricable from the bed in which he lay; and upon him and upon the pillow beside him lay that even coating of the patient and biding dust.

Then we noticed that in the second pillow was the indentation of a head. One of us lifted something from it, and leaning forward, that faint and invisible dust dry and acrid in the nostrils, we saw a long strand of iron-gray hair.

Questions

1. What is meaningful in the final detail that the strand of hair on the second pillow is *iron-gray?*
2. Who is the unnamed narrator? For whom does he profess to be speaking?
3. Why does "A Rose for Emily" seem better told from his point of view than if it were told (like John Updike's "A & P") from the point of view of the main character?
4. What foreshadowings of the discovery of the body of Homer Barron are we given earlier in the story? Share your experience in reading "A Rose for Emily": did the foreshadowings give away the ending for you? Did they heighten your interest?

5. What contrasts does the narrator draw between changing reality and Emily's refusal or inability to recognize change?

6. How do the character and background of Emily Grierson differ from those of Homer Barron? What general observations about the society that Faulkner depicts can be made from his portraits of these two characters and from his account of life in this one Mississippi town?

7. Does the story seem to you totally grim, or do you find any humor in it?

8. What do you infer to be the author's attitude toward Emily Grierson? Is she simply a murderous madwoman? Why do you suppose Faulkner calls his story "A Rose . . ."?

Edgar Allan Poe

The Tell-Tale Heart   (1843) 1850

Edgar Poe was born in Boston in January 1809, the second son of actors Eliza and David Poe. Edgar inherited his family's legacy of artistic talent, financial instability, and social inferiority (actors were not considered respectable in the nineteenth century), as well as his father's problems with alcohol. David Poe abandoned his family after the birth of Edgar's little sister, Rosalie, and Eliza died of tuberculosis in a Richmond, Virginia, boardinghouse before Edgar turned three. He was taken in by the wealthy John and Frances Allan of Richmond, whose name he added to his own. Allan educated Poe at first-rate schools, where he excelled in all subjects. But he grew into a moody adolescent, and his relationship with his foster father deteriorated.

Edgar Allan Poe

Poe's first year at the University of Virginia was marked by scholastic success, alcoholic binges, and gambling debts. Disgraced, he fled to Boston and joined the army under the name Edgar Perry. He performed well as an enlisted man and published his first collection of poetry, Tamerlane and Other Poems, *at the age of eighteen. After an abortive stint at West Point led to a final break with Allan, Poe embarked on a full-time literary career. A respected critic and editor, he sharply improved both the content and circulation of every magazine with which he was associated. But, morbidly sensitive to criticism, paranoid and belligerent when drunk, he left or was fired from every post he held. Poorly paid as both an editor and a writer, he earned almost nothing from the works that made him famous, such as "The Fall of the House of Usher" and "The Raven."*

After the break with his foster family, Poe rediscovered his own. From 1831, he lived with his father's widowed sister, Maria Clemm, and her daughter, Virginia. In 1836 Poe married this thirteen-year-old first cousin. These women provided him with much-needed emotional stability. However, like his mother, Poe's wife died of tuberculosis at age twenty-four, her demise doubtless hastened by poverty. Afterward, Poe's life came apart; his drinking intensified, as did his self-destructive tendencies. In October 1849 he died in mysterious circumstances, a few days after being found sick and incoherent on a Baltimore street.

True!—nervous—very, very dreadfully nervous I had been and am; but why *will* you say that I am mad? The disease had sharpened my senses—not destroyed—not dulled them. Above all was the sense of hearing acute. I heard all things in the heaven and in the earth. I heard many things in hell. How, then, am I mad? Hearken! and observe how healthily—how calmly, I can tell you the whole story.

It is impossible to say how first the idea entered my brain; but once conceived, it haunted me day and night. Object there was none. Passion there was none. I loved the old man. He had never wronged me. He had never given me insult. For his gold I had no desire. I think it was his eye! yes, it was this! One of his eyes resembled that of a vulture—a pale blue eye, with a film over it. Whenever it fell upon me, my blood ran cold; and so by degrees—very gradually—I made up my mind to take the life of the old man, and thus rid myself of the eye forever.

Now this is the point. You fancy me mad. Madmen know nothing. But you should have seen *me*. You should have seen how wisely I proceeded—with what caution—with what foresight—with what dissimulation I went to work! I was never kinder to the old man than during the whole week before I killed him. And every night, about midnight, I turned the latch of his door and opened it—oh, so gently! And then, when I had made an opening sufficient for my head, I put in a dark lantern, all closed, closed, so that no light shone out, and then I thrust in my head. Oh, you would have laughed to see how cunningly I thrust it in! I moved it slowly—very, very slowly, so that I might not disturb the old man's sleep. It took me an hour to place my whole head within the opening so far that I could see him as he lay upon his bed. Ha!—would a madman have been so wise as this? And then, when my head was well in the room, I undid the lantern cautiously—oh, so cautiously—cautiously (for the hinges creaked)—I undid it just so much that a single thin ray fell upon the vulture eye. And this I did for seven long nights—every night just at midnight—but I found the eye always closed; and so it was impossible to do the work; for it was not the old man who vexed me, but his Evil Eye. And every morning, when the day broke, I went boldly into the chamber, and spoke courageously to him, calling him by name in a hearty tone, and inquiring how he had passed the night. So you see he would have been a very profound old man, indeed, to suspect that every night, just at twelve, I looked in upon him while he slept.

Upon the eighth night I was more than usually cautious in opening the door. A watch's minute hand moves more quickly than did mine. Never before that night had I *felt* the extent of my own powers—of my sagacity. I could scarcely contain my feelings of triumph. To think that there I was, opening the door, little by little, and he not even to dream of my secret deeds or thoughts. I fairly chuckled at the idea; and perhaps he heard me; for he moved on the bed suddenly, as if startled. Now you may think that I drew back—but no. His room was as black as pitch with the thick darkness (for the shutters were close fastened, through fear of robbers), and so I knew that he could not see the opening of the door, and I kept pushing it on steadily, steadily.

I had my head in, and was about to open the lantern, when my thumb slipped upon the tin fastening, and the old man sprang up in the bed, crying out—"Who's there?"

5

I kept quite still and said nothing. For a whole hour I did not move a muscle, and in the meantime I did not hear him lie down. He was still sitting up in the bed, listening;—just as I have done, night after night, hearkening to the death watches° in the wall.

Presently I heard a slight groan, and I knew it was the groan of mortal terror. It was not a groan of pain or of grief—oh, no!—it was the low stifled sound that arises from the bottom of the soul when overcharged with awe. I knew the sound very well. Many a night, just at midnight, when all the world slept, it has welled up from my own bosom, deepening, with its dreadful echo, the terrors that distracted me. I say I knew it well. I knew what the old man felt, and pitied him, although I chuckled at heart. I knew that he had been lying awake ever since the first slight noise, when he had turned in the bed. His fears had been ever since growing upon him. He had been trying to fancy them causeless, but could not. He had been saying to himself—"It is nothing but the wind in the chimney—it is only a mouse crossing the floor," or "it is merely a cricket which has made a single chirp." Yes, he had been trying to comfort himself with these suppositions; but he had found all in vain. *All in vain;* because Death, in approaching him, had stalked with his black shadow before him, and enveloped the victim. And it was the mournful influence of the unperceived shadow that caused him to feel—although he neither saw nor heard—to *feel* the presence of my head within the room.

When I had waited a long time, very patiently, without hearing him lie down, I resolved to open a little—a very, very little crevice in the lantern. So I opened it—you cannot imagine how stealthily, stealthily—until, at length, a single dim ray, like the thread of the spider, shot from out of the crevice and fell upon the vulture eye.

It was open—wide, wide open—and I grew furious as I gazed upon it. I saw it with perfect distinctness—all a dull blue, with a hideous veil over it that chilled the very marrow in my bones; but I could see nothing else of the old man's face or person: for I had directed the ray as if by instinct, precisely upon the damned spot.

And now have I not told you that what you mistake for madness is but over-acuteness of the senses?—now, I say, there came to my ears a low, dull, quick sound, such as a watch makes when enveloped in cotton. I knew *that* sound well, too. It was the beating of the old man's heart. It increased my fury, as the beating of a drum stimulates the soldier into courage.

But even yet I refrained and kept still. I scarcely breathed. I held the lantern motionless. I tried how steadily I could maintain the ray upon the eye. Meantime the hellish tattoo of the heart increased. It grew quicker and quicker, and louder and louder every instant. The old man's terror *must* have been extreme! It grew louder, I say, louder every moment!—do you mark me well? I have told you that I am nervous: so I am. And now at the dead hour of the night, amid the dreadful silence of that old house, so strange a noise as this excited me to uncontrollable terror. Yet, for some minutes longer I refrained and stood still. But the beating grew louder, louder! I thought the heart must burst. And now a new anxiety seized me—the sound would be heard by a neighbor! The old man's hour had come! With a loud yell, I threw open the lantern and leaped into the room. He shrieked once—once only. In an instant I dragged him to the floor, and pulled the heavy bed over him. I then smiled gaily, to find the deed so far done. But, for many minutes, the heart beat on with a muffled sound. This, however, did not vex me; it would not be heard through the wall.

10

---

death watches: beetles that infest timbers. Their clicking sound was thought to be an omen of death.

At length it ceased. The old man was dead. I removed the bed and examined the corpse. Yes, he was stone, stone dead. I placed my hand upon the heart and held it there many minutes.

If still you think me mad, you will think so no longer when I describe the wise precautions I took for the concealment of the body. The night waned, and I worked hastily, but in silence. First of all I dismembered the corpse. I cut off the head and the arms and the legs.

I then took up three planks from the flooring of the chamber, and deposited all between the scantlings. I then replaced the boards so cleverly, so cunningly, that no human eye—not even *his*—could have detected anything wrong. There was nothing to wash out—no stain of any kind—no blood-spot whatever. I had been too wary for that. A tub had caught all—ha! ha!

When I had made an end of these labors, it was four o'clock—still dark as midnight. As the bell sounded the hour, there came a knocking at the street door. I went down to open it with a light heart,—for what had I *now* to fear? There entered three men, who introduced themselves, with perfect suavity, as officers of the police. A shriek had been heard by a neighbor during the night; suspicion of foul play had been aroused, information had been lodged at the police office, and they (the officers) had been deputed to search the premises.

I smiled,—for *what* had I to fear? I bade the gentlemen welcome. The shriek, I   15
said, was my own in a dream. The old man, I mentioned, was absent in the country. I took my visitors all over the house. I bade them search—search *well*. I led them, at length, to *his* chamber. I showed them his treasures, secure, undisturbed. In the enthusiasm of my confidence, I brought chairs into the room, and desired them *here* to rest from their fatigues, while I myself, in the wild audacity of my perfect triumph, placed my own seat upon the very spot beneath which reposed the corpse of the victim.

The officers were satisfied. My *manner* had convinced them. I was singularly at ease. They sat, and while I answered cheerily, they chatted of familiar things. But, ere long, I felt myself getting pale and wished them gone. My head ached, and I fancied a ringing in my ears: but still they sat and still chatted. The ringing became more distinct:—it continued and became more distinct: I talked more freely to get rid of the feeling: but it continued and gained definitiveness—until, at length, I found that the noise was *not* within my ears.

No doubt I now grew *very* pale:—but I talked more fluently, and with a heightened voice. Yet the sound increased—and what could I do? It was a *low, dull, quick sound—much such a sound as a watch makes when enveloped in cotton.* I gasped for breath—and yet the officers heard it not. I talked more quickly—more vehemently; but the noise steadily increased. I arose and argued about trifles, in a high key and with violent gesticulations; but the noise steadily increased. Why *would* they not be gone? I paced the floor to and fro with heavy strides, as if excited to fury by the observations of the men—but the noise steadily increased. Oh God! what *could* I do? I foamed—I raved—I swore! I swung the chair upon which I had been sitting, and grated it upon the boards, but the noise arose over all and continually increased. It grew louder—louder—*louder!* And still the men chatted pleasantly, and smiled. Was it possible they heard not? Almighty God!—no, no! They heard!—they suspected!—they *knew!*—they were making a mockery of my horror!—this I thought, and this I think. But anything was better than this agony! Anything was more tolerable than this derision! I could bear those hypocritical smiles no longer! I felt that I must scream or die!—and now—again!—hark! louder! louder! louder! *louder!—*

"Villains!" I shrieked, "dissemble no more! I admit the deed!—tear up the planks!—here, here!—it is the beating of his hideous heart!"

Questions

1. From what point of view is Poe's story told? Why is this point of view particularly effective for "The Tell-Tale Heart"?
2. Point to details in the story that identify its speaker as an unreliable narrator.
3. What do we know about the old man in the story? What motivates the narrator to kill him?
4. In spite of all his precautions, the narrator does not commit the perfect crime. What trips him up?
5. How do you account for the police officers' chatting calmly with the murderer instead of reacting to the sound that stirs the murderer into a frenzy?
6. See the student essays on this story in the chapter "Writing About a Story" later in the book. What do they point out that enlarges your own appreciation of Poe's art?

Virginia Woolf

A Haunted House   1921

Adeline Virginia Stephen Woolf (1882–1941) was born in London, the daughter of Sir Leslie Stephen, an influential critic and editor of the voluminous Dictionary of National Biography. *Virginia and her sister Vanessa (later Vanessa Bell) were largely self-educated in their father's extensive library while—in a distinction not lost on them—their brothers were sent to college. After their father's death in 1904, Virginia and Vanessa moved to Bloomsbury, a bohemian London neighborhood, and became the center of the "Bloomsbury Group" of progressive artists and intellectuals. Always in frail health, Virginia experienced episodes of mental disturbance. In 1912 she married Leonard Woolf, a journalist and novelist. In 1917 as therapy, they set up a hand-press in their home and started the Hogarth Press, which became one of the most*

Virginia Woolf

celebrated small presses of the century. In addition to Woolf's books, it issued works by T. S. Eliot, Katherine Mansfield, Robinson Jeffers, Edwin Arlington Robinson, and Sigmund Freud. Woolf's first novel was The Voyage Out *(1915); though realistic in technique, it foreshadowed the psychological depth and poetic force of her late work. In innovative novels such as* Mrs. Dalloway *(1925) and* To the Lighthouse *(1927), Woolf became one of the central Modernist writers in English and a pioneer of stream-of-consciousness narration, which portrays the random flow of thoughts and feelings through a character's mind. Her critical essays are collected in* The Common Reader *(1925, second series 1932); her long essay* A Room of One's Own *(1929) is a feminist classic. After several nervous breakdowns, Woolf, fearing for her sanity, drowned herself in 1941.*

Whatever hour you woke there was a door shutting. From room to room they went, hand in hand, lifting here, opening there, making sure—a ghostly couple.

"Here we left it," she said. And he added, "Oh, but here too!" "It's upstairs," she murmured. "And in the garden," he whispered. "Quietly," they said, "or we shall wake them."

But it wasn't that you woke us. Oh, no. "They're looking for it; they're drawing the curtain," one might say, and so read on a page or two. "Now they've found it," one would be certain, stopping the pencil on the margin. And then, tired of reading, one might rise and see for oneself, the house all empty, the doors standing open, only the wood pigeons bubbling with content and the hum of the threshing machine sounding from the farm. "What did I come in here for? What did I want to find?" My hands were empty. "Perhaps it's upstairs then?" The apples were in the loft. And so down again, the garden still as ever, only the book had slipped into the grass.

But they had found it in the drawing room. Not that one could ever see them. The window panes reflected apples, reflected roses; all the leaves were green in the glass. If they moved in the drawing room, the apple only turned its yellow side. Yet, the moment after, if the door was opened, spread about the floor, hung upon the walls, pendant from the ceiling—what? My hands were empty. The shadow of a thrush crossed the carpet; from the deepest wells of silence the wood pigeon drew its bubble of sound. "Safe, safe, safe," the pulse of the house beat softly. "The treasure buried; the room . . ." the pulse stopped short. Oh, was that the buried treasure?

A moment later the light had faded. Out in the garden then? But the trees spun darkness for a wandering beam of sun. So fine, so rare, coolly sunk beneath the surface the beam I sought always burnt behind the glass. Death was the glass; death was between us; coming to the woman first, hundreds of years ago, leaving the house, sealing all the windows; the rooms were darkened. He left it, left her, went North, went East, saw the stars turned in the Southern sky; sought the house, found it dropped beneath the Downs. "Safe, safe, safe," the pulse of the house beat gladly. "The Treasure yours."

The wind roars up the avenue. Trees stoop and bend this way and that. Moonbeams splash and spill wildly in the rain. But the beam of the lamp falls straight from the window. The candle burns stiff and still. Wandering through the house, opening the windows, whispering not to wake us, the ghostly couple seek their joy.

"Here we slept" she says. And he adds, "Kisses without number." "Waking in the morning—" "Silver between the trees—" "Upstairs—" "In the garden—" "When summer came—" "In winter snowtime—" The doors go shutting far in the distance, gently knocking like the pulse of a heart.

Nearer they come; cease at the doorway. The wind falls, the rain slides silver down the glass. Our eyes darken; we hear no steps beside us; we see no lady spread her ghostly cloak. His hands shield the lantern. "Look," he breathes. "Sound asleep. Love upon their lips."

Stooping, holding their silver lamp above us, long they look and deeply. Long they pause. The wind drives straightly; the flame stoops slightly. Wild beams of moonlight cross both floor and wall, and, meeting, stain the faces bent; the faces pondering; the faces that search the sleepers and seek their hidden joy.

"Safe, safe, safe," the heart of the house beats proudly. "Long years—" he sighs. "Again you found me." "Here," she murmurs, "sleeping; in the garden reading;

laughing, rolling apples in the loft. Here we left our treasure—" Stooping, their light lifts the lids upon my eyes. "Safe! safe! safe!" the pulse of the house beats wildly. Waking, I cry "Oh, is this *your* buried treasure? The light in the heart."

Questions

1. Who is telling this story?
2. Note Woolf's pronoun usage, especially in the story's opening paragraphs. Why does she deliberately shift among first-, second-, and third-person perspectives?
3. What does the narrator report that she herself could not have seen or heard? How can she tell us things that she couldn't possibly know?
4. "A Haunted House," according to critic David Daiches, is not a story at all, but "simply an exercise in the writing of fluid associative prose." What do you think? Can any elements we usually find in a story be found in "A Haunted House"?
5. What is the treasure that is being sought? Notice Woolf's use of "silver" at several points of the story. What is the real treasure in the house?
6. What are the implications of the repeated phrase "Safe, safe, safe"?

Eudora Welty

Why I Live at the P.O. 1941

Eudora Welty (1909–2001) was born in Jackson, Mississippi, daughter of an insurance company president. Like William Faulkner, another Mississippi writer, she stayed close to her roots for practically all her life, except for short sojourns at the University of Wisconsin, where she took her B.A., and in New York City, where she studied advertising. She lived most of her life in her childhood home in Jackson, within a stone's throw of the state capitol. Although Welty was a novelist distinguished for The Robber Bridegroom *(1942),* Delta Wedding *(1946),* The Ponder Heart *(1954),* Losing Battles *(1970), and* The Optimist's Daughter *(1972), many critics think her finest work was in the short-story form.* The Collected Stories of Eudora Welty *(1980) gathers the work*

Eudora Welty

of more than forty years. Welty's other books include a memoir, One Writer's Beginnings *(1984), and* The Eye of the Story *(1977), a book of sympathetic criticism on the fiction of other writers, including Willa Cather, Virginia Woolf, Katherine Anne Porter, and Isak Dinesen.* One Time, One Place, *a book of photographs of everyday life that Welty took in Mississippi during the Depression, was republished in a revised edition in 1996.*

I was getting along fine with Mama, Papa-Daddy, and Uncle Rondo until my sister Stella-Rondo just separated from her husband and came back home again. Mr. Whitaker! Of course I went with Mr. Whitaker first, when he first appeared here in China Grove, taking "Pose Yourself" photos, and Stella-Rondo broke us up. Told him I was one-sided. Bigger on one side than the other, which is a deliberate, calculated falsehood: I'm the same. Stella-Rondo is exactly twelve months to the day younger than I am and for that reason she's spoiled.

She's always had anything in the world she wanted and then she'd throw it away. Papa-Daddy gave her this gorgeous Add-a-Pearl necklace when she was eight years old and she threw it away playing baseball when she was nine, with only two pearls.

So as soon as she got married and moved away from home the first thing she did was separate! From Mr. Whitaker! This photographer with the popeyes she said she trusted. Came home from one of those towns up in Illinois and to our complete surprise brought this child of two.

Mama said she like to make her drop dead for a second. "Here you had this marvelous blonde child and never so much as wrote your mother a word about it," says Mama. "I'm thoroughly ashamed of you." But of course she wasn't.

Stella-Rondo just calmly takes off this *hat*. I wish you could see it. She says, 5
"Why, Mama, Shirley-T.'s adopted, I can prove it."

"How?" says Mama, but all I says was, "H'm!" There I was over the hot stove, trying to stretch two chickens over five people and a completely unexpected child into the bargain, without one moment's notice.

"What do you mean—'H'm!'?" says Stella-Rondo, and Mama says, "I heard that, Sister."

I said that oh, I didn't mean a thing, only that whoever Shirley-T. was, she was the spit-image of Papa-Daddy if he'd cut off his beard, which of course he'd never do in the world. Papa-Daddy's Mama's papa and sulks.

Stella-Rondo got furious! She said, "Sister, I don't need to tell you you got a lot of nerve and always did have and I'll thank you to make no future reference to my adopted child whatsoever."

"Very well," I said. "Very well, very well. Of course I noticed at once she looks 10
like Mr. Whitaker's side too. That frown. She looks like a cross between Mr. Whitaker and Papa-Daddy."

"Well, all I can say is she isn't."

"She looks exactly like Shirley Temple to me," says Mama, but Shirley-T. just ran away from her.

So the first thing Stella-Rondo did at the table was turn Papa-Daddy against me.

"Papa-Daddy," she says. He was trying to cut up his meat. "Papa-Daddy!" I was taken completely by surprise. Papa-Daddy is about a million years old and's got this long-long beard. "Papa-Daddy, Sister says she fails to understand why you don't cut off your beard."

So Papa Daddy l-a-y-s down his knife and fork! He's real rich. Mama says he is, 15
he says he isn't. So he says, "Have I heard correctly? You don't understand why I don't cut off my beard?"

"Why," I says, "Papa-Daddy, of course I understand, I did not say any such of a thing, the idea!"

He says, "Hussy!"

I says, "Papa-Daddy, you know I wouldn't any more want you to cut off your beard than the man in the moon. It was the farthest thing from my mind! Stella-Rondo sat there and made that up while she was eating breast of chicken."

But he says, "So the postmistress fails to understand why I don't cut off my beard. Which job I got you through my influence with the government. 'Bird's nest'—is that what you call it?"

Not that it isn't the next to smallest P.O. in the entire state of Mississippi.   20

I says, "Oh, Papa-Daddy," I says, "I didn't say any such of a thing, I never dreamed it was a bird's nest, I have always been grateful though this is the next to smallest P.O. in the state of Mississippi, and I do not enjoy being referred to as a hussy by my own grandfather."

But Stella-Rondo says, "Yes, you did say it too. Anybody in the world could of heard you, that had ears."

"Stop right there," says Mama, looking at *me*.

So I pulled my napkin straight back through the napkin ring and left the table.

As soon as I was out of the room Mama says, "Call her back, or she'll starve to   25
death," but Papa-Daddy says, "This is the beard I started growing on the Coast when I was fifteen years old." He would of gone on till nightfall if Shirley-T. hadn't lost the Milky Way she ate in Cairo.

So Papa-Daddy says, "I am going out and lie in the hammock, and you can all sit here and remember my words: I'll never cut off my beard as long as I live, even one inch, and I don't appreciate it in you at all." Passed right by me in the hall and went straight out and got in the hammock.

It would be a holiday. It wasn't five minutes before Uncle Rondo suddenly appeared in the hall in one of Stella-Rondo's flesh-colored kimonos, all cut on the bias, like something Mr. Whitaker probably thought was gorgeous.

"Uncle Rondo!" I says. "I didn't know who that was! Where are you going?"

"Sister," he says, "get out of my way, I'm poisoned."

"If you're poisoned stay away from Papa-Daddy," I says. "Keep out of the ham-   30
mock. Papa-Daddy will certainly beat you on the head if you come within forty miles of him. He thinks I deliberately said he ought to cut off his beard after he got me the P.O., and I've told him and told him and told him, and he acts like he just don't hear me. Papa-Daddy must of gone stone deaf."

"He picked a fine day to do it then," says Uncle Rondo, and before you could say "Jack Robinson" flew out in the yard.

What he'd really done, he'd drunk another bottle of that prescription. He does it every single Fourth of July as sure as shooting, and it's horribly expensive. Then he falls over in the hammock and snores. So he insisted on zigzagging right on out to the hammock, looking like a half-wit.

Papa-Daddy woke up with this horrible yell and right there without moving an inch he tried to turn Uncle Rondo against me. I heard every word he said. Oh, he told Uncle Rondo I didn't learn to read till I was eight years old and he didn't see how in the world I ever got the mail put up at the P.O., much less read it all, and he said if Uncle Rondo could only fathom the lengths he had gone to get me that job! And he said on the other hand he thought Stella-Rondo had a brilliant mind and deserved credit for getting out of town. All the time he was just lying there swinging as pretty as you please and looping out his beard, and poor Uncle Rondo was *pleading* with him to slow down the hammock, it was making him as dizzy as a witch to watch it. But that's what Papa-Daddy likes about a hammock. So Uncle Rondo was too dizzy to get turned against me for the time being. He's

Mama's only brother and is a good case of a one-track mind. Ask anybody. A certified pharmacist.

Just then I heard Stella-Rondo raising the upstairs window. While she was married she got this peculiar idea that it's cooler with the windows shut and locked. So she has to raise the window before she can make a soul hear her outdoors.

So she raises the window and says, "*Oh!*" You would have thought she was mortally wounded.

Uncle Rondo and Papa-Daddy didn't even look up, but kept right on with what they were doing. I had to laugh.

I flew up the stairs and threw the door open! I says, "What in the wide world's the matter, Stella-Rondo? You mortally wounded?"

"No," she says, "I am not mortally wounded but I wish you would do me the favor of looking out that window there and telling me what you see."

So I shade my eyes and look out the window.

"I see the front yard," I says.

"Don't you see any human beings?" she says.

"I see Uncle Rondo trying to run Papa-Daddy out of the hammock," I says. "Nothing more. Naturally, it's so suffocating-hot in the house, with all the windows shut and locked, everybody who cares to stay in their right mind will have to go out and get in the hammock before the Fourth of July is over."

"Don't you notice anything different about Uncle Rondo?" asks Stella-Rondo.

"Why, no, except he's got on some terrible-looking flesh-colored contraption I wouldn't be found dead in, is all I can see," I says.

"Never mind, you won't be found dead in it, because it happens to be part of my trousseau, and Mr. Whitaker took several dozen photographs of me in it," says Stella-Rondo. "What on earth could Uncle Rondo *mean* by wearing part of my trousseau out in the broad open daylight without saying so much as 'Kiss my foot,' *knowing* I only got home this morning after my separation and hung my negligee up on the bathroom door, just as nervous as I could be?"

"I'm sure I don't know, and what do you expect me to do about it?" I says. "Jump out the window?"

"No, I expect nothing of the kind. I simply declare that Uncle Rondo looks like a fool in it, that's all," she says. "It makes me sick to my stomach."

"Well, he looks as good as he can," I says. "As good as anybody in reason could." I stood up for Uncle Rondo, please remember. And I said to Stella-Rondo, "I think I would do well not to criticize so freely if I were you and came home with a two-year-old child I had never said a word about, and no explanation whatever about my separation."

"I asked you the instant I entered this house not to refer one more time to my adopted child, and you gave me your word of honor you would not," was all Stella-Rondo would say, and started pulling out every one of her eyebrows with some cheap Kress tweezers.

So I merely slammed the door behind me and went down and made some green-tomato pickle. Somebody had to do it. Of course Mama had turned both the niggers loose; she always said no earthly power could hold one anyway on the Fourth of July, so she wouldn't even try. It turned out that Jaypan fell in the lake and came within a very narrow limit of drowning.

So Mama trots in. Lifts up the lid and says, "H'm! Not very good for your Uncle Rondo in his precarious condition, I must say. Or poor little adopted Shirley-T. Shame on you!"

That made me tired. I says, "Well, Stella-Rondo had better thank her lucky stars it was her instead of me came trotting in with that very peculiar-looking child. Now if it had been me that trotted in from Illinois and brought a peculiar-looking child of two, I shudder to think of the reception I'd of got, much less controlled the diet of an entire family."

"But you must remember, Sister, that you were never married to Mr. Whitaker in the first place and didn't go up to Illinois to live," says Mama, shaking a spoon in my face. If you had I would have been just as overjoyed to see you and your little adopted girl as I was to see Stella-Rondo, when you wound up with your separation and came on back home."

"You would not," I says.

"Don't contradict me, I would," says Mama.   55

But I said she couldn't convince me though she talked till she was blue in the face. Then I said, "Besides, you know as well as I do that that child is not adopted."

"She most certainly is adopted," says Mama, stiff as a poker.

I says, "Why, Mama, Stella-Rondo had her just as sure as anything in this world, and just too stuck up to admit it."

"Why Sister," said Mama. "Here I thought we were going to have a pleasant Fourth of July, and you start right out not believing a word your own baby sister tells you!"

"Just like Cousin Annie Flo. Went to her grave denying the facts of life," I   60
remind Mama.

"I told you if you ever mentioned Annie Flo's name I'd slap your face," says Mama, and slaps my face.

"All right, you wait and see," I says.

"I," says Mama, "I prefer to take my children's word for anything when it's humanly possible." You ought to see Mama, she weighs two hundred pounds and has real tiny feet.

Just then something perfectly horrible occurred to me.

"Mama," I says, "can that child talk?" I simply had to whisper! "Mama, I wonder   65
if that child can be—you know—in any way? Do you realize," I says, "that she hasn't spoken one single, solitary word to a human being up to this minute? This is the way she looks," I says, and I looked like this.

Well, Mama and I just stood there and stared at each other. It was horrible!

"I remember well that Joe Whitaker frequently drank like a fish," says Mama. "I believed to my soul he drank *chemicals.*" And without another word she marches to the foot of the stairs and calls Stella-Rondo.

"Stella-Rondo? O-o-o-o-o! Stella-Rondo!"

"What?" says Stella-Rondo from upstairs. Not even the grace to get up off the bed.

"Can that child of yours talk?" asks Mama.   70

Stella-Rondo yells back, "Can she what?"

"Talk! Talk!" says Mama. "Burdyburdyburdyburdy!"

So Stella-Rondo yells back, "Who says she can't talk?"

"Sister says so," says Mama.

"You didn't have to tell me, I know whose word of honor don't mean a thing in   75
this house," says Stella-Rondo.

And in a minute the loudest Yankee voice I ever heard in my life yells out,
"OE'm Pop-OE the Sailor-r-r-r Ma-a-an!" and then somebody jumps up and down
in the upstairs hall. In another second the house would of fallen down.

"Not only talks, she can tap-dance!" calls Stella-Rondo. "Which is more than
some people I won't name can do."

"Why, the little precious darling thing!" Mama says, so surprised. "Just as smart
as she can be!" Starts talking baby talk right there. Then she turns on me. "Sister,
you ought to be thoroughly ashamed! Run upstairs this instant and apologize to
Stella-Rondo and Shirley-T."

"Apologize for what?" I says. "I merely wondered if the child was normal, that's
all. Now that she's proved she is, why, I have nothing further to say."

But Mama just turned on her heel and flew out, furious. She ran right upstairs   80
and hugged the baby. She believed it was adopted. Stella-Rondo hadn't done a thing
but turn her against me from upstairs while I stood there helpless over the hot stove.
So that made Mama, Papa-Daddy, and the baby all on Stella-Rondo's side.

Next, Uncle Rondo.

I must say that Uncle Rondo has been marvelous to me at various times in the
past and I was completely unprepared to be made to jump out of my skin, the way it
turned out. Once Stella-Rondo did something perfectly horrible to him—broke a
chain letter from Flanders Field°—and he took the radio back he had given her and
gave it to me. Stella-Rondo was furious! For six months we all had to call her Stella
instead of Stella-Rondo, or she wouldn't answer. I always thought Uncle Rondo had
all the brains of the entire family. Another time he sent me to Mammoth Cave,°
with all expenses paid.

But this would be the day he was drinking that prescription, the Fourth of July.

So at supper Stella-Rondo speaks up and says she thinks Uncle Rondo ought to
try to eat a little something. So finally Uncle Rondo said he would try a little cold
biscuits and ketchup, but that was all. So *she* brought it to him.

"Do you think it is wise to disport with ketchup in Stella-Rondo's flesh-colored   85
kimono?" I says. Trying to be considerate! If Stella-Rondo couldn't watch out for her
trousseau, somebody had to.

"Any objections?" asks Uncle Rondo, just about to pour out all the ketchup.

"Don't mind what she says, Uncle Rondo," says Stella-Rondo. "Sister has been
devoting this solid afternoon to sneering out my bedroom window at the way you
look."

"What's that?" says Uncle Rondo. Uncle Rondo has got the most terrible temper
in the world. Anything is liable to make him tear the house down if it comes at the
wrong time.

Flanders Field: an Allied military cemetery in Belgium for the dead of World War I, it was made
famous by a poem by John McCrae. The artificial red poppies still sold for charity on Veterans Day
commemorate the cemetery and poem.   *Mammoth Cave*: a network of natural underground caverns
in Kentucky.

So Stella-Rondo says, "Sister says, 'Uncle Rondo certainly does look like a fool in that pink kimono!'"

Do you remember who it was really said that?   90

Uncle Rondo spills out all the ketchup and jumps out of his chair and tears off the kimono and throws it down on the dirty floor and puts his foot on it. It had to be sent all the way to Jackson to the cleaners and re-pleated.

"So that's your opinion of your Uncle Rondo, is it?" he says. "I look like a fool, do I? Well, that's the last straw. A whole day in this house with nothing to do, and then to hear you come out with a remark like that behind my back!"

"I didn't say any such of a thing, Uncle Rondo," I says, "and I'm not saying who did, either. Why, I think you look all right. Just try to take care of yourself and not talk and eat at the same time," I says. "I think you better go lie down."

"Lie down my foot," says Uncle Rondo. I ought to of known by that he was fixing to do something perfectly horrible.

So he didn't do anything that night in the precarious state he was in—just   95
played Casino with Mama and Stella-Rondo and Shirley-T. and gave Shirley-T. a nickel with a head on both sides. It tickled her nearly to death, and she called him "Papa." But at 6:30 A.M. the next morning, he threw a whole five-cent package of some unsold one-inch firecrackers from the store as hard as he could into my bedroom and they every one went off. Not one bad one in the string. Anybody else, there'd be one that wouldn't go off.

Well, I'm just terribly susceptible to noise of any kind, the doctor has always told me I was the most sensitive person he had ever seen in his whole life, and I was simply prostrated. I couldn't eat! People tell me they heard it as far as the cemetery, and old Aunt Jep Patterson, that had been holding her own so good, thought it was Judgment Day and she was going to meet her whole family. It's usually so quiet here.

And I'll tell you it didn't take me any longer than a minute to make up my mind what to do. There I was with the whole entire house on Stella-Rondo's side and turned against me. If I have anything at all I have pride.

So I just decided I'd go straight down to the P.O. There's plenty of room there in the back, I says to myself.

Well! I made no bones about letting the family catch on to what I was up to. I didn't try to conceal it.

The first thing they knew, I marched in where they were all playing Old Maid   100
and pulled the electric oscillating fan out by the plug, and everything got real hot. Next I snatched the pillow I'd done the needlepoint on right off the davenport from behind Papa-Daddy. He went "Ugh!" I beat Stella-Rondo up the stairs and finally found my charm bracelet in her bureau drawer under a picture of Nelson Eddy.°

"So that's the way the land lies," says Uncle Rondo. There he was, piecing on the ham. "Well, Sister, I'll be glad to donate my army cot if you got any place to set it up, providing you'll leave right this minute and let me get some peace." Uncle Rondo was in France.

"Thank you kindly for the cot and 'peace' is hardly the word I would select if I had to resort to firecrackers at 6:30 A.M. in a young girl's bedroom," I says back to

Nelson Eddy: a popular singer (1901–1967) who appeared in romantic musical films during the Depression era.

him. "And as to where I intend to go, you seem to forget my position as postmistress of China Grove, Mississippi," I says. "I've always got the P.O."

Well, that made them all sit up and take notice.

I went out front and started digging up some four-o'clocks to plant around the P.O.

"Ah-ah-ah!" says Mama, raising the window. "Those happen to be my four-o'- 105 clocks. Everything planted in that star is mine. I've never known you to make any-thing grow in your life."

"Very well," I says. "But I take the fern. Even you, Mama, can't stand there and deny that I'm the one watered that fern. And I happen to know where I can send in a box top and get a packet of one thousand mixed seeds, no two the same kind, free."

"Oh, where?" Mama wants to know.

But I says, "Too late. You 'tend to your house, and I'll 'tend to mine. You hear things like that all the time if you know how to listen to the radio. Perfectly marvelous offers. Get anything you want free."

So I hope to tell you I marched in and got that radio, and they could of all bit a nail in two, especially Stella-Rondo, that it used to belong to, and she well knew she couldn't get it back, I'd sue for it like a shot. And I very politely took the sewing-machine motor I helped pay the most on to give Mama for Christmas back in 1929, and a good big calendar, with the first-aid remedies on it. The thermometer and the Hawaiian ukulele certainly were rightfully mine, and I stood on the step-ladder and got all my watermelon-rind preserves and every fruit and vegetable I'd put up, every jar. Then I began to pull the tacks out of the bluebird wall vases on the archway to the dining room.

"Who told you you could have those, Miss Priss?" says Mama, fanning as hard as 110 she could.

"I bought 'em and I'll keep track of 'em," I says. "I'll tack 'em up one on each side the post-office window, and you can see 'em when you come to ask me for your mail, if you're so dead to see 'em."

"Not I! I'll never darken the door to that post office again if I live to be a hun-dred," Mama says. "Ungrateful child! After all the money we spent on you at the Normal."°

"Me either," says Stella-Rondo. "You can just let my mail lie there and *rot*, for all I care. I'll never come and relieve you of a single, solitary piece."

"I should worry," I says. "And who you think's going to sit down and write you all those big fat letters and postcards, by the way? Mr. Whitaker? Just because he was the only man ever dropped down in China Grove and you got him—unfairly—is he going to sit down and write you a lengthy correspondence after you come home giving no rhyme nor reason whatsoever for your separation and no explanation for the presence of that child? I may not have your brilliant mind, but I fail to see it."

So Mama says, "Sister, I've told you a thousand times that Stella-Rondo simply 115 got homesick, and this child is far too big to be hers," and she says, "Now, why don't you just sit down and play Casino?"

Normal: normal school, a two-year college for the training of elementary school teachers.

Then Shirley-T. sticks out her tongue at me in this perfectly horrible way. She has no more manners than the man in the moon. I told her she was going to cross her eyes like that some day and they'd stick.

"It's too late to stop me now," I says. "You should have tried that yesterday. I'm going to the P.O. and the only way you can possibly see me is to visit me there."

So Papa-Daddy says, "You'll never catch me setting foot in that post office, even if I should take a notion into my head to write a letter some place." He says, "I won't have you reachin' out of that little old window with a pair of shears and cuttin' off any beard of mine. I'm too smart for you!"

"We all are," says Stella-Rondo.

But I said, "If you're so smart, where's Mr. Whitaker?"   120

So then Uncle Rondo says, "I'll thank you from now on to stop reading all the orders I get on postcards and telling everybody in China Grove what you think is the matter with them," but I says, "I draw my own conclusions and will continue in the future to draw them." I says, "If people want to write their inmost secrets on penny post-cards, there's nothing in the wide world you can do about it, Uncle Rondo."

"And if you think we'll ever *write* another postcard you're sadly mistaken," says Mama.

"Cutting off your nose to spite your face then," I says. "But if you're all determined to have no more to do with the U.S. mail, think of this: What will Stella-Rondo do now, if she wants to tell Mr. Whitaker to come after her?"

"Wah!" says Stella-Rondo. I knew she'd cry. She had a conniption fit right there in the kitchen.

"It will be interesting to see how long she holds out," I says. "And now—I am   125
leaving."

"Good-by," says Uncle Rondo.

"Oh, I declare," says Mama, "to think that a family of mine should quarrel on the Fourth of July, or the day after, over Stella-Rondo leaving old Mr. Whitaker and having the sweetest little adopted child! It looks like we'd all be glad!"

"Wah!" says Stella-Rondo, and has a fresh conniption fit.

"*He* left *her*—you mark my words," I says. "That's Mr. Whitaker. I know Mr. Whitaker. After all, I knew him first. I said from the beginning he'd up and leave her. I foretold every single thing that's happened."

"Where did he go?" asks Mama.   130

"Probably to the North Pole, if he knows what's good for him," I says.

But Stella-Rondo just bawled and wouldn't say another word. She flew to her room and slammed the door.

"Now look what you've gone and done, Sister," says Mama. "You go apologize."

"I haven't got time, I'm leaving," I says.

"Well, what are you waiting around for?" asks Uncle Rondo.   135

So I just picked up the kitchen clock and marched off, without saying "Kiss my foot," or anything, and never did tell Stella-Rondo good-by.

There was a nigger girl going along on a little wagon right in front.

"Nigger girl," I says, "come help me haul these things down the hill, I'm going to live in the post office."

Took her nine trips in her express wagon. Uncle Rondo came out on the porch and threw her a nickel.

*

And that's the last I've laid eyes on any of my family or my family laid eyes on 140
me for five solid days and nights. Stella-Rondo may be telling the most horrible tales
in the world about Mr. Whitaker, but I haven't heard them. As I tell everybody, I
draw my own conclusions.

But oh, I like it here. It's ideal, as I've been saying. You see, I've got everything
cater-cornered, the way I like it. Hear the radio? All the war news. Radio, sewing machine, book ends, ironing board and that great big piano lamp—peace, that's what I
like. Butter-bean vines planted all along the front where the strings are.

Of course, there's not much mail. My family are naturally the main people in
China Grove, and if they prefer to vanish from the face of the earth, for all the mail
they get or the mail they write, why, I'm not going to open my mouth. Some of the
folks here in town are taking up for me and some turned against me. I know which is
which. There are always people who will quit buying stamps just to get on the right
side of Papa-Daddy.

But here I am, and here I'll stay. I want the world to know I'm happy.

And if Stella-Rondo should come to me this minute, on bended knees, and
attempt to explain the incidents of her life with Mr. Whitaker, I'd simply put my
fingers in both my ears and refuse to listen.

Questions

1. Can we equate the narrator's voice with Welty's? What clues does the author give that
   Sister's opinions are not her own?
2. What statements does the narrator make that seem unreliable?
3. Describe Sister's personality. Is she slightly crazy or is her odd behavior a justified revolt
   against her family?
4. Sister uses the word "nigger" several times in the story, and she is clearly a racist. What
   does her attitude toward African Americans tell you about the time and place of the
   story?
5. Why does Sister fight so much with her family?

James Baldwin

Sonny's Blues   1957

*James Baldwin (1924–1987) was born in Harlem, in New York City. His father was a
Pentecostal minister, and the young Baldwin initially planned to become a clergyman.
While still in high school, he preached sermons in a storefront church. At seventeen,
however, he left home to live in Greenwich Village, where he worked at menial jobs and
began publishing articles in* Commentary *and the* Nation. *Later he embarked on a series of travels that eventually brought him to France. Baldwin soon regarded France as a
second home, a country in which he could avoid the racial discrimination he felt in
America. His first novel,* Go Tell It on the Mountain *(1953), which described a single day in the lives of the members of a Harlem church, immediately earned him a position as a leading African American writer. His next two novels,* Giovanni's Room
(1956) and Another Country *(1962), dealt with homosexual themes and drew criticism from some of his early champions. His collection of essays* Notes of a Native Son
*(1955) remains one of the key books of the civil rights movement. His short stories were
not collected until* Going to Meet the Man *was published in 1965. Although he spent
nearly forty years in France, Baldwin still considered himself an American. He was not*

an expatriate, he claimed, but a "commuter." He died in St. Paul de Vence, France, but was buried in Ardsley, New York.

I read about it in the paper, in the subway, on my way to work. I read it, and I couldn't believe it, and I read it again. Then perhaps I just stared at it, at the newsprint spelling out his name, spelling out the story. I stared at it in the swinging lights of the subway car, and in the faces and bodies of the people, and in my own face, trapped in the darkness which roared outside.

It was not to be believed and I kept telling myself that, as I walked from the subway station to the high school. And at the same time I couldn't doubt it. I was scared, scared for Sonny. He became real to me again. A great block of ice got settled in my belly and kept melting there slowly all day long, while I taught my classes algebra. It was a special kind of ice. It kept melting, sending trickles of ice water all up and down my veins, but it never got less. Sometimes it hardened and seemed to expand until I felt my guts were going to come spilling out or that I was going to choke or scream. This would always be at a moment when I was remembering some specific thing Sonny had once said or done.

When he was about as old as the boys in my classes his face had been bright and open, there was a lot of copper in it; and he'd had wonderfully direct brown eyes, and great gentleness and privacy. I wondered what he looked like now. He had been picked up, the evening before, in a raid on an apartment downtown, for peddling and using heroin.

I couldn't believe it: but what I mean by that is that I couldn't find any room for it anywhere inside me. I had kept it outside me for a long time. I hadn't wanted to know. I had had suspicions, but I didn't name them, I kept putting them away. I told myself that Sonny was wild, but he wasn't crazy. And he'd always been a good boy, he hadn't ever turned hard or evil or disrespectful, the way kids can, so quick, so quick, especially in Harlem. I didn't want to believe that I'd ever see my brother going down, coming to nothing, all that light in his face gone out, in the condition I'd already seen so many others. Yet it had happened and here I was, talking about algebra to a lot of boys who might, every one of them for all I knew, be popping off needles every time they went to the head. Maybe it did more for them than algebra could.

I was sure that the first time Sonny had ever had horse,° he couldn't have been much older than these boys were now. These boys, now, were living as we'd been living then, they were growing up with a rush and their heads bumped abruptly against the low ceiling of their actual possibilities. They were filled with rage. All they really knew were two darknesses, the darkness of their lives, which was now closing in on them, and the darkness of the movies, which had blinded them to that other darkness, and in which they now, vindictively, dreamed, at once more together than they were at any other time, and more alone.

When the last bell rang, the last class ended, I let out my breath. It seemed I'd been holding it for all that time. My clothes were wet—I may have looked as though I'd been sitting in a steam bath, all dressed up, all afternoon. I sat alone in the classroom a long time. I listened to the boys outside, downstairs, shouting and cursing and laughing. Their laughter struck me for perhaps the first time. It was not the joyous laughter which—God knows why—one associates with children. It was mocking and

horse: heroin.

insular, its intent to denigrate. It was disenchanted, and in this, also, lay the authority of their curses. Perhaps I was listening to them because I was thinking about my brother and in them I heard my brother. And myself.

One boy was whistling a tune, at once very complicated and very simple, it seemed to be pouring out of him as though he were a bird, and it sounded very cool and moving through all that harsh, bright air, only just holding its own through all those other sounds.

I stood up and walked over to the window and looked down into the courtyard. It was the beginning of the spring and the sap was rising in the boys. A teacher passed through them every now and again, quickly, as though he or she couldn't wait to get out of that courtyard, to get those boys out of their sight and off their minds. I started collecting my stuff. I thought I'd better get home and talk to Isabel.

The courtyard was almost deserted by the time I got downstairs. I saw this boy standing in the shadow of a doorway, looking just like Sonny. I almost called his name. Then I saw that it wasn't Sonny, but somebody we used to know, a boy from around our block. He'd been Sonny's friend. He'd never been mine, having been too young for me, and, anyway, I'd never liked him. And now, even though he was a grown-up man, he still hung around that block, still spent hours on the street corners, was always high and raggy. I used to run into him from time to time and he'd often work around to asking me for a quarter or fifty cents. He always had some real good excuse, too, and I always gave it to him, I don't know why.

But now, abruptly, I hated him. I couldn't stand the way he looked at me, partly like a dog, partly like a cunning child. I wanted to ask him what the hell he was doing in the school courtyard. | 10

He sort of shuffled over to me, and he said, "I see you got the papers. So you already know about it."

"You mean about Sonny? Yes, I already know about it. How come they didn't get you?"

He grinned. It made him repulsive and it also brought to mind what he'd looked like as a kid. "I wasn't there. I stay away from them people."

"Good for you." I offered him a cigarette and I watched him through the smoke. "You come all the way down here just to tell me about Sonny?"

"That's right." He was sort of shaking his head and his eyes looked strange, as | 15 though they were about to cross. The bright sun deadened his damp dark brown skin and it made his eyes look yellow and showed up the dirt in his kinked hair. He smelled funky. I moved a little away from him and I said, "Well, thanks. But I already know about it and I got to get home."

"I'll walk you a little ways," he said. We started walking. There were a couple of kids still loitering in the courtyard and one of them said goodnight to me and looked strangely at the boy beside me.

"What're you going to do?" he asked me. "I mean, about Sonny?"

"Look. I haven't seen Sonny for over a year. I'm not sure I'm going to do anything. Anyway, what the hell *can* I do?"

"That's right," he said quickly, "ain't nothing you can do. Can't much help old Sonny no more, I guess."

It was what I was thinking and so it seemed to me he had no right to say it. | 20

"I'm surprised at Sonny, though," he went on—he had a funny way of talking, he looked straight ahead as though he were talking to himself—"I thought Sonny was a smart boy, I thought he was too smart to get hung."

"I guess he thought so too," I said sharply, "and that's how he got hung. And how about you? You're pretty goddamn smart, I bet."

Then he looked directly at me, just for a minute. "I ain't smart," he said. "If I was smart, I'd have reached for a pistol a long time ago."

"Look. Don't tell *me* your sad story, if it was up to me, I'd give you one." Then I felt guilty—guilty, probably, for never having supposed that the poor bastard *had* a story of his own, much less a sad one, and I asked, quickly, "What's going to happen to him now?"

He didn't answer this. He was off by himself some place. "Funny thing," he said,   25
and from his tone we might have been discussing the quickest way to get to Brooklyn, "when I saw the papers this morning, the first thing I asked myself was if I had anything to do with it. I felt sort of responsible."

I began to listen more carefully. The subway station was on the corner, just before us, and I stopped. He stopped, too. We were in front of a bar and he ducked slightly, peering in, but whoever he was looking for didn't seem to be there. The juke box was blasting away with something black and bouncy and I half watched the barmaid as she danced her way from the juke box to her place behind the bar. And I watched her face as she laughingly responded to something someone said to her, still keeping time to the music. When she smiled one saw the little girl, one sensed the doomed, still-struggling woman beneath the battered face of the semi-whore.

"I never *give* Sonny nothing," the boy said finally, "but a long time ago I come to school high and Sonny asked me how it felt." He paused, I couldn't bear to watch him, I watched the barmaid, and I listened to the music which seemed to be causing the pavement to shake. "I told him it felt great." The music stopped, the barmaid paused and watched the juke box until the music began again. "It did."

All this was carrying me some place I didn't want to go. I certainly didn't want to know how it felt. It filled everything, the people, the houses, the music, the dark, quicksilver barmaid, with menace; and this menace was their reality.

"What's going to happen to him now?" I asked again.

"They'll send him away some place and they'll try to cure him." He shook his   30
head. "Maybe he'll even think he's kicked the habit. Then they'll let him loose"—he gestured, throwing his cigarette into the gutter. "That's all."

"What do you mean, that's *all?*"

But I knew what he meant.

"I *mean,* that's *all.*" He turned his head and looked at me, pulling down the corners of his mouth. "Don't you know what I mean?" he asked, softly.

"How the hell *would* I know what you mean?" I almost whispered it, I don't know why.

"That's right," he said to the air, "how would *he* know what I mean?" He turned to-   35
ward me again, patient and calm, and yet I somehow felt him shaking, shaking as though he were going to fall apart. I felt that ice in my guts again, the dread I'd felt all afternoon; and again I watched the barmaid, moving about the bar, washing glasses, and singing. "Listen. They'll let him out and then it'll just start all over again. That's what I mean."

"You mean—they'll let him out. And then he'll just start working his way back in again. You mean he'll never kick the habit. Is that what you mean?"

"That's right," he said, cheerfully. "*You* see what I mean."

"Tell me," I said at last, "why does he want to die? He must want to die, he's killing himself, why does he want to die?"

He looked at me in surprise. He licked his lips. "He don't want to die. He wants to live. Don't nobody want to die, ever."

Then I wanted to ask him—too many things. He could not have answered, or if he had, I could not have borne the answers. I started walking. "Well, I guess it's none of my business." 40

"It's going to be rough on old Sonny," he said. We reached the subway station. "This is your station?" he asked. I nodded. I took one step down. "Damn!" he said, suddenly. I looked up at him. He grinned again. "Damn it if I didn't leave all my money home. You ain't got a dollar on you, have you? Just for a couple of days, is all."

All at once something inside gave and threatened to come pouring out of me. I didn't hate him any more. I felt that in another moment I'd start crying like a child.

"Sure," I said. "Don't sweat." I looked in my wallet and didn't have a dollar, I only had a five. "Here," I said. "That hold you?"

He didn't look at it—he didn't want to look at it. A terrible closed look came over his face, as though he were keeping the number on the bill a secret from him and me. "Thanks," he said, and now he was dying to see me go. "Don't worry about Sonny. Maybe I'll write him or something."

"Sure," I said. "You do that. So long." 45

"Be seeing you," he said. I went on down the steps.

And I didn't write Sonny or send him anything for a long time. When I finally did, it was just after my little girl died, he wrote me back a letter which made me feel like a bastard.

Here's what he said:

Dear brother,

You don't know how much I needed to hear from you. I wanted to write you many a time but I dug how much I must have hurt you and so I didn't write. But now I feel like a man who's been trying to climb up out of some deep, real deep and funky hole and just saw the sun up there, outside. I got to get outside.

I can't tell you much about how I got here. I mean I don't know how to tell you. I guess I was afraid of something or I was trying to escape from something and you know I have never been very strong in the head (smile). I'm glad Mama and Daddy are dead and can't see what's happened to their son and I swear if I'd known what I was doing I would never have hurt you so, you and a lot of other fine people who were nice to me and who believed in me.

I don't want you to think it had anything to do with me being a musician. It's more than that. Or maybe less than that. I can't get anything straight in my head down here and I try not to think about what's going to happen to me when I get outside again. Sometime I think I'm going to flip and *never* get outside and sometime I think I'll come straight back. I tell you one thing, though, I'd rather blow my brains out than go through this again. But that's what they all say, so they tell me. If I tell you when I'm coming to New York and if you could meet me, I sure would appreciate it. Give my love to Isabel and the kids and I was sure sorry to hear about little Gracie. I wish I could be like Mama and say the Lord's will be done, but I don't know it seems to me that trouble is the one thing that never does get stopped and I don't know what good it does to blame it on the Lord. But maybe it does some good if you believe it.

Your brother,
Sonny

Then I kept in constant touch with him and I sent him whatever I could and I went to meet him when he came back to New York. When I saw him many things I thought I had forgotten came flooding back to me. This was because I had begun, finally, to wonder about Sonny, about the life that Sonny lived inside. This life, whatever it was, had made him older and thinner and it had deepened the distant stillness in which he had always moved. He looked very unlike my baby brother. Yet, when he smiled, when we shook hands, the baby brother I'd never known looked out from the depths of his private life, like an animal waiting to be coaxed into the light.

"How you been keeping?" he asked me.   50

"All right. And you?"

"Just fine." He was smiling all over his face. "It's good to see you again."

"It's good to see you."

The seven years' difference in our ages lay between us like a chasm: I wondered if these years would ever operate between us as a bridge. I was remembering, and it made it hard to catch my breath, that I had been there when he was born; and I had heard the first words he had ever spoken. When he started to walk, he walked from our mother straight to me. I caught him just before he fell when he took the first steps he ever took in this world.

"How's Isabel?"   55

"Just fine. She's dying to see you."

"And the boys?"

"They're fine, too. They're anxious to see their uncle."

"Oh, come on. You know they don't remember me."

"Are you kidding? Of course they remember you."   60

He grinned again. We got into a taxi. We had a lot to say to each other, far too much to know how to begin.

As the taxi began to move, I asked, "You still want to go to India?"

He laughed. "You still remember that. Hell, no. This place is Indian enough for me."

"It used to belong to them," I said.

And he laughed again. "They damn sure knew what they were doing when they   65
got rid of it."

Years ago, when he was around fourteen, he'd been all hipped on the idea of going to India. He read books about people sitting on rocks, naked, in all kinds of weather, but mostly bad, naturally, and walking barefoot through hot coals and arriving at wisdom. I used to say that it sounded to me as though they were getting away from wisdom as fast as they could. I think he sort of looked down on me for that.

"Do you mind," he asked, "if we have the driver drive alongside the park? On the west side—I haven't seen the city in so long."

"Of course not," I said. I was afraid that I might sound as though I were humoring him, but I hoped he wouldn't take it that way.

So we drove along, between the green of the park and the stony, lifeless elegance of hotels and apartment buildings, toward the vivid, killing streets of our childhood. These streets hadn't changed, though housing projects jutted up out of them now like rocks in the middle of a boiling sea. Most of the houses in which we had grown up had vanished, as had the stores from which we had stolen, the basements in which we had first tried sex, the rooftops from which we had hurled tin cans and bricks. But houses exactly like the houses of our past yet dominated the landscape, boys exactly like the boys we once had been found themselves smothering in these houses, came down into the streets for light and air and found themselves encircled by disaster. Some escaped the trap, most didn't. Those who got out always left something of themselves behind, as some animals amputate a leg and leave it in the trap. It might be said, perhaps, that I had escaped, after all, I was a school teacher; or that Sonny had, he hadn't lived in Harlem for years. Yet, as the cab moved uptown through streets which seemed, with a rush, to darken with dark people, and as I covertly studied Sonny's face, it came to me that what we both were seeking through our separate cab windows was that part of ourselves which had been left behind. It's always at the hour of trouble and confrontation that the missing member aches.

We hit 110th Street and started rolling up Lenox Avenue. And I'd known this avenue all my life, but it seemed to me again, as it had seemed on the day I'd first heard about Sonny's trouble, filled with a hidden menace which was its very breath of life.

"We almost there," said Sonny.

"Almost." We were both too nervous to say anything more.

We live in a housing project. It hasn't been up long. A few days after it was up it seemed uninhabitably new, now, of course, it's already rundown. It looks like a parody of the good, clean, faceless life—God knows the people who live in it do their best to make it a parody. The beat-looking grass lying around isn't enough to make their lives green, the hedges will never hold out the streets, and they know it. The big windows fool no one, they aren't big enough to make space out of no space. They don't bother with the windows, they watch the TV screen instead. The playground is most popular with the children who don't play at jacks, or skip rope, or roller skate, or swing, and they can be found in it after dark. We moved in partly because it's not too far from where I teach, and partly for the kids; but it's really just like the houses in which Sonny and I grew up. The same things happen, they'll have the same things to remember. The moment Sonny and I started into the house I had the feeling that I was simply bringing him back into the danger he had almost died trying to escape.

Sonny has never been talkative. So I don't know why I was sure he'd be dying to talk to me when supper was over the first night. Everything went fine, the oldest boy remembered him, and the youngest boy liked him, and Sonny had remembered to bring something for each of them; and Isabel, who is really much nicer than I am, more open and giving, had gone to a lot of trouble about dinner and was genuinely glad to see him. And she's always been able to tease Sonny in a way that I haven't. It was nice to see her face so vivid again and to hear her laugh and watch her make Sonny laugh. She wasn't, or, anyway, she didn't seem to be, at all uneasy or embarrassed. She chatted as though there were no subject which had to be avoided and she got Sonny past his first, faint stiffness. And thank God she was there, for I was filled with that icy dread again. Everything I did seemed awkward to me, and everything I said sounded freighted with hidden meaning. I was trying to remember everything I'd heard about dope addiction and I couldn't help watching Sonny for signs. I wasn't

70

doing it out of malice. I was trying to find out something about my brother. I was dying to hear him tell me he was safe.

"Safe!" my father grunted, whenever Mama suggested trying to move to a neighborhood which might be safer for children. "Safe, hell! Ain't no place safe for kids, nor nobody." 75

He always went on like this, but he wasn't, ever, really as bad as he sounded, not even on weekends, when he got drunk. As a matter of fact, he was always on the lookout for "something a little better," but he died before he found it. He died suddenly, during a drunken weekend in the middle of the war, when Sonny was fifteen. He and Sonny hadn't ever got on too well. And this was partly because Sonny was the apple of his father's eye. It was because he loved Sonny so much and was frightened for him, that he was always fighting with him. It doesn't do any good to fight with Sonny. Sonny just moves back, inside himself, where he can't be reached. But the principal reason that they never hit it off is that they were so much alike. Daddy was big and rough and loud-talking, just the opposite of Sonny, but they both had—that same privacy.

Mama tried to tell me something about this, just after Daddy died. I was home on leave from the army.

This was the last time I ever saw my mother alive. Just the same, this picture gets all mixed up in my mind with pictures I had of her when she was younger. The way I always see her is the way she used to be on a Sunday afternoon, say, when the old folks were talking after the big Sunday dinner. I always see her wearing pale blue. She'd be sitting on the sofa. And my father would be sitting in the easy chair, not far from her. And the living room would be full of church folks and relatives. There they sit, in chairs all around the living room, and the night is creeping up outside, but nobody knows it yet. You can see the darkness growing against the windowpanes and you hear the street noises every now and again, or maybe the jangling beat of a tambourine from one of the churches close by, but it's real quiet in the room. For a moment nobody's talking, but every face looks darkening, like the sky outside. And my mother rocks a little from the waist, and my father's eyes are closed. Everyone is looking at something a child can't see. For a minute they've forgotten the children. Maybe a kid is lying on the rug, half asleep. Maybe somebody's got a kid in his lap and is absent-mindedly stroking the kid's head. Maybe there's a kid, quiet and big-eyed, curled up in a big chair in the corner. The silence, the darkness coming, and the darkness in the faces frightens the child obscurely. He hopes that the hand which strokes his forehead will never stop—will never die. He hopes that there will never come a time when the old folks won't be sitting around the living room, talking about where they've come from, and what they've seen, and what's happened to them and their kinfolk.

But something deep and watchful in the child knows that this is bound to end, is already ending. In a moment someone will get up and turn on the light. Then the old folks will remember the children and they won't talk any more that day. And when light fills the room, the child is filled with darkness. He knows that every time this happens he's moved just a little closer to that darkness outside. The darkness outside is what the old folks have been talking about. It's what they've come from. It's what they endure. The child knows that they won't talk any more because if he knows too much about what's happened to *them*, he'll know too much too soon, about what's going to happen to *him*.

The last time I talked to my mother, I remember I was restless. I wanted to get 80
out and see Isabel. We weren't married then and we had a lot to straighten out
between us.

There Mama sat, in black, by the window. She was humming an old church
song, *Lord, you brought me from a long ways off.* Sonny was out somewhere. Mama
kept watching the streets.

"I don't know," she said, "if I'll ever see you again, after you go off from here. But
I hope you'll remember the things I tried to teach you."

"Don't talk like that," I said, and smiled. "You'll be here a long time yet."

She smiled, too, but she said nothing. She was quiet for a long time. And I said,
"Mama, don't you worry about nothing. I'll be writing all the time, and you be getting
the checks . . ."

"I want to talk to you about your brother," she said, suddenly. "If anything hap- 85
pens to me he ain't going to have nobody to look out for him."

"Mama," I said, "ain't nothing going to happen to you *or* Sonny. Sonny's all
right. He's a good boy and he's got good sense."

"It ain't a question of his being a good boy," Mama said, "nor of his having good
sense. It ain't only the bad ones, nor yet the dumb ones that gets sucked under." She
stopped, looking at me. "Your Daddy once had a brother," she said, and she smiled in
a way that made me feel she was in pain. "You didn't never know that, did you?"

"No," I said, "I never knew that," and I watched her face.

"Oh, yes," she said, "your Daddy had a brother." She looked out of the window
again. "I know you never saw your Daddy cry. But *I* did—many a time, through all
these years."

I asked her, "What happened to his brother? How come nobody's ever talked 90
about him?"

This was the first time I ever saw my mother look old.

"His brother got killed," she said, "when he was just a little younger than you are
now. I knew him. He was a fine boy. He was maybe a little full of the devil, but he
didn't mean nobody no harm."

Then she stopped and the room was silent, exactly as it had sometimes been on
those Sunday afternoons. Mama kept looking out into the streets.

"He used to have a job in the mill," she said, "and, like all young folks, he just
liked to perform on Saturday nights. Saturday nights, him and your father would drift
around to different places, go to dances and things like that, or just sit around with
people they knew, and your father's brother would sing, he had a fine voice, and play
along with himself on his guitar. Well, this particular Saturday night, him and your
father was coming home from some place, and they were both a little drunk and
there was a moon that night, it was bright like day. Your father's brother was feeling
kind of good, and he was whistling to himself, and he had his guitar slung over his
shoulder. They was coming down a hill and beneath them was a road that turned off
from the highway. Well, your father's brother, being always kind of frisky, decided to
run down this hill, and he did, with that guitar banging and clanging behind him,
and he ran across the road, and he was making water behind a tree. And your father
was sort of amused at him and he was still coming down the hill, kind of slow. Then
he heard a car motor and that same minute his brother stepped from behind the tree,
into the road, in the moonlight. And he started to cross the road. And your father
started to run down the hill, he says he don't know why. This car was full of white

men. They was all drunk, and when they seen your father's brother they let out a great whoop and holler and they aimed the car straight at him. They was having fun, they just wanted to scare him, the way they do sometimes, you know. But they was drunk. And I guess the boy, being drunk, too, and scared, kind of lost his head. By the time he jumped it was too late. Your father says he heard his brother scream when the car rolled over him, and he heard the wood of that guitar when it give, and he heard them strings go flying, and he heard them white men shouting, and the car kept on a-going and it ain't stopped till this day. And, time your father got down the hill, his brother weren't nothing but blood and pulp."

Tears were gleaming on my mother's face. There wasn't anything I could say. 95

"He never mentioned it," she said, "because I never let him mention it before you children. Your Daddy was like a crazy man that night and for many a night thereafter. He says he never in his life seen anything as dark as that road after the lights of that car had gone away. Weren't nothing, weren't nobody on that road, just your Daddy and his brother and that busted guitar. Oh, yes. Your Daddy never did really get right again. Till the day he died he weren't sure but that every white man he saw was the man that killed his brother."

She stopped and took out her handkerchief and dried her eyes and looked at me.

"I ain't telling you all this," she said, "to make you scared or bitter or to make you hate nobody. I'm telling you this because you got a brother. And the world ain't changed."

I guess I didn't want to believe this. I guess she saw this in my face. She turned away from me, toward the window again, searching those streets.

"But I praise my Redeemer," she said at last, "that He called your Daddy home 100 before me. I ain't saying it to throw no flowers at myself, but, I declare, it keeps me from feeling too cast down to know I helped your father get safely through this world. Your father always acted like he was the roughest, strongest man on earth. And everybody took him to be like that. But if he hadn't had *me* there—to see his tears!"

She was crying again. Still, I couldn't move. I said, "Lord, Lord, Mama, I didn't know it was like that."

"Oh, honey," she said, "there's a lot that you don't know. But you are going to find it out." She stood up from the window and came over to me. "You got to hold on to your brother," she said, "and don't let him fall, no matter what it looks like is happening to him and no matter how evil you gets with him. You going to be evil with him many a time. But don't you forget what I told you, you hear?"

"I won't forget," I said. "Don't you worry, I won't forget. I won't let nothing happen to Sonny."

My mother smiled as though she were amused at something she saw in my face. Then, "You may not be able to stop nothing from happening. But you got to let him know you's *there*."

Two days later I was married, and then I was gone. And I had a lot of things on 105 my mind and I pretty well forgot my promise to Mama until I got shipped home on a special furlough for her funeral.

And, after the funeral, with just Sonny and me alone in the empty kitchen, I tried to find out something about him.

"What do you want to do?" I asked him.

"I'm going to be a musician," he said.

For he had graduated, in the time I had been away, from dancing to the juke box to finding out who was playing what, and what they were doing with it, and he had bought himself a set of drums.

"You mean, you want to be a drummer?" I somehow had the feeling that being a   110 drummer might be all right for other people but not for my brother Sonny.

"I don't think," he said, looking at me very gravely, "that I'll ever be a good drummer. But I think I can play a piano."

I frowned. I'd never played the role of the older brother quite so seriously before, had scarcely ever, in fact, *asked* Sonny a damn thing. I sensed myself in the presence of something I didn't really know how to handle, didn't understand. So I made my frown a little deeper as I asked: "What kind of musician do you want to be?"

He grinned. "How many kinds do you think there are?"

"Be *serious*," I said.

He laughed, throwing his head back, and then looked at me. "I *am* serious."   115

"Well, then, for Christ's sake, stop kidding around and answer a serious question. I mean, do you want to be a concert pianist, you want to play classical music and all that, or—or what?" Long before I finished he was laughing again. "For Christ's *sake*, Sonny!"

He sobered, but with difficulty. "I'm sorry. But you sound so—*scared!*" and he was off again.

"Well, you may think it's funny now, baby, but it's not going to be so funny when you have to make your living at it, let me tell you *that*." I was furious because I knew he was laughing at me and I didn't know why.

"No," he said, very sober now, and afraid, perhaps, that he'd hurt me, "I don't want to be a classical pianist. That isn't what interests me. I mean"—he paused, looking hard at me, as though his eyes would help me to understand, and then gestured helplessly, as though perhaps his hand would help—"I mean, I'll have a lot of studying to do, and I'll have to study *everything*, but, I mean, I want to play *with*—jazz musicians." He stopped. "I want to play jazz," he said.

Well, the word had never before sounded as heavy, as real, as it sounded that   120 afternoon in Sonny's mouth. I just looked at him and I was probably frowning a real frown by this time. I simply couldn't see why on earth he'd want to spend his time hanging around nightclubs, clowning around on bandstands, while people pushed each other around a dance floor. It seemed—beneath him, somehow. I had never thought about it before, had never been forced to, but I suppose I had always put jazz musicians in a class with what Daddy called "goodtime people."

"Are you *serious?*"

"Hell, *yes*, I'm serious."

He looked more helpless than ever, and annoyed, and deeply hurt.

I suggested, helpfully: "You mean—like Louis Armstrong?"°

His face closed as though I'd struck him. "No. I'm not talking about none of that   125 old-time, down home crap."

"Well, look, Sonny, I'm sorry, don't get mad. I just don't altogether get it, that's all. Name somebody—you know, a jazz musician you admire."

Louis Armstrong: jazz trumpeter and vocalist (1900–1971) born in New Orleans. In the 1950s his music would have been considered conservative by progressive jazz fans.

"Bird."

"Who?"

"Bird! Charlie Parker!° Don't they teach you nothing in the goddamn army?"

I lit a cigarette. I was surprised and then a little amused to discover that I was 130
trembling. "I've been out of touch," I said. "You'll have to be patient with me. Now.
Who's this Parker character?"

"He's just one of the greatest jazz musicians alive," said Sonny, sullenly, his
hands in his pockets, his back to me. "Maybe *the* greatest," he added, bitterly, "that's
probably why *you* never heard of him."

"All right," I said, "I'm ignorant. I'm sorry. I'll go out and buy all the cat's records
right away, all right?"

"It don't," said Sonny, with dignity, "make any difference to me. I don't care
what you listen to. Don't do me no favors."

I was beginning to realize that I'd never seen him so upset before. With another
part of my mind I was thinking that this would probably turn out to be one of those
things kids go through and that I shouldn't make it seem important by pushing it too
hard. Still, I didn't think it would do any harm to ask: "Doesn't all this take a lot of
time? Can you make a living at it?"

He turned back to me and half leaned, half sat, on the kitchen table. "Every- 135
thing takes time," he said, "and—well, yes, sure, I can make a living at it. But what I
don't seem to be able to make you understand is that it's the only thing I want to do."

"Well, Sonny," I said, gently, "you know people can't always do exactly what
they *want* to do—"

"*No,* I don't know that," said Sonny, surprising me. "I think people *ought* to do
what they want to do, what else are they alive for?"

"You getting to be a big boy," I said desperately, "it's time you started thinking
about your future."

"I'm thinking about my future," said Sonny, grimly. "I think about it all the time."

I gave up. I decided, if he didn't change his mind, that we could always talk 140
about it later. "In the meantime," I said, "you got to finish school." We had already
decided that he'd have to move in with Isabel and her folks. I knew this wasn't the
ideal arrangement because Isabel's folks are inclined to be dicty° and they hadn't especially wanted Isabel to marry me. But I didn't know what else to do. "And we have
to get you fixed up at Isabel's."

There was a long silence. He moved from the kitchen table to the window.
"That's a terrible idea. You know it yourself."

"Do you have a *better* idea?"

He just walked up and down the kitchen for a minute. He was as tall as I was. He
had started to shave. I suddenly had the feeling that I didn't know him at all.

He stopped at the kitchen table and picked up my cigarettes. Looking at me
with a kind of mocking, amused defiance, he put one between his lips. "You
mind?"

"You smoking already?"

145

Charlie Parker: a jazz saxophonist (1920–1955) who helped create the progressive jazz style called
bebop. Parker was a heroin addict who died at an early age.   *dicty:* slang word for stylish, high-
class; snobbish.

He lit the cigarette and nodded, watching me through the smoke. "I just wanted to see if I'd have the courage to smoke in front of you." He grinned and blew a great cloud of smoke to the ceiling. "It was easy." He looked at my face. "Come on, now. I bet you was smoking at my age, tell the truth."

I didn't say anything but the truth was on my face, and he laughed. But now there was something very strained in his laugh. "Sure. And I bet that ain't all you was doing."

He was frightening me a little. "Cut the crap," I said. "We already decided that you was going to go and live at Isabel's. Now what's got into you all of a sudden?"

"*You* decided it," he pointed out. "*I* didn't decide nothing." He stopped in front of me, leaning against the stove, arms loosely folded. "Look, brother. I don't want to stay in Harlem no more, I really don't." He was very earnest. He looked at me, then over toward the kitchen window. There was something in his eyes I'd never seen before, some thoughtfulness, some worry all his own. He rubbed the muscle of one arm. "It's time I was getting out of here."

"Where do you want to *go*, Sonny?"   150

"I want to join the army. Or the navy, I don't care. If I say I'm old enough, they'll believe me."

Then I got mad. It was because I was so scared. "You must be crazy. You goddamn fool, what the hell do you want to go and join the *army* for?"

"I just told you. To get out of Harlem."

"Sonny, you haven't even finished *school*. And if you really want to be a musician, how do you expect to study if you're in the *army?*"

He looked at me, trapped, and in anguish. "There's ways. I might be able to work   155
out some kind of deal. Anyway, I'll have the G.I. Bill when I come out."

"*If* you come out." We stared at each other. "Sonny, please. Be reasonable. I know the setup is far from perfect. But we got to do the best we can."

"I ain't learning nothing in school," he said. "Even when I go." He turned away from me and opened the window and threw his cigarette out into the narrow alley. I watched his back. "At least, I ain't learning nothing you'd want me to learn." He slammed the window so hard I thought the glass would fly out, and turned back to me. "And I'm sick of the stink of these garbage cans!"

"Sonny," I said, "I know how you feel. But if you don't finish school now, you're going to be sorry later that you didn't." I grabbed him by the shoulders. "And you only got another year. It ain't so bad. And I'll come back and I swear I'll help you do *whatever* you want to do. Just try to put up with it till I come back. Will you please do that? For me?"

He didn't answer and he wouldn't look at me.

"Sonny. You hear me?"   160

He pulled away. "I hear you. But you never hear anything *I* say."

I didn't know what to say to that. He looked out of the window and then back at me. "OK," he said, and sighed. "I'll try."

Then I said, trying to cheer him up a little, "They got a piano at Isabel's. You can practice on it."

And as a matter of fact, it did cheer him up for a minute. "That's right," he said to himself. "I forgot that." His face relaxed a little. But the worry, the thoughtfulness, played on it still, the way shadows play on a face which is staring into the fire.

*

But I thought I'd never hear the end of that piano. At first, Isabel would write   165
me, saying how nice it was that Sonny was so serious about his music and how, as
soon as he came in from school, or wherever he had been when he was supposed to
be at school, he went straight to that piano and stayed there until suppertime. And,
after supper, he went back to that piano and stayed there until everybody went to
bed. He was at the piano all day Saturday and all day Sunday. Then he bought a
record player and started playing records. He'd play one record over and over again,
all day long sometimes, and he'd improvise along with it on the piano. Or he'd play
one section of the record, one chord, one change, one progression, then he'd do it on
the piano. Then back to the record. Then back to the piano.

Well, I really don't know how they stood it. Isabel finally confessed that it wasn't
like living with a person at all, it was like living with sound. And the sound didn't
make any sense to her, didn't make any sense to any of them—naturally. They began, in a way, to be afflicted by this presence that was living in their home. It was as
though Sonny were some sort of god, or monster. He moved in an atmosphere which
wasn't like theirs at all. They fed him and he ate, he washed himself, he walked in
and out of their door; he certainly wasn't nasty or unpleasant or rude, Sonny isn't any
of those things; but it was as though he were all wrapped up in some cloud, some fire,
some vision all his own; and there wasn't any way to reach him.

At the same time, he wasn't really a man yet, he was still a child, and they had to
watch out for him in all kinds of ways. They certainly couldn't throw him out. Neither did they dare to make a great scene about that piano because even they dimly
sensed, as I sensed, from so many thousands of miles away, that Sonny was at that
piano playing for his life.

But he hadn't been going to school. One day a letter came from the school board
and Isabel's mother got it—there had, apparently, been other letters but Sonny had
torn them up. This day, when Sonny came in, Isabel's mother showed him the letter
and asked where he'd been spending his time. And she finally got it out of him that
he'd been down in Greenwich Village, with musicians and other characters, in a
white girl's apartment. And this scared her and she started to scream at him and what
came up, once she began—though she denies it to this day—was what sacrifices they
were making to give Sonny a decent home and how little he appreciated it.

Sonny didn't play the piano that day. By evening, Isabel's mother had calmed
down but then there was the old man to deal with, and Isabel herself. Isabel says she
did her best to be calm but she broke down and started crying. She says she just
watched Sonny's face. She could tell, by watching him, what was happening with
him. And what was happening was that they penetrated his cloud, they had reached
him. Even if their fingers had been a thousand times more gentle than human fingers
ever are, he could hardly help feeling that they had stripped him naked and were
spitting on that nakedness. For he also had to see that his presence, that music,
which was life or death to him, had been torture for them and that they had endured
it, not at all for his sake, but only for mine. And Sonny couldn't take that. He can
take it a little better today than he could then but he's still not very good at it and,
frankly, I don't know anybody who is.

The silence of the next few days must have been louder than the sound of all the   170
music ever played since time began. One morning, before she went to work, Isabel
was in his room for something and she suddenly realized that all of his records were
gone. And she knew for certain that he was gone. And he was. He went as far as the

navy would carry him. He finally sent me a postcard from some place in Greece and that was the first I knew that Sonny was still alive. I didn't see him any more until we were both back in New York and the war had long been over.

He was a man by then, of course, but I wasn't willing to see it. He came by the house from time to time, but we fought almost every time we met. I didn't like the way he carried himself, loose and dreamlike all the time, and I didn't like his friends, and his music seemed to be merely an excuse for the life he led. It sounded just that weird and disordered.

Then we had a fight, a pretty awful fight, and I didn't see him for months. By and by I looked him up, where he was living, in a furnished room in the Village, and I tried to make it up. But there were lots of people in the room and Sonny just lay on his bed, and he wouldn't come downstairs with me, and he treated these other people as though they were his family and I weren't. So I got mad and then he got mad, and then I told him that he might just as well be dead as live the way he was living. Then he stood up and he told me not to worry about him any more in life, that he *was* dead as far as I was concerned. Then he pushed me to the door and the other people looked on as though nothing were happening, and he slammed the door behind me. I stood in the hallway, staring at the door. I heard somebody laugh in the room and then the tears came to my eyes. I started down the steps, whistling to keep from crying, I kept whistling to myself, *You going to need me, baby, one of these cold, rainy days.*

I read about Sonny's trouble in the spring. Little Grace died in the fall. She was a beautiful little girl. But she only lived a little over two years. She died of polio and she suffered. She had a slight fever for a couple of days, but it didn't seem like anything and we just kept her in bed. And we would certainly have called the doctor, but the fever dropped, she seemed to be all right. So we thought it had just been a cold. Then, one day, she was up, playing, Isabel was in the kitchen fixing lunch for the two boys when they'd come in from school, and she heard Grace fall down in the living room. When you have a lot of children you don't always start running when one of them falls, unless they start screaming or something. And, this time, Grace was quiet. Yet, Isabel says that when she heard that *thump* and then that silence, something happened in her to make her afraid. And she ran to the living room and there was little Grace on the floor, all twisted up, and the reason she hadn't screamed was that she couldn't get her breath. And when she did scream, it was the worst sound, Isabel says, that she'd ever heard in all her life, and she still hears it sometimes in her dreams. Isabel will sometimes wake me up with a low, moaning, strangled sound and I have to be quick to awaken her and hold her to me and where Isabel is weeping against me seems a mortal wound.

I think I may have written Sonny the very day that little Grace was buried. I was sitting in the living room in the dark, by myself, and I suddenly thought of Sonny. My trouble made his real.

One Saturday afternoon, when Sonny had been living with us, or, anyway, been 175 in our house, for nearly two weeks, I found myself wandering aimlessly about the living room, drinking from a can of beer, and trying to work up the courage to search Sonny's room. He was out, he was usually out whenever I was home, and Isabel had taken the children to see their grandparents. Suddenly I was standing still in front of the living room window, watching Seventh Avenue. The idea of searching Sonny's room made me still. I scarcely dared to admit to myself what I'd be searching for. I didn't know what I'd do if I found it. Or if I didn't.

On the sidewalk across from me, near the entrance to a barbecue joint, some people were holding an old-fashioned revival meeting. The barbecue cook, wearing a dirty white apron, his conked hair reddish and metallic in the pale sun, and a cigarette between his lips, stood in the doorway, watching them. Kids and older people paused in their errands and stood there, along with some older men and a couple of very tough-looking women who watched everything that happened on the avenue, as though they owned it, or were maybe owned by it. Well, they were watching this, too. The revival was being carried on by three sisters in black, and a brother. All they had were their voices and their Bibles and a tambourine. The brother was testifying and while he testified two of the sisters stood together, seeming to say, amen, and the third sister walked around with the tambourine outstretched and a couple of people dropped coins into it. Then the brother's testimony ended and the sister who had been taking up the collection dumped the coins into her palm and transferred them to the pocket of her long black robe. Then she raised both hands, striking the tambourine against the air, and then against one hand, and she started to sing. And the two other sisters and the brother joined in.

It was strange, suddenly, to watch, though I had been seeing these street meetings all my life. So, of course, had everybody else down there. Yet, they paused and watched and listened and I stood still at the window. *"Tis the old ship of Zion,"* they sang, and the sister with the tambourine kept a steady, jangling beat, *"it has rescued many a thousand!"* Not a soul under the sound of their voices was hearing this song for the first time, not one of them had been rescued. Nor had they seen much in the way of rescue work being done around them. Neither did they especially believe in the holiness of the three sisters and the brother, they knew too much about them, knew where they lived, and how. The woman with the tambourine, whose voice dominated the air, whose face was bright with joy, was divided by very little from the woman who stood watching her, a cigarette between her heavy, chapped lips, her hair a cuckoo's nest, her face scarred and swollen from many beatings, and her black eyes glittering like coal. Perhaps they both knew this, which was why, when, as rarely, they addressed each other, they addressed each other as Sister. As the singing filled the air the watching, listening faces underwent a change, the eyes focusing on something within; the music seemed to soothe a poison out of them; and time seemed, nearly, to fall away from the sullen, belligerent, battered faces, as though they were fleeing back to their first condition, while dreaming of their last. The barbecue cook half shook his head and smiled, and dropped his cigarette and disappeared into his joint. A man fumbled in his pockets for change and stood holding it in his hand impatiently, as though he had just remembered a pressing appointment further up the avenue. He looked furious. Then I saw Sonny, standing on the edge of the crowd. He was carrying a wide, flat notebook with a green cover, and it made him look, from where I was standing, almost like a schoolboy. The coppery sun brought out the copper in his skin, he was very faintly smiling, standing very still. Then the singing stopped, the tambourine turned into a collection plate again. The furious man dropped in his coins and vanished, so did a couple of the women, and Sonny dropped some change in the plate, looking directly at the woman with a little smile. He started across the avenue, toward the house. He has a slow, loping walk, something like the way Harlem hipsters walk, only he's imposed on this his own half-beat. I had never really noticed it before.

I stayed at the window, both relieved and apprehensive. As Sonny disappeared
from my sight, they began singing again. And they were still singing when his key
turned in the lock.

"Hey," he said.

"Hey, yourself. You want some beer?"   180

"No. Well, maybe." But he came up to the window and stood beside me, looking
out. "What a warm voice," he said.

They were singing *If I could only hear my mother pray again!*

"Yes," I said, "and she can sure beat that tambourine."

"But what a terrible song," he said, and laughed. He dropped his notebook on
the sofa and disappeared into the kitchen. "Where's Isabel and the kids?"

"I think they went to see their grandparents. You hungry?"   185

"No." He came back into the living room with his can of beer. "You want to
come some place with me tonight?"

I sensed, I don't know how, that I couldn't possibly say no. "Sure. Where?"

He sat down on the sofa and picked up his notebook and started leafing through
it. "I'm going to sit in with some fellows in a joint in the Village."

"You mean, you're going to play, tonight?"

"That's right." He took a swallow of his beer and moved back to the window. He   190
gave me a sidelong look. "If you can stand it."

"I'll try," I said.

He smiled to himself and we both watched as the meeting across the way broke
up. The three sisters and the brother, heads bowed, were singing *God be with you till
we meet again.* The faces around them were very quiet. Then the song ended. The
small crowd dispersed. We watched the three women and the lone man walk slowly
up the avenue.

"When she was singing before," said Sonny, abruptly, "her voice reminded me
for a minute of what heroin feels like sometimes—when it's in your veins. It makes
you feel sort of warm and cool at the same time. And distant. And—and sure." He
sipped his beer, very deliberately not looking at me. I watched his face. "It makes you
feel—in control. Sometimes you've got to have that feeling."

"Do you?" I sat down slowly in the easy chair.

"Sometimes." He went to the sofa and picked up his notebook again. "Some   195
people do."

"In order," I asked, "to play?" And my voice was very ugly, full of contempt and
anger.

"Well"—he looked at me with great, troubled eyes, as though, in fact, he hoped
his eyes would tell me things he could never otherwise say—"they *think* so. And *if*
they think so—!"

"And what do *you* think?" I asked.

He sat on the sofa and put his can of beer on the floor. "I don't know," he said,
and I couldn't be sure if he were answering my question or pursuing his thoughts.
His face didn't tell me. "It's not so much to *play.* It's to *stand* it, to be able to make it
at all. On any level." He frowned and smiled: "In order to keep from shaking to
pieces."

"But these friends of yours," I said, "they seem to shake themselves to pieces   200
pretty goddamn fast."

"Maybe." He played with the notebook. And something told me that I should
curb my tongue, that Sonny was doing his best to talk, that I should listen. "But of

course you only know the ones that've gone to pieces. Some don't—or at least they haven't *yet* and that's just about all *any* of us can say." He paused. "And then there are some who just live, really, in hell, and they know it and they see what's happening and they go right on. I don't know." He sighed, dropped the notebook, folded his arms. "Some guys, you can tell from the way they play, they on something *all* the time. And you can see that, well, it makes something real for them. But of course," he picked up his beer from the floor and sipped it and put the can down again, "they *want* to, too, you've got to see that. Even some of them that say they don't—*some*, not all."

"And what about you?" I asked—I couldn't help it. "What about you? Do *you* want to?"

He stood up and walked to the window and remained silent for a long time. Then he sighed. "Me," he said. Then: "While I was downstairs before, on my way here, listening to that woman sing, it struck me all of a sudden how much suffering she must have had to go through—to sing like that. It's *repulsive* to think you have to suffer that much."

I said: "But there's no way not to suffer—is there, Sonny?"

"I believe not," he said and smiled, "but that's never stopped anyone from try-   205
ing." He looked at me. "Has it?" I realized, with this mocking look, that there stood between us, forever, beyond the power of time or forgiveness, the fact that I had held silence—so long!—when he had needed human speech to help him. He turned back to the window. "No, there's no way not to suffer. But you try all kinds of ways to keep from drowning in it, to keep on top of it, and to make it seem—well, like *you*. Like you did something, all right, and now you're suffering for it. You know?" I said nothing. "Well you know," he said, impatiently, "why *do* people suffer? Maybe it's better to do something to give it a reason, *any* reason."

"But we just agreed," I said "that there's no way not to suffer. Isn't it better, then, just to—take it?"

"But nobody just takes it," Sonny cried, "that's what I'm telling you! *Everybody* tries not to. You're just hung up on the *way* some people try—it's not *your* way!"

The hair on my face began to itch, my face felt wet. "That's not true," I said, "that's not true. I don't give a damn what other people do, I don't even care how they suffer. I just care how *you* suffer." And he looked at me. "Please believe me," I said, "I don't want to see you—die—trying not to suffer."

"I won't," he said, flatly, "die trying not to suffer. At least, not any faster than anybody else."

"But there's no need," I said, trying to laugh, "is there? in killing yourself."   210

I wanted to say more, but I couldn't. I wanted to talk about will power and how life could be—well, beautiful. I wanted to say that it was all within; but was it? or, rather, wasn't that exactly the trouble? And I wanted to promise that I would never fail him again. But it would all have sounded—empty words and lies.

So I made the promise to myself and prayed that I would keep it.

"It's terrible sometimes, inside," he said, "that's what's the trouble. You walk these streets, black and funky and cold, and there's not really a living ass to talk to, and there's nothing shaking, and there's no way of getting it out—that storm inside. You can't talk it and you can't make love with it, and when you finally try to get with it and play it, you realize *nobody's* listening. So *you've* got to listen. You got to find a way to listen."

And then he walked away from the window and sat on the sofa again, as though all the wind had suddenly been knocked out of him. "Sometimes you'll do *anything* to play, even cut your mother's throat." He laughed and looked at me. "Or your brother's." Then he sobered. "Or your own." Then: "Don't worry. I'm all right now and I think I'll *be* all right. But I can't forget—where I've been. I don't mean just the physical place I've been, I mean where I've *been*. And *what* I've been."

"What have you been, Sonny?" I asked.   215

He smiled—but sat sideways on the sofa, his elbow resting on the back, his fingers playing with his mouth and chin, not looking at me. "I've been something I didn't recognize, didn't know I could be. Didn't know anybody could be." He stopped, looking inward, looking helplessly young, looking old. "I'm not talking about it now because I feel *guilty* or anything like that—maybe it would be better if I did, I don't know. Anyway, I can't really talk about it. Not to you, not to anybody," and now he turned and faced me. "Sometimes, you know, and it was actually when I was most *out* of the world, I felt that I was in it, that I was *with* it, really, and I could play or I didn't really have to *play*, it just came out of me, it was there. And I don't know how I played, thinking about it now, but I know I did awful things, those times, sometimes, to people. Or it wasn't that I *did* anything to them—it was that they weren't real." He picked up the beer can; it was empty; he rolled it between his palms: "And other times—well, I needed a fix, I needed to find a place to lean, I needed to clear a space to *listen*—and I couldn't find it, and I—went crazy, I did terrible things to *me*, I was terrible *for* me." He began pressing the beer can between his hands, I watched the metal begin to give. It glittered, as he played with it, like a knife, and I was afraid he would cut himself, but I said nothing. "Oh well. I can never tell you. I was all by myself at the bottom of something, stinking and sweating and crying and shaking, and I smelled it, you know? *my* stink, and I thought I'd die if I couldn't get away from it and yet, all the same, I knew that everything I was doing was just locking me in with it. And I didn't know," he paused, still flattening the beer can, "I didn't know, I still *don't* know, something kept telling me that maybe it was good to smell your own stink, but I didn't think that *that* was what I'd been trying to do—and—who can stand it?" and he abruptly dropped the ruined beer can, looking at me with a small, still smile, and then rose, walking to the window as though it were the lodestone rock. I watched his face, he watched the avenue. "I couldn't tell you when Mama died—but the reason I wanted to leave Harlem so bad was to get away from drugs. And then, when I ran away, that's what I was running from—really. When I came back, nothing had changed, I hadn't changed, I was just—older." And he stopped, drumming with his fingers on the windowpane. The sun had vanished, soon darkness would fall. I watched his face. "It can come again," he said, almost as though speaking to himself. Then he turned to me. "It can come again," he repeated. "I just want you to know that."

"All right," I said, at last. "So it can come again. All right."

He smiled, but the smile was sorrowful. "I had to try to tell you," he said.

"Yes," I said. "I understand that."

"You're my brother," he said, looking straight at me, and not smiling at all.   220

"Yes," I repeated, "yes. I understand that."

He turned back to the window, looking out. "All that hatred down there," he said, "all that hatred and misery and love. It's a wonder it doesn't blow the avenue apart."

We went to the only nightclub on a short, dark street, downtown. We squeezed through the narrow, chattering, jam-packed bar to the entrance of the big room, where the bandstand was. And we stood there for a moment, for the lights were very dim in this room and we couldn't see. Then, "Hello, boy," said a voice and an enormous black man, much older than Sonny or myself, erupted out of all that atmospheric lighting and put an arm around Sonny's shoulder. "I been sitting right here," he said, "waiting for you."

He had a big voice, too, and heads in the darkness turned toward us.

Sonny grinned and pulled a little away, and said, "Creole, this is my brother. I told you about him." 225

Creole shook my hand. "I'm glad to meet you, son," he said, and it was clear that he was glad to meet me *there*, for Sonny's sake. And he smiled, "You got a real musician in *your* family," and he took his arm from Sonny's shoulder and slapped him, lightly, affectionately, with the back of his hand.

"Well. Now I've heard it all," said a voice behind us. This was another musician, and a friend of Sonny's, a coal-black, cheerful-looking man, built close to the ground. He immediately began confiding to me, at the top of his lungs, the most terrible things about Sonny, his teeth gleaming like a lighthouse and his laugh coming up out of him like the beginning of an earthquake. And it turned out that everyone at the bar knew Sonny, or almost everyone; some were musicians, working there, or nearby, or not working, some were simply hangers-on, and some were there to hear Sonny play. I was introduced to all of them and they were all very polite to me. Yet, it was clear that, for them, I was only Sonny's brother. Here, I was in Sonny's world. Or, rather: his kingdom. Here, it was not even a question that his veins bore royal blood.

They were going to play soon and Creole installed me, by myself, at a table in a dark corner. Then I watched them, Creole, and the little black man, and Sonny, and the others, while they horsed around, standing just below the bandstand. The light from the bandstand spilled just a little short of them and, watching them laughing and gesturing and moving about, I had the feeling that they, nevertheless, were being most careful not to step into that circle of light too suddenly: that if they moved into the light too suddenly, without thinking, they would perish in flame. Then, while I watched, one of them, the small, black man, moved into the light and crossed the bandstand and started fooling around with his drums. Then—being funny and being, also, extremely ceremonious—Creole took Sonny by the arm and led him to the piano. A woman's voice called Sonny's name and a few hands started clapping. And Sonny, also being funny and being ceremonious, and so touched, I think, that he could have cried, but neither hiding it nor showing it, riding it like a man, grinned, and put both hands to his heart and bowed from the waist.

Creole then went to the bass fiddle and a lean, very bright-skinned brown man jumped up on the bandstand and picked up his horn. So there they were, and the atmosphere on the bandstand and in the room began to change and tighten. Someone stepped up to the microphone and announced them. Then there were all kinds of murmurs. Some people at the bar shushed others. The waitress ran around, frantically getting in the last orders, guys and chicks got closer to each other, and the lights on the bandstand, on the quartet, turned to a kind of indigo. Then they all looked different there. Creole looked about him for the last time, as though he were making certain that all his chickens were in the coop, and then he—jumped and struck the fiddle. And there they were.

All I know about music is that not many people ever really hear it. And even 230
then, on the rare occasions when something opens within, and the music enters,
what we mainly hear, or hear corroborated, are personal, private, vanishing
evocations. But the man who creates the music is hearing something else, is dealing
with the roar rising from the void and imposing order on it as it hits the air.
What is evoked in him, then, is of another order, more terrible because it has no
words, and triumphant, too, for that same reason. And his triumph, when he
triumphs, is ours. I just watched Sonny's face. His face was troubled, he was working
hard, but he wasn't with it. And I had the feeling that, in a way, everyone on the
bandstand was waiting for him, both waiting for him and pushing him along. But
as I began to watch Creole, I realized that it was Creole who held them all back.
He had them on a short rein. Up there, keeping the beat with his whole body,
wailing on the fiddle, with his eyes half closed, he was listening to everything,
but he was listening to Sonny. He was having a dialogue with Sonny. He wanted
Sonny to leave the shoreline and strike out for the deep water. He was Sonny's
witness that deep water and drowning were not the same thing—he had been
there, and he knew. And he wanted Sonny to know. He was waiting for Sonny to
do the things on the keys which would let Creole know that Sonny was in the
water.

And, while Creole listened, Sonny moved, deep within, exactly like someone in
torment. I had never before thought of how awful the relationship must be between
the musician and his instrument. He has to fill it, this instrument, with the breath of
life, his own. He has to make it do what he wants it to do. And a piano is just a piano.
It's made out of so much wood and wires and little hammers and big ones, and ivory.
While there's only so much you can do with it, the only way to find this out is to try;
to try and make it do everything.

And Sonny hadn't been near a piano for over a year. And he wasn't on much
better terms with his life, not the life that stretched before him now. He and the
piano stammered, started one way, got scared, stopped; started another way,
panicked, marked time, started again; then seemed to have found a direction,
panicked again, got stuck. And the face I saw on Sonny I'd never seen before.
Everything had been burned out of it, and, at the same time, things usually hidden
were being burned in, by the fire and fury of the battle which was occurring in him
up there.

Yet, watching Creole's face as they neared the end of the first set, I had the
feeling that something had happened, something I hadn't heard. Then they
finished, there was scattered applause, and then, without an instant's warning,
Creole started into something else, it was almost sardonic, it was *Am I Blue*. And,
as though he commanded, Sonny began to play. Something began to happen. And
Creole let out the reins. The dry, low, black man said something awful on the
drums, Creole answered, and the drums talked back. Then the horn insisted,
sweet and high, slightly detached perhaps, and Creole listened, commenting now
and then, dry, and driving, beautiful and calm and old. Then they all came
together again, and Sonny was part of the family again. I could tell this from his
face. He seemed to have found, right there beneath his fingers, a damn brand-new
piano. It seemed that he couldn't get over it. Then, for awhile, just being happy
with Sonny, they seemed to be agreeing with him that brand-new pianos certainly
were a gas.

Then Creole stepped forward to remind them that what they were playing was the blues. He hit something in all of them, he hit something in me, myself, and the music tightened and deepened, apprehension began to beat the air. Creole began to tell us what the blues were all about. They were not about anything very new. He and his boys up there were keeping it new, at the risk of ruin, destruction, madness, and death, in order to find new ways to make us listen. For, while the tale of how we suffer, and how we are delighted, and how we may triumph is never new, it always must be heard. There isn't any other tale to tell, it's the only light we've got in all this darkness.

And this tale, according to that face, that body, those strong hands on those 235 strings, has another aspect in every country, and a new depth in every generation. Listen, Creole seemed to be saying, listen. Now these are Sonny's blues. He made the little black man on the drums know it, and the bright, brown man on the horn. Creole wasn't trying any longer to get Sonny in the water. He was wishing him Godspeed.° Then he stepped back, very slowly, filling the air with the immense suggestion that Sonny speak for himself.

Then they all gathered around Sonny and Sonny played. Every now and again one of them seemed to say, amen. Sonny's fingers filled the air with life, his life. But that life contained so many others. And Sonny went all the way back, he really began with the spare, flat statement of the opening phrase of the song. Then he began to make it his. It was very beautiful because it wasn't hurried and it was no longer a lament. I seemed to hear with what burning he had made it his, with what burning we had yet to make it ours, how we could cease lamenting. Freedom lurked around us and I understood, at last, that he could help us to be free if we would listen, that he would never be free until we did. Yet, there was no battle in his face now. I heard what he had gone through, and would continue to go through until he came to rest in earth. He had made it his: that long line, of which we knew only Mama and Daddy. And he was giving it back, as everything must be given back, so that, passing through death, it can live forever. I saw my mother's face again, and felt, for the first time, how the stones of the road she had walked on must have bruised her feet. I saw the moon-lit road where my father's brother died. And it brought something else back to me, and carried me past it. I saw my little girl again and felt Isabel's tears again, and I felt my own tears begin to rise. And I was yet aware that this was only a moment, that the world waited outside, as hungry as a tiger, and that trouble stretched above us, longer than the sky.

Then it was over. Creole and Sonny let out their breath, both soaking wet, and grinning. There was a lot of applause and some of it was real. In the dark, the girl came by and I asked her to take drinks to the bandstand. There was a long pause, while they talked up there in the indigo light and after awhile I saw the girl put a Scotch and milk on top of the piano for Sonny. He didn't seem to notice it, but just before they started playing again, he sipped from it and looked toward me, and nodded. Then he put it back on top of the piano. For me, then, as they began to play again, it glowed and shook above my brother's head like the very cup of trembling.

---

wishing him Godspeed: wishing success.

Questions

1. From whose point of view is "Sonny's Blues" told? How do the narrator's values and experiences affect his view of the story?
2. What is the older brother's profession? Does it suggest anything about his personality?
3. How would this story change if it were told by Sonny?
4. What event prompts the narrator to write to his brother?
5. What does the narrator's mother ask him to do for Sonny? Does the older brother keep his promise?
6. The major characters in this story are called Mama, Daddy, and Sonny (the older brother is never named or even nicknamed). How do these names affect our sense of the story?
7. Reread the last four paragraphs and explain the significance of the statement "Now these are Sonny's blues." How has Sonny made this music his own?

■ WRITING *effectively*

James Baldwin on Writing

Race and the African American Writer   1955

James Baldwin

I know, in any case, that the most crucial time in my own development came when I was forced to recognize that I was a kind of bastard of the West; when I followed the line of my past I did not find myself in Europe but in Africa. And this meant that in some subtle way, in a really profound way, I brought to Shakespeare, Bach, Rembrandt, to the stones of Paris, to the cathedral at Chartres, and to the Empire State Building, a special attitude. These were not really my creations, they did not contain my history; I might search in them in vain forever for any reflection of myself. I was an interloper; this was not my heritage. At the same time I had no other heritage which I could possibly hope to use—I had certainly been unfitted for the jungle or the tribe. I would have to appropriate these white centuries, I would have to make them mine—I would have to accept my special attitude, my special place in this scheme—otherwise I would have no place in *any* scheme. What was the most difficult was the fact that I was forced to admit something I had always hidden from myself, which the American Negro has had to hide from himself as the price of his public progress; that I hated and feared the world. And this meant, not only that I thus gave the world an altogether murderous power over me, but also that in such a self-destroying limbo I could never hope to write.

One writes out of one thing only—one's own experience. Everything depends on how relentlessly one forces from this experience the last drop, sweet or bitter, it can possibly give. This is the only real concern of the artist, to recreate out of the disorder of life that order which is art. The difficulty then, for me, of being a Negro writer was the fact that I was, in effect, prohibited from examining my own experience too closely by the tremendous demands and the very real dangers of my social situation.

I don't think the dilemma outlined above is uncommon. I do think, since writers work in the disastrously explicit medium of language, that it goes a little way towards explaining why, out of the enormous resources of Negro speech and life, and despite the example of Negro music, prose written by Negroes has been generally speaking so pallid and so harsh. I have not written about being a Negro at such length because I expect that to be my only subject, but only because it was the gate I had to unlock before I could hope to write about anything else.

From "Autobiographical Notes"

THINKING ABOUT POINT OF VIEW

When we hear an outlandish piece of news, something that doesn't quite add up, we're well advised, as the saying goes, to consider the source. The same is true when we read a short story.

- **Consider who is telling the story.** A story's point of view determines how much confidence a reader should have in the events related. A story told from a third-person omniscient point of view generally provides a sense of authority and stability that makes the narrative seem reliable.
- **Ask why the narrator is telling the story.** The use of a first-person narrator, on the other hand, often suggests a certain bias, especially when the narrator relates events in which he or she has played a part. In such cases the narrator sometimes has an obvious interest in the audience's accepting his or her version of the story as truth.
- **Think about whether anything important is being left out of the story.** Is something of obvious importance to the situation not being reported? Understanding the limits of a narrator's point of view is key to interpreting what a story says.

CHECKLIST: Writing About Point of View

- ☐ How is the story narrated? Is it told in the third or the first person?
- ☐ If the story is told in the third person, is the point of view omniscient or does it confine itself to what is perceived by a particular character?
- ☐ What is gained by this choice?
- ☐ If the story is told by a first-person narrator, what is the speaker's main reason for telling the story? What does the narrator have to gain by making us believe his or her account?
- ☐ Does the first-person narrator fully understand his or her own motivations? Is there some important aspect of the narrator's character or situation that is being overlooked?
- ☐ Is there anything peculiar about the first-person narrator? Does this peculiarity create any suspicions about the narrator's accuracy or reliability?
- ☐ What does the narrator's perspective add? Would the story seem as memorable if related from another narrative angle?

WRITING ASSIGNMENT ON POINT OF VIEW

Choose a story from this book and analyze how point of view contributes to the story's overall meaning. Come up with a thesis sentence, and back up your argument with specific observations about the text. Incorporate at least three quotations, and document them, as explained in the writing chapters at the end of the book. Some stories that might lend themselves well to this assignment are "Sonny's Blues," "Cathedral," "The Tell-Tale Heart," and "Greasy Lake."

MORE TOPICS FOR WRITING

1. Retell the events in "A & P" from the point of view of one of the story's minor characters: Lengel, or Stokesie, or one of the girls. How does the story's emphasis change?
2. Here is another writing exercise to help you sense what a difference a point of view makes. Write a short statement from the point of view of William Faulkner's Homer Barron on "My Affair with Miss Emily."
3. Imagine a story such as "A & P" or "A Rose for Emily" told by an omniscient third-person narrator. Write several paragraphs about what would be lost (or gained) by such a change.
4. Choose any tale from "Stories for Further Reading," and, in a paragraph or two, describe how point of view colors the general meaning. If you like, you may argue that the story might be told more effectively from an alternate point of view.
5. Think back to a confrontation in your own life, and describe that event from a point of view contrary to your own. Try to imagine yourself inside your speaker's personality, and present the facts as that person would, as convincingly as you can.
6. With "Sonny's Blues" in mind, write about a family member or friend from your own point of view, allowing, as Baldwin does, an understanding of that person's perspective to slowly develop.
7. Tell the story of a confrontation—biographical or fictional—from the point of view of a minor character peripheral to the central action. You could, for instance, tell the story of a disastrous first date from the point of view of the unlucky waitress who serves the couple dinner.

▶ TERMS FOR *review*

Points of View

Total omniscience ▶ Point of view in which the narrator knows everything about all of the characters and events in a story. A narrator with total omniscience can move freely from one character to another. Generally, a totally omniscient narrative is written in the third person.

Limited or selective omniscience ▶ Point of view in which the narrator sees into the minds of some but not all of the characters. Most typically, limited omniscience sees through the eyes of one major or minor character.

Impartial omniscience ▶ Point of view employed when an omniscient narrator, who presents the thoughts and actions of the characters, does not judge them or comment on them.

Editorial omniscience ▶ Point of view employed when an omniscient narrator goes beyond reporting the thoughts of his characters to make a critical judgment or commentary, making explicit the narrator's own thoughts or attitudes.

Objective point of view ▶ Point of view in which the third-person narrator merely reports dialogue and action with little or no interpretation or access to the characters' minds.

Types of Narrators

Omniscient or all-knowing narrator ▶ A narrator who has the ability to move freely through the consciousness of any character. The omniscient narrator also has complete knowledge of all of the external events in a story.

Participant or first-person narrator ▶ A narrator who is a participant in the action. Such a narrator refers to himself or herself as "I" and may be a major or minor character in the story.

Observer ▶ A first-person narrator who is relatively detached from or plays only a minor role in the events described.

Nonparticipant or third-person narrator ▶ A narrator who does not appear in the story as a character but is usually capable of revealing the thoughts and motives of one or more characters.

Innocent or naive narrator ▶ A character who fails to understand all the implications of the story he or she tells. The innocent narrator—often a child or childlike adult—is frequently used by an author to generate irony, sympathy, or pity by creating a gap between what the narrator perceives and what the reader knows.

Unreliable narrator ▶ A narrator who—intentionally or unintentionally—relates events in a subjective or distorted manner. The author usually provides some indication early on in such stories that the narrator is not to be completely trusted.

Narrative Techniques

Interior monologue ▶ An extended presentation of a character's thoughts in a narrative. Usually written in the present tense and printed without quotation marks, an interior monologue reads as if the character were speaking aloud to himself or herself, for the reader to overhear.

Stream of consciousness ▶ A type of modern narration that uses various literary devices, especially interior monologue, in an attempt to duplicate the subjective and associative nature of human consciousness.

3

CHARACTER

*Show me a character without anxieties
and I will show you a boring book.*

—MARGARET ATWOOD

From popular fiction and drama, both classic and contemporary, we are acquainted with many stereotyped characters. Called **stock characters**, they are often known by some outstanding trait or traits: the *bragging* soldier of Greek and Roman comedy, the Prince *Charming* of fairy tales, the *mad* scientist of horror movies, the *fearlessly reckless* police detective of urban action films, the *brilliant but alcoholic* brain surgeon of medical thrillers on television. Stock characters are especially convenient for writers of commercial fiction: they require little detailed portraiture, for we already know them well. Most writers of the literary story, however, attempt to create characters who strike us not as stereotypes but as unique individuals. Although stock characters tend to have single dominant virtues and vices, characters in the finest contemporary short stories tend to have many facets, like people we meet.

A **character**, then, is presumably an imagined person who inhabits a story—although that simple definition may admit to a few exceptions. In George Stewart's novel *Storm*, the protagonist is the wind; in Richard Adams's *Watership Down*, the main characters are rabbits. But usually we recognize, in the main characters of a story, human personalities that become familiar to us. If the story seems "true to life," we generally find that its characters act in a reasonably consistent manner and that the author has provided them with **motivation**: sufficient reason to behave as they do. Should a character behave in a sudden and unexpected way, seeming to deny what we have been told about his or her nature or personality, we trust that there was a reason for this behavior and that sooner or later we will discover it.

In good fiction, characters sometimes change or develop. In *A Christmas Carol*, Charles Dickens tells how Ebenezer Scrooge, a tightfisted miser, reforms overnight, suddenly gives to the poor, and endeavors to assist his clerk's struggling family. But Dickens amply demonstrates why Scrooge had such a change of heart: four ghostly visitors, stirring kind memories the old miser had forgotten and also warning him of the probable consequences of his habits, provide the character (and hence the story) with adequate motivation.

TYPES OF CHARACTERS

To borrow the useful terms of the English novelist E. M. Forster, characters may seem **flat** or **round**, depending on whether a writer sketches or sculpts them. A flat character has only one outstanding trait or feature, or at most a few distinguishing marks: for example, the familiar stock character of the mad scientist, with his lust for absolute power and his crazily gleaming eyes. Flat characters, however, need not be stock characters: in all of literature there is probably only one Tiny Tim, though his functions in A Christmas Carol are mainly to invoke blessings and to remind others of their Christian duties.

Some writers, notably Balzac, who peopled his many novels with hosts of characters, try to distinguish the flat ones by giving each a single odd physical feature or mannerism—a nervous twitch, a piercing gaze, an obsessive fondness for oysters. Round characters, however, present us with more facets—that is, their authors portray them in greater depth and in more generous detail. Such a round character may appear to us only as he appears to the other characters in the story. If their views of him differ, we will see him from more than one side. In other stories, we enter a character's mind and come to know him through his own thoughts, feelings, and perceptions.

Flat characters tend to stay the same throughout a story, but round characters often change—learn or become enlightened, grow or deteriorate. In William Faulkner's "Barn Burning" (Chapter 5), the boy Sarty Snopes, driven to defy his proud and violent father, becomes at the story's end more knowing and more mature. (Some critics call a fixed character **static**; a changing one, **dynamic**.) This is not to damn a flat character as an inferior creation. In most fiction—even the greatest—minor characters tend to be flat instead of round. Why? Rounding them would cost time and space; and so enlarged, they might only distract us from the main characters.

"A character, first of all, is the noise of his name," according to novelist William Gass. Names, chosen artfully, can indicate natures. A simple illustration is the completely virtuous Squire Allworthy, the foster father in Tom Jones by Henry Fielding. Subtler, perhaps, is the custom of giving a character a name that makes an **allusion**: a reference to some famous person, place, or thing. For his central characters in Moby-Dick, Herman Melville chose names from the Old Testament, calling his tragic and domineering Ahab after a biblical tyrant who came to a bad end, and his wandering narrator Ishmael after a biblical outcast. Whether or not it includes such a reference, a good name often reveals the character of the character. Charles Dickens, a vigorous and richly suggestive christener, named a couple of shyster lawyers Dodgson and Fogg (suggesting dodging evasiveness and foglike obfuscation), and named two heartless educators, who grimly drill their schoolchildren in "hard facts," Gradgind and M'Choakumchild.

Hero Versus Antihero

Instead of a hero, many a recent novel has featured an **antihero**: a protagonist conspicuously lacking in one or more of the usual attributes of a traditional **hero**, bravery, skill, idealism, sense of purpose. The antihero is an ordinary, unglorious citizen of the modern world, usually drawn (according to the Irish short story writer Sean O'Faolain) as someone "groping, puzzled, cross, mocking, frustrated, and isolated."

If epic poets once drew their heroes as decisive leaders of their people, embodying their people's highest ideals, antiheroes tend to be loners, without admirable qualities, just barely able to survive. A gulf separates Leopold Bloom, antihero of

James Joyce's novel *Ulysses*, from the hero of the Greek *Odyssey*. In Homer's epic, Ulysses wanders the Mediterranean, battling monsters and overcoming enchantments. In Joyce's novel, Bloom wanders the littered streets of Dublin, peddling advertising space. Meursault, the title character of Albert Camus's novel *The Stranger*, is so alienated from his own life that he is unmoved at the news of his mother's death.

Many contemporary writers of fiction would deny even that people have definite selves to alter. Following Sigmund Freud and other modern psychologists, they assume that a large part of human behavior is shaped in the unconscious—that, for instance, a person might fear horses, not because of a basically timid nature, but because of unconscious memories of having been nearly trampled by a horse when a child. To some writers it now appears that personality is more vulnerable to change from such causes as age, disease, neurosis, psychic shock, or brainwashing than was once believed.

Characterization, as practiced by nineteenth-century novelists, almost entirely disappears in Franz Kafka's *The Castle*, whose protagonist has no home, no family, no definite appearance—not even a name, just the initial K. Characters are things of the past, insisted the modern French novelist Alain Robbe-Grillet. Still, nearly all writers of fiction go on portraying them.

Katherine Anne Porter

The Jilting of Granny Weatherall

1930

Katherine Anne Porter (1890–1980) was born in Indian Creek, Texas. Her mother died when she was two, and Porter was raised by a grandmother who surrounded the growing girl with books. At sixteen she ran away from school and soon married a railway clerk in Louisiana. Three years later, she divorced her husband and began supporting herself as a reporter in Chicago, Denver, and Fort Worth, and sometimes as an actress and ballad singer while traveling through the South. Sojourns in Europe and in Mexico supplied her with material for some of her finest stories. Her brilliant, sensitive short fiction, first collected in Flowering Judas *(1930), won her a high reputation. Her one novel,* Ship of Fools *(1962), with which she had struggled for twenty years, received harsh critical notices, but proved a commercial success. In 1965 her* Collected Stories *received a Pulitzer Prize and a National Book Award.*

Katherine Anne Porter
(© Jill Krementz, Inc.)

She flicked her wrist neatly out of Doctor Harry's pudgy careful fingers and pulled the sheet up to her chin. The brat ought to be in knee breeches. Doctoring around the country with spectacles on his nose! "Get along now, take your schoolbooks and go. There's nothing wrong with me."

Doctor Harry spread a warm paw like a cushion on her forehead where the forked green vein danced and made her eyelids twitch. "Now, now, be a good girl, and we'll have you up in no time."

"That's no way to speak to a woman nearly eighty years old just because she's down. I'd have you respect your elders, young man."

"Well, Missy, excuse me." Doctor Harry patted her cheek. "But I've got to warn you, haven't I? You're a marvel, but you must be careful or you're going to be good and sorry."

"Don't tell me what I'm going to be. I'm on my feet now, morally speaking. It's 5 Cornelia. I had to go to bed to get rid of her."

Her bones felt loose, and floated around in her skin, and Doctor Harry floated like a balloon around the foot of the bed. He floated and pulled down his waist-coat and swung his glasses on a cord. "Well, stay where you are, it certainly can't hurt you."

"Get along and doctor your sick," said Granny Weatherall. "Leave a well woman alone. I'll call for you when I want you. . . . Where were you forty years ago when I pulled through milk-leg and double pneumonia? You weren't even born. Don't let Cornelia lead you on," she shouted, because Doctor Harry appeared to float up to the ceiling and out. "I pay my own bills, and I don't throw my money away on nonsense!"

She meant to wave good-by, but it was too much trouble. Her eyes closed of themselves, it was like a dark curtain drawn around the bed. The pillow rose and floated under her, pleasant as a hammock in a light wind. She listened to the leaves rustling outside the window. No, somebody was swishing newspapers: no, Cornelia and Doctor Harry were whispering together. She leaped broad awake, thinking they whispered in her ear.

"She was never like this, *never* like this!" "Well, what can we expect?" "Yes, eighty years old. . . ."

Well, and what if she was? She still had ears. It was like Cornelia to whisper 10 around doors. She always kept things secret in such a public way. She was always be-ing tactful and kind. Cornelia was dutiful; that was the trouble with her. Dutiful and good: "So good and dutiful," said Granny, "that I'd like to spank her." She saw herself spanking Cornelia and making a fine job of it.

"What'd you say, Mother?"

Granny felt her face tying up in hard knots.

"Can't a body think, I'd like to know?"

"I thought you might want something."

"I do. I want a lot of things. First off, go away and don't whisper." 15

She lay and drowsed, hoping in her sleep that the children would keep out and let her rest a minute. It had been a long day. Not that she was tired. It was always pleasant to snatch a minute now and then. There was always so much to be done, let me see: tomorrow.

Tomorrow was far away and there was nothing to trouble about. Things were fin-ished somehow when the time came; thank God there was always a little margin over for peace: then a person could spread out the plan of life and tuck in the edges or-derly. It was good to have everything clean and folded away, with the hair brushes and tonic bottles sitting straight on the white embroidered linen: the day started without fuss and the pantry shelves laid out with rows of jelly glasses and brown jugs and white stone-china jars with blue whirligigs and words painted on them: coffee, tea, sugar, ginger, cinnamon, allspice: and the bronze clock with the lion on top nicely dusted off. The dust that lion could collect in twenty-four hours! The box in the attic with all those letters tied up, well, she'd have to go through that tomorrow.

All those letters—George's letters and John's letters and her letters to them both—lying around for the children to find afterwards made her uneasy. Yes, that would be tomorrow's business. No use to let them know how silly she had been once.

While she was rummaging around she found death in her mind and it felt clammy and unfamiliar. She had spent so much time preparing for death there was no need for bringing it up again. Let it take care of itself now. When she was sixty she had felt very old, finished, and went around making farewell trips to see her children and grandchildren, with a secret in her mind: This is the very last of your mother, children! Then she made her will and came down with a long fever. That was all just a notion like a lot of other things, but it was lucky too, for she had once for all got over the idea of dying for a long time. Now she couldn't be worried. She hoped she had better sense now. Her father had lived to be one hundred and two years old and had drunk a noggin of strong hot toddy on his last birthday. He told the reporters it was his daily habit, and he owed his long life to it. He had made quite a scandal and was very pleased about it. She believed she'd just plague Cornelia a little.

"Cornelia! Cornelia!" No footsteps, but a sudden hand on her cheek. "Bless you, where have you been?"

"Here, Mother."

"Well, Cornelia, I want a noggin of hot toddy." 20

"Are you cold, darling?"

"I'm chilly, Cornelia. Lying in bed stops the circulation. I must have told you that a thousand times."

Well, she could just hear Cornelia telling her husband that Mother was getting a little childish and they'd have to humor her. The thing that most annoyed her was that Cornelia thought she was deaf, dumb, and blind. Little hasty glances and tiny gestures tossed around her and over her head saying, "Don't cross her, let her have her way, she's eighty years old," and she sitting there as if she lived in a thin glass cage. Sometimes Granny almost made up her mind to pack up and move back to her own house where nobody could remind her every minute that she was old. Wait, wait, Cornelia, till your own children whisper behind your back!

In her day she had kept a better house and had got more work done. She 25 wasn't too old yet for Lydia to be driving eighty miles for advice when one of the children jumped the track, and Jimmy still dropped in and talked things over: "Now, Mammy, you've a good business head, I want to know what you think of this? . . ." Old. Cornelia couldn't change the furniture around without asking. Little things, little things! They had been so sweet when they were little. Granny wished the old days were back again with the children young and everything to be done over. It had been a hard pull, but not too much for her. When she thought of all the food she had cooked, and all the clothes she had cut and sewed, and all the gardens she had made—well, the children showed it. There they were, made out of her, and they couldn't get away from that. Sometimes she wanted to see John again and point to them and say, Well, I didn't do so badly, did I? But that would have to wait. That was for tomorrow. She used to think of him as a man, but now all the children were older than their father, and he would be a child beside her if she saw him now. It seemed strange and there was something wrong in the idea. Why, he couldn't possibly recognize her. She had fenced in a hundred acres once, digging the post holes herself and clamping the wires with just a negro boy to help. That changed a woman. John would be looking for a young woman with the peaked Spanish comb in her hair and the painted fan. Digging post holes changed a woman. Riding country roads in the winter when women had their babies was another thing: sitting up nights with sick horses and sick negroes and sick children and hardly ever losing one. John, I hardly ever lost one of them! John would see that in a minute, that would be something he could understand, she wouldn't have to explain anything!

It made her feel like rolling up her sleeves and putting the whole place to rights again. No matter if Cornelia was determined to be everywhere at once, there were a great many things left undone on this place. She would start tomorrow and do them. It was good to be strong enough for everything, even if all you made melted and changed and slipped under your hands, so that by the time you finished you almost forgot what you were working for. What was it I set out to do? she asked herself intently, but she could not remember. A fog rose over the valley, she saw it marching across the creek swallowing the trees and moving up the hill like an army of ghosts. Soon it would be at the near edge of the orchard, and then it was time to go in and light the lamps. Come in, children, don't stay out in the night air.

Lighting the lamps had been beautiful. The children huddled up to her and breathed like little calves waiting at the bars in the twilight. Their eyes followed the match and watched the flame rise and settle in a blue curve, then they moved away from her. The lamp was lit, they didn't have to be scared and hang on to mother any more. Never, never, never more. God, for all my life I thank Thee. Without Thee, my God, I could never have done it. Hail, Mary, full of grace.

I want you to pick all the fruit this year and see that nothing is wasted. There's always someone who can use it. Don't let good things rot for want of using. You waste life when you waste good food. Don't let things get lost. It's bitter to lose things. Now, don't let me get to thinking, not when I am tired and taking a little nap before supper. . . .

The pillow rose about her shoulders and pressed against her heart and the memory was being squeezed out of it: oh, push down the pillow, somebody: it would smother her if she tried to hold it. Such a fresh breeze blowing and such a green day with no threats in it. But he had not come, just the same. What does a woman do when she has put on the white veil and set out the white cake for a man and he doesn't come? She tried to remember. No, I swear he never harmed me but in that. He never harmed me but in that . . . and what if he did? There was the day, the day, but a whirl of dark smoke rose and covered it, crept up and over into the bright field where everything was planted so carefully in orderly rows. That was hell, she knew hell when she saw it. For sixty years she had prayed against remembering him and against losing her soul in the deep pit of hell, and now the two things were mingled in one and the thought of him was a smoky cloud from hell that moved and crept in her head when she had just got rid of Doctor Harry and was trying to rest a minute. Wounded vanity, Ellen, said a sharp voice in the top of her mind. Don't let your wounded vanity get the upper hand of you. Plenty of girls get jilted. You were jilted, weren't you? Then stand up to it. Her eyelids wavered and let in streamers of blue-gray light like tissue paper over her eyes. She must get up and pull the shades down or she'd never sleep. She was in bed again and the shades were not down. How could that happen? Better turn over, hide from the light, sleeping in the light gave you nightmares. "Mother, how do you feel now?" and a stinging wetness on her forehead. But I don't like having my face washed in cold water!

Hapsy? George? Lydia? Jimmy? No, Cornelia, and her features were swollen and   30
full of little puddles. "They're coming, darling, they'll all be here soon." Go wash your
face, child, you look funny.

Instead of obeying, Cornelia knelt down and put her head on the pillow. She
seemed to be talking but there was no sound. "Well, are you tongue-tied? Whose
birthday is it? Are you going to give a party?"

Cornelia's mouth moved urgently in strange shapes. "Don't do that, you bother
me, daughter."

"Oh, no, Mother. Oh, no. . . ."

Nonsense. It was strange about children. They disputed your every word. "No
what, Cornelia?"

"Here's Doctor Harry."   35

"I won't see that boy again. He just left three minutes ago."

"That was this morning, Mother. It's night now. Here's the nurse."

"This is Doctor Harry, Mrs. Weatherall. I never saw you look so young and
happy!"

"Ah, I'll never be young again—but I'd be happy if they'd let me lie in peace and
get rested."

She thought she spoke up loudly, but no one answered. A warm weight on her   40
forehead, a warm bracelet on her wrist, and a breeze went on whispering, trying to
tell her something. A shuffle of leaves in the everlasting hand of God. He blew on
them and they danced and rattled. "Mother, don't mind, we're going to give you a little hypodermic." "Look here, daughter, how do ants get in this bed? I saw sugar ants
yesterday." Did you send for Hapsy too?

It was Hapsy she really wanted. She had to go a long way back through a great
many rooms to find Hapsy standing with a baby on her arm. She seemed to herself to
be Hapsy also, and the baby on Hapsy's arm was Hapsy and himself and herself, all at
once, and there was no surprise in the meeting. Then Hapsy melted from within and
turned flimsy as gray gauze and the baby was a gauzy shadow, and Hapsy came up
close and said, "I thought you'd never come," and looked at her very searchingly and
said, "You haven't changed a bit!" They leaned forward to kiss, when Cornelia began
whispering from a long way off, "Oh, is there anything you want to tell me? Is there
anything I can do for you?"

Yes, she had changed her mind after sixty years and she would like to see
George. I want you to find George. Find him and be sure to tell him I forgot him. I
want him to know I had my husband just the same and my children and my house
like any other woman. A good house too and a good husband that I loved and fine
children out of him. Better than I hoped for even. Tell him I was given back everything he took away and more. Oh, no, oh, God, no, there was something else besides
the house and the man and the children. Oh, surely they were not all? What was it?
Something not given back. . . . Her breath crowded down under her ribs and grew
into a monstrous frightening shape with cutting edges; it bored up into her head, and
the agony was unbelievable: Yes, John, get the Doctor now, no more talk, my time
has come.

When this one was born it should be the last. The last. It should have been born
first, for it was the one she had truly wanted. Everything came in good time. Nothing
left out, left over. She was strong, in three days she would be as well as ever. Better. A
woman needed milk in her to have her full health.

"Mother, do you hear me?"

"I've been telling you—"   45

"Mother, Father Connolly's here."

"I went to Holy Communion only last week. Tell him I'm not so sinful as all that."

"Father just wants to speak to you."

He could speak as much as he pleased. It was like him to drop in and inquire about her soul as if it were a teething baby, and then stay on for a cup of tea and a round of cards and gossip. He always had a funny story of some sort, usually about an Irishman who made his little mistakes and confessed them, and the point lay in some absurd thing he would blurt out in the confessional showing his struggles between native piety and original sin. Granny felt easy about her soul. Cornelia, where are your manners? Give Father Connolly a chair. She had her secret comfortable understanding with a few favorite saints who cleared a straight road to God for her. All as surely signed and sealed as the papers for the new Forty Acres. Forever . . . heirs and assigns forever. Since the day the wedding cake was not cut, but thrown out and wasted. The whole bottom dropped out of the world, and there she was blind and sweating with nothing under her feet and the walls falling away. His hand had caught her under the breast, she had not fallen, there was the freshly polished floor with the green rug on it, just as before. He had cursed like a sailor's parrot and said, "I'll kill him for you." Don't lay a hand on him, for my sake leave something to God. "Now, Ellen, you must believe what I tell you. . . ."

So there was nothing, nothing to worry about any more, except sometimes in   50
the night one of the children screamed in a nightmare, and they both hustled out shaking and hunting for the matches and calling, "There, wait a minute, here we are!" John, get the doctor now, Hapsy's time has come. But there was Hapsy standing by the bed in a white cap. "Cornelia, tell Hapsy to take off her cap. I can't see her plain."

Her eyes opened very wide and the room stood out like a picture she had seen somewhere. Dark colors with the shadows rising towards the ceiling in long angles. The tall black dresser gleamed with nothing on it but John's picture, enlarged from a little one, with John's eyes very black when they should have been blue. You never saw him, so how do you know how he looked? But the man insisted the copy was perfect, it was very rich and handsome. For a picture, yes, but it's not my husband. The table by the bed had a linen cover and a candle and a crucifix. The light was blue from Cornelia's silk lampshades. No sort of light at all, just frippery. You had to live forty years with kerosene lamps to appreciate honest electricity. She felt very strong and she saw Doctor Harry with a rosy nimbus around him.

"You look like a saint, Doctor Harry, and I vow that's as near as you'll ever come to it."

"She's saying something."

"I heard you, Cornelia. What's all this carrying-on?"

"Father Connolly's saying—"   55

Cornelia's voice staggered and bumped like a cart in a bad road. It rounded corners and turned back again and arrived nowhere. Granny stepped up in the cart very lightly and reached for the reins, but a man sat beside her and she knew him by his hands, driving the cart. She did not look in his face, for she knew without seeing, but looked instead down the road where the trees leaned over and bowed to each other and a thousand birds were singing a Mass. She felt like singing too, but she put her hand in the bosom of her dress and pulled out a rosary, and Father Connolly murmured

Latin in a very solemn voice and tickled her feet. My God, will you stop that non-sense? I'm a married woman. What if he did run away and leave me to face the priest by myself? I found another a whole world better. I wouldn't have exchanged my hus-band for anybody except St. Michael himself, and you may tell him that for me with a thank you in the bargain.

Light flashed on her closed eyelids, and a deep roaring shook her. Cornelia, is that lightning? I hear thunder. There's going to be a storm. Close all the windows. Call the children in. . . . "Mother, here we are, all of us." "Is that you, Hapsy?" "Oh, no, I'm Lydia. We drove as fast as we could." Their faces drifted above her, drifted away. The rosary fell out of her hands and Lydia put it back. Jimmy tried to help, their hands fumbled together, and Granny closed two fingers around Jimmy's thumb. Beads wouldn't do, it must be something alive. She was so amazed her thoughts ran round and round. So, my dear Lord, this is my death and I wasn't even thinking about it. My children have come to see me die. But I can't, it's not time. Oh, I always hated surprises. I wanted to give Cornelia the amethyst set—Cornelia, you're to have the amethyst set, but Hapsy's to wear it when she wants, and, Doctor Harry, do shut up. Nobody sent for you. Oh, my dear Lord, do wait a minute. I meant to do some-thing about the Forty Acres, Jimmy doesn't need it and Lydia will later on, with that worthless husband of hers. I meant to finish the altar cloth and send six bottles of wine to Sister Borgia for her dyspepsia. I want to send six bottles of wine to Sister Borgia, Father Connolly, now don't let me forget.

Cornelia's voice made short turns and tilted over and crashed, "Oh, Mother, oh, Mother, oh, Mother. . . ."

"I'm not going, Cornelia. I'm taken by surprise. I can't go."

You'll see Hapsy again. What about her? "I thought you'd never come." Granny 60
made a long journey outward, looking for Hapsy. What if I don't find her? What then? Her heart sank down and down, there was no bottom to death, she couldn't come to the end of it. The blue light from Cornelia's lampshade drew into a tiny point in the center of her brain, it flickered and winked like an eye, quietly it flut-tered and dwindled. Granny lay curled down within herself, amazed and watchful, staring at the point of light that was herself; her body was now only a deeper mass of shadow in an endless darkness and this darkness would curl around the light and swallow it up. God, give a sign!

For the second time there was no sign. Again no bridegroom and the priest in the house. She could not remember any other sorrow because this grief wiped them all away. Oh, no, there's nothing more cruel than this—I'll never forgive it. She stretched herself with a deep breath and blew out the light.

Questions

1. In the very first paragraph, what does the writer tell us about Ellen (Granny) Weatherall?
2. What does the name of Weatherall have to do with Granny's nature (or her life story)? What other traits or qualities do you find in her?
3. "Her bones felt loose, and floated around in her skin, and Doctor Harry floated like a balloon" (paragraph 6). What do you understand from this statement? By what other remarks does the writer indicate Granny's condition? In paragraph 56, why does Father Connolly tickle Granny's feet? At what other moments in the story does she fail to understand what is happening, or confuse the present with the past?
4. Exactly what happened to Ellen Weatherall sixty years earlier? What effects did this event have on her?

5. In paragraph 49, whom do you guess to be the man who "cursed like a sailor's parrot"? In paragraph 56, whom do you assume to be the man driving the cart? Is the fact that these persons are not clearly labeled and identified a failure on the author's part?

6. What is stream of consciousness? Would you call "The Jilting of Granny Weatherall" a stream-of-consciousness story? Refer to the story in your reply.

7. Sum up the character of the daughter Cornelia.

8. Why doesn't Granny's last child, Hapsy, come to her mother's deathbed?

9. Would you call the character of Doctor Harry "flat" or "round"? Why is his flatness (or roundness) appropriate to the story?

10. How is this the story of another "jilting"? What similarities are there between that fateful day of sixty years ago (described in paragraphs 29, 49, and 61) and the moment when Granny is dying? This time, who is the "bridegroom" not in the house?

11. "This is the story of an eighty-year-old woman lying in bed, getting groggy, and dying. I can't see why it should interest anybody." How would you answer this critic?

Katherine Mansfield

Miss Brill   1922

Katherine Mansfield Beauchamp (1888–1923), who shortened her byline, was born into a sedate Victorian family in New Zealand, the daughter of a successful businessman. At fifteen, she emigrated to England to attend school and did not ever permanently return Down Under. In 1918, after a time of wild-oat sowing in bohemian London, she married the journalist and critic John Middleton Murry. All at once, Mansfield found herself struggling to define her sexual identity, to earn a living by her pen, to endure World War I (in which her brother was killed in action), and to survive the ravages of tuberculosis. She died at thirty-four, in France, at a spiritualist commune where she had sought to regain her health. Mansfield wrote no novels, but during her brief career concentrated on the short story, in which form of art she has few peers. Bliss (1920) *and* The Garden-*

Katherine Mansfield

Party and Other Stories (1922) were greeted with an acclaim that has continued; her collected short stories were published in 1937. Some of her stories celebrate life, others wryly poke fun at it. Many reveal, in ordinary lives, small incidents that open like doorways into significances.

Although it was so brilliantly fine—the blue sky powdered with gold and great spots of light like white wine splashed over the Jardins Publiques—Miss Brill was glad that she had decided on her fur. The air was motionless, but when you opened your mouth there was just a faint chill, like a chill from a glass of iced water before you sip, and now and again a leaf came drifting—from nowhere, from the sky. Miss Brill put up her hand and touched her fur. Dear little thing! It was nice to feel it again. She had taken it out of its box that afternoon, shaken out the moth-powder, given it a good brush, and rubbed the life back into the dim little eyes. "What has been happening to me?" said the sad little eyes. Oh, how sweet it was to see them snap at her again from the red eiderdown! . . . But the nose, which was of some black composi-tion, wasn't at all firm. It must have had a knock, somehow. Never mind—a little dab of black sealing-wax when the time came—when it was absolutely necessary. . . . Little rogue! Yes, she really felt like that about it. Little rogue biting its tail just by her left ear. She could have taken it off and laid it on her lap and stroked it. She felt a tingling in her hands and arms, but that came from walking, she supposed. And when she breathed, something light and sad—no, not sad, exactly—something gentle seemed to move in her bosom.

There were a number of people out this afternoon, far more than last Sunday. And the band sounded louder and gayer. That was because the Season had begun. For although the band played all year round on Sundays, out of season it was never the same. It was like some one playing with only the family to listen; it didn't care how it played if there weren't any strangers present. Wasn't the conductor wearing a new coat, too? She was sure it was new. He scraped with his foot and flapped his arms like a rooster about to crow, and the bandsmen sitting in the green rotunda blew out their cheeks and glared at the music. Now there came a little "flutey" bit—very pretty!—a little chain of bright drops. She was sure it would be repeated. It was; she lifted her head and smiled.

Only two people shared her "special" seat: a fine old man in a velvet coat, his hands clasped over a huge carved walking-stick, and a big old woman, sitting upright, with a roll of knitting on her embroidered apron. They did not speak. This was disap-pointing, for Miss Brill always looked forward to the conversation. She had become really quite expert, she thought, at listening as though she didn't listen, at sitting in other people's lives just for a minute while they talked round her.

She glanced, sideways, at the old couple. Perhaps they would go soon. Last Sunday, too, hadn't been as interesting as usual. An Englishman and his wife, he wearing a dreadful Panama hat and she button boots. And she'd gone on the whole time about how she ought to wear spectacles; she knew she needed them; but that it was no good getting any; they'd be sure to break and they'd never keep on. And he'd been so pa-tient. He'd suggested everything—gold rims, the kind that curved round your ears, little pads inside the bridge. No, nothing would please her. "They'll always be sliding down my nose!" Miss Brill wanted to shake her.

The old people sat on the bench, still as statues. Never mind, there was always the crowd to watch. To and fro, in front of the flower-beds and the band rotunda, the couples and groups paraded, stopped to talk, to greet, to buy a handful of flowers from the old beggar who had his tray fixed to the railings. Little children ran among them, swooping and laughing; little boys with big white silk bows under their chins, little girls, little French dolls, dressed up in velvet and lace. And sometimes a tiny stag-gerer came suddenly rocking into the open from under the trees, stopped, stared, as suddenly sat down "flop," until its small high-stepping mother, like a young hen, rushed scolding to its rescue. Other people sat on the benches and green chairs, but they were nearly always the same, Sunday after Sunday, and—Miss Brill had often noticed—there was something funny about nearly all of them. They were odd, silent, nearly all old, and from the way they stared they looked as though they'd just come from dark little rooms or even—even cupboards!

Behind the rotunda the slender trees with yellow leaves down drooping, and through them just a line of sea, and beyond the blue sky with gold-veined clouds.

Tum-tum-tum tiddle-um! tiddle-um! tum tiddley-um tum ta! blew the band.

Two young girls in red came by and two young soldiers in blue met them, and they laughed and paired and went off arm-in-arm. Two peasant women with funny straw hats passed, gravely, leading beautiful smoke-colored donkeys. A cold, pale nun hurried by. A beautiful woman came along and dropped her bunch of violets, and a little boy ran after to hand them to her, and she took them and threw them away as if they'd been poisoned. Dear me! Miss Brill didn't know whether to admire that or not! And now an ermine toque and a gentleman in grey met just in front of her. He was tall, stiff, dignified, and she was wearing the ermine toque she'd bought when her hair was yellow. Now everything, her hair, her face, even her eyes, was the same color as the shabby ermine, and her hand, in its cleaned glove, lifted to dab her lips, was a tiny yellowish paw. Oh, she was so pleased to see him—delighted! She rather thought they were going to meet that afternoon. She described where she'd been—everywhere, here, there, along by the sea. The day was so charming—didn't he agree? And wouldn't he, perhaps? . . . But he shook his head, lighted a cigarette, slowly breathed a great deep puff into her face, and, even while she was still talking and laughing, flicked the match away and walked on. The ermine toque was alone; she smiled more brightly than ever. But even the band seemed to know what she was feeling and played more softly, played tenderly, and the drum beat, "The Brute! The Brute!" over and over. What would she do? What was going to happen now? But as Miss Brill wondered, the ermine toque turned, raised her hand as though she'd seen some one else, much nicer, just over there, and pattered away. And the band changed again and played more quickly, more gaily than ever, and the old couple on Miss Brill's seat got up and marched away, and such a funny old man with long whiskers hobbled along in time to the music and was nearly knocked over by four girls walking abreast.

Oh, how fascinating it was! How she enjoyed it! How she loved sitting here, watching it all! It was like a play. It was exactly like a play. Who could believe the sky at the back wasn't painted? But it wasn't till a little brown dog trotted on solemn and then slowly trotted off, like a little "theatre" dog, a little dog that had been drugged, that Miss Brill discovered what it was that made it so exciting. They were all on the stage. They weren't only the audience, not only looking on; they were acting. Even she had a part and came every Sunday. No doubt somebody would have noticed if she hadn't been there; she was part of the performance after all. How strange she'd never thought of it like that before! And yet it explained why she made such a point of starting from home at just the same time each week—so as not to be late for the performance—and it also explained why she had quite a queer, shy feeling at telling her English pupils how she spent her Sunday afternoons. No wonder! Miss Brill nearly laughed out loud. She was on the stage. She thought of the old invalid gentleman to whom she read the newspaper four afternoons a week while he slept in the garden. She had got quite used to the frail head on the cotton pillow, the hollowed eyes, the open mouth and the high pinched nose. If he'd been dead she mightn't have noticed for weeks; she wouldn't have minded. But suddenly he knew he was having the paper read to him by an actress! "An actress!" The old head lifted; two points of light quivered in the old eyes. "An actress—are ye?" And Miss Brill smoothed the newspaper as though it were the manuscript of her part and said gently: "Yes, I have been an actress for a long time."

The band had been having a rest. Now they started again. And what they played 10
was warm, sunny, yet there was just a faint chill—a something, what was it?—not
sadness—no, not sadness—a something that made you want to sing. The tune lifted,
lifted, the light shone; and it seemed to Miss Brill that in another moment all of
them, all the whole company, would begin singing. The young ones, the laughing
ones who were moving together, they would begin, and the men's voices, very resolute and brave, would join them. And then she too, she too, and the others on the
benches—they would come in with a kind of accompaniment—something low, that
scarcely rose or fell, something so beautiful—moving . . . And Miss Brill's eyes filled
with tears and she looked smiling at all the other members of the company. Yes, we
understand, we understand, she thought—though what they understood she didn't
know.

Just at that moment a boy and a girl came and sat down where the old couple
had been. They were beautifully dressed; they were in love. The hero and heroine, of
course, just arrived from his father's yacht. And still soundlessly singing, still with
that trembling smile, Miss Brill prepared to listen.

"No, not now," said the girl. "Not here, I can't."

"But why? Because of that stupid old thing at the end there?" asked the boy.
"Why does she come here at all—who wants her? Why doesn't she keep her silly old
mug at home?"

"It's her fu-fur which is so funny," giggled the girl. "It's exactly like a fried whiting."

"Ah, be off with you!" said the boy in an angry whisper. Then: "Tell me, my 15
petite chérie—"

"No, not here," said the girl. "Not yet."

On her way home she usually bought a slice of honeycake at the baker's. It was
her Sunday treat. Sometimes there was an almond in her slice, sometimes not. It
made a great difference. If there was an almond it was like carrying home a tiny
present—a surprise—something that might very well not have been there. She
hurried on the almond Sundays and struck the match for the kettle in quite a dash-
ing way.

But today she passed the baker's boy, climbed the stairs, went into the little dark
room—her room like a cupboard—and sat down on the red eiderdown. She sat there
for a long time. The box that the fur came out of was on the bed. She unclasped the
necklet quickly; quickly, without looking, laid it inside. But when she put the lid on
she thought she heard something crying.

Questions

1. What details provide insight into Miss Brill's character and lifestyle?
2. What point of view is used in "Miss Brill"? How does this method improve the story?
3. Where and in what season does the story take place? Would the effect be the same if the story were set, say, in a remote Alaskan village in the winter?
4. What draws Miss Brill to the park every Sunday? What is the nature of the startling revelation that delights her on the day the story takes place?
5. Miss Brill's sense of herself is at least partly based on her attitudes toward others. Give instances of this tendency, showing also how it is connected with her drastic change of mood.
6. What explanations might there be for Miss Brill's thinking, in the last line of the story, that she "heard something crying"?

Naguib Mahfouz

The Lawsuit   1989

Translated by Denys Johnson-Davies

Naguib Mahfouz

Naguib Mahfouz (1911–2006) was born in Cairo, Egypt, where he spent his entire life and which served as the setting for his thirty-four novels and fourteen collections of short stories. His father was a civil servant, a path that Mahfouz himself would follow, spending most of his career in the Ministry of Culture. Mahfouz graduated from Cairo University in 1934 with a degree in philosophy but abandoned his postgraduate studies to pursue writing, concentrating so intently on this goal that he deferred marriage until 1943. Prose fiction was a relatively new genre in Arabic literature, and Mahfouz—who had read and admired many Western novelists, including Melville, Dostoyevsky, Balzac, and Camus— was enormously influential in modernizing its language, techniques, and subject matter. He planned a sequence of novels telling the entire history of Egypt, but after writing three novels set in the time of the Pharaohs he abandoned this project in favor of contemporary settings. Among his most important works are the Cairo Trilogy (Palace Walk, Palace of Desire, Sugar Street, *1956–57), depicting three generations of a middle-class Cairo family, and* Children of Gebelawi *(1959), an allegorical treatment of the development of Judaism, Christianity, and Islam. Considered blasphemous, this novel has not been published in the Arabic world, except in Lebanon. Mahfouz further alienated Islamic fundamentalists through his condemnation of the fatwa against Salman Rushdie for* The Satanic Verses *in 1989. Although Mahfouz regarded Rushdie's novel as offensive, he supported the author's freedom of expression. As a result of defending Rushdie, Mahfouz was stabbed in the neck by an Islamic fundamentalist. He recovered, but was left with permanent nerve damage that impaired his ability to write. In 1988 Mahfouz became the first Arabic writer to win the Nobel Prize in Literature. Though the award had little effect on his modest lifestyle, it had an immense impact on his literary fortunes: previously almost unknown outside the Arab world, he became a widely translated author with an international reputation.*

I found myself suddenly the subject of a lawsuit. My father's widow was demanding maintenance. Awakened from the depths of time, the past with its memories had invaded me. After reading the petition I exclaimed, "When did she go broke? Has she in her turn been robbed?"

"This woman robbed us and deprived us of our legal rights," I said to my lawyer.

I felt a strong desire to see her, not through any temptation to gloat over her but in order to see what effects time had had upon her. Today, like me, she was in her forties. Had her beauty withstood the passage of time? Was it holding out against poverty? If the lawsuit was not genuine, would she have stretched out a demanding hand to one of her enemies? On the other hand, if it was specious, why had she not stretched out her hand before? What a ravishing beauty she had been!

"My father married her," I told the lawyer, "when he was in his middle fifties and she a girl of twenty." A semiliterate, old-fashioned contractor, he did not deal with banks but stored his profits away in a large cupboard in his bedroom. We were happy about this so long as we were a single family. The announcement of the new marriage was like a bomb exploding among us—my mother, my elder brother, and myself, as well as my sisters in their various homes. The top floor was given over to my father, the bride, and the cupboard. We were struck dumb by her youth and beauty. My mother said in a quavering voice choked with weeping, "What a catastrophe! We'll end up without a bean."

My elder brother was illiterate and mentally retarded. He was without work, but considered himself a landowner. He flared up in a rage, declaring, "I'll defend myself to the very death."

Some of our relatives advised us to consult a lawyer, but my father threatened my mother with divorce if we were to entertain any such move. "I'm not gullible or an idiot, and no one's rights will be lost."

I was the one least affected by the disaster, partly because of my youth and partly because I was the only one in the family who wanted to study, hoping to enter the engineering college. Yet even so, I did not miss the significance of the facts—my father's age and that of his beautiful bride, and the fortune under threat. By way of smoothing things over, I would say, "I have confidence in my father."

"If we say nothing," my brother would say, "we'll find the cupboard empty."

I shared his fears but affected outwardly what I did not feel inwardly. All the time I felt that our oasis, which had appeared so tranquil, was being subjected to a wild wind and that on the horizon black clouds were gathering. My mother took refuge in silent anxiety, with each new day giving her warning of a bad outcome. As for my elder brother, he would brave the lion in his lair, pleading with his father. "I am the firstborn, uneducated as you can see, and without means of support, so give me my share."

"Do you want to inherit from me while I'm still alive? It's a disgrace for you to doubt me—no one's rights will be lost." But my brother would not calm down and would pester my father whenever they met. He would hurl threats at him from behind his back, and my mother would say that she was more worried about my brother than she was about the fortune.

For my part, I wondered whether my father, that capable master of his trade, the man who was such a meticulous accountant despite his illiteracy, would meet defeat at the hands of a pretty girl. Yet, without doubt, he was changing, slipping down little by little each day. He would take himself off to the Turkish baths twice a month, would clip his beard and trim his mustache every week, and would strut about in new clothes. Finally he took to dyeing his hair. Precious gifts embellished the bride's neck, bosom, and arms. Now there was a Chevrolet and a chauffeur waiting in front of our house.

My brother became more and more angry. "Where did he get her from?" he would say to me. Was it so impossible that she might get hold of the key and find her way to opening the cupboard? Would she not take from him something to secure her future? Did she not have the power to make him happy or to turn his life into one of misery and turmoil as she wished?

Arguments would develop between my brother and my father that would go beyond the bounds of propriety. My father would grow angry and spit in my brother's face. In an explosive outburst, my brother seized hold of a table lamp and hurled it at his father, drawing blood. Seeing the blood, my brother was scared, but even so persevered in his attempts to do Father in, with the cook and the chauffeur intervening. My father insisted on informing the police, and my brother was taken off to court and from there to prison, where he died after a year.

"How did she find the courage to bring her case?" I asked the lawyer.

"Necessity has its own rules." 15

In the midst of our alarm and our mourning for my brother, my mother and I heard the noise of something striking the floor above us. We hurried upstairs and found ourselves standing aghast over my father's body. As is usual in such circumstances, we asked ourselves again and again what could have happened, but no amount of questioning can bring back the dead. It seems that he had had a paralyzing stroke a whole day before his death without our knowing.

We waited till he had been buried and the rites of mourning were over, and then the family gathered together. My sisters, their husbands, and their husbands' parents were there, and the lawyer was present as well. We asked about the key to the cupboard, and the young widow answered quite simply that she knew nothing about it. Sometimes the mind boggles at the sheer brazenness of lying. But what could be done? We then came across the key, and the cupboard finally divulged its secrets, exhibiting to us with profound mockery a bundle of notes that did not exceed five thousand pounds. "Then where is the man's fortune?" everyone called out.

All eyes were fixed on the beautiful widow, who answered defiantly. We had recourse to the police, and there were investigations and searches. As my mother had predicted, we came out of it all "without a bean." The beautiful widow went off to her parents' house, and the curtain was brought down upon her and the inheritance. My mother died. I got a job, married, and achieved a notable success. I became oblivious of the past until the lawsuit brought me back to it.

"It's really the height of irony," I said to the lawyer, "that I should be required to pay maintenance to that woman."

His voice came to me from between the files on his desk. "The old story does on 20 the face of it appear worthy of being put forward, but what's the point of unearthing it when we have no evidence against her?"

"Even if the old story may not be open for discussion, it's a good starting point, whose effect should not be underrated."

"On the contrary, we would be providing the woman's lawyer with the chance to take the offensive and to attract sympathy for her."

"Sympathy?"

"Steady now. Let's think about it a bit objectively. An old man hoards his wealth in a cupboard in his bedroom. He then buys himself a beautiful girl of twenty when he's a man of fifty-five. Such and such happens to his family and such and such to his beautiful wife. Fine, who was to blame?" He was silent for a while, scowling, then continued. "Let's look at it from your side. You're a man who's earning and has a family, and the cost of living is unbearably high, and so on and so forth. . . . Let's content ourselves by settling on a reasonable sum for maintenance."

"Too bad!" I muttered. "She robbed us; then there was the death of my brother 25 and my mother's distress."

"I'm sorry about that, but she's as much a victim as you are. Even the fortune she made off with brought her to disaster. And now here she is begging."

Prompted by casual curiosity, I said, "It's as though you know something about her."

He shook his head with diplomatic vagueness. "A woman who couldn't have children, she was married and divorced several times when she was in her prime. In middle age she fell in love with a student, who, in his turn, robbed her and went off."

He did not divulge the sources of his information, but I surmised the logical progression of events. I experienced a feeling of gratification, which a sense of decency prevented me from showing.

On the day of the court session, I was again seized by a mysterious desire to set   30
eyes on her. I recognized her as she waited in front of the lawyers' room. I knew her by conjecture before actually recognizing her, for the beauty that had made away with our fortune and ruined us had completely vanished. She was fat, excessively and unacceptably so, and the charming freshness had leaked away from her face. What little beauty was left seemed insipid. A veneer of perpetual dejection acted like a screen between her and other people. Without giving the matter any thought, I went up to her, inclined my head in greeting, and said, "I remember you. . . perhaps you remember me?"

At first she gazed at me in surprise, then in confusion. She returned the greeting with a gesture of her covered head. "I'm sorry to cause you trouble," she said, as though apologizing, "but I am forced to do so."

I forgot what I wanted to say. In fact words failed me, and I felt an inner peace. "Don't worry—let the Lord do as He wills." I quietly moved away as I said to myself, "Why not? Even a farce must continue right to the final act."

Questions

1. What impressions do you form about the narrator after reading the first three paragraphs? Are those impressions confirmed or overturned as the story unfolds?
2. Would you call the narrator a round character or a flat one? Explain your reasons why.
3. In your judgment, do the members of the narrator's family behave rationally? If not, how would you characterize their actions?
4. How would you describe the behavior of the lawyer? Does he seem to be an effective advocate for his client's interests? Explain.
5. How does the narrator react to seeing his father's wife in the courtroom at the end of the story? How do his reactions influence his attitude toward the lawsuit?
6. What does the narrator mean by his comments in the last paragraph? What resolution of the case do you think he anticipates?

Raymond Carver

Cathedral   1983

Raymond Carver (1938–1988) was born in Clatskanie, Oregon. When he was three, his family moved to Yakima, Washington, where his father worked in a sawmill. In his early years Carver worked briefly at a lumber mill and at other unskilled jobs, including a stint as a tulip-picker. Married with two children before he was twenty, he experienced blue-collar desperation more intimately than most American writers, though he once quipped that, until he read critics' reactions to his works, he never realized that the characters in his stories "were so bad off." In 1963 Carver earned a degree from Humboldt State College (now California State University, Humboldt). He briefly attended the Writers' Workshop of the University of Iowa, but, needing to support his family, he returned to California, working for three years as a hospital custodian before finding a job editing textbooks. In 1967 he met Gordon Lish, the influential editor who would publish several of his stories in Esquire. *Under Lish's demanding tutelage, Carver learned to pare his fiction to the essentials. In the early 1970s, though plagued with bankruptcies, increasing dependency on alcohol, and marital problems, he taught at several universities.*

Carver's publishing career began with a volume of poems, Near Klamath *(1968). His books of short stories include* Will You Please Be Quiet, Please? *(1977),* What We Talk About When We Talk About Love *(1981),* Cathedral *(1983), and* Where I'm Calling From *(1988), which contained new and selected work. The compression of language he learned as a poet may in part account for the lean quality of his prose, often called "minimalist," a term Carver did not like. In his last decade Carver taught creative writing at Syracuse University, and lived with the poet Tess Gallagher, whom he married in 1988. He divided his final years between Syracuse and Port Angeles, Washington. Carver's personal victory in 1977 over decades of alcoholism underscored the many professional triumphs of his final decade. He once said, "I'm prouder of that, that I quit drinking, than I am of anything in my life." His reputation as a master craftsman of the contemporary short story was still growing when he died, after a struggle with lung cancer.*

This blind man, an old friend of my wife's, he was on his way to spend the night. His wife had died. So he was visiting the dead wife's relatives in Connecticut. He called my wife from his in-laws'. Arrangements were made. He would come by train, a five-hour trip, and my wife would meet him at the station. She hadn't seen him since she worked for him one summer in Seattle ten years ago. But she and the blind man had kept in touch. They made tapes and mailed them back and forth. I wasn't enthusiastic about his visit. He was no one I knew. And his being blind bothered me. My idea of blindness came from the movies. In the movies, the blind moved slowly and never laughed. Sometimes they were led by seeing-eye dogs. A blind man in my house was not something I looked forward to.

That summer in Seattle she had needed a job. She didn't have any money. The man she was going to marry at the end of the summer was in officers' training school. He didn't have any money, either. But she was in love with the guy, and he was in love with her, etc. She'd seen something in the paper: HELP WANTED—*Reading to Blind Man,* and a telephone number. She phoned and went over, was hired on the spot. She'd worked with this blind man all summer. She read stuff to him, case studies, reports, that sort of thing. She helped him organize his little office in the county social-service department. They'd become good friends, my wife and the blind man. How do I know these things? She told me. And she told me something else. On her last day in the office, the blind man asked if he could touch her face. She agreed to this. She told me he touched his fingers to every part of her face, her nose—even her neck! She never forgot it. She even tried to write a poem about it. She was always trying to write a poem. She wrote a poem or two every year, usually after something really important had happened to her.

When we first started going out together, she showed me the poem. In the poem, she recalled his fingers and the way they had moved around over her face. In the poem, she talked about what she had felt at the time, about what went through her mind when the blind man touched her nose and lips. I can remember I didn't think much of the poem. Of course, I didn't tell her that. Maybe I just don't understand poetry. I admit it's not the first thing I reach for when I pick up something to read.

Anyway, this man who'd first enjoyed her favors, the officer-to-be, he'd been her childhood sweetheart. So okay. I'm saying that at the end of the summer she let the blind man run his hands over her face, said good-bye to him, married her childhood etc., who was now a commissioned officer, and she moved away from Seattle. But they'd kept in touch, she and the blind man. She made the first contact after a year or so. She called him up one night from an Air Force base in Alabama. She wanted to talk. They talked. He asked her to send a tape and tell him about her life. She did this. She sent the tape. On the tape, she told the blind man about her husband and about their life together in the military. She told the blind man she loved her husband but she didn't like it where they lived and she didn't like it that he was part of the military-industrial thing. She told the blind man she'd written a poem and he was in it. She told him that she was writing a poem about what it was like to be an Air Force officer's wife. The poem wasn't finished yet. She was still writing it. The blind man made a tape. He sent her the tape. She made a tape. This went on for years. My wife's officer was posted to one base and then another. She sent tapes from Moody AFB, McGuire, McConnell, and finally Travis, near Sacramento, where one night she got to feeling lonely and cut off from people she kept losing in that moving-around life. She got to feeling she couldn't go it another step. She went in and swallowed all the pills and capsules in the medicine chest and washed them down with a bottle of gin. Then she got into a hot bath and passed out.

But instead of dying, she got sick. She threw up. Her officer—why should he have a name? he was the childhood sweetheart, and what more does he want?—came home from somewhere, found her, and called the ambulance. In time, she put it all on a tape and sent the tape to the blind man. Over the years, she put all kinds of stuff on tapes and sent the tapes off lickety-split. Next to writing a poem every year, I think it was her chief means of recreation. On one tape, she told the blind man she'd decided to live away from her officer for a time. On another tape, she told him about her divorce. She and I began going out, and of course she told her blind man about it. She told him everything, or so it seemed to me. Once she asked me if I'd like to hear the latest tape from the blind man. This was a year ago. I was on the tape, she said. So I said okay, I'd listen to it. I got us drinks and we settled down in the living room. We made ready to listen. First she inserted the tape into the player and adjusted a couple of dials. Then she pushed a lever. The tape squeaked and someone began to talk in this loud voice. She lowered the volume. After a few minutes of harmless chitchat, I heard my own name in the mouth of this stranger, this blind man I didn't even know! And then this: "From all you've said about him, I can only conclude—" But we were interrupted, a knock at the door, something, and we didn't ever get back to the tape. Maybe it was just as well. I'd heard all I wanted to.

Now this same blind man was coming to sleep in my house.

"Maybe I could take him bowling," I said to my wife. She was at the draining board doing scalloped potatoes. She put down the knife she was using and turned around.

"If you love me," she said, "you can do this for me. If you don't love me, okay. But if you had a friend, any friend, and the friend came to visit, I'd make him feel comfortable." She wiped her hands with the dish towel.

"I don't have any blind friends," I said.

"You don't have *any* friends," she said. "Period. Besides," she said, "goddamn it, his wife's just died! Don't you understand that? The man's lost his wife!"

I didn't answer. She'd told me a little about the blind man's wife. Her name was Beulah. Beulah! That's a name for a colored woman.

"Was his wife a Negro?" I asked.

"Are you crazy?" my wife said. "Have you just flipped or something?" She picked up a potato. I saw it hit the floor, then roll under the stove. "What's wrong with you?" she said. "Are you drunk?"

"I'm just asking," I said.

Right then my wife filled me in with more detail than I cared to know. I made a   15
drink and sat at the kitchen table to listen. Pieces of the story began to fall into place.

Beulah had gone to work for the blind man the summer after my wife had stopped working for him. Pretty soon Beulah and the blind man had themselves a church wedding. It was a little wedding—who'd want to go to such a wedding in the first place?—just the two of them, plus the minister and the minister's wife. But it was a church wedding just the same. It was what Beulah had wanted, he'd said. But even then Beulah must have been carrying the cancer in her glands. After they had been inseparable for eight years—my wife's word, *inseparable*—Beulah's health went into a rapid decline. She died in a Seattle hospital room, the blind man sitting beside the bed and holding on to her hand. They'd married, lived and worked together, slept to-gether—had sex, sure—and then the blind man had to bury her. All this without his having ever seen what the goddamned woman looked like. It was beyond my under-standing. Hearing this, I felt sorry for the blind man for a little bit. And then I found myself thinking what a pitiful life this woman must have led. Imagine a woman who could never see herself as she was seen in the eyes of her loved one. A woman who could go on day after day and never receive the smallest compliment from her beloved. A woman whose husband could never read the expression on her face, be it misery or something better. Someone who could wear makeup or not—what differ-ence to him? She could, if she wanted, wear green eye-shadow around one eye, a straight pin in her nostril, yellow slacks, and purple shoes, no matter. And then to slip off into death, the blind man's hand on her hand, his blind eyes streaming tears—I'm imagining now—her last thought maybe this: that he never even knew what she looked like, and she on an express to the grave. Robert was left with a small insurance policy and a half of a twenty-peso Mexican coin. The other half of the coin went into the box with her. Pathetic.

So when the time rolled around, my wife went to the depot to pick him up. With nothing to do but wait—sure, I blamed him for that—I was having a drink and watching the TV when I heard the car pull into the drive. I got up from the sofa with my drink and went to the window to have a look.

I saw my wife laughing as she parked the car. I saw her get out of the car and shut the door. She was still wearing a smile. Just amazing. She went around to the other side of the car to where the blind man was already starting to get out. This blind man, feature this, he was wearing a full beard! A beard on a blind man! Too much, I say. The blind man reached into the backseat and dragged out a suitcase. My wife took his arm, shut the car door, and, talking all the way, moved him down the drive and then up the steps to the front porch. I turned off the TV. I finished my drink, rinsed the glass, dried my hands. Then I went to the door.

My wife said, "I want you to meet Robert. Robert, this is my husband. I've told you all about him." She was beaming. She had this blind man by his coat sleeve.

The blind man let go of his suitcase and up came his hand.   20

I took it. He squeezed hard, held my hand, and then he let it go.

"I feel like we've already met," he boomed.

"Likewise," I said. I didn't know what else to say. Then I said, "Welcome. I've heard a lot about you." We began to move then, a little group, from the porch into the living room, my wife guiding him by the arm. The blind man was carrying his suitcase in his other hand. My wife said things like, "To your left here, Robert. That's right. Now watch it, there's a chair. That's it. Sit down right here. This is the sofa. We just bought this sofa two weeks ago."

I started to say something about the old sofa. I'd liked that old sofa. But I didn't say anything. Then I wanted to say something else, small-talk, about the scenic ride along the Hudson. How going *to* New York, you should sit on the right-hand side of the train, and coming *from* New York, the left-hand side.

"Did you have a good train ride?" I said. "Which side of the train did you sit on, 25 by the way?"

"What a question, which side!" my wife said. "What's it matter which side?" she said.

"I just asked," I said.

"Right side," the blind man said. "I hadn't been on a train in nearly forty years. Not since I was a kid. With my folks. That's been a long time. I'd nearly forgotten the sensation. I have winter in my beard now," he said. "So I've been told, anyway. Do I look distinguished, my dear?" the blind man said to my wife.

"You look distinguished, Robert," she said. "Robert," she said. "Robert, it's just so good to see you."

My wife finally took her eyes off the blind man and looked at me. I had the 30 feeling she didn't like what she saw. I shrugged.

I've never met, or personally known, anyone who was blind. This blind man was late forties, a heavy-set, balding man with stooped shoulders, as if he carried a great weight there. He wore brown slacks, brown shoes, a light-brown shirt, a tie, a sports coat. Spiffy. He also had this full beard. But he didn't use a cane and he didn't wear dark glasses. I'd always thought dark glasses were a must for the blind. Fact was, I wished he had a pair. At first glance, his eyes looked like anyone else's eyes. But if you looked close, there was something different about them. Too much white in the iris, for one thing, and the pupils seemed to move around in the sockets without his knowing it or being able to stop it. Creepy. As I stared at his face, I saw the left pupil turn in toward his nose while the other made an effort to keep in one place. But it was only an effort, for that eye was on the roam without his knowing it or wanting it to be.

I said, "Let me get you a drink. What's your pleasure? We have a little of everything. It's one of our pastimes."

"Bub, I'm a Scotch man myself," he said fast enough in this big voice.

"Right," I said. Bub! "Sure you are. I knew it."

He let his fingers touch his suitcase, which was sitting alongside the sofa. He was 35 taking his bearings. I didn't blame him for that.

"I'll move that up to your room," my wife said.

"No, that's fine," the blind man said loudly. "It can go up when I go up."

"A little water with the Scotch?" I said.

"Very little," he said.

"I knew it," I said. 40

He said, "Just a tad. The Irish actor, Barry Fitzgerald? I'm like that fellow. When I drink water, Fitzgerald said, I drink water. When I drink whiskey, I drink whiskey." My wife laughed. The blind man brought his hand up under his beard. He lifted his beard slowly and let it drop.

I did the drinks, three big glasses of Scotch with a splash of water in each. Then we made ourselves comfortable and talked about Robert's travels. First the long flight from the West Coast to Connecticut, we covered that. Then from Connecticut up here by train. We had another drink concerning that leg of the trip.

I remembered having read somewhere that the blind didn't smoke because, as speculation had it, they couldn't see the smoke they exhaled. I thought I knew that much and that much only about blind people. But this blind man smoked his cigarette down to the nubbin and then lit another one. This blind man filled his ashtray and my wife emptied it.

When we sat down at the table for dinner, we had another drink. My wife heaped Robert's plate with cube steak, scalloped potatoes, green beans. I buttered him up two slices of bread. I said, "Here's bread and butter for you." I swallowed some of my drink. "Now let us pray," I said, and the blind man lowered his head. My wife looked at me, her mouth agape. "Pray the phone won't ring and the food doesn't get cold," I said.

We dug in. We ate everything there was to eat on the table. We ate like there was no tomorrow. We didn't talk. We ate. We scarfed. We grazed that table. We were into serious eating. The blind man had right away located his foods, he knew just where everything was on his plate. I watched with admiration as he used his knife and fork on the meat. He'd cut two pieces of meat, fork the meat into his mouth, and then go all out for the scalloped potatoes, the beans next, and then he'd tear off a hunk of buttered bread and eat that. He'd follow this up with a big drink of milk. It didn't seem to bother him to use his fingers once in a while, either.

We finished everything, including half a strawberry pie. For a few moments, we sat as if stunned. Sweat beaded on our faces. Finally, we got up from the table and left the dirty plates. We didn't look back. We took ourselves into the living room and sank into our places again. Robert and my wife sat on the sofa. I took the big chair. We had us two or three more drinks while they talked about the major things that had come to pass for them in the past ten years. For the most part, I just listened. Now and then I joined in. I didn't want him to think I'd left the room, and I didn't want her to think I was feeling left out. They talked of things that had happened to them—to them!—these past ten years. I waited in vain to hear my name on my wife's sweet lips: "And then my dear husband came into my life"—something like that. But I heard nothing of the sort. More talk of Robert. Robert had done a little of everything, it seemed, a regular blind jack-of-all-trades. But most recently he and his wife had had an Amway distributorship, from which, I gathered, they'd earned their living, such as it was. The blind man was also a ham radio operator. He talked in his loud voice about conversations he'd had with fellow operators in Guam, in the Philippines, in Alaska, and even in Tahiti. He said he'd have a lot of friends there if he ever wanted to go visit those places. From time to time, he'd turn his blind face toward me, put his hand under his beard, ask me something. How long had I been in my present position? (Three years.) Did I like my work? (I didn't.) Was I going to stay with it? (What were the options?) Finally, when I thought he was beginning to run down, I got up and turned on the TV.

My wife looked at me with irritation. She was heading toward a boil. Then she looked at the blind man and said, "Robert, do you have a TV?"

The blind man said, "My dear, I have two TVs. I have a color set and a black-and-white thing, an old relic. It's funny, but if I turn the TV on, and I'm always turning it on, I turn on the color set. It's funny, don't you think?"

45

I didn't know what to say to that. I had absolutely nothing to say to that. No opinion. So I watched the news program and tried to listen to what the announcer was saying.

"This is a color TV," the blind man said. "Don't ask me how, but I can tell." 50

"We traded up a while ago," I said.

The blind man had another taste of his drink. He lifted his beard, sniffed it, and let it fall. He leaned forward on the sofa. He positioned his ashtray on the coffee table, then put the lighter to his cigarette. He leaned back on the sofa and crossed his legs at the ankles.

My wife covered her mouth, and then she yawned. She stretched. She said, "I think I'll go upstairs and put on my robe. I think I'll change into something else. Robert, you make yourself comfortable," she said.

"I'm comfortable," the blind man said.

"I want you to feel comfortable in this house," she said. 55

"I am comfortable," the blind man said.

After she'd left the room, he and I listened to the weather report and then to the sports roundup. By that time, she'd been gone so long I didn't know if she was going to come back. I thought she might have gone to bed. I wished she'd come back down-stairs. I didn't want to be left alone with a blind man. I asked him if he wanted an-other drink, and he said sure. Then I asked if he wanted to smoke some dope with me. I said I'd just rolled a number. I hadn't, but I planned to do so in about two shakes.

"I'll try some with you," he said.

"Damm right," I said. "That's the stuff."

"I got our drinks and sat down on the sofa with him. Then I rolled us two fat 60 numbers. I lit one and passed it. I brought it to his fingers. He took it and inhaled.

"Hold it as long as you can," I said. I could tell he didn't know the first thing.

My wife came back downstairs wearing her pink robe and her pink slippers.

"What do I smell?" she said.

"We thought we'd have us some cannabis," I said.

My wife gave me a savage look. Then she looked at the blind man and said, 65 "Robert, I didn't know you smoked."

He said, "I do now, my dear. There's a first time for everything. But I don't feel anything yet."

"This stuff is pretty mellow," I said. "This stuff is mild. It's dope you can reason with," I said. "It doesn't mess you up."

"Not much it doesn't, bub," he said, and laughed.

My wife sat on the sofa between the blind man and me. I passed her the num-ber. She took it and toked and then passed it back to me. "Which way is this going?" she said. Then she said, "I shouldn't be smoking this. I can hardly keep my eyes open as it is. That dinner did me in. I shouldn't have eaten so much."

"It was the strawberry pie," the blind man said. "That's what did it," he said, and 70 he laughed his big laugh. Then he shook his head.

"There's more strawberry pie," I said.

"Do you want some more, Robert?" my wife said.

"Maybe in a little while," he said.

We gave our attention to the TV. My wife yawned again. She said, "Your bed is made up when you feel like going to bed, Robert. I know you must have had a long day. When you're ready to go to bed, say so." She pulled his arm. "Robert?"

He came to and said, "I've had a real nice time. This beats tapes, doesn't it?"   75

I said, "Coming at you," and I put the number between his fingers. He inhaled, held the smoke, and then let it go. It was like he'd been doing it since he was nine years old.

"Thanks, bub," he said. "But I think this is all for me. I think I'm beginning to feel it," he said. He held the burning roach out for my wife.

"Same here," she said. "Ditto. Me, too." She took the roach and passed it to me. "I may just sit here for a while between you two guys with my eyes closed. But don't let me bother you, okay? Either one of you. If it bothers you, say so. Otherwise, I may just sit here with my eyes closed until you're ready to go to bed," she said. "Your bed's made up, Robert, when you're ready. It's right next to our room at the top of the stairs. We'll show you up when you're ready. You wake me up now, you guys, if I fall asleep." She said that and then she closed her eyes and went to sleep.

The news program ended. I got up and changed the channel. I sat back down on the sofa. I wished my wife hadn't pooped out. Her head lay across the back of the sofa, her mouth open. She'd turned so that her robe slipped away from her legs, exposing a juicy thigh. I reached to draw her robe back over her, and it was then that I glanced at the blind man. What the hell! I flipped the robe open again.

"You say when you want some strawberry pie," I said.   80

"I will," he said.

I said, "Are you tired? Do you want me to take you up to your bed? Are you ready to hit the hay?"

"Not yet," he said. "No, I'll stay up with you, bub. If that's all right. I'll stay up until you're ready to turn in. We haven't had a chance to talk. Know what I mean? I feel like me and her monopolized the evening." He lifted his beard and he let it fall. He picked up his cigarettes and his lighter.

"That's all right," I said. Then I said, "I'm glad for the company."

And I guess I was. Every night I smoked dope and stayed up as long as I could be-   85
fore I fell asleep. My wife and I hardly ever went to bed at the same time. When I did go to sleep, I had these dreams. Sometimes I'd wake up from one of them, my heart going crazy.

Something about the church and the Middle Ages was on the TV. Not your run-of-the-mill TV fare. I wanted to watch something else. I turned to the other channels. But there was nothing on them, either. So I turned back to the first channel and apologized.

"Bub, it's all right," the blind man said. "It's fine with me. Whatever you want to watch is okay. I'm always learning something. Learning never ends. It won't hurt me to learn something tonight. I got ears," he said.

We didn't say anything for a time. He was leaning forward with his head turned at me, his right ear aimed in the direction of the set. Very disconcerting. Now and then his eyelids drooped and then they snapped open again. Now and then he put his fingers into his beard and tugged, like he was thinking about something he was hearing on the television.

On the screen, a group of men wearing cowls was being set upon and tormented by men dressed in skeleton costumes and men dressed as devils. The men dressed as devils wore devil masks, horns, and long tails. This pageant was part of a procession. The Englishman who was narrating the thing said it took place in Spain once a year. I tried to explain to the blind man what was happening.

"Skeletons," he said. "I know about skeletons," he said, and he nodded.   90

The TV showed this one cathedral. Then there was a long, slow look at another one. Finally, the picture switched to the famous one in Paris, with its flying buttresses and its spires reaching up to the clouds. The camera pulled away to show the whole of the cathedral rising above the skyline.

There were times when the Englishman who was telling the thing would shut up, would simply let the camera move around the cathedrals. Or else the camera would tour the countryside, men in fields walking behind oxen. I waited as long as I could. Then I felt I had to say something. I said, "They're showing the outside of this cathedral now. Gargoyles. Little statues carved to look like monsters. Now I guess they're in Italy. Yeah, they're in Italy. There's paintings on the walls of this one church."

"Are those fresco paintings, bub?" he asked, and he sipped from his drink.

I reached for my glass. But it was empty. I tried to remember what I could remember. "You're asking me are those frescoes?" I said. "That's a good question. I don't know."

The camera moved to a cathedral outside Lisbon. The differences in the Por-   95
tuguese cathedral compared with the French and Italian were not that great. But they were there. Mostly the interior stuff. Then something occurred to me, and I said, "Something has occurred to me. Do you have any idea what a cathedral is? What they look like, that is? Do you follow me? If somebody says cathedral to you, do you have any notion what they're talking about? Do you know the difference between that and a Baptist church, say?"

He let the smoke dribble from his mouth. "I know they took hundreds of workers fifty or a hundred years to build," he said. "I just heard the man say that, of course. I know generations of the same families worked on a cathedral. I heard him say that, too. The men who began their life's work on them, they never lived to see the completion of their work. In that wise, bub, they're no different from the rest of us, right?" He laughed. Then his eyelids drooped again. His head nodded. He seemed to be snoozing. Maybe he was imagining himself in Portugal. The TV was showing another cathedral now. This one was in Germany. The Englishman's voice droned on. "Cathedrals," the blind man said. He sat up and rolled his head back and forth. "If you want the truth, bub, that's about all I know. What I just said. What I heard him say. But maybe you could describe one to me? I wish you'd do it. I'd like that. If you want to know, I really don't have a good idea."

I stared hard at the shot of the cathedral on the TV. How could I even begin to describe it? But say my life depended on it. Say my life was being threatened by an insane guy who said I had to do it or else.

I stared some more at the cathedral before the picture flipped off into the country-side. There was no use. I turned to the blind man and said, "To begin with, they're very tall." I was looking around the room for clues. "They reach way up. Up and up. Toward the sky. They're so big, some of them, they have to have these supports. To help hold them up, so to speak. These supports are called buttresses. They remind me of viaducts, for some reason. But maybe you don't know viaducts, either? Sometimes the cathedrals have devils and such carved into the front. Sometimes lords and ladies. Don't ask me why this is," I said.

He was nodding. The whole upper part of his body seemed to be moving back and forth.

"I'm not doing so good, am I?" I said.   100

He stopped nodding and leaned forward on the edge of the sofa. As he listened to me, he was running his fingers through his beard. I wasn't getting through to him, I could see that. But he waited for me to go on just the same. He nodded, like he was trying to encourage me. I tried to think what else to say. "They're really big," I said. "They're massive. They're built of stone. Marble, too, sometimes. In those olden days, when they built cathedrals, men wanted to be close to God. In those olden days, God was an important part of everyone's life. You could tell this from their cathedral-building. I'm sorry," I said, "but it looks like that's the best I can do for you. I'm just no good at it."

"That's all right, bub," the blind man said. "Hey, listen. I hope you don't mind my asking you. Can I ask you something? Let me ask you a simple question, yes or no. I'm just curious and there's no offense. You're my host. But let me ask if you are in any way religious? You don't mind my asking?"

I shook my head. He couldn't see that, though. A wink is the same as a nod to a blind man. "I guess I don't believe in it. In anything. Sometimes it's hard. You know what I'm saying?"

"Sure, I do," he said.

"Right," I said.   105

The Englishman was still holding forth. My wife sighed in her sleep. She drew a long breath and went on with her sleeping.

"You'll have to forgive me," I said. "But I can't tell you what a cathedral looks like. It just isn't in me to do it. I can't do any more than I've done."

The blind man sat very still, his head down, as he listened to me.

I said, "The truth is, cathedrals don't mean anything special to me. Nothing. Cathedrals. They're something to look at on late-night TV. That's all they are."

It was then that the blind man cleared his throat. He brought something up. He   110 took a handkerchief from his back pocket. Then he said, "I get it, bub. It's okay. It happens. Don't worry about it," he said. "Hey, listen to me. Will you do me a favor? I got an idea. Why don't you find us some heavy paper? And a pen. We'll do something. We'll draw one together. Get us a pen and some heavy paper. Go on, bub, get the stuff," he said.

So I went upstairs. My legs felt like they didn't have any strength in them. They felt like they did after I'd done some running. In my wife's room I looked around. I found some ballpoints in a little basket on her table. And then I tried to think where to look for the kind of paper he was talking about.

Downstairs, in the kitchen, I found a shopping bag with onion skins in the bottom of the bag. I emptied the bag and shook it. I brought it into the living room and sat down with it near his legs. I moved some things, smoothed the wrinkles from the bag, spread it out on the coffee table.

The blind man got down from the sofa and sat next to me on the carpet.

He ran his fingers over the paper. He went up and down the sides of the paper. The edges, even the edges. He fingered the corners.

"All right," he said. "All right, let's do her."   115

He found my hand, the hand with the pen. He closed his hand over my hand. "Go ahead, bub, draw," he said. "Draw. You'll see. I'll follow along with you. It'll be okay. Just begin now like I'm telling you. You'll see. Draw," the blind man said.

So I began. First I drew a box that looked like a house. It could have been the house I lived in. Then I put a roof on it. At either end of the roof, I drew spires. Crazy.

"Swell," he said. "Terrific. You're doing fine," he said. "Never thought anything like this could happen in your lifetime, did you, bub? Well, it's a strange life, we all know that. Go on now. Keep it up."

I put in windows with arches. I drew flying buttresses. I hung great doors. I couldn't stop. The TV station went off the air. I put down the pen and closed and opened my fingers. The blind man felt around over the paper. He moved the tips of his fingers over the paper, all over what I had drawn, and he nodded.

"Doing fine," the blind man said. 120

I took up the pen again, and he found my hand. I kept at it. I'm no artist. But I kept drawing just the same.

My wife opened up her eyes and gazed at us. She sat up on the sofa, her robe hanging open. She said, "What are you doing? Tell me, I want to know."

I didn't answer her.

The blind man said, "We're drawing a cathedral. Me and him are working on it. Press hard," he said to me. "That's right. That's good," he said. "Sure. You got it, bub, I can tell. You didn't think you could. But you can, can't you? You're cooking with gas now. You know what I'm saying? We're going to really have us something here in a minute. How's the old arm?" he said. "Put some people in there now. What's a cathedral without people?"

My wife said, "What's going on? Robert, what are you doing? What's going on?" 125

"It's all right," he said to her. "Close your eyes now," the blind man said to me. I did it. I closed them just like he said.

"Are they closed?" he said. "Don't fudge."

"They're closed," I said.

"Keep them that way," he said. He said, "Don't stop now. Draw." 130

So we kept on with it. His fingers rode my fingers as my hand went over the paper. It was like nothing else in my life up to now.

Then he said, "I think that's it. I think you got it," he said. "Take a look. What do you think?"

But I had my eyes closed. I thought I'd keep them that way for a little longer. I thought it was something I ought to do.

"Well?" he said. "Are you looking?"

My eyes were still closed. I was in my house. I knew that. But I didn't feel like I 135 was inside anything.

"It's really something," I said.

Questions

1. What details in "Cathedral" make clear the narrator's initial attitude toward blind people? What hints does the author give about the reasons for this attitude? At what point in the story do the narrator's preconceptions about blind people start to change?

2. For what reason does the wife keep asking Robert if he'd like to go to bed (paragraphs 74–78)? What motivates the narrator to make the same suggestion in paragraph 82? What effect does Robert's reply have on the narrator?

3. What makes the narrator start explaining what he's seeing on television?

4. How does the point of view contribute to the effectiveness of the story?

5. At the end, the narrator has an epiphany. How would you describe it?

6. Would you describe the narrator as an antihero? Use specific details from the story to back up your response.

7. Is the wife a flat or a round character? What about Robert? Support your conclusion about each of them.

8. In a good story, a character doesn't suddenly become a completely different sort of person. Find details early in the story that show the narrator's more sensitive side and thus help to make his development credible and persuasive.

■ WRITING *effectively*

Raymond Carver on Writing

Commonplace but Precise Language   1983

Raymond Carver

It's possible, in a poem or short story, to write about commonplace things and objects using commonplace but precise language, and to endow those things—a chair, a window curtain, a fork, a stone, a woman's earring—with immense, even startling power. It is possible to write a line of seemingly innocuous dialogue and have it send a chill along the reader's spine—the source of artistic delight, as Nabokov would have it. That's the kind of writing that most interests me. I hate sloppy or haphazard writing whether it flies under the banner of experimentation or else is just clumsily rendered realism. In Isaac Babel's wonderful short story, "Guy de Maupassant," the narrator has this to say about the writing of fiction: "No iron can pierce the heart with such force as a period put just at the right place." This too ought to go on a three-by-five.

Evan Connell said once that he knew he was finished with a short story when he found himself going through it and taking out commas and then going through the story again and putting commas back in the same places. I like that way of working on something. I respect that kind of care for what is being done. That's all we have, finally, the words, and they had better be the right ones, with the punctuation in the right places so that they can best say what they are meant to say. If the words are heavy with the writer's own unbridled emotions, or if they are imprecise and inaccurate for some reason—if the words are in any way blurred—the reader's eyes will slide right over them and nothing will be achieved.

From "On Writing"

THINKING ABOUT CHARACTER

Although readers usually consider plot the central element of fiction, writers usually remark that stories begin with characters.

- **Identify the most important character.** The central character is the one who must deal with the plot complications and the central crisis of the story. The choices made by this character communicate his or her attitudes as well as the story's themes.
- **Consider the ways the characters' personalities and values are communicated.** Note that the way characters speak can immediately reveal important things about their personalities, beliefs, and behavior. A single line of dialogue can tell the audience a great deal, as in an old film in which the comedian W. C. Fields confides, "A woman drove me to drink and I never even had the courtesy to thank her."
- **Consider how the story's action grows out of its central character.** A story's action usually grows out of the personality of its protagonist and the situation he or she faces. As novelist Phyllis Bottome observed, "If a writer is true to his characters, they will give him his plot."

CHECKLIST: Writing About Character

- ☐ Who is the main character or protagonist of the story?
- ☐ Make a quick list of the character's physical, mental, moral, or behavioral traits. Which seem especially significant to the action of the story?
- ☐ Does the main character have an antagonist in the story? How do they differ?
- ☐ Does the way the protagonist speaks reveal anything about his or her personality?
- ☐ If the story is told in the first person, what is revealed about how the protagonist views his or her surroundings?
- ☐ What is the character's primary motivation? Does this motivation seem reasonable to you?
- ☐ Does the protagonist fully understand his or her motivations?
- ☐ In what ways is the protagonist changed or tested by the events of the story?

WRITING ASSIGNMENT ON CHARACTER

Choose a story with a dynamic protagonist. (See the beginning of this chapter for a discussion of dynamic characters.) Write an essay exploring how that character evolves over the course of the story, providing evidence from the story to back up your argument. Some good story choices might be Faulkner's "Barn Burning," Carver's "Cathedral," Baldwin's "Sonny's Blues," and Mahfouz's "The Lawsuit."

MORE TOPICS FOR WRITING

1. Using a story from this book, write a short essay that explains why a protagonist takes a crucial life-changing action. What motivates this character to do something that seems bold or surprising? You might consider:
   - What motivates the narrator to overcome his instinctive antipathy to the blind man in "Cathedral"?
   - What motivates the older brother to write to Sonny during his incarceration in "Sonny's Blues"?
   - Why doesn't Miss Brill buy her usual slice of honeycake on her way home at the end of "Miss Brill"?
2. Choose a minor character from any of the stories in this book, and write briefly on what the story reveals about that person, reading closely for even the smallest of details. Is he or she a stock character? Why or why not?
3. Choose a story in which the main character has an obvious antagonist, such as "Cathedral," "Sonny's Blues," or "The Lawsuit." What role does this second character play in bringing the protagonist to a new awareness of life?
4. Choose a dynamic character from one of the stories you've read so far. Write a brief essay on how the events in the story relate to your chosen character's strengths or shortcomings.
5. Choose a favorite character from a television show you watch regularly. What details are provided (either in the show's dialogue or in its visuals) to communicate the personality of this character? Would you say this person is a stock character or a rounded one? Write a brief essay making a case for your position.
6. Browse through magazines and newspapers to find a picture of a person you can't identify. Cut out the picture. Create a character based on the picture. As many writers do, make a list of characteristics, from the large (her life's ambition) to the small (his favorite breakfast cereal). As you build your list, make sure your details add up to a rounded character.

▶ TERMS FOR *review*

Characterization ▶ The techniques a writer uses to create, reveal, or develop the characters in a narrative.

Character description ▶ An aspect of characterization through which the author overtly relates either physical or mental traits of a character. This description is almost invariably a sign of what lurks beneath the surface of the character.

Character development ▶ The process by which a character is introduced, advanced, and possibly transformed in a story.

Character motivation ▶ What a character in a narrative wants, the reasons an author provides for a character's actions. Motivation can be either *explicit* (these reasons are specifically stated in a story) or *implicit* (the reasons are only hinted at or partially revealed).

Flat character ▶ A term coined by English novelist E. M. Forster to describe a character with only one outstanding trait. Flat characters are rarely the central characters in a narrative and stay the same throughout a story.

Round character ▶ A term also coined by E. M. Forster to describe a complex character who is presented in depth in a narrative. Round characters are those who change significantly during the course of a narrative or whose full personalities are revealed gradually throughout the story.

Stock character ▶ A common or stereotypical character. Examples of stock characters are the mad scientist, the battle-scarred veteran, and the strong but silent cowboy.

4

SETTING

ELEMENTS OF SETTING

By the **setting** of a story, we mean its time and place. The word might remind you of the metal that holds a diamond in a ring, or of a *set* used in a play—perhaps a bare chair in front of a slab of painted canvas. But often, in an effective short story, setting may figure as more than mere background or underpinning. It can make things happen. It can prompt characters to act, bring them to realizations, or cause them to reveal their inmost natures.

Place

To be sure, the idea of setting includes the physical environment of a story: a house, a street, a city, a landscape, a region. (*Where* a story takes place is sometimes called its **locale**.) Physical places mattered so greatly to French novelist Honoré de Balzac that sometimes, before writing a story set in a particular town, he would visit that town, select a few houses, and describe them in detail, down to their very smells.

Time

In addition to place, setting may crucially involve the time of the story—the hour, year, or century. It might matter greatly that a story takes place at dawn, or on the day of the first moon landing. When we begin to read a historical novel, we are soon made aware that we aren't reading about life in the twenty-first century. In *The Scarlet Letter*, nineteenth-century author Nathaniel Hawthorne, by a long introduction and a vivid opening scene at a prison door, prepares us to witness events in the Puritan community of Boston in the earlier seventeenth century. This setting, together with scenes of Puritan times we recall from high school history, helps us understand what happens in the novel. We can appreciate the shocked agitation in town when a woman is accused of adultery: she has given illegitimate birth. Such an event might seem common today, but in the stern, God-fearing New England Puritan community, it was a flagrant defiance of church and state, which were all-powerful (and were all one). That reader will make no sense of *The Scarlet Letter* who ignores its setting—if it is even possible to ignore the setting, given how much attention Hawthorne pays to it.

The fact that Hawthorne's novel takes place in a time remote from our own leads us to expect different customs and different attitudes. Some critics and teachers regard the setting of a story as its whole society, including the beliefs and assumptions of its characters. Still, we suggest that for now you keep your working definition of *setting* simple. Call it time and place. If later you should feel that your definition needs widening and deepening, you can always expand it.

Weather

Besides time and place, setting may also include the weather, which in some stories may be crucial. Climate seems as substantial as any character in William Faulkner's "Dry September." After sixty-two rainless days, a long unbroken spell of late-summer heat has frayed every nerve in a small town and caused the main character, a hot-headed white supremacist, to feel more and more irritated. The weather, someone remarks, is "enough to make a man do anything." When a false report circulates that a white woman has been raped by a black man, the rumor, like a match flung into a dry field, ignites rage and provokes a lynching. Evidently, to understand the story we have to recognize its locale, a small town in Mississippi in the 1930s during an infernal heat wave. Fully to take in the meaning of Faulkner's story, we have to take in the setting in its entirety.

Atmosphere

Atmosphere is the dominant mood or feeling that pervades all parts of a literary work. Atmosphere refers to the total effect conveyed by the author's use of language, images, and physical setting. But as the term *atmosphere* suggests, aspects of the physical setting (place, time, and weather) are usually crucial elements in achieving the author's intention. In some stories, a writer will seem to draw a setting mainly to evoke atmosphere. In such a story, setting starts us feeling whatever the storyteller would have us feel. In "The Tell-Tale Heart," Poe's setting the action in an old, dark, lantern-lit house greatly contributes to our sense of unease—and so helps the story's effectiveness.

HISTORICAL FICTION

One obvious example of how time can become a major element of setting is in **historical fiction**, where the story is set in another time and place. In historical fiction the author usually tries to recreate a faithful picture of daily life during the period. The historical period might be long ago, such as ancient Rome in Robert Graves's novel *I, Claudius* (1934), or it may be more recent, as in the setting of early twentieth-century Britain in Ian McEwan's *Atonement* (2001). Historical fiction sometimes introduces well-known figures from the past. Thornton Wilder's *Ides of March* (1948) includes Julius Caesar and Cleopatra among its many characters. Ron Hansen's *Exiles* (2008) depicts the life of English poet Gerard Manley Hopkins. More often, historical fiction presents imaginary characters in a carefully reconstructed version of a particular period of the past. Part of the pleasure of reading this sort of fiction comes from experiencing the many details of another time, just as films carefully set in a particular historical moment, such as Ridley Scott's *Gladiator* (2000) and James Cameron's *Titanic* (1997), let us see meticulously recreated settings of another time and place.

REGIONALISM

Physical place, by the way, is especially vital to a **regional writer**, who usually sets stories (or other work) in one geographic area. Such a writer, often a native of the place, tries to bring it alive to readers who live elsewhere. William Faulkner, a distinguished regional writer, almost always sets his novels and stories in his native Mississippi. Though born in St. Louis, Kate Chopin became known as a regional writer because she wrote about Louisiana in many of her short stories and in her novel *The Awakening*. Willa Cather, for her novels of frontier Nebraska, sometimes is regarded as another outstanding regionalist (though she also set fiction in Quebec, the Southwest, and, in "Paul's Case," in Pittsburgh and New York).

There is often something arbitrary, however, about calling an author a regional writer. The label sometimes has a political tinge; it means that the author describes an area outside the political and economic centers of a society. In a sense, we might think of James Joyce as a regional writer, in that all his fiction takes place in the city of Dublin, but instead we usually call him an Irish author.

As such writers show, a place can profoundly affect the character of someone who grew up in it. Willa Cather is fond of portraying strong-minded, independent women, such as the heroine of her novel *My Antonía*, strengthened in part by years of coping with the hardships of life on the wind-lashed prairie.

NATURALISM

Some writers consider the social and economic setting the most important element in the story. They present social environment as the determining factor in human behavior. Their approach is called **naturalism**—fiction of grim realism, in which the writer observes human characters like a scientist observing ants, seeing them as the products and victims of environment and heredity. Naturalism was first consciously developed in fiction in the late nineteenth century by French novelist Émile Zola. Important American Naturalists include Jack London, Theodore Dreiser, and Stephen Crane. Dreiser's novel *The Financier* (1912) begins in a city setting. A young boy (who will grow up to be a ruthless industrialist) is watching a battle to the death between a lobster and a squid in a fish-market tank. Dented for the rest of his life by this grim scene, he decides that's exactly the way human society functions.

Setting usually operates more subtly than that fish tank. Often, setting and character will reveal each other. Recall how Faulkner, at the start of "A Rose for Emily," depicts Emily Grierson's house, once handsome but now "an eyesore among eyesores" surrounded by gas stations. Still standing, refusing to yield its old-time horse-and-buggy splendor to the age of the automobile, the house in "its stubborn and coquettish decay" embodies the character of its owner. In John Steinbeck's "The Chrysanthemums" (Chapter 7), the story begins with a fog that has sealed off a valley from the rest of the world—a fog like the lid on a pot. That physical setting helps convey the isolation and loneliness of the protagonist's situation.

But be warned: you'll meet stories in which setting appears hardly to matter. In W. Somerset Maugham's fable "The Appointment in Samarra," all we need to be told about the setting is that it is a marketplace in Baghdad. In that brief fable, the inevitability of death is the point, not an exotic setting. In this chapter, though, you will meet four fine stories in which setting, for one reason or another, counts greatly. Without it, none of these stories could take place.

Kate Chopin

The Storm   1898

Kate Chopin

Kate Chopin (1851–1904) was born Katherine O'Flaherty in St. Louis, daughter of an Irish immigrant grown wealthy in retailing. On his death, young Kate was raised by her mother's family: aristocratic Creoles, descendants of the French and Spaniards who had colonized Louisiana. Young Kate received a convent schooling, and at nineteen married Oscar Chopin, a Creole cotton broker from New Orleans. Later, the Chopins lived on a plantation near Cloutierville, Louisiana, a region whose varied people—Creoles, Cajuns, blacks—Kate Chopin was later to write about with loving care in Bayou Folk *(1894) and* A Night in Arcadia *(1897). The shock of her husband's sudden death in 1883, which left her with the raising of six children, seems to have plunged Kate Chopin into writing. She read and admired fine woman writers of her day, such as the Maine realist Sarah Orne Jewett. She also read Maupassant, Zola, and other new (and scandalous) French naturalist writers. She began to bring into American fiction some of their hard-eyed observation and their passion for telling unpleasant truths. Determined, in defiance of her times, frankly to show the sexual feelings of her characters, Chopin suffered from neglect and censorship. When her major novel,* The Awakening, *appeared in 1899, critics were outraged by her candid portrait of a woman who seeks sexual and professional independence. After causing such a literary scandal, Chopin was unable to get her later work published, and wrote little more before she died.* The Awakening *and many of her stories had to wait seven decades for a sympathetic audience.*

I

The leaves were so still that even Bibi thought it was going to rain. Bobinôt, who was accustomed to converse on terms of perfect equality with his little son, called the child's attention to certain somber clouds that were rolling with sinister intention from the west, accompanied by a sullen, threatening roar. They were at Friedheimer's store and decided to remain there till the storm had passed. They sat within the door on two empty kegs. Bibi was four years old and looked very wise.

"Mama'll be 'fraid, yes," he suggested with blinking eyes.

"She'll shut the house. Maybe she got Sylvie helpin' her this evenin'," Bobinôt responded reassuringly.

"No; she ent got Sylvie. Sylvie was helpin' her yistiday," piped Bibi.

Bobinôt arose and going across to the counter purchased a can of shrimps, of which Calixta was very fond. Then he returned to his perch on the keg and sat stolidly holding the can of shrimps while the storm burst. It shook the wooden store   5 and seemed to be ripping great furrows in the distant field. Bibi laid his little hand on his father's knee and was not afraid.

II

Calixta, at home, felt no uneasiness for their safety. She sat at a side window sewing furiously on a sewing machine. She was greatly occupied and did not notice the approaching storm. But she felt very warm and often stopped to mop her face on which the perspiration gathered in beads. She unfastened her white sacque at the throat. It began to grow dark, and suddenly realizing the situation she got up hurriedly and went about closing windows and doors.

Out on the small front gallery she had hung Bobinôt's Sunday clothes to air and she hastened out to gather them before the rain fell. As she stepped outside, Alcée Laballière rode in at the gate. She had not seen him very often since her marriage, and never alone. She stood there with Bobinôt's coat in her hands, and the big rain drops began to fall. Alcée rode his horse under the shelter of a side projection where the chickens had huddled and there were plows and a harrow piled up in the corner.

"May I come and wait on your gallery till the storm is over, Calixta?" he asked.

"Come 'long in, M'sieur Alcée."

His voice and her own startled her as if from a trance, and she seized Bobinôt's 10 vest. Alcée, mounting to the porch, grabbed the trousers and snatched Bibi's braided jacket that was about to be carried away by a sudden gust of wind. He expressed an intention to remain outside, but it was soon apparent that he might as well have been out in the open: the water beat in upon the boards in driving sheets, and he went inside, closing the door after him. It was even necessary to put something beneath the door to keep the water out.

"My! what a rain! It's good two years sence it rain like that," exclaimed Calixta as she rolled up a piece of bagging and Alcée helped her to thrust it beneath the crack.

She was a little fuller of figure than five years before when she married; but she had lost nothing of her vivacity. Her blue eyes still retained their melting quality; and her yellow hair, dishevelled by the wind and rain, kinked more stubbornly than ever about her ears and temples.

The rain beat upon the low, shingled roof with a force and clatter that threatened to break an entrance and deluge them there. They were in the dining room— the sitting room—the general utility room. Adjoining was her bed room, with Bibi's couch along side her own. The door stood open, and the room with its white, monumental bed, its closed shutters, looked dim and mysterious.

Alcée flung himself into a rocker and Calixta nervously began to gather up from the floor the lengths of a cotton sheet which she had been sewing.

"If this keeps up, *Dieu sait°* if the levees goin' to stan' it!" she exclaimed.   15

"What have you got to do with the levees?"

"I got enough to do! An' there's Bobinôt with Bibi out in that storm—if he only didn' left Friedheimer's!"

"Let us hope, Calixta, that Bobinôt's got sense enough to come in out of a cyclone."

She went and stood at the window with a greatly disturbed look on her face. She wiped the frame that was clouded with moisture. It was stiflingly hot. Alcée got up

Dieu sait: God only knows.

and joined her at the window, looking over her shoulder. The rain was coming down in sheets obscuring the view of far-off cabins and enveloping the distant wood in a gray mist. The playing of the lightning was incessant. A bolt struck a tall chinaberry tree at the edge of the field. It filled all visible space with a blinding glare and the crash seemed to invade the very boards they stood upon.

Calixta put her hands to her eyes, and with a cry, staggered backward. Alcée's arm encircled her, and for an instant he drew her close and spasmodically to him.   20

"*Bonté!*"° she cried, releasing herself from his encircling arm and retreating from the window, "the house'll go next! If I only knew w'ere Bibi was!" She would not compose herself; she would not be seated. Alcée clasped her shoulders and looked into her face. The contact of her warm, palpitating body when he had unthinkingly drawn her into his arms, had aroused all the old-time infatuation and desire for her flesh.

"Calixta," he said, "don't be frightened. Nothing can happen. The house is too low to be struck, with so many tall trees standing about. There! aren't you going to be quiet? say, aren't you?" He pushed her hair back from her face that was warm and steaming. Her lips were as red and moist as pomegranate seed. Her white neck and a glimpse of her full, firm bosom disturbed him powerfully. As she glanced up at him the fear in her liquid blue eyes had given place to a drowsy gleam that unconsciously betrayed a sensuous desire. He looked down into her eyes and there was nothing for him to do but gather her lips in a kiss. It reminded him of Assumption.°

"Do you remember—in Assumption, Calixta?" he asked in a low voice broken by passion. Oh! she remembered; for in Assumption he had kissed her and kissed and kissed her; until his senses would well nigh fail, and to save her he would resort to a desperate flight. If she was not an immaculate dove in those days, she was still inviolate; a passionate creature whose very defenselessness had made her defense, against which his honor forbade him to prevail. Now—well, now—her lips seemed in a manner free to be tasted, as well as her round, white throat and her whiter breasts.

They did not heed the crashing torrents, and the roar of the elements made her laugh as she lay in his arms. She was a revelation in that dim, mysterious chamber; as white as the couch she lay upon. Her firm, elastic flesh that was knowing for the first time its birthright, was like a creamy lily that the sun invites to contribute its breath and perfume to the undying life of the world.

The generous abundance of her passion, without guile or trickery, was like a white flame which penetrated and found response in depths of his own sensuous nature that had never yet been reached.   25

When he touched her breasts they gave themselves up in quivering ecstasy, inviting his lips. Her mouth was a fountain of delight. And when he possessed her, they seemed to swoon together at the very borderland of life's mystery.

He stayed cushioned upon her, breathless, dazed, enervated, with his heart beating like a hammer upon her. With one hand she clasped his head, her lips lightly touching his forehead. The other hand stroked with a soothing rhythm his muscular shoulders.

The growl of the thunder was distant and passing away. The rain beat softly upon the shingles, inviting them to drowsiness and sleep. But they dared not yield.

Bonté!: Heavens!   *Assumption*: a parish west of New Orleans.

The rain was over; and the sun was turning the glistening green world into a palace of gems. Calixta, on the gallery, watched Alcée ride away. He turned and smiled at her with a beaming face; and she lifted her pretty chin in the air and laughed aloud.

III

Bobinôt and Bibi, trudging home, stopped without at the cistern to make them-   30
selves presentable.

"My! Bibi, w'at will yo' mama say! You ought to be ashame'. You oughtn' put on those good pants. Look at 'em! An' that mud on yo' collar! How you got that mud on yo' collar, Bibi? I never saw such a boy!" Bibi was the picture of pathetic resignation. Bobinôt was the embodiment of serious solicitude as he strove to remove from his own person and his son's the signs of their tramp over heavy roads and through wet fields. He scraped the mud off Bibi's bare legs and feet with a stick and carefully re-moved all traces from his heavy brogans. Then, prepared for the worst—the meeting with an overscrupulous housewife, they entered cautiously at the back door.

Calixta was preparing supper. She had set the table and was dripping coffee at the hearth. She sprang up as they came in.

"Oh, Bobinôt! You back! My! but I was uneasy. W'ere you been during the rain? An' Bibi? he ain't wet? he ain't hurt?" She had clasped Bibi and was kissing him effu-sively. Bobinôt's explanations and apologies which he had been composing all along the way, died on his lips as Calixta felt him to see if he were dry, and seemed to ex-press nothing but satisfaction at their safe return.

"I brought you some shrimps, Calixta," offered Bobinôt, hauling the can from his ample side pocket and laying it on the table.

"Shrimps! Oh, Bobinôt! you too good fo' anything!" and she gave him a smack-   35
ing kiss on the cheek that resounded. "*J'vous réponds,*° we'll have feas' to night! umph-umph!"

Bobinôt and Bibi began to relax and enjoy themselves, and when the three seated themselves at table they laughed much and so loud that anyone might have heard them as far away as Laballière's.

IV

Alcée Laballière wrote to his wife, Clarisse, that night. It was a loving letter, full of tender solicitude. He told her not to hurry back, but if she and the babies liked it at Biloxi, to stay a month longer. He was getting on nicely; and though he missed them, he was willing to bear the separation a while longer—realizing that their health and pleasure were the first things to be considered.

V

As for Clarisse, she was charmed upon receiving her husband's letter. She and the babies were doing well. The society was agreeable; many of her old friends and acquaintances were at the bay. And the first free breath since her marriage seemed to restore the pleasant liberty of her maiden days. Devoted as she was to her husband, their intimate conjugal life was something which she was more than willing to forego for a while.

So the storm passed and everyone was happy.

J'vous réponds: Let me tell you.

Questions

1. Exactly where does Chopin's story take place? How can you tell?
2. What circumstances introduced in Part I turn out to have a profound effect on events in the story?
3. What details in "The Storm" emphasize the fact that Bobinôt loves his wife? What details reveal how imperfectly he comprehends her nature?
4. What general attitudes toward sex, love, and marriage does Chopin imply? Cite evidence to support your answer.
5. What meanings do you find in the title "The Storm"?
6. In the story as a whole, how do setting and plot reinforce each other?

Jack London

To Build a Fire   1910

Jack London

Jack London (1876–1916), born in San Francisco, won a large popular audience for his novels of the sea and the Yukon: The Call of the Wild *(1903),* The Sea-Wolf *(1904), and* White Fang *(1906). Like Ernest Hemingway, he was a writer who lived a strenuous life. In 1893, he marched cross-country in Coxey's Army, an organized protest of the unemployed; in 1897, he took part in the Klondike gold rush; and later, as a reporter, he covered the Russo-Japanese War and the Mexican Revolution. Son of an unmarried mother and a father who denied his paternity, London grew up in poverty. At fourteen, he began holding hard jobs: working in a canning factory and a jute-mill, serving as a deck hand, pirating oysters in San Francisco Bay. These experiences persuaded him to join the Socialist Labor Party and crusade for workers' rights. In his political novel* The Iron Heel *(1908), London envisions a grim totalitarian America. Like himself, the hero of his novel* Martin Eden *(1909) is a man of brief schooling who gains fame as a writer, works for a cause, loses faith in it, and finds life without meaning. Though endowed with immense physical energy—he wrote fifty volumes—London drank hard, spent fast, and played out early. While his reputation as a novelist may have declined since his own day, some of his short stories have lasted triumphantly.*

Day had broken cold and gray, exceedingly cold and gray, when the man turned aside from the main Yukon trail and climbed the high earth-bank, where a dim and little-travelled trail led eastward through the fat spruce timberland. It was a steep bank, and he paused for breath at the top, excusing the act to himself by looking at his watch. It was nine o'clock. There was no sun nor hint of sun, though there was not a cloud in the sky. It was a clear day, and yet there seemed an intangible pall over the face of things, a subtle gloom that made the day dark, and that was due to the absence of sun. This fact did not worry the man. He was used to the lack of sun. It had been days since he had seen the sun, and he knew that a few more days must pass before that cheerful orb, due south, would just peep above the sky line and dip immediately from view.

The man flung a look back along the way he had come. The Yukon lay a mile wide and hidden under three feet of ice. On top of this ice were as many feet of snow. It was all pure white, rolling in gentle undulations where the ice jams of the freeze-up had formed. North and south, as far as the eye could see, it was unbroken white, save for a dark hairline that curved and twisted from around the spruce-covered island to the south, and that curved and twisted away into the north, where it disappeared behind another spruce-covered island. This dark hairline was the trail—the main trail—that led south five hundred miles to the Chilcoot Pass, Dyea, and salt water; and that led north seventy miles to Dawson, and still on to the north a thousand miles to Nulato, and finally to St. Michael, on Bering Sea, a thousand miles and half a thousand more.

But all this—the mysterious, far-reaching hairline trail, the absence of sun from the sky, the tremendous cold, and the strangeness and weirdness of it all—made no impression on the man. It was not because he was long used to it. He was a newcomer in the land, a *chechaquo*, and this was his first winter. The trouble with him was that he was without imagination. He was quick and alert in the things of life, but only in the things, and not in the significances. Fifty degrees below zero meant eighty-odd degrees of frost. Such fact impressed him as being cold and uncomfortable, and that was all. It did not lead him to meditate upon his frailty as a creature of temperature, and upon man's frailty in general, able only to live within certain narrow limits of heat and cold; and from there on it did not lead him to the conjectural field of immortality and man's place in the universe. Fifty degrees below zero stood for a bite of frost that hurt and that must be guarded against by the use of mittens, ear flaps, warm moccasins, and thick socks. Fifty degrees below zero was to him just precisely fifty degrees below zero. That there should be anything more to it than that was a thought that never entered his head.

As he turned to go on, he spat speculatively. There was a sharp, explosive crackle that startled him. He spat again. And again, in the air, before it could fall to the snow, the spittle crackled. He knew that at fifty below spittle crackled on the snow, but this spittle had crackled in the air. Undoubtedly it was colder than fifty below—how much colder he did not know. But the temperature did not matter. He was bound for the old claim on the left fork of Henderson Creek, where the boys were already. They had come over across the divide from the Indian Creek country, while he had come the roundabout way to take a look at the possibilities of getting out logs in the spring from the islands in the Yukon. He would be in to camp by six o'clock; a bit after dark, it was true, but the boys would be there, a fire would be going, and a hot supper would be ready. As for lunch, he pressed his hand against the protruding bundle under his jacket. It was also under his shirt, wrapped up in a handkerchief and lying against the naked skin. It was the only way to keep the biscuits from freezing. He smiled agreeably to himself as he thought of those biscuits, each cut open and sopped in bacon grease, and each enclosing a generous slice of fried bacon.

He plunged in among the big spruce trees. The trail was faint. A foot of snow had fallen since the last sled had passed over, and he was glad he was without a sled, travelling light. In fact, he carried nothing but the lunch wrapped in the handkerchief. He was surprised, however, at the cold. It certainly was cold, he concluded, as he rubbed his numb nose and cheekbones with his mittened hand. He was a warm-whiskered

5

man, but the hair on his face did not protect the high cheekbones and the eager nose that thrust itself aggressively into the frosty air.

At the man's heels trotted a dog, a big native husky, the proper wolf dog, gray-coated and without any visible or temperamental difference from its brother, the wild wolf. The animal was depressed by the tremendous cold. It knew that it was no time for travelling. Its instinct told it a truer tale than was told to the man by the man's judgment. In reality, it was not merely colder than fifty below zero; it was colder than sixty below, than seventy below. It was seventy-five below zero. Since the freezing point is thirty-two above zero, it meant that one hundred and seven degrees of frost obtained. The dog did not know anything about thermometers. Possibly in its brain there was no sharp consciousness of a condition of very cold such as was in the man's brain. But the brute had its instinct. It experienced a vague but menacing apprehension that subdued it and made it slink along at the man's heels, and that made it question eagerly every unwonted movement of the man as if expecting him to go into camp or to seek shelter somewhere and build a fire. The dog had learned fire, and it wanted fire, or else to burrow under the snow and cuddle its warmth away from the air.

The frozen moisture of its breathing had settled on its fur in a fine powder of frost, and especially were its jowls, muzzle, and eyelashes whitened by its crystalled breath. The man's red beard and mustache were likewise frosted, but more solidly, the deposit taking the form of ice and increasing with every warm, moist breath he exhaled. Also, the man was chewing tobacco, and the muzzle of ice held his lips so rigidly that he was unable to clear his chin when he expelled the juice. The result was that a crystal beard of the color and solidity of amber was increasing its length on his chin. If he fell down it would shatter itself, like glass, into brittle fragments. But he did not mind the appendage. It was the penalty all tobacco chewers paid in that country, and he had been out before in two cold snaps. They had not been so cold as this, he knew, but by the spirit thermometer at Sixty Mile he knew they had been registered at fifty below and at fifty-five.

He held on through the level stretch of woods for several miles, crossed a wide flat, and dropped down a bank to the frozen bed of a small stream. This was Henderson Creek, and he knew he was ten miles from the forks. He looked at his watch. It was ten o'clock. He was making four miles an hour, and he calculated that he would arrive at the forks at half-past twelve. He decided to celebrate that event by eating his lunch there.

The dog dropped in again at his heels, with a tail drooping discouragement, as the man swung along the creek bed. The furrow of the old sled trail was plainly visible, but a dozen inches of snow covered the marks of the last runners. In a month no man had come up or down that silent creek. The man held steadily on. He was not much given to thinking, and just then particularly he had nothing to think about save that he would eat lunch at the forks and that at six o'clock he would be in camp with the boys. There was nobody to talk to; and, had there been, speech would have been impossible because of the ice muzzle on his mouth. So he continued monotonously to chew tobacco and to increase the length of his amber beard.

Once in a while the thought reiterated itself that it was very cold and that he had never experienced such cold. As he walked along he rubbed his cheekbones and nose with the back of his mittened hand. He did this automatically, now and again changing hands. But, rub as he would, the instant he stopped his cheekbones were numb, and the following instant the end of his nose went numb. He was sure to frost

10

his cheeks; he knew that, and experienced a pang of regret that he had not devised a nose strap of the sort Bud wore in cold snaps. Such a strap passed across the cheeks, as well, and saved them. But it didn't matter much, after all. What were frosted cheeks? A bit painful, that was all; they were never serious.

Empty as the man's mind was of thoughts, he was keenly observant, and he noticed the changes in the creek, the curves and bends and timber jams, and always he sharply noted where he placed his feet. Once, coming around a bend, he shied abruptly, like a startled horse, curved away from the place where he had been walking, and retreated several paces back along the trail. The creek he knew was frozen clear to the bottom—no creek could contain water in that arctic winter—but he knew also that there were springs that bubbled out from the hillsides and ran along under the snow and on top the ice of the creek. He knew that the coldest snaps never froze these springs, and he knew likewise their danger. They were traps. They hid pools of water under the snow that might be three inches deep, or three feet. Sometimes a skin of ice half an inch thick covered them, and in turn was covered by the snow. Sometimes there were alternate layers of water and ice skin, so that when one broke through he kept on breaking through for a while, sometimes wetting himself to the waist.

That was why he had shied in such panic. He had felt the give under his feet and heard the crackle of a snow-hidden ice skin. And to get his feet wet in such a temperature meant trouble and danger. At the very least it meant delay, for he would be forced to stop and build a fire, and under its protection to bare his feet while he dried his socks and moccasins. He stood and studied the creek bed and its banks, and decided that the flow of water came from the right. He reflected awhile, rubbing his nose and cheeks, then skirted to the left, stepping gingerly and testing the footing for each step. Once clear of the danger, he took a fresh chew of tobacco and swung along at his four-mile gait.

In the course of the next two hours he came upon several similar traps. Usually the snow above the hidden pools had a sunken, candied appearance that advertised the danger. Once again, however, he had a close call; and once, suspecting danger, he compelled the dog to go on in front. The dog did not want to go. It hung back until the man shoved it forward, and then it went quickly across the white, unbroken surface. Suddenly it broke through, floundered to one side, and got away to firmer footing. It had wet its forefeet and legs, and almost immediately the water that clung to it turned to ice. It made quick efforts to lick the ice off its legs, then dropped down in the snow and began to bite out the ice that had formed between the toes. This was a matter of instinct. To permit the ice to remain would mean sore feet. It did not know this. It merely obeyed the mysterious prompting that arose from the deep crypts of its being. But the man knew, having achieved a judgment on the subject, and he removed the mitten from his right hand and helped tear out the ice particles. He did not expose his fingers more than a minute, and was astonished at the swift numbness that smote them. It certainly was cold. He pulled on the mitten hastily, and beat the hand savagely across his chest.

At twelve o'clock the day was at its brightest. Yet the sun was too far south on its winter journey to clear the horizon. The bulge of the earth intervened between it and Henderson Creek, where the man walked under a clear sky at noon and cast no shadow. At half-past twelve, to the minute, he arrived at the forks of the creek. He was pleased at the speed he had made. If he kept it up, he would certainly be with the boys by six. He unbuttoned his jacket and shirt and drew forth his lunch.

The action consumed no more than a quarter of a minute, yet in that brief moment the numbness laid hold of the exposed fingers. He did not put the mitten on, but, instead, struck the fingers a dozen sharp smashes against his leg. Then he sat down on a snow-covered log to eat. The sting that followed upon the striking of his fingers against his leg ceased so quickly that he was startled. He had had no chance to take a bite of biscuit. He struck the fingers repeatedly and returned them to the mitten, baring the other hand for the purpose of eating. He tried to take a mouthful, but the ice muzzle prevented. He had forgotten to build a fire and thaw out. He chuckled at his foolishness, and as he chuckled he noted the numbness creeping into the exposed fingers. Also, he noted that the stinging which had first come to his toes when he sat down was already passing away. He wondered whether the toes were warm or numb. He moved them inside the moccasins and decided that they were numb.

He pulled the mitten on hurriedly and stood up. He was a bit frightened. He stamped up and down until the stinging returned into the feet. It certainly was cold, was his thought. That man from Sulphur Creek had spoken the truth when telling how cold it sometimes got in the country. And he had laughed at him at the time! That showed one must not be too sure of things. There was no mistake about it, it *was* cold. He strode up and down, stamping his feet and threshing his arms, until reassured by the returning warmth. Then he got out matches and proceeded to make a fire. From the undergrowth, where high water of the previous spring had lodged a supply of seasoned twigs, he got his firewood. Working carefully from a small beginning, he soon had a roaring fire, over which he thawed the ice from his face and in the protection of which he ate his biscuits. For the moment the cold of space was outwitted. The dog took satisfaction in the fire, stretching out close enough for warmth and far enough away to escape being singed. 15

When the man had finished, he filled his pipe and took his comfortable time over a smoke. Then he pulled on his mittens, settled the ear flaps of his cap firmly about his ears, and took the creek trail up the left fork. The dog was disappointed and yearned back toward the fire. This man did not know cold. Possibly all the generations of his ancestry had been ignorant of cold, of real cold, of cold one hundred and seven degrees below freezing point. But the dog knew; all its ancestry knew, and it had inherited the knowledge. And it knew that it was not good to walk abroad in such fearful cold. It was the time to lie snug in a hole in the snow and wait for a curtain of cloud to be drawn across the face of outer space whence this cold came. On the other hand, there was no keen intimacy between the dog and the man. The one was the toil slave of the other, and the only caresses it had ever received were the caresses of the whip lash and of harsh and menacing throat sounds that threatened the whip lash. So the dog made no effort to communicate its apprehension to the man. It was not concerned in the welfare of the man; it was for its own sake that it yearned back toward the fire. But the man whistled, and spoke to it with the sound of whip lashes, and the dog swung in at the man's heels and followed after.

The man took a chew of tobacco and proceeded to start a new amber beard. Also, his moist breath quickly powdered with white his mustache, eyebrows, and lashes. There did not seem to be so many springs on the left fork of the Henderson, and for half an hour the man saw no signs of any. And then it happened. At a place where there were no signs, where the soft, unbroken snow seemed to advertise solidity beneath, the man broke through. It was not deep. He wet himself halfway to the knees before he floundered out to the firm crust.

He was angry, and cursed his luck aloud. He had hoped to get into camp with the boys at six o'clock, and this would delay him an hour, for he would have to build a fire and dry out his footgear. This was imperative at that low temperature—he knew that much; and he turned aside to the bank, which he climbed. On top, tangled in the underbrush about the trunks of several small spruce trees, was a high-water deposit of dry firewood—sticks and twigs, principally, but also larger portions of seasoned branches and fine, dry, last year's grasses. He threw down several large pieces on top of the snow. This served for a foundation and prevented the young flame from drowning itself in the snow it otherwise would melt. The flame he got by touching a match to a small shred of birch bark that he took from his pocket. This burned even more readily than paper. Placing it on the foundation, he fed the young flame with wisps of dry grass and with the tiniest dry twigs.

He worked slowly and carefully, keenly aware of his danger. Gradually, as the flame grew stronger, he increased the size of the twigs with which he fed it. He squatted in the snow, pulling the twigs out from their entanglement in the brush and feeding directly to the flame. He knew there must be no failure. When it is seventy-five below zero, a man must not fail in his first attempt to build a fire—that is, if his feet are wet. If his feet are dry, and he fails, he can run along the trail for half a mile and restore his circulation. But the circulation of wet and freezing feet cannot be restored by running when it is seventy-five below. No matter how fast he runs, the wet feet will freeze the harder.

All this the man knew. The old-timer on Sulphur Creek had told him about it the previous fall, and now he was appreciating the advice. Already all sensation had gone out of his feet. To build the fire he had been forced to remove his mittens, and the fingers had quickly gone numb. His pace of four miles an hour had kept his heart pumping blood to the surface of his body and to all the extremities. But the instant he stopped, the action of the pump eased down. The cold of space smote the unprotected tip of the planet, and he, being on that unprotected tip, received the full force of the blow. The blood of his body recoiled before it. The blood was alive, like the dog, and like the dog it wanted to hide away and cover itself up from the fearful cold. So long as he walked four miles an hour, he pumped that blood, willy-nilly, to the surface; but now it ebbed away and sank down into the recesses of his body. The extremities were the first to feel its absence. His wet feet froze the faster, and his exposed fingers numbed the faster, though they had not yet begun to freeze. Nose and cheeks were already freezing, while the skin of all his body chilled as it lost its blood. 20

But he was safe. Toes and nose and cheeks would be only touched by the frost, for the fire was beginning to burn with strength. He was feeding it with twigs the size of his finger. In another minute he would be able to feed it with branches the size of his wrist, and then he could remove his wet footgear, and, while it dried, he could keep his naked feet warm by the fire, rubbing them at first, of course, with snow. The fire was a success. He was safe. He remembered the advice of the old-timer on Sulphur Creek, and smiled. The old-timer had been very serious in laying down the law that no man must travel alone in the Klondike after fifty below. Well, here he was; he had had the accident; he was alone; and he had saved himself. Those old-timers were rather womanish, some of them, he thought. All a man had to do was to keep his head, and he was all right. Any man who was a man could travel alone. But it was surprising, the rapidity with which his cheeks and nose were freezing. And he had not thought his fingers could go lifeless in so short a time. Lifeless they were, for he could scarcely make them move together to grip a twig, and they seemed remote from his body and from him. When he touched a twig, he had to look and see whether or not he had hold of it. The wires were pretty well down between him and his finger ends.

All of which counted for little. There was the fire, snapping and crackling and promising life with every dancing flame. He started to untie his moccasins. They were coated with ice; the thick German socks were like sheaths of iron halfway to the knees; and the moccasin strings were like rods of steel all twisted and knotted as by some conflagration. For a moment he tugged with his numb fingers, then, realizing the folly of it, he drew his sheath knife.

But before he could cut the strings, it happened. It was his own fault or, rather, his mistake. He should not have built the fire under the spruce tree. He should have built it in the open. But it had been easier to pull the twigs from the brush and drop them directly on the fire. Now the tree under which he had done this carried a weight of snow on its boughs. No wind had blown for weeks, and each bough was fully freighted. Each time he had pulled a twig he had communicated a slight agitation to the tree— an imperceptible agitation, so far as he was concerned, but an agitation sufficient to bring about the disaster. High up in the tree one bough capsized its load of snow. This fell on the boughs beneath, capsizing them. This process continued, spreading out and involving the whole tree. It grew like an avalanche, and it descended without warning upon the man and the fire, and the fire was blotted out! Where it had burned was a mantle of fresh and disordered snow.

The man was shocked. It was as though he had just heard his own sentence of death. For a moment he sat and stared at the spot where the fire had been. Then he grew very calm. Perhaps the old-timer on Sulphur Creek was right. If he had only had a trail mate he would have been in no danger now. The trail mate could have built the fire. Well, it was up to him to build the fire over again, and this second time there must be no failure. Even if he succeeded, he would most likely lose some toes. His feet must be badly frozen by now, and there would be some time before the second fire was ready.

Such were his thoughts, but he did not sit and think them. He was busy all the time they were passing through his mind. He made a new foundation for a fire, this time in the open, where no treacherous tree could blot it out. Next he gathered dry grasses and tiny twigs from the high-water flotsam. He could not bring his fingers together to pull them out, but he was able to gather them by the handful. In this way he got many rotten twigs and bits of green moss that were undesirable, but it was the best he could do. He worked methodically, even collecting an armful of the larger branches to be used later when the fire gathered strength. And all the while the dog sat and watched him, a certain yearning wistfulness in its eye, for it looked upon him as the fire provider, and the fire was slow in coming.

When all was ready, the man reached in his pocket for a second piece of birch bark. He knew the bark was there, and, though he could not feel it with his fingers, he could hear its crisp rustling as he fumbled for it. Try as he would, he could not clutch hold of it. And all the time, in his consciousness, was the knowledge that each instant his feet were freezing. This thought tended to put him in a panic, but he fought against it and kept calm. He pulled on his mittens with his teeth, and threshed his arms back and forth, beating his hands with all his might against his sides. He did this

25

sitting down, and he stood up to do it; and all the while the dog sat in the snow, its wolf brush of a tail curled around warmly over its forefeet, its sharp wolf ears pricked forward intently as it watched the man. And the man, as he beat and threshed with his arms and hands, felt a great surge of envy as he regarded the creature that was warm and secure in its natural covering.

After a time he was aware of the first faraway signals of sensation in his beaten fingers. The faint tingling grew stronger till it evolved into a stinging ache that was excruciating, but which the man hailed with satisfaction. He stripped the mitten from his right hand and fetched forth the birch bark. The exposed fingers were quickly going numb again. Next he brought out his bunch of sulphur matches. But the tremendous cold had already driven the life out of his fingers. In his effort to separate one match from the others, the whole bunch fell in the snow. He tried to pick it out of the snow, but failed. The dead fingers could neither touch nor clutch. He was very careful. He drove the thought of his freezing feet, and nose, and cheeks, out of his mind, devoting his whole soul to the matches. He watched, using the sense of vision in place of that of touch, and when he saw his fingers on each side the bunch, he closed them—that is, he willed to close them, for the wires were down, and the fingers did not obey. He pulled the mitten on the right hand, and beat it fiercely against his knee. Then, with both mittened hands, he scooped the bunch of matches, along with much snow, into his lap. Yet he was no better off.

After some manipulation he managed to get the bunch between the heels of his mittened hands. In this fashion he carried it to his mouth. The ice crackled and snapped when by a violent effort he opened his mouth. He drew the lower jaw in, curled the upper lip out of the way, and scraped the bunch with his upper teeth in order to separate a match. He succeeded in getting one, which he dropped on his lap. He was no better off. He could not pick it up. Then he devised a way. He picked it up in his teeth and scratched it on his leg. Twenty times he scratched before he succeeded in lighting it. As it flamed he held it with his teeth to the birch bark. But the burning brimstone went up his nostrils and into his lungs, causing him to cough spasmodically. The match fell into the snow and went out.

The old-timer on Sulphur Creek was right, he thought in the moment of controlled despair that ensued: after fifty below, a man should travel with a partner. He beat his hands, but failed in exciting any sensation. Suddenly he bared both hands, removing the mittens with his teeth. He caught the whole bunch between the heels of his hands. His arm muscles not being frozen enabled him to press the hand heels tightly against the matches. Then he scratched the bunch along his leg. It flared into flame, seventy sulphur matches at once! There was no wind to blow them out. He kept his head to one side to escape the strangling fumes, and held the blazing bunch to the birch bark. As he so held it, he became aware of sensation in his hand. His flesh was burning. He could smell it. Deep down below the surface he could feel it. The sensation developed into pain that grew acute. And still he endured it, holding the flame of the matches clumsily to the bark that would not light readily because his own burning hands were in the way, absorbing most of the flame.

At last, when he could endure no more, he jerked his hands apart. The blazing matches fell sizzling into the snow, but the birch bark was alight. He began laying dry grasses and the tiniest twigs on the flame. He could not pick and choose, for he had to lift the fuel between the heels of his hands. Small pieces of rotten wood and green moss clung to the twigs, and he bit them off as well as he could with his teeth. He cherished the flame carefully and awkwardly. It meant life, and it must not perish. The withdrawal of blood from the surface of his body now made him begin to shiver, and he grew more awkward. A large piece of green moss fell squarely on the little fire. He tried to poke it out with his fingers, but his shivering frame made him poke too far, and he disrupted the nucleus of the little fire, the burning grasses and tiny twigs separating and scattering. He tried to poke them together again, but in spite of the tenseness of the effort, his shivering got away from him, and the twigs were hopelessly scattered. Each twig gushed a puff of smoke and went out. The fire provider had failed. As he looked apathetically about him, his eyes chanced on the dog, sitting across the ruins of the fire from him, in the snow, making restless, hunching movements, slightly lifting one forefoot and then the other, shifting its weight back and forth on them with wistful eagerness.

The sight of the dog put a wild idea into his head. He remembered the tale of the man, caught in the blizzard, who killed a steer and crawled inside the carcass, and so was saved. He would kill the dog and bury his hands in the warm body until the numbness went out of them. Then he could build another fire. He spoke to the dog, calling it to him; but in his voice was a strange note of fear that frightened the animal, who had never known the man to speak in such a way before. Something was the matter, and its suspicious nature sensed danger—it knew not what danger, but somewhere, somehow, in its brain arose an apprehension of the man. It flattened its ears down at the sound of the man's voice, and its restless, hunching movements and the liftings and shiftings of its forefeet became more pronounced; but it would not come to the man. He got on his hands and knees and crawled toward the dog. This unusual posture again excited suspicion, and the animal sidled mincingly away.

The man sat up in the snow for a moment and struggled for calmness. Then he pulled on his mittens, by means of his teeth, and got upon his feet. He glanced down at first in order to assure himself that he was really standing up, for the absence of sensation in his feet left him unrelated to the earth. His erect position in itself started to drive the webs of suspicion from the dog's mind; and when he spoke peremptorily, with the sound of whip lashes in his voice, the dog rendered its customary allegiance and came to him. As it came within reaching distance, the man lost his control. His arms flashed out to the dog, and he experienced genuine surprise when he discovered that his hands could not clutch, that there was neither bend nor feeling in the fingers. He had forgotten for the moment that they were frozen and that they were freezing more and more. All this happened quickly, and before the animal could get away, he encircled its body with his arms. He sat down in the snow, and in this fashion held the dog, while it snarled and whined and struggled.

But it was all he could do, hold its body encircled in his arms and sit there. He realized that he could not kill the dog. There was no way to do it. With his helpless hands he could neither draw nor hold his sheath knife nor throttle the animal. He released it, and it plunged wildly away, with tail between its legs, and still snarling. It halted forty feet away and surveyed him curiously, with ears sharply pricked forward.

The man looked down at his hands in order to locate them, and found them hanging on the ends of his arms. It struck him as curious that one should have to use his eyes in order to find out where his hands were. He began threshing his arms back and forth, beating the mittened hands against his sides. He did this for five minutes, violently, and his heart pumped enough blood up to the surface to put a stop to his shivering. But no sensation was aroused in the hands. He had an impression that they hung like weights on the ends of his arms, but when he tried to run the impression down, he could not find it.

A certain fear of death, dull and oppressive, came to him. This fear quickly   35
became poignant as he realized that it was no longer a mere matter of freezing his fingers and toes, or of losing his hands and feet, but that it was a matter of life and death with the chances against him. This threw him into a panic, and he turned and ran up the creek bed along the old, dim trail. The dog joined in behind and kept up with him. He ran blindly, without intention, in fear such as he had never known in his life. Slowly, as he plowed and floundered through the snow, he began to see things again—the banks of the creek, the old timber jams, the leafless aspens, and the sky. The running made him feel better. He did not shiver. Maybe, if he ran on, his feet would thaw out; and anyway, if he ran far enough, he would reach camp and the boys. Without doubt he would lose some fingers and toes and some of his face; but the boys would take care of him, and save the rest of him when he got there. And at the same time there was another thought in his mind that said he would never get to the camp and the boys; that it was too many miles away, that the freezing had too great a start on him, and that he would soon be stiff and dead. This thought he kept in the background and refused to consider. Sometimes it pushed itself forward and demanded to be heard, but he thrust it back and strove to think of other things.

It struck him as curious that he could run at all on feet so frozen that he could not feel them when they struck the earth and took the weight of his body. He seemed to himself to skim along above the surface, and to have no connection with the earth. Somewhere he had once seen a winged Mercury, and he wondered if Mercury felt as he felt when skimming over the earth.

His theory of running until he reached the camp and the boys had one flaw in it: he lacked the endurance. Several times he stumbled, and finally he tottered, crumpled up, and fell. When he tried to rise, he failed. He must sit and rest, he decided, and next time he would merely walk and keep on going. As he sat and regained his breath, he noted that he was feeling quite warm and comfortable. He was not shivering, and it even seemed that a warm glow had come to his chest and trunk. And yet, when he touched his nose and cheeks, there was no sensation. Running would not thaw them out. Nor would it thaw out his hands and feet. Then the thought came to him that the frozen portions of his body must be extending. He tried to keep this thought down, to forget it, to think of something else; he was aware of the panicky feeling that it caused, and he was afraid of the panic. But the thought asserted itself, and persisted, until it produced a vision of his body totally frozen. This was too much, and he made another wild run along the trail. Once he slowed down to a walk, but the thought of the freezing extending itself made him run again.

And all the time the dog ran with him, at his heels. When he fell down a second time, it curled its tail over its forefeet and sat in front of him, facing him, curiously eager and intent. The warmth and security of the animal angered him, and he cursed it till it flattened down its ears appeasingly. This time the shivering came more quickly upon the man. He was losing in his battle with the frost. It was creeping into his body from all sides. The thought of it drove him on, but he ran no more than a hundred feet, when he staggered and pitched headlong. It was his last panic. When he had recovered his breath and control, he sat up and entertained in his mind the conception of meeting death with dignity. However, the conception did not come to him in such terms. His idea of it was that he had been making a fool of himself, running around like a chicken with its head cut off—such was the simile that occurred to him. Well, he was bound to freeze anyway, and he might as well take it decently. With this new-found peace of mind came the first glimmerings of drowsiness. A good idea, he thought, to sleep off to death. It was like taking an anesthetic. Freezing was not so bad as people thought. There were lots worse ways to die.

He pictured the boys finding his body next day. Suddenly he found himself with them, coming along the trail and looking for himself. And, still with them, he came around a turn in the trail and found himself lying in the snow. He did not belong with himself any more, for even then he was out of himself, standing with the boys and looking at himself in the snow. It certainly was cold, was his thought. When he got back to the States he could tell the folks what real cold was. He drifted on from this to a vision of the old-timer on Sulphur Creek. He could see him quite clearly, warm and comfortable, and smoking a pipe.

"You were right, old hoss; you were right," the man mumbled to the old-timer of 40 Sulphur Creek.

Then the man drowsed off into what seemed to him the most comfortable and satisfying sleep he had ever known. The dog sat facing him and waiting. The brief day drew to a close in a long, slow twilight. There were no signs of a fire to be made, and, besides, never in the dog's experience had it known a man to sit like that in the snow and make no fire. As the twilight drew on, its eager yearning for the fire mastered it, and with a great lifting and shifting of forefeet, it whined softly, then flattened its ears down in anticipation of being chidden by the man. But the man remained silent. Later the dog whined loudly. And still later it crept close to the man and caught the scent of death. This made the animal bristle and back away. A little longer it delayed, howling under the stars that leaped and danced and shone brightly in the cold sky. Then it turned and trotted up the trail in the direction of the camp it knew, where were the other food providers and fire providers.

Questions

1. Roughly how much of London's story is devoted to describing the setting? What particular details make it memorable?
2. To what extent does setting determine what happens in this story?
3. From what point of view is London's story told?
4. In "To Build a Fire" the man is never given a name. What is the effect of his being called simply "the man" throughout the story?
5. From the evidence London gives us, what stages are involved in the process of freezing to death? What does the story gain from London's detailed account of the man's experience with each successive stage?
6. What are the most serious mistakes the man makes? To what factors do you attribute these errors?

T. Coraghessan Boyle

Greasy Lake

1985

T. Coraghessan Boyle

T. Coraghessan Boyle (the T. stands for Tom) was born in 1948 in Peekskill, New York, the son of Irish immigrants. He grew up, he recalls, "as a sort of pampered punk" who did not read a book until he was eighteen. After a brief period as a high school teacher, he studied in the University of Iowa Writers' Workshop, submitting a collection of stories for his Ph.D. His stories in Esquire, Paris Review, the Atlantic, and other magazines quickly won him notice for their outrageous macabre humor and bizarre inventiveness. Boyle has published seven volumes of short stories, including Greasy Lake (1985), T.C. Boyle Stories (1998), and Tooth and Claw (2005). He has also published nine novels that are quite unlike anything else in contemporary American fiction. The subjects of some Boyle novels reveal his wide-ranging and idiosyncratic interests. Budding Prospects (1984) is a picaresque romp among adventurous marijuana growers. East Is East (1990) is a half-serious, half-comic story of a Japanese fugitive in an American writers' colony. The Road to Wellville (1993) takes place in 1907 in a sanitarium run by Dr. John Harvey Kellogg of corn flakes fame, with cameo appearances by Henry Ford, Thomas Edison, and Harvey Firestone. Boyle's most recent novel is The Women (2009). He lives in Southern California.

It's about a mile down on the dark side of Route 88.

—BRUCE SPRINGSTEEN

There was a time when courtesy and winning ways went out of style, when it was good to be bad, when you cultivated decadence like a taste. We were all dangerous characters then. We wore torn-up leather jackets, slouched around with toothpicks in our mouths, sniffed glue and ether and what somebody claimed was cocaine. When we wheeled our parents' whining station wagons out onto the street we left a patch of rubber half a block long. We drank gin and grape juice, Tango, Thunderbird, and Bali Hai. We were nineteen. We were bad. We read André Gide° and struck elaborate poses to show that we didn't give a shit about anything. At night, we went up to Greasy Lake.

Through the center of town, up the strip, past the housing developments and shopping malls, street lights giving way to the thin streaming illumination of the headlights, trees crowding the asphalt in a black unbroken wall: that was the way out to Greasy Lake. The Indians had called it Wakan, a reference to the clarity of its waters. Now it was fetid and murky, the mud banks glittering with broken glass and strewn with beer cans and the charred remains of bonfires. There was a single ravaged island a hundred yards from shore, so stripped of vegetation it looked as if the air force had strafed it. We went up to the lake because everyone went there, because we

---

André Gide: controversial French writer (1869–1951) whose novels, including *The Counterfeiters* and *Lafcadio's Adventures*, often show individuals in conflict with accepted morality.

wanted to snuff the rich scent of possibility on the breeze, watch a girl take off her clothes and plunge into the festering murk, drink beer, smoke pot, howl at the stars, savor the incongruous full-throated roar of rock and roll against the primeval susurrus of frogs and crickets. This was nature.

I was there one night, late, in the company of two dangerous characters. Digby wore a gold star in his right ear and allowed his father to pay his tuition at Cornell; Jeff was thinking of quitting school to become a painter/musician/head-shop proprietor. They were both expert in the social graces, quick with a sneer, able to manage a Ford with lousy shocks over a rutted and gutted blacktop road at eighty-five while rolling a joint as compact as a Tootsie Roll Pop stick. They could lounge against a bank of booming speakers and trade "man"s with the best of them or roll out across the dance floor as if their joints worked on bearings. They were slick and quick and they wore their mirror shades at breakfast and dinner, in the shower, in closets and caves. In short, they were bad.

I drove. Digby pounded the dashboard and shouted along with Toots & the Maytals while Jeff hung his head out the window and streaked the side of my mother's Bel Air with vomit. It was early June, the air soft as a hand on your cheek, the third night of summer vacation. The first two nights we'd been out till dawn, looking for something we never found. On this, the third night, we'd cruised the strip sixty-seven times, been in and out of every bar and club we could think of in a twenty-mile radius, stopped twice for bucket chicken and forty-cent hamburgers, debated going to a party at the house of a girl Jeff's sister knew, and chucked two dozen raw eggs at mailboxes and hitchhikers. It was 2:00 A.M.; the bars were closing. There was nothing to do but take a bottle of lemon-flavored gin up to Greasy Lake.

The taillights of a single car winked at us as we swung into the dirt lot with its tufts of weed and washboard corrugations; '57 Chevy, mint, metallic blue. On the far side of the lot, like the exoskeleton of some gaunt chrome insect, a chopper leaned against its kickstand. And that was it for excitement: some junkie halfwit biker and a car freak pumping his girlfriend. Whatever it was we were looking for, we weren't about to find it at Greasy Lake. Not that night.

But then all of a sudden Digby was fighting for the wheel. "Hey, that's Tony Lovett's car! Hey!" he shouted, while I stabbed at the brake pedal and the Bel Air nosed up to the gleaming bumper of the parked Chevy. Digby leaned on the horn, laughing, and instructed me to put my brights on. I flicked on the brights. This was hilarious. A joke. Tony would experience premature withdrawal and expect to be confronted by grim-looking state troopers with flashlights. We hit the horn, strobed the lights, and then jumped out of the car to press our witty faces to Tony's windows; for all we knew we might even catch a glimpse of some little fox's tit, and then we could slap backs with red-faced Tony, roughhouse a little, and go on to new heights of adventure and daring.

The first mistake, the one that opened the whole floodgate, was losing my grip on the keys. In the excitement, leaping from the car with the gin in one hand and a roach clip in the other, I spilled them in the grass—in the dark, rank, mysterious nighttime grass of Greasy Lake. This was a tactical error, as damaging and irreversible in its way as Westmoreland's decision to dig in at Khe Sanh.° I felt it like a jab of

5

Westmoreland's decision . . . Khe Sanh: General William C. Westmoreland commanded U.S. troops in Vietnam (1964–68). In late 1967 the North Vietnamese and Viet Cong forces attacked Khe Sanh (or Khesanh) with a show of strength, causing Westmoreland to expend great effort to defend a plateau of relatively little tactical importance.

intuition, and I stopped there by the open door, peering vaguely into the night that puddled up round my feet.

The second mistake—and this was inextricably bound up with the first—was identifying the car as Tony Lovett's. Even before the very bad character in greasy jeans and engineer boots ripped out of the driver's door, I began to realize that this chrome blue was much lighter than the robin's-egg of Tony's car, and that Tony's car didn't have rear-mounted speakers. Judging from their expressions, Digby and Jeff were privately groping toward the same inevitable and unsettling conclusion as I was.

In any case, there was no reasoning with this bad greasy character—clearly he was a man of action. The first lusty Rockette° kick of his steel-toed boot caught me under the chin, chipped my favorite tooth, and left me sprawled in the dirt. Like a fool, I'd gone down on one knee to comb the stiff hacked grass for the keys, my mind making connections in the most dragged-out, testudineous way, knowing that things had gone wrong, that I was in a lot of trouble, and that the lost ignition key was my grail and my salvation. The three or four succeeding blows were mainly absorbed by my right buttock and the tough piece of bone at the base of my spine.

Meanwhile, Digby vaulted the kissing bumpers and delivered a savage kung-fu blow to the greasy character's collarbone. Digby had just finished a course in martial arts for phys-ed credit and had spent the better part of the past two nights telling us apocryphal tales of Bruce Lee types and of the raw power invested in lightning blows shot from coiled wrists, ankles, and elbows. The greasy character was unimpressed. He merely backed off a step, his face like a Toltec mask, and laid Digby out with a single whistling roundhouse blow . . . but by now Jeff had got into the act, and I was beginning to extricate myself from the dirt, a tinny compound of shock, rage, and impotence wadded in my throat.

Jeff was on the guy's back, biting at his ear. Digby was on the ground, cursing. I went for the tire iron I kept under the driver's seat. I kept it there because bad characters always keep tire irons under the driver's seat, for just such an occasion as this. Never mind that I hadn't been involved in a fight since sixth grade, when a kid with a sleepy eye and two streams of mucus depending from his nostrils hit me in the knee with a Louisville slugger,° never mind that I'd touched the tire iron exactly twice before, to change tires: it was there. And I went for it.

I was terrified. Blood was beating in my ears, my hands were shaking, my heart turning over like a dirtbike in the wrong gear. My antagonist was shirtless, and a single cord of muscle flashed across his chest as he bent forward to peel Jeff from his back like a wet overcoat. "Motherfucker," he spat, over and over, and I was aware in that instant that all four of us—Digby, Jeff, and myself included—were chanting "motherfucker, motherfucker," as if it were a battle cry. (What happened next? the detective asks the murderer from beneath the turned-down brim of his porkpie hat. I don't know, the murderer says, something came over me. Exactly.)

Digby poked the flat of his hand in the bad character's face and I came at him like a kamikaze, mindless, raging, stung with humiliation—the whole thing, from the initial boot in the chin to this murderous primal instant involving no more than sixty hyperventilating, gland-flooding seconds—I came at him and brought the tire iron down across his ear. The effect was instantaneous, astonishing. He was a stunt man

10

Rockette: member of a dance troupe in the stage show at Radio City Music Hall, New York, famous for its ability to kick fast and high with wonderful coordination. *Louisville slugger*: a brand of baseball bat.

and this was Hollywood, he was a big grimacing toothy balloon and I was a man with a straight pin. He collapsed. Wet his pants. Went loose in his boots.

A single second, big as a zeppelin, floated by. We were standing over him in a circle, gritting our teeth, jerking our necks, our limbs and hands and feet twitching with glandular discharges. No one said anything. We just stared down at the guy, the car freak, the lover, the bad greasy character laid low. Digby looked at me; so did Jeff. I was still holding the tire iron, a tuft of hair clinging to the crook like dandelion fluff, like down. Rattled, I dropped it in the dirt, already envisioning the headlines, the pitted faces of the police inquisitors, the gleam of handcuffs, clank of bars, the big black shadows rising from the back of the cell . . . when suddenly a raw torn shriek cut through me like all the juice in all the electric chairs in the country.

It was the fox. She was short, barefoot, dressed in panties and a man's shirt.   15 "Animals!" she screamed, running at us with her fists clenched and wisps of blow-dried hair in her face. There was a silver chain round her ankle, and her toenails flashed in the glare of the headlights. I think it was the toenails that did it. Sure, the gin and the cannabis and even the Kentucky Fried may have had a hand in it, but it was the sight of those flaming toes that set us off—the toad emerging from the loaf in *Virgin Spring*,° lipstick smeared on a child; she was already tainted. We were on her like Bergman's deranged brothers—see no evil, hear none, speak none—panting, wheezing, tearing at her clothes, grabbing for flesh. We were bad characters, and we were scared and hot and three steps over the line—anything could have happened.

It didn't.

Before we could pin her to the hood of the car, our eyes masked with lust and greed and the purest primal badness, a pair of headlights swung into the lot. There we were, dirty, bloody, guilty, dissociated from humanity and civilization, the first of the Ur-crimes behind us, the second in progress, shreds of nylon panty and spandex brassiere dangling from our fingers, our flies open, lips licked—there we were, caught in the spotlight. Nailed.

We bolted. First for the car, and then, realizing we had no way of starting it, for the woods. I thought nothing. I thought escape. The headlights came at me like accusing fingers. I was gone.

Ram-bam-bam, across the parking lot, past the chopper and into the feculent undergrowth at the lake's edge, insects flying up in my face, weeds whipping, frogs and snakes and red-eyed turtles splashing off into the night: I was already ankle-deep in muck and tepid water and still going strong. Behind me, the girl's screams rose in intensity, disconsolate, incriminating, the screams of the Sabine women,° the Christian martyrs, Anne Frank° dragged from the garret. I kept going, pursued by those cries, imagining cops and bloodhounds. The water was up to my knees when I realized what I was doing: I was going to swim for it. Swim the breadth of Greasy Lake and hide myself in the thick clot of woods on the far side. They'd never find me there.

Virgin Spring: film by Swedish director Ingmar Bergman (1960).   *Sabine women:* members of an ancient tribe in Italy, according to legend, forcibly carried off by the early Romans under Romulus to be their wives. The incident is depicted in a famous painting, "The Rape of the Sabine Women," by seventeenth-century French artist Nicolas Poussin.   *Anne Frank:* German Jewish girl (1929–1945) whose diary written during the Nazi occupation of the Netherlands later became world-famous. She hid with her family in a secret attic in Amsterdam, but was caught by the Gestapo and sent to the concentration camp at Belsen, where she died.

I was breathing in sobs, in gasps. The water lapped at my waist as I looked out   20
over the moon-burnished ripples, the mats of algae that clung to the surface like
scabs. Digby and Jeff had vanished. I paused. Listened. The girl was quieter now,
screams tapering to sobs, but there were male voices, angry, excited, and the high-
pitched ticking of the second car's engine. I waded deeper, stealthy, hunted, the ooze
sucking at my sneakers. As I was about to take the plunge—at the very instant I
dropped my shoulder for the first slashing stroke—I blundered into something. Something unspeakable, obscene, something soft, wet, moss-grown. A patch of weed? A
log? When I reached out to touch it, it gave like a rubber duck, it gave like flesh.

In one of those nasty little epiphanies for which we are prepared by films and
TV and childhood visits to the funeral home to ponder the shrunken painted
forms of dead grandparents, I understood what it was that bobbed there so inad-
missibly in the dark. Understood, and stumbled back in horror and revulsion, my
mind yanked in six different directions (I was nineteen, a mere child, an infant,
and here in the space of five minutes I'd struck down one greasy character and
blundered into the waterlogged carcass of a second), thinking, The keys, the keys,
why did I have to go and lose the keys? I stumbled back, but the muck took hold of
my feet—a sneaker snagged, balance lost—and suddenly I was pitching face forward into the buoyant black mass, throwing out my hands in desperation while simultaneously conjuring the image of reeking frogs and muskrats revolving in slicks
of their own deliquescing juices. AAAAArrrgh! I shot from the water like a tor-
pedo, the dead man rotating to expose a mossy beard and eyes cold as the moon. I
must have shouted out, thrashing around in the weeds, because the voices behind
me suddenly became animated.

"What was that?"

"It's them, it's them: they tried to, tried to . . . *rape* me!" Sobs.

A man's voice, flat Midwestern accent. "You sons a bitches, we'll kill you!"

Frogs, crickets.   25

Then another voice, harsh, *r*-less, Lower East Side: "Motherfucker!" I recognized the verbal virtuosity of the bad greasy character in the engineer boots. Tooth
chipped, sneakers gone, coated in mud and slime and worse, crouching breathless in
the weeds waiting to have my ass thoroughly and definitively kicked and fresh from
the hideous stinking embrace of a three-days-dead-corpse, I suddenly felt a rush of
joy and vindication: the son of a bitch was alive! Just as quickly, my bowels turned to
ice. "Come on out of there, you pansy mothers!" the bad greasy character was
screaming. He shouted curses till he was out of breath.

The crickets started up again, then the frogs. I held my breath. All at once there
was a sound in the reeds, a swishing, a splash: thunk-a-thunk. They were throwing
rocks. The frogs fell silent. I cradled my head. Swish, swish, thunk-a-thunk. A wedge
of feldspar the size of a cue ball glanced off my knee. I bit my finger.

It was then that they turned to the car. I heard a door slam, a curse, and then the
sound of the headlights shattering—almost a good-natured sound, celebratory, like
corks popping from the necks of bottles. This was succeeded by the dull booming of
the fenders, metal on metal, and then the icy crash of the windshield. I inched forward, elbows and knees, my belly pressed to the muck, thinking of guerrillas and
commandos and *The Naked and the Dead.*° I parted the weeds and squinted the
length of the parking lot.

The Naked and the Dead: novel (1948) by Norman Mailer, about U.S. Army life in World War II.

The second car—it was a Trans-Am—was still running, its high beams washing the scene in a lurid stagy light. Tire iron flailing, the greasy bad character was laying into the side of my mother's Bel Air like an avenging demon, his shadow riding up the trunks of the trees. Whomp. Whomp. Whomp-whomp. The other two guys—blond types, in fraternity jackets—were helping out with tree branches and skull-sized boulders. One of them was gathering up bottles, rocks, muck, candy wrappers, used condoms, poptops, and other refuse and pitching it through the window on the driver's side. I could see the fox, a white bulb behind the windshield of the '57 Chevy. "Bobbie," she whined over the thumping, "come on." The greasy character paused a moment, took one good swipe at the left taillight, and then heaved the tire iron halfway across the lake. Then he fired up the '57 and was gone.

Blond head nodded at blond head. One said something to the other, too low for   30
me to catch. They were no doubt thinking that in helping to annihilate my mother's car they'd committed a fairly rash act, and thinking too that there were three bad characters connected with that very car watching them from the woods. Perhaps other possibilities occurred to them as well—police, jail cells, justices of the peace, reparations, lawyers, irate parents, fraternal censure. Whatever they were thinking, they suddenly dropped branches, bottles, and rocks and sprang for their car in unison, as if they'd choreographed it. Five seconds. That's all it took. The engine shrieked, the tires squealed, a cloud of dust rose from the rutted lot and then settled back on darkness.

I don't know how long I lay there, the bad breath of decay all around me, my jacket heavy as a bear, the primordial ooze subtly reconstituting itself to accommodate my upper thighs and testicles. My jaws ached, my knee throbbed, my coccyx was on fire. I contemplated suicide, wondered if I'd need bridgework, scraped the recesses of my brain for some sort of excuse to give my parents—a tree had fallen on the car, I was blinded by a bread truck, hit and run, vandals had got to it while we were playing chess at Digby's. Then I thought of the dead man. He was probably the only person on the planet worse off than I was. I thought about him, fog on the lake, insects chirring eerily, and felt the tug of fear, felt the darkness opening up inside me like a set of jaws. Who was he, I wondered, this victim of time and circumstance bobbing sorrowfully in the lake at my back. The owner of the chopper, no doubt, a bad older character come to this. Shot during a murky drug deal, drowned while drunkenly frolicking in the lake. Another headline. My car was wrecked; he was dead.

When the eastern half of the sky went from black to cobalt and the trees began to separate themselves from the shadows, I pushed myself up from the mud and stepped out into the open. By now the birds had begun to take over for the crickets, and dew lay slick on the leaves. There was a smell in the air, raw and sweet at the same time, the smell of the sun firing buds and opening blossoms. I contemplated the car. It lay there like a wreck along the highway, like a steel sculpture left over from a vanished civilization. Everything was still. This was nature.

I was circling the car, as dazed and bedraggled as the sole survivor of an air blitz, when Digby and Jeff emerged from the trees behind me. Digby's face was cross-hatched with smears of dirt; Jeff's jacket was gone and his shirt was torn across the shoulder. They slouched across the lot, looking sheepish, and silently came up beside me to gape at the ravaged automobile. No one said a word. After a while Jeff swung open the driver's door and began to scoop the broken glass and garbage off the seat. I looked at Digby. He shrugged. "At least they didn't slash the tires," he said.

It was true: the tires were intact. There was no windshield, the headlights were staved in, and the body looked as if it had been sledge-hammered for a quarter a shot at the county fair, but the tires were inflated to regulation pressure. The car was drivable. In silence, all three of us bent to scrape the mud and shattered glass from the interior. I said nothing about the biker. When we were finished, I reached in my pocket for the keys, experienced a nasty stab of recollection, cursed myself, and turned to search the grass. I spotted them almost immediately, no more than five feet from the open door, glinting like jewels in the first tapering shaft of sunlight. There was no reason to get philosophical about it: I eased into the seat and turned the engine over.

It was at that precise moment that the silver Mustang with the flame decals rumbled into the lot. All three of us froze; then Digby and Jeff slid into the car and slammed the door. We watched as the Mustang rocked and bobbed across the ruts and finally jerked to a halt beside the forlorn chopper at the far end of the lot. "Let's go," Digby said. I hesitated, the Bel Air wheezing beneath me. **35**

Two girls emerged from the Mustang. Tight jeans, stiletto heels, hair like frozen fur. They bent over the motorcycle, paced back and forth aimlessly, glanced once or twice at us, and then ambled over to where the reeds sprang up in a green fence round the perimeter of the lake. One of them cupped her hands to her mouth. "Al," she called. "Hey, Al!"

"Come on," Digby hissed. "Let's get out of here."

But it was too late. The second girl was picking her way across the lot, unsteady on her heels, looking up at us and then away. She was older—twenty-five or -six— and as she came closer we could see there was something wrong with her: she was stoned or drunk, lurching now and waving her arms for balance. I gripped the steering wheel as if it were the ejection lever of a flaming jet, and Digby spat out my name, twice, terse and impatient.

"Hi," the girl said.

We looked at her like zombies, like war veterans, like deaf-and-dumb pencil **40** peddlers.

She smiled, her lips cracked and dry. "Listen," she said, bending from the waist to look in the window, "you guys seen Al?" Her pupils were pinpoints, her eyes glass. She jerked her neck. "That's his bike over there—Al's. You seen him?"

Al. I didn't know what to say. I wanted to get out of the car and retch, I wanted to go home to my parents' house and crawl into bed. Digby poked me in the ribs. "We haven't seen anybody," I said.

The girl seemed to consider this, reaching out a slim veiny arm to brace herself against the car. "No matter," she said, slurring the *t*'s, "he'll turn up." And then, as if she'd just taken stock of the whole scene—the ravaged car and our battered faces, the desolation of the place—she said: "Hey, you guys look like some pretty bad characters—been fightin', huh?" We stared straight ahead, rigid as catatonics. She was fumbling in her pocket and muttering something. Finally she held out a handful of tablets in glassine wrappers: "Hey, you want to party, you want to do some of these with me and Sarah?"

I just looked at her. I thought I was going to cry. Digby broke the silence. "No, thanks," he said, leaning over me. "Some other time."

I put the car in gear and it inched forward with a groan, shaking off pellets of glass **45** like an old dog shedding water after a bath, heaving over the ruts on its worn springs, creeping toward the highway. There was a sheen of sun on the lake. I looked back. The girl was still standing there, watching us, her shoulders slumped, hand outstretched.

Questions

1. Around what year, would you say, was it that "courtesy and winning ways went out of style, when it was good to be bad, when you cultivated decadence like a taste"?
2. What is it about Digby and Jeff that inspires the narrator to call them "bad"?
3. Twice in "Greasy Lake"—in paragraphs 2 and 32—appear the words, "This was nature." What contrasts do you find between the "nature" of the narrator's earlier and later views?
4. What makes the narrator and his friends run off into the woods?
5. How does the young men's encounter with the two girls at the end of the story differ from their earlier encounter with the girl from the blue Chevy? How do you account for the difference? When at the end of the story the girl offers to party with the three friends, what makes the narrator say, "I thought I was going to cry"?
6. How important to what happens in this story is Greasy Lake itself? What details about the lake and its shores strike you as particularly memorable (whether funny, disgusting, or both)?

Amy Tan

A Pair of Tickets   1989

Amy Tan was born in Oakland, California, in 1952. Both of her parents were recent Chinese immigrants. Her father was an electrical engineer (as well as a Baptist minister); her mother was a vocational nurse. When her father and older brother both died of brain tumors, the fifteen-year-old Tan moved with her mother and younger brother to Switzerland, where she attended high school. On their return to the United States Tan attended Linfield College, a Baptist school in Oregon, but she eventually transferred to California State University at San Jose. At this time Tan and her mother argued about her future. The mother insisted her daughter pursue premedical studies in preparation for becoming a neurosurgeon, but Tan wanted to do something else. For six months the two did not speak to one another. Tan worked for IBM writing computer manuals and also wrote freelance business articles under a pseudonym. In 1987 she and her mother visited China together. This experience, which is reflected in "A Pair of Tickets," deepened Tan's sense of her Chinese American identity. "As soon as my feet touched China," she wrote, "I became Chinese." Soon after, she began writing her first novel, The Joy Luck Club *(1989), which consists of sixteen interrelated stories about a group of Chinese American mothers and their daughters. (The club of the title is a woman's social group.)* The Joy Luck Club *became both a critical success and a best seller, and was made into a movie in 1993. In 1991 Tan published her second novel,* The Kitchen God's Wife. *Her later novels include* The Bonesetter's Daughter *(2001) and* Saving Fish from Drowning *(2005). Tan performs with a "vintage garage" band called the Rock Bottom Remainders, which also includes, among others, Stephen King, Dave Barry, and Scott Turow. She lives outside San Francisco with her husband.*

The minute our train leaves the Hong Kong border and enters Shenzhen, China, I feel different. I can feel the skin on my forehead tingling, my blood rushing through a new course, my bones aching with a familiar old pain. And I think, My mother was right. I am becoming Chinese.

"Cannot be helped," my mother said when I was fifteen and had vigorously denied that I had any Chinese whatsoever below my skin. I was a sophomore at Galileo High in San Francisco, and all my Caucasian friends agreed: I was about as Chinese as they were. But my mother had studied at a famous nursing school in Shanghai, and she said she knew all about genetics. So there was no doubt in her mind, whether I agreed or not: Once you are born Chinese, you cannot help but feel and think Chinese.

"Someday you will see," said my mother. "It is in your blood, waiting to be let go."

And when she said this, I saw myself transforming like a werewolf, a mutant tag of DNA suddenly triggered, replicating itself insidiously into a *syndrome,*° a cluster of telltale Chinese behaviors, all those things my mother did to embarrass me—haggling with store owners, pecking her mouth with a toothpick in public, being color-blind to the fact that lemon yellow and pale pink are not good combinations for winter clothes.

But today I realize I've never really known what it means to be Chinese. I am thirty-six years old. My mother is dead and I am on a train, carrying with me her dreams of coming home. I am going to China.   5

We are first going to Guangzhou, my seventy-two-year-old father, Canning Woo, and I, where we will visit his aunt, whom he has not seen since he was ten years old. And I don't know whether it's the prospect of seeing his aunt or if it's because he's back in China, but now he looks like he's a young boy, so innocent and happy I want to button his sweater and pat his head. We are sitting across from each other, separated by a little table with two cold cups of tea. For the first time I can ever remember, my father has tears in his eyes, and all he is seeing out the train window is a sectioned field of yellow, green, and brown, a narrow canal flanking the tracks, low rising hills, and three people in blue jackets riding an ox-driven cart on this early October morning. And I can't help myself. I also have misty eyes, as if I had seen this a long, long time ago, and had almost forgotten.

In less than three hours, we will be in Guangzhou, which my guidebook tells me is how one properly refers to Canton these days. It seems all the cities I have heard of, except Shanghai, have changed their spellings. I think they are saying China has changed in other ways as well. Chungking is Chongqing. And Kweilin is Guilin. I have looked these names up, because after we see my father's aunt in Guangzhou, we will catch a plane to Shanghai, where I will meet my two half-sisters for the first time.

They are my mother's twin daughters from her first marriage, little babies she was forced to abandon on a road as she was fleeing Kweilin for Chungking in 1944. That was all my mother had told me about these daughters, so they had remained babies in my mind, all these years, sitting on the side of a road, listening to bombs whistling in the distance while sucking their patient red thumbs.

And it was only this year that someone found them and wrote with this joyful news. A letter came from Shanghai, addressed to my mother. When I first heard about this, that they were alive, I imagined my identical sisters transforming from little babies into six-year-old girls. In my mind, they were seated next to each other at a table, taking turns with the fountain pen. One would write a neat row of characters: *Dearest Mama. We are alive.* She would brush back her wispy bangs and hand the other sister the pen, and she would write: *Come get us. Please hurry.*

Of course they could not know that my mother had died three months before, suddenly, when a blood vessel in her brain burst. One minute she was talking to my father, complaining about the tenants upstairs, scheming how to evict them under the pretense that relatives from China were moving in. The next minute she was holding her head, her eyes squeezed shut, groping for the sofa, and then crumpling softly to the floor with fluttering hands.   10

---

syndrome: a group of symptoms that occur together as the sign of a particular disease or abnormality.

So my father had been the first one to open the letter, a long letter it turned out. And they did call her Mama. They said they always revered her as their true mother. They kept a framed picture of her. They told her about their life, from the time my mother last saw them on the road leaving Kweilin to when they were finally found.

And the letter had broken my father's heart so much—these daughters calling my mother from another life he never knew—that he gave the letter to my mother's old friend Auntie Lindo and asked her to write back and tell my sisters, in the gentlest way possible, that my mother was dead.

But instead Auntie Lindo took the letter to the Joy Luck Club and discussed with Auntie Ying and Auntie An-mei what should be done, because they had known for many years about my mother's search for her twin daughters, her endless hope. Auntie Lindo and the others cried over this double tragedy, of losing my mother three months before, and now again. And so they couldn't help but think of some miracle, some possible way of reviving her from the dead, so my mother could fulfill her dream.

So this is what they wrote to my sisters in Shanghai: "Dearest Daughters, I too have never forgotten you in my memory or in my heart. I never gave up hope that we would see each other again in a joyous reunion. I am only sorry it has been too long. I want to tell you everything about my life since I last saw you. I want to tell you this when our family comes to see you in China. . . ." They signed it with my mother's name.

It wasn't until all this had been done that they first told me about my sisters, the letter they received, the one they wrote back.

"They'll think she's coming, then," I murmured. And I had imagined my sisters now being ten or eleven, jumping up and down, holding hands, their pigtails bouncing, excited that their mother—*their* mother—was coming, whereas my mother was dead.

"How can you say she is not coming in a letter?" said Auntie Lindo. "She is their mother. She is your mother. You must be the one to tell them. All these years, they have been dreaming of her." And I thought she was right.

But then I started dreaming, too, of my mother and my sisters and how it would be if I arrived in Shanghai. All these years, while they waited to be found, I had lived with my mother and then had lost her. I imagined seeing my sisters at the airport. They would be standing on their tip-toes, looking anxiously, scanning from one dark head to another as we got off the plane. And I would recognize them instantly, their faces with the identical worried look.

"*Jyejye, Jyejye.* Sister, Sister. We are here," I saw myself saying in my poor version of Chinese.

"Where is Mama?" they would say, and look around, still smiling, two flushed and eager faces. "Is she hiding?" And this would have been like my mother, to stand behind just a bit, to tease a little and make people's patience pull a little on their hearts. I would shake my head and tell my sisters she was not hiding.

"Oh, that must be Mama, no?" one of my sisters would whisper excitedly, pointing to another small woman completely engulfed in a tower of presents. And that, too, would have been like my mother, to bring mountains of gifts, food, and toys for children—all bought on sale—shunning thanks, saying the gifts were nothing, and later turning the labels over to show my sisters, "Calvin Klein, 100% wool."

I imagined myself starting to say, "Sisters, I am sorry, I have come alone . . ." and before I could tell them—they could see it in my face—they were wailing, pulling their hair, their lips twisted in pain, as they ran away from me. And then I saw myself getting back on the plane and coming home.

15

20

After I had dreamed this scene many times—watching their despair turn from horror into anger—I begged Auntie Lindo to write another letter. And at first she refused.

"How can I say she is dead? I cannot write this," said Auntie Lindo with a stubborn look.

"But it's cruel to have them believe she's coming on the plane," I said. "When they see it's just me, they'll hate me." 25

"Hate you? Cannot be." She was scowling. "You are their own sister, their only family."

"You don't understand," I protested.

"What I don't understand?" she said.

And I whispered, "They'll think I'm responsible, that she died because I didn't appreciate her."

And Auntie Lindo looked satisfied and sad at the same time, as if this were true 30 and I had finally realized it. She sat down for an hour, and when she stood up she handed me a two-page letter. She had tears in her eyes. I realized that the very thing I had feared, she had done. So even if she had written the news of my mother's death in English, I wouldn't have had the heart to read it.

"Thank you," I whispered.

The landscape has become gray, filled with low flat cement buildings, old factories, and then tracks and more tracks filled with trains like ours passing by in the opposite direction. I see platforms crowded with people wearing drab Western clothes, with spots of bright colors: little children wearing pink and yellow, red and peach. And there are soldiers in olive green and red, and old ladies in gray tops and pants that stop mid-calf. We are in Guangzhou.

Before the train even comes to a stop, people are bringing down their belongings from above their seats. For a moment there is a dangerous shower of heavy suitcases laden with gifts to relatives, half-broken boxes wrapped in miles of string to keep the contents from spilling out, plastic bags filled with yarn and vegetables and packages of dried mushrooms, and camera cases. And then we are caught in a stream of people rushing, shoving, pushing us along, until we find ourselves in one of a dozen lines waiting to go through customs. I feel as if I were getting on the number 30 Stockton bus in San Francisco. I am in China, I remind myself. And somehow the crowds don't bother me. It feels right. I start pushing too.

I take out the declaration forms and my passport. "Woo," it says at the top, and below that, "June May," who was born in "California, U.S.A.," in 1951. I wonder if the customs people will question whether I'm the same person in the passport photo. In this picture, my chin-length hair is swept back and artfully styled. I am wearing false eyelashes, eye shadow, and lip liner. My cheeks are hollowed out by bronze blusher. But I had not expected the heat in October. And now my hair hangs limp with the humidity. I wear no makeup; in Hong Kong my mascara had melted into dark circles and everything else had felt like layers of grease. So today my face is plain, unadorned except for a thin mist of shiny sweat on my forehead and nose.

Even without makeup, I could never pass for true Chinese. I stand five-foot-six, 35 and my head pokes above the crowd so that I am eye level only with other tourists. My mother once told me my height came from my grandfather, who was a northerner, and may have even had some Mongol blood. "This is what your grandmother once told me," explained my mother. "But now it is too late to ask her. They are all dead, your grandparents, your uncles, and their wives and children, all killed in the war, when a bomb fell on our house. So many generations in one instant."

She had said this so matter-of-factly that I thought she had long since gotten over any grief she had. And then I wondered how she knew they were all dead.

"Maybe they left the house before the bomb fell," I suggested.

"No," said my mother. "Our whole family is gone. It is just you and I."

"But how do you know? Some of them could have escaped."

"Cannot be," said my mother, this time almost angrily. And then her frown was 40 washed over by a puzzled blank look, and she began to talk as if she were trying to remember where she had misplaced something. "I went back to that house. I kept looking up to where the house used to be. And it wasn't a house, just the sky. And below, underneath my feet, were four stories of burnt bricks and wood, all the life of our house. Then off to the side I saw things blown into the yard, nothing valuable. There was a bed someone used to sleep in, really just a metal frame twisted up at one corner. And a book, I don't know what kind, because every page had turned black. And I saw a teacup which was unbroken but filled with ashes. And then I found my doll, with her hands and legs broken, her hair burned off. . . . When I was a little girl, I had cried for that doll, seeing it all alone in the store window, and my mother had bought it for me. It was an American doll with yellow hair. It could turn its legs and arms. The eyes moved up and down. And when I married and left my family home, I gave the doll to my youngest niece, because she was like me. She cried if that doll was not with her always. Do you see? If she was in the house with that doll, her parents were there, and so everybody was there, waiting together, because that's how our family was."

The woman in the customs booth stares at my documents, then glances at me briefly, and with two quick movements stamps everything and sternly nods me along. And soon my father and I find ourselves in a large area filled with thousands of people and suitcases. I feel lost and my father looks helpless.

"Excuse me," I say to a man who looks like an American. "Can you tell me where I can get a taxi?" He mumbles something that sounds Swedish or Dutch.

"Syau Yen! Syau Yen!" I hear a piercing voice shout from behind me. An old woman in a yellow knit beret is holding up a pink plastic bag filled with wrapped trinkets. I guess she is trying to sell us something. But my father is staring down at this tiny sparrow of a woman, squinting into her eyes. And then his eyes widen, his face opens up and he smiles like a pleased little boy.

"Aiyi! Aiyi!" —Auntie Auntie!—he says softly.

"Syau Yen!" coos my great-aunt. I think it's funny she has just called my father 45 "Little Wild Goose." It must be his baby milk name, the name used to discourage ghosts from stealing children.

They clasp each other's hands—they do not hug—and hold on like this, taking turns saying, "Look at you! You are so old. Look how old you've become!" They are both crying openly, laughing at the same time, and I bite my lip, trying not to cry. I'm afraid to feel their joy. Because I am thinking how different our arrival in Shanghai will be tomorrow, how awkward it will feel.

Now Aiyi beams and points to a Polaroid picture of my father. My father had wisely sent pictures when he wrote and said we were coming. See how smart she was, she seems to intone as she compares the picture to my father. In the letter, my father had said we would call her from the hotel once we arrived, so this is a surprise, that they've come to meet us. I wonder if my sisters will be at the airport.

It is only then that I remember the camera. I had meant to take a picture of my father and his aunt the moment they met. It's not too late.

"Here, stand together over here," I say, holding up the Polaroid. The camera flashes and I hand them the snapshot. Aiyi and my father still stand close together, each of them holding a corner of the picture, watching as their images begin to form. They are almost reverentially quiet. Aiyi is only five years older than my father, which makes her around seventy-seven. But she looks ancient, shrunken, a mummified relic. Her thin hair is pure white, her teeth are brown with decay. So much for stories of Chinese women looking young forever, I think to myself.

Now Aiyi is crooning to me: "*Jandale.*" So big already. She looks up at me, at my full height, and then peers into her pink plastic bag—her gifts to us, I have figured out—as if she is wondering what she will give to me, now that I am so old and big. And then she grabs my elbow with her sharp pincerlike grasp and turns me around. A man and woman in their fifties are shaking hands with my father, everybody smiling and saying, "Ah! Ah!" They are Aiyi's oldest son and his wife, and standing next to them are four other people, around my age, and a little girl who's around ten. The introductions go by so fast, all I know is that one of them is Aiyi's grandson, with his wife, and the other is her granddaughter, with her husband. And the little girl is Lili, Aiyi's great-granddaughter.

Aiyi and my father speak the Mandarin dialect from their childhood, but the rest of the family speaks only the Cantonese of their village. I understand only Mandarin but can't speak it that well. So Aiyi and my father gossip unrestrained in Mandarin, exchanging news about people from their old village. And they stop only occasionally to talk to the rest of us, sometimes in Cantonese, sometimes in English.

"Oh, it is as I suspected," says my father, turning to me. "He died last summer." And I already understood this. I just don't know who this person, Li Gong, is. I feel as if I were in the United Nations and the translators had run amok.

"Hello," I say to the little girl. "My name is Jing-mei." But the little girl squirms to look away, causing her parents to laugh with embarrassment. I try to think of Cantonese words I can say to her, stuff I learned from friends in Chinatown, but all I can think of are swear words, terms for bodily functions, and short phrases like "tastes good," "tastes like garbage," and "she's really ugly." And then I have another plan: I hold up the Polaroid camera, beckoning Lili with my finger. She immediately jumps forward, places one hand on her hip in the manner of a fashion model, juts out her chest, and flashes me a toothy smile. As soon as I take the picture she is standing next to me, jumping and giggling every few seconds as she watches herself appear on the greenish film.

By the time we hail taxis for the ride to the hotel, Lili is holding tight onto my hand, pulling me along.

In the taxi, Aiyi talks nonstop, so I have no chance to ask her about the different sights we are passing by.

"You wrote and said you would come only for one day," says Aiyi to my father in an agitated tone. "One day! How can you see your family in one day! Toishan is many hours' drive from Guangzhou. And this idea to call us when you arrive. This is nonsense. We have no telephone."

My heart races a little. I wonder if Auntie Lindo told my sisters we would call from the hotel in Shanghai?

Aiyi continues to scold my father. "I was so beside myself, ask my son, almost turned heaven and earth upside down trying to think of a way! So we decided the best was for us to take the bus from Toishan and come into Guangzhou—meet you right from the start."

And now I am holding my breath as the taxi driver dodges between trucks and buses, honking his horn constantly. We seem to be on some sort of long freeway overpass, like a bridge above the city. I can see row after row of apartments, each floor cluttered with laundry hanging out to dry on the balcony. We pass a public bus, with people jammed in so tight their faces are nearly wedged against the window. Then I see the skyline of what must be downtown Guangzhou. From a distance, it looks like a major American city, with high rises and construction going on everywhere. As we slow down in the more congested part of the city, I see scores of little shops, dark inside, lined with counters and shelves. And then there is a building, its front laced with scaffolding made of bamboo poles held together with plastic strips. Men and women are standing on narrow platforms, scraping the sides, working without safety straps or helmets. Oh, would OSHA° have a field day here, I think.

Aiyi's shrill voice rises up again: "So it is a shame you can't see our village, our house. My sons have been quite successful, selling our vegetables in the free market. We had enough these last few years to build a big house, three stories, all of new brick, big enough for our whole family and then some. And every year, the money is even better. You Americans aren't the only ones who know how to get rich!" 60

The taxi stops and I assume we've arrived, but then I peer out at what looks like a grander version of the Hyatt Regency. "This is communist China?" I wonder out loud. And then I shake my head toward my father. "This must be the wrong hotel." I quickly pull out our itinerary, travel tickets, and reservations. I had explicitly instructed my travel agent to choose something inexpensive, in the thirty-to-forty-dollar range. I'm sure of this. And there it says on our itinerary: Garden Hotel, Huanshi Dong Lu. Well, our travel agent had better be prepared to eat the extra, that's all I have to say.

The hotel is magnificent. A bellboy complete with uniform and sharp-creased cap jumps forward and begins to carry our bags into the lobby. Inside, the hotel looks like an orgy of shopping arcades and restaurants all encased in granite and glass. And rather than be impressed, I am worried about the expense, as well as the appearance it must give Aiyi, that we rich Americans cannot be without our luxuries even for one night.

But when I step up to the reservation desk, ready to haggle over this booking mistake, it is confirmed. Our rooms are prepaid, thirty-four dollars each. I feel sheepish, and Aiyi and the others seem delighted by our temporary surroundings. Lili is looking wide-eyed at an arcade filled with video games.

Our whole family crowds into one elevator, and the bellboy waves, saying he will meet us on the eighteenth floor. As soon as the elevator door shuts, everybody becomes very quiet, and when the door finally opens again, everybody talks at once in what sounds like relieved voices. I have the feeling Aiyi and the others have never been on such a long elevator ride.

Our rooms are next to each other and are identical. The rugs, drapes, bedspreads are all in shades of taupe. There's a color television with remote-control panels built 65

OSHA: Occupational Safety and Health Administration, a U.S. federal agency that regulates and monitors workplace safety conditions.

into the lamp table between the two twin beds. The bathroom has marble walls and floors. I find a built-in wet bar with a small refrigerator stocked with Heineken beer, Coke Classic, and Seven-Up, mini-bottles of Johnnie Walker Red, Bacardi rum, and Smirnoff vodka, and packets of M & M's, honey-roasted cashews, and Cadbury chocolate bars. And again I say out loud, "This is communist China?"

My father comes into my room. "They decided we should just stay here and visit," he says, shrugging his shoulders. "They say, Less trouble that way. More time to talk."

"What about dinner?" I ask. I have been envisioning my first real Chinese feast for many days already, a big banquet with one of those soups steaming out of a carved winter melon, chicken wrapped in clay, Peking duck, the works.

My father walks over and picks up a room service book next to a *Travel & Leisure* magazine. He flips through the pages quickly and then points to the menu. "This is what they want," says my father.

So it's decided. We are going to dine tonight in our rooms, with our family, sharing hamburgers, french fries, and apple pie à la mode.

Aiyi and her family are browsing the shops while we clean up. After a hot ride   70
on the train, I'm eager for a shower and cooler clothes.

The hotel has provided little packets of shampoo which, upon opening, I discover is the consistency and color of hoisin sauce. This is more like it, I think. This is China. And I rub some in my damp hair.

Standing in the shower, I realize this is the first time I've been by myself in what seems like days. But instead of feeling relieved, I feel forlorn. I think about what my mother said, about activating my genes and becoming Chinese. And I wonder what she meant.

Right after my mother died, I asked myself a lot of things, things that couldn't be answered, to force myself to grieve more. It seemed as if I wanted to sustain my grief, to assure myself that I had cared deeply enough.

But now I ask the questions mostly because I want to know the answers. What was that pork stuff she used to make that had the texture of sawdust? What were the names of the uncles who died in Shanghai? What had she dreamt all these years about her other daughters? All the times when she got mad at me, was she really thinking about them? Did she wish I were they? Did she regret that I wasn't?

At one o'clock in the morning, I awake to tapping sounds on the window. I   75
must have dozed off and now I feel my body uncramping itself. I'm sitting on the floor, leaning against one of the twin beds. Lili is lying next to me. The others are asleep, too, sprawled out on the beds and floor. Aiyi is seated at a little table, looking very sleepy. And my father is staring out the window, tapping his fingers on the glass. The last time I listened my father was telling Aiyi about his life since he last saw her. How he had gone to Yenching University, later got a post with a newspaper in Chungking, met my mother there, a young widow. How they later fled together to Shanghai to try to find my mother's family house, but there was nothing there. And then they traveled eventually to Canton and then to Hong Kong, then Haiphong and finally to San Francisco. . . .

"Suyuan didn't tell me she was trying all these years to find her daughters," he is now saying in a quiet voice. "Naturally, I did not discuss her daughters with her. I thought she was ashamed she had left them behind."

"Where did she leave them?" asks Aiyi. "How were they found?"

I am wide awake now. Although I have heard parts of this story from my mother's friends.

"It happened when the Japanese took over Kweilin," says my father.

"Japanese in Kweilin?" says Aiyi. "That was never the case. Couldn't be. The Japanese never came to Kweilin." 80

"Yes, that is what the newspapers reported. I know this because I was working for the news bureau at the time. The Kuomintang often told us what we could say and could not say. But we knew the Japanese had come into Kwangsi Province. We had sources who told us how they had captured the Wuchang-Canton railway. How they were coming overland, making very fast progress, marching toward the provincial capital."

Aiyi looks astonished. "If people did not know this, how could Suyuan know the Japanese were coming?"

"An officer of the Kuomintang secretly warned her," explains my father. "Suyuan's husband also was an officer and everybody knew that officers and their families would be the first to be killed. So she gathered a few possessions and, in the middle of the night, she picked up her daughters and fled on foot. The babies were not even one year old."

"How could she give up those babies!" sighs Aiyi. "Twin girls. We have never had such luck in our family." And then she yawns again.

"What were they named?" she asks. I listen carefully. I had been planning on us- 85 ing just the familiar "Sister" to address them both. But now I want to know how to pronounce their names.

"They have their father's surname, Wang," says my father. "And their given names are Chwun Yu and Chwun Hwa."

"What do the names mean?" I ask.

"Ah." My father draws imaginary characters on the window. "One means 'Spring Rain,' the other 'Spring Flower,' " he explains in English, "because they born in the spring, and of course rain come before flower, same order these girls are born. Your mother like a poet, don't you think?"

I nod my head. I see Aiyi nod her head forward, too. But it falls forward and stays there. She is breathing deeply, noisily. She is asleep.

"And what does Ma's name mean?" I whisper. 90

"'Suyuan,'" he says, writing more invisible characters on the glass. "The way she write it in Chinese, it mean 'Long-Cherished Wish.' Quite a fancy name, not so ordinary like flower name. See this first character, it mean something like 'Forever Never Forgotten.' But there is another way to write 'Suyuan.' Sound exactly the same, but the meaning is opposite." His finger creates the brushstrokes of another character. "The first part look the same: 'Never Forgotten.' But the last part add to first part make the whole word mean 'Long-Held Grudge.' Your mother get angry with me, I tell her her name should be Grudge."

My father is looking at me, moist-eyed. "See, I pretty clever, too, hah?"

I nod, wishing I could find some way to comfort him. "And what about my name," I ask, "what does 'Jing-mei' mean?"

"Your name also special," he says. I wonder if any name in Chinese is not something special. "'Jing' like excellent *jing*. Not just good, it's something pure, essential, the best quality. *Jing* is good leftover stuff when you take impurities out of something like gold, or rice, or salt. So what is left—just pure essence. And 'Mei,' this is common *mei*, as in *meimei*, 'younger sister.'"

I think about this. My mother's long-cherished wish. Me, the younger sister who   95
was supposed to be the essence of the others. I feed myself with the old grief, wondering
how disappointed my mother must have been. Tiny Aiyi stirs suddenly, her head rolls
and then falls back, her mouth opens as if to answer my question. She grunts in her
sleep, tucking her body more closely into the chair.

"So why did she abandon those babies on the road?" I need to know, because
now I feel abandoned too.

"Long time I wondered this myself," says my father. "But then I read that letter
from her daughters in Shanghai now, and I talk to Auntie Lindo, all the others. And
then I knew. No shame in what she done. None."

"What happened?"

"Your mother running away—" begins my father.

"No, tell me in Chinese," I interrupt. "Really, I can understand."   100

He begins to talk, still standing at the window, looking into the night.

After fleeing Kweilin, your mother walked for several days trying to find a main
road. Her thought was to catch a ride on a truck or wagon, to catch enough rides
until she reached Chungking, where her husband was stationed.

She had sewn money and jewelry into the lining of her dress, enough, she
thought, to barter rides all the way. If I am lucky, she thought, I will not have to trade
the heavy gold bracelet and jade ring. These were things from her mother, your
grandmother.

By the third day, she had traded nothing. The roads were filled with people,
everybody running and begging for rides from passing trucks. The trucks rushed by,
afraid to stop. So your mother found no rides, only the start of dysentery pains in her
stomach.

Her shoulders ached from the two babies swinging from scarf slings. Blisters grew   105
on her palms from holding two leather suitcases. And then the blisters burst and began to bleed. After a while, she left the suitcases behind, keeping only the food and a
few clothes. And later she also dropped the bags of wheat flour and rice and kept
walking like this for many miles, singing songs to her little girls, until she was delirious with pain and fever.

Finally, there was not one more step left in her body. She didn't have the strength
to carry those babies any farther. She slumped to the ground. She knew she would die
of her sickness, or perhaps from thirst, from starvation, or from the Japanese, who she
was sure were marching right behind her.

She took the babies out of the slings and sat them on the side of the road, then
lay down next to them. You babies are so good, she said, so quiet. They smiled back,
reaching their chubby hands for her, wanting to be picked up again. And then she
knew she could not bear to watch her babies die with her.

She saw a family with three young children in a cart going by. "Take my babies, I
beg you," she cried to them. But they stared back with empty eyes and never stopped.

She saw another person pass and called out again. This time a man turned
around, and he had such a terrible expression—your mother said it looked like death
itself—she shivered and looked away.

When the road grew quiet, she tore open the lining of her dress, and stuffed jew-   110
elry under the shirt of one baby and money under the other. She reached into her
pocket and drew out the photos of her family, the picture of her father and mother,
the picture of herself and her husband on their wedding day. And she wrote on the

back of each the names of the babies and this same message: "Please care for these babies with the money and valuables provided. When it is safe to come, if you bring them to Shanghai, 9 Weichang Lu, the Li family will be glad to give you a generous reward. Li Suyuan and Wang Fuchi."

And then she touched each baby's cheek and told her not to cry. She would go down the road to find them some food and would be back. And without looking back, she walked down the road, stumbling and crying, thinking only of this one last hope, that her daughters would be found by a kindhearted person who would care for them. She would not allow herself to imagine anything else.

She did not remember how far she walked, which direction she went, when she fainted, or how she was found. When she awoke, she was in the back of a bouncing truck with several other sick people, all moaning. And she began to scream, thinking she was now on a journey to Buddhist hell. But the face of an American missionary lady bent over her and smiled, talking to her in a soothing language she did not understand. And yet she could somehow understand. She had been saved for no good reason, and it was now too late to go back and save her babies.

When she arrived in Chungking, she learned her husband had died two weeks before. She told me later she laughed when the officers told her this news, she was so delirious with madness and disease. To come so far, to lose so much and to find nothing.

I met her in a hospital. She was lying on a cot, hardly able to move, her dysentery had drained her so thin. I had come in for my foot, my missing toe, which was cut off by a piece of falling rubble. She was talking to herself, mumbling.

"Look at these clothes," she said, and I saw she had on a rather unusual dress for 115 wartime. It was silk satin, quite dirty, but there was no doubt it was a beautiful dress.

"Look at this face," she said, and I saw her dusty face and hollow cheeks, her eyes shining back. "Do you see my foolish hope?"

"I thought I had lost everything, except these two things," she murmured. "And I wondered which I would lose next. Clothes or hope? Hope or clothes?"

"But now, see here, look what is happening," she said, laughing, as if all her prayers had been answered. And she was pulling hair out of her head as easily as one lifts new wheat from wet soil.

It was an old peasant woman who found them. "How could I resist?" the peasant woman later told your sisters when they were older. They were still sitting obediently near where your mother had left them, looking like little fairy queens waiting for their sedan to arrive.

The woman, Mei Ching, and her husband, Mei Han, lived in a stone cave. There 120 were thousands of hidden caves like that in and around Kweilin so secret that the people remained hidden even after the war ended. The Meis would come out of their cave every few days and forage for food supplies left on the road, and sometimes they would see something that they both agreed was a tragedy to leave behind. So one day they took back to their cave a delicately painted set of rice bowls, another day a little footstool with a velvet cushion and two new wedding blankets. And once, it was your sisters.

They were pious people, Muslims, who believed the twin babies were a sign of double luck, and they were sure of this when, later in the evening, they discovered how valuable the babies were. She and her husband had never seen rings and bracelets like those. And while they admired the pictures, knowing the babies came from a good family, neither of them could read or write. It was not until many months later that Mei

Ching found someone who could read the writing on the back. By then, she loved these baby girls like her own.

In 1952 Mei Han, the husband, died. The twins were already eight years old, and Mei Ching now decided it was time to find your sisters' true family.

She showed the girls the picture of their mother and told them they had been born into a great family and she would take them back to see their true mother and grandparents. Mei Ching told them about the reward, but she swore she would refuse it. She loved these girls so much, she only wanted them to have what they were entitled to—a better life, a fine house, educated ways. Maybe the family would let her stay on as the girls' amah. Yes, she was certain they would insist.

Of course, when she found the place at 9 Weichang Lu, in the old French Concession, it was something completely different. It was the site of a factory building, recently constructed, and none of the workers knew what had become of the family whose house had burned down on that spot.

Mei Ching could not have known, of course, that your mother and I, her new husband, had already returned to that same place in 1945 in hopes of finding both her family and her daughters.

Your mother and I stayed in China until 1947. We went to many different cities—back to Kweilin, to Changsha, as far south as Kunming. She was always looking out of one corner of her eye for twin babies, then little girls. Later we went to Hong Kong, and when we finally left in 1949 for the United States, I think she was even looking for them on the boat. But when we arrived, she no longer talked about them. I thought, At last, they have died in her heart.

When letters could be openly exchanged between China and the United States, she wrote immediately to old friends in Shanghai and Kweilin. I did not know she did this. Auntie Lindo told me. But of course, by then, all the street names had changed. Some people had died, others had moved away. So it took many years to find a contact. And when she did find an old schoolmate's address and wrote asking her to look for her daughters, her friend wrote back and said this was impossible, like looking for a needle on the bottom of the ocean. How did she know her daughters were in Shanghai and not somewhere else in China? The friend, of course, did not ask, How do you know your daughters are still alive?

So her schoolmate did not look. Finding babies lost during the war was a matter of foolish imagination, and she had no time for that.

But every year, your mother wrote to different people. And this last year, I think she got a big idea in her head, to go to China and find them herself. I remember she told me, "Canning, we should go, before it is too late, before we are too old." And I told her we were already too old, it was already too late.

I just thought she wanted to be a tourist! I didn't know she wanted to go and look for her daughters. So when I said it was too late, that must have put a terrible thought in her head that her daughters might be dead. And I think this possibility grew bigger and bigger in her head, until it killed her.

Maybe it was your mother's dead spirit who guided her Shanghai schoolmate to find her daughters. Because after your mother died, the schoolmate saw your sisters, by chance, while shopping for shoes at the Number One Department Store on Nanjing Dong Road. She said it was like a dream, seeing these two women who looked so much alike, moving down the stairs together. There was something about their facial expressions that reminded the schoolmate of your mother.

She quickly walked over to them and called their names, which of course, they did not recognize at first, because Mei Ching had changed their names. But your mother's friend was so sure, she persisted. "Are you not Wang Chwun Yu and Wang Chwun Hwa?" she asked them. And then these double-image women became very excited, because they remembered the names written on the back of an old photo, a photo of a young man and woman they still honored, as their much-loved first parents, who had died and become spirit ghosts still roaming the earth looking for them.

At the airport, I am exhausted. I could not sleep last night. Aiyi had followed me into my room at three in the morning, and she instantly fell asleep on one of the twin beds, snoring with the might of a lumberjack. I lay awake thinking about my mother's story, realizing how much I have never known about her, grieving that my sisters and I had both lost her.

And now at the airport, after shaking hands with everybody, waving good-bye, I think about all the different ways we leave people in this world. Cheerily waving good-bye to some at airports, knowing we'll never see each other again. Leaving others on the side of the road, hoping that we will. Finding my mother in my father's story and saying good-bye before I have a chance to know her better.

Aiyi smiles at me as we wait for our gate to be called. She is so old. I put one arm around her and one around Lili. They are the same size, it seems. And then it's time. As we wave good-bye one more time and enter the waiting area, I get the sense I am going from one funeral to another. In my hand I'm clutching a pair of tickets to Shanghai. In two hours we'll be there.   135

The plane takes off. I close my eyes. How can I describe to them in my broken Chinese about our mother's life? Where should I begin?

"Wake up, we're here," says my father. And I awake with my heart pounding in my throat. I look out the window and we're already on the runway. It's gray outside.

And now I'm walking down the steps of the plane, onto the tarmac and toward the building. If only, I think, if only my mother had lived long enough to be the one walking toward them. I am so nervous I cannot even feel my feet. I am just moving somehow.

Somebody shouts, "She's arrived!" And then I see her. Her short hair. Her small body. And that same look on her face. She has the back of her hand pressed hard against her mouth. She is crying as though she had gone through a terrible ordeal and were happy it is over.

And I know it's not my mother, yet it is the same look she had when I was five   140 and had disappeared all afternoon, for such a long time, that she was convinced I was dead. And when I miraculously appeared, sleepy-eyed, crawling from underneath my bed, she wept and laughed, biting the back of her hand to make sure it was true.

And now I see her again, two of her, waving, and in one hand there is a photo, the Polaroid I sent them. As soon as I get beyond the gate, we run toward each other, all three of us embracing, all hesitations and expectations forgotten.

"Mama, Mama," we all murmur, as if she is among us.

My sisters look at me, proudly. "*Meimei jandale,*" says one sister proudly to the other. "Little Sister has grown up." I look at their faces again and I see no trace of my mother in them. Yet they still look familiar. And now I also see what part of me is Chinese. It is so obvious. It is my family. It is in our blood. After all these years, it can finally be let go.

*

My sisters and I stand, arms around each other, laughing and wiping the tears from each other's eyes. The flash of the Polaroid goes off and my father hands me the snapshot. My sisters and I watch quietly together, eager to see what develops.

The gray-green surface changes to the bright colors of our three images, sharp- 145
ening and deepening all at once. And although we don't speak, I know we all see it: Together we look like our mother. Her same eyes, her same mouth, open in surprise to see, at last, her long-cherished wish.

Questions

1. How is the external setting of "A Pair of Tickets" essential to what happens internally to the narrator in the course of this story?
2. How does the narrator's view of her father change by seeing him in a different setting?
3. In what ways does the narrator feel at home in China? In what ways does she feel foreign?
4. What do the narrator and her half-sisters have in common? How does this element relate to the theme of the story?
5. In what ways does the story explore specifically Chinese American experiences? In what other ways is the story grounded in universal family issues?

■ WRITING *effectively*

Amy Tan on Writing

Setting the Voice   1989

Lately, I've been giving more thought to the kind of English my mother speaks. Like oth-ers, I have described it to people as "broken" or "fractured" English. But I wince when I say that. It has always bothered me that I can think of no way to describe it other than "broken," as if it were damaged and needed to be fixed, as if it lacked a certain wholeness and soundness. I've heard other terms used, "limited English," for example. But they seem just as bad, as if everything is limited, including people's perceptions of the limited English speaker.

I know this for a fact, because when I was growing up, my mother's "limited" English limited *my* perception of her. I was ashamed of her English. I believed that her

Amy Tan

English reflected the quality of what she had to say. That is, because she expressed them imperfectly, her thoughts were imperfect. And I had plenty of empirical evidence to support me: the fact that people in department stores, at banks, and at restaurants did not take her seriously, did not give her good service, pretended not to under-stand her, or even acted as if they did not hear her.

• • •

But it wasn't until 1985 that I finally began to write fiction. And at first I wrote using what I thought to be wittily crafted sentences, sentences that would finally prove I had mastery over the English language. Here's an example from the first draft of a story that later made its way into *The Joy Luck Club*, but without this line: "That was my mental quandary in its nascent state." A terrible line, which I can barely pronounce.

Fortunately, for reasons I won't get into today, I later decided I should envision a reader for the stories I would write. And the reader I decided upon was my mother, because these were stories about mothers. So with this reader in mind—and in fact she did read my early drafts—I began to write stories using all the Englishes I grew up with: the English I spoke to my mother, which for lack of a better term might be described as "simple"; the English she used with me, which for lack of a better term might be described as "broken"; my translation of her Chinese, which could certainly be described as "watered down"; and what I imagined to be her translation of her Chinese if she could speak in perfect English, her internal language, and for that I sought to preserve the essence, but neither an English nor a Chinese structure. I wanted to capture what language ability tests can never reveal: her intent, her passion, her imagery, the rhythms of her speech and the nature of her thoughts.

Apart from what any critic had to say about my writing, I knew I had succeeded where it counted when my mother finished reading my book and gave me her verdict: "So easy to read."

From "Mother Tongue"

THINKING ABOUT SETTING

The time and place in which a story is set serve as more than mere backdrop. When preparing to write about a story, be sure to consider where and when it is set, and what role the setting plays.

- **Ask whether setting helps motivate the plot.** The external pressure of the setting is often the key factor that compels or invites the protagonist into action. Setting can play as large a role as plot and characters do by prompting a protagonist into an action he or she might not otherwise take.
- **Consider whether the external setting suggests the character's inner reality.** A particular setting can create a mood or provide clues to a protagonist's nature. To write about a story's setting, therefore, invites you to study not only the time and place but also their relation to the protagonist. Does the external reality provide a clue to the protagonist's inner reality?
- **Notice whether the setting changes as the plot progresses.** The settings in a story are not static. Characters can move from place to place, and their actions may bring them into significantly different external and internal places.

CHECKLIST: Writing About Setting

☐ Where does the story take place?

☐ What does the setting suggest about the characters' lives?

☐ Are there significant differences in the settings for different characters? What does this suggest about each person?

☐ When does the story take place? Is the time of year or time of day significant?

☐ Does the weather play a meaningful role in the story's action?

☐ What is the protagonist's relationship to the setting?

☐ Does the setting of the story in some way compel the protagonist into action?

☐ Does the story's time or place suggest something about the character of the protagonist?

☐ Does a change in setting during the story suggest some internal change in the protagonist?

WRITING ASSIGNMENT ON SETTING

Choose a story from this chapter, and explore how character and setting are interrelated. A possible topic would be to describe the significance of setting to the protagonist in "A Pair of Tickets" or "Greasy Lake." How does the setting of the climax of the story contribute to a change in the character's personal perspective?

MORE TOPICS FOR WRITING

1. "Greasy Lake" takes its title and epigraph from Bruce Springsteen's song "Spirit in the Night," about a carefree night at a lakeside party. If you're not familiar with it, you can find the lyrics on the Internet or download the song to get the full effect. Contrast the role setting plays in the story and in the song. What do you make of the fact that Boyle's story is so much darker than the song to which it refers?

2. Write about how setting functions as a kind of character in "To Build a Fire." Do the landscape and weather act as the antagonist in the story's plot?

3. Think of a place—on campus or beyond—to which you often return. If possible, go there. Make a list of every physical detail you can think of to describe that place. Then look the list over and write a paragraph on what sort of mood is suggested by it. If you were to describe your emotional connection to the place, which three details would you choose? Why?

4. Choose any story in this book, and pay careful attention to setting as you read it. Write several paragraphs reflecting on the following questions: What details in the story suggest the time and place in which it is set? Is setting central to the story? If the action were transplanted to some other place and time, how would the story change?

▶ TERMS FOR *review*

Setting ▶ The time and place of a story. The setting may also include the climate and even the social, psychological, or spiritual state of the characters.

Locale ▶ The location where a story takes place.

Atmosphere ▶ The dominant mood or feeling that pervades all or part of a literary work. Atmosphere is the total effect conveyed by the author's use of language, images, and physical setting.

Regionalism ▶ The literary representation of a specific locale that consciously uses the particulars of geography, custom, history, folklore, or speech. In regional narratives, the locale plays a crucial role in the presentation and progression of the story.

Naturalism ▶ A type of fiction in which the characters are presented as products or victims of environment and heredity. Naturalism is considered an extreme form of **realism** (the attempt to reproduce faithfully the surface appearance of life, especially that of ordinary people in everyday situations).

5

TONE AND STYLE

*Style has no fixed laws; it is changed by the usage
of the people, never the same for any length of time.*

—SENECA

In many Victorian novels it was customary for some commentator, presumably the author, to interrupt the story from time to time, remarking on the action, offering philosophical asides, or explaining the procedures to be followed in telling the story.

> Two hours later, Dorothea was seated in an inner room or boudoir of a handsome apartment in the Via Sistina. I am sorry to add that she was sobbing bitterly. . . .
>
> —George Eliot in *Middlemarch* (1873)

> But let the gentle-hearted reader be under no apprehension whatsoever. It is not destined that Eleanor shall marry Mr. Slope or Bertie Stanhope.
>
> —Anthony Trollope in *Barchester Towers* (1857)

Of course, the voice of this commentator was not identical with that of the "real-life" author—the one toiling over an inkpot, worrying about publication deadlines and whether the rent would be paid. At times the living author might have been far different in personality from that usually wise and cheerful intruder who kept addressing the reader of the book. Much of the time, to be sure, the author probably agreed with whatever attitudes this alter ego expressed. But, in effect, the author created the character of a commentator to speak for him or her and artfully sustained that character's voice throughout the novel.

Such intrusions, although sometimes useful to the "real" author and enjoyable to the reader, are today rare. Modern storytellers, carefully keeping out of sight, seldom comment on their plots and characters. Apparently they agree with Anton Chekhov that a writer should not judge the characters but should serve as their "impartial witness." And yet, no less definitely than Victorian novelists who introduced commentators, modern writers of effective stories no doubt have feelings toward their characters and events. The authors make us see these people in such a way that we, too, will care about them.

Although many modern writers have adopted Chekhov's "impartial" methods, they are rarely impartial witnesses. They merely embed their own feelings more deeply into the story so that those reactions emerge indirectly for the reader. For example, when at the beginning of the short story "In Exile" Chekhov introduces us to a character, he does so with a description that arouses sympathy:

> The Tartar was worn out and ill, and wrapping himself in his rags, he talked about how good it was in the province of Simbirsk, and what a beautiful and clever wife he had left at home. He was not more than twenty-five, and in the firelight his pale, sickly face and woebegone expression made him seem like a boy.

Other than the comparison of the Tartar to a child, the details in this passage seem mostly factual: the young man's illness, ragged clothes, facial expression, and topics of conversation. But these details form a portrait that stirs pity. By his selection of these imaginary details out of countless others that he might have included, Chekhov firmly directs our feelings about the Tartar, so miserable and pathetic in his sickness and his homesickness. We cannot know, of course, exactly what the living Chekhov felt; but at least we can be sure that we are supposed to share the compassion and tenderness of the narrator—Chekhov's impartial (but human) witness.

TONE

Not only the author's choice of details may lead us to infer his or her attitude, but also choice of characters, events, and situations, and choice of words. When the narrator of Joseph Conrad's *Heart of Darkness* comes upon an African outpost littered with abandoned machines and notices "a boiler wallowing in the grass," the exact word *wallowing* conveys an attitude: that there is something swinish about this scene of careless waste.

Whatever leads us to infer the author's attitude is commonly called **tone**. Like a tone of voice, the tone of a story may communicate amusement, anger, affection, sorrow, contempt. It implies the feelings of the author, so far as we can sense them. Those feelings may be similar to feelings expressed by the narrator of the story (or by any character), but sometimes they may be dissimilar, even sharply opposed. The characters in a story may regard an event as sad, but we sense that the author regards it as funny. To understand the tone of a story, then, is to understand some attitude more fundamental to the story than whatever attitudes the characters explicitly declare.

The tone of a story, like a tone of voice, may convey not simply one attitude, but a medley. Reading "A & P" (Chapter 1), we have mingled feelings about Sammy: delight in his wicked comments about other people and his skewering of hypocrisy; irritation at his smugness and condescension; admiration for his readiness to take a stand; sympathy for the pain of his disillusionment. Often the tone of a literary story will be too rich and complicated to sum up in one or two words. But to try to describe the tone of such a story may be a useful way to penetrate to its center and to grasp the whole of it.

STYLE

One of the clearest indications of the tone of a story is the **style** in which it is written. In general, style refers to the individual traits or characteristics of a piece of writing: to a writer's particular ways of managing words that we come to recognize as habitual or customary. A distinctive style marks the work of a fine writer: we can tell his or her work from that of anyone else. From one story to another, however, the writer may fittingly change style; and in some stories, style may be altered meaningfully as the story goes along. In his novel *As I Lay Dying,* William Faulkner changes narrators with every chapter, and he distinguishes the narrators one from another by giving each an individual style or manner of speaking. Though each narrator has his or her own style, the book as a whole demonstrates Faulkner's style as well. For instance, one chapter is written from the point of view of a small boy, Vardaman Bundren, member of a family of poor Mississippi tenant farmers, whose view of a horse in a barn reads like this:

> It is as though the dark were resolving him out of his integrity, into an unre-lated scattering of components—snuffings and stampings; smells of cooling flesh and ammoniac hair; an illusion of a co-ordinated whole of splotched hide and strong bones within which, detached and secret and familiar, an *is* different from my *is.*

How can a small boy unaccustomed to libraries use words like *integrity, components, illusion,* and *co-ordinated?* Elsewhere in the story, Vardaman says aloud, with no trace of literacy, "Hit was a-laying right there on the ground." Apparently, in the passage it is not the voice of the boy that we are hearing, but something resembling the voice of William Faulkner, elevated and passionate, expressing the boy's thoughts in a style that admits Faulknerian words.

DICTION

Usually, *style* indicates a mode of expression: the language a writer uses. In this sense, the notion of style includes such traits as the length and complexity of sentences, and **diction**, or choice of words: abstract or concrete, bookish ("unrelated scattering of components") or close to speech ("Hit was a-laying right there on the ground"). Involved in the idea of style, too, is any habitual use of imagery, patterns of sound, figures of speech, or other devices.

Several writers of realistic fiction, called **minimalists**—Ann Beattie, Raymond Carver, Bobbie Ann Mason—have written with a flat, laid-back, unemotional tone, in an appropriately bare, unadorned style. Minimalists seem to give nothing but facts drawn from ordinary life, sometimes in picayune detail. Here is a sample passage from Raymond Carver's story "A Small, Good Thing":

> She pulled into the driveway and cut the engine. She closed her eyes and leaned her head against the wheel for a minute. She listened to the ticking sounds the engine made as it began to cool. Then she got out of the car. She could hear the dog barking inside the house. She went to the front door, which was unlocked. She went inside and turned on lights and put on a ket-tle of water for tea. She opened some dog food and fed Slug on the back porch. The dog ate in hungry little smacks. It kept running into the kitchen to see that she was going to stay.

Explicit feeling and showy language are kept at a minimum here. Notice how Carver's diction relies on everyday words—most words of only one and two syllables. Taken out of context, this description may strike you as banal, as if the writer himself were bored; but it works effectively as a part of Carver's entire story. As in all good writing, the style here seems a faithful mirror of what is said in it. At its best, such writing achieves "a hard-won reduction, a painful stripping away of richness, a baring of bone."[1]

Two Examples of Style: Hemingway Versus Faulkner

To see what style means, compare the stories in this chapter by William Faulkner ("Barn Burning") and by Ernest Hemingway ("A Clean, Well-Lighted Place"). Faulkner frequently falls into a style in which a statement, as soon as it is uttered, is followed by another statement expressing the idea in a more emphatic way. Sentences are interrupted with parenthetical elements (asides, like this) thrust into them unexpectedly. At times, Faulkner writes of seemingly ordinary matters as if giving a speech in a towering passion. Here, from "Barn Burning," is a description of how a boy's father delivers a rug:

> "Don't you want me to help?" he whispered. His father did not answer and now he heard again that stiff foot striking the hollow portico with that wooden and clocklike deliberation, that outrageous overstatement of the weight it carried. The rug, hunched, not flung (the boy could tell that even in the darkness) from his father's shoulder struck the angle of wall and floor with a sound unbelievably loud, thunderous, then the foot again, unhurried and enormous; a light came on in the house and the boy sat, tense, breathing steadily and quietly and just a little fast, though the foot itself did not increase its beat at all, descending the steps now; now the boy could see him.

Faulkner is not merely indulging in language for its own sake. As you will find when you read the whole story, this rug delivery is vital to the story, and so too is the father's profound defiance—indicated by his walk. By devices of style—by *metaphor* and *simile* ("wooden and clocklike"), by exact qualification ("not flung"), by emphatic adjectives ("loud, thunderous")—Faulkner is carefully placing his emphases.

By the words he selects to describe the father's stride, Faulkner directs how we feel toward the man and perhaps also indicates his own wondering but skeptical attitude toward a character whose very footfall is "outrageous" and "enormous." (Fond of long sentences like the last one in the quoted passage, Faulkner remarked that there are sentences that need to be written in the way a circus acrobat pedals a bicycle on a high wire: rapidly, so as not to fall off.)

Hemingway's famous style includes both short sentences and long, but when the sentences are long, they tend to be relatively simple in construction. Hemingway likes long compound sentences (clause plus clause plus clause), sometimes joined with "and"s. He interrupts such a sentence with a dependent clause or a parenthetical element much less frequently than Faulkner does. The effect is like listening to speech:

> In the day time the street was dusty, but at night the dew settled the dust and the old man liked to sit late because he was deaf and now at night it was quiet and he felt the difference.

Hemingway is a master of swift, terse dialogue, and often casts whole scenes in the form of conversation. As if he were a closemouthed speaker unwilling to let his feelings loose, the narrator of a Hemingway story often addresses us in understatement, implying greater depths of feeling than he puts into words. Read the following story and you will see that its style and tone cannot be separated.

---

[1]Letter in the *New York Times Book Review*, 5 June 1988.

Ernest Hemingway

A Clean, Well-Lighted Place   1933

Ernest Hemingway (1899–1961), born in Oak Park, Illinois, bypassed college to be a cub reporter. In World War I, as an eighteen-year-old volunteer ambulance driver in Italy, he was wounded in action. In 1922 he settled in Paris, then aswarm with writers; he later recalled that time in A Moveable Feast *(1964). Hemingway won swift acclaim for his early stories,* In Our Time *(1925), and for his first, perhaps finest, novel,* The Sun Also Rises *(1926), portraying a "lost generation" of postwar American drifters in France and Spain.* For Whom the Bell Tolls *(1940) depicts life during the Spanish Civil War. Hemingway became a celebrity, often photographed as a marlin fisherman or a lion hunter. A fan of bullfighting, he wrote two nonfiction books on the subject:* Death in the Afternoon *(1932) and* The Dangerous Summer *(posthumously published in 1985). After World War II, with his fourth wife, journalist Mary Welsh, he made his home in Cuba, where he wrote* The Old Man and the Sea *(1952). The Nobel Prize in Literature came his way in 1954. In 1961, mentally distressed and physically ailing, he shot himself. Hemingway brought a hard-bitten realism to American fiction. His heroes live dangerously, by personal codes of honor, courage, and endurance. Hemingway's distinctively crisp, unadorned style left American literature permanently changed.*

It was late and every one had left the café except an old man who sat in the shadow the leaves of the tree made against the electric light. In the day time the street was dusty, but at night the dew settled the dust and the old man liked to sit late because he was deaf and now at night it was quiet and he felt the difference. The two waiters inside the café knew that the old man was a little drunk, and while he was a good client they knew that if he became too drunk he would leave without paying, so they kept watch on him.

"Last week he tried to commit suicide," one waiter said.

"Why?"

"He was in despair."

"What about?"

"Nothing."   5

"How do you know it was nothing?"

"He has plenty of money."

They sat together at a table that was close against the wall near the door of the café and looked at the terrace where the tables were all empty except where the old man sat in the shadow of the leaves of the tree that moved slightly in the wind. A girl and a soldier went by in the street. The street light shone on the brass number on his collar. The girl wore no head covering and hurried beside him.

"The guard will pick him up," one waiter said.   10

"What does it matter if he gets what he's after?"

"He had better get off the street now. The guard will get him. They went by five minutes ago."

The old man sitting in the shadow rapped on his saucer with his glass. The younger waiter went over to him.

"What do you want?"

The old man looked at him. "Another brandy," he said.   15

"You'll be drunk," the waiter said. The old man looked at him. The waiter went away.

"He'll stay all night," he said to his colleague. "I'm sleepy now. I never get into bed before three o'clock. He should have killed himself last week."

The waiter took the brandy bottle and another saucer from the counter inside the café and marched out to the old man's table. He put down the saucer and poured the glass full of brandy.

"You should have killed yourself last week," he said to the deaf man. The old man motioned with his finger. "A little more," he said. The waiter poured on into the glass so that the brandy slopped over and ran down the stem into the top saucer of the pile. "Thank you," the old man said. The waiter took the bottle back inside the café. He sat down at the table with his colleague again.

"He's drunk now," he said.   20

"He's drunk every night."°

"What did he want to kill himself for?"

"How should I know?"

"How did he do it?"

"He hung himself with a rope."   25

"Who cut him down?"

"His niece."

"Why did they do it?"

"Fear for his soul."

"How much money has he got?"   30

"He's got plenty."

"He must be eighty years old."

"Anyway I should say he was eighty."°

"I wish he would go home. I never get to bed before three o'clock. What kind of hour is that to go to bed?"

"He stays up because he likes it."   35

"He's lonely. I'm not lonely. I have a wife waiting in bed for me."

"He had a wife once too."

"A wife would be no good to him now."

"You can't tell. He might be better with a wife."

"His niece looks after him."   40

"I know. You said she cut him down."

"I wouldn't want to be that old. An old man is a nasty thing."

"Not always. This old man is clean. He drinks without spilling. Even now, drunk. Look at him."

"I don't want to look at him. I wish he would go home. He has no regard for those who must work."

The old man looked from his glass across the square, then over at the waiters.   45

"Another brandy," he said, pointing to his glass. The waiter who was in a hurry came over.

"Finished," he said, speaking with that omission of syntax stupid people employ when talking to drunken people or foreigners. "No more tonight. Close now."

"He's drunk now," he said. "He's drunk every night": The younger waiter perhaps says both these lines. A device of Hemingway's style is sometimes to have a character pause, then speak again—as often happens in actual speech.   *"He must be eighty years old." "Anyway I should say he was eighty"*: Is this another instance of the same character's speaking twice? Clearly, it is the younger waiter who says the next line, "I wish he would go home."

"Another," said the old man.

"No. Finished." The waiter wiped the edge of the table with a towel and shook his head.

The old man stood up, slowly counted the saucers, took a leather coin purse from   50
his pocket and paid for the drinks, leaving half a peseta tip.

The waiter watched him go down the street, a very old man walking unsteadily but with dignity.

"Why didn't you let him stay and drink?" the unhurried waiter asked. They were putting up the shutters. "It is not half-past two."

"I want to go home to bed."

"What is an hour?"

"More to me than to him."   55

"An hour is the same."

"You talk like an old man yourself. He can buy a bottle and drink at home."

"It's not the same."

"No, it is not," agreed the waiter with a wife. He did not wish to be unjust. He was only in a hurry.

"And you? You have no fear of going home before the usual hour?"   60

"Are you trying to insult me?"

"No, hombre, only to make a joke."

"No," the waiter who was in a hurry said, rising from pulling down the metal shutters. "I have confidence. I am all confidence."

"You have youth, confidence, and a job," the older waiter said. "You have every-thing."

"And what do you lack?"   65

"Everything but work."

"You have everything I have."

"No. I have never had confidence and I am not young."

"Come on. Stop talking nonsense and lock up."

"I am of those who like to stay late at the café," the older waiter said. "With all   70
those who do not want to go to bed. With all those who need a light for the night."

"I want to go home and into bed."

"We are of two different kinds," the older waiter said. He was not dressed to go home. "It is not only a question of youth and confidence although those things are very beautiful. Each night I am reluctant to close up because there may be some one who needs the café."

"Hombre, there are bodegas° open all night long."

"You do not understand. This is a clean and pleasant café. It is well lighted. The light is very good and also, now, there are shadows of the leaves."

"Good night," said the younger waiter.   75

"Good night," the other said. Turning off the electric light he continued the conversation with himself. It is the light of course but it is necessary that the place be clean and pleasant. You do not want music. Certainly you do not want music. Nor can you stand before a bar with dignity although that is all that is provided for these hours. What did he fear? It was not fear or dread. It was a nothing that he knew too well. It was all a nothing and a man was nothing too. It was only that and light was all it needed and a certain cleanness and order. Some lived in it and never felt it but

bodegas: wineshops.

he knew it all was nada y pues nada y nada y pues nada.° Our nada who art in nada, nada be thy name thy kingdom nada thy will be nada in nada as it is in nada. Give us this nada our daily nada and nada us our nada as we nada our nadas and nada us not into nada but deliver us from nada; pues nada. Hail nothing full of nothing, nothing is with thee. He smiled and stood before a bar with a shining steam pressure coffee machine.

"What's yours?" asked the barman.

"Nada."

"Otro loco más,"° said the barman and turned away.

"A little cup," said the waiter.   80

The barman poured it for him.

"The light is very bright and pleasant but the bar is unpolished," the waiter said.

The barman looked at him but did not answer. It was too late at night for conversation.

"You want another copita?"° the barman asked.

"No, thank you," said the waiter and went out. He disliked bars and bodegas. A   85
clean, well-lighted café was a very different thing. Now, without thinking further, he would go home to his room. He would lie in the bed and finally, with daylight, he would go to sleep. After all, he said to himself, it is probably only insomnia. Many must have it.

Questions

1. What besides insomnia makes the older waiter reluctant to go to bed? Comment especially on his meditation with its *nada* refrain. Why does he understand so well the old man's need for a café? What does the café represent for the two of them?

2. Compare the younger waiter and the older waiter in their attitudes toward the old man. Whose attitude do you take to be closer to that of the author? Even though Hemingway does not editorially state his own feelings, how does he make them clear to us?

3. Point to sentences that establish the style of the story. What is distinctive in them? What repetitions of words or phrases seem particularly effective? Does Hemingway seem to favor a simple or an erudite vocabulary?

4. What is the story's point of view? Discuss its appropriateness.

William Faulkner

Barn Burning   1939

William Faulkner (1897–1962) receives a capsule biography in Chapter 2, page 29, along with his story "A Rose for Emily." "Barn Burning" is among his many contributions to the history of Yoknapatawpha, an imaginary Mississippi county in which the Sartorises and the de Spains are landed aristocrats living by a code of honor and the Snopeses—most of them— are shiftless ne'er-do-wells.

The store in which the Justice of the Peace's court was sitting smelled of cheese. The boy, crouched on his nail keg at the back of the crowded room, knew he smelled cheese, and more: from where he sat he could see the ranked shelves close-packed

---

nada y pues . . . nada: nothing and then nothing and nothing and then nothing.   *Otro loco más:* another lunatic.   *copita:* little cup.

with the solid, squat, dynamic shapes of tin cans whose labels his stomach read, not from the lettering which meant nothing to his mind but from the scarlet devils and the silver curve of fish—this, the cheese which he knew he smelled and the hermetic meat which his intestines believed he smelled coming in intermittent gusts momentary and brief between the other constant one, the smell and sense just a little of fear because mostly of despair and grief, the old fierce pull of blood. He could not see the table where the Justice sat and before which his father and his father's enemy (*our enemy* he thought in that despair: *ourn! mine and hisn both! He's my father!*) stood, but he could hear them, the two of them that is, because his father had said no word yet:

"But what proof have you, Mr. Harris?"

"I told you. The hog got into my corn. I caught it up and sent it back to him. He had no fence that would hold it. I told him so, warned him. The next time I put the hog in my pen. When he came to get it I gave him enough wire to patch up his pen. The next time I put the hog up and kept it. I rode down to his house and saw the wire I gave him still rolled on to the spool in his yard. I told him he could have the hog when he paid me a dollar pound fee. That evening a nigger came with the dollar and got the hog. He was a strange nigger. He said, 'He say to tell you wood and hay kin burn.' I said, 'What?' 'That whut he say to tell you,' the nigger said. 'Wood and hay kin burn.' That night my barn burned. I got the stock out but I lost the barn."

"Where's the nigger? Have you got him?"

"He was a strange nigger, I tell you. I don't know what became of him."   5

"But that's not proof. Don't you see that's not proof?"

"Get that boy up here. He knows." For a moment the boy thought too that the man meant his older brother until Harris said, "Not him. The little one. The boy," and, crouching, small for his age, small and wiry like his father, in patched and faded jeans even too small for him, with straight, uncombed, brown hair and eyes gray and wild as storm scud, he saw the men between himself and the table part and become a lane of grim faces, at the end of which he saw the Justice, a shabby, collarless, graying man in spectacles, beckoning him. He felt no floor under his bare feet; he seemed to walk beneath the palpable weight of the grim turning faces. His father, still in his black Sunday coat donned not for the trial but for the moving, did not even look at him. *He aims for me to lie,* he thought, again with that frantic grief and despair. *And I will have to do hit.*

"What's your name, boy?" the Justice said.

"Colonel Sartoris Snopes," the boy whispered.

"Hey?" the Justice said. "Talk louder. Colonel Sartoris? I reckon anybody named   10
for Colonel Sartoris in this country can't help but tell the truth, can they?" The boy said nothing. *Enemy! Enemy!* he thought; for a moment he could not even see, could not see that the Justice's face was kindly nor discern that his voice was troubled when he spoke to the man named Harris: "Do you want me to question this boy?" But he could hear, and during those subsequent long seconds while there was absolutely no sound in the crowded little room save that of quiet and intent breathing it was as if he had swung outward at the end of a grape vine, over a ravine, and at the top of the swing had been caught in a prolonged instant of mesmerized gravity, weightless in time.

"No!" Harris said violently, explosively. "Damnation! Send him out of here!" Now time, the fluid world, rushed beneath him again, the voices coming to him again through the smell of cheese and sealed meat, the fear and despair and the old grief of blood:

"This case is closed. I can't find against you, Snopes, but I can give you advice. Leave this country and don't come back to it."

His father spoke for the first time, his voice cold and harsh, level, without emphasis: "I aim to. I don't figure to stay in a country among people who . . ." he said something unprintable and vile, addressed to no one.

"That'll do," the Justice said. "Take your wagon and get out of this country before dark. Case dismissed."

His father turned, and he followed the stiff black coat, the wiry figure walking a   15
little stiffly from where a Confederate provost's man's musket ball had taken him in the heel on a stolen horse thirty years ago, followed the two backs now, since his older brother had appeared from somewhere in the crowd, no taller than the father but thicker, chewing tobacco steadily, between the two lines of grim-faced men and out of the store and across the worn gallery and down the sagging steps and among the dogs and half-grown boys in the mild May dust, where as he passed a voice hissed:

"Barn burner!"

Again he could not see, whirling; there was a face in a red haze, moonlike, bigger than the full moon, the owner of it half again his size, he leaping in the red haze toward the face, feeling no blow, feeling no shock when his head struck the earth, scrabbling up and leaping again, feeling no blow this time either and tasting no blood, scrabbling up to see the other boy in full flight and himself already leaping into pursuit as his father's hand jerked him back, the harsh, cold voice speaking above him: "Go get in the wagon."

It stood in a grove of locusts and mulberries across the road. His two hulking sisters in their Sunday dresses and his mother and her sister in calico and sunbonnets were already in it, sitting on and among the sorry residue of the dozen and more movings which even the boy could remember—the battered stove, the broken beds and chairs, the clock inlaid with mother-of-pearl, which would not run, stopped at some fourteen minutes past two o'clock of a dead and forgotten day and time, which had been his mother's dowry. She was crying, though when she saw him she drew her sleeve across her face and began to descend from the wagon. "Get back," the father said.

"He's hurt. I got to get some water and wash his . . ."

"Get back in the wagon," his father said. He got in too, over the tail-gate. His   20
father mounted to the seat where the older brother already sat and struck the gaunt mules two savage blows with the peeled willow, but without heat. It was not even sadistic; it was exactly that same quality which in later years would cause his descendants to over-run the engine before putting a motor car into motion, striking and reining back in the same movement. The wagon went on, the store with its quiet crowd of grimly watching men dropped behind; a curve in the road hid it. *Forever* he thought. *Maybe he's done satisfied now, now that he has . . .* stopping himself, not to say it aloud even to himself. His mother's hand touched his shoulder.

"Does hit hurt?" she said.

"Naw," he said. "Hit don't hurt. Lemme be."

"Can't you wipe some of the blood off before hit dries?"

"I'll wash to-night," he said. "Lemme be, I tell you."

The wagon went on. He did not know where they were going. None of them   25
ever did or ever asked, because it was always somewhere, always a house of sorts waiting for them a day or two days or even three days away. Likely his father had already arranged to make a crop on another farm before he . . . Again he had to stop himself. He (the father) always did. There was something about his wolflike independence

and even courage when the advantage was at least neutral which impressed strangers, as if they got from his latent ravening ferocity not so much a sense of dependability as a feeling that his ferocious conviction in the rightness of his own actions would be of advantage to all whose interest lay with his.

That night they camped, in a grove of oaks and beeches where a spring ran. The nights were still cool and they had a fire against it, of a rail lifted from a nearby fence and cut into lengths—a small fire, neat, niggard almost, a shrewd fire; such fires were his father's habit and custom always, even in freezing weather. Older, the boy might have remarked this and wondered why not a big one; why should not a man who had not only seen the waste and extravagance of war, but who had in his blood an inherent voracious prodigality with material not his own, have burned everything in sight? Then he might have gone a step farther and thought that that was the reason: that niggard blaze was the living fruit of nights passed during those four years in the woods hiding from all men, blue and gray, with his strings of horses (captured horses, he called them). And older still, he might have divined the true reason: that the element of fire spoke to some deep mainspring of his father's being, as the element of steel or of powder spoke to other men, as the one weapon for the preservation of integrity, else breath were not worth the breathing, and hence to be regarded with respect and used with discretion.

But he did not think this now and he had seen those same niggard blazes all his life. He merely ate his supper beside it and was already half asleep over his iron plate when his father called him, and once more he followed the stiff back, the stiff and ruthless limp, up the slope and on to the starlit road where, turning, he could see his father against the stars but without face or depth—a shape black, flat, and bloodless as though cut from tin in the iron folds of the frockcoat which had not been made for him, the voice harsh like tin and without heat like tin:

"You were fixing to tell them. You would have told him." He didn't answer. His father struck him with the flat of his hand on the side of the head, hard but without heat, exactly as he had struck the two mules at the store, exactly as he would strike either of them with any stick in order to kill a horse fly, his voice without heat or anger: "You're getting to be a man. You got to learn. You got to learn to stick to your own blood or you ain't going to have any blood to stick to you. Do you think either of them, any man there this morning, would? Don't you know all they wanted was a chance to get at me because they knew I had them beat? Eh?" Later, twenty years later, he was to tell himself, "If I had said they wanted only truth, justice, he would have hit me again." But now he said nothing. He was not crying. He just stood there. "Answer me," his father said.

"Yes," he whispered. His father turned.

"Get on to bed. We'll be there tomorrow." 30

Tomorrow they were there. In the early afternoon the wagon stopped before a paintless two-room house identical almost with the dozen others it had stopped before even in the boy's ten years, and again, as on the other dozen occasions, his mother and aunt got down and began to unload the wagon, although his two sisters and his father and brother had not moved.

"Likely hit ain't fitten for hawgs," one of the sisters said.

"Nevertheless, fit it will and you'll hog it and like it," his father said. "Get out of them chairs and help your Ma unload."

The two sisters got down, big, bovine, in a flutter of cheap ribbons; one of them drew from the jumbled wagon bed a battered lantern, the other a worn broom. His father handed the reins to the older son and began to climb stiffly over the wheel. "When they get unloaded, take the team to the barn and feed them." Then he said, and at first the boy thought he was still speaking to his brother: "Come with me."

"Me?" he said.

35

"Yes," his father said. "You."

"Abner," his mother said. His father paused and looked back—the harsh level stare beneath the shaggy, graying, irascible brows.

"I reckon I'll have a word with the man that aims to begin to-morrow owning me body and soul for the next eight months."

They went back up the road. A week ago—or before last night, that is—he would have asked where they were going, but not now. His father had struck him before last night but never before had he paused afterward to explain why; it was as if the blow and the following calm, outrageous voice still rang, repercussed, divulging nothing to him save the terrible handicap of being young, the light weight of his few years, just heavy enough to prevent his soaring free of the world as it seemed to be ordered but not heavy enough to keep him footed solid in it, to resist it and try to change the course of its events.

Presently he could see the grove of oaks and cedars and the other flowering trees and shrubs where the house would be, though not the house yet. They walked beside a fence massed with honeysuckle and Cherokee roses and came to a gate swinging open between two brick pillars, and now, beyond a sweep of drive, he saw the house for the first time and at that instant he forgot his father and the terror and despair both, and even when he remembered his father again (who had not stopped) the terror and despair did not return. Because, for all the twelve movings, they had sojourned until now in a poor country, a land of small farms and fields and houses, and he had never seen a house like this before. *Hit's big as a courthouse* he thought quietly, with a surge of peace and joy whose reason he could not have thought into words, being too young for that: *They are safe from him. People whose lives are a part of this peace and dignity are beyond his touch, he no more to them than a buzzing wasp: capable of stinging for a little moment but that's all; the spell of this peace and dignity rendering even the barns and stable and cribs which belong to it impervious to the puny flames he might contrive . . .* this, the peace and joy, ebbing for an instant as he looked again at the stiff black back, the stiff and implacable limp of the figure which was not dwarfed by the house, for the reason that it had never looked big anywhere and which now, against the serene columned backdrop, had more than ever that impervious quality of something cut ruthlessly from tin, depthless, as though, sidewise to the sun, it would cast no shadow. Watching him, the boy remarked the absolutely undeviating course which his father held and saw the stiff foot come squarely down in a pile of fresh droppings where a horse had stood in the drive and which his father could have avoided by a simple change of stride. But it ebbed only a moment, though he could not have thought this into words either, walking on in the spell of the house, which he could even want but without envy, without sorrow, certainly never with that ravening and jealous rage which unknown to him walked in the ironlike black coat before him: *Maybe he will feel it too. Maybe it will even change him now from what maybe he couldn't help but be.*

40

They crossed the portico. Now he could hear his father's stiff foot as it came down on the boards with clocklike finality, a sound out of all proportion to the displacement of the body it bore and which was not dwarfed either by the white door before it, as though it had attained to a sort of vicious and ravening minimum not to be dwarfed by anything—the flat, wide, black hat, the formal coat of broadcloth which had once been black but which had now that friction-glazed greenish cast of the bodies of old house flies, the lifted sleeve which was too large, the lifted hand like a curled claw. The door opened so promptly that the boy knew the Negro must have been watching them all the time, an old man with neat grizzled hair, in a linen jacket, who stood barring the door with his body, saying, "Wipe yo foots, white man, fo you come in here. Major ain't home nohow."

"Get out of my way, nigger," his father said, without heat too, flinging the door back and the Negro also and entering, his hat still on his head. And now the boy saw the prints of the stiff foot on the doorjamb and saw them appear on the pale rug behind the machinelike deliberation of the foot which seemed to bear (or transmit) twice the weight which the body compassed. The Negro was shouting "Miss Lula! Miss Lula!" somewhere behind them, then the boy, deluged as though by a warm wave by a suave turn of the carpeted stair and a pendant glitter of chandeliers and a mute gleam of gold frames, heard the swift feet and saw her too, a lady—perhaps he had never seen her like before either—in a gray, smooth gown with lace at the throat and an apron tied at the waist and the sleeves turned back, wiping cake or biscuit dough from her hands with a towel as she came up the hall, looking not at his father at all but at the tracks on the blond rug with an expression of incredulous amazement.

"I tried," the Negro cried. "I tole him to . . ."

"Will you please go away?" she said in a shaking voice. "Major de Spain is not at home. Will you please go away?"

His father had not spoken again. He did not speak again. He did not even look at her. He just stood stiff in the center of the rug, in his hat, the shaggy iron-gray brows twitching slightly above the pebble-colored eyes as he appeared to examine the house with brief deliberation. Then with the same deliberation he turned; the boy watched him pivot on the good leg and saw the stiff foot drag around the arc of the turning, leaving a final long and fading smear. His father never looked at it, he never once looked down at the rug. The Negro held the door. It closed behind them, upon the hysteric and indistinguishable woman-wail. His father stopped at the top of the steps and scraped his boot clean on the edge of it. At the gate he stopped again. He stood for a moment, planted stiffly on the stiff foot, looking back at the house. "Pretty and white, ain't it?" he said. "That's sweat. Nigger sweat. Maybe it ain't white enough yet to suit him. Maybe he wants to mix some white sweat with it." 45

Two hours later the boy was chopping wood behind the house within which his mother and aunt and the two sisters (the mother and aunt, not the two girls, he knew that; even at this distance and muffled by walls the flat loud voices of the two girls emanated an incorrigible idle inertia) were setting up the stove to prepare a meal, when he heard the hooves and saw the linen-clad man on a fine sorrel mare, whom he recognized even before he saw the rolled rug in front of the Negro youth following on a fat bay carriage horse—a suffused, angry face vanishing, still at full gallop, beyond the corner of the house where his father and brother were sitting in the two tilted chairs; and a moment later, almost before he could have put the axe down, he heard the hooves again and watched the sorrel mare go back out of the yard, already galloping again. Then his father began to shout one of the sisters' names, who presently emerged backward from the kitchen door dragging the rolled rug along the ground by one end while the other sister walked behind it.

"If you ain't going to tote, go on and set up the wash pot," the first said.

"You, Sarty!" the second shouted. "Set up the wash pot!" His father appeared at the door, framed against that shabbiness, as he had been against that other bland perfection, impervious to either, the mother's anxious face at his shoulder.

"Go on," the father said. "Pick it up." The two sisters stooped, broad, lethargic; stooping, they presented an incredible expanse of pale cloth and a flutter of tawdry ribbons.

"If I thought enough of a rug to have to git hit all the way from France I wouldn't keep hit where folks coming in would have to tromp on hit," the first said. They raised the rug.

"Abner," the mother said. "Let me do it."

"You go back and git dinner," his father said. "I'll tend to this."

From the woodpile through the rest of the afternoon the boy watched them, the rug spread flat in the dust beside the bubbling wash pot, the two sisters stooping over it with that profound and lethargic reluctance, while the father stood over them in turn, implacable and grim, driving them though never raising his voice again. He could smell the harsh homemade lye they were using; he saw his mother come to the door once and look toward them with an expression not anxious now but very like despair; he saw his father turn, and he fell to with the axe and saw from the corner of his eye his father raise from the ground a flattish fragment of field stone and examine it and return to the pot, and this time his mother actually spoke: "Abner. Abner. Please don't. Please, Abner."

Then he was done too. It was dusk; the whippoorwills had already begun. He could smell coffee from the room where they would presently eat the cold food remaining from the mid-afternoon meal, though when he entered the house he realized they were having coffee again probably because there was a fire on the hearth, before which the rug now lay spread over the backs of the two chairs. The tracks of his father's foot were gone. Where they had been were now long, water-cloudy scoriations resembling the sporadic course of a lilliputian mowing machine.

It still hung there while they ate the cold food and then went to bed, scattered without order or claim up and down the two rooms, his mother in one bed, where his father would later lie, the older brother in the other, himself, the aunt, and the two sisters on pallets on the floor. But his father was not in bed yet. The last thing the boy remembered was the depthless, harsh silhouette of the hat and coat bending over the rug and it seemed to him that he had not even closed his eyes when the silhouette was standing over him, the fire almost dead behind it, the stiff foot prodding him awake. "Catch up the mule," his father said.

When he returned with the mule his father was standing in the back door, the rolled rug over his shoulder. "Ain't you going to ride?" he said.

"No. Give me your foot."

He bent his knee into his father's hand, the wiry, surprising power flowed smoothly, rising, he rising with it, on to the mule's bare back (they had owned a saddle once; the boy could remember it though not when or where) and with the same effortlessness his father swung the rug up in front of him. Now in the starlight they retraced the afternoon's path, up the dusty road rife with honeysuckle, through the gate and up the black tunnel of the drive to the lightless house, where he sat on the mule and felt the rough warp of the rug drag across his thighs and vanish.

"Don't you want me to help?" he whispered. His father did not answer and now he heard again that stiff foot striking the hollow portico with that wooden and clocklike deliberation, that outrageous overstatement of the weight it carried. The rug, hunched, not flung (the boy could tell that even in the darkness) from his father's shoulder struck the angle of wall and floor with a sound unbelievably loud, thunderous, then the foot again, unhurried and enormous; a light came on in the house and the boy sat, tense, breathing steadily and quietly and just a little fast, though the foot itself did not increase its beat at all, descending the steps now; now the boy could see him.

"Don't you want to ride now?" he whispered. "We kin both ride now," the light   60
within the house altering now, flaring up and sinking. *He's coming down the stairs now*, he thought. He had already ridden the mule up beside the horse block; presently his father was up behind him and he doubled the reins over and slashed the mule across the neck, but before the animal could begin to trot the hard, thin arm came around him, the hard, knotted hand jerking the mule back to a walk.

In the first red rays of the sun they were in the lot, putting plow gear on the mules. This time the sorrel mare was in the lot before he heard it at all, the rider collarless and even bareheaded, trembling, speaking in a shaking voice as the woman in the house had done, his father merely looking up once before stooping again to the hame he was buckling, so that the man on the mare spoke to his stooping back:

"You must realize you have ruined that rug. Wasn't there anybody here, any of your women . . ." he ceased, shaking, the boy watching him, the older brother leaning now in the stable door, chewing, blinking slowly and steadily at nothing apparently. "It cost a hundred dollars. But you never had a hundred dollars. You never will. So I'm going to charge you twenty bushels of corn against your crop. I'll add it in your contract and when you come to the commissary you can sign it. That won't keep Mrs. de Spain quiet but maybe it will teach you to wipe your feet off before you enter her house again."

Then he was gone. The boy looked at his father, who still had not spoken or even looked up again, who was now adjusting the logger-head in the hame.

"Pap," he said. His father looked at him—the inscrutable face, the shaggy brows beneath where the gray eyes glinted coldly. Suddenly the boy went toward him, fast, stopping as suddenly. "You done the best you could!" he cried. "If he wanted hit done different why didn't he wait and tell you how? He won't git no twenty bushels! He won't git none! We'll gather hit and hide hit! I kin watch . . ."

"Did you put the cutter back in that straight stock like I told you?"   65

"No, sir," he said.

"Then go do it."

That was Wednesday. During the rest of that week he worked steadily, at what was within his scope and some which was beyond it, with an industry that did not need to be driven nor even commanded twice; he had this from his mother, with the difference that some at least of what he did he liked to do, such as splitting wood with the half-size axe which his mother and aunt had earned, or saved money somehow, to present him with at Christmas. In company with the two older women (and on one afternoon, even one of the sisters), he built pens for the shoat and the cow which were a part of his father's contract with the landlord, and one afternoon, his father being absent, gone somewhere on one of the mules, he went to the field.

They were running a middle buster now, his brother holding the plow straight while he handled the reins, and walking beside the straining mule, the rich black soil shearing cool and damp against his bare ankles, he thought *Maybe this is the end of it. Maybe even that twenty bushels that seems hard to have to pay for just a rug will be a cheap price for him to stop forever and always from being what he used to be*; thinking, dreaming now, so that his brother had to speak sharply to him to mind the mule: *Maybe he even won't collect the twenty bushels. Maybe it will all add up and balance and vanish—corn, rug, fire; the terror and grief; the being pulled two ways like between two teams of horses— gone, done with for ever and ever.*

Then it was Saturday; he looked up from beneath the mule he was harnessing   70
and saw his father in the black coat and hat. "Not that," his father said. "The wagon gear." And then, two hours later, sitting in the wagon bed behind his father and brother on the seat, the wagon accomplished a final curve, and he saw the weathered paintless store with its tattered tobacco- and patent-medicine posters and the teth- ered wagons and saddle animals below the gallery. He mounted the gnawed steps be- hind his father and brother, and there again was the lane of quiet, watching faces for the three of them to walk through. He saw the man in spectacles sitting at the plank table and he did not need to be told this was a Justice of the Peace; he sent one glare of fierce, exultant, partisan defiance at the man in collar and cravat now, whom he had seen but twice before in his life, and that on a galloping horse, who now wore on his face an expression not of rage but of amazed unbelief which the boy could not have known was at the incredible circumstance of being sued by one of his own ten- ants, and came and stood against his father and cried at the Justice: "He ain't done it! He ain't burnt . . ."

"Go back to the wagon," his father said.

"Burnt?" the Justice said. "Do I understand this rug was burned too?"

"Does anybody here claim it was?" his father said. "Go back to the wagon." But he did not, he merely retreated to the rear of the room, crowded as that other had been, but not to sit down this time, instead, to stand pressing among the motionless bodies, listening to the voices:

"And you claim twenty bushels of corn is too high for the damage you did to the rug?"

"He brought the rug to me and said he wanted the tracks washed out of it. I   75
washed the tracks out and took the rug back to him."

"But you didn't carry the rug back to him in the same condition it was in before you made the tracks on it."

His father did not answer, and now for perhaps half a minute there was no sound at all save that of breathing, the faint, steady suspiration of complete and intent lis- tening.

"You decline to answer that, Mr. Snopes?" Again his father did not answer. "I'm going to find against you, Mr. Snopes. I'm going to find that you were responsible for the injury to Major de Spain's rug and hold you liable for it. But twenty bushels of corn seems a little high for a man in your circumstances to have to pay. Major de Spain claims it cost a hundred dollars. October corn will be worth about fifty cents. I figure that if Major de Spain can stand a ninety-five dollar loss on something he paid cash for, you can stand a five-dollar loss you haven't earned yet. I hold you in damages to Major de Spain to the amount of ten bushels of corn over and above your contract with him, to be paid to him out of your crop at gathering time. Court adjourned."

It had taken no time hardly, the morning was but half begun. He thought they would return home and perhaps back to the field, since they were late, far behind all other farmers. But instead his father passed on behind the wagon, merely indicating with his hand for the older brother to follow with it, and crossed the road toward the blacksmith shop opposite, pressing on after his father, overtaking him, speaking, whispering up at the harsh, calm face beneath the weathered hat: "He won't git no ten bushels either. He won't git one. We'll . . ." until his father glanced for an instant down at him, the face absolutely calm, the grizzled eyebrows tangled above the cold eyes, the voice almost pleasant, almost gentle:

"You think so? Well, we'll wait till October anyway." 80

The matter of the wagon—the setting of a spoke or two and the tightening of the tires—did not take long either, the business of the tires accomplished by driving the wagon into the spring branch behind the shop and letting it stand there, the mules nuzzling into the water from time to time, and the boy on the seat with the idle reins, looking up the slope and through the sooty tunnel of the shed where the slow hammer rang and where his father sat on an upended cypress bolt, easily, either talking or listening, still sitting there when the boy brought the dripping wagon up out of the branch and halted it before the door.

"Take them on to the shade and hitch," his father said. He did so and returned. His father and the smith and a third man squatting on his heels inside the door were talking, about crops and animals; the boy, squatting too in the ammoniac dust and hoof-parings and scales of rust, heard his father tell a long and unhurried story out of the time before the birth of the older brother even when he had been a professional horsetrader. And then his father came up beside him where he stood before a tattered last year's circus poster on the other side of the store, gazing rapt and quiet at the scarlet horses, the incredible poisings and convulsions of tulle and tights and the painted leers of comedians, and said, "It's time to eat."

But not at home. Squatting beside his brother against the front wall, he watched his father emerge from the store and produce from a paper sack a segment of cheese and divide it carefully and deliberately into three with his pocket knife and produce crackers from the same sack. They all three squatted on the gallery and ate, slowly, without talking; then in the store again, they drank from a tin dipper tepid water smelling of the cedar bucket and of living beech trees. And still they did not go home. It was a horse lot this time, a tall rail fence upon and along which men stood and sat and out of which one by one horses were led, to be walked and trotted and then cantered back and forth along the road while the slow swapping and buying went on and the sun began to slant westward, they—the three of them—watching and listening, the older brother with his muddy eyes and his steady, inevitable tobacco, the father commenting now and then on certain of the animals, to no one in particular.

It was after sundown when they reached home. They ate supper by lamplight, then, sitting on the doorstep, the boy watched the night fully accomplish, listening to the whippoorwills and the frogs, when he heard his mother's voice: "Abner! No! No! Oh, God. Oh, God. Abner!" and he rose, whirled, and saw the altered light through the door where a candle stub now burned in a bottle neck on the table and his father, still in the hat and coat, at once formal and burlesque as though dressed carefully for some shabby and ceremonial violence, emptying the reservoir of the lamp back into the five-gallon kerosene can from which it had been filled, while the mother tugged at his arm until he shifted the lamp to the other hand and flung her back, not savagely or viciously, just hard, into the wall, her hands flung out against the wall for balance, her mouth open and in her face the same quality of hopeless despair as had been in her voice. Then his father saw him standing in the door.

"Go to the barn and get that can of oil we were oiling the wagon with," he said. 85
The boy did not move. Then he could speak.

"What . . ." he cried. "What are you . . ."

"Go get that oil," his father said. "Go."

Then he was moving, running, outside the house, toward the stable: this the old habit, the old blood which he had not been permitted to choose for himself, which had been bequeathed him willy nilly and which had run for so long (and who knew where, battening on what of outrage and savagery and lust) before it came to him. *I could keep on,* he thought. *I could run on and on and never look back, never need to see his face again. Only I can't. I can't,* the rusted can in his hand now, the liquid sploshing in it as he ran back to the house and into it, into the sound of his mother's weeping in the next room, and handed the can to his father.

"Ain't you going to even send a nigger?" he cried. "At least you sent a nigger before!"

This time his father didn't strike him. The hand came even faster than the blow had, the same hand which had set the can on the table with almost excruciating care flashing from the can toward him too quick for him to follow it, gripping him by the back of his shirt and on to tiptoe before he had seen it quit the can, the face stooping at him in breathless and frozen ferocity, the cold, dead voice speaking over him to the older brother who leaned against the table, chewing with that steady, curious, sidewise motion of cows: 90

"Empty the can into the big one and go on. I'll catch up with you."

"Better tie him up to the bedpost," the brother said.

"Do like I told you," the father said. Then the boy was moving, his bunched shirt and the hard, bony hand between his shoulder-blades, his toes just touching the floor, across the room and into the other one, past the sisters sitting with spread heavy thighs in the two chairs over the cold hearth, and to where his mother and aunt sat side by side on the bed, the aunt's arm about his mother's shoulders.

"Hold him," the father said. The aunt made a startled movement. "Not you," the father said. "Lennie. Take hold of him. I want to see you do it." His mother took him by the wrist. "You'll hold him better than that. If he gets loose don't you know what he is going to do? He will go up yonder." He jerked his head toward the road. "Maybe I'd better tie him."

"I'll hold him," his mother whispered. 95

"See you do then." Then his father was gone, the stiff foot heavy and measured upon the boards, ceasing at last.

Then he began to struggle. His mother caught him in both arms, he jerking and wrenching at them. He would be stronger in the end, he knew that. But he had no time to wait for it. "Lemme go!" he cried. "I don't want to have to hit you!"

"Let him go!" the aunt said. "If he don't go, before God, I am going up there myself!"

"Don't you see I can't?" his mother cried. "Sarty! Sarty! No! No! Help me, Lizzie!"

Then he was free. His aunt grasped at him but it was too late. He whirled, running, his mother stumbled forward on to her knees behind him, crying to the nearer sister: "Catch him, Net! Catch him!" But that was too late too, the sister (the sisters were twins, born at the same time, yet either of them now gave the impression of being, encompassing as much living meat and volume and weight as any other two of the family) not yet having begun to rise from the chair, her head, face, alone merely turned, presenting to him in the flying instant an astonishing expanse of young female features untroubled by any surprise even, wearing only an expression of bovine interest. Then he was out of the room, out of the house, in the mild dust of the starlit 100 road and the heavy rifeness of honeysuckle, the pale ribbon unspooling with terrific slowness under his running feet, reaching the gate at last and turning in, running, his heart and lungs drumming, on up the drive toward the lighted house, the lighted door. He did not knock, he burst in, sobbing for breath, incapable for the moment of speech; he saw the astonished face of the Negro in the linen jacket without knowing when the Negro had appeared.

"De Spain!" he cried, panted. "Where's . . ." then he saw the white man too emerging from a white door down the hall. "Barn!" he cried. "Barn!"

"What?" the white man said. "Barn?"

"Yes!" the boy cried. "Barn!"

"Catch him!" the white man shouted.

But it was too late this time too. The Negro grasped his shirt, but the entire   105
sleeve, rotten with washing, carried away, and he was out that door too and in the drive again, and had actually never ceased to run even while he was screaming into the white man's face.

Behind him the white man was shouting, "My horse! Fetch my horse!" and he thought for an instant of cutting across the park and climbing the fence into the road, but he did not know the park nor how high the vine-massed fence might be and he dared not risk it. So he ran on down the drive, blood and breath roaring; presently he was in the road again though he could not see it. He could not hear either: the galloping mare was almost upon him before he heard her, and even then he held his course, as if the very urgency of his wild grief and need must in a moment more find him wings, waiting until the ultimate instant to hurl himself aside and into the weed-choked roadside ditch as the horse thundered past and on, for an instant in furious silhouette against the stars, the tranquil early summer night sky which, even before the shape of the horse and rider vanished, stained abruptly and violently upward: a long, swirling roar incredible and soundless, blotting the stars, and he springing up and into the road again, running again, knowing it was too late yet still running even after he heard the shot and, an instant later, two shots, pausing now without knowing he had ceased to run, crying, "Pap! Pap!", running again before he knew he had begun to run, stumbling, tripping over something and scrabbling up again without ceasing to run, looking backward over his shoulder at the glare as he got up, running on among the invisible trees, panting, sobbing, "Father! Father!"

At midnight he was sitting on the crest of a hill. He did not know it was midnight and he did not know how far he had come. But there was no glare behind him now and he sat now, his back toward what he had called home for four days anyhow, his face toward the dark woods which he would enter when breath was strong again, small, shaking steadily in the chill darkness, hugging himself into the remainder of his thin, rotten shirt, the grief and despair now no longer terror and fear but just grief and despair. *Father. My father*, he thought. "He was brave!" he cried suddenly, aloud but not loud, no more than a whisper. "He was! He was in the war! He was in Colonel Sartoris' cav'ry!" not knowing that his father had gone to that war a private in the fine old European sense, wearing no uniform, admitting the authority of and giving fidelity to no man or army or flag, going to war as Malbrouck° himself did: for booty—it meant nothing and less than nothing to him if it were enemy booty or his own.

Malbrouck: John Churchill, Duke of Marlborough (1650–1722), English general victorious in the Battle of Blenheim (1704), which triumph drove the French army out of Germany. The French called him Malbrouck, a name they found easier to pronounce.

The slow constellations wheeled on. It would be dawn and then sun-up after a while and he would be hungry. But that would be to-morrow and now he was only cold, and walking would cure that. His breathing was easier now and he decided to get up and go on, and then he found that he had been asleep because he knew it was almost dawn, the night almost over. He could tell that from the whippoorwills. They were everywhere now among the dark trees below him, constant and inflectioned and ceaseless, so that, as the instant for giving over to the day birds drew nearer and nearer, there was no interval at all between them. He got up. He was a little stiff, but walking would cure that too as it would the cold, and soon there would be the sun. He went on down the hill, toward the dark woods within which the liquid silver voices of the birds called unceasing—the rapid and urgent beating of the urgent and quiring heart of the late spring night. He did not look back.

Questions

1. After delivering his warning to Major de Spain, the boy Snopes does not actually witness what happens to his father and brother, or what happens to the Major's barn. But what do you assume happens? What evidence is given in the story?

2. What do you understand to be Faulkner's opinion of Abner Snopes? Make a guess, indicating details in the story that convey attitudes.

3. Which adjectives best describe the general tone of the story: *calm, amused, disinterested, scornful, marveling, excited, impassioned*? Point out passages that may be so described. What do you notice about the style in which these passages are written?

4. In tone and style, how does "Barn Burning" compare with Faulkner's story "A Rose for Emily" (Chapter 2)? To what do you attribute any differences?

5. Suppose that, instead of "Barn Burning," Faulkner had written a story told by Abner Snopes in the first person. Why would such a story need a style different from that of "Barn Burning"? (Suggestion: Notice Faulkner's descriptions of Abner Snopes's voice.)

6. Although "Barn Burning" takes place some thirty years after the Civil War, how does the war figure in it?

IRONY

If a friend declares, "Oh, sure, I just *love* to have four papers due on the same day," you detect that the statement contains **irony**. This is **verbal irony**, the most familiar kind, in which we understand the speaker's meaning to be far from the usual meaning of the words—in this case, quite the opposite. (When the irony is found, as here, in a somewhat sour statement tinged with mockery, it is called **sarcasm**.)

Irony, of course, occurs in writing as well as in conversation. When in a comic moment in Isaac Bashevis Singer's "Gimpel the Fool" the sexton announces, "The wealthy Reb Gimpel invites the congregation to a feast in honor of the birth of a son," the people at the synagogue burst into laughter. They know that Gimpel, in contrast to the sexton's words, is not a wealthy man but a humble baker; that the son is not his own but his wife's lover's; and that the birth brings no honor to anybody. Verbal irony, then, implies a contrast or discrepancy between what is *said* and what is *meant*.

Dramatic Irony

There are also times when the speaker, unlike the reader, does not realize the ironic dimension of his or her words; such instances are known as **dramatic irony**. The most famous example occurs in Sophocles' tragic drama *Oedipus the King*, when Oedipus vows to find and punish the murderer of King Laius, unaware that he himself is the man he seeks, and adds: "if by any chance / he proves to be an intimate of our house, / here at my hearth, with my full knowledge, / may the curse I just called down on him strike me!" Dramatic irony may also be used, of course, for lighter purposes: for example, Daisy Coble, the mother in Anne Tyler's "Teenage Wasteland," whose attitudes and moods shift constantly according to what others tell her, responds to the idea that *she* should be less strict with her son by saying, "But see, he's still so suggestible." Stories often contain other kinds of irony besides such verbal irony. A situation, for example, can be ironic if it contains some wry contrast or incongruity. In Jack London's "To Build a Fire" (Chapter 4), it is ironic that a freezing man, desperately trying to strike a match to light a fire and save himself, accidentally ignites all his remaining matches.

Irony as Point of View

An entire story may be told from an **ironic point of view**. Whenever we sense a sharp distinction between the narrator of a story and the author, irony is likely to occur—especially when the narrator is telling us something that we are clearly expected to doubt or to interpret very differently. In "A & P," Sammy (who tells his own story) makes many smug and cruel observations about the people around him; but the author makes clear to us that much of his superiority is based on immaturity and lack of self-knowledge. (This irony, by the way, does not negate the fact that Sammy makes some very telling comments about society's superficial values and rigid and judgmental attitudes, comments that Updike seems to endorse and wants us to endorse as well.) And when we read Hemingway's "A Clean, Well-Lighted Place," surely we feel that most of the time the older waiter speaks for the author. Though the waiter gives us a respectful, compassionate view of a lonely old man, and we don't doubt that the view is Hemingway's, still, in the closing lines of the story we are reminded that author and waiter are not identical. Musing on the sleepless night ahead of him, the waiter tries to shrug off his problem—"After all, it is probably only insomnia"—but the reader, who recalls the waiter's bleak view of *nada*, nothingness, knows that it certainly isn't mere insomnia that keeps him awake but a dread of solitude and death. At that crucial moment, Hemingway and the older waiter part company, and we perceive an ironic point of view, and also a verbal irony, "After all, it is probably only insomnia."

Cosmic Irony

Storytellers are sometimes fond of ironic twists of fate—developments that reveal a terrible distance between what people deserve and what they get, between what is and what ought to be. In the novels of Thomas Hardy, some hostile fate keeps playing tricks to thwart the main characters. In *Tess of the D'Urbervilles*, an all-important letter, thrust under a door, by chance slides beneath a carpet and is not received. Such an irony is sometimes called an **irony of fate** or a **cosmic irony**, for it suggests that some malicious fate (or other spirit in the universe) is deliberately frustrating human efforts. Evidently, there is an irony of fate in the servant's futile attempt to escape Death in the fable "The Appointment in Samarra," and perhaps in the flaring up of the all-precious matches in "To Build a Fire" as well. To notice an irony gives pleasure. It may move us to laughter, make us feel wonder, or arouse our sympathy. By so involving us, irony—whether in a statement, a situation, an unexpected event, or a point of view—can render a story more likely to strike us, to affect us, and to be remembered.

A famous example of O. Henry's irony is the following story, perhaps the best-known and most-loved of his many tales.

O. Henry (William Sydney Porter)

The Gift of the Magi

1906

O. Henry

William Sydney Porter (1862–1910), known to the world as O. Henry, was born in Greensboro, North Carolina. He began writing in his mid-twenties, contributing humorous sketches to various periodicals. In 1896 he was indicted for embezzlement from the First National Bank of Austin, Texas; he fled to Honduras before his trial, but returned when he found that his wife was terminally ill. He was convicted, and served three years of a five-year sentence; his guilt or innocence has never been definitively established. Released in 1901, he moved to New York the following year. Already a well-known writer, for the next three years he produced a story every week for the New York World while also contributing tales and sketches to magazines. Beginning with Cabbages and Kings *in 1904, his stories were published in nine highly successful collections in the few remaining years of his life, as well as in three posthumously issued volumes. Financial extravagance and alcoholism darkened his last days, culminating in his death from tuberculosis at the age of forty-seven. Ranked during his lifetime with Hawthorne and Poe, O. Henry is more likely now to be invoked in negative terms, for his sentimentality and especially for his reliance on frequently forced trick endings, but the most prestigious annual volume of the best American short fiction is still called* The O. Henry Prize Stories, *and the best of his own work is loved by millions of readers.*

One dollar and eighty-seven cents. That was all. And sixty cents of it was in pennies. Pennies saved one and two at a time by bulldozing the grocer and the vegetable man and the butcher until one's cheeks burned with the silent imputation of parsimony that such close dealing implied. Three times Della counted it. One dollar and eighty-seven cents. And the next day would be Christmas.

There was clearly nothing to do but flop down on the shabby little couch and howl. So Della did it. Which instigates the moral reflection that life is made up of sobs, sniffles, and smiles, with sniffles predominating.

While the mistress of the home is gradually subsiding from the first stage to the second, take a look at the home. A furnished flat at $8 per week. It did not exactly beggar description, but it certainly had that word on the lookout for the mendicancy squad.

In the vestibule below was a letter-box into which no letter would go, and an electric button from which no mortal finger could coax a ring. Also appertaining thereunto was a card bearing the name "Mr. James Dillingham Young."

The "Dillingham" had been flung to the breeze during a former period of prosperity when its possessor was being paid $30 per week. Now, when the income was shrunk to $20, the letters of "Dillingham" looked blurred, as though they were thinking seriously of contracting to a modest and unassuming D. But whenever Mr. James Dillingham Young came home and reached his flat above he was called "Jim" and greatly hugged by Mrs. James Dillingham Young, already introduced to you as Della. Which is all very good.

5

Della finished her cry and attended to her cheeks with the powder rag. She stood by the window and looked out dully at a grey cat walking a grey fence in a grey backyard. Tomorrow would be Christmas Day, and she had only $1.87 with which to buy Jim a present. She had been saving every penny she could for months, with this result. Twenty dollars a week doesn't go far. Expenses had been greater than she had calculated. They always are. Only $1.87 to buy a present for Jim. Her Jim. Many a happy hour she had spent planning for something nice for him. Something fine and rare and sterling—something just a little bit near to being worthy of the honor of being owned by Jim.

There was a pier-glass between the windows of the room. Perhaps you have seen a pier-glass in an $8 flat. A very thin and very agile person may, by observing his reflection in a rapid sequence of longitudinal strips, obtain a fairly accurate conception of his looks. Della, being slender, had mastered the art.

Suddenly she whirled from the window and stood before the glass. Her eyes were shining brilliantly, but her face had lost its color within twenty seconds. Rapidly she pulled down her hair and let it fall to its full length.

Now, there were two possessions of the James Dillingham Youngs in which they both took a mighty pride. One was Jim's gold watch that had been his father's and his grandfather's. The other was Della's hair. Had the Queen of Sheba lived in the flat across the airshaft, Della would have let her hair hang out the window some day to dry just to depreciate Her Majesty's jewels and gifts. Had King Solomon been the janitor, with all his treasures piled up in the basement, Jim would have pulled out his watch every time he passed, just to see him pluck at his beard from envy.

So now Della's beautiful hair fell about her, rippling and shining like a cascade of   10
brown waters. It reached below her knee and made itself almost a garment for her. And then she did it up again nervously and quickly. Once she faltered for a minute and stood still while a tear or two splashed on the worn red carpet.

On went her old brown jacket; on went her old brown hat. With a whirl of skirts and with the brilliant sparkle still in her eyes, she fluttered out the door and down the stairs to the street.

Where she stopped the sign read: "Mme. Sofronie. Hair Goods of All Kinds." One flight up Della ran, and collected herself, panting. Madame, large, too white, chilly, hardly looked the "Sofronie."

"Will you buy my hair?" asked Della.

"I buy hair," said Madame. "Take yer hat off and let's have a sight at the looks of it."

Down rippled the brown cascade.   15

"Twenty dollars," said Madame, lifting the mass with a practiced hand.

"Give it to me quick," said Della.

Oh, and the next two hours tripped by on rosy wings. Forget the hashed metaphor. She was ransacking the stores for Jim's present.

She found it at last. It surely had been made for Jim and no one else. There was no other like it in any of the stores, and she had turned all of them inside out. It was a platinum fob chain simple and chaste in design, properly proclaiming its value by substance alone and not by meretricious ornamentation—as all good things should do. It was even worthy of The Watch. As soon as she saw it she knew that it must be Jim's. It was like him. Quietness and value—the description applied to both. Twenty-one dollars they took from her for it, and she hurried home with the 87 cents. With that chain on his watch Jim might be properly anxious about the time in any company. Grand as the watch was, he sometimes looked at it on the sly on account of the old leather strap that he used in place of a chain.

When Della reached home her intoxication gave way a little to prudence and reason. She got out her curling irons and lighted the gas and went to work repairing the ravages made by generosity added to love. Which is always a tremendous task, dear friends—a mammoth task.

Within forty minutes her head was covered with tiny, close-lying curls that made her look wonderfully like a truant schoolboy. She looked at her reflection in the mirror long, carefully, and critically.

"If Jim doesn't kill me," she said to herself, "before he takes a second look at me, he'll say I look like a Coney Island chorus girl. But what could I do—oh! What could I do with a dollar and eighty-seven cents?"

At 7 o'clock the coffee was made and the frying-pan was on the back of the stove hot and ready to cook the chops.

Jim was never late. Della doubled the fob chain in her hand and sat on the corner of the table near the door that he always entered. Then she heard his step on the stair away down on the first flight, and she turned white for just a moment. She had a habit of saying little silent prayers about the simplest everyday things, and now she whispered: "Please God, make him think I am still pretty."

The door opened and Jim stepped in and closed it. He looked thin and very serious. Poor fellow, he was only twenty-two—and to be burdened with a family! He needed a new overcoat and he was without gloves.

Jim stopped inside the door, as immovable as a setter at the scent of quail. His eyes were fixed upon Della, and there was an expression in them that she could not read, and it terrified her. It was not anger, nor surprise, nor disapproval, nor horror, nor any of the sentiments that she had been prepared for. He simply stared at her fixedly with that peculiar expression on his face.

Della wriggled off the table and went for him.

"Jim, darling," she cried, "don't look at me that way. I had my hair cut off and sold because I couldn't have lived through Christmas without giving you a present. It'll grow out again—you won't mind, will you? I just had to do it. My hair grows awfully fast. Say 'Merry Christmas!' Jim, and let's be happy. You don't know what a nice—what a beautiful, nice gift I've got for you."

"You've cut off your hair?" asked Jim, laboriously, as if he had not arrived at that patent fact yet even after the hardest mental labor.

"Cut it off and sold it," said Della. "Don't you like me just as well, anyhow? I'm me without my hair, ain't I?"

Jim looked about the room curiously.

"You say your hair is gone?" he said, with an air almost of idiocy.

"You needn't look for it," said Della. "It's sold, I tell you—sold and gone, too. It's Christmas Eve, boy. Be good to me, for it went for you. Maybe the hairs of my head were numbered," she went on with a sudden serious sweetness, "but nobody could ever count my love for you. Shall I put the chops on, Jim?"

Out of his trance Jim seemed quickly to wake. He enfolded his Della. For ten seconds let us regard with discreet scrutiny some inconsequential object in the other direction. Eight dollars a week or a million a year—what is the difference? A mathematician or a wit would give you the wrong answer. The magi brought valuable gifts, but that was not among them. This dark assertion will be illuminated later on.

Jim drew a package from his overcoat pocket and threw it upon the table.

"Don't make any mistake, Dell," he said, "about me. I don't think there's anything in the way of a haircut or a shave or a shampoo that could make me like my girl any less. But if you'll unwrap that package you may see why you had me going a while at first."

White fingers and nimble tore at the string and paper. And then an ecstatic scream of joy; and then, alas! a quick feminine change to hysterical tears and wails, necessitating the immediate employment of all the comforting powers of the lord of the flat.

For there lay The Combs—the set of combs, side and back, that Della had worshipped for long in a Broadway window. Beautiful combs, pure tortoise shell, with jewelled rims—just the shade to wear in the beautiful vanished hair. They were expensive combs, she knew, and her heart had simply craved and yearned over them without the least hope of possession. And now, they were hers, but the tresses that should have adorned the coveted adornments were gone.

But she hugged them to her bosom, and at length she was able to look up with dim eyes and a smile and say: "My hair grows so fast, Jim!"

And then Della leaped up like a little singed cat and cried, "Oh, oh!"   40

Jim had not yet seen his beautiful present. She held it out to him eagerly upon her open palm. The dull precious metal seemed to flash with a reflection of her bright and ardent spirit.

"Isn't it a dandy, Jim? I hunted all over town to find it. You'll have to look at the time a hundred times a day now. Give me your watch. I want to see how it looks on it."

Instead of obeying, Jim tumbled down on the couch and put his hands under the back of his head and smiled.

"Dell," said he, "let's put our Christmas presents away and keep 'em a while. They're too nice to use just at present. I sold the watch to get the money to buy your combs. And now suppose you put the chops on."

The magi, as you know, were wise men—wonderfully wise men—who brought   45
gifts to the Babe in the manger. They invented the art of giving Christmas presents. Being wise, their gifts were no doubt wise ones, possibly bearing the privilege of exchange in case of duplication. And here I have lamely related to you the uneventful chronicle of two foolish children in a flat who most unwisely sacrificed for each other the greatest treasures of their house. But in a last word to the wise of these days let it be said that of all who give gifts these two were the wisest. Of all who give and receive gifts, such as they are wisest. Everywhere they are wisest. They are the magi.

Questions

1. How would you describe the style of this story? Does the author's tone tell you anything about his attitude toward the characters and events of the narrative?

2. What do the details in paragraph 7 tell you about Della and Jim's financial situation?

3. O. Henry tells us that Jim "needed a new overcoat and he was without gloves" (paragraph 25). Why do you think Della didn't buy him these things for Christmas instead of a watch chain?

4. "Eight dollars a week or a million a year—what is the difference? A mathematician or a wit would give you the wrong answer" (paragraph 34). What, in your view, is "the wrong answer," and why is it wrong? What might the right answer be?

5. What is ironic about the story's ending? Is this plot twist the most important element of the conclusion? If not, what is?

Ha Jin

Saboteur

2000

Ha Jin is the pen name of Xuefei Jin, who was born in Liaoning, China, in 1956. The son of a military officer and a worker, Jin grew up during the turbulent Cultural Revolution, a ten-year upheaval initiated by the Communist Party in 1966 to transform China into a Marxist workers' society by destroying all remnants of the nation's ancient past. During this period many schools and universities were closed and intellectuals were required to work in proletarian jobs. At fourteen, Jin joined the People's Liberation Army, where he remained for nearly six years, and later worked as a telegraph opera- tor for a railroad company. He then attended Heilongjiang University, where in 1981 he re- ceived a B.A. in English. After earning an M.A. in American literature from Shangdong

Ha Jin

University in 1984, Jin traveled to the United States to work on a Ph.D. at Brandeis University. He intended to return to China, but the Communist Party's violent suppression of the student movement in 1989 made him decide to stay in the United States and write only in English. "It's such a brutal government," he commented, "I was very angry, and I decided not to return to China." "Writing in English became my means of survival," he remarked, "of spending or wasting my life, of retrieving losses, mine, and those of others."

Jin has published three books of poetry and five novels, including Waiting *(1999, National Book Award),* War Trash *(2004, PEN/Faulkner Award), and* A Free Life *(2007). His first volume of short fiction,* Ocean of Words *(1996), was drawn from his ex- perience in the People's Liberation Army and won the PEN/Hemingway Award. He is a professor of English at Boston University.*

Mr. Chiu and his bride were having lunch in the square before Muji Train Sta- tion. On the table between them were two bottles of soda spewing out brown foam and two paper boxes of rice and sautéed cucumber and pork. "Let's eat," he said to her, and broke the connected ends of the chopsticks. He picked up a slice of streaky pork and put it into his mouth. As he was chewing, a few crinkles appeared on his thin jaw.

To his right, at another table, two railroad policemen were drinking tea and laughing; it seemed that the stout, middle-aged man was telling a joke to his young comrade, who was tall and of athletic build. Now and again they would steal a glance at Mr. Chiu's table.

The air smelled of rotten melon. A few flies kept buzzing above the couple's lunch. Hundreds of people were rushing around to get on the platform or to catch buses to downtown. Food and fruit vendors were crying for customers in lazy voices. About a dozen young women, representing the local hotels, held up plac- ards which displayed the daily prices and words as large as a palm, like FREE MEALS, AIR-CONDITIONING, and ON THE RIVER. In the center of the square stood a concrete statue of Chairman Mao, at whose feet peasants were napping, their backs on the warm granite and their faces toward the sunny sky. A flock of pigeons perched on the Chairman's raised hand and forearm.

The rice and cucumber tasted good, and Mr. Chiu was eating unhurriedly. His sallow face showed exhaustion. He was glad that the honeymoon was finally over and that he and his bride were heading back for Harbin. During the two weeks' vacation, he had been worried about his liver, because three months ago he had suffered from acute hepatitis; he was afraid he might have a relapse. But he had had no severe symptoms, despite his liver being still big and tender. On the whole he was pleased with his health, which could endure even the strain of a honeymoon; indeed, he was on the course of recovery. He looked at his bride, who took off her wire glasses, kneading the root of her nose with her fingertips. Beads of sweat coated her pale cheeks.

"Are you all right, sweetheart?" he asked.   5

"I have a headache. I didn't sleep well last night."

"Take an aspirin, will you?"

"It's not that serious. Tomorrow is Sunday and I can sleep in. Don't worry."

As they were talking, the stout policeman at the next table stood up and threw a bowl of tea in their direction. Both Mr. Chiu's and his bride's sandals were wet instantly.

"Hooligan!" she said in a low voice.   10

Mr. Chiu got to his feet and said out loud, "Comrade Policeman, why did you do this?" He stretched out his right foot to show the wet sandal.

"Do what?" the stout man asked huskily, glaring at Mr. Chiu while the young fellow was whistling.

"See, you dumped tea on our feet."

"You're lying. You wet your shoes yourself."

"Comrade Policemen, your duty is to keep order, but you purposely tortured us   15
common citizens. Why violate the law you are supposed to enforce?" As Mr. Chiu was speaking, dozens of people began gathering around.

With a wave of his hand, the man said to the young fellow, "Let's get hold of him!"

They grabbed Mr. Chiu and clamped handcuffs around his wrists. He cried, "You can't do this to me. This is utterly unreasonable."

"Shut up!" The man pulled out his pistol. "You can use your tongue at our headquarters."

The young fellow added, "You're a saboteur, you know that? You're disrupting public order."

The bride was too petrified to say anything coherent. She was a recent college   20
graduate, had majored in fine arts, and had never seen the police make an arrest. All she could say was, "Oh, please, please!"

The policemen were pulling Mr. Chiu, but he refused to go with them, holding the corner of the table and shouting, "We have a train to catch. We already bought the tickets."

The stout man punched him in the chest. "Shut up. Let your ticket expire." With the pistol butt he chopped Mr. Chiu's hands, which at once released the table. Together the two men were dragging him away to the police station.

Realizing he had to go with them, Mr. Chiu turned his head and shouted to his bride, "Don't wait for me here. Take the train. If I'm not back by tomorrow morning, send someone over to get me out."

She nodded, covering her sobbing mouth with her palm.

*

After removing his belt, they locked Mr. Chiu into a cell in the back of the Rail-   25
road Police Station. The single window in the room was blocked by six steel bars; it
faced a spacious yard, in which stood a few pines. Beyond the trees, two swings hung
from an iron frame, swaying gently in the breeze. Somewhere in the building a cleaver
was chopping rhythmically. There must be a kitchen upstairs, Mr. Chiu thought.

He was too exhausted to worry about what they would do to him, so he lay down on
the narrow bed and shut his eyes. He wasn't afraid. The Cultural Revolution was over already, and recently the Party had been propagating the idea that all citizens were equal
before the law. The police ought to be a law-abiding model for common people. As long
as he remained coolheaded and reasoned with them, they probably wouldn't harm him.

Late in the afternoon he was taken to the Interrogation Bureau on the second
floor. On his way there, in the stairwell, he ran into the middle-aged policeman who
had manhandled him. The man grinned, rolling his bulgy eyes and pointing his fingers
at him as if firing a pistol. Egg of a tortoise! Mr. Chiu cursed mentally.

The moment he sat down in the office, he burped, his palm shielding his mouth.
In front of him, across a long desk, sat the chief of the bureau and a donkey-faced
man. On the glass desktop was a folder containing information on his case. He felt it
bizarre that in just a matter of hours they had accumulated a small pile of writing
about him. On second thought he began to wonder whether they had kept a file on
him all the time. How could this have happened? He lived and worked in Harbin,
more than three hundred miles away, and this was his first time in Muji City.

The chief of the bureau was a thin, bald man who looked serene and intelligent.
His slim hands handled the written pages in the folder in the manner of a lecturing
scholar. To Mr. Chiu's left sat a young scribe, with a clipboard on his knee and a
black fountain pen in his hand.

"Your name?" the chief asked, apparently reading out the question from a form.   30

"Chiu Maguang."

"Age?"

"Thirty-four."

"Profession?"

"Lecturer."   35

"Work unit?"

"Harbin University."

"Political status?"

"Communist Party member."

The chief put down the paper and began to speak. "Your crime is sabotage, al-   40
though it hasn't induced serious consequences yet. Because you are a Party member,
you should be punished more. You have failed to be a model for the masses and you—"

"Excuse me, sir," Mr. Chiu cut him off.

"What?"

"I didn't do anything. Your men are the saboteurs of our social order. They threw
hot tea on my feet and on my wife's feet. Logically speaking, you should criticize
them, if not punish them."

"That statement is groundless. You have no witness. Why should I believe you?"
the chief said matter-of-factly.

"This is my evidence." He raised his right hand. "Your man hit my fingers with a   45
pistol."

"That doesn't prove how your feet got wet. Besides, you could have hurt your
fingers yourself."

"But I am telling the truth!" Anger flared up in Mr. Chiu. "Your police station owes me an apology. My train ticket has expired, my new leather sandals are ruined, and I am late for a conference in the provincial capital. You must compensate me for the damage and losses. Don't mistake me for a common citizen who would tremble when you sneeze. I'm a scholar, a philosopher, and an expert in dialectical materialism. If necessary, we will argue about this in *The Northeastern Daily*, or we will go to the highest People's Court in Beijing. Tell me, what's your name?" He got carried away with his harangue, which was by no means trivial and had worked to his advantage on numerous occasions.

"Stop bluffing us," the donkey-faced man broke in. "We have seen a lot of your kind. We can easily prove you are guilty. Here are some of the statements given by eyewitnesses." He pushed a few sheets of paper toward Mr. Chiu.

Mr. Chiu was dazed to see the different handwritings, which all stated that he had shouted in the square to attract attention and refused to obey the police. One of the witnesses had identified herself as a purchasing agent from a shipyard in Shanghai. Something stirred in Mr. Chiu's stomach, a pain rising to his rib. He gave out a faint moan.

"Now you have to admit you are guilty," the chief said. "Although it's a serious crime, we won't punish you severely, provided you write out a self-criticism and promise that you won't disrupt the public order again. In other words, your release will depend on your attitude toward this crime." 50

"You're daydreaming," Mr. Chiu cried. "I won't write a word, because I'm innocent. I demand that you provide me with a letter of apology so I can explain to my university why I'm late."

Both the interrogators smiled contemptuously. "Well, we've never done that," said the chief, taking a puff of his cigarette.

"Then make this a precedent."

"That's unnecessary. We are pretty certain that you will comply with our wishes." The chief blew a column of smoke toward Mr. Chiu's face.

At the tilt of the chief's head, two guards stepped forward and grabbed the criminal by the arms. Mr. Chiu meanwhile went on saying, "I shall report you to the Provincial Administration. You'll have to pay for this! You are worse than the Japanese military police." 55

They dragged him out of the room.

After dinner, which consisted of a bowl of millet porridge, a corn bun, and a piece of pickled turnip, Mr. Chiu began to have a fever, shaking with a chill and sweating profusely. He knew that the fire of anger had gotten into his liver and that he was probably having a relapse. No medicine was available, because his briefcase had been left with his bride. At home it would have been time for him to sit in front of their color TV, drinking jasmine tea and watching the evening news. It was so lonesome in here. The orange bulb above the single bed was the only source of light, which enabled the guards to keep him under surveillance at night. A moment ago he had asked them for a newspaper or a magazine to read, but they turned him down.

Through the small opening on the door noises came in. It seemed that the police on duty were playing cards or chess in a nearby office; shouts and laughter could be heard now and then. Meanwhile, an accordion kept coughing from a remote corner in the building. Looking at the ballpoint and the letter paper left for him by the guards when they took him back from the Interrogation Bureau, Mr. Chiu remembered the old saying, "When a scholar runs into soldiers, the more he argues, the muddier his point becomes." How ridiculous this whole thing was. He ruffled his thick hair with his fingers.

He felt miserable, massaging his stomach continually. To tell the truth, he was more upset than frightened, because he would have to catch up with his work once he was back home—a paper that was due at the printers next week, and two dozen books he ought to read for the courses he was going to teach in the fall.

A human shadow flitted across the opening. Mr. Chiu rushed to the door and shouted through the hole, "Comrade Guard, Comrade Guard!" 60

"What do you want?" a voice rasped.

"I want you to inform your leaders that I'm very sick. I have heart disease and hepatitis. I may die here if you keep me like this without medication."

"No leader is on duty on the weekend. You have to wait till Monday."

"What? You mean I'll stay in here tomorrow?"

"Yes." 65

"Your station will be held responsible if anything happens to me."

"We know that. Take it easy, you won't die."

It seemed illogical that Mr. Chiu slept quite well that night, though the light above his head had been on all the time and the straw mattress was hard and infested with fleas. He was afraid of ticks, mosquitoes, cockroaches—any kind of insect but fleas and bedbugs. Once, in the countryside, where his school's faculty and staff had helped the peasants harvest crops for a week, his colleagues had joked about his flesh, which they said must have tasted nonhuman to fleas. Except for him, they were all afflicted with hundreds of bites.

More amazing now, he didn't miss his bride a lot. He even enjoyed sleeping alone, perhaps because the honeymoon had tired him out and he needed more rest.

The backyard was quiet on Sunday morning. Pale sunlight streamed through the 70
pine branches. A few sparrows were jumping on the ground, catching caterpillars and ladybugs. Holding the steel bars, Mr. Chiu inhaled the morning air, which smelled meaty. There must have been an eatery or a cooked-meat stand nearby. He reminded himself that he should take this detention with ease. A sentence that Chairman Mao had written to a hospitalized friend rose in his mind: "Since you are already in here, you may as well stay and make the best of it."

His desire for peace of mind originated in his fear that his hepatitis might get worse. He tried to remain unperturbed. However, he was sure that his liver was swelling up, since the fever still persisted. For a whole day he lay in bed, thinking about his paper on the nature of contradictions. Time and again he was overwhelmed by anger, cursing aloud, "A bunch of thugs!" He swore that once he was out, he would write an article about this experience. He had better find out some of the policemen's names.

It turned out to be a restful day for the most part; he was certain that his university would send somebody to his rescue. All he should do now was remain calm and wait patiently. Sooner or later the police would have to release him, although they had no idea that he might refuse to leave unless they wrote him an apology. Damn those hoodlums, they had ordered more than they could eat!

When he woke up on Monday morning, it was already light. Somewhere a man was moaning; the sound came from the backyard. After a long yawn, and kicking off the tattered blanket, Mr. Chiu climbed out of bed and went to the window. In the middle of the yard, a young man was fastened to a pine, his wrists handcuffed around the trunk from behind. He was wriggling and swearing loudly, but there was no sight of anyone else in the yard. He looked familiar to Mr. Chiu.

Mr. Chiu squinted his eyes to see who it was. To his astonishment, he recognized the man, who was Fenjin, a recent graduate from the Law Department at Harbin

University. Two years ago Mr. Chiu had taught a course in Marxist materialism, in which Fenjin had enrolled. Now, how on earth had this young devil landed here?

Then it dawned on him that Fenjin must have been sent over by his bride. What a stupid woman! A bookworm, who only knew how to read foreign novels! He had expected that she would contact the school's Security Section, which would for sure send a cadre here. Fenjin held no official position; he merely worked in a private law firm that had just two lawyers; in fact, they had little business except for some detective work for men and women who suspected their spouses of having extramarital affairs. Mr. Chiu was overcome with a wave of nausea.

Should he call out to let his student know he was nearby? He decided not to, because he didn't know what had happened. Fenjin must have quarreled with the police to incur such a punishment. Yet this could never have occurred if Fenjin hadn't come to his rescue. So no matter what, Mr. Chiu had to do something. But what could he do?

It was going to be a scorcher. He could see purple steam shimmering and rising from the ground among the pines. Poor devil, he thought, as he raised a bowl of corn glue to his mouth, sipped, and took a bite of a piece of salted celery.

When a guard came to collect the bowl and the chopsticks, Mr. Chiu asked him what had happened to the man in the backyard. "He called our boss 'bandit,'" the guard said. "He claimed he was a lawyer or something. An arrogant son of a rabbit."

Now it was obvious to Mr. Chiu that he had to do something to help his rescuer. Before he could figure out a way, a scream broke out in the backyard. He rushed to the window and saw a tall policeman standing before Fenjin, an iron bucket on the ground. It was the same young fellow who had arrested Mr. Chiu in the square two days before. The man pinched Fenjin's nose, then raised his hand, which stayed in the air for a few seconds, then slapped the lawyer across the face. As Fenjin was groaning, the man lifted up the bucket and poured water on his head.

"This will keep you from getting sunstroke, boy. I'll give you some more every hour," the man said loudly.

Fenjin kept his eyes shut, yet his wry face showed that he was struggling to hold back from cursing the policeman, or, more likely, that he was sobbing in silence. He sneezed, then raised his face and shouted, "Let me go take a piss."

"Oh, yeah?" the man bawled. "Pee in your pants."

Still Mr. Chiu didn't make any noise, gripping the steel bars with both hands, his fingers white. The policeman turned and glanced at the cell's window; his pistol, partly holstered, glittered in the sun. With a snort he spat his cigarette butt to the ground and stamped it into the dust.

Then the door opened and the guards motioned Mr. Chiu to come out. Again they took him upstairs to the Interrogation Bureau.

The same men were in the office, though this time the scribe was sitting there empty-handed. At the sight of Mr. Chiu the chief said, "Ah, here you are. Please be seated."

After Mr. Chiu sat down, the chief waved a white silk fan and said to him, "You may have seen your lawyer. He's a young man without manners, so our director had him taught a crash course in the backyard."

"It's illegal to do that. Aren't you afraid to appear in a newspaper?"

"No, we are not, not even on TV. What else can you do? We are not afraid of any story you make up. We call it fiction. What we do care about is that you cooperate with us. That is to say, you must admit your crime."

"What if I refuse to cooperate?"

"Then your lawyer will continue his education in the sunshine."

A swoon swayed Mr. Chiu, and he held the arms of the chair to steady himself. A numb pain stung him in the upper stomach and nauseated him, and his head was throbbing. He was sure that the hepatitis was finally attacking him. Anger was flaming up in his chest; his throat was tight and clogged.

The chief resumed, "As a matter of fact, you don't even have to write out your self-criticism. We have your crime described clearly here. All we need is your signature."

Holding back his rage, Mr. Chiu said, "Let me look at that."

With a smirk the donkey-faced man handed him a sheet which carried these words:

I hereby admit that on July 13 I disrupted public order at Muji Train Station, and that I refused to listen to reason when the railroad police issued their warning. Thus I myself am responsible for my arrest. After two days' detention, I have realized the reactionary nature of my crime. From now on, I shall continue to educate myself with all my effort and shall never commit this kind of crime again.

A voice started screaming in Mr. Chiu's ears, "Lie, lie!" But he shook his head   95
and forced the voice away. He asked the chief, "If I sign this, will you release both my lawyer and me?"

"Of course, we'll do that." The chief was drumming his fingers on the blue folder—their file on him.

Mr. Chiu signed his name and put his thumbprint under his signature.

"Now you are free to go," the chief said with a smile, and handed him a piece of paper to wipe his thumb with.

Mr. Chiu was so sick that he couldn't stand up from the chair at first try. Then he doubled his effort and rose to his feet. He staggered out of the building to meet his lawyer in the backyard, having forgotten to ask for his belt back. In his chest he felt as though there were a bomb. If he were able to, he would have razed the entire police station and eliminated all their families. Though he knew he could do nothing like that, he made up his mind to do something.

"I'm sorry about this torture, Fenjin," Mr. Chiu said when they met.   100

"It doesn't matter. They are savages." The lawyer brushed a patch of dirt off his jacket with trembling fingers. Water was still dribbling from the bottoms of his trouser legs.

"Let's go now," the teacher said.

The moment they came out of the police station, Mr. Chiu caught sight of a tea stand. He grabbed Fenjin's arm and walked over to the old woman at the table. "Two bowls of black tea," he said and handed her a one-yuan note.

After the first bowl, they each had another one. Then they set out for the train station. But before they walked fifty yards, Mr. Chiu insisted on eating a bowl of tree-ear soup at a food stand. Fenjin agreed. He told his teacher, "You mustn't treat me like a guest."

"No, I want to eat something myself."   105

As if dying of hunger, Mr. Chiu dragged his lawyer from restaurant to restaurant near the police station, but at each place he ordered no more than two bowls of food. Fenjin wondered why his teacher wouldn't stay at one place and eat his fill.

Mr. Chiu bought noodles, wonton, eight-grain porridge, and chicken soup, respectively, at four restaurants. While eating, he kept saying through his teeth, "If only I could kill all the bastards!" At the last place he merely took a few sips of the soup without tasting the chicken cubes and mushrooms.

Fenjin was baffled by his teacher, who looked ferocious and muttered to himself mysteriously, and whose jaundiced face was covered with dark puckers. For the first time Fenjin thought of Mr. Chiu as an ugly man.

Within a month over eight hundred people contracted acute hepatitis in Muji. Six died of the disease, including two children. Nobody knew how the epidemic had started.

Questions

1. Why is Mr. Chiu in Muji?
2. In the story's second paragraph, two railroad policemen are sitting next to Mr. Chiu and his wife. Why do you think they are laughing and looking at the newlywed couple?
3. With what specific crime is Mr. Chiu charged? Is he guilty?
4. What is Mr. Chiu's initial reaction to his arrest?
5. Why does Mr. Chiu initially refuse to sign a confession? Why does he eventually sign it?
6. What is ironic about Mr. Chiu's arrest? What is ironic about his ultimate confession?
7. When does Mr. Chiu decide to revenge himself on the police?
8. Is Mr. Chiu's revenge justified? Are the effects of his revenge proportionate to his own suffering?
9. What is ironic about the story's title? Who is the saboteur?

■ WRITING *effectively*

Ernest Hemingway on Writing

The Direct Style

1964

"When you write," he [Hemingway] said, "your object is to convey every sensation, sight, feeling, emotion, to the reader. So you have to work over what you write. If you use a pencil, you get three different views of it to see if you are getting it across the way you want to. First, when you read it over, then when it is typed, and again in proof. And it keeps it fluid longer so that you can improve it easier."

"How do you ever learn to convey every sensation, sight and feeling to the reader? Just keep working at it for forty-odd years the way you have? Are there any tricks?"

"No. The hardest trade in the world to do is the writing of straight, honest prose about human beings. But there are ways you can train yourself."

"How?"

Ernest Hemingway

"When you walk into a room and you get a certain feeling or emotion, remember back until you see exactly what it was that gave you the emotion. Remember what the noises and smells were and what was said. Then write it down, making it clear so the reader will see it too and have the same feeling you had. And watch people, observe, try to put yourself in somebody else's head. If two men argue, don't just think who is right and who is wrong. Think what both their sides are. As a man, you know who is right and who is wrong; you have to judge. As a writer, you should not judge, you should understand."

From "An Afternoon with Hemingway" by Edward Stafford

THINKING ABOUT TONE AND STYLE

If you look around a crowded classroom, you will notice—consciously or not—the styles of your fellow students. The way they dress, talk, and even sit conveys information about their attitudes. A haircut, T-shirt, tattoo, or piece of jewelry all silently say something. Similarly, a writer's style—his or her own distinct voice—can give the reader crucial extra information. To analyze a writer's style, think about:

- **Diction: Consider the flavor of words chosen by the author for a particular story.** In "A Clean, Well-Lighted Place," for example, Hemingway favors simple, unemotional, and descriptive language, whereas in "The Storm," Chopin uses extravagant and emotionally charged diction. Each choice reveals something important about the story.
- **Sentence structure: Look for patterns in a story's sentence structure.** Hemingway is famous for his short, clipped sentences, which often repeat certain key words. Faulkner, however, favors complex, elaborate syntax that immerses the reader in the emotion of the narrative.
- **Tone: Try to determine the writer's attitude toward the story he or she is telling.** In "The Gospel According to Mark," Borges uses dispassionate restraint to present a central irony, a tragic misunderstanding that will doom his protagonist. Tan's "A Pair of Tickets," by contrast, creates a tone of hushed excitement and direct emotional involvement.
- **Organization: Examine the order in which information is presented.** Borges tells his story in a straightforward, chronological manner, which eventually makes it possible for us to appreciate the tale's complex undercurrents. Other stories (for example, Atwood's "Happy Endings") present the narrative's events in more complicated and surprising ways.

CHECKLIST: Writing About Tone and Style

- ☐ Does the writer use word choice in a distinctive way?
- ☐ Is the diction unusual in any way?
- ☐ Does the author tend toward long or short—even fragmented—sentences?
- ☐ How would you characterize the writer's voice? Is it formal or casual? Distant or intimate? Impassioned or restrained?
- ☐ Can the narrator's words be taken at face value? Is there anything ironic about the narrator's voice?
- ☐ How does the writer arrange the material? Is information delivered chronologically, or is the organization more complex?
- ☐ What is the writer's attitude toward the material?

WRITING ASSIGNMENT ON TONE AND STYLE

Examine a short story with a style you admire. Write an essay in which you analyze the author's approach toward diction, sentence structure, tone, and organization. How do these elements work together to create a certain mood? How does that mood contribute to the story's meaning? If your chosen story has a first-person narrator, how do stylistic choices help to create a sense of that particular character?

MORE TOPICS FOR WRITING

1. Write a brief analysis of irony in either "Saboteur," "The Gift of the Magi," or "The Jilting of Granny Weatherall." What sorts of irony does your story employ?

2. Consider a short story in which the narrator is the central character, perhaps "A & P," "Greasy Lake," "Araby," "I Stand Here Ironing," or "Cathedral." In a brief essay, show how the character of the narrator determines the style of the story. Examine language in particular—words or phrases, slang expressions, figures of speech, local or regional usage.

3. Write a page in which you describe eating a meal in the company of others. Using sensory details, convey a sense of the setting, the quality of the food, and the presence of your dining companions. Now rewrite your paragraph as Ernest Hemingway. Finally, rewrite it as William Faulkner.

4. In a paragraph, describe a city street as seen through the eyes of a college graduate who has just moved to the city to start a new career. Now describe that same street in the voice of an old woman walking home from the hospital where her husband has just died. Finally, describe the street in the voice of a teenage runaway. In each paragraph, refrain from identifying your character or saying anything about his or her circumstances. Simply present the street as each character would perceive it.

▶ TERMS FOR *review*

Tone ▶ The attitude toward a subject conveyed in a literary work. No single stylistic device creates tone; it is the net result of the various elements an author brings to creating the work's feeling and manner.

Style ▶ All the distinctive ways in which an author uses language to create a literary work. An author's style depends on his or her characteristic use of diction, imagery, tone, syntax, and figurative language.

Diction ▶ Word choice or vocabulary. Diction refers to the class of words that an author decides is appropriate to use in a particular work.

Irony ▶ A literary device in which a discrepancy of meaning is masked beneath the surface of the language. Irony is present when a writer says one thing but means something quite the opposite.

Dramatic irony ▶ Where the reader understands the implication and meaning of a situation and may foresee the oncoming disaster or triumph while the character does not.

Cosmic irony or irony of fate ▶ A type of situational irony that emphasizes the discrepancy between what characters deserve and what they get, between a character's aspirations and the treatment he or she receives at the hands of fate.

Verbal irony ▶ A statement in which the speaker or writer says the opposite of what is really meant. For example, a friend might say, "How graceful!" after you trip clumsily on a stair.

Sarcasm ▶ A conspicuously bitter form of irony in which the ironic statement is designed to hurt or mock its target.

6

THEME

*They say great themes make great novels . . . but
what these young writers don't understand is that
there is no greater theme than men and women.*

—JOHN O'HARA

The **theme** of a story is whatever general idea or insight the entire story reveals. In some stories the theme is unmistakable. At the end of Aesop's fable about the council of the mice that can't decide who will bell the cat, the theme is stated in the moral: *It is easier to propose a thing than to carry it out.* In a work of commercial fiction, too, the theme (if any) is usually obvious. Consider a typical detective thriller in which, say, a rookie police officer trained in scientific methods of crime detection sets out to solve a mystery sooner than his or her rival, a veteran sleuth whose only laboratory is carried under his hat. Perhaps the veteran solves the case, leading to the conclusion (and the theme), "The old ways are the best ways after all." Another story by the same writer might dramatize the same rivalry but reverse the outcome, having the rookie win, thereby reversing the theme: "The times are changing! Let's shake loose from old-fashioned ways." In such commercial entertainments, a theme is like a length of rope with which the writer, patently and mechanically, trusses the story neatly (usually too neatly) into meaningful shape.

PLOT VERSUS THEME

In literary fiction, a theme is seldom so obvious. That is, a theme need not be a moral or a message; it may be what the events add up to, what the story is about. When we come to the end of a finely wrought short story such as Ernest Hemingway's "A Clean, Well-Lighted Place" (Chapter 5), it may be easy to sum up the plot—to say what happens—but it is more difficult to sum up the story's main idea. Evidently, Hemingway relates events—how a younger waiter gets rid of an old man and how an older waiter then goes to a coffee bar—but in themselves these events seem relatively slight, though the story as a whole seems large (for its size) and full of meaning. A **summary**, a brief condensation of the main idea or plot of a literary work, may be helpful, but it tends to focus on the surface events of a story. A theme aims for a deeper and more comprehensive statement of its larger meaning.

For the meaning, we must look to other elements in the story besides what happens in it. It is clear that Hemingway is most deeply interested in the thoughts and feelings of the older waiter, the character who has more and more to say as the story progresses, until at the end the story is entirely confined to his thoughts and perceptions. What is meaningful in these thoughts and perceptions? The older waiter understands the old man and sympathizes with his need for a clean, well-lighted place. If we say that, we are still talking about what happens in the story, though we have gone beyond merely recording its external events. But a theme is usually stated in *general* words. Another try: "Solitary people who cannot sleep need a cheerful, orderly place where they can drink with dignity." That's a little better. We have indicated, at least, that Hemingway's story is about more than just an old man and a couple of waiters. But what about the older waiter's meditation on *nada*, nothingness? Coming near the end of the story, it is given great emphasis, and probably no good statement of Hemingway's theme can leave it out. Still another try at a statement: "Solitary people need a place of refuge from their terrible awareness that their lives (or, perhaps, human lives) are essentially meaningless." Neither this nor any other statement of the story's theme is unarguably right, but at least the sentence helps the reader to bring into focus one primary idea that Hemingway seems to be driving at.

When we finish reading "A Clean, Well-Lighted Place," we feel that there is such a theme, a unifying vision, even though we cannot reduce it absolutely to a tag. Like some freshwater lake alive with creatures, Hemingway's story is a broad expanse, reflecting in many directions. No wonder that many readers will view it in different ways.

Moral inferences may be drawn from the story, no doubt, for Hemingway is indirectly giving us advice about properly regarding and sympathizing with the lonely, the uncertain, and the old. But the story doesn't set forth a lesson that we are supposed to put into practice. One could argue that "A Clean, Well-Lighted Place" contains *several* themes, and other statements could be made to include Hemingway's views of love, of communication between people, of dignity. Great short stories, like great symphonies, frequently have more than one theme.

THEME AS UNIFYING DEVICE

In many a fine short story, theme is the center, the moving force, the principle of unity. Clearly, such a theme is something other than the characters and events of its story. To say of James Joyce's "Araby" (Chapter 12) that it is about a boy who goes to a bazaar to buy a gift for a young woman, only to arrive too late, is to summarize plot, not theme. (The theme *might* be put, "The illusions of a romantic youth are vulnerable," or it might be put in any of a few hundred other ways.) Although the title of Shirley Jackson's "The Lottery" (Chapter 7), with its hint of the lure of easy riches, may arouse pleasant expectations, which the neutral tone of the narrative does nothing to dispel, the theme—the larger realization that the story leaves us with—has to do with the ways in which cruel and insensitive attitudes can come to seem like normal and natural ones.

Sometimes you will hear it said that the theme of a story (say, Faulkner's "Barn Burning") is "loss of innocence" or "initiation into maturity," or that the theme of some other story (Hurston's "Sweat," for instance) is "the revolt of the downtrodden." This is to use *theme* in a larger and more abstract sense than we use it here. Although such general descriptions of theme can be useful—as in sorting a large number of stories into rough categories—we suggest that, in the beginning, you look for whatever truth or insight you think the writer of a story reveals. Try to sum it up *in a sentence*. By doing so, you will find yourself looking closely at the story, trying to define its principal meaning.

FINDING THE THEME

You may find it helpful, in making a sentence-statement of theme, to consider these questions:

1. Look back once more at the title of the story. From what you have read, what does it indicate?
2. Does the main character change in any way over the course of the story? Does this character arrive at any eventual realization or understanding? Are you left with any realization or understanding you did not have before?
3. Does the author make any general observations about life or human nature? Do the characters make any? (Caution: Characters now and again will utter opinions with which the reader is not necessarily supposed to agree.)
4. Does the story contain any especially curious objects, mysterious flat characters, significant animals, repeated names, song titles, or whatever, that hint at meanings larger than such things ordinarily have? In literary stories, such symbols may point to central themes.
5. When you have worded your statement of theme, have you cast it into general language, not just given a plot summary?
6. Does your statement hold true for the story as a whole, not for just part of it?

In distilling a statement of theme from a rich and complicated story, we have, of course, no more encompassed the whole story than a paleontologist taking a plaster mold of a petrified footprint has captured a living brontosaurus. A writer (other than a fabulist) does not usually set out with theme in hand, determined to make every detail in the story work to demonstrate it. Well then, the skeptical reader may ask, if only *some* stories have themes, if those themes may be hard to sum up, and if readers will probably disagree in their summations, why bother to state themes? Isn't it too much trouble? Surely it is, unless the effort to state a theme ends in pleasure and profit. Trying to sum up the point of a story in our own words is merely one way to make ourselves better aware of whatever we may have understood vaguely and tentatively. Attempted with loving care, such statements may bring into focus our scattered impressions of a rewarding story, may help to clarify and hold fast whatever wisdom the storyteller has offered us.

Stephen Crane

The Open Boat   1897

Stephen Crane (1871–1900) was born in Newark, New Jersey, a Methodist minister's fourteenth and last child. After flunking out of both Lafayette College and Syracuse University, he became a journalist in New York, specializing in the grim lives of the down-and-out, such as the characters of his early self-published novel Maggie: A Girl of the Streets *(1893). Restlessly generating material for stories, Crane trekked to the Southwest, New Orleans, and Mexico. "The Open Boat" is based on personal experience. En route to Havana to*

Stephen Crane
(Courtesy of the Newark Public Library)

report on the Cuban revolution for the New York Press, Crane was shipwrecked when the SS Commodore *sank in heavy seas east of New Smyrna, Florida, on January 2, 1897. He escaped in a ten-foot lifeboat with the captain and two members of the crew. Later that year, Crane moved into a stately home in England with Cora Taylor, former madam of a Florida brothel, hobnobbed with literary greats, and lived beyond his means. Hounded by creditors, afflicted by tuberculosis, he died in Germany at twenty-eight. Crane has been called the first writer of American realism. His classic novel* The Red Badge of Courage *(1895) gives an imagined but convincing account of a young Union soldier's initiation into battle. A handful of his short stories appear immortal. He was also an original poet, writing terse, sardonic poems in open forms, considered radical at the time. In his short life, Crane greatly helped American literature to come of age.*

A tale intended to be after the fact:
Being the experience of four men from the sunk steamer Commodore

I

None of them knew the c'olor of the sky. Their eyes glanced level, and were fastened upon the waves that swept toward them. These waves were of the hue of slate, save for the tops, which were of foaming white, and all of the men knew the colors of the sea. The horizon narrowed and widened, and dipped and rose, and at all times its edge was jagged with waves that seemed thrust up in points like rocks.

Many a man ought to have a bathtub larger than the boat which here rode upon the sea. These waves were most wrongfully and barbarously abrupt and tall, and each froth-top was a problem in small-boat navigation.

The cook squatted in the bottom, and looked with both eyes at the six inches of gunwale which separated him from the ocean. His sleeves were rolled over his fat forearms, and the two flaps of his unbuttoned vest dangled as he bent to bail out the boat. Often he said, "Gawd! that was a narrow clip." As he remarked it he invariably gazed eastward over the broken sea.

The oiler, steering with one of the two oars in the boat, sometimes raised himself suddenly to keep clear of water that swirled in over the stern. It was a thin little oar, and it seemed often ready to snap.

The correspondent,° pulling at the other oar, watched the waves and wondered why he was there.   5

The injured captain, lying in the bow, was at this time buried in that profound dejection and indifference which comes, temporarily at least, to even the bravest and most enduring when, willy-nilly, the firm fails, the army loses, the ship goes down. The mind of the master of a vessel is rooted deep in the timbers of her, though he command for a day or a decade; and this captain had on him the stern impression of a scene in the grays of dawn of seven turned faces, and later a stump of a topmast with a white ball on it, that slashed to and fro at the waves, went low and lower, and down. Thereafter there was something strange in his voice. Although steady, it was deep with mourning, and of a quality beyond oration or tears.

"Keep 'er a little more south, Billie," said he.

---

correspondent: foreign correspondent, newspaper reporter.

"A little more south, sir," said the oiler in the stern.

A seat in this boat was not unlike a seat upon a bucking broncho, and by the same token a broncho is not much smaller. The craft pranced and reared and plunged like an animal. As each wave came, and she rose for it, she seemed like a horse making at a fence outrageously high. The manner of her scramble over these walls of water is a mystic thing, and, moreover, at the top of them were ordinarily these problems in white water, the foam racing down from the summit of each wave requiring a new leap, and a leap from the air. Then, after scornfully bumping a crest, she would slide and race and splash down a long incline, and arrive bobbing and nodding in front of the next menace.

A singular disadvantage of the sea lies in the fact that after successfully surmounting one wave you discover that there is another behind it just as important and just as nervously anxious to do something effective in the way of swamping boats. In a ten-foot dinghy one can get an idea of the resources of the sea in the line of waves that is not probable to the average experience, which is never at sea in a dinghy. As each slaty wall of water approached, it shut all else from the view of the men in the boat, and it was not difficult to imagine that this particular wave was the final outburst of the ocean, the last effort of the grim water. There was a terrible grace in the move of the waves, and they came in silence, save for the snarling of the crests.

In the wan light the faces of the men must have been gray. Their eyes must have glinted in strange ways as they gazed steadily astern. Viewed from a balcony, the whole thing would doubtless have been weirdly picturesque. But the men in the boat had no time to see it, and if they had had leisure, there were other things to occupy their minds. The sun swung steadily up the sky, and they knew it was broad day because the color of the sea changed from slate to emerald green streaked with amber lights, and the foam was like tumbling snow. The process of the breaking day was unknown to them. They were aware only of this effect upon the color of the waves that rolled toward them.

In disjointed sentences the cook and the correspondent argued as to the difference between a life-saving station and a house of refuge. The cook had said: "There's a house of refuge just north of the Mosquito Inlet Light, and as soon as they see us they'll come off in their boat and pick us up."

"As soon as who see us?" said the correspondent.

"The crew," said the cook.

"Houses of refuge don't have crews," said the correspondent. "As I understand them, they are only places where clothes and grub are stored for the benefit of shipwrecked people. They don't carry crews."

"Oh, yes, they do," said the cook.

"No, they don't," said the correspondent.

"Well, we're not there yet, anyhow," said the oiler, in the stern.

"Well," said the cook, "perhaps it's not a house of refuge that I'm thinking of as being near Mosquito Inlet Light; perhaps it's a life-saving station."

"We're not there yet," said the oiler in the stern.

II

As the boat bounced from the top of each wave the wind tore through the hair of the hatless men, and as the craft plopped her stern down again the spray slashed past them. The crest of each of these waves was a hill, from the top of which the men surveyed for a moment a broad tumultuous expanse, shining and wind-riven. It was probably splendid, it was probably glorious, this play of the free sea, wild with lights of emerald and white and amber.

"Bully good thing it's an on-shore wind," said the cook. "If not, where would we be? Wouldn't have a show."

"That's right," said the correspondent.

The busy oiler nodded his assent.

Then the captain, in the bow, chuckled in a way that expressed humor, contempt,   25
tragedy, all in one. "Do you think we've got much of a show now, boys?" said he.

Whereupon the three were silent, save for a trifle of hemming and hawing. To express any particular optimism at this time they felt to be childish and stupid, but they all doubtless possessed this sense of the situation in their minds. A young man thinks doggedly at such times. On the other hand, the ethics of their condition was decidedly against any open suggestion of hopelessness. So they were silent.

"Oh, well," said the captain, soothing his children, "we'll get ashore all right."

But there was that in his tone which made them think; so the oiler quoth, "Yes! if this wind holds."

The cook was bailing. "Yes! if we don't catch hell in the surf."

Canton-flannel gulls flew near and far. Sometimes they sat down on the sea,   30
near patches of brown seaweed that rolled over the waves with a movement like carpets on a line in a gale. The birds sat comfortably in groups, and they were envied by some in the dinghy, for the wrath of the sea was no more to them than it was to a covey of prairie chickens a thousand miles inland. Often they came very close and stared at the men with black bead-like eyes. At these times they were uncanny and sinister in their unblinking scrutiny, and the men hooted angrily at them, telling them to be gone. One came, and evidently decided to alight on the top of the captain's head. The bird flew parallel to the boat and did not circle, but made short sidelong jumps in the air in chicken-fashion. His black eyes were wistfully fixed upon the captain's head. "Ugly brute," said the oiler to the bird. "You look as if you were made with a jacknife." The cook and the correspondent swore darkly at the creature. The captain naturally wished to knock it away with the end of the heavy painter, but he did not dare do it, because anything resembling an emphatic gesture would have capsized this freighted boat; and so, with his open hand, the captain gently and carefully waved the gull away. After it had been discouraged from the pursuit the captain breathed easier on account of his hair, and others breathed easier because the bird struck their minds at this time as being somehow gruesome and ominous.

In the meantime the oiler and the correspondent rowed. And also they rowed. They sat together in the same seat, and each rowed an oar. Then the oiler took both oars; then the correspondent took both oars; then the oiler; then the correspondent. They rowed and they rowed. The very ticklish part of the business was when the time came for the reclining one in the stern to take his turn at the oars. By the very last star of truth, it is easier to steal eggs from under a hen than it was to change seats in the dinghy. First the man in the stern slid his hand along the thwart and moved with care, as if he were of Sèvres.° Then the man in the rowing-seat slid his hand along the other thwart. It was all done with the

---

Sèvres: chinaware made in this French town.

most extraordinary care. As the two sidled past each other, the whole party kept watchful eyes on the coming wave, and the captain cried: "Look out, now! Steady, there!"

The brown mats of seaweed that appeared from time to time were like islands, bits of earth. They were travelling, apparently, neither one way nor the other. They were, to all intents, stationary. They informed the men in the boat that it was making progress slowly toward the land.

The captain, rearing cautiously in the bow after the dinghy soared on a great swell, said that he had seen the lighthouse at Mosquito Inlet. Presently the cook remarked that he had seen it. The correspondent was at the oars then, and for some reason he too wished to look at the lighthouse; but his back was toward the far shore, and the waves were important, and for some time he could not seize an opportunity to turn his head. But at last there came a wave more gentle than the others, and when at the crest of it he swiftly scoured the western horizon.

"See it?" said the captain.

"No," said the correspondent, slowly; "I didn't see anything." 35

"Look again," said the captain. He pointed. "It's exactly in that direction."

At the top of another wave the correspondent did as he was bid, and this time his eyes chanced on a small, still thing on the edge of the swaying horizon. It was precisely like the point of a pin. It took an anxious eye to find a lighthouse so tiny.

"Think we'll make it, Captain?"

"If this wind holds and the boat don't swamp, we can't do much else," said the captain.

The little boat, lifted by each towering sea and splashed viciously by the crests, 40 made progress that in the absence of seaweed was not apparent to those in her. She seemed just a wee thing wallowing, miraculously top up, at the mercy of five oceans. Occasionally a great spread of water, like white flames, swarmed into her.

"Bail her, cook," said the captain, serenely.

"All right, Captain," said the cheerful cook.

III

It would be difficult to describe the subtle brotherhood of men that was here established on the seas. No one said that it was so. No one mentioned it. But it dwelt in the boat, and each man felt it warm him. They were a captain, an oiler, a cook, and a correspondent, and they were friends—friends in a more curiously iron-bound degree than may be common. The hurt captain, lying against the water-jar in the bow, spoke always in a low voice and calmly; but he could never command a more ready and swiftly obedient crew than the motley three of the dinghy. It was more than a mere recognition of what was best for the common safety. There was surely in it a quality that was personal and heartfelt. And after this devotion to the commander of the boat, there was this comradeship, that the correspondent, for instance, who had been taught to be cynical of men, knew even at the time was the best experience of his life. But no one said that it was so. No one mentioned it.

"I wish we had a sail," remarked the captain. "We might try my overcoat on the end of an oar, and give you two boys a chance to rest." So the cook and the correspondent held the mast and spread wide the overcoat; the oiler steered; and the little boat made good way with her new rig. Sometimes the oiler had to scull sharply to keep a sea from breaking into the boat, but otherwise sailing was a success.

Meanwhile the lighthouse had been growing slowly larger. It had now almost as-   45
sumed color, and appeared like a little gray shadow on the sky. The man at the oars
could not be prevented from turning his head rather often to try for a glimpse of this
little gray shadow.

At last, from the top of each wave, the men in the tossing boat could see land.
Even as the lighthouse was an upright shadow on the sky, this land seemed but a long
black shadow on the sea. It certainly was thinner than paper. "We must be about opposite New Smyrna," said the cook, who had coasted this shore often in schooners.
"Captain, by the way, I believe they abandoned that life-saving station there about a
year ago."

"Did they?" said the captain.

The wind slowly died away. The cook and the correspondent were not now
obliged to slave in order to hold high the oar. But the waves continued their old im-
petuous swooping at the dinghy, and the little craft, no longer under way, struggled
woundily over them. The oiler or the correspondent took the oars again.

Shipwrecks are apropos of nothing. If men could only train for them and have
them occur when the men had reached pink condition, there would be less drowning
at sea. Of the four in the dinghy none had slept any time worth mentioning for two
days and two nights previous to embarking in the dinghy, and in the excitement of
clambering about the deck of a foundering ship they had also forgotten to eat heartily.

For these reasons, and for others, neither the oiler nor the correspondent was   50
fond of rowing at this time. The correspondent wondered ingenuously how in the
name of all that was sane could there be people who thought it amusing to row a
boat. It was not an amusement; it was a diabolical punishment, and even a genius of
mental aberrations could never conclude that it was anything but a horror to the
muscles and crime against the back. He mentioned to the boat in general how the
amusement of rowing struck him, and the weary-faced oiler smiled in full sympathy.
Previously to the foundering, by the way, the oiler had worked double watch in the
engine-room of the ship.

"Take her easy now, boys," said the captain. "Don't spend yourselves. If we have
to run a surf you'll need all your strength, because we'll sure have to swim for it. Take
your time."

Slowly the land arose from the sea. From a black line it became a line of black
and a line of white—trees and sand. Finally the captain said that he could make out a
house on the shore. "That's the house of refuge, sure," said the cook. "They'll see us
before long, and come out after us."

The distant lighthouse reared high. "The keeper ought to be able to make us out
now, if he's looking through a glass," said the captain. "He'll notify the life-saving
people."

"None of those other boats could have got ashore to give word of the wreck," said
the oiler, in a low voice, "else the life-boat would be out hunting us."

Slowly and beautifully the land loomed out of the sea. The wind came again. It   55
had veered from the northeast to the southeast. Finally a new sound struck the ears of
the men in the boat. It was the low thunder of the surf on the shore. "We'll never be
able to make the lighthouse now," said the captain. "Swing her head a little more
north, Billie."

"A little more north, sir," said the oiler.

Whereupon the little boat turned her nose once more down the wind, and all
but the oarsman watched the shore grow. Under the influence of this expansion

doubt and direful apprehension were leaving the minds of the men. The management of the boat was still most absorbing, but it could not prevent a quiet cheerfulness. In an hour, perhaps, they would be ashore.

Their backbones had become thoroughly used to balancing in the boat, and they now rode this wild colt of a dinghy like circus men. The correspondent thought that he had been drenched to the skin, but happening to feel in the top pocket of his coat, he found therein eight cigars. Four of them were soaked with seawater; four were perfectly scatheless. After a search, somebody produced three dry matches; and thereupon the four waifs rode impudently in their little boat and, with an assurance of an impending rescue shining in their eyes, puffed at the big cigars, and judged well and ill of all men. Everybody took a drink of water.

IV

"Cook," remarked the captain, "there don't seem to be any signs of life about your house of refuge."

"No," replied the cook. "Funny they don't see us!" 60

A broad stretch of lowly coast lay before the eyes of the men. It was of low dunes topped with dark vegetation. The roar of the surf was plain, and sometimes they could see the white lip of a wave as it spun up the beach. A tiny house was blocked out black upon the sky. Southward, the slim lighthouse lifted its little gray length.

Tide, wind, and waves were swinging the dinghy northward. "Funny they don't see us," said the men.

The surf's roar was here dulled, but its tone was nevertheless thunderous and mighty. As the boat swam over the great rollers the men sat listening to this roar. "We'll swamp sure," said everybody.

It is fair to say here that there was not a life-saving station within twenty miles in either direction; but the men did not know this fact, and in consequence they made dark and opprobrious remarks concerning the eyesight of the nation's life-savers. Four scowling men sat in the dinghy and surpassed records in the invention of epithets.

"Funny they don't see us." 65

The light-heartedness of a former time had completely faded. To their sharpened minds it was easy to conjure pictures of all kinds of incompetency and blindness and, indeed, cowardice. There was the shore of the populous land, and it was bitter and bitter to them that from it came no sign.

"Well," said the captain, ultimately, "I suppose we'll have to make a try for ourselves. If we stay out here too long, we'll none of us have strength left to swim after the boat swamps."

And so the oiler, who was at the oars, turned the boat straight for the shore. There was a sudden tightening of muscles. There was some thinking.

"If we don't all get ashore," said the captain—"if we don't all get ashore, I suppose you fellows know where to send news of my finish?"

They then briefly exchanged some addresses and admonitions. As for the reflec- 70 tions of the men, there was a great deal of rage in them. Perchance they might be formulated thus: "If I am going to be drowned—if I am going to be drowned—if I am going to be drowned, why, in the name of the seven mad gods who rule the sea, was I allowed to come thus far and contemplate sand and trees? Was I brought here merely to have my nose dragged away as I was about to nibble the sacred cheese of life? It is preposterous. If this old ninny-woman, Fate, cannot do better than this, she should be deprived of the management of men's fortunes. She is an old hen who knows not her intention. If she has decided to drown me, why did she not do it in the beginning and save me all this trouble? The whole affair is absurd. . . . But no; she cannot mean to drown me. She dare not drown me. She cannot drown me. Not after all this work." Afterward the man might have had an impulse to shake his fist at the clouds. "Just you drown me, now, and then hear what I call you!"

The billows that came at this time were more formidable. They seemed always just about to break and roll over the little boat in a turmoil of foam. There was a preparatory and long growl in the speech of them. No mind unused to the sea would have concluded that the dinghy could ascend these sheer heights in time. The shore was still afar. The oiler was a wily surfman. "Boys," he said swiftly, "she won't live three minutes more, and we're too far out to swim. Shall I take her to sea again, Captain?

"Yes; go ahead!" said the captain.

This oiler, by a series of quick miracles and fast and steady oarsmanship, turned the boat in the middle of the surf and took her safely to sea again.

There was a considerable silence as the boat bumped over the furrowed sea to deeper water. Then somebody in gloom spoke: "Well, anyhow, they must have seen us from the shore by now."

The gulls went in slanting flight up the wind toward the gray, desolate east. A   75
squall, marked by dingy clouds and clouds brick-red, like smoke from a burning build-ing, appeared from the southeast.

"What do you think of those life-saving people? Ain't they peaches?"

"Funny they haven't seen us."

"Maybe they think we're out here for sport! Maybe they think we're fishin'. Maybe they think we're damned fools."

It was a long afternoon. A changed tide tried to force them southward, but wind and wave said northward. Far ahead, where coast-line, sea, and sky formed their mighty angle, there were little dots which seemed to indicate a city on the shore.

"St. Augustine?"   80
The captain shook his head. "Too near Mosquito Inlet."

And the oiler rowed, and then the correspondent rowed; then the oiler rowed. It was a weary business. The human back can become the seat of more aches and pains than are registered in books for the composite anatomy of a regiment. It is a limited area, but it can become the theatre of innumerable muscular conflicts, tangles, wrenches, knots, and other comforts.

"Did you ever like to row, Billie?" asked the correspondent.

"No," said the oiler; "hang it!"

When one exchanged the rowing-seat for a place in the bottom of the boat, he   85
suffered a bodily depression that caused him to be careless of everything save an obligation to wiggle one finger. There was cold sea-water swashing to and fro in the boat, and he lay in it. His head, pillowed on a thwart, was within an inch of the swirl of a wave-crest, and sometimes a particularly obstreperous sea came inboard and drenched him once more. But these matters did not annoy him. It is almost certain that if the boat had capsized he would have tumbled comfortably upon the ocean as if he felt sure that it was a great soft mattress.

"Look! There's a man on the shore!"

"Where?"

"There! See 'im? See 'im?"

"Yes, sure! He's walking along."

"Now he's stopped. Look! He's facing us!"   90

"He's waving at us!"

"So he is! By thunder!"

"Ah, now we're all right! Now we're all right! There'll be a boat out here for us
in half an hour."

"He's going on. He's running. He's going up to that house there."

The remote beach seemed lower than the sea, and it required a searching glance   95
to discern the little black figure. The captain saw a floating stick, and they rowed to
it. A bath towel was by some weird chance in the boat, and, tying this on the stick,
the captain waved it. The oarsman did not dare turn his head, so he was obliged to
ask questions.

"What's he doing now?"

"He's standing still again. He's looking, I think. . . . There he goes again. Toward
the house. . . . Now he's stopped again."

"Is he waving at us?"

"No, not now; he was, though."

"Look! There comes another man!"   100

"He's running."

"Look at him go, would you!"

"Why, he's on a bicycle. Now he's met the other man. They're both waving at
us. Look!"

"There comes something up the beach."

"What the devil is that thing?"   105

"Why, it looks like a boat."

"Why, certainly, it's a boat."

"No; it's on wheels."

"Yes, so it is. Well, that must be the life-boat. They drag them along shore on a
wagon."

"That's the life-boat, sure."   110

"No, by God, it's—it's an omnibus."

"I tell you it's a life-boat."

"It is not! It's an omnibus. I can see it plain. See? One of the these big hotel
omnibuses."

"By thunder, you're right. It's an omnibus, sure as fate. What do you suppose
they are doing with an omnibus? Maybe they are going around collecting the life-
crew, hey?"

"That's it, likely. Look! There's a fellow waving a little black flag. He's standing   115
on the steps of the omnibus. There come those other two fellows. Now they're all talking together. Look at the fellow with the flag. Maybe he ain't waving it!"

"That ain't a flag, is it? That's his coat. Why, certainly, that's his coat."

"So it is; it's his coat. He's taken it off and is waving it around his head. But
would you look at him swing it!"

"Oh, say, there isn't any life-saving station there. That's just a winter-
resort hotel omnibus that has brought over some of the boarders to see us drown."

"What's that idiot with the coat mean? What's he signalling, anyhow?"

"It looks as if he were trying to tell us to go north. There must be a life-saving   120
station up there."

"No; he thinks we're fishing. Just giving us a merry hand. See? Ah, there, Willie!"

"Well, I wish I could make something out of those signals. What do you suppose he means?"

"He don't mean anything; he's just playing."

"Well, if he'd just signal us to try the surf again, or to go to sea and wait, or go north, or go south, or go to hell, there would be some reason in it. But look at him! He just stands there and keeps his coat revolving like a wheel. The ass!"

"There come more people."   125

"Now there's quite a mob. Look! Isn't that a boat?"

"Where? Oh, I see where you mean. No, that's no boat."

"That fellow is still waving his coat."

"He must think we like to see him do that. Why don't he quit it? It don't mean anything."

"I don't know. I think he is trying to make us go north. It must be that there's a   130
life-saving station there somewhere."

"Say, he ain't tired yet. Look at 'im wave!"

"Wonder how long he can keep that up. He's been revolving his coat ever since he caught sight of us. He's an idiot. Why aren't they getting men to bring a boat out? A fishing boat—one of those big yawls—could come out here all right. Why don't he do something?"

"Oh, it's all right now."

"They'll have a boat out here for us in less than no time, now that they've seen us."

A faint yellow tone came into the sky over the low land. The shadows on the sea   135
slowly deepened. The wind bore coldness with it, and the men began to shiver.

"Holy smoke!" said one, allowing his voice to express his impious mood, "If we keep on monkeying out here! If we've got to flounder out here all night!"

"Oh, we'll never have to stay here all night! Don't you worry. They've seen us now, and it won't be long before they'll come chasing out after us."

The shore grew dusky. The man waving a coat blended gradually into this gloom, and it swallowed in the same manner the omnibus and the group of people. The spray, when it dashed uproariously over the side, made the voyagers shrink and swear like men who were being branded.

"I'd like to catch the chump who waved the coat. I feel like socking him one, just for luck."

"Why? What did he do?"   140

"Oh, nothing, but then he seemed so damned cheerful."

In the meantime the oiler rowed, and then the correspondent rowed, and then the oiler rowed. Gray-faced and bowed forward, they mechanically, turn by turn, plied the leaden oars. The form of the lighthouse had vanished from the southern horizon, but finally a pale star appeared, just lifting from the sea. The streaked saffron in the west passed before the all-merging darkness, and the sea to the east was black. The land had vanished, and was expressed only by the low and drear thunder of the surf.

"If I am going to be drowned—if I am going to be drowned—if I am going to be drowned, why, in the name of the seven mad gods who rule the sea, was I allowed to come thus far and contemplate sand and trees? Was I brought here merely to have my nose dragged away as I was about to nibble the sacred cheese of life?"

The patient captain, drooped over the water-jar, was sometimes obliged to speak to the oarsman.

"Keep her head up! Keep her head up!"   145

"Keep her head, up, sir." The voices were weary and low.

This was surely a quiet evening. All save the oarsman lay heavily and listlessly in the boat's bottom. As for him, his eyes were just capable of noting the tall black waves that swept forward in a most sinister silence, save for an occasional subdued growl of a crest.

The cook's head was on a thwart, and he looked without interest at the water under his nose. He was deep in other scenes. Finally he spoke. "Billie," he murmured, dreamfully, "what kind of pie do you like best?"

V

"Pie!" said the oiler and the correspondent, agitatedly. "Don't talk about those things, blast you!"

"Well," said the cook, "I was just thinking about ham sandwiches, and—" 150

A night on the sea in an open boat is a long night. As darkness settled finally, the shine of the light, lifting from the sea in the south, changed to full gold. On the northern horizon a new light appeared, a small bluish gleam on the edge of the waters. These two lights were the furniture of the world. Otherwise there was nothing but waves.

Two men huddled in the stern, and distances were so magnificent in the dinghy that the rower was enabled to keep his feet partly warm by thrusting them under his companions. Their legs indeed extended far under the rowing-seat until they touched the feet of the captain forward. Sometimes, despite the efforts of the tired oarsman, a wave came piling into the boat, an icy wave of the night, and the chilling water soaked them anew. They would twist their bodies for a moment and groan, and sleep the dead sleep once more, while the water in the boat gurgled about them as the craft rocked.

The plan of the oiler and the correspondent was for one to row until he lost the ability, and then arouse the other from his sea-water couch in the bottom of the boat.

The oiler plied the oars until his head drooped forward and the overpowering sleep blinded him; and he rowed yet afterward. Then he touched a man in the bottom of the boat, and called his name. "Will you spell me for a little while?" he said meekly.

"Sure, Billie," said the correspondent, awaking and dragging himself to a sitting 155 position. They exchanged places carefully, and the oiler, cuddling down in the sea-water at the cook's side, seemed to go to sleep instantly.

The particular violence of the sea had ceased. The waves came without snarling. The obligation of the man at the oars was to keep the boat headed so that the tilt of the roller would not capsize her, and to preserve her from filling when the crests rushed past. The black waves were silent and hard to be seen in the darkness. Often one was almost upon the boat before the oarsman was aware.

In a low voice the correspondent addressed the captain. He was not sure that the captain was awake, although this iron man seemed to be always awake. "Captain, shall I keep her making for that light north, sir?"

The same steady voice answered him. "Yes. Keep it about two points off the port bow."

The cook had tied a life-belt around himself in order to get even the warmth which this clumsy cork contrivance could donate, and he seemed almost stove-like when a rower, whose teeth invariably chattered wildly as soon as he ceased his labor, dropped down to sleep.

The correspondent, as he rowed, looked down at the two men sleeping under- 160
foot. The cook's arm was around the oiler's shoulders, and, with their fragmentary
clothing and haggard faces, they were the babes of the sea—a grotesque rendering of
the old babes in the wood.

Later he must have grown stupid at his work, for suddenly there was a growling
of water, and a crest came with a roar and a swash into the boat, and it was a wonder
that it did not set the cook afloat in his life-belt. The cook continued to sleep, but
the oiler sat up, blinking his eyes and shaking with the new cold.

"Oh, I'm awful sorry, Billie," said the correspondent, contritely.

"That's all right, old boy," said the oiler, and lay down again and was asleep.

Presently it seemed that even the captain dozed, and the correspondent thought
that he was the one man afloat on all the oceans. The wind had a voice as it came
over the waves, and it was sadder than the end.

There was a long, loud swishing astern of the boat, and a gleaming trail of phos- 165
phorescence, like blue flame, was furrowed on the black waters. It might have been
made by a monstrous knife.

Then there came a stillness, while the correspondent breathed with open mouth
and looked at the sea.

Suddenly there was another swish and another long flash of bluish light, and this
time it was alongside the boat, and might almost have been reached with an oar. The
correspondent saw an enormous fin speed like a shadow through the water, hurling
the crystalline spray and leaving the long glowing trail.

The correspondent looked over his shoulder at the captain. His face was hidden,
and he seemed to be asleep. He looked at the babes of the sea. They certainly were
asleep. So, being bereft of sympathy, he leaned a little way to one side and swore
softly into the sea.

But the thing did not then leave the vicinity of the boat. Ahead or astern, on
one side or the other, at intervals long or short, fled the long sparkling streak, and
there was to be heard the *whirroo* of the dark fin. The speed and power of the thing
was greatly to be admired. It cut the water like a gigantic and keen projectile.

The presence of this biding thing did not affect the man with the same horror 170
that it would if he had been a picnicker. He simply looked at the sea dully and swore
in an undertone.

Nevertheless, it is true that he did not wish to be alone with the thing. He
wished one of his companions to awake by chance and keep him company with it.
But the captain hung motionless over the water-jar, and the oiler and the cook in the
bottom of the boat were plunged in slumber.

VI

"If I am going to be drowned—if I am going to be drowned—if I am going to be
drowned, why, in the name of the seven mad gods who rule the sea, was I allowed to
come thus far and contemplate sand and trees?"

During this dismal night, it may be remarked that a man would conclude that
it was really the intention of the seven mad gods to drown him, despite the abominable injustice of it. For it was certainly an abominable injustice to drown a man
who had worked so hard, so hard. The man felt it would be a crime most unnatural.
Other people had drowned at sea since galleys swarmed with painted sails, but
still—

When it occurs to a man that nature does not regard him as important, and that she feels she would not maim the universe by disposing of him, he at first wishes to throw bricks at the temple, and he hates deeply the fact that there are no bricks and no temples. Any visible expression of nature would surely be pelleted with his jeers.

Then, if there be no tangible thing to hoot, he feels, perhaps, the desire to 175 confront a personification and indulge in pleas, bowed to one knee, and with hands supplicant, saying, "Yes, but I love myself."

A high cold star on a winter's night is the word he feels that she says to him. Thereafter he knows the pathos of his situation.

The men in the dinghy had not discussed these matters, but each had, no doubt, reflected upon them in silence and according to his mind. There was seldom any expression upon their faces save the general one of complete weariness. Speech was devoted to the business of the boat.

To chime the notes of his emotion, a verse mysteriously entered the correspondent's head. He had even forgotten that he had forgotten this verse, but it suddenly was in his mind.

> A soldier of the Legion lay dying in Algiers;
> There was lack of woman's nursing, there was dearth of woman's tears;
> But a comrade stood beside him, and he took that comrade's hand,
> And he said, "I never more shall see my own, my native land."°

In his childhood the correspondent had been made acquainted with the fact that a soldier of the Legion lay dying in Algiers, but he had never regarded the fact as important. Myriads of his school-fellows had informed him of the soldier's plight, but the dinning had naturally ended by making him perfectly indifferent. He had never considered it his affair that a soldier of the Legion lay dying in Algiers, nor had it appeared to him as a matter for sorrow. It was less to him than the breaking of a pencil's point.

Now, however, it quaintly came to him as a human, living thing. It was no 180 longer merely a picture of a few throes in the breast of a poet, meanwhile drinking tea and warming his feet at the grate; it was an actuality—stern, mournful, and fine.

The correspondent plainly saw the soldier. He lay on the sand with his feet out straight and still. While his pale left hand was upon his chest in an attempt to thwart the going of his life, the blood came between his fingers. In the far Algerian distance, a city of low square forms was set against a sky that was faint with the last sunset hues. The correspondent, plying the oars and dreaming of the slow and slower movements of the lips of the soldier, was moved by a profound and perfectly impersonal comprehension. He was sorry for the soldier of the Legion who lay dying in Algiers.

The thing which had followed the boat and waited had evidently grown bored at the delay. There was no longer to be heard the slash of the cutwater, and there was no longer the flame of the long trail. The light in the north still glimmered, but it was apparently no nearer to the boat. Sometimes the boom of the surf rang in the correspondent's ears, and he turned the craft seaward then and rowed harder. Southward, some one had evidently built a watch-fire on the beach. It was too low and too far to be seen, but it made a shimmering, roseate reflection upon the bluff in back of it, and this could be discerned from the boat. The wind came stronger,

---

A soldier of the Legion . . . native land: The correspondent remembers a Victorian ballad about a German dying in the French Foreign Legion, "Bingen on the Rhine" by Caroline Norton.

and sometimes a wave suddenly raged out like a mountain cat, and there was to be seen the sheen and sparkle of a broken crest.

The captain, in the bow, moved on his water-jar and sat erect. "Pretty long night," he observed to the correspondent. He looked at the shore. "Those life-saving people take their time."

"Did you see that shark playing around?"

"Yes, I saw him. He was a big fellow, all right." 185

"Wish I had known you were awake."

Later the correspondent spoke into the bottom of the boat.

"Billie!" There was a slow and gradual disentanglement. "Billie, will you spell me?"

"Sure," said the oiler.

As soon as the correspondent touched the cold, comfortable sea-water in the 190 bottom of the boat and had huddled close to the cook's life-belt he was deep in sleep, despite the fact that his teeth played all the popular airs. This sleep was so good to him that it was but a moment before he heard a voice call his name in a tone that demonstrated the last stages of exhaustion. "Will you spell me?"

"Sure, Billie."

The light in the north had mysteriously vanished, but the correspondent took his course from the wide-awake captain.

Later in the night they took the boat farther out to sea, and the captain directed the cook to take one oar at the stern and keep the boat facing the seas. He was to call out if he should hear the thunder of the surf. This plan enabled the oiler and the correspondent to get respite together. "We'll give those boys a chance to get into shape again," said the captain. They curled down and, after a few preliminary chatterings and trembles, slept once more the dead sleep. Neither knew they had bequeathed to the cook the company of another shark, or perhaps the same shark.

As the boat caroused on the waves, spray occasionally bumped over the side and gave them a fresh soaking, but this had no power to break their repose. The ominous slash of the wind and the water affected them as it would have affected mummies.

"Boys," said the cook, with the notes of every reluctance in his voice, "she's 195 drifted in pretty close. I guess one of you had better take her to sea again." The correspondent, aroused, heard the crash of the toppled crests.

As he was rowing, the captain gave him some whisky and water, and this steadied the chills out of him. "If I ever get ashore and anybody shows me even a photograph of an oar—"

At last there was a short conversation.

"Billie! . . . Billie, will you spell me?"

"Sure," said the oiler.

VII

When the correspondent again opened his eyes, the sea and sky were each of the 200 gray hue of the dawning. Later, carmine and gold was painted upon the waters. The morning appeared finally, in its splendor, with a sky of pure blue, and the sunlight flamed on the tips of the waves.

On the distant dunes were set many little black cottages, and a tall white windmill reared above them. No man, nor dog, nor bicycle appeared on the beach. The cottages might have formed a deserted village.

The voyagers scanned the shore. A conference was held in the boat. "Well," said the captain, "if no help is coming, we might better try a run through the surf right away. If we stay out here much longer we will be too weak to do anything for ourselves at all." The others silently acquiesced in this reasoning. The boat was headed for the beach. The correspondent wondered if none ever ascended the tall wind-tower, and if they never looked seaward. This tower was a giant, standing with its back to the plight of the ants. It represented in a degree, to the correspondent, the serenity of nature amid the struggles of the individual—nature in the wind, and nature in the vision of men. She did not seem cruel to him then, nor beneficent, nor treacherous, nor wise. But she was indifferent, flatly indifferent. It is, perhaps, plausible that a man in this situation, impressed with the unconcern of the universe, should see the innumerable flaws of life, and have them taste wickedly in his mind, and wish for another chance. A distinction between right and wrong seems absurdly clear to him, then, in this new ignorance of the grave-edge, and he understands that if he were given another opportunity he would mend his conduct and his words, and be better and brighter during an introduction or at a tea.

"Now, boys," said the captain, "she is going to swamp sure. All we can do is to work her in as far as possible, and then when she swamps, pile out and scramble for the beach. Keep cool now, and don't jump until she swamps sure."

The oiler took the oars. Over his shoulders he scanned the surf. "Captain," he said, "I think I'd better bring her about and keep her head-on to the seas and back her in."

"All right, Billie," said the captain. "Back her in." The oiler swung the boat 205 then, and, seated in the stern, the cook and the correspondent were obliged to look over their shoulders to contemplate the lonely and indifferent shore.

The monstrous inshore rollers heaved the boat high until the men were again enabled to see the white sheets of water scudding up the slanted beach. "We won't get in very close," said the captain. Each time a man could wrest his attention from the rollers, he turned his glance toward the shore, and in the expression of the eyes during this contemplation there was a singular quality. The correspondent, observing the others, knew that they were not afraid, but the full meaning of their glances was shrouded.

As for himself, he was too tired to grapple fundamentally with the fact. He tried to coerce his mind into thinking of it, but the mind was dominated at this time by the muscles, and the muscles said they did not care. It merely occurred to him that if he should drown it would be a shame.

There were no hurried words, no pallor, no plain agitation. The men simply looked at the shore. "Now, remember to get well clear of the boat when you jump," said the captain.

Seaward the crest of a roller suddenly fell with a thunderous crash, and the long white comber came roaring down upon the boat.

"Steady now," said the captain. The men were silent. They turned their eyes 210 from the shore to the comber and waited. The boat slid up the incline, leaped at the furious top, bounced over it, and swung down the long back of the wave. Some water had been shipped, and the cook bailed it out.

But the next crest crashed also. The tumbling, boiling flood of white water caught the boat and whirled it almost perpendicular. Water swarmed in from all sides. The correspondent had his hands on the gunwale at this time, and when the

water entered at that place he swiftly withdrew his fingers, as if he objected to
wetting them.

The little boat, drunken with this weight of water, reeled and snuggled deeper
into the sea.

"Bail her out, cook! Bail her out!" said the captain.

"All right, Captain," said the cook.

"Now, boys, the next one will do for us sure," said the oiler. "Mind to jump clear   215
of the boat."

The third wave moved forward, huge, furious, implacable. It fairly swallowed the
dinghy, and almost simultaneously the men tumbled into the sea. A piece of life-belt
had lain in the bottom of the boat, and as the correspondent went overboard he held
this to his chest with his left hand.

The January water was icy, and he reflected immediately that it was colder than
he had expected to find it off the coast of Florida. This appeared to his dazed mind
as a fact important enough to be noted at the time. The coldness of the water was
sad; it was tragic. This fact was somehow mixed and confused with his opinion of his
own situation, so that it seemed almost a proper reason for tears. The water was
cold.

When he came to the surface he was conscious of little but the noisy water. Afterward he saw his companions in the sea. The oiler was ahead in the race. He was
swimming strongly and rapidly. Off to the correspondent's left, the cook's great
white and corked back bulged out of the water; and in the rear the captain was hanging with his one good hand to the keel of the overturned dinghy.

There is a certain immovable quality to a shore, and the correspondent wondered
at it amid the confusion of the sea.

It seemed also very attractive; but the correspondent knew that it was a long   220
journey, and he paddled leisurely. The piece of life-preserver lay under him, and
sometimes he whirled down the incline of a wave as if he were on a hand-sled.

But finally he arrived at a place in the sea where travel was beset with difficulty.
He did not pause swimming to inquire what manner of current had caught him, but
there his progress ceased. The shore was set before him like a bit of scenery on a
stage, and he looked at it and understood with his eyes each detail of it.

As the cook passed, much farther to the left, the captain was calling to him,
"Turn over on your back, cook! Turn over on your back and use the oar."

"All right, sir." The cook turned on his back, and, paddling with an oar, went
ahead as if he were a canoe.

Presently the boat also passed to the left of the correspondent, with the captain
clinging with one hand to the keel. He would have appeared like a man raising himself to look over a board fence if it were not for the extraordinary gymnastics of the
boat. The correspondent marvelled that the captain could still hold to it.

They passed on nearer to shore—the oiler, the cook, the captain—and following   225
them went the water-jar, bouncing gaily over the seas.

The correspondent remained in the grip of this strange new enemy—a current. The
shore, with its white slope of sand and its green bluff topped with little silent cottages,
was spread like a picture before him. It was very near to him then, but he was impressed
as one who, in a gallery, looks at a scene from Brittany or Algiers.

He thought: "I am going to drown? Can it be possible? Can it be possible? Can
it be possible?" Perhaps an individual must consider his own death to be the final
phenomenon of nature.

But later a wave perhaps whirled him out of this small deadly current, for he found suddenly that he could again make progress toward the shore. Later still he was aware that the captain, clinging with one hand to the keel of the dinghy, had his face turned away from the shore and toward him, and was calling his name. "Come to the boat! Come to the boat!"

In his struggle to reach the captain and the boat, he reflected that when one gets properly wearied drowning must really be a comfortable arrangement—a cessation of hostilities accompanied by a large degree of relief; and he was glad of it, for the main thing in his mind for some moments had been horror of the temporary agony. He did not wish to be hurt.

Presently he saw a man running along the shore. He was undressing with most 230 remarkable speed. Coat, trousers, shirt, everything flew magically off him.

"Come to the boat!" called the captain.

"All right, Captain." As the correspondent paddled, he saw the captain let himself down to bottom and leave the boat. Then the correspondent performed his one little marvel of the voyage. A large wave caught him and flung him with ease and supreme speed completely over the boat and far beyond it. It struck him even then as an event in gymnastics and a true miracle of the sea. An overturned boat in the surf is not a plaything to a swimming man.

The correspondent arrived in water that reached only to his waist, but his condition did not enable him to stand for more than a moment. Each wave knocked him into a heap, and the undertow pulled at him.

Then he saw the man who had been running and undressing, and undressing and running, come bounding into the water. He dragged ashore the cook, and then waded toward the captain; but the captain waved him away and sent him to the correspondent. He was naked—naked as a tree in winter; but a halo was about his head, and he shone like a saint. He gave a strong pull, and a long drag, and a bully heave at the correspondent's hand. The correspondent, schooled in the minor formulae, said, "Thanks, old man." But suddenly the man cried, "What's that?" He pointed a swift finger. The correspondent said, "Go."

In the shallows, face downward, lay the oiler. His forehead touched sand that 235 was periodically, between each wave, clear of the sea.

The correspondent did not know all that transpired afterward. When he achieved safe ground he fell, striking the sand with each particular part of his body. It was as if he had dropped from a roof, but the thud was grateful to him.

It seems that instantly the beach was populated with men with blankets, clothes, and flasks, and women with coffee-pots and all the remedies sacred to their minds. The welcome of the land to the men from the sea was warm and generous; but a still and dripping shape was carried slowly up the beach, and the land's welcome for it could only be the different and sinister hospitality of the grave.

When it came night, the white waves paced to and fro in the moonlight, and the wind brought the sound of the great sea's voice to the men on the shore, and they felt that they could then be interpreters.

Questions

1. In actuality, Crane, the captain of the *Commodore*, and the two crew members spent nearly thirty hours in the open boat. William Higgins, the oiler, was drowned as Crane describes. Does a knowledge of these facts in any way affect your response to

the story? Would you admire the story less—or more—if you believed it to be pure fiction?

2. Sum up the personalities of each of the four men in the boat: captain, cook, oiler, and correspondent.

3. What is the point of view of the story?

4. In paragraph 9, we are told that as each wave came, the boat "seemed like a horse making at a fence outrageously high." Point to other vivid similes or figures of speech. What do they contribute to the story's effectiveness?

5. Notice some of the ways in which Crane, as a storyteller conscious of plot, builds suspense. What enemies or obstacles do the men in the boat confront? What is the effect of the episode of the men who wave from the beach (paragraphs 86–141)? What is the climax of the story? (If you need to be refreshed on the meaning of *climax*, see the discussion of plot in Chapter 1.)

6. In paragraph 70 (and again in paragraph 143), the men wonder, "Was I brought here merely to have my nose dragged away as I was about to nibble the sacred cheese of life?" What variety of irony do you find in this quotation?

7. Why does the scrap of verse about the soldier dying in Algiers (paragraph 178) suddenly come to mean so much to the correspondent?

8. What theme in "The Open Boat" seems most important to you? Where is it stated?

9. What secondary themes also enrich the story? See for instance paragraph 43 (the thoughts on comradeship).

10. How do you define *heroism?* Who is a hero in "The Open Boat"?

Alice Munro

How I Met My Husband   1974

Alice Munro, one of the most widely admired contemporary Canadian writers, was born of farm parents in 1931 in Wingham, in southwestern Ontario, an area in which she has spent most of her life. Its small-town people figure in many of her stories. For two years, she attended the University of Western Ontario, but dropped out at twenty, after her first marriage. The mother of three daughters, Munro is a particularly sensitive explorer of the relations between parents and children, yet she ranges widely in choosing her themes. She has published twelve remarkable collections of short fiction, including Dance of the Happy Shades *(1968),* The Beggar Maid *(1982),* The Love of a Good Woman *(1998), and* The View from Castle Rock *(2006). Munro's* Selected Stories *appeared in 1996, comfirming her position as one of the greatest living masters of short fiction. Three of her books have*

Alice Munro

won Canada's prestigious Governor General's Literary Award; in the United States she has won the National Book Critics Circle Award. The short story is her true medium, and she has declared her preference for "the story that will zero in and give you intense, but not connected, moments of experience."

We heard the plane come over at noon, roaring through the radio news, and we were sure it was going to hit the house, so we all ran out into the yard. We saw it come in over the treetops, all red and silver, the first close-up plane I ever saw. Mrs. Peebles screamed.

"Crash landing," their little boy said. Joey was his name.

"It's okay," said Dr. Peebles. "He knows what he's doing." Dr. Peebles was only an animal doctor, but had a calming way of talking, like any doctor.

This was my first job—working for Dr. and Mrs. Peebles, who had bought an old house out on the Fifth Line, about five miles out of town. It was just when the trend was starting of town people buying up old farms, not to work them but to live on them.

We watched the plane land across the road, where the fairgrounds used to be. It did make a good landing field, nice and level for the old race track, and the barns and display sheds torn down now for scrap lumber so there was nothing in the way. Even the old grandstand bays had burned.

"All right," said Mrs. Peebles, snappy as she always was when she got over her nerves. "Let's go back in the house. Let's not stand here gawking like a set of farmers."

She didn't say that to hurt my feelings. It never occurred to her.

I was just setting the dessert down when Loretta Bird arrived, out of breath, at the screen door.

"I thought it was going to crash into the house and kill youse all!"

She lived on the next place and the Peebleses thought she was a country-woman, they didn't know the difference. She and her husband didn't farm, he worked on the roads and had a bad name for drinking. They had seven children and couldn't get credit at the HiWay Grocery. The Peebleses made her welcome, not knowing any better, as I say, and offered her dessert.

Dessert was never anything to write home about, at their place. A dish of Jell-O or sliced bananas or fruit out of a tin. "Have a house without a pie, be ashamed until you die," my mother used to say, but Mrs. Peebles operated differently.

Loretta Bird saw me getting the can of peaches.

"Oh, never mind," she said. "I haven't got the right kind of a stomach to trust what comes out of those tins, I can only eat home canning."

I could have slapped her. I bet she never put down fruit in her life.

"I know what he's landed here for," she said. "He's got permission to use the fair-grounds and take people up for rides. It costs a dollar. It's the same fellow who was over at Palmerston° last week and was up the lakeshore before that. I wouldn't go up, if you paid me."

"I'd jump at the chance," Dr. Peebles said. "I'd like to see this neighborhood from the air."

Mrs. Peebles said she would just as soon see it from the ground. Joey said he wanted to go and Heather did, too. Joey was nine and Heather was seven.

"Would you, Edie?" Heather said.

I said I didn't know. I was scared, but I never admitted that, especially in front of children I was taking care of.

"People are going to be coming out here in their cars raising dust and trampling your property, if I was you I would complain," Loretta said. She hooked her legs around the chair rung and I knew we were in for a lengthy visit. After Dr. Peebles went back to his office or out on his next call and Mrs. Peebles went for her nap, she

Palmerston: a town in southern Ontario, Canada.

would hang around me while I was trying to do the dishes. She would pass remarks about the Peebleses in their own house.

"She wouldn't find time to lay down in the middle of the day, if she had seven kids like I got."

She asked me did they fight and did they keep things in the dresser drawer not to have babies with. She said it was a sin if they did. I pretended I didn't know what she was talking about.

I was fifteen and away from home for the first time. My parents had made the effort and sent me to high school for a year, but I didn't like it. I was shy of strangers and the work was hard, they didn't make it nice for you or explain the way they do now. At the end of the year the averages were published in the paper, and mine came out at the very bottom, 37 percent. My father said that's enough and I didn't blame him. The last thing I wanted, anyway, was to go on and end up teaching school. It happened the very day the paper came out with my disgrace in it, Dr. Peebles was staying at our place for dinner, having just helped one of the cows have twins, and he said I looked smart to him and his wife was looking for a girl to help. He said she felt tied down, with the two children, out in the country. I guess she would, my mother said, being polite, though I could tell from her face she was wondering what on earth it would be like to have only two children and no barn work, and then to be complaining.

When I went home I would describe to them the work I had to do, and it made everybody laugh. Mrs. Peebles had an automatic washer and dryer, the first I ever saw. I have had those in my own home for such a long time now it's hard to remember how much of a miracle it was to me, not having to struggle with the wringer and hang up and haul down. Let alone not having to heat water. Then there was practically no baking. Mrs. Peebles said she couldn't make pie crust, the most amazing thing I ever heard a woman admit. I could, of course, and I could make light biscuits and a white cake and dark cake, but they didn't want it, she said they watched their figures. The only thing I didn't like about working there, in fact, was feeling half hungry a lot of the time. I used to bring back a box of doughnuts made out at home, and hide them under my bed. The children found out, and I didn't mind sharing, but I thought I better bind them to secrecy.

The day after the plane landed Mrs. Peebles put both children in the car and   25
drove over to Chesley, to get their hair cut. There was a good woman then at Chesley for doing hair. She got hers done at the same place, Mrs. Peebles did, and that meant they would be gone a good while. She had to pick a day Dr. Peebles wasn't going out into the country, she didn't have her own car. Cars were still in short supply then, after the war.

I loved being left in the house alone, to do my work at leisure. The kitchen was all white and bright yellow, with fluorescent lights. That was before they ever thought of making the appliances all different colors and doing the cupboards like dark old wood and hiding the lighting. I loved light. I loved the double sink. So would anybody new-come from washing dishes in a dishpan with a rag-plugged hole on an oilcloth-covered table by light of a coal-oil lamp. I kept everything shining.

The bathroom too. I had a bath in there once a week. They wouldn't have minded if I took one oftener, but to me it seemed like asking too much, or maybe risking making it less wonderful. The basin and the tub and the toilet were all pink, and there were glass doors with flamingoes painted on them, to shut off the tub. The light had a rosy cast and the mat sank under your feet like snow, except that it was warm. The mirror was three-way. With the mirror all steamed up and the air like a perfume cloud, from things I was allowed to use, I stood up on the side of the tub and admired myself naked, from three directions. Sometimes I thought about the way we lived out at home and the way we lived here and how one way was so hard to imagine when you were living the other way. But I thought it was still a lot easier, living the way we lived at home, to picture something like this, the painted flamingoes and the warmth and the soft mat, than it was anybody knowing only things like this to picture how it was the other way. And why was that?

I was through my jobs in no time, and had the vegetables peeled for supper and sitting in cold water besides. Then I went into Mrs. Peebles' bedroom. I had been in there plenty of times, cleaning, and I always took a good look in her closet, at the clothes she had hanging there. I wouldn't have looked in her drawers, but a closet is open to anybody. That's a lie. I would have looked in drawers, but I would have felt worse doing it and been more scared she could tell.

Some clothes in her closet she wore all the time, I was quite familiar with them. Others she never put on, they were pushed to the back. I was disappointed to see no wedding dress. But there was one long dress I could just see the skirt of, and I was hungering to see the rest. Now I took note of where it hung and lifted it out. It was satin, a lovely weight on my arm, light bluish-green in color, almost silvery. It had a fitted, pointed waist and a full skirt and an off-the-shoulder fold hiding the little sleeves.

Next thing was easy. I got out of my own things and slipped it on. I was slimmer   30 at fifteen than anybody would believe who knows me now and the fit was beautiful. I didn't, of course, have a strapless bra on, which was what it needed, I just had to slide my straps down my arms under the material. Then I tried pinning up my hair, to get the effect. One thing led to another. I put on rouge and lipstick and eyebrow pencil from her dresser. The heat of the day and the weight of the satin and all the excitement made me thirsty, and I went out to the kitchen, got-up as I was, to get a glass of ginger ale with ice cubes from the refrigerator. The Peebleses drank ginger ale, or fruit drinks, all day, like water, and I was getting so I did too. Also there was no limit on ice cubes, which I was so fond of I would even put them in a glass of milk.

I turned from putting the ice tray back and saw a man watching me through the screen. It was the luckiest thing in the world I didn't spill the ginger ale down the front of me then and there.

"I never meant to scare you. I knocked but you were getting the ice out, you didn't hear me."

I couldn't see what he looked like, he was dark the way somebody is pressed up against a screen door with the bright daylight behind them. I only knew he wasn't from around here.

"I'm from the plane over there. My name is Chris Watters and what I was wondering was if I could use that pump."

There was a pump in the yard. That was the way the people used to get their water.   35 Now I noticed he was carrying a pail.

"You're welcome," I said. "I can get it from the tap and save you pumping." I guess I wanted him to know we had piped water, didn't pump ourselves.

"I don't mind the exercise." He didn't move, though, and finally he said, "Were you going to a dance?"

Seeing a stranger there had made me entirely forget how I was dressed.

"Or is that the way ladies around here generally get dressed up in the afternoon?"
I didn't know how to joke back then. I was too embarrassed.

40

"You live here? Are you the lady of the house?"

"I'm the hired girl."

Some people change when they find that out, their whole way of looking at you and speaking to you changes, but his didn't.

"Well, I just wanted to tell you you look very nice. I was so surprised when I looked in the door and saw you. Just because you looked so nice and beautiful."

I wasn't even old enough then to realize how out of the common it is, for a man
to say something like that to a woman, or somebody he is treating like a woman. For a man to say a word like *beautiful*. I wasn't old enough to realize or to say anything back, or in fact to do anything but wish he would go away. Not that I didn't like him, but just that it upset me so, having him look at me, and me trying to think of something to say.

45

He must have understood. He said good-bye, and thanked me, and went and started filling his pail from the pump. I stood behind the Venetian blinds in the dining room, watching him. When he had gone, I went into the bedroom and took the dress off and put it back in the same place. I dressed in my own clothes and took my hair down and washed my face, wiping it on Kleenex, which I threw in the wastebasket.

The Peebleses asked me what kind of man he was. Young, middle-aged, short, tall? I couldn't say.

"Good-looking?" Dr. Peebles teased me.

I couldn't think a thing but that he would be coming to get his water again, he would be talking to Dr. or Mrs. Peebles, making friends with them, and he would mention seeing me that first afternoon, dressed up. Why not mention it? He would think it was funny. And no idea of the trouble it would get me into.

After supper the Peebleses drove into town to go to a movie. She wanted to go somewhere with her hair fresh done. I sat in my bright kitchen wondering what to do, knowing I would never sleep. Mrs. Peebles might not fire me, when she found out, but it would give her a different feeling about me altogether. This was the first place I ever worked but I already had picked up things about the way people feel when you are working for them. They like to think you aren't curious. Not just that you aren't dishonest, that isn't enough. They like to feel you don't notice things, that you don't think or wonder about anything but what they liked to eat and how they liked things ironed, and so on. I don't mean they weren't kind to me, because they were. They had me eat my meals with them (to tell the truth I expected to, I didn't know there were families who don't) and sometimes they took me along in the car. But all the same.

50

I went up and checked on the children being asleep and then I went out. I had to do it. I crossed the road and went in the old fairgrounds gate. The plane looked unnatural sitting there, and shining with the moon. Off at the far side of the fairgrounds where the bush was taking over, I saw his tent.

He was sitting outside it smoking a cigarette. He saw me coming.

"Hello, were you looking for a plane ride? I don't start taking people up till tomorrow." Then he looked again and said, "Oh, it's you. I didn't know you without your long dress on."

My heart was knocking away, my tongue was dried up. I had to say something. But I couldn't. My throat was closed and I was like a deaf-and-dumb.

"Did you want a ride? Sit down. Have a cigarette." 55

I couldn't even shake my head to say no, so he gave me one.

"Put it in your mouth or I can't light it. It's a good thing I'm used to shy ladies."

I did. It wasn't the first time I had smoked a cigarette, actually. My girlfriend out home, Muriel Lowe, used to steal them from her brother.

"Look at your hand shaking. Did you just want to have a chat, or what?"

In one burst I said, "I wisht you wouldn't say anything about that dress." 60

"What dress? Oh, the long dress."

"It's Mrs. Peebles'."

"Whose? Oh, the lady you work for? She wasn't home so you got dressed up in her dress, eh? You got dressed up and played queen. I don't blame you. You're not smoking the cigarette right. Don't just puff. Draw it in. Did anybody ever show you how to inhale? Are you scared I'll tell on you? Is that it?"

I was so ashamed at having to ask him to connive this way I couldn't nod. I just looked at him and he saw *yes.*

"Well I won't. I won't in the slightest way mention it or embarrass you. I give 65 you my word of honor."

Then he changed the subject, to help me out, seeing I couldn't even thank him.

"What do you think of this sign?"

It was a board sign lying practically at my feet.

SEE THE WORLD FROM THE SKY. ADULTS $1.00, CHILDREN 50¢. QUALIFIED PILOT.

"My old sign was getting pretty beat up, I thought I'd make a new one. That's 70 what I've been doing with my time today."

The lettering wasn't all that handsome, I thought. I could have done a better one in half an hour.

"I'm not an expert at sign making."

"It's very good," I said.

"I don't need it for publicity, word of mouth is usually enough. I turned away two carloads tonight. I felt like taking it easy. I didn't tell them ladies were dropping in to visit me."

Now I remembered the children and I was scared again, in case one of them had 75 waked up and called me and I wasn't there.

"Do you have to go so soon?"

I remembered some manners. "Thank you for the cigarette."

"Don't forget. You have my word of honor."

I tore off across the fairgrounds, scared I'd see the car heading home from town. My sense of time was mixed up, I didn't know how long I'd been out of the house. But it was all right, it wasn't late, the children were asleep. I got in my bed myself and lay thinking what a lucky end to the day, after all, and among things to be grateful for I could be grateful Loretta Bird hadn't been the one who caught me.

The yard and borders didn't get trampled, it wasn't as bad as that. All the same it 80 seemed very public, around the house. The sign was on the fairgrounds gate. People came mostly after supper but a good many in the afternoon, too. The Bird children all came without fifty cents between them and hung on the gate. We got used to the excitement of the plane coming in and taking off, it wasn't excitement anymore. I never went over, after that one time, but would see him when he came to get his water. I would be out on the steps doing sitting-down work, like preparing vegetables, if I could.

"Why don't you come over? I'll take you up in my plane."

"I'm saving my money," I said, because I couldn't think of anything else.

"For what? For getting married?"

I shook my head.

"I'll take you up for free if you come sometime when it's slack. I thought you would come, and have another cigarette." 85

I made a face to hush him, because you never could tell when the children would be sneaking around the porch, or Mrs. Peebles herself listening in the house. Sometimes she came out and had a conversation with him. He told her things he hadn't bothered to tell me. But then I hadn't thought to ask. He told her he had been in the war, that was where he learned to fly a plane, and how he couldn't settle down to ordinary life, this was what he liked. She said she couldn't imagine anybody liking such a thing. Though sometimes, she said, she was almost bored enough to try anything herself, she wasn't brought up to living in the country. It's all my husband's idea, she said. This was news to me.

"Maybe you ought to give flying lessons," she said.

"Would you take them?"

She just laughed.

Sunday was a busy flying day in spite of it being preached against from two pulpits. We were all sitting out watching. Joey and Heather were over on the fence with the Bird kids. Their father had said they could go, after their mother saying all week they couldn't. 90

A car came down the road past the parked cars and pulled up right in the drive. It was Loretta Bird who got out, all importance, and on the driver's side another woman got out, more sedately. She was wearing sunglasses.

"This is a lady looking for the man that flies the plane," Loretta Bird said. "I heard her inquire in the hotel coffee shop where I was having a Coke and I brought her out."

"I'm sorry to bother you," the lady said. "I'm Alice Kelling, Mr. Watters' fiancée."

This Alice Kelling had on a pair of brown and white checked slacks and a yellow top. Her bust looked to me rather low and bumpy. She had a worried face. Her hair had had a permanent, but had grown out, and she wore a yellow band to keep it off her face. Nothing in the least pretty or even young-looking about her. But you could tell from how she talked she was from the city, or educated, or both.

Dr. Peebles stood up and introduced himself and his wife and me and asked her to be seated. 95

"He's up in the air right now, but you're welcome to sit and wait. He gets his water here and he hasn't been yet. He'll probably take his break about five."

"That is him, then?" said Alice Kelling, wrinkling and straining at the sky.

"He's not in the habit of running out on you, taking a different name?" Dr. Peebles laughed. He was the one, not his wife, to offer iced tea. Then she sent me into the kitchen to fix it. She smiled. She was wearing sunglasses too.

"He never mentioned his fiancée," she said.

I loved fixing iced tea with lots of ice and slices of lemon in tall glasses. I ought to have mentioned before, Dr. Peebles was an abstainer, at least around the house, or I wouldn't have been allowed to take the place. I had to fix a glass for Loretta Bird too, though it galled me, and when I went out she had settled in my lawn chair, leaving me the steps. 100

"I knew you was a nurse when I first heard you in that coffee shop."

"How would you know a thing like that?"

"I get my hunches about people. Was that how you met him, nursing?"

"Chris? Well yes. Yes, it was."

"Oh, were you overseas?" said Mrs. Peebles.   105

"No, it was before he went overseas. I nursed him when he was stationed at Centralia and had a ruptured appendix. We got engaged and then he went overseas. My, this is refreshing, after a long drive."

"He'll be glad to see you," Dr. Peebles said. "It's a rackety kind of life, isn't it, not staying one place long enough to really make friends."

"Youse've had a long engagement," Loretta Bird said.

Alice Kelling passed that over. "I was going to get a room at the hotel, but when I was offered directions I came on out. Do you think I could phone them?"

"No need," Dr. Peebles said. "You're five miles away from him if you stay at the   110 hotel. Here, you're right across the road. Stay with us. We've got rooms on rooms, look at this big house."

Asking people to stay, just like that, is certainly a country thing, and maybe seemed natural to him now, but not to Mrs. Peebles, from the way she said, oh yes, we have plenty of room. Or to Alice Kelling, who kept protesting, but let herself be worn down. I got the feeling it was a temptation to her, to be that close. I was trying for a look at her ring. Her nails were painted red, her fingers were freckled and wrinkled. It was a tiny stone. Muriel Lowe's cousin had one twice as big.

Chris came to get his water, late in the afternoon just as Dr. Peebles had predicted. He must have recognized the car from a way off. He came smiling.

"Here I am chasing after you to see what you're up to," called Alice Kelling. She got up and went to meet him and they kissed, just touched, in front of us.

"You're going to spend a lot on gas that way," Chris said.

Dr. Peebles invited Chris to stay for supper, since he had already put up the sign   115 that said: NO MORE RIDES TILL 7 P.M. Mrs. Peebles wanted it served in the yard, in spite of the bugs. One thing strange to anybody from the country is this eating outside. I had made a potato salad earlier and she had made a jellied salad, that was one thing she could do, so it was just a matter of getting those out, and some sliced meat and cucumbers and fresh leaf lettuce. Loretta Bird hung around for some time saying, "Oh, well, I guess I better get home to those yappers," and, "It's so nice just sitting here, I sure hate to get up," but nobody invited her, I was relieved to see, and finally she had to go.

That night after rides were finished Alice Kelling and Chris went off somewhere in her car. I lay awake till they got back. When I saw the car lights sweep my ceiling I got up to look down on them through the slats of my blind. I don't know what I thought I was going to see. Muriel Lowe and I used to sleep on her front veranda and watch her sister and her sister's boy friend saying good night. Afterward we couldn't get to sleep, for longing for somebody to kiss us and rub against us and we would talk about suppose you were out in a boat with a boy and he wouldn't bring you in to shore unless you did it, or what if somebody got you trapped in a barn, you would have to, wouldn't you, it wouldn't be your fault. Muriel said her two girl cousins used to try with a toilet paper roll that one of them was a boy. We wouldn't do anything like that; just lay and wondered.

All that happened was that Chris got out of the car on one side and she got out on the other and they walked off separately—him toward the fairgrounds and her toward the house. I got back in bed and imagined about me coming home with him, not like that.

Next morning Alice Kelling got up late and I fixed a grapefruit for her the way I had learned and Mrs. Peebles sat down with her to visit and have another cup of coffee. Mrs. Peebles seemed pleased enough now, having company. Alice Kelling said she guessed she better get used to putting in a day just watching Chris take off and come down, and Mrs. Peebles said she didn't know if she should suggest it because Alice Kelling was the one with the car, but the lake was only twenty-five miles away and what a good day for a picnic.

Alice Kelling took her up on the idea and by eleven o'clock they were in the car, with Joey and Heather and a sandwich lunch I had made. The only thing was that Chris hadn't come down, and she wanted to tell him where they were going.

"Edie'll go over and tell him," Mrs. Peebles said. "There's no problem."   120

Alice Kelling wrinkled her face and agreed.

"Be sure and tell him we'll be back by five!"

I didn't see that he would be concerned about knowing this right away, and I thought of him eating whatever he ate over there, alone, cooking on his camp stove, so I got to work and mixed up a crumb cake and baked it, in between the other work I had to do; then, when it was a bit cooled, wrapped it in a tea towel. I didn't do anything to myself but take off my apron and comb my hair. I would like to have put some makeup on, but I was too afraid it would remind him of the way he first saw me, and that would humiliate me all over again.

He had come and put another sign on the gate: NO RIDES THIS P.M. APOLOGIES. I worried that he wasn't feeling well. No sign of him outside and the tent flap was down. I knocked on the pole.

"Come in," he said, in a voice that would just as soon have said *Stay out*.   125

I lifted the flap.

"Oh, it's you. I'm sorry. I didn't know it was you."

He had been just sitting on the side of the bed, smoking. Why not at least sit and smoke in the fresh air?

"I brought a cake and hope you're not sick," I said.

"Why would I be sick? Oh—that sign. That's all right. I'm just tired of talking to   130 people. I don't mean you. Have a seat." He pinned back the tent flap. "Get some fresh air in here."

I sat on the edge of the bed, there was no place else. It was one of those foldup cots, really; I remembered and gave him his fiancée's message.

He ate some of the cake. "Good."

"Put the rest away for when you're hungry later."

"I'll tell you a secret. I won't be around here much longer."

"Are you getting married?"

"Ha ha. What time did you say they'd be back?"   135

"Five o'clock."

"Well, by that time this place will have seen the last of me. A plane can get further than a car." He unwrapped the cake and ate another piece of it, absent-mindedly.

"Now you'll be thirsty."

"There's some water in the pail."   140

"It won't be very cold. I could bring some fresh. I could bring some ice from the refrigerator."

"No," he said. "I don't want you to go. I want a nice long time of saying good-bye to you."

He put the cake away carefully and sat beside me and started those little kisses, so soft, I can't ever let myself think about them, such kindness in his face and lovely kisses, all over my eyelids and neck and ears, all over, then me kissing back as well as I could (I had only kissed a boy on a dare before, and kissed my own arms for practice) and we lay back on the cot and pressed together, just gently, and he did some other things, not bad things or not in a bad way. It was lovely in the tent, that smell of grass and hot tent cloth with the sun beating down on it, and he said, "I wouldn't do you any harm for the world." Once, when he had rolled on top of me and we were sort of rocking together on the cot, he said softly, "Oh, no," and freed himself and jumped up and got the water pail. He splashed some of it on his neck and face, and the little bit left, on me lying there.

"That's to cool us off, miss."

When we said good-bye I wasn't at all sad, because he held my face and said,   145
"I'm going to write you a letter. I'll tell you where I am and maybe you can come and see me. Would you like that? Okay then. You wait." I was really glad I think to get away from him, it was like he was piling presents on me I couldn't get the pleasure of till I considered them alone.

No consternation at first about the plane being gone. They thought he had taken somebody up, and I didn't enlighten them. Dr. Peebles had phoned he had to go to the country, so there was just us having supper, and then Loretta Bird thrusting her head in the door and saying, "I see he's took off."

"What?" said Alice Kelling, and pushed back her chair.

"The kids come and told me this afternoon he was taking down his tent. Did he think he'd run through all the business there was around here? He didn't take off without letting you know, did he?"

"He'll send me word," Alice Kelling said. "He'll probably phone tonight. He's terribly restless, since the war."

"Edie, he didn't mention to you, did he?" Mrs. Peebles said. "When you took   150
over the message?"

"Yes," I said. So far so true.

"Well why didn't you say?" All of them were looking at me. "Did he say where he was going?"

"He said he might try Bayfield," I said. What made me tell such a lie? I didn't intend it.

"Bayfield, how far is that?" said Alice Kelling.

Mrs. Peebles said, "Thirty, thirty-five miles."   155

"That's not far. Oh, well, that's really not far at all. It's on the lake, isn't it?"

You'd think I'd be ashamed of myself, setting her on the wrong track. I did it to give him more time, whatever time he needed. I lied for him, and also, I have to admit, for me. Women should stick together and not do things like that. I see that now, but didn't then. I never thought of myself as being in any way like her, or coming to the same troubles, ever.

She hadn't taken her eyes off me. I thought she suspected my lie.

"When did he mention this to you?"

"Earlier."   160

"When you were over at the plane?"

"Yes."

"You must've stayed and had a chat." She smiled at me, not a nice smile. "You must've stayed and had a little visit with him."

"I took a cake," I said, thinking that telling some truth would spare me telling the rest.

"We didn't have a cake," said Mrs. Peebles rather sharply.   165

"I baked one."

Alice Kelling said, "That was very friendly of you."

"Did you get permission," said Loretta Bird. "You never know what these girls'll do next," she said. "It's not they mean harm so much, as they're ignorant."

"The cake is neither here nor there," Mrs. Peebles broke in. "Edie, I wasn't aware you knew Chris that well."

I didn't know what to say.   170

"I'm not surprised," Alice Kelling said in a high voice. "I knew by the look of her as soon as I saw her. We get them at the hospital all the time." She looked hard at me with her stretched smile. "Having their babies. We have to put them in a special ward because of their diseases. Little country tramps. Fourteen and fifteen years old. You should see the babies they have, too."

"There was a bad woman here in town had a baby that pus was running out of its eyes," Loretta Bird put in.

"Wait a minute," said Mrs. Peebles. "What is this talk? Edie. What about you and Mr. Watters? Were you intimate with him?"

"Yes," I said. I was thinking of us lying on the cot and kissing, wasn't that intimate? And I would never deny it.

They were all one minute quiet, even Loretta Bird.   175

"Well," said Mrs. Peebles. "I am surprised. I think I need a cigarette. This is the first of any such tendencies I've seen in her," she said, speaking to Alice Kelling, but Alice Kelling was looking at me.

"Loose little bitch." Tears ran down her face. "Loose little bitch, aren't you? I knew as soon as I saw you. Men despise girls like you. He just made use of you and went off, you know that, don't you? Girls like you are just nothing, they're just public conveniences, just filthy little rags!"

"Oh, now," said Mrs. Peebles.

"Filthy," Alice Kelling sobbed. "Filthy little rags!"

"Don't get yourself upset," Loretta Bird said. She was swollen up with pleasure at   180
being in on this scene. "Men are all the same."

"Edie, I'm very surprised," Mrs. Pebbles said. "I thought your parents were so strict. You don't want to have a baby, do you?"

I'm still ashamed of what happened next. I lost control, just like a six-year-old, I started howling. "You don't get a baby from just doing that!"

"You see. Some of them are that ignorant," Loretta Bird said.

But Mrs. Peebles jumped up and caught my arms and shook me.

"Calm down. Don't get hysterical. Calm down. Stop crying. Listen to me. Listen. 185
I'm wondering, if you know what being intimate means. Now tell me. What did you think it meant?"

"Kissing," I howled.

She let go. "Oh, Edie. Stop it. Don't be silly. It's all right. It's all a misunder-standing. Being intimate means a lot more than that. Oh, I *wondered*."

"She's trying to cover up, now," said Alice Kelling. "Yes. She's not so stupid. She sees she got herself in trouble."

"I believe her," Mrs. Peebles said. "This is an awful scene."

"Well there is one way to find out," said Alice Kelling, getting up. "After all, I am a nurse." 190

Mrs. Peebles drew a breath and said, "No. No. Go to your room, Edie. And stop that noise. This is too disgusting."

I heard the car start in a little while. I tried to stop crying, pulling back each wave as it started over me. Finally I succeeded, and lay heaving on the bed.

Mrs. Peebles came and stood in the doorway.

"She's gone," she said. "That Bird woman too. Of course, you know you should never have gone near that man and that is the cause of all this trouble. I have a headache. As soon as you can, go and wash your face in cold water and get at the dishes and we will not say any more about this."

Nor we didn't. I didn't figure out till years later the extent of what I had been 195 saved from. Mrs. Peebles was not very friendly to me afterward, but she was fair. Not very friendly is the wrong way of describing what she was. She had never been very friendly. It was just that now she had to see me all the time and it got on her nerves, a little.

As for me, I put it all out of my mind like a bad dream and concentrated on waiting for my letter. The mail came every day except Sunday, between one-thirty and two in the afternoon, a good time for me because Mrs. Peebles was always having her nap. I would get the kitchen all cleaned and then go up to the mailbox and sit in the grass, waiting. I was perfectly happy, waiting. I forgot all about Alice Kelling and her misery and awful talk and Mrs. Peebles and her chilliness and the embarrassment of whether she told Dr. Peebles and the face of Loretta Bird, getting her fill of other people's troubles. I was always smiling when the mailman got there, and continued smiling even after he gave me the mail and I saw today wasn't the day. The mailman was a Carmichael. I knew by his face because there are a lot of Carmichaels living out by us and so many of them have a sort of sticking-out top lip. So I asked his name (he was a young man, shy, but good-humored, anybody could ask him anything) and then I said, "I knew by your face!" He was pleased by that and always glad to see me and got a little less shy. "You've got the smile I've been waiting for all day!" he used to holler out the car window.

It never crossed my mind for a long time a letter might not come. I believed in it coming just like I believed the sun would rise in the morning. I just put off my hope from day to day, and there was the goldenrod out around the mailbox and the children gone back to school, and the leaves turning, and I was wearing a sweater when I went to wait. One day walking back with the hydro bill stuck in my hand, that was all, looking across at the fairgrounds with the full-blown milkweed and dark teasels, so much like fall, it just struck me: *No letter was ever going to come.* It was an impossible idea to get used to. No, not impossible. If I thought about Chris's face when he said he was going to write me, it was impossible, but if I forgot that and thought about the actual tin mailbox, empty, it was plain and true. I kept on going to meet the mail, but my heart was heavy now like a lump of lead. I only smiled because I thought of the mailman counting on it, and he didn't have an easy life, with the winter driving ahead.

Till it came to me one day there were women doing this with their lives, all over. There were women just waiting and waiting by mailboxes for one letter or another. I imagined me making this journey day after day and year after year, and my hair starting to get gray, and I thought, I was never made to go on like that. So I stopped meeting the mail. If there were women all through life waiting, and women busy and not waiting, I knew which I had to be. Even though there might be things the second kind of women have to pass up and never know about, it still is better.

I was surprised when the mailman phoned the Peebleses' place in the evening and asked for me. He said he missed me. He asked if I would like to go to Goderich, where some well-known movie was on, I forget now what. So I said yes, and I went out with him for two years and he asked me to marry him, and we were engaged a year more while I got my things together, and then we did marry. He always tells the children the story of how I went after him by sitting by the mailbox every day, and naturally I laugh and let him, because I like for people to think what pleases them and makes them happy.

Questions

1. What is your attitude toward Edie, the narrator—sympathy, condescension, disapproval, or something more complicated? Explain.
2. What aspects of Mrs. Peebles and her life does Edie admire or envy? What things about Mrs. Peebles does she find off-putting?
3. Why does Edie dislike Loretta Bird so much?
4. Reread the description of Alice Kelling in paragraph 94. What details does Edie notice about her, and why are these qualities important to Edie?
5. It is interesting that the story contains no description of Chris Watters's personal appearance. Why not, do you think? What are the things about him that really matter to Edie?
6. The twist at the end of the story may remind you of "The Gift of the Magi." Is there here, as there is in O. Henry's tale, more to the conclusion than just a clever surprise?
7. How would you state the theme of this story? Explain.

Luke 15:11–32

The Parable of the Prodigal Son   (Authorized or King James Version, 1611)

And he said, A certain man had two sons: And the younger of them said to his father, Father, give me the portion of goods that falleth to me. And he divided unto them his living. And not many days after the younger son gathered all together, and took his journey into a far country, and there wasted his substance with riotous living. And when he had spent all, there arose a mighty famine in that land; and he began to be in want. And he went and joined himself to a citizen of that country; and he sent him into his fields to feed swine. And he would fain have filled his belly with the husks that the swine did eat: and no man gave unto him. And when he came to himself, he said, How many hired servants of my father's have bread enough and to spare, and I perish with hunger! I will arise and go to my father, and will say unto him, Father I have sinned against heaven, and before thee, and am no more worthy to be called thy son; make me as one of thy hired servants. And he arose, and came to his father. But when he was yet a great way off, his father saw him, and had compassion, and ran, and fell on his neck, and kissed him. And the son said unto him, Father I have sinned against heaven, and in thy sight, and am no more worthy to be called thy son. But the father said to his servants, Bring forth the best robe, and put it on him; and put a ring on his hand, and shoes on his feet: And bring hither the fatted calf, and kill it; and let us eat, and be merry: For this my son was dead, and is alive again; he was lost, and is found. And they began to be merry. Now his elder son was in the field: and he came and drew nigh to the house, he heard music and dancing. And he called one of the servants, and asked what these things meant. And he said unto him, Thy brother is come; and thy father hath killed the fatted calf, because he hath received him safe and sound. And he was angry, and would not go in: therefore came his father out, and entreated him. And he answering said to his father, Lo, these many years do I serve thee, neither transgressed I at any time thy commandment; and yet thou never gavest me a kid, that I might make merry with my friends: But as soon as this thy son was come, which hath devoured thy living with harlots, thou hast killed for him the fatted calf. And he said unto him, Son thou art ever with me, and all that I have is thine. It was meet that we should make merry, and be glad: for this thy brother was dead, and is alive again; and was lost, and is found.

Questions

1. This story has traditionally been called "The Parable of the Prodigal Son." What does *prodigal* mean? Which of the two brothers is prodigal?
2. What position does the younger son expect when he returns to his father's house? What does the father give him?
3. When the older brother sees the celebration for his younger brother's return, he grows angry. He makes a very reasonable set of complaints to his father. He has indeed been a loyal and moral son, but what virtue does the older brother lack?
4. Is the father fair to the elder son? Explain your answer.
5. Theologians have discussed this parable's religious significance for two thousand years. What, in your own words, is the human theme of the story?

Kurt Vonnegut Jr.

Harrison Bergeron   1961

Kurt Vonnegut Jr. (1922–2007) was born in Indianapolis. During the Depression his father, a well-to-do architect, had virtually no work, and the family lived in reduced circumstances. Vonnegut attended Cornell University, where he majored in chemistry and was also managing editor of the daily student newspaper. In 1943 he enlisted in the U.S. Army. During the Battle of the Bulge he was captured by German troops and interned as a prisoner of war in Dresden, where he survived the massive Allied firebombing, which killed tens of thousands of people, mostly civilians. (The firebombing of Dresden became the central incident in Vonnegut's best-selling 1969 novel, Slaughterhouse-Five.) *After the war, Vonnegut worked as a reporter and later as a public relations man for General Electric in Schenectady, New York. He quit his job in 1951 to write full-time after publishing several science fiction stories in national magazines. His first novel,* Player Piano, *appeared in 1952, followed by* Sirens of Titan *(1959) and his first bestseller,* Cat's Cradle *(1963)—all now considered classics of literary science fiction. Among his many other books are* Mother Night *(1961),* Jailbird *(1979), and a book of biographical essays,* A Man Without a Country *(2005). His short fiction is collected in* Welcome to the Monkey House *(1968) and* Bagombo Snuff Box *(1999). Vonnegut is a singular figure in modern American fiction. An ingenious comic writer, he combined the popular genre of science fiction with the literary tradition of dark satire—a combination splendidly realized in "Harrison Bergeron."*

The year was 2081, and everybody was finally equal. They weren't only equal before God and the law. They were equal every which way. Nobody was smarter than anybody else. Nobody was better looking than anybody else. Nobody was stronger or quicker than anybody else. All this equality was due to the 211th, 212th, and 213th Amendments to the Constitution, and to the unceasing vigilance of agents of the United States Handicapper General.

Some things about living still weren't quite right, though. April, for instance, still drove people crazy by not being springtime. And it was in that clammy month that the H-G men took George and Hazel Bergeron's fourteen-year-old son, Harrison, away.

It was tragic, all right, but George and Hazel couldn't think about it very hard. Hazel had a perfectly average intelligence, which meant she couldn't think about anything except in short bursts. And George, while his intelligence was way above normal, had a little mental handicap radio in his ear. He was required by law to wear it at all times. It was tuned to a government transmitter. Every twenty seconds or so, the transmitter would send out some sharp noise to keep people like George from taking unfair advantage of their brains.

George and Hazel were watching television. There were tears on Hazel's cheeks, but she'd forgotten for the moment what they were about.

On the television screen were ballerinas.   5

A buzzer sounded in George's head. His thoughts fled in panic, like bandits from a burglar alarm.

"That was a real pretty dance, that dance they just did," said Hazel.

"Huh?" said George.

"That dance—it was nice," said Hazel.

"Yup," said George. He tried to think a little about the ballerinas. They weren't   10
really very good—no better than anybody else would have been, anyway. They were burdened with sashweights and bags of birdshot, and their faces were masked, so that no one, seeing a free and graceful gesture or a pretty face, would feel like something the cat drug in. George was toying with the vague notion that maybe dancers shouldn't be handicapped. But he didn't get very far with it before another noise in his ear radio scattered his thoughts.

George winced. So did two out of the eight ballerinas.

Hazel saw him wince. Having no mental handicap herself, she had to ask George what the latest sound had been.

"Sounded like somebody hitting a milk bottle with a ball peen hammer," said George.

"I'd think it would be real interesting, hearing all the different sounds," said Hazel, a little envious. "All the things they think up."

"Um," said George.   15

"Only, if I was Handicapper General, you know what I would do?" said Hazel. Hazel, as a matter of fact, bore a strong resemblance to the Handicapper General, a woman named Diana Moon Glampers. "If I was Diana Moon Glampers," said Hazel, "I'd have chimes on Sunday—just chimes. Kind of in honor of religion."

"I could think, if it was just chimes," said George.

"Well—maybe make 'em real loud," said Hazel. "I think I'd make a good Handicapper General."

"Good as anybody else," said George.

"Who knows better'n I do what normal is?" said Hazel.   20

"Right," said George. He began to think glimmeringly about his abnormal son who was now in jail, about Harrison, but a twenty-one-gun salute in his head stopped that.

"Boy!" said Hazel, "that was a doozy, wasn't it?"

It was such a doozy that George was white and trembling, and tears stood on the rims of his red eyes. Two of the eight ballerinas had collapsed to the studio floor, were holding their temples.

"All of a sudden you look so tired," said Hazel. "Why don't you stretch out on the sofa, so's you can rest your handicap bag on the pillows, honeybunch." She was referring to the forty-seven pounds of birdshot in a canvas bag, which was padlocked around George's neck. "Go on and rest the bag for a little while," she said. "I don't care if you're not equal to me for a while."

George weighed the bag with his hands. "I don't mind it," he said. "I don't notice   25
it any more. It's just a part of me."

"You been so tired lately—kind of wore out," said Hazel. "If there was just some way we could make a little hole in the bottom of the bag, and just take out a few of them lead balls. Just a few."

"Two years in prison and two thousand dollars fine for every ball I took out," said George. "I don't call that a bargain."

"If you could just take a few out when you came home from work," said Hazel. "I mean—you don't compete with anybody around here. You just set around."

"If I tried to get away with it," said George, "then other people'd get away with it—and pretty soon we'd be right back to the dark ages again, with everybody competing against everybody else. You wouldn't like that, would you?"

"I'd hate it," said Hazel.   30

"There you are," said George. "The minute people start cheating on laws, what do you think happens to society?"

If Hazel hadn't been able to come up with an answer to this question, George couldn't have supplied one. A siren was going off in his head.

"Reckon it'd fall all apart," said Hazel.

"What would?" said George blankly.

"Society," said Hazel uncertainly. "Wasn't that what you just said?"   35

"Who knows?" said George.

The television program was suddenly interrupted for a news bulletin. It wasn't clear at first as to what the bulletin was about, since the announcer, like all announcers, had a serious speech impediment. For about half a minute, and in a state of high excitement, the announcer tried to say, "Ladies and gentlemen—"

He finally gave up, handed the bulletin to a ballerina to read.

"That's all right—" Hazel said of the announcer, "he tried. That's the big thing. He tried to do the best he could with what God gave him. He should get a nice raise for trying so hard."

"Ladies and gentlemen—" said the ballerina, reading the bulletin. She must have   40
been extraordinarily beautiful, because the mask she wore was hideous. And it was easy to see that she was the strongest and most graceful of all the dancers, for her handicap bags were as big as those worn by two-hundred-pound men.

And she had to apologize at once for her voice, which was a very unfair voice for a woman to use. Her voice was a warm, luminous, timeless melody. "Excuse me—" she said, and she began again, making her voice absolutely uncompetitive.

"Harrison Bergeron, age fourteen," she said in a grackle squawk, "has just escaped from jail, where he was held on suspicion of plotting to overthrow the government. He is a genius and an athlete, is under-handicapped, and should be regarded as extremely dangerous."

A police photograph of Harrison Bergeron was flashed on the screen upside down, then sideways, upside down again, then right side up. The picture showed the full length of Harrison against a background calibrated in feet and inches. He was exactly seven feet tall.

The rest of Harrison's appearance was Halloween and hardware. Nobody had ever borne heavier handicaps. He had outgrown hindrances faster than the H-G men could think them up. Instead of a little ear radio for a mental handicap, he wore a tremendous pair of earphones, and spectacles with thick wavy lenses. The spectacles were intended to make him not only half blind, but to give him whanging headaches besides.

Scrap metal was hung all over him. Ordinarily, there was a certain symmetry, a 45
military neatness to the handicaps issued to strong people, but Harrison looked like a walking junkyard. In the race of life, Harrison carried three hundred pounds.

And to offset his good looks, the H-G men required that he wear at all times a red rubber ball for a nose, keep his eyebrows shaved off, and cover his even white teeth with black caps at snaggle-tooth random.

"If you see this boy," said the ballerina, "do not—I repeat, do not—try to reason with him."

There was the shriek of a door being torn from its hinges.

Screams and barking cries of consternation came from the television set. The photograph of Harrison Bergeron on the screen jumped again and again, as though dancing to the tune of an earthquake.

George Bergeron correctly identified the earthquake, and well he might have— 50
for many was the time his own home had danced to the same crashing tune. "My God—" said George, "that must be Harrison!"

The realization was blasted from his mind instantly by the sound of an automobile collision in his head.

When George could open his eyes again, the photograph of Harrison was gone. A living, breathing Harrison filled the screen.

Clanking, clownish, and huge, Harrison stood in the center of the studio. The knob of the uprooted studio door was still in his hand. Ballerinas, technicians, musicians, and announcers cowered on their knees before him, expecting to die.

"I am the Emperor!" cried Harrison. "Do you hear? I am the Emperor! Everybody must do what I say at once!" He stamped his foot and the studio shook.

"Even as I stand here—" he bellowed, "crippled, hobbled, sickened—I am a greater 55
ruler than any man who ever lived! Now watch me become what I *can* become!"

Harrison tore the straps of his handicap harness like wet tissue paper, tore straps guaranteed to support five thousand pounds.

Harrison's scrap-iron handicaps crashed to the floor.

Harrison thrust his thumbs under the bar of the padlock that secured his head harness. The bar snapped like celery. Harrison smashed his headphones and spectacles against the wall.

He flung away his rubber-ball nose, revealed a man that would have awed Thor, the god of thunder.

"I shall now select my Empress!" he said, looking down on the cowering 60
people. "Let the first woman who dares rise to her feet claim her mate and her throne!"

A moment passed, and then a ballerina arose, swaying like a willow.

Harrison plucked the mental handicap from her ear, snapped off her physical handicaps with marvelous delicacy. Last of all, he removed her mask.

She was blindingly beautiful.

"Now—" said Harrison, taking her hand, "shall we show the people the meaning of the word dance? Music!" he commanded.

The musicians scrambled back into their chairs, and Harrison stripped them of their handicaps, too. "Play your best," he told them, "and I'll make you barons and dukes and earls."

The music began. It was normal at first—cheap, silly, false. But Harrison snatched two musicians from their chairs, waved them like batons as he sang the music as he wanted it played. He slammed them back into their chairs.

The music began again and was much improved.

Harrison and his Empress merely listened to the music for a while—listened gravely, as though synchronizing their heartbeats with it.

They shifted their weights to their toes.

Harrison placed his big hands on the girl's tiny waist, letting her sense the weightlessness that would soon be hers.

And then, in an explosion of joy and grace, into the air they sprang!

Not only were the laws of the land abandoned, but the law of gravity and the laws of motion as well.

They reeled, whirled, swiveled, flounced, capered, gamboled, and spun.

They leaped like deer on the moon.

The studio ceiling was thirty feet high, but each leap brought the dancers nearer to it.

It became their obvious intention to kiss the ceiling.

They kissed it.

And then, neutralizing gravity with love and pure will, they remained suspended in air inches below the ceiling, and they kissed each other for a long, long time.

It was then that Diana Moon Glampers, the Handicapper General, came into the studio with a double-barreled ten-gauge shotgun. She fired twice, and the Emperor and the Empress were dead before they hit the floor.

Diana Moon Glampers loaded the gun again. She aimed it at the musicians and told them they had ten seconds to get their handicaps back on.

It was then that the Bergerons' television tube burned out.

Hazel turned to comment about the blackout to George. But George had gone out into the kitchen for a can of beer.

George came back in with the beer, paused while a handicap signal shook him up. And then he sat down again. "You been crying?" he said to Hazel.

"Yup," she said.

"What about?" he said.

"I forget," she said. "Something real sad on television."

"What was it?" he said.

"It's all kind of mixed up in my mind," said Hazel.

"Forget sad things," said George.

"I always do," said Hazel.

"That's my girl," said George. He winced. There was the sound of a rivetting gun in his head.

"Gee—I could tell that one was a doozy," said Hazel.

"You can say that again," said George.

"Gee—" said Hazel, "I could tell that one was a doozy."

Questions

1. What tendencies in present-day American society is Vonnegut satirizing? Does the story argue *for* anything? How would you sum up its theme?

2. Is Diana Moon Glampers a "flat" or a "round" character? (If you need to review these terms, see the discussion of character in Chapter 3.) Would you call Vonnegut's characterization of her "realistic"? If not, why doesn't it need to be?

3. From what point of view is the story told? Why is it more effective than if Harrison Bergeron had told his own story in the first person?

4. Two sympathetic critics of Vonnegut's work, Karen and Charles Wood, have said of his stories: "Vonnegut proves repeatedly . . . that men and women remain fundamentally the same, no matter what technology surrounds them." Try applying this comment to "Harrison Bergeron." Do you agree?

5. Stanislaw Lem, Polish author of *Solaris* and other novels, once made this thoughtful criticism of many of his contemporaries among science fiction writers:

> The revolt against the machine and against civilization, the praise of the "aesthetic" nature of catastrophe, the dead-end course of human civilization—these are their foremost problems, the intellectual content of their works. Such SF is as it were *a priori* vitiated by pessimism, in the sense that anything that may happen will be for the worse. ("The Time-Travel Story and Related Matters of SF Structuring," *Science Fiction Studies* 1 [1974], 143–54.)

How might Lem's objection be raised against "Harrison Bergeron"? In your opinion, does it negate the value of Vonnegut's story?

■ WRITING *effectively*

Kurt Vonnegut Jr. on Writing

The Themes of Science Fiction   1971, 1973

Interviewer: You talked a lot about the difficulties you had when you first began. For instance, I think you gave one of the reasons for using the science fiction form as the fact that you were a professional writer and had to do something which was popular.

Vonnegut: In the beginning I was writing about what concerned me, and what was all around me was machinery. I myself had had some training in engineering and chemistry rather than in the arts and I was working for General Electric in a big factory city, Schenectady. So the first book I wrote was about Schenectady, which is full of machinery and engineers. And I was classified as a science fiction writer. Well, in the past, science fiction writers have been beneath the attention of any serious critic. That is, far

Kurt Vonnegut Jr.

above you are the people dealing with the really important, beautiful issues and using great skills and so forth. It used to be that if you were a science fiction writer you really didn't belong in the arts at all, and other artists wouldn't talk to you. You just had this scruffy little gang of your own.

• • •

Interviewer: What attracted you to using the form [of science fiction] yourself?

Vonnegut: . . . I saw a milling machine for cutting the rotors on jet engines, gas turbines. This was a very expensive thing for a machinist to do, to cut what is essentially one of those Brancusi forms. So they had a computer-operated milling machine built to cut the blades, and I was fascinated by that. This was in 1949 and the guys who were working on it were foreseeing all sorts of machines being run by little boxes and punched cards. *Player Piano* was my response to the implications of having everything run by little boxes. The idea of doing that, you know, made sense, perfect sense. To have a little clicking box make all the decisions wasn't a vicious thing to do. But it was too bad for the human beings who got their dignity from their jobs.

Interviewer: So science fiction seemed like the best way to write about your thoughts on the subject.

Vonnegut: There was no avoiding it, since General Electric Company *was* science fiction.

From interviews with Laurie Clancy and David Standish

THINKING ABOUT THEME

A clear, precise statement about a story's theme can serve as a promising thesis for a writing assignment. After you read a short story, you will probably have some vague sense of its theme—the central unifying idea, or the point of the story. How do you hone that vague sense of theme into a sharp and intriguing thesis?

- **Start by making a list of all the story's possible themes.** If you are discussing Stephen Crane's "The Open Boat," your list might look like this:

  > Man versus nature
  > Life-and-death struggle
  > Camaraderie of people in crisis
  > Blindness of fate
  > Courage in face of danger
  > Bravery not enough

- **Determine which points seem most important; then formulate a single sentence in which you combine them.** For Crane, you might have circled "man versus nature," "blindness of fate," and "bravery not enough," and your summary might be: "The central theme of 'The Open Boat' is nature's indifference to the fate of even the most courageous individuals."

- **Try to capture the story's essence in a single sentence.** Remember, your goal is to transcend a mere one-sentence plot summary. How can you clearly express the central theme in a few words?

CHECKLIST: Writing About Theme

- ☐ List as many possible themes as you can.
- ☐ Circle the two or three most important points and try to combine them into a sentence.
- ☐ Relate particular details of the story to the theme you have spelled out. Consider plot details, dialogue, setting, point of view, title—any elements that seem especially pertinent.
- ☐ Check whether all the elements of the story fit your thesis.
- ☐ Have you missed an important aspect of the story? Or, have you chosen to focus on a secondary idea, overlooking the central one?
- ☐ If necessary, rework your thesis until it applies to every element in the story.

WRITING ASSIGNMENT ON THEME

Choose a story that catches your attention, and go through the steps outlined above to develop a strong thesis sentence about the story's theme. Then flesh out your argument into an essay, supporting your thesis with evidence from the text, including quotations. Some good story choices might be "A Clean, Well-Lighted Place," "The Chrysanthemums," "A Good Man Is Hard to Find," and "The Lottery."

MORE TOPICS FOR WRITING

1. Define the central theme of "Harrison Bergeron." Is Vonnegut's early 1960s vision of the future still relevant today? Why or why not?
2. Think of a social trend that worries you. With "Harrison Bergeron" in mind, write a brief science fiction parable to warn against this danger to society. Try to pick a less familiar or surprising trend instead of one of the hot-button social issues that immediately pop into your mind.
3. "To Build a Fire" and "The Open Boat" both address the theme of a human being pitted against indifferent nature. Contrast the stories' approaches to this theme. How do the tones of the stories differ? How do these tonal differences help to communicate theme?
4. What does "How I Met My Husband" have to say about first love? Back up your response with specific evidence from the story.
5. Write a brief personal narrative about your first crush. Use dialogue and sensory detail to capture a sense of time, place, and the personalities involved. Your narrative should have a thematic focus—for example, the sting of first love, or its many delights.
6. A recent *Time* magazine article describes a young California woman who distanced herself from her Chinese heritage until reading *The Joy Luck Club* "turned her into a 'born-again Asian.' It gave her new insights into why her mom was so hard on her and why the ways she showed love—say, through food—were different from those of the families [she] saw on TV, who seemed to say 'I love you' all day long." Have you ever had a similar experience, in which something you read gave you a better understanding of a loved one, or even yourself?

▶ TERMS FOR *review*

Summary ▶ A brief condensation of the main idea or plot of a literary work. A summary is similar to a paraphrase, but less detailed.

Theme ▶ The main idea or larger meaning of a work of literature. A theme may be a message or a moral, but it is more likely to be a central, unifying insight or viewpoint.

7

SYMBOL

*All you have to do is close your eyes
and wait for the symbols.*

—TENNESSEE WILLIAMS

In F. Scott Fitzgerald's novel *The Great Gatsby*, a huge pair of bespectacled eyes stares across a wilderness of ash heaps, from a billboard advertising the services of an oculist. Repeatedly entering into the story, the advertisement comes to mean more than simply the availability of eye examinations. Fitzgerald has a character liken it to the eyes of God; he hints that some sad, compassionate spirit is brooding as it watches the passing procession of humanity. Such an object is a **symbol**: in literature, a person, place, or thing that suggests more than its literal meaning. Symbols generally do not "stand for" any one meaning, nor for anything absolutely definite; they point, they hint, or, as Henry James put it, they cast long shadows. To take a large example: in Herman Melville's *Moby-Dick,* the great white whale of the book's title apparently means more than the literal dictionary-definition meaning of an aquatic mammal. He also suggests more than the devil, to whom some of the characters liken him. The great whale, as the story unfolds, comes to imply an amplitude of meanings, among them the forces of nature and the whole created universe.

ALLEGORY

This indefinite multiplicity of meanings is characteristic of a symbolic story and distinguishes it from an **allegory**, a story in which persons, places, and things form a system of clearly labeled equivalents. In a simple allegory, characters and other elements often stand for other definite meanings, which are often abstractions. You will meet such a character in another story in this book, Nathaniel Hawthorne's "Young Goodman Brown." This tale's main female character, Faith, represents the religious virtue suggested by her name. Supreme allegories are found in some biblical parables ("The Kingdom of Heaven is like a man who sowed good seed in his field . . . ," Matthew 13:24–30).

A classic allegory is the medieval play *Everyman*, whose hero represents us all, and who, deserted by false friends called Kindred and Goods, faces the judgment of God accompanied only by a faithful friend called Good Deeds. In John Bunyan's seventeenth-century allegory *Pilgrim's Progress*, the protagonist, Christian, struggles along the difficult road toward salvation, meeting along the way persons such as Mr. Worldly Wiseman, who directs him into a more comfortable path (a wrong turn), and the residents of a town called Fair Speech, among them a hypocrite named Mr. Facing-both-ways. Not all allegories are simple: Dante's *Divine Comedy*, written during the Middle Ages, continues to reveal new meanings to careful readers. Allegory was much beloved in the Middle Ages, but in contemporary fiction it is rare. One modern instance is George Orwell's long fable *Animal Farm*, in which (among its double meanings) barnyard animals stand for human victims and totalitarian oppressors.

SYMBOLS

Symbols in fiction are not generally abstract terms such as *love* or *truth*, but are likely to be perceptible objects (or worded descriptions that cause us to imagine them). In William Faulkner's "A Rose for Emily" (Chapter 2), Miss Emily's invisible watch ticking at the end of a golden chain not only indicates the passage of time, but also suggests that time passes without even being noticed by the watch's owner, and the golden chain carries suggestions of wealth and authority. Objects (and creatures) that seem insignificant in themselves can take on a symbolic importance in the larger context: in Jhumpa Lahiri's "Interpreter of Maladies" (Chapter 12) the piece of gum that Mrs. Das gives Mr. Kapasi—"As soon as Mr. Kapasi put the gum in his mouth a thick sweet liquid burst onto his tongue"—underscores her effect on his slumbering senses.

Often the symbols we meet in fiction are inanimate objects, but other things also may function symbolically. In James Joyce's "Araby" (Chapter 12), the very name of the bazaar, Araby—the poetic name for Arabia—suggests magic, romance, and *The Arabian Nights*; its syllables (the narrator tells us) "cast an Eastern enchantment over me." Even a locale, or a feature of physical topography, can provide rich suggestions. Recall Ernest Hemingway's "A Clean, Well-Lighted Place" (Chapter 5), in which the café is not merely a café, but an island of refuge from night, chaos, loneliness, old age, and impending death.

Symbolic Characters

In some novels and stories, symbolic characters make brief cameo appearances. Such characters often are not well-rounded and fully known, but are seen fleetingly and remain slightly mysterious. In *Heart of Darkness*, a short novel by Joseph Conrad, a steamship company that hires men to work in the Congo maintains in its waiting room two women who knit black wool—like the classical Fates. Usually such a symbolic character is more a portrait than a person—or somewhat portraitlike, as Faulkner's Miss Emily, who twice appears at a window of her house "like the carven torso of an idol in a niche." Though Faulkner invests Miss Emily with life and vigor, he also clothes her in symbolic hints: she seems almost to personify the vanishing aristocracy of the antebellum South, still maintaining a black servant and being ruthlessly betrayed by a moneymaking Yankee. Sometimes a part of a character's body or an attribute may convey symbolic meaning: a baleful eye, as in Edgar Allan Poe's "The Tell-Tale Heart" (Chapter 2).

Symbolic Acts

Much as a symbolic whale holds more meaning than an ordinary whale, a **symbolic act** is a gesture with larger significance than usual. For the boy's father in Faulkner's "Barn Burning" (Chapter 5), the act of destroying a barn is no mere act of spite, but an expression of his profound hatred for anything not belonging to him. Faulkner adds that burning a barn reflects the father's memories of the "waste and extravagance of war," and further adds that "the element of fire spoke to some deep mainspring" in his being. A symbolic act, however, doesn't have to be a gesture as large as starting a conflagration. Before setting out in pursuit of the great white whale, Melville's Captain Ahab in *Moby-Dick* deliberately snaps his tobacco pipe and throws it away, as if to suggest (among other things) that he will let no pleasure or pastime distract him from his vengeance.

Why do writers have to symbolize—why don't they tell us outright? One advantage of a symbol is that it is so compact, and yet so fully laden. Both starkly concrete and slightly mysterious, like Miss Emily's invisible ticking watch, it may impress us with all the force of something beheld in a dream or in a nightmare. The watch suggests, among other things, the slow and invisible passage of time. What this symbol says, it says more fully and more memorably than could be said, perhaps, in a long essay on the subject.

To some extent (it may be claimed), all stories are symbolic. Merely by holding up for our inspection these characters and their actions, the writer lends them *some* special significance. But this is to think of *symbol* in an extremely broad and inclusive way. For the usual purposes of reading a story and understanding it, there is probably little point in looking for symbolism in every word, in every stick or stone, in every striking of a match, in every minor character. Still, to be on the alert for symbols when reading fiction is perhaps wiser than to ignore them. Not to admit that symbolic meanings may be present, or to refuse to think about them, would be another way to misread a story—or to read no further than its outer edges.

RECOGNIZING SYMBOLS

How, then, do you recognize a symbol in fiction when you meet it? Fortunately, the storyteller often gives the symbol particular emphasis. It may be mentioned repeatedly throughout the story; it may even supply the story with a title ("Barn Burning," "A Clean, Well-Lighted Place," "Araby"). At times, a crucial symbol will open a story or end it. Unless an object, act, or character is given some such special emphasis and importance, we may generally feel safe in taking it at face value. Probably it isn't a symbol if it points clearly and unmistakably toward some one meaning, like a whistle in a factory, whose blast at noon means lunch. But an object, an act, or a character is surely symbolic (and almost as surely displays high literary art) if, when we finish the story, we realize that it was that item—that gigantic eye; that clean, well-lighted café; that burning of a barn—which led us to the author's theme, the essential meaning.

John Steinbeck

The Chrysanthemums   1938

John Steinbeck (1902–1968) was born in Salinas, California, in the fertile valley he remembers in "The Chrysanthemums." Off and on, he attended Stanford University, then sojourned in New York as a reporter and a bricklayer. After years of struggle to earn his living by fiction, Steinbeck reached a large audience with Tortilla Flat *(1935), a loosely woven novel portraying Mexican Americans in Monterey with fondness and sympathy. Great acclaim greeted* The Grapes of Wrath *(1939), the story of a family of Oklahoma farmers who, ruined by dust storms in the 1930s, join a mass migration to California. In 1962 he became the seventh American to win the Nobel Prize in Literature, but critics have never placed Steinbeck on the*

John Steinbeck

same high shelf as Faulkner and Hemingway. He wrote much, not all good, and yet his best work adds up to an impressive total. Besides The Grapes of Wrath, *it includes* In Dubious Battle *(1936), a novel of an apple-pickers' strike;* Of Mice and Men *(1937), a powerful short novel of comradeship between a hobo and a retarded man; and the short stories in* The Long Valley *(1938). Throughout the fiction he wrote in his prime, Steinbeck maintains an appealing sympathy for the poor and downtrodden, the lonely and dispossessed.*

The high grey-flannel fog of winter closed off the Salinas Valley° from the sky and from all the rest of the world. On every side it sat like a lid on the mountains and made of the great valley a closed pot. On the broad, level land floor the gang plows bit deep and left the black earth shining like metal where the shares had cut. On the foothill ranches across the Salinas River, the yellow stubble fields seemed to be bathed in pale cold sunshine, but there was no sunshine in the valley now in December. The thick willow scrub along the river flamed with sharp and positive yellow leaves.

It was a time of quiet and of waiting. The air was cold and tender. A light wind blew up from the southwest so that the farmers were mildly hopeful of a good rain before long; but fog and rain do not go together.

Across the river, on Henry Allen's foothill ranch there was little work to be done, for the hay was cut and stored and the orchards were plowed up to receive the rain deeply when it should come. The cattle on the higher slopes were becoming shaggy and rough-coated.

Elisa Allen, working in her flower garden, looked down across the yard and saw Henry, her husband, talking to two men in business suits. The three of them stood by the tractor shed, each man with one foot on the side of the little Fordson. They smoked cigarettes and studied the machine as they talked.

Elisa watched them for a moment and then went back to her work. She was   5
thirty-five. Her face was lean and strong and her eyes were as clear as water. Her figure looked blocked and heavy in her gardening costume, a man's black hat pulled

Salinas Valley: south of San Francisco in the Coast Ranges region of California.

low down over her eyes, clodhopper shoes, a figured print dress almost completely covered by a big corduroy apron with four big pockets to hold the snips, the trowel and scratcher, the seeds and the knife she worked with. She wore heavy leather gloves to protect her hands while she worked.

She was cutting down the old year's chrysanthemum stalks with a pair of short and powerful scissors. She looked down toward the men by the tractor shed now and then. Her face was eager and mature and handsome; even her work with the scissors was over-eager, over-powerful. The chrysanthemum stems seemed too small and easy for her energy.

She brushed a cloud of hair out of her eyes with the back of her glove, and left a smudge of earth on her cheek in doing it. Behind her stood the neat white farm house with red geraniums close-banked around it as high as the windows. It was a hard-swept looking little house with hard-polished windows, and a clean mud-mat on the front steps.

Elisa cast another glance toward the tractor shed. The strangers were getting into their Ford coupe. She took off a glove and put her strong fingers down into the forest of new green chrysanthemum sprouts that were growing around the old roots. She spread the leaves and looked down among the close-growing stems. No aphids were there, no sowbugs or snails or cutworms. Her terrier fingers destroyed such pests before they could get started.

Elisa started at the sound of her husband's voice. He had come near quietly, and he leaned over the wire fence that protected her flower garden from cattle and dogs and chickens.

"At it again," he said. "You've got a strong new crop coming."   10

Elisa straightened her back and pulled on the gardening glove again. "Yes. They'll be strong this coming year." In her tone and on her face there was a little smugness.

"You've got a gift with things," Henry observed. "Some of those yellow chrysanthemums you had this year were ten inches across. I wish you'd work out in the orchard and raise some apples that big."

Her eyes sharpened. "Maybe I could do it, too. I've a gift with things, all right. My mother had it. She could stick anything in the ground and make it grow. She said it was having planters' hands that knew how to do it."

"Well, it sure works with flowers," he said.

"Henry, who were those men you were talking to?"   15

"Why, sure, that's what I came to tell you. They were from the Western Meat Company. I sold those thirty head of three-year-old steers. Got nearly my own price, too."

"Good," she said. "Good for you."

"And I thought," he continued, "I thought how it's Saturday afternoon, and we might go into Salinas for dinner at a restaurant, and then to a picture show—to celebrate, you see."

"Good," she repeated. "Oh, yes. That will be good."

Henry put on his joking tone. "There's fights tonight. How'd you like to go to   20
the fights?"

"Oh, no," she said breathlessly. "No, I wouldn't like fights."

"Just fooling, Elisa. We'll go to a movie. Let's see. It's two now. I'm going to take Scotty and bring down those steers from the hill. It'll take us maybe two hours. We'll go in town about five and have dinner at the Cominos Hotel. Like that?"

"Of course I'll like it. It's good to eat away from home."

"All right, then. I'll go get up a couple of horses."

She said, "I'll have plenty of time to transplant some of these sets, I guess."   25

She heard her husband calling Scotty down by the barn. And a little later she saw the two men ride up the pale yellow hillside in search of the steers.

There was a little square sandy bed kept for rooting the chrysanthemums. With her trowel she turned the soil over and over, and smoothed it and patted it firm. Then she dug ten parallel trenches to receive the sets. Back at the chrysanthemum bed she pulled out the little crisp shoots, trimmed off the leaves of each one with her scissors and laid it on a small orderly pile.

A squeak of wheels and plod of hoofs came from the road. Elisa looked up. The country road ran along the dense bank of willows and cottonwoods that bordered the river, and up this road came a curious vehicle, curiously drawn. It was an old spring-wagon, with a round canvas top on it like the cover of a prairie schooner. It was drawn by an old bay horse and a little grey-and-white burro. A big stubble-bearded man sat between the cover flaps and drove the crawling team. Underneath the wagon, between the hind wheels, a lean and rangy mongrel dog walked sedately. Words were painted on the canvas, in clumsy, crooked letters. "Pots, pans, knives, sisors, lawn mores, Fixed." Two rows of articles, and the triumphantly definitive "Fixed" below. The black paint had run down in little sharp points beneath each letter.

Elisa, squatting on the ground, watched to see the crazy, loose-jointed wagon pass by. But it didn't pass. It turned into the farm road in front of her house, crooked old wheels skirling and squeaking. The rangy dog darted from between the wheels and ran ahead. Instantly the two ranch shepherds flew out at him. Then all three stopped, and with stiff and quivering tails, with taut straight legs, with ambassadorial dignity, they slowly circled, sniffing daintily. The caravan pulled up to Elisa's wire fence and stopped. Now the newcomer dog, feeling out-numbered, lowered his tail and retired under the wagon with raised hackles and bared teeth.

The man on the wagon seat called out, "That's a bad dog in a fight when he gets   30 started."

Elisa laughed. "I see he is. How soon does he generally get started?"

The man caught up her laughter and echoed it heartily. "Sometimes not for weeks and weeks," he said. He climbed stiffly down, over the wheel. The horse and the donkey drooped like unwatered flowers.

Elisa saw that he was a very big man. Although his hair and beard were greying, he did not look old. His worn black suit was wrinkled and spotted with grease. The laughter had disappeared from his face and eyes the moment his laughing voice ceased. His eyes were dark, and they were full of the brooding that gets in the eyes of teamsters and of sailors. The calloused hands he rested on the wire fence were cracked, and every crack was a black line. He took off his battered hat.

"I'm off my general road, ma'am," he said. "Does this dirt road cut over across the river to the Los Angeles highway?"

Elisa stood up and shoved the thick scissors in her apron pocket. "Well, yes, it   35 does, but it winds around and then fords the river. I don't think your team could pull through the sand."

He replied with some asperity, "It might surprise you what them beasts can pull through."

"When they get started?" she asked.

He smiled for a second. "Yes. When they get started."

"Well," said Elisa, "I think you'll save time if you go back to the Salinas road and pick up the highway there."

He drew a big finger down the chicken wire and made it sing. "I ain't in any 40 hurry, ma'am. I go from Seattle to San Diego and back every year. Takes all my time. About six months each way. I aim to follow nice weather."

Elisa took off her gloves and stuffed them in the apron pocket with the scissors. She touched the under edge of her man's hat, searching for fugitive hairs. "That sounds like a nice kind of a way to live," she said.

He leaned confidentially over the fence. "Maybe you noticed the writing on my wagon. I mend pots and sharpen knives and scissors. You got any of them things to do?"

"Oh, no," she said quickly. "Nothing like that." Her eyes hardened with resistance.

"Scissors is the worst thing," he explained. "Most people just ruin scissors trying to sharpen 'em, but I know how. I got a special tool. It's a little bobbit kind of thing, and patented. But it sure does the trick."

"No. My scissors are all sharp." 45

"All right, then. Take a pot," he continued earnestly, "a bent pot, or a pot with a hole. I can make it like new so you don't have to buy no new ones. That's a saving for you."

"No," she said shortly. "I tell you I have nothing like that for you to do."

His face fell to an exaggerated sadness. His voice took on a whining undertone. "I ain't had a thing to do today. Maybe I won't have no supper tonight. You see I'm off my regular road. I know folks on the highway clear from Seattle to San Diego. They save their things for me to sharpen up because they know I do it so good and save them money."

"I'm sorry," Elisa said irritably. "I haven't anything for you to do."

His eyes left her face and fell to searching the ground. They roamed about until 50 they came to the chrysanthemum bed where she had been working. "What's them plants, ma'am?"

The irritation and resistance melted from Elisa's face. "Oh, those are chrysanthemums, giant whites and yellows. I raise them every year, bigger than anybody around here."

"Kind of a long-stemmed flower? Looks like a quick puff of colored smoke?" he asked.

"That's it. What a nice way to describe them."

"They smell kind of nasty till you get used to them," he said.

"It's a good bitter smell," she retorted, "not nasty at all." 55

He changed his tone quickly. "I like the smell myself."

"I had ten-inch blooms this year," she said.

The man leaned farther over the fence. "Look. I know a lady down the road a piece, has got the nicest garden you ever seen. Got nearly every kind of flower but no chrysanthemums. Last time I was mending a copper-bottom washtub for her (that's a hard job but I do it good), she said to me, 'If you ever run acrost some nice chrysanthemums I wish you'd try to get me a few seeds.' That's what she told me."

Elisa's eyes grew alert and eager. "She couldn't have known much about chrysanthemums. You *can* raise them from seed, but it's much easier to root the little sprouts you see there."

"Oh," he said. "I s'pose I can't take none to her, then." 60

"Why yes you can," Elisa cried. "I can put some in damp sand, and you can carry them right along with you. They'll take root in the pot if you keep them damp. And then she can transplant them."

"She'd sure like to have some, ma'am. You say they're nice ones?"

"Beautiful," she said. "Oh, beautiful." Her eyes shone. She tore off the battered hat and shook out her dark pretty hair. "I'll put them in a flower pot, and you can take them right with you. Come into the yard."

While the man came through the picket gate Elisa ran excitedly along the geranium-bordered path to the back of the house. And she returned carrying a big red flower pot. The gloves were forgotten now. She kneeled on the ground by the starting bed and dug up the sandy soil with her fingers and scooped it into the bright new flower pot. Then she picked up the little pile of shoots she had prepared. With her strong fingers she pressed them in the sand and tamped around them with her knuckles. The man stood over her. "I'll tell you what to do," she said. "You remember so you can tell the lady."

"Yes, I'll try to remember." 65

"Well, look. These will take root in about a month. Then she must set them out, about a foot apart in good rich earth like this, see?" She lifted a handful of dark soil for him to look at. "They'll grow fast and tall. Now remember this: In July tell her to cut them down, about eight inches from the ground."

"Before they bloom?" he asked.

"Yes, before they bloom." Her face was tight with eagerness. "They'll grow right up again. About the last of September the buds will start."

She stopped and seemed perplexed. "It's the budding that takes the most care," she said hesitantly. "I don't know how to tell you." She looked deep into his eyes, searchingly. Her mouth opened a little, and she seemed to be listening. "I'll try to tell you," she said. "Did you ever hear of planting hands?"

"Can't say I have, ma'am." 70

"Well, I can only tell you what it feels like. It's when you're picking off the buds you don't want. Everything goes right down into your fingertips. You watch your fingers work. They do it themselves. You can feel how it is. They pick and pick the buds. They never make a mistake. They're with the plant. Do you see? Your fingers and the plant. You can feel that, right up your arm. They know. They never make a mistake. You can feel it. When you're like that you can't do anything wrong. Do you see that? Can you understand that?"

She was kneeling on the ground looking up at him. Her breast swelled passionately.

The man's eyes narrowed. He looked away self-consciously. "Maybe I know," he said. "Sometimes in the night in the wagon there—"

Elisa's voice grew husky. She broke in on him, "I've never lived as you do, but I know what you mean. When the night is dark—why, the stars are sharp-pointed, and there's quiet. Why, you rise up and up! Every pointed star gets driven into your body. It's like that. Hot and sharp and—lovely."

Kneeling there, her hand went out toward his legs in the greasy black trousers. 75 Her hesitant fingers almost touched the cloth. Then her hand dropped to the ground. She crouched low like a fawning dog.

He said, "It's nice, just like you say. Only when you don't have no dinner, it ain't."

She stood up then, very straight, and her face was ashamed. She held the flower pot out to him and placed it gently in his arms. "Here. Put it in your wagon, on the seat, where you can watch it. Maybe I can find something for you to do."

At the back of the house she dug in the can pile and found two old and battered aluminum saucepans. She carried them back and gave them to him. "Here, maybe you can fix these."

His manner changed. He became professional. "Good as new I can fix them." At the back of his wagon he set a little anvil, and out of an oily tool box dug a small machine hammer. Elisa came through the gate to watch him while he pounded out the dents in the kettles. His mouth grew sure and knowing. At a difficult part of the work he sucked his under-lip.

"You sleep right in the wagon?" Elisa asked.   80

"Right in the wagon, ma'am. Rain or shine I'm dry as a cow in there."

"It must be nice," she said. "It must be very nice. I wish women could do such things."

"It ain't the right kind of a life for a woman."

Her upper lip raised a little, showing her teeth. "How do you know? How can you tell?" she said.

"I don't know, ma'am," he protested. "Of course I don't know. Now here's your   85
kettles, done. You don't have to buy no new ones."

"How much?"

"Oh, fifty cents'll do. I keep my prices down and my work good. That's why I have all them satisfied customers up and down the highway."

Elisa brought him a fifty-cent piece from the house and dropped it in his hand. "You might be surprised to have a rival some time. I can sharpen scissors, too. And I can beat the dents out of little pots. I could show you what a woman might do."

He put his hammer back in the oily box and shoved the little anvil out of sight. "It would be a lonely life for a woman, ma'am, and a scarey life, too, with animals creeping under the wagon all night." He climbed over the singletree, steadying himself with a hand on the burro's white rump. He settled himself in the seat, picked up the lines. "Thank you kindly, ma'am," he said. "I'll do like you told me; I'll go back and catch the Salinas road."

"Mind," she called, "if you're long in getting there, keep the sand damp."   90

"Sand, ma'am? . . . Sand? Oh, sure. You mean around the chrysanthemums. Sure I will." He clucked his tongue. The beasts leaned luxuriously into their collars. The mongrel dog took his place between the back wheels. The wagon turned and crawled out the entrance road and back the way it had come, along the river.

Elisa stood in front of her wire fence watching the slow progress of the caravan. Her shoulders were straight, her head thrown back, her eyes half-closed, so that the scene came vaguely into them. Her lips moved silently, forming the words "Good-bye—good-bye." Then she whispered, "That's a bright direction. There's a glowing there." The sound of her whisper startled her. She shook herself free and looked about to see whether anyone had been listening. Only the dogs had heard. They lifted their heads toward her from their sleeping in the dust, and then stretched out their chins and settled asleep again. Elisa turned and ran hurriedly into the house.

In the kitchen she reached behind the stove and felt the water tank. It was full of hot water from the noonday cooking. In the bathroom she tore off her soiled clothes and flung them into the corner. And then she scrubbed herself with a little block of pumice, legs and thighs, loins and chest and arms, until her skin was scratched and red. When she had dried herself she stood in front of a mirror in her bedroom and looked at her body. She tightened her stomach and threw out her chest. She turned and looked over her shoulder at her back.

After a while she began to dress, slowly. She put on her newest underclothing and her nicest stockings and the dress which was the symbol of her prettiness. She worked carefully on her hair, penciled her eyebrows and rouged her lips.

Before she was finished she heard the little thunder of hoofs and the shouts of   95
Henry and his helper as they drove the red steers into the corral. She heard the gate bang shut and set herself for Henry's arrival.

His step sounded on the porch. He entered the house calling, "Elisa, where are you?"

"In my room, dressing. I'm not ready. There's hot water for your bath. Hurry up. It's getting late."

When she heard him splashing in the tub, Elisa laid his dark suit on the bed, and shirt and socks and tie beside it. She stood his polished shoes on the floor beside the bed. Then she went to the porch and sat primly and stiffly down. She looked toward the river road where the willow-line was still yellow with frosted leaves so that under the high grey fog they seemed a thin band of sunshine. This was the only color in the grey afternoon. She sat unmoving for a long time. Her eyes blinked rarely.

Henry came banging out of the door, shoving his tie inside his vest as he came. Elisa stiffened and her face grew tight. Henry stopped short and looked at her. "Why—why, Elisa. You look so nice!"

"Nice? You think I look nice? What do you mean by 'nice'?"   100

Henry blundered on. "I don't know. I mean you look different, strong and happy."

"I am strong? Yes, strong. What do you mean 'strong'?"

He looked bewildered. "You're playing some kind of a game," he said helplessly. "It's a kind of a play. You look strong enough to break a calf over your knee, happy enough to eat it like a watermelon."

For a second she lost her rigidity. "Henry! Don't talk like that. You didn't know what you said." She grew complete again. "I'm strong," she boasted. "I never knew before how strong."

Henry looked down toward the tractor shed, and when he brought his eyes back   105
to her, they were his own again. "I'll get out the car. You can put on your coat while I'm starting."

Elisa went into the house. She heard him drive to the gate and idle down his motor, and then she took a long time to put on her hat. She pulled it here and pressed it there. When Henry turned the motor off she slipped into her coat and went out.

The little roadster bounced along on the dirt road by the river, raising the birds and driving the rabbits into the brush. Two cranes flapped heavily over the willow-line and dropped into the river-bed.

Far ahead on the road Elisa saw a dark speck. She knew.

She tried not to look as they passed it, but her eyes would not obey. She whispered to herself sadly, "He might have thrown them off the road. That wouldn't have been much trouble, not very much. But he kept the pot," she explained. "He had to keep the pot. That's why he couldn't get them off the road."

The roadster turned a bend and she saw the caravan ahead. She swung full   110
around toward her husband so she could not see the little covered wagon and the mismatched team as the car passed them.

In a moment it was over. The thing was done. She did not look back.

She said loudly, to be heard above the motor, "It will be good, tonight, a good dinner."

"Now you're changed again," Henry complained. He took one hand from the wheel and patted her knee. "I ought to take you in to dinner oftener. It would be good for both of us. We get so heavy out on the ranch."

"Henry," she asked, "could we have wine at dinner?"

"Sure we could. Say! That will be fine."   115

She was silent for a while; then she said, "Henry, at those prize fights, do the men hurt each other very much?"

"Sometimes a little, not often. Why?"

"Well, I've read how they break noses, and blood runs down their chests. I've read how the fighting gloves get heavy and soggy with blood."

He looked around at her. "What's the matter, Elisa? I didn't know you read things like that." He brought the car to a stop, then turned to the right over the Salinas River bridge.

"Do any women ever go to the fights?" she asked.   120

"Oh, sure, some. What's the matter, Elisa? Do you want to go? I don't think you'd like it, but I'll take you if you really want to go."

She relaxed limply in the seat. "Oh, no. No. I don't want to go. I'm sure I don't." Her face was turned away from him. "It will be enough if we can have wine. It will be plenty." She turned up her coat collar so he could not see that she was crying weakly—like an old woman.

Questions

1. When we first meet Elisa Allen in her garden, with what details does Steinbeck delineate her character for us?

2. Elisa works inside a "wire fence that protected her flower garden from cattle and dogs and chickens" (paragraph 9). What does this wire fence suggest?

3. How would you describe Henry and Elisa's marriage? Cite details from the story.

4. With what motive does the traveling salesman take an interest in Elisa's chrysanthemums? What immediate effect does his interest have on Elisa?

5. For what possible purpose does Steinbeck give us such a detailed account of Elisa's preparations for her evening out? Notice her tearing off her soiled clothes and her scrubbing her body with pumice (paragraphs 93–94).

6. Of what significance to Elisa is the sight of the contents of the flower pot discarded in the road? Notice that, as her husband's car overtakes the covered wagon, Elisa averts her eyes; and then Steinbeck adds, "In a moment it was over. The thing was done. She did not look back" (paragraph 111). Explain this passage.

7. How do you interpret Elisa's asking for wine with dinner? How do you account for her new interest in prizefights?

8. In a sentence, try to state this short story's theme.

9. Why are Elisa Allen's chrysanthemums so important to this story? Sum up what you understand them to mean.

John Cheever

The Swimmer   1964

John Cheever (1912–1982) was born in Quincy, Massachusetts. His parents had been modestly prosperous, but their livelihood declined substantially and was finally dashed by the 1929 stock market crash. Cheever was sent away to Thayer Academy, a prep school, where he was a poor student. When he was expelled at eighteen, he wrote a story about the incident that was published in the New Republic *(1930). Cheever never finished high school or attended college, dedicating himself instead to writing.*

John Cheever

Cheever's stories, most of which appeared in the New Yorker, *often deal with the ordinary lives of middle-class characters living in Manhattan or its suburbs. Although his stories are realistic in plot and setting, they also often contain an underlying religious vision—exploring themes of guilt, grace, and redemption. Cheever's novels include* The Wapshot Chronicle *(1957), which won the National Book Award;* Bullet Park *(1969); and* Falconer *(1977). The Stories of John Cheever (1978), selected works from his five volumes of short fiction, won the Pulitzer Prize and National Book Critics Circle Award. After Cheever's death, his notebooks and letters revealed how tortured his life had been by sex and alcohol. While some early reviewers regarded Cheever's popular stories as "New Yorker fiction" (satiric views of middle-class life), critics now see the psychological and religious vision underlying his work. Once undervalued, Cheever is now generally regarded as one of the finest American short-story writers of the twentieth century.*

It was one of those midsummer Sundays when everyone sits around saying, "I *drank* too much last night." You might have heard it whispered by the parishioners leaving church, heard it from the lips of the priest himself, struggling with his cassock in the *vestiarium:* heard it from the golf links and the tennis courts, heard it from the wildlife preserve where the leader of the Audubon group was suffering from a terrible hangover. "I *drank* too much," said Donald Westerhazy. "We all *drank* too much," said Lucinda Merrill. "It must have been the wine," said Helen Westerhazy. "I *drank* too much of that claret."

This was at the edge of the Westerhazys' pool. The pool, fed by an artesian well with a high iron content, was a pale shade of green. It was a fine day. In the west there was a massive stand of cumulus cloud so like a city seen from a distance—from the bow of an approaching ship—that it might have had a name. Lisbon. Hackensack. The sun was hot. Neddy Merrill sat by the green water, one hand in it, one around a glass of gin. He was a slender man—he seemed to have the especial slenderness of youth—and while he was far from young he had slid down his banister that morning and given the bronze backside of Aphrodite on the hall table a smack, as he jogged toward the smell of coffee in his dining room. He might have been compared to a summer's day, particularly the last hours of one, and while he lacked a tennis racket or a sail bag the impression was definitely one of youth, sport, and clement weather. He had been swimming and now he was breathing deeply, stertorously as if he could gulp into his lungs the components of that moment, the heat of the sun, the intenseness of his pleasure. It all seemed to flow into his chest. His own house stood in Bullet Park, eight miles to the south, where his four beautiful daughters would have had their lunch and might be playing tennis. Then it occurred to him that by taking a dogleg to the southwest he could reach his home by water.

His life was not confining and the delight he took in this observation could not be explained by its suggestion of escape. He seemed to see, with a cartographer's eye, that string of swimming pools, that quasi-subterranean stream that curved across the county. He had made a discovery, a contribution to modern geography; he would name the stream Lucinda after his wife. He was not a practical joker nor was he a fool but he was determinedly original and had a vague and modest idea of himself as a legendary figure. The day was beautiful and it seemed to him that a long swim might enlarge and celebrate its beauty.

He took off a sweater that was hung over his shoulders and dove in. He had an inexplicable contempt for men who did not hurl themselves into pools. He swam a choppy crawl, breathing either with every stroke or every fourth stroke and counting somewhere well in the back of his mind the one-two one-two of a flutter kick. It was not a serviceable stroke for long distances but the domestication of swimming had saddled the sport with some customs and in his part of the world a crawl was customary. To be embraced and sustained by the light green water was less a pleasure, it seemed, than the resumption of a natural condition, and he would have liked to swim without trunks, but this was not possible, considering his project. He hoisted himself up on the far curb—he never used the ladder—and started across the lawn. When Lucinda asked where he was going he said he was going to swim home.

The only maps and charts he had to go by were remembered or imaginary but   5 these were clear enough. First there were the Grahams, the Hammers, the Lears, the Howlands, and the Crosscups. He would cross Ditmar Street to the Bunkers and come, after a short portage, to the Levys, the Welchers, and the public pool in Lancaster. Then there were the Hallorans, the Sachses, the Biswangers, Shirley Adams, the Gilmartins, and the Clydes. The day was lovely, and that he lived in a world so generously supplied with water seemed like a clemency, a beneficence. His heart was high and he ran across the grass. Making his way home by an uncommon route gave him the feeling that he was a pilgrim, an explorer, a man with a destiny, and he knew that he would find friends all along the way; friends would line the banks of the Lucinda River.

He went through a hedge that separated the Westerhazys' land from the Grahams', walked under some flowering apple trees, passed the shed that housed their pump and filter, and came out at the Grahams' pool. "Why, Neddy," Mrs. Graham said, "what a marvelous surprise. I've been trying to get you on the phone all morning. Here, let me get you a drink." He saw then, like any explorer, that the hospitable customs and traditions of the natives would have to be handled with diplomacy if he was ever going to reach his destination. He did not want to mystify or seem rude to the Grahams nor did he have the time to linger there. He swam the length of their pool and joined them in the sun and was rescued, a few minutes later, by the arrival of two carloads of friends from Connecticut. During the uproarious reunions he was able to slip away. He went down by the front of the Grahams' house, stepped over a thorny hedge, and crossed a vacant lot to the Hammers'. Mrs. Hammer, looking up from her roses, saw him swim by although she wasn't quite sure who it was. The Lears heard him splashing past the open windows of their living room. The Howlands and the Crosscups were away.

After leaving the Howlands' he crossed Ditmar Street and started for the Bunkers', where he could hear, even at that distance, the noise of a party.

The water refracted the sound of voices and laughter and seemed to suspend it in midair. The Bunkers' pool was on a rise and he climbed some stairs to a terrace where twenty-five or thirty men and women were drinking. The only person in the water was Rusty Towers, who floated there on a rubber raft. Oh, how bonny and lush were the banks of the Lucinda River! Prosperous men and women gathered by the sapphire-colored waters while caterer's men in white coats passed them cold gin. Overhead a red de Haviland trainer was circling around and around and around in the sky with something like the glee of a child in a swing. Ned felt a passing affection for the scene, a tenderness for the gathering, as if it was something he might touch. In the distance he heard thunder. As soon as Enid Bunker saw him she began to scream: "Oh, look who's here! What a marvelous surprise! When Lucinda said you couldn't come I thought I'd *die*." She made her way to him through the crowd, and when they had finished kissing she led him to the bar, a progress that was slowed by the fact that he stopped to kiss eight or ten other women and shake the hands of as many men. A smiling bartender he had seen at a hundred parties gave him a gin and tonic and he stood by the bar for a moment, anxious not to get stuck in any conversation that would delay his voyage. When he seemed about to be surrounded he dove in and swam close to the side to avoid colliding with Rusty's raft. At the far end of the pool he bypassed the Tomlinsons with a broad smile and jogged up the garden path. The gravel cut his feet but this was the only unpleasantness. The party was confined to the pool, and as he went toward the house he heard the brilliant, watery sound of voices fade, heard the noise of a radio from the Bunkers' kitchen, where someone was listening to a ball game. Sunday afternoon. He made his way through the parked cars and down the grassy border of their driveway to Alewives Lane. He did not want to be seen on the road in his bathing trunks but there was no traffic and he made the short distance to the Levys' driveway, marked with a PRIVATE PROPERTY sign and a green tube for *The New York Times*. All the doors and windows of the big house were open but there were no signs of life; not even a dog barked. He went around the side of the house to the pool and saw that the Levys had only recently left. Glasses and bottles and dishes of nuts were on a table at the deep end, where there was a bathhouse or gazebo, hung with Japanese lanterns. After swimming the pool he got himself a glass and poured a drink. It was his fourth or fifth drink and he had swum nearly half the length of the Lucinda River. He felt tired, clean, and pleased at that moment to be alone; pleased with everything.

It would storm. The stand of cumulus cloud—that city—had risen and darkened, and while he sat there he heard the percussiveness of thunder again. The de Haviland trainer was still circling overhead and it seemed to Ned that he could almost hear the pilot laugh with pleasure in the afternoon; but when there was another peal of thunder he took off for home. A train whistle blew and he wondered what time it had gotten to be. Four? Five? He thought of the provincial station at that hour, where a waiter, his tuxedo concealed by a raincoat, a dwarf with some flowers wrapped in newspaper, and a woman who had been crying would be waiting for the local. It was suddenly growing dark; it was that moment when the pin-headed birds seem to organize their song into some acute and knowledgeable recognition of the storm's approach. Then there was a fine noise of rushing water from the crown of an oak at his back, as if a spigot there had been turned. Then the noise of fountains came from the crowns of all the tall trees. Why did he love storms, what was the meaning of his excitement when the door sprang open and the rain wind fled rudely up the stairs, why had the simple task of shutting the windows of an old house seemed fitting and urgent, why did the first watery notes of a storm wind have for him the unmistakable sound of good news, cheer, glad tidings? Then there was an explosion, a smell of cordite, and rain lashed the Japanese lanterns that Mrs. Levy had bought in Kyoto the year before last, or was it the year before that?

He stayed in the Levys' gazebo until the storm had passed. The rain had cooled the air and he shivered. The force of the wind had stripped a maple of its red and yellow leaves and scattered them over the grass and the water. Since it was midsummer the tree must be blighted, and yet he felt a peculiar sadness at this sign of autumn. He braced his shoulders, emptied his glass, and started for the Welchers' pool. This meant crossing the Lindleys' riding ring and he was surprised to find it overgrown with grass and all the jumps dismantled. He wondered if the Lindleys had sold their horses or gone away for the summer and put them out to board. He seemed to remember having heard something about the Lindleys and their horses but the memory was unclear. On he went, barefoot through the wet grass, to the Welchers', where he found their pool was dry.

This breach in his chain of water disappointed him absurdly, and he felt like some explorer who seeks a torrential headwater and finds a dead stream. He was disappointed and mystified. It was common enough to go away for the summer but no one ever drained his pool. The Welchers had definitely gone away. The pool furniture was folded, stacked, and covered with a tarpaulin. The bathhouse was locked. All the windows of the house were shut, and when he went around to the driveway in front he saw a FOR SALE sign nailed to the tree. When had he last heard from the Welchers—when, that is, had he and Lucinda last regretted an invitation to dine with them? It seemed only a week or so ago. Was his memory failing or had he so disciplined it in the repression of unpleasant facts that he had damaged his sense of the truth? Then in the distance he heard the sound of a tennis game. This cheered him, cleared away all his apprehensions and let him regard the overcast sky and the cold air with indifference. This was the day that Neddy Merrill swam across the county. That was the day! He started off then for his most difficult portage.

Had you gone for a Sunday afternoon ride that day you might have seen him, close to naked, standing on the shoulders of Route 424, waiting for a chance to cross. You might have wondered if he was the victim of foul play, had his car broken down, or was he merely a fool. Standing barefoot in the deposits of the highway—beer cans, rags, and blowout patches—exposed to all kinds of ridicule, he seemed pitiful. He had known when he started that this was a part of his journey—it had been on his maps—but confronted with the lines of traffic, worming through the summery light, he found himself unprepared. He was laughed at, jeered at, a beer can was thrown at him, and he had no dignity or humor to bring to the situation. He could have gone back, back to the Westerhazys', where Lucinda would still be sitting in the sun. He had signed nothing, vowed nothing, pledged nothing, not even to himself. Why, believing as he did, that all human obduracy was susceptible to common sense, was he unable to turn back? Why was he determined to complete his journey even if it meant putting his life in danger? At what point had this prank, this joke, this piece of horseplay become serious? He could not go back, he could not even recall with any clearness the green water at the Westerhazys', the sense of inhaling the day's components, the friendly and relaxed voices saying that

10

they had *drunk* too much. In the space of an hour, more or less, he had covered a distance that made his return impossible.

An old man, tooling down the highway at fifteen miles an hour, let him get to the middle of the road, where there was a grass divider. Here he was exposed to the ridicule of the northbound traffic, but after ten or fifteen minutes he was able to cross. From here he had only a short walk to the Recreation Center at the edge of the village of Lancaster, where there were some handball courts and a public pool.

The effect of the water on voices, the illusion of brilliance and suspense, was the same here as it had been at the Bunkers' but the sounds here were louder, harsher, and more shrill, and as soon as he entered the crowded enclosure he was confronted with regimentation. "ALL SWIMMERS MUST TAKE A SHOWER BEFORE USING THE POOL. ALL SWIMMERS MUST USE THE FOOTBATH. ALL SWIMMERS MUST WEAR THEIR IDENTIFI-CATION DISKS." He took a shower, washed his feet in a cloudy and bitter solution, and made his way to the edge of the water. It stank of chlorine and looked to him like a sink. A pair of lifeguards in a pair of towers blew police whistles at what seemed to be regular intervals and abused the swimmers through a public address system. Neddy remembered the sapphire water at the Bunkers' with longing and thought that he might contaminate himself—damage his own prosperousness and charm— by swimming in this murk, but he reminded himself that he was an explorer, a pil-grim, and that this was merely a stagnant bend in the Lucinda River. He dove, scowling with distaste, into the chlorine and had to swim with his head above water to avoid collisions, but even so he was bumped into, splashed, and jostled. When he got to the shallow end both lifeguards were shouting at him: "Hey, you, you without the identification disk, get outa the water." He did, but they had no way of pursuing him and he went through the reek of suntan oil and chlorine out through the hurri-cane fence and passed the handball courts. By crossing the road he entered the wooded part of the Halloran estate. The woods were not cleared and the footing was treacherous and difficult until he reached the lawn and the clipped beech hedge that encircled their pool.

The Hallorans were friends, an elderly couple of enormous wealth who seemed to bask in the suspicion that they might be Communists. They were zealous reformers but they were not Communists, and yet when they were accused, as they sometimes were, of subversion, it seemed to gratify and excite them. Their beech hedge was yel-low and he guessed this had been blighted like the Levys' maple. He called hullo, hullo, to warn the Hallorans of his approach, to palliate his invasion of their privacy. The Hallorans, for reasons that had never been explained to him, did not wear bathing suits. No explanations were in order, really. Their nakedness was a detail in their uncompromising zeal for reform and he stepped politely out of his trunks before he went through the opening in the hedge.

Mrs. Halloran, a stout woman with white hair and a serene face, was reading the *Times*. Mr. Halloran was taking beech leaves out of the water with a scoop. They seemed not surprised or displeased to see him. Their pool was perhaps the oldest in the county, a fieldstone rectangle, fed by a brook. It had no filter or pump and its waters were the opaque gold of the stream. 15

"I'm swimming across the county," Ned said.

"Why, I didn't know one could," exclaimed Mrs. Halloran.

"Well, I've made it from the Westerhazys'," Ned said. "That must be about four miles."

He left his trunks at the deep end, walked to the shallow end, and swam this stretch. As he was pulling himself out of the water he heard Mrs. Halloran say, "We've been *terribly* sorry to hear about all your misfortunes, Neddy."

"My misfortunes?" Ned asked. "I don't know what you mean."   20

"Why we heard that you'd sold the house and that your poor children. . . ."

"I don't recall having sold the house," Ned said, "and the girls are at home."

"Yes," Mrs. Halloran sighed. "Yes. . . ." Her voice filled the air with an unseasonable melancholy and Ned spoke briskly. "Thank you for the swim."

"Well, have a nice trip," said Mrs. Halloran.

Beyond the hedge he pulled on his trunks and fastened them. They were loose   25
and he wondered if, during the space of an afternoon, he could have lost some weight. He was cold and he was tired and the naked Hallorans and their dark water had depressed him. The swim was too much for his strength but how could he have guessed this, sliding down the banister that morning and sitting in the Westerhazys' sun? His arms were lame. His legs felt rubbery and ached at the joints. The worst of it was the cold in his bones and the feeling that he might never be warm again. Leaves were falling down around him and he smelled wood smoke on the wind. Who would be burning wood at this time of the year?

He needed a drink. Whiskey would warm him, pick him up, carry him through the last of his journey, refresh his feeling that it was original and valorous to swim across the county. Channel swimmers took brandy. He needed a stimulant. He crossed the lawn in front of the Hallorans' house and went down a little path to where they had built a house for their only daughter, Helen, and her husband, Eric Sachs. The Sachses' pool was small and he found Helen and her husband there.

"Oh, *Neddy*," Helen said. "Did you lunch at Mother's?"

"Not *really*," Ned said. "I *did* stop to see your parents." This seemed to be explanation enough. "I'm terribly sorry to break in on you like this but I've taken a chill and I wonder if you'd give me a drink."

"Why, I'd *love* to," Helen said, "but there hasn't been anything in this house to drink since Eric's operation. That was three years ago."

Was he losing his memory, had his gift for concealing painful facts let him forget   30
that he had sold his house, that his children were in trouble, and that his friend had been ill? His eyes slipped from Eric's face to his abdomen, where he saw three pale, sutured scars, two of them at least a foot long. Gone was his navel, and what, Neddy thought, would the roving hand, bed-checking one's gifts at 3 A.M., make of a belly with no navel, no link to birth, this breach in the succession?

"I'm sure you can get a drink at the Biswangers'," Helen said. "They're having an enormous do. You can hear it from here. Listen!"

She raised her head and from across the road, the lawns, the gardens, the woods, the fields, he heard again the brilliant noise of voices over water. "Well, I'll get wet," he said, still feeling that he had no freedom of choice about his means of travel. He dove into the Sachses' cold water, and gasping, close to drowning, made his way from one end of the pool to the other. "Lucinda and I want *terribly* to see you," he said over his shoulder, his face set toward the Biswangers'. "We're sorry it's been so long and we'll call you *very* soon."

He crossed some fields to the Biswangers' and the sounds of revelry there. They would be honored to give him a drink, they would be happy to give him a drink. The Biswangers invited him and Lucinda for dinner four times a year, six weeks in advance.

They were always rebuffed and yet they continued to send out their invitations, unwilling to comprehend the rigid and undemocratic realities of their society. They were the sort of people who discussed the price of things at cocktails, exchanged market tips during dinner, and after dinner told dirty stories to mixed company. They did not belong to Neddy's set—they were not even on Lucinda's Christmas card list. He went toward their pool with feelings of indifference, charity, and some unease, since it seemed to be getting dark and these were the longest days of the year. The party when he joined it was noisy and large. Grace Biswanger was the kind of hostess who asked the optometrist, the veterinarian, the real-estate dealer, and the dentist. No one was swimming and the twilight, reflected on the water of the pool, had a wintry gleam. There was a bar and he started for this. When Grace Biswanger saw him she came toward him, not affectionately as he had every right to expect, but bellicosely.

"Why, this party has everything," she said loudly, "including a gate crasher."

She could not deal him a social blow—there was no question about this and he 35
did not flinch. "As a gate crasher," he asked politely, "do I rate a drink?"

"Suit yourself," she said. "You don't seem to pay much attention to invitations."

She turned her back on him and joined some guests, and he went to the bar and ordered a whiskey. The bartender served him but he served him rudely. His was a world in which the caterer's men kept the social score, and to be rebuffed by a part-time barkeep meant that he had suffered some loss of social esteem. Or perhaps the man was new and uninformed. Then he heard Grace at his back say: "They went for broke overnight—nothing but income—and he showed up drunk one Sunday and asked us to loan him five thousand dollars. . . ." She was always talking about money. It was worse than eating your peas off a knife. He dove into the pool, swam its length, and went away.

The next pool on his list, the last but two, belonged to his old mistress, Shirley Adams. If he had suffered any injuries at the Biswangers' they would be cured here. Love—sexual roughhouse in fact—was the supreme elixir, the pain killer, the brightly colored pill that would put the spring back into his step, the joy of life in his heart. They had had an affair last week, last month, last year. He couldn't remember. It was he who had broken it off, his was the upper hand, and he stepped through the gate of the wall that surrounded her pool with nothing so considered as self-confidence. It seemed in a way to be his pool, as the lover, particularly the illicit lover, enjoys the possessions of his mistress with an authority unknown to holy matrimony. She was there, her hair the color of brass, but her figure, at the edge of the lighted, cerulean water, excited in him no profound memories. It had been, he thought, a lighthearted affair, although she had wept when he broke it off. She seemed confused to see him and he wondered if she was still wounded. Would she, God forbid, weep again?

"What do you want?" she asked.

"I'm swimming across the county."

"Good Christ. Will you ever grow up?"

What's the matter?"

"If you've come here for money," she said, "I won't give you another cent."

"You could give me a drink."

"I could but I won't. I'm not alone."

"Well, I'm on my way."

He dove in and swam the pool, but when he tried to haul himself up onto the curb he found that the strength in his arms and shoulders had gone, and he paddled to the ladder and climbed out. Looking over his shoulder he saw, in the lighted bathhouse, a young man. Going out onto the dark lawn he smelled chrysanthemums or marigolds—some stubborn autumnal fragrance—on the night air, strong as gas. Looking overhead he saw that the stars had come out, but why should he seem to see Andromeda, Cepheus, and Cassiopeia? What had become of the constellations of midsummer? He began to cry.

It was probably the first time in his adult life that he had ever cried, certainly the first time in his life that he had ever felt so miserable, cold, tired, and bewildered. He could not understand the rudeness of the caterer's barkeep or the rudeness of a mistress who had come to him on her knees and showered his trousers with tears. He had swum too long, he had been immersed too long, and his nose and his throat were sore from the water. What he needed then was a drink, some company, and some clean, dry clothes, and while he could have cut directly across the road to his home he went on to the Gilmartins' pool. Here, for the first time in his life, he did not dive but went down the steps into the icy water and swam a hobbled sidestroke that he might have learned as a youth. He staggered with fatigue on his way to the Clydes' and paddled the length of their pool, stopping again and again with his hand on the curb to rest. He climbed up the ladder and wondered if he had the strength to get home. He had done what he wanted, he had swum the county, but he was so stupefied with exhaustion that his triumph seemed vague. Stooped, holding on to the gateposts for support, he turned up the driveway of his own house.

The place was dark. Was it so late that they had all gone to bed? Had Lucinda stayed at the Westerhazys' for supper? Had the girls joined her there or gone someplace else? Hadn't they agreed, as they usually did on Sunday, to regret all their invitations and stay at home? He tried the garage doors to see what cars were in but the doors were locked and rust came off the handles onto his hands. Going toward the house, he saw the force of the thunderstorm had knocked one of the rain gutters loose. It hung down over the front door like an umbrella rib, but it could be fixed in the morning. The house was locked, and he thought that the stupid cook or the stupid maid must have locked the place up until he remembered that it had been some time since they had employed a maid or a cook. He shouted, pounded on the door, tried to force it with his shoulder, and then, looking in at the windows, saw that the place was empty.

Questions

1. How is setting used symbolically in the story? Focus on such details as the change in weather and specific locales such as the highway and the public pool.
2. How is Neddy Merrill presented in the beginning of the story (especially paragraphs 2 and 3)? How would you describe the narrator's tone, and what does that tone communicate about the narrator's attitude toward Neddy?
3. At what point do you begin to realize that all is not what it appears to be on the surface? What textual details lead you to that realization?
4. How does Cheever communicate the passing of time and Neddy's aging? Cite specific passages from the story to back up your answer.
5. Does Neddy himself function symbolically in the story? If so, what might he be a symbol of?
6. In paragraph 3, Neddy decides that "he would name the stream Lucinda after his wife." What does that decision suggest at the beginning of the story? What does it suggest at the end?

Ursula K. Le Guin

The Ones Who Walk Away from Omelas   1975

Ursula Kroeber Le Guin was born in 1929 on St.
Ursula's Day (October 21) in Berkeley, California,
the only daughter and youngest child of Theodora
Kroeber, a folklorist, and Alfred Kroeber, a
renowned anthropologist. Le Guin attended
Radcliffe College, where she graduated Phi Beta
Kappa, and then entered Columbia University to
do graduate work in French and Italian literature.
While completing her M.A., she wrote her first
stories. On a Fulbright fellowship to France, she
met Charles Le Guin, a professor of French his-
tory, whom she married in Paris in 1953. Over
the next decade Le Guin reared three children and
worked on her writing in private.

Ursula K. Le Guin

 In the early sixties Le Guin began publishing
in both science fiction pulp magazines and acade-
mic journals. In 1966 her first novel, Rocannon's World, *was published as an Ace science*
fiction paperback original—hardly a respectable format for the debut of one of America's
premier writers. In 1968 Le Guin published A Wizard of Earthsea, *the first novel in her*
Earthsea Trilogy, now considered a classic of children's literature. The next two volumes,
The Tombs of Atuan *(1971), which won a Newbery citation, and* The Farthest Shore
(1972), which won a National Book Award, brought Le Guin mainstream acclaim.

 Le Guin's novels The Left Hand of Darkness *(1969) and* The Dispossessed *(1974)*
won both the Hugo and the Nebula awards, science fiction's two most prized honors. She
also twice won the Hugo for best short story, including the 1974 award for "The Ones Who
Walk Away from Omelas." Le Guin has published more than thirty novels and volumes of
short stories. She lives in Portland, Oregon.

 One of the few science fiction writers whose work has earned general critical acclaim,
Le Guin belongs most naturally in the company of major novelists of ideas such as Aldous
Huxley, George Orwell, and Anthony Burgess, who have used the genre of science fiction
to explore the possible consequences of ideological rather than technological change. Le Guin
has been especially concerned with issues of social justice and equality. In her short stories—
such as "The Ones Who Walk Away from Omelas"—she creates complex imaginary
civilizations, envisioned with anthropological authority, and her aim is less to imagine alien
cultures than to explore humanity.

  With a clamor of bells that set the swallows soaring, the Festival of Summer
came to the city. Omelas bright-towered by the sea. The rigging of the boats in har-
bor sparkled with flags. In the streets between houses with red roofs and painted
walls, between old moss-grown gardens and under avenues of trees, past great parks
and public buildings, processions moved. Some were decorous: old people in long stiff
robes of mauve and grey, grave master workmen, quiet, merry women carrying their
babies and chatting as they walked. In other streets the music beat faster, a shimmering of gong and tambourine, and the people went dancing, the procession was a
dance. Children dodged in and out, their high calls rising like the swallows' crossing

flights over the music and the singing. All the processions wound towards the north side of the city, where on the great water-meadow called the Green Fields boys and girls, naked in the bright air, with mud-stained feet and ankles and long, lithe arms, exercised their restive horses before the race. The horses wore no gear at all but a halter without bit. Their manes were braided with streamers of silver, gold, and green. They flared their nostrils and pranced and boasted to one another; they were vastly excited, the horse being the only animal who has adopted our ceremonies as his own. Far off to the north and west the mountains stood up half encircling Omelas on her bay. The air of morning was so clear that the snow still crowning the Eighteen Peaks burned with white-gold fire across the miles of sunlit air, under the dark blue of the sky. There was just enough wind to make the banners that marked the racecourse snap and flutter now and then. In the silence of the broad green meadows one could hear the music winding through the city streets, farther and nearer and ever approaching, a cheerful faint sweetness of the air that from time to time trembled and gathered together and broke out into the great joyous clanging of the bells.

Joyous! How is one to tell about joy? How describe the citizens of Omelas?

They were not simple folk, you see, though they were happy. But we do not say the words of cheer much any more. All smiles have become archaic. Given a description such as this one tends to make certain assumptions. Given a description such as this one tends to look next for the King, mounted on a splendid stallion and surrounded by his noble knights, or perhaps in a golden litter borne by great-muscled slaves. But there was no king. They did not use swords, or keep slaves. They were not barbarians. I do not know the rules and laws of their society, but I suspect that they were singularly few. As they did without monarchy and slavery, so they also got on without the stock exchange, the advertisement, the secret police, and the bomb. Yet I repeat that these were not simple folk, not dulcet shepherds, noble savages, bland utopians. They were not less complex than us. The trouble is that we have a bad habit, encouraged by pedants and sophisticates, of considering happiness as something rather stupid. Only pain is intellectual, only evil interesting. This is the treason of the artist: a refusal to admit the banality of evil and the terrible boredom of pain. If you can't lick 'em, join 'em. If it hurts, repeat it. But to praise despair is to condemn delight, to embrace violence is to lose hold of everything else. We have almost lost hold; we can no longer describe a happy man, nor make any celebration of joy. How can I tell you about the people of Omelas? They were not naïve and happy children—though their children were, in fact, happy. They were mature, intelligent, passionate adults whose lives were not wretched. O miracle! but I wish I could describe it better. I wish I could convince you. Omelas sounds in my words like a city in a fairy tale, long ago and far away, once upon a time. Perhaps it would be best if you imagined it as your own fancy bids, assuming it will rise to the occasion, for certainly I cannot suit you all. For instance, how about technology? I think that there would be no cars or helicopters in and above the streets; this follows from the fact that the people of Omelas are happy people. Happiness is based on a just discrimination of what is necessary, what is neither necessary nor destructive, and what is destructive. In the middle category, however—that of the unnecessary but undestructive, that of comfort, luxury, exuberance, etc.—they could perfectly well have central heating, subway trains, washing machines, and all kinds of marvelous devices not yet invented here, floating light-sources, fuelless power, a cure for the common cold. Or they could have none of that: it doesn't matter. As you like it. I incline to think that people from towns up and down the coast have

been coming in to Omelas during the last days before the Festival on very fast little trains and double-decked trams, and that the train station of Omelas is actually the handsomest building in town, though plainer than the magnificent
Farmers' Market. But even granted trains, I fear that Omelas so far strikes some of
you as goody-goody. Smiles, bells, parades, horses, bleh. If so, please add an orgy.
If an orgy would help, don't hesitate. Let us not, however, have temples from
which issue beautiful nude priests and priestesses already half in ecstasy and ready
to copulate with any man or woman, lover or stranger, who desires union with
the deep godhead of the blood, although that was my first idea. But really it
would be better not to have any temples in Omelas—at least, not manned temples. Religion yes, clergy no. Surely the beautiful nudes can just wander about, offering themselves like divine soufflés to the hunger of the needy and the rapture of
the flesh. Let them join the processions. Let tambourines be struck above the copu-
lations, and the glory of desire be proclaimed upon the gongs, and (a not unimportant point) let the offspring of these delightful rituals be beloved and looked after
by all. One thing I know there is none of in Omelas is guilt. But what else should
there be? I thought at first there were no drugs, but that is puritanical. For those
who like it, the faint insistent sweetness of *drooz* may perfume the ways of the
city, *drooz* which first brings a great lightness and brilliance to the mind and
limbs, and then after some hours a dreamy languor, and wonderful visions at last
of the very arcana and inmost secrets of the Universe, as well as exciting the
pleasure of sex beyond all belief; and it is not habit-forming. For more modest
tastes I think there ought to be beer. What else, what else belongs in the joyous
city? The sense of victory, surely, the celebration of courage. But as we did without clergy, let us do without soldiers. The joy built upon successful slaughter is not
the right kind of joy; it will not do; it is fearful and it is trivial. A boundless and
generous contentment, a magnanimous triumph felt not against some outer enemy
but in communion with the finest and fairest in the souls of all men everywhere
and the splendor of the world's summer: this is what swells the hearts of the people
of Omelas, and the victory they celebrate is that of life. I really don't think many
of them need to take *drooz*.

Most of the processions have reached the Green Fields by now. A marvelous
smell of cooking goes forth from the red and blue tents of the provisioners. The faces
of small children are amiably sticky; in the benign grey beard of a man a couple of
crumbs of rich pastry are entangled. The youths and girls have mounted their horses
and are beginning to group around the starting line of the course. An old woman,
small, fat, and laughing, is passing out flowers from a basket, and tall young men wear
her flowers in their shining hair. A child of nine or ten sits at the edge of the crowd,
alone, playing on a wooden flute. People pause to listen, and they smile, but they do
not speak to him, for he never ceases playing and never sees them, his dark eyes
wholly rapt in the sweet, thin magic of the tune.

He finishes, and slowly lowers his hands holding the wooden flute.   5

As if that little private silence were the signal, all at once a trumpet sounds from
the pavilion near the starting line: imperious, melancholy, piercing. The horses rear
on their slender legs, and some of them neigh in answer. Sober-faced, the young riders stroke the horses' necks and soothe them, whispering, "Quiet, quiet, there my
beauty, my hope. . . ." They begin to form in rank along the starting line. The crowds
along the racecourse are like a field of grass and flowers in the wind. The Festival of
Summer has begun.

Do you believe? Do you accept the festival, the city, the joy? No? Then let me describe one more thing.

In a basement under one of the beautiful public buildings of Omelas, or perhaps in the cellar of one of its spacious private homes, there is a room. It has one locked door, and no window. A little light seeps in dustily between cracks in the boards, secondhand from a cobwebbed window somewhere across the cellar. In one corner of the little room a couple of mops, with stiff, clotted, foul-smelling heads, stand near a rusty bucket. The floor is dirt, a little damp to the touch, as cellar dirt usually is. The room is about three paces long and two wide: a mere broom closet or disused tool room. In the room a child is sitting. It could be a boy or a girl. It looks about six, but actually is nearly ten. It is feeble-minded. Perhaps it was born defective, or perhaps it has become imbecile through fear, malnutrition, and neglect. It picks its nose and occasionally fumbles vaguely with its toes or genitals, as it sits hunched in the corner farthest from the bucket and the two mops. It is afraid of the mops. It finds them horrible. It shuts its eyes, but it knows the mops are still standing there; and the door is locked; and nobody will come. The door is always locked; and nobody ever comes, except that sometimes—the child has no understanding of time or interval—sometimes the door rattles terribly and opens, and a person, or several people, are there. One of them may come in and kick the child to make it stand up. The others never come close, but peer in at it with frightened, disgusted eyes. The food bowl and the water jug are hastily filled, the door is locked, the eyes disappear. The people at the door never say anything, but the child, who has not always lived in the tool room, and can remember sunlight and its mother's voice, sometimes speaks. "I will be good," it says. "Please let me out. I will be good!" They never answer. The child used to scream for help at night, and cry a good deal, but now it only makes a kind of whining, "eh-haa, eh-haa," and it speaks less and less often. It is so thin there are no calves to its legs; its belly protrudes; it lives on a half-bowl of corn meal and grease a day. It is naked. Its buttocks and thighs are a mass of festered sores, as it sits in its own excrement continually.

They all know it is there, all the people of Omelas. Some of them have come to see it, others are content merely to know it is there. They all know that it has to be there. Some of them understand why, and some do not, but they all understand that their happiness, the beauty of their city, the tenderness of their friendships, the health of their children, the wisdom of their scholars, the skill of their makers, even the abundance of their harvest and the kindly weathers of their skies, depend wholly on this child's abominable misery.

This is usually explained to children when they are between eight and twelve, 10 whenever they seem capable of understanding; and most of those who come to see the child are young people, though often enough an adult comes, or comes back, to see the child. No matter how well the matter has been explained to them, these young spectators are always shocked and sickened at the sight. They feel disgust, which they had thought themselves superior to. They feel anger, outrage, impotence, despite all the explanations. They would like to do something for the child. But there is nothing they can do. If the child were brought up into the sunlight out of that vile place, if it were cleaned and fed and comforted, that would be a good thing, indeed; but if it were done, in that day and hour all the prosperity and beauty and delight of Omelas would wither and be destroyed. Those are the terms. To exchange all the goodness and grace of every life in Omelas for that single, small improvement: to throw away the happiness of thousands for the chance of the happiness of one: that would be to let guilt within the walls indeed.

The terms are strict and absolute; there may not even be a kind word spoken to the child.

Often the young people go home in tears, or in a tearless rage, when they have seen the child and faced this terrible paradox. They may brood over it for weeks or years. But as time goes on they begin to realize that even if the child could be released, it would not get much good of its freedom: a little vague pleasure of warmth and food, no doubt, but little more. It is too degraded and imbecile to know any real joy. It has been afraid too long ever to be free of fear. Its habits are too uncouth for it to respond to humane treatment. Indeed, after so long it would probably be wretched without walls about it to protect it, and darkness for its eyes, and its own excrement to sit in. Their tears at the bitter injustice dry when they begin to perceive the terrible justice of reality, and to accept it. Yet it is their tears and anger, the trying of their generosity and the acceptance of their helplessness, which are perhaps the true source of the splendor of their lives. Theirs is no vapid, irresponsible happiness. They know that they, like the child, are not free. They know compassion. It is the existence of the child, and their knowledge of its existence, that makes possible the nobility of their architecture, the poignancy of their music, the profundity of their science. It is because of the child that they are so gentle with children. They know that if the wretched one were not there snivelling in the dark, the other one, the flute-player, could make no joyful music as the young riders line up in their beauty for the race in the sunlight of the first morning of summer.

Now do you believe in them? Are they not more credible? But there is one more thing to tell, and this is quite incredible.

At times one of the adolescent girls or boys who go to see the child does not go home to weep or rage, does not, in fact, go home at all. Sometimes also a man or woman much older falls silent for a day or two, and then leaves home. These people go out into the street, and walk down the street alone. They keep walking, and walk straight out of the city of Omelas, through the beautiful gates. They keep walking across the farmlands of Omelas. Each one goes alone, youth or girl, man or woman. Night falls; the traveler must pass down village streets, between the houses with yellow-lit windows, and on out into the darkness of the fields. Each alone, they go west or north, toward the mountains. They go on. They leave Omelas, they walk ahead into the darkness, and they do not come back. The place they go towards is a place even less imaginable to most of us than the city of happiness. I cannot describe it at all. It is possible that it does not exist. But they seem to know where they are going, the ones who walk away from Omelas.

Questions

1. Does the narrator live in Omelas? What do we know about the narrator's society?
2. What is the narrator's opinion of Omelas? Does the author seem to share that opinion?
3. What is the narrator's attitude toward "the ones who walk away from Omelas"? Would the narrator have been one of those who walked away?
4. How do you account for the narrator's willingness to let us readers add anything we like to the story?—"If an orgy would help, don't hesitate" (paragraph 3). Doesn't Ursula Le Guin care what her story includes?
5. What is suggested by the locked, dark cellar in which the child sits? What other details in the story are suggestive enough to be called symbolic?
6. Do you find in the story any implied criticism of our own society?

Shirley Jackson

The Lottery 1948

*Shirley Jackson (1919–1965), a native of San Francisco, moved in her teens to Rochester, New York. She started college at the University of Rochester, but had to drop out, stricken by severe depression, a problem that was to recur at intervals throughout her life. Later she graduated from Syracuse University. With her husband, Stanley Edgar Hyman, a literary critic, she settled in Bennington, Vermont, in a sprawling house built in the nineteenth century. There Jackson conscientiously set herself to produce a fixed number of words each day. She wrote novels—*The Road Through the Wall *(1948)— and three psychological thrillers—*Hangsaman *(1951),* The Haunting of Hill House *(1959), and* We Have Always Lived in the Castle *(1962). She wrote light, witty articles for* Good Housekeeping *and other popular magazines about the horrors of housekeeping and rearing four children, collected in* Life Among the Savages *(1953) and* Raising Demons *(1957); but she claimed to have written these only for money. When "The Lottery" appeared in the* New Yorker *in 1948, that issue of the magazine quickly sold out. Her purpose in writing the story, Jackson declared, had been "to shock the story's readers with a graphic demonstration of the pointless violence and general inhumanity in their own lives."*

The morning of June 27th was clear and sunny, with the fresh warmth of a full-summer day; the flowers were blossoming profusely and the grass was richly green. The people of the village began to gather in the square, between the post office and the bank, around ten o'clock; in some towns there were so many people that the lottery took two days and had to be started on June 26th, but in this village, where there were only about three hundred people, the whole lottery took less than two hours, so it could begin at ten o'clock in the morning and still be through in time to allow the villagers to get home for noon dinner.

The children assembled first, of course. School was recently over for the summer, and the feeling of liberty sat uneasily on most of them; they tended to gather together quietly for a while before they broke into boisterous play, and their talk was still of the classroom and the teacher, of books and reprimands. Bobby Martin had already stuffed his pockets full of stones, and the other boys soon followed his example, selecting the smoothest and roundest stones; Bobby and Harry Jones and Dickie Delacroix—the villagers pronounced this name "Dellacroy"—eventually made a great pile of stones in one corner of the square and guarded it against the raids of the other boys. The girls stood aside, talking among themselves, looking over their shoulders at the boys, and the very small children rolled in the dust or clung to the hands of their older brothers or sisters.

Soon the men began to gather, surveying their own children, speaking of planting and rain, tractors and taxes. They stood together, away from the pile of stones in the corner, and their jokes were quiet and they smiled rather than laughed. The women, wearing faded house dresses and sweaters, came shortly after their menfolk. They greeted one another and exchanged bits of gossip as they went to join their husbands. Soon the women, standing by their husbands, began to call to their children, and the children came reluctantly, having to be called four or five times. Bobby Martin ducked under his mother's grasping hand and ran, laughing, back to the pile of stones. His father spoke up sharply, and Bobby came quickly and took his place between his father and his oldest brother.

The lottery was conducted—as were the square dances, the teenage club, the Halloween program—by Mr. Summers, who had time and energy to devote to civic activities. He was a roundfaced, jovial man and he ran the coal business, and people were sorry for him, because he had no children and his wife was a scold. When he arrived in the square, carrying the black wooden box, there was a murmur of conversation among the villagers and he waved and called, "Little late today, folks." The postmaster, Mr. Graves, followed him, carrying a three-legged stool, and the stool was put in the center of the square and Mr. Summers set the black box down on it. The villagers kept their distance, leaving a space between themselves and the stool, and when Mr. Summers said, "Some of you fellows want to give me a hand?" there was a hesitation before two men, Mr. Martin and his oldest son, Baxter, came forward to hold the box steady on the stool while Mr. Summers stirred up the papers inside it.

The original paraphernalia for the lottery had been lost long ago, and the black box now resting on the stool had been put into use even before Old Man Warner, the oldest man in town, was born. Mr. Summers spoke frequently to the villagers about making a new box, but no one liked to upset even as much tradition as was represented by the black box. There was a story that the present box had been made with some pieces of the box that had preceded it, the one that had been constructed when the first people settled down to make a village here. Every year, after the lottery, Mr. Summers began talking again about a new box, but every year the subject was allowed to fade off without anything's being done. The black box grew shabbier each year; by now it was no longer completely black but splintered badly along one side to show the original wood color, and in some places faded or stained.

Mr. Martin and his oldest son, Baxter, held the black box securely on the stool until Mr. Summers had stirred the papers thoroughly with his hand. Because so much of the ritual had been forgotten or discarded, Mr. Summers had been successful in having slips of paper substituted for the chips of wood that had been used for generations. Chips of wood, Mr. Summers had argued, had been all very well when the village was tiny, but now that the population was more than three hundred and likely to keep on growing, it was necessary to use something that would fit more easily into the black box. The night before the lottery, Mr. Summers and Mr. Graves made up the slips of paper and put them in the box, and it was then taken to the safe of Mr. Summers's coal company and locked up until Mr. Summers was ready to take it to the square next morning. The rest of the year, the box was put away, sometimes one place, sometimes another; it had spent one year in Mr. Graves's barn and another year underfoot in the post office, and sometimes it was set on a shelf in the Martin grocery and left there.

There was a great deal of fussing to be done before Mr. Summers declared the lottery open. There were lists to make up—of heads of families, heads of households in each family, members of each household in each family. There was the proper swearing-in of Mr. Summers by the postmaster, as the official of the lottery; at one time, some people remembered, there had been a recital of some sort, performed by the official of the lottery, a perfunctory, tuneless chant that had been rattled off duly each year; some people believed that the official of the lottery used to stand just so when he said or sang it, others believed that he was supposed to walk among the people, but years and years ago this part of the ritual had been allowed to lapse. There had been, also, a ritual salute, which the official of the lottery had had to use in addressing each person who came up to draw from the box, but this also had changed with time, until now it was felt necessary only

5

for the official to speak to each person approaching. Mr. Summers was very good at all this; in his clean white shirt and blue jeans, with one hand resting carelessly on the black box, he seemed very proper and important as he talked interminably to Mr. Graves and the Martins.

Just as Mr. Summers finally left off talking and turned to the assembled villagers, Mrs. Hutchinson came hurriedly along the path to the square, her sweater thrown over her shoulders, and slid into place in the back of the crowd. "Clean forgot what day it was," she said to Mrs. Delacroix, who stood next to her, and they both laughed softly. "Thought my old man was out back stacking wood," Mrs. Hutchinson went on, "and then I looked out the window and the kids were gone, and then I remembered it was the twenty-seventh and came a-running." She dried her hands on her apron, and Mrs. Delacroix said, "You're in time, though. They're still talking away up there."

Mrs. Hutchinson craned her neck to see through the crowd and found her husband and children standing near the front. She tapped Mrs. Delacroix on the arm as a farewell and began to make her way through the crowd. The people separated good-humoredly to let her through; two or three people said, in voices just loud enough to be heard across the crowd, "Here comes your Missus, Hutchinson," and "Bill, she made it after all." Mrs. Hutchinson reached her husband, and Mr. Summers, who had been waiting, said cheerfully, "Thought we were going to have to get on without you, Tessie." Mrs. Hutchinson said, grinning, "Wouldn't have me leave m'dishes in the sink, now would you, Joe?" and soft laughter ran through the crowd as the people stirred back into position after Mrs. Hutchinson's arrival.

"Well, now," Mr. Summers said soberly, "guess we better get started, get this over 10 with, so's we can go back to work. Anybody ain't here?"

"Dunbar," several people said. "Dunbar, Dunbar."

Mr. Summers consulted his list. "Clyde Dunbar," he said. "That's right. He's broke his leg, hasn't he? Who's drawing for him?"

"Me, I guess," a woman said, and Mr. Summers turned to look at her. "Wife draws for her husband," Mr. Summers said. "Don't you have a grown boy to do it for you, Janey?" Although Mr. Summers and everyone else in the village knew the answer perfectly well, it was the business of the official of the lottery to ask such questions formally. Mr. Summers waited with an expression of polite interest while Mrs. Dunbar answered.

"Horace's not but sixteen yet," Mrs. Dunbar said regretfully. "Guess I gotta fill in for the old man this year."

"Right," Mr. Summers said. He made a note on the list he was holding. Then he 15 asked, "Watson boy drawing this year?"

A tall boy in the crowd raised his hand. "Here," he said. "I'm drawing for m'mother and me." He blinked his eyes nervously and ducked his head as several voices in the crowd said things like "Good fellow, Jack," and "Glad to see your mother's got a man to do it."

"Well," Mr. Summers said, "guess that's everyone. Old Man Warner make it?"

"Here," a voice said, and Mr. Summers nodded.

A sudden hush fell on the crowd as Mr. Summers cleared his throat and looked at the list. "All ready?" he called. "Now, I'll read the names—heads of families first—and the men come up and take a paper out of the box. Keep the paper folded in your hand without looking at it until everyone has had a turn. Everything clear?"

The people had done it so many times that they only half listened to the direc-   20
tions; most of them were quiet, wetting their lips, not looking around. Then Mr.
Summers raised one hand high and said, "Adams." A man disengaged himself from the
crowd and came forward. "Hi, Steve," Mr. Summers said, and Mr. Adams said, "Hi,
Joe." They grinned at one another humorlessly and nervously. Then Mr. Adams
reached into the black box and took out a folded paper. He held it firmly by one corner
as he turned and went hastily back to his place in the crowd, where he stood a little
apart from his family, not looking down at his hand.

"Allen," Mr. Summers said. "Anderson. . . . Bentham."

"Seems like there's no time at all between lotteries any more," Mrs. Delacroix
said to Mrs. Graves in the back row. "Seems like we got through with the last one
only last week."

"Time sure goes fast," Mrs. Graves said.

"Clark. . . . Delacroix."

"There goes my old man," Mrs. Delacroix said. She held her breath while her   25
husband went forward.

"Dunbar," Mr. Summers said, and Mrs. Dunbar went steadily to the box while
one of the women said, "Go on, Janey," and another said, "There she goes."

"We're next," Mrs. Graves said. She watched while Mr. Graves came around
from the side of the box, greeted Mr. Summers gravely, and selected a slip of paper
from the box. By now, all through the crowd there were men holding the small folded
papers in their large hands, turning them over and over nervously. Mrs. Dunbar and
her two sons stood together, Mrs. Dunbar holding the slip of paper.

"Harburt. . . . Hutchinson."

"Get up there, Bill," Mrs. Hutchinson said, and the people near her laughed.

"Jones."   30

"They do say," Mr. Adams said to Old Man Warner, who stood next to him,
"that over in the north village they're talking of giving up the lottery."

Old Man Warner snorted. "Pack of crazy fools," he said. "Listening to the young
folks, nothing's good enough for *them*. Next thing you know, they'll be wanting to go
back to living in caves, nobody work any more, live *that* way for a while. Used to be a
saying about 'Lottery in June, corn be heavy soon.' First thing you know, we'd all be
eating stewed chickweed and acorns. There's *always* been a lottery," he added petu-
lantly. "Bad enough to see young Joe Summers up there joking with everybody."

"Some places have already quit lotteries," Mrs. Adams said.

"Nothing but trouble in *that*," Old Man Warner said stoutly. "Pack of young fools."

"Martin." And Bobby Martin watched his father go forward. "Overdyke. . . . Percy."   35

"I wish they'd hurry," Mrs. Dunbar said to her older son. "I wish they'd hurry."

"They're almost through," her son said.

"You get ready to run tell Dad," Mrs. Dunbar said.

Mr. Summers called his own name and then stepped forward precisely and
selected a slip from the box. Then he called, "Warner."

"Seventy-seventh year I been in the lottery," Old Man Warner said as he went   40
through the crowd. "Seventy-seventh time."

"Watson." The tall boy came awkwardly through the crowd. Someone said,
"Don't be nervous, Jack," and Mr. Summers said, "Take your time, son."

"Zanini."

After that, there was a long pause, a breathless pause, until Mr. Summers, holding his slip of paper in the air, said, "All right, fellows." For a minute, no one moved,

and then all the slips of paper were opened. Suddenly, all the women began to speak at once, saying, "Who is it?" "Who's got it?" "Is it the Dunbars?" "Is it the Watsons?" Then the voices began to say, "It's Hutchinson. It's Bill." "Bill Hutchinson's got it."

"Go tell your father," Mrs. Dunbar said to her older son.

People began to look around to see the Hutchinsons. Bill Hutchinson was standing quiet, staring down at the paper in his hand. Suddenly, Tessie Hutchinson shouted to Mr. Summers, "You didn't give him time enough to take any paper he wanted. I saw you. It wasn't fair!"

"Be a good sport, Tessie," Mrs. Delacroix called, and Mrs. Graves said, "All of us took the same chance."

"Shut up, Tessie," Bill Hutchinson said.

"Well, everyone," Mr. Summers said, "that was done pretty fast, and now we've got to be hurrying a little more to get done in time." He consulted his next list. "Bill," he said, "you draw for the Hutchinson family. You got any other households in the Hutchinsons?"

"There's Don and Eva," Mrs. Hutchinson yelled. "Make them take their chance!"

"Daughters draw with their husbands' families, Tessie," Mr. Summers said gently. "You know that as well as anyone else."

"It wasn't fair," Tessie said.

"I guess not, Joe," Bill Hutchinson said regretfully. "My daughter draws with her husband's family, that's only fair. And I've got no other family except the kids."

"Then, as far as drawing for families is concerned, it's you," Mr. Summers said in explanation, "and as far as drawing for households is concerned, that's you, too. Right?"

"Right," Bill Hutchinson said.

"How many kids, Bill?" Mr. Summers asked formally.

"Three," Bill Hutchinson said. "There's Bill, Jr., and Nancy, and little Dave. And Tessie and me."

"All right, then," Mr. Summers said. "Harry, you got their tickets back?"

Mr. Graves nodded and held up the slips of paper. "Put them in the box, then," Mr. Summers directed. "Take Bill's and put it in."

"I think we ought to start over," Mrs. Hutchinson said, as quietly as she could. "I tell you it wasn't *fair*. You didn't give him time enough to choose. *Everybody* saw that."

Mr. Graves had selected the five slips and put them in the box, and he dropped all the papers but those onto the ground, where the breeze caught them and lifted them off.

"Listen, everybody," Mrs. Hutchinson was saying to the people around her.

"Ready, Bill?" Mr. Summers asked, and Bill Hutchinson, with one quick glance around at his wife and children, nodded.

"Remember," Mr. Summers said, "take the slips and keep them folded until each person has taken one. Harry, you help little Dave." Mr. Graves took the hand of the little boy, who came willingly with him up to the box. "Take a paper out of the box, Davy," Mr. Summers said. Davy put his hand into the box and laughed. "Take just *one* paper," Mr. Summers said. "Harry, you hold it for him." Mr. Graves took the child's hand and removed the folded paper from the tight fist and held it while little Dave stood next to him and looked up at him wonderingly.

"Nancy next," Mr. Summers said. Nancy was twelve, and her school friends breathed heavily as she went forward, switching her skirt, and took a slip daintily from the box. "Bill, Jr.," Mr. Summers said, and Billy, his face red and his feet over-large, nearly knocked the box over as he got a paper out. "Tessie," Mr. Summers said. She hesitated for a minute, looking around defiantly, and then set her lips and went up to the box. She snatched a paper out and held it behind her.

"Bill," Mr. Summers said, and Bill Hutchinson reached into the box and felt   65
around, bringing his hand out at last with the slip of paper in it.

The crowd was quiet. A girl whispered, "I hope it's not Nancy," and the sound of the whisper reached the edges of the crowd.

"It's not the way it used to be," Old Man Warner said clearly. "People ain't the way they used to be."

"All right," Mr. Summers said. "Open the papers. Harry, you open little Dave's."

Mr. Graves opened the slip of paper and there was a general sigh through the crowd as he held it up and everyone could see that it was blank. Nancy and Bill, Jr., opened theirs at the same time, and both beamed and laughed, turning around to the crowd and holding their slips of paper above their heads.

"Tessie," Mr. Summers said. There was a pause, and then Mr. Summers looked at   70
Bill Hutchinson, and Bill unfolded his paper and showed it. It was blank.

"It's Tessie," Mr. Summers said, and his voice was hushed. "Show us her paper, Bill."

Bill Hutchinson went over to his wife and forced the slip of paper out of her hand. It had a black spot on it, the black spot Mr. Summers had made the night before with the heavy pencil in the coal-company office. Bill Hutchinson held it up, and there was a stir in the crowd.

"All right, folks," Mr. Summers said, "Let's finish quickly."

Although the villagers had forgotten the ritual and lost the original black box, they still remembered to use stones. The pile of stones the boys had made earlier was ready; there were stones on the ground with the blowing scraps of paper that had come out of the box. Mrs. Delacroix selected a stone so large she had to pick it up with both hands and turned to Mrs. Dunbar. "Come on," she said. "Hurry up."

Mrs. Dunbar had small stones in both hands, and she said, gasping for breath, "I   75
can't run at all. You'll have to go ahead and I'll catch up with you."

The children had stones already, and someone gave little Davy Hutchinson a few pebbles.

Tessie Hutchinson was in the center of a cleared space by now, and she held her hands out desperately as the villagers moved in on her. "It isn't fair," she said. A stone hit her on the side of the head.

Old Man Warner was saying, "Come on, come on, everyone." Steve Adams was in the front of the crowd of villagers, with Mrs. Graves beside him.

"It isn't fair, it isn't right," Mrs. Hutchinson screamed, and then they were upon her.

Questions

1. Where do you think "The Lottery" takes place? What purpose do you suppose the writer has in making this setting appear so familiar and ordinary?
2. What details in paragraphs 2 and 3 foreshadow the ending of the story?
3. Take a close look at Jackson's description of the black wooden box (paragraph 5) and of the black spot on the fatal slip of paper (paragraph 72). What do these objects suggest to you? Are there any other symbols in the story?
4. What do you understand to be the writer's own attitude toward the lottery and the stoning? Exactly what in the story makes her attitude clear to us?

5. What do you make of Old Man Warner's saying, "Lottery in June, corn be heavy soon" (paragraph 32)?
6. What do you think Shirley Jackson is driving at? Consider each of the following interpretations and, looking at the story, see if you can find any evidence for it:

> Jackson takes a primitive fertility rite and playfully transfers it to a small town in North America.

> Jackson, writing her story soon after World War II, indirectly expresses her horror at the Holocaust. She assumes that the massacre of the Jews was carried out by unwitting, obedient people, like these villagers.

> Jackson is satirizing our own society, in which men are selected for the army by lottery.

> Jackson is just writing a memorable story that signifies nothing at all.

■ WRITING *effectively*

Shirley Jackson on Writing

Biography of a Story   (1960) 1968

My agent did not care for the story, but—as she said in her note at the time—her job was to sell it, not to like it. She sent it at once to the *New Yorker*, and about a week after the story had been written I received a telephone call from the fiction editor of the *New Yorker*; it was quite clear that he did not really care for the story, either, but the *New Yorker* was going to buy it. He asked for one change—that the date mentioned in the story be changed to coincide with the date of the issue of the magazine in which the story would appear, and I said of course. He then asked, hesitantly, if I had any particular interpretation of my own for the story; Mr. Harold Ross, then the editor of the *New Yorker*, was not altogether sure that he understood the story, and wondered if I cared to enlarge upon its meaning. I said no.

Shirley Jackson

Mr. Ross, he said, thought that the story might be puzzling to some people, and in case anyone telephoned the magazine, as sometimes happened, or wrote in asking about the story, was there anything in particular I wanted them to say? No, I said, nothing in particular; it was just a story I wrote.

I had no more preparation than that. I went on picking up the mail every morning, pushing my daughter up and down the hill in her stroller, anticipating pleasurably the check from the *New Yorker*, and shopping for groceries. The weather stayed nice and it looked as though it was going to be a good summer. Then, on June 28, the *New Yorker* came out with my story.

Things began mildly enough with a note from a friend at the *New Yorker:* "Your story has kicked up quite a fuss around the office," he wrote. I was flattered; it's nice to think that your friends notice what you write. Later that day there was a call from one of the magazine's editors; they had had a couple of people phone in about my story, he said, and was there anything I particularly wanted him to say if there were any more calls? No, I said, nothing particular; anything he chose to say was perfectly all right with me; it was just a story.

I was further puzzled by a cryptic note from another friend: "Heard a man talking about a story of yours on the bus this morning," she wrote. "Very exciting. I wanted to tell him I knew the author, but after I heard what he was saying I decided I'd better not."

One of the most terrifying aspects of publishing stories and books is the realization that they are going to be read, and read by strangers. I had never fully realized this before, although I had of course in my imagination dwelt lovingly upon the thought of millions and millions of people who were going to be uplifted and enriched and delighted by the stories I wrote. It had simply never occurred to me that these millions and millions of people might be so far from being uplifted that they would sit down and write me letters I was downright scared to open; of the three-hundred-odd letters that I received that summer I can count only thirteen that spoke kindly to me, and they were mostly from friends. Even my mother scolded me: "Dad and I did not care at all for your story in the *New Yorker*," she wrote sternly; "it does seem, dear, that this gloomy kind of story is what all you young people think about these days. Why don't you write something to cheer people up?"

By mid-July I had begun to perceive that I was very lucky indeed to be safely in Vermont, where no one in our small town had ever heard of the *New Yorker*, much less read my story. Millions of people, and my mother, had taken a pronounced dislike to me.

The magazine kept no track of telephone calls, but all letters addressed to me care of the magazine were forwarded directly to me for answering, and all letters addressed to the magazine—some of them addressed to Harold Ross personally; these were the most vehement—were answered at the magazine and then the letters were sent me in great batches, along with carbons of the answers written at the magazine. I have all the letters still, and if they could be considered to give any accurate cross section of the reading public, or the reading public of the *New Yorker*, or even the reading public of one issue of the *New Yorker*, I would stop writing now.

Judging from these letters, people who read stories are gullible, rude, frequently illiterate, and horribly afraid of being laughed at. Many of the writers were positive that the *New Yorker* was going to ridicule them in print; and the most cautious letters were headed, in capital letters: NOT FOR PUBLICATION or PLEASE DO NOT PRINT THIS LETTER, or, at best, THIS LETTER MAY BE PUBLISHED AT YOUR USUAL RATES OF PAYMENT. Anonymous letters, of which there were a few, were destroyed. The *New Yorker* never published any comment of any kind about the story in the magazine, but did issue one publicity release saying that the story had received more mail than any piece of fiction they had ever published; this was after the newspapers had gotten into the act, in midsummer, with a front-page story in the San Francisco *Chronicle* begging to know what the story meant, and a series of columns in New York and Chicago papers pointing out that *New Yorker* subscriptions were being canceled right and left.

Curiously, there are three main themes which dominate the letters of that first summer—three themes which might be identified as bewilderment, speculation, and plain old-fashioned abuse. In the years since then, during which the story has been anthologized, dramatized, televised, and even—in one completely mystifying transformation—made into a ballet, the tenor of letters I receive has changed. I am addressed more politely, as a rule, and the letters largely confine themselves to questions like what does this story mean? The general tone of the early letters, however, was a kind of wide-eyed, shocked innocence. People at first were not so much concerned with what the story meant; what they wanted to know was where these lotteries were held, and whether they could go there and watch.

From *Come Along with Me*

THINKING ABOUT SYMBOLS

One danger in analyzing a story's symbolism is the temptation to read symbolic meaning into *everything*. An image acquires symbolic resonance because it is organically important to the actions and emotions of the story.

- **Consider a symbolic object's relevance to the plot.** What events, characters, and ideas are associated with it? It also helps to remember that some symbols arrive with cultural baggage. Any great white whale that swims into a work of contemporary fiction will inevitably summon up the symbolic associations of Melville's Moby Dick.
- **Ask yourself what the symbol means to the protagonist of your story.** Writers don't simply assign arbitrary meanings to items in their stories; generally, a horse is a horse, and a hammer is just a hammer. Sometimes, though, an object means something more to a character. Think of the flowers in "The Chrysanthemums."
- **Remember: in literature, few symbols are hidden.** Don't go on a symbol hunt. As you read or reread a story, any real symbol will usually find you. If an object appears time and again, or is tied inextricably to the story's events, it is likely to suggest something beyond itself. When an object, an action, or a place has emotional or intellectual power beyond its literal importance, then it is a genuine symbol.

CHECKLIST: Writing About Symbols

- ☐ Which objects, actions, or places seem unusually significant?
- ☐ List the specific objects, people, and ideas with which a particular symbol is associated.
- ☐ Locate the exact place in the story where the symbol links itself to the other thing.
- ☐ Ask whether each symbol comes with ready-made cultural associations.
- ☐ Avoid far-fetched interpretations. Focus first on the literal things, places, and actions in the story.
- ☐ Don't make a symbol mean too much or too little. Don't limit it to one narrow association or claim it summons up many different things.
- ☐ Be specific. Identify the exact place in the story where a symbol takes on a deeper meaning.

WRITING ASSIGNMENT ON SYMBOLS

From the stories in this book, choose one with a strong central symbol. Explain how the symbol helps to communicate the story's meaning, citing specific moments in the text. Here is an example of a paper written on that topic by Samantha L. Brown, a student of Melinda Barth's at El Camino College.

SAMPLE STUDENT PAPER

Brown 1

Samantha L. Brown
Professor Barth
English 210
26 May 2009

An Analysis of the Symbolism in Steinbeck's
"The Chrysanthemums"

In a work of literature a symbol is something that suggests more than its surface meaning. In his short story "The Chrysanthemums," John Steinbeck uses the flowers of the title for both realistic and symbolic purposes. On the realistic level, the chrysanthemums advance the plot because they are the basis for the story's central action. They also help define the character of Elisa, provide a greater understanding of the setting, and play a vital part in revealing the story's theme.

The chrysanthemums provide the reader with insight into Elisa. When we first see her, she is in her flower garden working with her chrysanthemums. She is putting a great deal of energy into the relatively simple job of tending to the flowers. Elisa and her husband, Henry, have no children. They do not appear to have a very intense or passionate relationship. He praises her skill at growing flowers, but says that he wishes she would work in the orchard and grow larger apples for him. His interests are practical and financial. The beauty of the flowers, which also symbolizes her beauty as a woman, is not important to him.

"The Chrysanthemums" is set in rural Monterey, California, in the 1930s. The ranch where Elisa and Henry live is in an isolated area. The flower garden is isolated from the rest of the ranch. The reader sees that Elisa is unhappy and frustrated, emotionally isolated from her husband and the life of their ranch.

Thesis sentence

Clarification and elaboration of thesis

Topic sentence

Development of thesis

Textual evidence

Further development of thesis

Brown 2

The flower garden is also surrounded by a wire fence, which symbolizes Elisa's feelings of being fenced in. She shows such feelings later in the story when she envies the free and easy life of the tinker and wishes that women could live that way.

The symbolic significance of the chrysanthemums is especially brought out in Elisa's conversation with the tinker. At first she resists his attempts to repair something for her, but then she responds to him because he admires her flowers. When he describes them in a poetic-sounding way, she feels she has met someone like herself that she can share an emotional bond with. The feelings he arouses in her are passionate—even sexual, as we see when she stops herself from reaching out and touching his pants. This is also shown after he leaves, when she takes off her mannish gardening clothes, bathes, and looks at her body in the mirror.

The last and most painful symbolic use of the flowers comes toward the end of the story, when Elisa and her husband are driving into town for their evening out. Even before she can see it clearly, she knows that the speck by the side of the road is the chrysanthemum sprouts she gave the tinker to give to the (probably fictitious) woman he told her about. This is so upsetting to her that she turns around toward her husband so as not to see the tinker again as the car passes his wagon.

If we read the story only on the surface level, we won't be able to understand why Elisa is so upset. So a cunning traveler has manipulated her love of flowers to soften her up into giving him some work. Maybe he made a fool of her, but it's in the middle of the Depression, and he has to eat, too. What's the big deal? Only when we understand the symbolic importance of the chrysanthemums do we understand why this is so painful for her. She had felt that someone understood her, maybe even felt that life was richer in possibilities than it had seemed. This illusion is shattered, however, when she sees the plant sprouts. The discarded, dying plants symbolize her diminished life, her failure to find anyone who can understand her needs and feelings.

The chrysanthemums are vital to Steinbeck's presentation of the theme. At the beginning, Elisa is presented as a strong woman, strong enough to break the back of a calf. At the end, she is seen huddled like an old woman, crying weakly. The newly revealed Elisa is not the strong woman that she or her husband thought she was. It wasn't until she saw the discarded plant sprouts that she felt the sting of her rejection and isolation. Until that moment, her

Textual evidence

Further development of thesis

Textual evidence

Topic sentence announces culmination of thesis

Topic sentence on significance of symbolism

Elaboration of significance of symbolism

Elaboration of how symbol reveals theme

Brown 3

Conclusion sums up main idea without simply restating it

gardening had protected—or at least distracted—her from her loneliness, isolation, and feelings of inadequacy. Finally, the theme emerges from our understanding of this woman and the importance of her chrysanthemums. Understanding Steinbeck's symbolism, therefore, is essential to understanding how the story works.

MORE TOPICS FOR WRITING

1. Choose a story from this chapter. Describe your experience of reading that story, and of encountering its symbols. At what point did the main symbol's meaning become clear? What in the story indicated the larger importance of that symbol?

2. From any story in this book, select an object, or place, or action that seems clearly symbolic. How do you know? Now select an object, place, or action from the same story that clearly seems to signify no more than itself. How can you tell?

3. Analyze the symbolism in a story from "Stories for Further Reading." Some good choices might be "Dead Men's Path," "The Story of an Hour," and "Where Are You Going, Where Have You Been?" Choose a symbol that recurs over the course of the story, and look closely at each appearance it makes. How does the story's use of the symbol evolve?

4. In an essay of 600 to 800 words, compare and contrast the symbolic use of the scapegoat in "The Lottery" and "The Ones Who Walk Away from Omelas."

▶ TERMS FOR *review*

Symbol ▶ A person, place, or thing in a narrative that suggests meanings beyond its literal sense. Symbol is related to allegory, but it works more complexly. A symbol often contains multiple meanings and associations.

Conventional symbol ▶ A literary symbol that has a conventional or customary meaning for most readers—for example, a black cat crossing a path or a young bride in a white dress.

Symbolic act ▶ An action whose significance goes well beyond its literal meaning. In literature, symbolic acts often involve some conscious or unconscious ritual element such as rebirth, purification, forgiveness, vengeance, or initiation.

Allegory ▶ A narrative in which the literal events (persons, places, and things) consistently point to a parallel sequence of symbolic equivalents. This narrative strategy is often used to dramatize abstract ideas, historical events, religious systems, or political issues. An allegory has two levels of meaning: a literal level that tells a surface story and a symbolic level in which the abstract ideas unfold.

8

READING LONG STORIES AND NOVELS

The novel is the one bright book of life.

—D. H. LAWRENCE

Among the forms of imaginative literature in our language, the novel has been the favorite of both writers and readers for more than two hundred years. Broadly defined, a **novel** is a book-length fictional story in prose, whose author tries to create the sense that while we read, we experience actual life.

This sense of actuality, also found in artful short stories, may be the quality that sets the novel apart from other long prose narratives. Why do we not apply the name *novel* to, for instance, *Gulliver's Travels*? In his marvel-filled account of Lemuel Gulliver's voyages among pygmies, giants, civilized horses, and noxious humanoid swine, Jonathan Swift does not seem primarily to care if we find his story credible. Though he arrays the adventures of Gulliver in painstaking detail (and, ironically, has Gulliver swear to the truth of them), Swift neither attempts nor achieves a convincing illusion of life. For his book is a fantastic satire that finds resemblances between noble horses and man's reasoning faculties, between debased apes and man's kinship with the beasts.

ORIGINS OF THE NOVEL

Unlike other major literary forms—drama, lyric, ballad, and epic—the novel is a relative newcomer. Originally, the drama in ancient Greece came alive only when actors performed it; the epic or heroic poem (from the classic *Iliad* through the Old English *Beowulf*), only when a bard sang or chanted it. But the English novel came to maturity in literate times, in the eighteenth century, and by its nature was something different: a story to be communicated silently in printed books, at whatever moment and at whatever pace (whether quickly or slowly and meditatively) the reader desired.

Some definitions of the novel would more strictly define the form. "The Novel is a picture of real life and manners, and of the time in which it was written," declared Clara Reeve in 1785. By so specifying that the novel depicts life in the present day, the critic was probably observing the derivation of the word *novel*. Akin to the French word for "news" (*nouvelles*), it comes from the Italian *novella* ("something new and small"), a term applied to a newly made story taking place in recent times, and not a traditional story taking place long ago.

Romances

The novel, which is principally a realistic form, is often contrasted with the other major prose tradition of narrative, the **romance**. In general terms, romance is a narrative mode that employs exotic adventure and idealized emotion rather than realistic depiction of character and action. In the romantic mode—out of which most popular genre fictions develop—people, actions, and events are depicted more as we wish them to be (heroes are very brave, villains are very bad) than as the complex entities they usually are. Medieval romances (in both prose and verse) presented chivalric tales of kings, knights, and aristocratic ladies. Modern romances, emerging in the nineteenth century, were represented by adventure novels such as Sir Walter Scott's *Ivanhoe* which embodied the symbolic quests and idealized characters of earlier, chivalric tales in slightly more realistic terms, a tradition carried on in contemporary popular works such as the *Stars Wars* and James Bond films.

Novels Versus Romances

Also drawing a line between novel and romance, Nathaniel Hawthorne, in his preface to *The House of the Seven Gables* (1851), restricted the novel "not merely to the possible, but to the probable and ordinary course of man's experience." A romance had no such limitations. Such a definition would deny the name of *novel* to any fantastic or speculative story—to, say, the Gothic novel and the science fiction novel. Carefully bestowed, the labels *novel* and *romance* may be useful to distinguish between the true-to-life story of usual people in ordinary places (such as George Eliot's *Silas Marner* or Amy Tan's *The Joy Luck Club*) and the larger-than-life story of daring deeds and high adventure, set in the past or future or in some timeless land (such as Walter Scott's *Ivanhoe* or J. R. R. Tolkien's *The Lord of the Rings*). This sense of the actual is, perhaps, the hallmark of a novel, whether or not the events it relates are literally possible.

A student shouldn't worry too much about the differences between the novel and romance. In everyday conversation people usually refer to any book-length fictional narratives as "novels." The important thing to remember is that there are two fundamentally different ways of telling a story. The novelistic method stresses the everyday, realistic aspects. The romantic method stresses the aspects of adventure, surprise, and wish fulfillment. It is particularly interesting to see the rare occasions when authors deliberately stray across the boundary between the two modes. In Franz Kafka's *The Metamorphosis*, for example, the story begins with a fantastic premise—Gregor Samsa wakes to discover himself turned into a giant insect. This bizarre transformation would seem the very stuff of romance, but after the first sentence Kafka tells the story in the most matter-of-fact and realistic way. The stunning quality of Kafka's masterpiece comes from his novelistic manner of telling his seemingly unrealistic tale.

Novels and Journalism

Since both the novel and journalism try to capture the fabric of everyday life, there has long been a close relationship between the two literary forms. Many novelists, among them Ernest Hemingway, Stephen Crane, and Jack London, began their writing careers as cub reporters. Ambrose Bierce was the most influential newspaper satirist of his day.

The two modes of writing, however, remain different. "Literature is the art of writing something that will be read twice," commented critic and novelist Cyril

Connolly, "journalism what will be grasped at once." Journalism greatly influences how novelists depict the world around them. Stephen Crane's "The Open Boat" (Chapter 6) began as a newspaper account of his actual experiences in a small row-boat after the sinking of the *Commodore* in 1897. A journalist might have been content with such a gripping first-person story of surviving a shipwreck, but a great fiction writer has the gift of turning personal bad luck into art, and Crane eventually created a masterpiece of fiction based on fact.

NOVELISTIC METHODS

Many early novels were told in the form of letters. Sometimes these **epistolary novels** contained letters by only one character; often they contained letters exchanged by several of the characters in the book. By casting his novel *Pamela* (1740) into the form of personal letters, Samuel Richardson helped give the story the appearance of being not invented but discovered from real documents. Alice Walker's *The Color Purple* (1982) is a more recent epistolary novel, though some of the letters that tell the story are addressed to God.

Another method favored by novelists is to write as though setting down a memoir or an autobiography. Daniel Defoe, whose skill in feigning such memoirs was phenomenal, succeeded in writing the supposedly true confessions of a woman retired from a life of crime, *Moll Flanders* (1722), and in maintaining a vivid truthfulness:

> Going through Aldersgate Street, there was a pretty little child who had been at a dancing-school, and was going home all alone: and my prompter, like a true devil, set me upon this innocent creature. I talked to it, and it prattled to me again, and I took it by the hand and led it along till I came to a paved alley that goes into Bartholomew Close, and I led it in there. The child said that was not its way home. I said, "Yes, my dear, it is; I'll show you the way home." The child had a little necklace on of gold beads, and I had my eye upon that, and in the dark of the alley I stooped, pretending to mend the child's clog that was loose, and took off her necklace, and the child never felt it, and so led the child on again. Here, I say, the devil put me upon killing the child in the dark alley, that it might not cry, but the very thought frighted me so that I was ready to drop down; but I turned the child about and bade it go back again. . . . The last affair left no great concern upon me, for as I did the poor child no harm, I only said to myself, I had given the parents a just reproof for their negligence in leaving the poor little lamb to come home by itself, and it would teach them to take more care of it another time.

What could sound more like the voice of an experienced child-robber than this manner of excusing her crime, and even justifying it?

Some novelists place great emphasis on research and notetaking. James A. Michener, the internationally best-selling author of novels such as *Centennial* (which tracks life in Colorado from prehistory through modern times) and *Chesapeake* (which describes 400 years of events on Maryland's Eastern Shore), started work on a book by studying everything available about his chosen subject. He also traveled to locations that might appear in the book, interviewed local people, and compiled immense amounts of scientific, historical, and cultural data. Research alone, however, is not enough to produce a novel. A novel grows to completion only through the slow mental process of creation, selection, and arrangement. But raw facts can sometimes provide a beginning. Many novels started when the author read some arresting episode in a newspaper or magazine. Theodore Dreiser's impressive study of a murder, *An American Tragedy* (1925), for example, was inspired by a journalist's account of a real-life case.

Nonfiction Novels

In the 1960s there was a great deal of talk about the **nonfiction novel**, in which the author presents actual people and events in story form. The vogue of the nonfiction novel was created by Truman Capote's *In Cold Blood* (1966), which depicts an actual multiple murder and the resulting trial in Kansas. Capote traveled to the scene of the crime and interviewed all of the principal parties, including the murderers. Norman Mailer wrote a similar novel, *The Executioner's Song* (1979), chronicling the life and death of Gary Gilmore, the Utah murderer who demanded his own execution. More recently, John Berendt's darkly comic 1994 account of the upper class and under class of Savannah, Georgia, *Midnight in the Garden of Good and Evil* (which also centers on a murder and the subsequent trial), revived interest in the form.

Perhaps the name "nonfiction novel" (Capote's term for it) is newer than the form. In the past, writers of autobiography have cast their memoirs into what looks like novel form: Richard Wright in *Black Boy* (1945), William Burroughs in *Junkie* (1953). Derived from his reporting, John Hersey's *Hiroshima* (1946) reconstructs the lives of six survivors of the atom bomb as if they were fictional. In reading such works we may nearly forget we are reading literal truth, so well do the techniques of the novel lend an air of immediacy to remembered facts.

Historical Novels

A familiar kind of fiction that claims a basis in fact is the **historical novel**, a detailed reconstruction of life in another time, perhaps in another place. In some historical novels the author attempts a faithful picture of daily life in another era, as does Robert Graves in *I, Claudius* (1934), a novel of patrician Rome. More often, history is a backdrop for an exciting story of love and heroic adventure. Nathaniel Hawthorne's *The Scarlet Letter* (set in Puritan Boston) and Stephen Crane's *The Red Badge of Courage* (set on the battlefields of the Civil War) are historical novels in that their authors lived considerably later than the scenes and events that they depicted, and strove for truthfulness, by imaginative means.

Other Types of Novels

Other varieties of novel will be familiar to anyone who browses in bookstores: the mystery or detective novel, the Western novel, the science fiction novel, and other enduring types. Novels are sometimes said to belong to a category if they contain some recognizable kind of structure or theme. Such a category is the **Bildungsroman** (German for a "novel of growth and development"), sometimes called the **apprenticeship novel** after its classic example, *Wilhelm Meister's Apprenticeship* (1796) by Johann Wolfgang von Goethe. This is the kind of novel in which a youth struggles toward maturity, seeking, perhaps, some consistent worldview or philosophy of life. Sometimes the apprenticeship novel is evidently derived from the author's recollection of his own early life: James Joyce's *A Portrait of the Artist as a Young Man* (1916) and Tobias Wolff's *Old School* (2003).

Picaresques

In a **picaresque** (another famous category), a likable scoundrel wanders through adventures, living by his wits, duping the straight citizenry. The name comes from Spanish: *pícaro*, "rascal" or "rogue." The classic picaresque novel is the anonymous Spanish *Life of Lazarillo de Tormes* (1554), imitated by many English writers, among them Henry Fielding in his story of a London thief and racketeer, *Jonathan Wild* (1743). Mark Twain's *Huckleberry Finn* (1885) owes something to the tradition; like early picaresque novels, it is told in episodes rather than in one all-unifying plot and is narrated in the first person by a hero at odds with respectable society ("dismal regular and decent," Huck Finn calls it). In Twain's novel, however, the traveling swindlers who claim to be a duke and a dauphin are much more typical rogues of picaresque fiction than Huck himself, an honest innocent. Modern novels worthy of the name include Saul Bellow's *The Adventures of Augie March* (1953), J. P. Donleavy's *The Ginger Man* (1965), Erica Jong's *Fanny* (1981), and Seth Morgan's *Homeboy* (1990).

Short Novels and Novellas

The term **short novel** (or **novella**) mainly describes the size of a narrative; it refers to a narrative midway in length between a short story and a novel. (E. M. Forster once said that a novel should be at least 50,000 words in length, and most editors and publishers would agree with that definition.) Generally a short novel, like a short story, focuses on just one or two characters; but, unlike a short story, it has room to examine them in great depth and detail. A short novel also often explores its characters over a greater period of time.

Many writers, such as Thomas Mann, Henry James, Joseph Conrad, and Willa Cather, favored the novella as a perfect medium between the necessary compression of the short story and the potential sprawl of the novel. Franz Kafka's famous novella *The Metamorphosis* is included in this book. When the term **novelette** is used, it usually refers (often disapprovingly) to a short novel written for a popular magazine, especially in such fields as science fiction, romance, the Western, and horror.

READING NOVELS

Trying to perceive a novel as a whole, we may find it helpful to look for the same elements that we have noticed in reading short stories. By asking ourselves leading questions, we may be drawn more deeply into the novel's world, and may come to recognize and appreciate the techniques of the novelist. Does the novel have themes, or an overall theme? Who is its main character? What is the author's kind of narrative voice? How would we describe the tone, style, and use of irony? Why is this novel written from one point of view rather than from another? If the novel in question is large and thickly populated, it may help to read it with a pencil and take brief notes. Forced to put the novel aside and later return to it, we may find that the notes refresh the memory. Once our reading of a novel is finished and we prepare to discuss it or write about it, it may be a good idea to browse through it again, rereading brief portions. This method of overall browsing may also help when first approaching a bulky and difficult novel. Just as an explorer mapping unfamiliar territory may find it best to begin by taking an aerial view of it, so too the reader approaching an exceptionally thick and demanding novel may wish, at the start, to look for its general shape. There is, of course, no shortcut to novel reading, and probably the best method is to settle in comfort and read the book through: with your own eyes, not with the borrowed glasses of literary criticism.

The Future of the Novel

The death of the novel has been frequently announced. Competition from television, DVDs, video games, and the Internet, some critics claim, will overwhelm the habit of reading; the public is lazy and will follow the easiest route available for entertainment. But in England and America television and films have been sending people back in vast numbers to the books they dramatize. Jane Austen has never lacked readers, but films such as *Pride and Prejudice, Emma, Persuasion,* and *Sense and Sensibility* (not to mention *Clueless,* a teenage version of *Emma* set in Beverly Hills, or *Bride and Prejudice,* a singing and dancing Bollywood treatment set in modern-day India) made her one of the world's best-selling novelists. Stylish adaptations of Philip K. Dick's offbeat science fiction, including *Blade Runner, Total Recall,* and *Minority Report,* have created a cult for his once neglected work. Sometimes Hollywood even helps bring a good book into print. No one would publish Thomas M. Disch's sophisticated children's novella *The Brave Little Toaster,* until Walt Disney turned it into a cartoon movie. A major publisher then not only rushed it into print, but commissioned a sequel.

Meanwhile, each year new novels by the hundreds continue to appear, their authors wistfully looking for a public. Some of these books reach a mass audience. To forecast the end of the novel seems risky, for the novel exercises the imagination of the beholder. At any hour, at a touch of the hand, it opens and (with no warmup) begins to speak. Once printed, it consumes no further energy. Often so small that it may be carried in a pocket, it may yet survive by its ability to contain multitudes (a "capacious vessel," Henry James called it): a thing that is both a work of art and an amazingly compact system for the storage and retrieval of imagined life.

Leo Tolstoy

The Death of Ivan Ilych   1886

Translated by Louise and Aylmer Maude

The complex and contradictory Leo Nikolaevich Tolstoy (1828–1910) is generally considered the greatest Russian novelist. Born on his aristocratic family's country estate, Yasnaya Polyana, in central Russia, he was orphaned at nine and raised by his aunts. At sixteen, Tolstoy entered Kazan University to study law, but soon returned to the family estate. The young count took off for St. Petersburg and Moscow, where he led a profligate life—carefully listing his moral transgressions in his diary. In 1851 Tolstoy joined the army and fought in the Caucasus. It was there that he completed his first book, Childhood *(1852), a lyrical memoir. Having served in the Crimean War, he left the army in 1856 to become a writer.*

Leo Tolstoy

For the next half century the brilliant and perpetually dissatisfied Tolstoy tried to settle in Yasnaya Polyana, but frequently escaped to St. Petersburg and Western Europe. In 1862 he wed Sonya Bers, an intellectual middle-class woman. Initially happy, the marriage was eventually undermined by the sex-obsessed and guilt-ridden Tolstoy, who engaged in many infidelities (which were sometimes followed by the author's unsuccessful renunciations of sex). Despite its many problems, the marriage produced thirteen children. At Yasnaya Polyana, Tolstoy wrote his two greatest novels, the six-volume War and Peace *(1863–1869), which depicts the lives of five aristocratic Russian families during the Napoleonic Wars, and* Anna Karenina *(1877), which tells the tragic story of a woman led by romantic illusions into a destructive adulterous liaison. As Tolstoy grew older, he became obsessed with early Christianity. He formulated his own version of Christ's teachings, stressing simplicity, love, nonviolence, and community property. Excommunicated by the Orthodox Church, the count, who now dressed in peasant clothing, preached his "Christian anarchism" to the Russian intelligentsia in streams of books and pamphlets. Upset by his ruined marriage and his inability to renounce his personal wealth, the eighty-two-year-old Tolstoy fled home one night to enter a monastery. He died of pneumonia a few days later in a provincial railway station.*

Tolstoy is one of the great masters of European Realism. His fame came early and has never been seriously challenged. Much of his fiction examines a tragic predicament of human existence—the difficult search for truth and justice in a world of limited knowledge and ethical imperfection. Tolstoy resolutely believed in the moral development of humanity, but was also painfully aware of the obstacles to genuine progress. His gripping novella The Death of Ivan Ilych *dramatizes Tolstoy's central spiritual concerns. His antiheroic Everyman faces death with the horrifying realization that he has not lived a correct or meaningful life.*

I

During an interval in the Melvinski trial in the large building of the Law Courts, the members and public prosecutor met in Ivan Egorovich Shebek's private room, where the conversation turned on the celebrated Krasovski case. Fëdor Vasilievich warmly maintained that it was not subject to their jurisdiction, Ivan Egorovich maintained the contrary, while Peter Ivanovich, not having entered into the discussion at the start, took no part in it but looked through the *Gazette* which had just been handed in.

"Gentlemen," he said, "Ivan Ilych has died!"

"You don't say so!"

"Here, read it yourself," replied Peter Ivanovich, handing Fëdor Vasilievich the paper still damp from the press. Surrounded by a black border were the words: "Praskovya Fëdorovna Golovina, with profound sorrow, informs relatives and friends of the demise of her beloved husband Ivan Ilych Golovin, Member of the Court of Justice, which occurred on February the 4th of this year 1882. The funeral will take place on Friday at one o'clock in the afternoon."

Ivan Ilych had been a colleague of the gentlemen present and was liked by them all. He had been ill for some weeks with an illness said to be incurable. His post had been kept open for him, but there had been conjectures that in case of his death Alexeev might receive his appointment, and that either Vinnikov or Shtabel would succeed Alexeev. So on receiving the news of Ivan Ilych's death the first thought of each of the gentlemen in that private room was of the changes and promotions it might occasion among themselves or their acquaintances.

"I shall be sure to get Shtabel's place or Vinnikov's," thought Fëdor Vasilievich. "I was promised that long ago, and the promotion means an extra eight hundred rubles a year for me besides the allowance."

"Now I must apply for my brother-in-law's transfer from Kaluga," thought Peter Ivanovich. "My wife will be very glad, and then she won't be able to say that I never do anything for her relations."

"I thought he would never leave his bed again," said Peter Ivanovich aloud. "It's very sad."

"But what really was the matter with him?"

"The doctors couldn't say—at least they could, but each of them said something   10
different. When last I saw him I thought he was getting better."

"And I haven't been to see him since the holidays. I always meant to go."

"Had he any property?"

"I think his wife had a little—but something quite trifling."

"We shall have to go to see her, but they live so terribly far away."

"Far away from you, you mean. Everything's far away from your place."   15

"You see, he never can forgive my living on the other side of the river," said Peter Ivanovich, smiling at Shebek. Then, still talking of the distances between different parts of the city, they returned to the Court.

Besides considerations as to the possible transfers and promotions likely to result from Ivan Ilych's death, the mere fact of the death of a near acquaintance aroused, as usual, in all who heard of it the complacent feeling that "it is he who is dead and not I."

Each one thought or felt, "Well, he's dead but I'm alive!" But the more intimate of Ivan Ilych's acquaintances, his so-called friends, could not help thinking also that they would now have to fulfil the very tiresome demands of propriety by attending the funeral service and paying a visit of condolence to the widow.

Fëdor Vasilievich and Peter Ivanovich had been his nearest acquaintances. Peter Ivanovich had studied law with Ivan Ilych and had considered himself to be under obligations to him.

Having told his wife at dinner-time of Ivan Ilych's death and of his conjecture   20
that it might be possible to get her brother transferred to their circuit, Peter Ivanovich sacrificed his usual nap, put on his evening clothes, and drove to Ivan Ilych's house.

At the entrance stood a carriage and two cabs. Leaning against the wall in the hall downstairs near the cloak-stand was a coffin-lid covered with cloth of gold, ornamented with gold cord and tassels, that had been polished up with metal powder. Two ladies in black were taking off their fur cloaks. Peter Ivanovich recognized one of them as Ivan Ilych's sister, but the other was a stranger to him. His colleague Schwartz was just coming downstairs, but on seeing Peter Ivanovich enter he stopped and winked at him, as if to say: "Ivan Ilych has made a mess of things—not like you and me."

Schwartz's face with his Piccadilly whiskers and his slim figure in evening dress had as usual an air of elegant solemnity which contrasted with the playfulness of his character and had a special piquancy here, or so it seemed to Peter Ivanovich.

Peter Ivanovich allowed the ladies to precede him and slowly followed them upstairs. Schwartz did not come down but remained where he was, and Peter Ivanovich understood that he wanted to arrange where they should play bridge that evening. The ladies went upstairs to the widow's room, and Schwartz with seriously compressed lips but a playful look in his eyes, indicated by a twist of his eyebrows the room to the right where the body lay.

Peter Ivanovich, like everyone else on such occasions, entered feeling uncertain what he would have to do. All he knew was that at such times it is always safe to cross oneself. But he was not quite sure whether one should make obeisances while doing so. He therefore adopted a middle course. On entering the room he began crossing himself and made a slight movement resembling a bow. At the same time, as far as the motion of his head and arm allowed, he surveyed the room. Two young men—apparently nephews, one of whom was a high-school pupil—were leaving the room, crossing themselves as they did so. An old woman was standing motionless, and a lady with strangely arched eyebrows was saying something to her in a whisper. A vigorous, resolute Church Reader, in a frock-coat, was reading something in a loud voice with an expression that precluded any contradiction. The butler's assistant, Gerasim, stepping lightly in front of Peter Ivanovich, was strewing something on the floor. Noticing this, Peter Ivanovich was immediately aware of a faint odor of a decomposing body.

The last time he had called on Ivan Ilych, Peter Ivanovich had seen Gerasim in   25
the study. Ivan Ilych had been particularly fond of him and he was performing the duty of a sick nurse.

Peter Ivanovich continued to make the sign of the cross, slightly inclining his head in an intermediate direction between the coffin, the Reader, and the icons on the table in a corner of the room. Afterwards, when it seemed to him that this movement of his arm in crossing himself had gone on too long, he stopped and began to look at the corpse.

The dead man lay, as dead men always lie, in a specially heavy way, his rigid limbs sunk in the soft cushions of the coffin, with the head forever bowed on the pillow. His yellow waxen brow with bald patches over his sunken temples was thrust up in the way peculiar to the dead, the protruding nose seeming to press on the upper lip. He was much changed and had grown even thinner since Peter Ivanovich had last seen him, but, as is always the case with the dead, his face was handsomer and above all more dignified than when he was alive. The expression on the face said that what was necessary had been accomplished, and accomplished rightly. Besides this there was in that expression a reproach and a warning to the living. This warning seemed to Peter Ivanovich out of place, or at least not applicable to him. He felt a certain discomfort and so he hurriedly crossed himself once more and turned and went out the door—too hurriedly and too regardless of propriety, as he himself was aware.

Schwartz was waiting for him in the adjoining room with legs spread wide apart and both hands toying with his top-hat behind his back. The mere sight of that playful, well-groomed, and elegant figure refreshed Peter Ivanovich. He felt that Schwartz was above all these happenings and would not surrender to any depressing influences. His very look said that this incident of a church service for Ivan Ilych could not be a sufficient reason for infringing the order of the session—in other words, that it would certainly not prevent his unwrapping a new pack of cards and shuffling them that evening while a footman placed four fresh candles on the table: in fact, that there was no reason for supposing that this incident would hinder their spending the evening agreeably. Indeed he said this in a whisper as Peter Ivanovich passed him, proposing that they should meet for a game at Fëdor Vasilievich's. But apparently Peter Ivanovich was not destined to play bridge that evening. Praskovya Fëdorovna (a short, fat woman who despite all efforts to the contrary had continued to broaden steadily from her shoulders downwards and who had the same extraordinarily arched eyebrows as the lady who had been standing by the coffin), dressed all in black, her head covered with lace, came out of her own room with some other ladies, conducted them to the room where the dead body lay, and said: "The service will begin immediately. Please go in."

Schwartz, making an indefinite bow, stood still, evidently neither accepting nor declining this invitation. Praskovya Fëdorovna, recognizing Peter Ivanovich, sighed, went close up to him, took his hand, and said: "I know you were a true friend to Ivan Ilych . . ." and looked at him awaiting some suitable response. And Peter Ivanovich knew that, just as it had been the right thing to cross himself in that room, so what he had to do here was to press her hand, sigh, and say, "Believe me. . . ." So he did all this and as he did it felt that the desired result had been achieved: that both he and she were touched.

"Come with me. I want to speak to you before it begins," said the widow. "Give me your arm."   30

Peter Ivanovich gave her his arm and they went to the inner rooms, passing Schwartz, who winked at Peter Ivanovich compassionately.

"That does for our bridge! Don't object if we find another player. Perhaps you can cut in when you do escape," said his playful look.

Peter Ivanovich sighed still more deeply and despondently, and Praskovya Fëdorovna pressed his arm gratefully. When they reached the drawing-room, uphol-stered in pink cretonne and lighted by a dim lamp, they sat down at the table—she on a sofa and Peter Ivanovich on a low pouffe, the springs of which yielded spas-modically under his weight. Praskovya Fëdorovna had been on the point of warn-ing him to take another seat, but felt that such a warning was out of keeping with her present condition and so changed her mind. As he sat down on the pouffe Peter Ivanovich recalled how Ivan Ilych had arranged this room and had consulted him regarding this pink cretonne with green leaves. The whole room was full of furniture and knick-knacks, and on her way to the sofa the lace of the widow's black shawl caught on the carved edge of the table. Peter Ivanovich rose to detach it, and the springs of the pouffe, relieved of his weight, rose also and gave him a push. The widow began detaching her shawl herself, and Peter Ivanovich again sat down, suppressing the rebellious springs of the pouffe under him. But the widow had not quite freed herself and Peter Ivanovich got up again, and again the pouffe rebelled and even creaked. When this was all over she took out a clean cambric handkerchief and began to weep. The episode with the shawl and the struggle with the pouffe had cooled Peter Ivanovich's emotions and he sat there with a sullen look on his face. This awkward situation was interrupted by Sokolov, Ivan Ilych's butler, who came to report that the plot in the cemetery that Praskovya Fëdorovna had chosen would cost two hundred rubles. She stopped weeping and, looking at Peter Ivanovich with the air of a victim, remarked in French that it was very hard for her. Peter Ivanovich made a silent gesture signifying his full conviction that it must indeed be so.

"Please smoke," she said in a magnanimous yet crushed voice, and turned to discuss with Sokolov the price of the plot for the grave.

Peter Ivanovich while lighting his cigarette heard her inquiring very circumstan-tially into the prices of different plots in the cemetery and finally decide which she would take. When that was done she gave instructions about engaging the choir. Sokolov then left the room.   35

"I look after everything myself," she told Peter Ivanovich, shifting the albums that lay on the table; and noticing that the table was endangered by his cigarette-ash, she immediately passed him an ashtray, saying as she did so: "I consider it an affectation to say that my grief prevents my attending to practical affairs. On the contrary, if anything can—I won't say console me, but—distract me, it is seeing to everything concerning him." She again took out her handkerchief as if preparing to cry, but suddenly, as if mastering her feeling, she shook herself and began to speak calmly. "But there is something I want to talk to you about."

Peter Ivanovich bowed, keeping control of the springs of the pouffe, which immediately began quivering under him.

"He suffered terribly the last few days."

"Did he?" said Peter Ivanovich.

"Oh, terribly! He screamed unceasingly, not for minutes but for hours. For the last three days he screamed incessantly. It was unendurable. I cannot understand how I bore it; you could hear him three rooms off. Oh, what I have suffered!"   40

"Is it possible that he was conscious all that time?" asked Peter Ivanovich.

"Yes," she whispered. "To the last moment. He took leave of us a quarter of an hour before he died, and asked us to take Volodya away."

The thought of the suffering of this man he had known so intimately, first as a merry little boy, then as a school-mate, and later as a grown-up colleague, suddenly struck Peter Ivanovich with horror, despite an unpleasant consciousness of his own and this woman's dissimulation. He again saw that brow, and that nose pressing down on the lip, and felt afraid for himself.

"Three days of frightful suffering and then death! Why, that might suddenly, at any time, happen to me," he thought, and for a moment felt terrified. But—he did not himself know how—the customary reflection at once occurred to him that this had happened to Ivan Ilych and not to him, and that it should not and could not happen to him, and that to think that it could would be yielding to depression which he ought not to do, as Schwartz's expression plainly showed. After which reflection Peter Ivanovich felt reassured, and began to ask with interest about the details of Ivan Ilych's death, as though death was an accident natural to Ivan Ilych but certainly not to himself.

After many details of the really dreadful physical sufferings Ivan Ilych had endured (which details he learnt only from the effect those sufferings had produced on Praskovya Fëdorovna's nerves) the widow apparently found it necessary to get to business.   45

"Oh, Peter Ivanovich, how hard it is! How terribly, terribly hard!" and she again began to weep.

Peter Ivanovich sighed and waited for her to finish blowing her nose. When she had done so he said, "Believe me . . ." and she again began talking and brought out what was evidently her chief concern with him—namely, to question him as to how she could obtain a grant of money from the government on the occasion of her husband's death. She made it appear that she was asking Peter Ivanovich's advice about her pension, but he soon saw that she already knew about that to the minutest detail, more even than he did himself. She knew how much could be got out of the government in consequence of her husband's death, but wanted to find out whether she could not possibly extract something more. Peter Ivanovich tried to think of some means of doing so, but after reflecting for a while and, out of propriety, condemning the government for its niggardliness, he said he thought that nothing more could be got. Then she sighed and evidently began to devise means of getting rid of her visitor. Noticing this, he put out his cigarette, rose, pressed her hand, and went out into the anteroom.

In the dining-room where the clock stood that Ivan Ilych had liked so much and had bought at an antique shop, Peter Ivanovich met a priest and a few acquaintances who had come to attend the service, and he recognized Ivan Ilych's daughter, a handsome young woman. She was in black and her slim figure appeared slimmer than ever. She had a gloomy, determined, almost angry expression, and bowed to Peter Ivanovich as though he were in some way to blame. Behind her, with the same offended look, stood a wealthy young man, an examining magistrate, whom Peter Ivanovich also knew and who was her fiancé, as he had heard. He bowed mournfully to them and was about to pass into the death-chamber, when from under the stairs appeared the figure of Ivan Ilych's schoolboy son, who was extremely like his father. He seemed a little Ivan Ilych, such as Peter Ivanovich remembered when they studied law together. His tear-stained eyes had in them the look that is seen in the eyes of boys of thirteen or fourteen who are not pure-minded. When he saw Peter Ivanovich he scowled morosely and shamefacedly. Peter Ivanovich nodded to him and entered the death-chamber. The service began: candles, groans, incense, tears, and sobs. Peter Ivanovich stood looking gloomily down at his feet. He did not look once at the dead man, did not yield to any depressing influence, and was one of the first to leave the room. There was no one in the anteroom, but Gerasim darted out of the dead man's room, rummaged with his strong hands among the fur coats to find Peter Ivanovich's, and helped him on with it.

"Well, friend Gerasim," said Peter Ivanovich, so as to say something. "It's a sad affair, isn't it?"

"It's God's will. We shall all come to it some day," said Gerasim, displaying his   50
teeth—the even, white teeth of a healthy peasant—and, like a man in the thick of urgent work, he briskly opened the front door, called the coachman, helped Peter Ivanovich into the sledge, and sprang back to the porch as if in readiness for what he had to do next.

Peter Ivanovich found the fresh air particularly pleasant after the smell of incense, the dead body, and carbolic acid.

"Where to, sir?" asked the coachman.

"It's not too late even now . . . I'll call round on Fëdor Vasilievich."

He accordingly drove there and found them just finishing the first rubber, so that it was quite convenient for him to cut in.

II

Ivan Ilych's life had been most simple and most ordinary and therefore most   55
terrible.

He had been a member of the Court of Justice, and died at the age of forty-five. His father had been an official who after serving in various ministries and departments in Petersburg had made the sort of career which brings men to positions from which by reason of their long service they cannot be dismissed, though they are obviously unfit to hold any responsible position, and for whom therefore posts are specially created, which, though fictitious, carry salaries of from six to ten thousand rubles that are not fictitious, and in receipt of which they live on to a great age.

Such was the Privy Councillor and superfluous member of various superfluous institutions, Ilya Epimovich Golovin.

He had three sons, of whom Ivan Ilych was the second. The eldest son was following in his father's footsteps only in another department, and was already approaching that stage in the service at which a similar sinecure would be reached. The third son was a failure. He had ruined his prospects in a number of positions and was now serving in the railway department. His father and brothers, and still more their wives, not merely disliked meeting him, but avoided remembering his existence unless compelled to do so. His sister had married Baron Greff, a Petersburg official of her father's type. Ivan Ilych was *le phénix de la famille°* as people said. He was neither as cold and formal as his elder brother nor as wild as the younger, but was a happy mean between them—an intelligent, polished, lively, and agreeable man. He had studied with his younger brother at the School of Law, but the latter had failed to complete the course and was expelled when he was in the fifth class. Ivan Ilych finished the course well. Even when he was at the School of Law he was just what he remained for the rest of his life: a capable, cheerful, good-natured, and sociable man, though strict in the fulfillment of what he considered to be his duty: and he considered his duty to be what was so considered by those in authority. Neither as a boy nor as a man was he a toady, but from early youth was by nature attracted to people of high station as a fly is drawn to the light, assimilating their ways and views of life and establishing friendly relations with them. All the enthusiasms of childhood and youth passed without leaving much trace on him; he succumbed to sensuality, to vanity, and latterly among the highest classes to liberalism, but always within limits which his instinct unfailingly indicated to him as correct.

At school he had done things which had formerly seemed to him very horrid and made him feel disgusted with himself when he did them; but when later on he saw that such actions were done by people of good position and that they did not regard them as wrong, he was able not exactly to regard them as right, but to forget about them entirely or not be at all troubled at remembering them.

Having graduated from the School of Law and qualified for the tenth rank of the civil service, and having received money from his father for his equipment, Ivan Ilych ordered himself clothes at Scharmer's, the fashionable tailor, hung a medallion inscribed *respice finem°* on his watch-chain, took leave of his professor and the prince who was patron of the school, had a farewell dinner with his comrades at Donon's first-class restaurant, and with his new and fashionable portmanteau, linen, clothes, shaving and other toilet appliances, and a traveling rug all purchased at the best shops, he set off for one of the provinces where through his father's influence, he had been attached to the Governor as an official for special service.

In the province Ivan Ilych soon arranged as easy and agreeable a position for himself as he had had at the School of Law. He performed his official tasks, made his career, and at the same time amused himself pleasantly and decorously. Occasionally he paid official visits to country districts, where he behaved with dignity both to his superiors and inferiors, and performed the duties entrusted to him, which related chiefly to the sectarians,° with an exactness and incorruptible honesty of which he could not but feel proud.

In official matters, despite his youth and taste for frivolous gaiety, he was exceedingly reserved, punctilious, and even severe; but in society he was often amusing

le phénix de la famille: French for "the prize of the family."   *respice finem:* Latin for "Think of the end (of your life)."   *sectarians:* dissenters from the Orthodox Church.

and witty, and always good-natured, correct in his manner, and *bon enfant*,° as the Governor and his wife—with whom he was like one of the family—used to say of him.

In the province he had an affair with a lady who made advances to the elegant young lawyer, and there was also a milliner; and there were carousals with aides-de-camp who visited the district, and after-supper visits to a certain outlying street of doubtful reputation; and there was too some obsequiousness to his chief and even to his chief's wife, but all this was done with such a tone of good breeding that no hard names could be applied to it. It all came under the heading of the French saying: *"Il faut que jeunesse se passe."*° It was all done with clean hands, in clean linen, with French phrases, and above all among people of the best society and consequently with the approval of people of rank.

So Ivan Ilych served for five years and then came a change in his official life. The new and reformed judicial institutions were introduced, and new men were needed. Ivan Ilych became such a new man. He was offered the post of examining magistrate, and he accepted it though the post was in another province and obliged him to give up the connections he had formed and to make new ones. His friends met to give him a send-off; they had a group-photograph taken and presented him with a silver cigarette-case, and he set off to his new post.

As examining magistrate Ivan Ilych was just as *comme il faut*° and decorous a man, inspiring general respect and capable of separating his official duties from his private life, as he had been when acting as an official on special service. His duties now as examining magistrate were far more interesting and attractive than before. In his former position it had been pleasant to wear an undress uniform made by Scharmer, and to pass through the crowd of petitioners and officials who were timorously awaiting an audience with the Governor, and who envied him as with free and easy gait he went straight into his chief's private room to have a cup of tea and a cigarette with him. But not many people had then been directly dependent on him—only police officials and the sectarians when he went on special missions—and he liked to treat them politely, almost as comrades, as if he were letting them feel that he who had the power to crush them was treating them in this simple, friendly way. There were then but few such people. But now, as an examining magistrate, Ivan Ilych felt that everyone without exception, even the most important and self-satisfied, was in his power, and that he need only write a few words on a sheet of paper with a certain heading, and this or that important, self-satisfied person would be brought before him in the role of an accused person or a witness, and if he did not choose to allow him to sit down, would have to stand before him and answer his questions. Ivan Ilych never abused his power; he tried on the contrary to soften its expression, but the consciousness of it and of the possibility of softening its effect, supplied the chief interest and attraction of his office. In his work itself, especially in his examinations, he very soon acquired a method of eliminating all considerations irrelevant to the legal aspect of the case, and reducing even the most complicated case to a form in which it would be presented on paper only in its externals, completely excluding his personal opinion of the matter, while above all observing every prescribed formality. The work was new and Ivan Ilych was one of the first men to apply the new Code of 1864.°

65

bon enfant: French for "a well-behaved child."   *"Il faut que jeunesse se passe"*: "Youth doesn't last." *comme il faut:* "as required," rule-abiding.   *Code of 1864:* The emancipation of the serfs in 1861 was followed by a thorough all-round reform of judicial proceedings. [Translators' note.]

On taking up the post of examining magistrate in a new town, he made new acquaintances and connections, placed himself on a new footing, and assumed a somewhat different tone. He took up an attitude of rather dignified aloofness towards the provincial authorities, but picked out the best circle of legal gentlemen and wealthy gentry living in the town and assumed a tone of slight dissatisfaction with the government, of moderate liberalism, and of enlightened citizenship. At the same time, without at all altering the elegance of his toilet, he ceased shaving his chin and allowed his beard to grow as it pleased.

Ivan Ilych settled down very pleasantly in this new town. The society there, which inclined towards opposition to the Governor, was friendly, his salary was larger, and he began to play *vint*,° which he found added not a little to the pleasure of life, for he had a capacity for cards, played good-humoredly, and calculated rapidly and astutely, so that he usually won.

After living there for two years he met his future wife, Praskovya Fëdorovna Mikhel, who was the most attractive, clever, and brilliant girl of the set in which he moved, and among other amusements and relaxations from his labors as examining magistrate, Ivan Ilych established light and playful relations with her.

While he had been an official on special service he had been accustomed to dance, but now as an examining magistrate it was exceptional for him to do so. If he danced now, he did it as if to show that though he served under the reformed order of things, and had reached the fifth official rank, yet when it came to dancing he could do it better than most people. So at the end of an evening he sometimes danced with Praskovya Fëdorovna, and it was chiefly during these dances that he captivated her. She fell in love with him. Ivan Ilych had at first no definite intention of marrying, but when the girl fell in love with him he said to himself: "Really, why shouldn't I marry?"

Praskovya Fëdorovna came of a good family, was not bad-looking, and had some little property. Ivan Ilych might have aspired to a more brilliant match, but even this was good. He had his salary, and she, he hoped, would have an equal income. She was well connected, and was a sweet, pretty, and thoroughly correct young woman. To say that Ivan Ilych married because he fell in love with Praskovya Fëdorovna and found that she sympathized with his views of life would be as incorrect as to say that he married because his social circle approved of the match. He was swayed by both these considerations: the marriage gave him personal satisfaction, and at the same time it was considered the right thing by the most highly placed of his associates.

So Ivan Ilych got married.

The preparations for marriage and the beginning of married life, with its conjugal caresses, the new furniture, new crockery, and new linen, were very pleasant until his wife became pregnant—so that Ivan Ilych had begun to think that marriage would not impair the easy, agreeable, gay, and always decorous character of his life, approved of by society and regarded by himself as natural, but would even improve it. But from the first months of his wife's pregnancy, something new, unpleasant, depressing, and unseemly, and from which there was no way of escape, unexpectedly showed itself.

His wife, without any reason—*de gaieté de coeur*° as Ivan Ilych expressed it to himself—began to disturb the pleasure and propriety of their life. She began to be

70

jealous without any cause, expected him to devote his whole attention to her, found fault with everything, and made coarse and ill-mannered scenes.

At first Ivan Ilych hoped to escape from the unpleasantness of this state of affairs by the same easy and decorous relation to life that had served him heretofore: he tried to ignore his wife's disagreeable moods, continued to live in his usual easy and pleasant way, invited friends to his house for a game of cards, and also tried going out to his club or spending his evenings with friends. But one day his wife began upbraiding him so vigorously, using such coarse words, and continued to abuse him every time he did not fulfil her demands, so resolutely and with such evident determination not to give way till he submitted—that is, till he stayed at home and was bored just as she was—that he became alarmed. He now realized that matrimony—at any rate with Praskovya Fëdorovna—was not always conducive to the pleasures and amenities of life, but on the contrary often infringed both comfort and propriety, and that he must therefore entrench himself against such infringement. And Ivan Ilych began to seek for means of doing so. His official duties were the one thing that imposed upon Praskovya Fëdorovna, and by means of his official work and the duties attached to it he began struggling with his wife to secure his own independence.

With the birth of their child, the attempts to feed it and the various failures in   75
doing so, and with the real and imaginary illnesses of mother and child, in which Ivan Ilych's sympathy was demanded but about which he understood nothing, the need of securing for himself an existence outside his family life became still more imperative.

As his wife grew more irritable and exacting and Ivan Ilych transferred the center of gravity of his life more and more to his official work, so did he grow to like his work better and became more ambitious than before.

Very soon, within a year of his wedding, Ivan Ilych had realized that marriage, though it may add some comforts to life, is in fact a very intricate and difficult affair towards which in order to perform one's duty, that is, to lead a decorous life approved of by society, one must adopt a definite attitude just as towards one's official duties.

And Ivan Ilych evolved such an attitude towards married life. He only required of it those conveniences—dinner at home, housewife, and bed—which it could give him, and above all that propriety of external forms required by public opinion. For the rest he looked for light-hearted pleasure and propriety, and was very thankful when he found them, but if he met with antagonism and querulousness he at once retired into his separate fenced-off world of official duties, where he found satisfaction.

Ivan Ilych was esteemed a good official, and after three years was made Assistant Public Prosecutor. His new duties, their importance, the possibility of indicting and imprisoning anyone he chose, the publicity his speeches received, and the success he had in all these things, made his work still more attractive.

More children came. His wife became more and more querulous and ill-tempered,   80
but the attitude Ivan Ilych had adopted towards his home life rendered him almost impervious to her grumbling.

After seven years' service in that town he was transferred to another province as Public Prosecutor. They moved, but were short of money and his wife did not like the place they moved to. Though the salary was higher the cost of living was greater, besides which two of their children died and family life became still more unpleasant for him.

Praskovya Fëdorovna blamed her husband for every inconvenience they encountered in their new home. Most of the conversations between husband and wife, especially as to the children's education, led to topics which recalled former disputes, and those disputes were apt to flare up again at any moment. There remained only those rare periods of amorousness which still came to them at times but did not last long. These were islets at which they anchored for a while and then again set out upon that ocean of veiled hostility which showed itself in their aloofness from one another. This aloofness might have grieved Ivan Ilych had he considered that it ought not to exist, but he now regarded the position as normal, and even made it the goal at which he aimed in family life. His aim was to free himself more and more from those unpleasantnesses and to give them a semblance of harmlessness and propriety. He attained this by spending less and less time with his family, and when obliged to be at home he tried to safeguard his position by the presence of outsiders. The chief thing, however, was that he had his official duties. The whole interest of his life now centered in the official world and that interest absorbed him. The consciousness of his power, being able to ruin anybody he wished to ruin, the importance, even the external dignity of his entry into court, or meetings with his subordinates, his success with superiors and inferiors, and above all his masterly handling of cases, of which he was conscious—all this gave him pleasure and filled his life, together with chats with his colleagues, dinners, and bridge. So that on the whole Ivan Ilych's life continued to flow as he considered it should do—pleasantly and properly.

So things continued for another seven years. His eldest daughter was already sixteen, another child had died, and only one son was left, a schoolboy and a subject of dissension. Ivan Ilych wanted to put him in the School of Law, but to spite him Praskovya Fëdorovna entered him at the High School. The daughter had been educated at home and had turned out well: the boy did not learn badly either.

III

So Ivan Ilych lived for seventeen years after his marriage. He was already a Public Prosecutor of long standing, and had declined several proposed transfers while awaiting a more desirable post, when an unanticipated and unpleasant occurrence quite upset the peaceful course of his life. He was expecting to be offered the post of presiding judge in a University town, but Happe somehow came to the front and obtained the appointment instead. Ivan Ilych became irritable, reproached Happe, and quarreled both with him and with his immediate superiors—who became colder to him and again passed him over when other appointments were made.

This was in 1880, the hardest year of Ivan Ilych's life. It was then that it became evident on the one hand that his salary was insufficient for them to live on, and on the other that he had been forgotten, and not only this, but that what was for him the greatest and most cruel injustice appeared to others a quite ordinary occurrence. Even his father did not consider it his duty to help him. Ivan Ilych felt himself abandoned by everyone, and that they regarded his position with a salary of 3,500 rubles as quite normal and even fortunate. He alone knew that with the consciousness of the injustices done him, with his wife's incessant nagging, and with the debts he had contracted by living beyond his means, his position was far from normal.

In order to save money that summer he obtained leave of absence and went with his wife to live in the country at her brother's place.

In the country, without his work, he experienced *ennui* for the first time in his life, and not only *ennui* but intolerable depression, and he decided that it was impossible to go on living like that, and that it was necessary to take energetic measures.

Having passed a sleepless night pacing up and down the veranda, he decided to go to Petersburg and bestir himself, in order to punish those who had failed to appreciate him and to get transferred to another ministry.

Next day, despite many protests from his wife and her brother, he started for Petersburg with the sole object of obtaining a post with a salary of five thousand rubles a year. He was no longer bent on any particular department, or tendency, or kind of activity. All he now wanted was an appointment to another post with a salary of five thousand rubles, either in the administration, in the banks, with the railways, in one of the Empress Marya's Institutions,° or even in the customs—but it had to carry with it a salary of five thousand rubles and be in a ministry other than that in which they had failed to appreciate him.

And this quest of Ivan Ilych's was crowned with remarkable and unexpected suc-   90
cess. At Kursk an acquaintance of his, F. I. Ilyin, got into the first-class carriage, sat down beside Ivan Ilych, and told him of a telegram just received by the Governor of Kursk announcing that a change was about to take place in the ministry: Peter Ivanovich was to be superseded by Ivan Semënovich.

The proposed change, apart from its significance for Russia, had a special significance for Ivan Ilych, because by bringing forward a new man, Peter Petrovich, and consequently his friend Zachar Ivanovich, it was highly favorable for Ivan Ilych, since Zachar Ivanovich was a friend and colleague of his.

In Moscow this news was confirmed, and on reaching Petersburg Ivan Ilych found Zachar Ivanovich and received a definite promise of an appointment in his former department of Justice.

A week later he telegraphed to his wife: "Zachar in Miller's place. I shall receive appointment on presentation of report."

Thanks to this change of personnel, Ivan Ilych had unexpectedly obtained an appointment in his former ministry which placed him two stages above his former colleagues besides giving him five thousand rubles salary and three thousand five hundred rubles for expenses connected with his removal. All his ill humor towards his former enemies and the whole department vanished, and Ivan Ilych was completely happy.

He returned to the country more cheerful and contented than he had been for a   95
long time. Praskovya Fëdorovna also cheered up and a truce was arranged between them. Ivan Ilych told of how he had been fêted by everybody in Petersburg, how all those who had been his enemies were put to shame and now fawned on him, how envious they were of his appointment, and how much everybody in Petersburg had liked him.

Praskovya Fëdorovna listened to all this and appeared to believe it. She did not contradict anything, but only made plans for their life in the town to which they were going. Ivan Ilych saw with delight that these plans were his plans, that he and his wife agreed, and that, after a stumble, his life was regaining its due and natural character of pleasant lightheartedness and decorum.

Ivan Ilych had come back for a short time only, for he had to take up his new duties on the 10th of September. Moreover, he needed time to settle into the new place, to move all his belongings from the province, and to buy and order many additional things: in a word, to make such arrangements as he had resolved on, which were almost exactly what Praskovya Fëdorovna too had decided on.

Empress Marya's Institutions: orphanages.

Now that everything had happened so fortunately, and that he and his wife were at one in their aims and moreover saw so little of one another, they got on together better than they had done since the first years of marriage. Ivan Ilych had thought of taking his family away with him at once, but the insistence of his wife's brother and her sister-in-law, who had suddenly become particularly amiable and friendly to him and his family, induced him to depart alone.

So he departed, and the cheerful state of mind induced by his success and by the harmony between his wife and himself, the one intensifying the other, did not leave him. He found a delightful house, just the thing both he and his wife had dreamt of. Spacious, lofty reception rooms in the old style, a convenient and dignified study, rooms for his wife and daughter, a study for his son—it might have been specially built for them. Ivan Ilych himself superintended the arrangements, chose the wallpapers, supplemented the furniture (preferably with antiques which he considered particularly *comme il faut*), and supervised the upholstering. Everything progressed and progressed and approached the ideal he had set himself: even when things were only half completed they exceeded his expectations. He saw what a refined and elegant character, free from vulgarity, it would all have when it was ready. On falling asleep he pictured to himself how the reception-room would look. Looking at the yet unfinished drawing-room he could see the fireplace, the screen, the what-not, the little chairs dotted here and there, the dishes and plates on the walls, and the bronzes, as they would be when everything was in place. He was pleased by the thought of how his wife and daughter, who shared his taste in this matter, would be impressed by it. They were certainly not expecting as much. He had been particularly successful in finding, and buying cheaply, antiques which gave a particularly aristocratic character to the whole place. But in his letters he intentionally understated everything in order to be able to surprise them. All this so absorbed him that his new duties—though he liked his official work—interested him less than he had expected. Sometimes he even had moments of absentmindedness during the Court Sessions, and would consider whether he should have straight or curved cornices for his curtains. He was so interested in it all that he often did things himself, rearranging the furniture, or rehanging the curtains. Once when mounting a stepladder to show the upholsterer, who did not understand, how he wanted the hangings draped, he made a false step and slipped, but being a strong and agile man he clung on and only knocked his side against the knob of the window frame. The bruised place was painful but the pain soon passed, and he felt particularly bright and well just then. He wrote: "I feel fifteen years younger." He thought he would have everything ready by September, but it dragged on till mid-October. But the result was charming not only in his eyes but to everyone who saw it.

In reality it was just what is usually seen in the houses of people of moderate means who want to appear rich, and therefore succeed only in resembling others like themselves: there were damasks, dark wood, plants, rugs, and dull and polished bronzes—all the things people of a certain class have in order to resemble other people of that class. His house was so like the others that it would never have been noticed, but to him it all seemed to be quite exceptional. He was very happy when he met his family at the station and brought them to the newly furnished house all lit up, where a footman in a white tie opened the door into the hall decorated with plants, and when they went on into the drawing-room and the study uttering exclamations of delight. He conducted them everywhere, drank in their praises eagerly, and beamed with pleasure. At tea that evening, when Praskovya Fëdorovna among other things asked him about his fall, he laughed and showed them how he had gone flying and had frightened the upholsterer.

"It's a good thing I'm a bit of an athlete. Another man might have been killed, but I merely knocked myself, just here; it hurts when it's touched, but it's passing off already—it's only a bruise."

So they began living in their new home—in which, as always happens, when they got thoroughly settled in they found they were just one room short—and with the increased income, which as always was just a little (some five hundred rubles) too little, but it was all very nice.

Things went particularly well at first, before everything was finally arranged and while something had still to be done: this thing bought, that thing ordered, another thing moved, and something else adjusted. Though there were some disputes between husband and wife, they were both so well satisfied and had so much to do that it all passed off without any serious quarrels. When nothing was left to arrange it became rather dull and something seemed to be lacking, but they were then making acquaintances, forming habits, and life was growing fuller.

Ivan Ilych spent his mornings at the law courts and came home to dinner, and at first he was generally in a good humor, though he occasionally became irritable just on account of his house. (Every spot on the tablecloth or the upholstery, and every broken window-blind string, irritated him. He had devoted so much trouble to arranging it all that every disturbance of it distressed him.) But on the whole his life ran its course as he believed life should do: easily, pleasantly, and decorously.

He got up at nine, drank his coffee, read the paper, and then put on his undress uniform and went to the law courts. There the harness in which he worked had already been stretched to fit him and he donned it without a hitch: petitioners, inquiries at the chancery, the chancery itself, and the sittings public and administrative. In all this the thing was to exclude everything fresh and vital, which always disturbs the regular course of official business, and to admit only official relations with people, and then only on official grounds. A man would come, for instance, wanting some information. Ivan Ilych, as one in whose sphere the matter did not lie, would have nothing to do with him: but if the man had some business with him in his official capacity, something that could be expressed on officially stamped paper, he would do everything, positively everything he could within the limits of such relations, and in doing so would maintain the semblance of friendly human relations, that is, would observe the courtesies of life. As soon as the official relations ended, so did everything else. Ivan Ilych possessed this capacity to separate his real life from the official side of affairs and not mix the two, in the highest degree, and by long practice and natural aptitude had brought it to such a pitch that sometimes, in the manner of a virtuoso, he would even allow himself to let the human and official relations mingle. He let himself do this just because he felt that he could at any time he chose resume the strictly official attitude again and drop the human relation. And he did it all easily, pleasantly, correctly, and even artistically. In the intervals between the sessions he smoked, drank tea, chatted a little about politics, a little about general topics, a little about cards, but most of all about official appointments. Tired, but with the feelings of a virtuoso—one of the first violins who has played his part in an orchestra with precision—he would return home to find that his wife and daughter had been out paying calls, or had a visitor, and that his son had been to school, had done his homework with his tutor, and was duly learning what is taught at High Schools. Everything was as it should be. After dinner, if they had no visitors, Ivan Ilych sometimes read a book that was being much discussed at the time, and in the evening settled down to work, that is, read official papers, compared the depositions of witnesses, and noted paragraphs of the Code applying to them. This was neither dull nor amusing. It was dull when he might have been playing bridge, but if no bridge was available it was at any rate better than doing nothing or sitting with his wife. Ivan Ilych's chief pleasure was giving little dinners to which he invited men and women of good social position, and just as his drawing-room resembled all other drawing-rooms so did his enjoyable little parties resemble all other such parties.

Once they even gave a dance. Ivan Ilych enjoyed it and everything went off well, except that it led to a violent quarrel with his wife about the cakes and sweets. Praskovya Fëdorovna had made her own plans, but Ivan Ilych insisted on getting everything from an expensive confectioner and ordered too many cakes, and the quarrel occurred because some of those cakes were left over and the confectioner's bill came to forty-five rubles. It was a great and disagreeable quarrel. Praskovya Fëdorovna called him "a fool and an imbecile," and he clutched at his head and made angry allusions to divorce.

But the dance itself had been enjoyable. The best people were there, and Ivan Ilych had danced with Princess Trufonova, a sister of the distinguished founder of the Society "Bear My Burden."

The pleasures connected with his work were pleasures of ambition; his social pleasures were those of vanity; but Ivan Ilych's greatest pleasure was playing bridge. He acknowledged that whatever disagreeable incident happened in his life, the pleasure that beamed like a ray of light above everything else was to sit down to bridge with good players, not noisy partners, and of course to four-handed bridge (with five players it was annoying to have to stand out, though one pretended not to mind), to play a clever and serious game (when the cards allowed it), and then to have supper and drink a glass of wine. After a game of bridge, especially if he had won a little (to win a large sum was unpleasant), Ivan Ilych went to bed in specially good humor.

So they lived. They formed a circle of acquaintances among the best people and were visited by people of importance and by young folk. In their views as to their acquaintances, husband, wife, and daughter were entirely agreed, and tacitly and unanimously kept at arm's length and shook off the various shabby friends and relations who, with much show of affection, gushed into the drawing-room with its Japanese plates on the walls. Soon these shabby friends ceased to obtrude themselves and only the best people remained in the Golovins' set.

Young men made up to Lisa, and Petrishchev, an examining magistrate and [110] Dmitri Ivanovich Petrishchev's son and sole heir, began to be so attentive to her that Ivan Ilych had already spoken to Praskovya Fëdorovna about it, and considered whether they should not arrange a party for them, or get up some private theatricals.

So they lived, and all went well, without change, and life flowed pleasantly.

IV

They were all in good health. It could not be called ill health if Ivan Ilych sometimes said that he had a queer taste in his mouth and felt some discomfort in his left side.

But this discomfort increased and, though not exactly painful, grew into a sense of pressure in his side accompanied by ill humor. And his irritability became worse and worse and began to mar the agreeable, easy, and correct life that had established itself in the Golovin family. Quarrels between husband and wife became more and more frequent, and soon the ease and amenity disappeared and even the decorum was barely maintained. Scenes again became frequent, and very few of those islets remained on which husband and wife could meet without an explosion. Praskovya Fëdorovna now had good reason to say that her husband's temper was trying. With characteristic exaggeration she said he had always had a dreadful temper, and that it had needed all her good nature to put up with it for twenty years. It was true that now the quarrels were started by him. His bursts of temper always came just before dinner, often just as he began to eat his soup. Sometimes he noticed that a plate or dish was chipped, or the food was not right, or his son put his elbow on the table, or his daughter's hair was not done as he liked it, and for all this he blamed Praskovya Fëdorovna. At first she retorted and said disagreeable things to him, but once or twice he fell into such a rage at the beginning of dinner that she realized it was due to some physical derangement brought on by taking food, and so she restrained herself and did not answer, but only hurried to get the dinner over. She regarded this self-restraint as highly praiseworthy. Having come to the conclusion that her husband had a dreadful temper and made her life miserable, she began to feel sorry for herself, and the more she pitied herself the more she hated her husband. She began to wish he would die; yet she did not want him to die because then his salary would cease. And this irritated her against him still more. She considered herself dreadfully unhappy just because not even his death could save her, and though she concealed her exasperation, that hidden exasperation of hers increased his irritation also.

After one scene in which Ivan Ilych had been particularly unfair and after which he had said in explanation that he certainly was irritable but that it was due to his not being well, she said that if he was ill it should be attended to, and insisted on his going to see a celebrated doctor.

He went. Everything took place as he had expected and as it always does. There was the usual waiting and the important air assumed by the doctor, with which he was so familiar (resembling that which he himself assumed in court), and the sounding and listening, and the questions which called for answers that were foregone conclusions and were evidently unnecessary, and the look of importance which implied that "if only you put yourself in our hands we will arrange everything—we know indubitably how it has to be done, always in the same way for everybody alike." It was all just as it was in the law courts. The doctor put on just the same air towards him as he himself put on towards an accused person.   115

The doctor said that so-and-so indicated that there was so-and-so inside the patient, but if the investigation of so-and-so did not confirm this, then he must assume that and that. If he assumed that and that, then . . . and so on. To Ivan Ilych only one question was important: was his case serious or not? But the doctor ignored that inappropriate question. From his point of view it was not the one under consideration, the real question was to decide between a floating kidney, chronic catarrh, or appendicitis. It was not a question of Ivan Ilych's life or death, but one between a floating kidney and appendicitis. And that question the doctor solved brilliantly, as it seemed to Ivan Ilych, in favor of the appendix, with the reservation that should an examination of the urine give fresh indications the matter would be reconsidered. All this was just what Ivan Ilych had himself brilliantly accomplished a thousand times in dealing with men on trial. The doctor summed up just as brilliantly, looking over his spectacles triumphantly and even gaily at the accused. From the doctor's summing up Ivan Ilych concluded that things were bad, but that for the doctor, and perhaps for everybody else, it was a matter of indifference, though for him it was bad. And this conclusion struck him painfully, arousing in him a great feeling of pity for himself and of bitterness towards the doctor's indifference to a matter of such importance.

He said nothing of this, but rose, placed the doctor's fee on the table, and remarked with a sigh: "We sick people probably often put inappropriate questions. But tell me, in general, is this complaint dangerous, or not? . . ."

The doctor looked at him sternly over his spectacles with one eye, as if to say: "Prisoner, if you will not keep to the questions put to you, I shall be obliged to have you removed from the court."

"I have already told you what I consider necessary and proper. The analysis may show something more." And the doctor bowed.

Ivan Ilych went out slowly, seated himself disconsolately in his sledge, and drove home. All the way home he was going over what the doctor had said, trying to translate those complicated, obscure, scientific phrases into plain language and find in them an answer to the question: "Is my condition bad? Is it very bad? Or is there as yet nothing much wrong?" And it seemed to him that the meaning of what the doctor had said was that it was very bad. Everything in the streets seemed depressing. The cabmen, the houses, the passers-by, and the shops, were dismal. His ache, this dull gnawing ache that never ceased for a moment, seemed to have acquired a new and more serious significance from the doctor's dubious remarks. Ivan Ilych now watched it with a new and oppressive feeling.

He reached home and began to tell his wife about it. She listened, but in the middle of his account his daughter came in with her hat on, ready to go out with her mother. She sat down reluctantly to listen to this tedious story, but could not stand it long, and her mother too did not hear him to the end.

"Well, I am very glad," she said. "Mind now to take your medicine regularly. Give me the prescription and I'll send Gerasim to the chemist's." And she went to get ready to go out.

While she was in the room Ivan Ilych had hardly taken time to breathe, but he sighed deeply when she left it.

"Well," he thought, "perhaps it isn't so bad after all."

He began taking his medicine and following the doctor's directions, which had been altered after the examination of the urine. But then it happened that there was a contradiction between the indications drawn from the examination of the urine and the symptoms that showed themselves. It turned out that what was happening differed from what the doctor had told him, and that he had either forgotten, or blundered, or hidden something from him. He could not, however, be blamed for that, and Ivan Ilych still obeyed his orders implicitly and at first derived some comfort from doing so.

From the time of his visit to the doctor, Ivan Ilych's chief occupation was the exact fulfillment of the doctor's instructions regarding hygiene and the taking of medicine, and the observation of his pain and his excretions. His chief interests came to be people's ailments and people's health. When sickness, deaths, or recoveries were mentioned in his presence, especially when the illness resembled his own, he listened with agitation which he tried to hide, asked questions, and applied what he heard to his own case.

The pain did not grow less, but Ivan Ilych made efforts to force himself to think that he was better. And he could do this so long as nothing agitated him. But as soon as he had any unpleasantness with his wife, any lack of success in his official work, or held bad cards at bridge, he was at once acutely sensible of his disease. He had formerly borne such mischances, hoping soon to adjust what was wrong, to master it and attain success, or make a grand slam. But now every mischance upset him and plunged him into despair. He would say to himself: "There now, just as I was beginning to get better and the medicine had begun to take effect, comes this accursed misfortune, or unpleasantness. . . ." And he was furious with the mishap, or with the people who were causing the unpleasantness and killing him, for he felt that this fury was killing him but could not restrain it. One would have thought that it should have been clear to him that this exasperation with circumstances and people aggravated his illness, and that he ought therefore to ignore unpleasant occurrences. But he drew the very opposite conclusion: he said that he needed peace, and he watched for everything that might disturb it and became irritable at the slightest infringement of it. His condition was rendered worse by the fact that he read medical books and consulted doctors. The progress of his disease was so gradual that he could deceive himself when comparing one day with another—the difference was so slight. But when he consulted the doctors it seemed to him that he was getting worse, and even very rapidly. Yet despite this he was continually consulting them.

That month he went to see another celebrity, who told him almost the same as the first had done but put his questions rather differently, and the interview with this celebrity only increased Ivan Ilych's doubts and fears. A friend of a friend of his, a very good doctor, diagnosed his illness again quite differently from the others, and though he predicted recovery, his questions and suppositions bewildered Ivan Ilych still more and increased his doubts. A homeopathist diagnosed the disease in yet another way, and prescribed medicine which Ivan Ilych took secretly for a week. But after a week, not feeling any improvement and having lost confidence both in the former doctor's treatment and in this one's, he became still more despondent. One day a lady acquaintance mentioned a cure effected by a wonder-working icon. Ivan Ilych caught himself listening attentively and beginning to believe that it had occurred. This incident alarmed him. "Has my mind really weakened to such an extent?" he asked himself. "Nonsense! It's all rubbish. I mustn't give way to nervous fears but having chosen a doctor must keep strictly to his treatment. That is what I will do. Now it's all settled. I won't think about it, but will follow the treatment seriously till summer, and then we shall see. From now there must be no more of this wavering!" This was easy to say but impossible to carry out. The pain in his side oppressed him and seemed to grow worse and more incessant, while the taste in his mouth grew stranger and stranger. It seemed to him that his breath had a disgusting smell, and he was conscious of a loss of appetite and strength. There was no deceiving himself: something terrible, new, and more important than anything before in his life, was taking place within him of which he alone was aware. Those about him did not understand or would not understand it, but thought everything in the world was going on as usual. That tormented Ivan Ilych more than anything. He saw that his household, especially his wife and daughter who were in a perfect whirl of visiting, did not understand anything of it and were annoyed that he was so depressed and so exacting, as if he were to blame for it. Though they tried to disguise it he saw that he was an obstacle in their path, and that his wife had adopted a definite line in regard to his illness and kept to it regardless of anything he said or did. Her attitude was this: "You know," she would say to her friends, "Ivan Ilych can't do as other people do, and keep to the treatment prescribed for him. One day he'll take his drops and keep strictly to his diet and go to bed in good time, but the next day unless I watch him he'll suddenly forget his medicine, eat sturgeon—which is forbidden—and sit up playing cards till one o'clock in the morning."

"Oh, come, when was that?" Ivan Ilych would ask in vexation. "Only once at Peter Ivanovich's."

"And yesterday with Shebek."

"Well, even if I hadn't stayed up, this pain would have kept me awake."

"Be that as it may you'll never get well like that, but will always make us wretched."

Praskovya Fëdorovna's attitude to Ivan Ilych's illness, as she expressed it both to others and to him, was that it was his own fault and was another of the annoyances he caused her. Ivan Ilych felt that this opinion escaped her involuntarily—but that did not make it easier for him.

At the law courts too, Ivan Ilych noticed, or thought he noticed, a strange attitude towards himself. It sometimes seemed to him that people were watching him inquisitively as a man whose place might soon be vacant. Then again, his friends would suddenly begin to chaff him in a friendly way about his low spirits, as if the awful, horrible, and unheard-of thing that was going on within him, incessantly gnawing at him and irresistibly drawing him away, was a very agreeable subject for jests. Schwartz in particular irritated him by his jocularity, vivacity, and *savoir-faire*, which reminded him of what he himself had been ten years ago.

Friends came to make up a set and they sat down to cards. They dealt, bending the new cards to soften them, and he sorted the diamonds in his hand and found he had seven. His partner said "No trumps" and supported him with two diamonds. What more could be wished for? It ought to be jolly and lively. They would make a grand slam. But suddenly Ivan Ilych was conscious of that gnawing pain, that taste in his mouth, and it seemed ridiculous that in such circumstances he should be pleased to make a grand slam.

He looked at his partner Mikhail Mikhaylovich, who rapped the table with his strong hand and instead of snatching up the tricks pushed the cards courteously and indulgently towards Ivan Ilych that he might have the pleasure of gathering them up without the trouble of stretching out his hand for them. "Does he think I am too weak to stretch out my arm?" thought Ivan Ilych, and forgetting what he was doing he over-trumped his partner, missing the grand slam by three tricks. And what was most awful of all was that he saw how upset Mikhail Mikhaylovich was about it but did not himself care. And it was dreadful to realize why he did not care.

They all saw that he was suffering, and said: "We can stop if you are tired. Take a rest." Lie down? No, he was not at all tired, and he finished the rubber. All were gloomy and silent. Ivan Ilych felt that he had diffused this gloom over them and could not dispel it. They had supper and went away, and Ivan Ilych was left alone with the consciousness that his life was poisoned and was poisoning the lives of others, and that this poison did not weaken but penetrated more and more deeply into his whole being.

With this consciousness, and with physical pain besides the terror, he must go to bed, often to lie awake the greater part of the night. Next morning he had to get up again, dress, go to the law courts, speak, and write; or if he did not go out, spend at home those twenty-four hours a day each of which was a torture. And he had to live thus all alone on the brink of an abyss, with no one who understood or pitied him.

V

So one month passed and then another. Just before the New Year his brother-in-law came to town and stayed at their house. Ivan Ilych was at the law courts and

Praskovya Fëdorovna had gone shopping. When Ivan Ilych came home and entered his study he found his brother-in-law there—a healthy, florid man—unpacking his portmanteau himself. He raised his head on hearing Ivan Ilych's footsteps and looked up at him for a moment without a word. That stare told Ivan Ilych everything. His brother-in-law opened his mouth to utter an exclamation of surprise but checked himself, and that action confirmed it all.

"I have changed, eh?"   140

"Yes, there is a change."

And after that, try as he would to get his brother-in-law to return to the subject of his looks, the latter would say nothing about it. Praskovya Fëdorovna came home and her brother went out to her. Ivan Ilych locked the door and began to examine himself in the glass, first full face, then in profile. He took up a portrait of himself taken with his wife, and compared it with what he saw in the glass. The change in him was immense. Then he bared his arms to the elbow, looked at them, drew the sleeves down again, sat down on an ottoman, and grew blacker than night.

"No, no, this won't do!" he said to himself, and jumped up, went to the table, took up some law papers, and began to read them, but could not continue. He unlocked the door and went into the reception-room. The door leading to the draw-ing-room was shut. He approached it on tiptoe and listened.

"No, you are exaggerating!" Praskovya Fëdorovna was saying.

"Exaggerating! Don't you see it? Why, he's a dead man! Look at his eyes—there's   145
no light in them. But what is it that is wrong with him?"

"No one knows. Nikolaevich said something, but I don't know what. And Leshchetitsky° said quite the contrary . . ."

Ivan Ilych walked away, went to his own room, lay down, and began musing: "The kidney, a floating kidney." He recalled all the doctors had told him of how it detached itself and swayed about. And by an effort of imagination he tried to catch that kidney and arrest it and support it. So little was needed for this, it seemed to him. "No, I'll go to see Peter Ivanovich° again." He rang, ordered the carriage, and got ready to go.

"Where are you going, Jean?" asked his wife, with a specially sad and exception-ally kind look.

This exceptionally kind look irritated him. He looked morosely at her.

"I must go to see Peter Ivanovich."   150

He went to see Peter Ivanovich, and together they went to see his friend, the doctor. He was in, and Ivan Ilych had a long talk with him.

Reviewing the anatomical and physiological details of what in the doctor's opin-ion was going on inside him, he understood it all.

There was something, a small thing, in the vermiform appendix. It might all come right. Only stimulate the energy of one organ and check the activity of an-other, then absorption would take place and everything would come right. He got home rather late for dinner, ate his dinner, and conversed cheerfully, but could not for a long time bring himself to go back to work in his room. At last, however, he went to his study and did what was necessary, but the consciousness that he had put something aside—an important, intimate matter which he would revert to when his work was done—never left him. When he had finished his work he remembered that

---

Nikolaevich, Leshchetitsky: two doctors, the latter a celebrated specialist. [Translators' note.]   *Peter Ivanovich:* That was the friend whose friend was a doctor. [Translators' note.]

this intimate matter was the thought of his vermiform appendix. But he did not give himself up to it, and went to the drawing-room for tea. There were callers there, including the examining magistrate who was a desirable match for his daughter, and they were conversing, playing the piano, and singing. Ivan Ilych, as Praskovya Fëdorovna remarked, spent that evening more cheerfully than usual, but he never for a moment forgot that he had postponed the important matter of the appendix. At eleven o'clock he said good-night and went to his bedroom. Since his illness he had slept alone in a small room next to his study. He undressed and took up a novel by Zola, but instead of reading it he fell into thought, and in his imagination that desired improvement in the vermiform appendix occurred. There was the absorption and evacuation and the re-establishment of normal activity. "Yes, that's it!" he said to himself. "One need only assist nature, that's all." He remembered his medicine, rose, took it, and lay down on his back watching for the beneficent action of the medicine and for it to lessen the pain. "I need only take it regularly and avoid all injurious influences. I am already feeling better, much better." He began touching his side: it was not painful to the touch. "There, I really don't feel it. It's much better already." He put out the light and turned on his side . . . "The appendix is getting better, absorption is occurring." Suddenly he felt the old, familiar, dull, gnawing pain, stubborn and serious. There was the same familiar loathsome taste in his mouth. His heart sank and he felt dazed. "My God! My God!" he muttered. "Again, again! and it will never cease." And suddenly the matter presented itself in a quite different aspect. "Vermiform appendix! Kidney!" he said to himself. "It's not a question of appendix or kidney, but of life and . . . death. Yes, life was there and now it is going, going and I cannot stop it. Yes. Why deceive myself? Isn't it obvious to everyone but me that I'm dying, and that it's only a question of weeks, days . . . it may happen this moment. There was light and now there is darkness. I was here and now I'm going there! Where?" A chill came over him, his breathing ceased, and he felt only the throbbing of his heart.

"When I am not, what will there be? There will be nothing. Then where shall I be when I am no more? Can this be dying? No, I don't want to!" He jumped up and tried to light the candle, felt for it with trembling hands, dropped candle and candlestick on the floor, and fell back on his pillow.

"What's the use? It makes no difference," he said to himself, staring with wide-open eyes into the darkness. "Death. Yes, death. And none of them knows or wishes to know it, and they have no pity for me. Now they are playing." (He heard through the door the distant sound of a song and its accompaniment.) "It's all the same to them, but they will die too! Fools! I first, and they later, but it will be the same for them. And now they are merry . . . the beasts!"

Anger choked him and he was agonizingly, unbearably miserable. "It is impossible that all men have been doomed to suffer this awful horror!" He raised himself.

"Something must be wrong. I must calm myself—must think it all over from the beginning." And he again began thinking. "Yes, the beginning of my illness: I knocked my side, but I was still quite well that day and the next. It hurt a little, then rather more. I saw the doctors, then followed despondency and anguish, more doctors, and I drew nearer to the abyss. My strength grew less and I kept coming nearer and nearer, and now I have wasted away and there is no light in my eyes. I think of the appendix—but this is death! I think of mending the appendix, and all the while here is death! Can it really be death?" Again terror seized him and he gasped for breath. He leant down and began feeling for the matches, pressing with his elbow

155

on the stand beside the bed. It was in his way and hurt him, he grew furious with it, pressed on it still harder, and upset it. Breathless and in despair he fell on his back, expecting death to come immediately.

Meanwhile the visitors were leaving. Praskovya Fëdorovna was seeing them off. She heard something fall and came in.

"What has happened?"

"Nothing. I knocked it over accidentally."   160

She went out and returned with a candle. He lay there panting heavily, like a man who has run a thousand yards, and stared upwards at her with a fixed look.

"What is it, Jean?"

"No . . . o . . . thing. I upset it." ("Why speak of it? She won't understand," he thought.)

And in truth she did not understand. She picked up the stand, lit his candle, and hurried away to see another visitor off. When she came back he still lay on his back, looking upwards.

"What is it? Do you feel worse?"   165

"Yes."

She shook her head and sat down.

"Do you know, Jean, I think we must ask Leshchetitsky to come and see you here."

This meant calling in the famous specialist, regardless of expense. He smiled malignantly and said "No." She remained a little longer and then went up to him and kissed his forehead.

While she was kissing him he hated her from the bottom of his soul and with   170
difficulty refrained from pushing her away.

"Good-night. Please God you'll sleep."

"Yes."

VI

Ivan Ilych saw that he was dying, and he was in continual despair.

In the depth of his heart he knew he was dying, but not only was he not accustomed to the thought, he simply did not and could not grasp it.

The syllogism he had learnt from Kiesewetter's Logic: "Caius is a man, men are   175
mortal, therefore Caius is mortal," had always seemed to him correct as applied to Caius, but certainly not as applied to himself. That Caius—man in the abstract—was mortal, was perfectly correct, but he was not Caius, not an abstract man, but a creature quite, quite separate from all others. He had been little Vanya, with a mamma and a papa, with Mitya and Volodya, with the toys, a coachman and a nurse, afterwards with Katenka and with all the joys, griefs, and delights of childhood, boyhood, and youth. What did Caius know of the smell of that striped leather ball Vanya had been so fond of? Had Caius kissed his mother's hand like that, and did the silk of her dress rustle so for Caius? Had he rioted like that at school when the pastry was bad? Had Caius been in love like that? Could Caius preside at a session as he did? "Caius really was mortal, and it was right for him to die; but for me, little Vanya, Ivan Ilych, with all my thoughts and emotions, it's altogether a different matter. It cannot be that I ought to die. That would be too terrible."

Such was his feeling.

"If I had to die like Caius I should have known it was so. An inner voice would have told me so, but there was nothing of the sort in me and I and all my friends felt that our case was quite different from that of Caius. And now here it is!" he said to himself. "It can't be. It's impossible! But here it is. How is this? How is one to understand it?"

He could not understand it, and tried to drive this false, incorrect, morbid thought away and to replace it by other proper and healthy thoughts. But that thought, and not the thought only but the reality itself, seemed to come and confront him.

And to replace that thought he called up a succession of others, hoping to find in them some support. He tried to get back into the former current of thoughts that had once screened the thought of death from him. But strange to say, all that had formerly shut off, hidden, and destroyed his consciousness of death, no longer had that effect. Ivan Ilych now spent most of his time in attempting to re-establish that old current. He would say to himself: "I will take up my duties again—after all I used to live by them." And banishing all doubts he would go to the law courts, enter into conversation with his colleagues, and sit carelessly as was his wont, scanning the crowd with a thoughtful look and leaning both his emaciated arms on the arms of his oak chair; bending over as usual to a colleague and drawing his papers nearer he would interchange whispers with him, and then suddenly raising his eyes and sitting erect would pronounce certain words and open the proceedings. But suddenly in the midst of those proceedings the pain in his side, regardless of the stage the proceedings had reached, would begin its own gnawing work. Ivan Ilych would turn his attention to it and try to drive the thought of it away, but without success. It would come and stand before him and look at him, and he would be petrified and the light would die out of his eyes, and he would again begin asking himself whether It alone was true. And his colleagues and subordinates would see with surprise and distress that he, the brilliant and subtle judge, was becoming confused and making mistakes. He would shake himself, try to pull himself together, manage somehow to bring the sitting to a close, and return home with the sorrowful consciousness that his judicial labors could not as formerly hide from him what he wanted them to hide, and could not deliver him from It. And what was worst of all was that It drew his attention to itself not in order to make him take some action but only that he should look at It, look it straight in the face: look at it and, without doing anything, suffer inexpressibly.

And to save himself from this condition Ivan Ilych looked for consolation—new screens—and new screens were found and for a while seemed to save him, but then they immediately fell to pieces or rather became transparent, as if It penetrated them and nothing could veil It.

In these latter days he would go into the drawing-room he had arranged—that drawing-room where he had fallen and for the sake of which (how bitterly ridiculous it seemed) he had sacrificed his life—for he knew that his illness originated with that knock. He would enter and see that something had scratched the polished table. He would look for the cause of this and find that it was the bronze ornamentation of an album, that had got bent. He would take up the expensive album which he had lovingly arranged, and feel vexed with his daughter and her friends for their untidiness—for the album was torn here and there and some of the photographs turned upside down. He would put it carefully in order and bend the ornamentation back into position. Then it would occur to him to place all those things in another corner of the room, near the plants. He would call the footman, but his daughter or wife would come to help him. They would not agree, and his wife would contradict

180

him, and he would dispute and grow angry. But that was all right, for then he did not think about *It*. *It* was invisible.

But then, when he was moving something himself, his wife would say: "Let the servants do it. You will hurt yourself again." And suddenly *It* would flash through the screen and he would see it. It was just a flash, and he hoped it would disappear, but he would involuntarily pay attention to his side. "It sits there as before, gnawing just the same!" And he could no longer forget *It*, but could distinctly see it looking at him from behind the flowers. "What is it all for?"

"It really is so! I lost my life over that curtain as I might have done when storming a fort. Is that possible? How terrible and how stupid. It can't be true! It can't, but it is."

He would go to his study, lie down, and again be alone with *It*: face to face with *It*. And nothing could be done with *It* except to look at it and shudder.

VII

How it happened it is impossible to say because it came about step by step, unnoticed, but in the third month of Ivan Ilych's illness, his wife, his daughter, his son, his acquaintances, the doctors, the servants, and above all he himself, were aware that the whole interest he had for other people was whether he would soon vacate his place, and at last release the living from the discomfort caused by his presence and be himself released from his sufferings. 185

He slept less and less. He was given opium and hypodermic injections of morphine, but this did not relieve him. The dull depression he experienced in a somnolent condition at first gave him a little relief, but only as something new, afterwards it became as distressing as the pain itself or even more so.

Special foods were prepared for him by the doctors' orders, but all those foods became increasingly distasteful and disgusting to him.

For his excretions also special arrangements had to be made, and this was a torment to him every time—a torment from the uncleanliness, the unseemliness, and the smell, and from knowing that another person had to take part in it.

But just through this most unpleasant matter, Ivan Ilych obtained comfort. Gerasim, the butler's young assistant, always came in to carry the things out. Gerasim was a clean, fresh peasant lad, grown stout on town food and always cheerful and bright. At first the sight of him, in his clean Russian peasant costume, engaged on that disgusting task embarrassed Ivan Ilych.

Once when he got up from the commode too weak to draw up his trousers, he dropped into a soft armchair and looked with horror at his bare, enfeebled thighs with the muscles so sharply marked on them. 190

Gerasim with a firm light tread, his heavy boots emitting a pleasant smell of tar and fresh winter air, came in wearing a clean Hessian apron, the sleeves of his print shirt tucked up over his strong, bare young arms; and refraining from looking at his sick master out of consideration for his feelings, and restraining the joy of life that beamed from his face, he went up to the commode.

"Gerasim!" said Ivan Ilych in a weak voice.

Gerasim started, evidently afraid he might have committed some blunder, and with a rapid movement turned his fresh, kind, simple young face which just showed the first downy signs of a beard.

"Yes, sir?"

"That must be very unpleasant for you. You must forgive me. I am helpless." 195

"Oh, why, sir," and Gerasim's eyes beamed and he showed his glistening white teeth, "what's a little trouble? It's a case of illness with you, sir."

And his deft strong hands did their accustomed task, and he went out of the room stepping lightly. Five minutes later he as lightly returned.

Ivan Ilych was still sitting in the same position in the armchair.

"Gerasim," he said when the latter had replaced the freshly washed utensil. "Please come here and help me." Gerasim went up to him. "Lift me up. It is hard for me to get up, and I have sent Dmitri away."

Gerasim went up to him, grasped his master with his strong arms deftly but gently,   200
in the same way that he stepped—lifted him, supported him with one hand, and with the other drew up his trousers and would have set him down again, but Ivan Ilych asked to be led to the sofa. Gerasim, without an effort and without apparent pressure, led him, almost lifting him, to the sofa, and placed him on it.

"Thank you. How easily and well you do it all!"

Gerasim smiled again and turned to leave the room. But Ivan Ilych felt his presence such a comfort that he did not want to let him go.

"One thing more, please move up that chair. No, the other one—under my feet. It is easier for me when my feet are raised."

Gerasim brought the chair, set it down gently in place, and raised Ivan Ilych's legs on to it. It seemed to Ivan Ilych that he felt better while Gerasim was holding up his legs.

"It's better when my legs are higher," he said. "Place that cushion under them."   205

Gerasim did so. He again lifted the legs and placed them, and again Ivan Ilych felt better while Gerasim held his legs. When he set them down Ivan Ilych fancied he felt worse.

"Gerasim," he said. "Are you busy now?"

"Not at all, sir," said Gerasim, who had learnt from the townsfolk how to speak to gentlefolk.

"What have you still to do?"

"What have I to do? I've done everything except chopping the logs for tomor-   210
row."

"Then hold my legs up a bit higher, can you?"

"Of course I can. Why not?" And Gerasim raised his master's legs higher and Ivan Ilych thought that in that position he did not feel any pain at all.

"And how about the logs?"

"Don't trouble about that, sir. There's plenty of time."

Ivan Ilych told Gerasim to sit down and hold his legs, and began to talk to him.   215
And strange to say it seemed to him that he felt better while Gerasim held his legs up.

After that Ivan Ilych would sometimes call Gerasim and get him to hold his legs on his shoulders, and he liked talking to him. Gerasim did it all easily, willingly, simply, and with a good nature that touched Ivan Ilych. Health, strength, and vitality in other people were offensive to him, but Gerasim's strength and vitality did not mortify but soothed him.

What tormented Ivan Ilych most was the deception, the lie, which for some reason they all accepted, that he was not dying but was simply ill, and that he only need keep quiet and undergo a treatment and then something very good would result. He, however, knew that do what they would nothing would come of it, only still more agonizing suffering and death. This deception tortured him—their not wishing to admit what they all knew and what he knew, but wanting to lie to him concerning his terrible condition, and wishing and forcing him to participate in that lie. Those lies—lies enacted over him on the eve of his death and destined to degrade this awful, solemn act to the level of their visitings, their curtains, their sturgeon for dinner—were a terrible agony for Ivan Ilych. And strangely enough, many times when they were going through their antics over him he had been within a hairbreadth of calling out to them: "Stop lying! You know and I know that I am dying. Then at least stop lying about it!" But he had never had the spirit to do it. The awful, terrible act of his dying was, he could see, reduced by those about him to the level of a casual, unpleasant, and almost indecorous incident (as if someone entered a drawing-room diffusing an unpleasant odor) and this was done by that very decorum which he had served all his life long. He saw that no one felt for him, because no one even wished to grasp his position. Only Gerasim recognized it and pitied him. And so Ivan Ilych felt at ease only with him. He felt comforted when Gerasim supported his legs (sometimes all night long) and refused to go to bed, saying: "Don't you worry, Ivan Ilych. I'll get sleep enough later on," or when he suddenly became familiar and exclaimed: "If you weren't sick it would be another matter, but as it is, why should I grudge a little trouble?" Gerasim alone did not lie; everything showed that he alone understood the facts of the case and did not consider it necessary to disguise them, but simply felt sorry for his emaciated and enfeebled master. Once when Ivan Ilych was sending him away he even said straight out: "We shall all of us die, so why should I grudge a little trouble?"—expressing the fact that he did not think his work burdensome, because he was doing it for a dying man and hoped someone would do the same for him when his time came.

Apart from this lying, or because of it, what most tormented Ivan Ilych was that no one pitied him as he wished to be pitied. At certain moments after prolonged suffering he wished most of all (though he would have been ashamed to confess it) for someone to pity him as a sick child is pitied. He longed to be petted and comforted. He knew he was an important functionary, that he had a beard turning grey, and that therefore what he longed for was impossible, but still he longed for it. And in Gerasim's attitude towards him there was something akin to what he wished for, and so that attitude comforted him. Ivan Ilych wanted to weep, wanted to be petted and cried over, and then his colleague Shebek would come, and instead of weeping and being petted, Ivan Ilych would assume a serious, severe, and profound air, and by force of habit would express his opinion on a decision of the Court of Cassation and would stubbornly insist on that view. This falsity around him and within him did more than anything else to poison his last days.

VIII

It was morning. He knew it was morning because Gerasim had gone, and Peter the footman had come and put out the candles, drawn back one of the curtains, and begun quietly to tidy up. Whether it was morning or evening, Friday or Sunday, made no difference, it was all just the same: the gnawing, unmitigated, agonizing pain, never ceasing for an instant, the consciousness of life inexorably waning but not yet extinguished, the approach of that ever dreaded and hateful Death which was the only reality, and always the same falsity. What were days, weeks, hours, in such a case?

"Will you have some tea, sir?"

"He wants things to be regular, and wishes the gentlefolk to drink tea in the morning," thought Ivan Ilych, and only said "No."

220

"Wouldn't you like to move onto the sofa, sir?"

"He wants to tidy up the room, and I'm in the way. I am uncleanliness and disorder," he thought, and said only:

"No, leave me alone."

The man went on bustling about. Ivan Ilych stretched out his hand. Peter came 225 up, ready to help.

"What is it, sir?"

"My watch."

Peter took the watch which was close at hand and gave it to his master.

"Half-past eight. Are they up?"

"No, sir, except Vasily Ivanovich" (the son) "who has gone to school. Praskovya 230 Fëdorovna ordered me to wake her if you asked for her. Shall I do so?"

"No, there's no need to." "Perhaps I'd better have some tea," he thought, and added aloud: "Yes, bring me some tea."

Peter went to the door, but Ivan Ilych dreaded being left alone. "How can I keep him here? Oh yes, my medicine." "Peter, give me my medicine." "Why not? Perhaps it may still do me some good." He took a spoonful and swallowed it. "No, it won't help. It's all tomfoolery, all deception," he decided as soon as he became aware of the familiar, sickly, hopeless taste. "No, I can't believe in it any longer. But the pain, why this pain? If it would only cease just for a moment!" And he moaned. Peter turned towards him. "It's all right. Go and fetch me some tea."

Peter went out. Left alone Ivan Ilych groaned not so much with pain, terrible though that was, as from mental anguish. Always and forever the same, always these endless days and nights. If only it would come quicker! If only *what* would come quicker? Death, darkness? . . . No, no! Anything rather than death!

When Peter returned with the tea on a tray, Ivan Ilych stared at him for a time in perplexity, not realizing who and what he was. Peter was disconcerted by that look and his embarrassment brought Ivan Ilych to himself.

"Oh, tea! All right, put it down. Only help me to wash and put on a clean shirt." 235

And Ivan Ilych began to wash. With pauses for rest, he washed his hands and then his face, cleaned his teeth, brushed his hair, and looked in the glass. He was terrified by what he saw, especially by the limp way in which his hair clung to his pallid forehead.

While his shirt was being changed he knew that he would be still more frightened at the sight of his body, so he avoided looking at it. Finally he was ready. He drew on a dressing-gown, wrapped himself in a plaid, and sat down in the armchair to take his tea. For a moment he felt refreshed, but soon as he began to drink the tea he was again aware of the same taste, and the pain also returned. He finished it with an effort, and then lay down stretching out his legs, and dismissed Peter.

Always the same. Now a spark of hope flashes up, then a sea of despair rages, and always pain; always pain, always despair, and always the same. When alone he had a dreadful and distressing desire to call someone, but he knew beforehand that with others present it would be still worse. "Another dose of morphine—to lose consciousness. I will tell him, the doctor, that he must think of something else. It's impossible, impossible, to go on like this."

An hour and another pass like that. But now there is a ring at the door bell. Perhaps it's the doctor? It is. He comes in fresh, hearty, plump, and cheerful, with that look on his face that seems to say: "There now, you're in a panic about something, but we'll arrange it all for you directly!" The doctor knows this expression is out of place here, but he has put it on once for all and can't take it off—like a man who has put on a frock-coat in the morning to pay a round of calls.

The doctor rubs his hands vigorously and reassuringly. 240

"Brr! How cold it is! There's such a sharp frost; just let me warm myself!" he says, as if it were only a matter of waiting till he was warm, and then he would put everything right.

"Well now, how are you?"

Ivan Ilych feels that the doctor would like to say: "Well, how are our affairs?" but that even he feels that this would not do, and says instead: "What sort of a night have you had?"

Ivan Ilych looks at him as much as to say: "Are you really never ashamed of lying?" But the doctor does not wish to understand this question, and Ivan Ilych says: "Just as terrible as ever. The pain never leaves me and never subsides. If only something . . ."

"Yes, you sick people are always like that. . . . There, now I think I am warm 245 enough. Even Praskovya Fëdorovna, who is so particular, could find no fault with my temperature. Well, now I can say good-morning," and the doctor presses his patient's hand.

Then, dropping his former playfulness, he begins with a most serious face to examine the patient, feeling his pulse and taking his temperature, and then begins the sounding and auscultation.

Ivan Ilych knows quite well and definitely that all this is nonsense and pure deception, but when the doctor, getting down on his knee, leans over him, putting his ear first higher then lower, and performs various gymnastic movements over him with a significant expression on his face, Ivan Ilych submits to it all as he used to submit to the speeches of the lawyers, though he knew very well that they were all lying and why they were lying.

The doctor, kneeling on the sofa, is still sounding him when Praskovya Fëdorovna's silk dress rustles at the door and she is heard scolding Peter for not having let her know of the doctor's arrival.

She comes in, kisses her husband, and at once proceeds to prove that she has been up a long time already, and only owing to a misunderstanding failed to be there when the doctor arrived.

Ivan Ilych looks at her, scans her all over, sets against her the whiteness and 250 plumpness and cleanness of her hands and neck, the gloss of her hair, and the sparkle of her vivacious eyes. He hates her with his whole soul. And the thrill of hatred he feels for her makes him suffer from her touch.

Her attitude towards him and his disease is still the same. Just as the doctor had adopted a certain relation to his patient which he could not abandon, so had she formed one towards him—that he was not doing something he ought to do and was himself to blame, and that she reproached him lovingly for this—and she could not now change that attitude.

"You see he doesn't listen to me and doesn't take his medicine at the proper time. And above all he lies in a position that is no doubt bad for him—with his legs up."

She described how he made Gerasim hold his legs up.

The doctor smiled with a contemptuous affability that said: "What's to be done? These sick people do have foolish fancies of that kind, but we must forgive them."

When the examination was over the doctor looked at his watch, and then 255 Praskovya Fëdorovna announced to Ivan Ilych that it was of course as he pleased, but she had sent today for a celebrated specialist who would examine him and have a consultation with Michael Danilovich (their regular doctor).

"Please don't raise any objections. I am doing this for my own sake," she said ironically, letting it be felt that she was doing it all for his sake and only said this to leave him no right to refuse. He remained silent, knitting his brows. He felt that he was so surrounded and involved in a mesh of falsity that it was hard to unravel anything.

Everything she did for him was entirely for her own sake, and she told him she was doing for herself what she actually was doing for herself, as if that was so incredible that he must understand the opposite.

At half-past eleven the celebrated specialist arrived. Again the sounding began and the significant conversations in his presence and in another room, about the kidneys and the appendix, and the questions and answers, with such an air of importance that again, instead of the real question of life and death which now alone confronted him, the question arose of the kidney and appendix which were not behaving as they ought to and would now be attacked by Michael Danilovich and the specialist and forced to amend their ways.

The celebrated specialist took leave of him with a serious though not hopeless look, and in reply to the timid question Ivan Ilych, with eyes glistening with fear and hope, put to him as to whether there was a chance of recovery, said that he could not vouch for it but there was a possibility. The look of hope with which Ivan Ilych watched the doctor out was so pathetic that Praskovya Fëdorovna, seeing it, even wept as she left the room to hand the doctor his fee.

The gleam of hope kindled by the doctor's encouragement did not last long. The same room, the same pictures, curtains, wallpaper, medicine bottles, were all there, and the same aching suffering body, and Ivan Ilych began to moan. They gave him a subcutaneous injection and he sank into oblivion. 260

It was twilight when he came to. They brought him his dinner and he swallowed some beef tea with difficulty, and then everything was the same again and night was coming on.

After dinner, at seven o'clock, Praskovya Fëdorovna came into the room in evening dress, her full bosom pushed up by her corset, and with traces of powder on her face. She had reminded him in the morning that they were going to the theater. Sarah Bernhardt was visiting the town and they had a box, which he had insisted on their taking. Now he had forgotten about it and her toilet offended him, but he concealed his vexation when he remembered that he had himself insisted on their securing a box and going because it would be an instructive and aesthetic pleasure for the children.

Praskovya Fëdorovna came in, self-satisfied but yet with a rather guilty air. She sat down and asked how he was, but, as he saw, only for the sake of asking and not in order to learn about it, knowing that there was nothing to learn—and then went on to what she really wanted to say: that she would not on any account have gone but that the box had been taken and Helen and their daughter were going, as well as Petrishchev (the examining magistrate, their daughter's fiancé), and that it was out of the question to let them go alone; but that she would have much preferred to sit with him for a while; and he must be sure to follow the doctor's orders while she was away.

"Oh, and Fëdor Petrovich" (the fiancé) "would like to come in. May he? And Lisa?"

"All right."

265

Their daughter came in in full evening dress, her fresh young flesh exposed (making a show of that very flesh which in his own case caused so much suffering), strong, healthy, evidently in love, and impatient with illness, suffering, and death, because they interfered with her happiness.

Fëdor Petrovich came in too, in evening dress, his hair curled *à la Capoul,*° a tight stiff collar round his long sinewy neck, an enormous white shirtfront, and narrow black trousers tightly stretched over his strong thighs. He had one white glove tightly drawn on, and was holding his opera hat in his hand.

Following him the schoolboy crept in unnoticed, in a new uniform, poor little fellow, and wearing gloves. Terribly dark shadows showed under his eyes, the meaning of which Ivan Ilych knew well.

His son had always seemed pathetic to him, and now it was dreadful to see the boy's frightened look of pity. It seemed to Ivan Ilych that Vasya was the only one besides Gerasim who understood and pitied him.

They all sat down and again asked how he was. A silence followed. Lisa asked   270
her mother about the opera-glasses, and there was an altercation between mother and daughter as to who had taken them and where they had been put. This occasioned some unpleasantness.

Fëdor Petrovich inquired of Ivan Ilych whether he had ever seen Sarah Bernhardt. Ivan Ilych did not at first catch the question, but then replied: "No, have you seen her before?"

"Yes, in *Adrienne Lecouvreur.*"

Praskovya Fëdorovna mentioned some rôles in which Sarah Bernhardt was particularly good. Her daughter disagreed. Conversation sprang up as to the elegance and realism of her acting—the sort of conversation that is always repeated and is always the same.

In the midst of the conversation Fëdor Petrovich glanced at Ivan Ilych and became silent. The others also looked at him and grew silent. Ivan Ilych was staring with glittering eyes straight before him, evidently indignant with them. This had to be rectified, but it was impossible to do so. The silence had to be broken, but for a time no one dared to break it and they all became afraid that the conventional deception would suddenly become obvious and the truth become plain to all. Lisa was the first to pluck up courage and break that silence, but by trying to hide what everybody was feeling, she betrayed it.

"Well, if we are going it's time to start," she said, looking at her watch, a present   275
from her father, and with a faint and significant smile at Fëdor Petrovich relating to something known only to them. She got up with a rustle of her dress.

They all rose, said good-night, and went away.

When they had gone it seemed to Ivan Ilych that he felt better; the falsity had gone with them. But the pain remained—that same pain and that same fear that made everything monotonously alike, nothing harder and nothing easier. Everything was worse.

Again minute followed minute and hour followed hour. Everything remained the same and there was no cessation. And the inevitable end of it all became more and more terrible.

"Yes, send Gerasim here," he replied to a question Peter asked.

à la Capoul: imitating the hairdo of Victor Capoul, a contemporary French singer.

IX

His wife returned late at night. She came in on tiptoe, but he heard her, opened 280
his eyes, and made haste to close them again. She wished to send Gerasim away and to
sit with him herself, but he opened his eyes and said: "No, go away."

"Are you in great pain?"

"Always the same."

"Take some opium."

He agreed and took some. She went away.

Till about three in the morning he was in a state of stupefied misery. It seemed to 285
him that he and his pain were being thrust into a narrow, deep black sack, but though
they were pushed further and further in they could not be pushed to the bottom. And
this, terrible enough in itself, was accompanied by suffering. He was frightened yet
wanted to fall through the sack, he struggled but yet cooperated. And suddenly he
broke through, fell, and regained consciousness. Gerasim was sitting at the foot of the
bed dozing quietly and patiently, while he himself lay with his emaciated stockinged
legs resting on Gerasim's shoulders; the same shaded candle was there and the same
unceasing pain.

"Go away, Gerasim," he whispered.

"It's all right, sir. I'll stay a while."

"No. Go away."

He removed his legs from Gerasim's shoulders, turned sideways onto his arm,
and felt sorry for himself. He only waited till Gerasim had gone into the next room
and then restrained himself no longer but wept like a child. He wept on account of
his helplessness, his terrible loneliness, the cruelty of man, the cruelty of God, and
the absence of God.

"Why hast Thou done all this? Why hast Thou brought me here? Why, why dost 290
Thou torment me so terribly?"

He did not expect an answer and yet wept because there was no answer and
could be none. The pain grew more acute, but he did not stir and did not call. He
said to himself: "Go on! Strike me! But what is it for? What have I done to Thee?
What is it for?"

Then he grew quiet and not only ceased weeping but even held his breath and
became all attention. It was as though he was listening not to an audible voice but to
the voice of his soul, to the current of thoughts arising within him.

"What is it you want?" was the first clear conception capable of expression in
words, that he heard.

"What do you want? What do you want?" he repeated to himself.

"What do I want? To live and not to suffer," he answered. 295

And again he listened with such concentrated attention that even his pain did
not distract him.

"To live? How?" asked his inner voice.

"Why, to live as I used to—well and pleasantly."

"As you lived before, well and pleasantly?" the voice repeated.

And in imagination he began to recall the best moments of his pleasant life. But 300
strange to say none of those best moments of his pleasant life now seemed at all what
they had then seemed—none of them except the first recollections of childhood. There,
in childhood, there had been something really pleasant with which it would be possible
to live if it could return. But the child who had experienced that happiness existed no
longer, it was like a reminiscence of somebody else.

As soon as the period began which had produced the present Ivan Ilych, all that had then seemed joys now melted before his sight and turned into something trivial and often nasty.

And the further he departed from childhood and the nearer he came to the present the more worthless and doubtful were the joys. This began with the School of Law. A little that was really good was still found there—there was lightheartedness, friendship, and hope. But in the upper classes there had already been fewer of such good moments. Then during the first years of his official career, when he was in the service of the Governor, some pleasant moments again occurred: they were the memories of love for a woman. Then all became confused and there was still less of what was good; later on again there was still less that was good, and the further he went the less there was. His marriage, a mere accident, then the disenchantment that followed it, his wife's bad breath and the sensuality and hypocrisy; then that deadly official life and those preoccupations about money, a year of it, and two, and ten, and twenty, and always the same thing. And the longer it lasted the more deadly it became. "It is as if I had been going downhill while I imagined I was going up. And that is really what it was. I was going up in public opinion, but to the same extent life was ebbing away from me. And now it is all done and there is only death."

"Then what does it mean? Why? It can't be that life is so senseless and horrible. But if it really has been so horrible and senseless, why must I die and die in agony? There is something wrong!"

"Maybe I did not live as I ought to have done," it suddenly occurred to him. "But how could that be, when I did everything properly?" he replied, and immediately dismissed from his mind this, the sole solution of all the riddles of life and death, as something quite impossible.

"Then what do you want now? To live? Live how? Live as you lived in the law 305 courts when the usher proclaimed 'The judge is coming!' The judge is coming, the judge!" he repeated to himself. "Here he is, the judge. But I am not guilty!" he exclaimed angrily. "What is it for?" And he ceased crying, but turning his face to the wall continued to ponder on the same question: Why, and for what purpose, is there all this horror? But however much he pondered he found no answer. And whenever the thought occurred to him, as it often did, that it all resulted from his not having lived as he ought to have done, he at once recalled the correctness of his whole life and dismissed so strange an idea.

X

Another fortnight passed. Ivan Ilych now no longer left his sofa. He would not lie in bed but lay on the sofa, facing the wall nearly all the time. He suffered ever the same unceasing agonies and in his loneliness pondered always on the same insoluble question: "What is this? Can it be that it is Death?" And the inner voice answered: "Yes, it is Death."

"Why these sufferings?" And the voice answered, "For no reason—they just are so." Beyond and besides this there was nothing.

From the very beginning of his illness, ever since he had first been to see the doctor, Ivan Ilych's life had been divided between two contrary and alternating moods: now it was despair and the expectation of this uncomprehended and terrible death, and now hope and an intently interested observation of the functioning of his organs. Now before his eyes there was only a kidney or an intestine that temporarily evaded its duty, and now only that incomprehensible and dreadful death from which it was impossible to escape.

These two states of mind had alternated from the very beginning of his illness, but the further it progressed the more doubtful and fantastic became the conception of the kidney, and the more real the sense of impending death.

He had but to call to mind what he had been three months before and what he was now, to call to mind with what regularity he had been going downhill, for every possibility of hope to be shattered.

Latterly during that loneliness in which he found himself as he lay facing the back of the sofa, a loneliness in the midst of a populous town and surrounded by numerous acquaintances and relations but that yet could not have been more complete anywhere—either at the bottom of the sea or under the earth—during that terrible loneliness Ivan Ilych had lived only in memories of the past. Pictures of his past rose before him one after another. They always began with what was nearest in time and then went back to what was most remote—to his childhood—and rested there. If he thought of the stewed prunes that had been offered him that day, his mind went back to the raw shrivelled French plums of his childhood, their peculiar flavor and the flow of saliva when he sucked their stones, and along with the memory of that taste came a whole series of memories of those days: his nurse, his brother, and their toys. "No, I mustn't think of that. . . . It is too painful," Ivan Ilych said to himself, and brought himself back to the present—to the button on the back of the sofa and the creases in its morocco. "Morocco is expensive, but it does not wear well: there had been a quarrel about it. It was a different kind of quarrel and a different kind of morocco that time when we tore father's portfolio and were punished, and mamma brought us some tarts. . . ." And again his thoughts dwelt on his childhood, and again it was painful and he tried to banish them and fix his mind on something else.

Then again together with that chain of memories another series passed through his mind—of how his illness had progressed and grown worse. There also the further back he looked the more life there had been. There had been more of what was good in life and more of life itself. The two merged together. "Just as the pain went on getting worse and worse, so my life grew worse and worse," he thought. "There is one bright spot there at the back, at the beginning of life, and afterwards all becomes blacker and blacker and proceeds more and more rapidly—in inverse ratio to the square of the distance from death," thought Ivan Ilych. And the example of a stone falling downwards with increasing velocity entered his mind. Life, a series of increasing sufferings, flies further and further towards its end—the most terrible suffering. "I am flying. . . ." He shuddered, shifted himself, and tried to resist, but was already aware that resistance was impossible, and again, with eyes weary of gazing but unable to cease seeing what was before them, he stared at the back of the sofa and waited—awaiting that dreadful fall and shock and destruction.

"Resistance is impossible!" he said to himself. "If I could only understand what it is all for! But that too is impossible. An explanation would be possible if it could be said that I have not lived as I ought to. But it is impossible to say that," and he remembered all the legality, correctitude, and propriety of his life. "That at any rate can certainly not be admitted," he thought, and his lips smiled ironically as if someone could see that smile and be taken in by it. "There is no explanation! Agony, death. . . . What for?"

XI

Another two weeks went by in this way and during that fortnight an event occurred that Ivan Ilych and his wife had desired. Petrishchev formally proposed. It

happened in the evening. The next day Praskovya Fëdorovna came into her husband's room considering how best to inform him of it, but that very night there had
been a fresh change for the worse in his condition. She found him still lying on the
sofa but in a different position. He lay on his back, groaning and staring fixedly
straight in front of him.

She began to remind him of his medicines, but he turned his eyes towards her   315
with such a look that she did not finish what she was saying; so great an animosity, to
her in particular, did that look express.

"For Christ's sake let me die in peace!" he said.

She would have gone away, but just then their daughter came in and went up to
say good morning. He looked at her as he had done at his wife, and in reply to her
inquiry about his health said dryly that he would soon free them all of himself. They
were both silent and after sitting with him for a while went away.

"Is it our fault?" Lisa said to her mother. "It's as if we were to blame! I am sorry
for papa, but why should we be tortured?"

The doctor came at his usual time. Ivan Ilych answered "Yes" and "No," never
taking his angry eyes from him, and at last said: "You know you can do nothing for
me, so leave me alone."

"We can ease your sufferings."   320

"You can't even do that. Let me be."

The doctor went into the drawing-room and told Praskovya Fëdorovna that the
case was very serious and that the only resource left was opium to allay her husband's
sufferings, which must be terrible.

It was true, as the doctor said, that Ivan Ilych's physical sufferings were terrible,
but worse than the physical sufferings were his mental sufferings, which were his
chief torture.

His mental sufferings were due to the fact that one night, as he looked at
Gerasim's sleepy, good-natured face with its prominent cheekbones, the question
suddenly occurred to him: "What if my whole life has really been wrong?"

It occurred to him that what had appeared perfectly impossible before, namely   325
that he had not spent his life as he should have done, might after all be true. It
occurred to him that his scarcely perceptible attempts to struggle against what was
considered good by the most highly placed people, those scarcely noticeable impulses
which he had immediately suppressed, might have been the real thing, and all the
rest false. And his professional duties and the whole arrangement of his life and of his
family, and all his social and official interests, might all have been false. He tried to
defend all those things to himself and suddenly felt the weakness of what he was
defending. There was nothing to defend.

"But if that is so," he said to himself, "and I am leaving this life with the consciousness that I have lost all that was given me and it is impossible to rectify it—
what then?"

He lay on his back and began to pass his life in review in quite a new way. In the
morning when he saw first his footman, then his wife, then his daughter, and then the
doctor, their every word and movement confirmed to him the awful truth that had
been revealed to him during the night. In them he saw himself—all that for which he
had lived—and saw clearly that it was not real at all, but a terrible and huge deception
which had hidden both life and death. This consciousness intensified his physical suffering tenfold. He groaned and tossed about, and pulled at his clothing which choked
and stifled him. And he hated them on that account.

He was given a large dose of opium and became unconscious, but at noon his sufferings began again. He drove everybody away and tossed from side to side.

His wife came to him and said:

"Jean, my dear, do this for me. It can't do any harm and often helps. Healthy people often do it."

He opened his eyes wide.

"What? Take communion? Why? It's unnecessary! However . . ."

She began to cry.

"Yes, do, my dear. I'll send for our priest. He is such a nice man."

"All right. Very well," he muttered.

When the priest came and heard his confession, Ivan Ilych was softened and seemed to feel a relief from his doubts and consequently from his sufferings, and for a moment there came a ray of hope. He again began to think of the vermiform appendix and the possibility of correcting it. He received the sacrament with tears in his eyes.

When they laid him down again afterwards he felt a moment's ease, and the hope that he might live awoke in him again. He began to think of the operation that had been suggested to him. "To live! I want to live!" he said to himself.

His wife came in to congratulate him after his communion, and when uttering the usual conventional words she added:

"You feel better, don't you?"

Without looking at her he said "Yes."

Her dress, her figure, the expression of her face, the tone of her voice, all revealed the same thing. "This is wrong, it is not as it should be. All you have lived for and still live for is falsehood and deception, hiding life and death from you." And as soon as he admitted that thought, his hatred and his agonizing physical suffering again sprang up, and with that suffering a consciousness of the unavoidable, approaching end. And to this was added a new sensation of grinding shooting pain and a feeling of suffocation.

The expression of his face when he uttered that "yes" was dreadful. Having uttered it, he looked her straight in the eyes, turned on his face with a rapidity extraordinary in his weak state and shouted:

"Go away! Go away and leave me alone!"

XII

From that moment the screaming began that continued for three days, and was so terrible that one could not hear it through two closed doors without horror. At the moment he answered his wife he realized that he was lost, that there was no return, that the end had come, the very end, and his doubts were still unsolved and remained doubts.

"Oh! Oh! Oh!" he cried in various intonations. He had begun by screaming "I won't!" and continued screaming on the letter O.

For three whole days, during which time did not exist for him, he struggled in that black sack into which he was being thrust by an invisible, resistless force. He struggled as a man condemned to death struggles in the hands of the executioner, knowing that he cannot save himself. And every moment he felt that despite all his efforts he was drawing nearer and nearer to what terrified him. He felt that his agony was due to his being thrust into that black hole and still more to his not being able to get right into it. He was hindered from getting into it by his conviction that his life had been a good one. That very justification of his life held him fast and prevented his moving forward, and it caused him most torment of all.

Suddenly some force struck him in the chest and side, making it still harder to breathe, and he fell through the hole and there at the bottom was a light. What had happened to him was like the sensation one sometimes experiences in a railway carriage when one thinks one is going backwards while one is really going forwards and suddenly becomes aware of the real direction.

"Yes, it was all not the right thing," he said to himself, "but that's no matter. It can be done. But what *is* the right thing?" he asked himself, and suddenly grew quiet.

This occurred at the end of the third day, two hours before his death. Just then his schoolboy son had crept softly in and gone up to the bedside. The dying man was still screaming desperately and waving his arms. His hand fell on the boy's head, and the boy caught it, pressed it to his lips, and began to cry.

At that very moment Ivan Ilych fell through and caught sight of the light, and   350 it was revealed to him that though his life had not been what it should have been, this could still be rectified. He asked himself, "What *is* the right thing?" and grew still, listening. Then he felt that someone was kissing his hand. He opened his eyes, looked at his son, and felt sorry for him. His wife came up to him and he glanced at her. She was gazing at him open-mouthed, with undried tears on her nose and cheek and a despairing look on her face. He felt sorry for her too.

"Yes, I am making them wretched," he thought. "They are sorry, but it will be better for them when I die." He wished to say this but had not the strength to utter it. "Besides, why speak? I must act," he thought. With a look at his wife he indicated his son and said: "Take him away . . . sorry for him . . . sorry for you too. . . ." He tried to add, "Forgive me," but said "forgo" and waved his hand, knowing that He whose understanding mattered would understand.

And suddenly it grew clear to him that what had been oppressing him and would not leave him was all dropping away at once from two sides, from ten sides, and from all sides. He was sorry for them, he must act so as not to hurt them: release them and free himself from these sufferings. "How good and how simple!" he thought. "And the pain?" he asked himself. "What has become of it? Where are you, pain?"

He turned his attention to it.

"Yes, here it is. Well, what of it? Let the pain be."

"And death . . . where is it?"   355

He sought his former accustomed fear of death and did not find it. "Where is it? What death?" There was no fear because there was no death.

In place of death there was light.

"So that's what it is!" he suddenly exclaimed aloud. "What joy!"

To him all this happened in a single instant, and the meaning of that instant did not change. For those present his agony continued for another two hours. Something rattled in his throat, his emaciated body twitched, then the gasping and rattle became less and less frequent.

"It is finished!" said someone near him.   360

He heard these words and repeated them in his soul.

"Death is finished," he said to himself. "It is no more!"

He drew in a breath, stopped in the midst of a sigh, stretched out, and died.

Questions

1. Sum up the reactions of Ivan Ilych's colleagues to the news of his death. What is implied in Tolstoy's calling them not friends, but "nearest acquaintances"?
2. What comic elements do you find in the account of the wake that Peter Ivanovich attends?

3. In Tolstoy's description of the corpse and its expression (paragraph 27), what details seem especially revealing and meaningful?

4. Do you think Tolstoy would have improved the story if he had placed the events in chronological order? What would be lost if the opening scene of Ivan Ilych's colleagues at the law courts and the wake scene were to be given last?

5. Would you call Ivan Ilyich, when we first meet him, a religious man? Sum up his goals in life, his values, and his attitudes.

6. By what "virtues" and abilities does Ivan Ilych rise through the ranks? While he continues to succeed in his career, what happens to his marriage?

7. "Every spot on the tablecloth or the upholstery, and every broken window-blind string, irritated him. He had devoted so much trouble to arranging it all that every disturbance of it distressed him" (paragraph 104). What do you make of this passage? What is its tone? Does the narrator sympathize with Ivan Ilych's attachment to his possessions?

8. Consider the account of Ivan Ilych's routine in paragraph 105 ("He got up at nine . . ."). What elements of a full life, what higher satisfactions, does this routine omit?

9. What caused Ivan Ilych's illness? How would it probably be diagnosed today? What is the narrator's attitude toward Ivan Ilych's doctors?

10. In what successive stages does Tolstoy depict Ivan Ilych's growing isolation as his progressive illness sets him more and more apart?

11. What are we apparently supposed to admire in the character and conduct of the servant Gerasim?

12. What do you understand from the statement that Ivan Ilych's justification of his life "prevented his moving forward, and it caused him most torment of all" (paragraph 346)?

13. What is memorable in the character of Ivan Ilych's schoolboy son? Why is he crucial to the story? (Suggestion: Look closely at paragraphs 349–350.)

14. What realization allows Ivan Ilych to triumph over pain? Why does he die peacefully?

15. The writer Henri Troyat has said that through the story of Ivan Ilych we imagine what our own deaths will be. Is it possible to identify with an aging, selfish, worldly, nineteenth-century Russian judge?

Franz Kafka

The Metamorphosis   1915

Translated by John Siscoe

Franz Kafka (1883–1924) was born into a German-speaking Jewish family in Prague, Czechoslovakia (then part of the Austro-Hungarian empire). He was the only surviving son of a domineering, successful father. After earning a law degree, Kafka worked as a claims investigator for the state accident insurance company. He worked on his stories at night, especially during his frequent bouts of insomnia. He never married, and lived mostly with his parents. Kafka was such a careful and self-conscious writer that he found it difficult to finish his work and send it out for publication. During his lifetime he published only a few thin volumes of short fiction, most notably The Metamorphosis *(1915) and* In the Penal

Franz Kafka

Colony (1919). He never finished to his own satisfaction any of his three novels (all published posthumously): The Trial (1925), The Castle (1926), and Amerika (1927). As
Kafka was dying of tuberculosis, he begged his friend and literary executor Max Brod to
burn his uncompleted manuscripts. Brod pondered this request but luckily didn't obey.
Kafka's two major novels, The Trial and The Castle, both depict huge, remote, bumbling,
irresponsible bureaucracies in whose power the individual feels helpless and blind. Kafka's
works appear startlingly prophetic to readers looking back on them in the later light of Stalin-
ism, World War II, and the Holocaust. His haunting vision of an alienated modern world
led the poet W. H. Auden to remark at midcentury, "Had one to name the author who
comes nearest to bearing the same kind of relation to our age as Dante, Shakespeare, and
Goethe bore to theirs, Kafka is the first one would think of." The Metamorphosis, which
arguably has the most famous opening sentence in twentieth-century literature, shows
Kafka's dreamlike fiction at its most brilliant and most disturbing.

I

When Gregor Samsa awoke one morning from troubled dreams, he found himself transformed in his bed into a monstrous insect. He was lying on his back, which
was hard, as if plated in armor, and when he lifted his head slightly he could see his
belly: rounded, brown, and divided into stiff arched segments; on top of it the blanket, about to slip off altogether, still barely clinging. His many legs, which seemed
pathetically thin when compared to the rest of his body, flickered helplessly before
his eyes.

"What's happened to me?" he thought. It was no dream. His room, a normal
though somewhat small human bedroom, lay quietly within its four familiar walls.
Above the table on which his unpacked fabric samples were spread—Samsa was a
traveling salesman—hung the picture he had recently cut out of an illustrated magazine and had set in a lovely gilt frame. It showed a lady wearing a fur hat and a fur
stole, sitting upright, and thrusting out to the viewer a thick fur muff, into which her
whole forearm had disappeared.

Gregor's glance then fell on the window, and the overcast sky—one could hear
raindrops drumming on the tin sheeting of the windowsill—made him feel profoundly sad. "What if I went back to sleep for a while and forgot all this nonsense,"
he thought. But that wasn't to be, for he was used to sleeping on his right side and
in his present state was unable to get into that position. No matter how hard he
threw himself to his right, he would immediately roll onto his back again. He must
have tried a hundred times, shutting his eyes so as not to see his wriggling legs, not
stopping until he began to feel in his side a slight dull pain that he had never felt
before.

"My God," he thought, "what an exhausting job I've chosen! Always on the go,
day in and day out. There are far more worries on the road than at the office, what
with the constant travel, the nuisance of making your train connections, the
wretched meals eaten at odd hours, and the casual acquaintances you meet only in
passing, never to see again, never to become intimate friends. To hell with it all!" He
felt a slight itch on the surface of his belly. Slowly he shoved himself on his back
closer to the bedpost so that he could lift his head more easily. He found the place
where it itched. It was covered with small white spots he did not understand. He
started to touch it with one of his legs, but pulled back immediately, for the contact
sent a cold shiver through him.

He slid back down to his former position. "Getting up this early," he thought, ₅
"would turn anyone into an idiot. A man needs his sleep. Other salesmen live like
harem women. For example, when I get back to the hotel in the morning to write
up the sales I've made, these gentlemen are sitting down to breakfast. If I tried
that with my director, I'd be fired on the spot. Actually, that might not be such a
bad idea. If I didn't have to curb my tongue because of my parents, I'd have given
notice long ago. I'd have gone up to the director and told him from the bottom of
my heart exactly what I thought. That would have knocked him from his desk! It's
an odd way to run things, this sitting high at a desk and talking down to employees, especially when, since the director is hard of hearing, they have to approach
so near. Well, there's hope yet; as soon as I've saved enough money to pay back
what my parents owe him—that should take another five or six years—I'll go do it
for sure. Then, I'll cut myself completely free. Right now, though, I'd better get up,
as my train leaves at five."

He looked at the alarm clock ticking on top of the chest of drawers. "God
Almighty!" he thought. It was half past six and the hands were quietly moving forward,
it was later than half past, it was nearly a quarter to seven. Hadn't the alarm clock gone
off? You could see from the bed that it had been correctly set for four o'clock; of course
it must have gone off. Yes, but could he really have slept peacefully through that
ear-splitting racket? Well, if he hadn't slept peacefully, he'd slept deeply all the
same. But what was he to do now? The next train left at seven, to make it he would
have to rush like mad, and his samples weren't even packed, and he himself wasn't
feeling particularly spry or alert. And even if he were to make the train, there would
be no avoiding a scene with the director. The office messenger would've been waiting for the five o'clock train and would've long since reported his not showing up.
The messenger, dim-witted and lacking a will of his own, was a tool of the director.
Well, what if he were to call in sick? But that would look embarrassing and suspicious
since in his five years with the firm Gregor had not been sick once. The director himself was sure to come over with the health insurance doctor, would upbraid his parents for their son's laziness, and would cut short all excuses by deferring to the doctor,
who believed that everyone in the world was a perfectly healthy layabout. And really,
would he be so wrong in this case? Apart from a drowsiness that was hard to account
for after such a long sleep, Gregor really felt quite well, and in fact was exceptionally
hungry.

As he was thinking all this at top speed, without being able to make up his mind
to get out of bed—the alarm clock had just struck a quarter to seven—a cautious tap
sounded on the door behind his head. "Gregor," said a voice—it was his mother—
"it's a quarter to seven. Don't you have a train to catch?" That gentle voice! Gregor
was shocked when he heard his own voice answering hers; unmistakably his own
voice, true, but mixed in with it, like an undertone, a miserable squeaking that
allowed the words to be clearly heard only for a moment before rising up, reverberating, to drown out their meaning, so that no one could be sure if he had heard them
correctly. Gregor wanted to answer fully and give a complete explanation, but under
the circumstances he merely said, "Yes, yes, thank you, Mother, I'm just getting up."
Through the wooden door between them the change in Gregor's voice was probably
not obvious, for his mother, quietly accepting his words, shuffled away. However, this
brief exchange had made the rest of the family aware that Gregor, surprisingly, was
still in the house, and already at one of the side doors his father was knocking, softly,
yet with his fist. "Gregor, Gregor," he called, "what's the matter?" Before long he

called once more in a deeper voice, "Gregor? Gregor?" From the other side door came the sound of his sister's voice, gentle and plaintive. "Gregor, aren't you feeling well? Is there anything I can get you?" Gregor answered the two of them at the same time: "I'm almost ready." He tried hard to keep his voice from sounding strange by enunciating the words with great care, and by inserting long pauses between the words. His father went back to his breakfast but his sister whispered, "Gregor, please, open the door." But Gregor had no intention of opening the door, and was thankful for having formed, while traveling, the prudent habit of keeping all his doors locked at night, even at home.

What he wanted to do now was to get up quietly and calmly, to get dressed, and above all to eat his breakfast. Only then would he think about what to do next, for he understood that mulling things over in bed would lead him nowhere. He remembered how often in the past he had felt some small pain in bed, perhaps caused by lying in an uncomfortable position, which as soon as he had gotten up had proven to be purely imaginary, and he looked forward to seeing how this morning's fancies would gradually fade and disappear. As for the change in his voice, he hadn't the slightest doubt that it was nothing more than the first sign of a severe cold, an occupational hazard of traveling salesmen.

Throwing off the blanket was easy enough; he had only to puff himself up a little and it slipped right off. But the next part was difficult, especially as he was so unusually wide. He would have needed arms and legs to lift himself up; instead he had only these numerous little legs that never stopped moving and over which he had no control at all. As soon as he tried to bend one of them it would straighten itself out, and if he finally succeeded in making it do as he wished, all the others, as if set free, would waggle about in a high degree of painful agitation. "But what's the point of lying uselessly in bed?" Gregor said to himself.

He thought that he might start by easing the lower part of his body out of bed first, but this lower part, which incidentally he hadn't yet seen and of which he couldn't form a clear picture, turned out to be very difficult to budge—it went so slowly. When finally, almost in a frenzy, he gathered his strength and pushed forward desperately, he miscalculated his direction and bumped sharply against the post at the foot of the bed, and the searing pain he felt told him that, for right now at least, it was exactly this lower part of his body that was perhaps the most tender. 10

So he tried getting the top part of his body out first, and cautiously turned his head towards the side of the bed. This proved easy enough, and eventually, despite its breadth and weight the bulk of his body slowly followed the turning of his head. But when he finally got his head out over the edge of the bed he felt too afraid to go any farther, for if he were to let himself fall from this position only a miracle would prevent him from hurting his head. And it was precisely now, at all costs, that he must not lose consciousness; he would be better off staying in bed.

But when after repeating his efforts he lay, sighing, in his former position, and once more watched his little legs struggling with one another more furiously than ever, if that were possible, and saw no way of bringing calm and order into this mindless confusion, he again told himself that it was impossible to stay in bed and that the wisest course would be to stake everything on the hope, however slight, of getting away from the bed. At the same time he didn't forget to remind himself that the calmest of calm reflection was much better than frantic resolutions. During this time he kept his eyes fixed as firmly as possible on the window, but unfortunately the morning fog, which shrouded even the other side of the narrow street, gave him little comfort and cheer. "Already seven o'clock," he said to himself when the alarm clock chimed again, "already seven and still such a thick fog." And for some time he lay still, breathing quietly, as if in the hope that utter stillness would bring all things back to how they really and normally were.

But then he said to himself: "I must make sure that I'm out of bed before it strikes a quarter past seven. Anyway, by then someone from work will have come to check on me, since the office opens before seven." And he immediately set the whole length of his body rocking with a rhythmic motion in order to swing out of bed. If he tumbled out this way he could prevent his head from being injured by keeping it tilted upward as he fell. His back seemed to be hard; the fall onto the carpet would probably not hurt it. His greatest worry was the thought of the loud crash he was bound to make; it would probably cause anxiety, if not outright fear, on the other side of the doors. Yet he had to take the chance.

When Gregor was already half out of bed—his new technique made it more of a game than a struggle, since all he had to do was to edge himself across by rocking back and forth—it struck him how simple it would be if he could get someone to help him. Two strong people—he thought of his father and the maid—would be more than enough. All they would have to do would be to slip their arms under his curved back, lift him out of bed, bend down with their burden, and then wait patiently while he flipped himself right side up onto the floor, where, one might hope, his little legs would acquire some purpose. Well then, aside from the fact that the doors were locked, wouldn't it be a good idea to call for help? In spite of his misery, he could not help smiling at the thought.

He had reached the point where, if he rocked any harder, he was in danger of los-   15
ing his balance, and very soon he would have to commit himself, because in five minutes it would be a quarter past seven—when the doorbell rang. "It's someone from the office," he said to himself, and almost froze, while his little legs danced even faster. For a moment everything remained quiet. "They won't open the door," Gregor said to himself, clutching at an absurd sort of hope. But then, of course, the maid, as usual, went with her firm tread to the door and opened it. Gregor had only to hear the visitor's first word of greeting to know at once who it was—the office manager himself. Why was Gregor condemned to work for a firm where the most insignificant failure to appear instantly provoked the deepest suspicion? Were the employees, one and all, nothing but scoundrels? Wasn't there among them one man who was true and loyal, who if, one morning, he were to waste an hour or so of the firm's time, would become so conscience-stricken as to be driven out of his mind and actually rendered incapable of leaving his bed? Wouldn't it have been enough to send an office boy to ask—that is, if such prying were necessary at all? Did the office manager have to come in person, and thus demonstrate to an entire family of innocent people that he was the only one wise enough to properly investigate this suspicious affair? And it was more from the anxiety caused by these thoughts than by any act of will that Gregor swung himself out of bed with all his might. There was a loud thump, but not really a crash. The carpet broke his fall somewhat, and his back too was more elastic than he had thought, so there was only a muffled thud that was relatively unobtrusive. However, he had not lifted his head carefully enough and had banged it; he twisted it and rubbed it against the carpet in frustration and pain.

"Something fell down in there," said the office manager in the room on the left. Gregor tried to imagine whether something like what had happened to him today might one day happen to the office manager; really, one had to admit that it was possible. But as if in a blunt reply to this question the office manager took several determined steps in the next room and his patent leather boots creaked. From the room on the right his sister was whispering to let him know what was going on: "Gregor, the office manager is here." "I know," said Gregor to himself, but he didn't dare speak loudly enough for his sister to hear him.

"Gregor," his father now said from the room on the left, "the office manager is here and he wants to know why you weren't on the early train. We don't know what to tell him. Besides, he wants to speak to you in person. So please open the door. I'm sure he'll be kind enough to excuse any untidiness in your room." "Good morning, Mr. Samsa," the manager was calling out amiably. "He isn't feeling well," said his mother to the manager, while his father was still speaking at the door. "He's not well, sir, believe me. Why else would Gregor miss his train? The boy thinks of nothing but his work. It nearly drives me to distraction the way he never goes out in the evening; he's been here the last eight days, and every single evening he's stayed at home. He just sits here at the table with us quietly reading the newspapers or looking over train schedules. The only enjoyment he gets is when he's working away with his fretsaw.° For example, he spent two or three evenings cutting out a little picture frame, you'd be surprised at how pretty it is, it's hanging in his room, you'll see it in a minute as soon as Gregor opens the door. By the way, I'm glad you've come, sir, we would've never have gotten him to unlock the door by ourselves, he's so stubborn; and I'm sure he's sick, even though he wouldn't admit it this morning." "I'm coming right now," said Gregor, slowly and carefully and not moving an inch for fear of missing a single word of the conversation. "I can't imagine any other explanation, madam," said the office manager, "I hope it's nothing serious. But on the other hand businessmen such as ourselves—fortunately or unfortunately—very often have to ignore any minor indisposition, since the demands of business come first." "So, can the office manager come in now?" asked Gregor's father impatiently, once more knocking on the door. "No," said Gregor. In the room on the left there was an embarrassed silence; in the room on the right his sister began to sob.

But why didn't his sister go and join the others? Probably because she had just gotten out of bed and hadn't even begun to dress yet. Then why was she crying? Because he was in danger of losing his job, and because the director would start once again dunning his parents for the money they owed him? Yet surely these were matters one didn't need to worry about just now. Gregor was still here, and hadn't the slightest intention of deserting the family. True, at the moment he was lying on the carpet, and no one aware of his condition could seriously expect him to let the office manager in. But this minor discourtesy, for which in good time an appropriate excuse could easily be found, was unlikely to result in Gregor's being fired on the spot. And it seemed to Gregor far more sensible for them now to leave him in peace than to bother him with their tears and entreaties. But the uncertainty that preyed upon them excused their behavior.

"Mr. Samsa," the office manager now called in a louder voice, "what's the matter with you? You've barricaded yourself in your room, giving only yes or no answers, causing your parents a great deal of needless grief and neglecting—I mention this only in passing—neglecting your business responsibilities to an unbelievable degree. I am speaking now in the name of your parents and of your director, and I beg you in

---

fretsaw: saw with a long, narrow, fine-toothed blade, for cutting thin wooden boards or metal plates into patterns.

all seriousness to give me a complete explanation at once. I'm amazed at you, simply amazed. I took you for a calm and reliable person, and now all at once you seem determined to make a ridiculous spectacle of yourself. Earlier this morning the director did suggest to me a possible explanation for your disappearance—I'm referring to the sums of cash that were recently entrusted to you—but I practically swore on my solemn word of honor that this could not be. However, now when I see how incredibly stubborn you are, I no longer have the slightest desire to defend you. And your position with the firm is by no means secure. I came intending to tell you all this in private, but since you're so pointlessly wasting my time I don't see why your parents shouldn't hear it as well. For some time now your work has left much to be desired. We are aware, of course, that this is not the prime season for doing business; but a season for doing no business at all—that, Mr. Samsa, does not and must not exist."

"But sir," Gregor called out distractedly, forgetting everything else in his excite- 20 ment, "I'm on the verge of opening the door right now. A slight indisposition, a dizzy spell, has prevented me from getting up. I'm still in bed. But I'm feeling better already. I'm getting up now. Please be patient for just a moment. It seems I'm not quite as well as I thought. But really I'm all right. Something like this can come on so suddenly! Only last night I was feeling fine, as my parents can tell you, or actually I did have a slight premonition. I must have shown some sign of it. Oh, why didn't I report it to the office! But one always thinks one can get better without having to stay at home. Please, sir, have mercy on my parents! None of what you've just accused me of has any basis in fact; no one has even spoken a word to me about it. Perhaps you haven't seen the latest orders I've sent in. Anyway, I can still make the eight o'clock train. Don't let me keep you, sir, I'll be showing up at the office very soon. Please be kind enough to inform them, and convey my best wishes to the director."

And while hurriedly blurting all this out, hardly knowing what he was saying, Gregor had reached the chest of drawers easily enough, perhaps because of the practice he had already gotten in bed, and was now trying to use it to lift himself upright. For he actually wanted to open the door, actually intended to show himself, and to talk with the manager; he was eager to find out what the others, who now wanted to see him so much, would say at the sight of him. If they recoiled in horror then he would take no further responsibility and could remain peaceably where he was. But if they took it all in stride then he too had no reason to be upset, and, if he hurried, could even get to the station by eight. The first few times, he slipped down the polished surface of the chest, but finally with one last heave he stood upright. He no longer paid attention to the burning pains in his abdomen, no matter how they hurt. Then, allowing himself to fall against the backrest of a nearby chair, he clung to its edges with his little legs. Now he was once more in control of himself; he fell silent, and was able to hear what the manager was saying.

"Did you understand a single word?" the office manager was asking his parents. "He's not trying to make fools of us, is he?" "My God," cried his mother, already in tears, "maybe he's seriously ill and we're tormenting him. Grete! Grete!" she shouted then. "Mother?" called his sister from the other side. They were calling to each other across Gregor's room. "You must go to the doctor at once. Gregor is sick. Go get the doctor now. Did you hear how Gregor was speaking?" "That was the voice of an animal," said the manager in a tone that was noticeably restrained compared to his mother's shrillness. "Anna! Anna!" his father shouted through the hall to the kitchen, clapping his hands, "get a locksmith and hurry!" And the two girls, their skirts rustling, were already running down the hall—how could his sister have gotten dressed so quickly?—and were pulling the front door open. There was no sound of its being shut; evidently they had left it standing open, as is the custom in houses stricken by some great sorrow.

But Gregor now felt much calmer. Though the words he spoke were apparently no longer understandable, they seemed clear enough to him, even clearer than before, perhaps because his hearing had grown accustomed to their sound. In any case, people were now convinced that something was wrong with him, and were ready to help him. The confidence and assurance with which these first measures had been taken comforted him. He felt himself being drawn back into the human circle and hoped for marvelous and astonishing results from both doctor and locksmith, without really drawing a distinction between them. To ready his voice for the crucial discussion that was now almost upon him, to make it sound as clear as possible, he coughed slightly, as quietly as he could, since for all he knew it might sound different from human coughing. Meanwhile in the next room there was utter silence. Perhaps his parents and the manager were sitting at the table, whispering; perhaps they were, all of them, leaning against the door, listening.

Gregor slowly advanced on the door, pushing the chair in front of him. Then he let go of it, grabbed onto the door for support—the pads at the end of his little legs were somewhat sticky—and, leaning against it, rested for a moment after his efforts. Then he started to turn the key in the lock with his mouth. Unfortunately, he didn't really have any teeth—how was he going to grip the key?—but to make up for that he clearly had very powerful jaws; with their help he was in fact able to start turning the key, paying no attention to the fact that he was surely hurting them somehow, for a brown liquid poured out of his mouth, flowed over the key, and dripped onto the floor. "Listen," said the manager on the other side of the door, "he's turning the key." This was a great encouragement to Gregor, but they should all have been cheering him on, his mother and his father too. "Come on, Gregor," they should have been shouting, "keep at it, hold on to that key!" And, imagining that they were all intently following his efforts, he grimly clamped his jaws on the key with all his might. As the key continued to turn he danced around the lock, holding himself by his mouth alone, either hanging onto the key or pressing down on it with the full weight of his body, as the situation required. The sharper sound of the lock as it finally snapped free woke Gregor up completely. With a sigh of relief he said to himself, "So I didn't need the locksmith after all," and he pressed his head down on the handle to open one wing of the double door.

Because he had to pull the wing in towards him, even when it stood wide open he remained hidden from view. He had to edge slowly around this wing and to do it very carefully or he would fall flat on his back as he made his entrance. He was still busy carrying out this maneuver, with no time to notice anything else, when he heard the manager give a loud "Oh!"—it sounded like a gust of wind—and now he could see him, standing closest to the door, his hand over his open mouth, slowly backing away as if propelled by the relentless pressure of some invisible force. His mother—in spite of the manager's presence, she was standing there with her hair still unpinned and sticking out in all directions—first folded her hands and looked at Gregor's father, then took two steps forward and sank to the floor, her skirts billowing out all around her and her face completely buried in her breast. His father, glowering, clenched his fist, as if he intended to drive Gregor back into his room; then he looked around the living room with uncertainty, covered his eyes with his hands, and wept so hard his great chest shook.

25

Now Gregor made no attempt to enter the living room, but leaned against the locked wing of the double door, so that only half of his body was visible, with his head above it cocked to one side, peering at the others. Meanwhile the daylight had grown much brighter; across the street one could clearly see a section of the endless, dark gray building opposite—it was a hospital—with a row of uniform windows starkly punctuating its facade. The rain was still falling, but only in large, visibly separate drops that looked as though they were being flung, one by one, onto the earth. On the table the breakfast dishes were set out in lavish profusion, for breakfast was the most important meal of the day for Gregor's father, who lingered over it for hours while reading various newspapers. Hanging on the opposite wall was a photograph of Gregor from his army days, showing him as a lieutenant, with his hand on his sword and his carefree smile demanding respect for his bearing and his rank. The door to the hall stood open, and as the front door was open too, one could see the landing beyond and the top of the stairs going down.

"Well," said Gregor, who was perfectly aware that he was the only one who had kept his composure, "I'll go now and get dressed, pack up my samples, and be on my way. You will, you will let me go, won't you? You can see, sir, that I'm not stubborn and I'm willing to work; the life of a traveling salesman is hard, but I couldn't live without it. Where are you going, sir? To the office? You are? Will you give an honest report about all this? A man may be temporarily unable to work, but that's just the time to remember the service he has rendered in the past, and to bear in mind that later on, when the present problem has been resolved, he is sure to work with even more energy and diligence than before. As you know very well, I am deeply obligated to the director. At the same time, I'm responsible for my parents and my sister. I'm in a tight spot right now, but I'll get out of it. Don't make things more difficult for me than they already are. Stand up for me at the office! People don't like traveling salesmen, I know. They think they make scads of money and lead lives of luxury. And there's no compelling reason for them to revise this prejudice. But you, sir, have a better understanding of things than the rest of the staff, a better understanding, if I may say so, than even the director himself, who, since he is the owner, can be easily swayed against an employee. You also know very well that a traveling salesman, who is away from the office for most of the year, can so easily fall victim to gossip and bad luck and groundless accusations, against which he is powerless to defend himself since he knows nothing about them until, returning home exhausted from his journeys, he suffers personally from evil consequences that can no longer be traced back to their origins. Sir, please don't go away without giving me some word to show that you think that I'm at least partly right!"

But the office manager had turned away at Gregor's first words, and was looking at him now over one twitching shoulder, his mouth agape. And during Gregor's speech he didn't stand still for even a moment, but without once taking his eyes off him kept edging towards the door, yet very slowly, as if there were some secret injunction against his leaving the room. He was already in the hall, and from the suddenness with which he took his last step out of the living room, one might have thought he had burned the sole of his foot. But once in the hall, he stretched out his right hand as far as possible in the direction of the staircase, as if some supernatural rescuer awaited him there.

Gregor realized that he could not let the manager leave in this frame of mind, or his position with the firm would be in extreme jeopardy. His parents were incapable of clearly grasping this; over the years they had come to believe that Gregor was set for life with this firm, and besides they were now so preoccupied with their immediate problems that they had lost the ability to foresee events. But Gregor had this ability. The manager must be overtaken, calmed, swayed, and finally convinced; the future of Gregor and of his family depended on it! If only his sister were here—she was perceptive; she had already begun to cry while Gregor was still lying calmly on his back. And surely the manager, that ladies' man, would've listened to her; she would've shut the door behind them and in the hall talked him out of his fright. But his sister wasn't there, and he would have to handle this himself. And forgetting that he had no idea what his powers of movement were, and forgetting as well that once again his words would possibly, even probably, be misunderstood, he let go of the door, pushed his way through the opening, and started towards the manager, who by now was on the landing, clinging in a ridiculous manner to the banister with both hands. But as Gregor reached out for support, he immediately fell down with a little cry onto his numerous legs. The moment this happened he felt, for the first time that morning, a sense of physical well-being. His little legs had solid ground under them, and, he noticed with joy, they were at his command, and were even eager to carry him in whatever direction he might desire; and he already felt sure that the final recovery from all his misery was at hand. But at that very moment, as he lay on the floor rocking with suppressed motion, not far from his mother and just opposite her, she, who had seemed so completely overwhelmed, leapt to her feet, stretched her arms out wide, spread her fingers, and cried, "Help! For God's sake, help!" She then craned her neck forward as if to see Gregor better, but at the same time, inconsistently, backed away from him. Forgetting that the table with all its dishes was behind her, she sat down on it, and, as if in a daze when she bumped into it, seemed utterly unaware that the large coffee pot next to her had tipped over and was pouring out a flood of coffee onto the carpet.

"Mother, Mother," said Gregor gently, looking up at her. For the moment he 30 had completely forgotten the office manager; on the other hand, he couldn't resist snapping his jaws a few times at the sight of the streaming coffee. This made his mother scream again; she ran from the table and into the outstretched arms of his father, who came rushing to her. But Gregor had no time now for his parents. The manager had already reached the staircase; with his chin on the banister railing, he was looking back for the last time. Gregor darted forward, to be as sure as possible of catching up with him, but the manager must have guessed his intention, for he sprinted down several steps and disappeared. He was still yelling "Oohh!" and the sound echoed throughout the stairwell.

Unfortunately the manager's escape seemed to make his father, who until now had seemed reasonably calm, lose all sense of proportion. Instead of running after the man himself, or at least not interfering with Gregor's pursuit, he grabbed with his right hand the manager's cane, which he had left behind, together with his hat and overcoat, on the chair; with his left hand he snatched up a large newspaper from the table. He began stamping his feet and waving the cane and newspaper in order to drive Gregor back into his room. Nothing Gregor said made any difference, indeed, nothing he said was even understood. No matter how humbly he lowered his head his father only stamped the louder. Behind his father his mother, despite the cold, had flung open a window and was leaning far outside it, her face in her hands. A strong breeze from the street blew across the room to the stairwell, the window curtains billowed inwards, the newspapers fluttered on the table, stray pages skittered across the floor. His father, hissing like a savage, mercilessly drove him back. But as

Gregor had had no practice in walking backwards, it was a very slow process. If he had been given a chance to turn around then he would've gotten back into his room at once, but he was afraid that the length of time it would take him to turn around would exasperate his father and that at any moment the cane in his father's hand might deal him a fatal blow on his back or his head. In the end, though, he had no choice, for he noticed to his horror that while moving backwards he couldn't even keep a straight course. And so, looking back anxiously, he began turning around as quickly as possible, which in reality was very slowly. Perhaps his father divined his good intentions, for he did not interfere, and even helped to direct the maneuver from afar with the tip of his cane. If only he would stop that unbearable hissing! It made Gregor completely lose his concentration. He had turned himself almost all the way around when, confused by this hissing, he made a mistake and started turning back the wrong way. But when at last he'd succeeded in getting his head in front of the doorway, he found that his body was too wide to make it through. Of course his father, in the state he was in, couldn't even begin to consider opening the other wing of the door to let Gregor in. His mind was on one thing only: to drive Gregor back into this room as quickly as possible. He would never have permitted the complicated preparations necessary for Gregor to haul himself upright and in that way perhaps slip through. Instead, making even more noise, he urged Gregor forward as if the way were clear. To Gregor the noise behind him no longer sounded like the voice of merely one father; this really wasn't a joke, and Gregor squeezed himself into the doorway, heedless of the consequences. One side of his body lifted up, he was pitched at an angle in the doorway; the other side was scraped raw, ugly blotches stained the white door. Soon he was stuck fast and couldn't have moved any further by himself. On one side his little legs hung trembling in the air, while those on the other were painfully crushed against the floor—when, from behind, his father gave him a hard blow that was truly a deliverance, and bleeding profusely, he flew far into his room. Behind him the door was slammed shut with the cane, and then at last everything was still.

II

It was already dusk when Gregor awoke from a deep, almost comatose sleep. Surely, even if he hadn't been disturbed he would've soon awakened by himself, since he'd rested and slept long enough; yet it seemed to him that he'd been awakened by the sound of hurried steps and the furtive closing of the hallway door. The light from the electric streetlamps cast pale streaks here and there on the ceiling and the upper part of the furniture, but down below, where Gregor was, it was dark. Groping awkwardly with the feelers which he was only now beginning to appreciate, he slowly pushed himself over to the door to see what had been going on there. His left side felt as if it were one long, painfully tightening scar, and he was actually limping on his two rows of legs. One little leg, moreover, had been badly hurt during the morning's events—it was nearly miraculous that only one had been hurt—and it trailed along lifelessly.

Only when he reached the door did he realize what had impelled him forward—the smell of something to eat. For there stood a bowl full of fresh milk, in which floated small slices of white bread. He could almost have laughed for joy, since he was even hungrier now than he'd been during the morning, and he immediately dipped his head into the milk, almost up to his eyes. But he soon drew it back in disappointment; not only did he find it difficult to eat because of the soreness in his left side—and he was capable of eating only if his whole gasping body cooperated—but also because he didn't like the milk at all, although it had once been his favorite drink, which, no doubt, was why his sister had brought it in. In fact, he turned away from the bowl almost in disgust, and crawled back to the middle of the room.

In the living room, as Gregor could see through the crack in the door, the gaslight had been lit. But while this was the hour when his father would usually be reading the afternoon paper in a loud voice to his mother and sometimes to his sister as well, now there wasn't a sound to be heard. Well, perhaps this custom of reading aloud, which his sister was always telling him about or mentioning in her letters, had recently been discontinued. Still, though the apartment was completely silent, it was scarcely deserted. "What a quiet life the family's been leading," said Gregor to himself, and, staring fixedly into the darkness, he felt a genuine pride at having been able to provide his parents and his sister with such a life in such a nice apartment. But what if all this calm, prosperity, and contentment were to end in horror? So as not to give in to such thoughts, Gregor set himself in motion, and he crawled up and down the room.

Once during the long evening first one of the side doors and then the other was 35 opened a crack and then quickly shut. Someone, it seemed, had wanted to come in but then had thought better of it. Gregor now stationed himself so as to somehow get the hesitant visitor to come in or at least to find out who it might be. But the door did not open again and he waited in vain. That morning when the doors had been locked, everyone had wanted to come in, but now after he'd unlocked one of the doors himself—and the others had evidently been unlocked during the day—nobody came in, and the keys, too, were now on the outside.

It was late at night before the light was put out in the living room, and it was easy for Gregor to tell that his parents and sister had stayed up all the while, since he could plainly hear the three of them as they tiptoed away. As it was obvious that no one would be visiting Gregor before morning, he had plenty of time in which to contemplate, undisturbed, how best to rearrange his life. But the open, high-ceilinged room in which he was forced to lie flat on the floor filled him with a dread which he couldn't account for—since it was, after all, the room he had lived in for the past five years. Almost unthinkingly, and not without a faint sense of shame, he scurried under the couch. There, although his back was slightly cramped and he could no longer raise his head, he immediately felt very much at home, and his only regret was that his body was too wide to fit completely under the couch.

There he spent the rest of the night, now in a doze from which hunger pangs kept awakening him with a start, now preoccupied with worries and vague hopes, all of which, however, led to the same conclusion: that for the time being he must remain calm and, by being patient and showing every consideration, try to help his family bear the burdens that his present condition had placed upon them.

Early the next morning—the night was barely over—Gregor got an opportunity to test the strength of his newly-made resolutions, because his sister, who was almost fully dressed, opened the hallway door and looked in expectantly. She didn't see him at first, but when she spotted him underneath the couch—well, my God, he had to be somewhere, he couldn't just fly away—she was so surprised that she lost her self-control and slammed the door shut again. But, as if she felt sorry for her behavior, she opened it again right away and tiptoed in, as if she were in the presence of someone who was very ill, or who was a stranger. Gregor had moved his head forward almost to the edge of the couch and was watching her. Would she notice that he'd let the milk sit there, and not from lack of hunger, and would she bring him some other food that was more to his taste? If she wasn't going to do it on her own, he'd sooner starve than call her attention to it, although in fact he was feeling a tremendous urge to dash out from under the couch, fling himself at his sister's feet, and beg her for something good to eat. But his sister immediately noticed to her astonishment that the bowl was still full, with only a little milk spilt around it. She picked up the bowl at once—not, it's true, with her bare hands but using a rag—and carried it out. Gregor was extremely curious to find out what she would bring in its place, and he speculated at length as to what it might be. But he never would have guessed what his sister, in the goodness of her heart, actually did. She brought him a wide range of choices, all spread out on an old newspaper. There were old, half-rotten vegetables; bones left over from dinner, covered with a congealed white sauce; some raisins and almonds; a piece of cheese which Gregor two days ago had declared inedible; a slice of plain bread, a slice of bread and butter, and a slice with butter and salt. In addition to all this she replaced the bowl, now evidently reserved for Gregor, filled this time with water. And out of a sense of delicacy, since she knew that Gregor wouldn't eat in front of her, she left in a hurry, even turning the key in the lock in order that Gregor might know that he was free to make himself as comfortable as possible. Gregor's legs whirred as they propelled him toward the food. Besides, his wounds must have healed completely, for he no longer felt handicapped, which amazed him. He thought of how, a month ago, he'd cut his finger slightly with his knife and how only the day before yesterday that little wound had still hurt. "Am I less sensitive now?" he wondered, greedily sucking on the cheese, to which, above all the other dishes, he was immediately and strongly attracted. Tears of joy welled up in his eyes as he devoured the cheese, the vegetables, and the sauce. The fresh foods, on the other hand, were not to his liking; in fact, he couldn't stand to smell them and he actually dragged the food he wanted to eat a little way off. He'd long since finished eating, and was merely lying lazily in the same spot, when his sister began to slowly turn the key in the lock as a signal for him to withdraw. He got up at once, although he'd almost fallen asleep, and scurried back under the couch. But it took a great deal of self-control for him to remain under the couch even for the brief time his sister was in the room, for his heavy meal had swollen his body to some extent and he could scarcely breathe in that confined space. Between little fits of suffocation he stared with slightly bulging eyes as his unsuspecting sister took a broom and swept away not only the scraps of what he'd eaten, but also the food that he'd left untouched—as if these too were no longer any good—and hurriedly dumped everything into a bucket, which she covered with a wooden lid and carried away. She'd hardly turned her back before Gregor came out from under the couch to stretch and puff himself out.

So this was how Gregor was fed each day, once in the morning when his parents and the maid were still asleep, and again after the family's midday meal, while his parents took another brief nap and his sister could send the maid away on some errand or other. His parents didn't want Gregor to starve any more than his sister did, but perhaps for them to be directly involved in his feeding was more than they could bear, or perhaps his sister wanted to shield them even from what might prove to be no more than a minor discomfort, for they were surely suffering enough as it was.

Gregor was unable to discover what excuses had served to get rid of the doctor 40 and the locksmith that first morning. Since the others couldn't understand what he said it never occurred to them, not even to his sister, that he could understand them, so when his sister was in the room, he had to be satisfied with occasionally hearing her sighs and her appeals to the saints. Only later, after she began to get used to the situation—of course she could never become completely used to it—would Gregor sometimes hear a remark that was intended to be friendly or could be so interpreted. "He really liked it today," she'd say when Gregor had polished off a good portion, and when the opposite was the case, which began to happen more and more often, she'd say almost sadly, "Once again, he didn't touch a thing."

But while Gregor wasn't able to get any news directly, he could overhear a considerable amount from the adjoining rooms, and as soon as he would hear the sound of voices he would immediately run to the appropriate door and press his whole body against it. In the early days especially, there wasn't a conversation that didn't in some way, if only indirectly, refer to him. For two whole days, at every meal, the family discussed what they should do, and they kept on doing so between meals as well, for at least two members of the family were now always at home, probably because nobody wanted to be in the apartment alone, and it would be unthinkable to leave it empty. Furthermore, on the very first day the cook—it wasn't completely clear how much she knew of what had happened—had on her knees begged Gregor's mother to dismiss her immediately, and when she said her goodbyes a quarter of an hour later, she thanked them for her dismissal with tears in her eyes, as if this had been the greatest favor ever bestowed on her in the house, and without having to be asked she made a solemn vow never to breathe a word of this to anyone.

So now his sister, together with his mother, had to do all the cooking as well, though in fact this wasn't too much of a chore, since the family ate practically nothing. Gregor kept hearing them vainly urging one another to eat, without receiving any reply except "No thanks, I've had enough," or some similar remark. They didn't seem to drink anything, either. His sister would often ask his father if he'd like some beer, and would gladly offer to go out and get it herself. When he wouldn't respond she'd say, in order to remove any hesitation on his part, that she could always send the janitor's wife, but at that point the father would finally utter an emphatic "No" and that would be the end of the matter.

It was on the very first day that his father gave a full account, to both mother and sister, of the family's financial situation and prospects. Every now and then he would get up from the table and take a receipt or notebook from out of the small safe he'd salvaged from the collapse of his business five years before. He could be heard opening the complicated lock and then securing it again after taking out whatever he'd been looking for. The account that his father gave, or at least part of it, was the first encouraging news that Gregor had heard since being imprisoned. He'd always had the impression that his father had failed to save a penny from the ruin of his business; at least his father had never told him otherwise, and Gregor, for that matter, had never asked him about it. At that time Gregor's only concern had been to do his utmost to make the family forget as quickly as possible the business failure that had plunged them all into a state of total despair. And so he had set to work with tremendous zeal, and had risen almost overnight from junior clerk to become a traveling salesman, which naturally opened up completely new financial opportunities so that in no time at all his success was instantly translated, by way of commissions, into hard cash, which could be laid out on the table under the eyes of his astonished and delighted family. Those had been wonderful times, and they had never returned, at least not with the same glory, even though later on Gregor had been earning enough to pay the entire family's expenses, and in fact had been doing so. They'd simply gotten used to it, both family and Gregor; they had gratefully accepted the money, and he had given it gladly, but no special warmth went with it. Gregor had remained close only to his sister, and it was his secret plan that she, who unlike Gregor loved music and could play the violin with deep feeling, should next year attend the Conservatory, despite the expense which, great as it was, would have to be met in some way. During Gregor's brief stays in the city the subject of the Conservatory would often come up in his conversations with his sister, but always only as a beautiful dream that wasn't meant to come true. His parents weren't happy to hear even these innocent remarks, but Gregor's ideas on the subject were firm and he had intended to make a solemn announcement on Christmas Eve.

Such were the thoughts, so futile in his present condition, that ran through his mind as he stood there, pressed against the door, listening. Sometimes he would grow so thoroughly weary that he couldn't listen any more and would carelessly let his head bump against the door, and though he'd pull it back immediately, even the slight noise he'd made would be heard in the next room, causing everyone to fall silent. "What's he up to now?" his father would say after a pause, obviously looking at the door, and only then would the interrupted conversation gradually be resumed.

Gregor now learned with considerable thoroughness—for his father tended to 45
repeat his explanations several times, partly because he hadn't dealt with these matters in a long time, and partly because his mother didn't understand everything the first time through—that despite their catastrophic ruin a certain amount of capital, a very small amount, it's true, had survived intact from the old days, and thanks to the interest being untouched had even increased slightly. And what was more, the money which Gregor had been bringing home every month—he'd kept only a small sum for himself—hadn't been completely spent and had grown into a tidy sum. Gregor nodded eagerly behind his door, delighted to hear of this unexpected foresight and thrift. Of course he might have been able to use this extra money to pay off more of his father's debt to the director, and thus have brought nearer the day when he could quit his current job, but, given the present circumstances, things were better the way his father had arranged them.

Now the sum of this money wasn't nearly large enough for the family to live off the interest; the principal might support them for a year, or two at the most, but that was all. So this was really only a sum that was not to be touched, but saved instead for emergencies. As for money to live on—that would have to be earned. Though Gregor's father was indeed still healthy, nevertheless he was an old man who hadn't worked for five years and one from whom not too much should be expected in any case. During those five years, the first ones of leisure in his hard-working but unsuccessful life, he had put on a lot of weight and consequently had grown somewhat sluggish. And as for Gregor's elderly mother, was she supposed to start bringing in money, burdened as she was by her asthma which made it a strain for her to even walk across the apartment and which kept her gasping for breath every other day on the couch by the open window? Or should his sister go to work instead—she who though seventeen was still a child and one moreover whom it would be cruel to deprive of the life she'd led up until now, a life of wearing pretty clothes, sleeping late, helping around the house, enjoying a few modest pleasures, and above all playing the violin? At first, whenever their conversation turned to the need to earn money, Gregor would let go of the door and fling himself down on the cool leather couch which stood beside it, for he felt hot with grief and shame.

Often he would lie there all night long, not sleeping a wink, scratching at the leather couch for hours. Or, undaunted by the great effort it required, he would push the chair over to the window. Then he would crawl up to the sill and, propped up by the chair, would lean against the pane, apparently inspired by some memory of the sense of freedom that gazing out a window used to give him. For in truth objects only a short distance away were now, each day, becoming more indistinct; the hospital across the street, which he used to curse because he could see it all too clearly, was now completely outside his field of vision, and if he hadn't known for a fact that he lived on Charlotte Street—a quiet but nevertheless urban street—he could have imagined that he was looking out his window at a wasteland where gray sky and gray earth had indistinguishably merged as one. His observant sister needed only to notice twice that the armchair had been moved to the window. From then on, whenever she cleaned the room, she carefully placed the chair back by the window, and even began leaving the inner casement open.

If only Gregor had been able to speak to his sister and thank her for everything she'd had to do for him, he could have borne her kindnesses more easily, but as it was they were painful to him. Of course his sister tried her best to ease the general embarrassment, and naturally as time passed she grew better and better at it. But Gregor too, over time, gained a clearer sense of what was involved. Even the way in which she entered the room was a torture to him. No sooner had she stepped in when—not even pausing to shut the door, despite the care she normally would take in sparing others the sight of Gregor's room—she would run straight over to the window and tear it open with impatient fingers, almost as if she were suffocating, and she would remain for some time by the window, even in the coldest weather, breathing deeply. Twice a day she would terrify Gregor with all this noise and rushing around. He would cower under the couch the entire time, knowing full well that she surely would have spared him this if only she could have stood being in the room with him with the windows closed.

Once, about a month after Gregor's metamorphosis—so there was really no particular reason for his sister to be upset by his appearance—she came in earlier than usual and caught Gregor as he gazed out the window, terrifying in his stillness. It wouldn't have surprised Gregor if she'd decided not to come in, since his position prevented her from opening the window right away, but not only did she not come in, she actually jumped back and shut the door—a stranger might have thought that Gregor had been planning to ambush her and bite her. Of course he immediately hid under the couch, but he had to wait until noon before she came back, and this time she seemed much more nervous than usual. In this way he came to realize that the sight of him disgusted her, and likely would always disgust her, and that she probably had to steel herself not to run away at the sight of even the tiny portion of his body that stuck out from under the couch. So, one day, to spare her even this, he carried the bedsheet on his back over to the couch—it took him four hours—and spread it so that he was completely covered and his sister wouldn't be able to see him even if she bent down. If she felt this sheet wasn't necessary then of course she could remove it, since obviously Gregor wasn't shutting himself away so completely in order to amuse himself. But she left the sheet alone, and Gregor even thought that he caught a look of gratitude when he cautiously lifted the sheet a little with his head in order to see how his sister was taking to this new arrangement.

During the first two weeks, his parents couldn't bring themselves to come in to see him, and he frequently heard them remarking how much they appreciated his sister's efforts, whereas previously they'd often been annoyed with her for being, in their eyes, somewhat useless. But now both father and mother had fallen into the habit of waiting outside Gregor's door while his sister cleaned up the room, and as soon as she emerged

50

she would have to tell them every detail of the room's condition, what Gregor had eaten, how he'd behaved this time, and whether he'd perhaps shown a little improvement. It wasn't long before his mother began to want to visit Gregor, but his father and sister were at first able to dissuade her by rational arguments to which Gregor listened with great care, and with which he thoroughly agreed. But as time went by she had to be restrained by force, and when she cried out "Let me go to Gregor, he's my unhappy boy! Don't you understand that I have to go to him?" Gregor began to think that it might be a good idea if his mother did come in after all, not every day, naturally, but, say, once a week. She was really a much more capable person than his sister, who, for all her courage, was still only a child and had perhaps taken on such a difficult task only out of a childish impulsiveness.

Gregor's wish to see his mother was soon fulfilled. During the day Gregor didn't want to show himself at the window, if only out of consideration for his parents. But his few square meters of floor gave him little room to crawl around in, he found it hard to lie still even at night, and eating soon ceased to give him any pleasure. So in order to distract himself he fell into the habit of crawling all over the walls and the ceiling. He especially enjoyed hanging from the ceiling; it was completely different from lying on the floor. He could breathe more freely, a faint pulsing coursed through his body, and in his state of almost giddy absentmindedness up there, Gregor would sometimes, to his surprise, lose his grip and tumble onto the floor. But now, of course, since he had much better control over his body, even such a great fall didn't hurt him. His sister noticed right away the new pastime Gregor had discovered for himself—he'd left sticky traces where he'd been crawling—and so she got it into her head to provide Gregor with as much room as possible to crawl around in by removing all the furniture that was in the way—especially the chest of drawers and the desk. But she couldn't manage this by herself; she didn't dare ask her father for help; the maid wouldn't be of any use, for while this girl, who was around sixteen, was brave enough to stay on after the cook had left, she'd asked to be allowed to always keep the kitchen door locked, opening it only when specifically asked to do so. This left his sister with no choice but, one day when her father was out, to ask her mother for help. And indeed, her mother followed her with joyful, excited cries, although she fell silent when they reached the door to Gregor's room. Naturally his sister first made sure that everything in the room was as it should be; only then did she let her mother come in. Gregor had hurriedly pulled his sheet even lower and had folded it more tightly and it really did look as if it had been casually tossed over the couch. This time Gregor also refrained from peeking out from under the sheet; he denied himself the pleasure of seeing his mother for now and was simply glad that she'd come after all. "Come on in, he's nowhere in sight," said his sister, apparently leading his mother in by the hand. Now Gregor could hear the two delicate women moving the heavy chest of drawers away from its place, his sister stubbornly insisting on doing the hardest work, ignoring the warnings of her mother, who was afraid her daughter would overstrain herself. The work took a very long time. After struggling for over a quarter of an hour, his mother suggested that they might leave the chest where it was; in the first place, it was just too heavy, they'd never be done before his father came home and they'd have to leave it in the middle of the room, blocking Gregor's movements in every direction; in the second place, it wasn't at all certain that they were doing Gregor a favor in removing the furniture. It seemed to her that the opposite was true, the sight of the bare walls broke her heart; and why shouldn't Gregor feel the same since he'd been used to this furniture for so long and would feel abandoned in the empty room? "And wouldn't it look as if," his mother concluded very softly—in fact, she'd been almost whispering the entire time, as if she wanted to prevent Gregor, whose exact whereabouts she didn't know, from hearing the sound of her voice (she was convinced that he couldn't understand her words)—"as if by removing his furniture we were telling him that we'd given up all hope of his getting better, and were callously leaving him to his own devices? I think the best course would be to try to keep the room exactly the way it was, so that when Gregor does come back to us he'll find everything the same, making it easier for him to forget what has happened in the meantime."

When he heard his mother's words, Gregor realized that, over the past two months, the lack of having anyone to converse with, together with the monotonous life within the family, must have befuddled his mind; there wasn't any other way he could explain to himself how he could have ever seriously wanted his room cleared out. Did he really want this warm room of his, so comfortably furnished with family heirlooms, transformed into a lair where he'd be perfectly free to crawl around in every direction, but only at the cost of simultaneously forgetting his human past, swiftly and utterly? Just now he'd been on the brink of forgetting, and only his mother's voice, which he hadn't heard for so long, had brought him back. Nothing should be removed; everything must stay. He couldn't do without the furniture's soothing influence on his state of mind, and if the furniture were to impede his senselessly crawling around, that wouldn't be a loss but rather a great advantage.

But unfortunately his sister thought otherwise. She'd become accustomed, and not without some justification, to assuming the role of the acknowledged expert whenever she and her parents discussed Gregor's affairs; so her mother's advice was enough for her to insist now not merely on her original plan of moving the chest and the desk, but on the removal of every bit of furniture except for the indispensable couch. Her resolve, to be sure, didn't stem merely from childish stubbornness or from the self-confidence she had recently and unexpectedly gained at such great cost. For in fact she'd noticed that while Gregor needed plenty of room to crawl around in, on the other hand, as far as she could tell, he never used the furniture at all. Perhaps too, the sentimental enthusiasm of girls her age, which they indulge themselves in at every opportunity, now tempted Grete to make Gregor's situation all the more terrifying so that she might be able to do more for him. No one but Grete would ever be likely to enter a room where Gregor ruled the bare walls all alone.

And so she refused to give in to her mother, who in any case, from the sheer anxiety caused by being in Gregor's room, seemed unsure of herself. She soon fell silent and began as best she could to help her daughter remove the chest of drawers. Well, if he must, then Gregor could do without the chest, but the desk had to stay. And no sooner had the two women, groaning and squeezing, gotten the chest out of the room than Gregor poked his head out from under the couch to see how he might intervene as tactfully as possible. But unfortunately it was his mother who came back first, leaving Grete in the next room, gripping the chest with her arms and rocking it back and forth without, of course, being able to budge it from the spot. His mother wasn't used to the sight of him—it might make her sick; so Gregor, frightened, scuttled backwards to the far end of the couch, but he couldn't prevent the front of the sheet from stirring slightly. That was enough to catch his mother's attention. She stopped, stood still for a moment, and then went back to Grete.

Gregor kept telling himself that nothing unusual was happening, that only a few pieces of furniture were being moved around. But he soon had to admit that all this 55 coming and going of the two women, their little calls to one another, the scraping of the furniture across the floor, affected him as if it were some gigantic commotion rushing in on him from every side, and though he tucked in his head and legs and pressed his body against the floor, he had to accept the fact that he wouldn't be able to stand it much longer. They were cleaning out his room, taking away from him everything that he loved; already they'd carried off his chest, where he kept his fretsaw and his other tools; now they were trying to pry his writing desk loose—it was practically embedded in the floor—the same desk where he'd always done his homework when he'd been a student at business school, in high school, and even in elementary school. He really no longer had any time left in which to weigh the good intentions of these two women whose existence, for that matter, he'd almost forgotten, since they were so exhausted by now that they worked in silence, the only sound being that of their weary, plodding steps.

And so, while the women were in the next room, leaning against the desk and trying to catch their breath, he broke out, changing his direction four times—since he really didn't know what to rescue first—when he saw, hanging conspicuously on the otherwise bare wall, the picture of the lady all dressed in furs. He quickly crawled up to it and pressed himself against the glass, which held him fast, soothing his hot belly. Now that Gregor completely covered it, this picture at least wasn't about to be carried away by anyone. He turned his head towards the living room door, so that he could watch the women when they returned.

They hadn't taken much of a rest and were already coming back. Grete had put her arm around her mother and was almost carrying her. "Well, what should we take next?" said Grete, looking around. And then her eyes met Gregor's, looking down at her from the wall. Probably only because her mother was there, she kept her composure, bent her head down to her mother to prevent her from glancing around, and said, though in a hollow, quavering voice: "Come on, let's go back to the living room for a minute." To Gregor, her intentions were obvious: she wanted to get his mother to safety and then chase him down from the wall. Well, just let her try! He clung to his picture and he wasn't going to give it up. He'd rather fly at Grete's face.

But Grete's words had made her mother even more anxious; she stepped aside, glimpsed the huge brown blotch on the flowered wallpaper, and before she fully understood that what she was looking at was Gregor, she cried out, "Oh God, oh God!" in a hoarse scream of a voice, and, as if giving up completely, fell with outstretched arms across the couch, and lay there without moving. "You! Gregor!" cried his sister, raising her fist and glaring at him. These were the first words she had addressed directly to him since his metamorphosis. She ran into the next room to get some spirits to revive her mother from her faint. Gregor also wanted to help—he could rescue the picture another time—but he was stuck to the glass and had to tear himself free. He then scuttled into the next room as if to give some advice, as he used to, to his sister. Instead, he had to stand behind her uselessly while she rummaged among various little bottles. When she turned around she was startled, a bottle fell to the floor, a splinter of glass struck Gregor in the face, some sort of corrosive medicine splashed on him, and Grete, without further delay, grabbing as many of the little bottles as she could carry, ran inside with them to her mother, and slammed the door shut behind her with her foot. Now Gregor was cut off from his mother, who was perhaps near death because of him. He didn't dare open the door for fear of scaring his sister, who had to remain with his mother. There wasn't anything for him to do but wait; and so, tormented by guilt and anxiety, he began crawling. He crawled over everything, walls, furniture, and ceiling, until finally, in despair, the room beginning to spin around him, he collapsed onto the middle of the large table.

A short time passed; Gregor lay there stupefied. Everything was quiet around him; perhaps that was a good sign. Then the doorbell rang. The maid, of course, stayed locked up in her kitchen, so Grete had to answer the door. His father was back. "What's happened?" were his first words. Grete's expression must've told him everything. Her answers came in muffled tones—she was obviously burying her face in her father's chest. "Mother fainted, but she's better now. Gregor's broken loose." "I knew it," her father said. "I told you this would happen, but you women refuse to listen." It was clear to Gregor that his father had put the worst construction on Grete's all too brief account and had assumed that Gregor was guilty of some violent act. That meant that he must calm his father down, since he had neither the time nor the ability to explain things to him. So he fled to the door of his room and pressed himself against it in order that his father might see, as soon as he entered the living room, that Gregor had every intention of returning immediately to his own room and there was no need to force him back. All they had to do was to open the door and he would disappear at once.

But his father wasn't in the mood to notice such subtleties; "Ah!" he roared as he entered, in a voice that sounded at once furious and gleeful. Gregor turned his head from the door and lifted it towards his father. He really hadn't imagined that his father would look the way he did standing before him now; true, Gregor had become too absorbed lately by his new habit of crawling to bother about whatever else might be going on in the apartment, and he should have anticipated that there would be some changes. And yet, and yet, could this really be his father? Was this the same man who used to lie sunk in bed, exhausted, whenever Gregor would set out on one of his business trips; who would greet him upon his return in the evening while sitting in his bathrobe in the armchair; who was hardly capable of getting to his feet, and to show his joy could only lift up his arms; and who, on those rare times when the whole family went out for a walk—on the occasional Sunday or on a legal holiday—used to painfully shuffle along between Gregor and his mother, who were slow walkers themselves, and yet he was always slightly slower than they, wrapped up in his old overcoat, carefully planting his crook-handled cane before him with every step, and almost invariably stopping and gathering his escort around him whenever he wanted to say something? Now, however, he held himself very erect, dressed up in a closely-fitting blue uniform with gold buttons, of the kind worn by bank messengers. His heavy chin thrust out over the stiff collar of his jacket; his black eyes stared, sharp and bright, from under his bushy eyebrows; his white hair, once so rumpled, was combed flat, it gleamed, and the part was meticulously exact. He tossed his cap—which bore a gold monogram, probably that of some bank—in an arc across the room so that it landed on the couch, and with his hands in his pockets, the tails of his uniform's long jacket flung back, his face grim, he went after Gregor. He probably didn't know himself what he was going to do, but he lifted his feet unusually high, and Gregor was amazed at the immense size of the soles of his boots. However, Gregor didn't dwell on these reflections, for he had known from the very first day of his new life that his father considered only the strictest measures to be appropriate in dealing with him. So he ran ahead of his father, stopped when he stood still, and scurried on again when he made the slightest move. In this way they circled the room several times without anything decisive happening; in fact, their movements, because of their slow tempo, did not suggest those of a chase. So

60

Gregor kept to the floor for the time being, especially since he was afraid that his father might consider any flight to the walls or ceiling to be particularly offensive. All the same, Gregor had to admit that he wouldn't be able to keep up even this pace for long, since whenever his father took a single step, Gregor had to perform an entire series of movements. He was beginning to get winded, since even in his former life his lungs had never been strong. As he kept staggering on like this, so weary he could barely keep his eyes open, since he was saving all his strength for running; not even thinking, dazed as he was, that there might be any other way to escape than by running; having almost forgotten that he was free to use the walls, though against these walls, admittedly, were placed bits of intricately carved furniture, bristling with spikes and sharp corners—suddenly something sailed overhead, hit the floor nearby, and rolled right in front of him. It was an apple; at once a second one came flying after it. Gregor stopped, petrified with fear; it was useless to keep on running, for his father had decided to bombard him. He had filled his pockets with the fruit from the bowl on the sideboard and now he was throwing one apple after another, for now at least without bothering to take good aim. These little red apples, colliding with one another, rolled around on the floor as if electrified. One weakly-thrown apple grazed Gregor's back, rolling off without causing harm. But another one that came flying immediately afterwards actually imbedded itself in Gregor's back. Gregor wanted to drag himself onward, as if this shocking and unbelievable pain might disappear if he could only keep moving, but he felt as if he were nailed to the spot, and he splayed himself out in the utter confusion of his senses. With his last glance he saw the door of his room burst open, and his mother, wearing only her chemise—his sister had removed her dress to help her breathe after she'd fainted—rush out, followed by his screaming sister. He saw his mother run toward his father, her loosened underskirts slipping one by one onto the floor. Stumbling over her skirts she flung herself upon his father, embraced him, was as one with him—but now Gregor's sight grew dim—and with her arms clasped around his father's neck, begged for Gregor's life.

III

Gregor's serious wound, which made him suffer for over a month—the apple remained imbedded in his flesh as a visible reminder, no one having the courage to remove it—seemed to have persuaded even his father that Gregor, despite his present pathetic and disgusting shape, was a member of the family who shouldn't be treated as an enemy. On the contrary, familial duty required them to swallow their disgust and to endure him, to endure him and nothing more.

And though his wound probably had caused Gregor to suffer a permanent loss of mobility, and though it now took him, as if he were some disabled war veteran, many a long minute to creep across his room—crawling above ground level was out of the question—yet in return for this deterioration of his condition he was granted a compensation which satisfied him completely: each day around dusk the living room door—which he was in the habit of watching closely for an hour or two ahead of time—was opened, and lying in the darkness of his room, invisible from the living room, he could see the whole family sitting at the table lit by the lamp and could listen to their conversation as if by general consent, instead of the way he'd done before.

True, these were no longer the lively conversations of old, those upon which Gregor had mused somewhat wistfully as he'd settled wearily into his damp bed in some tiny hotel room. Things were now very quiet for the most part. Soon after dinner his father would fall asleep in his armchair, while his mother and sister would admonish each other to be quiet; his mother, bending forward under the light, would sew fine lingerie for a fashion store; his sister, who had found work as a salesgirl, would study shorthand and French in the evenings, hoping to obtain a better job in the future. Sometimes his father would wake up, as if he hadn't the slightest idea that he'd been asleep, and would say to his mother, "Look how long you've been sewing again today!" and then would fall back to sleep, while his mother and sister would exchange weary smiles.

With a kind of perverse obstinacy his father refused to take off his messenger's uniform even in the apartment; while his robe hung unused on the clothes hook, he would sleep fully dressed in his chair, as if he were always ready for duty and were waiting even here for the voice of his superior. As a result his uniform, which hadn't been new in the first place, began to get dirty in spite of all his mother and sister could do to care for it, and Gregor would often spend entire evenings gazing at this garment covered with stains and with its constantly polished buttons gleaming, in which the old man would sit, upright and uncomfortable, yet peacefully asleep.

As soon as the clock would strike ten, his mother would try to awaken his father   65
with soft words of encouragement and then persuade him to go to bed, for this wasn't any place in which to get a decent night's sleep, and his father badly needed his rest, since he had to be at work at six in the morning. But with the stubbornness that had possessed him ever since he'd become a bank messenger he would insist on staying at the table a little while longer, though he invariably would fall asleep again, and then it was only with the greatest difficulty that he could be persuaded to trade his chair for bed. No matter how much mother and sister would urge him on with little admonishments, he'd keep shaking his head for a good fifteen minutes, his eyes closed, and wouldn't get up. Gregor's mother would tug at his sleeve, whisper sweet words into his ear; and his sister would leave her homework to help her mother, but it was all useless. He only sank deeper into his armchair. Not until the two women would lift him up by the arms would he open his eyes, look now at one, now at the other, and usually say, "What a life. So this is the peace of my old age." And leaning on the two women he would get up laboriously, as if he were his own greatest burden, and would allow the women to lead him to the door, where, waving them aside, he continued on his own, while Gregor's mother abandoned her sewing and her sister her pen so that they might run after his father and continue to look after him.

Who in this overworked and exhausted family had time to worry about Gregor any more than was absolutely necessary? Their resources grew more limited; the maid was now dismissed after all; a gigantic bony cleaning woman with white hair fluttering about her head came in the mornings and evenings to do the roughest work; Gregor's mother took care of everything else, in addition to her sewing. It even happened that certain pieces of family jewelry which his mother and sister had worn with such pleasure at parties and celebrations in days gone by, were sold, as Gregor found out one evening by listening to a general discussion of the prices they'd gone for. But their greatest complaint was that they couldn't give up the apartment, which was too big for their current needs, since no one could figure out how they would move Gregor. But Gregor understood clearly enough that it wasn't simply consideration for him which prevented them moving, since he could have easily been transported in a suitable crate equipped with a few air holes. The main reason preventing them from moving was their utter despair and the feeling that they had been struck by a misfortune far greater than any that had ever visited their friends and relatives. What the world demands of the poor they did to the utmost: his father fetched breakfast for the bank's minor officials, his mother sacrificed herself for the underwear of strangers, his sister ran back and forth behind the counters at the beck and call of customers; but they lacked the strength for anything beyond this. And the wound in Gregor's back began to ache once more when his mother and sister, after putting his father to bed, returned to the room, ignored their work, and sat huddled together cheek to cheek, and his mother said, "Close that door, Grete," so that Gregor was back in the dark, while in the next room the women wept together or simply stared at the table with dry eyes.

Gregor spent the days and nights almost entirely without sleep. Sometimes he imagined that the next time the door opened he would once again assume control of the family's affairs, as he'd done in the old days. Now, after a long absence, there reappeared in his thoughts the director and the manager, the salesmen and the apprentices, the remarkably stupid errand runner, two or three friends from other firms, a chambermaid at one of the provincial hotels—a sweet, fleeting memory—a cashier at a hat store whom he'd courted earnestly but too slowly—they all came to him mixed up with strangers and with people whom he'd already forgotten. But instead of helping him and his family they were all unapproachable, and he was glad when they faded away. At other times he was in no mood to worry about his family; he was utterly filled with rage at how badly he was being treated, and although he couldn't imagine anything that might tempt his appetite, he nevertheless tried to think up ways of getting into the pantry to take what was rightfully his, even if he wasn't hungry. No longer bothering to consider what Gregor might like as a treat, his sister, before she hurried off to work in the morning and after lunch, would shove any sort of food into Gregor's room with her foot. In the evening, regardless of whether the food had been picked at, or—as was more often the case—left completely untouched, she would sweep it out with a swish of the broom. Nowadays she would clean the room in the evening, and she couldn't have done it any faster. Streaks of grime ran along the walls, balls of dust and dirt lay here and there on the floor. At first, whenever his sister would come in, Gregor would station himself in some corner that was particularly objectionable, as if his presence there might serve as a reproach to her. But he probably could have remained there for weeks without her mending her ways; she obviously could see the dirt as clearly as he could, but she'd made up her mind to leave it. At the same time she made certain—with a touchiness that was completely new to her and which indeed was infecting the entire family—that the cleaning of Gregor's room was to remain her prerogative. On one occasion Gregor's mother had subjected his room to a thorough cleaning, which she managed to accomplish only with the aid of several buckets of water—all this dampness being a further annoyance to Gregor, who lay flat, unhappy, and motionless on the couch. But his mother's punishment was not long in coming. For that evening, as soon as Gregor's sister noticed the difference in his room, she ran, deeply insulted, into the living room, and without regard for his mother's uplifted, beseeching hands, burst into a fit of tears. Both parents—the father, naturally, had been startled out of his armchair—at first looked on with helpless amazement, and then they joined in, the father on his right side blaming the mother: she shouldn't have interfered with the sister's cleaning of the room, while on his left side yelling at the sister that she'd never be allowed to clean Gregor's room again. The mother was trying to drag the father, who was half out of his mind, into their bedroom while the sister, shaking with sobs, pounded the table with her little fists, and Gregor hissed loudly with rage because not one of them had thought to close the door and spare him this scene and this commotion.

But even if his sister, worn out by her job at the store, had gotten tired of taking care of Gregor as she once had, it wasn't really necessary for his mother to take her place so that Gregor wouldn't be neglected. For now the cleaning woman was there. This ancient widow, whose powerful bony frame had no doubt helped her through the hard times in her long life, wasn't at all repelled by Gregor. Without being the least bit inquisitive, she had once, by chance, opened the door to Gregor's room and at the sight of Gregor—who, taken completely by surprise, began running back and forth although no one was chasing him—stood there in amazement, her hands folded over her belly. From then on, morning and evening, she never failed to open his door a crack and peek in on him. At first she also would call him to her, using phrases she probably meant to be friendly, such as "Come on over here, you old dung beetle!" or "Just look at that old dung beetle!" Gregor wouldn't respond to such forms of address, but would remain motionless where he was as if the door had never been opened. If only this cleaning woman, instead of pointlessly disturbing him whenever she felt like it, had been given orders to clean his room every day! Once, early in the morning, when a heavy rain, perhaps a sign of the already approaching spring, was beating against the window panes, Gregor became so exasperated when the cleaning woman started in with her phrases that he made as if to attack her, though, of course, in a slow and feeble manner. But instead of being frightened, the cleaning woman simply picked up a chair by the door and, lifting it high in the air, stood there with her mouth wide open. Obviously she didn't plan on shutting it until the chair in her hands had first come crashing down on Gregor's back. "So you're not going through with it?" she asked as Gregor turned back while she calmly set the chair down again in the corner.

By now Gregor was eating next to nothing. Only when he happened to pass by the food set out for him would he take a bite, hold it in his mouth for hours, and then spit most of it out again. At first he imagined that it was his anguish at the state of his room that kept him from eating, but it was those very changes to which he had quickly become accustomed. The family had fallen into the habit of using the room to store things for which there wasn't any place anywhere else, and there were many of these things now, since one room in the apartment had been rented to three boarders. These serious gentlemen—all three of them had full beards, as Gregor once noted, peering through a crack in the door—had a passion for neatness, not only in their room but since they were now settled in as boarders, throughout the entire apartment, and especially in the kitchen. They couldn't abide useless, let alone dirty, junk. Besides, they'd brought most of their own household goods along with them. This meant that many objects were now superfluous, which, while clearly without any resale value, couldn't just be thrown out either. All these things ended up in Gregor's room, and so did the ash bucket and the garbage can from the kitchen. Anything that wasn't being used at the moment was simply tossed into Gregor's room by the cleaning woman, who was always in a tremendous hurry. Fortunately, Gregor generally saw only the object in question and the hand that held it. Perhaps the cleaning woman intended to come back for these things when she had the time, or perhaps she planned on throwing them all out, but in fact there they remained, wherever they'd happened to land, except for Gregor's disturbing them as he squeezed his way through the junk pile. At first he did so simply because he was forced to, since there wasn't any other space to crawl in, but later he took a growing pleasure in these rambles even though they left him dead tired and so sad that he would lie motionless for hours. Since the boarders would sometimes have their dinner at home in the shared living room, on those evenings the door between that room and Gregor's would remain shut. But Gregor didn't experience the door's not being open as a hardship; in fact there had been evenings when he'd ignored the open door and had lain, unnoticed by the family, in the darkest corners of his room. But one time the cleaning woman left the door slightly ajar, and it remained ajar when the boarders came in that evening and the lamp was lit. They sat down at the head of the table, where Gregor, his mother and his father had sat in the old days; they unfolded their napkins, and picked up their knives and forks. At once his mother appeared at the kitchen door carrying a platter of meat and right behind her came his sister carrying a platter piled high with potatoes. The steaming food gave off a thick vapor. The platters were set down in front of the boarders, who bent over them as if to examine them before eating, and in fact the one sitting in the middle, who was apparently looked up to as an authority by the other two, cut into a piece of meat while it was still on the platter, evidently to determine if it was tender enough or whether perhaps it should be sent back to the kitchen. He was satisfied, and both mother and daughter, who'd been watching anxiously, breathed a sigh of relief and began to smile.

The family itself ate in the kitchen. Even so, before going to the kitchen his father came into the living room, bowed once and, cap in hand, walked around the table. The boarders all rose together and mumbled something into their beards. When they were once more alone, they ate in almost complete silence. It seemed strange to Gregor that, out of all the noises produced by eating, he distinctly heard the sound of their teeth chewing; it was as if he were being told you needed teeth in order to eat and that even with the most wonderful toothless jaws, you wouldn't be able to accomplish a thing. "Yes, I'm hungry enough," Gregor told himself sadly, "but not for those things. How well these boarders feed themselves, while I waste away." 70

That very evening—during this whole time Gregor couldn't once remember hearing the violin—the sound of violin playing came from the kitchen. The boarders had already finished their dinner, the one in the middle had pulled out a newspaper, handed one sheet each to the other two, and now they were leaning back, reading and smoking. When the violin began to play, they noticed it, stood up, and tiptoed to the hall doorway where they stood together in a tight group. They must have been heard in the kitchen for his father called, "Does the playing bother you, gentlemen? We can stop it at once." "On the contrary," said the gentleman in the middle, "wouldn't the young lady like to come and play in here where it's much more roomy and comfortable?" "Why, certainly," called Gregor's father, as if he were the violinist. Soon his father came in carrying the music stand, his mother the sheet music, and his sister the violin. His sister calmly got everything ready for playing; his parents—who had never rented out rooms before and so were overly polite to the boarders—didn't even dare to sit down in their own chairs. His father leaned against the door, slipping his right hand between the buttons of his uniform's jacket, which he'd kept buttoned up; but his mother was offered a chair by one of the gentlemen, and, leaving it where he happened to have placed it, she sat off to one side, in the corner.

His sister began to play; his father and mother, on either side, closely followed the movements of her hands. Gregor, attracted by the playing, had moved a little farther forward and already had his head in the living room. He was hardly surprised that recently he'd shown so little concern for others, although in the past he'd taken pride in being considerate. Now more than ever he had good reason to remain hidden, since he was completely covered with the dust that lay everywhere in his room and was stirred up by the slightest movement. Moreover, threads, hairs, and scraps of food clung to his back and sides, his indifference to everything was much too great for him to have gotten onto his back and rubbed himself clean against the carpet, as he had once done several times a day. And despite his condition he wasn't ashamed to edge his way a little further across the spotless living room floor.

To be sure, no one took any notice of him. The family was completely absorbed by the violin-playing. The boarders, however, who had at first placed themselves, their hands in their pockets, much too close to the music stand—close enough for every one of them to have followed the score, which surely must have flustered his sister—soon retreated to the window, muttering to one another, with their heads lowered. And there they remained while his father watched them anxiously. It seemed all too obvious that they had been disappointed in their hopes of hearing good or entertaining violin-playing; they had had enough of the entire performance, and it was only out of politeness that they continued to let their peace be disturbed. It was especially obvious, by the way they blew their smoke out of their mouths and noses—it floated upwards to the ceiling—just how ill at ease they were. And yet his sister was playing so beautifully. Her face was inclined to one side, and her sad eyes carefully followed the notes of the music. Gregor crawled forward a little farther, keeping his head close to the floor so that their eyes might possibly meet. Was he an animal, that music could move him so? He felt that he was being shown the way to an unknown nourishment he yearned for. He was determined to press on until he reached his sister, to tug at her skirt, and to let her know in this way that she should bring her violin into his room, for no one here would honor her playing as he would. He would never let her out of his room again, at least not for as long as he lived; at last his horrifying appearance would be useful; he would be at every door of his room at once, hissing and spitting at the attackers. His sister, however, wouldn't be forced to remain with him, she would do so of her own free will. She would sit beside him on the couch, leaning towards him and listening as he confided that he had firmly intended to send her to the Conservatory, and if the misfortune hadn't intervened, he would've announced this to everyone last Christmas—for hadn't Christmas come and gone by now?—without paying the slightest attention to any objection. After this declaration his sister would be so moved that she would burst into tears, and Gregor would lift himself up to her shoulder and kiss her on her neck, which, since she had started her job, she had kept bare, without ribbon or collar.

"Mr. Samsa!" cried the middle gentleman to Gregor's father, and without wasting another word pointed with his index finger at Gregor, who was slowly advancing. The violin stopped, the middle gentleman, shaking his head, smiled first at his friend and then looked at Gregor again. Instead of driving Gregor away, his father seemed to think it more important to soothe the boarders, although they weren't upset at all and appeared to consider Gregor more entertaining than the violin-playing. His father rushed over to them and with outstretched arms tried to herd them back into their room and at the same time block their view of Gregor with his body. Now they actually got a little angry—it wasn't clear whether this was due to his father's behavior or to their dawning realization that they had had all along, without knowing it, a next-door neighbor like Gregor. They demanded explanations from his father, raised their own arms now as well, tugged nervously at their beards, and only slowly backed away toward their room. Meanwhile his sister had managed to overcome the bewildered state into which she'd fallen when her playing had been so abruptly interrupted, and after some moments spent holding the violin and bow in her slackly dangling hands and staring at the score as if she were still playing, she suddenly pulled herself together, placed her instrument on her mother's lap—she was still sitting in her chair with her lungs heaving, gasping for breath—and ran into the next room, which the boarders, under pressure from her father, were ever more swiftly approaching. One could see pillows and blankets flying high in the air and then neatly arranging themselves under his sister's practical hands. Before the gentlemen had even reached their room, she had finished making the beds and had slipped out.

Once again a perverse stubbornness seemed to grip Gregor's father, to the extent   75
that he forgot to pay his tenants the respect still due them. He kept on pushing and shoving until the middle gentleman, who was already standing in the room's doorway, brought him up short with a thunderous stamp of his foot. "I hereby declare," he said, raising his hand and looking around for Gregor's mother and sister as well, "that considering the disgusting conditions prevailing in this apartment and in this family"—here he suddenly spat on the floor— "I'm giving immediate notice. Naturally I'm not going to pay a penny for the time I've spent here; on the contrary, I shall be seriously considering bringing some sort of action against you with claims that—I assure you—will be very easy to substantiate." He stopped speaking and stared ahead of him, as if expecting something. And indeed his two friends chimed right in, saying "We're giving immediate notice too." Whereupon he grabbed the doorknob and slammed the door shut with a crash.

Gregor's father, groping his way and staggering forward, collapsed into his armchair; it looked as if he were stretching himself out for his usual evening nap, but his heavily drooping head, looking as if it had lost all means of support, showed that he was anything but asleep. All this time Gregor had lain quietly right where the boarders had first seen him. His disappointment over the failure of his plan, and perhaps also the weakness caused by eating so little for so long, made movement an impossibility. He feared with some degree of certainty that at the very next moment the whole catastrophe would fall on his head, and he waited. He wasn't even startled when the violin slipped from his mother's trembling fingers and fell off her lap with a reverberating clatter.

"Dear parents," said his sister, pounding the table with her hand by way of preamble, "we can't go on like this. Maybe you don't realize it, but I do. I refuse to utter my brother's name in the presence of this monster, and so all I have to say is: we've got to try to get rid of it. We've done everything humanly possible to take care of it and put up with it; I don't think anyone can blame us in the least."

"She's absolutely right," said his father to himself. His mother, still trying to catch her breath, with a wild look in her eyes, began to cough, her cupped hand muffling the sound.

His sister rushed over to his mother and held her forehead. His father seemed to have been led to more definite thoughts by Grete's words; he was sitting up straight and toying with his messenger's cap, which lay on the table among the dishes left over from the boarders' dinner. From time to time he would glance over at Gregor's motionless form.

"We must try to get rid of it," said his sister, speaking only to her father since her   80
mother's coughing was such that she was incapable of hearing a word. "It will be the death of you both. I can see it coming. People who have to work as hard as we do can't stand this constant torture at home. I can't stand it anymore either." And she

burst out sobbing so violently that her tears ran down onto her mother's face, where she wiped them away mechanically with her hand.

"But, my child," said her father with compassion and remarkable understanding, "what should we do?"

Gregor's sister could only shrug her shoulders as a sign of the helplessness that had overcome her while she wept, in contrast to her earlier self-confidence.

"If he could understand us," said her father tentatively; Gregor's sister, through her tears, shook her hand violently to indicate how impossible that was.

"If he could understand us," repeated her father, closing his eyes so as to take in his daughter's belief that this was impossible, "then perhaps we might be able to reach some agreement with him, but the way things are—"

"He's got to go," cried Gregor's sister, "it's the only way, Father. You just have to get rid of the idea that this is Gregor. Our real misfortune is having believed it for so long. But how can it be Gregor? If it were, he would've realized a long time ago that it's impossible for human beings to live with a creature like that, and he would've left on his own accord. Then we would've lost a brother, but we'd have been able to go on living and honor his memory. But the way things are, this animal persecutes us, drives away our boarders, obviously it wants to take over the whole apartment and make us sleep in the gutter. Look, Father," she suddenly screamed, "he's at it again!" And in a panic which Gregor found incomprehensible his sister abandoned his mother, and actually pushing herself from the chair as if she would rather sacrifice her mother than remain near Gregor, she rushed behind her father, who, startled by this behavior, got up as well, half raising his arms in front of Grete as if to protect her. 85

Gregor hadn't the slightest desire to frighten anyone, least of all his sister. He had merely started to turn around in order to go back to his room, a procedure which admittedly looked strange, since in his weakened condition he had to use his head to help him in this difficult maneuver, several times raising it and then knocking it against the floor. He stopped and looked around. His good intentions seemed to have been understood; the panic had only been temporary. Now, silent and sad, they all looked at him. His mother lay in her armchair with her legs outstretched and pressed together, her eyes almost closed from exhaustion. His father and sister sat side by side, and his sister had put her arm around her father's neck.

"Now maybe they'll let me turn around," thought Gregor, resuming his efforts. He couldn't stop panting from the strain, and he also had to rest from time to time. At least no one harassed him and he was left alone. When he had finished turning around, he immediately began to crawl back in a straight line. He was amazed at the distance between him and his room and couldn't understand how, weak as he was, he'd covered the same stretch of ground only a little while ago almost without being aware of it. Completely intent on crawling rapidly, he scarcely noticed that neither a word nor an exclamation came from his family to interrupt his progress. Only when he reached the doorway did he turn his head; not all the way, for he felt his neck growing stiff, but enough to see that behind him all was as before except that his sister had gotten to her feet. His last glimpse was of his mother, who by now was fast asleep.

He was barely inside the room before the door was slammed shut, bolted, and locked. Gregor was so frightened by the sudden noise behind him that his little legs collapsed underneath him. It was his sister who had been in such a hurry. She'd been standing there, ready and waiting, and then had sprung swiftly forward, before

Gregor had even heard her coming. "At last!" she cried to her parents as she turned the key in the lock.

"And now?" Gregor asked himself, looking around in the darkness. He soon discovered that he was no longer able to move. This didn't surprise him; rather it seemed to him strange that until now he'd actually been able to propel himself with these thin little legs. In other respects he felt relatively comfortable. It was true that his entire body ached, but the pain seemed to him to be growing fainter and fainter and soon would go away altogether. The rotten apple in his back and the inflamed area around it, completely covered with fine dust, hardly bothered him anymore. He recalled his family with deep emotion and love. His own belief that he must disappear was, if anything, even firmer than his sister's. He remained in this state of empty and peaceful reflection until the tower clock struck three in the morning. He could still just sense the general brightening outside his window. Then, involuntarily, his head sank all the way down, and from his nostrils came his last feeble breath.

Early that morning, when the cleaning woman appeared—out of sheer energy and impatience she always slammed all the doors, no matter how often she'd been asked not to, so hard that sleep was no longer possible anywhere in the apartment once she'd arrived—she didn't notice anything peculiar when she paid Gregor her usual brief visit. She thought that he was lying there so still on purpose, pretending that his feelings were hurt; she considered him to be very clever. As she happened to be holding a long broom, she tried to tickle Gregor with it from the doorway. When this too had no effect, she became annoyed and jabbed it into Gregor a little, and it was only when she shoved him from his place without meeting resistance that she began to take notice. Quickly realizing how things stood, she opened her eyes wide, gave a soft whistle, and without wasting any time she tore open the bedroom door and yelled at the top of her lungs into the darkness: "Come and look, it's had it, it's lying there, dead and done for."

Mr. and Mrs. Samsa sat up in their marriage bed, trying to absorb the shock the cleaning woman had given them and yet at first unable to comprehend the meaning of her words. Then they quickly climbed out of bed, Mr. Samsa on one side, Mrs. Samsa on the other. Mr. Samsa threw a blanket over his shoulders, Mrs. Samsa wore only her nightgown; dressed in this fashion they entered Gregor's room. Meanwhile the door to the living room, where Grete had been sleeping since the boarders' arrival, opened as well. Grete was fully dressed, as if she'd never gone to bed, and the pallor of her face seemed to confirm this. "Dead?" asked Mrs. Samsa and looked inquiring at the cleaning woman, although she could have checked for herself, or guessed at the truth without having to investigate. "That's for sure," said the cleaning woman, and to prove it she pushed Gregor's corpse a good way to one side with her broom. Mrs. Samsa made a move as if to stop her, then let it go. "Well," said Mr. Samsa, "now thanks be to God." He crossed himself, and the three women followed his example. Grete, who never took her eyes off the corpse, said, "Just look how thin he was. It's been a long time since he's eaten anything. The food came out just as it was when it came in." Indeed, Gregor's body was completely flat and dry; this was only now obvious because the body was no longer raised on its little legs and nothing else distracted the eye.

"Come to our room with us for a little while, Grete," said Mrs. Samsa with a sad smile, and Grete, not without a look back at the corpse, followed her parents into the bedroom. The cleaning woman shut the door and opened the windows

90

wide. Although it was early in the morning, there was a certain mildness in the fresh air. After all, these were the last days of March.

The three boarders came out of their rooms and looked around in amazement for their breakfast; they had been forgotten. "Where's our breakfast?" the middle gentleman asked the cleaning woman in a sour tone. But she put her finger to her lips, and then quickly and quietly beckoned to the gentlemen to enter Gregor's room. So they did, and, with their hands in the pockets of their somewhat threadbare jackets, they stood in a circle around Gregor's corpse in the now sunlit room.

At that point the bedroom door opened and Mr. Samsa, wearing his uniform, appeared with his wife on one arm and his daughter on the other. They all looked a little tearful; from time to time Grete would press her face against her father's sleeve.

"Leave my home at once," Mr. Samsa told the three gentlemen, pointing to the door without letting go of the women. "What do you mean?" said the middle gentleman, who, somewhat taken aback, smiled a sugary smile. The other two held their hands behind their backs, and kept rubbing them together as if cheerfully anticipating a major argument which they were bound to win. "I mean just what I say," replied Mr. Samsa, and advanced in a line with his two companions directly on the middle boarder. At first this gentleman stood still, looking at the floor as if the thoughts inside his head were arranging themselves in a new pattern. "Well, so we'll be off," he then said, looking up at Mr. Samsa as if, suddenly overcome with humility, he was asking permission for even this decision. Mr. Samsa, his eyes glowering, merely gave him a few brief nods. With that the gentleman, taking long strides, actually set off in the direction of the hall; his two friends, who had been listening for some time with their hands quite still, now went hopping right along after him, as if they were afraid that Mr. Samsa might reach the hall before them and cut them off from their leader. Once in the hall the three of them took their hats from the coat rack, pulled their canes from the umbrella stand, bowed silently, and left the apartment. Impelled by a suspicion that would turn out to be utterly groundless, Mr. Samsa led the two women out onto the landing; leaning against the banister railing they watched the three gentlemen as they marched slowly but steadily down the long staircase, disappearing at every floor when the staircase made a turn and then after a few moments reappearing once again. The lower they descended the more the Samsas' interest in them waned; and when a butcher's boy with a basket on his head came proudly up the stairs towards the gentlemen and then swept on past them, Mr. Samsa and the women quickly left the banister and, as if relieved, returned to the apartment.

They decided to spend this day resting and going for a walk; not only did they deserve this break from work, they absolutely needed it. And so they sat down at the table to write their three letters excusing themselves, Mr. Samsa to the bank manager, Mrs. Samsa to her employer, and Grete to the store's owner. While they were writing, the cleaning woman came by to say that she was leaving now, since her morning's work was done. At first the three letter writers merely nodded without looking up, but when the cleaning woman made no move to go, they looked up at her, annoyed. "Well?" asked Mr. Samsa. The cleaning woman stood in the doorway, smiling as if she had some wonderful news for the family, news she wasn't about to share until they came right out and asked her to. The little ostrich feathers in her hat, which stood up nearly straight in the air and which had irritated Mr. Samsa the entire time she had worked for them, swayed gently in every direction. "What can we do for you?" asked Mrs. Samsa, whom the cleaning woman respected the most. "Well," the cleaning woman replied, with such good-humored laughter that she had

95

to pause before continuing, "you don't have to worry about getting rid of that thing in the next room. It's already been taken care of." Mrs. Samsa and Grete bent over their letters as if they intended to keep on writing; Mr. Samsa, who realized that the cleaning woman was about to go into the details, stopped her firmly with an out-stretched hand. Seeing that she wasn't going to be allowed to tell her story, she suddenly remembered that she was in a great hurry; clearly insulted, she called out, "Bye, everybody," whirled around wildly, and left the apartment with a terrible slamming of doors.

"She'll be dismissed tonight," said Mr. Samsa, but without getting a reply from his wife or his daughter, for the cleaning woman seemed to have ruined their tenuous peace of mind. They got up, went to the window, and remained there holding each other tightly. Mr. Samsa turned around in his chair toward them and watched them quietly for some time. Then he called out, "Come on now, come over here. Let those old troubles alone. And have a little consideration for me, too." The two women promptly obeyed him, hurried over to him, caressed him, and quickly finished their letters.

Then all three of them left the apartment together, something they hadn't done in months, and took a streetcar out to the open country on the outskirts of the city. Their car, which they had all to themselves, was completely bathed in warm sunlight. Leaning comfortably back in their seats they discussed their prospects for the future, which on closer inspection seemed to be not so bad, since all three of them had jobs which—though they'd never asked one another about them in any detail—were in each case very advantageous and promising. Of course the greatest immediate improvement in their situation would quickly come about when they found a new apartment, one that was smaller, cheaper, and in every way easier to maintain than their current one, which Gregor had chosen for them. As they were talking on in this way, it occurred to both Mr. and Mrs. Samsa, almost simultaneously, as they watched their daughter become more and more vivacious, that in spite of all the recent troubles that had turned her cheeks pale, she had blossomed into a pretty and shapely girl. Growing quieter now, communicating almost unconsciously through glances, they reflected that soon it would be time to find her a good husband. And it was as if in confirmation of their new dreams and good intentions that at the end of their ride their daughter got up first and stretched her young body.

Questions

1. What was Gregor's occupation before his transformation? How did he come to his particular job? What keeps him working for his firm?
2. When Gregor wakes to discover he has become a gigantic insect, he is mostly intent on the practical implications of his metamorphosis—how to get out of bed, how to get to his job, and so on. He never wonders why or how he has been changed. What does this odd reaction suggest about Gregor?
3. When Gregor's parents first see the gigantic insect (paragraph 25), do they recognize it as their son? What do their initial reactions suggest about their attitude toward their son?
4. How does each family member react to Gregor after his transformation? How do these reactions differ from one another? What do they have in common?
5. What things about Gregor have been changed? What seems to have remained the same? List specific qualities.
6. *The Metamorphosis* takes place almost entirely in the Samsa family apartment. How does the story's setting shape its themes?
7. Which family member first decides that the family must "get rid of" the insect? What rationale is given? In what specific ways does the family's decision affect Gregor?

8. How does the family react to Gregor's death?
9. Does Grete change in the course of the story? If so, how does she change?
10. In what ways is Gregor's metamorphosis symbolic?

■ WRITING *effectively*

Franz Kafka on Writing

Discussing *The Metamorphosis* c. 1920

My friend Alfred Kämpf . . . admired Kafka's story *The Metamorphosis*. He described the author as "a new, more profound and therefore more significant Edgar Allan Poe."

During a walk with Franz Kafka on the Altstädter Ring° I told him about this new admirer of his, but aroused neither interest nor understanding. On the contrary, Kafka's expression showed that any discussion of his book was distasteful to him. I, however, was filled with a zeal for discoveries, and so I was tactless.

"The hero of the story is called Samsa," I said. "It sounds like a cryptogram for Kafka. Five letters in each word. The S in the word Samsa has the same position as the K in the word Kafka. The A . . ."

Kafka interrupted me.

"It is not a cryptogram. Samsa is not merely Kafka, and nothing else. *The Metamorphosis* is not a confession, although it is—in a certain sense—an indiscretion."

"I know nothing about that."

"Is it perhaps delicate and discreet to talk about the bugs in one's own family?"

"It isn't usual in good society."

"You see what bad manners I have."

Kafka smiled. He wished to dismiss the subject. But I did not wish to.

"It seems to me that the distinction between good and bad manners hardly applies here," I said. "*The Metamorphosis* is a terrible dream, a terrible conception."

Kafka stood still.

"The dream reveals the reality, which conception lags behind. That is the horror of life—the terror of art. But now I must go home."

From *Conversations with Kafka* by Gustav Janouch

THINKING ABOUT LONG STORIES AND NOVELS

Writing about a long story or novella may seem overwhelming. There can seem to be so much to analyze and consider. You may despair of being able to master the material and discuss it coherently, but if you focus your attention on some central concerns, you will be surprised at how easily you can develop and express your responses to the work.

■ **Be aware that characters in a longer narrative often have more complex personalities.** In a short story, characters are often presented in terms of two

---

Altstädter Ring: a major street in Prague.

or three basic personality traits. But in a long story or novella, characters are usually drawn with more depth and shading—and sometimes even contradictory elements—to their personalities. In reading a long story, you should be alert to all the different aspects of a character's nature.

- **Consider that a longer narrative allows for more development.** Often the intention of a short story is to reveal a personality or a situation as it is, much in the manner of showing a snapshot or drawing back a curtain. But a longer story requires movement and development to sustain the reader's interest. As you read, notice the—often subtle—changes that may take place in the protagonist as he or she initiates or otherwise experiences the events of the narrative.

- **Review the work.** As a long story or novella unfolds, your recollections of the earlier parts of the text may be pushed aside as new events and situations occur. A first-rate work of fiction will yield a wealth of interconnections of language, images, actions, and ideas. After you finish reading the work, by going through the text again you may often see much more in the story than you did the first time around.

CHECKLIST: Writing About Long Stories and Novels

- ☐ What is the protagonist's situation at the beginning of the work?
- ☐ What is the protagonist's main objective at the beginning?
- ☐ What changes take place in the protagonist's situation as the narrative proceeds?
- ☐ How does the protagonist react to these changes? How does his or her response to stress reveal the protagonist's basic nature?
- ☐ Who are the story's other important characters, and what are their relationships to the protagonist?
- ☐ Can anyone be described as an antagonist?
- ☐ Compare and contrast the beginning of the story with its conclusion.
- ☐ Don't try to put everything in your essay. The longer and more involved the text is, the more important it is to focus on the main points and be selective in the choice of textual details.
- ☐ Try to put your ideas in some logical order.
- ☐ Outline the main points of your argument to see clearly what is relevant to that argument and what is not.

WRITING ASSIGNMENT FOR A RESEARCH PAPER

This challenging assignment for a research paper comes from Professor Michael Cass of Mercer University. He asked his students to select the fiction writer whose work impressed them most. Each student had to write a paper defending that author's claim to literary greatness and research the author, using at least five critical sources. The student had to present clear reasons why the author was a major writer and to support the argument with both examples from the writer's work and statements from critics. Choose an author from this book whose greatness you would defend. Here is a short research paper by a student in Professor Cass's class, Stephanie Crowe, who discussed why she believed that Franz Kafka was a great writer.

SAMPLE STUDENT RESEARCH PAPER

Stephanie Crowe

Professor Cass

English 120

21 November 2009

Kafka's Greatness

Introduction of essay topic

Although most of his major works remained unfinished and unpublished at his untimely death in 1924, Franz Kafka has gradually come to be considered one of the great writers of the twentieth century. By 1977, well over ten thousand

Citation of secondary source

works of commentary had appeared on Kafka, and many more have been written since then (Goodden 2). According to critic Peter Heller, Kafka represents the

Quotation from secondary source integrated into sentence

"mainstream of German literary and intellectual tradition," a nihilistic tradition which extends from Goethe and Lessing to the present (289).

Topic sentence on Kafka as influence

Not only is Kafka generally considered one of the greatest fiction writers of the modern era, he is also indisputably one of the most influential. In his 1989 study, *After Kafka*, Shimon Sandbank discusses Kafka's influence on a dozen modern writers, including Sartre, Camus, Beckett, Borges, and Ionesco. His effects on these writers differ. Some borrow his understated, almost passive prose style while others adopt his recurrent images and themes. Whatever the specific elements they use, however, Kafka's ability to influence these writers is another measure of his stature.

Great literature often gives us the stories and images to understand our own age, a process that necessarily includes understanding our deepest

Assumptions explained

problems. The twentieth century, to borrow a phrase from W. H. Auden, was mostly an "Age of Anxiety." Most modern people are no longer bound to follow the occupations, behaviors, and beliefs of their parents, but they gain this newfound freedom at the expense of a constant, difficult search for identity. The personal quest for meaningful identity often leads to despair. This "existential crisis" is the basis for many contemporary problems including the decline of religion, the rise of totalitarianism, the breakdown of social identity, and the decay of traditional family structure.

Topic sentence on Kafka's relationship to his time

Kafka's works dramatize these problems memorably because they provide us with myths, images, stories, and situations that describe the particular crises of the early twentieth century. When faced with the modern challenge of not having a predetermined social or religious identity, Kafka's characters

Crowe 2

desperately attempt to find certainty. The problem, however, is that they are usually afraid to do anything decisive because everything is uncertain. Auden observed:

> Far from being confident of success, the Kafka hero is convinced from the start that he is doomed to fail, as he is also doomed, being who he is, to make prodigious and unending efforts to reach it [the goal]. Indeed, the mere desire to reach the goal is itself a proof, not that he is one of the elect, but that he is under a special curse. (162)

Quotation from secondary source, set off from text

One way that Kafka memorably dramatizes the modern struggle for identity is by reversing the traditional quest story. In a quest story, the hero knows the goal that he wants to achieve and has some confidence that he will be able to achieve it. As he tries to reach the goal, he must overcome various enemies and obstacles. "In a typical Kafka story, on the other hand, the goal is peculiar to the hero himself: he has no competitors" (Auden 162). His question then becomes not a practical "Can I succeed?" but instead a vague and problematic "What should I do?" Unable to answer this question satisfactorily, the hero becomes increasingly alienated from his own surroundings. This alienation is yet another symptom of "the inhumanity of modern society" that Kafka so memorably portrayed (Kuna 62).

Topic sentence elaborates on how Kafka's work reflects his time

Verbatim quotation from secondary source

Kafka also distinguishes himself as a great writer because he created a distinctive style that effectively dramatizes modern problems. Although Kafka's fiction often describes extreme situations, his prose usually seems strangely calm and detached. He uses "clear and simple language" that paints "concrete pictures of human beings, pictures that, in a sense, have to speak for themselves" (Cooper 19). These haunting images (the unreachable castle, the unknown laws, the unspecified trial) dramatize the mysterious struggles of the characters.

Topic sentence on relationship between Kafka's era and his style

Kafka also uses his style to separate himself from his characters, a technique that develops a contrast between the calmness of his style and the nervous desperation of his characters (Heller 237). For example, the opening of Kafka's novella *The Metamorphosis*, which is perhaps the most famous first sentence in modern fiction, describes an outrageous event—a young man who wakes up transformed into a giant bug—in a strangely matter-of-fact tone. This contrast is important because it reminds us of the desperation of modern man imprisoned in a world he can neither understand nor control.

Topic sentence on Kafka's style incorporates critical view

Crowe 3

Topic sentence on Kafka's style of ambiguity

Perhaps the most interesting feature of Kafka's style is his ability to create works that cannot be explained by a single interpretation. Because he allows his pictures to "speak for themselves," "Kafka's texts have been subject to a variety of widely divergent approaches" (Heller 236). Another critic, speaking directly of *The Metamorphosis*, agrees: "Gregor's transformation has a double meaning: it is both an escape from his oppressive life and a representation or even an intensification of it" (Goldfarb). Therefore, no single interpretation can adequately explain an entire work of Kafka's. Most interpretations may illuminate particular moments in a work, but inevitably they lead to a dead end when pressed to explain the whole narrative. Whether one is reading on a social, moral, psychological, metaphysical, theological, or existential level, Kafka "tends to suspend all distinction and thus to revert to total ambiguity" (Heller 285). According to Heller, this characteristic mysteriousness becomes "the epitome of his art" (230).

Topic sentence on Kafka's complexity

Auden believed that the impossibility of interpreting Kafka's work is essential in defining him as an important and influential writer. He says that "Kafka is a great, perhaps the greatest, master of the pure parable, a literary genre about which a critic can say very little worth saying" (159). Since the meaning of a parable is different for each individual, critics cannot explain them without revealing their own visions and values. Kafka develops stories with important symbols that are easily identified; attempting to interpret these symbols, however, only leads to frustration.

Topic sentence on Kafka's central theme incorporates quotation from secondary source

The frustration that comes from trying to interpret Kafka's works exemplifies his recurrent, and particularly twentieth-century, theme, which Peter Heller has described as man's "ever frustrated, ever defeated striving for self-realization in an inhuman human universe in which he is alienated from himself and from the world he lives in" (305). Kafka uses his characteristic difficult symbolism and ambiguity, along with his theme of hopelessness and despair, as a common thread that binds all of his works together.

Topic sentence on tone

Kafka's book *The Great Wall of China* contains several short pieces which have a slightly less desperate tone than that of *The Metamorphosis*. Many of the stories in *The Great Wall of China*, however, still present the theme of hopelessness. In the reflection entitled "The Problem of Our Laws," Kafka examines the origins and legitimacy of law. This parable begins with the narrator stating, "Our laws are not generally known; they are kept secret by the

Quotation from primary source

small group of nobles who rule us" (147). Next, the narrator goes through a

Crowe 4

laborious process of rationally questioning why only the nobility knows the laws, whether the laws really exist, and whether it will ever be possible for common men to know the laws. He finally concludes that the only way to know the law would be a quiet revolution that ends nobility. But even this solution, he realizes, is futile. The nobility cannot be eliminated because they provide the only order that exists. While this parable makes several interesting points, its structure is essentially static. The narrator ends where he began—trapped in an unknowable world.

One of Kafka's unfinished novels, *The Trial*, also concentrates on the unknown symbol of the Law. In the novel, Joseph K. is arrested for a crime that no one ever knows. Joseph, like most of Kafka's characters, is a common man with an uneventful life who admits that he knows little of the Law. The drama of the novel is the protagonist's hopeless attempts to master an unknown and impossible situation. Joseph K.'s life itself becomes a trial, although he is never sentenced. Finally, one year after his arrest, two men come and murder him. Instead of trying to understand the Law, "In the end he appears to accept the verdict as a release from the condition of despair," and "dies like an animal, without comprehending the rationale of the Law which condemns him" (Heller 280-81). Like many men, before his death K. is struggling to discover his identity in relation to the Law that governs him; however, K.'s hopeless life ends with a pointless murder.

> *Topic sentence on theme*

Kafka's other great, unfinished novel, *The Castle*, also concentrates on the theme of unknowability and despair. Instead of trying to understand the Law, K. in *The Castle* has another impossible quest, his attempt to enter the castle of the local ruler to report for duty as a land surveyor. His constant efforts, however, prove futile. As in *The Trial*, the protagonist is at the mercy of an arbitrary and unknowable Law:

> *Topic sentence on theme*

> In many ways the castle functions like a secret court system: the officials decide and carry out policies that are conceived as stipulations of law; they lean on their law books, try to serve the law, and know the clandestine ways of law. Many decisions are arrived at arbitrarily and remain secret; even legal actions such as an official indictment can be kept hidden for some time. (Heidsieck 3)

Only when K. lies on his deathbed does a call from the castle come, giving him permission to live in the town. Once again, the protagonist suffers hopelessly and dies in despair.

Crowe 5

While *The Trial* emphasizes political and psychological themes characteristic of the twentieth century, *The Castle* focuses on the religious identity crisis. *The Metamorphosis* examines similar themes of identity on a personal and family level. All of these works focus on modern humanity's difficult struggle to define its place in existence.

Conclusion sums up argument

Kafka, through his works, accurately describes the modern condition of many by using memorable images and a distinctive style. This characteristic style influenced many twentieth-century writers and readers. While difficult and somewhat bleak, Kafka's often ambiguous, yet understated dramatizations of man's condition, along with his lasting influence, form the foundation of his greatness.

Thesis sentence makes debatable claim

Crowe 6

Works Cited

Auden, W. H. "The I Without a Self." *The Dyer's Hand*. New York: Random, 1989. 159–70. Print.

Cooper, Gabriele Bon Natzmer. *Kafka and Language: In the Stream of Thoughts and Life*. Riverside, CA: Ariadne, 1991. Print.

Goldfarb, Sheldon. "Critical Essay on *The Metamorphosis*." *Short Stories for Students*. Ed. Jennifer Smith. Vol. 12. Detroit: Gale, 2001. N. pag. *Literature Resource Center*. Gale. Web. 19 September 2009.

Goodden, Christina. "Points of Departure." *The Kafka Debate: New Perspectives for Our Time*. Ed. Angel Flores. New York: Gordian, 1988. 2–9. Print.

Heidsieck, Arnold. "Community, Delusion and Anti-Semitism in Kafka's *The Castle*." *German Studies Program*. German Dept., U of Southern California, n.d. Web. 19 September 2009. <http://www.usc.edu/dept/LAS/german/track/heidsiec/KafkaAntisemitism/KafkaAntisemitism.pdf>.

Heller, Peter. "Kafka: The Futility of Striving." *Dialectics and Nihilism*. Amherst: U of Massachusetts P, 1966. 227–306. Print.

Kafka, Franz. "The Problem of Our Laws." *The Great Wall of China*. New York: Schocken, 1946. 147–49. Print.

Crowe 7

Kuna, Franz. *Franz Kafka: Literature as Corrective Punishment*. Bloomington: Indiana UP, 1974. Print.

Sandbank, Shimon. *After Kafka: The Influence of Kafka's Fiction*. Athens: U of Georgia P, 1989. Print.

MORE TOPICS FOR WRITING

1. What do Ivan Ilych and Gregor Samsa have in common? In what ways are their lives and deaths dissimilar?

2. Choose a thematic concern of either *The Death of Ivan Ilych* or *The Metamorphosis*; some possibilities are work, romantic love, and the family. Develop a thesis about what your story has to say on your chosen theme. Now choose three key moments from the story to back up your argument. Make your case in a medium-length paper (600 to 1,000 words); be sure to quote as needed from the text.

3. In one carefully thought-out paragraph, sum up what you believe Tolstoy is saying in *The Death of Ivan Ilych*.

4. Compare Tolstoy's short novel with another story of spiritual awakening: Flannery O'Connor's "Revelation" or "A Good Man Is Hard to Find." In each, what brings about the enlightenment of the central character?

5. Is *The Metamorphosis* a horror story? What elements does Kafka's story share with horror fiction or films you have known? How does *The Metamorphosis* differ?

6. Compare and contrast Gregor Samsa's relationships with the people in his life to Miss Emily's relationships with those around her in "A Rose for Emily."

7. Explore how Gregor Samsa's metamorphosis into a giant insect is symbolic of his earlier life and relations with his family. (For a discussion of literary symbols, see Chapter 7, "Symbol.")

8. Write a metamorphosis story of your own. Imagine a character who turns overnight into something quite other than himself or herself. As you describe that character's struggles, try for a mix of tragedy and grotesque comedy, as found in *The Metamorphosis*.

► TERMS FOR *review*

Novel ► An extended work of fictional prose narrative. The term *novel* usually implies a book-length narrative.

Novella ► In modern terms, a prose narrative longer than a short story but shorter than a novel. Unlike a short story, a novella is long enough to be published independently as a brief book.

Romance ► In general terms, romance is a narrative mode that employs exotic adventure and idealized emotion rather than realistic depiction of character and action. In the romantic mode, people, actions, and events are depicted more as we wish them to be (heroes are very brave, villains are very bad) than in the complex forms in which they usually exist. Most popular fiction genres—such as mystery, horror, adventure, science fiction—develop from this mode.

Historical fiction ▶ A type of fiction in which the narrative is set in another time or place. In historical fiction, the author often attempts to recreate a faithful picture of daily life during the period. While it may depict real historical figures, more often it places imaginary characters in a carefully reconstructed version of a particular era.

Nonfiction novel ▶ A genre in which actual events are presented as a novel-length story, using the techniques of fiction.

Picaresque ▶ A type of narrative, usually a novel, that presents the life of a likable scoundrel at odds with respectable society. The narrator of a picaresque was originally a *pícaro* (Spanish for "rascal" or "rogue") who recounts his or her adventures tricking the rich and gullible. This type of narrative rarely has a tightly constructed plot, and the episodes or adventures follow in a loose chronological order.

Epistolary novel ▶ Novel in which the story is told by way of letters written by one or more of the characters. This form often lends an authenticity to the story, an illusion that the author may have discovered these letters, even though they are a product of the author's imagination.

Bildungsroman ▶ German for "novel of growth and development." Sometimes called an **apprenticeship novel,** this genre depicts a youth who struggles toward maturity and the forming of a worldview or philosophy of life.

9   LATIN AMERICAN FICTION

Writing is nothing more than a guided dream.

—JORGE LUIS BORGES

Before the middle of the twentieth century Latin America produced a number of highly talented novelists, but their work had relatively little impact outside their region—and often little impact beyond their own individual nations. For the most part, these novels fit into the tradition of realism that dominated European literature in the late nineteenth century, and often pursued a social agenda, emphasizing the economic and geographical characteristics that were unique to the writer's own country. It was relatively rare for the fiction of any individual nation to be published or even to circulate in the other countries of Spanish America. One author who transcended these limits was the Guatemalan novelist Miguel Ángel Asturias (1899–1974), who is credited with introducing some of the techniques of Modernism into Latin American fiction and who would go on to win the Nobel Prize in Literature in 1967.

But even Asturias felt that Latin American literature, while powerful, remained provincial. In a 1970 interview he said, "To believe that we Latin Americans are going to teach Europeans to reflect, to philosophize, to write egocentric or psychological novels, to believe that we are already a mature enough society to produce a Proust or a Goethe—that would be daydreaming and self-deception." His remarks exemplified the marginality still felt by most Latin American writers of his generation.

"EL BOOM"

Asturias underestimated the growing influence and appeal of Latin American literature. By 1970 Latin American fiction had begun to capture international attention. A new generation of fiction writers had emerged who had been profoundly influenced by the great Modernists of American, British, and European literature. In their hands, formal literary style relaxed to incorporate common speech, sudden shifts of tone, and extravagant wordplay. Characterization became more complex and multilayered, and instead of straightforward, realist narrative there were now often fractured time sequences and fantastic events. These young writers were the catalysts of an explosion of creativity—commonly referred to as **"El Boom"**—that transformed Latin America into one of the centers of modern world fiction.

One of the pioneering figures of the movement was the Mexican writer Carlos Fuentes; Chilean novelist Jose Donoso would later write of Fuentes's 1959 novel *Where the Air Is Clear*: "Reading it was a cataclysm for me. Until then, I had been governed by a paralyzing good taste, and for me, the politics and forces giving shape to our history were matters of hometown gossip on the level of friendly phone calls, never on the level of myths, invasions, or idolatries." Other writers prominently associated with the Boom were Julio Cortázar of Argentina, whose experimental novel *Hopscotch* (1963) attracted widespread international attention, and Mario Vargas Llosa of Peru, who also achieved an international reputation with *The Time of the Hero* (1963) and *Aunt Julia and the Scriptwriter* (1977). But its best-known and most influential figure is the Colombian novelist Gabriel García Márquez, whose *One Hundred Years of Solitude* (1967) is the defining text both of "El Boom" and of the genre known as *magic realism*.

MAGIC REALISM

Magic realism (*el realismo magical*) was a term coined in 1949 by the Cuban novelist Alejo Carpentier to describe the matter-of-fact combination of the fantastic and everyday in Latin American fiction. Magic realism has now become the standard name for a major trend in contemporary fiction that stretches from Latin American works such as García Márquez's *One Hundred Years of Solitude* and Octavio Paz's "My Life with the Wave," to *norteamericana* novels such as Mark Helprin's *Winter's Tale* (1983) and Asian works such as Salman Rushdie's *Midnight's Children* (1981). In all cases the term refers to the tendency among contemporary fiction writers to mix the magical and mundane in an overall context of realistic narration.

If the term *magic realism* is relatively new, what it describes has been around since the early development of the novel and short story as modern literary forms. One already sees the key elements of magic realism in *Gulliver's Travels* (1726), which factually narrates the fabulous adventures of an English surgeon. Likewise Nikolai Gogol's short story "The Nose" (1842), in which a minor Czarist bureaucrat's nose takes off to pursue its own career in St. Petersburg, fulfills virtually every requirement of this purportedly contemporary style. One finds similar precedents in Charles Dickens, Honoré de Balzac, Fyodor Dostoyevsky, Guy de Maupassant, Franz Kafka, and others. Seen from a historical perspective, therefore, magic realism is a vital contemporary manifestation of a venerable fictive impulse.

The possibilities of storytelling will always hover between the opposing poles of realism and romance. Until recently most English-language critics almost exclusively favored the realist mode—their emphasis reflected what F. R. Leavis called the "Great Tradition" of the psychological and social realist novel. This tradition encompassed Jane Austen, George Eliot, Henry James, Edith Wharton, Joseph Conrad, Virginia Woolf, D. H. Lawrence, Willa Cather, and early James Joyce. These British and American critics would hardly have imagined that a radically different kind of fiction was being developed beyond their ken in places like Argentina, Colombia, and Peru. By the time García Márquez and his fellow members of the Boom in Latin American fiction came to maturity, the reemergence of the fantastic heritage in fiction seemed nearly as revolutionary as the region's politics.

All of the main features of Latin American magic realism can be found in García Márquez's "A Very Old Man with Enormous Wings," which appeared in his 1972 book

The Incredible and Sad Tale of Innocent Eréndira and Her Heartless Grandmother, written soon after *One Hundred Years of Solitude*. As a young law student, García Márquez
read Kafka's *The Metamorphosis*. It proved a decisive encounter, and the influence is
not hard to observe in the early stories, which so often present bizarre incidents
unfolding in ordinary circumstances. If Kafka reinvented the animal fable by placing
it in the everyday modern world, García Márquez reset it in the unfamiliar landscape
of the Third World. If Kafka made spiritual issues more mysterious by surrounding
them with bureaucratic procedure, his Colombian follower changed our perception
of Latin America by insisting that in this New World visionary romanticism was
merely reportage. García Márquez also had another crucial mentor closer at hand—
the Argentinean master, Jorge Luis Borges.

Only thirty years García Márquez's senior, Borges had quietly redrawn the
imaginative boundaries of Latin American fiction, though his work appeared only
sporadically in English translation until the early 1960s. Almost single-handedly he
had rehabilitated the fantastic tale for literary fiction. Significantly, Borges expressed
his sophisticated fictions in popular rather than experimental forms—the fable, the
detective story, the supernatural tale, the gaucho legend. Intellectually and tem-
peramentally, Borges was a true citizen of the world; both bookish and playful by nature, he was widely read in European literature and was influenced by an impressive
range of writers, including—among many others—Cervantes, Poe, Kafka, and
Robert Louis Stevenson. Possessed of an essentially ironic sensibility, he was also
strongly influenced by the late-nineteenth-century Symbolist movement—both of
which tendencies can be found in "The Gospel According to Mark." He was the
first great postmodernist storyteller, and he found an eager apprentice in García
Márquez, who developed these innovative notions in different and usually more
expansive forms.

AFTER THE BOOM

Like Borges, the Mexican author Octavio Paz was older than the writers of the
Boom and had been publishing for decades before their careers began. Paz originally made his mark as a poet, but in the later decades of the twentieth century he
gradually established himself as one of the dominant figures of Latin American literature with a series of prose works that incorporated history, biography, psychology, literary theorizing, and spiritual meditation. As the critic Ilan Stavans has said
of him: "Paz was never a best-selling author on the scale of Stephen King, but his
influence on our culture and his endurance are infinitely wider and more durable."
Along with Borges, Paz helped make Latin American literature more inclusive and
cosmopolitan.

One of the most frequently raised criticisms of the Boom is its heavily male
emphasis, in terms of both the authors themselves and the characters in their novels.
More recent years have seen the emergence of important female authors, including
the Chilean Isabel Allende, a writer in the tradition of magical realism whose novel
The House of the Spirits (1982) was an international best-seller, and the Mexican Inés
Arredondo, whose subtle and moving short stories—of which "The Shunammite" is
an outstanding example—explore the psychology of women and their place in society. In the wake of the Boom, Latin American literature is notably richer, deeper,
and more diverse than ever before. If someone were to slightly modify the Englishman
Sydney Smith's early nineteenth-century sneer at the literature of the United States

and ask "Who reads a Latin American book?," the answer would be, anyone who wants to be in touch with some of the most original, exciting, and important literature in the world today.

Jorge Luis Borges

The Gospel According to Mark   1970

Translated by Andrew Hurley

Jorge Luis Borges

Jorge Luis Borges (1899–1986), an outstanding modern writer of Latin America, was born in Buenos Aires into a family prominent in Argentine history. His father, with whom he had a very close relationship, was a lawyer and teacher. Borges grew up bilingual, learning English from his English grandmother and receiving his early education from an English tutor. In later years, he would translate work by Poe, Melville, Whitman, Faulkner, and others into Spanish. Caught in Europe by the outbreak of World War I, Borges lived in Switzerland—where he learned French and taught himself German—and later Spain, where he joined the Ultraists, a group of experimental poets who renounced realism. On returning to Argentina, he edited a poetry magazine printed in the form of a poster and affixed to city walls. In his early writings, Borges favored the style of Criollismo (regionalism), but by the mid-1930s he had begun to take a more cosmopolitan and internationalist approach; in this same period, his principal literary emphasis began to shift from poetry to fiction. In 1946, for his opposition to the regime of Colonel Juan Perón, Borges was forced to resign his post as a librarian and was mockingly offered a job as a chicken inspector. In 1955, after Perón was deposed, Borges became director of the National Library and professor of English literature at the University of Buenos Aires. A sufferer since childhood from poor eyesight, Borges eventually went blind. His eye problems may have encouraged him to work mainly in short, highly crafted forms: stories, essays, fables, and lyric poems full of elaborate music. His short stories, in Ficciones (1944), El hacedor (1960; translated as Dreamtigers, 1964), and Labyrinths (1962), have been admired worldwide.

The incident took place on the Los Alamos ranch, south of the small town of Junín, in late March of 1928. Its protagonist was a medical student named Baltasar Espinosa. We might define him for the moment as a Buenos Aires youth much like many others, with no traits worthier of note than the gift for public speaking that had won him more than one prize at the English school° in Ramos Mejía and an almost unlimited goodness. He didn't like to argue; he preferred that his interlocutor rather than he himself be right. And though he found the chance twists and turns of gambling interesting, he was a poor gambler, because he didn't like to win. He was intelligent and open to learning, but he was lazy; at thirty-three he had not yet completed the last requirements for his degree. (The work he still owed, incidentally, was for his

English school: a prep school that emphasized English (well-to-do Argentineans of this era wanted their children to learn English).

favorite class.) His father, like all the gentlemen of his day a freethinker,° had instructed Espinosa in the doctrines of Herbert Spencer,° but once, before he set off on a trip to Montevideo, his mother had asked him to say the Lord's Prayer every night and make the sign of the cross, and never in all the years that followed did he break that promise. He did not lack courage; one morning, with more indifference than wrath, he had traded two or three blows with some of his classmates that were trying to force him to join a strike at the university. He abounded in debatable habits and opinions, out of a spirit of acquiescence: his country mattered less to him than the danger that people in other countries might think the Argentines still wore feathers; he venerated France but had contempt for the French; he had little respect for Americans but took pride in the fact that there were skyscrapers in Buenos Aires; he thought that the gauchos° of the plains were better horsemen than the gauchos of the mountains. When his cousin Daniel invited him to spend the summer at Los Alamos, he immediately accepted—not because he liked the country but out of a natural desire to please, and because he could find no good reason for saying no.

The main house at the ranch was large and a bit run-down; the quarters for the foreman, a man named Gutre, stood nearby. There were three members of the Gutre family: the father, the son (who was singularly rough and unpolished), and a girl of uncertain paternity. They were tall, strong, and bony, with reddish hair and Indian features. They rarely spoke. The foreman's wife had died years before.

In the country, Espinosa came to learn things he hadn't known, had never even suspected; for example, that when you're approaching a house there's no reason to gallop and that nobody goes out on a horse unless there's a job to be done. As the summer wore on, he learned to distinguish birds by their call.

Within a few days, Daniel had to go to Buenos Aires to close a deal on some livestock. At the most, he said, the trip would take a week. Espinosa, who was already a little tired of his cousin's *bonnes fortunes* and his indefatigable interest in the vagaries of men's tailoring, stayed behind on the ranch with his textbooks. The heat was oppressive, and not even nightfall brought relief. Then one morning toward dawn, he was awakened by thunder. Wind lashed the casuarina trees. Espinosa heard the first drops of rain and gave thanks to God. Suddenly the wind blew cold. That afternoon, the Salado overflowed.

The next morning, as he stood on the porch looking out over the flooded plains, Baltasar Espinosa realized that the metaphor equating the pampas with the sea was not, at least that morning, an altogether false one, though Hudson° had noted that the sea seems the grander of the two because we view it not from horseback or our own height, but from the deck of a ship. The rain did not let up; the Gutres, helped (or hindered) by the city dweller, saved a good part of the livestock, though many animals were drowned. There were four roads leading to the ranch; all were under water. On the third day, when a leaking roof threatened the foreman's house, Espinosa gave the Gutres a room at the back of the main house, alongside the toolshed. The move brought Espinosa and the Gutres closer, and they began to eat together in the large dining room. Conversation was not easy; the Gutres, who knew so much about things in the country, did not know how to explain them. One night Espinosa asked them if people still remembered

5

---

freethinker: person who rejects traditional beliefs, especially religious dogma, in favor of rational inquiry. *Herbert Spencer:* a British philosopher (1820–1903) who championed the theory of evolution. *gaucho:* a South American cowboy. *W. H. Hudson:* an English naturalist and author (1841–1922) who wrote extensively about South America.

anything about the Indian raids, back when the military command for the frontier had been in Junín. They told him they did, but they would have given the same answer if he had asked them about the day Charles I° had been beheaded. Espinosa recalled that his father used to say that all the cases of longevity that occur in the country are the result of either poor memory or a vague notion of dates—gauchos quite often know neither the year they were born in nor the name of the man that fathered them.

In the entire house, the only reading material to be found were several copies of a farming magazine, a manual of veterinary medicine, a deluxe edition of the romantic verse drama *Tabaré*, a copy of *The History of the Shorthorn in Argentina*, several erotic and detective stories, and a recent novel that Espinosa had not read—*Don Segundo Sombra*, by Ricardo Güiraldes. In order to put some life into the inevitable after-dinner attempt at conversation, Espinosa read a couple of chapters of the novel to the Gutres, who did not know how to read or write. Unfortunately, the foreman had been a cattle drover himself, and he could not be interested in the adventures of another such a one. It was easy work, he said; they always carried along a pack mule with everything they might need. If he had not been a cattle drover, he announced, he'd never have seen Lake Gómez, or the Bragado River, or even the Núñez ranch, in Chacabuco. . . .

In the kitchen there was a guitar; before the incident I am narrating, the laborers would sit in a circle and someone would pick up the guitar and strum it, though never managing actually to play it. That was called "giving it a strum."

Espinosa, who was letting his beard grow out, would stop before the mirror to look at his changed face; he smiled to think that he'd soon be boring the fellows in Buenos Aires with his stories about the Salado overrunning its banks. Curiously, he missed places in the city he never went, and would never go: a street corner on Cabrera where a mailbox stood; two cement lions on a porch on Calle Jujuy a few blocks from the Plaza del Once; a tile-floored corner grocery-store-and-bar (whose location he couldn't quite remember). As for his father and his brothers, by now Daniel would have told them that he had been isolated—the word was etymologically precise—by the floodwaters.

Exploring the house still cut off by the high water, he came upon a Bible printed in English. On its last pages the Guthries (for that was their real name) had kept their family history. They had come originally from Inverness° and had arrived in the New World—doubtlessly as peasant laborers—in the early nineteenth century; they had intermarried with Indians. The chronicle came to an end in the eighteen-seventies; they no longer knew how to write. Within a few generations they had forgotten their English; by the time Espinosa met them, even Spanish gave them some difficulty. They had no faith, though in their veins, alongside the superstitions of the pampas, there still ran a dim current of the Calvinist's harsh fanaticism. Espinosa mentioned his find to them, but they hardly seemed to hear him.

He leafed through the book, and his fingers opened it to the first verses of the Gospel According to St. Mark. To try his hand at translating, and perhaps to see if they might understand a little of it, he decided that that would be the text he read the Gutres after dinner. He was surprised that they listened first attentively and then with mute fascination. The presence of gold letters on the binding may have given it increased authority. "It's in their blood," he thought. It also occurred to him that   10

Charles I: King of England, beheaded in 1649. *Inverness:* a county in Scotland.

throughout history, humankind has told two stories: the story of a lost ship sailing the Mediterranean seas in quest of a beloved isle, and the story of a god who allows himself to be crucified on Golgotha. He recalled his elocution classes in Ramos Mejía, and he rose to his feet to preach the parables.

In the following days, the Gutres would wolf down the spitted beef and canned sardines in order to arrive sooner at the Gospel.

The girl had a little lamb; it was her pet, and she prettied it with a sky blue ribbon. One day it cut itself on a piece of barbed wire; to stanch the blood, the Gutres were about to put spiderwebs on the wound, but Espinosa treated it with pills. The gratitude awakened by that cure amazed him. At first, he had not trusted the Gutres and had hidden away in one of his books the two hundred forty pesos he'd brought; now, with Daniel gone, he had taken the master's place and begun to give timid orders, which were immediately followed. The Gutres would trail him through the rooms and along the hallway, as though they were lost. As he read, he noticed that they would sweep away the crumbs he had left on the table. One afternoon, he surprised them as they were discussing him in brief, respectful words. When he came to the end of the Gospel According to St. Mark, he started to read another of the three remaining gospels, but the father asked him to reread the one he'd just finished, so they could understand it better. Espinosa felt they were like children, who prefer repetition to variety or novelty. One night he dreamed of the Flood (which is not surprising) and was awakened by the hammering of the building of the Ark, but he told himself it was thunder. And in fact the rain, which had let up for a while, had begun again; it was very cold. The Gutres told him the rain had broken through the roof of the toolshed; when they got the beams repaired, they said, they'd show him where. He was no longer a stranger, a foreigner, and they all treated him with respect; he was almost spoiled. None of them liked coffee, but there was always a little cup for him, with spoonfuls of sugar stirred in.

That second storm took place on a Tuesday. Thursday night there was a soft knock on his door; because of his doubts about the Gutres he always locked it. He got up and opened the door; it was the girl. In the darkness he couldn't see her, but he could tell by her footsteps that she was barefoot, and afterward, in the bed, that she was naked—that in fact she had come from the back of the house that way. She did not embrace him, or speak a word; she lay down beside him and she was shivering. It was the first time she had lain with a man. When she left, she did not kiss him; Espinosa realized that he didn't even know her name. Impelled by some sentiment he did not attempt to understand, he swore that when he returned to Buenos Aires, he'd tell no one of the incident.

The next day began like all the others, except that the father spoke to Espinosa to ask whether Christ had allowed himself to be killed in order to save all mankind. Espinosa, who was a freethinker like his father but felt obliged to defend what he had read them, paused.

"Yes," he finally replied. "To save all mankind from hell."   15

"What *is* hell?" Gutre then asked him.

"A place underground where souls will burn in fire forever."

"And those that drove the nails will also be saved?"

"Yes," replied Espinosa, whose theology was a bit shaky. (He had worried that the foreman wanted to have a word with him about what had happened last night with his daughter.)

After lunch they asked him to read the last chapters again.   20

Espinosa had a long siesta that afternoon, although it was a light sleep, interrupted by persistent hammering and vague premonitions. Toward evening he got up and went out into the hall.

"The water's going down," he said, as though thinking out loud. "It won't be long now."

"Not long now," repeated Gutre, like an echo.

The three of them had followed him. Kneeling on the floor, they asked his blessing. Then they cursed him, spat on him, and drove him to the back of the house. The girl was weeping. Espinosa realized what awaited him on the other side of the door. When they opened it, he saw the sky. A bird screamed; *it's a goldfinch,* Espinosa thought. There was no roof on the shed; they had torn down the roof beams to build the Cross.

Questions

1. What is about to happen to Baltasar Espinosa at the end of this story?
2. How old is Espinosa? What is ironic about his age?
3. What is the background of the Gutre family? How did they come to own an English Bible? Why is it ironic that they own this book?
4. The narrator claims that the protagonist, Espinosa, has only two noteworthy qualities: an almost unlimited kindness and a capacity for public speaking. How do these qualities become important in the story?
5. When Espinosa begins reading the Gospel of Saint Mark to the Gutres, what changes in their behavior does he notice?
6. What other action does Espinosa perform that earns the Gutres's gratitude?
7. Reread the last paragraph. Why is it ironic that the Gutres ask Espinosa's blessing and the daughter weeps?
8. Why do the Gutres kill Espinosa? What do they hope to gain?
9. Is the significance of Espinosa's death entirely ironic? Or does he resemble Christ in any important respect?

Octavio Paz

My Life with the Wave   1951

Translated by Eliot Weinberger

Octavio Paz (1914–1998) was born in Mexico City. His grandfather, a journalist and novelist, had fought alongside Benito Juarez in resistance to the French occupation of Mexico in the 1860s. His father, a lawyer, had fought for the revolution and had been the private secretary of peasant guerrilla leader Emiliano Zapata. Paz grew up in his grandfather's large but decaying house, and spent much of his time in its library of more than 6,000 volumes. He went to Spain in 1937, intending to fight on the Loyalist side in the Spanish Civil War, but found his leftist ideals severely tested by what he witnessed there, and he gradually adopted a centrist political

Octavio Paz

position that rejected both extremes of right-wing dictatorship and Marxist revolution; his intellectual honesty would later bring him many enemies when he became an early critic of the Castro regime in Cuba. Paz joined the Mexican foreign service in 1945; over the course of his diplomatic career, he held postings in San Francisco, New York, Tokyo, Geneva, and Delhi, but in 1968, after six years as Mexico's ambassador to India, he resigned in protest over his government's brutal suppression of student demonstrations. He then supported himself by teaching at Cambridge, Harvard, the University of Texas, and elsewhere.

Beginning in 1933 and continuing steadily thereafter, Paz published the many volumes of poetry that are the cornerstone of his achievement and the basis of his worldwide reputation. His work, which has been translated by such eminent poets as Elizabeth Bishop, Denise Levertov, John Frederick Nims, and Charles Tomlinson, has its fullest representation in English in The Collected Poems of Octavio Paz 1957–1987. While immersed in his own culture and national ethos, as demonstrated in The Labyrinth of Solitude (1950), Paz was a profound internationalist as well: The Bow and the Lyre (1956), a study of the poetic process, and Convergences: Essays on Art and Literature (1987) range impressively from ancient to modern times, from the old world to the new. In 1990, Paz was awarded the Nobel Prize in Literature, becoming the only Mexican-born writer to have attained that honor.

When I left that sea, a wave moved ahead of the others. She was tall and light. In spite of the shouts of the others who grabbed her by her floating clothes, she clutched my arm and went off with me leaping. I didn't want to say anything to her, because it hurt me to shame her in front of her friends. Besides, the furious stares of the elders paralyzed me. When we got to town, I explained to her that it was impossible, that life in the city was not what she had been able to imagine with the ingenuity of a wave that had never left the sea. She watched me gravely. "No, your decision is made. You can't go back." I tried sweetness, hardness, irony. She cried, screamed, hugged, threatened. I had to apologize.

The next day my troubles began. How could we get on the train without being seen by the conductor, the passengers, the police? Certainly the rules say nothing in respect to the transport of waves on the railroad, but this same reserve was an indication of the severity with which our act would be judged. After much thought I arrived at the station an hour before departure, took my seat, and, when no one was looking, emptied the water tank for the passengers; then, carefully, poured in my friend.

The first incident came about when the children of a nearby couple declared their noisy thirst. I stopped them and promised them refreshments and lemonade. They were at the point of accepting when another thirsty passenger approached. I was about to invite her also, but the stare of her companion stopped me. The lady took a paper cup, approached the tank, and turned the faucet. Her cup was barely half full when I leaped between the woman and my friend. She looked at me astonished. While I apologized, one of the children turned the faucet again. I closed it violently. The lady brought the cup to her lips:

"Agh, this water is salty."

The boy echoed her. Various passengers rose. The husband called the conductor: 5

"This man put salt in the water."

The conductor called the Inspector:

"So you put substances in the water?"

The Inspector in turn called the police:

"So you poisoned the water?"   10

The police in turn called the Captain:

"So you're the poisoner?"

The captain called three agents. The agents took me to an empty car amid the stares and whispers of the passengers. At the next station they took me off and pushed and dragged me to the jail. For days no one spoke to me, except during the long interrogations. When I explained my story no one believed me, not even the jailer, who shook his head, saying: "The case is grave, truly grave. You didn't want to poison the children?" One day they brought me before the Magistrate.

"Your case is difficult," he repeated. "I will assign you to the Penal Judge."

A year passed. Finally they judged me. As there were no victims, my sentence   15
was light. After a short time, my day of liberty arrived.

The Chief of the Prison called me in:

"Well, now you're free. You were lucky. Lucky there were no victims. But don't do it again, because the next time won't be so short . . ."

And he stared at me with the same grave stare with which everyone watched me.

The same afternoon I took the train and after hours of uncomfortable traveling arrived in Mexico City. I took a cab home. At the door of my apartment I heard laughter and singing. I felt a pain in my chest, like the smack of a wave of surprise when surprise smacks us across the chest: my friend was there, singing and laughing as always.

"How did you get back?"   20

"Simple: in the train. Someone, after making sure that I was only salt water, poured me in the engine. It was a rough trip: soon I was a white plume of vapor, soon I fell in a fine rain on the machine. I thinned out a lot. I lost many drops."

Her presence changed my life. The house of dark corridors and dusty furniture was filled with air, with sun, with sounds and green and blue reflections, a numerous and happy populace of reverberations and echoes. How many waves is one wave, and how it can make a beach or a rock or jetty out of a wall, a chest, a forehead that it crowns with foam! Even the abandoned corners, the abject corners of dust and debris were touched by her light hands. Everything began to laugh and everywhere shined with teeth. The sun entered the old rooms with pleasure and stayed in my house for hours, abandoning the other houses, the district, the city, the country. And some nights, very late, the scandalized stars watched it sneak from my house.

Love was a game, a perpetual creation. All was beach, sand, a bed of sheets that were always fresh. If I embraced her, she swelled with pride, incredibly tall, like the liquid stalk of a poplar; and soon that thinness flowered into a fountain of white feathers, into a plume of smiles that fell over my head and back and covered me with whiteness. Or she stretched out in front of me, infinite as the horizon, until I too became horizon and silence. Full and sinuous, it enveloped me like music or some giant lips. Her present was a going and coming of caresses, of murmurs, of kisses. Entered in her waters, I was drenched to the socks and in a wink of an eye I found myself up above, at the height of vertigo, mysteriously suspended, to fall like a stone and feel myself gently deposited on the dryness, like a feather. Nothing is comparable to sleeping in those waters, to wake pounded by a thousand happy light lashes, by a thousand assaults that withdraw laughing.

But never did I reach the center of her being. Never did I touch the nakedness of pain and of death. Perhaps it does not exist in waves, that secret site that renders a woman vulnerable and mortal, that electric button where all interlocks, twitches, and straightens out to then swoon. Her sensibility, like that of women, spread in ripples, only they weren't concentric ripples, but rather eccentric, spreading each time farther, until they touched other galaxies. To love her was to extend to remote contacts, to vibrate with far-off stars we never suspected. But her center . . . no, she had no center, just an emptiness as in a whirlwind, that sucked me in and smothered me.

Stretched out side by side, we exchanged confidences, whispers, smiles. Curled up, she fell on my chest and there unfolded like a vegetation of murmurs. She sang in my ear, a little snail. She became humble and transparent, clutching my feet like a small animal, calm water. She was so clear I could read all of her thoughts. Certain nights her skin was covered with phosphorescence and to embrace her was to embrace a piece of night tattooed with fire. But she also became black and bitter. At unexpected hours she roared, moaned, twisted. Her groans woke the neighbors. Upon hearing her, the sea wind would scratch at the door of the house or rave in a loud voice on the roof. Cloudy days irritated her; she broke furniture, said bad words, covered me with insults and green and gray foam. She spat, cried, swore, prophesied. Subject to the moon, to the stars, to the influence of the light of other worlds, she changed her moods and appearance in a way that I thought fantastic, but it was as fatal as the tide.

She began to miss solitude. The house was full of snails and conches, of small sailboats that in her fury she had shipwrecked (together with the others, laden with images, that each night left my forehead and sank in her ferocious or pleasant whirlwinds). How many little treasures were lost in that time! But my boats and the silent song of the snails was not enough. I had to install in the house a colony of fish. I confess that it was not without jealousy that I watched them swimming in my friend, caressing her breasts, sleeping between her legs, adorning her hair with light flashes of color.

Among all those fish there were a few particularly repulsive and ferocious ones, little tigers from the aquarium, the large fixed eyes and jagged and bloodthirsty mouths. I don't know by what aberration my friend delighted in playing with them, shamelessly showing them a preference whose significance I preferred to ignore. She passed long hours confined with those horrible creatures. One day I couldn't stand it any more; I threw open the door and launched after them. Agile and ghostly they escaped my hands while she laughed and pounded me until I fell. I thought I was drowning. And when I was at the point of death, and purple, she deposited me on the bank and began to kiss me, saying I don't know what things. I felt very weak, fatigued, and humiliated. And at the same time her voluptuousness made me close my eyes, because her voice was sweet and she spoke to me of the delicious death of the drowned. When I recovered, I began to fear and hate her.

I had neglected my affairs. Now I began to visit friends and renew old and dear relations. I met an old girlfriend. Making her swear to keep my secret, I told her of my life with the wave. Nothing moves women so much as the possibility of saving a man. My redeemer employed all of her arts, but what could a woman, master of a limited number of souls and bodies, do in front of my friend who was always changing—and always identical to herself in her incessant metamorphoses.

Winter came. The sky turned gray. Fog fell on the city. Frozen drizzle rained. My friend cried every night. During the day she isolated herself, quiet and sinister, stuttering a single syllable, like an old woman who grumbles in a corner. She became cold; to sleep with her was to shiver all night and to feel freeze, little by little, the blood, the bones, the thoughts. She turned deep, impenetrable, restless. I left frequently and my absences were each time more prolonged. She, in her corner, howled loudly. With teeth like steel and a corrosive tongue she gnawed the walls, crumbled them. She passed the nights in mourning, reproaching me. She had nightmares, deliriums of the sun, of warm beaches. She dreamt of the pole and of changing into a great block of ice, sailing beneath black skies in nights long as months. She insulted me. She cursed and laughed, filled the house with guffaws and phantoms. She called up the monsters of the depths, blind ones, quick ones, blunt. Charged with electricity, she carbonized all she touched; full of acid, she dissolved whatever she brushed against. Her sweet embraces became knotty cords that strangled me. And her body, greenish and elastic, was an implacable whip that lashed, lashed, lashed. I fled. The horrible fish laughed with ferocious smiles.

There in the mountains, among the tall pines and precipices, I breathed the cold 30 thin air like a thought of liberty. At the end of a month I returned. I had decided. It had been so cold that over the marble of the chimney, next to the extinct fire, I found a statue of ice. I was unmoved by her weary beauty. I put her in a big canvas sack and went out to the streets with the sleeper on my shoulders. In a restaurant in the outskirts I sold her to a waiter friend who immediately began to chop her into little pieces, which he carefully deposited in the buckets where bottles are chilled.

Questions

1. "My Life with the Wave" is a fantastic story, but the plot still in some ways resembles a conventional human love affair. In what ways is it like a love story between two people?
2. Does Paz ever explicitly state why the wave left the sea? What details does he give to reveal her motivation?
3. How is the wave different from an ordinary woman? How is she similar?
4. Why does the narrator begin to love the wave?
5. When does the narrator cease loving her? Why do his feelings change so radically from earlier?
6. Is the narrator justified in dispatching the frozen wave? Do his actions represent a symbolic murder or simply the final break-up between two lovers?
7. If the wave is a symbol, what symbolic associations does she suggest?

Gabriel García Márquez

A Very Old Man with Enormous Wings   1968

Translated by Gregory Rabassa

Gabriel García Márquez, among the most eminent of living Latin American writers, was born in 1928 in Aracataca, a Caribbean port in Colombia, one of sixteen children of an impoverished telegraph operator. For a time he studied law in Bogotá, then became a newspaper reporter. Although he never joined the Communist Party, García Márquez outspokenly advocated many left-wing proposals for reform. In 1954, despairing of any prospect for political change, he left Colombia to live in Mexico City. Though at nineteen he had already completed a book of short stories, La hojorasca (Leaf Storm), *he waited until 1955 to publish it. Soon he began to build a towering reputation among readers of Spanish. His celebrated novel* Cien años de soledad (1967), *published in English as* One Hundred Years of Solitude (1969), *traces the history of a Colombian family through six generations. Called by Chilean poet Pablo Neruda "the greatest revelation in the Spanish language since* Don Quixote," *the book has sold more than thirty million copies in thirty-five languages. In 1982 García Márquez was awarded the Nobel Prize in Literature. His fiction, rich in myth and invention, has reminded American readers of the work of William Faulkner, another explorer of his native ground; indeed, García Márquez has called Faulkner "my master." His later novels include* Love in the Time of Cholera *(1988),* The General in His Labyrinth *(1990),* Of Love and Other Demons *(1995), and* Memories of My Melancholy Whores *(2005). His* Collected Stories *was published in 1994.* Living to Tell the Tale *(2003), the first volume of an autobiographical trilogy, traces the author's life up to the beginning of his journalistic career, and offers many insights into the sources and techniques of his works of fiction. García Márquez still lives in Mexico City.*

A Tale for Children

On the third day of rain they had killed so many crabs inside the house that Pelayo had to cross his drenched courtyard and throw them into the sea, because the newborn child had a temperature all night and they thought it was due to the stench. The world had been sad since Tuesday. Sea and sky were a single ash-gray thing and the sands of the beach, which on March nights glimmered like powdered light, had become a stew of mud and rotten shellfish. The light was so weak at noon that when Pelayo was coming back to the house after throwing away the crabs, it was hard for him to see what it was that was moving and groaning in the rear of the courtyard. He had to go very close to see that it was an old man, a very old man, lying face down in the mud, who, in spite of his tremendous efforts, couldn't get up, impeded by his enormous wings.

Frightened by that nightmare, Pelayo ran to get Elisenda, his wife, who was putting compresses on the sick child, and he took her to the rear of the courtyard. They both looked at the fallen body with mute stupor. He was dressed like a ragpicker. There were only a few faded hairs left on his bald skull and very few teeth in his mouth, and his pitiful condition of a drenched great-grandfather had taken away any sense of grandeur he might have had. His huge buzzard wings, dirty and half-plucked, were forever entangled in the mud. They looked at him so long and so closely that Pelayo and Elisenda very soon overcame their surprise and in the end found him familiar. Then they dared speak to him, and he answered in an incomprehensible dialect with a strong sailor's voice. That was how they skipped over the inconvenience of the wings and quite intelligently concluded that he was a lonely castaway from some foreign ship wrecked by the storm. And yet, they called in a neighbor woman who knew everything about life and death to see him, and all she needed was one look to show them their mistake.

"He's an angel," she told them. "He must have been coming for the child, but the poor fellow is so old that the rain knocked him down."

On the following day everyone knew that a flesh-and-blood angel was held captive in Pelayo's house. Against the judgment of the wise neighbor woman, for whom angels in those times were the fugitive survivors of a celestial conspiracy, they did not have the heart to club him to death. Pelayo watched over him all afternoon from the kitchen, armed with his bailiff's club, and before going to bed he dragged him out of the mud and locked him up with the hens in the wire chicken coop. In the middle of the night, when the rain stopped, Pelayo and Elisenda were still killing crabs. A short time afterward the child woke up without a fever and with a desire to eat. Then they felt magnanimous and decided to put the angel on a raft with fresh water and provisions for three days and leave him to his fate on the high seas. But when they went out into the courtyard with the first light of dawn, they found the whole neighborhood in front of the chicken coop having fun with the angel, without the slightest reverence, tossing him things to eat through the openings in the wire as if he weren't a super-natural creature but a circus animal.

Father Gonzaga arrived before seven o'clock, alarmed at the strange news. By that time onlookers less frivolous than those at dawn had already arrived and they were making all kinds of conjectures concerning the captive's future. The simplest among them thought that he should be named mayor of the world. Others of sterner mind felt that he should be promoted to the rank of five-star general in order to win all wars. Some visionaries hoped that he could be put to stud in order to implant on earth a race of winged wise men who could take charge of the universe. But Father Gonzaga, before becoming a priest, had been a robust woodcutter. Standing by the wire, he reviewed his catechism in an instant and asked them to open the door so that he could take a close look at that pitiful man who looked more like a huge decrepit hen among the fascinated chickens. He was lying in a corner drying his open wings in the sunlight among the fruit peels and breakfast leftovers that the early risers had thrown him. Alien to the impertinences of the world, he only lifted his antiquarian eyes and murmured something in his dialect when Father Gonzaga went into the chicken coop and said good morning to him in Latin. The parish priest had his first suspicion of an impostor when he saw that he did not understand the language of God or know how to greet His ministers. Then he noticed that seen close up he was much too human: he had an unbearable smell of the outdoors, the back side of his wings was strewn with parasites and his main feathers had been mistreated by terrestrial winds, and nothing about him measured up to the proud dignity of angels. Then he came out of the chicken coop and in a brief sermon warned the curious against the risks of being ingenuous. He reminded them that the devil had the bad habit of making use of carni-val tricks in order to confuse the unwary. He argued that if wings were not the essen-tial element in determining the difference between a hawk and an airplane, they were even less so in the recognition of angels. Nevertheless, he promised to write a letter to his bishop so that the latter would write to his primate so that the latter would write to the Supreme Pontiff in order to get the final verdict from the highest courts.

His prudence fell on sterile hearts. The news of the captive angel spread with such rapidity that after a few hours the courtyard had the bustle of a marketplace and they had to call in troops with fixed bayonets to disperse the mob that was about to knock the house down. Elisenda, her spine all twisted from sweeping up so much marketplace trash, then got the idea of fencing in the yard and charging five cents admission to see the angel.

The curious came from far away. A traveling carnival arrived with a flying acro-bat who buzzed over the crowd several times, but no one paid any attention to him because his wings were not those of an angel but, rather, those of a sidereal bat. The most unfortunate invalids on earth came in search of health: a poor woman who since childhood had been counting her heartbeats and had run out of numbers; a Portuguese man who couldn't sleep because the noise of the stars disturbed him; a sleepwalker who got up at night to undo the things he had done while awake; and many others with less serious ailments. In the midst of that shipwreck disorder that made the earth tremble, Pelayo and Elisenda were happy with fatigue, for in less than a week they had crammed their rooms with money and the line of pilgrims waiting their turn to enter still reached beyond the horizon.

The angel was the only one who took no part in his own act. He spent his time trying to get comfortable in his borrowed nest, befuddled by the hellish heat of the oil lamps and sacramental candles that had been placed along the wire. At first they tried to make him eat some mothballs, which, according to the wisdom of the wise neighbor woman, were the food prescribed for angels. But he turned them down, just as he turned down the papal lunches that the penitents brought him, and they never found out whether it was because he was an angel or because he was an old man that in the end ate nothing but eggplant mush. His only supernatural virtue seemed to be patience. Especially during the first days, when the hens pecked at him, searching for the stellar parasites that proliferated in his wings, and the cripples pulled out feathers to touch their defective parts with, and even the most merciful threw stones at him, trying to get him to rise so they could see him standing. The only time they succeeded in arousing him was when they burned his side with an iron for branding steers, for he had been motionless for so many hours that they thought he was dead. He awoke with a start, ranting in his hermetic language and with tears in his eyes, and he flapped his wings a couple of times, which brought on a whirlwind of chicken dung and lunar dust and a gale of panic that did not seem to be of this world. Although many thought that his reaction had been one not of rage but of pain, from then on they were careful not to annoy him, because the majority understood that his passivity was not that of a hero taking his ease but that of a cataclysm in repose.

Father Gonzaga held back the crowd's frivolity with formulas of maidservant inspiration while awaiting the arrival of a final judgment on the nature of the captive. But the mail from Rome showed no sense of urgency. They spent their time finding out if the prisoner had a navel, if his dialect had any connection with Aramaic, how many times he could fit on the head of a pin,° or whether he wasn't just a Norwegian with wings. Those meager letters might have come and gone until the end of time if a providential event had not put an end to the priest's tribulations.

It so happened that during those days, among so many other carnival attractions,   10 there arrived in town the traveling show of the woman who had been changed into a spider for having disobeyed her parents. The admission to see her was not only less than the admission to see the angel, but people were permitted to ask her all manner of questions about her absurd state and to examine her up and down so that no one would ever doubt the truth of her horror. She was a frightful tarantula the size of a ram and with the head of a sad maiden. What was most heart-rending, however, was not her outlandish shape but the sincere affliction with which she recounted the details of her misfortune. While still practically a child she had sneaked out of her parents' house to go to a dance, and while she was coming back through the woods after having danced all night without permission, a fearful thunderclap rent the sky in two and through the crack came the lightning bolt of brimstone that changed her into a spider. Her only nourishment came from the meatballs that charitable souls chose to toss into her mouth. A spectacle like that, full of so much human truth and with such a fearful lesson, was bound to defeat without even trying that of a haughty angel who scarcely deigned to look at mortals. Besides, the few miracles attributed to the angel showed a certain mental disorder, like the blind man who didn't recover his sight but grew three new teeth, or the paralytic who didn't get to walk but almost won the lottery, and the leper whose sores sprouted sunflowers. Those consolation miracles, which were more like mocking fun, had already ruined the angel's reputation when the woman who had

---

fit on the head of a pin: this allusion refers to the famous medieval arguments about how many angels (who had no physical bodies) could dance on the head of a pin.

been changed into a spider finally crushed him completely. That was how Father Gonzaga was cured forever of his insomnia and Pelayo's courtyard went back to being as empty as during the time it had rained for three days and crabs walked through the bedrooms.

The owners of the house had no reason to lament. With the money they saved they built a two-story mansion with balconies and gardens and high netting so that crabs wouldn't get in during the winter, and with iron bars on the windows so that angels wouldn't get in. Pelayo also set up a rabbit warren close to town and gave up his job as bailiff for good, and Elisenda bought some satin pumps with high heels and many dresses of iridescent silk, the kind worn on Sunday by the most desirable women in those times. The chicken coop was the only thing that didn't receive any attention. If they washed it down with creolin° and burned tears of myrrh inside it every so often, it was not in homage to the angel but to drive away the dungheap stench that still hung everywhere like a ghost and was turning the new house into an old one. At first, when the child learned to walk, they were careful that he not get too close to the chicken coop. But then they began to lose their fears and got used to the smell, and before the child got his second teeth he'd gone inside the chicken coop to play, where the wires were falling apart. The angel was no less standoffish with him than with other mortals, but he tolerated the most ingenious infamies with the patience of a dog who had no illusions. They both came down with chicken pox at the same time. The doctor who took care of the child couldn't resist the temptation to listen to the angel's heart, and he found so much whistling in the heart and so many sounds in his kidneys that it seemed impossible for him to be alive. What surprised him most, however, was the logic of his wings. They seemed so natural on that completely human organism that he couldn't understand why other men didn't have them too.

When the child began school it had been some time since the sun and rain had caused the collapse of the chicken coop. The angel went dragging himself about here and there like a stray dying man. They would drive him out of the bedroom with a broom and a moment later find him in the kitchen. He seemed to be in so many places at the same time that they grew to think that he'd been duplicated, that he was reproducing himself all through the house, and the exasperated and unhinged Elisenda shouted that it was awful living in that hell full of angels. He could scarcely eat and his antiquarian eyes had also become so foggy that he went about bumping into posts. All he had left were the bare cannulae° of his last feathers. Pelayo threw a blanket over him and extended him the charity of letting him sleep in the shed, and only then did they notice that he had a temperature at night, and was delirious with the tongue twisters of an old Norwegian. That was one of the few times they became alarmed, for they thought he was going to die and not even the wise neighbor woman had been able to tell them what to do with dead angels.

And yet he not only survived his worst winter, but seemed improved with the first sunny days. He remained motionless for several days in the farthest corner of the courtyard, where no one would see him, and at the beginning of December some large, stiff feathers began to grow on his wings, the feathers of a scarecrow, which looked more like another misfortune of decrepitude. But he must have

---

creolin: a type of cleaning product.   *cannulae:* the Latin word for tubes; it refers to the tubelike quills that attach feathers to a body.

known the reason for those changes, for he was quite careful that no one should notice them, that no one should hear the sea chanteys that he sometimes sang under the stars. One morning Elisenda was cutting some bunches of onions for lunch when a wind that seemed to come from the high seas blew into the kitchen. Then she went to the window and caught the angel in his first attempts at flight. They were so clumsy that his fingernails opened a furrow in the vegetable patch and he was on the point of knocking the shed down with the ungainly flapping that slipped on the light and couldn't get a grip on the air. But he did manage to gain altitude. Elisenda let out a sigh of relief, for herself and for him, when she saw him pass over the last houses, holding himself up in some way with the risky flapping of a senile vulture. She kept watching him even when she was through cutting the onions and she kept on watching until it was no longer possible for her to see him, because then he was no longer an annoyance in her life but an imaginary dot on the horizon of the sea.

Questions

1. How would you describe the *tone* of this story? What does that tone contribute to your understanding of the story's larger intentions?

2. The earliest and most pervasive assumption made about the old man is that he is an angel. Other than his wings, is there anything angelic about him?

3. How would you characterize Father Gonzaga? Use textual references to back up your conclusions.

4. Consider the specific ailments that are assigned to the "most unfortunate invalids on earth" (paragraph 7). What seems to you to be the point of the author's mockery here?

5. What changes has the old man's presence brought to the lives of Pelayo and his family?

6. Given those changes, why is Elisenda glad to see the old man go away at the end of the story?

Inés Arredondo

The Shunammite   1965

Translated by Alberto Manguel

Inés Arredondo (1928–1989) was born in Culiacán, the capital and largest city of the state of Sinaloa, Mexico, the daughter of a doctor. In 1947 she enrolled in the National Autonomous University of Mexico, but in the following year experienced a spiritual and emotional crisis that brought her close to suicide. In 1953 she married the writer Tomas Segovia; the union, which produced three children, was troubled, leading to separation in 1962 and divorce three years later. In 1972 she married Carlos Ruiz Sanchez, a physician. Throughout her adult life, financial necessity caused Arredondo to work at a variety of jobs—librarian, editor, translator, and professor (including guest lectureships at Indiana University and Purdue University in 1966).

Inés Arredondo

Because of spinal problems she was forced to undergo five operations and was ultimately confined to a wheelchair. Beginning in 1965, she published several small volumes of short fiction (the collected edition of her work runs to fewer than four hundred pages), which brought her several awards and established her reputation as a major writer. "The Shunammite" was filmed, with a screenplay by Arredondo, as a segment in a 1965 Mexican movie called Amor Amor Amor, and was the basis for a 1991 opera by Marcela Rodríguez. Underground River and Other Stories (1996) presents twelve of her stories in an English translation.

So they sought for a fair damsel throughout all the coasts of Israel,
and found Abishag, a Shunammite,° and brought her to the king.
*   And the damsel was very fair, and cherished the king,*
and ministered to him; but the king knew her not.

—1 KINGS 1:3–4

The summer had been a fiery furnace. The last summer of my youth.

Tense, concentrated in the arrogance that precedes combustion, the city shone in a dry and dazzling light. I stood in the very midst of the light, dressed in mourning, proud, feeding the flames with my blonde hair, alone. Men's sly glances slid over my body without soiling it, and my haughty modesty forced them to barely nod at me, full of respect. I was certain of having the power to dominate passions, to purify anything in the scorching air that surrounded but did not singe me.

Nothing changed when I received the telegram; the sadness it brought me did not affect in the least my feelings towards the world. My uncle Apolonio was dying at the age of seventy-odd years and wanted to see me. I had lived as a daughter in his house for many years and I sincerely felt pain at the thought of his inevitable death. All this was perfectly normal, and not a single omen, not a single shiver made me suspect anything. Quickly I made arrangements for the journey, in the very same untouchable midst of the motionless summer.

I arrived at the village during the hour of siesta.

Walking down the empty streets with my small suitcase, I fell to daydreaming,   5 in that dusky zone between reality and time, born of the excessive heat. I was not remembering; I was almost reliving things as they had been. "Look, Licha, the amapas° are blooming again." The clear voice, almost childish. "I want you to get yourself a dress like that of Margarita Ibarra to wear on the sixteenth." I could hear her, feel her walking by my side, her shoulders bent a little forwards, light in spite of her plumpness, happy and old. I carried on walking in the company of my aunt Panchita, my mother's sister. "Well, my dear, if you *really* don't like Pepe . . . but he's such a *nice* boy." Yes, she had used those exact words, here, in front of

Abishag, the Shunammite: Among the tasks Abishag was called upon to perform for the aged and dying King David was to lie in bed with him and warm him with her body; as the last clause of the epigraph indicates, there was no sexual contact between them.   *amapa:* a small tree that is covered, when in bloom, by masses of yellow, pink, or purple tubular flowers.

Tichi Valenzuela's window, with her gay smile, innocent and impish. I walked a little further, where the paving stones seemed to fade away in the haze, and when the bells rang, heavy and real, ending the siesta and announcing the Rosary, I opened my eyes and gave the village a good, long look: it was not the same. The *amapas* had not bloomed and I was crying, in my mourning dress, at the door of my uncle's house.

The front gate was open, as always, and at the end of the courtyard rose the bougainvillea. As always: but not the same. I dried my tears, and felt that I was not arriving: I was leaving. Everything looked motionless, pinioned in my memory, and the heat and the silence seemed to wither it all. My footsteps echoed with a new sound, and María came out to greet me.

"Why didn't you let us know? We'd have sent . . ."

We went straight into the sick man's room. As I entered, I felt cold. Silence and gloom preceded death.

"Luisa, is that you?"

The dear voice was dying out and would soon be silent forever.   10

"I'm here, uncle."

"God be praised! I won't die alone."

"Don't say that; you'll soon be much better."

He smiled sadly; he knew I was lying but he did not want to make me cry.

"Yes, my daughter. Yes. Now have a rest, make yourself at home and then come   15
and keep me company. I'll try to sleep a little."

Shriveled, wizened, toothless, lost in the immense bed and floating senselessly in whatever was left of his life, he was painful to be with, like something superfluous, out of place, like so many others at the point of death. Stepping out of the overheated passageway, one would take a deep breath, instinctively, hungry for light and air.

I began to nurse him and I felt happy doing it. This house was *my* house, and in the morning, while tidying up, I would sing long-forgotten songs. The peace that surrounded me came perhaps from the fact that my uncle no longer awaited death as something imminent and terrible, but instead let himself be carried by the passing days towards a more or less distant or nearby future, with the unconscious tenderness of a child. He would go over his past life with great pleasure and enjoy imagining that he was bequeathing me his images, as grandparents do with their children.

"Bring me that small chest, there, in the large wardrobe. Yes, that one. The key is underneath the mat, next to Saint Anthony. Bring the key as well."

And his sunken eyes would shine once again at the sight of all his treasures.

"Look: this necklace—I gave it to your aunt for our tenth wedding anniversary. I   20
bought it in Mazatlán from a Polish jeweler who told me God-knows-what story about an Austrian princess, and asked an impossible price for it. I brought it back hidden in my pistol-holder and didn't sleep a wink in the stagecoach—I was so afraid someone would steal it!"

The light of dusk made the young, living stones glitter in his calloused hands.

"This ring, so old, belonged to my mother; look carefully at the miniature in the other room and you'll see her wearing it. Cousin Begoña would mutter behind her back that a sweetheart of hers . . . "

The ladies in the portraits would move their lips and speak, once again, would breathe again—all these ladies he had seen, he had touched. I would picture them in my mind and understand the meaning of these jewels.

"Have I told you about the time we traveled to Europe, in 1908, before the Revolution?° You had to take a ship to Colima. And in Venice your aunt Panchita fell in love with a certain pair of earrings. They were much too expensive, and I told her so. 'They are fit for a queen.' Next day I bought them for her. You just can't imagine what it was like because all this took place long, long before you were born, in 1908, in Venice, when your aunt was so young, so . . . "

"Uncle, you're getting tired, you should rest." 25

"You're right, I'm tired. Leave me a while and take the small chest to your room. It's yours."

"But, uncle . . . "

"It's all yours, that's all! I trust I can give away whatever I want!"

His voice broke into a sob: the illusion was vanishing and he found himself again on the point of dying, of saying goodbye to the things he had loved. He turned to the wall and I left with the box in my hands, not knowing what to do.

On other occasions he would tell me about "the year of the famine," or "the year 30 of the yellow corn," or "the year of the plague," and very old tales of murderers and ghosts. Once he even tried to sing a *corrido*° from his youth, but it shattered in his jagged voice. He was leaving me his life, and he was happy.

The doctor said that yes, he could see some recovery, but that we were not to raise our hopes, there was no cure, it was merely a matter of a few days more or less.

One afternoon of menacing dark clouds, when I was bringing in the clothes hanging out to dry in the courtyard, I heard María cry out. I stood still, listening to her cry as if it were a peal of thunder, the first of the storm to come. Then silence, and I was left alone in the courtyard, motionless. A bee buzzed by and the rain did not fall. No one knows as well as I do how awful a foreboding can be, a premonition hanging above a head turned towards the sky.

"Lichita, he's dying! He's gasping for air!"

"Go get the doctor . . . No! I'll go. But call doña Clara to stay with you till I'm back."

"And the priest, fetch the priest." 35

I ran, I ran away from that unbearable moment, blunt and asphyxiating. I ran, hurried back, entered the house, made coffee; I greeted the relatives who began to arrive dressed in half-mourning; I ordered candles; I asked for a few holy relics; I kept on feverishly trying to fulfill my only obligation at the time, to be with my uncle. I asked the doctor: he had given him an injection, so as not to leave anything untried, but he knew it was useless. I saw the priest arrive with the Eucharist, even then I lacked the courage to enter. I knew I would regret it afterwards. "Thank God, now I won't die alone"—but I couldn't. I covered my face with my hands and prayed.

The priest came and touched my shoulder. I thought that all was over and I shivered.

"He's calling you. Come in."

I don't know how I reached the door. Night had fallen and the room, lit by a bedside lamp, seemed enormous. The furniture, larger than life, looked black, and a

the Revolution: the Mexican Revolution, which toppled the dictator Porfirio Díaz and led to a decade of political unrest and civil war, began in 1910. *corrido*: a kind of narrative ballad; *corridos* were originally about romantic love, but at the time of the Revolution they were frequently political in nature.

strange clogging atmosphere hung about the bed. Trembling, I felt I was inhaling death.

"Stand next to him," said the priest.   40

I obeyed, moving towards the foot of the bed, unable to look even at the sheets.

"Your uncle's wish, unless you say otherwise, is to marry you *in articulo mortis*,° so that you may inherit his possessions. Do you accept?"

I stifled a cry of horror. I opened my eyes wide enough to let in the whole terrible room. "Why does he want to drag me into his grave?" I felt death touching my skin. "Luisa . . . "

It was uncle Apolonio. Now I had to look at him. He could barely mouth the words,   45
his jaw seemed slack and he spoke moving his face like that of a ventriloquist's doll.

"Please."

And he fell silent with exhaustion.

I could take no more. I left the room. That was not my uncle, it did not even look like him. Leave everything to me, yes, but not only his possessions, his stories, his life. I didn't want it, his life, his death. I didn't want it. When I opened my eyes I was standing once again in the courtyard and the sky was still overcast. I breathed in deeply, painfully.

"Already?" the relatives drew near to ask, seeing me so distraught.

I shook my head. Behind me, the priest explained.   50

"Don Apolonio wants to marry her with his last breath, so that she may inherit him."

"And you won't?" the old servant asked anxiously. "Don't be silly, no one deserves it more than you. You were a daughter to them, and you have worked very hard looking after him. If you don't marry him, the cousins in Mexico City will leave you without a cent. Don't be silly!"

"It's a fine gesture on his part."

"And afterwards you'll be left a rich widow, as untouched as you are now." A young cousin laughed nervously.

"It's a considerable fortune, and I, as your uncle several times removed, would   55
advise you to . . . "

"If you think about it, not accepting shows a lack of both charity and humility."

"That's true, that's absolutely true."

I did not want to give an old man his last pleasure, a pleasure I should, after all, be thankful for, because my youthful body, of which I felt so proud, had not dwelt in any of the regions of death. I was overcome by nausea. That was my last clear thought that night. I woke from a kind of hypnotic slumber as they forced me to hold his hand covered in cold sweat. I felt nauseous again, but said "yes."

I remember vaguely that they hovered over me all the time, talking all at once, taking me over there, bringing me over here, making me sign, making me answer. The taste of that night—a taste that has stayed with me for the rest of my life—was that of an evil ring-around-the-rosies turning vertiginously around me, while everyone laughed and sang grotesquely

This is the way the widow is wed,
The widow is wed, the widow is wed

in articulo mortis: "at the point of death." Such marriages were allowed to take place without the usual formalities and were considered binding even if, as here, the dying party subsequently recovered.

while I stood, a slave, in the middle. Something inside me hurt, and I could not lift my eyes.

When I came to my senses, all was over, and on my hand shone the braided ring 60 which I had seen so many times on my aunt Panchita's finger: there had been no time for anything else.

The guests began to leave.

"If you need me, don't hesitate to call. In the meantime give him these drops every six hours."

"May God bless you and give you strength."

"Happy honeymoon," whispered the young cousin in my ear, with a nasty laugh.

I returned to the sickbed. "Nothing has changed, nothing has changed." My fear 65 certainly had not changed. I convinced María to stay and help me look after uncle Apolonio. I only calmed down once I saw dawn was breaking. It had started to rain, but without thunder or lightning, very still.

It kept on drizzling that day and the next, and the day after. Four days of anguish. Nobody came to visit, nobody other than the doctor and the priest. On days like these no one goes out, everyone stays indoors and waits for life to start again. These are the days of the spirit, sacred days.

If at least the sick man had needed plenty of attention my hours would have seemed shorter, but there was little that could be done for him.

On the fourth night María went to bed in a room close by, and I stayed alone with the dying man. I was listening to the monotonous rain and praying unconsciously, half asleep and unafraid, waiting. My fingers stopped turning the rosary, and as I held the beads I could feel through my fingertips a peculiar warmth, a warmth both alien and intimate, the warmth we leave in things and which is returned to us transformed, a comrade, a brother foreshadowing the warmth of others, a warmth both unknown and recollected, never quite grasped and yet inhabiting the core of my bones. Softly, deliciously, my nerves relaxed, my fingers felt light, I fell asleep.

I must have slept many hours: it was dawn when I woke up. I knew because the lights had been switched off and the electric plant stops working at two in the morning. The room, barely lit by an oil lamp at the feet of the Holy Virgin on the chest of drawers, made me think of the wedding night, *my* wedding night. It was so long ago, an empty eternity.

From the depth of the gloomy darkness don Apolonio's broken and tired breathing 70 reached me. There he still was, not the man himself, simply the persistent and incomprehensible shred that hangs on, with no goal, with no apparent motive. Death is frightening, but life mingled with death, soaked in death, is horrible in a way that owes little to either life or death. Silence, corruption of the flesh, the stench, the monstrous transformation, the final vanishing act, all this is painful, but it reaches a climax and then gives way, dissolves into the earth, into memory, into history. But not this: this arrangement worked out between life and death—echoed in the useless exhaling and inhaling—could carry on forever. I would hear him trying to clear his anaesthetized throat and it occurred to me that air was not entering that body, or rather, that it was not a human body breathing the air: it was a machine, puffing and panting, stopping in a curious game, a game to kill time without end. That thing was no human being: it was somebody playing with huffs and snores. And the horror of it all won me over: I began to breathe to the rhythm of his panting; to inhale, stop suddenly, choke, breathe, choke again, unable to control myself, until I realized I had been deceived by what I thought was the sense of the game. What I really felt was the pain and shortness of breath of an animal in pain. But I kept on, on, until there was one single breathing, one single inhuman breath, one single agony. I felt calmer, terrified but calmer: I had lifted the barrier, I could let myself go and simply wait for the common end. It seemed to me that by abandoning myself, by giving myself up unconditionally, the end would happen quickly, would not be allowed to continue. It would have fulfilled its purpose and its persistent search in the world.

Not a hint of farewell, not a glimmer of pity towards me. I carried on the mortal game for a long, long while, from someplace where time had ceased to matter.

The shared breathing became less agitated, more peaceful, but also weaker. I seemed to be drifting back. I felt so tired I could barely move, exhaustion nestling in forever inside my body. I opened my eyes. Nothing had changed.

No: far away, in the shadows, is a rose. Alone, unique, alive. There it is, cut out against the darkness, clear as day, with its fleshy, luminous petals, shining. I look at it and my hand moves and I remember its touch and the simple act of putting it in a vase. I looked at it then, but I only understand it now. I stir, I blink, and the rose is still there, in full bloom, identical to itself.

I breathe freely, with my own breath. I pray, I remember, I doze off, and the untouched rose mounts guard over the dawning light and my secret. Death and hope suffer change.

And now day begins to break and in the clean sky I see that at last the days of rain are over. I stay at the window a long time, watching everything change in the sun. A strong ray enters and the suffering seems a lie. Unjustified bliss fills my lungs and unwittingly I smile. I turn to the rose as if to an accomplice but I can't find it: the sun has withered it.

Clear days came again, and maddening heat. The people went to work, and sang, but don Apolonio would not die; in fact he seemed to get better. I kept on looking after him, but no longer in a cheerful mood—my eyes downcast, I turned the guilt I felt into hard work. My wish, now clearly, was that it all end, that he die. The fear, the horror I felt looking at him, at his touch, his voice, were unjustified because the link between us was not real, could never be real, and yet he felt like a dead weight upon me. Through politeness and shame I wanted to get rid of it.

Yes, don Apolonio was visibly improving. Even the doctor was surprised and offered no explanation.

On the very first morning I sat him up among the pillows, I noticed that certain look in my uncle's eyes. The heat was stifling and I had to lift him all by myself. Once I had propped him up I noticed: the old man was staring as if dazed at my heaving chest, his face distorted and his trembling hands unconsciously moving towards me. I drew back instinctively and turned my head away.

"Please close the blinds, it's too hot."

His almost dead body was growing warm.

"Come here, Luisa, sit by my side. Come."

"Yes, uncle." I sat, my knees drawn up, at the foot of the bed, without looking at him.

"Polo, you must call me Polo, after all we are closer relatives now." There was mockery in the tone of his voice.

"Yes, uncle."

"Polo, Polo." His voice was again sweet and soft. "You'll have a lot to forgive me. I'm old and sick, and a man in my condition is like a child."

"Yes."

"Let's see. Try saying, 'Yes, Polo.'"

"Yes, Polo."

The name on my lips seemed to me an aberration, made me nauseated.

Polo got better, but became fussy and irritable. I realized he was fighting to be the   90
man he once had been, and yet the resurrected self was not the same, but another.

"Luisa, bring me . . . Luisa, give me . . . Luisa, plump up my pillows . . . pour me
some water . . . prop up my leg . . . "

He wanted me to be there all day long, always by his side, seeing to his needs,
touching him. And the fixed look and distorted face kept coming back, more and
more frequently, growing over his features like a mask.

"Pick up my book. It fell underneath the bed, on this side."

I kneeled and stuck my head and almost half my body underneath the bed, and
had to stretch my arm as far as it would go, to reach it. At first I thought it had been
my own movements, or maybe the bedclothes, but once I had the book in my hand
and was shuffling to get out, I froze, stunned by what I had long foreseen, even
expected: the outburst, the scream, the thunder. A rage never before felt raced
through me when the realization of what was happening reached my consciousness,
when his shaking hand, taking advantage of my amazement, became surer and heavier, and enjoyed itself, adventuring with no restraints, feeling and exploring my
thighs—a fleshless hand glued to my skin, fingering my body with delight, a dead
hand searching impatiently between my legs, a bodyless hand.

I rose as quickly as I could, my face burning with shame and determination, but   95
when I saw him I forgot myself and entered like an automation into the nightmare.
Polo was laughing softly through his toothless mouth. And then, suddenly serious,
with a coolness that terrified me, he said:

"What? Aren't you my wife before God and men? Come here, I'm cold, heat my
bed. But first take off your dress, you don't want to get it creased."

What followed, I know, is my story, my life, but I can barely remember it; like a
disgusting dream I can't even tell whether it was long or short. Only one thought
kept me sane during the early days: "This can't go on, it can't go on." I imagined that
God would not allow it, would prevent it in some way or another. He, personally,
God, would interfere. Death, once dreaded, seemed my only hope. Not Apolonio's—
he was a demon of death—but mine, the just and necessary death for my corrupted
flesh. But nothing happened. Everything stayed on, suspended in time, without
future. Then, one morning, taking nothing with me, I left.

It was useless. Three days later they let me know that my husband was dying, and
they called me back. I went to see the father confessor and told him my story.

"What keeps him alive is lust, the most horrible of all sins. This isn't life, Father,
it's death. Let him die!"

"He would die in despair. I can't allow it."   100

"And I?"

"I understand, but if you don't go to him, it would be like murder. Try not to
arouse him, pray to the Blessed Virgin, and keep your mind on your duties."

I went back. And lust drew him out of the grave once more.

Fighting, endlessly fighting, I managed, after several years, to overcome my
hatred, and finally, at the very end, I even conquered the beast: Apolonio died in
peace, sweetly, his old self again.

But I was not able to go back to who I was. Now wickedness, malice, shine in the   105
eyes of the men who look at me, and I feel I have become an occasion of sin for all, I,
the vilest of harlots. Alone, a sinner, totally engulfed by the never-ending flames of
this cruel summer which surrounds us all, like an army of ants.

Questions

1. The story begins—and ends—with references to the summer heat, and there are several
   days of rain after the marriage takes place. Is this just scene-setting, or is there a larger significance to the descriptions?
2. How would you characterize Luisa—her sense of herself, her attitude toward men, her
   feelings about her uncle—at the beginning of the story?
3. How do the priest and Luisa's other relatives respond to don Apolonio's request to marry
   her? How does Luisa herself react? Why does she agree to do it?
4. Luisa says of don Apolonio: "I realized he was fighting to be the man he once had been,
   and yet the resurrected self was not the same, but another" (paragraph 90). What differences do you see in him before and after his "resurrection"?
5. Speaking to the priest near the end of the story, Luisa describes lust as "the most horrible
   of all sins." Do you think that we are intended to agree with this assessment? Why or why
   not?
6. At the very end, Luisa says: "I feel I have become an occasion of sin for all . . . the vilest of
   harlots . . . a sinner. . . ." Do you think that we are intended to agree with *this* assessment?

■ WRITING *effectively*

Gabriel García Márquez on Writing

My Beginnings as a Writer   1981

Interviewer: How did you start writing?

García Márquez: By drawing. By drawing
cartoons. Before I could read or write I used
to draw comics at school and at home. The
funny thing is that I now realize that when I
was in high school I had the reputation of
being a writer, though I never in fact wrote
anything. If there was a pamphlet to be written or a letter of petition, I was the one to do
it because I was supposedly the writer. When
I entered college I happened to have a very
good literary background in general, considerably above the average of my friends. At
the university in Bogotá, I started making
new friends and acquaintances, who introduced me to contemporary writers. One
night a friend lent me a book of short stories
by Franz Kafka. I went back to the *pension*

Gabriel García Márquez

where I was staying and began to read *The Metamorphosis*. The first line almost
knocked me off the bed. I was so surprised. The first line reads, "As Gregor Samsa

awoke that morning from uneasy dreams, he found himself transformed in his bed into a gigantic insect. . . . " When I read the line I thought to myself that I didn't know anyone was allowed to write things like that. If I had known, I would have started writing a long time ago. So I immediately started writing short stories. They were totally intellectual short stories because I was writing them on the basis of my literary experience and had not yet found the link between literature and life. The stories were published in the literary supplement of the newspaper *El Espectador* in Bogotá and they did have a certain success at the time—probably because nobody in Colombia was writing intellectual short stories. What was being written then was mostly about life in the countryside and social life. When I wrote my first short stories I was told they had Joycean influences.

Interviewer: Had you read Joyce at that time?

García Márquez: I had never read Joyce, so I started reading *Ulysses*. I read it in the only Spanish edition available. Since then, after having read *Ulysses* in English as well as a very good French translation, I can see that the original Spanish translation was very bad. But I did learn something that was to be very useful to me in my future writing—the technique of the interior monologue. I later found this in Virginia Woolf, and I like the way she uses it better than Joyce. Although I later realized that the person who invented this interior monologue was the anonymous writer of the *Lazarillo de Tormes*.°

From *Paris Review* interview with Peter H. Stone

TOPICS FOR WRITING ABOUT "THE GOSPEL ACCORDING TO MARK"

1. The long opening paragraph of "The Gospel According to Mark" tells a great deal about the background and personality of Baltasar Espinosa. Write a brief essay in which you consider how the character traits described there foreshadow the story's events.

2. Have you ever been involved in a misunderstanding that was caused by excessive literal-mindedness, your own or someone else's? Write a description of the incident, including how it was resolved, if at all.

3. What larger point do you think Borges is making about his protagonist's final fate, especially in light of Espinosa's attitudes toward religious belief? Back up your conclusions with references to the text.

TOPICS FOR WRITING ABOUT "MY LIFE WITH THE WAVE"

1. Suppose that a friend to whom you had recommended "My Life with the Wave" came back to you and said, "That story was just stupid; it made no sense at all." How would you argue against this attitude?

2. The incident on the train, with all its escalations and repercussions (paragraphs 3–18), is very funny, but is there also an ominous, perhaps Kafkaesque quality to it, one that might

---

Lazarillo de Tormes: Life of Lazarillo de Tormes (1554), the anonymous Spanish novel credited as the original picaresque novel, a story of a likable scoundrel who wanders through adventures, living by his wits, at odds with respectable society.

find analogies in contemporary attitudes—or is it all just a joke? Discuss this point, explaining your conclusions.

3. One critic has suggested that the theme of "My Life with the Wave" is the impossibility of sustained romantic or sexual passion. Defend or disagree with that statement.

4. Using "My Life with the Wave" as a model, write a narrative of your relationship with a possession—a book or CD, a piece of clothing or jewelry, a car—as if you were describing the stages of a love affair, from initial attraction and desire to final disillusionment and break-up.

TOPICS FOR WRITING ABOUT "A VERY OLD MAN WITH ENORMOUS WINGS"

1. As is said earlier in this chapter, all of the main features of Latin American magic realism can be found in García Márquez's "A Very Old Man with Enormous Wings." Develop this theme in a brief essay, with detailed reference to both the story itself and the components of magic realism.

2. Are you familiar with Franz Kafka's *The Metamorphosis*? If so, discuss the presentation of the spider woman in paragraph 10 of "A Very Old Man with Enormous Wings" as a parody of the Kafka work.

3. Write an essay in which you discuss what you understand the meaning of the story to be. Refer as specifically as possible to the text of the story to back up your arguments.

TOPICS FOR WRITING ABOUT "THE SHUNAMMITE"

1. "The Shunammite" makes some observations about how women are perceived by the larger culture and—partly as a consequence of that—how they perceive themselves. How applicable are those observations to contemporary American society?

2. Do you find it credible that Luisa would behave as submissively as she does throughout the story, even when she is asked to do things she strongly objects to? Refer to the text to substantiate your conclusions.

3. Write a brief essay in which you agree or disagree with the following proposition: "The meaning of this story is very simple: Men are animals."

► TERMS FOR *review*

Magic (or magical) realism ► A type of contemporary narrative in which the magical and the mundane are mixed in an overall context of realistic storytelling; the term was originally used to describe the matter-of-fact combination of the fantastic and the everyday in Latin American fiction.

"El Boom" ► An explosion of creativity in the 1960s—marked by stylistic extravagance, complex characterization, fractured time sequences, and fantastic events—that transformed Latin America into one of the centers of modern world fiction.

10 CRITICAL CASEBOOK
Flannery O'Connor

Flannery O'Connor and her *Self-Portrait with Pheasant Cock*, 1962.

*The main concern of the fiction writer is with mystery
as it is incarnated in real life.*

—FLANNERY O'CONNOR

FLANNERY O'CONNOR

Mary Flannery O'Connor (1925–1964) was born in Savannah, Georgia, but spent most of her life in the small town of Milledgeville. While attending Georgia State College for Women, she won a local reputation for her fledgling stories and satiric cartoons. After graduating in 1945, she went on to study at the University of Iowa, where she earned an M.F.A. in 1947. Diagnosed in 1950 with disseminated lupus, the same incurable illness that had killed her father, O'Connor returned home and spent the last decade of her life living with her mother in Milledgeville. Back on the family dairy farm, she wrote, maintained an extensive literary correspondence, raised peacocks, and underwent medical treatment. When her illness occasionally went into a period of remission, she made trips to lecture and read her stories to college audiences. Her health declined rapidly after surgery early in 1964 for an unrelated complaint. She died at thirty-nine.

O'Connor is unusual among modern American writers in the depth of her Christian vision. A devout Roman Catholic, she attended mass daily while growing up and living in the largely Protestant South. As a latter-day satirist in the manner of Jonathan Swift, O'Connor levels the eye of an uncompromising moralist on the violence and spiritual disorder of the modern world, focusing on what she calls "the action of grace in territory held largely by the devil." She is sometimes called a "Southern Gothic" writer because of her fascination with grotesque incidents and characters. Throughout her career she depicted the South as a troubled region in which the social, racial, and religious status quo that had existed since before the Civil War was coming to a violent end. Despite the inherent seriousness of her religious and social themes, O'Connor's mordant and frequently outrageous humor is everywhere apparent. Her combination of profound vision and dark comedy is the distinguishing characteristic of her literary sensibilities.

O'Connor's published work includes two short novels, Wise Blood *(1952) and* The Violent Bear It Away *(1960), and two collections of short stories,* A Good Man Is Hard to Find *(1955) and* Everything That Rises Must Converge, *published posthumously in 1965. A collection of essays and miscellaneous prose,* Mystery and Manners *(1969), and her selected letters,* The Habit of Being *(1979), reveal an innate cheerfulness and engaging personal warmth that are not always apparent in her fiction.* The Complete Stories of Flannery O'Connor *was posthumously awarded the National Book Award in 1971.*

STORIES

A Good Man Is Hard to Find
1955

The grandmother didn't want to go to Florida. She wanted to visit some of her connections in east Tennessee and she was seizing at every chance to change Bailey's mind. Bailey was the son she lived with, her only boy. He was sitting on the edge of his chair at the table, bent over the orange sports section of the *Journal*. "Now look here, Bailey," she said, "see here, read this," and she stood with one hand on her thin hip and the other rattling the newspaper at his bald head. "Here this fellow that calls himself The Misfit is aloose from the Federal Pen and headed toward Florida and you read here what it says he did to these people. Just you read it. I wouldn't take my children in any direction with a criminal like that aloose in it. I couldn't answer to my conscience if I did."

Bailey didn't look up from his reading so she wheeled around then and faced the children's mother, a young woman in slacks, whose face was as broad and innocent as a cabbage and was tied around with a green head-kerchief that had two points on the top like rabbit's ears. She was sitting on the sofa, feeding the baby his apricots out of a jar. "The children have been to Florida before," the old lady said. "You all ought to take them somewhere else for a change so they would see different parts of the world and be broad. They never have been to east Tennessee."

The children's mother didn't seem to hear her but the eight-year-old boy, John Wesley, a stocky child with glasses, said, "If you don't want to go to Florida, why dontcha stay at home?" He and the little girl, June Star, were reading the funny papers on the floor.

"She wouldn't stay at home to be queen for a day," June Star said without raising her yellow head.

"Yes and what would you do if this fellow, The Misfit, caught you?" the grand-   5
mother said.

"I'd smack his face," John Wesley said.

"She wouldn't stay at home for a million bucks," June Star said. "Afraid she'd miss something. She has to go everywhere we go."

"All right, Miss," the grandmother said. "Just remember that the next time you want me to curl your hair."

June Star said her hair was naturally curly.

The next morning the grandmother was the first one in the car, ready to go. She   10
had her big black valise that looked like the head of a hippopotamus in one corner, and underneath it she was hiding a basket with Pitty Sing, the cat, in it. She didn't intend for the cat to be left alone in the house for three days because he would miss her too much and she was afraid he might brush against one of the gas burners and accidentally asphyxiate himself. Her son, Bailey, didn't like to arrive at a motel with a cat.

She sat in the middle of the back seat with John Wesley and June Star on either side of her. Bailey and the children's mother and the baby sat in front and they left Atlanta at eight forty-five with the mileage on the car at 55890. The grandmother wrote this down because she thought it would be interesting to say how many miles they had been when they got back. It took them twenty minutes to reach the outskirts of the city.

The old lady settled herself comfortably, removing her white cotton gloves and putting them up with her purse on the shelf in front of the back window. The children's mother still had on slacks and still had her hair tied up in a green kerchief, but the grandmother had on a navy blue straw sailor hat with a bunch of white violets on the brim and a navy blue dress with a small white dot in the print. Her collars and cuffs were white organdy trimmed with lace and at her neckline she had pinned a purple spray of cloth violets containing a sachet. In case of an accident, anyone seeing her dead on the highway would know at once that she was a lady.

She said she thought it was going to be a good day for driving, neither too hot nor too cold, and she cautioned Bailey that the speed limit was fifty-five miles an hour and that the patrolmen hid themselves behind billboards and small clumps of trees and sped out after you before you had a chance to slow down. She pointed out interesting details of the scenery: Stone Mountain; the blue granite that in some places came up to both sides of the highway; the brilliant red clay banks slightly streaked with purple; and the various crops that made rows of green lace-work on the ground. The trees were full of silver-white sunlight and the meanest of them sparkled. The children were reading comic magazines and their mother had gone back to sleep.

"Let's go through Georgia fast so we won't have to look at it much," John Wesley said.

"If I were a little boy," said the grandmother, "I wouldn't talk about my native state that way. Tennessee has the mountains and Georgia has the hills."

15

"Tennessee is just a hillbilly dumping ground," John Wesley said, "and Georgia is a lousy state too."

"You said it," June Star said.

"In my time," said the grandmother, folding her thin veined fingers, "children were more respectful of their native states and their parents and everything else. People did right then. Oh look at the cute little pickaninny!" she said and pointed to a Negro child standing in the door of a shack. "Wouldn't that make a picture, now?" she asked and they all turned and looked at the little Negro out of the back window. He waved.

"He didn't have any britches on," June Star said.

"He probably didn't have any," the grandmother explained. "Little niggers in the country don't have things like we do. If I could paint, I'd paint that picture," she said.

20

The children exchanged comic books.

The grandmother offered to hold the baby and the children's mother passed him over the front seat to her. She set him on her knee and bounced him and told him about the things they were passing. She rolled her eyes and screwed up her mouth and stuck her leathery thin face into his smooth bland one. Occasionally he gave her a faraway smile. They passed a large cotton field with five or six graves fenced in the middle of it, like a small island. "Look at the graveyard!" the grandmother said, pointing it out. "That was the old family burying ground. That belonged to the plantation."

"Where's the plantation?" John Wesley asked.

"Gone With the Wind," said the grandmother. "Ha. Ha."

When the children finished all the comic books they had brought, they opened the lunch and ate it. The grandmother ate a peanut butter sandwich and an olive and would not let the children throw the box and the paper napkins out the window. When there was nothing else to do they played a game by choosing a cloud and making the other two guess what shape it suggested. John Wesley took one the shape of a cow and June Star guessed a cow and John Wesley said, no, an automobile, and June Star said he didn't play fair, and they began to slap each other over the grandmother.

25

The grandmother said she would tell them a story if they would keep quiet. When she told a story, she rolled her eyes and waved her head and was very dramatic. She said once when she was a maiden lady she had been courted by a Mr. Edgar Atkins Teagarden from Jasper, Georgia. She said he was a very good-looking man and a gentleman and that he brought her a watermelon every Saturday afternoon with his initials cut in it, E. A. T. Well, one Saturday, she said, Mr. Teagarden brought the watermelon and there was nobody at home and he left it on the front porch and returned in his buggy to Jasper, but she never got the watermelon, she said, because a nigger boy ate it when he saw the initials, E. A. T.! This story tickled John Wesley's funny bone and he giggled and giggled but June Star didn't think it was any good. She said she wouldn't marry a man that just brought her a watermelon on Saturday. The grandmother said she would have done well to marry Mr. Teagarden because he was a gentleman and had bought Coca-Cola stock when it first came out and that he had died only a few years ago, a very wealthy man.

They stopped at The Tower for barbecued sandwiches. The Tower was a part stucco and part wood filling station and dance hall set in a clearing outside of

Timothy. A fat man named Red Sammy Butts ran it and there were signs stuck here and there on the building and for miles up and down the highway saying, TRY RED SAMMY'S FAMOUS BARBECUE. NONE LIKE FAMOUS RED SAMMY'S! RED SAM! THE FAT BOY WITH THE HAPPY LAUGH. A VETERAN! RED SAMMY'S YOUR MAN!

Red Sammy was lying on the bare ground outside The Tower with his head under a truck while a gray monkey about a foot high, chained to a small chinaberry tree, chattered nearby. The monkey sprang back into the tree and got on the highest limb as soon as he saw the children jump out of the car and run toward him.

Inside, The Tower was a long dark room with a counter at one end and tables at the other and dancing space in the middle. They all sat down at a board table next to the nickelodeon and Red Sam's wife, a tall burnt-brown woman with hair and eyes lighter than her skin, came and took their order. The children's mother put a dime in the machine and played "The Tennessee Waltz," and the grandmother said that tune always made her want to dance. She asked Bailey if he would like to dance but he only glared at her. He didn't have a naturally sunny disposition like she did and trips made him nervous. The grandmother's brown eyes were very bright. She swayed her head from side to side and pretended she was dancing in her chair. June Star said play something she could tap to so the children's mother put in another dime and played a fast number and June Star stepped out onto the dance floor and did her tap routine.

"Ain't she cute?" Red Sam's wife said, leaning over the counter. "Would you like to come be my little girl?" 30

"No I certainly wouldn't," June Star said. "I wouldn't live in a broken-down place like this for a million bucks!" and she ran back to the table.

"Ain't she cute?" the woman repeated, stretching her mouth politely.

"Arn't you ashamed?" hissed the grandmother.

Red Sam came in and told his wife to quit lounging on the counter and hurry up with these people's order. His khaki trousers reached just to his hip bones and his stomach hung over them like a sack of meal swaying under his shirt. He came over and sat down at a table nearby and let out a combination sigh and yodel. "You can't win," he said. "You can't win," and he wiped his sweating red face off with a gray handkerchief. "These days you don't know who to trust," he said. "Ain't that the truth?"

"People are certainly not nice like they used to be," said the grandmother. 35

"Two fellers come in here last week," Red Sammy said, "driving a Chrysler. It was a old beat-up car but it was a good one and these boys looked all right to me. Said they worked at the mill and you know I let them fellers charge the gas they bought? Now why did I do that?"

"Because you're a good man!" the grandmother said at once.

"Yes'm, I suppose so," Red Sam said as if he were struck with this answer.

His wife brought the orders, carrying the five plates all at once without a tray, two in each hand and one balanced on her arm. "It isn't a soul in this green world of God's that you can trust," she said. "And I don't count nobody out of that, not nobody," she repeated, looking at Red Sammy.

"Did you read about that criminal, The Misfit, that's escaped?" asked the grand- 40 mother.

"I wouldn't be a bit surprised if he didn't attact this place right here," said the woman. "If he hears about it being here, I wouldn't be none surprised to see him. If he hears it's two cent in the cash register, I wouldn't be a-tall surprised if he . . ."

"That'll do," Red Sam said. "Go bring these people their Co'-Colas," and the woman went off to get the rest of the order.

"A good man is hard to find," Red Sammy said. "Everything is getting terrible. I remember the day you could go off and leave your screen door unlatched. Not no more."

He and the grandmother discussed better times. The old lady said that in her opinion Europe was entirely to blame for the way things were now. She said the way Europe acted you would think we were made of money and Red Sam said it was no use talking about it, she was exactly right. The children ran outside into the white sunlight and looked at the monkey in the lacy chinaberry tree. He was busy catching fleas on himself and biting each one carefully between his teeth as if it were a delicacy.

They drove off again into the hot afternoon. The grandmother took cat naps and woke up every five minutes with her own snoring. Outside of Toombsboro she woke up and recalled an old plantation that she had visited in this neighborhood once when she was a young lady. She said the house had six white columns across the front and that there was an avenue of oaks leading up to it and two little wooden trellis arbors on either side in front where you sat down with your suitor after a stroll in the garden. She recalled exactly which road to turn off to get to it. She knew that Bailey would not be willing to lose any time looking at an old house, but the more she talked about it, the more she wanted to see it once again and find out if the little twin arbors were still standing. "There was a secret panel in this house," she said craftily, not telling the truth but wishing that she were, "and the story went that all the family silver was hidden in it when Sherman° came through but it was never found . . ."

"Hey!" John Wesley said. "Let's go see it! We'll find it! We'll poke all the woodwork and find it! Who lives there? Where do you turn off at? Hey, Pop, can't we turn off there?"

"We never have seen a house with a secret panel!" June Star shrieked. "Let's go to the house with the secret panel! Hey Pop, can't we go see the house with the secret panel!"

"It's not far from here, I know," the grandmother said. "It wouldn't take over twenty minutes."

Bailey was looking straight ahead. His jaw was as rigid as a horseshoe. "No," he said.

The children began to yell and scream that they wanted to see the house with the secret panel. John Wesley kicked the back of the front seat and June Star hung over her mother's shoulder and whined desperately into her ear that they never had any fun even on their vacation, that they could never do what THEY wanted to do. The baby began to scream and John Wesley kicked the back of the seat so hard that his father could feel the blows in his kidney.

"All right!" he shouted and drew the car to a stop at the side of the road. "Will you all shut up? Will you all just shut up for one second? If you don't shut up, we won't go anywhere."

"It would be very educational for them," the grandmother murmured.

"All right," Bailey said, "but get this: this is the only time we're going to stop for anything like this. This is the one and only time."

Sherman: General William Tecumseh Sherman, Union commander, whose troops burned Atlanta in 1864, then made a devastating march to the sea.

"The dirt road that you have to turn down is about a mile back," the grandmother directed. "I marked it when we passed."

"A dirt road," Bailey groaned.   55

After they had turned around and were headed toward the dirt road, the grandmother recalled other points about the house, the beautiful glass over the front doorway and the candle-lamp in the hall. John Wesley said that the secret panel was probably in the fireplace.

"You can't go inside this house," Bailey said. "You don't know who lives there."

"While you all talk to the people in front, I'll run around behind and get in a window," John Wesley suggested.

"We'll all stay in the car," his mother said.

They turned onto the dirt road and the car raced roughly along in a swirl of pink   60
dust. The grandmother recalled the times when there were no paved roads and thirty miles was a day's journey. The dirt road was hilly and there were sudden washes in it and sharp curves on dangerous embankments. All at once they would be on a hill, looking down over the blue tops of trees for miles around, then the next minute, they would be in a red depression with the dust-coated trees looking down on them.

"This place had better turn up in a minute," Bailey said, "or I'm going to turn around."

The road looked as if no one had traveled on it for months.

"It's not much farther," the grandmother said and just as she said it, a horrible thought came to her. The thought was so embarrassing that she turned red in the face and her eyes dilated and her feet jumped up, upsetting her valise in the corner. The instant the valise moved, the newspaper top she had over the basket under it rose with a snarl and Pitty Sing, the cat, sprang onto Bailey's shoulder.

The children were thrown to the floor and their mother, clutching the baby, was thrown out the door onto the ground; the old lady was thrown into the front seat. The car turned over once and landed right-side-up in a gulch off the side of the road. Bailey remained in the driver's seat with the cat—gray-striped with a broad white face and an orange nose—clinging to his neck like a caterpillar.

As soon as the children saw they could move their arms and legs, they scrambled   65
out of the car, shouting, "We've had an ACCIDENT!" The grandmother was curled up under the dashboard, hoping she was injured so that Bailey's wrath would not come down on her all at once. The horrible thought she had had before the accident was that the house she had remembered so vividly was not in Georgia but in Tennessee.

Bailey removed the cat from his neck with both hands and flung it out the window against the side of a pine tree. Then he got out of the car and started looking for the children's mother. She was sitting against the side of the red gutted ditch, holding the screaming baby, but she only had a cut down her face and a broken shoulder. "We've had an ACCIDENT!" the children screamed in a frenzy of delight.

"But nobody's killed," June Star said with disappointment as the grandmother limped out of the car, her hat still pinned to her head but the broken front brim standing up at a jaunty angle and the violet spray hanging off the side. They all sat down in the ditch, except the children, to recover from the shock. They were all shaking.

"Maybe a car will come along," said the children's mother hoarsely.

"I believe I have injured an organ," said the grandmother, pressing her side, but no one answered her. Bailey's teeth were clattering. He had on a yellow sport shirt with bright blue parrots designed in it and his face was as yellow as the shirt.

The grandmother decided that she would not mention that the house was in Tennessee.

The road was about ten feet above and they could see only the tops of the trees on the other side of it. Behind the ditch they were sitting in there were more woods, tall and dark and deep. In a few minutes they saw a car some distance away on top of a hill, coming slowly as if the occupants were watching them. The grandmother stood up and waved both her arms dramatically to attract their attention. The car continued to come on slowly, disappeared around a bend and appeared again, moving even slower, on top of the hill they had gone over. It was a big black battered hearse-like automobile. There were three men in it.

It came to a stop just over them and for some minutes, the driver looked down with a steady expressionless gaze to where they were sitting, and didn't speak. Then he turned his head and muttered something to the other two and they got out. One was a fat boy in black trousers and a red sweat shirt with a silver stallion embossed on the front of it. He moved around on the right side of them and stood staring, his mouth partly open in a kind of loose grin. The other had on khaki pants and a blue striped coat and a gray hat pulled down very low, hiding most of his face. He came around slowly on the left side. Neither spoke.

The driver got out of the car and stood by the side of it, looking down at them. He was an older man than the other two. His hair was just beginning to gray and he wore silver-rimmed spectacles that gave him a scholarly look. He had a long creased face and didn't have on any shirt or undershirt. He had on blue jeans that were too tight for him and was holding a black hat and a gun. The two boys also had guns.

"We've had an ACCIDENT!" the children screamed.

The grandmother had the peculiar feeling that the bespectacled man was someone she knew. His face was as familiar to her as if she had known him all her life but she could not recall who he was. He moved away from the car and began to come down the embankment, placing his feet carefully so that he wouldn't slip. He had on tan and white shoes and no socks, and his ankles were red and thin. "Good afternoon," he said. "I see you all had you a little spill."

"We turned over twice!" said the grandmother.

"Oncet," he corrected. "We seen it happen. Try their car and see will it run, Hiram," he said quietly to the boy with the gray hat.

"What you got that gun for?" John Wesley asked. "Whatcha gonna do with that gun?"

"Lady," the man said to the children's mother, "would you mind calling them children to sit down by you? Children make me nervous. I want all you all to sit down right together there where you're at."

"What are you telling US what to do for?" June Star asked.

Behind them the line of woods gaped like a dark open mouth. "Come here," said their mother.

"Look here now," Bailey began suddenly, "we're in a predicament! We're in . . ."

The grandmother shrieked. She scrambled to her feet and stood staring. "You're The Misfit!" she said. "I recognized you at once!"

"Yes'm," the man said, smiling slightly as if he were pleased in spite of himself to be known, "but it would have been better for all of you, lady, if you hadn't of reckernized me."

Bailey turned his head sharply and said something to his mother that shocked even the children. The old lady began to cry and The Misfit reddened.

"Lady," he said, "don't you get upset. Sometimes a man says things he don't   85
mean. I don't reckon he meant to talk to you thataway."

"You wouldn't shoot a lady, would you?" the grandmother said and removed a
clean handkerchief from her cuff and began to slap at her eyes with it.

The Misfit pointed the toe of his shoe into the ground and made a little hole and
then covered it up again. "I would hate to have to," he said.

"Listen," the grandmother almost screamed, "I know you're a good man. You
don't look a bit like you have common blood. I know you must come from nice people!"

"Yes mam," he said, "finest people in the world." When he smiled he showed a
row of strong white teeth. "God never made a finer woman than my mother and my
daddy's heart was pure gold," he said. The boy with the red sweat shirt had come
around behind them and was standing with his gun at his hip. The Misfit squatted
down on the ground. "Watch them children, Bobby Lee," he said. "You know they
make me nervous." He looked at the six of them huddled together in front of him
and he seemed to be embarrassed as if he couldn't think of anything to say. "Ain't a
cloud in the sky," he remarked, looking up at it. "Don't see no sun but don't see no
cloud neither."

"Yes, it's a beautiful day," said the grandmother. "Listen," she said, "you shouldn't   90
call yourself The Misfit because I know you're a good man at heart. I can just look at
you and tell."

"Hush!" Bailey yelled. "Hush! Everybody shut up and let me handle this!" He was
squatting in the position of a runner about to sprint forward but he didn't move.

"I pre-chate that, lady," The Misfit said and drew a little circle in the ground
with the butt of his gun.

"It'll take a half a hour to fix this here car," Hiram called, looking over the raised
hood of it.

"Well, first you and Bobby Lee get him and that little boy to step over yonder
with you," The Misfit said, pointing to Bailey and John Wesley. "The boys want to
ast you something," he said to Bailey. "Would you mind stepping back in them woods
there with them?"

"Listen," Bailey began, "we're in a terrible predicament! Nobody realizes what   95
this is," and his voice cracked. His eyes were as blue and intense as the parrots in his
shirt and he remained perfectly still.

The grandmother reached up to adjust her hat brim as if she were going to the
woods with him but it came off in her hand. She stood staring at it and after a second
she let it fall on the ground. Hiram pulled Bailey up by the arm as if he were assisting
an old man. John Wesley caught hold of his father's hand and Bobby Lee followed.
They went off toward the woods and just as they reached the dark edge, Bailey turned
and supporting himself against a gray naked pine trunk, he shouted, "I'll be back in a
minute, Mamma, wait on me!"

"Come back this instant!" his mother shrilled but they all disappeared into the
woods.

"Bailey Boy!" the grandmother called in a tragic voice but she found she was
looking at The Misfit squatting on the ground in front of her. "I just know you're a
good man," she said desperately. "You're not a bit common!"

"Nome, I ain't a good man," The Misfit said after a second as if he had considered her statement carefully, "but I ain't the worst in the world neither. My daddy
said I was a different breed of dog from my brothers and sisters. 'You know,' Daddy

said, 'it's some that can live their whole life out without asking about it and it's others has to know why it is, and this boy is one of the latters. He's going to be into
everything!'" He put on his black hat and looked up suddenly and then away deep
into the woods as if he were embarrassed again. "I'm sorry I don't have on a shirt
before you ladies," he said, hunching his shoulders slightly. "We buried our clothes
that we had on when we escaped and we're just making do until we can get better.
We borrowed these from some folks we met," he explained.

"That's perfectly all right," the grandmother said. "Maybe Bailey has an extra   100
shirt in his suitcase."

"I'll look and see terrectly," The Misfit said.

"Where are they taking him?" the children's mother screamed.

"Daddy was a card himself," The Misfit said. "You couldn't put anything over
on him. He never got in trouble with the Authorities though. Just had the knack of
handling them."

"You could be honest too if you'd only try," said the grandmother. "Think how
wonderful it would be to settle down and live a comfortable life and not have to
think about somebody chasing you all the time."

The Misfit kept scratching in the ground with the butt of his gun as if he were   105
thinking about it. "Yes'm, somebody is always after you," he murmured.

The grandmother noticed how thin his shoulder blades were just behind his hat
because she was standing up looking down on him. "Do you ever pray?" she asked.

He shook his head. All she saw was the black hat wiggle between his shoulder
blades. "Nome," he said.

There was a pistol shot from the woods, followed closely by another. Then silence.
The old lady's head jerked around. She could hear the wind move through the tree tops
like a long satisfied insuck of breath. "Bailey Boy!" she called.

"I was a gospel singer for a while," The Misfit said. "I been most everything. Been
in the arm service, both land and sea, at home and abroad, been twict married, been an
undertaker, been with the railroads, plowed Mother Earth, been in a tornado, seen a
man burnt alive oncet," and he looked up at the children's mother and the little girl
who were sitting close together, their faces white and their eyes glassy; "I even seen a
woman flogged," he said.

"Pray, pray," the grandmother began, "pray, pray . . ."   110

"I never was a bad boy that I remember of," The Misfit said in an almost dreamy
voice, "but somewheres along the line I done something wrong and got sent to the
penitentiary. I was buried alive," and he looked up and held her attention to him by a
steady stare.

"That's when you should have started to pray," she said. "What did you do to get
sent to the penitentiary that first time?"

"Turn to the right, it was a wall," The Misfit said, looking up again at the cloudless sky. "Turn to the left, it was a wall. Look up it was a ceiling, look down it was a
floor. I forget what I done, lady. I set there and set there, trying to remember what it
was I done and I ain't recalled it to this day. Oncet in a while, I would think it was
coming to me, but it never come."

"Maybe they put you in by mistake," the old lady said vaguely.

"Nome," he said. "It wasn't no mistake. They had the papers on me."   115

"You must have stolen something," she said.

The Misfit sneered slightly. "Nobody had nothing I wanted," he said. "It was a
head-doctor at the penitentiary said what I had done was kill my daddy but I known

that for a lie. My daddy died in nineteen ought nineteen of the epidemic flu and I never had a thing to do with it. He was buried in the Mount Hopewell Baptist churchyard and you can go there and see for yourself."

"If you would pray," the old lady said, "Jesus would help you."

"That's right," The Misfit said.

"Well then, why don't you pray?" she asked trembling with delight suddenly.   120

"I don't want no hep," he said. "I'm doing all right by myself."

Bobby Lee and Hiram came ambling back from the woods. Bobby Lee was dragging a yellow shirt with bright blue parrots in it.

"Thow me that shirt, Bobby Lee," The Misfit said. The shirt came flying at him and landed on his shoulder and he put it on. The grandmother couldn't name what the shirt reminded her of. "No, lady," The Misfit said while he was buttoning it up, "I found out the crime don't matter. You can do one thing or you can do another, kill a man or take a tire off his car, because sooner or later you're going to forget what it was you done and just be punished for it."

The children's mother had begun to make heaving noises as if she couldn't get her breath. "Lady," he asked, "would you and that little girl like to step off yonder with Bobby Lee and Hiram and join your husband?"

"Yes, thank you," the mother said faintly. Her left arm dangled helplessly and she   125 was holding the baby, who had gone to sleep, in the other. "Hep that lady up, Hiram," The Misfit said as she struggled to climb out of the ditch, "and Bobby Lee, you hold onto that little girl's hand."

"I don't want to hold hands with him," June Star said. "He reminds me of a pig."

The fat boy blushed and laughed and caught her by the arm and pulled her off into the woods after Hiram and her mother.

Alone with The Misfit, the grandmother found that she had lost her voice. There was not a cloud in the sky nor any sun. There was nothing around her but woods. She wanted to tell him that he must pray. She opened and closed her mouth several times before anything came out. Finally she found herself saying, "Jesus. Jesus," meaning, Jesus will help you, but the way she was saying it, it sounded as if she might be cursing.

"Yes'm," The Misfit said as if he agreed. "Jesus thown everything off balance. It was the same case with Him as with me except He hadn't committed any crime and they could prove I had committed one because they had the papers on me. Of course," he said, "they never shown me my papers. That's why I sign myself now. I said long ago, you get you a signature and sign everything you do and keep a copy of it. Then you'll know what you done and you can hold up the crime to the punishment and see do they match and in the end you'll have something to prove you ain't been treated right. I call myself The Misfit," he said, "because I can't make what all I done wrong fit what all I gone through in punishment."

There was a piercing scream from the woods, followed closely by a pistol report.   130 "Does it seem right to you, lady, that one is punished a heap and another ain't punished at all?"

"Jesus!" the old lady cried. "You've got good blood! I know you wouldn't shoot a lady! I know you come from nice people! Pray! Jesus, you ought not to shoot a lady. I'll give you all the money I've got!"

"Lady," The Misfit said, looking beyond her far into the woods, "there never was a body that give the undertaker a tip."

There were two more pistol reports and the grandmother raised her head like a parched old turkey hen crying for water and called, "Bailey Boy, Bailey Boy!" as if her heart would break.

"Jesus was the only One that ever raised the dead," The Misfit continued, "and He shouldn't have done it. He thown everything off balance. If He did what He said, then it's nothing for you to do but thow away everything and follow Him, and if He didn't, then it's nothing for you to do but enjoy the few minutes you got left the best way you can—by killing somebody or burning down his house or doing some other meanness to him. No pleasure but meanness," he said and his voice had become almost a snarl.

"Maybe He didn't raise the dead," the old lady mumbled, not knowing what she 135 was saying and feeling so dizzy that she sank down in the ditch with her legs twisted under her.

"I wasn't there so I can't say He didn't," The Misfit said. "I wisht I had of been there," he said, hitting the ground with his fist. "It ain't right I wasn't there because if I had of been there I would of known. Listen lady," he said in a high voice, "if I had of been there I would of known and I wouldn't be like I am now." His voice seemed about to crack and the grandmother's head cleared for an instant. She saw the man's face twisted close to her own as if he were going to cry and she murmured, "Why you're one of my babies. You're one of my own children!" She reached out and touched him on the shoulder. The Misfit sprang back as if a snake had bitten him and shot her three times through the chest. Then he put his gun down on the ground and took off his glasses and began to clean them.

Hiram and Bobby Lee returned from the woods and stood over the ditch, looking down at the grandmother who half sat and half lay in a puddle of blood with her legs crossed under her like a child's and her face smiling up at the cloudless sky.

Without his glasses, The Misfit's eyes were red-rimmed and pale and defenseless-looking. "Take her off and thow her where you thown the others," he said, picking up the cat that was rubbing itself against his leg.

"She was a talker, wasn't she?" Bobby Lee said, sliding down the ditch with a yodel.

"She would of been a good woman," The Misfit said, "if it had been somebody 140 there to shoot her every minute of her life."

"Some fun!" Bobby Lee said.

"Shut up, Bobby Lee," The Misfit said. "It's no real pleasure in life."

Questions

1. How early in the story does O'Connor foreshadow what will happen in the end? What further hints does she give us along the way? How does the scene at Red Sammy's Barbecue advance the story toward its conclusion?

2. When we first meet the grandmother, what kind of person is she? What do her various remarks reveal about her? Does she remain a static character, or does she change in any way as the story goes on?

3. When the grandmother's head clears for an instant (paragraph 138), what does she suddenly understand? Reread this passage carefully and prepare to discuss what it means.

4. What do we learn from the conversation between The Misfit and the grandmother while the others go out to the woods? How would you describe The Misfit's outlook on the world? Compare it with the author's, from whatever you know about Flannery O'Connor and from the story itself.

5. How would you respond to a reader who complained, "The title of this story is just an obvious platitude"?

Revelation 1965

The doctor's waiting room, which was very small, was almost full when the Turpins entered and Mrs. Turpin, who was very large, made it look even smaller by her presence. She stood looming at the head of the magazine table set in the center of it, a living demonstration that the room was inadequate and ridiculous. Her little bright black eyes took in all the patients as she sized up the seating situation. There was one vacant chair and a place on a sofa occupied by a blond child in a dirty blue romper who should have been told to move over and make room for the lady. He was five or six, but Mrs. Turpin saw at once that no one was going to tell him to move over. He was slumped down in the seat, his arms idle at his sides and his eyes idle in his head; his nose ran unchecked.

Mrs. Turpin put a firm hand on Claud's shoulder and said in a voice that included anyone who wanted to listen, "Claud, you sit in that chair there," and gave him a push down into the vacant one. Claud was florid and bald and sturdy, somewhat shorter than Mrs. Turpin, but he sat down as if he were accustomed to doing what she told him to.

Mrs. Turpin remained standing. The only man in the room besides Claud was a lean stringy old fellow with a rusty hand spread out on each knee, whose eyes were closed as if he were asleep or dead or pretending to be so as not to get up and offer her his seat. Her gaze settled agreeably on a well-dressed grey-haired lady whose eyes met hers and whose expression said: if that child belonged to me, he would have some manners and move over—there's plenty of room there for you and him too.

Claud looked up with a sigh and made as if to rise.

"Sit down," Mrs. Turpin said. "You know you're not supposed to stand on that leg. He has an ulcer on his leg," she explained.   5

Claud lifted his foot onto the magazine table and rolled his trouser leg up to reveal a purple swelling on a plump marble-white calf.

"My!" the pleasant lady said. "How did you do that?"

"A cow kicked him," Mrs. Turpin said.

"Goodness!" said the lady.

Claud rolled his trouser leg down.   10

"Maybe the little boy would move over," the lady suggested, but the child did not stir.

"Somebody will be leaving in a minute," Mrs. Turpin said. She could not understand why a doctor—with as much money as they made charging five dollars a day to just stick their head in the hospital door and look at you—couldn't afford a decent-sized waiting room. This one was hardly bigger than a garage. The table was cluttered with limp-looking magazines and at one end of it there was a big green glass ash tray full of cigaret butts and cotton wads with little blood spots on them. If she had had anything to do with the running of the place, that would have been emptied every so often. There were no chairs against the wall at the head of the room. It had a rectangular-shaped panel in it that permitted a view of the office where the nurse came and went and the secretary listened to the radio. A plastic fern in a gold pot sat in the opening and trailed its fronds down almost to the floor. The radio was softly playing gospel music.

Just then the inner door opened and a nurse with the highest stack of yellow hair Mrs. Turpin had ever seen put her face in the crack and called for the next patient. The woman sitting beside Claud grasped the two arms of her chair and hoisted herself up; she pulled her dress free from her legs and lumbered through the door where the nurse had disappeared.

Mrs. Turpin eased into the vacant chair, which held her tight as a corset. "I wish I could reduce," she said, and rolled her eyes and gave a comic sigh.

"Oh, *you* aren't fat," the stylish lady said. 15

"Ooooo I am too," Mrs. Turpin said. "Claud he eats all he wants to and never weighs over one hundred and seventy-five pounds, but me I just look at something good to eat and I gain some weight," and her stomach and shoulders shook with laughter. "You can eat all you want to, can't you, Claud?" she asked, turning to him.

Claud only grinned.

"Well, as long as you have such a good disposition," the stylish lady said, "I don't think it makes a bit of difference what size you are. You just can't beat a good disposition."

Next to her was a fat girl of eighteen or nineteen, scowling into a thick blue book which Mrs. Turpin saw was entitled *Human Development*. The girl raised her head and directed her scowl at Mrs. Turpin as if she did not like her looks. She appeared annoyed that anyone should speak while she tried to read. The poor girl's face was blue with acne and Mrs. Turpin thought how pitiful it was to have a face like that at that age. She gave the girl a friendly smile but the girl only scowled the harder. Mrs. Turpin herself was fat but she had always had good skin, and, though she was forty-seven years old, there was not a wrinkle in her face except around her eyes from laughing too much.

Next to the ugly girl was the child, still in exactly the same position, and next 20 to him was a thin leathery old woman in a cotton print dress. She and Claud had three sacks of chicken feed in their pump house that was in the same print. She had seen from the first that the child belonged with the old woman. She could tell by the way they sat—kind of vacant and white-trashy, as if they would sit there until Doomsday if nobody called and told them to get up. And at right angles but next to the well-dressed pleasant lady was a lank-faced woman who was certainly the child's mother. She had on a yellow sweat shirt and wine-colored slacks, both gritty-looking, and the rims of her lips were stained with snuff. Her dirty yellow hair was tied behind with a little piece of red paper ribbon. Worse than niggers any day, Mrs. Turpin thought.

The gospel hymn playing was, "When I looked up and He looked down," and Mrs. Turpin, who knew it, supplied the last line mentally, "And wona these days I know I'll we-eara crown."

Without appearing to, Mrs. Turpin always noticed people's feet. The well-dressed lady had red and grey suede shoes to match her dress. Mrs. Turpin had on her good black patent leather pumps. The ugly girl had on Girl Scout shoes and heavy socks. The old woman had on tennis shoes and the white-trashy mother had on what appeared to be bedroom slippers, black straw with gold braid threaded through them—exactly what you would have expected her to have on.

Sometimes at night when she couldn't go to sleep, Mrs. Turpin would occupy herself with the question of who she would have chosen to be if she couldn't have been herself. If Jesus had said to her before he made her, "There's only two places available for you. You can either be a nigger or white-trash," what would she have said? "Please, Jesus, please," she would have said, "just let me wait until there's another place available," and he would have said, "No, you have to go right now and I have only those two places so make up your mind." She would have wiggled and squirmed and begged and pleaded but it would have been no use and finally she would have said, "All right, make me a nigger then—but that don't mean a trashy one." And he would have made her a neat clean respectable Negro woman, herself but black.

Next to the child's mother was a red-headed youngish woman, reading one of the magazines and working a piece of chewing gum, hell for leather, as Claud would say. Mrs. Turpin could not see the woman's feet. She was not white-trash, just common. Sometimes Mrs. Turpin occupied herself at night naming the classes of people. On the bottom of the heap were most colored people, not the kind she would have been if she had been one, but most of them; then next to them—not above, just away from— were the white-trash; then above them were the home-owners, and above them the home-and-land owners, to which she and Claud belonged. Above she and Claud were people with a lot of money and much bigger houses and much more land. But here the complexity of it would begin to bear in on her, for some of the people with a lot of money were common and ought to be below she and Claud and some of the people who had good blood had lost their money and had to rent and then there were colored people who owned their homes and land as well. There was a colored dentist in town who had two red Lincolns and a swimming pool and a farm with registered white-face cattle on it. Usually by the time she had fallen asleep all the classes of people were moiling and roiling around in her head, and she would dream they were all crammed in together in a box car, being ridden off to be put in a gas oven.

"That's a beautiful clock," she said and nodded to her right. It was a big wall   25
clock, the face encased in a brass sunburst.

"Yes, it's very pretty," the stylish lady said agreeably. "And right on the dot too," she added, glancing at her watch.

The ugly girl beside her cast an eye upward at the clock, smirked, then looked directly at Mrs. Turpin and smirked again. Then she returned her eyes to her book. She was obviously the lady's daughter because, although they didn't look anything alike as to disposition, they both had the same shape of face and the same blue eyes. On the lady they sparkled pleasantly but in the girl's seared face they appeared alternately to smolder and to blaze.

What if Jesus had said, "All right, you can be white-trash or a nigger or ugly"!

Mrs. Turpin felt an awful pity for the girl, though she thought it was one thing to be ugly and another to act ugly.

The woman with the snuff-stained lips turned around in her chair and looked up at   30
the clock. Then she turned back and appeared to look a little to the side of Mrs. Turpin. There was a cast in one of her eyes. "You want to know wher you can get you one of themther clocks?" she asked in a loud voice.

"No, I already have a nice clock," Mrs. Turpin said. Once somebody like her got a leg in the conversation, she would be all over it.

"You can get you one with green stamps," the woman said. "That's most likely wher he got hisn. Save you up enough, you can get you most anythang. I got me some joo'ry."

Ought to have got you a wash rag and some soap, Mrs. Turpin thought.

"I get contour sheets with mine," the pleasant lady said.

The daughter slammed her book shut. She looked straight in front of her,   35
directly through Mrs. Turpin and on through the yellow curtain and the plate glass window which made the wall behind her. The girl's eyes seemed lit all of a sudden with a peculiar light, an unnatural light like night road signs give. Mrs. Turpin turned her head to see if there was anything going on outside that she should see, but she could not see anything. Figures passing cast only a pale shadow through the curtain. There was no reason the girl should single her out for her ugly looks.

"Miss Finley," the nurse said, cracking the door. The gum-chewing woman got up and passed in front of her and Claud and went into the office. She had on red high-heeled shoes.

Directly across the table, the ugly girl's eyes were fixed on Mrs. Turpin as if she had some very special reason for disliking her.

"This is wonderful weather, isn't it?" the girl's mother said.

"It's good weather for cotton if you can get the niggers to pick it," Mrs. Turpin said, "but niggers don't want to pick cotton any more. You can't get the white folks to pick it and now you can't get the niggers—because they got to be right up there with the white folks."

"They gonna *try* anyways," the white-trash woman said, leaning forward.   40

"Do you have one of those cotton-picking machines?" the pleasant lady asked.

"No," Mrs. Turpin said, "they leave half the cotton in the field. We don't have much cotton anyway. If you want to make it farming now, you have to have a little of everything. We got a couple of acres of cotton and a few hogs and chickens and just enough white-face that Claud can look after them himself."

"One thang I don't want," the white-trash woman said, wiping her mouth with the back of her hands. "Hogs. Nasty stinking things, a-gruntin and a-rootin all over the place."

Mrs. Turpin gave her the merest edge of her attention. "Our hogs are not dirty and they don't stink," she said. "They're cleaner than some children I've seen. Their feet never touch the ground. We have a pig-parlor—that's where you raise them on concrete," she explained to the pleasant lady, "and Claud scoots them down with the hose every afternoon and washes off the floor." Cleaner by far than that child right there, she thought. Poor nasty little thing. He had not moved except to put the thumb of his dirty hand into his mouth.

The woman turned her face away from Mrs. Turpin. "I know I wouldn't scoot   45 down no hog with no hose," she said to the wall.

You wouldn't have no hog to scoot down, Mrs. Turpin said to herself.

"A-gruntin and a-rootin and a-groanin," the woman muttered.

"We got a little of everything," Mrs. Turpin said to the pleasant lady. "It's no use in having more than you can handle yourself with help like it is. We found enough niggers to pick our cotton this year but Claud he has to go after them and take them home again in the evening. They can't walk that half a mile. No they can't. I tell you," she said and laughed merrily, "I sure am tired of buttering up niggers, but you got to love em if you want em to work for you. When they come in the morning, I run out and I say, 'Hi yawl this morning?' and when Claud drives them off to the field I just wave to beat the band and they just wave back." And she waved her hand rapidly to illustrate.

"Like you read out of the same book," the lady said, showing she understood perfectly.

"Child, yes," Mrs. Turpin said. "And when they come in from the field, I run out   50 with a bucket of icewater. That's the way it's going to be from now on," she said. "You may as well face it."

"One thang I know," the white-trash woman said. "Two thangs I ain't going to do: love no niggers or scoot down no hog with no hose." And she let out a bark of contempt.

The look that Mrs. Turpin and the pleasant lady exchanged indicated they both understood that you had to *have* certain things before you could *know* certain things.

But every time Mrs. Turpin exchanged a look with the lady, she was aware that the ugly girl's peculiar eyes were still on her, and she had trouble bringing her attention back to the conversation.

"When you got something," she said, "you got to look after it." And when you ain't got a thing but breath and britches, she added to herself, you can afford to come to town every morning and just sit on the Court House coping and spit.

A grotesque revolving shadow passed across the curtain behind her and was thrown palely on the opposite wall. Then a bicycle clattered down against the outside of the building. The door opened and a colored boy glided in with a tray from the drug store. It had two large red and white paper cups on it with tops on them. He was a tall, very black boy in discolored white pants and a green nylon shirt. He was chewing gum slowly, as if to music. He set the tray down in the office opening next to the fern and stuck his head through to look for the secretary. She was not in there. He rested his arms on the ledge and waited, his narrow bottom stuck out, swaying slowly to the left and right. He raised a hand over his head and scratched the base of his skull.

"You see that button there, boy?" Mrs. Turpin said. "You can punch that and   55
she'll come. She's probably in the back somewhere."

"Is thas right?" the boy said agreeably, as if he had never seen the button before. He leaned to the right and put his finger on it. "She sometime out," he said and twisted around to face his audience, his elbows behind him on the counter. The nurse appeared and he twisted back again. She handed him a dollar and he rooted in his pocket and made the change and counted it out to her. She gave him fifteen cents for a tip and he went out with the empty tray. The heavy door swung to slowly and closed at length with the sound of suction. For a moment no one spoke.

"They ought to send all them niggers back to Africa," the white-trash woman said. "That's wher they come from in the first place."

"Oh, I couldn't do without my good colored friends," the pleasant lady said.

"There's a heap of things worse than a nigger," Mrs. Turpin agreed. "It's all kinds of them just like it's all kinds of us."

"Yes, and it takes all kinds to make the world go round," the lady said in her   60
musical voice.

As she said it, the raw-complexioned girl snapped her teeth together. Her lower lip turned downwards and inside out, revealing the pale pink inside of her mouth. After a second it rolled back up. It was the ugliest face Mrs. Turpin had ever seen anyone make and for a moment she was certain that the girl had made it at her. She was looking at her as if she had known and disliked her all her life—all of Mrs. Turpin's life, it seemed too, not just all the girl's life. Why, girl, I don't even know you, Mrs. Turpin said silently.

She forced her attention back to the discussion. "It wouldn't be practical to send them back to Africa," she said. "They wouldn't want to go. They got it too good here."

"Wouldn't be what they wanted—if I had anythang to do with it," the woman said.

"It wouldn't be a way in the world you could get all the niggers back over there," Mrs. Turpin said. "They'd be hiding out and lying down and turning sick on you and wailing and hollering and raring and pitching. It wouldn't be a way in the world to get them over there."

"They got over here," the trashy woman said. "Get back like they got over."   65

"It wasn't so many of them then," Mrs. Turpin explained.

The woman looked at Mrs. Turpin as if here was an idiot indeed but Mrs. Turpin was not bothered by the look, considering where it came from.

"Nooo," she said, "they're going to stay here where they can go to New York and marry white folks and improve their color. That's what they all want to do, every one of them, improve their color."

"You know what comes of that, don't you?" Claud asked.

"No, Claud, what?" Mrs. Turpin said.

Claud's eyes twinkled. "White-faced niggers," he said with never a smile.

Everybody in the office laughed except the white-trash and the ugly girl. The girl gripped the book in her lap with white fingers. The trashy woman looked around her from face to face as if she thought they were all idiots. The old woman in the feed sack dress continued to gaze expressionless across the floor at the hightop shoes of the man opposite her, the one who had been pretending to be asleep when the Turpins came in. He was laughing heartily, his hands still spread out on his knees. The child had fallen to the side and was lying now almost face down in the old woman's lap.

While they recovered from their laughter, the nasal chorus on the radio kept the room from silence.

"You go to blank blank
And I'll go to mine
But we'll all blank along
To-geth-ther,
And all along the blank
We'll hep eachother out
Smile-ling in any kind of
Weath-ther!"

Mrs. Turpin didn't catch every word but she caught enough to agree with the spirit of the song and it turned her thoughts sober. To help anybody out that needed it was her philosophy of life. She never spared herself when she found somebody in need, whether they were white or black, trash or decent. And of all she had to be thankful for, she was most thankful that this was so. If Jesus had said, "You can be high society and have all the money you want and be thin and svelte-like, but you can't be a good woman with it," she would have had to say, "Well don't make me that then. Make me a good woman and it don't matter what else, how fat or how ugly or how poor!" Her heart rose. He had not made her a nigger or white-trash or ugly! He had made her herself and given her a little of everything. Jesus, thank you! she said. Thank you thank you thank you! Whenever she counted her blessings she felt as buoyant as if she weighed one hundred and twenty-five pounds instead of one hundred and eighty.

"What's wrong with your little boy?" the pleasant lady asked the white-trashy woman.

"He has a ulcer," the woman said proudly. "He ain't give me a minute's peace since he was born. Him and her are just alike," she said, nodding at the old woman, who was running her leathery fingers through the child's pale hair. "Look like I can't get nothing down them two but Co' Cola and candy."

That's all you try to get down em, Mrs. Turpin said to herself. Too lazy to light the fire. There was nothing you could tell her about people like them that she didn't know already. And it was not just that they didn't have anything. Because if you gave them everything, in two weeks it would all be broken or filthy or they would have chopped it up for lightwood. She knew all this from her own experience. Help them you must, but help them you couldn't.

All at once the ugly girl turned her lips inside out again. Her eyes were fixed like two drills on Mrs. Turpin. This time there was no mistaking that there was something urgent behind them.

Girl, Mrs. Turpin exclaimed silently, I haven't done a thing to you! The girl 80 might be confusing her with somebody else. There was no need to sit by and let herself be intimidated. "You must be in college," she said boldly, looking directly at the girl. "I see you reading a book there."

The girl continued to stare and pointedly did not answer.

Her mother blushed at this rudeness. "The lady asked you a question, Mary Grace," she said under her breath.

"I have ears," Mary Grace said.

The poor mother blushed again. "Mary Grace goes to Wellesley College," she explained. She twisted one of the buttons on her dress. "In Massachusetts," she added with a grimace. "And in the summer she just keeps right on studying. Just reads all the time, a real book worm. She's done real well at Wellesley; she's taking English and Math and History and Psychology and Social Studies," she rattled on, "and I think it's too much. I think she ought to get out and have fun."

The girl looked as if she would like to hurl them all through the plate glass 85 window.

"Way up north," Mrs. Turpin murmured and thought, well, it hasn't done much for her manners.

"I'd almost rather to have him sick," the white-trash woman said, wrenching the attention back to herself. "He's so mean when he ain't. Look like some children just take natural to meanness. It's some gets bad when they get sick but he was the opposite. Took sick and turned good. He don't give me no trouble now. It's me waitin to see the doctor," she said.

If I was going to send anybody back to Africa, Mrs. Turpin thought, it would be your kind, woman. "Yes, indeed," she said aloud, but looking up at the ceiling, "it's a heap of things worse than a nigger." And dirtier than a hog, she added to herself.

"I think people with bad dispositions are more to be pitied than anyone on earth," the pleasant lady said in a voice that was decidedly thin.

"I thank the Lord he has blessed me with a good one," Mrs. Turpin said. "The 90 day has never dawned that I couldn't find something to laugh at."

"Not since she married me anyways," Claud said with a comical straight face.

Everybody laughed except the girl and the white-trash.

Mrs. Turpin's stomach shook. "He's such a caution," she said, "that I can't help but laugh at him."

The girl made a loud ugly noise through her teeth.

Her mother's mouth grew thin and straight. "I think the worst thing in the 95 world," she said, "is an ungrateful person. To have everything and not appreciate it. I know a girl," she said, "who has parents who would give her anything, a little brother who loves her dearly, who is getting a good education, who wears the best clothes, but who can never say a kind word to anyone, who never smiles, who just criticizes and complains all day long."

"Is she too old to paddle?" Claud asked.

The girl's face was almost purple.

"Yes," the lady said, "I'm afraid there's nothing to do but leave her to her folly. Some day she'll wake up and it'll be too late."

"It never hurt anyone to smile," Mrs. Turpin said. "It just makes you feel better all over."

"Of course," the lady said sadly, "but there are just some people you can't tell 100 anything to. They can't take criticism."

"If it's one thing I am," Mrs. Turpin said with feeling, "it's grateful. When I think who all I could have been besides myself and what all I got, a little of everything, and a good disposition besides, I just feel like shouting, 'Thank you, Jesus, for making everything the way it is!' It could have been different!" For one thing, somebody else could have got Claud. At the thought of this, she was flooded with gratitude and a terrible pang of joy ran through her. "Oh thank you, Jesus, Jesus, thank you!" she cried aloud.

The book struck her directly over her left eye. It struck almost at the same instant that she realized the girl was about to hurl it. Before she could utter a sound, the raw face came crashing across the table toward her, howling. The girl's fingers sank like clamps into the soft flesh of her neck. She heard the mother cry out and Claud shout, "Whoa!" There was an instant when she was certain that she was about to be in an earthquake.

All at once her vision narrowed and she saw everything as if it were happening in a small room far away, or as if she were looking at it through the wrong end of a telescope. Claud's face crumpled and fell out of sight. The nurse ran in, then out, then in again. Then the gangling figure of the doctor rushed out of the inner door. Magazines flew this way and that as the table turned over. The girl fell with a thud and Mrs. Turpin's vision suddenly reversed itself and she saw everything large instead of small. The eyes of the white-trashy woman were staring hugely at the floor. There the girl, held down on one side by the nurse and on the other by her mother, was wrenching and turning in their grasp. The doctor was kneeling astride her, trying to hold her arm down. He managed after a second to sink a long needle into it.

Mrs. Turpin felt entirely hollow except for her heart which swung from side to side as if it were agitated in a great empty drum of flesh.

"Somebody that's not busy call for the ambulance," the doctor said in the off- 105 hand voice young doctors adopt for terrible occasions.

Mrs. Turpin could not have moved a finger. The old man who had been sitting next to her skipped nimbly into the office and made the call, for the secretary still seemed to be gone.

"Claud!" Mrs. Turpin called.

He was not in his chair. She knew she must jump up and find him but she felt like some one trying to catch a train in a dream, when everything moves in slow motion and the faster you try to run the slower you go.

"Here I am," a suffocated voice, very unlike Claud's, said.

He was doubled up in the corner on the floor, pale as paper, holding his leg. She 110 wanted to get up and go to him but she could not move. Instead, her gaze was drawn slowly downward to the churning face on the floor, which she could see over the doctor's shoulder.

The girl's eyes stopped rolling and focused on her. They seemed a much lighter blue than before, as if a door that had been tightly closed behind them was now open to admit light and air.

Mrs. Turpin's head cleared and her power of motion returned. She leaned forward until she was looking directly into the fierce brilliant eyes. There was no doubt in her mind that the girl did know her, knew her in some intense and personal way, beyond time and place and condition. "What you got to say to me?" she asked hoarsely and held her breath, waiting, as for a revelation.

The girl raised her head. Her gaze locked with Mrs. Turpin's. "Go back to hell where you came from, you old wart hog," she whispered. Her voice was low but clear.

Her eyes burned for a moment as if she saw with pleasure that her message had struck its target.

Mrs. Turpin sank back in her chair.

After a moment the girl's eyes closed and she turned her head wearily to the side.   115

The doctor rose and handed the nurse the empty syringe. He leaned over and put both hands for a moment on the mother's shoulders, which were shaking. She was sitting on the floor, her lips pressed together, holding Mary Grace's hand in her lap. The girl's fingers were gripped like a baby's around her thumb. "Go on to the hospital," he said. "I'll call and make the arrangements."

"Now let's see that neck," he said in a jovial voice to Mrs. Turpin. He began to inspect her neck with his first two fingers. Two little moon-shaped lines like pink fish bones were indented over her windpipe. There was the beginning of an angry red swelling above her eye. His fingers passed over this also.

"Lea' me be," she said thickly and shook him off. "See about Claud. She kicked him."

"I'll see about him in a minute," he said and felt her pulse. He was a thin grey-haired man, given to pleasantries. "Go home and have yourself a vacation the rest of the day," he said and patted her on the shoulder.

Quit your pattin me, Mrs. Turpin growled to herself.   120

"And put an ice pack over that eye," he said. Then he went and squatted down beside Claud and looked at his leg. After a moment he pulled him up and Claud limped after him into the office.

Until the ambulance came, the only sounds in the room were the tremulous moans of the girl's mother, who continued to sit on the floor. The white-trash woman did not take her eyes off the girl. Mrs. Turpin looked straight ahead at nothing. Presently the ambulance drew up, a long dark shadow, behind the curtain. The attendants came in and set the stretcher down beside the girl and lifted her expertly onto it and carried her out. The nurse helped the mother gather up her things. The shadow of the ambulance moved silently away and the nurse came back in the office.

"That ther girl is going to be a lunatic, ain't she?" the white-trash woman asked the nurse, but the nurse kept on to the back and never answered her.

"Yes, she's going to be a lunatic," the white-trash woman said to the rest of them.

"Po' critter," the old woman murmured. The child's face was still in her lap. His   125 eyes looked idly out over her knees. He had not moved during the disturbance except to draw one leg up under him.

"I thank Gawd," the white-trash woman said fervently, "I ain't a lunatic."

Claud came limping out and the Turpins went home.

As their pick-up truck turned into their own dirt road and made the crest of the hill, Mrs. Turpin gripped the window ledge and looked out suspiciously. The land sloped gracefully down through a field dotted with lavender weeds and at the start of the rise their small yellow frame house, with its little flower beds spread out around it like a fancy apron, sat primly in its accustomed place between two giant hickory trees. She would not have been startled to see a burnt wound between two blackened chimneys.

Neither of them felt like eating so they put on their house clothes and lowered the shade in the bedroom and lay down, Claud with his leg on a pillow and herself with a damp washcloth over her eye. The instant she was flat on her back, the image of a razor-backed hog with warts on its face and horns coming out behind its ears snorted into her head. She moaned, a low quiet moan.

"I am not," she said tearfully, "a wart hog. From hell." But the denial had no force. 130
The girl's eyes and her words, even the tone of her voice, low but clear, directed only to
her, brooked no repudiation. She had been singled out for the message, though there
was trash in the room to whom it might justly have been applied. The full force of this
fact struck her only now. There was a woman there who was neglecting her own child
but she had been overlooked. The message had been given to Ruby Turpin, a respectable, hard-working, church-going woman. The tears dried. Her eyes began to burn
instead with wrath.

She rose on her elbow and the washcloth fell into her hand. Claud was lying on his
back, snoring. She wanted to tell him what the girl had said. At the same time, she did
not wish to put the image of herself as a wart hog from hell into his mind.

"Hey, Claud," she muttered and pushed his shoulder.

Claud opened one pale baby blue eye.

She looked into it warily. He did not think about anything. He just went his way.

"Wha, whasit?" he said and closed the eye again. 135

"Nothing," she said. "Does your leg pain you?"

"Hurts like hell," Claud said.

"It'll quit terreckly," she said and lay back down. In a moment Claud was snoring
again. For the rest of the afternoon they lay there. Claud slept. She scowled at the
ceiling. Occasionally she raised her fist and made a small stabbing motion over her
chest as if she was defending her innocence to invisible guests who were like the
comforters of Job, reasonable-seeming but wrong.

About five-thirty Claud stirred. "Got to go after those niggers," he sighed, not
moving.

She was looking straight up as if there were unintelligible handwriting on the 140
ceiling. The protuberance over her eye had turned a greenish-blue. "Listen here," she
said.

"What?"

"Kiss me."

Claud leaned over and kissed her loudly on the mouth. He pinched her side and
their hands interlocked. Her expression of ferocious concentration did not change.
Claud got up, groaning and growling, and limped off. She continued to study the
ceiling.

She did not get up until she heard the pick-up truck coming back with the
Negroes. Then she rose and thrust her feet in her brown oxfords, which she did not
bother to lace, and stumped out onto the back porch and got her red plastic bucket.
She emptied a tray of ice cubes into it and filled it half full of water and went out into
the back yard. Every afternoon after Claud brought the hands in, one of the boys
helped him put out hay and the rest waited in the back of the truck until he was
ready to take them home. The truck was parked in the shade under one of the hickory trees.

"Hi yawl this evening?" Mrs. Turpin asked grimly, appearing with the bucket 145
and the dipper. There were three women and a boy in the truck.

"Us doin nicely," the oldest woman said. "Hi you doin?" and her gaze stuck immediately on the dark lump on Mrs. Turpin's forehead. "You done fell down, ain't you?"
she asked in a solicitous voice. The old woman was dark and almost toothless. She had
on an old felt hat of Claud's set back on her head. The other two women were younger
and lighter and they both had new bright green sun hats. One of them had hers on her
head; the other had taken hers off and the boy was grinning beneath it.

Mrs. Turpin set the bucket down on the floor of the truck. "Yawl hep your-selves," she said. She looked around to make sure Claud had gone. "No. I didn't fall down," she said, folding her arms. "It was something worse than that."

"Ain't nothing bad happen to you!" the old woman said. She said it as if they all knew Mrs. Turpin was protected in some special way by Divine Providence. "You just had you a little fall."

"We were in town at the doctor's office for where the cow kicked Mr. Turpin," Mrs. Turpin said in a flat tone that indicated they could leave off their foolishness. "And there was this girl there. A big fat girl with her face all broke out. I could look at that girl and tell she was peculiar but I couldn't tell how. And me and her mama were just talking and going along and all of a sudden WHAM! She throws this big book she was reading at me and . . ."

"Naw!" the old woman cried out.   150

"And then she jumps over the table and commences to choke me."

"Naw!" they all exclaimed, "naw!"

"Hi come she do that?" the old woman asked. "What ail her?"

Mrs. Turpin only glared in front of her.

"Somethin ail her," the old woman said.   155

"They carried her off in an ambulance," Mrs. Turpin continued, "but before she went she was rolling on the floor and they were trying to hold her down to give her a shot and she said something to me." She paused. "You know what she said to me?"

"What she say?" they asked.

"She said," Mrs. Turpin began, and stopped, her face very dark and heavy. The sun was getting whiter and whiter, blanching the sky overhead so that the leaves of the hickory tree were black in the face of it. She could not bring forth the words. "Something real ugly," she muttered.

"She sho shouldn't said nothin ugly to you," the old woman said. "You so sweet. You the sweetest lady I know."

"She pretty too," the one with the hat on said.   160

"And stout," the other one said. "I never knowed no sweeter white lady."

"That's the truth befo' Jesus," the old woman said. "Amen! You des as sweet and pretty as you can be."

Mrs. Turpin knew just exactly how much Negro flattery was worth and it added to her rage. "She said," she began again and finished this time with a fierce rush of breath, "that I was an old wart hog from hell."

There was an astounded silence.

"Where she at?" the youngest woman cried in a piercing voice.   165

"Lemme see her. I'll kill her!"

"I'll kill her with you!" the other one cried.

"She b'long in the sylum," the old woman said emphatically. "You the sweetest white lady I know."

"She pretty too," the other two said. "Stout as she can be and sweet. Jesus satisfied with her!"

"Deed he is," the old woman declared.   170

Idiots! Mrs. Turpin growled to herself. You could never say anything intelligent to a nigger. You could talk at them but not with them. "Yawl ain't drunk your water," she said shortly. "Leave the bucket in the truck when you're finished with it. I got more to do than just stand around and pass the time of day," and she moved off and into the house.

She stood for a moment in the middle of the kitchen. The dark protuberance over her eye looked like a miniature tornado cloud which might any moment sweep across the horizon of her brow. Her lower lip protruded dangerously. She squared her massive shoulders. Then she marched into the front of the house and out the side door and started down the road to the pig parlor. She had the look of a woman going single-handed, weaponless, into battle.

The sun was a deep yellow now like a harvest moon and was riding westward very fast over the far tree line as if it meant to reach the hogs before she did. The road was rutted and she kicked several good-sized stones out of her path as she strode along. The pig parlor was on a little knoll at the end of a lane that ran off from the side of the barn. It was a square of concrete as large as a small room, with a board fence about four feet high around it. The concrete floor sloped slightly so that the hog wash could drain off into a trench where it was carried to the field for fertilizer. Claud was standing on the outside, on the edge of the concrete, hanging onto the top board, hosing down the floor inside. The hose was connected to the faucet of a water trough nearby.

Mrs. Turpin climbed up beside him and glowered down at the hogs inside. There were seven long-snouted bristly shoats in it—tan with liver-colored spots—and an old sow a few weeks off from farrowing. She was lying on her side grunting. The shoats were running about shaking themselves like idiot children, their little slit pig eyes searching the floor for anything left. She had read that pigs were the most intelligent animal. She doubted it. They were supposed to be smarter than dogs. There had even been a pig astronaut. He had performed his assignment perfectly but died of a heart attack afterwards because they left him in his electric suit, sitting upright throughout his examination when naturally a hog should be on all fours.

A-gruntin and a-rootin and a-groanin. 175

"Gimme that hose," she said, yanking it away from Claud. "Go on and carry them niggers home and then get off that leg."

"You look like you might have swallowed a mad dog," Claud observed, but he got down and limped off. He paid no attention to her humors.

Until he was out of earshot, Mrs. Turpin stood on the side of the pen, holding the hose and pointing the stream of water at the hind quarters of any shoat that looked as if it might try to lie down. When he had had time to get over the hill, she turned her head slightly and her wrathful eyes scanned the path. He was nowhere in sight. She turned back again and seemed to gather herself up. Her shoulders rose and she drew in her breath.

"What do you send me a message like that for?" she said in a low fierce voice, barely above a whisper but with the force of a shout in its concentrated fury. "How am I a hog and me both? How am I saved and from hell too?" Her free fist was knotted and with the other she gripped the hose, blindly pointing the stream of water in and out of the eye of the old sow whose outraged squeal she did not hear.

The pig parlor commanded a view of the back pasture where their twenty beef 180 cows were gathered around the hay-bales Claud and the boy had put out. The freshly cut pasture sloped down to the highway. Across it was their cotton field and beyond that a dark green dusty wood which they owned as well. The sun was behind the wood, very red, looking over the paling of trees like a farmer inspecting his own hogs.

"Why me?" she rumbled. "It's no trash around here, black or white, that I haven't given to. And break my back to the bone every day working. And do for the church."

She appeared to be the right size woman to command the arena before her. "How am I a hog?" she demanded. "Exactly how am I like them?" and she jabbed the stream of water at the shoats. "There was plenty of trash there. It didn't have to be me."

"If you like trash better, go get yourself some trash then," she railed. "You could have made me trash. Or a nigger. If trash is what you wanted why didn't you make me trash?" She shook her fist with the hose in it and a watery snake appeared momentarily in the air. "I could quit working and take it easy and be filthy," she growled. "Lounge about the sidewalks all day drinking root beer. Dip snuff and spit in every puddle and have it all over my face. I could be nasty.

"Or you could have made me a nigger. It's too late for me to be a nigger," she said with deep sarcasm, "but I could act like one. Lay down in the middle of the road and stop traffic. Roll on the ground."

In the deepening light everything was taking on a mysterious hue. The pasture 185 was growing a peculiar glassy green and the streak of highway had turned lavender. She braced herself for a final assault and this time her voice rolled out over the pasture. "Go on," she yelled, "call me a hog! Call me a hog again. From hell. Call me a wart hog from hell. Put that bottom rail on top. There'll still be a top and bottom!"

A garbled echo returned to her.

A final surge of fury shook her and she roared, "Who do you think you are?"

The color of everything, field and crimson sky, burned for a moment with a transparent intensity. The question carried over the pasture and across the highway and the cotton field and returned to her clearly like an answer from beyond the wood.

She opened her mouth but no sound came out of it.

A tiny truck, Claud's, appeared on the highway, heading rapidly out of sight. Its 190 gears scraped thinly. It looked like a child's toy. At any moment a bigger truck might smash into it and scatter Claud's and the niggers' brains all over the road.

Mrs. Turpin stood there, her gaze fixed on the highway, all her muscles rigid, until in five or six minutes the truck reappeared, returning. She waited until it had had time to turn into their own road. Then like a monumental statue coming to life, she bent her head slowly and gazed, as if through the very heart of mystery, down into the pig parlor at the hogs. They had settled all in one corner around the old sow who was grunting softly. A red glow suffused them. They appeared to pant with a secret life.

Until the sun slipped finally behind the tree line, Mrs. Turpin remained there with her gaze bent to them as if she were absorbing some abysmal life-giving knowledge. At last she lifted her head. There was only a purple streak in the sky, cutting through a field of crimson and leading, like an extension of the highway, into the descending dusk. She raised her hands from the side of the pen in a gesture hieratic and profound. A visionary light settled in her eyes. She saw the streak as a vast swinging bridge extending upward from the earth through a field of living fire. Upon it a vast horde of souls were rumbling toward heaven. There were whole companies of white-trash, clean for the first time in their lives, and bands of black niggers in white robes, and battalions of freaks and lunatics shouting and clapping and leaping like frogs. And bringing up the end of the procession was a tribe of people whom she recognized at once as those who, like herself and Claud, had always had a little of everything and the God-given wit to use it right. She leaned forward to observe them closer. They were marching behind the others with great dignity, accountable as they had always been for good order and common sense and respectable behavior. They alone were on key. Yet she could see by their shocked and altered faces that even their virtues were being burned away. She lowered her hands and gripped the rail of the hog pen, her eyes small but fixed unblinkingly on what lay ahead. In a moment the vision faded but she remained where she was, immobile.

At length she got down and turned off the faucet and made her slow way on the darkening path to the house. In the woods around her the invisible cricket choruses had struck up, but what she heard were the voices of the souls climbing upward into the starry field and shouting hallelujah.

Questions

1. How does Mrs. Turpin see herself before Mary Grace calls her a wart hog?
2. What is the narrator's attitude toward Mrs. Turpin in the beginning of the story? How can you tell? Does this attitude change, or stay the same, at the end?
3. Describe the relationship between Mary Grace and her mother. What annoying platitudes does the mother mouth? Which of Mrs. Turpin's opinions seem especially to anger Mary Grace?
4. Sketch the plot of the story. What moment or event do you take to be the crisis, or turning point? What is the climax? What is the conclusion?
5. What do you infer from Mrs. Turpin's conversation with the black farm workers? Is she their friend? Why does she now find their flattery unacceptable ("Jesus satisfied with her")?
6. When, near the end of the story, Mrs. Turpin roars "Who do you think you are?" an echo "returned to her clearly like an answer from beyond the wood" (paragraph 188). Explain.
7. What is the final revelation given to Mrs. Turpin? (To state it is to state the theme of the story.) What new attitude does the revelation impart? (How is Mrs. Turpin left with a new vision of humanity?)
8. Other stories in this book contain revelations: "Young Goodman Brown," "The Gospel According to Mark." If you have read them, try to sum up the supernatural revelation made to the central character in each story. In each, is the revelation the same as a statement of the story's main theme?

Parker's Back[1]   1965

Parker's wife was sitting on the front porch floor, snapping beans. Parker was sitting on the step, some distance away, watching her sullenly. She was plain, plain. The skin on her face was thin and drawn as tight as the skin on an onion and her eyes were gray and sharp like the points of two icepicks. Parker understood why he had married her—he couldn't have got her any other way—but he couldn't understand why he stayed with her now. She was pregnant and pregnant women were not his favorite kind. Nevertheless, he stayed as if she had him conjured. He was puzzled and ashamed of himself.

The house they rented sat alone save for a single tall pecan tree on a high embankment overlooking a highway. At intervals a car would shoot past below and his wife's eyes would swerve suspiciously after the sound of it and then come back to rest on the newspaper full of beans in her lap. One of the things she did not approve of was automobiles. In addition to her other bad qualities, she was forever sniffing up sin. She did not smoke or dip, drink whiskey, use bad language or paint her face, and God knew some paint would have improved it, Parker thought. Her being against color, it was the more remarkable she had married him. Sometimes he supposed that

---

[1]"Parker's Back" was the last story Flannery O'Connor wrote, and was published the year after her death.

she had married him because she meant to save him. At other times he had a suspicion that she actually liked everything she said she didn't. He could account for her one way or another; it was himself he could not understand.

She turned her head in his direction and said, "It's no reason you can't work for a man. It don't have to be a woman."

"Aw shut your mouth for a change," Parker muttered.

If he had been certain she was jealous of the woman he worked for he would have been pleased but more likely she was concerned with the sin that would result if he and the woman took a liking to each other. He had told her that the woman was a hefty young blonde; in fact she was nearly seventy years old and too dried up to have an interest in anything except getting as much work out of him as she could. Not that an old woman didn't sometimes get an interest in a young man, particularly if he was as attractive as Parker felt he was, but this old woman looked at him the same way she looked at her old tractor—as if she had to put up with it because it was all she had. The tractor had broken down the second day Parker was on it and she had set him at once to cutting bushes, saying out of the side of her mouth to the nigger, "Everything he touches, he breaks." She also asked him to wear his shirt when he worked; Parker had removed it even though the day was not sultry; he put it back on reluctantly.

This ugly woman Parker married was his first wife. He had had other women but he had planned never to get himself tied up legally. He had first seen her one morning when his truck broke down on the highway. He had managed to pull it off the road into a neatly swept yard on which sat a peeling two-room house. He got out and opened the hood of the truck and began to study the motor. Parker had an extra sense that told him when there was a woman nearby watching him. After he had leaned over the motor a few minutes, his neck began to prickle. He cast his eye over the empty yard and porch of the house. A woman he could not see was either nearby beyond a clump of honeysuckle or in the house, watching him out the window.

Suddenly Parker began to jump up and down and fling his hand about as if he had mashed it in the machinery. He doubled over and held his hand close to his chest. "God dammit!" he hollered, "Jesus Christ in hell! Jesus God Almighty damm! God dammit to hell!" he went on, flinging out the same few oaths over and over as loud as he could.

Without warning a terrible bristly claw slammed the side of his face and he fell backwards on the hood of the truck. "You don't talk no filth here!" a voice close to him shrilled.

Parker's vision was so blurred that for an instant he thought he had been attacked by some creature from above, a giant hawk-eyed angel wielding a hoary weapon. As his sight cleared, he saw before him a tall raw-boned girl with a broom.

"I hurt my hand," he said. "I HURT my hand." He was so incensed that he forgot that he hadn't hurt his hand. "My hand may be broke," he growled although his voice was still unsteady.

"Lemme see it," the girl demanded.

Parker stuck out his hand and she came closer and looked at it. There was no mark on the palm and she took the hand and turned it over. Her own hand was dry and hot and rough and Parker felt himself jolted back to life by her touch. He looked more closely at her. I don't want nothing to do with this one, he thought.

The girl's sharp eyes peered at the back of the stubby reddish hand she held. There emblazoned in red and blue was a tattooed eagle perched on a cannon.

Parker's sleeve was rolled to the elbow. Above the eagle a serpent was coiled about a shield and in the spaces between the eagle and the serpent there were hearts, some with arrows through them. Above the serpent there was a spread hand of cards. Every space on the skin of Parker's arm, from wrist to elbow, was covered in some loud design. The girl gazed at this with an almost stupefied smile of shock, as if she had accidentally grasped a poisonous snake; she dropped the hand.

"I got most of my other ones in foreign parts," Parker said. "These here I mostly got in the United States. I got my first one when I was only fifteen year old."

"Don't tell me," the girl said, "I don't like it. I ain't got any use for it."   15

"You ought to see the ones you can't see," Parker said and winked.

Two circles of red appeared like apples on the girl's cheeks and softened her appearance. Parker was intrigued. He did not for a minute think that she didn't like the tattoos. He had never yet met a woman who was not attracted to them.

Parker was fourteen when he saw a man in a fair, tattooed from head to foot. Except for his loins which were girded with a panther hide, the man's skin was patterned in what seemed from Parker's distance—he was near the back of the tent, standing on a bench—a single intricate design of brilliant color. The man, who was small and sturdy, moved about on the platform, flexing his muscles so that the arabesque of men and beasts and flowers on his skin appeared to have a subtle motion of its own. Parker was filled with emotion, lifted up as some people are when the flag passes. He was a boy whose mouth habitually hung open. He was heavy and earnest, as ordinary as a loaf of bread. When the show was over, he had remained standing on the bench, staring where the tattooed man had been, until the tent was almost empty.

Parker had never before felt the least motion of wonder in himself. Until he saw the man at the fair, it did not enter his head that there was anything out of the ordinary about the fact that he existed. Even then it did not enter his head, but a peculiar unease settled in him. It was as if a blind boy had been turned so gently in a different direction that he did not know his destination had been changed.

He had his first tattoo some time after—the eagle perched on the cannon. It was   20
done by a local artist. It hurt very little, just enough to make it appear to Parker to be worth doing. This was peculiar too for before he had thought that only what did not hurt was worth doing. The next year he quit school because he was sixteen and could. He went to the trade school for a while, then he quit the trade school and worked for six months in a garage. The only reason he worked at all was to pay for more tattoos. His mother worked in a laundry and could support him, but she would not pay for any tattoo except her name on a heart, which he had put on, grumbling. However, her name was Betty Jean and nobody had to know it was his mother. He found out that the tattoos were attractive to the kind of girls he liked but who had never liked him before. He began to drink beer and get in fights. His mother wept over what was becoming of him. One night she dragged him off to a revival with her, not telling him where they were going. When he saw the big lighted church, he jerked out of her grasp and ran. The next day he lied about his age and joined the navy.

Parker was large for the tight sailor's pants but the silly white cap, sitting low on his forehead, made his face by contrast look thoughtful and almost intense. After a month or two in the navy, his mouth ceased to hang open. His features hardened into the features of a man. He stayed in the navy five years and seemed a natural part of the grey mechanical ship, except for his eyes, which were the same pale slate-color as the ocean and reflected the immense spaces around him as if they were a microcosm of the mysterious sea. In port Parker wandered about comparing the run-down places he was in to Birmingham, Alabama. Everywhere he went he picked up more tattoos.

He had stopped having lifeless ones like anchors and crossed rifles. He had a tiger and a panther on each shoulder, a cobra coiled about a torch on his chest, hawks on his thighs, Elizabeth II and Philip over where his stomach and liver were respectively. He did not care much what the subject was so long as it was colorful; on his abdomen he had a few obscenities but only because that seemed the proper place for them. Parker would be satisfied with each tattoo about a month, then something about it that had attracted him would wear off. Whenever a decent-sized mirror was available, he would get in front of it and study his overall look. The effect was not of one intricate arabesque of colors but of something haphazard and botched. A huge dissatisfaction would come over him and he would go off and find another tattooist and have another space filled up. The front of Parker was almost completely covered but there were no tattoos on his back. He had no desire for one anywhere he could not readily see it him-self. As the space on the front of him for tattoos decreased, his dissatisfaction grew and became general.

After one of his furloughs, he didn't go back to the navy but remained away without official leave, drunk, in a rooming house in a city he did not know. His dis-satisfaction, from being chronic and latent, had suddenly become acute and raged in him. It was as if the panther and the lion and the serpents and the eagles and the hawks had penetrated his skin and lived inside him in a raging warfare. The navy caught up with him, put him in the brig for nine months and then gave him a dis-honorable discharge.

After that Parker decided that country air was the only kind fit to breathe. He rented the shack on the embankment and bought the old truck and took various jobs which he kept as long as it suited him. At the time he met his future wife, he was buying apples by the bushel and selling them for the same price by the pound to isolated homesteaders on back country roads.

"All that there," the woman said, pointing to his arm, "is no better than what a   25
fool Indian would do. It's a heap of vanity." She seemed to have found the word she wanted. "Vanity of vanities," she said.

Well what the hell do I care what she thinks of it? Parker asked himself, but he was plainly bewildered. "I reckon you like one of these better than another anyway," he said, dallying until he thought of something that would impress her. He thrust the arm back at her. "Which you like best?"

"None of them," she said, "but the chicken is not as bad as the rest."

"What chicken?" Parker almost yelled.

She pointed to the eagle.

"That's an eagle," Parker said. "What fool would waste their time having a   30
chicken put on themself?"

"What fool would have any of it?" the girl said and turned away. She went slowly back to the house and left him there to get going. Parker remained for almost five minutes, looking agape at the dark door she had entered.

The next day he returned with a bushel of apples. He was not one to be outdone by anything that looked like her. He liked women with meat on them, so you didn't feel their muscles, much less their old bones. When he arrived, she was sitting on the top step and the yard was full of children, all as thin and poor as herself; Parker remembered it was Saturday. He hated to be making up to a woman when there were children around, but it was fortunate he had brought the bushel of apples off the truck. As the children approached him to see what he carried, he gave each child an apple and told it to get lost; in that way he cleared out the whole crowd.

The girl did nothing to acknowledge his presence. He might have been a stray pig or goat that had wandered into the yard and she too tired to take up the broom and send it off. He set the bushel of apples down next to her on the step. He sat down on a lower step.

"Hep yourself," he said, nodding at the basket; then he lapsed into silence.

She took an apple quickly as if the basket might disappear if she didn't make   35
haste. Hungry people made Parker nervous. He had always had plenty to eat himself. He grew very uncomfortable. He reasoned he had nothing to say so why should he say it? He could not think now why he had come or why he didn't go before he wasted another bushel of apples on the crowd of children. He supposed they were her brothers and sisters.

She chewed the apple slowly but with a kind of relish of concentration, bent slightly but looking out ahead. The view from the porch stretched off across a long incline studded with iron weed and across the highway to a vast vista of hills and one small mountain. Long views depressed Parker. You look out into space like that and you begin to feel as if someone were after you, the navy or the government or religion.

"Who them children belong to, you?" he said at length.

"I ain't married yet," she said. "They belong to momma." She said it as if it were only a matter of time before she would be married.

Who in God's name would marry her? Parker thought.

A large barefooted woman with a wide gap-toothed face appeared in the door   40
behind Parker. She had apparently been there for several minutes.

"Good evening," Parker said.

The woman crossed the porch and picked up what was left of the bushel of apples. "We thank you," she said and returned with it into the house.

"That your old woman?" Parker muttered.

The girl nodded. Parker knew a lot of sharp things he could have said like "You got my sympathy," but he was gloomily silent. He just sat there, looking at the view. He thought he must be coming down with something.

"If I pick up some peaches tomorrow I'll bring you some," he said.   45

"I'll be much obliged to you," the girl said.

Parker had no intention of taking any basket of peaches back there but the next day he found himself doing it. He and the girl had almost nothing to say to each other. One thing he did say was, "I ain't got any tattoo on my back."

"What you got on it?" the girl said.

"My shirt," Parker said. "Haw."

"Haw, haw," the girl said politely.   50

Parker thought he was losing his mind. He could not believe for a minute that he was attracted to a woman like this. She showed not the least interest in anything but what he brought until he appeared the third time with two cantaloups. "What's your name?" she asked.

"O. E. Parker," he said.

"What does the O. E. stand for?"

"You can just call me O. E.," Parker said. "Or Parker. Don't nobody call me by my name."

"What's it stand for?" she persisted.   55

"Never mind," Parker said. "What's yours?"

"I'll tell you when you tell me what them letters are the short of," she said. There was just a hint of flirtatiousness in her tone and it went rapidly to Parker's head. He had never revealed the name to any man or woman, only to the files of the navy and the government, and it was on his baptismal record which he got at the age of a month; his mother was a Methodist. When the name leaked out of the navy files, Parker narrowly missed killing the man who used it.

"You'll go blab it around," he said.

"I'll swear I'll never tell nobody," she said. "On God's holy word I swear it."

Parker sat for a few minutes in silence. Then he reached for the girl's neck, drew   60
her ear close to his mouth and revealed the name in a low voice.

"Obadiah," she whispered. Her face slowly brightened as if the name came as a sign to her. "Obadiah," she said.

The name still stank in Parker's estimation.

"Obadiah Elihue," she said in a reverent voice.

"If you call me that aloud, I'll bust your head open," Parker said. "What's yours?"

"Sarah Ruth Cates," she said.   65

"Glad to meet you, Sarah Ruth," Parker said.

Sarah Ruth's father was a Straight Gospel preacher but he was away, spreading it in Florida. Her mother did not seem to mind his attention to the girl so long as he brought a basket of something with him when he came. As for Sarah Ruth herself, it was plain to Parker after he had visited three times that she was crazy about him. She liked him even though she insisted that pictures on the skin were vanity of vanities and even after hearing him curse, and even after she had asked him if he was saved and he had replied that he didn't see it was anything in particular to save him from. After that, inspired, Parker had said, "I'd be saved enough if you was to kiss me."

She scowled. "That ain't being saved," she said.

Not long after that she agreed to take a ride in his truck. Parker parked it on a deserted road and suggested to her that they lie down together in the back of it.

"Not until after we're married," she said—just like that.   70

"Oh that ain't necessary," Parker said and as he reached for her, she thrust him away with such force that the door of the truck came off and he found himself flat on his back on the ground. He made up his mind then and there to have nothing further to do with her.

They were married in the County Ordinary's office because Sarah Ruth thought churches were idolatrous. Parker had no opinion about that one way or the other. The Ordinary's office was lined with cardboard file boxes and record books with dusty yellow slips of paper hanging on out of them. The Ordinary was an old woman with red hair who had held office for forty years and looked as dusty as her books. She married them from behind the iron-grill of a stand-up desk and when she finished, she said with a flourish, "Three dollars and fifty cents and till death do you part!" and yanked some forms out of a machine.

Marriage did not change Sarah Ruth a jot and it made Parker gloomier than ever. Every morning he decided he had had enough and would not return that night; every night he returned. Whenever Parker couldn't stand the way he felt, he would have another tattoo, but the only surface left on him now was his back. To see a tattoo on his own back he would have to get two mirrors and stand between them in just the correct position and this seemed to Parker a good way to make an idiot of himself. Sarah Ruth who, if she had had better sense, could have enjoyed a tattoo on his back, would not even look at the ones he had elsewhere. When he attempted to point out especial details of them, she would shut her eyes tight and turn her back as well. Except in total darkness, she preferred Parker dressed and with his sleeves rolled down.

"At the judgement seat of God, Jesus is going to say to you, 'What you been doing all your life besides have pictures drawn all over you?'" she said.

"You don't fool me none," Parker said, "you're just afraid that hefty girl I work for'll   75
like me so much she'll say, 'Come on, Mr. Parker, let's you and me . . .'"

"You're tempting sin," she said, "and at the judgement seat of God you'll have to answer for that too. You ought to go back to selling the fruits of the earth."

Parker did nothing much when he was at home but listen to what the judgement seat of God would be like for him if he didn't change his ways. When he could, he broke in with tales of the hefty girl he worked for. "'Mr. Parker,'" he said she said, 'I hired you for your brains.'" (She had added, "So why don't you use them?")

"And you should have seen her face the first time she saw me without my shirt," he said. "'Mr. Parker,' she said, 'you're a walking panner-rammer!'" This had, in fact, been her remark but it had been delivered out of one side of her mouth.

Dissatisfaction began to grow so great in Parker that there was no containing it outside of a tattoo. It had to be his back. There was no help for it. A dim half-formed inspiration began to work in his mind. He visualized having a tattoo put there that Sarah Ruth would not be able to resist—a religious subject. He thought of an open book with HOLY BIBLE tattooed under it and an actual verse printed on the page. This seemed just the thing for a while; then he began to hear her say, "Ain't I already got a real Bible? What you think I want to read the same verse over and over for when I can read it all?" He needed something better even than the Bible! He thought about it so much that he began to lose sleep. He was already losing flesh—Sarah Ruth just threw food in the pot and let it boil. Not knowing for certain why he continued to stay with a woman who was both ugly and pregnant and no cook made him generally nervous and irritable, and he developed a little tic in the side of his face.

Once or twice he found himself turning around abruptly as if someone were   80
trailing him. He had had a granddaddy who had ended in the state mental hospital, although not until he was seventy-five, but as urgent as it might be for him to get a tattoo, it was just as urgent that he get exactly the right one to bring Sarah Ruth to heel. As he continued to worry over it, his eyes took on a hollow preoccupied expression. The old woman he worked for told him that if he couldn't keep his mind on what he was doing, she knew where she could find a fourteen-year-old colored boy who could. Parker was too preoccupied even to be offended. At any time previous, he would have left her then and there, saying drily, "Well, you go ahead on and get him then."

Two or three mornings later he was baling hay with the old woman's sorry baler and her broken down tractor in a large field, cleared save for one enormous old tree standing in the middle of it. The old woman was the kind who would not cut down a large old tree because it was a large old tree. She had pointed it out to Parker as if he didn't have eyes and told him to be careful not to hit it as the machine picked up hay near it. Parker began at the outside of the field and made circles inward toward it. He had to get off the tractor every now and then and untangle the baling cord or kick a rock out of the way. The old woman had told him to carry the rocks to the edge of the field, which he did when she was there watching. When he thought he could make it, he ran over them. As he circled the field his mind was on a suitable design for his back. The sun, the size of a golf ball, began to switch regularly from in front to behind him, but he appeared to see it both places as if he had eyes in the back of his head. All at once he saw the tree reaching out to grasp him. A ferocious thud propelled him into the air, and he heard himself yelling in an unbelievably loud voice, "GOD ABOVE!"

He landed on his back while the tractor crashed upside down into the tree and burst into flame. The first thing Parker saw were his shoes, quickly being eaten by the fire; one was caught under the tractor, the other was some distance away, burning by itself. He was not in them. He could feel the hot breath of the burning tree on his face. He scrambled backwards, still sitting, his eyes cavernous, and if he had known how to cross himself he would have done it.

His truck was on a dirt road at the edge of the field. He moved toward it, still sitting, still backwards, but faster and faster; halfway to it he got up and began a kind of forward-bent run from which he collapsed on his knees twice. His legs felt like two old rusted rain gutters. He reached the truck finally and took off in it, zigzagging up the road. He drove past his house on the embankment and straight for the city, fifty miles distant.

Parker did not allow himself to think on the way to the city. He only knew that there had been a great change in his life, a leap forward into a worse unknown, and that there was nothing he could do about it. It was for all intents accomplished.

The artist had two large cluttered rooms over a chiropodist's office on a back street. Parker, still barefooted, burst silently in on him at a little after three in the afternoon. The artist, who was about Parker's own age—twenty-eight—but thin and bald, was behind a small drawing table, tracing a design in green ink. He looked up with an annoyed glance and did not seem to recognize Parker in the hollow-eyed creature before him.   85

"Let me see the book you got with all the pictures of God in it," Parker said breathlessly. "The religious one."

The artist continued to look at him with his intellectual, superior stare. "I don't put tattoos on drunks," he said.

"You know me!" Parker cried indignantly. "I'm O. E. Parker! You done work for me before and I always paid!"

The artist looked at him another moment as if he were not altogether sure. "You've fallen off some," he said. "You must have been in jail."

"Married," Parker said.   90

"Oh," said the artist. With the aid of mirrors the artist had tattooed on the top of his head a miniature owl, perfect in every detail. It was about the size of a half-dollar and served him as a show piece. There were cheaper artists in town but Parker had never wanted anything but the best. The artist went over to a cabinet at the back of the room and began to look over some art books. "Who are you interested in?" he said, "saints, angels, Christs or what?"

"God," Parker said.

"Father, Son or Spirit?"

"Just God," Parker said impatiently. "Christ. I don't care. Just so it's God."

The artist returned with a book. He moved some papers off another table and   95
put the book down on it and told Parker to sit down and see what he liked. "The
up-to-date ones are in the back," he said.

Parker sat down with the book and wet his thumb. He began to go through
it, beginning at the back where the up-to-date pictures were. Some of them he
recognized—The Good Shepherd, Forbid Them Not, The Smiling Jesus, Jesus the
Physician's Friend, but he kept turning rapidly backwards and the pictures became
less and less reassuring. One showed a gaunt green dead face streaked with blood.
One was yellow with sagging purple eyes. Parker's heart began to beat faster and
faster until it appeared to be roaring inside him like a great generator. He flipped the
pages quickly, feeling that when he reached the one ordained, a sign would come. He
continued to flip through until he had almost reached the front of the book. On one
of the pages a pair of eyes glanced at him swiftly. Parker sped on, then stopped. His
heart too appeared to cut off; there was absolute silence. It said as plainly as if silence
were a language itself, GO BACK.

Parker returned to the picture—the haloed head of a flat stern Byzantine Christ
with all-demanding eyes. He sat there trembling; his heart began slowly to beat again
as if it were being brought to life by a subtle power.

"You found what you want?" the artist asked.

Parker's throat was too dry to speak. He got up and thrust the book at the artist,
opened at the picture.

"That'll cost you plenty," the artist said. "You don't want all those little blocks   100
though, just the outline and some better features."

"Just like it is," Parker said, "just like it is or nothing."

"It's your funeral," the artist said, "but I don't do that kind of work for nothing."

"How much?" Parker asked.

"It'll take maybe two days work."

"How much?" Parker said.   105

"On time or cash?" the artist asked. Parker's other jobs had been on time, but he
had paid.

"Ten down and ten for every day it takes," the artist said.

Parker drew ten dollar bills out of his wallet; he had three left in.

"You come back in the morning," the artist said, putting the money in his own
pocket. "First I'll have to trace that out of the book."

"No no!" Parker said. "Trace it now or gimme my money back," and his eyes   110
blared as if he were ready for a fight.

The artist agreed. Any one stupid enough to want a Christ on his back, he reasoned, would be just as likely as not to change his mind the next minute, but once
the work was begun he could hardly do so.

While he worked on the tracing, he told Parker to go wash his back at the sink
with the special soap he used there. Parker did it and returned to pace back and forth
across the room, nervously flexing his shoulders. He wanted to go look at the picture
again but at the same time he did not want to. The artist got up finally and had
Parker lie down on the table. He swabbed his back with ethyl chloride and then
began to outline the head on it with his iodine pencil. Another hour passed before he
took up his electric instrument. Parker felt no particular pain. In Japan he had had a
tattoo of the Buddha done on his upper arm with ivory needles; in Burma, a little
brown root of a man had made a peacock on each of his knees using thin pointed
sticks, two feet long; amateurs had worked on him with pins and soot. Parker was

usually so relaxed and easy under the hand of the artist that he often went to sleep, but this time he remained awake, every muscle taut.

At midnight the artist said he was ready to quit. He propped one mirror, four feet square, on a table by the wall and took a smaller mirror off the lavatory wall and put it in Parker's hands. Parker stood with his back to the one on the table and moved the other until he saw a flashing burst of color reflected from his back. It was almost completely covered with little red and blue and ivory and saffron squares; from them he made out the lineaments of the face—a mouth, the beginning of heavy brows, a straight nose, but the face was empty; the eyes had not yet been put in. The impression for the moment was almost as if the artist had tricked him and done the Physician's Friend.

"It don't have eyes," Parker cried out.

"That'll come," the artist said, "in due time. We have another day to go on it yet." 115

Parker spent the night on a cot at the Haven of Light Christian Mission. He found these the best places to stay in the city because they were free and included a meal of sorts. He got the last available cot and because he was still barefooted, he accepted a pair of second-hand shoes which, in his confusion, he put on to go to bed; he was still shocked from all that had happened to him. All night he lay awake in the long dormitory of cots with lumpy figures on them. The only light was from a phosphorescent cross glowing at the end of the room. The tree reached out to grasp him again, then burst into flame; the shoe burned quietly by itself; the eyes in the book said to him distinctly GO BACK and at the same time did not utter a sound. He wished that he were not in this city, not in this Haven of Light Mission, not in a bed by himself. He longed miserably for Sarah Ruth. Her sharp tongue and icepick eyes were the only comfort he could bring to mind. He decided he was losing it. Her eyes appeared soft and dilatory compared with the eyes in the book, for even though he could not summon up the exact look of those eyes, he could still feel their penetration. He felt as though, under their gaze, he was as transparent as the wing of a fly.

The tattooist had told him not to come until ten in the morning, but when he arrived at that hour, Parker was sitting in the dark hallway on the floor, waiting for him. He had decided upon getting up that, once the tattoo was on him, he would not look at it, that all his sensations of the day and night before were those of a crazy man and that he would return to doing things according to his own sound judgement.

The artist began where he left off. "One thing I want to know," he said presently as he worked over Parker's back, "why do you want this on you? Have you gone and got religion? Are you saved?" he asked in a mocking voice.

Parker's throat felt salty and dry. "Naw," he said, "I ain't got no use for none of that. A man can't save his self from whatever it is he don't deserve none of my sympathy." These words seemed to leave his mouth like wraiths and to evaporate at once as if he had never uttered them.

"Then why . . ." 120

"I married this woman that's saved," Parker said. "I never should have done it. I ought to leave her. She's done gone and got pregnant."

"That's too bad," the artist said. "Then it's her making you have this tattoo."

"Naw," Parker said, "she don't know nothing about it. It's a surprise for her."

"You think she'll like it and lay off you a while?"

"She can't hep herself," Parker said. "She can't say she don't like the looks of 125 God." He decided he had told the artist enough of his business. Artists were all right in their place but he didn't like them poking their noses into the affairs of regular people. "I didn't get no sleep last night," he said. "I think I'll get some now."

That closed the mouth of the artist but it did not bring him any sleep. He lay there, imagining how Sarah Ruth would be struck speechless by the face on his back and every now and then this would be interrupted by a vision of the tree of fire and his empty shoe burning beneath it.

The artist worked steadily until nearly four o'clock, not stopping to have lunch, hardly pausing with the electric instrument except to wipe the dripping dye off Parker's back as he went along. Finally he finished. "You can get up and look at it now," he said.

Parker sat up but he remained on the edge of the table.

The artist was pleased with his work and wanted Parker to look at it at once. Instead Parker continued to sit on the edge of the table, bent forward slightly but with a vacant look. "What ails you?" the artist said. "Go look at it."

"Ain't nothing ail me," Parker said in a sudden belligerent voice. "That tattoo   130
ain't going nowhere. It'll be there when I get there." He reached for his shirt and began gingerly to put it on.

The artist took him roughly by the arm and propelled him between the two mirrors. "Now *look*," he said, angry at having his work ignored.

Parker looked, turned white and moved away. The eyes in the reflected face continued to look at him—still, straight, all-demanding, enclosed in silence.

"It was your idea, remember," the artist said. "I would have advised something else."

Parker said nothing. He put on his shirt and went out the door while the artist shouted, "I'll expect all of my money!"

Parker headed toward a package shop on the corner. He bought a pint of whiskey   135
and took it into a nearby alley and drank it all in five minutes. Then he moved on to a pool hall nearby which he frequented when he came to the city. It was a well-lighted barn-like place with a bar up one side and gambling machines on the other and pool tables in the back. As soon as Parker entered, a large man in a red and black checkered shirt hailed him by slapping him on the back and yelling, "Yeyyyyyy boy! O. E. Parker!"

Parker was not yet ready to be struck on the back. "Lay off," he said, "I got a fresh tattoo there."

"What you got this time?" the man asked and then yelled to a few at the machines. "O. E.'s got him another tattoo."

"Nothing special this time," Parker said and slunk over to a machine that was not being used.

"Come on," the big man said, "let's have a look at O. E.'s tattoo," and while Parker squirmed in their hands, they pulled up his shirt. Parker felt all the hands drop away instantly and his shirt fell again like a veil over the face. There was a silence in the pool room which seemed to Parker to grow from the circle around him until it extended to the foundations under the building and upward through the beams in the roof.

Finally some one said, "Christ!" Then they all broke into noise at once. Parker   140
turned around, an uncertain grin on his face.

"Leave it to O. E.!" the man in the checkered shirt said. "That boy's a real card!"

"Maybe he's gone and got religion," some one yelled.

"Not on your life," Parker said.

"O. E.'s got religion and is witnessing for Jesus, ain't you, O. E.?" a little man with a piece of cigar in his mouth said wryly. "An o-riginal way to do it if I ever saw one."

"Leave it to Parker to think of a new one!" the fat man said.   145

"Yyeeeeeeyyyyyyy boy!" someone yelled and they all began to whistle and curse in compliment until Parker said, "Aaa shut up."

"What'd you do it for?" somebody asked.

"For laughs," Parker said. "What's it to you?"

"Why ain't you laughing then?" somebody yelled. Parker lunged into the midst of them and like a whirlwind on a summer's day there began a fight that raged amid overturned tables and swinging fists until two of them grabbed him and ran to the door with him and threw him out. Then a calm descended on the pool hall as nerve shattering as if the long barn-like room were the ship from which Jonah had been cast into the sea.

Parker sat for a long time on the ground in the alley behind the pool hall,   150
examining his soul. He saw it as a spider web of facts and lies that was not at all important to him but which appeared to be necessary in spite of his opinion. The eyes that were now forever on his back were eyes to be obeyed. He was as certain of it as he had ever been of anything. Throughout his life, grumbling and sometimes curs-ing, often afraid, once in rapture, Parker had obeyed whatever instinct of this kind had come to him—in rapture when his spirit had lifted at the sight of the tattooed man at the fair, afraid when he had joined the navy, grumbling when he had married Sarah Ruth.

The thought of her brought him slowly to his feet. She would know what he had to do. She would clear up the rest of it, and she would at least be pleased. It seemed to him that, all along, that was what he wanted, to please her. His truck was still parked in front of the building where the artist had his place, but it was not far away. He got in it and drove out of the city and into the country night. His head was almost clear of liquor and he observed that his dissatisfaction was gone, but he felt not quite like himself. It was as if he were himself but a stranger to himself, driving into a new country though everything he saw was familiar to him, even at night.

He arrived finally at the house on the embankment, pulled the truck under the pecan tree and got out. He made as much noise as possible to assert that he was still in charge here, that his leaving her for a night without word meant nothing except it was the way he did things. He slammed the car door, stamped up the two steps and across the porch and rattled the door knob. It did not respond to his touch. "Sarah Ruth!" he yelled, "let me in."

There was no lock on the door and she had evidently placed the back of a chair against the knob. He began to beat on the door and rattle the knob at the same time.

He heard the bed springs screak and bent down and put his head to the keyhole, but it was stopped up with paper. "Let me in!" he hollered, bamming on the door again. "What you got me locked out for?

A sharp voice close to the door said, "Who's there?"   155

"Me," Parker said, "O. E."

He waited a moment.

"Me," he said impatiently, "O. E."

Still no sound from inside.

He tried once more. "O. E.," he said, bamming the door two or three more times. 160
"O. E. Parker. You know me."

There was a silence. Then the voice said slowly, "I don't know no O. E."

"Quit fooling," Parker pleaded. "You ain't got any business doing me this way. It's me, old O. E., I'm back. You ain't afraid of me."

"Who's there?" the same unfeeling voice said.

Parker turned his head as if he expected someone behind him to give him the answer. The sky had lightened slightly and there were two or three streaks of yellow floating above the horizon. Then as he stood there, a tree of light burst over the skyline.

Parker fell back against the door as if he had been pinned there by a lance.   165

"Who's there?" the voice from inside said and there was a quality about it now that seemed final. The knob rattled and the voice said peremptorily, "Who's there, I ast you?"

Parker bent down and put his mouth near the stuffed keyhole. "Obadiah," he whispered and all at once he felt the light pouring through him, turning his spider web soul into a perfect arabesque of colors, a garden of trees and birds and beasts.

"Obadiah Elihue!" he whispered.

The door opened and he stumbled in. Sarah Ruth loomed there, hands on her hips. She began at once, "That was no hefty blonde woman you was working for and you'll have to pay her every penny on her tractor you busted up. She don't keep insurance on it. She came here and her and me had us a long talk and I . . ."

Trembling, Parker set about lighting the kerosene lamp.   170

"What's the matter with you, wasting that kerosene this near daylight?" she demanded. "I ain't got to look at you."

A yellow glow enveloped them. Parker put the match down and began to unbutton his shirt.

"And you ain't going to have none of me this near morning," she said.

"Shut your mouth," he said quietly. "Look at this and then I don't want to hear no more out of you." He removed the shirt and turned his back to her.

"Another picture," Sarah Ruth growled. "I might have known you was off after   175 putting some more trash on yourself."

Parker's knees went hollow under him. He wheeled around and cried, "Look at it! Don't just say that! *Look* at it!"

"I done looked," she said.

"Don't you know who it is?" he cried in anguish.

"No, who is it?" Sarah Ruth said. "It ain't anybody I know."

"It's him," Parker said.   180

"Him who?"

"God!" Parker cried.

"God? God don't look like that!"

"What do you know how he looks?" Parker moaned. "You ain't seen him."

"He don't *look*," Sarah Ruth said. "He's a spirit. No man shall see his face."   185

"Aw listen," Parker groaned, "this is just a picture of him."

"Idolatry!" Sarah Ruth screamed. "Idolatry! Enflaming yourself with idols under every green tree! I can put up with lies and vanity but I don't want no idolator in this house!" and she grabbed up the broom and began to thrash him across the shoulders with it.

Parker was too stunned to resist. He sat there and let her beat him until she had nearly knocked him senseless and large welts had formed on the face of the tattooed Christ. Then he staggered up and made for the door.

She stamped the broom two or three times on the floor and went to the window and shook it out to get the taint of him off it. Still gripping it, she looked toward the pecan tree and her eyes hardened still more. There he was—who called himself Obadiah Elihue—leaning against the tree, crying like a baby.

Questions

1. Why, in your judgment, did Parker marry Sarah Ruth? Why did she marry him?

2. At the end of the second paragraph, the author says of Parker and Sarah Ruth: "He could account for her one way or another; it was himself he could not understand." How accurate is each part of this assumption?

3. What does Parker's employer think of him? How valid is her estimation?

4. What is the basis of Parker's fascination with tattooing? What kinds of feelings usually prompt him to get a new tattoo?

5. "Long views depressed Parker. You look out into space like that and you begin to feel as if someone were after you, the navy or the government or religion" (paragraph 36). What insights does this statement give us into Parker's character—and, consequently, into his behavior?

6. What motivates Parker to get the tattoo on his back? How does he expect Sarah Ruth to respond to it?

7. While waiting for the "artist" to finish the "God" tattoo, Parker feels that "his sensations of the day and night before were those of a crazy man and that he would return to doing things according to his own sound judgement" (paragraph 117). How much self-awareness does this observation demonstrate?

8. When the artist asks him if he's "gone and got religion," Parker says, "I ain't got no use for none of that. A man can't save his self from whatever it is he don't deserve none of my sympathy" (paragraph 119). What does this attitude illustrate about Parker's personality? By his own standard, how much of his own sympathy does he deserve?

9. Why does Sarah Ruth refuse to recognize Parker by his initials? What is the significance of his whispering his name through the keyhole, and what effect does doing so have on him?

FLANNERY O'CONNOR ON WRITING

Flannery O'Connor at her mother's Georgia farm where she raised peacocks; c. 1962.

Excerpt from "On Her Own Work": Insights into "A Good Man Is Hard to Find"

1963

A story really isn't any good unless it successfully resists paraphrase, unless it hangs on and expands in the mind. Properly, you analyze to enjoy, but it's equally true that to analyze with any discrimination, you have to have enjoyed already, and I think that the best reason to hear a story read is that it should stimulate that primary enjoyment.

I don't have any pretensions to being an Aeschylus or Sophocles and providing you in this story with a cathartic experience out of your mythic background, though this story I'm going to read certainly calls up a good deal of the South's mythic background, and it should elicit from you a degree of pity and terror, even though its way of being serious is a comic one. I do think, though, that like the Greeks you should know what is going to happen in this story so that any element of suspense in it will be transferred from its surface to its interior.

I would be most happy if you had already read it, happier still if you knew it well, but since experience has taught me to keep my expectations along these lines modest, I'll tell you that this is the story of a family of six which, on its way driving to Florida, gets wiped out by an escaped convict who calls himself the Misfit. The family is made up of the Grandmother and her son, Bailey, and his children, John Wesley and June Star and the baby, and there is also the cat and the children's mother. The cat is named Pitty Sing, and the Grandmother is taking him with them, hidden in a basket.

Now I think it behooves me to try to establish with you the basis on which reason operates in this story. Much of my fiction takes its character from a reasonable use of the unreasonable, though the reasonableness of my use of it may not always be apparent. The assumptions that underlie this use of it, however, are those of the central Christian mysteries. These are assumptions to which a large part of the modern audience takes exception. About this I can only say that there are perhaps other ways than my own in which this story could be read, but none other by which it could have been written. Belief, in my own case anyway, is the engine that makes perception operate.

The heroine of this story, the Grandmother, is in the most significant position life offers the Christian. She is facing death. And to all appearances she, like the rest of us, is not too well prepared for it. She would like to see the event postponed. Indefinitely.

I've talked to a number of teachers who use this story in class and who tell their students that the Grandmother is evil, that in fact, she's a witch, even down to the cat. One of these teachers told me that his students, and particularly his Southern students, resisted this interpretation with a certain bemused vigor, and he didn't understand why. I had to tell him that they resisted it because they all had grandmothers or great-aunts just like her at home, and they knew, from personal experience, that the old lady lacked comprehension, but that she had a good heart. The Southerner is usually tolerant of those weaknesses that proceed from innocence, and he knows that a taste for self-preservation can be readily combined with the missionary spirit.

This same teacher was telling his students that morally the Misfit was several cuts above the Grandmother. He had a really sentimental attachment to the Misfit. But then a prophet gone wrong is almost always more interesting than your grandmother, and you have to let people take their pleasures where they find them.

It is true that the old lady is a hypocritical old soul; her wits are no match for the Misfit's, nor is her capacity for grace equal to his; yet I think the unprejudiced reader will feel that the Grandmother has a special kind of triumph in this story which instinctively we do not allow to someone altogether bad.

I often ask myself what makes a story work, and what makes it hold up as a story, and I have decided that it is probably some action, some gesture of a character that is unlike any other in the story, one which indicates where the real heart of the story lies. This would have to be an action or a gesture which was both totally right and totally unexpected; it would have to be one that was both in character and beyond character; it would have to suggest both the world and eternity. The action or gesture I'm talking about would have to be on the anagogical level, that is, the level which has to do with the Divine life and our participation in it. It would be a gesture that transcended any neat allegory that might have been intended or any pat moral categories a reader could make. It would be a gesture which somehow made contact with mystery.

There is a point in this story where such a gesture occurs. The Grandmother is at last alone, facing the Misfit. Her head clears for an instant and she realizes, even in her limited way, that she is responsible for the man before her and joined to him by ties of kinship which have their roots deep in the mystery she has been merely prattling about so far. And at this point, she does the right thing, she makes the right gesture.

I find that students are often puzzled by what she says and does here, but I think myself that if I took out this gesture and what she says with it, I would have no story. What was left would not be worth your attention. Our age not only does not have a very sharp eye for the almost imperceptible intrusions of grace, it no longer has much feeling for the nature of the violences which precede and follow them. The devil's greatest wile, Baudelaire has said, is to convince us that he does not exist.

I suppose the reasons for the use of so much violence in modern fiction will differ with each writer who uses it, but in my own stories I have found that violence is strangely capable of returning my characters to reality and preparing them to accept their moment of grace. Their heads are so hard that almost nothing else will do the work. This idea, that reality is something to which we must be returned at considerable cost, is one which is seldom understood by the casual reader, but it is one which is implicit in the Christian view of the world.

I don't want to equate the Misfit with the devil. I prefer to think that, however unlikely this may seem, the old lady's gesture, like the mustard-seed, will grow to be a great crow-filled tree in the Misfit's heart, and will be enough of a pain to him there to turn him into the prophet he was meant to become. But that's another story.

This story has been called grotesque, but I prefer to call it literal. A good story is literal in the same sense that a child's drawing is literal. When a child draws, he doesn't intend to distort but to set down exactly what he sees, and as his gaze is direct, he sees the lines that create motion. Now the lines of motion that interest the writer are usually invisible. They are lines of spiritual motion. And in this story you should be on the lookout for such things as the action of grace in the Grandmother's soul, and not for the dead bodies.

We hear many complaints about the prevalence of violence in modern fiction, and it is always assumed that this violence is a bad thing and meant to be an end in itself. With the serious writer, violence is never an end in itself. It is the extreme situation that best reveals what we are essentially, and I believe these are times when writers are more interested in what we are essentially than in the tenor of our daily lives. Violence is a force which can be used for good or evil, and among other things taken by it is the kingdom of heaven. But regardless of what can be taken by it, the man in the violent situation reveals those qualities least dispensable in his personality, those qualities which are all he will have to take into eternity with him; and since the characters in this story are all on the verge of eternity, it is appropriate to think of what they take with them. In any case, I hope that if you consider these points in connection with the story, you will come to see it as something more than an account of a family murdered on the way to Florida.

From "On Her Own Work"

On Her Catholic Faith   1955

I write the way I do because (not though) I am a Catholic. This is a fact and nothing covers it like the bald statement. However, I am a Catholic peculiarly possessed of the modern consciousness, the thing Jung describes as unhistorical, solitary, and guilty. To possess this within the Church is to bear a burden, the necessary burden for the conscious Catholic. It's to feel the contemporary situation at the ultimate level. I think

that the Church is the only thing that is going to make the terrible world we are coming to endurable; the only thing that makes the Church endurable is that it is somehow
the body of Christ and that on this we are fed. It seems to be a fact that you suffer as
much from the Church as for it but if you believe in the divinity of Christ, you have to
cherish the world at the same time that you struggle to endure it. This may explain the
lack of bitterness in the stories.

From a letter (July 20, 1955) in The Habit of Being

Excerpt from "The Grotesque in Southern Fiction": The Serious Writer and the Tired Reader   1960

Those writers who speak for and with their age are able to do so with a great deal
more ease and grace than those who speak counter to prevailing attitudes. I once
received a letter from an old lady in California who informed me that when the tired
reader comes home at night, he wishes to read something that will lift up his heart.
And it seems her heart had not been lifted up by anything of mine she had read. I
think that if her heart had been in the right place, it would have been lifted up.

You may say that the serious writer doesn't have to bother about the tired
reader, but he does, because they are all tired. One old lady who wants her heart
lifted up wouldn't be so bad, but you multiply her two hundred and fifty thousand
times and what you get is a book club. I used to think it should be possible to write
for some supposed elite, for the people who attend the universities and sometimes
know how to read, but I have since found that though you may publish your stories
in *Botteghe Oscure*,° if they are any good at all, you are eventually going to get a letter from some old lady in California, or some inmate of the Federal Penitentiary or
the state insane asylum or the local poorhouse, telling you where you have failed to
meet his needs.

And his need, of course, is to be lifted up. There is something in us, as storytellers and as listeners to stories, that demands the redemptive act, that demands
that what falls at least be offered the chance to be restored. The reader of today
looks for this motion, and rightly so, but what he has forgotten is the cost of it. His
sense of evil is diluted or lacking altogether and so he has forgotten the price of
restoration. When he reads a novel, he wants either his senses tormented or his spirits raised. He wants to be transported, instantly, either to a mock damnation or a
mock innocence.

I am often told that the model of balance for the novelist should be Dante, who
divided his territory up pretty evenly between hell, purgatory, and paradise. There
can be no objection to this, but also there can be no reason to assume that the result
of doing it in these times will give us the balanced picture that it gave in Dante's.
Dante lived in the 13th century when that balance was achieved in the faith of his
age. We live now in an age which doubts both fact and value, which is swept this way
and that by momentary convictions. Instead of reflecting a balance from the world
around him, the novelist now has to achieve one from a felt balance inside himself.
There are ages when it is possible to woo the reader; there are others when something
more drastic is necessary.

Botteghe Oscure: a distinguished and expensive literary magazine published in Rome from 1949 to 1960
by the Princess Marguerite Caetani for a small, sophisticated audience.

There is no literary orthodoxy that can be prescribed as settled for the fiction writer, not even that of Henry James who balanced the elements of traditional realism and romance so admirably within each of his novels. But this much can be said. The great novels we get in the future are not going to be those that the public thinks it wants, or those that critics demand. They are going to be the kind of novels that interest the novelist. And the novels that interest the novelist are those that have not already been written. They are those that put the greatest demands on him, that require him to operate at the maximum of his intelligence and his talents, and to be true to the particularities of his own vocation. The direction of many of us will be toward concentration and the distortion that is necessary to get our vision across; it will be more toward poetry than toward the traditional novel.

The problem for such a novelist will be to know how far he can distort without destroying, and in order not to destroy, he will have to descend far enough into himself to reach those underground springs that give life to his work. This descent into himself will, at the same time, be a descent into his region. It will be a descent through the darkness of the familiar into a world where, like the blind man cured in the gospels, he sees men as if they were trees, but walking. This is the beginning of vision, and I feel it is a vision which we in the South must at least try to understand if we want to participate in the continuance of a vital Southern literature. I hate to think that in twenty years Southern writers too may be writing about men in grey flannel suits and may have lost their ability to see that these gentlemen are even greater freaks than what we are writing about now. I hate to think of the day when the Southern writer will satisfy the tired reader.

From "The Grotesque in Southern Fiction"

Yearbook Cartoons   1944

Untitled linoleum block cartoons by O'Connor for the yearbook at Georgia State College.

CRITICS ON FLANNERY O'CONNOR

J. O. Tate

A Good Source Is Not So Hard to Find: The Real Life Misfit   1980

The mounting evidence of O'Connor's use of items from the Milledgeville and Atlanta newspapers will interest those who realize that these sources, in and of themselves, have nothing to do with the Gothic, the grotesque, the American Romance tradition, Southwestern humor, Southern literature, adolescent aggression, the New Hermeneutics, the anxiety of influence, structuralism, pentecostal Gnosticism, medieval theology, Christian humanism, existentialism, or the Roman Catholic Church.

I. On "The Misfit" as Name and Word

The text of an Atlanta *Constitution* article of November 6, 1952, p. 29, identifies for us the source of a celebrated sobriquet. This newspaper reference was reprinted in *The Flannery O'Connor Bulletin*, Volume III, Autumn 1974. The headline says enough: "'The Misfit' Robs Office, Escapes With $150." Flannery O'Connor took a forgotten criminal's alias and used it for larger purposes: *her* Misfit was out of place in a grander way than the original. But we should not forget O'Connor's credentials as "a literalist of the imagination." There is always "a little lower layer." She meant to mock pop psychology by exploiting the original Misfit's exploitation of a sociopsychological "excuse" for aberrant behavior. But even a little lower: the original meaning of the word "misfit" has to do with clothing. We should not fail, therefore, to note that The Misfit's "borrowed" blue jeans are too tight. He leaves the story, of course, wearing Bailey's shirt.

II. On the Identity and Destiny of the Original Misfit

By November 15, 1952, The Misfit had been apprehended; he had also advanced himself to page three of the Atlanta *Journal*. The Misfit was a twenty-five-year old named James C. Yancey. He "was found to be of unsound mind" and committed to the state mental hospital at—Milledgeville. Where else?

*III. On The Misfit's Notoriety, Peregrinations, Good Manners, Eye-glasses,
    Companions, and Mental Hygiene*

The original Misfit was, as criminals go, small potatoes. He was an unambitious thief, no more. O'Connor took nothing from him but his imposing signature.

'The Misfit' Robs Office, Escapes With $150

A bandit who told his victims he was "The Misfit," held up the Atlanta Federal Savings and Loan Association office at 22 Marietta St., N. W., and escaped with $150 cash in a daring daylight raid Wednesday afternoon.

The man was described as being 30 years old, six feet tall and 175 pounds in weight. He carried a nickel-steel .32-caliber revolver, according to J. F. Clemmer, assistant vice-president of the company.

Clemmer told Det. Y. H. Allen the man shoved an envelope through the window where a cashier, Mrs. Beverly Bradshaw of 1919 Sylvan Ridge Dr., S. W., was at work. A crudely lettered message on the envelope read: "Put $150 in here and don't say anything. I have a gun, and I am 'The Misfit.'"

Mrs. Bradshaw ducked behind the counter, Clemmer said. Clemmer told another cashier to "do whatever the man wanted." Then he told the robber he'd "better go—we're protected by the FBI." The bandit then fled on Marietta St.

Detectives said the description of the man tallied with that of one who Tuesday night held up a hotel clerk at 87 Harris St., N. W., and fled with $50. FBI agents joined Atlanta police in a search.

The article in the Atlanta *Constitution*, November 6, 1952, that provided Flannery O'Connor with the criminal nickname "The Misfit."

But it just so happens that there was another well-publicized criminal aloose in Tennessee and Georgia just before the time that O'Connor appropriated the Misfit's name. This other hold-up artist had four important qualities in common with *her* Misfit. First, he inspired a certain amount of terror through several states. Second, he had, or claimed to have, a certain *politesse*. Third, he wore spectacles. Fourth, he had two accomplices, in more than one account.

James Francis ("Three-Gun") Hill, the sinister celebrity of the front pages, much more closely resembles the object of the grandmother's warnings than the original Misfit. Various articles tell of "a fantastic record of 26 kidnappings in four states, as many robberies, 10 car thefts, and a climactic freeing of four Florida convicts from a prison gang—all in two kaleidoscopic weeks." He had advanced "from an obscure hoodlum to top billing as a public enemy" (The Atlanta *Constitution*, November 1, p. 1). Such headlines as the grandmother had in mind screamed of Hill (though not in the sports section that Bailey was reading): "Maniac's Gang Terrorizes Hills" (*Constitution*, October 24, p. 2, from Sparta, Tenn.); "Search for Kidnap-Robbery Trio Centers in Atlanta and Vicinity" (October 25, p. 1, from Atlanta); "Chattanooga Is Focal Point for Manhunt" (October 27, p. 26); "2nd of Terror Gang Seized In Florida/Pal Said Still In Atlanta Area" (October 29, p. 32); "Self-Styled 3-Gun Maniac Frees 4 Road Gang Convicts at Gunpoint" (October 31, p. 1, from Bartow, Florida). It is quite clear that O'Connor, imagining through the grandmother's point of view, was, like the newspapers, assuming an Atlanta locale and orientation. The southward trip was in the same direction as Hill's last run.

The article of October 24 gives us a bit of color: "A fantastic band of highwaymen, led by a self-styled 'maniac' who laughed weirdly while he looted his victims, spread terror through the Cumberland hills today. . . . [The leader] boasted that he had escaped from the Utah State Prison and 'killed two people' . . . 'They call me a three-gun maniac, and brother, they got the picture straight,' the head bandit was quoted by victims." The October 31 article hints at the rustic setting of O'Connor's story: "The escapees and Hill . . . drove up a dead-end road and abandoned the car. They fled into thick woods on foot. . . ."

The *Constitution* of November 1 speaks of Hill on the front page as "the bespectacled, shrunken-cheeked highwayman." A later article gives us, as it gave O'Connor, a clue to her Misfit's respectful modes of address ("Good afternoon . . . I pre-chate that, lady . . . Nome . . . I'm sorry I don't have on a shirt before you ladies . . . Yes'm . . ."): We read of the trial of "Accused kidnapper, James Francis (Three-Gun) Hill, who says he's a 'gentleman-bandit' because 'I didn't cuss in front of ladies. . . .'" This Associated Press wire story from Chattanooga was on page 26 of the November 13 Atlanta *Journal*.

The *Constitution* of the same date says "Hearing Delayed for 'Maniac' Hill and 2 Cronies," and goes on to mention "James Francis Hill, self-styled 'three-gun maniac.'" We may observe that both Yancey and Hill were referred to in the newspapers as "self-styled," an arresting phrase perhaps to an author attuned to extravagances of self. I think we may also recognize here the genesis of Hiram and Bobby Lee.

The result of Hill's plea of guilty was perhaps not as forthright as his intention: "'Maniac' Hill Is Adjudged Incompetent" (*Constitution*, November 18). Like Yancey, The Misfit, Hill was sent to a mental institution—in Tennessee, this time. (His cronies were sentenced to jail.) The diagnosis of both Yancey and Hill as mentally ill may have suggested O'Connor's Misfit's experiences with the "head-doctor."

IV. On the Misfit, Memory, and Guilt

The fictional Misfit was not easily freudened: he knew perfectly well that he had not killed his daddy. Yet he insisted there was no balance between guilt and punishment—if memory served.

The issues of accuracy of memory, consciousness of guilt, and conscience were also raised in an odd "human-interest" story that was published in those same days when O'Connor was gathering so much material from the newspapers. The Misfit's claim that he was punished for crimes he did not remember may have been inspired by this account of a man who was *not* punished for a crime he *did* remember—but remembered wrongly.

The *Journal* of November 5, 1952 carried the article, written from Brookhaven, New York, on page 12: "'Murder' Didn't Happen, House Painter Free." Louis Roberts had shot a policeman in 1928; he assumed he had killed him. Over twenty years later, his conscience finally forced him to confess. When his tale was investigated, it was discovered that the policeman had survived after all. There was no prosecution for, as an authority was quoted as saying, "His conscience has punished him enough."

From "A Good Source Is Not So Hard to Find"

Mary Jane Schenck (b. 1944)

Deconstructing "A Good Man Is Hard to Find" 1988

"A Good Man Is Hard to Find" presents a masterful portrait of a woman who creates a self and a world through language. From the outset, the grandmother relies on "texts" to structure her reality. The newspaper article about The Misfit mentioned in the opening paragraph of the story is a written text which has a particular status in the narrative. It refers to events outside and prior to the primary *récit*, but it stands as an unrecognized prophecy of the events which occur at the end. For Bailey, the newspaper story is not important or meaningful, and for the grandmother it does not represent a real threat but is part of a ploy to get her own way. It is thus the first one of her "fictions," one which ironically comes true. The grandmother's whole personality is built upon the fictions she tells herself and her family. Although she knows Bailey would object if she brought her cat on the trip, the grandmother sneaks the cat into the car, justifying her behavior by imagining "he would miss her too much and she was afraid he might brush himself against one of the gas burners and accidentally asphyxiate himself." She also carefully cultivates a fiction about the past when people were good and when "children were more respectful of their native states and their parents and everything else." As she tells Red Sam at the Tower when they stop to eat, "People are certainly not nice like they used to be."

The grandmother reads fictional stories to the children, tells them ostensibly true stories, and provides a continual gloss on the physical world they are passing. "Little niggers in the country don't have things like we do. If I could paint, I'd paint that picture." Lacking that skill, the grandmother nevertheless verbally "creates" a whole universe as they ride along. "'Look at the graveyard!' the grandmother said, pointing it out. 'That was the old family burying ground. That belonged to the plantation.'" She creates the stories behind the visual phenomena she sees and explains relationships between events or her own actions which have no logic other than that which she lends them.

Her most important fiction is, of course, the story of the old plantation house which becomes more of an imperative as she tells it. The more she talks about it, the more she wants to see it again, so she does not hesitate to self-consciously lie about it. "'There was a secret panel in this house,' she said craftily, not telling the truth but wishing she were." At this point we see clearly the performative quality of the grandmother's language. At first it motivates her own desire, then spills over onto the children, finally culminating in their violent outburst of screaming and kicking to get their father to stop the car. The performative quality of her language becomes even more crucial when she realizes that she has fantasized the location of the house. She does not admit it, but her thoughts manifest themselves physically: "The thought was so embarrassing that she turned red in the face and her eyes dilated and her feet jumped up, upsetting her valise in the corner." Of course, it is her physical action which frees the cat and causes the accident. After the accident, she again fictionalizes about her condition, hoping she is injured so she can deflect Bailey's anger, and she cannot even manage to tell the truth about the details of the accident.

The scene with The Misfit is the apogee of the grandmother's use of "fictions" to explain and control reality, attempts that are thwarted by her encounter with a character who understands there is no reality behind her words. When the grandmother recognizes The Misfit, he tells her it would have been better if she hadn't, but she has *named* him, thus forcing him to become what is behind his self-selected name. In a desperate attempt to cope with the threat posed by the murderer, the grandmother runs through her litany of convenient fictions. She believes that there are class distinctions ("I know you're a good man. You don't look a bit like you have common blood"), that appearance reflects reality ("You shouldn't call yourself The Misfit because I know you're a good man at heart. I can just look at you and tell"), that redemption can be achieved through work ("You could be honest too if you'd only try. . . . Think how wonderful it would be to settle down . . ."), and finally, that prayer will change him ("'Pray, pray,' she commanded him").

From "Deconstructing Meaning in Two Short Stories by Flannery O'Connor"

Louise S. Cowan (b. 1916)

The Character of Mrs. Turpin in "Revelation" 2005

O'Connor held that serious writers cannot produce their works simply from their own ideas and conscious convictions; rather, if they are to produce anything of value, they must submit to a larger body of customs and manners of which they are a part. "As far as the creation of a body of fiction is concerned," she writes, "the social is superior to the purely personal." The writer whose themes are religious particularly needs a region where the themes find a response in the life of the people. "What the Southern Catholic writer is apt to find when he descends within his imagination is not Catholic life but the life of his region in which he is both native and alien." For O'Connor, then, the South presented the region to which she could devote her genius. It was out of step with the rest of the nation, since it was still largely agrarian, retaining in the early twentieth century traces in it of an older worldview. Further, as she saw, it still had a "folk," both white and black, who maintained an outlook fundamentally religious. It was likely to be from these groups that the prophetic figures in her fiction could emerge. In the South the general conception of man is still, O'Connor maintained, theological:

> The Bible is known by the ignorant as well as the educated and it is always the *mythos* which the poor hold in common that is most valuable to the fiction writer. When the poor hold sacred history in common, they have ties to the universal and the holy which allows the meaning of their every action to be heightened and seen under the aspect of eternity.

• • •

"Revelation"

The short story "Revelation," which won first prize in the 1964 O. Henry Awards, is one of O'Connor's last-written pieces and one of her most accomplished. It is about her familiar theme of Pharisaism;° and the epiphany with which it ends is no less devastating for occurring while the protagonist, Mrs. Turpin, is hosing down one of her prize hogs.

O'Connor's favorite target is the respectable, moral person who has lived a good and sensible life. The main character in "Revelation," Ruby Turpin, is such a figure, innocently falling into the pattern of self-satisfaction that finally assumes God himself must be impressed with her virtue. It is a mistake, however, to construe O'Connor's keen portrayals as pitiless. Her pharisaical characters are unaware of their self-love; they conduct themselves with kindness and courtesy, as good decent people should do. Mrs. Turpin in "Revelation" is such a naively self-righteous person, convinced that her righteousness makes her a special friend of Jesus. One of O'Connor's worries about the story "Revelation," as a matter of fact, was that people would think she was disapproving of Mrs. Turpin. "You got to be a very big woman to shout at the Lord across a hog pen," she wrote in a letter to a friend.

Ruby Turpin is one of O'Connor's masterpieces. Essentially good-hearted, she is blind to her own pride and self-satisfaction. She passes judgment on everyone she meets, sometimes occupying herself with naming over the classes of people. "On the bottom of the heap were most colored people . . . then next to them, not above, just away from—were the white trash, then above them the home-owners, and above them the home-and-land owners to which she and Claud belonged." She naively congratulates herself on having been born as who she is, a good respectable white woman who, with her husband, makes do with what they have and takes care of their property. But there are people who own more property—and people over them, and some of them are not morally good; so Mrs. Turpin's neat little scale of measurement becomes blurry and leaves her puzzled.

The crucial event in Ruby Turpin's life begins in a doctor's office. . . . She has been singled out, she knows, for a message. And, afterwards, the more she thinks about it in her isolation (for she can't bring herself to ask her husband about it; and the black servants who work for her merely flatter her), the more the incident seems to have some sort of divine import. "The message had been given to Ruby Turpin, a respectable, hard-working, church-going woman." Angry, she makes her way to the hogpen; and as she is watering down a white sow she begins her questioning of God that turns into a challenge: "Go on, call me a hog! Call me a hog again. From hell. Call me a wart hog from hell." And finally the blasphemous, "Who do you think you are?"

Pharisaism: hypocritical self-righteousness.

It is this direct challenge to the Almighty that produces the real revelation for Ruby Turpin. And in the vision that she receives, the question she had always stumbled over—the complexity of categorizing the classes of people—is answered, with a revelation at once grotesque and sublime.

From "Passing by the Dragon: Flannery O'Connor's Art of Revelation"

Kathleen Feeley (b. 1929)

The Mystery of Divine Direction: "Parker's Back"   1972

In the last story O'Connor wrote, "Parker's Back," she explores the mystery of divine direction. Unlikely candidate for God's election though he is, O. E. Parker is "chosen," and the story illuminates the communication of that choice and the effect that it has on his life. God leads Parker to understand his destiny through a strange combination of circumstances: his attraction to tattoos and his marriage to a woman who abhors them. This story achieves a goal set by a statement which O'Connor marked in her copy of Emmanuel Mounier's *The Character of Man:* "To draw mystery into the light of day, without losing its strength and fascination, is the highest achievement either of art or of thought." The "light of day" is the absolute credibility of this story; the "mystery" is God's way with man.

A "peculiar unease" which settles in Parker when he is fourteen years old is the first indication of God's designs upon him. At a fair he sees a man tattooed from head to foot; when the man flexes his muscles, the pattern of men and beasts and flowers on his skin appears to have a subtle motion of its own. After this vision fills his eyes, Parker is never the same; the "unease" in him can be satisfied only by tattoos, which he gets, one after the other, all over his body, for the next fourteen years. But the "unease" remains. Each tattoo dispels it for a time, but always it returns. He longs to see on his own body the "moving arabesque of color" that fills his imagination, but when he examines himself in a mirror, he sees only "something haphazard and blotched." It seems as if his desire can never be satisfied, for, when the story opens, he has only one body-space left, and that a place he cannot see—his back.

• • •

One can see in Parker's openness to life's mystery and in Sarah Ruth's certainty about life the difference between the many who are "called" and the few who are "chosen." Trusting exclusively in a literal interpretation of Scripture, Sarah Ruth follows the narrow path to salvation which excludes any other means of apprehending God. Her eyes, "gray and sharp like the points of two icepicks," reveal her determined character. Parker's mind bends toward mystery. Since the time he was initially drawn to the mystery of moving color on the body of the tattooed man, he has been responsive to the inner promptings of his spirit, even if he does not understand them. From that time, his life has had a mysterious orientation; "it was as if a blind boy had been turned so gently in a different direction that he did not know his destination had been changed." This openness to mystery is reflected in his eyes, "which were the same pale slate-color as the ocean and reflected the immense spaces around him as if they were a microcosm of the mysterious sea." Parker, aware of mystery, is open to the power of grace. Confronted with mystery, Sarah Ruth closes her heart. After raising welts on the face of the Christ tattooed on her husband's back and driving him out of the house, she looks out of the window at him sobbing against a tree, and "her eyes hardened still more." Parker had thought that his wife would like his tattoo because "she can't say she don't like the looks of God." But his wife has a narrow conception of Divinity. With her enraged assertion that "God don't look like that! . . . He don't *look.* . . . He's a spirit. No man shall see his face," she cuts herself off from grace.

From *Flannery O'Connor: Voice of the Peacock*

■ WRITING *effectively*

TOPICS FOR WRITING

1. Read three stories by Flannery O'Connor, or any one of the writers who appear in this book. Identify a theme or idea common to all three stories. Write an essay describing how your chosen author treats this theme. Support your argument with evidence from all three stories.

2. Compare and contrast a pair of characters from two different stories who feel conceptually related. Good choices might be Sarah Ruth from "Parker's Back," Mary Grace or Mrs. Turpin from "Revelation," and the grandmother in "A Good Man Is Hard to Find." Do these characters play similar roles in their respective stories?

3. All three stories are about revelations of one kind or another. How do these three revelations relate to each other? Back up your argument with evidence from the three stories.

4. In the excerpt from "On Her Own Work," O'Connor writes:

> I often ask myself what makes a story work, and what makes it hold up as a story, and I have decided that it is probably some action, some gesture of a character that is unlike any other in the story, one which indicates where the real heart of the story lies. This would have to be an action or a gesture which was both totally right and totally unexpected; it would have to be one that was both in character and beyond character; it would have to suggest both the world and eternity. . . . It would be a gesture which somehow made contact with mystery.

   While O'Connor is speaking specifically about "A Good Man Is Hard to Find," her words can be applied to her other stories. Choose a gesture from "Revelation" or "Parker's Back" that fits this description, and explain your choice.

5. In 750 to 1,000 words, comment on O'Connor's use of humor. How does comedy help her say what she has to say?

11

CRITICAL CASEBOOK
Three Stories in Depth

Nathaniel Hawthorne ▪ *Young Goodman Brown*
Charlotte Perkins Gilman ▪ *The Yellow Wallpaper*
Alice Walker ▪ *Everyday Use*

NATHANIEL HAWTHORNE

Nathaniel Hawthorne (1804–1864) was born in the clipper-ship seaport of Salem, Massachusetts, son of a merchant captain (who died when the future novelist was only four years old) and great-great-grandson of a magistrate involved in the notorious Salem witchcraft trials. Hawthorne takes a keen interest in New England's sin-and-brimstone Puritan past in many of his stories, especially "Young Goodman Brown," and in the classic novel The Scarlet Letter (1850), his deepest exploration of his major themes of conscience, sin, and guilt. In 1825 Hawthorne graduated from Bowdoin College; one of his classmates—and his lifelong best friend—was Franklin Pierce, who in 1852 would be elected president of the United States. After college, Hawthorne lived at home and trained to be a writer. His first novel, Fanshawe

Nathaniel Hawthorne

(1828), begun while he was still an undergraduate, was published anonymously and at his own expense. During this period, Hawthorne also experienced great difficulty in trying to publish his short fiction, both in magazines and in book form, until the appearance of Twice-Told Tales (1837). In 1841, he was appointed to a position in the Boston Custom House; in the following year he married Sophia Peabody. The newlyweds settled in the Old Manse in Concord, Massachusetts. Three more novels followed: The House of the Seven Gables (1851, the story of a family curse, tinged with nightmarish humor), The Blithedale Romance (1852, drawn from his short, irritating stay at a Utopian commune, Brook Farm), and The Marble Faun (1860, inspired by a stay in Italy). When Franklin Pierce ran for president, Hawthorne wrote his campaign biography. After taking office, Pierce appointed his old friend American

consul at Liverpool, England. Depressed by ill health and the terrible toll of the Civil War, Hawthorne died suddenly while on a tour with Pierce of New Hampshire's White Mountains. With his contemporary Edgar Allan Poe, Hawthorne transformed the American short story from popular magazine filler into a major literary form.

Young Goodman Brown   (1835) 1846

Young Goodman° Brown came forth, at sunset, into the street of Salem village,° but put his head back, after crossing the threshold, to exchange a parting kiss with his young wife. And Faith, as the wife was aptly named, thrust her own pretty head into the street, letting the wind play with the pink ribbons of her cap, while she called to Goodman Brown.

"Dearest heart," whispered she, softly and rather sadly, when her lips were close to his ear, "pray thee, put off your journey until sunrise, and sleep in your own bed to-night. A lone woman is troubled with such dreams and such thoughts, that she's afraid of herself, sometimes. Pray, tarry with me this night, dear husband, of all nights in the year!"

"My love and my Faith," replied young Goodman Brown, "of all nights in the year, this one night must I tarry away from thee. My journey, as thou callest it, forth and back again, must needs be done 'twixt now and sunrise. What, my sweet, pretty wife, dost thou doubt me already, and we but three months married!"

"Then, God bless you!" said Faith, with the pink ribbons, "and may you find all well, when you come back."

"Amen!" cried Goodman Brown. "Say thy prayers, dear Faith, and go to bed at   5
dusk, and no harm will come to thee."

So they parted; and the young man pursued his way, until, being about to turn the corner by the meeting-house, he looked back, and saw the head of Faith still peeping after him, with a melancholy air, in spite of her pink ribbons.

"Poor little Faith!" thought he, for his heart smote him. "What a wretch am I, to leave her on such an errand! She talks of dreams, too. Methought, as she spoke, there was trouble in her face, as if a dream had warned her what work is to be done to-night. But, no, no! 'twould kill her to think it. Well; she's a blessed angel on earth; and after this one night, I'll cling to her skirts and follow her to Heaven."

With this excellent resolve for the future, Goodman Brown felt himself justified in making more haste on his present evil purpose. He had taken a dreary road, darkened by all the gloomiest trees of the forest, which barely stood aside to let the narrow path creep through, and closed immediately behind. It was all as lonely as could be; and there is this peculiarity in such a solitude, that the traveller knows not who may be concealed by the innumerable trunks and the thick boughs overhead; so that, with lonely footsteps, he may yet be passing through an unseen multitude.

"There may be a devilish Indian behind every tree," said Goodman Brown, to himself; and he glanced fearfully behind him, as he added, "What if the devil himself should be at my very elbow!"

His head being turned back, he passed a crook of the road, and looking forward   10
again, beheld the figure of a man, in grave and decent attire, seated at the foot of an

---

Goodman: title given by Puritans to a male head of a household; a farmer or other ordinary citizen.
Salem village: in England's Massachusetts Bay Colony.

old tree. He arose, at Goodman Brown's approach, and walked onward, side by side with him.

"You are late, Goodman Brown," said he. "The clock of the Old South was striking as I came through Boston; and that is full fifteen minutes agone."°

"Faith kept me back awhile," replied the young man, with a tremor in his voice, caused by the sudden appearance of his companion, though not wholly unexpected.

It was now deep dusk in the forest, and deepest in that part of it where these two were journeying. As nearly as could be discerned, the second traveller was about fifty years old, apparently in the same rank of life as Goodman Brown, and bearing a considerable resemblance to him, though perhaps more in expression than features. Still, they might have been taken for father and son. And yet, though the elder person was as simply clad as the younger, and as simple in manner too, he had an indescribable air of one who knew the world, and would not have felt abashed at the governor's dinner-table, or in King William's court,° were it possible that his affairs should call him thither. But the only thing about him, that could be fixed upon as remarkable, was his staff, which bore the likeness of a great black snake, so curiously wrought, that it might almost be seen to twist and wriggle itself, like a living serpent. This, of course, must have been an ocular deception, assisted by the uncertain light.

"Come, Goodman Brown!" cried his fellow-traveller, "this is dull pace for the beginning of a journey. Take my staff, if you are so soon weary."

"Friend," said the other, exchanging his slow pace for a full stop, "having kept covenant by meeting thee here, it is my purpose now to return whence I came. I have scruples, touching the matter thou wot'st° of."   15

"Sayest thou so?" replied he of the serpent, smiling apart. "Let us walk on, nevertheless, reasoning as we go, and if I convince thee not, thou shalt turn back. We are but a little way in the forest, yet."

"Too far, too far!" exclaimed the goodman, unconsciously resuming his walk. "My father never went into the woods on such an errand, nor his father before him. We have been a race of honest men and good Christians, since the days of the martyrs.° And shall I be the first of the name of Brown, that ever took this path, and kept—"

"Such company, thou wouldst say," observed the elder person, interpreting his pause. "Well said, Goodman Brown! I have been as well acquainted with your family as with ever a one among the Puritans; and that's no trifle to say. I helped your grandfather, the constable, when he lashed the Quaker woman so smartly through the streets of Salem. And it was I that brought your father a pitch-pine knot, kindled at my own hearth, to set fire to an Indian village, in King Philip's war.° They were my good friends,

---

full fifteen minutes agone: Apparently this mystery man has traveled in a flash from Boston's Old South Church all the way to the woods beyond Salem—as the crow flies, a good sixteen miles. *King William's court:* back in England, where William III reigned from 1689 to 1702. *wot'st:* know. *days of the martyrs:* a time when many forebears of the New England Puritans had given their lives for religious convictions—when Mary I (Mary Tudor, nicknamed "Bloody Mary"), queen of England from 1553 to 1558, briefly reestablished the Roman Catholic Church in England and launched a campaign of persecution against Protestants. *King Philip's war:* Metacomet, or King Philip (as the English called him), chief of the Wampanoag Indians, had led a bitter, widespread uprising of several New England tribes (1675–78). Metacomet died in the war, as did one out of every ten white male colonists.

both; and many a pleasant walk have we had along this path, and returned merrily after midnight. I would fain be friends with you, for their sake."

"If it be as thou sayest," replied Goodman Brown, "I marvel they never spoke of these matters. Or, verily, I marvel not, seeing that the least rumor of the sort would have driven them from New England. We are a people of prayer, and good works, to boot, and abide no such wickedness."

"Wickedness or not," said the traveller with the twisted staff, "I have a very general acquaintance here in New England. The deacons of many a church have drunk the communion wine with me; the selectmen, of divers towns, make me their chairman; and a majority of the Great and General Court are firm supporters of my interest. The governor and I, too—but these are state-secrets."   20

"Can this be so!" cried Goodman Brown, with a stare of amazement at his undisturbed companion. "Howbeit, I have nothing to do with the governor and council; they have their own ways, and are no rule for a simple husbandman, like me. But, were I to go on with thee, how should I meet the eye of that good old man, our minister, at Salem village? Oh, his voice would make me tremble, both Sabbath-day and lecture-day!"°

Thus far, the elder traveller had listened with due gravity, but now burst into a fit of irrepressible mirth, shaking himself so violently, that his snake-like staff actually seemed to wriggle in sympathy.

"Ha! ha! ha!" shouted he, again and again; then composing himself, "Well, go on, Goodman Brown, go on; but pray thee, don't kill me with laughing!"

"Well, then, to end the matter at once," said Goodman Brown, considerably nettled, "there is my wife, Faith. It would break her dear little heart; and I'd rather break my own!"

"Nay, if that be the case," answered the other, "e'en go thy ways, Goodman Brown. I would not, for twenty old women like the one hobbling before us, that Faith should come to any harm."   25

As he spoke, he pointed his staff at a female figure on the path, in whom Goodman Brown recognized a very pious and exemplary dame, who had taught him his catechism, in youth, and was still his moral and spiritual adviser, jointly with the minister and Deacon Gookin.

"A marvel, truly, that Goody° Cloyse should be so far in the wilderness, at nightfall!" said he. "But, with your leave, friend, I shall take a cut through the woods, until we have left this Christian woman behind. Being a stranger to you, she might ask whom I was consorting with, and whither I was going."

"Be it so," said his fellow-traveller. "Betake you to the woods, and let me keep the path."

Accordingly, the young man turned aside, but took care to watch his companion, who advanced softly along the road, until he had come within a staff's length of the old dame. She, meanwhile, was making the best of her way, with singular speed for so aged a woman, and mumbling some indistinct words, a prayer, doubtless, as she

---

lecture-day: a weekday when everyone had to go to church to hear a sermon or Bible-reading. *Goody:* short for Goodwife, title for a married woman of ordinary station. In his story, Hawthorne borrows from history the names of two "Goodys"—Goody Cloyse and Goody Cory—and one unmarried woman, Martha Carrier. In 1692 Hawthorne's great-great-grandfather John Hathorne, a judge in the Salem witchcraft trials, had condemned all three to be hanged.

went. The traveller put forth his staff, and touched her withered neck with what seemed the serpent's tail.

"The devil!" screamed the pious old lady.

"Then Goody Cloyse knows her old friend?" observed the traveller, confronting her, and leaning on his writhing stick.

"Ah, forsooth, and is it your worship, indeed?" cried the good dame. "Yea, truly is it, and in the very image of my old gossip,° Goodman Brown, the grandfather of the silly fellow that now is. But—would your worship believe it?—my broomstick hath strangely disappeared, stolen, as I suspect, by that unhanged witch, Goody Cory, and that, too, when I was all anointed with the juice of smallage and cinquefoil and wolf's bane—"°

"Mingled with fine wheat and the fat of a new-born babe," said the shape of old Goodman Brown.

"Ah, your worship knows the receipt,"° cried the old lady, cackling aloud. "So, as I was saying, being all ready for the meeting, and no horse to ride on, I made up my mind to foot it; for they tell me, there is a nice young man to be taken into communion to-night. But now your good worship will lend me your arm, and we shall be there in a twinkling."

"That can hardly be," answered her friend. "I may not spare you my arm, Goody Cloyse, but here is my staff, if you will."

So saying, he threw it down at her feet, where, perhaps, it assumed life, being one of the rods which its owner had formerly lent to the Egyptian Magi.° Of this fact, however, Goodman Brown could not take cognizance. He had cast up his eyes in astonishment, and looking down again, beheld neither Goody Cloyse nor the serpentine staff, but his fellow-traveller alone, who waited for him as calmly as if nothing had happened.

"That old woman taught me my catechism!" said the young man; and there was a world of meaning in this simple comment.

They continued to walk onward, while the elder traveller exhorted his companion to make good speed and persevere in the path, discoursing so aptly, that his arguments seemed rather to spring up in the bosom of his auditor, than to be suggested by himself. As they went, he plucked a branch of maple, to serve for a walking-stick, and began to strip it of the twigs and little boughs, which were wet with evening dew. The moment his fingers touched them, they became strangely withered and dried up, as with a week's sunshine. Thus the pair proceeded, at a good free pace, until suddenly, in a gloomy hollow of the road, Goodman Brown sat himself down on the stump of a tree, and refused to go any farther.

"Friend," said he, stubbornly, "my mind is made up. Not another step will I budge on this errand. What if a wretched old woman do choose to go to the devil, when I thought she was going to Heaven! Is that any reason why I should quit my dear Faith, and go after her?"

"You will think better of this, by-and-by," said his acquaintance, composedly. "Sit here and rest yourself awhile; and when you feel like moving again, there is my staff to help you along."

30

35

40

---

gossip: friend or kinsman.   *smallage and cinquefoil and wolf's bane:* wild plants—here, ingredients for a witch's brew.   *receipt:* recipe.   *Egyptian Magi:* In the Bible, Pharaoh's wise men and sorcerers who by their magical powers changed their rods into live serpents. (This incident, part of the story of Moses and Aaron, is related in Exodus 7:8–12.)

Without more words, he threw his companion the maple stick, and was as speedily out of sight, as if he had vanished into the deepening gloom. The young man sat a few moments, by the road-side, applauding himself greatly, and thinking with how clear a conscience he should meet the minister, in his morning-walk, nor shrink from the eye of good old Deacon Gookin. And what calm sleep would be his, that very night, which was to have been spent so wickedly, but purely and sweetly now, in the arms of Faith! Amidst these pleasant and praiseworthy meditations, Goodman Brown heard the tramp of horses along the road, and deemed it advisable to conceal himself within the verge of the forest, conscious of the guilty purpose that had brought him thither, though now so happily turned from it.

On came the hoof-tramps and the voices of the riders, two grave old voices, conversing soberly as they drew near. These mingled sounds appeared to pass along the road, within a few yards of the young man's hiding-place; but owing, doubtless, to the depth of the gloom, at that particular spot, neither the travellers nor their steeds were visible. Though their figures brushed the small boughs by the way-side, it could not be seen that they intercepted, even for a moment, the faint gleam from the strip of bright sky, athwart which they must have passed. Goodman Brown alternately crouched and stood on tip-toe, pulling aside the branches, and thrusting forth his head as far as he durst, without discerning so much as a shadow. It vexed him the more, because he could have sworn, were such a thing possible, that he recognized the voices of the minister and Deacon Gookin, jogging along quietly, as they were wont to do, when bound to some ordination or ecclesiastical council. While yet within hearing, one of the riders stopped to pluck a switch.

"Of the two, reverend Sir," said the voice like the deacon's, "I had rather miss an ordination-dinner than to-night's meeting. They tell me that some of our community are to be here from Falmouth and beyond, and others from Connecticut and Rhode Island; besides several of the Indian powows,° who, after their fashion, know almost as much deviltry as the best of us. Moreover, there is a goodly young woman to be taken into communion."

"Mighty well, Deacon Gookin!" replied the solemn old tones of the minister. "Spur up, or we shall be late. Nothing can be done, you know, until I get on the ground."

The hoofs clattered again, and the voices, talking so strangely in the empty   45
air, passed on through the forest, where no church had ever been gathered, nor solitary Christian prayed. Whither, then, could these holy men be journeying, so deep into the heathen wilderness? Young Goodman Brown caught hold of a tree, for support, being ready to sink down on the ground, faint and overburdened with the heavy sickness of his heart. He looked up to the sky, doubting whether there really was a Heaven above him. Yet, there was the blue arch, and the stars brightening in it.

"With Heaven above, and Faith below, I will yet stand firm against the devil!" cried Goodman Brown.

While he still gazed upward, into the deep arch of the firmament, and had lifted his hands to pray, a cloud, though no wind was stirring, hurried across the zenith, and hid the brightening stars. The blue sky was still visible, except directly overhead,

---

powows: Indian priests or medicine men.

where this black mass of cloud was sweeping swiftly northward. Aloft in the air, as if from the depths of the cloud, came a confused and doubtful sound of voices. Once, the listener fancied that he could distinguish the accents of town's-people of his own, men and women, both pious and ungodly, many of whom he had met at the communion-table, and had seen others rioting at the tavern. The next moment, so indistinct were the sounds, he doubted whether he had heard aught but the murmur of the old forest, whispering without a wind. Then came a stronger swell of those familiar tones, heard daily in the sunshine, at Salem village, but never, until now, from a cloud of night. There was one voice, of a young woman, uttering lamentations, yet with an uncertain sorrow, and entreating for some favor, which, perhaps, it would grieve her to obtain. And all the unseen multitude, both saints and sinners, seemed to encourage her onward.

"Faith!" shouted Goodman Brown, in a voice of agony and desperation; and the echoes of the forest mocked him, crying—"Faith! Faith!" as if bewildered wretches were seeking her, all through the wilderness.

The cry of grief, rage, and terror, was yet piercing the night, when the unhappy husband held his breath for a response. There was a scream, drowned immediately in a louder murmur of voices, fading into far-off laughter, as the dark cloud swept away, leaving the clear and silent sky above Goodman Brown. But something fluttered lightly down through the air, and caught on the branch of a tree. The young man seized it, and beheld a pink ribbon.

"My Faith is gone!" cried he, after one stupefied moment. "There is no good on earth; and sin is but a name. Come, devil! for to thee is this world given." 50

And maddened with despair, so that he laughed loud and long, did Goodman Brown grasp his staff and set forth again, at such a rate, that he seemed to fly along the forest-path, rather than to walk or run. The road grew wilder and drearier, and more faintly traced, and vanished at length, leaving him in the heart of the dark wilderness, still rushing onward, with the instinct that guides mortal man to evil. The whole forest was peopled with frightful sounds; the creaking of the trees, the howling of wild beasts, and the yell of Indians; while, sometimes, the wind tolled like a distant church-bell, and sometimes gave a broad roar around the traveller, as if all Nature were laughing him to scorn. But he was himself the chief horror of the scene, and shrank not from its other horrors.

"Ha! ha! ha!" roared Goodman Brown, when the wind laughed at him. "Let us hear which will laugh loudest! Think not to frighten me with your deviltry! Come witch, come wizard, come Indian powow, come devil himself! and here comes Goodman Brown. You may as well fear him as he fear you!"

In truth, all through the haunted forest, there could be nothing more frightful than the figure of Goodman Brown. On he flew, among the black pines, brandishing his staff with frenzied gestures, now giving vent to an inspiration of horrid blasphemy, and now shouting forth such laughter, as set all the echoes of the forest laughing like demons around him. The fiend in his own shape is less hideous, than when he rages in the breast of man. Thus sped the demoniac on his course, until, quivering among the trees, he saw a red light before him, as when the felled trunks and branches of a clearing have been set on fire, and throw up their lurid blaze against the sky, at the hour of midnight. He paused, in a lull of the tempest that had driven him onward, and heard the swell of what seemed a hymn, rolling solemnly from a distance, with the weight of many voices. He knew the tune; it was a familiar one in the choir of the village meeting-house. The verse died heavily away, and was lengthened by a chorus, not of human voices, but of all the sounds of the benighted wilderness, pealing in awful harmony together. Goodman Brown cried out; and his cry was lost to his own ear, by its unison with the cry of the desert.

In the interval of silence, he stole forward, until the light glared full upon his eyes. At one extremity of an open space, hemmed in by the dark wall of the forest, arose a rock, bearing some rude, natural resemblance either to an altar or a pulpit, and surrounded by four blazing pines, their tops aflame, their stems untouched, like candles at an evening meeting. The mass of foliage, that had overgrown the summit of the rock, was all on fire, blazing high into the night, and fitfully illuminating the whole field. Each pendent twig and leafy festoon was in a blaze. As the red light arose and fell, a numerous congregation alternately shone forth, then disappeared in shadow, and again grew, as it were, out of the darkness, peopling the heart of the solitary woods at once.

"A grave and dark-clad company!" quoth Goodman Brown.   55

In truth, they were such. Among them, quivering to-and-fro, between gloom and splendor, appeared faces that would be seen, next day, at the council-board of the province, and others which, Sabbath after Sabbath, looked devoutly heavenward, and benignantly over the crowded pews, from the holiest pulpits in the land. Some affirm that the lady of the governor was there. At least, there were high dames well known to her, and wives of honored husbands, and widows, a great multitude, and ancient maidens, all of excellent repute, and fair young girls, who trembled, lest their mothers should espy them. Either the sudden gleams of light, flashing over the obscure field, bedazzled Goodman Brown, or he recognized a score of the church-members of Salem village, famous for their especial sanctity. Good old Deacon Gookin had arrived, and waited at the skirts of that venerable saint, his revered pastor. But, irreverently consorting with these grave, reputable, and pious people, these elders of the church, these chaste dames and dewy virgins, there were men of dissolute lives and women of spotted fame, wretches given over to all mean and filthy vice, and suspected even of horrid crimes. It was strange to see, that the good shrank not from the wicked, nor were the sinners abashed by the saints. Scattered, also, among their pale-faced enemies, were the Indian priests, or powows, who had often scared their native forest with more hideous incantations than any known to English witchcraft.

"But, where is Faith?" thought Goodman Brown; and, as hope came into his heart, he trembled.

Another verse of the hymn arose, a slow and mournful strain, such as the pious love, but joined to words which expressed all that our nature can conceive of sin, and darkly hinted at far more. Unfathomable to mere mortals is the lore of fiends. Verse after verse was sung, and still the chorus of the desert swelled between, like the deepest tone of a mighty organ. And, with the final peal of that dreadful anthem, there came a sound, as if the roaring wind, the rushing streams, the howling beasts, and every other voice of the unconverted wilderness, were mingling and according with the voice of guilty man, in homage to the prince of all. The four blazing pines threw up a loftier flame, and obscurely discovered shapes and visages of horror on the smoke-wreaths, above the impious assembly. At the same moment, the fire on the rock shot redly forth, and formed a glowing arch above its base, where now appeared a figure. With reverence be it spoken, the figure bore no slight similitude, both in garb and manner, to some grave divine of the New England churches.

"Bring forth the converts!" cried a voice, that echoed through the field and rolled into the forest.

At the word, Goodman Brown stepped forth from the shadow of the trees, and approached the congregation, with whom he felt a loathful brotherhood, by the sympathy of all that was wicked in his heart. He could have well nigh sworn, that the shape of his own dead father beckoned him to advance, looking downward from a smoke-wreath, while a woman, with dim features of despair, threw out her hand to warn him back. Was it his mother? But he had no power to retreat one step, nor to resist, even in thought, when the minister and good old Deacon Gookin seized his arms, and led him to the blazing rock. Thither came also the slender form of a veiled female, led between Goody Cloyse, that pious teacher of the catechism, and Martha Carrier, who had received the devil's promise to be queen of hell. A rampant hag was she! And there stood the proselytes,° beneath the canopy of fire.

"Welcome, my children," said the dark figure, "to the communion of your race! Ye have found, thus young, your nature and your destiny. My children, look behind you!"

They turned; and flashing forth, as it were, in a sheet of flame, the fiend-worshippers were seen; the smile of welcome gleamed darkly on every visage.

"There," resumed the sable form, "are all whom ye have reverenced from youth. Ye deemed them holier than yourselves, and shrank from your own sin, contrasting it with their lives of righteousness, and prayerful aspirations heavenward. Yet, here are they all, in my worshipping assembly! This night it shall be granted you to know their secret deeds; how hoary-bearded elders of the church have whispered wanton words to the young maids of their households; how many a woman, eager for widow's weeds, has given her husband a drink at bedtime, and let him sleep his last sleep in her bosom; how beardless youths have made haste to inherit their fathers' wealth; and how fair damsels—blush not, sweet ones!—have dug little graves in the garden, and bidden me, the sole guest, to an infant's funeral. By the sympathy of your human hearts for sin, ye shall scent out all the places—whether in church, bed-chamber, street, field, or forest—where crime has been committed, and shall exult to behold the whole earth one stain of guilt, one mighty bloodspot. Far more than this! It shall be yours to penetrate, in every bosom, the deep mystery of sin, the fountain of all wicked arts, and which inexhaustibly supplies more evil impulses than human power—than my power, at its utmost!—can make manifest in deeds. And now, my children, look upon each other."

They did so; and, by the blaze of the hell-kindled torches, the wretched man beheld his Faith, and the wife her husband, trembling before that unhallowed altar.

"Lo! there ye stand, my children," said the figure, in a deep and solemn tone, almost sad, with its despairing awfulness, as if his once angelic nature could yet mourn for our miserable race. "Depending upon one another's hearts, ye had still hoped, that virtue were not all a dream. Now are ye undeceived! Evil is the nature of mankind. Evil must be your only happiness. Welcome, again, my children, to the communion of your race!"

"Welcome!" repeated the fiend-worshippers, in one cry of despair and triumph.

And there they stood, the only pair, as it seemed, who were yet hesitating on the verge of wickedness, in this dark world. A basin was hollowed, naturally, in the rock. Did it contain water, reddened by the lurid light? or was it blood? or, perchance, a

proselytes: new converts.

liquid flame? Herein did the Shape of Evil dip his hand, and prepare to lay the mark of baptism upon their foreheads, that they might be partakers of the mystery of sin, more conscious of the secret guilt of others, both in deed and thought, than they could now be of their own. The husband cast one look at his pale wife, and Faith at him. What polluted wretches would the next glance show them to each other, shuddering alike at what they disclosed and what they saw!

"Faith! Faith!" cried the husband. "Look up to Heaven, and resist the Wicked one!"

Whether Faith obeyed, he knew not. Hardly had he spoken, when he found himself amid calm night and solitude, listening to a roar of the wind, which died heavily away through the forest. He staggered against the rock and felt it chill and damp, while a hanging twig, that had been all on fire, besprinkled his cheek with the coldest dew.

The next morning, young Goodman Brown came slowly into the street of Salem village, staring around him like a bewildered man. The good old minister was taking a walk along the grave-yard, to get an appetite for breakfast and meditate his sermon, and bestowed a blessing, as he passed, on Goodman Brown. He shrank from the venerable saint, as if to avoid an anathema.° Old Deacon Goodkin was at domestic worship, and the holy words of his prayer were heard through the open window. "What God doth the wizard pray to?" quoth Goodman Brown. Goody Cloyse, that excellent old Christian, stood in the early sunshine, at her own lattice, catechizing a little girl, who had brought her a pint of morning's milk. Goodman Brown snatched away the child, as from the grasp of the fiend himself. Turning the corner by the meeting-house, he spied the head of Faith, with the pink ribbons, gazing anxiously forth, and bursting into such joy at sight of him, that she skipt along the street, and almost kissed her husband before the whole village. But, Goodman Brown looked sternly and sadly into her face, and passed on without a greeting.

Had Goodman Brown fallen asleep in the forest, and only dreamed a wild dream of a witch-meeting?

Be it so, if you will. But, alas! it was a dream of evil omen for young Goodman Brown. A stern, a sad, a darkly meditative, a distrustful, if not a desperate man, did he become, from the night of that fearful dream. On the Sabbath-day, when the congregation were singing a holy psalm, he could not listen, because an anthem of sin rushed loudly upon his ear, and drowned all the blessed strain. When the minister spoke from the pulpit, with power and fervid eloquence, and, with his hand on the open Bible, of the sacred truths of our religion, and of saint-like lives and triumphant deaths, and of future bliss or misery unutterable, then did Goodman Brown turn pale, dreading, lest the roof should thunder down upon the gray blasphemer and his hearers. Often, awakening suddenly at midnight, he shrank from the bosom of Faith, and at morning or even-tide, when the family knelt down at prayer, he scowled, and muttered to himself, and gazed sternly at his wife, and turned away. And when he had lived long, and was borne to his grave, a hoary corpse, followed by Faith, an aged woman, and children and grandchildren, a goodly procession, besides neighbors, not a few, they carved no hopeful verse upon his tombstone; for his dying hour was gloom.

anathema: an official curse, a decree that casts one out of a church and bans him from receiving the sacraments.

Questions

1. Hawthorne's story is set in Salem, Massachusetts. What historical associations does this setting suggest to the reader?

2. Why is Brown's new bride Faith "aptly named" according to the narrator? What does the name "Goodman Brown" suggest about the character of the protagonist?

3. Is there any significance to the fact that the old man in the woods seems to resemble Brown?

4. As Brown and the stranger proceed deeper into the woods, what does Brown find out that troubles him? When the pink ribbon flutters to the ground, as though fallen from something airborne (paragraph 49), what does Brown assume? What effect does this event have upon his determination to resist the devil?

5. Is it significant that most of the story's action take place at night and in the woods?

6. What is the nature of the ceremony going on in the woods? What is being transacted between the old man and the townspeople?

7. What power does the devil promise to give his communicants (paragraph 63)?

8. Is Brown's experience in the woods real? If not, what other explanation can you provide?

9. What would be lost if the last three paragraphs of the tale were omitted?

10. If the story is an allegory, summarize the symbolical drama enacted in it.

NATHANIEL HAWTHORNE ON WRITING

Reflections on Truth and Clarity in Literature   (1837–1863)

I have another great difficulty, in the lack of materials; for I have seen so little of the world, that I have nothing but thin air to concoct my stories of, and it is not easy to give a lifelike semblance to such shadowy stuff. Sometimes, through a peep-hole, I have caught a glimpse of the real world; and the two or three articles, in which I have portrayed such glimpses, please me better than the others.

From a letter to Henry Wadsworth Longfellow, June 4, 1837

Every day of my life makes me feel more and more how seldom a fact is accurately stated; how, almost invariably, when a story has passed through the mind of a third person, it becomes, so far as regards the impression that it makes in further repetitions, little better than a falsehood, and this, too, though the narrator be the most truth-seeking person in existence. . . . Is truth a fantasy which we are to pursue forever and never grasp?

From a letter to his wife, Sophia Peabody, May 1, 1841

I am glad you think my style plain. I never, in any one page or paragraph, aimed at making it anything else, or giving it any other merit—and I wish people would leave off talking about its beauty. If it have any, it is only pardonable as being unintentional. The greatest possible merit of style is, of course, to make the mere words absolutely disappear into the thought.

From a letter to editor Evert A. Duyckinck, April 27, 1851

Upon my honor, I am not quite sure that I entirely comprehend my own meaning, in some of these blasted allegories; but I remember that I always had a meaning—or at least thought I had. I am a good deal changed since those times; and, to tell you the truth, my past self is not very much to my taste, as I see myself in this book.

From a letter to his publisher, James T. Fields, April 13, 1854

[Y]ou attribute to me a superiority which I do not dream of asserting. A reader, who can fully understand and appreciate a work, possesses all the faculties of the writer who produced it—except a knack of expression, by which the latter is enabled to give definite shape to an idea or sentiment which he and his appreciative reader possess in common. Thus the advantage on the author's part is but a slight one, and the more truth and wisdom he writes, the smaller is his individual share in it.

From a letter to Robert J. Poney, September 28, 1863

The Obscurest Man in American Letters   1851

The author of *Twice-Told Tales* has a claim to one distinction, which, as none of his literary brethren will care about disputing it with him, he need not be afraid to mention. He was, for a good many years, the obscurest man of letters in America.

These stories were published in Magazines and Annuals, extending over a period of ten or twelve years, and comprising the whole of the writer's young manhood, without making (so far as he has ever been aware) the slightest impression on the Public. One or two among them—"The Rill from the Town-Pump" in perhaps a greater degree than any other—had a pretty wide newspaper-circulation; as for the rest, he has no grounds for supposing, that, on their first appearance, they met with the good or evil fortune to be read by anybody. Throughout the time above-specified, he had no incitement to literary effort in a reasonable prospect of reputation or profit; nothing but the pleasure itself of composition—an enjoyment not at all amiss in its way, and perhaps essential to the merit of the work in hand, but which, in the long run, will hardly keep the chill out of a writer's heart, or the numbness out of his fingers. To this total lack of sympathy, at the age when his mind would naturally have been most effervescent, the Public owe it, (and it is certainly an effect not to be regretted, on either part,) that the Author can show nothing for the thought and industry of that portion of his life, save the forty sketches, or thereabouts, included in these volumes.

From the preface to the 1851 edition of *Twice-Told Tales*

CRITICS ON HAWTHORNE

Herman Melville (1819–1891)

Excerpt from a Review of *Mosses from an Old Manse*   1850

[W]ith whatever motive, playful or profound, Nathaniel Hawthorne has chosen to entitle his pieces in the manner he has, it is certain, that some of them are directly calculated to deceive—egregiously deceive, the superficial skimmer of pages. To be downright and candid once more, let me cheerfully say, that two of these titles did dolefully dupe no less an eagle-eyed reader than myself; and that, too, after I had been impressed with a sense of the great depth and breadth of this American man. "Who in the name of thunder" (as the country-people say in this neighborhood) "who in the name of thunder," would anticipate any marvel in a piece entitled "Young Goodman Brown"? You would of course suppose that it was a simple little tale, intended as a supplement to "Goody Two Shoes." Whereas, it is deep as Dante; nor can you finish it, without addressing the author in his own words—"It is yours to penetrate, in every bosom, the deep mystery of sin." And with Young Goodman, too, in allegorical pursuit of his Puritan wife, you cry out in your anguish,—

> "Faith!" shouted Goodman Brown, in a voice of agony and desperation; and the echoes of the forest mocked him, crying—"Faith! Faith!" as if bewildered wretches were seeking her all through the wilderness.

From "Hawthorne and His Mosses"

Edgar Allan Poe (1809–1849)

The Genius of Hawthorne's Short Stories   1842

Were we called upon however to designate that class of composition which, next to [a short lyric poem] should best fulfill the demands of high genius—should offer it the most advantageous field of exertion—we should unhesitatingly speak of the prose tale, as Mr. Hawthorne has here exemplified it. We allude to the short prose narrative, requiring from a half-hour to one or two hours in its perusal. The ordinary novel is objectionable, from its length, for reasons already stated in substance. As it cannot be read at one sitting, it deprives itself, of course, of the immense force derivable from *totality*. Worldly interests intervening during the pauses of perusal, modify, annul, or counteract, in a greater or less degree, the impressions of the book. But simple cessation in reading, would, of itself, be sufficient to destroy the true unity. In the brief tale, however, the author is enabled to carry out the fullness of his intention, be it what it may. During the hour of perusal the soul of the reader is at the writer's control. There are no external or extrinsic influences—resulting from weariness or interruption.

A skillful literary artist has constructed a tale. If wise, he has not fashioned his thoughts to accommodate his incidents; but having conceived, with deliberate care, a certain unique or single *effect* to be wrought out, he then invents such incidents—he then combines such events as may best aid him in establishing this preconceived effect. If his very initial sentence tend not to the outbringing of this effect, then he has failed in his first step. In the whole composition there should be no word written, of which the tendency, direct or indirect, is not to the one pre-established design. And by such means, with such care and skill, a picture is at length painted which leaves in the mind of him who contemplates it with a kindred art, a sense of the fullest satisfaction. The idea of the tale has been presented unblemished, because undisturbed; and this is an end unattainable by the novel. Undue brevity is just as exceptionable here as in the poem; but undue length is yet more to be avoided.

• • •

Of Mr. Hawthorne's Tales we would say, emphatically, that they belong to the highest region of Art—an Art subservient to genius of a very lofty order. We had supposed, with good reason for so supposing, that he had been thrust into his present position by one of the impudent *cliques* which beset our literature, and whose pretensions it is our full purpose to expose at the earliest opportunity; but we have been most agreeably mistaken. We know of few compositions which the critic can more honestly commend than these "Twice-Told Tales." As Americans, we feel proud of the book.

Mr. Hawthorne's distinctive trait is invention, creation, imagination, originality—a trait which, in the literature of fiction, is positively worth all the rest. But the nature of originality, so far as regards its manifestation in letters, is but imperfectly understood. The inventive or original mind as frequently displays itself in novelty of *tone* as in novelty of matter. Mr. Hawthorne is original at *all* points.

From a review of *Twice-Told Tales* by Nathaniel Hawthorne

CRITICS ON "YOUNG GOODMAN BROWN"

Film adaption of Hawthorne, 1926.

Richard H. Fogle (1911–1995)

Ambiguity in "Young Goodman Brown"   1945

"Young Goodman Brown" is generally felt to be one of Hawthorne's more difficult tales, from the ambiguity of the conclusions which may be drawn from it. Its hero, a naive young man who accepts both society in general and his fellow-men as individuals at their own valuation, is in one terrible night presented with the vision of human Evil, and is ever afterwards "A stern, a sad, a darkly meditative, a distrustful, if not a desperate man . . . ," whose "dying hour was gloom." So far we are clear enough, but there are confusing factors. In the first place, are the events of the night merely subjective, a dream; or do they actually occur? Again, at the crucial point in his ordeal Goodman Brown summons the strength to cry to his wife Faith, "look up to heaven, and resist the evil one." It would appear from this that he has successfully resisted the supreme temptation—but evidently he is not therefore saved. Henceforth, "On the Sabbath-day, when the congregation were singing a holy psalm, he could not listen, because an anthem of sin rushed loudly upon his ear, and drowned all the blessed strain." On the other hand, he is not wholly lost, for in the sequel he is only at intervals estranged from "the bosom of Faith." Has Hawthorne himself failed to control the implications of his allegory?

I should say rather that these ambiguities of meaning are intentional, an integral part of his purpose. Hawthorne wishes to propose, not flatly that man is primarily evil, but instead the gnawing doubt lest this should indeed be true. "Come, devil! for to thee is this world given," exclaims Goodman Brown at the height of his agony, but he finds strength to resist the devil, and in the ambiguous conclusion he does not entirely reject his former faith. His trial, then, comes not from the certainty but the dread of Evil. Hawthorne poses the dangerous question of the relations of Good and Evil in man, but withholds his answer. Nor does he permit himself to settle whether the events of the night of trial are real or the mere figment of a dream.

From "Ambiguity and Clarity in Hawthorne's 'Young Goodman Brown'"

Paul J. Hurley (1931–2003)

Evil Wherever He Looks

1966

Has Goodman Brown really been subjected to visions which imply the universal prevalence of evil? Has the faith of a good man been destroyed by a revelation of the world's sinfulness? It would seem not. If one accepts the fact that Hawthorne gives us no valid grounds to believe in the reality of Goodman Brown's visions and voices, he must either believe, as Fogle does, that Hawthorne feared his own knowledge of the world's evil; or he must treat those events as emanations from Brown's subconscious which intimate the corruption of Brown's own mind. Why do the young man's visions of evil concern only Goody Cloyse, the minister, Deacon Gookin, and his wife? One answer, of course, is that they represent an exceptional piety which makes their participation in evil dramatically more effective. But if Hawthorne's theme concerns the universality of human sinfulness, should we not see a wider manifestation of that evil? The only scene in which such a manifestation occurs is the Devil's communion, but that takes place *after* Goodman Brown has declared his loss of faith; and the scene of that vision, Hawthorne tells us, was "in the heart of the dark wilderness," a setting whose significance is so inescapable that Conrad would later echo Hawthorne's words (unknowingly?) in the title of one of his novels.

A more significant reason for Hawthorne's choice of those four characters occurs to us if we return to a consideration of their relationship to Goodman Brown. They are the four people in Salem village to whom he is morally responsible. Goody Cloyse "had taught him his catechism in youth, and was still his moral and spiritual advisor, jointly with the minister and Deacon Gookin." His wife is an even more important representative of the forces of morality and virtue. It seems obvious that they are the four people whose respectability must destroyed before Goodman Brown can fully commit himself to a belief in the wickedness of the world. . . .

The most striking quality of the paragraph which describes Goodman Brown's return to the village of Salem is its tone. No longer are there any suggestions of the weird and incredible. The dreamlike quality of Brown's adventure in the forest is replaced by purposefully direct and forthright narration. Life proceeds in the village as it always has. Only Goodman Brown has changed. If the events of the night before had been real, or even symbolic of reality, would not Hawthorne have indicated in some way a shared knowledge between Goodman Brown and the townsfolk whom he sees? Hawthorne has told us that Brown did not know whether his wife obeyed his cry to look up to heaven. Nonetheless, he passes her without a greeting when she runs to meet him. His own distrust and suspicion have assured him that she is sinful, even though, as Hawthorne is careful to note, she is wearing the pink ribbons which Goodman Brown thought he had grasped from the air. Nor is there any change in anyone else. The minister seeks to bless Goodman Brown, but the young man shrinks from him; Deacon Gookin is praying and even though Goodman Brown can hear "the holy words of his prayer," he still thinks him a wizard. Goody Cloyse is catechizing a young girl, and Goodman Brown snatches the child from the old woman's arms. The corruption of his mind and heart is complete; Goodman Brown sees evil wherever he looks. He sees it because he wants to see it.

If Hawthorne had wished to intimate that the events of the night were real, it would hardly do to confuse us with suggestions about dreams (unless, as Fogle thinks, this was Hawthorne's method of escaping the implications of his own insight into man's depravity). A more acceptable interpretation of the ambiguity of the story is to see in it Hawthorne's suggestion that the incredible incidents in the forest were the product of an ego-induced fantasy, the self-justification of a diseased mind. It seems clear that these incidents were not experienced; they were willed. The important point, however, is that Goodman Brown has accepted them as truth; and the acceptance of evil as the final truth about man has turned him into "A stern, a sad, a darkly meditative, a distrustful" human being. Goodman Brown does not become aware of his own kinship with evil; he does not see sinfulness in himself but only in others. That, perhaps, is his most awful sin. He has lost not only faith in his fellow men but his compassion for them. And so it is that "On the Sabbath-day, when the congregation were singing a holy psalm, he could not listen, because an anthem of sin rushed loudly upon his ear, and drowned all the blessed strain." Hawthorne never tells us that the anthem, loud and fearful as it must have been, ever reached the ears of any but young Goodman Brown.

From "Young Goodman Brown's 'Heart of Darkness'"

Nancy Bunge (b. 1942)

Complacency and Community   1993

"Young Goodman Brown" not only presents the issue of the Salem witch trials, but a number of its characters have the names of Salem residents charged with witchcraft, and its major action takes place in the noisy pasture historical documents of the period designate as a witches' gathering place. Hawthorne does not simply provide a record of the time, he uses history to examine issues of community and individualism explaining both the madness in Salem and much subsequent madness.

Ostensibly, this tale indicts arrogant individualism. Young Goodman Brown, either in dream or in fact, almost joins a witches' sabbath in the forest. He turns away at the last moment because he does not want to confess his evil. Ironically, his exemplary behavior produces a life of isolation and gloom: "A stern, a sad, a darkly meditative, a distrustful, if not a desperate man, did he become, from the night of that fearful dream." He despises his townspeople because he believes they participated in the evil ceremony he resisted. He sees nothing but their sinfulness. His wife, Faith, particularly offends him: "Often, awakening suddenly at midnight, he shrank from the bosom of Faith, and at morning or even-tide, when the family knelt down at prayer, he scowled, and muttered to himself, and gazed sternly at his wife, and turned away." Brown has a classic case of projection. Unable to deal with his own frailty, he sees and hates it in everyone else. So the tale seems to celebrate humility.

But Brown learns complacency from his community. He lives in a society that ruthlessly judges evil in everyone else. He resists the demonic figure who urges him towards the witches' sabbath because he suspects that acting out his sinful impulses will bring dishonor on his family. The devil laughs at Brown's innocence: "I have been as well acquainted with your family as with ever a one among the Puritans; and that's no trifle to say. I helped your grandfather, the constable, when he lashed the Quaker woman so smartly through the streets of Salem. And it was I that brought your father a pitch-pine knot, kindled at my own hearth, to set fire to an Indian village, in King Philip's war." In other words, Puritan "goodness" has justified gross violations of people the Puritans perceived as bad, such as Quakers and Native Americans. Brown's decision to declare himself good and assign all the evil to others has strong community history.

The tale also calls into question the quality of Brown's present social and family life since Brown functions as a beloved father and prized citizen, even though he despises everyone: "He had lived long, and was borne to his grave, a hoary corpse, followed by Faith, an aged woman, and children and grandchildren, a goodly procession, besides neighbors, not a few."

So, although this tale condemns arrogance and recommends community, it acknowledges the difficulties of distinguishing real and apparent solidarity. People long to belong and they almost inevitably attempt to win acceptance by following socially approved patterns. But this faith in their family, society, or nation assumes that convention grows from wisdom, not habit. Those willing to resist society's self-righteousness may achieve the humility necessary to genuine fellowship, but they will have trouble making themselves understood. On the other hand, the community will support those who ask no questions. Societies encourage conformity because the assumption that this state, unlike all others, rests on a bedrock of truth, cannot survive examination. So behavior deviating from this complacency needs speedy and forceful correction.

From *Nathaniel Hawthorne: A Study of the Short Fiction*

CHARLOTTE PERKINS GILMAN

Charlotte Perkins Gilman (1860–1935) was born in Hartford, Connecticut. Her father was the writer Frederick Beecher Perkins (a nephew of reformer-novelist Harriet Beecher Stowe, author of Uncle Tom's Cabin, *and abolitionist minister Henry Ward Beecher), but he abandoned the family shortly after his daughter's birth. Raised in meager surroundings, the young Gilman adopted her intellectual Beecher aunts as role models. Because she and her mother moved from one relation to another, Gilman's early education was neglected—at fifteen, she had had only four years of schooling. In 1878 she studied commercial art at the Rhode Island School of Design. In 1884 she married Walter Stetson, an artist. After the birth of her one daughter, she experienced a severe depression. The rest cure her doctor prescribed became the basis of her most famous story, "The Yellow Wallpaper." This tale combines standard ele-*

Charlotte Perkins Gilman

ments of Gothic fiction (the isolated country mansion, the brooding atmosphere of the room, the aloof but dominating husband) with the fresh clarity of Gilman's feminist perspective. Gilman's first marriage ended in an amicable divorce. A celebrated essayist and public speaker, she became an important early figure in American feminism. Her study Women and Economics *(1898) stressed the importance of both sexes having a place in the working world. Her feminist-Utopian novel* Herland *(1915) describes a thriving nation of women without men. In 1900 Gilman married a second time—this time, more happily—to her cousin George Houghton Gilman. Following his sudden death in 1934, Gilman discovered she had inoperable breast cancer. After finishing her autobiography, she killed herself with chloroform in Pasadena, California.*

The Yellow Wallpaper   1892

It is very seldom that mere ordinary people like John and myself secure ancestral halls for the summer.

A colonial mansion, a hereditary estate, I would say a haunted house and reach the height of romantic felicity—but that would be asking too much of fate!

Still I will proudly declare that there is something queer about it.

Else, why should it be let so cheaply? And why have stood so long untenanted?

John laughs at me, of course, but one expects that.   5

John is practical in the extreme. He has no patience with faith, an intense horror of superstition, and he scoffs openly at any talk of things not to be felt and seen and put down in figures.

John is a physician, and *perhaps*—(I would not say it to a living soul, of course, but this is dead paper and a great relief to my mind)—*perhaps* that is one reason I do not get well faster.

You see, he does not believe I am sick! And what can one do?

If a physician of high standing, and one's own husband, assures friends and relatives that there is really nothing the matter with one but temporary nervous depression—a slight hysterical tendency—what is one to do?

My brother is also a physician, and also of high standing, and he says the same thing.

So I take phosphates or phosphites—whichever it is—and tonics, and air and exercise, and journeys, and am absolutely forbidden to "work" until I am well again.

Personally, I disagree with their ideas.

Personally, I believe that congenial work, with excitement and change, would do me good.

But what is one to do?

I did write for a while in spite of them; but it *does* exhaust me a good deal—having to be so sly about it, or else meet with heavy opposition.

I sometimes fancy that in my condition, if I had less opposition and more society and stimulus—but John says the very worst thing I can do is to think about my condition, and I confess it always makes me feel bad.

So I will let it alone and talk about the house.

The most beautiful place! It is quite alone, standing well back from the road, quite three miles from the village. It makes me think of English places that you read about, for there are hedges and walls and gates that lock, and lots of separate little houses for the gardeners and people.

There is a *delicious* garden! I never saw such a garden—large and shady, full of box-bordered paths, and lined with long grape-covered arbors with seats under them.

There were greenhouses, but they are all broken now.

There was some legal trouble, I believe, something about the heirs and co-heirs; anyhow, the place has been empty for years.

That spoils my ghostliness, I am afraid, but I don't care—there is something strange about the house—I can feel it.

I even said so to John one moonlight evening, but he said what I felt was a *draught*, and shut the window.

I get unreasonably angry with John sometimes. I'm sure I never used to be so sensitive. I think it is due to this nervous condition.

But John says if I feel so I shall neglect proper self-control; so I take pains to control myself—before him, at least, and that makes me very tired.

I don't like our room a bit. I wanted one downstairs that opened onto the piazza and had roses all over the window, and such pretty old-fashioned chintz hangings! But John would not hear of it.

He said there was only one window and not room for two beds, and no near room for him if he took another.

He is very careful and loving, and hardly lets me stir without special direction.

I have a schedule prescription for each hour in the day; he takes all care from me, and so I feel basely ungrateful not to value it more.

He said he came here solely on my account, that I was to have perfect rest and all the air I could get. "Your exercise depends on your strength, my dear," said he, "and your food somewhat on your appetite; but air you can absorb all the time." So we took the nursery at the top of the house.

It is a big, airy room, the whole floor nearly, with windows that look all ways, and air and sunshine galore. It was a nursery first, and then playroom and gymnasium,

I should judge, for the windows are barred for little children, and there are rings and things in the walls.

The paint and paper look as if a boys' school had used it. It is stripped off—the paper—in great patches all around the head of my bed, about as far as I can reach, and in a great place on the other side of the room low down. I never saw a worse paper in my life. One of those sprawling, flamboyant patterns committing every artistic sin.

It is dull enough to confuse the eye in following, pronounced enough constantly to irritate and provoke study, and when you follow the lame uncertain curves for a little distance they suddenly commit suicide—plunge off at outrageous angles, destroy themselves in unheard-of contradictions.

The color is repellent, almost revolting: a smouldering unclean yellow, strangely faded by the slow-turning sunlight. It is a dull yet lurid orange in some places, a sickly sulphur tint in others.

No wonder the children hated it! I should hate it myself if I had to live in this room long. 35

There comes John, and I must put this away—he hates to have me write a word.

We have been here two weeks, and I haven't felt like writing before, since that first day.

I am sitting by the window now, up in this atrocious nursery, and there is nothing to hinder my writing as much as I please, save lack of strength.

John is away all day, and even some nights when his cases are serious.

I am glad my case is not serious! 40

But these nervous troubles are dreadfully depressing.

John does not know how much I really suffer. He knows there is no *reason* to suffer, and that satisfies him.

Of course it is only nervousness. It does weigh on me so not to do my duty in any way!

I meant to be such a help to John, such a real rest and comfort, and here I am a comparative burden already!

Nobody would believe what an effort it is to do what little I am able—to dress and entertain, and order things. 45

It is fortunate Mary is so good with the baby. Such a dear baby!

And yet I *cannot* be with him, it makes me so nervous.

I suppose John never was nervous in his life. He laughs at me so about this wallpaper!

At first he meant to repaper the room, but afterward he said that I was letting it get the better of me, and that nothing was worse for a nervous patient than to give way to such fancies.

He said that after the wallpaper was changed it would be the heavy bedstead, 50 and then the barred windows, and then that gate at the head of the stairs, and so on.

"You know the place is doing you good," he said, "and really, dear, I don't care to renovate the house just for a three months' rental."

"Then do let us go downstairs," I said. "There are such pretty rooms there."

Then he took me in his arms and called me a blessed little goose, and said he would go down to the cellar, if I wished, and have it whitewashed into the bargain.

But he is right enough about the beds and windows and things.

It is as airy and comfortable a room as anyone need wish, and, of course, I would 55 not be so silly as to make him uncomfortable just for a whim.

I'm really getting quite fond of the big room, all but that horrid paper.

Out of one window I can see the garden—those mysterious deep-shaded arbors, the riotous old-fashioned flowers, and bushes and gnarly trees.

Out of another I get a lovely view of the bay and a little private wharf belonging to the estate. There is a beautiful shaded lane that runs down there from the house. I always fancy I see people walking in these numerous paths and arbors, but John has cautioned me not to give way to fancy in the least. He says that with my imaginative power and habit of story-making, a nervous weakness like mine is sure to lead to all manner of excited fancies, and that I ought to use my will and good sense to check the tendency. So I try.

I think sometimes that if I were only well enough to write a little it would relieve the press of ideas and rest me.

But I find I get pretty tired when I try. 60

It is so discouraging not to have any advice and companionship about my work. When I get really well, John says we will ask Cousin Henry and Julia down for a long visit; but he says he would as soon put fireworks in my pillow-case as to let me have those stimulating people about now.

I wish I could get well faster.

But I must not think about that. This paper looks to me as if it *knew* what a vicious influence it had!

There is a recurrent spot where the pattern lolls like a broken neck and two bulbous eyes stare at you upside down.

I get positively angry with the impertinence of it and the everlastingness. Up 65 and down and sideways they crawl, and those absurd unblinking eyes are everywhere. There is one place where two breadths didn't match, and the eyes go all up and down the line, one a little higher than the other.

I never saw so much expression in an inanimate thing before, and we all know how much expression they have! I used to lie awake as a child and get more entertainment and terror out of blank walls and plain furniture than most children could find in a toy-store.

I remember what a kindly wink the knobs of our big old bureau used to have, and there was one chair that always seemed like a strong friend.

I used to feel that if any of the other things looked too fierce I could always hop into that chair and be safe.

The furniture in this room is no worse than inharmonious, however, for we had to bring it all from downstairs. I suppose when this was used as a playroom they had to take the nursery things out, and no wonder! I never saw such ravages as the children have made here.

The wallpaper, as I said before, is torn off in spots, and it sticketh closer than a 70 brother—they must have had perseverance as well as hatred.

Then the floor is scratched and gouged and splintered, the plaster itself is dug out here and there, and this great heavy bed, which is all we found in the room, looks as if it had been through the wars.

But I don't mind it a bit—only the paper.

There comes John's sister. Such a dear girl as she is, and so careful of me! I must not let her find me writing.

She is a perfect and enthusiastic housekeeper, and hopes for no better profession. I verily believe she thinks it is the writing which made me sick!

But I can write when she is out, and see her a long way off from these windows. 75

There is one that commands the road, a lovely shaded winding road, and one that just looks off over the country. A lovely country, too, full of great elms and velvet meadows.

This wallpaper has a kind of sub-pattern in a different shade, a particularly irritating one, for you can only see it in certain lights, and not clearly then.

But in the places where it isn't faded and where the sun is just so—I can see a strange, provoking, formless sort of figure that seems to skulk about behind that silly and conspicuous front design.

There's sister on the stairs!

Well, the Fourth of July is over! The people are all gone, and I am tired out. John   80
thought it might do me good to see a little company, so we just had Mother and Nellie and the children down for a week.

Of course I didn't do a thing. Jennie sees to everything now.

But it tired me all the same.

John says if I don't pick up faster he shall send me to Weir Mitchell° in the fall.

But I don't want to go there at all. I had a friend who was in his hands once, and she says he is just like John and my brother, only more so!

Besides, it is such an undertaking to go so far.   85

I don't feel as if it was worthwhile to turn my hand over for anything, and I'm getting dreadfully fretful and querulous.

I cry at nothing, and cry most of the time.

Of course I don't when John is here, or anybody else, but when I am alone.

And I am alone a good deal just now. John is kept in town very often by serious cases, and Jennie is good and lets me alone when I want her to.

So I walk a little in the garden or down that lovely lane, sit on the porch under   90
the roses, and lie down up here a good deal.

I'm getting really fond of the room in spite of the wallpaper. Perhaps *because* of the wallpaper.

It dwells in my mind so!

I lie here on this great immovable bed—it is nailed down, I believe—and follow that pattern about by the hour. It is as good as gymnastics, I assure you. I start, we'll say, at the bottom, down in the corner over there where it has not been touched, and I determine for the thousandth time that I *will* follow that pointless pattern to some sort of a conclusion.

I know a little of the principle of design, and I know this thing was not arranged on any laws of radiation,° or alternation, or repetition, or symmetry, or anything else that I ever heard of.

It is repeated, of course, by the breadths, but not otherwise.   95

Looked at in one way, each breadth stands alone; the bloated curves and flourishes—a kind of "debased Romanesque" with *delirium tremens*—go waddling up and down in isolated columns of fatuity.

Weir Mitchell (1829–1914): famed nerve specialist who actually treated the author, Charlotte Perkins Gilman, for nervous prostration with his well-known "rest cure." (The cure was not successful.) Also the author of *Diseases of the Nervous System, Especially of Women* (1881).   *laws of radiation:* a principle of design in which all elements are arranged in some circular pattern around a center.

But, on the other hand, they connect diagonally, and the sprawling outlines run off in great slanting waves of optic horror, like a lot of wallowing sea-weeds in full chase.

The whole thing goes horizontally, too, at least it seems so, and I exhaust myself trying to distinguish the order of its going in that direction.

They have used a horizontal breadth for a frieze, and that adds wonderfully to the confusion.

There is one end of the room where it is almost intact, and there, when the crosslights fade and the low sun shines directly upon it, I can almost fancy radiation after all—the interminable grotesque seems to form around a common center and rush off in headlong plunges of equal distraction.

It makes me tired to follow it. I will take a nap, I guess.

I don't know why I should write this.

I don't want to.

I don't feel able.

And I know John would think it absurd. But I *must* say what I feel and think in some way—it is such a relief!

But the effort is getting to be greater than the relief.

Half the time now I am awfully lazy, and lie down ever so much. John says I mustn't lose my strength, and has me take cod liver oil and lots of tonics and things, to say nothing of ale and wines and rare meat.

Dear John! He loves me very dearly, and hates to have me sick. I tried to have a real earnest reasonable talk with him the other day, and tell him how I wish he would let me go and make a visit to Cousin Henry and Julia.

But he said I wasn't able to go, nor able to stand it after I got there; and I did not make out a very good case for myself, for I was crying before I had finished.

It is getting to be a great effort for me to think straight. Just this nervous weakness, I suppose.

And dear John gathered me up in his arms, and just carried me upstairs and laid me on the bed, and sat by me and read to me till it tired my head.

He said I was his darling and his comfort and all he had, and that I must take care of myself for his sake, and keep well.

He says no one but myself can help me out of it, that I must use my will and self-control and not let any silly fancies run away with me.

There's one comfort—the baby is well and happy, and does not have to occupy this nursery with the horrid wallpaper.

If we had not used it, that blessed child would have! What a fortunate escape! Why, I wouldn't have a child of mine, an impressionable little thing, live in such a room for worlds.

I never thought of it before, but it is lucky that John kept me here after all; I can stand it so much easier than a baby, you see.

Of course I never mention it to them any more—I am too wise—but I keep watch for it all the same.

There are things in the wallpaper that nobody knows about but me, or ever will.

Behind that outside pattern the dim shapes get clearer every day.

It is always the same shape, only very numerous.

And it is like a woman stooping down and creeping about behind that pattern. I don't like it a bit. I wonder—I begin to think—I wish John would take me away from here!

It is so hard to talk with John about my case, because he is so wise, and because he loves me so.

But I tried it last night.

It was moonlight. The moon shines in all around just as the sun does.

I hate to see it sometimes, it creeps so slowly, and always comes in by one   125 window or another.

John was asleep and I hated to waken him, so I kept still and watched the moonlight on that undulating wallpaper till I felt creepy.

The faint figure behind seemed to shake the pattern, just as if she wanted to get out.

I got up softly and went to feel and see if the paper *did* move, and when I came back John was awake.

"What is it, little girl?" he said. "Don't go walking about like that—you'll get cold."

I thought it was a good time to talk, so I told him that I really was not gaining   130 here, and that I wished he would take me away.

"Why, darling!" said he. "Our lease will be up in three weeks, and I can't see how to leave before.

"The repairs are not done at home, and I cannot possibly leave town just now. Of course, if you were in any danger, I could and would, but you really are better, dear, whether you can see it or not. I am a doctor, dear, and I know. You are gaining flesh and color, your appetite is better, I feel really much easier about you."

"I don't weigh a bit more," said I, "nor as much; and my appetite may be better in the evening when you are here but it is worse in the morning when you are away!"

"Bless her little heart!" said he with a big hug. "She shall be as sick as she pleases! But now let's improve the shining hours by going to sleep, and talk about it in the morning!"

"And you won't go away?" I asked gloomily.   135

"Why, how can I, dear? It is only three weeks more and then we will take a nice little trip for a few days while Jennie is getting the house ready. Really, dear, you are better!"

"Better in body perhaps—" I began, and stopped short, for he sat up straight and looked at me with such a stern, reproachful look that I could not say another word.

"My darling," said he, "I beg you, for my sake and for our child's sake, as well as for your own, that you will never for one instant let that idea enter your mind! There is nothing so dangerous, so fascinating, to a temperament like yours. It is a false and foolish fancy. Can you trust me as a physician when I tell you so?"

So of course I said no more on that score, and we went to sleep before long. He thought I was asleep first, but I wasn't, and lay there for hours trying to decide whether that front pattern and the back pattern really did move together or separately.

On a pattern like this, by daylight, there is a lack of sequence, a defiance of law,   140 that is a constant irritant to a normal mind.

The color is hideous enough, and unreliable enough, and infuriating enough, but the pattern is torturing.

You think you have mastered it, but just as you get well under way in following, it turns a back-somersault and there you are. It slaps you in the face, knocks you down, and tramples upon you. It is like a bad dream.

The outside pattern is a florid arabesque,° reminding one of a fungus. If you can imagine a toadstool in joints, an interminable string of toadstools, budding and sprouting in endless convolutions—why, that is something like it.

That is, sometimes!

There is one marked peculiarity about this paper, a thing nobody seems to notice   145
but myself, and that is that it changes as the light changes.

When the sun shoots in through the east window—I always watch for that first long, straight ray—it changes so quickly that I never can quite believe it.

That is why I watch it always.

By moonlight—the moon shines in all night when there is a moon—I wouldn't know it was the same paper.

At night in any kind of light, in twilight, candlelight, lamplight, and worst of all by moonlight, it becomes bars! The outside pattern, I mean, and the woman behind it is as plain as can be.

I didn't realize for a long time what the thing was that showed behind, that dim   150
sub-pattern, but now I am quite sure it is a woman.

By daylight she is subdued, quiet. I fancy it is the pattern that keeps her so still. It is so puzzling. It keeps me quiet by the hour.

I lie down ever so much now. John says it is good for me, and to sleep all I can.

Indeed he started the habit by making me lie down for an hour after each meal.

It is a very bad habit, I am convinced, for you see, I don't sleep.

And that cultivates deceit, for I don't tell them I'm awake—oh, no!   155

The fact is I am getting a little afraid of John.

He seems very queer sometimes, and even Jennie has an inexplicable look.

It strikes me occasionally, just as a scientific hypothesis, that perhaps it is the paper!

I have watched John when he did not know I was looking, and come into the room suddenly on the most innocent excuses, and I've caught him several times *looking at the paper!* And Jennie too. I caught Jennie with her hand on it once.

She didn't know I was in the room, and when I asked her in a quiet, a very quiet   160
voice, with the most restrained manner possible, what she was doing with the paper, she turned around as if she had been caught stealing, and looked quite angry—asked me why I should frighten her so!

Then she said that the paper stained everything it touched, that she had found yellow smooches° on all my clothes and John's and she wished we would be more careful!

Did not that sound innocent? But I know she was studying that pattern, and I am determined that nobody shall find it out but myself!

Life is very much more exciting now than it used to be. You see, I have something more to expect, to look forward to, to watch. I really do eat better, and am more quiet than I was.

John is so pleased to see me improve! He laughed a little the other day, and said I seemed to be flourishing in spite of my wallpaper.

I turned it off with a laugh. I had no intention of telling him it was *because* of the   165
wallpaper—he would make fun of me. He might even want to take me away.

arabesque: a type of ornamental style (Arabic in origin) that uses flowers, foliage, fruit, or other figures to create an intricate pattern of interlocking shapes and lines.   *smooches:* smudges or smears.

I don't want to leave now until I have found it out. There is a week more, and I think that will be enough.

I'm feeling so much better!

I don't sleep much at night, for it is so interesting to watch developments; but I sleep a good deal during the daytime.

In the daytime it is tiresome and perplexing.

There are always new shoots on the fungus, and new shades of yellow all over it. 170 I cannot keep count of them, though I have tried conscientiously.

It is the strangest yellow, that wallpaper! It makes me think of all the yellow things I ever saw—not beautiful ones like buttercups, but old, foul, bad yellow things.

But there is something else about that paper—the smell! I noticed it the moment we came into the room, but with so much air and sun it was not bad. Now we have had a week of fog and rain, and whether the windows are open or not, the smell is here.

It creeps all over the house.

I find it hovering in the dining-room, skulking in the parlor, hiding in the hall, lying in wait for me on the stairs.

It gets into my hair. 175

Even when I go to ride, if I turn my head suddenly and surprise it—there is that smell!

Such a peculiar odor, too! I have spent hours in trying to analyze it, to find what it smelled like.

It is not bad—at first—and very gentle, but quite the subtlest, most enduring odor I ever met.

In this damp weather it is awful. I wake up in the night and find it hanging over me.

It used to disturb me at first. I thought seriously of burning the house—to reach 180 the smell.

But now I am used to it. The only thing I can think of that it is like is the *color* of the paper! A yellow smell.

There is a very funny mark on this wall, low down, near the mopboard. A streak that runs round the room. It goes behind every piece of furniture, except the bed, a long, straight, even *smooch*, as if it had been rubbed over and over.

I wonder how it was done and who did it, and what they did it for. Round and round and round—round and round and round—it makes me dizzy!

I really have discovered something at last.

Through watching so much at night, when it changes so, I have finally found 185 out.

The front pattern *does* move—and no wonder! The woman behind shakes it!

Sometimes I think there are a great many women behind, and sometimes only one, and she crawls around fast, and her crawling shakes it all over.

Then in the very bright spots she keeps still, and in the very shady spots she just takes hold of the bars and shakes them hard.

And she is all the time trying to climb through. But nobody could climb through that pattern—it strangles so; I think that is why it has so many heads.

They get through and then the pattern strangles them off and turns them upside 190 down, and makes their eyes white!

If those heads were covered or taken off it would not be half so bad.

I think that woman gets out in the daytime!

And I'll tell you why—privately—I've seen her!

I can see her out of every one of my windows!

It is the same woman, I know, for she is always creeping, and most women do not 195
creep by daylight.

I see her in that long shaded lane, creeping up and down. I see her in those dark
grape arbors, creeping all round the garden.

I see her on that long road under the trees, creeping along, and when a carriage
comes she hides under the blackberry vines.

I don't blame her a bit. It must be very humiliating to be caught creeping by daylight!

I always lock the door when I creep by daylight. I can't do it at night, for I know
John would suspect something at once.

And John is so queer now that I don't want to irritate him. I wish he would take 200
another room! Besides, I don't want anybody to get that woman out at night but
myself.

I often wonder if I could see her out of all the windows at once.

But, turn as fast as I can, I can only see out of one at one time.

And though I always see her, she *may* be able to creep faster than I can turn! I
have watched her sometimes away off in the open country, creeping as fast as a cloud
shadow in a wind.

If only that top pattern could be gotten off from the under one! I mean to try it,
little by little.

I have found out another funny thing, but I shan't tell it this time! It does not do 205
to trust people too much.

There are only two more days to get this paper off, and I believe John is beginning to notice. I don't like the look in his eyes.

And I heard him ask Jennie a lot of professional questions about me. She had a
very good report to give.

She said I slept a good deal in the daytime.

John knows I don't sleep very well at night, for all I'm so quiet!

He asked me all sorts of questions too, and pretended to be very loving and kind. 210

As if I couldn't see through him!

Still, I don't wonder he acts so, sleeping under this paper for three months.

It only interests me, but I feel sure John and Jennie are affected by it.

Hurrah! This is the last day, but it is enough. John is to stay in town over night,
and won't be out until this evening.

Jennie wanted to sleep with me—the sly thing; but I told her I should undoubt- 215
edly rest better for a night all alone.

That was clever, for really I wasn't alone a bit! As soon as it was moonlight and
that poor thing began to crawl and shake the pattern, I got up and ran to help her.

I pulled and she shook. I shook and she pulled, and before morning we had
peeled off yards of that paper.

A strip about as high as my head and half around the room.

And then when the sun came and that awful pattern began to laugh at me, I
declared I would finish it today!

We go away tomorrow, and they are moving all my furniture down again to leave 220
things as they were before.

Jennie looked at the wall in amazement, but I told her merrily that I did it out of
pure spite at the vicious thing.

She laughed and said she wouldn't mind doing it herself, but I must not get tired.
How she betrayed herself that time!

But I am here, and no person touches this paper but me—not *alive!*

She tried to get me out of the room—it was too patent! But I said it was so quiet 225
and empty and clean now that I believed I would lie down again and sleep all I could,
and not to wake me even for dinner—I would call when I woke.

So now she is gone, and the servants are gone, and the things are gone, and there
is nothing left but that great bedstead nailed down, with the canvas mattress we
found on it.

We shall sleep downstairs tonight, and take the boat home tomorrow.

I quite enjoy the room, now it is bare again.

How those children did tear about here!

This bedstead is fairly gnawed! 230

But I must get to work.

I have locked the door and thrown the key down into the front path.

I don't want to go out, and I don't want to have anybody come in, till John
comes.

I want to astonish him.

I've got a rope up here that even Jennie did not find. If that woman does get out, 235
and tries to get away, I can tie her!

But I forgot I could not reach far without anything to stand on!

This bed will *not* move!

I tried to lift and push it until I was lame, and then I got so angry I bit off a little
piece at one corner—but it hurt my teeth.

Then I peeled off all the paper I could reach standing on the floor. It sticks horribly and the pattern just enjoys it! All those strangled heads and bulbous eyes and
waddling fungus growths just shriek with derision!

I am getting angry enough to do something desperate. To jump out of the win- 240
dow would be admirable exercise, but the bars are too strong even to try.

Besides I wouldn't do it. Of course not. I know well enough that a step like that
is improper and might be misconstrued.

I don't like to *look* out of the windows even—there are so many of those creeping
women, and they creep so fast.

I wonder if they all come out of that wallpaper as I did!

But I am securely fastened now by my well-hidden rope—you don't get *me* out in
the road there!

I suppose I shall have to get back behind the pattern when it comes night, and 245
that is hard!

It is so pleasant to be out in this great room and creep around as I please!

I don't want to go outside. I won't, even if Jennie asks me to.

For outside you have to creep on the ground, and everything is green instead of
yellow.

But here I can creep smoothly on the floor, and my shoulder just fits in that long
smooch around the wall, so I cannot lose my way.

Why, there's John at the door! 250

It is no use, young man, you can't open it!

How he does call and pound!

Now he's crying to Jennie for an axe.

It would be a shame to break down that beautiful door!

"John, dear!" said I in the gentlest voice. "The key is down by the front steps, un-   255
der a plantain leaf!"

That silenced him for a few moments.

Then he said, very quietly indeed, "Open the door, my darling!"

"I can't," said I. "The key is down by the front door under a plantain leaf!" And then
I said it again, several times, very gently and slowly, and said it so often that he had to go
and see, and he got it of course, and came in. He stopped short by the door.

"What is the matter?" he cried. "For God's sake, what are you doing!"

I kept on creeping just the same, but I looked at him over my shoulder.   260

"I've got out at last," said I, "in spite of you and Jane. And I've pulled off most of
the paper, so you can't put me back!"

Now why should that man have fainted? But he did, and right across my path by
the wall, so that I had to creep over him every time!

Questions

1. Several times at the beginning of the story, the narrator says such things as "What is one to do?" and "What can one do?" What do these comments refer to? What, if anything, do they suggest about women's roles at the time the story was written?

2. The narrator says, "I get unreasonably angry with John sometimes" (paragraph 24). How unreasonable is her anger at him? What does the fact that she feels it is unreasonable say about her?

3. What do her changing feelings about the wallpaper tell us about the changes in her condition?

4. "It is so hard to talk with John about my case, because he is so wise, and because he loves me so" (paragraph 122). His wisdom is, to say the least, open to question, but what about his love? Do you think he suffers merely from a failure of perception, or is there a failure of affection as well? Explain your response.

5. Where precisely in the story do you think it becomes clear that she has begun to hallucinate?

6. What does the woman behind the wallpaper represent? Why does the narrator come to identify with her?

7. How ill does the narrator seem at the beginning of the story? How ill does she seem at the end? How do you account for the change in her condition?

CHARLOTTE PERKINS GILMAN ON WRITING

Why I Wrote "The Yellow Wallpaper"   1913

Many and many a reader has asked that. When the story first came out, in the *New England Magazine* about 1891, a Boston physician made protest in *The Transcript.* Such a story ought not to be written, he said; it was enough to drive anyone mad to read it.

Another physician, in Kansas I think, wrote to say that it was the best description of incipient insanity he had ever seen, and—begging my pardon—had I been there?

Now the story of the story is this: For many years I suffered from a severe and continuous nervous breakdown tending to melancholia—and beyond. During about the third year of this trouble I went, in devout faith and some faint stir of hope, to a noted specialist in nervous diseases, the best known in the country. This wise man put me to bed and applied the rest cure, to which a still-good physique responded so promptly that he concluded there was nothing much the matter with me, and sent me home with solemn advice to "live as domestic a life as far as possible," to "have but two hours' intellectual life a day," and "never to touch pen, brush, or pencil again" as long as I lived. This was in 1887.

I went home and obeyed those directions for some three months, and came so near the borderline of utter mental ruin that I could see over.

Then, using the remnants of intelligence that remained, and helped by a wise friend, I cast the noted specialist's advice to the winds and went to work again—work, the normal life of every human being; work, in which is joy and growth and service, without which one is a pauper and a parasite—ultimately recovering some measure of power.

Being naturally moved to rejoicing by this narrow escape, I wrote "The Yellow Wallpaper," with its embellishments and additions, to carry out the ideal (I never had hallucinations or objections to my mural decorations) and sent a copy to the physician who so nearly drove me mad. He never acknowledged it.

The little book is valued by alienists and as a good specimen of one kind of literature. It has, to my knowledge, saved one woman from a similar fate—so terrifying her family that they let her out into normal activity and she recovered.

But the best result is this. Many years later I was told that the great specialist had admitted to friends of his that he had altered his treatment of neurasthenia since reading "The Yellow Wallpaper."

It was not intended to drive people crazy, but to save people from being driven crazy, and it worked.

From *The Forerunner*, October 1913

Whatever Is
1903

Whatever is we only know
As in our minds we find it so;
   No staring fact is half so clear
   As one dim, preconceived idea—
No matter how the fact may glow.   5

Vainly may Truth her trumpet blow
To stir our minds; like heavy dough
   They stick to what they think—won't hear
     Whatever is.

Our ancient myths in solid row   10
Stand up—we simply have to go
   And choke each fiction old and dear
   Before the modest facts appear;
Then we may grasp, reluctant, slow,
     Whatever is.   15

The Nervous Breakdown of Women 1916

[A]s a hindrance they [women] have to meet something which men have never met—the cold and cruel opposition of the other sex. In every step of their long upward path men have had women with them, never against them. In hardship, in privation, in danger, in the last test of religious martyrdom, in the pains and terrors of warfare, in rebellions and revolutions, men have had women with them. Individual women have no doubt been a hindrance to individual men, and the economic dependence of women is a drag upon men's freedom of action; but at no step of man's difficult advance has he had to meet the scorn, the neglect, the open vilification of massed womanhood.

No one has seemed to notice the cost of this great artificial barrier to the advance of woman, the effect upon her nervous system of opposition and abuse from the quarter where nature and tradition had taught her to expect aid and comfort. She has had to keep pace with him in meeting the demands of our swiftly changing times. She has had to meet the additional demands of her own even more swiftly changing conditions. And she has had to do this in the face not only of the organized opposition of the other sex, entrenched in secure possession of all the advantageous positions of church and state, buttressed by law and custom, fully trained and experienced, and holding all the ammunition—the "sinews of war"—the whole money power of the world; but besides this her slow, difficult, conscientious efforts to make the changes she knew were right, or which were forced upon her by conditions, have too often cost her man's love, respect and good will.

This is a heavy price to pay for progress.

We should be more than gentle with the many women who cannot yet meet it.

We should be more than grateful for those strong men who are more human than male, who can feel, think and act above the limitations of their sex, and who have helped women in their difficult advance.

Also we should deeply honor those great women of the last century, who met all demands, paid every exaction, faced all opposition and made the way easier for us now.

But we should not be surprised at the "nervous breakdown" of some women, nor attribute it to weakness.

Only the measureless strength of the mother sex could have enabled women to survive the sufferings of yesterday and to meet the exactions of today.

From *The Forerunner*, July–August 1916

CRITICS ON "THE YELLOW WALLPAPER"

A Massachusetts hospital for the insane in the era of Charlotte Perkins Gilman's "The Yellow Wallpaper."

Juliann Fleenor (b. 1942)

Gender and Pathology in "The Yellow Wallpaper" 1983

Although it is not generally known, Gilman wrote at least two other Gothic stories around the same time as "The Yellow Wallpaper." All three were published in the *New England Magazine*. At the time that "The Rocking Chair" and "The Giant Wistaria" were written, Gilman and her young daughter, Katherine, were living in the warmth of Pasadena, separated from her husband, Charles Walter Stetson. Gilman later noted in her papers: "'The Yellow Wallpaper' was written in two days, with the thermometer at one hundred and three in Pasadena, Ca." Her husband was living on the east coast, and, perhaps coincidentally, all three stories appear to be set in a nameless eastern setting, one urban and two rural. All three display similar themes, and all three are evidence that the conflict, central to Gilman's Gothic fiction and later to her autobiography, was a conflict with the mother, with mother-hood, and with creation.

In all three stories women are confined within the home; it is their prison, their insane asylum, even their tomb. A sense of the female isolation which Gilman felt, of exclusion from the public world of work and of men, is contained in the anecdote related by Zona Gale in her introduction to Gilman's autobiography. After watching the approach of several locomotives to a train platform in a small town in Wisconsin, Gilman said, "'All that, . . . and women have no part in it. Everything done by men, working together, while women worked on alone within their four walls!'" Female exclusion, women denied the opportunity to work, or their imprisonment behind four walls, led to madness. Her image, interestingly, does not suggest a female subculture of women working together; Gilman was

working against her own culture's definition of women, and her primary antagonists were women like her own mother.

Diseased maternity is explicit in Gilman's third Gothic story. The yellow wallpaper symbolizes more than confinement, victimization, and the inability to write.
It suggests a disease within the female self. When the narrator peels the wallpaper
off, "It sticks horribly and the pattern just enjoys it! All those strangled heads and
bulbous eyes and waddling fungus growths just shriek with derision." This passage
describes more than the peeling of wallpaper: the "strangled heads and bulbous eyes
and waddling fungus" imply something strange and terrible about birth and death
conjoined, about female procreation, and about female physiology. Nature is perverted here, too. The narrator thinks of "old, foul, bad yellow things." The smell
"creeps all over the house." She finds it "hovering in the dining-room, skulking in
the parlor, hiding in the hall, lying in wait for me on the stairs." Finally, "it gets into
my hair."

The paper stains the house in a way that suggests the effect of afterbirth. The
house, specifically this room, becomes more than a symbol of a repressive society;
it represents the physical self of the narrator as well. She is disgusted, perhaps
awed, perhaps frightened of her own bodily processes. The story establishes a sense
of fear and disgust, the skin crawls and grows clammy with the sense of physiological fear that Ellen Moers refers to as the Female Gothic.

My contention is that one of the major themes in the story, punishment for
becoming a mother (as well as punishment for being female), is supported by the
absence of the child. The child is taken away from the mother, almost in punishment, as was the child in "The Giant Wistaria." This differs from Gilman's experience; she had been told to keep her child with her at all times. In both the story
and in Gilman's life, a breakdown occurs directly after the birth of a child. The
narrator is confined as if she had committed a crime. Maternity—the creation of a
child—is combined with writing—the creation of writing—in a way that suggests
they are interrelated and perhaps symbiotic, as are the strange toadstools behind
the wallpaper.

The pathological nature of both experiences is not surprising, given the treatment Gilman received, and given the fact that maternity reduced women to mothers
and not writers. Childbirth has long been a rite of passage for women. But the question is, where does that passage lead? Becoming a mother leads to a child-like state.
The narrator becomes the absent child.

From "The Gothic Prism"

Sandra M. Gilbert (b. 1936)
and Susan Gubar (b. 1944)

Imprisonment and Escape: The Psychology of Confinement   1979

["The Yellow Wallpaper" is a] striking story of female confinement and escape, a
paradigmatic tale which (like *Jane Eyre*) seems to tell *the* story that all literary
women would tell if they could speak their "speechless woe." "The Yellow Wallpaper," which Gilman herself called "a description of a case of nervous breakdown,"
recounts in the first person the experiences of a woman who is evidently suffering
from a severe postpartum psychosis. Her husband, a censorious and paternalistic

physician, is treating her according to methods by which S. Weir Mitchell, a famous "nerve specialist," treated Gilman herself for a similar problem. He has confined her to a large garret room in an "ancestral hall" he has rented, and he has forbidden her to touch pen to paper until she is well again, for he feels, says the narrator, "that with my imaginative power and habit of story-making, a nervous weakness like mine is sure to lead to all manner of excited fancies, and that I ought to use my will and good sense to check the tendency."

The cure, of course, is worse than the disease, for the sick woman's mental condition deteriorates rapidly. "I think sometimes that if I were only well enough to write a little it would relieve the press of ideas and rest me," she remarks, but literally confined in a room she thinks is a one-time nursery because it has "rings and things" in the walls, she is literally locked away from creativity. The "rings and things," although reminiscent of children's gymnastic equipment, are really the paraphernalia of confinement, like the gate at the head of the stairs, instruments that definitively indicate her imprisonment. Even more tormenting, however, is the room's wallpaper: a sulfurous yellow paper, torn off in spots, and patterned with "lame uncertain curves" that "plunge off at outrageous angles" and "destroy themselves in unheard-of contradictions." Ancient, smoldering, "unclean" as the oppressive structures of the society in which she finds herself, this paper surrounds the narrator like an inexplicable text, censorious and overwhelming as her physician husband, haunting as the "hereditary estate" in which she is trying to survive. Inevitably she studies its suicidal implications—and inevitably, because of her "imaginative power and habit of story-making," she revises it, projecting her own passion for escape into its otherwise incomprehensible hieroglyphics. "This wallpaper," she decides, at a key point in her story,

> has a kind of sub-pattern in a different shade, a particularly irritating one, for you can only see it in certain lights, and not clearly then.
>
> But in the places where it isn't faded and where the sun is just so—I can see a strange, provoking, formless sort of figure that seems to skulk about behind that silly and conspicuous front design.

As time passes, this figure concealed behind what corresponds (in terms of what we have been discussing) to the facade of the patriarchal text becomes clearer and clearer. By moonlight the pattern of the wallpaper "becomes bars! The outside pattern I mean, and the woman behind it is as plain as can be." And eventually, as the narrator sinks more deeply into what the world calls madness, the terrifying implications of both the paper and the figure imprisoned behind the paper begin to permeate—that is, to *haunt*—the rented ancestral mansion in which she and her husband are immured. The "yellow smell" of the paper "creeps all over the house," drenching every room in its subtle aroma of decay. And the woman creeps too— through the house, in the house, and out of the house, in the garden and "on that long road under the trees." Sometimes, indeed, the narrator confesses, "I think there are a great many women" both behind the paper and creeping in the garden,

> and sometimes only one, and she crawls around fast, and her crawling shakes [the paper] all over. . . . And she is all the time trying to climb through. But nobody could climb through that pattern—it strangles so; I think that is why it has so many heads.

Eventually it becomes obvious to both reader and narrator that the figure creeping through and behind the wallpaper is both the narrator and the narrator's double. By the end of the story, moreover, the narrator has enabled this double to escape from her textual/architectural confinement: "I pulled and she shook, I shook and she pulled, and before morning we had peeled off yards of that paper." Is the message of the tale's conclusion mere madness? Certainly the righteous Doctor John—whose name links him to the anti-hero of Charlotte Bronte's *Villette*—has been temporarily defeated, or at least momentarily stunned. "Now why should that man have fainted?" the narrator ironically asks as she creeps around her attic. But John's unmasculine swoon of surprise is the least of the triumphs Gilman imagines for her madwoman. More significant are the madwoman's own imaginings and creations, mirages of health and freedom with which her author endows her like a fairy godmother showering gold on a sleeping heroine. The woman from behind the wallpaper creeps away, for instance, creeps fast and far on the long road, in broad daylight. "I have watched her sometimes away off in the open country," says the narrator, "creeping as fast as a cloud shadow in a high wind."

Indistinct and yet rapid, barely perceptible but inexorable, the progress of that cloud shadow is not unlike the progress of nineteenth-century literary women out of the texts defined by patriarchal poetics into the open spaces of their own authority. That such an escape from the numb world behind the patterned walls of the text was a flight from disease into health was quite clear to Gilman herself. When "The Yellow Wallpaper" was published she sent it to Weir Mitchell, whose strictures had kept her from attempting the pen during her own breakdown, thereby aggravating her illness, and she was delighted to learn, years later, that "he had changed his treatment of nervous prostration since reading" her story. "If that is a fact," she declared, "I have not lived in vain."

From *The Madwoman in the Attic*

Elizabeth Ammons

Biographical Echoes in "The Yellow Wallpaper"   1991

"The Yellow Wallpaper" probably had deep roots in Gilman's childhood. In her autobiography, the account she gives of her growing up focuses on the misery of her mother, a woman who adored her husband and loved having babies, only to have her husband leave and her babies grow up. Deserted, Gilman's mother—in the daughter's telling—grew bitter and fiercely repressed, deciding not to show any affection for her daughter in order to toughen the child. Life, as Gilman's mother had come to know it, brought women terrible disappointment and denial. Only in the dead of night would she allow herself to hug her daughter.

As a story about her mother, the early portions of Gilman's autobiography construct a family drama in which sexual desire in a woman leads to babies and death. (According to Gilman, her mother was warned that one more pregnancy would kill her, at which point the father left the family.) On the other hand, denial of sexual desire, the celibate life that Mary Fitch Perkins knew when her husband left, resulted in furious repression and frustration. Either way, female sexual desire, motherhood, and masculine power were bitterly entangled for Gilman's mother, who even after years of separation and rejection remained her husband's prisoner, calling for him on her deathbed. Looked at from the child's point of view, Charlotte Perkins Gilman clearly both admired and hated her father. Frederick Beecher Perkins's power over his wife was so strong that she had to stamp out all that was free and physical and warm in herself, and try to do the same to her daughter. In a sense the woman on her knees at the end of "The Yellow Wallpaper," the prisoner of a charming man and an ugly empty domestic life that she cannot escape, is Gilman's mother as the child experienced her while growing up—humiliated, angry, crushed.

• • •

The drama of patriarchal control in "The Yellow Wallpaper" is the same one that Charlotte Perkins Gilman felt as a child, saw in her mother's life, and then experienced again herself as a young wife and mother. The story is not limited to just one stage of her life as a woman, but applies potentially to all stages, from childhood to old age. It is not, moreover, simply a story about the desire for escape from male control. It is also a story about the desire to escape to a female world, a desire to unite with the mother, indeed with all women creeping and struggling in growing numbers, through the paper, behind the wall.

From *Conflicting Stories: American Women Writers*
at the Turn into the Twentieth Century

ALICE WALKER

Alice Walker, a leading black writer and social
activist, was born in 1944 in Eatonton, Georgia,
the youngest of eight children. Her father, a
sharecropper and dairy farmer, usually earned
about $300 a year; her mother helped by work-
ing as a maid. Both entertained their children by
telling stories. When Alice Walker was eight,
she was accidentally struck by a pellet from a
brother's BB gun. She lost the sight of one eye
because the Walkers had no car to rush her to
the hospital. Later she attended Spelman College in
Atlanta and finished college at Sarah Lawrence
College on a scholarship. While working for the
civil rights movement in Mississippi, she met a
young lawyer, Melvyn Leventhal. In 1967 they
settled in Jackson, Mississippi, the first legally
married interracial couple in town. They re-

Alice Walker

turned to New York in 1974 and were later divorced. First known as a poet, Walker has pub-
lished seven books of her verse. She also has edited a collection of the work of the then-neglected
black writer Zora Neale Hurston, and has written a study of Langston Hughes. In a collection
of essays, In Search of Our Mothers' Gardens: Womanist Prose *(1983), she recalls her*
mother and addresses her own daughter. (By womanist she means "black feminist.") But the
largest part of Walker's reading audience knows her fiction: three story collections, including
In Love and Trouble *(1973), from which "Everyday Use" is taken, and her many novels.*
Her best-known novel, The Color Purple *(1982), won a Pulitzer Prize and was made into a*
film by Steven Spielberg in 1985. Her recent novels include By the Light of My Father's
Smile *(1998) and* Now Is the Time to Open Your Heart *(2004). Walker now lives in*
Northern California.

Everyday Use   1973

for your grandmama

I will wait for her in the yard that Maggie and I made so clean and wavy yesterday afternoon. A yard like this is more comfortable than most people know. It is not
just a yard. It is like an extended living room. When the hard clay is swept clean as a
floor and the fine sand around the edges lined with tiny, irregular grooves, anyone
can come and sit and look up into the elm tree and wait for the breezes that never
come inside the house.

Maggie will be nervous until after her sister goes: she will stand hopelessly in
corners, homely and ashamed of the burn scars down her arms and legs, eyeing
her sister with a mixture of envy and awe. She thinks her sister has held life
always in the palm of one hand, that "no" is a word the world never learned to
say to her.

You've no doubt seen those TV shows where the child who has "made it" is
confronted, as a surprise, by her own mother and father, tottering in weakly from

backstage. (A pleasant surprise, of course: What would they do if parent and child came on the show only to curse out and insult each other?) On TV mother and child embrace and smile into each other's faces. Sometimes the mother and father weep, the child wraps them in her arms and leans across the table to tell how she would not have made it without their help. I have seen these programs.°

Sometimes I dream a dream in which Dee and I are suddenly brought together on a TV program of this sort. Out of a dark and soft-seated limousine I am ushered into a bright room filled with many people. There I meet a smiling, gray, sporty man like Johnny Carson who shakes my hand and tells me what a fine girl I have. Then we are on the stage and Dee is embracing me with tears in her eyes. She pins on my dress a large orchid, even though she has told me once that she thinks orchids are tacky flowers.

In real life I am a large, big-boned woman with rough, man-working hands. In the winter I wear flannel nightgowns to bed and overalls during the day. I can kill and clean a hog as mercilessly as a man. My fat keeps me hot in zero weather. I can work outside all day, breaking ice to get water for washing. I can eat pork liver cooked over the open fire minutes after it comes steaming from the hog. One winter I knocked a bull calf straight in the brain between the eyes with a sledge hammer and had the meat hung up to chill before nightfall. But of course all this does not show on television. I am the way my daughter would want me to be: a hundred pounds lighter, my skin like an uncooked barley pancake. My hair glistens in the hot bright lights. Johnny Carson has much to do to keep up with my quick and witty tongue.

But that is a mistake. I know even before I wake up. Who ever knew a Johnson with a quick tongue? Who can even imagine me looking a strange white man in the eye? It seems to me I have talked to them always with one foot raised in flight, with my head turned in whichever way is farthest from them. Dee, though. She would always look anyone in the eye. Hesitation was no part of her nature.

"How do I look, Mama?" Maggie says, showing just enough of her thin body enveloped in pink skirt and red blouse for me to know she's there, almost hidden by the door.

"Come out into the yard," I say.

Have you ever seen a lame animal, perhaps a dog run over by some careless person rich enough to own a car, sidle up to someone who is ignorant enough to be kind to him? That is the way my Maggie walks. She has been like this, chin on chest, eyes on ground, feet in shuffle, ever since the fire that burned the other house to the ground.

Dee is lighter than Maggie, with nicer hair and a fuller figure. She's a woman now, though sometimes I forget. How long ago was it that the other house burned? Ten, twelve years? Sometimes I can still hear the flames and feel Maggie's arms sticking to me, her hair smoking and her dress falling off her in little black papery flakes. Her eyes seemed stretched open, blazed open by the flames reflected in them. And Dee. I see her standing off under the sweet gum tree she used to dig gum out of; a look of concentration on her face as she watched the last dingy gray board of the house fall in toward the red-hot brick chimney. Why don't you do a dance around the ashes? I'd wanted to ask her. She had hated the house that much.

these programs: On the NBC television show *This Is Your Life*, people were publicly and often tearfully reunited with friends, relatives, and teachers they had not seen in years.

I used to think she hated Maggie, too. But that was before we raised the money, the church and me, to send her to Augusta to school. She used to read to us without pity; forcing words, lies, other folks' habits, whole lives upon us two, sitting trapped and ignorant underneath her voice. She washed us in a river of make-believe, burned us with a lot of knowledge we didn't necessarily need to know. Pressed us to her with the serious way she read, to shove us away at just the moment, like dimwits, we seemed about to understand.

Dee wanted nice things. A yellow organdy dress to wear to her graduation from high school; black pumps to match a green suit she'd made from an old suit somebody gave me. She was determined to stare down any disaster in her efforts. Her eyelids would not flicker for minutes at a time. Often I fought off the temptation to shake her. At sixteen she had a style of her own: and knew what style was.

I never had an education myself. After second grade the school was closed down. Don't ask me why: in 1927 colored asked fewer questions than they do now. Sometimes Maggie reads to me. She stumbles along good-naturedly but can't see well. She knows she is not bright. Like good looks and money, quickness passed her by. She will marry John Thomas (who has mossy teeth in an earnest face) and then I'll be free to sit here and I guess just sing church songs to myself. Although I never was a good singer. Never could carry a tune. I was always better at a man's job. I used to love to milk till I was hoofed in the side in '49. Cows are soothing and slow and don't bother you, unless you try to milk them the wrong way.

I have deliberately turned my back on the house. It is three rooms, just like the one that burned, except the roof is tin; they don't make shingle roofs any more. There are no real windows, just some holes cut in the sides, like the portholes in a ship, but not round and not square, with rawhide holding the shutters up on the outside. This house is in a pasture, too, like the other one. No doubt when Dee sees it she will want to tear it down. She wrote me once that no matter where we "choose" to live, she will manage to come see us. But she will never bring her friends. Maggie and I thought about this and Maggie asked me, "Mama, when did Dee ever *have* any friends?"

She had a few. Furtive boys in pink shirts hanging about on washday after school. Nervous girls who never laughed. Impressed with her they worshiped the well-turned phrase, the cute shape, the scalding humor that erupted like bubbles in lye. She read to them.   15

When she was courting Jimmy T she didn't have much time to pay to us, but turned all her faultfinding power on him. He *flew* to marry a cheap city girl from a family of ignorant flashy people. She hardly had time to recompose herself.

When she comes I will meet—but there they are!

Maggie attempts to make a dash for the house, in her shuffling way, but I stay her with my hand. "Come back here," I say. And she stops and tries to dig a well in the sand with her toe.

It is hard to see them clearly through the strong sun. But even the first glimpse of leg out of the car tells me it is Dee. Her feet were always neat-looking, as if God himself had shaped them with a certain style. From the other side of the car comes a short, stocky man. Hair is all over his head a foot long and hanging from his chin like a kinky mule tail. I hear Maggie suck in her breath. "Uhnnnh," is what it sounds like. Like when you see the wriggling end of a snake just in front of your foot on the road. "Uhnnnh."

Dee next. A dress down to the ground, in this hot weather. A dress so loud it   20
hurts my eyes. There are yellows and oranges enough to throw back the light of the
sun. I feel my whole face warming from the heat waves it throws out. Earrings, too,
gold and hanging down to her shoulders. Bracelets dangling and making noises when
she moves her arm up to shake the folds of the dress out of her armpits. The dress is
loose and flows, and as she walks closer, I like it. I hear Maggie go "Uhnnnh" again. It
is her sister's hair. It stands straight up like the wool on a sheep. It is black as night
and around the edges are two long pigtails that rope about like small lizards disappearing behind her ears.

"Wa-su-zo-Tean-o!"° she says, coming on in that gliding way the dress makes her
move. The short stocky fellow with the hair to his navel is all grinning and he follows
up with "Asalamalakim,° my mother and sister!" He moves to hug Maggie but she
falls back, right up against the back of my chair. I feel her trembling there and when
I look up I see the perspiration falling off her chin.

"Don't get up," says Dee. Since I am stout it takes something of a push. You
can see me trying to move a second or two before I make it. She turns, showing
white heels through her sandals, and goes back to the car. Out she peeks next with
a Polaroid. She stoops down quickly and lines up picture after picture of me sitting
there in front of the house with Maggie cowering behind me. She never takes a
shot without making sure the house is included. When a cow comes nibbling
around the edge of the yard she snaps it and me and Maggie *and* the house. Then
she puts the Polaroid in the back seat of the car, and comes up and kisses me on the
forehead.

Meanwhile Asalamalakim is going through the motions with Maggie's hand.
Maggie's hand is as limp as a fish, and probably as cold, despite the sweat, and she
keeps trying to pull it back. It looks like Asalamalakim wants to shake hands but
wants to do it fancy. Or maybe he don't know how people shake hands. Anyhow, he
soon gives up on Maggie.

"Well," I say. "Dee."

"No, Mama," she says. "Not 'Dee,' Wangero Leewanika Kemanjo!"   25

"What happened to 'Dee'?" I wanted to know.

"She's dead," Wangero said. "I couldn't bear it any longer, being named after the
people who oppress me."

"You know as well as me you was named after your aunt Dicie," I said. Dicie is
my sister. She named Dee. We called her "Big Dee" after Dee was born.

"But who was *she* named after?" asked Wangero.

"I guess after Grandma Dee," I said.   30

"And who was she named after?" asked Wangero.

"Her mother," I said, and saw Wangero was getting tired. "That's about as far
back as I can trace it," I said. Though, in fact, I probably could have carried it back
beyond the Civil War through the branches.

"Well," said Asalamalakim, "there you are."

"Uhnnnh," I heard Maggie say.

"There I was not," I said, "before 'Dicie' cropped up in our family, so why should   35
I try to trace it that far back?"

Wa-su-zo-Tean-o!: salutation in Swahili, an African language. Notice that Dee has to sound it out,
syllable by syllable.   *Asalamalakim:* salutation in Arabic: "Peace be upon you."

He just stood there grinning, looking down on me like somebody inspecting a Model A car.° Every once in a while he and Wangero sent eye signals over my head.

"How do you pronounce this name?" I asked.

"You don't have to call me by it if you don't want to," said Wangero.

"Why shouldn't I?" I asked. "If that's what you want us to call you, we'll call you."

"I know it might sound awkward at first," said Wangero.   40

"I'll get used to it," I said. "Ream it out again."

Well, soon we got the name out of the way. Asalamalakim had a name twice as long and three times as hard. After I tripped over it two or three times he told me to just call him Hakim-a-barber. I wanted to ask him was he a barber, but I didn't really think he was, so I didn't ask.

"You must belong to those beef-cattle peoples down the road," I said. They said "Asalamalakim" when they met you, too, but they didn't shake hands. Always too busy: feeding the cattle, fixing the fences, putting up salt-lick shelters, throwing down hay. When the white folks poisoned some of the herd the men stayed up all night with rifles in their hands. I walked a mile and a half just to see the sight.

Hakim-a-barber said, "I accept some of their doctrines, but farming and raising cattle is not my style." (They didn't tell me, and I didn't ask, whether Wangero (Dee) had really gone and married him.)

We sat down to eat and right away he said he didn't eat collards and pork was   45
unclean. Wangero, though, went on through the chitlins and corn bread, the greens and everything else. She talked a blue streak over the sweet potatoes. Everything delighted her. Even the fact that we still used the benches her daddy made for the table when we couldn't afford to buy chairs.

"Oh, Mama!" she cried. Then turned to Hakim-a-barber. "I never knew how lovely these benches are. You can feel the rump prints," she said, running her hands underneath her and along the bench. Then she gave a sigh and her hand closed over Grandma Dee's butter dish. "That's it!" she said. "I knew there was something I wanted to ask you if I could have." She jumped up from the table and went over in the corner where the churn stood, the milk in it clabber° by now. She looked at the churn and looked at it.

"This churn top is what I need," she said. "Didn't Uncle Buddy whittle it out of a tree you all used to have?"

"Yes," I said.

"Uh huh," she said happily. "And I want the dasher, too."

"Uncle Buddy whittle that, too?" asked the barber.   50

Dee (Wangero) looked up at me.

"Aunt Dee's first husband whittled the dash," said Maggie so low you almost couldn't hear her. "His name was Henry, but they called him Stash."

"Maggie's brain is like an elephant's," Wangero said, laughing. "I can use the churn top as a centerpiece for the alcove table," she said, sliding a plate over the churn, "and I'll think of something artistic to do with the dasher."

When she finished wrapping the dasher the handle stuck out. I took it for a moment in my hands. You didn't even have to look close to see where hands pushing the dasher up and down to make butter had left a kind of sink in the wood. In fact, there were a lot of small sinks; you could see where thumbs and fingers had sunk into

Model A car: popular low-priced automobile introduced by the Ford Motor Company in 1927.
clabber: sour milk or buttermilk.

the wood. It was beautiful light yellow wood, from a tree that grew in the yard where Big Dee and Stash had lived.

After dinner Dee (Wangero) went to the trunk at the foot of my bed and started 55 rifling through it. Maggie hung back in the kitchen over the dishpan. Out came Wangero with two quilts. They had been pieced by Grandma Dee and then Big Dee and me had hung them on the quilt frames on the front porch and quilted them. One was in the Lone Star pattern. The other was Walk Around the Mountain. In both of them were scraps of dresses Grandma Dee had worn fifty and more years ago. Bits and pieces of Grandpa Jarrell's paisley shirts. And one teeny faded blue piece, about the size of a penny matchbox, that was from Great Grandpa Ezra's uniform that he wore in the Civil War.

"Mama," Wangero said sweet as a bird. "Can I have these old quilts?"

I heard something fall in the kitchen, and a minute later the kitchen door slammed.

"Why don't you take one or two of the others?" I asked. "These old things was just done by me and Big Dee from some tops your grandma pieced before she died."

"No," said Wangero. "I don't want those. They are stitched around the borders by machine."

"That'll make them last better," I said. 60

"That's not the point," said Wangero. "These are all pieces of dresses Grandma used to wear. She did all this stitching by hand. Imagine!" She held the quilts securely in her arms, stroking them.

"Some of the pieces, like those lavender ones, come from old clothes her mother handed down to her," I said, moving up to touch the quilts. Dee (Wangero) moved back just enough so that I couldn't reach the quilts. They already belonged to her.

"Imagine!" she breathed again, clutching them closely to her bosom.

"The truth is," I said, "I promised to give them quilts to Maggie, for when she marries John Thomas."

She gasped like a bee had stung her. 65

"Maggie can't appreciate these quilts!" she said. "She'd probably be backward enough to put them to everyday use."

"I reckon she would," I said. "God knows I been saving 'em for long enough with nobody using 'em. I hope she will!" I didn't want to bring up how I had offered Dee (Wangero) a quilt when she went away to college. Then she had told me they were old-fashioned, out of style.

"But they're *priceless!*" she was saying now, furiously; for she has a temper. "Maggie would put them on the bed and in five years they'd be in rags. Less than that!"

"She can always make some more," I said. "Maggie knows how to quilt."

Dee (Wangero) looked at me with hatred. "You just will not understand. The 70 point is these quilts, *these* quilts!"

"Well," I said, stumped. "What would *you* do with them?"

"Hang them," she said. As if that was the only thing you *could* do with quilts.

Maggie by now was standing in the door. I could almost hear the sound her feet made as they scraped over each other.

"She can have them, Mama," she said, like somebody used to never winning anything, or having anything reserved for her. "I can 'member Grandma Dee without the quilts."

I looked at her hard. She had filled her bottom lip with checkerberry snuff and it 75 gave her face a kind of dopey, hangdog look. It was Grandma Dee and Big Dee who taught her how to quilt herself. She stood there with her scarred hands hidden in the folds of her skirt. She looked at her sister with something like fear but she wasn't mad at her. This was Maggie's portion. This was the way she knew God to work.

When I looked at her like that something hit me in the top of my head and ran down to the soles of my feet. Just like when I'm in church and the spirit of God touches me and I get happy and shout. I did something I never had done before: hugged Maggie to me, then dragged her on into the room, snatched the quilts out of Miss Wangero's hands and dumped them into Maggie's lap. Maggie just sat there on my bed with her mouth open.

"Take one or two of the others," I said to Dee.

But she turned without a word and went out to Hakim-a-barber.

"You just don't understand," she said, as Maggie and I came out to the car.

"What don't I understand?" I wanted to know.   80

"Your heritage," she said. And then she turned to Maggie, kissed her, and said, "You ought to try to make something of yourself, too, Maggie. It's really a new day for us. But from the way you and Mama still live you'd never know it."

She put on some sunglasses that hid everything above the tip of her nose and her chin.

Maggie smiled; maybe at the sunglasses. But a real smile, not scared. After we watched the car dust settle I asked Maggie to bring me a dip of snuff. And then the two of us sat there just enjoying, until it was time to go in the house and go to bed.

Questions

1. What is the basic conflict in "Everyday Use"?
2. What is the tone of Walker's story? By what means does the author communicate it?
3. From whose point of view is "Everyday Use" told? What does the story gain from being told from this point of view—instead of, say, from the point of view of Dee (Wangero)?
4. What does the narrator of the story feel toward Dee? What seems to be Dee's present attitude toward her mother and sister?
5. What do you take to be the author's attitude toward each of her characters? How does she convey it?
6. What levels of meaning do you find in the story's title?
7. Contrast Dee's attitude toward her heritage with the attitudes of her mother and sister. How much truth is there in Dee's accusation that her mother and sister don't understand their heritage?
8. Does the knowledge that "Everyday Use" was written by a black writer in any way influence your reactions to it? Explain.

ALICE WALKER ON WRITING

The Black Woman Writer in America   1973

Interview by John O'Brien

Interviewer: Why do you think that the black woman writer has been so ignored in America? Does she have even more difficulty than the black male writer, who perhaps has just begun to gain recognition?

Walker: There are two reasons why the black woman writer is not taken as seriously as the black male writer. One is that she's a woman. Critics seem unusually ill-equipped to intelligently discuss and analyze the works of black women. Generally, they do not even make the attempt; they prefer, rather, to talk about the lives of black women writers, not about what they write. And, since black women writers are not—it would seem—very likable—until recently they were the least willing worshipers of male supremacy—comments about them tend to be cruel.

In Nathan Huggins's very readable book, *Harlem Renaissance,* he hardly refers to Zora Neale Hurston's work, except negatively. He quotes from Wallace Thurman's novel, *Infants of the Spring,* at length, giving us the words of a character, "Sweetie Mae Carr," who is allegedly based on Zora Neale Hurston. "Sweetie Mae" is a writer noted more "for her ribald wit and personal effervescence than for any actual literary work. She was a great favorite among those whites who went in for Negro prodigies." Mr. Huggins goes on for several pages, never quoting Zora Neale Hurston herself, but rather the opinions of others about her character. He does say that she was "a master of dialect," but adds that "Her greatest weakness was carelessness or indifference to her art."

Having taught Zora Neale Hurston, and of course, having read her work myself, I am stunned. Personally, I do not care if Zora Hurston was fond of her white women friends. When she was a child in Florida, working for nickels and dimes, two white women helped her escape. Perhaps this explains it. But even if it doesn't, so what? Her work, far from being done carelessly, is done (especially in *Their Eyes Were Watching God*) almost too perfectly. She took the trouble to capture the beauty of rural black expression. She saw poetry where other writers merely saw failure to cope with English. She was so at ease with her blackness it never occurred to her that she should act one way among blacks and another among whites (as her more sophisticated black critics apparently did).

It seems to me that black writing has suffered, because even black critics have assumed that a book that deals with the relationships between members of a black family—or between a man and a woman—is less important than one that has white people as a primary antagonist. The consequences of this is that many of our books by "major" writers (always male) tell us little about the culture, history, or future, imagination, fantasies, etc., of black people, and a lot about isolated (often improbable) or limited encounters with a nonspecific white world. Where is the book, by an American black person (aside from *Cane*), that equals Elechi Amadi's *The Concubine,* for example? A book that exposes the *subconscious* of a people, because the people's dreams, imaginings, rituals, legends, etc., are known to be important, are known to contain the accumulated collective reality of the people themselves. Or, in *The Radiance of the King,* the white person is shown to be the outsider he is, because the culture he enters into in Africa *itself* [expels] him. Without malice, but as nature expels what does not suit. The white man is mysterious, a force to be reckoned with, but he is not glorified to such an extent that the Africans turn their attention away from themselves and their own imagination and culture. Which is what often happens with "protest literature." The superficial becomes—for a time—the deepest reality, and replaces the still waters of the collective subconscious.

When my own novel was published, a leading black monthly admitted (the editor did) that the book itself was never read; but the magazine ran an item stating that a *white* reviewer had praised the book (which was, in itself, an indication that the book was no good—such went the logic) and then hinted that the reviewer had liked my book because of my life-style. When I wrote to the editor to complain, he wrote me a small sermon on the importance of my "image," of what is "good" for others to see. Needless to say, what others "see" of me is the least of my worries, and I assumed that "others" are intelligent enough to recover from whatever shocks my presence might cause.

Women writers are supposed to be intimidated by male disapprobation. What they write is not important enough to be read. How they live, however, their "image," they owe to the race. Read the reason Zora Neale Hurston gave for giving up her writing. See what "image" the Negro press gave her, innocent as she was. I no longer read articles or reviews unless they are totally about the work. I trust that someday a generation of men and women will arise who will forgive me for such wrong as I do not agree I do, and will read my work because it is a true account of my feelings, my perceptions, and my imagination, and because it will reveal something to them of their own selves. They will also be free to toss it—and me—out of a high window. They can do what they like.

From *Interviews with Black Writers*

Reflections on Writing and Women's Lives   (mid-1990s) 2004

Interview by William R. Ferris

If you think of the early stories, it's true that the women end badly, but it's because they belong to the generation of my mother and grandmother, when they were suspended because they had nowhere to go. All of them couldn't be Bessie Smith or Billie Holiday, so they ended up doing all kinds of destructive things. Most of that generation didn't have any fame or glory. But notice that all of those women are much older than I am. They exist in an historical place that is removed from my generation of women. . . . I wrote about these women in *In Search of Our Mothers' Gardens*. The women who have not had anything, have been, almost of necessity, self-destructive. They've just been driven insane. And the ones who have managed have been the ones who could focus their enormous energies on art forms that were not necessarily recognized as art forms—on quilting, on flowers, on making things. It's a very human need, to make things, to create. To think that women didn't need that—that by having a baby you fulfill your whole function— is absurd and demeaning.

From *Southern Cultures*

CRITICS ON "EVERYDAY USE"

Lone Star quilt pattern: "Out came Wangero with two quilts. . . . One was in the Lone Star pattern" (paragraph 55).

Barbara T. Christian (1943–2000)

"Everyday Use" and the Black Power Movement   1994

"Everyday Use" is, in part, Alice Walker's response to the concept of heritage as articulated by the black movements of the 1960s. In that period, many African Americans, disappointed by the failure of integration, gravitated to the philosophy of cultural nationalism as the means to achieve liberation. In contrast to the veneration of Western ideas and ideals by many integrationists of the 1950s, Black Power ideologues emphasized the African cultural past as the true heritage of African Americans. The acknowledgment and appreciation of that heritage, which had too often been denigrated by African Americans themselves as well as by Euro-Americans, was a major tenet of the revolutionary movements of the period. Many blacks affirmed their African roots by changing their "slave names" to African names, and by wearing Afro styles and African clothing. Yet, ideologues of the period also lambasted older African Americans, opposing them to the lofty mythical models of the ancient past. These older men and women, they claimed, had become Uncle Toms and Aunt Jemimas who displayed little awareness of their culture and who, as a result of their slave past, had internalized the white man's view of blacks. So while these 1960s ideologues extolled an unknown ancient history, they denigrated the known and recent past. The tendency to idealize an ancient African past while ignoring the recent African American past still persists in the Afrocentric movements of the 1990s.

    In contrast to that tendency, Walker's "Everyday Use" is dedicated to "your grandmama." And the story is told by a woman many African Americans would recognize as their grandmama, that supposedly backward Southern ancestor the cultural nationalists of the North probably visited during the summers of their youth and probably considered behind the times. Walker stresses those physical qualities which suggest such a person, qualities often demeaned by cultural nationalists. For this grandmama, like the stereotypical mammy of slavery, is "a large big-boned woman with rough, man-working hands," who wears "flannel nightgowns to bed and overalls during the day," and whose "fat keeps [her] hot in zero weather." Nor is this grandmama politically conscious according to the fashion of the day; she never had an education after the second grade, she knows nothing about African names, and she eats pork. In having the grandmama tell this story, Walker gives voice to an entire maternal ancestry often silenced by the political rhetoric of the period. Indeed, Walker tells us in "In Search of Our Mothers' Gardens" that her writing is part of her mother's legacy to her, that many of her stories are based on stories *her* mother told her. Thus, Walker's writing is her way of breaking silences and stereotypes about her grandmothers', mothers', sisters' lives. In effect, her work is a literary continuation of a distinctly oral tradition in which African American women have been and still are pivotal participants.

Alice Walker is well aware of the restrictions of the African American Southern past, for she is the eighth child of Georgia sharecroppers. Born in 1944, she grew up during the period when, as she put it, apartheid existed in America. For in the 1940s and 1950s, when segregation was the law of the South, opportunities for economic and social advancement were legally denied to Southern blacks. Walker was fortunate to come to adulthood during the social and political movements of the late fifties and sixties. Of her siblings, only she, and a slightly older sister, Molly, were able even to imagine the possibility of moving beyond the poverty of their parents. It is unlikely that Alice Walker would have been able to go to college—first at Spelman, the African American women's college in Atlanta, and then at Sarah Lawrence, the white women's college near New York City—if it had not been for the changes that came about as a result of the Civil Rights Movement. Nor is it likely that she, a Southern black woman from a poor family, would have been able to become the writer that she did without the changes resulting from the ferment of the Black and Women's Movements of the 1960s and early 1970s.

While Walker was a participant in these movements, she was also one of their most astute critics. As a Southerner, she was aware of the ways in which black Southern culture was often thought of as backward by predominantly Northern Black Power ideologues, even as they proclaimed their love for black people. She was also acutely aware of the ways in which women were oppressed within the Black Power Movement itself, even as the very culture its participants revered was so often passed on by women. Walker had also visited Africa during her junior year of college and had personally experienced the gap between the Black Power advocates' idealization of Africa and the reality of the African societies she visited.

• • •

Names are extremely important in African and African American culture as a means of indicating a person's spirit. During the 1960s Walker criticized the tendency among some African Americans to give up the names their parents gave them—names which embodied the history of their recent past—for African names that did not relate to a single person they knew. Hence the grandmama in "Everyday Use" is amazed that Dee would give up her name for the name Wangero. For Dee was the name of her great-grandmother, a woman who had kept her family together against great odds. Wangero might have sounded authentically African but it had no relationship to a person she knew, nor to the personal history that had sustained her.

• • •

In "Everyday Use," by contrasting a sister who has the opportunity to go to college with a sister who stays at home, Walker reminds us of the challenges that contemporary African American women face as they discover what it means to be truly educated. The same concern appears in many of her works. For example, in "For My Sister Molly Who in the Fifties," she explores the conflicts that can result from an education that takes a woman away from her cultural source. Like Molly, Dee/Wangero in "Everyday Use" is embarrassed by her folk. She has been to the North, wears an Afro, and knows the correct political rhetoric of the 1960s, but she has little regard for her relatives who have helped to create that heritage. Thus, she does not know how to quilt and can only conceive of her family's quilts as priceless artifacts, as things, which she intends to hang on her wall as a means of demonstrating to others that she has "heritage." On the other hand, Maggie, the supposedly uneducated sister, who has been nowhere beyond the supposedly uneducated black South, loves and understands her family and can appreciate its history. She knows how to quilt and would put the precious quilts to "everyday use," which is precisely what, Walker suggests, one needs to do with one's heritage. For Maggie, the quilts are an embodiment of the spirit her folks have passed on to her.

From introduction to Everyday Use

Houston A. Baker (b. 1943)
and Charlotte Pierce-Baker (b. 1943)

Stylish vs. Sacred in "Everyday Use"   1985

The Johnson women, who populate the generations represented in Walker's short story "Everyday Use," are inhabitants of southern cabins who have always worked with "scraps" and seen what they could make of them. The result of their labor has been a succession of mothers and daughters surviving the ignominies of Jim Crow life and passing on ancestral blessings to descendants. The guardians of the Johnson homestead when the story commences are the mother—"a large, big-boned woman with rough, man-working hands"—and her daughter Maggie, who has remained with her "chin on chest, eyes on ground, feet in shuffle, ever since the fire that burned the other house to the ground" ten or twelve years ago. The mood at the story's beginning is one of ritualistic "waiting": "I will wait for her in the yard that Maggie and I made so clean and wavy yesterday afternoon." The subject awaited is the other daughter, Dee. Not only has the yard (as ritual ground) been prepared for the arrival of a goddess, but the sensibilities and costumes of Maggie and her mother have been appropriately attuned for the occasion. The mother daydreams of television shows where parents and children are suddenly—and pleasantly—reunited, banal shows where chatty hosts oversee tearful reunions. In her fantasy, she weighs a hundred pounds less, is several shades brighter in complexion, and possesses a devastatingly quick tongue. She returns abruptly to real life meditation, reflecting on her own heroic, agrarian accomplishments in slaughtering hogs and cattle and preparing their meat for winter nourishment. She is a robust provider who has gone to the people of her church and raised money to send her light-complexioned, lithe-figured, and ever-dissatisfied daughter Dee to college. Today, as she waits in the purified yard, she notes the stark differences between Maggie and Dee and recalls how the "last dingy gray board of the house [fell] in toward the red-hot brick chimney" when her former domicile burned. Maggie was scarred horribly by the fire, but Dee, who had hated the house with an intense fury, stood "off under the sweet gum tree . . . a look of concentration on her face." A scarred and dull Maggie, who has been kept at home and confined to everyday offices, has but one reaction to the fiery and vivacious arrival of her sister: "I hear Maggie suck in her breath. 'Uhnnnh,' is what it sounds like. Like when you see the wriggling end of a snake just in front of your foot on the road. 'Uhnnnh.'"

Indeed, the question raised by Dee's energetic arrival is whether there are words adequate to her flair, her brightness, her intense colorfulness of style which veritably blocks the sun. She wears "a dress so loud it hurts my eyes. There are yellows and oranges enough to throw back the light of the sun. I feel my whole face warming from the heat waves it throws out." Dee is both serpent and fire introduced with bursting esprit into the calm pasture that contains the Johnsons' tin-roofed, three-room, windowless shack and grazing cows. She has joined the radical, black nationalists of the 1960s and 1970s, changing her name from Dee to Wangero and cultivating a suddenly fashionable, or stylish, interest in what she passionately describes as her "heritage." If there is one quality that Dee (Wangero) possesses in abundance, it is "style": "At sixteen she had a style of her own: and knew what style was."

But in her stylishness, Dee is not an example of the indigenous rapping and styling out of Afro-America. Rather, she is manipulated by the style-makers, the fashion designers whose semiotics the French writer Roland Barthes has so aptly characterized. "Style" for Dee is the latest vogue—the most recent fantasy perpetuated by American media. When she left for college, her mother had tried to give her a quilt whose making began with her grandmother Dee, but the bright daughter felt such patched coverings were "old-fashioned and out of style." She has returned at the commencement of "Everyday Use," however, as one who now purports to know the value of the work of black women as holy patchers.

The dramatic conflict of the story surrounds the definition of holiness. The ritual purification of earth and expectant atmosphere akin to that of Beckett's famous drama ("I will wait for her in the yard that Maggie and I made so clean and wavy yesterday afternoon.") prepare us for the narrator's epiphanic experience at the story's conclusion.

Near the end of "Everyday Use," the mother (who is the tale's narrator) realizes that Dee (a.k.a. Wangero) is a *fantasy* child, a perpetrator and victim of: "words, lies, other folks's habits." The energetic daughter is as frivolously careless of other people's lives as the fiery conflagration that she had watched ten years previously. Assured by the makers of American fashion that "black" is currently "beautiful," she has conformed her own "style" to that notion. Hers is a trendy "blackness" cultivated as "art" and costume. She wears "a dress down to the ground . . . bracelets dangling and making noises when she moves her arm up to shake the folds of the dress out of her armpits." And she says of quilts she has removed from a trunk at the foot of her mother's bed: "Maggie can't appreciate these quilts! She'd probably be backward enough to put them to everyday use." "Art" is, thus, juxtaposed with "everyday use" in Walker's short story, and the fire goddess Dee, who has achieved literacy only to burn "us with a lot of knowledge we didn't necessarily need to know," is revealed as a perpetuator of institutional theories of aesthetics.

• • •

Quilts designed for everyday use, pieced wholes defying symmetry and pattern, are signs of the scarred generations of women who have always been alien to a world of literate words and stylish fantasies. The crafted fabric of Walker's story is the very weave of blues and jazz traditions in the Afro-American community, daringly improvisational modes that confront breaks in the continuity of melody (or theme) by riffing. The asymmetrical quilts of southern black women are like the off-centered stomping of the jazz solo or the innovative musical showmanship of the blues interlude. They speak a world in which the deceptively shuffling Maggie is capable of a quick change into goddess, an unlikely holy figure whose dues are paid in full. Dee's anger at her mother is occasioned principally by the mother's insistence that paid dues make Maggie a more likely bearer of sacredness, tradition, and true value than the "brighter" sister. "You just don't understand," she says to her mother. Her assessment is surely correct where institutional theories and systems of "art" are concerned. The mother's cognition contains no categories for framed art. The mother works according to an entirely different scale of use and value, finally assigning proper weight to the virtues of Maggie and to the ancestral importance of the pieced quilts that she has kept out of use for so many years. Smarting, perhaps, from Dee's designation of the quilts as "old-fashioned," the mother has buried the covers away in a trunk. At the end of Walker's story, however, she has become aware of her own mistaken value judgments, and she pays homage that is due to Maggie. The unlikely daughter is a *griot*° of the vernacular who remembers actors and events in a distinctively black "historical" drama.

Before Dee departs, she "put on some sunglasses that hid everything above the tip of her nose and her chin." Maggie smiles at the crude symbolism implicit in this act, for she has always known that her sister saw "through a glass darkly." But it is the mother's conferral of an ancestral blessing (signaled by her deposit of the quilts in Maggie's lap) that constitutes the occasion for the daughter's first "real smile." Maggie knows that it is only communal recognition by elders of the tribe that confers ancestral privileges on succeeding generations. The mother's holy recognition of the scarred daughter's sacred status as quilter is the best gift of a hard-pressed womankind to the fragmented goddess of the present.

At the conclusion of "Everyday Use," which is surely a fitting precursor to *The Color Purple*, with its sewing protagonist and its scenes of sisterly quilting, Maggie and her mother relax in the ritual yard after the dust of Dee's departing car has settled. They dip snuff in the manner of African confreres sharing cola nuts. The moment is past when a putatively "new" generation has confronted scenes of black, everyday life. A change has taken place, but it is a change best described by Amiri Baraka's designation for Afro-American music's various styles and discontinuities. The change in Walker's story is the "changing same." What has been reaffirmed at the story's conclusion is the value of the quiltmaker's motion and strategy in the precincts of a continuously undemocratic South.

From "Patches: Quilts and Community in
Alice Walker's 'Everyday Use'"

---

griot: African storyteller, guardian of the people's history [authors' note].

Elaine Showalter (b. 1941)

Quilt as Metaphor in "Everyday Use"   1991

For Alice Walker, piecing and quilting have come to represent both the aesthetic heritage of Afro-American women and the model for what she calls a "Womanist," or black feminist, writing of reconciliation and connection; in her essay "In Search of Our Mothers' Gardens," Walker identified the quilt as a major form of creative expression for black women in the South. "In the Smithsonian Institution in Washington, D.C.," Walker writes,

> there hangs a quilt unlike another in the world. In fanciful, inspired, and yet simple and identifiable figures, it portrays the story of the Crucifixion . . . Though it follows no known pattern of quiltmaking, and though it is made of bits and pieces of worthless rags, it is obviously the work of a person of powerful imagination and deep spiritual feeling. Below this quilt I saw a note that says it was made by "an anonymous Black woman in Alabama a hundred years ago."

The quilt Walker is describing from memory is in fact one of two extant narrative quilts by Harriet Powers (1836–1911), born a slave in Georgia. The Powers quilt at the Smithsonian illustrates Bible stories, while the one in the Boston Museum of Fine Arts mingles Bible tales with folklore and astronomical events such as shooting stars and meteor showers.[1] For Walker, genuine imagination and feeling can be recognized without the legitimacy conferred by the labels of "art" or the approval of museums. Paradoxically this heritage survives because it has been preserved in museums; but it can be a living art only if it is practiced.

The theme of Walker's quilt aesthetic is most explicitly presented in her early story "Everyday Use." Like much of her work, it uses a contrast between two sisters to get at the meaning of the concept of "heritage": a privileged one who escapes from Southern black culture, and a suffering one who stays or is left behind. The younger daughter, Maggie, has stayed at home since she was horribly scarred in a house fire ten years before. Dee is the bright and confident sister, the one with "faultfinding power." Dee has learned fast how to produce herself: "At sixteen she had a style of her own: and knew what style was." Now having chosen the style of radical black nationalism, her name changed to "Wangero," and spouting Swahili, Dee returns to claim her heritage from her mother in the form of "folk art": the worn benches made by her father, the butter churn whittled by an uncle, and especially the quilts pieced by her grandmother. "Maggie can't appreciate these quilts," Dee exclaims. "She'd probably be backward enough to put them to everyday use." Walker thus establishes a contrast between "everyday use" and "institutional theories of aesthetics."[2] In a moment of epiphanic insight, the mother, who has always been intimidated by Dee's intelligence and sophistication, decides to give the quilts to Maggie. "She can always make some more," the mother responds. "Maggie knows how to quilt." Maggie cannot speak glibly about her "heritage" or about "priceless" artifacts, but, unlike Dee, she understands the quilt as a process rather than as a commodity; she can read its meaning in a way Dee never will, because she knows the contexts of its pieces, and loves the women who have made it. The meaning of an aesthetic heritage, according

---

[1]See Marie Jean Adams, "The Harriet Powers Pictorial Quilts," *Black Art* 3 (1982) 12–28.
[2]Houston A. Baker and Charlotte Pierce-Baker, "Patches: Quilts and Community in Alice Walker's 'Everyday Use.'" *Southern Review* 21:3 (Summer 1985) 716.

to Walker's story, lies in continual renewal rather than in the rhetoric of nostalgia or appreciation. In writing *The Color Purple,* Walker herself took up quilt-making as well as using it as a central metaphor in the novel.

From *Sister's Choice: Tradition and Change in American Women's Writing*

■ WRITING *effectively*

TOPICS FOR WRITING ABOUT "YOUNG GOODMAN BROWN"

1. It is sometimes suggested that "Young Goodman Brown" is a story about an innocent young man who becomes disillusioned about human nature. How innocent is Goodman Brown at the beginning of the tale? Use details from the text to back up your conclusion.

2. Have you ever had to come to terms with the discovery of weakness or wrongdoing on the part of someone you admired? What was your initial reaction? What ultimate change was there, if any, in your feelings about that person?

3. The most hotly debated aspect of "Young Goodman Brown" is, of course, whether the events in the forest actually took place. Does it matter to your understanding and appreciation of the story that the issue be settled one way or the other? Why or why not?

4. At the end of the tale, Goodman Brown is withdrawn and isolated from everyone around him, including his wife and children. Is he a better person than everyone else, or a worse one? Refer as specifically as possible to the text itself in explaining the reasons for your conclusion.

TOPICS FOR WRITING ABOUT "THE YELLOW WALLPAPER"

1. "The Yellow Wallpaper" is cast in the form of the journal written by its central character. Consider how the use of this narrative device enriches—or impoverishes—the story.

2. Thomas L. Erskine and Connie L. Richards have written of "the aesthetic problem with much of Gilman's literary work; often her sociopolitical agenda overwhelms the characters, who become one-dimensional mouthpieces for different ideas. Propaganda all too often threatens art." Discuss whether or not you think these concerns apply to "The Yellow Wallpaper."

3. Think of a contemporary issue that involves women's feelings of being confined or thwarted by the male power structure. Then write a brief treatment of that issue in the style of "The Yellow Wallpaper."

4. Discuss the larger implications of the conclusion of "The Yellow Wallpaper." In the end, has the narrator triumphed by escaping her oppression, or has she been crushed by it?

TOPICS FOR WRITING ABOUT "EVERYDAY USE"

1. Write a brief version of the encounter in "Everyday Use" from Dee's point of view. Is it possible to present a nonironic affirmation of her values over those of her mother and sister? Why or why not?

2. Have you grown apart from a friend or relative with whom you once had a close relationship? Imagine an encounter with that person, and write a first-person description of it from the other person's point of view.

3. Alice Walker has suggested that one of her principal intentions in her writing is "nurturing and healing the reader." Is "nurturing and healing" one of the primary aims of "Everyday Use"?

4. How does the use of a first-person narrator function in "Everyday Use"? Are there places in which the reader is expected to understand more than the narrator does, or is everything that she says and sees to be accepted at face value?

STORIES FOR FURTHER READING

The novel tends to tell us everything, whereas the short story tells us only one thing and that intensely.

—V. S. PRITCHETT

Chinua Achebe

Dead Men's Path (1953) 1972

Chinua Achebe was born in Ogidi, a village in eastern Nigeria, in 1930. His father was a missionary schoolteacher, and Achebe had a devout Christian upbringing. A member of the Ibo tribe, the future writer grew up speaking Igbo, but at the age of eight, he began learning English. He went abroad to study at London University but returned to Africa to complete his B.A. at the University College of Ibadan in 1953. Achebe worked for years in Nigerian radio. Shortly after Nigeria's independence from Great Britain in 1963, civil war broke out, and the new nation split in two. Achebe left his job to join the Ministry of Information for Biafra, the new country created from eastern Nigeria. It was not until 1970 that the bloody

Chinua Achebe

civil war ended. Approximately one million Ibos lay dead from war, disease, and starvation as the defeated Biafrans reunited with Nigeria. Achebe is often considered Africa's premier novelist. His novels include Things Fall Apart *(1958),* No Longer at Ease *(1962),* A Man of the People *(1966), and* Anthills of the Savannah *(1987). His short stories have been collected in* Girls At War *(1972). He has also published poetry, children's stories, and several volumes of essays, the most recent of which is* Home and Exile *(2000). In 1990 Achebe suffered massive injuries in a car accident outside Lagos that left him paralyzed from the waist down. He currently teaches at Bard College in upstate New York. In 1999 he visited Nigeria again after a deliberate nine-year absence to protest government dictatorship, and his homecoming became a national event. In 2007 he was awarded the second Man Booker International Prize for his lifetime contribution to world literature.*

Michael Obi's hopes were fulfilled much earlier than he had expected. He was appointed headmaster of Ndume Central School in January 1949. It had always been an unprogressive school, so the Mission authorities decided to send a young and energetic man to run it. Obi accepted this responsibility with enthusiasm. He had many wonderful ideas and this was an opportunity to put them into practice. He had had sound secondary school education which designated him a "pivotal teacher" in the official records and set him apart from the other headmasters in the mission field. He was outspoken in his condemnation of the narrow views of these older and often less-educated ones.

"We shall make a good job of it, shan't we?" he asked his young wife when they first heard the joyful news of his promotion.

"We shall do our best," she replied. "We shall have such beautiful gardens and everything will be just *modern* and delightful . . ." In their two years of married life she had become completely infected by his passion for "modern methods" and his denigration of "these old and superannuated people in the teaching field who would be better employed as traders in the Onitsha market." She began to see herself already as the admired wife of the young headmaster, the queen of the school.

The wives of the other teachers would envy her position. She would set the fashion in everything . . . Then, suddenly, it occurred to her that there might not be other wives. Wavering between hope and fear, she asked her husband, looking anxiously at him.

"All our colleagues are young and unmarried," he said with enthusiasm which for once she did not share. "Which is a good thing," he continued.   5

"Why?"

"Why? They will give all their time and energy to the school."

Nancy was downcast. For a few minutes she became skeptical about the new school; but it was only for a few minutes. Her little personal misfortune could not blind her to her husband's happy prospects. She looked at him as he sat folded up in a chair. He was stoop-shouldered and looked frail. But he sometimes surprised people with sudden bursts of physical energy. In his present posture, however, all his bodily strength seemed to have retired behind his deep-set eyes, giving them an extraordinary power of penetration. He was only twenty-six, but looked thirty or more. On the whole, he was not unhandsome.

"A penny for your thoughts, Mike," said Nancy after a while, imitating the woman's magazine she read.

"I was thinking what a grand opportunity we've got at last to show these people   10
how a school should be run."

Ndume School was backward in every sense of the word. Mr. Obi put his whole life into the work, and his wife hers too. He had two aims. A high standard of teaching was insisted upon, and the school compound was to be turned into a place of beauty. Nancy's dream-gardens came to life with the coming of the rains, and blossomed. Beautiful hibiscus and allamanda hedges in brilliant red and yellow marked out the carefully tended school compound from the rank neighborhood bushes.

One evening as Obi was admiring his work he was scandalized to see an old woman from the village hobble right across the compound, through a marigold flower-bed and the hedges. On going up there he found faint signs of an almost disused path from the village across the school compound to the bush on the other side.

"It amazes me," said Obi to one of his teachers who had been three years in the school, "that you people allowed the villagers to make use of this footpath. It is simply incredible." He shook his head.

"The path," said the teacher apologetically, "appears to be very important to them. Although it is hardly used, it connects the village shrine with their place of burial."

"And what has that got to do with the school?" asked the headmaster.   15

"Well, I don't know," replied the other with a shrug of the shoulders. "But I remember there was a big row some time ago when we attempted to close it."

"That was some time ago. But it will not be used now," said Obi as he walked away. "What will the Government Education Officer think of this when he comes to inspect the school next week? The villagers might, for all I know, decide to use the schoolroom for a pagan ritual during the inspection."

Heavy sticks were planted closely across the path at the two places where it entered and left the school premises. These were further strengthened with barbed wire.

Three days later the village priest of *Ani* called on the headmaster. He was an old man and walked with a slight stoop. He carried a stout walking-stick which he usually tapped on the floor, by way of emphasis, each time he made a new point in his argument.

"I have heard," he said after the usual exchange of cordialities, "that our ancestral   20
footpath has recently been closed . . ."

"Yes," replied Mr. Obi. "We cannot allow people to make a highway of our school compound."

"Look here, my son," said the priest bringing down his walking-stick, "this path was here before you were born and before your father was born. The whole life of this village depends on it. Our dead relatives depart by it and our ancestors visit us by it. But most important, it is the path of children coming in to be born . . ."

Mr. Obi listened with a satisfied smile on his face.

"The whole purpose of our school," he said finally, "is to eradicate just such beliefs as that. Dead men do not require footpaths. The whole idea is just fantastic. Our duty is to teach your children to laugh at such ideas."

"What you say may be true," replied the priest, "but we follow the practices of   25
our fathers. If you reopen the path we shall have nothing to quarrel about. What I always say is: let the hawk perch and let the eagle perch." He rose to go.

"I am sorry," said the young headmaster. "But the school compound cannot be a thoroughfare. It is against our regulations. I would suggest your constructing another path, skirting our premises. We can even get our boys to help in building it. I don't suppose the ancestors will find the little detour too burdensome."

"I have no more words to say," said the old priest, already outside.

Two days later a young woman in the village died in childbed. A diviner was immediately consulted and he prescribed heavy sacrifices to propitiate ancestors insulted by the fence.

Obi woke up next morning among the ruins of his work. The beautiful hedges were torn up not just near the path but right round the school, the flowers trampled to death and one of the school buildings pulled down . . . That day, the white Supervisor came to inspect the school and wrote a nasty report on the state of the premises but more seriously about the "tribal-war situation developing between the school and the village, arising in part from the misguided zeal of the new headmaster."

Sherman Alexie

This Is What It Means to Say Phoenix, Arizona   1993

Sherman Alexie

Sherman Alexie was born in 1966 on the Spokane Indian Reservation in Wellpinit, Washington. Hydrocephalic at birth, he underwent surgery at the age of six months. At first he was expected not to survive; when that prognosis proved wrong, it was predicted, again wrongly, that he would be severely retarded. Alexie attended Gonzaga University in Spokane and graduated from the University of Washington with a degree in American studies. His first book, a collection of poems called The Business of Fancydancing, *appeared in 1991, and he has published prolifically since then, averaging a book a year. He is the author of ten volumes of poetry and two novels for young adults, as well as three collections of stories—*The Lone Ranger and Tonto Fistfight in Heaven *(1993),* The Toughest Indian in the World *(2000), and* Ten Little Indians *(2003)— and three novels—*Reservation Blues *(1995),* Indian Killer *(1996), and* Flight *(2007). In addition to his writing, Alexie won the World Heavyweight Poetry Bout competition an unprecedented four consecutive times (1998–2001); he has appeared on television discussion programs hosted by Bill Maher, Bill Moyers, and Jim Lehrer (a 1998 "Dialogue on Race" whose participants also included President Bill Clinton); he has performed frequently as a stand-up comedian; and he co-produced and wrote the 1998 feature film* Smoke Signals, *based on "This Is What It Means to Say Phoenix, Arizona." Alexie lives with his wife and two sons in Seattle, Washington.*

Just after Victor lost his job at the BIA,° he also found out that his father had died of a heart attack in Phoenix, Arizona. Victor hadn't seen his father in a few years, only talked to him on the telephone once or twice, but there still was a genetic pain, which was soon to be pain as real and immediate as a broken bone.

Victor didn't have any money. Who does have money on a reservation, except the cigarette and fireworks salespeople? His father had a savings account waiting to be claimed, but Victor needed to find a way to get to Phoenix. Victor's mother was just as poor as he was, and the rest of his family didn't have any use at all for him. So Victor called the Tribal Council.

"Listen," Victor said. "My father just died. I need some money to get to Phoenix to make arrangements."

"Now, Victor," the council said. "You know we're having a difficult time financially."

"But I thought the council had special funds set aside for stuff like this."   5

"Now, Victor, we do have some money available for the proper return of tribal members' bodies. But I don't think we have enough to bring your father all the way back from Phoenix."

BIA: Bureau of Indian Affairs, a federal agency responsible for management of Indian lands and concerns.

"Well," Victor said. "It ain't going to cost all that much. He had to be cremated. Things were kind of ugly. He died of a heart attack in his trailer and nobody found him for a week. It was really hot, too. You get the picture."

"Now, Victor, we're sorry for your loss and the circumstances. But we can really only afford to give you one hundred dollars."

"That's not even enough for a plane ticket."

"Well, you might consider driving down to Phoenix." 10

"I don't have a car. Besides, I was going to drive my father's pickup back up here."

"Now, Victor," the council said. "We're sure there is somebody who could drive you to Phoenix. Or is there somebody who could lend you the rest of the money?"

"You know there ain't nobody around with that kind of money."

"Well, we're sorry, Victor, but that's the best we can do."

Victor accepted the Tribal Council's offer. What else could he do? So he signed 15 the proper papers, picked up his check, and walked over to the Trading Post to cash it.

While Victor stood in line, he watched Thomas Builds-the-Fire standing near the magazine rack, talking to himself. Like he always did. Thomas was a storyteller that nobody wanted to listen to. That's like being a dentist in a town where everybody has false teeth.

Victor and Thomas Builds-the-Fire were the same age, had grown up and played in the dirt together. Ever since Victor could remember, it was Thomas who always had something to say.

Once, when they were seven years old, when Victor's father still lived with the family, Thomas closed his eyes and told Victor this story: "Your father's heart is weak. He is afraid of his own family. He is afraid of you. Late at night he sits in the dark. Watches the television until there's nothing but that white noise. Sometimes he feels like he wants to buy a motorcycle and ride away. He wants to run and hide. He doesn't want to be found."

Thomas Builds-the-Fire had known that Victor's father was going to leave, knew it before anyone. Now Victor stood in the Trading Post with a one-hundred-dollar check in his hand, wondering if Thomas knew that Victor's father was dead, if he knew what was going to happen next.

Just then Thomas looked at Victor, smiled, and walked over to him. 20

"Victor, I'm sorry about your father," Thomas said.

"How did you know about it?" Victor asked.

"I heard it on the wind. I heard it from the birds. I felt it in the sunlight. Also, your mother was just in here crying."

"Oh," Victor said and looked around the Trading Post. All the other Indians stared, surprised that Victor was even talking to Thomas. Nobody talked to Thomas anymore because he told the same damn stories over and over again. Victor was embarrassed, but he thought that Thomas might be able to help him. Victor felt a sudden need for tradition.

"I can lend you the money you need," Thomas said suddenly. "But you have to 25 take me with you."

"I can't take your money," Victor said. "I mean, I haven't hardly talked to you in years. We're not really friends anymore."

"I didn't say we were friends. I said you had to take me with you."

"Let me think about it."

Victor went home with his one hundred dollars and sat at the kitchen table. He held his head in his hands and thought about Thomas Builds-the-Fire, remembered little details, tears and scars, the bicycle they shared for a summer, so many stories.

*

Thomas Builds-the-Fire sat on the bicycle, waited in Victor's yard. He was ten 30
years old and skinny. His hair was dirty because it was the Fourth of July.

"Victor," Thomas yelled. "Hurry up. We're going to miss the fireworks."

After a few minutes, Victor ran out of his house, jumped the porch railing, and
landed gracefully on the sidewalk.

"And the judges award him a 9.95, the highest score of the summer," Thomas
said, clapped, laughed.

"That was perfect, cousin," Victor said. "And it's my turn to ride the bike."

Thomas gave up the bike and they headed for the fairgrounds. It was nearly dark 35
and the fireworks were about to start.

"You know," Thomas said. "It's strange how us Indians celebrate the Fourth of
July. It ain't like it was *our* independence everybody was fighting for."

"You think about things too much," Victor said. "It's just supposed to be fun.
Maybe Junior will be there."

"Which Junior? Everybody on this reservation is named Junior."

And they both laughed.

The fireworks were small, hardly more than a few bottle rockets and a fountain. 40
But it was enough for two Indian boys. Years later, they would need much more.

Afterwards, sitting in the dark, fighting off mosquitoes, Victor turned to Thomas
Builds-the-Fire.

"Hey," Victor said. "Tell me a story."

Thomas closed his eyes and told this story: "There were these two Indian boys who
wanted to be warriors. But it was too late to be warriors in the old way. All the horses
were gone. So the two Indian boys stole a car and drove to the city. They parked the
stolen car in front of the police station and then hitchhiked back home to the reservation. When they got back, all their friends cheered and their parents' eyes shone
with pride. *You were very brave,* everybody said to the two Indian boys. *Very brave.*"

"Ya-hey," Victor said. "That's a good one. I wish I could be a warrior."

"Me, too," Thomas said. 45

They went home together in the dark, Thomas on the bike now, Victor on foot.
They walked through shadows and light from streetlamps.

"We've come a long ways," Thomas said. "We have outdoor lighting."

"All I need is the stars," Victor said. "And besides, you still think about things
too much."

They separated then, each headed for home, both laughing all the way.

Victor sat at his kitchen table. He counted his one hundred dollars again and 50
again. He knew he needed more to make it to Phoenix and back. He knew he needed
Thomas Builds-the-Fire. So he put his money in his wallet and opened the front door
to find Thomas on the porch.

"Ya-hey, Victor," Thomas said. "I knew you'd call me."

Thomas walked into the living room and sat down on Victor's favorite chair.

"I've got some money saved up," Thomas said. "It's enough to get us down there,
but you have to get us back."

"I've got this hundred dollars," Victor said. "And my dad had a savings account
I'm going to claim."

"How much in your dad's account?" 55

"Enough. A few hundred."

"Sounds good. When we leaving?"

When they were fifteen and had long since stopped being friends, Victor and Thomas got into a fistfight. That is, Victor was really drunk and beat Thomas up for no reason at all. All the other Indian boys stood around and watched it happen. Junior was there and so were Lester, Seymour, and a lot of others. The beating might have gone on until Thomas was dead if Norma Many Horses hadn't come along and stopped it.

"Hey, you boys," Norma yelled and jumped out of her car. "Leave him alone."

If it had been someone else, even another man, the Indian boys would've just ig- 60 nored the warnings. But Norma was a warrior. She was powerful. She could have picked up any two of the boys and smashed their skulls together. But worse than that, she would have dragged them all over to some tipi and made them listen to some elder tell a dusty old story.

The Indian boys scattered, and Norma walked over to Thomas and picked him up.

"Hey, little man, are you okay?" she asked.

Thomas gave her a thumbs up.

"Why they always picking on you?"

Thomas shook his head, closed his eyes, but no stories came to him, no words or 65 music. He just wanted to go home, to lie in his bed and let his dreams tell his stories for him.

Thomas Builds-the-Fire and Victor sat next to each other in the airplane, coach section. A tiny white woman had the window seat. She was busy twisting her body into pretzels. She was flexible.

"I have to ask," Thomas said, and Victor closed his eyes in embarrassment.

"Don't," Victor said.

"Excuse me, miss," Thomas asked. "Are you a gymnast or something?"

"There's no something about it," she said. "I was first alternate on the 1980 70 Olympic team."

"Really?" Thomas asked.

"Really."

"I mean, you used to be a world-class athlete?" Thomas asked.

"My husband still thinks I am."

Thomas Builds-the-Fire smiled. She was a mental gymnast, too. She pulled her 75 leg straight up against her body so that she could've kissed her kneecap.

"I wish I could do that," Thomas said.

Victor was ready to jump out of the plane. Thomas, that crazy Indian storyteller with ratty old braids and broken teeth, was flirting with a beautiful Olympic gymnast. Nobody back home on the reservation would ever believe it.

"Well," the gymnast said. "It's easy. Try it."

Thomas grabbed at his leg and tried to pull it up into the same position as the gymnast. He couldn't even come close, which made Victor and the gymnast laugh.

"Hey," she asked. "You two are Indian, right?" 80

"Full-blood," Victor said.

"Not me," Thomas said. "I'm half magician on my mother's side and half clown on my father's."

They all laughed.

"What are your names?" she asked.

"Victor and Thomas." 85

"Mine is Cathy. Pleased to meet you all."

The three of them talked for the duration of the flight. Cathy the gymnast complained about the government, how they screwed the 1980 Olympic team by boycotting.°

"Sounds like you all got a lot in common with Indians," Thomas said.

Nobody laughed.

After the plane landed in Phoenix and they had all found their way to the termi- 90 nal, Cathy the gymnast smiled and waved good-bye.

"She was really nice," Thomas said.

"Yeah, but everybody talks to everybody on airplanes," Victor said. "It's too bad we can't always be that way."

"You always used to tell me I think too much," Thomas said. "Now it sounds like you do."

"Maybe I caught it from you."

"Yeah." 95

Thomas and Victor rode in a taxi to the trailer where Victor's father died.

"Listen," Victor said as they stopped in front of the trailer. "I never told you I was sorry for beating you up that time."

"Oh, it was nothing. We were just kids and you were drunk."

"Yeah, but I'm still sorry."

"That's all right." 100

Victor paid for the taxi and the two of them stood in the hot Phoenix summer. They could smell the trailer.

"This ain't going to be nice," Victor said. "You don't have to go in."

"You're going to need help."

Victor walked to the front door and opened it. The stink rolled out and made them both gag. Victor's father had lain in that trailer for a week in hundred-degree temperatures before anyone found him. And the only reason anyone found him was because of the smell. They needed dental records to identify him. That's exactly what the coroner said. They needed dental records.

"Oh, man," Victor said. "I don't know if I can do this." 105

"Well, then don't."

"But there might be something valuable in there."

"I thought his money was in the bank."

"It is. I was talking about pictures and letters and stuff like that."

"Oh," Thomas said as he held his breath and followed Victor into the trailer. 110

When Victor was twelve, he stepped into an underground wasp nest. His foot was caught in the hole, and no matter how hard he struggled, Victor couldn't pull free. He might have died there, stung a thousand times, if Thomas Builds-the-Fire had not come by.

---

they screwed the 1980 Olympic team by boycotting: in an international movement led by the United States at the direction of President Jimmy Carter, some sixty nations boycotted the 1980 Summer Olympic Games in Moscow as a protest against the Soviet invasion of Afghanistan in December 1979.

"Run," Thomas yelled and pulled Victor's foot from the hole. They ran then, hard as they ever had, faster than Billy Mills, faster than Jim Thorpe,° faster than the wasps could fly.

Victor and Thomas ran until they couldn't breathe, ran until it was cold and dark outside, ran until they were lost and it took hours to find their way home. All the way back, Victor counted his stings.

"Seven," Victor said. "My lucky number."

Victor didn't find much to keep in the trailer. Only a photo album and a stereo. 115
Everything else had that smell stuck in it or was useless anyway.

"I guess this is all," Victor said. "It ain't much."

"Better than nothing," Thomas said.

"Yeah, and I do have the pickup."

"Yeah," Thomas said. "It's in good shape."

"Dad was good about that stuff." 120

"Yeah, I remember your dad."

"Really?" Victor asked. "What do you remember?"

Thomas Builds-the-Fire closed his eyes and told this story: "I remember when I had this dream that told me to go to Spokane, to stand by the Falls in the middle of the city and wait for a sign. I knew I had to go there but I didn't have a car. Didn't have a license. I was only thirteen. So I walked all the way, took me all day, and I finally made it to the Falls. I stood there for an hour waiting. Then your dad came walking up. *What the hell are you doing here?* he asked me. I said, *Waiting for a vision.* Then your father said, *All you're going to get here is mugged.* So he drove me over to Denny's, bought me dinner, and then drove me home to the reservation. For a long time I was mad because I thought my dreams had lied to me. But they didn't. Your dad was my vision. *Take care of each other* is what my dreams were saying. *Take care of each other.*"

Victor was quiet for a long time. He searched his mind for memories of his father, found the good ones, found a few bad ones, added it all up, and smiled.

"My father never told me about finding you in Spokane," Victor said. 125

"He said he wouldn't tell anybody. Didn't want me to get in trouble. But he said I had to watch out for you as part of the deal."

"Really?"

"Really. Your father said you would need the help. He was right."

"That's why you came down here with me, isn't it?" Victor asked.

"I came because of your father." 130

Victor and Thomas climbed into the pickup, drove over to the bank, and claimed the three hundred dollars in the savings account.

Thomas Builds-the-Fire could fly.

Billy Mills . . . Jim Thorpe: William Mervin "Billy" Mills (born 1938), a member of the Sioux tribe, won a gold medal in the 10,000-meter run at the 1964 Summer Olympic Games in Tokyo, Japan. Jacobus Franciscus "Jim" Thorpe (1888–1953), of the Sac and Fox tribe, is widely regarded as one of the greatest American athletes of the twentieth century; he won gold medals in the pentathlon and decathlon at the 1912 Summer Olympic Games in Stockholm, Sweden. He also played professional football, baseball, and basketball.

Once, he jumped off the roof of the tribal school and flapped his arms like a crazy eagle. And he flew. For a second, he hovered, suspended above all the other Indian boys who were too smart or too scared to jump.

"He's flying," Junior yelled, and Seymour was busy looking for the trick wires or mirrors. But it was real. As real as the dirt when Thomas lost altitude and crashed to the ground.

He broke his arm in two places.   135

"He broke his wing," Victor chanted, and the other Indian boys joined in, made it a tribal song.

"He broke his wing, he broke his wing, he broke his wing," all the Indian boys chanted as they ran off, flapping their wings, wishing they could fly, too. They hated Thomas for his courage, his brief moment as a bird. Everybody has dreams about flying. Thomas flew.

One of his dreams came true for just a second, just enough to make it real.

Victor's father, his ashes, fit in one wooden box with enough left over to fill a cardboard box.

"He always was a big man," Thomas said.   140

Victor carried part of his father and Thomas carried the rest out to the pickup. They set him down carefully behind the seats, put a cowboy hat on the wooden box and a Dodgers cap on the cardboard box. That's the way it was supposed to be.

"Ready to head back home," Victor asked.

"It's going to be a long drive."

"Yeah, take a couple days, maybe."

"We can take turns," Thomas said.   145

"Okay," Victor said, but they didn't take turns. Victor drove for sixteen hours straight north, made it halfway up Nevada toward home before he finally pulled over.

"Hey, Thomas," Victor said. "You got to drive for a while."

"Okay."

Thomas Builds-the-Fire slid behind the wheel and started off down the road. All through Nevada, Thomas and Victor had been amazed at the lack of animal life, at the absence of water, of movement.

"Where is everything?" Victor had asked more than once.   150

Now when Thomas was finally driving they saw the first animal, maybe the only animal in Nevada. It was a long-eared jackrabbit.

"Look," Victor yelled. "It's alive."

Thomas and Victor were busy congratulating themselves on their discovery when the jackrabbit darted out into the road and under the wheels of the pickup.

"Stop the goddamn car," Victor yelled, and Thomas did stop, backed the pickup to the dead jackrabbit.

"Oh, man, he's dead," Victor said as he looked at the squashed animal.   155

"Really dead."

"The only thing alive in this whole state and we just killed it."

"I don't know," Thomas said. "I think it was suicide."

Victor looked around the desert, sniffed the air, felt the emptiness and loneliness, and nodded his head.

"Yeah," Victor said. "It had to be suicide."   160

"I can't believe this," Thomas said. "You drive for a thousand miles and there ain't even any bugs smashed on the windshield. I drive for ten seconds and kill the only living thing in Nevada."

"Yeah," Victor said. "Maybe I should drive."

"Maybe you should."

Thomas Builds-the-Fire walked through the corridors of the tribal school by himself. Nobody wanted to be anywhere near him because of all those stories. Story after story.

Thomas closed his eyes and this story came to him: "We are all given one thing 165 by which our lives are measured, one determination. Mine are the stories which can change or not change the world. It doesn't matter which as long as I continue to tell the stories. My father, he died on Okinawa in World War II, died fighting for this country, which had tried to kill him for years. My mother, she died giving birth to me, died while I was still inside her. She pushed me out into the world with her last breath. I have no brothers or sisters. I have only my stories which came to me before I even had the words to speak. I learned a thousand stories before I took my first thousand steps. They are all I have. It's all I can do."

Thomas Builds-the-Fire told his stories to all those who would stop and listen. He kept telling them long after people had stopped listening.

Victor and Thomas made it back to the reservation just as the sun was rising. It was the beginning of a new day on earth, but the same old shit on the reservation.

"Good morning," Thomas said.

"Good morning."

The tribe was waking up, ready for work, eating breakfast, reading the newspa- 170 per, just like everybody else does. Willene LeBret was out in her garden wearing a bathrobe. She waved when Thomas and Victor drove by.

"Crazy Indians made it," she said to herself and went back to her roses.

Victor stopped the pickup in front of Thomas Builds-the-Fire's HUD house.° They both yawned, stretched a little, shook dust from their bodies.

"I'm tired," Victor said.

"Of everything," Thomas added.

They both searched for words to end the journey. Victor needed to thank 175 Thomas for his help, for the money, and make the promise to pay it all back.

"Don't worry about the money," Thomas said. "It don't make any difference any- how."

"Probably not, enit?"

"Nope."

Victor knew that Thomas would remain the crazy storyteller who talked to dogs and cars, who listened to the wind and pine trees. Victor knew that he couldn't really be friends with Thomas, even after all that had happened. It was cruel but it was real. As real as the ashes, as Victor's father, sitting behind the seats.

"I know how it is," Thomas said. "I know you ain't going to treat me any better than 180 you did before. I know your friends would give you too much shit about it."

Victor was ashamed of himself. Whatever happened to the tribal ties, the sense of community? The only real thing he shared with anybody was a bottle and broken dreams. He owed Thomas something, anything.

"Listen," Victor said and handed Thomas the cardboard box which contained half of his father. "I want you to have this."

HUD house: housing subsidized by the U.S. Department of Housing and Urban Development.

Thomas took the ashes and smiled, closed his eyes, and told this story: "I'm going to travel to Spokane Falls one last time and toss these ashes into the water. And your father will rise like a salmon, leap over the bridge, over me, and find his way home. It will be beautiful. His teeth will shine like silver, like a rainbow. He will rise, Victor, he will rise."

Victor smiled.

"I was planning on doing the same thing with my half," Victor said. "But I didn't   185 imagine my father looking anything like a salmon. I thought it'd be like cleaning the attic or something. Like letting things go after they've stopped having any use."

"Nothing stops, cousin," Thomas said. "Nothing stops."

Thomas Builds-the-Fire got out of the pickup and walked up his driveway. Victor started the pickup and began the drive home.

"Wait," Thomas yelled suddenly from his porch. "I just got to ask one favor."

Victor stopped the pickup, leaned out the window, and shouted back. "What do you want?"

"Just one time when I'm telling a story somewhere, why don't you stop and   190 listen?" Thomas asked.

"Just once?"

"Just once."

Victor waved his arms to let Thomas know that the deal was good. It was a fair trade, and that was all Victor had ever wanted from his whole life. So Victor drove his father's pickup toward home while Thomas went into his house, closed the door behind him, and heard a new story come to him in the silence afterwards.

Margaret Atwood

Happy Endings   1983

Born in Ottawa, Ontario, in 1939, Margaret Eleanor Atwood was the daughter of an entomologist and spent her childhood summers in the forests of northern Quebec, where her father carried out research. Atwood began writing at the age of five and had already seriously entertained thoughts of becoming a professional writer before she finished high school. She graduated from the University of Toronto in 1961, and later did graduate work at Radcliffe and Harvard. Atwood first gained prominence as a poet. Her first full-length collection of poems, The Circle Game *(1966), was awarded a Governor General's Award, Canada's most prestigious literary honor, and she has since published nearly twenty volumes of verse. Atwood also began to write fiction seriously in graduate school, and her short stories were first collected in* Dancing Girls *(1977), followed by numerous additional collections, most recently* Moral Disorder *(2006).*

Margaret Atwood

A dedicated feminist, Atwood's works of fiction explore the complex relations between the sexes, most incisively in The Handmaid's Tale *(1986), a futuristic novel about a world in which gender roles are ruthlessly enforced by a society based on religious fundamentalism. In the same year that* The Handmaid's Tale *appeared, Atwood was named Woman of the Year by* Ms. *magazine. Subsequent novels include* Cat's Eye *(1988),* The Robber Bride *(1993),* The Blind Assassin *(2000), and* The Year of the Flood *(2009). Atwood has served as writer-in-residence at universities in Canada, the United States, and Europe, and she has been widely in demand for appearances at symposia devoted to literature and women's issues.*

John and Mary meet.
What happens next?
If you want a happy ending, try A.

A

John and Mary fall in love and get married. They both have worthwhile and remunerative jobs which they find stimulating and challenging. They buy a charming house. Real estate values go up. Eventually, when they can afford live-in help, they have two children, to whom they are devoted. The children turn out well. John and Mary have a stimulating and challenging sex life and worthwhile friends. They go on fun vacations together. They retire. They both have hobbies which they find stimulating and challenging. Eventually they die. This is the end of the story.

B

Mary falls in love with John but John doesn't fall in love with Mary. He merely   5
uses her body for selfish pleasure and ego gratification of a tepid kind. He comes to her apartment twice a week and she cooks him dinner, you'll notice that he doesn't even consider her worth the price of a dinner out, and after he's eaten the dinner he fucks her and after that he falls asleep, while she does the dishes so he won't think she's untidy, having all those dirty dishes lying around, and puts on fresh lipstick so she'll look good when he wakes up, but when he wakes up he doesn't even notice, he puts on his socks and his shorts and his pants and his shirt and his tie and his shoes, the reverse order from the one in which he took them off. He doesn't take off Mary's clothes, she takes them off herself, she acts as if she's dying for it every time, not because she likes sex exactly, she doesn't, but she wants John to think she does because if they do it often enough surely he'll get used to her, he'll come to depend on her and they will get married, but John goes out the door with hardly so much as a goodnight and three days later he turns up at six o'clock and they do the whole thing over again.

Mary gets rundown. Crying is bad for your face, everyone knows that and so does Mary but she can't stop. People at work notice. Her friends tell her John is a rat, a pig, a dog, he isn't good enough for her, but she can't believe it. Inside John, she thinks, is another John, who is much nicer. This other John will emerge like a butterfly from a cocoon, a Jack from a box, a pit from a prune, if the first John is only squeezed enough.

One evening John complains about the food. He has never complained about the food before. Mary is hurt.

Her friends tell her they've seen him in a restaurant with another woman, whose name is Madge. It's not even Madge that finally gets to Mary; it's the restaurant. John has never taken Mary to a restaurant. Mary collects all the sleeping pills and aspirins she can find, and takes them and a half a bottle of sherry. You can see what kind of a woman she is by the fact that it's not even whiskey. She leaves a note for John. She hopes he'll discover her and get her to the hospital in time and repent and then they can get married, but this fails to happen and she dies.

John marries Madge and everything continues as in A.

C

John, who is an older man, falls in love with Mary, and Mary, who is only twenty-two, feels sorry for him because he's worried about his hair falling out. She sleeps with him even though she's not in love with him. She met him at work. She's in love with someone called James, who is twenty-two also and not yet ready to settle down. 10

John on the contrary settled down long ago: this is what is bothering him. John has a steady, respectable job and is getting ahead in his field, but Mary isn't impressed by him, she's impressed by James, who has a motorcycle and a fabulous record collection. But James is often away on his motorcycle, being free. Freedom isn't the same for girls, so in the meantime Mary spends Thursday evenings with John. Thursdays are the only days John can get away.

John is married to a woman called Madge and they have two children, a charming house which they bought just before the real estate values went up, and hobbies which they find stimulating and challenging, when they have the time. John tells Mary how important she is to him, but of course, he can't leave his wife because a commitment is a commitment. He goes on about this more than is necessary and Mary finds it boring, but older men can keep it up longer so on the whole she has a fairly good time.

One day James breezes in on his motorcycle with some top-grade California hybrid and James and Mary get higher than you'd believe possible and they climb into bed. Everything becomes very underwater, but along comes John, who has a key to Mary's apartment. He finds them stoned and entwined. He's hardly in any position to be jealous, considering Madge, but nevertheless he's overcome with despair. Finally he's middle-aged, in two years he'll be bald as an egg and he can't stand it. He purchases a handgun, saying he needs it for target practice—this is the thin part of the plot, but it can be dealt with later—and shoots the two of them and himself.

Madge, after a suitable period of mourning, marries an understanding man called Fred and everything continues as in A, but under different names.

D

Fred and Madge have no problems. They get along exceptionally well and are good at working out any little difficulties that may arise. But their charming house is by the seashore and one day a giant tidal wave approaches. Real estate values go down. The rest of the story is about what caused the tidal wave and how they escape from it. They do, though thousands drown, but Fred and Madge are virtuous and lucky. Finally on high ground they clasp each other, wet and dripping and grateful, and continue as in A. 15

E

Yes, but Fred has a bad heart. The rest of the story is about how kind and understanding they both are until Fred dies. Then Madge devotes herself to charity work until the end of A. If you like, it can be "Madge," "cancer," "guilty and confused," and "bird watching."

F

If you think this is all too bourgeois, make John a revolutionary and Mary a counterespionage agent and see how far that gets you. Remember, this is Canada.

You'll still end up with A, though in between you may get a lustful brawling saga of passionate involvement, a chronicle of our times, sort of.

You'll have to face it, the endings are the same however you slice it. Don't be deluded by any other endings, they're all fake, either deliberately fake, with malicious intent to deceive, or just motivated by excessive optimism if not by downright sentimentality.

The only authentic ending is the one provided here:

John and Mary die. John and Mary die. John and Mary die.   20

So much for endings. Beginnings are always more fun. True connoisseurs, however, are known to favor the stretch in between, since it's the hardest to do anything with.

That's about all that can be said for plots, which anyway are just one thing after another, a what and a what and a what.

Now try How and Why.

Ambrose Bierce

An Occurrence at Owl Creek Bridge   1891

Ambrose Bierce (1842–1914?) was born in Horse Cave Creek, Ohio, the youngest child of nine in an impoverished farm family. A year at Kentucky Military Academy was his only formal schooling. Enlisting as a drummer boy in the Union Army, Bierce saw action at Shiloh and Chickamauga, took part in Sherman's March to the Sea, and came out of the army a brevet major. Then he became a writer, later an editor, for San Francisco newspapers. For a while Bierce thrived. He and his wife, on her ample dowry, lived five years in London, where Bierce wrote for London papers, honed his style, and cultivated his wit. But his wife left him, his two sons died (one of gunfire and the other of alcoholism), and late in life Bierce

Ambrose Bierce

came to deserve his nickname "Bitter Bierce." In 1913, at seventy-one, he trekked off to Mexico and vanished without a trace, although one report had him riding with the forces of revolutionist Pancho Villa. Bierce, who regarded the novel as "a short story padded," favored shorter lengths: short story, fable, newspaper column, aphorism. Sardonically, in The Devil's Dictionary (1911), *he defines diplomacy as "the patriotic art of lying for one's country" and saint as "a dead sinner revised and edited." Master of both realism and the ghost story, he collected his best Civil War fiction, including "An Occurrence at Owl Creek Bridge," in* Tales of Soldiers and Civilians (1891), *later retitled* In the Midst of Life.

I

A man stood upon a railroad bridge in northern Alabama, looking down into the swift water twenty feet below. The man's hands were behind his back, the wrists bound with a cord. A rope closely encircled his neck. It was attached to a stout cross-timber above his head and the slack fell to the level of his knees. Some loose boards laid upon the sleepers supporting the metals of the railway supplied a footing for him and his executioners—two private soldiers of the Federal army, directed by a sergeant who in civil life may have been a deputy sheriff. At a short remove upon the same temporary platform was an officer in the uniform of his rank, armed. He was a captain. A sentinel at each end of the bridge stood with his rifle in the position known as "support," that is to say, vertical in front of the left shoulder, the hammer resting on the forearm thrown straight across the chest—a formal and unnatural position, enforcing an erect carriage of the body. It did not appear to be the duty of these two men to know what was occurring at the center of the bridge; they merely blockaded the two ends of the foot planking that traversed it.

Beyond one of the sentinels nobody was in sight; the railroad ran straight away into a forest for a hundred yards, then, curving, was lost to view. Doubtless there was an outpost farther along. The other bank of the stream was open ground—a gentle acclivity topped with a stockade of vertical tree trunks, loop-holed for rifles, with a single embrasure through which protruded the muzzle of a brass cannon commanding the bridge. Midway of the slope between bridge and fort were the spectators—a single company of infantry in line, at "parade rest," the butts of the rifles on the ground, the barrels inclining slightly backward against the right shoulder, the hands crossed upon the stock. A lieutenant stood at the right of the line, the point of his sword upon the ground, his left hand resting upon his right. Excepting the group of four at the center of the bridge, not a man moved. The company faced the bridge, staring stonily, motionless. The sentinels, facing the banks of the stream, might have been statues to adorn the bridge. The captain stood with folded arms, silent, observing the work of his subordinates, but making no sign. Death is a dignitary who when he comes announced is to be received with formal manifestations of respect, even by those most familiar with him. In the code of military etiquette silence and fixity are forms of deference.

The man who was engaged in being hanged was apparently about thirty-five years of age. He was a civilian, if one might judge from his habit, which was that of a planter. His features were good—a straight nose, firm mouth, broad forehead, from which his long, dark hair was combed straight back, falling behind his ears to the collar of his well-fitting frock-coat. He wore a mustache and pointed beard, but no whiskers; his eyes were large and dark gray, and had a kindly expression which one would hardly have expected in one whose neck was in the hemp. Evidently this was no vulgar assassin. The liberal military code makes provision for hanging many kinds of persons, and gentlemen are not excluded.

The preparations being complete, the two private soldiers stepped aside and each drew away the plank upon which he had been standing. The sergeant turned to the captain, saluted and placed himself immediately behind that officer, who in turn moved apart one pace. These movements left the condemned man and the sergeant standing on the two ends of the same plank, which spanned three of the cross-ties of the bridge. The end upon which the civilian stood almost, but not quite, reached a fourth. This plank had been held in place by the weight of the captain; it was now held by that of the sergeant. At a signal from the former the latter would step aside, the plank would tilt and the condemned man go down between two ties. The arrangement commended itself to his judgment as simple and effective. His face had not been covered nor his eyes bandaged. He looked a moment at his "unsteadfast footing," then let his gaze wander to the swirling water of the stream racing madly beneath his feet. A piece of dancing driftwood caught his attention and his eyes followed it down the current. How slowly it appeared to move! What a sluggish stream!

He closed his eyes in order to fix his last thoughts upon his wife and children. The water, touched to gold by the early sun, the brooding mists under the banks at some distance down the stream, the fort, the soldiers, the piece of drift—all had distracted him. And now he became conscious of a new disturbance. Striking through the thought of his dear ones was a sound which he could neither ignore nor understand, a sharp, distinct, metallic percussion like the stroke of a blacksmith's hammer upon the anvil; it had the same ringing quality. He wondered what it was, and whether immeasurably distant or near by—it seemed both. Its recurrence was regular, but as slow as the tolling of a death knell. He awaited each stroke with impatience and—he knew not why—apprehension. The intervals of silence grew progressively longer; the delays became maddening. With their greater infrequency the sounds increased in strength and sharpness. They hurt his ear like the thrust of a knife; he feared he would shriek. What he heard was the ticking of his watch.

He unclosed his eyes and saw again the water below him. "If I could free my hands," he thought, "I might throw off the noose and spring into the stream. By diving I could evade the bullets and, swimming vigorously, reach the bank, take to the woods and get away home. My home, thank God, is as yet outside their lines; my wife and little ones are still beyond the invader's farthest advance."

As these thoughts, which have here to be set down in words, were flashed into the doomed man's brain rather than evolved from it the captain nodded to the sergeant. The sergeant stepped aside.

II

Peyton Farquhar was a well-to-do planter, of an old and highly respected Alabama family. Being a slave owner and like other slave owners a politician he was naturally an original secessionist and ardently devoted to the Southern cause. Circumstances of an imperious nature, which it is unnecessary to relate here, had prevented him from taking service with the gallant army that had fought the disastrous campaigns ending with the fall of Corinth, and he chafed under the inglorious restraint, longing for the release of his energies, the larger life of the soldier, the opportunity for distinction. That opportunity, he felt, would come, as it comes to all in war time. Meanwhile he did what he could. No service was too humble to him to perform in aid of the South, no adventure too perilous for him to undertake if consistent with the character of a civilian who was at heart a soldier, and who in good faith and without too much qualification assented to at least a part of the frankly villainous dictum that all is fair in love and war.

One evening while Farquhar and his wife were sitting on a rustic bench near the entrance to his grounds, a gray-clad soldier rode up to the gate and asked for a drink of water. Mrs. Farquhar was only too happy to serve him with her own white hands. While she was fetching the water her husband approached the dusty horseman and inquired eagerly for news from the front.

"The Yanks are repairing the railroads," said the man, "and are getting ready for another advance. They have reached the Owl Creek bridge, put it in order and built a stockade on the north bank. The commandant has issued an order, which is posted everywhere, declaring that any civilian caught interfering with the railroad, its bridges, tunnels or trains will be summarily hanged. I saw the order."

"How far is it to the Owl Creek bridge?" Farquhar asked.

"About thirty miles."

"Is there no force on this side the creek?"

"Only a picket post half a mile out, on the railroad, and a single sentinel at this end of the bridge."

"Suppose a man—a civilian and student of hanging—should elude the picket post and perhaps get the better of the sentinel," said Farquhar, smiling, "what could he accomplish?"   15

The soldier reflected. "I was there a month ago," he replied. "I observed that the flood of last winter had lodged a great quantity of driftwood against the wooden pier at this end of the bridge. It is now dry and would burn like tow."

The lady had now brought the water, which the soldier drank. He thanked her ceremoniously, bowed to her husband and rode away. An hour later, after nightfall, he repassed the plantation, going northward in the direction from which he had come. He was a Federal scout.

III

As Peyton Farquhar fell straight downward through the bridge he lost consciousness and was as one already dead. From this state he was awakened—ages later, it seemed to him—by the pain of a sharp pressure upon his throat, followed by a sense of suffocation. Keen, poignant agonies seemed to shoot from his neck downward through every fiber of his body and limbs. These pains appeared to flash along well-defined lines of ramification and to beat with an inconceivably rapid periodicity. They seemed like streams of pulsating fire heating him to an intolerable temperature. As to his head, he was conscious of nothing but a feeling of fulness—of congestion. These sensations were unaccompanied by thought. The intellectual part of his nature was already effaced; he had power only to feel, and feeling was torment. He was conscious of motion. Encompassed in a luminous cloud, of which he was now merely the fiery heart, without material substance, he swung through unthinkable arcs of oscillation, like a vast pendulum. Then all at once, with terrible suddenness, the light about him shot upward with the noise of a loud plash; a frightful roaring was in his ears, and all was cold and dark. The power of thought was restored; he knew that the rope had broken and he had fallen into the stream. There was no additional strangulation; the noose about his neck was already suffocating him and kept the water from his lungs. To die of hanging at the bottom of a river!—the idea seemed to him ludicrous. He opened his eyes in the darkness and saw above him a gleam of light, but how distant, how inaccessible! He was still sinking, for the light became fainter and fainter until it was a mere glimmer. Then it began to grow and brighten, and he knew that he was rising toward the surface—knew it with reluctance, for he was now very comfortable. "To be hanged and drowned," he thought, "that is not so bad; but I do not wish to be shot. No; I will not be shot; that is not fair."

He was not conscious of an effort, but a sharp pain in his wrist apprised him that he was trying to free his hands. He gave the struggle his attention, as an idler might observe the feat of a juggler, without interest in the outcome. What splendid effort!—what magnificent, what superhuman strength! Ah, that was a fine endeavor! Bravo! The cord fell away; his arms parted and floated upward, the hands dimly seen on each side in the growing light. He watched them with a new interest as first one and then the other pounced upon the noose at his neck. They tore it away and thrust it fiercely aside, its undulations resembling those of a water-snake. "Put it back, put it back!" He thought he shouted these words to his hands, for the undoing of the noose had been succeeded by the direst pang that he had yet experienced. His neck ached horribly; his brain was on fire; his heart, which had been fluttering faintly, gave a great leap, trying to force itself out at his mouth. His whole body was racked and wrenched with an insupportable anguish! But his disobedient hands gave no heed to the command. They beat the water vigorously with quick, downward strokes, forcing him to the surface. He felt his head emerge; his eyes were blinded by the sunlight; his chest expanded convulsively, and with a supreme and crowning agony his lungs engulfed a great draught of air, which instantly he expelled in a shriek!

He was now in full possession of his physical senses. They were, indeed, preternatu- 20 rally keen and alert. Something in the awful disturbance of his organic system had so ex- alted and refined them that they made record of things never before perceived. He felt the ripples upon his face and heard their separate sounds as they struck. He looked at the forest on the bank of the stream, saw the individual trees, the leaves and the veining of each leaf—saw the very insects upon them: the locusts, the brilliant-bodied flies, the gray spiders stretching their webs from twig to twig. He noted the prismatic colors in all the dewdrops upon a million blades of grass. The humming of the gnats that danced above the eddies of the stream, the beating of the dragon-flies' wings, the strokes of the water-spiders' legs, like oars which had lifted their boat—all these made audible music. A fish slid along beneath his eyes and he heard the rush of its body parting the water.

He had come to the surface facing down the stream; in a moment the visible world seemed to wheel slowly round, himself the pivotal point, and he saw the bridge, the fort, the soldiers upon the bridge, the captain, the sergeant, the two privates, his executioners. They were in silhouette against the blue sky. They shouted and gesticu- lated, pointing at him. The captain had drawn his pistol, but did not fire; the others were unarmed. Their movements were grotesque and horrible, their forms gigantic.

Suddenly he heard a sharp report and something struck the water smartly within a few inches of his head, spattering his face with spray. He heard a second report, and saw one of the sentinels with his rifle at his shoulder, a light cloud of blue smoke ris- ing from the muzzle. The man in the water saw the eye of the man on the bridge gaz- ing into his own through the sights of the rifle. He observed that it was a gray eye and remembered having read that gray eyes were keenest, and that all famous marksmen had them. Nevertheless, this one had missed.

A counter-swirl had caught Farquhar and turned him half round; he was again looking into the forest on the bank opposite the fort. The sound of a clear, high voice in a monotonous singsong now rang out behind him and came across the water with a distinctness that pierced and subdued all other sounds, even the beating of the rip- ples in his ears. Although no soldier, he had frequented camps enough to know the dread significance of that deliberate, drawling, aspirated chant; the lieutenant on shore was taking a part in the morning's work. How coldly and pitilessly—with what an even, calm intonation, presaging, and enforcing tranquility in the men—with what accurately measured intervals fell those cruel words:

"Attention, company! . . . Shoulder arms! . . . Ready! . . . Aim! . . . Fire!"

Farquhar dived—dived as deeply as he could. The water roared in his ears like 25 the voice of Niagara, yet he heard the dulled thunder of the volley and, rising again toward the surface, met shining bits of metal, singularly flattened, oscillating slowly downward. Some of them touched him on the face and hands, then fell away, continuing their descent. One lodged between his collar and neck; it was uncomfortably warm and he snatched it out.

As he rose to the surface, gasping for breath, he saw that he had been a long time under water; he was perceptibly farther down stream—nearer to safety. The soldiers had almost finished reloading; the metal ramrods flashed all at once in the sunshine as they were drawn from the barrels, turned in the air, and thrust into their sockets. The two sentinels fired again, independently and ineffectually.

The hunted man saw all this over his shoulder; he was now swimming vigorously with the current. His brain was as energetic as his arms and legs; he thought with the rapidity of lightning.

"The officer," he reasoned, "will not make that martinet's error a second time. It is as easy to dodge a volley as a single shot. He has probably already given the command to fire at will. God help me, I cannot dodge them all!"

An appalling plash within two yards of him was followed by a loud, rushing sound, *diminuendo*,° which seemed to travel back through the air to the fort and died in an explosion which stirred the very river to its deeps! A rising sheet of water curved over him, fell down upon him, blinded him, strangled him! The cannon had taken a hand in the game. As he shook his head free from the commotion of the smitten water he heard the deflected shot humming through the air ahead, and in an instant it was cracking and smashing the branches in the forest beyond.

"They will not do that again," he thought; "the next time they will use a charge   30
of grape. I must keep my eye upon the gun; the smoke will apprise me—the report arrives too late; it lags behind the missile. That is a good gun."

Suddenly he felt himself whirled round and round—spinning like a top. The water, the banks, the forests, the now distant bridge, fort and men—all were commingled and blurred. Objects were represented by their colors only; circular horizontal streaks of color—that was all he saw. He had been caught in a vortex and was being whirled on with a velocity of advance and gyration that made him giddy and sick. In a few moments he was flung upon the gravel at the foot of the left bank of the stream—the southern bank—and behind a projecting point which concealed him from his enemies. The sudden arrest of his motion, the abrasion of one of his hands on the gravel, restored him, and he wept with delight. He dug his fingers into the sand, threw it over himself in handfuls and audibly blessed it. It looked like diamonds, rubies, emeralds; he could think of nothing beautiful which it did not resemble. The trees upon the bank were giant garden plants; he noted a definite order in their arrangement, inhaled the fragrance of their blooms. A strange, roseate light shone through the spaces among their trunks and the wind made in their branches the music of aeolian harps. He had no wish to perfect his escape—was content to remain in that enchanting spot until retaken.

A whiz and rattle of grapeshot among the branches high above his head roused him from his dream. The baffled cannoneer had fired him a random farewell. He sprang to his feet, rushed up the sloping bank, and plunged into the forest.

All that day he traveled, laying his course by the rounding sun. The forest seemed interminable; nowhere did he discover a break in it, not even a woodman's road. He had not known that he lived in so wild a region. There was something uncanny in the revelation.

By nightfall he was fatigued, footsore, famishing. The thought of his wife and children urged him on. At last he found a road which led him in what he knew to be the right direction. It was as wide and straight as a city street, yet it seemed untraveled. No fields bordered it, no dwelling anywhere. Not so much as the barking of a dog suggested human habitation. The black bodies of the trees formed a straight wall on both sides,

---

diminuendo: diminishing (Italian); a term from music indicating a gradual decrease in loudness or force.

terminating on the horizon in a point, like a diagram in a lesson in perspective. Overhead, as he looked up through this rift in the wood, shone great golden stars looking unfamiliar and grouped in strange constellations. He was sure they were arranged in some order which had a secret and malign significance. The wood on either side was full of singular noises, among which—once, twice, and again—he distinctly heard whispers in an unknown tongue.

His neck was in pain and lifting his hand to it he found it horribly swollen. He 35 knew that it had a circle of black where the rope had bruised it. His eyes felt congested; he could no longer close them. His tongue was swollen with thirst; he relieved its fever by thrusting it forward from between his teeth into the cold air. How softly the turf had carpeted the untraveled avenue—he could no longer feel the roadway beneath his feet!

Doubtless, despite his suffering, he had fallen asleep while walking, for now he sees another scene—perhaps he has merely recovered from a delirium. He stands at the gate of his own home. All is as he left it, and all bright and beautiful in the morning sunshine. He must have traveled the entire night. As he pushes open the gate and passes up the wide white walk, he sees a flutter of female garments; his wife, looking fresh and cool and sweet, steps down from the veranda to meet him. At the bottom of the steps she stands waiting, with a smile of ineffable joy, an attitude of matchless grace and dignity. Ah, how beautiful she is! He springs forward with extended arms. As he is about to clasp her he feels a stunning blow upon the back of the neck; a blinding white light blazes all about him with a sound like the shock of a cannon—then all is darkness and silence!

Peyton Farquhar was dead; his body, with a broken neck, swung gently from side to side beneath the timbers of the Owl Creek bridge.

Willa Cather

Paul's Case   1905

Willa Cather (1876–1947) was born in Gore, Virginia, but at nine moved to Webster County, Nebraska, where pioneer sod houses still clung to the windswept plains. There, mainly in the town of Red Cloud, she grew up among Scandinavians, Czechs, Bohemians, and other immigrant settlers, for whom she felt a quick kinship: they too had been displaced from their childhood homes. After graduation from the University of Nebraska, Cather went east to spend ten years in Pittsburgh, where the story "Paul's Case" opens. (When she wrote the story, she was a high school teacher of Latin and English and a music critic for a newspaper.) Then, because her early stories had attracted notice, New York beckoned. A job on the staff of McClure's led to her becoming managing editor of that popular magazine. Her early novels of Nebraska won immense popularity: O

Willa Cather

Pioneers! *(1913),* My Ántonia *(1918), and* A Lost Lady *(1923). In her later novels Cather explores other regions of the North American past: in* Death Comes to the

Archbishop (1927), frontier New Mexico; in Shadows on the Rock (1931), seventeenth-century Quebec. She does not romanticize the rugged lives of farm people on the plains, or glamorize village life. Often, as in The Song of the Lark (1915), the story of a Colorado girl who becomes an opera singer, she depicts a small town as stifling. With remarkable skill, she may tell a story from a man's point of view, but her favorite characters are likely to be women of strong will who triumph over obstacles.

It was Paul's afternoon to appear before the faculty of the Pittsburgh High School to account for his various misdemeanors. He had been suspended a week ago, and his father had called at the Principal's office and confessed his perplexity about his son. Paul entered the faculty room suave and smiling. His clothes were a trifle outgrown and the tan velvet on the collar of his open overcoat was frayed and worn; but for all that there was something of the dandy about him, and he wore an opal pin in his neatly knotted black four-in-hand, and a red carnation in his buttonhole. This latter adornment the faculty somehow felt was not properly significant of the contrite spirit befitting a boy under the ban of suspension.

Paul was tall for his age and very thin, with high, cramped shoulders and a narrow chest. His eyes were remarkable for a certain hysterical brilliancy and he continually used them in a conscious, theatrical sort of way, peculiarly offensive in a boy. The pupils were abnormally large, as though he were addicted to belladonna, but there was a glassy glitter about them which that drug does not produce.

When questioned by the Principal as to why he was there, Paul stated, politely enough, that he wanted to come back to school. This was a lie, but Paul was quite accustomed to lying; found it, indeed, indispensable for overcoming friction. His teachers were asked to state their respective charges against him, which they did with such a rancor and aggrievedness as evinced that this was not a usual case. Disorder and impertinence were among the offenses named, yet each of his instructors felt that it was scarcely possible to put into words the real cause of the trouble, which lay in a sort of hysterically defiant manner of the boy's; in the contempt which they all knew he felt for them, and which he seemingly made not the least effort to conceal. Once, when he had been making a synopsis of a paragraph at the blackboard, his English teacher had stepped to his side and attempted to guide his hand. Paul had started back with a shudder and thrust his hands violently behind him. The astonished woman could scarcely have been more hurt and embarrassed had he struck at her. The insult was so involuntary and definitely personal as to be unforgettable. In one way and another, he had made all his teachers, men and women alike, conscious of the same feeling of physical aversion. In one class he habitually sat with his hand shading his eyes; in another he always looked out of the window during the recitation; in another he made a running commentary on the lecture, with humorous intention.

His teachers felt this afternoon that his whole attitude was symbolized by his shrug and his flippantly red carnation flower, and they fell upon him without mercy, his English teacher leading the pack. He stood through it smiling, his pale lips parted over his white teeth. (His lips were continually twitching, and he had a habit of raising his eyebrows that was contemptuous and irritating to the last degree.) Older boys than Paul had broken down and shed tears under that baptism of fire, but his set smile did not once desert him, and his only sign of discomfort was the nervous trembling of the fingers that toyed with the buttons of his overcoat, and an occasional jerking of the other hand that held his hat. Paul was always smiling, always glancing about him, seeming to feel that people might be watching him and trying to detect something. This conscious expression, since it was as far as possible from boyish mirthfulness, was usually attributed to insolence or "smartness."

As the inquisition proceeded, one of his instructors repeated an impertinent re-   5
mark of the boy's, and the Principal asked him whether he thought that a courteous speech to have made a woman. Paul shrugged his shoulders slightly and his eyebrows twitched.

"I don't know," he replied. "I didn't mean to be polite or impolite, either. I guess it's a sort of way I have of saying things regardless."

The Principal, who was a sympathetic man, asked him whether he didn't think that a way it would be well to get rid of. Paul grinned and said he guessed so. When he was told that he could go, he bowed gracefully and went out. His bow was but a repetition of the scandalous red carnation.

His teachers were in despair, and his drawing master voiced the feeling of them all when he declared there was something about the boy which none of them understood. He added: "I don't really believe that smile of his comes altogether from insolence; there's something sort of haunted about it. The boy is not strong, for one thing. I happen to know that he was born in Colorado, only a few months before his mother died out there of a long illness. There is something wrong about the fellow."

The drawing master had come to realize that, in looking at Paul, one saw only his white teeth and the forced animation of his eyes. One warm afternoon the boy had gone to sleep at his drawing-board, and his master had noted with amazement what a white, blue-veined face it was; drawn and wrinkled like an old man's about the eyes, the lips twitching even in his sleep, and stiff with a nervous tension that drew them back from his teeth.

His teachers left the building dissatisfied and unhappy; humiliated to have felt so   10
vindictive toward a mere boy, to have uttered this feeling in cutting terms, and to have set each other on, as it were, in the gruesome game of intemperate reproach. Some of them remembered having seen a miserable street cat set at bay by a ring of tormentors.

As for Paul, he ran down the hill whistling the Soldiers' Chorus from *Faust,*° looking wildly behind him now and then to see whether some of his teachers were not there to writhe under his light-heartedness. As it was now late in the afternoon and Paul was on duty that evening as usher at Carnegie Hall,° he decided that he would not go home to supper. When he reached the concert hall the doors were not yet open and, as it was chilly outside, he decided to go up into the picture gallery— always deserted at this hour—where there were some of Raffaelli's° gay studies of Paris streets and an airy blue Venetian scene or two that always exhilarated him. He was delighted to find no one in the gallery but the old guard, who sat in one corner, a newspaper on his knee, a black patch over one eye and the other closed. Paul possessed himself of the place and walked confidently up and down, whistling under his breath. After a while he sat down before a blue Rico° and lost himself. When he bethought him to look at his watch, it was after seven o'clock, and he rose with a

---

Faust: tragic grand opera (1859) by French composer Charles Gounod.   *Carnegie Hall:* concert hall endowed by Pittsburgh steel manufacturer Andrew Carnegie, not to be confused with the better-known Carnegie Hall in New York City.   *Raffaelli:* Jean-Francois Raffaelli (1850–1921), painter and graphic artist, native and lifelong resident of Paris, attained great popularity for his paintings and drawings of that city.   *Rico:* (flourished 1500–1550), painter of the Byzantine school, a native of Crete.

start and ran downstairs, making a face at Augustus, peering out from the cast-room,° and an evil gesture at the Venus of Milo as he passed her on the stairway.

When Paul reached the ushers' dressing-room half-a-dozen boys were there already, and he began excitedly to tumble into his uniform. It was one of the few that at all approached fitting, and Paul thought it very becoming—though he knew that the tight, straight coat accentuated his narrow chest, about which he was exceedingly sensitive. He was always considerably excited while he dressed, twanging all over to the tuning of the strings and the preliminary flourishes of the horns in the music-room; but tonight he seemed quite beside himself, and he teased and plagued the boys until, telling him that he was crazy, they put him down on the floor and sat on him.

Somewhat calmed by his suppression, Paul dashed out to the front of the house to seat the early comers. He was a model usher; gracious and smiling he ran up and down the aisles; nothing was too much trouble for him; he carried messages and brought programmes as though it were his greatest pleasure in life, and all the people in his section thought him a charming boy, feeling that he remembered and admired them. As the house filled, he grew more and more vivacious and animated, and the color came to his cheeks and lips. It was very much as though this were a great reception and Paul were the host. Just as the musicians came out to take their places, his English teacher arrived with checks for the seats which a prominent manufacturer had taken for the season. She betrayed some embarrassment when she handed Paul the tickets, and a hauteur° which subsequently made her feel very foolish. Paul was startled for a moment, and had the feeling of wanting to put her out; what business had she here among all these fine people and gay colors? He looked her over and decided that she was not appropriately dressed and must be a fool to sit downstairs in such togs. The tickets had probably been sent her out of kindness, he reflected as he put down a seat for her, and she had about as much right to sit there as he had.

When the symphony began Paul sank into one of the rear seats with a long sigh of relief, and lost himself as he had done before the Rico. It was not that symphonies, as such, meant anything in particular to Paul, but the first sigh of the instruments seemed to free some hilarious and potent spirit within him; something that struggled there like the Genius° in the bottle found by the Arab fisherman. He felt a sudden zest of life; the lights danced before his eyes and the concert hall blazed into unimaginable splendor. When the soprano soloist came on, Paul forgot even the nastiness of his teacher's being there and gave himself up to the peculiar stimulus such personages always had for him. The soloist chanced to be a German woman, by no means in her first youth, and the mother of many children; but she wore an elaborate gown and a tiara, and above all she had that indefinable air of achievement, that world-shine upon her, which, in Paul's eyes, made her a veritable queen of Romance.

After a concert was over Paul was always irritable and wretched until he got to sleep, and tonight he was even more than usually restless. He had the feeling of not

15

Augustus . . . cast-room: Paul mocks a plaster cast of the Vatican Museum's famous statue of the first Roman emperor (63 B.C.–A.D. 14), whom an unknown sculptor posed sternly pointing an index finger at his beholders.   *hauteur:* haughtiness.   *Genius:* genie in a tale from *The Arabian Nights*.

being able to let down, of its being impossible to give up this delicious excitement which was the only thing that could be called living at all. During the last number he withdrew and, after hastily changing his clothes in the dressing-room, slipped out to the side door where the soprano's carriage stood. Here he began pacing rapidly up and down the walk, waiting to see her come out.

Over yonder the Schenley, in its vacant stretch, loomed big and square through the fine rain, the windows of its twelve stories glowing like those of a lighted cardboard house under a Christmas tree. All the actors and singers of the better class stayed there when they were in the city, and a number of the big manufacturers of the place lived there in the winter. Paul had often hung about the hotel, watching the people go in and out, longing to enter and leave schoolmasters and dull care behind him forever.

At last the singer came out, accompanied by the conductor, who helped her into her carriage and closed the door with a cordial *auf wiedersehen*° which set Paul to wondering whether she were not an old sweetheart of his. Paul followed the carriage over to the hotel, walking so rapidly as not to be far from the entrance when the singer alighted and disappeared behind the swinging glass doors that were opened by a negro in a tall hat and a long coat. In the moment that the door was ajar it seemed to Paul that he, too, entered. He seemed to feel himself go after her up the steps, into the warm, lighted building, into an exotic, a tropical world of shiny, glistening surfaces and basking ease. He reflected upon the mysterious dishes that were brought into the dining-room, the green bottles in buckets of ice, as he had seen them in the supper party pictures of the *Sunday World* supplement. A quick gust of wind brought the rain down with sudden vehemence, and Paul was startled to find that he was still outside in the slush of the gravel driveway; that his boots were letting in the water and his scanty overcoat was clinging wet about him; that the lights in front of the concert hall were out, and that the rain was driving in sheets between him and the orange glow of the windows above him. There it was, what he wanted—tangibly before him, like the fairy world of a Christmas pantomime, but mocking spirits stood guard at the doors, and, as the rain beat in his face, Paul wondered whether he were destined always to shiver in the black night outside, looking up at it.

He turned and walked reluctantly toward the car tracks. The end had to come sometime; his father in his night-clothes at the top of the stairs, explanations that did not explain, hastily improvised fictions that were forever tripping him up, his upstairs room and its horrible yellow wall-paper, the creaking bureau with the greasy plush collar-box, and over his painted wooden bed the pictures of George Washington and John Calvin,° and the framed motto, "Feed my Lambs," which had been worked in red worsted by his mother.

Half an hour later, Paul alighted from his car and went slowly down one of the side streets off the main thoroughfare. It was a highly respectable street, where all the houses were exactly alike, and where businessmen of moderate means begot and reared large families of children, all of whom went to Sabbath-school and learned the shorter catechism, and were interested in arithmetic; all of whom were as exactly

auf wiedersehen: German equivalent of *au revoir,* or "here's to seeing you again." *John Calvin:* French Protestant theologian of the Reformation (1509–1564) whose teachings are the basis of Presbyterianism.

alike as their homes, and of a piece with the monotony in which they lived. Paul never went up Cordelia Street without a shudder of loathing. His home was next to the house of the Cumberland° minister. He approached it tonight with the nerveless sense of defeat, the hopeless feeling of sinking back forever into ugliness and commonness that he had always had when he came home. The moment he turned into Cordelia Street he felt the waters close above his head. After each of these orgies of living, he experienced all the physical depression which follows a debauch; the loathing of respectable beds, of common food, of a house penetrated by kitchen odors; a shuddering repulsion for the flavorless, colorless mass of every-day existence; a morbid desire for cool things and soft lights and fresh flowers.

The nearer he approached the house, the more absolutely unequal Paul felt to the   20
sight of it all; his ugly sleeping chamber; the cold bathroom with the grimy zinc tub, the cracked mirror, the dripping spigots; his father, at the top of the stairs, his hairy legs sticking out from his night-shirt, his feet thrust into carpet slippers. He was so much later than usual that there would certainly be inquiries and reproaches. Paul stopped short before the door. He felt that he could not be accosted by his father tonight; that he could not toss again on that miserable bed. He would not go in. He would tell his father that he had no car fare, and it was raining so hard he had gone home with one of the boys and stayed all night.

Meanwhile, he was wet and cold. He went around to the back of the house and tried one of the basement windows, found it open, raised it cautiously, and scrambled down the cellar wall to the floor. There he stood, holding his breath, terrified by the noise he had made, but the floor above him was silent, and there was no creak on the stairs. He found a soap-box, and carried it over to the soft ring of light that streamed from the furnace door, and sat down. He was horribly afraid of rats, so he did not try to sleep, but sat looking distrustfully at the dark, still terrified lest he might have awakened his father. In such reactions, after one of the experiences which made days and nights out of the dreary blanks of the calendar, when his senses were deadened, Paul's head was always singularly clear. Suppose his father had heard him getting in at the window and had come down and shot him for a burglar? Then, again, suppose his father had come down, pistol in hand, and he had cried out in time to save himself, and his father had been horrified to think how nearly he had killed him? Then, again, suppose a day should come when his father would remember that night, and wish there had been no warning cry to stay his hand? With this last supposition Paul entertained himself until daybreak.

The following Sunday was fine; the sodden November chill was broken by the last flash of autumnal summer. In the morning Paul had to go to church and Sabbath-school, as always. On seasonable Sunday afternoons the burghers of Cordelia Street always sat out on their front "stoops," and talked to their neighbors on the next stoop, or called to those across the street in neighborly fashion. The men usually sat on gay cushions placed upon the steps that led down to the sidewalk, while the women, in their Sunday "waists," sat in rockers on the cramped porches, pretending to be greatly at their ease. The children played in the streets; there were so many of them that the place resembled the recreation grounds of a kindergarten. The men on the steps—all in their shirt sleeves, their vests unbuttoned—sat with their legs

Cumberland: The minister, a Cumberland Presbyterian, belongs to a frontier denomination that had splintered away from the Presbyterian Church and whose ministers were ordained after a briefer training.

well apart, their stomachs comfortably protruding, and talked of the prices of things, or told anecdotes of the sagacity of their various chiefs and overlords. They occasionally looked over the multitude of squabbling children, listened affectionately to their high-pitched, nasal voices, smiling to see their own proclivities reproduced in their offspring, and interspersed their legends of the iron kings with remarks about their sons' progress at school, their grades in arithmetic, and the amounts they had saved in their toy banks.

On this last Sunday of November, Paul sat all the afternoon on the lowest step of his "stoop," staring into the street, while his sisters, in their rockers, were talking to the minister's daughters next door about how many shirt-waists they had made in the last week, and how many waffles some one had eaten at the last church supper. When the weather was warm, and his father was in a particularly jovial frame of mind, the girls made lemonade, which was always brought out in a red-glass pitcher, ornamented with forget-me-nots in blue enamel. This the girls thought very fine, and the neighbors always joked about the suspicious color of the pitcher.

Today Paul's father sat on the top step, talking to a young man who shifted a restless baby from knee to knee. He happened to be the young man who was daily held up to Paul as a model, and after whom it was his father's dearest hope that he would pattern. This young man was of a ruddy complexion, with a compressed, red mouth, and faded, near-sighted eyes, over which he wore thick spectacles, with gold bows that curved about his ears. He was clerk to one of the magnates of a great steel corporation, and was looked upon in Cordelia Street as a young man with a future. There was a story that, some five years ago—he was now barely twenty-six—he had been a trifle dissipated but in order to curb his appetites and save the loss of time and strength that a sowing of wild oats might have entailed, he had taken his chief's advice oft reiterated to his employees, and at twenty-one had married the first woman whom he could persuade to share his fortunes. She happened to be an angular school-mistress, much older than he, who also wore thick glasses, and who had now borne him four children, all near-sighted, like herself.

The young man was relating how his chief, now cruising in the Mediterranean, 25 kept in touch with all the details of the business, arranging his office hours on his yacht just as though he were at home, and "knocking off work enough to keep two stenographers busy." His father told, in turn, the plan his corporation was considering, of putting in an electric railway plant at Cairo. Paul snapped his teeth; he had an awful apprehension that they might spoil it all before he got there. Yet he rather liked to hear these legends of the iron kings, that were told and retold on Sundays and holidays; these stories of palaces in Venice, yachts on the Mediterranean, and high play at Monte Carlo appealed to his fancy, and he was interested in the triumphs of these cash boys who had become famous, though he had no mind for the cash-boy stage.

After supper was over, and he had helped to dry the dishes, Paul nervously asked his father whether he could go to George's to get some help in his geometry, and still more nervously asked for car fare. This latter request he had to repeat, as his father, on principle, did not like to hear requests for money, whether much or little. He asked Paul whether he could not go to some boy who lived nearer, and told him that he ought not to leave his school work until Sunday; but he gave him the dime. He was not a poor man, but he had a worthy ambition to come up in the world. His only reason for allowing Paul to usher was, that he thought a boy ought to be earning a little.

Paul bounded upstairs, scrubbed the greasy odor of the dish-water from his hands with the ill-smelling soap he hated, and then shook over his fingers a few drops of violet water from the bottle he kept hidden in his drawer. He left the house with his geometry conspicuously under his arm, and the moment he got out of Cordelia Street and boarded a downtown car, he shook off the lethargy of two deadening days, and began to live again.

The leading juvenile of the permanent stock company which played at one of the downtown theatres was an acquaintance of Paul's, and the boy had been invited to drop in at the Sunday-night rehearsals whenever he could. For more than a year Paul had spent every available moment loitering about Charley Edwards's dressing-room. He had won a place among Edward's following not only because the young actor, who could not afford to employ a dresser, often found him useful, but because he recognized in Paul something akin to what churchmen term "vocation."

It was at the theatre and at Carnegie Hall that Paul really lived; the rest was but a sleep and a forgetting. This was Paul's fairy tale, and it had for him all the allurement of a secret love. The moment he inhaled the gassy, painty, dusty odor behind the scenes, he breathed like a prisoner set free, and felt within him the possibility of doing or saying splendid, brilliant, poetic things. The moment the cracked orchestra beat out the overture from *Martha*,° or jerked at the serenade from *Rigoletto*,° all stupid and ugly things slid from him, and his senses were deliciously, yet delicately fired.

Perhaps it was because, in Paul's world, the natural nearly always wore the guise of   30
ugliness, that a certain element of artificiality seemed to him necessary in beauty. Perhaps it was because his experience of life elsewhere was so full of Sabbath-school picnics, petty economies, wholesome advice as to how to succeed in life, and the unescapable odors of cooking, that he found this existence so alluring, these smartly-clad men and women so attractive, that he was so moved by these starry apple orchards that bloomed perennially under the limelight.

It would be difficult to put it strongly enough how convincingly the stage entrance of that theatre was for Paul the actual portal of Romance. Certainly none of the company ever suspected it, least of all Charley Edwards. It was very like the old stories that used to float about London of fabulously rich Jews, who had subterranean halls there, with palms, and fountains, and soft lamps and richly apparelled women who never saw the disenchanting light of London day. So, in the midst of that smoke-palled city, enamored of figures and grimy toil, Paul had his secret temple, his wishing carpet, his bit of blue-and-white Mediterranean shore bathed in perpetual sunshine.

Several of Paul's teachers had a theory that his imagination had been perverted by garish fiction, but the truth was that he scarcely ever read at all. The books at home were not such as would either tempt or corrupt a youthful mind, and as for reading the novels that some of his friends urged upon him—well, he got what he wanted much more quickly from music; any sort of music, from an orchestra to a barrel organ. He needed only the spark, the indescribable thrill that made his imagination master of his senses, and he could make plots and pictures enough of his own. It was equally true that he was not stage struck—not, at any rate, in the usual acceptation of that expression. He had no desire to become an actor, any more than he had to become a musician. He felt no necessity to do any of these things; what he wanted

Martha: grand opera about romance among English aristocrats (1847) by German composer Friedrich von Flotow.   *Rigoletto*: tragic grand opera (1851) by Italian composer Giuseppe Verdi.

was to see, to be in the atmosphere, float on the wave of it, to be carried out, blue league after blue league, away from everything.

After a night behind the scenes, Paul found the school-room more than ever repulsive; the bare floors and naked walls; the prosy men who never wore frock coats, or violets in their buttonholes; the women with their dull gowns, shrill voices, and pitiful seriousness about prepositions that govern the dative. He could not bear to have the other pupils think, for a moment, that he took these people seriously; he must convey to them that he considered it all trivial, and was there only by way of a jest, anyway. He had autograph pictures of all the members of the stock company which he showed his classmates, telling them the most incredible stories of his familiarity with these people, of his acquaintance with the soloists who came to Carnegie Hall, his suppers with them and the flowers he sent them. When these stories lost their effect, and his audience grew listless, he became desperate and would bid all the boys good-bye, announcing that he was going to travel for a while; going to Naples, to Venice, to Egypt. Then, next Monday, he would slip back, conscious and nervously smiling; his sister was ill, and he should have to defer his voyage until spring.

Matters went steadily worse with Paul at school. In the itch to let his instructors know how heartily he despised them and their homilies, and how thoroughly he was appreciated elsewhere, he mentioned once or twice that he had no time to fool with theorems; adding—with a twitch of the eyebrows and a touch of that nervous bravado which so perplexed them—that he was helping the people down at the stock company; they were old friends of his.

The upshot of the matter was that the Principal went to Paul's father, and Paul was taken out of school and put to work. The manager at Carnegie Hall was told to get another usher in his stead; the door-keeper at the theatre was warned not to admit him to the house; and Charley Edwards remorsefully promised the boy's father not to see him again. 35

The members of the stock company were vastly amused when some of Paul's stories reached them—especially the women. They were hardworking women, most of them supporting indigent husbands or brothers, and they laughed rather bitterly at having stirred the boy to such fervid and florid inventions. They agreed with the faculty and with his father that Paul's was a bad case.

The east-bound train was ploughing through a January snow-storm; the dull dawn was beginning to show gray when the engine whistled a mile out of Newark. Paul started up from the seat where he had lain curled in uneasy slumber, rubbed the breath-misted window glass with his hand, and peered out. The snow was whirling in curling eddies above the white bottom lands, and the drifts lay already deep in the fields and along the fences, while here and there the long dead grass and dried weed stalks protruded black above it. Lights shone from the scattered houses, and a gang of laborers who stood beside the track waved their lanterns.

Paul had slept very little, and he felt grimy and uncomfortable. He had made the all-night journey in a day coach, partly because he was ashamed, dressed as he was, to go into a Pullman, and partly because he was afraid of being seen there by some Pittsburgh business man, who might have noticed him in Denny & Carson's office. When the whistle awoke him, he clutched quickly at his breast pocket, glancing about him with an uncertain smile. But the little, clay-bespattered Italians were still sleeping, the slatternly women across the aisle were in open-mouthed oblivion, and even the crumby, crying babies were for the nonce stilled. Paul settled back to struggle with his impatience as best as he could.

When he arrived at the Jersey City station, he hurried through his breakfast, manifestly ill at ease and keeping a sharp eye about him. After he reached the Twenty-third Street station,° he consulted a cabman, and had himself driven to a men's furnishing establishment that was just opening for the day. He spent upward of two hours there, buying with endless reconsidering and great care. His new street suit he put on in the fitting-room; the frock coat and dress clothes he had bundled into the cab with his linen. Then he drove to a hatter's and a shoe house. His next errand was at Tiffany's, where he selected his silver and a new scarf-pin. He would not wait to have his silver marked, he said. Lastly, he stopped at a trunk shop on Broadway, and had his purchases packed into various travelling bags.

It was a little after one-o'clock when he drove up to the Waldorf, and after set-   40
tling with the cabman, went into the office. He registered from Washington; said his mother and father had been abroad, and that he had come down to await the arrival of their steamer. He told his story plausibly and had no trouble, since he volunteered to pay for them in advance, in engaging his rooms; a sleeping-room, sitting-room and bath.

Not once, but a hundred times Paul had planned this entry into New York. He had gone over every detail of it with Charley Edwards, and in his scrap book at home there were pages of description about New York hotels, cut from the Sunday papers. When he was shown to his sitting-room on the eighth floor, he saw at a glance that everything was as it should be; there was but one detail in his mental picture that the place did not realize, so he rang for the bell boy and sent him down for flowers. He moved about nervously until the boy returned, putting away his new linen and fingering it delightedly as he did so. When the flowers came, he put them hastily into water, and then tumbled into a hot bath. Presently he came out of his white bathroom, resplendent in his new silk underwear, and playing with the tassels of his red robe. The snow was whirling so fiercely outside his windows that he could scarcely see across the street, but within the air was deliciously soft and fragrant. He put the violets and jonquils on the taboret beside the couch, and threw himself down, with a long sigh, covering himself with a Roman blanket. He was thoroughly tired; he had been in such haste, he had stood up to such a strain, covered so much ground in the last twenty-four hours, that he wanted to think how it had all come about. Lulled by the sound of the wind, the warm air, and the cool fragrance of the flowers, he sank into deep, drowsy retrospection.

It had been wonderfully simple; when they had shut him out of the theatre and concert hall, when they had taken away his bone, the whole thing was virtually determined. The rest was a mere matter of opportunity. The only thing that at all surprised him was his own courage—for he realized well enough that he had always been tormented by fear, a sort of apprehensive dread that, of late years, as the meshes of the lies he had told closed about him, had been pulling the muscles of his body tighter and tighter. Until now, he could not remember the time when he had not been dreading something. Even when he was a little boy, it was always there—behind him, or before, or on either side. There had always been the shadowed corner, the dark place into which he dared not look, but from which something seemed always to be watching him—and Paul had done things that were not pretty to watch, he knew.

Twenty-third Street station: The scene is now New York City.

But now he had a curious sense of relief, as though he had at last thrown down the gauntlet to the thing in the corner.

Yet it was but a day since he had been sulking in the traces; but yesterday afternoon that he had been sent to the bank with Denny & Carson's deposit, as usual—but this time he was instructed to leave the book to be balanced. There was above two thousand dollars in checks, and nearly a thousand in the bank notes which he had taken from the book and quietly transferred to his pocket. At the bank he had made out a new deposit slip. His nerves had been steady enough to permit of his returning to the office, where he had finished his work and asked for a full day's holiday tomorrow, Saturday, giving a perfectly reasonable pretext. The bank book, he knew, would not be returned before Monday or Tuesday, and his father would be out of town for the next week. From the time he slipped the bank notes into his pocket until he boarded the night train for New York, he had not known a moment's hesitation. It was not the first time Paul had steered through treacherous waters.

How astonishingly easy it had all been; here he was, the thing done; and this time there would be no awakening, no figure at the top of the stairs. He watched the snow flakes whirling by his window until he fell asleep.   45

When he awoke, it was three o'clock in the afternoon. He bounded up with a start; half of one of his precious days gone already! He spent more than an hour in dressing, watching every stage of his toilet carefully in the mirror. Everything was quite perfect; he was exactly the kind of boy he had always wanted to be.

When he went downstairs, Paul took a carriage and drove up Fifth Avenue toward the Park. The snow had somewhat abated; carriages and tradesmen's wagons were hurrying soundlessly to and fro in the winter twilight; boys in woollen mufflers were shovelling off the doorsteps; the avenue stages made fine spots of color against the white street. Here and there on the corners were stands, with whole flower gardens blooming under glass cases, against the sides of which the snow flakes stuck and melted; violets, roses, carnations, lilies of the valley—somewhat vastly more lovely and alluring that they blossomed thus unnaturally in the snow. The Park itself was a wonderful stage winter-piece.

When he returned, the pause of the twilight had ceased, and the tune of the streets had changed. The snow was falling faster, lights streamed from the hotels that reared their dozen stories fearlessly up into the storm, defying the raging Atlantic winds. A long, black stream of carriages poured down the avenue, intersected here and there by other streams, tending horizontally. There were a score of cabs about the entrance of his hotel, and his driver had to wait. Boys in livery were running in and out of the awning stretched across the sidewalk, up and down the red velvet carpet laid from the door to the street. Above, about, within it all was the rumble and roar, the hurry and toss of thousands of human beings as hot for pleasure as himself, and on every side of him towered the glaring affirmation of the omnipotence of wealth.

The boy set his teeth and drew his shoulders together in a spasm of realization: the plot of all dramas, the text of all romances, the nerve-stuff of all sensations was whirling about him like the snow flakes. He burnt like a faggot in a tempest.

When Paul went down to dinner, the music of the orchestra came floating up   50 the elevator shaft to greet him. His head whirled as he stepped into the thronged corridor, and he sank back into one of the chairs against the wall to get his breath. The lights, the chatter, the perfumes, the bewildering medley of color—he had, for a moment, the feeling of not being able to stand it. But only for a moment;

these were his own people, he told himself. He went slowly about the corridors, through the writing-rooms, smoking-rooms, reception-rooms, as though he were exploring the chambers of an enchanted palace, built and peopled for him alone.

When he reached the dining-room he sat down at a table near a window. The flowers, the white linen, the many-colored wine glasses, the gay toilettes of the women, the low popping of corks, the undulating repetitions of the *Blue Danube* from the orchestra, all flooded Paul's dream with bewildering radiance. When the roseate tinge of his champagne was added—that cold, precious, bubbling stuff that creamed and foamed in his glass—Paul wondered that there were honest men in the world at all. This was what all the world was fighting for, he reflected; this was what all the struggle was about. He doubted the reality of his past. Had he ever known a place called Cordelia Street, a place where fagged-looking businessmen got on the early car; mere rivets in a machine they seemed to Paul—sickening men, with combings of children's hair always hanging to their coats, and the smell of cooking in their clothes. Cordelia Street—Ah! that belonged to another time and country; had he not always been thus, had he not sat here night after night, from as far back as he could remember, looking pensively over just such shimmering textures, and slowly twirling the stem of a glass like this one between his thumb and middle finger? He rather thought he had.

He was not in the least abashed or lonely. He had no especial desire to meet or to know any of these people; all he demanded was the right to look on and conjecture, to watch the pageant. The mere stage properties were all he contended for. Nor was he lonely later in the evening, in his loge at the Metropolitan. He was now entirely rid of his nervous misgivings, of his forced aggressiveness, of the imperative desire to show himself different from his surroundings. He felt now that his surroundings explained him. Nobody questioned the purple; he had only to wear it passively. He had only to glance down at his attire to reassure himself that here it would be impossible for anyone to humiliate him.

He found it hard to leave his beautiful sitting-room to go to bed that night, and sat long watching the raging storm from his turret window. When he went to sleep it was with the lights turned on in his bedroom; partly because of his old timidity, and partly so that, if he should wake in the night, there would be no wretched moment of doubt, no horrible suspicion of yellow wall-paper, or of Washington and Calvin above his bed.

Sunday morning the city was practically snow-bound. Paul breakfasted late, and in the afternoon he fell in with a wild San Francisco boy, a freshman at Yale, who said he had run down for a "little flyer" over Sunday. The young man offered to show Paul the night side of the town, and the two boys went out together after dinner, not returning to the hotel until seven o'clock the next morning. They had started out in the confiding warmth of a champagne friendship, but their parting in the elevator was singularly cool. The freshman pulled himself together to make his train, and Paul went to bed. He awoke at two o'clock in the afternoon, very thirsty and dizzy, and rang for ice-water, coffee, and the Pittsburgh papers.

On the part of the hotel management, Paul excited no suspicion. There was this to be said for him, that he wore his spoils with dignity and in no way made himself conspicuous. Even under the glow of his wine he was never boisterous, though he found the stuff like a magician's wand for wonder-building. His chief greediness lay in his ears and eyes, and his excesses were not offensive ones. His dearest pleasures were the gray winter twilights in his sitting-room; his quiet enjoyment of his flowers, his clothes, his wide divan, his cigarette, and his sense of power. He could not remember a time when he had felt so at peace with himself. The mere release from the necessity of petty lying, lying every day and every day, restored his self-respect. He had never lied for pleasure, even at school; but to be noticed and admired, to assert his difference from other Cordelia Street boys; and he felt a good deal more manly, more honest, even, now that he had no need for boastful pretensions, now that he could, as his actor friends used to say, "dress the part." It was characteristic that remorse did not occur to him. His golden days went by without a shadow, and he made each as perfect as he could.

On the eighth day after his arrival in New York, he found the whole affair exploited in the Pittsburgh papers, exploited with a wealth of detail which indicated that local news of a sensational nature was at a low ebb. The firm of Denny & Carson announced that the boy's father had refunded the full amount of the theft, and that they had no intention of prosecuting. The Cumberland minister had been interviewed, and expressed his hope of yet reclaiming the motherless lad, and his Sabbath-school teacher declared that she would spare no effort to that end. The rumor had reached Pittsburgh that the boy had been seen in a New York hotel, and his father had gone East to find him and bring him home.

Paul had just come in to dress for dinner; he sank into a chair, weak to the knees, and clasped his head in his hands. It was to be worse than jail, even; the tepid waters of Cordelia Street were to close over him finally and forever. The gray monotony stretched before him in hopeless, unrelieved years; Sabbath-school, Young People's Meeting, the yellow-papered room, the damp dish-towels; it all rushed back upon him with a sickening vividness. He had the old feeling that the orchestra had suddenly stopped, the sinking sensation that the play was over. The sweat broke out on his face, and he sprang to his feet, looked about him with his white, conscious smile, and winked at himself in the mirror. With something of the old childish belief in miracles with which he had so often gone to class, all his lessons unlearned, Paul dressed and dashed whistling down the corridor to the elevator.

He had no sooner entered the dining-room and caught the measure of the music than his remembrance was lightened by his old elastic power of claiming the moment, mounting with it, and finding it all sufficient. The glare and glitter about him, the mere scenic accessories had again, and for the last time, their old potency. He would show himself that he was game, he would finish the thing splendidly. He doubted, more than ever, the existence of Cordelia Street, and for the first time he drank his wine recklessly. Was he not, after all, one of those fortunate beings born to the purple, was he not still himself and in his own place? He drummed a nervous accompaniment to the Pagliacci music and looked about him, telling himself over and over that it had paid.

He reflected drowsily, to the swell of the music and the chill sweetness of his wine, that he might have done it more wisely. He might have caught an outbound steamer and been well out of their clutches before now. But the other side of the world had seemed too far away and too uncertain then; he could not have waited for it; his need had been too sharp. If he had to choose over again, he would do the same thing tomorrow. He looked affectionately about the dining-room, now gilded with a soft mist. Ah, it had paid indeed!

Paul was awakened next morning by a painful throbbing in his head and feet. 60
He had thrown himself across the bed without undressing, and had slept with his

shoes on. His limbs and hands were lead heavy, and his tongue and throat were parched and burnt. There came upon him one of those fateful attacks of clear-headedness that never occurred except when he was physically exhausted and his nerves hung loose. He lay still and closed his eyes and let the tide of things wash over him.

His father was in New York; "stopping at some joint or other," he told himself. The memory of successive summers on the front stoop fell upon him like a weight of black water. He had not a hundred dollars left; and he knew now, more than ever, that money was everything, the wall that stood between all he loathed and all he wanted. The thing was winding itself up; he had thought of that on his first glorious day in New York, and had even provided a way to snap the thread. It lay on his dress-ing-table now; he had got it out last night when he came blindly up from dinner, but the shiny metal hurt his eyes, and he disliked the looks of it.

He rose and moved about with a painful effort, succumbing now and again to attacks of nausea. It was the old depression exaggerated; all the world had become Cordelia Street. Yet somehow he was not afraid of anything, was absolutely calm; perhaps because he had looked into the dark corner at last and knew. It was bad enough, what he saw there, but somehow not so bad as his long fear of it had been. He saw everything clearly now. He had a feeling that he had made the best of it, that he had lived the sort of life he was meant to live, and for half an hour he sat staring at the revolver. But he told himself that was not the way, so he went downstairs and took a cab to the ferry.

When Paul arrived at Newark, he got off the train and took another cab, direct-ing the driver to follow the Pennsylvania tracks out of the town. The snow lay heavy on the roadways and had drifted deep in the open fields. Only here and there the dead grass or dried weed stalks projected, singularly black, above it. Once well into the country, Paul dismissed the carriage and walked, floundering along the tracks, his mind a medley of irrelevant things. He seemed to hold in his brain an actual picture of everything he had seen that morning. He remembered every feature of both his drivers, of the toothless old woman from whom he had bought the red flowers in his coat, the agent from whom he had got his ticket, and all of his fellow-passengers on the ferry. His mind, unable to cope with vital matters near at hand, worked feverishly and deftly at sorting and grouping these images. They made for him a part of the ugliness of the world, of the ache in his head, and the bitter burning on his tongue. He stooped and put a handful of snow into his mouth as he walked, but that, too, seemed hot. When he reached a little hillside, where the tracks ran through a cut some twenty feet below him, he stopped and sat down.

The carnations in his coat were drooping with the cold, he noticed; their red glory all over. It occurred to him that all the flowers he had seen in the glass cases that first night must have gone the same way, long before this. It was only one splendid breath they had, in spite of their brave mockery at the winter outside the glass; and it was a losing game in the end, it seemed, this revolt against the homilies by which the world is run. Paul took one of the blossoms carefully from his coat and scooped a little hole in the snow, where he covered it up. Then he dozed a while, from his weak con-dition, seemingly insensible to the cold.

The sound of an approaching train awoke him, and he started to his feet,   65
remembering only his resolution, and afraid lest he should be too late. He stood watching the approaching locomotive, his teeth chattering, his lips drawn away from them in a frightened smile; once or twice he glanced nervously sidewise, as though he

were being watched. When the right moment came, he jumped. As he fell, the folly of his haste occurred to him with merciless clearness, the vastness of what he had left undone. There flashed through his brain, clearer than ever before, the blue of Adriatic water, the yellow of Algerian sands.

He felt something strike his chest, and that his body was being thrown swiftly through the air, on and on, immeasurably far and fast, while his limbs were gently relaxed. Then, because the picture making mechanism was crushed, the disturbing visions flashed into black, and Paul dropped back into the immense design of things.

Anton Chekhov

The Lady with the Pet Dog

1899

Translated by Avrahm Yarmolinsky

Anton Chekhov (1860–1904), one of the Russian writers who helped shape modern fiction, is remembered especially for his plays and short stories. Born in the provincial town of Taganrog, the grandson of a serf who had bought his own freedom, Chekhov as a boy worked in his father's general store, a hangout for vodka-drinking storytellers. As a young man, he studied at Moscow University and became a doctor of medicine. To earn money while a medical student, he wrote his first stories for magazines. By 1886 his work had become so celebrated that he gave up medicine for writing, though continuing to treat sick peasants at his home without fee and to work in clinics during times of famine and epidemic. From 1896 to 1904 Chekhov wrote his great plays for the Moscow Art

Anton Chekhov

Theater, where they were directed by the influential director Konstantin Stanislavsky: The Seagull, The Cherry Orchard, Uncle Vanya, *and* The Three Sisters. *Chekhov's last years were brightened by his marriage to Olga Knipper, a star of the theater company. He died at forty-four, after a long struggle against tuberculosis.*

I

A new person, it was said, had appeared on the esplanade:° a lady with a pet dog. Dmitry Dmitrich Gurov, who had spent a fortnight at Yalta° and had got used to the place, had also begun to take an interest in new arrivals. As he sat in Vernet's confectionery shop, he saw, walking on the esplanade, a fair-haired young woman of medium height, wearing a beret; a white Pomeranian was trotting behind her.

And afterwards he met her in the public garden and in the square several times a day. She walked alone, always wearing the same beret and always with the white dog; no one knew who she was and everyone called her simply "the lady with the pet dog."

---

esplanade: a walkway or promenade along the shore.   *Yalta:* a port city on the Black Sea, a popular seaside resort for wealthy Russians.

"If she is here alone without husband or friends," Gurov reflected, "it wouldn't be a bad thing to make her acquaintance."

He was under forty, but he already had a daughter twelve years old, and two sons at school. They had found a wife for him when he was very young, a student in his second year, and by now she seemed half as old again as he. She was a tall, erect woman with dark eyebrows, stately and dignified and, as she said of herself, intellectual. She read a great deal, used simplified spelling in her letters, called her husband, not Dmitry, but Dimitry, while he privately considered her of limited intelligence, narrow-minded, dowdy, was afraid of her, and did not like to be at home. He had begun being unfaithful to her long ago—had been unfaithful to her often and, probably for that reason, almost always spoke ill of women, and when they were talked of in his presence used to call them "the inferior race."

It seemed to him that he had been sufficiently tutored by bitter experience to call them what he pleased, and yet he could not have lived without "the inferior race" for two days together. In the company of men he was bored and ill at ease, he was chilly and uncommunicative with them; but when he was among women he felt free, and knew what to speak to them about and how to comport himself; and even to be silent with them was no strain on him. In his appearance, in his character, in his whole make-up there was something attractive and elusive that disposed women in his favor and allured them. He knew that, and some force seemed to draw him to them, too.

Oft-repeated and really bitter experience had taught him long ago that with decent people—particularly Moscow people—who are irresolute and slow to move, every affair which at first seems a light and charming adventure inevitably grows into a whole problem of extreme complexity, and in the end a painful situation is created. But at every new meeting with an interesting woman this lesson of experience seemed to slip from his memory, and he was eager for life, and everything seemed so simple and diverting.

One evening while he was dining in the public garden the lady in the beret walked up without haste to take the next table. Her expression, her gait, her dress, and the way she did her hair told him that she belonged to the upper class, that she was married, that she was in Yalta for the first time and alone, and that she was bored there. The stories told of the immorality in Yalta are to a great extent untrue; he despised them, and knew that such stories were made up for the most part by persons who would have been glad to sin themselves if they had had the chance; but when the lady sat down at the next table three paces from him, he recalled these stories of easy conquests, of trips to the mountains, and the tempting thought of a swift, fleeting liaison, a romance with an unknown woman of whose very name he was ignorant suddenly took hold of him.

He beckoned invitingly to the Pomeranian, and when the dog approached him, shook his finger at it. The Pomeranian growled; Gurov threatened it again.

The lady glanced at him and at once dropped her eyes.

"He doesn't bite," she said and blushed.

"May I give him a bone?" he asked; and when she nodded he inquired affably, "Have you been in Yalta long?"

"About five days."

"And I am dragging out the second week here."

There was a short silence.

"Time passes quickly, and yet it is so dull here!" she said, not looking at him.

"It's only the fashion to say it's dull here. A provincial will live in Belyov or Zhizdra and not be bored, but when he comes here it's 'Oh, the dullness! Oh, the dust!' One would think he came from Granada."

She laughed. Then both continued eating in silence, like strangers, but after dinner they walked together and there sprang up between them the light banter of people who are free and contented, to whom it does not matter where they go or what they talk about. They walked and talked of the strange light on the sea: the water was a soft, warm, lilac color, and there was a golden band of moonlight upon it. They talked of how sultry it was after a hot day. Gurov told her that he was a native of Moscow, that he had studied languages and literature at the university, but had a post in a bank; that at one time he had trained to become an opera singer but had given it up, that he owned two houses in Moscow. And he learned from her that she had grown up in Petersburg, but had lived in S_____ since her marriage two years previously, that she was going to stay in Yalta for about another month, and that her husband, who needed a rest, too, might perhaps come to fetch her. She was not certain whether her husband was a member of a Government Board or served on a Zemstvo Council,° and this amused her. And Gurov learned that her name was Anna Sergeyevna.

Afterwards in his room at the hotel he thought about her—and was certain that he would meet her the next day. It was bound to happen. Getting into bed he recalled that she had been a schoolgirl only recently, doing lessons like his own daughter; he thought how much timidity and angularity there was still in her laugh and her manner of talking with a stranger. It must have been the first time in her life that she was alone in a setting in which she was followed, looked at, and spoken to for one secret purpose alone, which she could hardly fail to guess. He thought of her slim, delicate throat, her lovely gray eyes.

"There's something pathetic about her, though," he thought, and dropped off.

II

A week had passed since they had struck up an acquaintance. It was a holiday. It was close indoors, while in the street the wind whirled the dust about and blew people's hats off. One was thirsty all day, and Gurov often went into the restaurant and offered Anna Sergeyevna a soft drink or ice cream. One did not know what to do with oneself.

In the evening when the wind had abated they went out on the pier to watch the steamer come in. There were a great many people walking about the dock; they had come to welcome someone and they were carrying bunches of flowers. And two peculiarities of a festive Yalta crowd stood out: the elderly ladies were dressed like young ones and there were many generals.

Owing to the choppy sea, the steamer arrived late, after sunset, and it was a long time tacking about before it put in at the pier. Anna Sergeyevna peered at the steamer and the passengers through her lorgnette as though looking for acquaintances, and whenever she turned to Gurov her eyes were shining. She talked a great deal and asked questions jerkily, forgetting the next moment what she had asked; then she lost her lorgnette in the crush.

The festive crowd began to disperse; it was now too dark to see people's faces; there was no wind any more, but Gurov and Anna Sergeyevna still stood as though

20

Zemstvo Council: the elected council for local administration in Czarist Russia, the equivalent of a county administration.

waiting to see someone else come off the steamer. Anna Sergeyevna was silent now, and sniffed her flowers without looking at Gurov.

"The weather has improved this evening," he said. "Where shall we go now? Shall we drive somewhere?"

She did not reply. 25

Then he looked at her intently, and suddenly embraced her and kissed her on the lips, and the moist fragrance of her flowers enveloped him; and at once he looked round him anxiously, wondering if anyone had seen them.

"Let us go to your place," he said softly. And they walked off together rapidly.

The air in her room was close and there was the smell of the perfume she had bought at the Japanese shop. Looking at her, Gurov thought: "What encounters life offers!" From the past he preserved the memory of carefree, good-natured women whom love made gay and who were grateful to him for the happiness he gave them, however brief it might be; and of women like his wife who loved without sincerity, with too many words, affectedly, hysterically, with an expression that it was not love or passion that engaged them but something more significant; and of two or three others, very beautiful, frigid women, across whose faces would suddenly flit a rapacious expression—an obstinate desire to take from life more than it could give, and these were women no longer young, capricious, unreflecting, domineering, unintelligent, and when Gurov grew cold to them their beauty aroused his hatred, and the lace on their lingerie seemed to him to resemble scales.

But here there was the timidity, the angularity of inexperienced youth, a feeling of awkwardness; and there was a sense of embarrassment, as though someone had suddenly knocked at the door. Anna Sergeyevna, "the lady with the pet dog," treated what had happened in a peculiar way, very seriously, as though it were her fall—so it seemed, and this was odd and inappropriate. Her features drooped and faded, and her long hair hung down sadly on either side of her face; she grew pensive and her dejected pose was that of a Magdalene in a picture by an old master.

"It's not right," she said. "You don't respect me now, you first of all." 30

There was a watermelon on the table. Gurov cut himself a slice and began eating it without haste. They were silent for at least half an hour.

There was something touching about Anna Sergeyevna; she had the purity of a well-bred, naive woman who has seen little of life. The single candle burning on the table barely illuminated her face, yet it was clear that she was unhappy.

"Why should I stop respecting you, darling?" asked Gurov. "You don't know what you're saying."

"God forgive me," she said, and her eyes filled with tears. "It's terrible."

"It's as though you were trying to exonerate yourself." 35

"How can I exonerate myself? No. I am a bad, low woman; I despise myself and I have no thought of exonerating myself. It's not my husband but myself I have deceived. And not only just now; I have been deceiving myself for a long time. My husband may be a good, honest man, but he is a flunkey! I don't know what he does, what his work is, but I know he is a flunkey! I was twenty when I married him. I was tormented by curiosity; I wanted something better. 'There must be a different sort of life,' I said to myself. I wanted to live! To live, to live! Curiosity kept eating at me—you don't understand, but I swear to God I could no longer control myself; something was going on in me; I could not be held back. I told my husband I was ill, and came here. And here I have been walking about as though in a daze, as though I were mad; and now I have become a vulgar, vile woman whom anyone may despise."

Gurov was already bored with her; he was irritated by her naive tone, by her repentance, so unexpected and so out of place, but for the tears in her eyes he might have thought she was joking or play-acting.

"I don't understand, my dear," he said softly. "What do you want?"

She hid her face on his breast and pressed close to him.

"Believe me, believe me, I beg you," she said, "I love honesty and purity, and sin   40
is loathsome to me; I don't know what I'm doing. Simple people say, 'The Evil One has led me astray.' And I may say of myself now that the Evil One has led me astray."

"Quiet, quiet," he murmured.

He looked into her fixed, frightened eyes, kissed her, spoke to her softly and affectionately, and by degrees she calmed down, and her gaiety returned; both began laughing.

Afterwards when they went out there was not a soul on the esplanade. The town with its cypresses looked quite dead, but the sea was still sounding as it broke upon the beach; a single launch was rocking on the waves and on it a lantern was blinking sleepily.

They found a cab and drove to Oreanda.

"I found out your surname in the hall just now; it was written on the board—von   45
Dideritz," said Gurov. "Is your husband German?"

"No; I believe his grandfather was German, but he is Greek Orthodox himself."

At Oreanda they sat on a bench not far from the church, looked down at the sea, and were silent. Yalta was barely visible through the morning mist; white clouds rested motionlessly on the mountaintops. The leaves did not stir on the trees, cicadas twanged, and the monotonous muffled sound of the sea that rose from below spoke of the peace, the eternal sleep awaiting us. So it rumbled below when there was no Yalta, no Oreanda here; so it rumbles now, and it will rumble as indifferently and as hollowly when we are no more. And in this constancy, in this complete indifference to the life and death of each of us, there lies, perhaps, a pledge of our eternal salvation, of the unceasing advance of life upon earth, of unceasing movement towards perfection. Sitting beside a young woman who in the dawn seemed so lovely, Gurov, soothed and spellbound by these magical surroundings—the sea, the mountains, the clouds, the wide sky—thought how everything is really beautiful in this world when one reflects: everything except what we think or do ourselves when we forget the higher aims of life and our own human dignity.

A man strolled up to them—probably a guard—looked at them and walked away. And this detail, too, seemed so mysterious and beautiful. They saw a steamer arrive from Feodosia, its lights extinguished in the glow of dawn.

"There is dew on the grass," said Anna Sergeyevna, after a silence.

"Yes, it's time to go home."   50

They returned to the city.

Then they met every day at twelve o'clock on the esplanade, lunched and dined together, took walks, admired the sea. She complained that she slept badly, that she had palpitations, asked the same questions, troubled now by jealousy and now by the fear that he did not respect her sufficiently. And often in the square or the public garden, when there was no one near them, he suddenly drew her to him and kissed her passionately. Complete idleness, these kisses in broad daylight exchanged furtively in dread of someone's seeing them, the heat, the smell of the sea, and the continual flitting before his eyes of idle, well-dressed, well-fed people, worked a complete change in him; he kept telling Anna Sergeyevna how beautiful she was, how seductive, was urgently passionate; he would not move a step away from her, while she was often pensive and continually pressed him to confess that he did not respect her, did not love her in the least, and saw in her nothing but a common woman. Almost every evening rather late they drove somewhere out of town, to Oreanda or to the waterfall; and the excursion was always a success, the scenery invariably impressed them as beautiful and magnificent.

They were expecting her husband, but a letter came from him saying that he had eye-trouble, and begging his wife to return home as soon as possible. Anna Sergeyevna made haste to go.

"It's a good thing I am leaving," she said to Gurov. "It's the hand of Fate!"

She took a carriage to the railway station, and he went with her. They were   55
driving the whole day. When she had taken her place in the express, and when the second bell had rung, she said, "Let me look at you once more—let me look at you again. Like this."

She was not crying but was so sad that she seemed ill and her face was quivering.

"I shall be thinking of you—remembering you," she said. "God bless you; be happy. Don't remember evil against me. We are parting forever—it has to be, for we ought never to have met. Well, God bless you."

The train moved off rapidly, its lights soon vanished, and a minute later there was no sound of it, as though everything had conspired to end as quickly as possible that sweet trance, that madness. Left alone on the platform, and gazing into the dark distance, Gurov listened to the twang of the grasshoppers and the hum of the telegraph wires, feeling as though he had just waked up. And he reflected, musing, that there had now been another episode or adventure in his life, and it, too, was at an end, and nothing was left of it but a memory. He was moved, sad, and slightly remorseful: this young woman whom he would never meet again had not been happy with him; he had been warm and affectionate with her, but yet in his manner, his tone, and his caresses there had been a shade of light irony, the slightly coarse arrogance of a happy male who was, besides, almost twice her age. She had constantly called him kind, exceptional, high-minded; obviously he had seemed to her different from what he really was, so he had involuntarily deceived her.

Here at the station there was already a scent of autumn in the air; it was a chilly evening.

"It is time for me to go north, too," thought Gurov as he left the platform. "High   60
time!"

III

At home in Moscow the winter routine was already established; the stoves were heated, and in the morning it was still dark when the children were having breakfast and getting ready for school, and the nurse would light the lamp for a short time. There were frosts already. When the first snow falls, on the first day the sleighs are out, it is pleasant to see the white earth, the white roofs; one draws easy, delicious breaths, and the season brings back the days of one's youth. The old limes and birches, white with hoar-frost, have a good-natured look; they are closer to one's heart than cypresses and palms, and near them one no longer wants to think of mountains and the sea.

Gurov, a native of Moscow, arrived there on a fine frosty day, and when he put on his fur coat and warm gloves and took a walk along Petrovka, and when on Saturday night he heard the bells ringing, his recent trip and the places he had visited lost all charm for him. Little by little he became immersed in Moscow life, greedily read three newspapers a day, and declared that he did not read the Moscow papers on principle. He already felt a longing for restaurants, clubs, formal dinners, anniversary celebrations, and it flattered him to entertain distinguished lawyers and actors, and to play cards with a professor at the physicians' club. He could eat a whole portion of meat stewed with pickled cabbage and served in a pan, Moscow style.

A month or so would pass and the image of Anna Sergeyevna, it seemed to him, would become misty in his memory, and only from time to time he would dream of her with her touching smile as he dreamed of others. But more than a month went by, winter came into its own, and everything was still clear in his memory as though he had parted from Anna Sergeyevna only yesterday. And his memories glowed more and more vividly. When in the evening stillness the voices of his children preparing their lessons reached his study, or when he listened to a song or to an organ playing in a restaurant, or when the storm howled in the chimney, suddenly everything would rise up in his memory: what had happened on the pier and the early morning with the mist on the mountains, and the steamer coming from Feodosia, and the kisses. He would pace about his room a long time, remembering and smiling; then his memories passed into reveries, and in his imagination the past would mingle with what was to come. He did not dream of Anna Sergeyevna, but she followed him about everywhere and watched him. When he shut his eyes he saw her before him as though she were there in the flesh, and she seemed to him lovelier, younger, tenderer than she had been, and he imagined himself a finer man than he had been in Yalta. Of evenings she peered out at him from the bookcase, from the fireplace, from the corner—he heard her breathing, the caressing rustle of her clothes. In the street he followed the women with his eyes, looking for someone who resembled her.

Already he was tormented by a strong desire to share his memories with someone. But in his home it was impossible to talk of his love, and he had no one to talk to outside; certainly he could not confide in his tenants or in anyone at the bank. And what was there to talk about? He hadn't loved her then, had he? Had there been anything beautiful, poetical, edifying, or simply interesting in his relations with Anna Sergeyevna? And he was forced to talk vaguely of love, of women, and no one guessed what he meant; only his wife would twitch her black eyebrows and say, "The part of a philanderer does not suit you at all, Dimitry."

One evening, coming out of the physicians' club with an official with whom he had been playing cards, he could not resist saying: 65

"If you only knew what a fascinating woman I became acquainted with at Yalta!"

The official got into his sledge and was driving away, but turned suddenly and shouted:

"Dmitry Dmitrich!"

"What is it?"

"You were right this evening: the sturgeon was a bit high."   70

These words, so commonplace, for some reason moved Gurov to indignation, and struck him as degrading and unclean. What savage manners, what mugs! What stupid nights, what dull, humdrum days! Frenzied gambling, gluttony, drunkenness, continual talk always about the same thing! Futile pursuits and conversations always about the same topics take up the better part of one's time, the better part of one's strength, and in the end there is left a life clipped and wingless, an absurd mess, and there is no escaping or getting away from it—just as though one were in a madhouse or a prison.

Gurov, boiling with indignation, did not sleep all night. And he had a headache all the next day. And the following nights too he slept badly; he sat up in bed, thinking, or paced up and down his room. He was fed up with his children, fed up with the bank; he had no desire to go anywhere or to talk of anything.

In December during the holidays he prepared to take a trip and told his wife he was going to Petersburg to do what he could for a young friend—and he set off for S_____. What for? He did not know, himself. He wanted to see Anna Sergeyevna and talk with her, to arrange a rendezvous if possible.

He arrived at S_____ in the morning, and at the hotel took the best room, in which the floor was covered with gray army cloth, and on the table there was an inkstand, gray with dust and topped by a figure on horseback, its hat in its raised hand and its head broken off. The porter gave him the necessary information: von Dideritz lived in a house of his own on Staro-Goncharnaya Street, not far from the hotel: he was rich and lived well and kept his own horses; everyone in the town knew him. The porter pronounced the name: "Dridiritz."

Without haste Gurov made his way to Staro-Goncharnaya Street and found the house. Directly opposite the house stretched a long gray fence studded with nails.

"A fence like that would make one run away," thought Gurov, looking now at the fence, now at the windows of the house.

He reflected: this was a holiday, and the husband was apt to be at home. And in any case, it would be tactless to go into the house and disturb her. If he were to send her a note, it might fall into her husband's hands, and that might spoil everything. The best thing was to rely on chance. And he kept walking up and down the street and along the fence, waiting for the chance. He saw a beggar go in at the gate and heard the dogs attack him; then an hour later he heard a piano, and the sound came to him faintly and indistinctly. Probably it was Anna Sergeyevna playing. The front door opened suddenly, and an old woman came out, followed by the familiar white Pomeranian. Gurov was on the point of calling to the dog, but his heart began beating violently, and in his excitement he could not remember the Pomeranian's name.

He kept walking up and down, and hated the gray fence more and more, and by now he thought irritably that Anna Sergeyevna had forgotten him, and was perhaps already diverting herself with another man, and that that was very natural in a young woman who from morning till night had to look at that damn fence. He went back to his hotel room and sat on the couch for a long while, not knowing what to do, then he had dinner and a long nap.

"How stupid and annoying all this is!" he thought when he woke and looked at the dark windows: it was already evening. "Here I've had a good sleep for some reason. What am I going to do at night?"

He sat on the bed, which was covered with a cheap gray blanket of the kind seen in hospitals, and he twitted himself in his vexation:

"So there's your lady with the pet dog. There's your adventure. A nice place to cool your heels in."

That morning at the station a playbill in large letters had caught his eye. *The Geisha* was to be given for the first time. He thought of this and drove to the theater.

"It's quite possible that she goes to first nights," he thought.

The theater was full. As in all provincial theaters, there was a haze above the chandelier, the gallery was noisy and restless; in the front row, before the beginning of the performance the local dandies were standing with their hands clasped behind their backs; in the Governor's box the Governor's daughter, wearing a boa, occupied the front seat, while the Governor himself hid modestly behind the portiere and only his hands were visible; the curtain swayed; the orchestra was a long time tuning up. While the audience was coming in and taking their seats, Gurov scanned the faces eagerly.

Anna Sergeyevna, too, came in. She sat down in the third row, and when Gurov   85
looked at her his heart contracted, and he understood clearly that in the whole world there was no human being so near, so precious, and so important to him; she, this lit-tle, undistinguished woman, lost in a provincial crowd, with a vulgar lorgnette in her hand, filled his whole life now, was his sorrow and his joy, the only happiness that he now desired for himself, and to the sounds of the bad orchestra, of the miserable local violins, he thought how lovely she was. He thought and dreamed.

A young man with small side-whiskers, very tall and stooped, came in with Anna Sergeyevna and sat down beside her; he nodded his head at every step and seemed to be bowing continually. Probably this was the husband whom at Yalta, in an access of bitter feeling, she had called a flunkey. And there really was in his lanky figure, his side-whiskers, his small bald patch, something of a flunkey's retiring man-ner; his smile was mawkish, and in his buttonhole there was an academic badge like a waiter's number.

During the first intermission the husband went out to have a smoke; she remained in her seat. Gurov, who was also sitting in the orchestra, went up to her and said in a shaky voice, with a forced smile:

"Good evening!"

She glanced at him and turned pale, then looked at him again in horror, unable to believe her eyes, and gripped the fan and the lorgnette tightly together in her hands, evidently trying to keep herself from fainting. Both were silent. She was sit-ting, he was standing, frightened by her distress and not daring to take a seat beside her. The violins and the flute that were being tuned up sang out. He suddenly felt frightened: it seemed as if all the people in the boxes were looking at them. She got up and went hurriedly to the exit; he followed her, and both of them walked blindly along the corridors and up and down stairs, and figures in the uniforms prescribed for magistrates, teachers, and officials of the Department of Crown Lands, all wearing badges, flitted before their eyes, as did also ladies, and fur coats on hangers; they were conscious of drafts and the smell of stale tobacco. And Gurov, whose heart was beat-ing violently, thought:

"Oh, Lord! Why are these people here and this orchestra!"   90

And at that instant he suddenly recalled how when he had seen Anna Sergeyevna off at the station he had said to himself that all was over between them and that they would never meet again. But how distant the end still was!

On the narrow, gloomy staircase over which it said "To the Amphitheatre," she stopped.

"How you frightened me!" she said, breathing hard, still pale and stunned. "Oh, how you frightened me! I am barely alive. Why did you come? Why?"

"But do understand, Anna, do understand—" he said hurriedly, under his breath. "I implore you, do understand—"

She looked at him with fear, with entreaty, with love; she looked at him intently,   95
to keep his features more distinctly in her memory.

"I suffer so," she went on, not listening to him. "All this time I have been think-ing of nothing but you; I live only by the thought of you. And I wanted to forget, to forget; but why, oh, why have you come?"

On the landing above them two high school boys were looking down and smoking, but it was all the same to Gurov; he drew Anna Sergeyevna to him and began kissing her face and hands.

"What are you doing, what are you doing!" she was saying in horror, pushing him away. "We have lost our senses. Go away today; go away at once—I conjure you by all that is sacred, I implore you—People are coming this way!"

Someone was walking up the stairs.

"You must leave," Anna Sergeyevna went on in a whisper. "Do you hear, Dmitry   100
Dmitrich? I will come and see you in Moscow. I have never been happy; I am unhappy now, and I never, never shall be happy, never! So don't make me suffer still more! I swear I'll come to Moscow. But now let us part. My dear, good, precious one, let us part!"

She pressed his hand and walked rapidly downstairs, turning to look round at him, and from her eyes he could see that she really was unhappy. Gurov stood for a while, listening, then when all grew quiet, he found his coat and left the theater.

IV

And Anna Sergeyevna began coming to see him in Moscow. Once every two or three months she left S_____, telling her husband that she was going to consult a doctor about a woman's ailment from which she was suffering—and her husband did and did not believe her. When she arrived in Moscow she would stop at the Slavyansky Bazar Hotel, and at once send a man in a red cap to Gurov. Gurov came to see her, and no one in Moscow knew of it.

Once he was going to see her in this way on a winter morning (the messenger had come the evening before and not found him in). With him walked his daughter, whom he wanted to take to school; it was on the way. Snow was coming down in big wet flakes.

"It's three degrees above zero,° and yet it's snowing," Gurov was saying to his daughter. "But this temperature prevails only on the surface of the earth; in the upper layers of the atmosphere there is quite a different temperature."

"And why doesn't it thunder in winter, papa?"   105

He explained that, too. He talked, thinking all the while that he was on his way to a rendezvous, and no living soul knew of it, and probably no one would ever know. He had two lives, an open one, seen and known by all who needed to know it, full of conventional truth and conventional falsehood, exactly like the lives of his friends and acquaintances; and another life that went on in secret. And through some strange, perhaps accidental, combination of circumstances, everything that was of interest and importance to him, everything that was essential to him, everything about which he felt sincerely and did not deceive himself, everything that constituted the core of his life, was going on concealed from others; while all that was false, the shell in which he hid to cover the truth—his work at the bank, for instance, his discussions at the club, his references to the "inferior race," his appearances at anniversary celebrations with his wife—all that went on in the open. Judging others by himself, he did not believe what he saw, and always fancied that every man led his real, most interesting life under cover of secrecy as

---

three degrees above zero: the Russian temperature is measured in Celsius degrees; the Fahrenheit equivalent would be about thirty-seven degrees.

under cover of night. The personal life of every individual is based on secrecy, and perhaps it is partly for that reason that civilized man is so nervously anxious that personal privacy should be respected.

Having taken his daughter to school, Gurov went on to the Slavyansky Bazar Hotel. He took off his fur coat in the lobby, went upstairs, and knocked gently at the door. Anna Sergeyevna, wearing his favorite gray dress, exhausted by the journey and by waiting, had been expecting him since the previous evening. She was pale, and looked at him without a smile, and had hardly entered when she flung herself on his breast. That kiss was a long, lingering one, as though they had not seen one another for two years.

"Well, darling, how are you getting on there?" he asked. "What news?"

"Wait; I'll tell you in a moment—I can't speak."

She could not speak; she was crying. She turned away from him, and pressed her 110
handkerchief to her eyes.

"Let her have her cry; meanwhile I'll sit down," he thought, and he seated himself in an armchair.

Then he rang and ordered tea, and while he was having his tea she remained standing at the window with her back to him. She was crying out of sheer agitation, in the sorrowful consciousness that their life was so sad; that they could only see each other in secret and had to hide from people like thieves! Was it not a broken life?

"Come, stop now, dear!" he said.

It was plain to him that this love of theirs would not be over soon, that the end of it was not in sight. Anna Sergeyevna was growing more and more attached to him. She adored him, and it was unthinkable to tell her that their love was bound to come to an end some day; besides, she would not have believed it!

He went up to her and took her by the shoulders, to fondle her and say some- 115
thing diverting, and at that moment he caught sight of himself in the mirror.

His hair was already beginning to turn gray. And it seemed odd to him that he had grown so much older in the last few years, and lost his looks. The shoulders on which his hands rested were warm and heaving. He felt compassion for this life, still so warm and lovely, but probably already about to begin to fade and wither like his own. Why did she love him so much? He always seemed to women different from what he was, and they loved in him not himself, but the man whom their imagination created and whom they had been eagerly seeking all their lives; and afterwards, when they saw their mistake, they loved him nevertheless. And not one of them had been happy with him. In the past he had met women, come together with them, parted from them, but he had never once loved; it was anything you please, but not love. And only now when his head was gray he had fallen in love, really, truly—for the first time in his life.

Anna Sergeyevna and he loved each other as people do who are very close and intimate, like man and wife, like tender friends; it seemed to them that Fate itself had meant them for one another, and they could not understand why he had a wife and she a husband; and it was as though they were a pair of migratory birds, male and female, caught and forced to live in different cages. They forgave each other what they were ashamed of in their past, they forgave everything in the present, and felt that this love of theirs had altered them both.

Formerly in moments of sadness he had soothed himself with whatever logical arguments came into his head, but now he no longer cared for logic; he felt profound compassion, he wanted to be sincere and tender.

"Give it up now, my darling," he said. "You've had your cry; that's enough. Let us have a talk now, we'll think up something."

Then they spent a long time taking counsel together, they talked of how to avoid the necessity for secrecy, for deception, for living in different cities, and not seeing one another for long stretches of time. How could they free themselves from these intolerable fetters?   120

"How? How?" he asked, clutching his head. "How?"

And it seemed as though in a little while the solution would be found, and then a new and glorious life would begin; and it was clear to both of them that the end was still far off, and that what was to be most complicated and difficult for them was only just beginning.

Kate Chopin

The Story of an Hour   1894

Kate Chopin (1851–1904) demonstrates again, as in "The Storm" in Chapter 4, her ability to write short stories of compressed intensity. For a brief biography and a portrait see page 110.

Knowing that Mrs. Mallard was afflicted with a heart trouble, great care was taken to break to her as gently as possible the news of her husband's death.

It was her sister Josephine who told her, in broken sentences; veiled hints that revealed in half concealing. Her husband's friend Richards was there, too, near her. It was he who had been in the newspaper office when intelligence of the railroad disaster was received, with Brently Mallard's name leading the list of "killed." He had only taken the time to assure himself of its truth by a second telegram, and had hastened to forestall any less careful, less tender friend in bearing the sad message.

She did not hear the story as many women have heard the same, with a paralyzed inability to accept its significance. She wept at once, with sudden, wild abandonment, in her sister's arms. When the storm of grief had spent itself she went away to her room alone. She would have no one follow her.

There stood, facing the open window, a comfortable, roomy armchair. Into this she sank, pressed down by a physical exhaustion that haunted her body and seemed to reach into her soul.

She could see in the open square before her house the tops of trees that were all aquiver with the new spring life. The delicious breath of rain was in the air. In the street below a peddler was crying his wares. The notes of a distant song which some one was singing reached her faintly, and countless sparrows were twittering in the eaves.   5

There were patches of blue sky showing here and there through the clouds that had met and piled one above the other in the west facing her window.

She sat with her head thrown back upon the cushion of the chair, quite motionless, except when a sob came up into her throat and shook her, as a child who has cried itself to sleep continues to sob in its dreams.

She was young, with a fair, calm face, whose lines bespoke repression and even a certain strength. But now there was a dull stare in her eyes, whose gaze was fixed away off yonder on one of those patches of blue sky. It was not a glance of reflection, but rather indicated a suspension of intelligent thought.

There was something coming to her and she was waiting for it, fearfully. What was it? She did not know; it was too subtle and elusive to name. But she felt it, creeping out of the sky, reaching toward her through the sounds, the scents, the color that filled the air.

Now her bosom rose and fell tumultuously. She was beginning to recognize this thing that was approaching to possess her, and she was striving to beat it back with her will—as powerless as her two white slender hands would have been.

When she abandoned herself a little whispered word escaped her slightly parted lips. She said it over and over under her breath: "free, free, free!" The vacant stare and the look of terror that had followed it went from her eyes. They stayed keen and bright. Her pulses beat fast, and the coursing blood warmed and relaxed every inch of her body.

She did not stop to ask if it were not a monstrous joy that held her. A clear and exalted perception enabled her to dismiss the suggestion as trivial.

She knew that she would weep again when she saw the kind, tender hands folded in death; the face that had never looked save with love upon her, fixed and gray and dead. But she saw beyond that bitter moment a long procession of years to come that would belong to her absolutely. And she opened and spread her arms out to them in welcome.

There would be no one to live for her during those coming years; she would live for herself. There would be no powerful will bending hers in that blind persistence with which men and women believe they have a right to impose a private will upon a fellow-creature. A kind intention or a cruel intention made the act seem no less a crime as she looked upon it in that brief moment of illumination.

And yet she had loved him—sometimes. Often she had not. What did it matter! What could love, the unsolved mystery, count for in face of this possession of self-assertion which she suddenly recognized as the strongest impulse of her being!

"Free! Body and soul free!" she kept whispering.

Josephine was kneeling before the closed door with her lips to the keyhole, imploring for admission. "Louise, open the door! I beg; open the door—you will make yourself ill. What are you doing, Louise? For heaven's sake open the door."

"Go away. I am not making myself ill." No; she was drinking in a very elixir of life through that open window.

Her fancy was running riot along those days ahead of her. Spring days, and summer days, and all sorts of days that would be her own. She breathed a quick prayer that life might be long. It was only yesterday she had thought with a shudder that life might be long.

She arose at length and opened the door to her sister's importunities. There was a feverish triumph in her eyes, and she carried herself unwittingly like a goddess of Victory. She clasped her sister's waist, and together they descended the stairs. Richards stood waiting for them at the bottom.

Some one was opening the front door with a latchkey. It was Brently Mallard who entered, a little travel-stained, composedly carrying his grip-sack and umbrella. He had been far from the scene of the accident, and did not even know there had been one. He stood amazed at Josephine's piercing cry; at Richards' quick motion to screen him from the view of his wife.

But Richards was too late.

When the doctors came they said she had died of heart disease—of joy that kills.

Sandra Cisneros

The House on Mango Street
1984

Sandra Cisneros was born in Chicago in 1954. The child of a Mexican father and a Mexican American mother, she was the only daughter in a family of seven children. She attended Loyola University of Chicago and then received a master's degree from the University of Iowa Writers' Workshop. She has instructed high-school dropouts, but more recently she has taught as a visiting writer at numerous universities, including the University of California at Irvine and at Berkeley, and the University of Michigan. Her honors include fellowships from the National Endowment for the Arts and the MacArthur Foundation. Cisneros's first published work was poetry: Bad Boys *(1980), followed by* My Wicked Wicked Ways *(1987) and* Loose Woman *(1994). Her fiction collections,* The*

Sandra Cisneros

House on Mango Street *(1984) and* Women Hollering Creek *(1991), however, earned her a broader audience. She has also published a bilingual children's book,* Hairs: Pelitos *(1994), and a novel,* Caramelo *(2002). Cisneros currently lives in San Antonio, Texas.*

We didn't always live on Mango Street. Before that we lived on Loomis on the third floor, and before that we lived on Keeler. Before Keeler it was Paulina, and before that I can't remember. But what I remember most is moving a lot. Each time it seemed there'd be one more of us. By the time we got to Mango Street we were six—Mama, Papa, Carlos, Kiki, my sister Nenny, and me.

The house on Mango Street is ours, and we don't have to pay rent to anybody, or share the yard with the people downstairs, or be careful not to make too much noise, and there isn't a landlord banging on the ceiling with a broom. But even so, it's not the house we'd thought we'd get.

We had to leave the flat on Loomis quick. The water pipes broke and the landlord wouldn't fix them because the house was too old. We had to leave fast. We were using the washroom next door and carrying water over in empty milk gallons. That's why Mama and Papa looked for a house, and that's why we moved into the house on Mango Street, far away, on the other side of town.

They always told us that one day we would move into a house, a real house that would be ours for always so we wouldn't have to move each year. And our house would have running water and pipes that worked. And inside it would have real stairs, not hallway stairs, but stairs inside like the houses on T.V. And we'd have a basement and at least three washrooms so when we took a bath we wouldn't have to tell everybody. Our house would be white with trees around it, a great big yard and grass growing without a fence. This was the house Papa talked about when he held a lottery ticket and this was the house Mama dreamed up in the stories she told us before we went to bed.

But the house on Mango Street is not the way they told it at all. It's small and red with tight steps in front and windows so small you'd think they were holding
5

their breath. Bricks are crumbling in places, and the front door is so swollen you have to push hard to get in. There is no front yard, only four little elms the city planted by the curb. Out back is a small garage for the car we don't own yet and a small yard that looks smaller between the two buildings on either side. There are stairs in our house, but they're ordinary hallway stairs, and the house has only one washroom. Everybody has to share a bedroom—Mama and Papa, Carlos and Kiki, me and Nenny.

Once when we were living on Loomis, a nun from my school passed by and saw me playing out front. The laundromat downstairs had been boarded up because it had been robbed two days before and the owner had painted on the wood YES WE'RE OPEN so as not to lose business.

Where do you live? she asked.

There, I said pointing up to the third floor.

You live *there?*

There. I had to look to where she pointed—the third floor, the paint peeling,   10
wooden bars Papa had nailed on the windows so we wouldn't fall out. You live *there?* The way she said it made me feel like nothing. *There.* I lived *there.* I nodded.

I knew then I had to have a house. A real house. One I could point to. But this isn't it. The house on Mango Street isn't it. For the time being, Mama says. Temporary, says Papa. But I know how those things go.

Ralph Ellison

Battle Royal   1952

Ralph Ellison (1914–1994) was born in Oklahoma City. His father, a small business owner who sold ice and coal, died when the future author was only three. Ellison's mother, a religious woman of strong convictions, worked as a maid to support her two sons. She also stressed the importance of education. Planning to be a composer, Ellison entered the Tuskegee Institute in 1933. Reading T. S. Eliot's poem The Waste Land, *however, helped focus his interest on literature. In 1936 he moved to New York to find a summer job to pay for his senior year's tuition. He never left. In Harlem Ellison met many black writers, including Langston Hughes and Richard Wright, and he soon began publishing short stories, poems, and reviews. In 1952 Ellison published his only novel,* Invisible Man, *which won the National Book Award for fiction*

Ralph Ellison

and has gradually come to be recognized as a contemporary American masterpiece. Over the next forty years Ellison tried to finish a second novel, a project that was delayed by the author's obsessive drive for perfection. He eventually published eight sections of the work, but it remained unfinished. A 368-page version of the novel, edited by John F. Callahan from more than 2,000 pages of manuscript, appeared in 1999 as Juneteenth. *Other posthumous publications were* The Collected Essays *(1995)—which gathered Ellison's two published books of essays,* Shadow and Act *(1964) and* Going to the Territory *(1986), along with much other material—and* Flying Home *(1996), thirteen short stories written between 1937 and 1954. For years Ellison taught at New York University. He published "Battle Royal" as a short story in 1948, and later revised it as the first chapter of* Invisible Man *(where it is preceded by a short prologue).*

It goes a long way back, some twenty years. All my life I had been looking for something, and everywhere I turned someone tried to tell me what it was. I accepted their answers too, though they were often in contradiction and even self-contradictory. I was naïve. I was looking for myself and asking everyone except myself questions which I, and only I, could answer. It took me a long time and much painful boomeranging of my expectations to achieve a realization everyone else appears to have been born with: That I am nobody but myself. But first I had to discover that I am an invisible man!

And yet I am no freak of nature, nor of history. I was in the cards, other things having been equal (or unequal) eighty-five years ago. I am not ashamed of my grand-parents for having been slaves. I am only ashamed of myself for having at one time been ashamed. About eighty-five years ago they were told they were free, united with others of our country in everything pertaining to the common good, and, in every-thing social, separate like the fingers of the hand. And they believed it. They exulted in it. They stayed in their place, worked hard, and brought up my father to do the same. But my grandfather is the one. He was an odd old guy, my grandfather, and I am told I take after him. It was he who caused the trouble. On his deathbed he called my father to him and said, "Son, after I'm gone I want you to keep up the good fight. I never told you, but our life is a war and I have been a traitor all my born days, a spy in the enemy's country ever since I give up my gun back in the Reconstruction. Live with your head in the lion's mouth. I want you to overcome 'em with yeses, under-mine 'em with grins, agree 'em to death and destruction, let 'em swoller you till they vomit or bust wide open." They thought the old man had gone out of his mind. He had been the meekest of men. The younger children were rushed from the room, the shades drawn and the flame of the lamp turned so low that it sputtered on the wick like the old man's breathing. "Learn it to the younguns," he whispered fiercely; then he died.

But my folks were more alarmed over his last words than over his dying. It was as though he had not died at all, his words caused so much anxiety. I was warned em-phatically to forget what he had said and, indeed, this is the first time it has been mentioned outside the family circle. It had a tremendous effect upon me, however. I could never be sure of what he meant. Grandfather had been a quiet old man who never made any trouble, yet on his deathbed he had called himself a traitor and a spy, and he had spoken of his meekness as a dangerous activity. It became a constant puz-zle which lay unanswered in the back of my mind. And whenever things went well for me I remembered my grandfather and felt guilty and uncomfortable. It was as though I was carrying out his advice in spite of myself. And to make it worse, everyone loved me for it. I was praised by the most lily-white men of the town. I was considered an example of desirable conduct—just as my grandfather had been. And what puzzled me was that the old man had defined it as *treachery*. When I was praised for my conduct I felt a guilt that in some way I was doing something that was really against the wishes of the white folks, that if they had understood they would have desired me to act just the opposite, that I should have been sulky and mean, and that that really would have been what they wanted, even though they were fooled and thought they wanted me to act as I did. It made me afraid that some day they would look upon me as a traitor and I would be lost. Still I was more afraid to act any other way because they didn't like that at all. The old man's words were like a curse. On my graduation day I delivered an oration in which I showed that humility was the secret, indeed, the very essence of progress. (Not that I believed this—how could I, remembering my grandfather?—I only believed that it worked.) It was a great success. Everyone praised me and I was invited to give the speech at a gathering of the town's leading white citizens. It was a triumph for the whole community.

It was in the main ballroom of the leading hotel. When I got there I discovered that it was on the occasion of a smoker, and I was told that since I was to be there anyway I might as well take part in the battle royal to be fought by some of my schoolmates as part of the entertainment. The battle royal came first.

All of the town's big shots were there in their tuxedoes, wolfing down the buffet foods, drinking beer and whiskey and smoking black cigars. It was a large room with a high ceiling. Chairs were arranged in neat rows around three sides of a portable boxing ring. The fourth side was clear, revealing a gleaming space of polished floor. I had some misgivings over the battle royal, by the way. Not from a distaste for fighting, but because I didn't care too much for the other fellows who were to take part. They were tough guys who seemed to have no grandfather's curse worrying their minds. No one could mistake their toughness. And besides, I suspected that fighting a battle royal might detract from the dignity of my speech. In those pre-invisible days I visualized myself as a potential Booker T. Washington. But the other fellows didn't care too much for me either, and there were nine of them. I felt superior to them in my way, and I didn't like the manner in which we were all crowded together into the servants' elevator. Nor did they like my being there. In fact, as the warmly lighted floors flashed past the elevator we had words over the fact that I, by taking part in the fight, had knocked one of their friends out of a night's work.

We were led out of the elevator through a rococo hall into an anteroom and told to get into our fighting togs. Each of us was issued a pair of boxing gloves and ushered out into the big mirrored hall, which we entered looking cautiously about us and whispering, lest we might accidentally be heard above the noise of the room. It was foggy with cigar smoke. And already the whiskey was taking effect. I was shocked to see some of the most important men of the town quite tipsy. They were all there—bankers, lawyers, judges, doctors, fire chiefs, teachers, merchants. Even one of the more fashionable pastors. Something we could not see was going on up front. A clarinet was vibrating sensuously and the men were standing up and moving eagerly forward. We were a small tight group, clustered together, our bare upper bodies touching and shining with anticipatory sweat; while up front the big shots were becoming increasingly excited over something we still could not see. Suddenly I heard the school superintendent, who had told me to come, yell, "Bring up the shines, gentlemen! Bring up the little shines!"

We were rushed up to the front of the ballroom, where it smelled even more strongly of tobacco and whiskey. Then we were pushed into place. I almost wet my pants. A sea of faces, some hostile, some amused, ringed around us, and in the center, facing us, stood a magnificent blonde—stark naked. There was dead silence. I felt a blast of cold air chill me. I tried to back away, but they were behind me and around me. Some of the boys stood with lowered heads, trembling. I felt a wave of irrational guilt and fear. My teeth chattered, my skin turned to goose flesh, my knees knocked.

Yet I was strongly attracted and looked in spite of myself. Had the price of looking been blindness, I would have looked. The hair was yellow like that of a circus kewpie doll, the face heavily powdered and rouged, as though to form an abstract mask, the eyes hollow and smeared a cool blue, the color of a baboon's butt. I felt a desire to spit upon her as my eyes brushed slowly over her body. Her breasts were firm and round as the domes of East Indian temples, and I stood so close as to see the fine skin texture and beads of pearly perspiration glistening like dew around the pink and erected buds of her nipples. I wanted at one and the same time to run from the room, to sink through the floor, or go to her and cover her from my eyes and the eyes of the others with my body; to feel the soft thighs, to caress her and destroy her, to love her and to murder her, to hide from her, and yet to stroke where below the small American flag tattooed upon her belly her thighs formed a capital V. I had a notion that of all in the room she saw only me with her impersonal eyes.

And then she began to dance, a slow sensuous movement; the smoke of a hundred cigars clinging to her like the thinnest of veils. She seemed like a fair bird-girl girdled in veils calling to me from the angry surface of some gray and threatening sea. I was transported. Then I became aware of the clarinet playing and the big shots yelling at us. Some threatened us if we looked and others if we did not. On my right I saw one boy faint. And now a man grabbed a silver pitcher from a table and stepped close as he dashed ice water upon him and stood him up and forced two of us to support him as his head hung and moans issued from his thick bluish lips. Another boy began to plead to go home. He was the largest of the group, wearing dark red fighting trunks much too small to conceal the erection which projected from him as though in answer to the insinuating low-registered moaning of the clarinet. He tried to hide himself with his boxing gloves.

And all the while the blonde continued dancing, smiling faintly at the big shots who watched her with fascination, and faintly smiling at our fear. I noticed a certain merchant who followed her hungrily, his lips loose and drooling. He was a large man who wore diamond studs in a shirtfront which swelled with the ample paunch underneath, and each time the blonde swayed her undulating hips he ran his hand through the thin hair of his bald head and, with his arms upheld, his posture clumsy like that of an intoxicated panda, wound his belly in a slow and obscene grind. This creature was completely hypnotized. The music had quickened. As the dancer flung herself about with a detached expression on her face, the men began reaching out to touch her. I could see their beefy fingers sink into the soft flesh. Some of the others tried to stop them and she began to move around the floor in graceful circles, as they gave chase, slipping and sliding over the polished floor. It was mad. Chairs went crashing, drinks were spilt, as they ran laughing and howling after her. They caught her just as she reached a door, raised her from the floor, and tossed her as college boys are tossed at a hazing, and above her red, fixed-smiling lips I saw the terror and disgust in her eyes, almost like my own terror and that which I saw in some of the other boys. As I watched, they tossed her twice and her soft breasts seemed to flatten against the air and her legs flung wildly as she spun. Some of the more sober ones helped her to escape. And I started off the floor, heading for the anteroom with the rest of the boys.

Some were still crying and in hysteria. But as we tried to leave we were stopped and ordered to get into the ring. There was nothing to do but what we were told. All ten of us climbed under the ropes and allowed ourselves to be blindfolded with broad bands of white cloth. One of the men seemed to feel a bit sympathetic and tried to cheer us up as we stood with our backs against the ropes. Some of us tried to grin. "See that boy over there?" one of the men said. "I want you to run across at the bell and give it to him right in the belly. If you don't get him, I'm going to get you. I don't like his looks." Each of us was told the same. The blindfolds were put on. Yet even then I had been going over my speech. In my mind each word was as bright as flame. I felt the cloth pressed into place, and frowned so that it would be loosened when I relaxed.

But now I felt a sudden fit of blind terror. I was unused to darkness. It was as though I had suddenly found myself in a dark room filled with poisonous cotton-mouths. I could hear the bleary voices yelling insistently for the battle royal to begin.

"Get going in there!"

"Let me at that big nigger!"

I strained to pick up the school superintendent's voice, as though to squeeze some security out of that slightly more familiar sound.

"Let me at those black sonsabitches!" someone yelled.   15

"No, Jackson, no!" another voice yelled. "Here, somebody, help me hold Jack."

"I want to get at that ginger-colored nigger. Tear him limb from limb," the first voice yelled.

I stood against the ropes trembling. For in those days I was what they called ginger-colored, and he sounded as though he might crunch me between his teeth like a crisp ginger cookie.

Quite a struggle was going on. Chairs were being kicked about and I could hear voices grunting as with terrific effort. I wanted to see, to see more desperately than ever before. But the blindfold was as tight as a thick skin-puckering scab and when I raised my gloved hands to push the layers of white aside a voice yelled, "Oh, no you don't, black bastard! Leave that alone!"

"Ring the bell before Jackson kills him a coon!" someone boomed in the sudden   20
silence. And I heard the bell clang and the sound of the feet scuffling forward.

A glove smacked against my head. I pivoted, striking out stiffly as someone went past, and felt the jar ripple along the length of my arm to my shoulder. Then it seemed as though all nine of the boys had turned upon me at once. Blows pounded me from all sides while I struck out as best I could. So many blows landed upon me that I wondered if I were not the only blindfolded fighter in the ring, or if the man called Jackson hadn't succeeded in getting me after all.

Blindfolded, I could no longer control my motions. I had no dignity. I stumbled about like a baby or a drunken man. The smoke had become thicker and with each new blow it seemed to sear and further restrict my lungs. My saliva became like hot bitter glue. A glove connected with my head, filling my mouth with warm blood. It was everywhere. I could not tell if the moisture I felt upon my body was sweat or blood. A blow landed hard against the nape of my neck. I felt myself going over, my head hitting the floor. Streaks of blue light filled the black world behind the blindfold. I lay prone, pretending that I was knocked out, but felt myself seized by hands and yanked to my feet. "Get going, black boy! Mix it up!" My arms were like lead, my head smarting from blows. I managed to feel my way to the ropes and held on, trying to catch my breath. A glove landed in my mid-section and I went over again, feeling as though the smoke had become a knife jabbed into my guts. Pushed this way and that by the legs milling around me, I finally pulled erect and discovered that I could see the black, sweat-washed forms weaving in the smoky-blue atmosphere like drunken dancers weaving to the rapid drum-like thuds of blows.

Everyone fought hysterically. It was complete anarchy. Everybody fought everybody else. No group fought together for long. Two, three, four, fought one, then turned to fight each other, were themselves attacked. Blows landed below the belt and in the kidney, with the gloves open as well as closed, and with my eye partly opened now there was not so much terror. I moved carefully, avoiding blows, although not too many to attract attention, fighting group to group. The boys groped about like blind, cautious crabs crouching to protect their mid-sections, their heads pulled in short against their shoulders, their arms stretched nervously before them, with their fists testing the smoke-filled air like the knobbed feelers of hypersensitive snails. In one corner I glimpsed a boy violently punching the air and heard him scream in pain as he smashed his hand against a ring post. For a second I saw him bent over holding his hand, then going down as a blow caught his unprotected head. I played one group against the other, slipping in and throwing a punch then stepping out of range while pushing the others into the melee to take the blows blindly aimed at me. The smoke was agonizing and there were no rounds, no bells at three minute intervals to relieve our exhaustion. The room spun round me, a swirl of lights, smoke, sweating bodies surrounded by tense white faces. I bled from both nose and mouth, the blood spattering upon my chest.

The men kept yelling, "Slug him, black boy! Knock his guts out!"

"Uppercut him! Kill him! Kill that big boy!"   25

Taking a fake fall, I saw a boy going down heavily beside me as though we were felled by a single blow, saw a sneaker-clad foot shoot into his groin as the two who had knocked him down stumbled upon him. I rolled out of range, feeling a twinge of nausea.

The harder we fought the more threatening the men became. And yet, I had begun to worry about my speech again. How would it go? Would they recognize my ability? What would they give me?

I was fighting automatically when suddenly I noticed that one after another of the boys was leaving the ring. I was surprised, filled with panic, as though I had been left alone with an unknown danger. Then I understood. The boys had arranged it among themselves. It was the custom for the two men left in the ring to slug it out for the winner's prize. I discovered this too late. When the bell sounded two men in tuxedoes leaped into the ring and removed the blindfold. I found myself facing Tatlock, the biggest of the gang. I felt sick at my stomach. Hardly had the bell stopped ringing in my ears than it clanged again and I saw him moving swiftly toward me. Thinking of nothing else to do I hit him smash on the nose. He kept coming, bringing the rank sharp violence of stale sweat. His face was a black blank of a face, only his eyes alive— with hate of me and aglow with a feverish terror from what had happened to us all. I became anxious. I wanted to deliver my speech and he came at me as though he meant to beat it out of me. I smashed him again and again, taking his blows as they came. Then on a sudden impulse I struck him lightly and we clinched. I whispered, "Fake like I knocked you out, you can have the prize."

"I'll break your behind," he whispered hoarsely.

"For *them?*"   30

"For *me*, sonofabitch!"

They were yelling for us to break it up and Tatlock spun me half around with a blow, and as a joggled camera sweeps in a reeling scene, I saw the howling red faces crouching tense beneath the cloud of blue-gray smoke. For a moment the world wavered, unraveled, flowed, then my head cleared and Tatlock bounced before me.

That fluttering shadow before my eyes was his jabbing left hand. Then falling forward, my head against his damp shoulder, I whispered,

"I'll make it five dollars more."

"Go to hell!"

But his muscles relaxed a trifle beneath my pressure and I breathed, "Seven?" 35

"Give it to your ma," he said, ripping me beneath the heart.

And while I still held him I butted him and moved away. I felt myself bombarded with punches. I fought back with hopeless desperation. I wanted to deliver my speech more than anything else in the world, because I felt that only these men could judge truly my ability, and now this stupid clown was ruining my chances. I began fighting carefully now, moving in to punch him and out again with my greater speed. A lucky blow to his chin and I had him going too—until I heard a loud voice yell, "I got my money on the big boy."

Hearing this, I almost dropped my guard. I was confused: Should I try to win against the voice out there? Would not this go against my speech, and was not this a moment for humility, for nonresistance? A blow to my head as I danced about sent my right eye popping like a jack-in-the-box and settled my dilemma. The room went red as I fell. It was a dream fall, my body languid and fastidious as to where to land, until the floor became impatient and smashed up to meet me. A moment later I came to. An hypnotic voice said FIVE emphatically. And I lay there, hazily watching a dark red spot of my own blood shaping itself into a butterfly, glistening and soaking into the soiled gray world of the canvas.

When the voice drawled TEN I was lifted up and dragged to a chair. I sat dazed. My eye pained and swelled with each throb of my pounding heart and I wondered if now I would be allowed to speak. I was wringing wet, my mouth still bleeding. We were grouped along the wall now. The other boys ignored me as they congratulated Tatlock and speculated as to how much they would be paid. One boy whimpered over his smashed hand. Looking up front, I saw attendants in white jackets rolling the portable ring away and placing a small square rug in the vacant space surrounded by chairs. Perhaps, I thought, I will stand on the rug to deliver my speech.

Then the M.C. called to us. "Come on up here boys and get your money." 40

We ran forward to where the men laughed and talked in their chairs, waiting. Everyone seemed friendly now.

"There it is on the rug," the man said. I saw the rug covered with coins of all dimensions and a few crumpled bills. But what excited me, scattered here and there, were the gold pieces.

"Boys, it's all yours," the man said. "You get all you grab."

"That's right, Sambo," a blond man said, winking at me confidentially.

I trembled with excitement, forgetting my pain. I would get the gold and the 45
bills, I thought. I would use both hands. I would throw my body against the boys nearest me to block them from the gold.

"Get down around the rug now," the man commanded, "and don't anyone touch it until I give the signal."

"This ought to be good," I heard.

As told, we got around the square rug on our knees. Slowly the man raised his freckled hand as we followed it upward with our eyes.

I heard, "These niggers look like they're about to pray!"

Then, "Ready," the man said. "Go!" 50

I lunged for a yellow coin lying on the blue design of the carpet, touching it and sending a surprised shriek to join those rising around me. I tried frantically to remove my hand but could not let go. A hot, violent force tore through my body, shaking me like a wet rat. The rug was electrified. The hair bristled up on my head as I shook myself free. My muscles jumped, my nerves jangled, writhed. But I saw that this was not stopping the other boys. Laughing in fear and embarrassment, some were holding back and scooping up the coins knocked off by the painful contortions of others. The men roared above us as we struggled.

"Pick it up, goddamnit, pick it up!" someone called like a bass-voiced parrot. "Go on, get it!"

I crawled rapidly around the floor, picking up the coins, trying to avoid the coppers and to get greenbacks and the gold. Ignoring the shock by laughing, as I brushed the coins off quickly, I discovered that I could contain the electricity—a contradiction, but it works. Then the men began to push us onto the rug. Laughing embarrassedly, we struggled out of their hands and kept after the coins. We were all wet and slippery and hard to hold. Suddenly I saw a boy lifted into the air, glistening with sweat like a circus seal, and dropped, his wet back landing flush upon the charged rug, heard him yell and saw him literally dance upon his back, his elbows beating a frenzied tattoo upon the floor, his muscles twitching like the flesh of a horse stung by many flies. When he finally rolled off, his face was gray and no one stopped him when he ran from the floor amid booming laughter.

"Get the money," the M.C. called. "That's good hard American cash!"

And we snatched and grabbed, snatched and grabbed. I was careful not to come 55 too close to the rug now, and when I felt the hot whiskey breath descend upon me like a cloud of foul air I reached out and grabbed the leg of a chair. It was occupied and I held on desperately.

"Leggo, nigger! Leggo!"

The huge face wavered down to mine as he tried to push me free. But my body was slippery and he was too drunk. It was Mr. Colcord, who owned a chain of movie houses and "entertainment palaces." Each time he grabbed me I slipped out of his hands. It became a real struggle. I feared the rug more than I did the drunk, so I held on, surprising myself for a moment by trying to topple *him* upon the rug. It was such an enormous idea that I found myself actually carrying it out. I tried not to be obvious, yet when I grabbed his leg, trying to tumble him out of the chair, he raised up roaring with laughter, and, looking at me with soberness dead in the eye, kicked me viciously in the chest. The chair leg flew out of my hand and I felt myself going and rolled. It was as though I had rolled through a bed of hot coals. It seemed a whole century would pass before I would roll free, a century in which I was seared through the deepest levels of my body to the fearful breath within me and the breath seared and heated to the point of explosion. It'll all be over in a flash, I thought as I rolled clear. It'll all be over in a flash.

But not yet, the men on the other side were waiting, red faces swollen as though from apoplexy as they bent forward in their chairs. Seeing their fingers coming toward me I rolled away as a fumbled football rolls off the receiver's fingertips, back into the coals. That time I luckily sent the rug sliding out of place and heard the coins ringing against the floor and the boys scuffling to pick them up and the M.C. calling, "All right, boys, that's all. Go get dressed and get your money."

I was limp as a dish rag. My back felt as though it had been beaten with wires.

When we had dressed the M.C. came in and gave us each five dollars, except   60
Tatlock, who got ten for being the last in the ring. Then he told us to leave. I was not
to get a chance to deliver my speech, I thought. I was going out into the dim alley in
despair when I was stopped and told to go back. I returned to the ballroom, where the
men were pushing back their chairs and gathering in small groups to talk.

The M.C. knocked on a table for quiet. "Gentlemen," he said, "we almost forgot
an important part of the program. A most serious part, gentlemen. This boy was
brought here to deliver a speech which he made at his graduation yesterday . . ."

"Bravo!"

"I'm told that he is the smartest boy we've got out there in Greenwood. I'm told
that he knows more big words than a pocket-sized dictionary."

Much applause and laughter.

"So now, gentlemen, I want you to give him your attention."   65

There was still laughter as I faced them, my mouth dry, my eyes throbbing. I began slowly, but evidently my throat was tense, because they began shouting, "Louder!
Louder!"

"We of the younger generation extol the wisdom of that great leader and educa-
tor," I shouted, "who first spoke these flaming words of wisdom: 'A ship lost at sea for
many days suddenly sighted a friendly vessel. From the mast of the unfortunate vessel
was seen a signal: "Water, water; we die of thirst!" The answer from the friendly vessel came back: "Cast down your bucket where you are." The captain of the distressed
vessel, at last heeding the injunction, cast down his bucket, and it came up full of
fresh sparkling water from the mouth of the Amazon River.' And like him I say, and
in his words, 'To those of my race who depend upon bettering their condition in a
foreign land, or who underestimate the importance of cultivating friendly relations
with the Southern white man, who is his next-door neighbor, I would say: "Cast
down your bucket where you are"—cast it down in making friends in every manly
way of the people of all races by whom we are surrounded . . .'"

I spoke automatically and with such fervor that I did not realize that the men
were still talking and laughing until my dry mouth, filling up with blood from the cut,
almost strangled me. I coughed, wanting to stop and go to one of the tall brass, sand-
filled spittoons to relieve myself, but a few of the men, especially the superintendent,
were listening and I was afraid. So I gulped it down, blood, saliva and all, and continued. (What powers of endurance I had during those days! What enthusiasm! What a
belief in the rightness of things!) I spoke even louder in spite of the pain. But still
they talked and still they laughed, as though deaf with cotton in dirty ears. So I spoke
with greater emotional emphasis. I closed my ears and swallowed blood until I was
nauseated. The speech seemed a hundred times as long as before, but I could not
leave out a single word. All had to be said, each memorized nuance considered, rendered. Nor was that all. Whenever I uttered a word of three or more syllables a group
of voices would yell for me to repeat it. I used the phrase "social responsibility" and
they yelled:

"What's that word you say, boy?"

"Social responsibility," I said.   70

"What?"

"Social . . ."

"Louder."

". . . responsibility."

"More!" 75

"Respon—"

"Repeat!"

"—sibility."

The room filled with the uproar of laughter until, no doubt, distracted by having to gulp down my blood, I made a mistake and yelled a phrase I had often seen denounced in newspaper editorials, heard debated in private.

"Social . . ." 80

"What?" they yelled.

". . . equality—"

The laughter hung smokelike in the sudden stillness. I opened my eyes, puzzled. Sounds of displeasure filled the room. The M.C. rushed forward. They shouted hostile phrases at me. But I did not understand.

A small dry mustached man in the front row blared out, "Say that slowly, son!"

"What, sir?" 85

"What you just said!"

"Social responsibility, sir," I said.

"You weren't being smart, were you, boy?" he said, not unkindly.

"No, sir!"

"You sure that about 'equality' was a mistake?" 90

"Oh, yes, sir," I said. "I was swallowing blood."

"Well, you had better speak more slowly so we can understand. We mean to do right by you, but you've got to know your place at all times. All right, now, go on with your speech."

I was afraid. I wanted to leave but I wanted also to speak and I was afraid they'd snatch me down.

"Thank you, sir," I said, beginning where I had left off, and having them ignore me as before.

Yet when I finished there was a thunderous applause. I was surprised to see the 95 superintendent come forth with a package wrapped in white tissue paper, and, gesturing for quiet, address the men.

"Gentlemen, you see that I did not overpraise the boy. He makes a good speech and some day he'll lead his people in the proper paths. And I don't have to tell you that that is important in these days and times. This is a good, smart boy, and so to encourage him in the right direction, in the name of the Board of Education I wish to present him a prize in the form of this . . ."

He paused, removing the tissue paper and revealing a gleaming calfskin brief case.

". . . in the form of this first-class article from Shad Whitmore's shop."

"Boy," he said, addressing me, "take this prize and keep it well. Consider it a badge of office. Prize it. Keep developing as you are and some day it will be filled with important papers that will help shape the destiny of your people."

I was so moved that I could hardly express my thanks. A rope of bloody saliva 100 forming a shape like an undiscovered continent drooled upon the leather and I wiped it quickly away. I felt an importance that I had never dreamed.

"Open it and see what's inside," I was told.

My fingers a-tremble, I complied, smelling fresh leather and finding an official-looking document inside. It was a scholarship to the state college for Negroes. My eyes filled with tears and I ran awkwardly off the floor.

I was overjoyed; I did not even mind when I discovered the gold pieces I had scrambled for were brass pocket tokens advertising a certain make of automobile.

When I reached home everyone was excited. Next day the neighbors came to congratulate me. I even felt safe from grandfather, whose deathbed curse usually spoiled my triumphs. I stood beneath his photograph with my brief case in hand and smiled triumphantly into his stolid black peasant's face. It was a face that fascinated me. The eyes seemed to follow everywhere I went.

That night I dreamed I was at a circus with him and that he refused to laugh at 105 the clowns no matter what they did. Then later he told me to open my brief case and read what was inside and I did, finding an official envelope stamped with the state seal; and inside the envelope I found another and another, endlessly, and I thought I would fall of weariness. "Them's years," he said. "Now open that one." And I did and in it I found an engraved stamp containing a short message in letters of gold. "Read it," my grandfather said. "Out loud."

"To Whom It May Concern," I intoned. "Keep This Nigger-Boy Running."

I awoke with the old man's laughter ringing in my ears.

Zora Neale Hurston

Sweat

1926

Zora Neale Hurston (1901?–1960) was born in Eatonville, Florida, but no record of her actual date of birth exists (best guesses range from 1891 to 1901). Hurston was one of eight children. Her father, a carpenter and Baptist preacher, was also the three-term mayor of Eatonville, the first all-black town incorporated in the United States. When Hurston's mother died in 1912, the father moved the children from one relative to another. Consequently, Hurston never finished grammar school, although in 1918 she began taking classes at Howard University, paying her way through school by working as a manicurist and maid. While at Howard, she published her first story. In early 1925 she moved to New York, arriving with "$1.50, no

Zora Neale Hurston

job, no friends, and a lot of hope." She soon became an important member of the Harlem Renaissance, a group of young black artists (including Langston Hughes, Countee Cullen, Jean Toomer, and Claude McKay) who sought "spiritual emancipation" for African Americans by exploring black heritage and identity in the arts. Hurston eventually became, according to critic Laura Zaidman, "the most prolific black American woman writer of her time." In 1925 she became the first African American student at Barnard College, where she completed a B.A. in anthropology. Hurston's most famous story, "Sweat," appeared in the only issue of Fire!!, a 1926 avant-garde Harlem Renaissance magazine edited by Hurston, Hughes, and Wallace Thurman. This powerful story of an unhappy marriage turned murderous was particularly noteworthy for having the characters speak in the black country dialect of Hurston's native Florida. Hurston achieved only modest success during her lifetime, despite the publication of her memorable novel Their Eyes Were Watching God *(1937) and her many contributions to the study of African American folklore. She died, poor and*

*neglected, in a Florida welfare home and was buried in an unmarked grave. In 1973 novelist
Alice Walker erected a gravestone for her carved with the words:*

> *Zora Neale Hurston*
> *"A Genius of the South"*
> *1901–1960*
> *Novelist, Folklorist*
> *Anthropologist*

I

It was eleven o'clock of a Spring night in Florida. It was Sunday. Any other
night, Delia Jones would have been in bed for two hours by this time. But she was a
washwoman, and Monday morning meant a great deal to her. So she collected the
soiled clothes on Saturday when she returned the clean things. Sunday night after
church, she sorted and put the white things to soak. It saved her almost a half-day's
start. A great hamper in the bedroom held the clothes that she brought home. It was
so much neater than a number of bundles lying around.

She squatted on the kitchen floor beside the great pile of clothes, sorting them into
small heaps according to color, and humming a song in a mournful key, but wondering
through it all where Sykes, her husband, had gone with her horse and buckboard.°

Just then something long, round, limp, and black fell upon her shoulders and
slithered to the floor beside her. A great terror took hold of her. It softened her knees
and dried her mouth so that it was a full minute before she could cry out or move.
Then she saw that it was the big bull whip her husband liked to carry when he drove.

She lifted her eyes to the door and saw him standing there bent over with
laughter at her fright. She screamed at him.

"Sykes, what you throw dat whip on me like dat? You know it would skeer me—   5
looks just like a snake, an' you knows how skeered Ah is of snakes."

"Course Ah knowed it! That's how come Ah done it." He slapped his leg with
his hand and almost rolled on the ground in his mirth. "If you such a big fool dat you
got to have a fit over a earth worm or a string, Ah don't keer how bad Ah skeer you."

"You ain't got no business doing it. Gawd knows it's a sin. Some day Ah'm gointuh drop dead from some of yo' foolishness. 'Nother thing, where you been wid mah
rig? Ah feeds dat pony. He ain't fuh you to be drivin' wid no bull whip."

"You sho' is one aggravatin' nigger woman!" he declared and stepped into the
room. She resumed her work and did not answer him at once. "Ah done tole you
time and again to keep them white folks' clothes outa dis house."

He picked up the whip and glared at her. Delia went on with her work. She went
out into the yard and returned with a galvanized tub and set it on the wash-bench.
She saw that Sykes had kicked all of the clothes together again, and now stood in her
way truculently, his whole manner hoping, *praying,* for an argument. But she walked
calmly around him and commenced to re-sort the things.

"Next time, Ah'm gointer kick 'em outdoors," he threatened as he struck a   10
match along the leg of his corduroy breeches.

Delia never looked up from her work, and her thin, stooped shoulders sagged further.

"Ah ain't for no fuss t'night Sykes. Ah just come from taking sacrament at the
church house."

---

buckboard: a four-wheeled open carriage with the seat resting on a spring platform.

He snorted scornfully. "Yeah, you just come from de church house on a Sunday night, but heah you is gone to work on them clothes. You ain't nothing but a hypocrite. One of them amen-corner Christians—sing, whoop, and shout, then come home and wash white folks' clothes on the Sabbath."

He stepped roughly upon the whitest pile of things, kicking them helter-skelter as he crossed the room. His wife gave a little scream of dismay, and quickly gathered them together again.

"Sykes, you quit grindin' dirt into these clothes! How can Ah git through by   15
Sat'day if Ah don't start on Sunday?"

"Ah don't keer if you never git through. Anyhow, Ah done promised Gawd and a couple of other men, Ah ain't gointer have it in mah house. Don't gimme no lip neither, else Ah'll throw 'em out and put mah fist up side yo' head to boot."

Delia's habitual meekness seemed to slip from her shoulders like a blown scarf. She was on her feet; her poor little body, her bare knuckly hands bravely defying the strapping hulk before her.

"Looka heah, Sykes, you done gone too fur. Ah been married to you fur fifteen years, and Ah been takin' in washin' fur fifteen years. Sweat, sweat, sweat! Work and sweat, cry and sweat, pray and sweat!"

"What's that got to do with me?" he asked brutally.

"What's it got to do with you, Sykes? Mah tub of suds is filled yo' belly with vit-   20
tles more times than yo' hands is filled it. Mah sweat is done paid for this house and Ah reckon Ah kin keep on sweatin' in it."

She seized the iron skillet from the stove and struck a defensive pose, which act surprised him greatly, coming from her. It cowed him and he did not strike her as he usually did.

"Naw you won't," she panted, "that ole snaggle-toothed black woman you runnin' with ain't comin' heah to pile up on *mah* sweat and blood. You ain't paid for nothin' on this place, and Ah'm gointer stay right heah till Ah'm toted out foot foremost."

"Well, you better quit gittin' me riled up, else they'll be totin' you out sooner than you expect. Ah'm so tired of you Ah don't know whut to do. Gawd! How Ah hates skinny wimmen!"

A little awed by this new Delia, he sidled out of the door and slammed the back gate after him. He did not say where he had gone, but she knew too well. She knew very well that he would not return until nearly daybreak also. Her work over, she went on to bed but not to sleep at once. Things had come to a pretty pass!

She lay awake, gazing upon the debris that cluttered their matrimonial trail. Not   25
an image left standing along the way. Anything like flowers had long ago been drowned in the salty stream that had been pressed from her heart. Her tears, her sweat, her blood. She had brought love to the union and he had brought a longing after the flesh. Two months after the wedding, he had given her the first brutal beating. She had the memory of his numerous trips to Orlando with all of his wages when he had returned to her penniless, even before the first year had passed. She was young and soft then, but now she thought of her knotty, muscled limbs, her harsh knuckly hands, and drew herself up into an unhappy little ball in the middle of the big feather bed. Too late now to hope for love, even if it were not Bertha it would be someone else. This case differed from the others only in that she was bolder than the others. Too late for everything except her little home. She had built it for her old days, and planted one by one the trees and flowers there. It was lovely to her, lovely.

Somehow, before sleep came, she found herself saying aloud: "Oh well, whatever goes over the Devil's back, is got to come under his belly. Sometime or ruther, Sykes, like everybody else, is gointer reap his sowing." After that she was able to build a spiritual earthworks° against her husband. His shells could no longer reach her. AMEN. She went to sleep and slept until he announced his presence in bed by kicking her feet and rudely snatching the covers away.

"Gimme some kivah heah, an' git yo' damn foots over on yo' own side! Ah oughter mash you in yo' mouf fuh drawing dat skillet on me."

Delia went clear to the rail without answering him. A triumphant indifference to all that he was or did.

II

The week was full of work for Delia as all other weeks, and Saturday found her behind her little pony, collecting and delivering clothes.

It was a hot, hot day near the end of July. The village men on Joe Clarke's porch even chewed cane listlessly. They did not hurl the cane-knots as usual. They let them dribble over the edge of the porch. Even conversation had collapsed under the heat. 30

"Heah come Delia Jones," Jim Merchant said, as the shaggy pony came 'round the bend of the road toward them. The rusty buckboard was heaped with baskets of crisp, clean laundry.

"Yep," Joe Lindsay agreed. "Hot or col', rain or shine, jes'ez reg'lar ez de weeks roll roun' Delia carries 'em an' fetches 'em on Sat'day."

"She better if she wanter eat," said Moss. "Syke Jones ain't wuth de shot an' powder hit would tek tuh kill 'im. Not to *huh* he ain't."

"He sho' ain't," Walter Thomas chimed in. "It's too bad, too, cause she wuz a right pretty li'l trick when he got huh. Ah'd uh mah'ied huh mahself if he hadnter beat me to it."

Delia nodded briefly at the men as she drove past. 35

"Too much knockin' will ruin *any* 'oman. He done beat huh 'nough tuh kill three women, let 'lone change they looks," said Elijah Moseley. "How Syke kin stommuck dat big black greasy Mogul he's layin' roun' wid, gits me. Ah swear dat eight-rock couldn't kiss a sardine can Ah done thowed out de back do' 'way las' yeah."

"Aw, she's fat, thass how come. He's allus been crazy 'bout fat women," put in Merchant. "He'd a' been tied up wid one long time ago if he could a' found one tuh have him. Did Ah tell yuh 'bout him come sidlin' roun' *mah* wife—bringin' her a basket uh peecans outa his yard fuh a present? Yessir, mah wife! She tol' him tuh take 'em right straight back home, 'cause Delia works so hard ovah dat washtub she reckon everything on de place taste lak sweat an' soapsuds. Ah jus' wisht Ah'd a' caught 'im 'roun' dere! Ah'd a' made his hips ketch on fiah down dat shell road."

"Ah know he done it, too. Ah sees 'im grinnin' at every 'oman dat passes," Walter Thomas said. "But even so, he useter eat some mighty big hunks uh humble pie tuh git dat li'l 'oman he got. She wuz ez pritty ez a speckled pup! Dat wuz fifteen years ago. He useter be so skeered uh losin' huh, she could make him do some parts of a husband's duty. Dey never wuz de same in de mind."

"There oughter be a law about him," said Lindsay. "He ain't fit tuh carry guts tuh a bear."

---

spiritual earthworks: earthworks are military fortifications made of earth; here Hurston uses it metaphorically to mean Delia's emotional defenses.

Clarke spoke for the first time. "Tain't no law on earth dat kin make a man be   40
decent if it ain't in 'im. There's plenty men dat takes a wife lak dey do a joint uh
sugar-cane. It's round, juicy, an' sweet when dey gits it. But dey squeeze an' grind,
squeeze an' grind an' wring tell dey wring every drop uh pleasure dat's in 'em out.
When dey's satisfied dat dey is wrung dry, dey treats 'em jes' lak dey do a cane-chew.
Dey thows 'em away. Dey knows whut dey is doin' while dey is at it, an' hates theirselves fuh it but they keeps on hangin' after huh tell she's empty. Den dey hates huh
fuh bein' a cane-chew an' in de way."

"We oughter take Syke an' dat stray 'oman uh his'n down in Lake Howell swamp
an' lay on de rawhide till they cain't say Lawd a' mussy. He allus wuz uh ovahbearin
niggah, but since dat white 'oman from up north done teached 'im how to run a automobile, he done got too biggety to live—an' we oughter kill 'im," Old Man Anderson
advised.

A grunt of approval went around the porch. But the heat was melting their civic
virtue and Elijah Moseley began to bait Joe Clarke.

"Come on, Joe, git a melon outa dere an' slice it up for yo' customers. We'se all
sufferin' wid de heat. De bear's done got *me!*"

"Thass right, Joe, a watermelon is jes' whut Ah needs tuh cure de eppizudicks,"
Walter Thomas joined forces with Moseley. "Come on dere, Joe. We all is steady customers an' you ain't set us up in a long time. Ah chooses dat long, bowlegged Floridy
favorite."

"A god, an' be dough. You all gimme twenty cents and slice away," Clarke   45
retorted. "Ah needs a col' slice m'self. Heah, everybody chip in. Ah'll lend y'all mah
meat knife."

The money was all quickly subscribed and the huge melon brought forth. At that
moment, Sykes and Bertha arrived. A determined silence fell on the porch and the
melon was put away again.

Merchant snapped down the blade of his jackknife and moved toward the store
door.

"Come on in, Joe, an' gimme a slab uh sow belly an' uh pound uh coffee—almost
fuhgot 'twas Sat'day. Got to git on home." Most of the men left also.

Just then Delia drove past on her way home, as Sykes was ordering magnificently
for Bertha. It pleased him for Delia to see.

"Git whutsoever yo' heart desires, Honey. Wait a minute, Joe. Give huh two   50
bottles uh strawberry soda-water, uh quart parched ground-peas, an' a block uh
chewin' gum."

With all this they left the store, with Sykes reminding Bertha that this was his
town and she could have it if she wanted it.

The men returned soon after they left, and held their watermelon feast.

"Where did Syke Jones git da 'oman from nohow?" Lindsay asked.

"Ovah Apopka. Guess dey musta been cleanin' out de town when she lef'. She
don't look lak a thing but a hunk uh liver wid hair on it."

"Well, she sho' kin squall," Dave Carter contributed. "When she gits ready tuh   55
laff, she jes' opens huh mouf an' latches it back tuh de las' notch. No ole granpa
alligator down in Lake Bell ain't got nothin' on huh."

III

Bertha had been in town three months now. Sykes was still paying her room-
rent at Della Lewis'—the only house in town that would have taken her in. Sykes

took her frequently to Winter Park to "stomps." He still assured her that he was the swellest man in the state.

"Sho' you kin have dat li'l ole house soon's Ah git dat 'oman outadere. Everything b'longs tuh me an' you sho' kin have it. Ah sho' 'bominates uh skinny 'oman. Lawdy, you sho' is got one portly shape on you! You kin git *anything* you wants. Dis is *mah* town an' you sho' kin have it."

Delia's work-worn knees crawled over the earth in Gethsemane° and up the rocks of Calvary° many, many times during these months. She avoided the villagers and meeting places in her efforts to be blind and deaf. But Bertha nullified this to a degree, by coming to Delia's house to call Sykes out to her at the gate.

Delia and Sykes fought all the time now with no peaceful interludes. They slept and ate in silence. Two or three times Delia had attempted a timid friendliness, but she was repulsed each time. It was plain that the breaches must remain agape.

The sun had burned July to August. The heat streamed down like a million hot   60
arrows, smiting all things living upon the earth. Grass withered, leaves browned, snakes went blind in shedding, and men and dogs went mad. Dog days!

Delia came home one day and found Sykes there before her. She wondered, but started to go on into the house without speaking, even though he was standing in the kitchen door and she must either stoop under his arm or ask him to move. He made no room for her. She noticed a soap box beside the steps, but paid no particular attention to it, knowing that he must have brought it there. As she was stooping to pass under his outstretched arm, he suddenly pushed her backward, laughingly.

"Look in de box dere, Delia, Ah done brung yuh somethin'!"

She nearly fell upon the box in her stumbling, and when she saw what it held, she all but fainted outright.

"Syke! Syke, mah Gawd! You take dat rattlesnake 'way from heah! You *gottuh.* Oh, Jesus, have mussy!"

"Ah ain't got tuh do nuthin' uh de kin'—fact is Ah ain't got tuh do nothin'   65
but die. Tain't no use uh you puttin' on airs makin' out lak you skeered uh dat snake—he's gointer stay right heah tell he die. He wouldn't bite me cause Ah knows how tuh handle 'im. Nohow he wouldn't risk breakin' out his fangs 'gin yo skinny laigs."

"Naw, now Syke, don't keep dat thing 'round tryin' tuh skeer me tuh death. You knows Ah'm even feared uh earth worms. Thass de biggest snake Ah evah did see. Kill 'im, Syke, please."

"Doan ast me tuh do nothin' fuh yuh. Goin' 'round tryin' tuh be so damn asterperious.° Naw, Ah ain't gonna kill it. Ah think uh damn sight mo' uh him dan you! Dat's a nice snake an' anybody doan lak 'im kin jes' hit de grit."

The village soon heard that Sykes had the snake, and came to see and ask questions.

"How de hen-fire did you ketch dat six-foot rattler, Syke?" Thomas asked.

"He's full uh frogs so he cain't hardly move, thass how Ah eased up on 'im. But   70
Ah'm a snake charmer an' knows how tuh handle 'em. Shux, dat ain't nothin'. Ah could ketch one eve'y day if Ah so wanted tuh."

Gethsemane: the garden outside Jerusalem that was the scene of Jesus' agony and arrest (see Matthew 26:36–57); hence, a scene of great suffering.   *Calvary:* the hill outside Jerusalem where Jesus was crucified.   *asterperious:* haughty.

"Whut he needs is a heavy hick'ry club leaned real heavy on his head. Dat's de bes' way tuh charm a rattlesnake."

"Naw, Walt, y'all jes' don't understand dese diamon' backs lak Ah do," said Sykes in a superior tone of voice.

The village agreed with Walter, but the snake stayed on. His box remained by the kitchen door with its screen wire covering. Two or three days later it had digested its meal of frogs and literally came to life. It rattled at every movement in the kitchen or the yard. One day as Delia came down the kitchen steps she saw his chalky-white fangs curved like scimitars hung in the wire meshes. This time she did not run away with averted eyes as usual. She stood for a long time in the doorway in a red fury that grew bloodier for every second that she regarded the creature that was her torment.

That night she broached the subject as soon as Sykes sat down to the table.

"Syke, Ah wants you tuh take dat snake 'way fum heah. You done starved me an' Ah put up widcher, you done beat me an Ah took dat, but you done kilt all mah insides bringin' dat varmint heah." 75

Sykes poured out a saucer full of coffee and drank it deliberately before he answered her.

"A whole lot Ah keer 'bout how you feels inside uh out. Dat snake ain't goin' no damn wheah till Ah gits ready fuh 'im tuh go. So fur as beatin' is concerned, yuh ain't took near all dat you gointer take ef yuh stay 'round *me*."

Delia pushed back her plate and got up from the table. "Ah hates you, Sykes," she said calmly. "Ah hates you tuh de same degree dat Ah useter love yuh. Ah done took an' took till mah belly is full up tuh mah neck. Dat's de reason Ah got mah letter fum de church an' moved mah membership tuh Woodbridge—so Ah don't haftuh take no sacrament wid yuh. Ah don't wantuh see yuh 'round me atall. Lay 'round wid dat 'oman all yuh wants tuh, but gwan 'way fum me an' mah house. Ah hates yuh lak uh suck-egg dog."

Sykes almost let the huge wad of corn bread and collard greens he was chewing fall out of his mouth in amazement. He had a hard time whipping himself up to the proper fury to try to answer Delia.

"Well, Ah'm glad you does hate me. Ah'm sho' tiahed uh you hangin' ontuh me. Ah don't want yuh. Look at yuh stringey ole neck! Yo' rawbony laigs an' arms is enough tuh cut uh man tuh death. You looks jes' lak de devvul's doll-baby tuh *me*. You cain't hate me no worse dan Ah hates you. Ah been hatin' *you* fuh years." 80

"Yo' ole black hide don't look lak nothin' tuh me, but uh passle uh wrinkled up rubber, wid yo' big ole yeahs flappin' on each side lak uh paih uh buzzard wings. Don't think Ah'm gointuh be run 'way fum mah house neither. Ah'm goin' tuh de white folks 'bout *you*, mah young man, de very nex' time you lay yo' han's on me. Mah cup is done run ovah." Delia said this with no signs of fear and Sykes departed from the house, threatening her, but made not the slightest move to carry out any of them.

That night he did not return at all, and the next day being Sunday, Delia was glad she did not have to quarrel before she hitched up her pony and drove the four miles to Woodbridge.

She stayed to the night service—"love feast"—which was very warm and full of spirit. In the emotional winds her domestic trials were borne far and wide so that she sang as she drove homeward,

> *Jurden water,° black an' col*
> *Chills de body, not de soul*
> *An' Ah wantah cross Jurden in uh calm time.*

She came from the barn to the kitchen door and stopped.

"Whut's de mattah, ol' Satan, you ain't kickin' up yo' racket?" She addressed the snake's box. Complete silence. She went on into the house with a new hope in its birth struggles. Perhaps her threat to go to the white folks had frightened Sykes! Perhaps he was sorry! Fifteen years of misery and suppression had brought Delia to the place where she would hope *anything* that looked towards a way over or through her wall of inhibitions.

She felt in the match-safe behind the stove at once for a match. There was only one there.   85

"Dat niggah wouldn't fetch nothin' heah tuh save his rotten neck, but he kin run thew whut Ah brings quick enough. Now he done toted off nigh on tuh haff uh box uh matches. He done had dat 'oman heah in mah house, too."

Nobody but a woman could tell how she knew this even before she struck the match. But she did and it put her into a new fury.

Presently she brought in the tubs to put the white things to soak. This time she decided she need not bring the hamper out of the bedroom; she would go in there and do the sorting. She picked up the pot-bellied lamp and went in. The room was small and the hamper stood hard by the foot of the white iron bed. She could sit and reach through the bedposts—resting as she worked.

"*Ah wantah cross Jurden in uh calm time.*" She was singing again. The mood of the "love feast" had returned. She threw back the lid of the basket almost gaily. Then, moved by both horror and terror, she sprang back toward the door. *There lay the snake in the basket!* He moved sluggishly at first, but even as she turned round and round, jumped up and down in an insanity of fear, he began to stir vigorously. She saw him pouring his awful beauty from the basket upon the bed, then she seized the lamp and ran as fast as she could to the kitchen. The wind from the open door blew out the light and the darkness added to her terror. She sped to the darkness of the yard, slamming the door after her before she thought to set down the lamp. She did not feel safe even on the ground, so she climbed up in the hay barn.

There for an hour or more she lay sprawled upon the hay a gibbering wreck.   90

Finally she grew quiet, and after that came coherent thought. With this stalked through her a cold, bloody rage. Hours of this. A period of introspection, a space of retrospection, then a mixture of both. Out of this an awful calm.

"Well, Ah done de bes' Ah could. If things ain't right, Gawd knows tain't mah fault."

She went to sleep—a twitch sleep—and woke up to a faint gray sky. There was a loud hollow sound below. She peered out. Sykes was at the wood-pile, demolishing a wire-covered box.

He hurried to the kitchen door, but hung outside there some minutes before he entered, and stood some minutes more inside before he closed it after him.

Jurden water: black Southern dialect for the River Jordan, which represents the last boundary before entering heaven. It comes from the Old Testament, when the Jews had to cross the River Jordan to reach the Promised Land.

The gray in the sky was spreading. Delia descended without fear now, and 95
crouched beneath the low bedroom window. The drawn shade shut out the dawn,
shut in the night. But the thin walls held back no sound.

"Dat ol' scratch° is woke up now!" She mused at the tremendous whirr inside,
which every woodsman knows, is one of the sound illusions. The rattler is a ventriloquist. His whirr sounds to the right, to the left, straight ahead, behind, close under
foot—everywhere but where it is. Woe to him who guesses wrong unless he is prepared
to hold up his end of the argument! Sometimes he strikes without rattling at all.

Inside, Sykes heard nothing until he knocked a pot lid off the stove while trying
to reach the match-safe in the dark. He had emptied his pockets at Bertha's.

The snake seemed to wake up under the stove and Sykes made a quick leap into
the bedroom. In spite of the gin he had had, his head was clearing now.

"Mah Gawd!" he chattered, "ef Ah could on'y strack uh light!"

The rattling ceased for a moment as he stood paralyzed. He waited. It seemed 100
that the snake waited also.

"Oh, fuh de light! Ah thought he'd be too sick"—Sykes was muttering to himself
when the whirr began again, closer, right underfoot this time. Long before this,
Sykes' ability to think had been flattened down to primitive instinct and he leaped—
onto the bed.

Outside Delia heard a cry that might have come from a maddened chimpanzee, a
stricken gorilla. All the terror, all the horror, all the rage that man possibly could express, without a recognizable human sound.

A tremendous stir inside there, another series of animal screams, the intermittent whirr of the reptile. The shade torn violently down from the window, letting in
the red dawn, a huge brown hand seizing the window stick, great dull blows upon the
wooden floor punctuating the gibberish of sound long after the rattle of the snake
had abruptly subsided. All this Delia could see and hear from her place beneath the
window, and it made her ill. She crept over to the four-o'clocks and stretched herself
on the cool earth to recover.

She lay there. "Delia, Delia!" She could hear Sykes calling in a most despairing
tone as one who expected no answer. The sun crept on up, and he called. Delia could
not move—her legs had gone flabby. She never moved, he called, and the sun kept
rising.

"Mah Gawd!" She heard him moan, "Mah Gawd fum Heben!" She heard 105
him stumbling about and got up from her flower-bed. The sun was growing warm.
As she approached the door she heard him call out hopefully, "Delia, is dat you
Ah heah?"

She saw him on his hands and knees as soon as she reached the door. He crept
an inch or two toward her—all that he was able, and she saw his horribly swollen
neck and his one open eye shining with hope. A surge of pity too strong to support
bore her away from that eye that must, could not, fail to see the tubs. He would see
the lamp. Orlando with its doctors was too far. She could scarcely reach the chinaberry tree, where she waited in the growing heat while inside she knew the cold river
was creeping up and up to extinguish that eye which must know by now that she
knew.

---

scratch: a folk expression for the devil.

James Joyce

Araby

1914

James Joyce (1882–1941) quit Ireland at twenty to spend his mature life in voluntary exile on the continent, writing of nothing but Dublin, where he was born. In Trieste, Zurich, and Paris, he supported his family with difficulty, sometimes teaching in Berlitz language schools, until his writing won him fame and wealthy patrons. At first Joyce met difficulty in getting his work printed and circulated. Publication of Dubliners *(1914), the collection of stories that includes "Araby," was delayed seven years because its prospective Irish publisher feared libel suits. (The book depicts local citizens, some of them recognizable, and views Dubliners mostly as a thwarted, self-deceived lot.) A Portrait of*

James Joyce

the Artist as a Young Man *(1916), a novel of thinly veiled autobiography, recounts a young intellectual's breaking away from country, church, and home. Joyce's immense comic novel* Ulysses *(1922), a parody of the Odyssey, spans eighteen hours in the life of a wandering Jew, a Dublin seller of advertising. Frank about sex but untitillating, the book was banned at one time by the U.S. Post Office. Joyce's later work stepped up its demands on readers. The challenging* Finnegans Wake *(1939), if read aloud, sounds as though a learned comic poet were sleep-talking, jumbling several languages. Joyce was an innovator whose bold experiments showed many other writers possibilities in fiction that had not earlier been imagined.*

North Richmond Street, being blind,° was a quiet street except at the hour when the Christian Brothers' School set the boys free. An uninhabited house of two stories stood at the blind end, detached from its neighbors in a square ground. The other houses of the street, conscious of decent lives within them, gazed at one another with brown imperturbable faces.

The former tenant of our house, a priest, had died in the back drawing-room. Air, musty from having been long enclosed, hung in all the rooms, and the waste room behind the kitchen was littered with old useless papers. Among these I found a few paper-covered books, the pages of which were curled and damp: *The Abbot*, by Walter Scott, *The Devout Communicant* and *The Memoirs of Vidocq*.° I liked the last best because its leaves were yellow. The wild garden behind the house contained a central apple-tree and a few straggling bushes under one of which I found the late tenant's rusty bicycle-pump. He had been a very charitable priest: in his will he had left all his money to institutions and the furniture of his house to his sister.

When the short days of winter came dusk fell before we had well eaten our dinners. When we met in the street the houses had grown somber. The space of sky above us was the color of ever-changing violet and towards it the lamps of the street

being blind: being a dead-end street.   *The Abbot . . . Vidocq*: a popular historical romance (1820); a book of pious meditations by an eighteenth-century English Franciscan, Pacificus Baker; and the autobiography of François-Jules Vidocq (1775–1857), a criminal who later turned detective.

lifted their feeble lanterns. The cold air stung us and we played till our bodies glowed. Our shouts echoed in the silent street. The career of our play brought us through the dark muddy lanes behind the houses where we ran the gantlet of the rough tribes from the cottages, to the back doors of the dark dripping gardens where odors arose from the ashpits, to the dark odorous stables where a coachman smoothed and combed the horse or shook music from the buckled harness. When we returned to the street light from the kitchen windows had filled the areas. If my uncle was seen turning the corner we hid in the shadow until we had seen him safely housed. Or if Mangan's sister° came out on the doorstep to call her brother in to his tea we watched her from our shadow peer up and down the street. We waited to see whether she would remain or go in and, if she remained, we left our shadow and walked up to Mangan's steps resignedly. She was waiting for us, her figure defined by the light from the half-opened door. Her brother always teased her before he obeyed and I stood by the railings looking at her. Her dress swung as she moved her body and the soft rope of her hair tossed from side to side.

Every morning I lay on the floor in the front parlor watching her door. The blind was pulled down within an inch of the sash so that I could not be seen. When she came out on the doorstep my heart leaped. I ran to the hall, seized my books and followed her. I kept her brown figure always in my eye and, when we came near the point at which our ways diverged, I quickened my pace and passed her. This happened morning after morning. I had never spoken to her, except for a few casual words, and yet her name was like a summons to all my foolish blood.

Her image accompanied me even in places the most hostile to romance. On Saturday evenings when my aunt went marketing I had to go to carry some of the parcels. We walked through the flaring streets, jostled by drunken men and bargaining women, amid the curses of laborers, the shrill litanies of shopboys who stood on guard by the barrels of pigs' cheeks, the nasal chanting of street-singers, who sang a *come-all-you* about O'Donovan Rossa,° or a ballad about the troubles in our native land. These noises converged in a single sensation of life for me: I imagined that I bore my chalice safely through a throng of foes. Her name sprang to my lips at moments in strange prayers and praises which I myself did not understand. My eyes were often full of tears (I could not tell why) and at times a flood from my heart seemed to pour itself out into my bosom. I thought little of the future. I did not know whether I would ever speak to her or not or, if I spoke to her, how I could tell her of my confused adoration. But my body was like a harp and her words and gestures were like fingers running upon the wires.

One evening I went into the back drawing-room in which the priest had died. It was a dark rainy evening and there was no sound in the house. Through one of the broken panes I heard the rain impinge upon the earth, the fine incessant needles of water playing in the sodden beds. Some distant lamp or lighted window gleamed below me. I was thankful that I could see so little. All my senses seemed to desire to veil themselves and, feeling that I was about to slip from them, I pressed the palms of my hands together until they trembled, murmuring: *O love! O love!* many times.

5

Mangan's sister: an actual young woman in this story, but the phrase recalls Irish poet James Clarence Mangan (1803–1849) and his best-known poem, "Dark Rosaleen," which personifies Ireland as a beautiful woman for whom the poet yearns. *come-all-you about O'Donovan Rossa:* the street singers earned their living by singing timely songs that usually began, "Come all you gallant Irishmen / And listen to my song." Their subject, also called Dynamite Rossa, was a popular hero jailed by the British for advocating violent rebellion.

At last she spoke to me. When she addressed the first words to me I was so confused that I did not know what to answer. She asked me was I going to *Araby*. I forget whether I answered yes or no. It would be a splendid bazaar, she said; she would love to go.

—And why can't you? I asked.

While she spoke she turned a silver bracelet round and round her wrist. She could not go, she said, because there would be a retreat that week in her convent.° Her brother and two other boys were fighting for their caps and I was alone at the railings. She held one of the spikes, bowing her head towards me. The light from the lamp opposite our door caught the white curve of her neck, lit up her hair that rested there and, falling, lit up the hand upon the railing. It fell over one side of her dress and caught the white border of a petticoat, just visible as she stood at ease.

—It's well for you, she said.   10

—If I go, I said, I will bring you something.

What innumerable follies laid waste my waking and sleeping thoughts after that evening! I wished to annihilate the tedious intervening days. I chafed against the work of school. At night in my bedroom and by day in the classroom her image came between me and the page I strove to read. The syllables of the word *Araby* were called to me through the silence in which my soul luxuriated and cast an Eastern enchantment over me. I asked for leave to go to the bazaar on Saturday night. My aunt was surprised and hoped it was not some Freemason° affair. I answered few questions in class. I watched my master's face pass from amiability to sternness; he hoped I was not beginning to idle. I could not call my wandering thoughts together. I had hardly any patience with the serious work of life which, now that it stood between me and my desire, seemed to me child's play, ugly monotonous child's play.

On Saturday morning I reminded my uncle that I wished to go to the bazaar in the evening. He was fussing at the hallstand, looking for the hatbrush, and answered me curtly:

—Yes, boy, I know.

As he was in the hall I could not go into the front parlor and lie at the window. I   15
left the house in bad humor and walked slowly towards the school. The air was pitilessly raw and already my heart misgave me.

When I came home to dinner my uncle had not yet been home. Still it was early. I sat staring at the clock for some time and, when its ticking began to irritate me, I left the room. I mounted the staircase and gained the upper part of the house. The high cold empty gloomy rooms liberated me and I went from room to room singing. From the front window I saw my companions playing below in the street. Their cries reached me weakened and indistinct and, leaning my forehead against the cool glass, I looked over at the dark house where she lived. I may have stood there for an hour, seeing nothing but the brown-clad figure cast by my imagination, touched discreetly by the lamplight at the curved neck, at the hand upon the railings and at the border below the dress.

When I came downstairs again I found Mrs. Mercer sitting at the fire. She was an old garrulous woman, a pawnbroker's widow, who collected used stamps for some pious purpose. I had to endure the gossip of the tea-table. The meal was prolonged

---

a retreat . . . in her convent: a week devoted to religious observances more intense than usual, at the convent school Miss Mangan attends; probably she will have to listen to a number of hellfire sermons. *Freemason:* Catholics in Ireland viewed the Masonic order as a Protestant conspiracy against them.

beyond an hour and still my uncle did not come. Mrs. Mercer stood up to go: she was sorry she couldn't wait any longer, but it was after eight o'clock and she did not like to be out late, as the night air was bad for her. When she had gone I began to walk up and down the room, clenching my fists. My aunt said:

—I'm afraid you may put off your bazaar for this night of Our Lord.

At nine o'clock I heard my uncle's latchkey in the halldoor. I heard him talking to himself and heard the hallstand rocking when it had received the weight of his overcoat. I could interpret these signs. When he was midway through his dinner I asked him to give me the money to go to the bazaar. He had forgotten.

—The people are in bed and after their first sleep now, he said.   20

I did not smile. My aunt said to him energetically:

—Can't you give him the money and let him go? You've kept him late enough as it is.

My uncle said he was very sorry he had forgotten. He said he believed in the old saying: *All work and no play makes Jack a dull boy*. He asked me where I was going and, when I had told him a second time he asked me did I know *The Arab's Farewell to His Steed*.° When I left the kitchen he was about to recite the opening lines of the piece to my aunt.

I held a florin tightly in my hands as I strode down Buckingham Street towards the station. The sight of the streets thronged with buyers and glaring with gas recalled to me the purpose of my journey. I took my seat in a third-class carriage of a deserted train. After an intolerable delay the train moved out of the station slowly. It crept onward among ruinous houses and over the twinkling river. At Westland Row Station a crowd of people pressed to the carriage doors; but the porters moved them back, saying that it was a special train for the bazaar. I remained alone in the bare carriage. In a few minutes the train drew up beside an improvised wooden platform. I passed out on to the road and saw by the lighted dial of a clock that it was ten minutes to ten. In front of me was a large building which displayed the magical name.

I could not find any sixpenny entrance and, fearing that the bazaar would be   25
closed, I passed in quickly through a turnstile, handing a shilling to a weary-looking man. I found myself in a big hall girdled at half its height by a gallery. Nearly all the stalls were closed and the greater part of the hall was in darkness. I recognized a silence like that which pervades a church after a service. I walked into the center of the bazaar timidly. A few people were gathered about the stalls which were still open. Before a curtain, over which the words *Café Chantant*° were written in colored lamps, two men were counting money on a salver.° I listened to the fall of the coins.

Remembering with difficulty why I had come I went over to one of the stalls and examined porcelain vases and flowered tea-sets. At the door of the stall a young lady was talking and laughing with two young gentlemen. I remarked their English accents and listened vaguely to their conversation.

—O, I never said such a thing!

—O, but you did!

—O, but I didn't!

The Arab's Farewell to His Steed: This sentimental ballad by a popular poet, Caroline Norton (1808–1877), tells the story of a nomad of the desert who, in a fit of greed, sells his beloved horse, then regrets the loss, flings away the gold he had received, and takes back his horse. Notice the echo of "Araby" in the song title.   *Café Chantant*: name for a Paris nightspot featuring topical songs. *salver*: a tray like that used in serving Holy Communion.

—Didn't she say that?   30
—Yes. I heard her.
—O, there's a . . . fib!

Observing me the young lady came over and asked me did I wish to buy anything. The tone of her voice was not encouraging; she seemed to have spoken to me
out of a sense of duty. I looked humbly at the great jars that stood like eastern guards
at either side of the dark entrance to the stall and murmured:

—No, thank you.

The young lady changed the position of one of the vases and went back to the   35
two young men. They began to talk of the same subject. Once or twice the young
lady glanced at me over her shoulder.

I lingered before her stall, though I knew my stay was useless, to make my interest in her wares seem the more real. Then I turned away slowly and walked down the
middle of the bazaar. I allowed the two pennies to fall against the sixpence in my
pocket. I heard a voice call from one end of the gallery that the light was out. The
upper part of the hall was now completely dark.

Gazing up into the darkness I saw myself as a creature driven and derided by vanity;
and my eyes burned with anguish and anger.

Franz Kafka

Before the Law   1919

Translated by John Siscoe

*Franz Kafka (1883–1924) receives a brief biography on page 301, along with his classic
novella* The Metamorphosis. *The ironic and devastating parable "Before the Law" contains the distilled essence of what we mean by the term "Kafkaesque."*

Before the Law stands a doorkeeper. To this doorkeeper comes a man from the
country who asks to be admitted to the Law. But the doorkeeper says that he can't
let the man in just now. The man thinks this over and then asks if he will be allowed
to enter later. "It's possible," answers the doorkeeper, "but not just now." Since the
door to the Law stands open as usual and the doorkeeper steps aside, the man bends
down to look through the doorway into the interior. Seeing this, the doorkeeper
laughs and says: "If you find it so compelling, then try to enter despite my prohibi-
tion. But bear in mind that I am powerful. And I am only the lowest doorkeeper. In
hall after hall, keepers stand at every door. The mere sight of the third one is more
than even I can bear." These are difficulties which the man from the country has not
expected; the Law, he thinks, should be always available to everyone. But when he
looks more closely at the doorkeeper in his furred robe, with his large pointed nose
and his long, thin, black Tartar beard, he decides that it would be better to wait until he receives permission to enter. The doorkeeper gives him a stool and allows him
to sit down beside the door. There he sits for days and years. He makes many attempts to be let in, and wearies the doorkeeper with his pleas. The doorkeeper often
questions him casually about his home and many other matters, but the questions are
asked with indifference, the way important men might ask them, and always conclude with the statement the man can't be admitted at this time. The man, who has
equipped himself with many things for his journey, spends all that he has, regardless

of value, in order to bribe the doorkeeper. The doorkeeper accepts it all, though saying each time as he does so, "I'm taking this only so that you won't feel that you haven't tried everything." During these long years the man watches the doorkeeper almost continuously. He forgets about the other doorkeepers, and imagines that this first one is the sole obstacle barring his way to the Law. In the early years he loudly bewails his misfortune; later, as he grows old, he merely grumbles to himself. He becomes childish, and since during his long study of the doorkeeper he has gotten to know even the fleas in the fur collar, he begs these fleas to help him change the doorkeeper's mind. At last his eyesight grows dim and he cannot tell whether it is really growing darker or whether his eyes are simply deceiving him. Yet in the darkness he can now perceive that radiance that streams inextinguishably from the door of the Law. Now his life is nearing its end. Before he dies, all his experiences during this long time coalesce in his mind into a single question, one which he has never yet asked the doorkeeper. He beckons to the doorkeeper, for he can no longer raise his stiffening body. The doorkeeper has to bend low to hear him, since the difference in size between them has increased very much to the man's disadvantage. "What do you want to know now?" asks the doorkeeper, "you are insatiable." "Surely everyone strives to reach the Law," says the man, "why then is it that in all these years no one has come seeking admittance but me?" The doorkeeper realizes that the man has reached his end and that his hearing is failing so he yells in his ear: "No one but you could have been admitted here, since this entrance was meant for you alone. Now I am going to shut it."

Jamaica Kincaid

Girl

1983

Jamaica Kincaid was born Elaine Potter Richardson in 1949 in St. John's, capital of the West Indian island nation of Antigua (she adopted the name Jamaica Kincaid in 1973 because of her family's disapproval of her writing). In 1965 she was sent to Westchester County, New York, to work as an au pair (or "servant," as she prefers to describe it). She attended Franconia College in New Hampshire, but did not complete a degree. Kincaid worked as a staff writer for the New Yorker for nearly twenty years; Talk Stories (2001) is a collection of seventy-seven short pieces that she wrote for the magazine. She won wide attention for At the Bottom of the River (1983), the volume of her stories that includes "Girl." In 1985 she published Annie John, an interlocking cycle of short stories about growing up in Antigua. Lucy (1990) was her

Jamaica Kincaid

first novel; it was followed by The Autobiography of My Mother (1996) and Mr. Potter (2002), novels inspired by the lives of her parents. Kincaid is also the author of A Small Place (1988), a memoir of her homeland and meditation on the destructiveness of colonialism, and My Brother (1997), a reminiscence of her brother Devon, who died of AIDS at thirty-three. Her most recent work is Among Flowers: A Walk in the Himalaya (2005), a travel book.

A naturalized U.S. citizen, Kincaid has said of her adopted country: "It's given me a place to be myself—but myself as I was formed somewhere else." She is currently a visiting lecturer at Harvard University.

Wash the white clothes on Monday and put them on the stone heap; wash the color clothes on Tuesday and put them on the clothesline to dry; don't walk barehead in the hot sun; cook pumpkin fritters in very hot sweet oil; soak your little cloths right after you take them off; when buying cotton to make yourself a nice blouse, be sure that it doesn't have gum on it, because that way it won't hold up well after a wash; soak salt fish overnight before you cook it; is it true that you sing benna° in Sunday school?; always eat your food in such a way that it won't turn someone else's stomach; on Sundays try to walk like a lady and not like the slut you are so bent on becoming; don't sing benna in Sunday school; you mustn't speak to wharf-rat boys, not even to give directions; don't eat fruits on the street—flies will follow you; *but I don't sing benna on Sundays at all and never in Sunday school;* this is how to sew on a button; this is how to make a buttonhole for the button you have just sewed on; this is how to hem a dress when you see the hem coming down and so to prevent yourself from looking like the slut I know you are so bent on becoming; this is how you iron your father's khaki shirt so that it doesn't have a crease; this is how you iron your father's khaki pants so that they don't have a crease; this is how you grow okra—far from the house, because okra tree harbors red ants; when you are growing dasheen, make sure it gets plenty of water or else it makes your throat itch when you are eating it; this is how you sweep a corner; this is how you sweep a whole house; this is how you sweep a yard; this is how you smile to someone you don't like too much; this is how you smile to someone you don't like at all; this is how you smile to someone you like completely; this is how you set a table for tea; this is how you set a table for dinner; this is how you set a table for dinner with an important guest; this is how you set a table for lunch; this is how you set a table for breakfast; this is how to behave in the presence of men who don't know you very well, and this way they won't recognize immediately the slut I have warned you against becoming; be sure to wash every day, even if it is with your own spit; don't squat down to play marbles—you are not a boy, you know; don't pick people's flowers—you might catch something; don't throw stones at blackbirds, because it might not be a blackbird at all; this is how to make a bread pudding; this is how to make doukona; this is how to make pepper pot; this is how to make a good medicine for a cold; this is how to make a good medicine to throw away a child before it even becomes a child; this is how to catch a fish; this is how to throw back a fish you don't like, and that way something bad won't fall on you; this is how to bully a man; this is how a man bullies you; this is how to love a man, and if this doesn't work there are other ways, and if they don't work don't feel too bad about giving up; this is how to spit up in the air if you feel like it, and this is how to move quick so that it doesn't fall on you; this is how to make ends meet; always squeeze bread to make sure it's fresh; *but what if the baker won't let me feel the bread?;* you mean to say that after all you are really going to be the kind of woman who the baker won't let near the bread?

benna: Kincaid defined this word, for two editors who inquired, as meaning "songs of the sort your parents didn't want you to sing, at first calypso and later rock and roll" (quoted by Sylvan Barnet and Marcia Stubbs, *The Little Brown Reader*, 2nd ed. [Boston: Little, 1980] 74).

Jhumpa Lahiri

Interpreter of Maladies

1999

Jhumpa Lahiri was born in London in 1967 and grew up in Rhode Island. Her father, a librarian, and her mother, a teacher, had emigrated from their native India, to which Lahiri has made a number of extended visits. After writing a great deal of fiction as a child and teenager, she wrote none at all during her college years. She graduated from Barnard College with a B.A. in English literature, and after all her graduate school applications had been rejected, she went to work as a research assistant for a nonprofit organization. She began staying late after work to use her office computer to write short stories, on the strength of which she was accepted into the creative writing program at Boston University. Earning an M.A. in creative writing, Lahiri

Jhumpa Lahiri

stayed on to complete an M.A. in English, an M.A. in comparative literature and the arts, and a Ph.D. in Renaissance studies. "In the process," she has said, "it became clear to me that I was not meant to be a scholar. It was something I did out of a sense of duty and practicality, but it was never something I loved." Lahiri's first book of stories, Interpreter of Maladies, *was published in 1999 to excellent reviews and won the Pulitzer Prize for fiction. Its title story was also selected for both an O. Henry Award and publication in* The Best American Short Stories. *Her first novel,* The Namesake (2003), *was made into a film (2006) directed by Mira Nair. Her second collection of stories,* Unaccustomed Earth (2008), *also received glowing reviews, and debuted at Number 1 on the* New York Times Book Review *Best-Seller List. Lahiri has taught creative writing at Boston University and the Rhode Island School of Design. She lives in New York.*

At the tea stall Mr. and Mrs. Das bickered about who should take Tina to the toilet. Eventually Mrs. Das relented when Mr. Das pointed out that he had given the girl her bath the night before. In the rearview mirror Mr. Kapasi watched as Mrs. Das emerged slowly from his bulky white Ambassador, dragging her shaved, largely bare legs across the back seat. She did not hold the little girl's hand as they walked to the rest room.

They were on their way to see the Sun Temple at Konarak. It was a dry, bright Saturday, the mid-July heat tempered by a steady ocean breeze, ideal weather for sightseeing. Ordinarily Mr. Kapasi would not have stopped so soon along the way, but less than five minutes after he'd picked up the family that morning in front of Hotel Sandy Villa, the little girl had complained. The first thing Mr. Kapasi had noticed when he saw Mr. and Mrs. Das, standing with their children under the portico of the hotel, was that they were very young, perhaps not even thirty. In addition to Tina they had two boys, Ronny and Bobby, who appeared very close in age and had teeth covered in a network of flashing silver wires. The family looked Indian but dressed as foreigners did, the children in stiff, brightly colored clothing and caps with translucent visors. Mr. Kapasi was accustomed to foreign tourists; he was assigned to them regularly because he could speak English. Yesterday he had driven an elderly couple from Scotland, both with spotted faces and fluffy white hair so thin it exposed their sunburnt scalps. In comparison, the tanned, youthful faces of Mr. and Mrs. Das were all the more striking. When he'd introduced himself, Mr. Kapasi had pressed his palms together in greeting, but Mr. Das squeezed hands like an American so that Mr. Kapasi felt it in his elbow. Mrs. Das, for her part, had flexed one side of her mouth, smiling dutifully at Mr. Kapasi, without displaying any interest in him.

As they waited at the tea stall, Ronny, who looked like the older of the two boys, clambered suddenly out of the back seat, intrigued by a goat tied to a stake in the ground.

"Don't touch it," Mr. Das said. He glanced up from his paperback tour book, which said "INDIA" in yellow letters and looked as if it had been published abroad. His voice, somehow tentative and a little shrill, sounded as though it had not yet settled into maturity.

"I want to give it a piece of gum," the boy called back as he trotted ahead.   5

Mr. Das stepped out of the car and stretched his legs by squatting briefly to the ground. A clean-shaven man, he looked exactly like a magnified version of Ronny. He had a sapphire blue visor, and was dressed in shorts, sneakers, and a T-shirt. The camera slung around his neck, with an impressive telephoto lens and numerous buttons and markings, was the only complicated thing he wore. He frowned, watching as Ronny rushed toward the goat, but appeared to have no intention of intervening. "Bobby, make sure that your brother doesn't do anything stupid."

"I don't feel like it," Bobby said, not moving. He was sitting in the front seat beside Mr. Kapasi, studying a picture of the elephant god taped to the glove compartment.

"No need to worry," Mr. Kapasi said. "They are quite tame." Mr. Kapasi was forty-six years old, with receding hair that had gone completely silver, but his butterscotch complexion and his unlined brow, which he treated in spare moments to dabs of lotus-oil balm, made it easy to imagine what he must have looked like at an earlier age. He wore gray trousers and a matching jacket-style shirt, tapered at the waist, with short sleeves and a large pointed collar, made of a thin but durable synthetic material. He had specified both the cut and the fabric to his tailor—it was his preferred uniform for giving tours because it did not get crushed during his long hours behind the wheel. Through the windshield he watched as Ronny circled around the goat, touched it quickly on its side, then trotted back to the car.

"You left India as a child?" Mr. Kapasi asked when Mr. Das had settled once again into the passenger seat.

"Oh, Mina and I were both born in America," Mr. Das announced with an air of   10 sudden confidence. "Born and raised. Our parents live here now, in Assansol.° They retired. We visit them every couple years." He turned to watch as the little girl ran toward the car, the wide purple bows of her sundress flopping on her narrow brown shoulders. She was holding to her chest a doll with yellow hair that looked as if it had been chopped, as a punitive measure, with a pair of dull scissors. "This is Tina's first trip to India, isn't it, Tina?"

"I don't have to go to the bathroom anymore," Tina announced.

"Where's Mina?" Mr. Das asked.

Mr. Kapasi found it strange that Mr. Das should refer to his wife by her first name when speaking to the little girl. Tina pointed to where Mrs. Das was purchasing

Assansol: a city in the state of West Bengal in northeastern India.

something from one of the shirtless men who worked at the tea stall. Mr. Kapasi heard one of the shirtless men sing a phrase from a popular Hindi love song as Mrs. Das walked back to the car, but she did not appear to understand the words of the song, for she did not express irritation, or embarrassment, or react in any other way to the man's declarations.

He observed her. She wore a red-and-white-checkered skirt that stopped above her knees, slip-on shoes with a square wooden heel, and a close-fitting blouse styled like a man's undershirt. The blouse was decorated at chest-level with a calico appliqué in the shape of a strawberry. She was a short woman, with small hands like paws, her frosty pink fingernails painted to match her lips, and was slightly plump in her figure. Her hair, shorn only a little longer than her husband's, was parted far to one side. She was wearing large dark brown sunglasses with a pinkish tint to them, and carried a big straw bag, almost as big as her torso, shaped like a bowl, with a water bottle poking out of it. She walked slowly, carrying some puffed rice tossed with peanuts and chili peppers in a large packet made from newspapers. Mr. Kapasi turned to Mr. Das.

"Where in America do you live?" 15

"New Brunswick, New Jersey."

"Next to New York?"

"Exactly. I teach middle school there."

"What subject?"

"Science. In fact, every year I take my students on a trip to the Museum of 20 Natural History in New York City. In a way we have a lot in common, you could say, you and I. How long have you been a tour guide, Mr. Kapasi?"

"Five years."

Mrs. Das reached the car. "How long's the trip?" she asked, shutting the door.

"About two and a half hours," Mr. Kapasi replied.

At this Mrs. Das gave an impatient sigh, as if she had been traveling her whole life without pause. She fanned herself with a folded Bombay film magazine written in English.

"I thought that the Sun Temple is only eighteen miles north of Puri," Mr. Das 25 said, tapping on the tour book.

"The roads to Konarak are poor. Actually it is a distance of fifty-two miles," Mr. Kapasi explained.

Mr. Das nodded, readjusting the camera strap where it had begun to chafe the back of his neck.

Before starting the ignition, Mr. Kapasi reached back to make sure the cranklike locks on the inside of each of the back doors were secured. As soon as the car began to move the little girl began to play with the lock on her side, clicking it with some effort forward and backward, but Mrs. Das said nothing to stop her. She sat a bit slouched at one end of the back seat, not offering her puffed rice to anyone. Ronny and Tina sat on either side of her, both snapping bright green gum.

"Look," Bobby said as the car began to gather speed. He pointed with his finger to the tall trees that lined the road. "Look."

"Monkeys!" Ronny shrieked. "Wow!" 30

They were seated in groups along the branches, with shining black faces, silver bodies, horizontal eyebrows, and crested heads. Their long gray tails dangled like a series of ropes among the leaves. A few scratched themselves with black leathery hands, or swung their feet, staring as the car passed.

"We call them the hanuman," Mr. Kapasi said. "They are quite common in the area."

As soon as he spoke, one of the monkeys leaped into the middle of the road, causing Mr. Kapasi to brake suddenly. Another bounced onto the hood of the car, then sprang away. Mr. Kapasi beeped his horn. The children began to get excited, sucking in their breath and covering their faces partly with their hands. They had never seen monkeys outside of a zoo, Mr. Das explained. He asked Mr. Kapasi to stop the car so that he could take a picture.

While Mr. Das adjusted his telephoto lens, Mrs. Das reached into her straw bag and pulled out a bottle of colorless nail polish, which she proceeded to stroke on the tip of her index finger.

The little girl stuck out a hand. "Mine too. Mommy, do mine too."   35

"Leave me alone," Mrs. Das said, blowing on her nail and turning her body slightly. "You're making me mess up."

The little girl occupied herself by buttoning and unbuttoning a pinafore on the doll's plastic body.

"All set," Mr. Das said, replacing the lens cap.

The car rattled considerably as it raced along the dusty road, causing them all to pop up from their seats every now and then, but Mrs. Das continued to polish her nails. Mr. Kapasi eased up on the accelerator, hoping to produce a smoother ride. When he reached for the gearshift the boy in front accommodated him by swinging his hairless knees out of the way. Mr. Kapasi noted that this boy was slightly paler than the other children. "Daddy, why is the driver sitting on the wrong side in this car, too?" the boy asked.

"They all do that here, dummy," Ronny said.   40

"Don't call your brother a dummy," Mr. Das said. He turned to Mr. Kapasi. "In America, you know . . . it confuses them."

"Oh yes, I am well aware," Mr. Kapasi said. As delicately as he could, he shifted gears again, accelerating as they approached a hill in the road. "I see it on *Dallas*,° the steering wheels are on the left-hand side."

"What's *Dallas?*" Tina asked, banging her now naked doll on the seat behind Mr. Kapasi.

"It went off the air," Mr. Das explained. "It's a television show."

They were all like siblings, Mr. Kapasi thought as they passed a row of date trees.   45
Mr. and Mrs. Das behaved like an older brother and sister, not parents. It seemed that they were in charge of the children only for the day; it was hard to believe they were regularly responsible for anything other than themselves. Mr. Das tapped on his lens cap, and his tour book, dragging his thumbnail occasionally across the pages so that they made a scraping sound. Mrs. Das continued to polish her nails. She had still not removed her sunglasses. Every now and then Tina renewed her plea that she wanted her nails done, too, and so at one point Mrs. Das flicked a drop of polish on the little girl's finger before depositing the bottle back inside her straw bag.

"Isn't this an air-conditioned car?" she asked, still blowing on her hand. The window on Tina's side was broken and could not be rolled down.

"Quit complaining," Mr. Das said. "It isn't so hot."

"I told you to get a car with air-conditioning," Mrs. Das continued. "Why do you do this, Raj, just to save a few stupid rupees. What are you saving us, fifty cents?"

Dallas: extremely popular 1980s television drama centered on the professional and romantic affairs of unscrupulous oil baron J. R. Ewing and his family.

Their accents sounded just like the ones Mr. Kapasi heard on American television programs, though not like the ones on *Dallas*.

"Doesn't it get tiresome, Mr. Kapasi, showing people the same thing every day?" Mr. Das asked, rolling down his own window all the way. "Hey, do you mind stopping the car. I just want to get a shot of this guy." 50

Mr. Kapasi pulled over to the side of the road as Mr. Das took a picture of a barefoot man, his head wrapped in a dirty turban, seated on top of a cart of grain sacks pulled by a pair of bullocks.° Both the man and the bullocks were emaciated. In the back seat Mrs. Das gazed out another window, at the sky, where nearly transparent clouds passed quickly in front of one another.

"I look forward to it, actually," Mr. Kapasi said as they continued on their way. "The Sun Temple is one of my favorite places. In that way it is a reward for me. I give tours on Fridays and Saturdays only. I have another job during the week."

"Oh? Where?" Mr. Das asked.

"I work in a doctor's office."

"You're a doctor?" 55

"I am not a doctor. I work with one. As an interpreter."

"What does a doctor need an interpreter for?"

"He has a number of Gujarati patients. My father was Gujarati, but many people do not speak Gujarati in this area, including the doctor. And so the doctor asked me to work in his office, interpreting what the patients say."

"Interesting. I've never heard of anything like that," Mr. Das said.

Mr. Kapasi shrugged. "It is a job like any other." 60

"But so romantic," Mrs. Das said dreamily, breaking her extended silence. She lifted her pinkish brown sunglasses and arranged them on top of her head like a tiara. For the first time, her eyes met Mr. Kapasi's in the rearview mirror: pale, a bit small, their gaze fixed but drowsy.

Mr. Das craned to look at her. "What's so romantic about it?"

"I don't know. Something." She shrugged, knitting her brows together for an instant. "Would you like a piece of gum, Mr. Kapasi?" she asked brightly. She reached into her straw bag and handed him a small square wrapped in green-and-white-striped paper. As soon as Mr. Kapasi put the gum in his mouth a thick sweet liquid burst onto his tongue.

"Tell us more about your job, Mr. Kapasi," Mrs. Das said.

"What would you like to know, madame?" 65

"I don't know," she shrugged, munching on some puffed rice and licking the mustard oil from the corners of her mouth. "Tell us a typical situation." She settled back in her seat, her head tilted in a patch of sun, and closed her eyes. "I want to picture what happens."

"Very well. The other day a man came in with a pain in his throat."

"Did he smoke cigarettes?"

"No. It was very curious. He complained that he felt as if there were long pieces of straw stuck in his throat. When I told the doctor he was able to prescribe the proper medication."

"That's so neat." 70

"Yes," Mr. Kapasi agreed after some hesitation.

"So these patients are totally dependent on you," Mrs. Das said. She spoke slowly, as if she were thinking aloud. "In a way, more dependent on you than the doctor."

bullocks: young or castrated bulls; steer.

"How do you mean? How could it be?"

"Well, for example, you could tell the doctor that the pain felt like a burning, not straw. The patient would never know what you had told the doctor, and the doctor wouldn't know that you had told the wrong thing. It's a big responsibility."

"Yes, a big responsibility you have there, Mr. Kapasi," Mr. Das agreed.   75

Mr. Kapasi had never thought of his job in such complimentary terms. To him it was a thankless occupation. He found nothing noble in interpreting people's maladies, assiduously translating the symptoms of so many swollen bones, countless cramps of bellies and bowels, spots on people's palms that changed color, shape, or size. The doctor, nearly half his age, had an affinity for bell-bottom trousers and made humorless jokes about the Congress party.° Together they worked in a stale little infirmary where Mr. Kapasi's smartly tailored clothes clung to him in the heat, in spite of the blackened blades of a ceiling fan churning over their heads.

The job was a sign of his failings. In his youth he'd been a devoted scholar of foreign languages, the owner of an impressive collection of dictionaries. He had dreamed of being an interpreter for diplomats and dignitaries, resolving conflicts between people and nations, settling disputes of which he alone could understand both sides. He was a self-educated man. In a series of notebooks, in the evenings before his parents settled his marriage, he had listed the common etymologies of words, and at one point in his life he was confident that he could converse, if given the opportunity, in English, French, Russian, Portuguese, and Italian, not to mention Hindi, Bengali, Orissi, and Gujarati. Now only a handful of European phrases remained in his memory, scattered words for things like saucers and chairs. English was the only non-Indian language he spoke fluently anymore. Mr. Kapasi knew it was not a remarkable talent. Sometimes he feared that his children knew better English than he did, just from watching television. Still, it came in handy for the tours.

He had taken the job as an interpreter after his first son, at the age of seven, contracted typhoid—that was how he had first made the acquaintance of the doctor. At the time Mr. Kapasi had been teaching English in a grammar school, and he bartered his skills as an interpreter to pay the increasingly exorbitant medical bills. In the end the boy had died one evening in his mother's arms, his limbs burning with fever, but then there was the funeral to pay for, and the other children who were born soon enough, and the newer, bigger house, and the good schools and tutors, and the fine shoes and the television, and the countless other ways he tried to console his wife and to keep her from crying in her sleep, and so when the doctor offered to pay him twice as much as he earned at the grammar school, he accepted. Mr. Kapasi knew that his wife had little regard for his career as an interpreter. He knew it reminded her of the son she'd lost, and that she resented the other lives he helped, in his own small way, to save. If ever she referred to his position, she used the phrase "doctor's assistant," as if the process of interpretation were equal to taking someone's temperature, or changing a bedpan. She never asked him about the patients who came to the doctor's office, or said that his job was a big responsibility.

For this reason it flattered Mr. Kapasi that Mrs. Das was so intrigued by his job. Unlike his wife, she had reminded him of its intellectual challenges. She had also used the word "romantic." She did not behave in a romantic way toward her husband, and yet she had used the word to describe him. He wondered if Mr. and Mrs.

the Congress party: India's governing party for five decades after independence in 1947, widely perceived as corrupt.

Das were a bad match, just as he and his wife were. Perhaps they, too, had little in common apart from three children and a decade of their lives. The signs he recognized from his own marriage were there—the bickering, the indifference, the protracted silences. Her sudden interest in him, an interest she did not express in either her husband or her children, was mildly intoxicating. When Mr. Kapasi thought once again about how she had said "romantic," the feeling of intoxication grew.

He began to check his reflection in the rearview mirror as he drove, feeling grateful that he had chosen the gray suit that morning and not the brown one, which tended to sag a little in the knees. From time to time he glanced through the mirror at Mrs. Das. In addition to glancing at her face he glanced at the strawberry between her breasts, and the golden brown hollow in her throat. He decided to tell Mrs. Das about another patient, and another: the young woman who had complained of a sensation of raindrops in her spine, the gentleman whose birthmark had begun to sprout hairs. Mrs. Das listened attentively, stroking her hair with a small plastic brush that resembled an oval bed of nails, asking more questions, for yet another example. The children were quiet, intent on spotting more monkeys in the trees, and Mr. Das was absorbed by his tour book, so it seemed like a private conversation between Mr. Kapasi and Mrs. Das. In this manner the next half hour passed, and when they stopped for lunch at a roadside restaurant that sold fritters and omelette sandwiches, usually something Mr. Kapasi looked forward to on his tours so that he could sit in peace and enjoy some hot tea, he was disappointed. As the Das family settled together under a magenta umbrella fringed with white and orange tassels, and placed their orders with one of the waiters who marched about in tricornered caps, Mr. Kapasi reluctantly headed toward a neighboring table.

"Mr. Kapasi, wait. There's room here," Mrs. Das called out. She gathered Tina onto her lap, insisting that he accompany them. And so, together, they had bottled mango juice and sandwiches and plates of onions and potatoes deep-fried in grahamflour batter. After finishing two omelette sandwiches Mr. Das took more pictures of the group as they ate.

"How much longer?" he asked Mr. Kapasi as he paused to load a new roll of film in the camera.

"About half an hour more."

By now the children had gotten up from the table to look at more monkeys perched in a nearby tree, so there was a considerable space between Mrs. Das and Mr. Kapasi. Mr. Das placed the camera to his face and squeezed one eye shut, his tongue exposed at one corner of his mouth. "This looks funny. Mina, you need to lean in closer to Mr. Kapasi."

She did. He could smell a scent on her skin, like a mixture of whiskey and rosewater. He worried suddenly that she could smell his perspiration, which he knew had collected beneath the synthetic material of his shirt. He polished off his mango juice in one gulp and smoothed his silver hair with his hands. A bit of the juice dripped onto his chin. He wondered if Mrs. Das had noticed.

She had not. "What's your address, Mr. Kapasi?" she inquired, fishing for something inside her straw bag.

"You would like my address?"

"So we can send you copies," she said. "Of the pictures." She handed him a scrap of paper which she had hastily ripped from a page of her film magazine. The blank portion was limited, for the narrow strip was crowded by lines of text and a tiny picture of a hero and heroine embracing under a eucalyptus tree.

The paper curled as Mr. Kapasi wrote his address in clear, careful letters. She would write to him, asking about his days interpreting at the doctor's office, and he would respond eloquently, choosing only the most entertaining anecdotes, ones that would make her laugh out loud as she read them in her house in New Jersey. In time she would reveal the disappointment of her marriage, and he his. In this way their friendship would grow, and flourish. He would possess a picture of the two of them, eating fried onions under a magenta umbrella, which he would keep, he decided, safely tucked between the pages of his Russian grammar. As his mind raced, Mr. Kapasi experienced a mild and pleasant shock. It was similar to a feeling he used to experience long ago when, after months of translating with the aid of a dictionary, he would finally read a passage from a French novel, or an Italian sonnet, and understand the words, one after another, unencumbered by his own efforts. In those moments Mr. Kapasi used to believe that all was right with the world, that all struggles were rewarded, that all of life's mistakes made sense in the end. The promise that he would hear from Mrs. Das now filled him with the same belief.

When he finished writing his address Mr. Kapasi handed her the paper, but as 90 soon as he did so he worried that he had either misspelled his name, or accidentally reversed the numbers of his postal code. He dreaded the possibility of a lost letter, the photograph never reaching him, hovering somewhere in Orissa,° close but ultimately unattainable. He thought of asking for the slip of paper again, just to make sure he had written his address accurately, but Mrs. Das had already dropped it into the jumble of her bag.

They reached Konarak at two-thirty. The temple, made of sandstone, was a massive pyramid-like structure in the shape of a chariot. It was dedicated to the great master of life, the sun, which struck three sides of the edifice as it made its journey each day across the sky. Twenty-four giant wheels were carved on the north and south sides of the plinth. The whole thing was drawn by a team of seven horses, speeding as if through the heavens. As they approached, Mr. Kapasi explained that the temple had been built between A.D. 1243 and 1255, with the efforts of twelve hundred artisans, by the great ruler of the Ganga dynasty, King Narasimhadeva the First, to commemorate his victory against the Muslim army.

"It says the temple occupies about a hundred and seventy acres of land," Mr. Das said, reading from his book.

"It's like a desert," Ronny said, his eyes wandering across the sand that stretched on all sides beyond the temple.

"The Chandrabhaga River once flowed one mile north of here. It is dry now," Mr. Kapasi said, turning off the engine.

They got out and walked toward the temple, posing first for pictures by the pair 95 of lions that flanked the steps. Mr. Kapasi led them next to one of the wheels of the chariot, higher than any human being, nine feet in diameter.

"'The wheels are supposed to symbolize the wheel of life,'" Mr. Das read. "'They depict the cycle of creation, preservation, and achievement of realization.' Cool." He turned the page of his book. "'Each wheel is divided into eight thick and thin spokes, dividing the day into eight equal parts. The rims are carved with designs of birds and animals, whereas the medallions in the spokes are carved with women in luxurious poses, largely erotic in nature.'"

Orissa: a state on the southwest border of West Bengal.

What he referred to were the countless friezes of entwined naked bodies, making love in various positions, women clinging to the necks of men, their knees wrapped eternally around their lovers' thighs. In addition to these were assorted scenes from daily life, of hunting and trading, of deer being killed with bows and arrows and marching warriors holding swords in their hands.

It was no longer possible to enter the temple, for it had filled with rubble years ago, but they admired the exterior, as did all the tourists Mr. Kapasi brought there, slowly strolling along each of its sides. Mr. Das trailed behind, taking pictures. The children ran ahead, pointing to figures of naked people, intrigued in particular by the Nagamithunas, the half-human, half-serpentine couples who were said, Mr. Kapasi told them, to live in the deepest waters of the sea. Mr. Kapasi was pleased that they liked the temple, pleased especially that it appealed to Mrs. Das. She stopped every three or four paces, staring silently at the carved lovers, and the processions of elephants, and the topless female musicians beating on two-sided drums.

Though Mr. Kapasi had been to the temple countless times, it occurred to him, as he, too, gazed at the topless women, that he had never seen his own wife fully naked. Even when they had made love she kept the panels of her blouse hooked together, the string of her petticoat knotted around her waist. He had never admired the backs of his wife's legs the way he now admired those of Mrs. Das, walking as if for his benefit alone. He had, of course, seen plenty of bare limbs before, belonging to the American and European ladies who took his tours. But Mrs. Das was different. Unlike the other women, who had an interest only in the temple, and kept their noses buried in a guidebook, or their eyes behind the lens of a camera, Mrs. Das had taken an interest in him.

Mr. Kapasi was anxious to be alone with her, to continue their private conversation, yet he felt nervous to walk at her side. She was lost behind her sunglasses, ignoring her husband's requests that she pose for another picture, walking past her children as if they were strangers. Worried that he might disturb her, Mr. Kapasi walked ahead, to admire, as he always did, the three life-sized bronze avatars of Surya, the sun god, each emerging from its own niche on the temple facade to greet the sun at dawn, noon, and evening. They wore elaborate headdresses, their languid, elongated eyes closed, their bare chests draped with carved chains and amulets. Hibiscus petals, offerings from previous visitors, were strewn at their gray-green feet. The last statue, on the northern wall of the temple, was Mr. Kapasi's favorite. This Surya had a tired expression, weary after a hard day of work, sitting astride a horse with folded legs. Even his horse's eyes were drowsy. Around his body were smaller sculptures of women in pairs, their hips thrust to one side.

"Who's that?" Mrs. Das asked. He was startled to see that she was standing beside him.

"He is the Astachala-Surya," Mr. Kapasi said. "The setting sun."

"So in a couple of hours the sun will set right here?" She slipped a foot out of one of her square-heeled shoes, rubbed her toes on the back of her other leg.

"That is correct."

She raised her sunglasses for a moment, then put them back on again. "Neat."

Mr. Kapasi was not certain exactly what the word suggested, but he had a feeling it was a favorable response. He hoped that Mrs. Das had understood Surya's beauty, his power. Perhaps they would discuss it further in their letters. He would explain things to her, things about India, and she would explain things to him about America. In its own way this correspondence would fulfill his dream, of serving as an interpreter between nations. He looked at her straw bag, delighted that his address lay nestled among its contents. When he pictured her so many thousands of miles away he plummeted, so much so that he had an overwhelming urge to wrap his arms around her, to freeze with her, even for an instant, in an embrace witnessed by his favorite Surya. But Mrs. Das had already started walking.

"When do you return to America?" he asked, trying to sound placid.

"In ten days."

He calculated: A week to settle in, a week to develop the pictures, a few days to compose her letter, two weeks to get to India by air. According to his schedule, allowing room for delays, he would hear from Mrs. Das in approximately six weeks' time.

The family was silent as Mr. Kapasi drove them back, a little past four-thirty, to   110
Hotel Sandy Villa. The children had bought miniature granite versions of the chariot's wheels at a souvenir stand, and they turned them round in their hands. Mr. Das continued to read his book. Mrs. Das untangled Tina's hair with her brush and divided it into two little ponytails.

Mr. Kapasi was beginning to dread the thought of dropping them off. He was not prepared to begin his six-week wait to hear from Mrs. Das. As he stole glances at her in the rearview mirror, wrapping elastic bands around Tina's hair, he wondered how he might make the tour last a little longer. Ordinarily he sped back to Puri using a shortcut, eager to return home, scrub his feet and hands with sandalwood soap, and enjoy the evening newspaper and a cup of tea that his wife would serve him in silence. The thought of that silence, something to which he'd long been resigned, now oppressed him. It was then that he suggested visiting the hills at Udayagiri and Khandagiri, where a number of monastic dwellings were hewn out of the ground, facing one another across a defile. It was some miles away, but well worth seeing, Mr. Kapasi told them.

"Oh yeah, there's something mentioned about it in this book," Mr. Das said. "Built by a Jain° king or something."

"Shall we go then?" Mr. Kapasi asked. He paused at a turn in the road. "It's to the left."

Mr. Das turned to look at Mrs. Das. Both of them shrugged.

"Left, left," the children chanted.   115

Mr. Kapasi turned the wheel, almost delirious with relief. He did not know what he would do or say to Mrs. Das once they arrived at the hills. Perhaps he would tell her what a pleasing smile she had. Perhaps he would compliment her strawberry shirt, which he found irresistibly becoming. Perhaps, when Mr. Das was busy taking a picture, he would take her hand.

He did not have to worry. When they got to the hills, divided by a steep path thick with trees, Mrs. Das refused to get out of the car. All along the path, dozens of monkeys were seated on stones, as well as on the branches of the trees. Their hind legs were stretched out in front and raised to shoulder level, their arms resting on their knees.

"My legs are tired," she said, sinking low in her seat. "I'll stay here."

"Why did you have to wear those stupid shoes?" Mr. Das said. "You won't be in the pictures."

Jain: an adherent of Jainism, a dualistic, ascetic religion founded in the sixth century B.C. in revolt against the Hindu caste system.

"Pretend I'm there." 120

"But we could use one of these pictures for our Christmas card this year. We didn't get one of all five of us at the Sun Temple. Mr. Kapasi could take it."

"I'm not coming. Anyway, those monkeys give me the creeps."

"But they're harmless," Mr. Das said. He turned to Mr. Kapasi. "Aren't they?"

"They are more hungry than dangerous," Mr. Kapasi said. "Do not provoke them with food, and they will not bother you."

Mr. Das headed up the defile with the children, the boys at his side, the little girl 125 on his shoulders. Mr. Kapasi watched as they crossed paths with a Japanese man and woman, the only other tourists there, who paused for a final photograph, then stepped into a nearby car and drove away. As the car disappeared out of view some of the monkeys called out, emitting soft whooping sounds, and then walked on their flat black hands and feet up the path. At one point a group of them formed a little ring around Mr. Das and the children. Tina screamed in delight. Ronny ran in circles around his father. Bobby bent down and picked up a fat stick on the ground. When he extended it, one of the monkeys approached him and snatched it, then briefly beat the ground.

"I'll join them," Mr. Kapasi said, unlocking the door on his side. "There is much to explain about the caves."

"No. Stay a minute," Mrs. Das said. She got out of the back seat and slipped in beside Mr. Kapasi. "Raj has his dumb book anyway." Together, through the windshield, Mrs. Das and Mr. Kapasi watched as Bobby and the monkey passed the stick back and forth between them.

"A brave little boy," Mr. Kapasi commented.

"It's not so surprising," Mrs. Das said.

"No?" 130

"He's not his."

"I beg your pardon?"

"Raj's. He's not Raj's son."

Mr. Kapasi felt a prickle on his skin. He reached into his shirt pocket for the small tin of lotus-oil balm he carried with him at all times, and applied it to three spots on his forehead. He knew that Mrs. Das was watching him, but he did not turn to face her. Instead he watched as the figures of Mr. Das and the children grew smaller, climbing up the steep path, pausing every now and then for a picture, surrounded by a growing number of monkeys.

"Are you surprised?" The way she put it made him choose his words with care. 135

"It's not the type of thing one assumes," Mr. Kapasi replied slowly. He put the tin of lotus-oil balm back in his pocket.

"No, of course not. And no one knows, of course. No one at all. I've kept it a secret for eight whole years." She looked at Mr. Kapasi, tilting her chin as if to gain a fresh perspective. "But now I've told you."

Mr. Kapasi nodded. He felt suddenly parched, and his forehead was warm and slightly numb from the balm. He considered asking Mrs. Das for a sip of water, then decided against it.

"We met when we were very young," she said. She reached into her straw bag in search of something, then pulled out a packet of puffed rice. "Want some?"

"No, thank you." 140

She put a fistful in her mouth, sank into the seat a little, and looked away from Mr. Kapasi, out the window on her side of the car. "We married when we were still in college. We were in high school when he proposed. We went to the same college, of course. Back then we couldn't stand the thought of being separated, not for a day, not for a minute. Our parents were best friends who lived in the same town. My entire life I saw him every weekend, either at our house or theirs. We were sent upstairs to play together while our parents joked about our marriage. Imagine! They never caught us at anything, though in a way I think it was all more or less a setup. The things we did those Friday and Saturday nights, while our parents sat downstairs drinking tea . . . I could tell you stories, Mr. Kapasi."

As a result of spending all her time in college with Raj, she continued, she did not make many close friends. There was no one to confide in about him at the end of a difficult day, or to share a passing thought or a worry. Her parents now lived on the other side of the world, but she had never been very close to them, anyway. After marrying so young she was overwhelmed by it all, having a child so quickly, and nursing, and warming up bottles of milk and testing their temperature against her wrist while Raj was at work, dressed in sweaters and corduroy pants, teaching his students about rocks and dinosaurs. Raj never looked cross or harried, or plump as she had become after the first baby.

Always tired, she declined invitations from her one or two college girlfriends, to have lunch or shop in Manhattan. Eventually the friends stopped calling her, so that she was left at home all day with the baby, surrounded by toys that made her trip when she walked or wince when she sat, always cross and tired. Only occasionally did they go out after Ronny was born, and even more rarely did they entertain. Raj didn't mind; he looked forward to coming home from teaching and watching television and bouncing Ronny on his knee. She had been outraged when Raj told her that a Punjabi° friend, someone whom she had once met but did not remember, would be staying with them for a week for some job interviews in the New Brunswick area.

Bobby was conceived in the afternoon, on a sofa littered with rubber teething toys, after the friend learned that a London pharmaceutical company had hired him, while Ronny cried to be freed from his playpen. She made no protest when the friend touched the small of her back as she was about to make a pot of coffee, then pulled her against his crisp navy suit. He made love to her swiftly, in silence, with an expertise she had never known, without the meaningful expressions and smiles Raj always insisted on afterward. The next day Raj drove the friend to JFK. He was married now, to a Punjabi girl, and they lived in London still, and every year they exchanged Christmas cards with Raj and Mina, each couple tucking photos of their families into the envelopes. He did not know that he was Bobby's father. He never would.

"I beg your pardon, Mrs. Das, but why have you told me this information?"   145
Mr. Kapasi asked when she had finally finished speaking, and had turned to face him once again.

"For God's sake, stop calling me Mrs. Das. I'm twenty-eight. You probably have children my age."

"Not quite." It disturbed Mr. Kapasi to learn that she thought of him as a parent. The feeling he had had toward her, that had made him check his reflection in the rearview mirror as they drove, evaporated a little.

"I told you because of your talents." She put the packet of puffed rice back into her bag without folding over the top.

Punjabi: a native of Punjab, a state in northwest India.

"I don't understand," Mr. Kapasi said.

"Don't you see? For eight years I haven't been able to express this to anybody,   150
not to friends, certainly not to Raj. He doesn't even suspect it. He thinks I'm still in
love with him. Well, don't you have anything to say?"

"About what?"

"About what I've just told you. About my secret, and about how terrible it makes
me feel. I feel terrible looking at my children, and at Raj, always terrible. I have terrible
urges, Mr. Kapasi, to throw things away. One day I had the urge to throw everything I
own out the window, the television, the children, everything. Don't you think it's un-
healthy?"

He was silent.

"Mr. Kapasi, don't you have anything to say? I thought that was your job."

"My job is to give tours, Mrs. Das."   155

"Not that. Your other job. As an interpreter."

"But we do not face a language barrier. What need is there for an interpreter?"

"That's not what I mean. I would never have told you otherwise. Don't you realize what it means for me to tell you?"

"What does it mean?"

"It means that I'm tired of feeling so terrible all the time. Eight years, Mr. Kapasi,   160
I've been in pain eight years. I was hoping you could help me feel better, say the right
thing. Suggest some kind of remedy."

He looked at her, in her red plaid skirt and strawberry T-shirt, a woman not yet
thirty, who loved neither her husband nor her children, who had already fallen out of
love with life. Her confession depressed him, depressed him all the more when he
thought of Mr. Das at the top of the path, Tina clinging to his shoulders, taking pictures of ancient monastic cells cut into the hills to show his students in America,
unsuspecting and unaware that one of his sons was not his own. Mr. Kapasi felt
insulted that Mrs. Das should ask him to interpret her common, trivial little secret.
She did not resemble the patients in the doctor's office, those who came glassy-eyed
and desperate, unable to sleep or breathe or urinate with ease, unable, above all, to
give words to their pains. Still, Mr. Kapasi believed it was his duty to assist Mrs. Das.
Perhaps he ought to tell her to confess the truth to Mr. Das. He would explain that
honesty was the best policy. Honesty, surely, would help her feel better, as she'd put it.
Perhaps he would offer to preside over the discussion, as a mediator. He decided to
begin with the most obvious question, to get to the heart of the matter, and so he
asked, "Is it really pain you feel, Mrs. Das, or is it guilt?"

She turned to him and glared, mustard oil thick on her frosty pink lips. She
opened her mouth to say something, but as she glared at Mr. Kapasi some certain
knowledge seemed to pass before her eyes, and she stopped. It crushed him; he knew
at that moment that he was not even important enough to be properly insulted. She
opened the car door and began walking up the path, wobbling a little on her square
wooden heels, reaching into her straw bag to eat handfuls of puffed rice. It fell
through her fingers, leaving a zigzagging trail, causing a monkey to leap down from a
tree and devour the little white grains. In search of more, the monkey began to follow
Mrs. Das. Others joined him, so that she was soon being followed by about half a
dozen of them, their velvety tails dragging behind.

Mr. Kapasi stepped out of the car. He wanted to holler, to alert her in some way,
but he worried that if she knew they were behind her, she would grow nervous. Perhaps she would lose her balance. Perhaps they would pull at her bag or her hair. He

began to jog up the path, taking a fallen branch in his hand to scare away the
monkeys. Mrs. Das continued walking, oblivious, trailing grains of puffed rice.
Near the top of the incline, before a group of cells fronted by a row of squat stone
pillars, Mr. Das was kneeling on the ground focusing the lens of his camera. The
children stood under the arcade, now hiding, now emerging from view.

"Wait for me," Mrs. Das called out. "I'm coming."

Tina jumped up and down. "Here comes Mommy!"   165

"Great," Mr. Das said without looking up. "Just in time. We'll get Mr. Kapasi
to take a picture of the five of us."

Mr. Kapasi quickened his pace, waving his branch so that the monkeys scampered
away, distracted, in another direction.

"Where's Bobby?" Mrs. Das asked when she stopped.

Mr. Das looked up from the camera. "I don't know. Ronny, where's Bobby?"

Ronny shrugged, "I thought he was right here."   170

"Where is he?" Mrs. Das repeated sharply. "What's wrong with all of you?"

They began calling his name, wandering up and down the path a bit. Because
they were calling, they did not initially hear the boy's screams. When they found
him, a little farther down the path under a tree, he was surrounded by a group of
monkeys, over a dozen of them, pulling at his T-shirt with their long black fingers.
The puffed rice Mrs. Das had spilled was scattered at his feet, raked over by the monkeys' hands. The boy was silent, his body frozen, swift tears running down his startled
face. His bare legs were dusty and red with welts from where one of the monkeys
struck him repeatedly with the stick he had given to it earlier.

"Daddy, the monkey's hurting Bobby," Tina said.

Mr. Das wiped his palms on the front of his shorts. In his nervousness he accidentally pressed the shutter on his camera; the whirring noise of the advancing film
excited the monkeys, and the one with the stick began to beat Bobby more intently.
"What are we supposed to do? What if they start attacking?"

"Mr. Kapasi," Mrs. Das shrieked, noticing him standing to one side. "Do some-   175
thing, for God's sake, do something!"

Mr. Kapasi took his branch and shooed them away, hissing at the ones that
remained, stomping his feet to scare them. The animals retreated slowly, with a measured gait, obedient but unintimidated. Mr. Kapasi gathered Bobby in his arms and
brought him back to where his parents and siblings were standing. As he carried him
he was tempted to whisper a secret into the boy's ear. But Bobby was stunned, and
shivering with fright, his legs bleeding slightly where the stick had broken the skin.
When Mr. Kapasi delivered him to his parents, Mr. Das brushed some dirt off the
boy's T-shirt and put the visor on him the right way. Mrs. Das reached into her straw
bag to find a bandage which she taped over the cut on his knee. Ronny offered his
brother a fresh piece of gum. "He's fine. Just a little scared, right, Bobby?" Mr. Das
said, patting the top of his head.

"God, let's get out of here," Mrs. Das said. She folded her arms across the strawberry
on her chest. "This place gives me the creeps."

"Yeah. Back to the hotel, definitely," Mr. Das agreed.

"Poor Bobby," Mrs. Das said. "Come here a second. Let Mommy fix your hair."
Again she reached into her straw bag, this time for her hairbrush, and began to run it
around the edges of the translucent visor. When she whipped out the hairbrush, the
slip of paper with Mr. Kapasi's address on it fluttered away in the wind. No one but
Mr. Kapasi noticed. He watched as it rose, carried higher and higher by the breeze,

into the trees where the monkeys now sat, solemnly observing the scene below. Mr. Kapasi observed it too, knowing that this was the picture of the Das family he would preserve forever in his mind.

D. H. Lawrence

The Rocking-Horse Winner   1933

David Herbert Lawrence (1885–1930) was born in Nottinghamshire, England, child of a coal miner and a schoolteacher who hated her husband's toil and vowed that her son should escape it. He took up fiction writing, attaining early success. During World War I, Lawrence and his wife were unjustly suspected of treason (he because of his pacifism, she because of her aristocratic German birth). After the armistice they left England and, seeking a climate healthier for Lawrence, who suffered from tuberculosis, wandered in Italy, France, Australia, Mexico, and the American Southwest.

D. H. Lawrence

Lawrence is an impassioned spokesman for our unconscious instinctive natures, which we moderns (he argues) have neglected in favor of our overweening intellects. In Lady Chatterley's Lover *(1928), he strove to restore explicit sexuality to English fiction. The book, which today seems tame and repetitious, was long banned in Britain and the United States. Deeper Lawrence novels include* Sons and Lovers *(1913), a veiled account of his breaking away from his fiercely possessive mother;* The Rainbow *(1915);* Women in Love *(1921); and* The Plumed Serpent *(1926), about a revival of pagan religion in Mexico. Besides fiction, Lawrence left a rich legacy of poetry, essays, criticism (*Studies in Classic American Literature, *1923, is especially shrewd and funny), and travel writing. Lawrence exerted deep influence on others, both by the message in his work and by his personal magnetism.*

There was a woman who was beautiful, who started with all the advantages, yet she had no luck. She married for love, and the love turned to dust. She had bonny children, yet she felt they had been thrust upon her, and she could not love them. They looked at her coldly, as if they were finding fault with her. And hurriedly she felt she must cover up some fault in herself. Yet what it was that she must cover up she never knew. Nevertheless, when her children were present, she always felt the center of her heart go hard. This troubled her, and in her manner she was all the more gentle and anxious for her children, as if she loved them very much. Only she herself knew that at the center of her heart was a hard little place that could not feel love, no, not for anybody. Everybody else said of her: "She is such a good mother. She adores her children." Only she herself, and her children themselves, knew it was not so. They read it in each other's eyes.

There were a boy and two little girls. They lived in a pleasant house, with a garden, and they had discreet servants, and felt themselves superior to anyone in the neighborhood.

Although they lived in style, they felt always an anxiety in the house. There was never enough money. The mother had a small income, and the father had a small income, but not nearly enough for the social position which they had to keep up. The father went into town to some office. But though he had good prospects, these prospects never materialized. There was always the grinding sense of the shortage of money, though the style was always kept up.

At last the mother said: "I will see if *I* can't make something." But she did not know where to begin. She racked her brains, and tried this thing and the other, but could not find anything successful. The failure made deep lines come into her face. Her children were growing up, they would have to go to school. There must be more money, there must be more money. The father, who was always very handsome and expensive in his tastes, seemed as if he never *would* be able to do anything worth doing. And the mother, who had a great belief in herself, did not succeed any better, and her tastes were just as expensive.

And so the house came to be haunted by the unspoken phrase: *There must be*   5
more money! There must be more money! The children could hear it all the time, though nobody said it aloud. They heard it at Christmas, when the expensive and splendid toys filled the nursery. Behind the shining modern rocking-horse, behind the smart doll's house, a voice would start whispering: "There *must* be more money! There *must* be more money!" And the children would stop playing, to listen for a moment. They would look into each other's eyes, to see if they had all heard. And each one saw in the eyes of the other two that they too had heard. "There *must* be more money! There *must* be more money!"

It came whispering from the springs of the still-swaying rocking-horse, and even the horse, bending his wooden, champing head, heard it. The big doll, sitting so pink and smirking in her new pram, could hear it quite plainly, and seemed to be smirking all the more self-consciously because of it. The foolish puppy, too, that took the place of the teddy-bear, he was looking so extraordinarily foolish for no other reason but that he heard the secret whisper all over the house: "There *must* be more money!"

Yet nobody ever said it aloud. The whisper was everywhere, and therefore no one spoke it. Just as no one ever says: "We are breathing!" in spite of the fact that breath is coming and going all the time.

"Mother," said the boy Paul one day, "why don't we keep a car of our own? Why do we always use uncle's, or else a taxi?"

"Because we're the poor members of the family," said the mother.

"But why *are* we, mother?"   10

"Well—I suppose," she said slowly and bitterly, "it's because your father has no luck."

The boy was silent for some time.

"Is luck money, mother?" he asked rather timidly.

"No, Paul. Not quite. It's what causes you to have money."

"Oh!" said Paul vaguely. "I thought when Uncle Oscar said *filthy lucker*, it meant   15
money."

"*Filthy lucre* does mean money," said the mother. "But it's lucre, not luck."

"Oh!" said the boy. "Then what *is* luck, mother?"

"It's what causes you to have money. If you're lucky you have money. That's why it's better to be born lucky than rich. If you're rich, you may lose your money. But if you're lucky, you will always get more money."

"Oh! Will you? And is father not lucky?"

"Very unlucky, I should say," she said bitterly.   20

The boy watched her with unsure eyes.

"Why?" he asked.

"I don't know. Nobody ever knows why one person is lucky and another unlucky."

"Don't they? Nobody at all? Does *nobody* know?"

"Perhaps God. But He never tells."   25

"He ought to, then. And aren't you lucky either, mother?"

"I can't be, if I married an unlucky husband."

"But by yourself, aren't you?"

"I used to think I was, before I married. Now I think I am very unlucky indeed."

"Why?"   30

"Well—never mind! Perhaps I'm not really," she said.

The child looked at her to see if she meant it. But he saw, by the lines of her mouth, that she was only trying to hide something from him.

"Well, anyhow," he said stoutly, "I'm a lucky person."

"Why?" said his mother, with a sudden laugh.

He stared at her. He didn't even know why he had said it.   35

"God told me," he asserted, brazening it out.

"I hope He did, dear!" she said, again with a laugh, but rather bitter.

"He did, mother!"

"Excellent!" said the mother, using one of her husband's exclamations.

The boy saw she did not believe him; or, rather, that she paid no attention to his   40
assertion. This angered him somewhat, and made him want to compel her attention.

He went off by himself, vaguely, in a childish way, seeking for the clue to "luck." Absorbed, taking no heed of other people, he went about with a sort of stealth, seeking inwardly for luck. He wanted luck, he wanted it, he wanted it. When the two girls were playing dolls in the nursery, he would sit on his big rocking-horse, charging madly into space, with a frenzy that made the little girls peer at him uneasily. Wildly the horse careered, the waving dark hair of the boy tossed, his eyes had a strange glare in them. The little girls dared not speak to him.

When he had ridden to the end of his mad little journey, he climbed down and stood in front of his rocking-horse, staring fixedly into its lowered face. Its red mouth was slightly open, its big eye was wide and glassy-bright.

"Now!" he would silently command the snorting steed. "Now, take me to where there is luck! Now take me!"

And he would slash the horse on the neck with the little whip he had asked Uncle Oscar for. He *knew* the horse could take him to where there was luck, if only he forced it. So he would mount again, and start on his furious ride, hoping at last to get there. He knew he could get there.

"You'll break your horse, Paul!" said the nurse.   45

"He's always riding like that! I wish he'd leave off!" said his elder sister Joan.

But he only glared down on them in silence. Nurse gave him up. She could make nothing of him. Anyhow he was growing beyond her.

One day his mother and his Uncle Oscar came in when he was on one of his furious rides. He did not speak to them.

"Hallo, you young jockey! Riding a winner?" said his uncle.

"Aren't you growing too big for a rocking-horse? You're not a very little boy any   50
longer, you know," said his mother.

But Paul only gave a blue glare from his big, rather close-set eyes. He would speak to nobody when he was in full tilt. His mother watched him with an anxious expression on her face.

At last he suddenly stopped forcing his horse into the mechanical gallop and slid down.

"Well, I got there!" he announced fiercely, his blue eyes still flaring, and his sturdy long legs straddling apart.

"Where did you get to?" asked his mother.

"Where I wanted to go," he flared back at her.   55

"That's right, son!" said Uncle Oscar. "Don't you stop till you get there. What's the horse's name?"

"He doesn't have a name," said the boy.

"Gets on without all right?" asked the uncle.

"Well, he has different names. He was called Sansovino last week."

"Sansovino, eh? Won the Ascot. How did you know his name?"   60

"He always talks about horse-races with Bassett," said Joan.

The uncle was delighted to find that his small nephew was posted with all the racing news. Bassett, the young gardener, who had been wounded in the left foot in the war and had got his present job through Oscar Cresswell, whose batman° he had been, was a perfect blade of the "turf." He lived in the racing events, and the small boy lived with him.

Oscar Cresswell got it all from Bassett.

"Master Paul comes and asks me, so I can't do more than tell him, sir," said Bassett, his face terribly serious, as if he were speaking of religious matters.

"And does he ever put anything on a horse he fancies?"   65

"Well—I don't want to give him away—he's a young sport, a fine sport, sir. Would you mind asking him himself? He sort of takes a pleasure in it, and perhaps he'd feel I was giving him away, sir, if you don't mind."

Bassett was serious as a church.

The uncle went back to his nephew and took him off for a ride in the car.

"Say, Paul, old man, do you ever put anything on a horse?" the uncle asked.

The boy watched the handsome man closely.   70

"Why, do you think I oughtn't to?" he parried.

"Not a bit of it. I thought perhaps you might give me a tip for the Lincoln."

The car sped on into the country, going down to Uncle Oscar's place in Hampshire.

"Honor bright?" said the nephew.

"Honor bright, son!" said the uncle.   75

"Well, then, Daffodil."

"Daffodil! I doubt it, sonny. What about Mirza?"

"I only know the winner," said the boy. "That's Daffodil."

"Daffodil, eh?"

There was a pause. Daffodil was an obscure horse comparatively.   80

"Uncle!"

"Yes, son?"

"You won't let it go any further, will you? I promised Bassett."

"Bassett be damned, old man! What's he got to do with it?"

"We're partners. We've been partners from the first. Uncle, he lent me my first   85
five shillings, which I lost. I promised him, honor bright, it was only between me and him; only you gave me that ten-shilling note I started winning with, so I thought you were lucky. You won't let it go any further, will you?"

---

batman: an enlisted man who serves as valet to a cavalry officer.

The boy gazed at his uncle from those big, hot, blue eyes, set rather close together. The uncle stirred and laughed uneasily.

"Right you are, son! I'll keep your tip private. Daffodil, eh? How much are you putting on him?"

"All except twenty pounds," said the boy. "I keep that in reserve."

The uncle thought it a good joke.

"You keep twenty pounds in reserve, do you, you young romancer? What are you 90 betting, then?"

"I'm betting three hundred," said the boy gravely. "But it's between you and me, Uncle Oscar! Honor bright?"

The uncle burst into a roar of laughter.

"It's between you and me all right, you young Nat Gould,"° he said, laughing. "But where's your three hundred?"

"Bassett keeps it for me. We're partners."

"You are, are you! And what is Bassett putting on Daffodil?" 95

"He won't go quite as high as I do, I expect. Perhaps he'll go a hundred and fifty."

"What, pennies?" laughed the uncle.

"Pounds," said the child, with a surprised look at his uncle. "Bassett keeps a bigger reserve than I do."

Between wonder and amusement Uncle Oscar was silent. He pursued the matter no further, but he determined to take his nephew with him to the Lincoln races.

"Now, son," he said, "I'm putting twenty on Mirza, and I'll put five for you on 100 any horse you fancy. What's your pick?"

"Daffodil, uncle."

"No, not the fiver on Daffodil!"

"I should if it was my own fiver," said the child.

"Good! Good! Right you are! A fiver for me and a fiver for you on Daffodil."

The child had never been to a race-meeting before, and his eyes were blue fire. 105 He pursed his mouth tight, and watched. A Frenchman just in front had put his money on Lancelot. Wild with excitement, he flayed his arms up and down, yelling "*Lancelot! Lancelot!*" in his French accent.

Daffodil came in first, Lancelot second, Mirza third. The child, flushed and with eyes blazing, was curiously serene. His uncle brought him four five-pound notes, four to one.

"What am I to do with these?" he cried, waving them before the boy's eyes.

"I suppose we'll talk to Bassett," said the boy. "I expect I have fifteen hundred now; and twenty in reserve; and this twenty."

His uncle studied him for some moments.

"Look here, son!" he said. "You're not serious about Bassett and that fifteen hundred, 110 are you?"

"Yes, I am. But it's between you and me, uncle. Honor bright!"

"Honor bright all right, son! But I must talk to Bassett."

"If you'd like to be a partner, uncle, with Bassett and me, we could all be partners. Only, you'd have to promise, honor bright, uncle, not to let it go beyond us three. Bassett and I are lucky, and you must be lucky, because it was your ten shillings I started winning with . . ."

Nat Gould: celebrated English gambler of the 1920s.

Uncle Oscar took both Bassett and Paul into Richmond Park for an afternoon, and there they talked.

"It's like this, you see, sir," Bassett said. "Master Paul would get me talking about 115 racing events, spinning yarns, you know, sir. And he was always keen on knowing if I'd made or if I'd lost. It's about a year since, now, that I put five shillings on Blush of Dawn for him: and we lost. Then the luck turned, and with that ten shillings he had from you: that we put on Singhalese. And since that time, it's been pretty steady, all things considering. What do you say, Master Paul?"

"We're all right when we're sure," said Paul. "It's when we're not quite sure that we go down."

"Oh, but we're careful then," said Bassett.

"But when are you *sure?*" smiled Uncle Oscar.

"It's Master Paul, sir," said Bassett, in a secret, religious voice. "It's as if he had it from heaven. Like Daffodil, now, for the Lincoln. That was as sure as eggs."

"Did you put anything on Daffodil?" asked Oscar Cresswell. 120

"Yes, sir. I made my bit."

"And my nephew?"

Bassett was obstinately silent, looking at Paul.

"I made twelve hundred, didn't I, Bassett? I told uncle I was putting three hundred on Daffodil."

"That's right," said Bassett, nodding. 125

"But where's the money?" asked the uncle.

"I keep it safe locked up, sir. Master Paul he can have it any minute he likes to ask for it."

"What, fifteen hundred pounds?"

"And twenty! And *forty*, that is, with the twenty he made on the course."

"It's amazing!" said the uncle. 130

"If Master Paul offers you to be partners, sir, I would, if I were you: if you'll excuse me," said Bassett.

Oscar Cresswell thought about it.

"I'll see the money," he said.

They drove home again, and, sure enough, Bassett came round to the garden-house with fifteen hundred pounds in notes. The twenty pounds reserve was left with Joe Glee, in the Turf Commission deposit.

"You see, it's all right, uncle, when I'm *sure!* Then we go strong, for all we're 135 worth. Don't we, Bassett!"

"We do that, Master Paul."

"And when are you sure?" said the uncle, laughing.

"Oh, well, sometimes I'm *absolutely* sure, like about Daffodil," said the boy; "and sometimes I have an idea; and sometimes I haven't even an idea, have I, Bassett? Then we're careful, because we mostly go down."

"You do, do you! And when you're sure, like about Daffodil, what makes you sure, sonny?"

"Oh, well, I don't know," said the boy uneasily. "I'm sure, you know, uncle; 140 that's all."

"It's as if he had it from heaven, sir," Bassett reiterated.

"I should say so!" said the uncle.

But he became a partner. And when the Leger was coming on, Paul was "sure" about Lively Spark, which was a quite inconsiderable horse. The boy insisted on putting a thousand on the horse, Bassett went for five hundred, and Oscar Cresswell two hundred. Lively Spark came in first, and the betting had been ten to one against him. Paul had made ten thousand.

"You see," he said, "I was absolutely sure of him."

Even Oscar Cresswell had cleared two thousand.   145

"Look here, son," he said, "this sort of thing makes me nervous."

"It needn't, uncle! Perhaps I shan't be sure again for a long time."

"But what are you going to do with your money?" asked the uncle.

"Of course," said the boy, "I started it for mother. She said she had no luck, because father is unlucky, so I thought if *I* was lucky, it might stop whispering."

"What might stop whispering?"   150

"Our house. I *hate* our house for whispering."

"What does it whisper?"

"Why—why"—the boy fidgeted—"why, I don't know. But it's always short of money, you know, uncle."

"I know it, son, I know it."

"You know people send mother writs, don't you, uncle?"   155

"I'm afraid I do," said the uncle.

"And then the house whispers, like people laughing at you behind your back. It's awful, that is! I thought if I was lucky—"

"You might stop it," added the uncle.

The boy watched him with big blue eyes, that had an uncanny cold fire in them, and he said never a word.

"Well, then!" said the uncle. "What are we doing?"   160

"I shouldn't like mother to know I was lucky," said the boy.

"Why not, son?"

"She'd stop me."

"I don't think she would."

"Oh!"—and the boy writhed in an odd way—"I *don't* want her to know, uncle."   165

"All right, son! We'll manage it without her knowing."

They managed it very easily. Paul, at the other's suggestion, handed over five thousand pounds to his uncle, who deposited it with the family lawyer, who was then to inform Paul's mother that a relative had put five thousand pounds into his hands, which sum was to be paid out a thousand pounds at a time, on the mother's birthday, for the next five years.

"So she'll have a birthday present of a thousand pounds for five successive years," said Uncle Oscar. "I hope it won't make it all the harder for her later."

Paul's mother had her birthday in November. The house had been "whispering" worse than ever lately, and, even in spite of his luck, Paul could not bear up against it. He was very anxious to see the effect of the birthday letter, telling his mother about the thousand pounds.

When there were no visitors, Paul now took his meals with his parents, as he was   170
beyond the nursery control. His mother went into town nearly every day. She had discovered that she had an odd knack of sketching furs and dress materials, so she worked secretly in the studio of a friend who was the chief "artist" for the leading drapers. She drew the figures of ladies in furs and ladies in silk and sequins for the newspaper advertisements. This young woman artist earned several thousand pounds a year, but Paul's mother only made several hundreds, and she was again dissatisfied. She so wanted to be first in something, and she did not succeed, even in making sketches for drapery advertisements.

She was down to breakfast on the morning of her birthday. Paul watched her face as she read her letters. He knew the lawyer's letter. As his mother read it, her face hardened and became more expressionless. Then a cold, determined look came on her mouth. She hid the letter under the pile of others, and said not a word about it.

"Didn't you have anything nice in the post for your birthday, mother?" said Paul.

"Quite moderately nice," she said, her voice cold and absent.

She went away to town without saying more.

But in the afternoon Uncle Oscar appeared. He said Paul's mother had had a 175 long interview with the lawyer, asking if the whole five thousand could not be advanced at once, as she was in debt.

"What do you think, uncle?" said the boy.

"I leave it to you, son."

"Oh, let her have it, then! We can get some more with the other," said the boy.

"A bird in the hand is worth two in the bush, laddie!" said Uncle Oscar.

"But I'm sure to *know* for the Grand National; or the Lincolnshire; or else the 180 Derby. I'm sure to know for *one* of them," said Paul.

So Uncle Oscar signed the agreement, and Paul's mother touched the whole five thousand. Then something very curious happened. The voices in the house suddenly went mad, like a chorus of frogs on a spring evening. There were certain new furnishings, and Paul had a tutor. He was *really* going to Eton, his father's school, in the following autumn. There were flowers in the winter, and a blossoming of the luxury Paul's mother had been used to. And yet the voices in the house, behind the sprays of mimosa and almond blossom, and from under the piles of iridescent cushions, simply trilled and screamed in a sort of ecstasy: "There *must* be more money! Oh-h-h; there *must* be more money. Oh, now, now-w! Now-w-w—there *must* be more money!—more than ever! More than ever!"

It frightened Paul terribly. He studied away at his Latin and Greek with his tutor. But his intense hours were spent with Bassett. The Grand National had gone by: he had not "known," and had lost a hundred pounds. Summer was at hand. He was in agony for the Lincoln. But even for the Lincoln he didn't "know," and he lost fifty pounds. He became wild-eyed and strange, as if something were going to explode in him.

"Let it alone, son! Don't you bother about it!" urged Uncle Oscar. But it was as if the boy couldn't really hear what his uncle was saying.

"I've got to know for the Derby! I've got to know for the Derby!" the child reiterated, his big blue eyes blazing with a sort of madness.

His mother noticed how overwrought he was. 185

"You'd better go to the seaside. Wouldn't you like to go now to the seaside, instead of waiting? I think you'd better," she said, looking down at him anxiously, her heart curiously heavy because of him.

But the child lifted his uncanny blue eyes.

"I couldn't possibly go before the Derby, mother!" he said. "I couldn't possibly!"

"Why not?" she said, her voice becoming heavy when she was opposed. "Why not? You can still go from the seaside to see the Derby with your Uncle Oscar, if that's what you wish. No need for you to wait here. Besides, I think you care too much about these races. It's a bad sign. My family has been a gambling family, and you won't know till you grow up how much damage it has done. But it has done damage. I shall have to send Bassett away, and ask Uncle Oscar not to talk racing to you, unless you promise to be reasonable about it: go away to the seaside and forget it. You're all nerves!"

"I'll do what you like, mother, so long as you don't send me away till after the 190
Derby," the boy said.

"Send you away from where? Just from this house?"

"Yes," he said, gazing at her.

"Why, you curious child, what makes you care about this house so much, suddenly?
I never knew you loved it."

He gazed at her without speaking. He had a secret within a secret, something he
had not divulged, even to Bassett or to his Uncle Oscar.

But his mother, after standing undecided and a little bit sullen for some moments, 195
said:

"Very well, then! Don't go to the seaside till after the Derby, if you don't wish it.
But promise me you won't let your nerves go to pieces. Promise you won't think so
much about horse-racing and *events,* as you call them!"

"Oh, no," said the boy casually. "I won't think much about them, mother. You
needn't worry. I wouldn't worry, mother, if I were you."

"If you were me and I were you," said his mother, "I wonder what we *should* do!"

"But you know you needn't worry, mother, don't you?" the boy repeated.

"I should be awfully glad to know it," she said wearily. 200

"Oh, well, you *can,* you know. I mean, you *ought* to know you needn't worry,"
he insisted.

"Ought I? Then I'll see about it," she said.

Paul's secret of secrets was his wooden horse, that which had no name. Since he
was emancipated from a nurse and a nursery-governess, he had had his rocking-horse
removed to his own bedroom at the top of the house.

"Surely, you're too big for a rocking-horse!" his mother had remonstrated.

"Well, you see, mother, till I can have a *real* horse, I like to have *some* sort of 205
animal about," had been his quaint answer.

"Do you feel he keeps you company?" she laughed.

"Oh, yes! He's very good, he always keeps me company, when I'm there,"
said Paul.

So the horse, rather shabby, stood in an arrested prance in the boy's bedroom.

The Derby was drawing near, and the boy grew more and more tense. He hardly
heard what was spoken to him, he was very frail, and his eyes were really uncanny.
His mother had sudden strange seizures of uneasiness about him. Sometimes, for half
an hour, she would feel a sudden anxiety about him that was almost anguish. She
wanted to rush to him at once, and know he was safe.

Two nights before the Derby, she was at a big party in town, when one of her 210
rushes of anxiety about her boy, her first-born, gripped her heart till she could hardly
speak. She fought with the feeling, might and main, for she believed in common
sense. But it was too strong. She had to leave the dance and go downstairs to telephone to the country. The children's nursery-governess was terribly surprised and
startled at being rung up in the night.

"Are the children all right, Miss Wilmot?"

"Oh, yes, they are quite all right."

"Master Paul? Is he all right?"

"He went to bed as right as a trivet. Shall I run up and look at him?"

"No," said Paul's mother reluctantly. "No! Don't trouble. It's all right. Don't 215
sit up. We shall be home fairly soon." She did not want her son's privacy intruded
upon.

"Very good," said the governess.

It was about one-o'clock when Paul's mother and father drove up to their house. All was still. Paul's mother went to her room and slipped off her white fur cloak. She had told her maid not to wait up for her. She heard her husband downstairs, mixing a whisky and soda.

And then, because of the strange anxiety at her heart, she stole upstairs to her son's room. Noiselessly she went along the upper corridor. Was there a faint noise? What was it?

She stood, with arrested muscles, outside his door, listening. There was a strange, heavy, and yet not loud noise. Her heart stood still. It was a soundless noise, yet rushing and powerful. Something huge, in violent, hushed motion. What was it? What in God's name was it? She ought to know. She felt that she knew the noise. She knew what it was.

Yet she could not place it. She couldn't say what it was. And on and on it went, 220 like a madness.

Softly, frozen with anxiety and fear, she turned the door-handle.

The room was dark. Yet in the space near the window, she heard and saw something plunging to and fro. She gazed in fear and amazement.

Then suddenly she switched on the light, and saw her son, in his green pajamas, madly surging on the rocking-horse. The blaze of light suddenly lit him up, as he urged the wooden horse, and lit her up, as she stood, blonde, in her dress of pale green and crystal, in the doorway.

"Paul!" she cried. "Whatever are you doing?"

"It's Malabar!" he screamed, in a powerful, strange voice. "It's Malabar!" 225

His eyes blazed at her for one strange and senseless second, as he ceased urging his wooden horse. Then he fell with a crash to the ground, and she, all her tormented motherhood flooding upon her, rushed to gather him up.

But he was unconscious, and unconscious he remained, with some brain-fever. He talked and tossed, and his mother sat stonily by his side.

"Malabar! It's Malabar! Bassett, Bassett, I *know*! It's Malabar!"

So the child cried, trying to get up and urge the rocking-horse that gave him his inspiration.

"What does he mean by Malabar?" asked the heart-frozen mother. 230

"I don't know," said the father stonily.

"What does he mean by Malabar?" she asked her brother Oscar.

"It's one of the horses running for the Derby," was the answer.

And, in spite of himself, Oscar Cresswell spoke to Bassett, and himself put a thousand on Malabar: at fourteen to one.

The third day of the illness was critical: they were waiting for a change. The boy, 235 with his rather long, curly hair, was tossing ceaselessly on the pillow. He neither slept nor regained consciousness, and his eyes were like blue stones. His mother sat, feeling her heart had gone, turned actually into a stone.

In the evening, Oscar Cresswell did not come, but Bassett sent a message, saying could he come up for one moment, just one moment? Paul's mother was very angry at the intrusion, but on second thoughts she agreed. The boy was the same. Perhaps Bassett might bring him to consciousness.

The gardener, a shortish fellow with a little brown moustache and sharp little brown eyes, tiptoed into the room, touched his imaginary cap to Paul's mother, and stole to the bedside, staring with glittering, smallish eyes, at the tossing, dying child.

"Master Paul!" he whispered. "Master Paul! Malabar came in first all right, a clean win. I did as you told me. You've made over seventy thousand pounds, you have; you've got over eighty thousand. Malabar came in all right, Master Paul."

"Malabar! Malabar! Did I say Malabar, mother? Did I say Malabar? Do you think I'm lucky, mother? I knew Malabar, didn't I? Over eighty thousand pounds! I call that lucky, don't you, mother? Over eighty thousand pounds! I knew, didn't I know I knew? Malabar came in all right. If I ride my horse till I'm sure, then I tell you, Bassett, you can go as high as you like. Did you go for all you were worth, Bassett?"

"I went a thousand on it, Master Paul."

"I never told you, mother, that if I can ride my horse, and *get there*, then I'm absolutely sure—oh, absolutely! Mother, did I ever tell you? I *am* lucky!"

240

"No, you never did," said his mother.

But the boy died in the night.

And even as he lay dead, his mother heard her brother's voice saying to her: "My God, Hester, you're eighty-odd thousand to the good, and a poor devil of a son to the bad. But, poor devil, poor devil, he's best gone out of a life where he rides his rocking-horse to find a winner."

Bobbie Ann Mason

Shiloh
1982

Bobbie Ann Mason, one of the leading voices in the new Southern fiction, was born in 1940 in Mayfield, Kentucky, growing up on a dairy farm in a region of western Kentucky whose people often appear in her stories. After her graduation from the University of Kentucky, she wrote for popular magazines, including Movie Life *and* TV Star Parade, *then began teaching college, taking her Ph.D. at the University of Connecticut and writing the critical studies* Nabokov's Garden *(1974) and* The Girl Sleuth: A Feminist Guide to the Bobbsey Twins, Nancy Drew, and Their Sisters *(1975). Her other nonfiction books include* Clear Springs *(1999), a family memoir, and* Elvis Presley *(2003), a biography in the Penguin Lives series. Her first fiction collection,* Shiloh and Other Stories *(1982),*

Bobbie Ann Mason

received wide attention; it was followed by Midnight Magic: Selected Stories of Bobbie Ann Mason *(1998),* Zigzagging Down a Wild Trail *(2001), and* Nancy Culpepper *(2006). She has published four novels,* In Country *(1985),* Spence + Lila *(1988),* Feather Crowns *(1993), and* An Atomic Romance *(2005). Mason has also supplied many unsigned contributions to the "Talk of the Town" feature in the* New Yorker. *She is a professor of English at the University of Kentucky.*

Leroy Moffitt's wife, Norma Jean, is working on her pectorals. She lifts three-pound dumbbells to warm up, then progresses to a twenty-pound barbell. Standing with her legs apart, she reminds Leroy of Wonder Woman.

"I'd give anything if I could just get these muscles to where they're real hard," says Norma Jean. "Feel this arm. It's not as hard as the other one."

"That's 'cause you're right-handed," says Leroy, dodging as she swings the barbell in an arc.

"Do you think so?"

"Sure."

5

Leroy is a truckdriver. He injured his leg in a highway accident four months ago, and his physical therapy, which involves weights and a pulley, prompted Norma Jean to try building herself up. Now she is attending a body-building class. Leroy has been collecting temporary disability since his tractor-trailer jackknifed in Missouri, badly twisting his left leg in its socket. He has a steel pin in his hip. He will probably not be able to drive his rig again. It sits in the backyard, like a gigantic bird that has flown home to roost. Leroy has been home in Kentucky for three months, and his leg is almost healed, but the accident frightened him and he does not want to drive any more long hauls. He is not sure what to do next. In the meantime, he makes things from craft kits. He started by building a miniature log cabin from notched Popsicle sticks. He varnished it and placed it on the TV set, where it remains. It reminds him of a rustic Nativity scene. Then he tried string art (sailing ships on black velvet), a macramé owl kit, a snap-together B-17 Flying Fortress, and a lamp made out of a model truck, with a light fixture screwed in the top of the cab. At first the kits were diversions, something to kill time, but now he is thinking about building a full-scale log house from a kit. It would be considerably cheaper than building a regular house, and besides, Leroy has grown to appreciate how things are put together. He has begun to realize that in all the years he was on the road he never took time to examine anything. He was always flying past scenery.

"They won't let you build a log cabin in any of the new subdivisions," Norma Jean tells him.

"They will if I tell them it's for you," he says, teasing her. Ever since they were married, he has promised Norma Jean he would build her a new home one day. They have always rented, and the house they live in is small and nondescript. It does not even feel like a home, Leroy realizes now.

Norma Jean works at the Rexall drugstore, and she has acquired an amazing amount of information about cosmetics. When she explains to Leroy the three stages of complexion care, involving creams, toners, and moisturizers, he thinks happily of other petroleum products—axle grease, diesel fuel. This is a connection between him and Norma Jean. Since he has been home, he has felt unusually tender about his wife and guilty over his long absences. But he can't tell what she feels about him. Norma Jean has never complained about his traveling; she has never made hurt remarks, like calling his truck a "widow-maker." He is reasonably certain she has been faithful to him, but he wishes she would celebrate his permanent home-coming more happily. Norma Jean is often startled to find Leroy at home, and he thinks she seems a little disappointed about it. Perhaps he reminds her too much of the early days of their marriage, before he went on the road. They had a child who died as an infant, years ago. They never speak about their memories of Randy, which have almost faded, but now that Leroy is home all the time, they sometimes feel awkward around each other, and Leroy wonders if one of them should mention the child. He has the feeling that they are waking up out of a dream together—that they must create a new marriage, start afresh. They are lucky they are still married. Leroy has read that for most people losing a child destroys the marriage—or else he heard this on *Donahue*. He can't always remember where he learns things anymore.

At Christmas, Leroy bought an electric organ for Norma Jean. She used to play   10
the piano when she was in high school. "It don't leave you," she told him once. "It's like riding a bicycle."

The new instrument had so many keys and buttons that she was bewildered by it at first. She touched the keys tentatively, pushed some buttons, then pecked out "Chopsticks." It came out in an amplified fox-trot rhythm, with marimba sounds.

"It's an orchestra!" she cried.

The organ had a pecan-look finish and eighteen preset chords, with optional flute, violin, trumpet, clarinet, and banjo accompaniments. Norma Jean mastered the organ almost immediately. At first she played Christmas songs. Then she bought *The Sixties Songbook* and learned every tune in it, adding variations to each with the rows of brightly colored buttons.

"I didn't like these old songs back then," she said. "But I have this crazy feeling I missed something."

"You didn't miss a thing," said Leroy.   15

Leroy likes to lie on the couch and smoke a joint and listen to Norma Jean play "Can't Take My Eyes Off You" and "I'll Be Back." He is back again. After fifteen years on the road, he is finally settling down with the woman he loves. She is still pretty. Her skin is flawless. Her frosted curls resemble pencil trimmings.

Now that Leroy has come home to stay, he notices how much the town has changed. Subdivisions are spreading across western Kentucky like an oil slick. The sign at the edge of town says "Pop: 11,500"—only seven hundred more than it said twenty years before. Leroy can't figure out who is living in all the new houses. The farmers who used to gather around the courthouse square on Saturday afternoons to play checkers and spit tobacco juice have gone. It has been years since Leroy has thought about the farmers, and they have disappeared without his noticing.

Leroy meets a kid named Stevie Hamilton in the parking lot at the new shopping center. While they pretend to be strangers meeting over a stalled car, Stevie tosses an ounce of marijuana under the front seat of Leroy's car. Stevie is wearing orange jogging shoes and a T-shirt that says CHATTAHOOCHEE SUPER-RAT. His father is a prominent doctor who lives in one of the expensive subdivisions in a new white-columned brick house that looks like a funeral parlor. In the phone book under his name there is a separate number, with the listing "Teenagers."

"Where do you get this stuff?" asks Leroy. "From your pappy?"

"That's for me to know and you to find out," Stevie says. He is slit-eyed and skinny.   20

"What else you got?"

"What you interested in?"

"Nothing special. Just wondered."

Leroy used to take speed on the road. Now he has to go slowly. He needs to be mellow. He leans back against the car and says, "I'm aiming to build me a log house, soon as I get time. My wife, though, I don't think she likes the idea."

"Well, let me know when you want me again," Stevie says. He has a cigarette in   25
his cupped palm, as though sheltering it from the wind. He takes a long drag, then stomps it on the asphalt and slouches away.

Stevie's father was two years ahead of Leroy in high school. Leroy is thirty-four. He married Norma Jean when they were both eighteen, and their child Randy was born a few months later, but he died at the age of four months and three days. He would be about Stevie's age now. Norma Jean and Leroy were at the drive-in, watching a double feature (*Dr. Strangelove* and *Lover Come Back*), and the baby was sleeping in the back seat. When the first movie ended, the baby was dead. It was the sudden infant death syndrome. Leroy remembers handing Randy to a nurse at the emergency room, as though he were offering her a large doll as a present. A dead baby feels like a sack of flour. "It just happens sometimes," said the doctor, in what Leroy always recalls as a nonchalant tone. Leroy can hardly remember the child anymore, but he still sees vividly a scene from *Dr. Strangelove°* in which the President of the United States was talking in a folksy voice on the hot line to the Soviet premier about the bomber accidentally headed toward Russia. He was in the War Room, and the world map was lit up. Leroy remembers Norma Jean standing catatonically beside him in the hospital and himself thinking: Who is this strange girl? He had forgotten who she was. Now scientists are saying that crib death is caused by a virus. Nobody knows anything, Leroy thinks. The answers are always changing.

When Leroy gets home from the shopping center, Norma Jean's mother, Mabel Beasley, is there. Until this year, Leroy has not realized how much time she spends with Norma Jean. When she visits, she inspects the closets and then the plants, informing Norma Jean when a plant is droopy or yellow. Mabel calls the plants "flowers," although there are never any blooms. She also notices if Norma Jean's laundry is piling up. Mabel is a short, overweight woman whose tight, brown-dyed curls look more like a wig than the actual wig she sometimes wears. Today she has brought Norma Jean an off-white dust ruffle she made for the bed; Mabel works in a custom-upholstery shop.

"This is the tenth one I made this year," Mabel says. "I got started and couldn't stop."

"It's real pretty," says Norma Jean.

"Now we can hide things under the bed," says Leroy, who gets along with his   30
mother-in-law primarily by joking with her. Mabel has never really forgiven him for disgracing her by getting Norma Jean pregnant. When the baby died, she said that fate was mocking her.

"What's that thing?" Mabel says to Leroy in a loud voice, pointing to a tangle of yarn on a piece of canvas.

Leroy holds it up for Mabel to see. "It's my needlepoint," he explains. "This is a *Star Trek* pillow cover."

"That's what a woman would do," says Mabel. "Great day in the morning!"

"All the big football players on TV do it," he says.

"Why, Leroy, you're always trying to fool me. I don't believe you for one minute.   35
You don't know what to do with yourself—that's the whole trouble. Sewing!"

"I'm aiming to build us a log house," says Leroy. "Soon as my plans come."

"Like *heck* you are," says Norma Jean. She takes Leroy's needlepoint and shoves it into a drawer. "You have to find a job first. Nobody can afford to build now anyway."

Mabel straightens her girdle and says, "I still think before you get tied down y'all ought to take a little run to Shiloh."

"One of these days, Mama," Norma Jean says impatiently.

Mabel is talking about Shiloh, Tennessee. For the past few years, she has been   40
urging Leroy and Norma Jean to visit the Civil War battleground there. Mabel went

---

Dr. Strangelove: Stanley Kubrick's classic 1964 suspense comedy film about a mad U.S. general who launches an unauthorized nuclear attack on Russia.

there on her honeymoon—the only real trip she ever took. Her husband died of a perforated ulcer when Norma Jean was ten, but Mabel, who was accepted into the United Daughters of the Confederacy in 1975, is still preoccupied with going back to Shiloh.

"I've been to kingdom come and back in that truck out yonder," Leroy says to Mabel, "but we never yet set foot in that battleground. Ain't that something? How did I miss it?"

"It's not even that far," Mabel says.

After Mabel leaves, Norma Jean reads to Leroy from a list she has made. "Things you could do," she announces. "You could get a job as a guard at Union Carbide, where they'd let you set on a stool. You could get one at the lumberyard. You could do a little carpenter work, if you want to build so bad. You could—"

"I can't do something where I'd have to stand up all day."

"You ought to try standing up all day behind a cosmetics counter. It's amazing 45
that I have strong feet, coming from two parents that never had strong feet at all." At the moment Norma Jean is holding on to the kitchen counter, raising her knees one at a time as she talks. She is wearing two-pound ankle weights.

"Don't worry," says Leroy. "I'll do something."

"You could truck calves to slaughter for somebody. You wouldn't have to drive any big old truck for that."

"I'm going to build you this house," says Leroy. "I want to make you a real home."

"I don't want to live in any log cabin."

"It's not a cabin. It's a house." 50

"I don't care. It looks like a cabin."

"You and me together could lift those logs. It's just like lifting weights."

Norma Jean doesn't answer. Under her breath, she is counting. Now she is marching through the kitchen. She is doing goose steps.°

Before his accident, when Leroy came home he used to stay in the house with Norma Jean, watching TV in bed and playing cards. She would cook fried chicken, picnic ham, chocolate pie—all his favorites. Now he is home alone much of the time. In the mornings, Norma Jean disappears, leaving a cooling place in the bed. She eats a cereal called Body Buddies, and she leaves the bowl on the table, with the soggy tan balls floating in a milk puddle. He sees things about Norma Jean that he never realized before. When she chops onions, she stares off into a corner, as if she can't bear to look. She puts on her house slippers almost precisely at nine o'clock every evening and nudges her jogging shoes under the couch. She saves bread heels for the birds. Leroy watches the birds at the feeder. He notices the peculiar way goldfinches fly past the window. They close their wings, then fall, then spread their wings to catch and lift themselves. He wonders if they close their eyes when they fall. Norma Jean closes her eyes when they are in bed. She wants the lights turned out. Even then, he is sure she closes her eyes.

He goes for long drives around town. He tends to drive a car rather carelessly. 55
Power steering and an automatic shift make a car feel so small and inconsequential that his body is hardly involved in the driving process. His injured leg stretches out

---

goose steps: a stiff-kneed, straight-legged marching step used in military parades. Used here as an exercise routine.

comfortably. Once or twice he has almost hit something, but even the prospect of an accident seems minor in a car. He cruises the new subdivisions, feeling like a criminal rehearsing for a robbery. Norma Jean is probably right about a log house being inappropriate here in the new subdivision. All the houses look grand and complicated. They depress him.

One day when Leroy comes home from a drive he finds Norma Jean in tears. She is in the kitchen making a potato and mushroom-soup casserole, with grated cheese topping. She is crying because her mother caught her smoking.

"I didn't hear her coming. I was standing here puffing away pretty as you please," Norma Jean says, wiping her eyes.

"I knew it would happen sooner or later," says Leroy, putting his arm around her.

"She don't know the meaning of the word 'knock,'" says Norma Jean. "It's a wonder she hadn't caught me years ago."

"Think of it this way," Leroy says. "What if she caught me with a joint?"   60

"You better not let her!" Norma Jean shrieks. "I'm warning you, Leroy Moffitt!"

"I'm just kidding. Here, play me a tune. That'll help you relax."

Norma Jean puts the casserole in the oven and sets the timer. Then she plays a ragtime tune, with horns and banjo, as Leroy lights up a joint and lies on the couch, laughing to himself about Mabel's catching him at it. He thinks of Stevie Hamilton—a doctor's son pushing grass. Everything is funny. The whole town seems crazy and small. He is reminded of Virgil Mathis, a boastful policeman Leroy used to shoot pool with. Virgil recently led a drug bust in a back room at a bowling alley, where he seized ten thousand dollars' worth of marijuana. The newspaper had a picture of him holding up the bags of grass and grinning widely. Right now, Leroy can imagine Virgil breaking down the door and arresting him with a lungful of smoke. Virgil would probably have been alerted to the scene because of all the racket Norma Jean is making. Now she sounds like a hard-rock band. Norma Jean is terrific. When she switches to a Latin-rhythm version of "Sunshine Superman," Leroy hums along. Norma Jean's foot goes up and down, up and down.

"Well, what do you think?" Leroy says, when Norma Jean pauses to search through her music.

"What do I think about what?"   65

His mind has gone blank. Then he says, "I'll sell my rig and build us a house." That wasn't what he wanted to say. He wanted to know what she thought—what she *really* thought—about them.

"Don't start in on that again," says Norma Jean. She begins playing "Who'll Be the Next in Line?"

Leroy used to tell hitchhikers his whole life story—about his travels, his hometown, the baby. He would end with a question: "Well, what do you think?" It was just a rhetorical question. In time, he had the feeling that he'd been telling the same story over and over to the same hitchhikers. He quit talking to hitchhikers when he realized how his voice sounded—whining and self-pitying, like some teenage-tragedy song. Now Leroy has the sudden impulse to tell Norma Jean about himself, as if he had just met her. They have known each other so long they have forgotten a lot about each other. They could become reacquainted. But when the oven timer goes off and she runs to the kitchen, he forgets why he wants to do this.

The next day, Mabel drops by. It is Saturday and Norma Jean is cleaning. Leroy is studying the plans of his log house, which have finally come in the mail. He has them spread out on the table—big sheets of stiff blue paper, with diagrams and numbers printed in white. While Norma Jean runs the vacuum, Mabel drinks coffee. She sets her coffee cup on a blueprint.

"I'm just waiting for time to pass," she says to Leroy, drumming her fingers on the table. 70

As soon as Norma Jean switches off the vacuum, Mabel says in a loud voice, "Did you hear about the datsun dog that killed the baby?"

Norma Jean says, "The word is 'dachshund.'"

"They put the dog on trial. It chewed the baby's legs off. The mother was in the next room all the time." She raises her voice. "They thought it was neglect."

Norma Jean is holding her ears. Leroy manages to open the refrigerator and get some Diet Pepsi to offer Mabel. Mabel still has some coffee and she waves away the Pepsi.

"Datsuns are like that," Mabel says. "They're jealous dogs. They'll tear a place to pieces if you don't keep an eye on them." 75

"You better watch out what you're saying, Mabel," says Leroy.

"Well, facts is facts."

Leroy looks out the window at his rig. It is like a huge piece of furniture gathering dust in the backyard. Pretty soon it will be an antique. He hears the vacuum cleaner. Norma Jean seems to be cleaning the living room rug again.

Later, she says to Leroy, "She just said that about the baby because she caught me smoking. She's trying to pay me back."

"What are you talking about?" Leroy says, nervously shuffling blueprints. 80

"You know good and well," Norma Jean says. She is sitting in a kitchen chair with her feet up and her arms wrapped around her knees. She looks small and helpless. She says, "The very idea, her bringing up a subject like that! Saying it was neglect."

"She didn't mean that," Leroy says.

"She might not have *thought* she meant it. She always says things like that. You don't know how she goes on."

"But she didn't really mean it. She was just talking."

Leroy opens a king-sized bottle of beer and pours it into two glasses, dividing it carefully. He hands a glass to Norma Jean and she takes it from him mechanically. For a long time, they sit by the kitchen window watching the birds at the feeder. 85

Something is happening. Norma Jean is going to night school. She has graduated from her six-week body-building course and now she is taking an adult-education course in composition at Paducah Community College. She spends her evenings outlining paragraphs.

"First, you have a topic sentence," she explains to Leroy. "Then you divide it up. Your secondary topic has to be connected to your primary topic."

To Leroy, this sounds intimidating. "I never was any good in English," he says.

"It makes a lot of sense."

"What are you doing this for, anyhow?" 90

She shrugs. "It's something to do." She stands up and lifts her dumbbells a few times.

"Driving a rig, nobody cared about my English."

"I'm not criticizing your English."

Norma Jean used to say, "If I lose ten minutes' sleep, I just drag all day." Now she stays up late, writing compositions. She got a B on her first paper—a how-to theme on soup-based casseroles. Recently Norma Jean has been cooking unusual foods—tacos, lasagna, Bombay chicken. She doesn't play the organ anymore, though her second paper was called "Why Music Is Important to Me." She sits at the kitchen table, concentrating on her outlines, while Leroy plays with his log house plans, practicing with a set of Lincoln Logs. The thought of getting a truckload of notched, numbered logs scares him, and he wants to be prepared. As he and Norma Jean work together at the kitchen table, Leroy has the hopeful thought that they are sharing something, but he knows he is a fool to think this. Norma Jean is miles away. He knows he is going to lose her. Like Mabel, he is just waiting for time to pass.

One day, Mabel is there before Norma Jean gets home from work, and Leroy finds 95 himself confiding in her. Mabel, he realizes, must know Norma Jean better than he does.

"I don't know what's got into that girl," Mabel says. "She used to go to bed with the chickens. Now you say she's up all hours. Plus her a-smoking. I like to died."

"I want to make her this beautiful home," Leroy says, indicating the Lincoln Logs. "I don't think she even wants it. Maybe she was happier with me gone."

"She don't know what to make of you, coming home like this."

"Is that it?"

Mabel takes the roof off his Lincoln Log cabin. "You couldn't get *me* in a log 100 cabin," she says. "I was raised in one. It's no picnic, let me tell you."

"They're different now," says Leroy.

"I tell you what," Mabel says, smiling oddly at Leroy.

"What?"

"Take her on down to Shiloh. Y'all need to get out together, stir a little. Her brain's all balled up over them books."

Leroy can see traces of Norma Jean's features in her mother's face. Mabel's worn face 105 has the texture of crinkled cotton, but suddenly she looks pretty. It occurs to Leroy that Mabel has been hinting all along that she wants them to take her with them to Shiloh.

"Let's all go to Shiloh," he says. "You and me and her. Come Sunday."

Mabel throws up her hand in protest. "Oh, no, not me. Young folks want to be by theirselves."

When Norma Jean comes in with groceries, Leroy says excitedly, "Your mama here's been dying to go to Shiloh for thirty-five years. It's about time we went, don't you think?"

"I'm not going to butt in on anybody's second honeymoon," Mabel says.

"Who's going on a honeymoon, for Christ's sake?" Norma Jean says loudly. 110

"I never raised no daughter of mine to talk that-a-way," Mabel says.

"You ain't seen nothing yet," says Norma Jean. She starts putting away boxes and cans, slamming cabinet doors.

"There's a log cabin at Shiloh," Mabel says. "It was there during the battle. There's bullet holes in it."

"When are you going to *shut up* about Shiloh, Mama?" asks Norma Jean.

"I always thought Shiloh was the prettiest place, so full of history," Mabel 115 goes on. "I just hoped y'all could see it once before I die, so you could tell me about it." Later, she whispers to Leroy, "You do what I said. A little change is what she needs."

"Your name means 'the king,'" Norma Jean says to Leroy that evening. He is trying to get her to go to Shiloh, and she is reading a book about another century.

"Well, I reckon I ought to be right proud."

"I guess so."

"Am I still king around here?"

Norma Jean flexes her biceps and feels them for hardness. "I'm not fooling   120
around with anybody, if that's what you mean," she says.

"Would you tell me if you were?"

"I don't know."

"What does *your* name mean?"

"It was Marilyn Monroe's real name."

"No kidding!"   125

"Norma comes from the Normans. They were invaders," she says. She closes her
book and looks hard at Leroy. "I'll go to Shiloh with you if you'll stop staring at me."

On Sunday, Norma Jean packs a picnic and they go to Shiloh. To Leroy's relief
Mabel says she does not want to come with them. Norma Jean drives, and Leroy, sitting beside her, feels like some boring hitchhiker she has picked up. He tries some
conversation, but she answers him in monosyllables. At Shiloh, she drives aimlessly
through the park, past bluffs and trails and steep ravines. Shiloh is an immense place,
and Leroy cannot see it as a battleground. It is not what he expected. He thought it
would look like a golf course. Monuments are everywhere, showing through the thick
clusters of trees. Norma Jean passes the log cabin Mabel mentioned. It is surrounded
by tourists looking for bullet holes.

"That's not the kind of log house I've got in mind," says Leroy apologetically.

"I know *that*."

"This is a pretty place. Your mama was right."   130

"It's O.K.," says Norma Jean. "Well, we've seen it. I hope she's satisfied."

They burst out laughing together.

At the park museum, a movie on Shiloh is shown every half hour, but they decide that they don't want to see it. They buy a souvenir Confederate flag for Mabel,
and then they find a picnic spot near the cemetery. Norma Jean has brought a picnic
cooler, with pimiento sandwiches, soft drinks, and Yodels. Leroy eats a sandwich
and then smokes a joint, hiding it behind the picnic cooler. Norma Jean has quit
smoking altogether. She is picking cake crumbs from the cellophane wrapper, like a
fussy bird.

Leroy says, "So the boys in gray ended up in Corinth. The Union soldiers zapped
'em finally. April 7, 1862."

They both know that he doesn't know any history. He is just talking about some   135
of the historical plaques they have read. He feels awkward, like a boy on a date with
an older girl. They are still just making conversation.

"Corinth is where Mama eloped to," says Norma Jean.

They sit in silence and stare at the cemetery for the Union dead and, beyond, at
a tall cluster of trees. Campers are parked nearby, bumper to bumper, and small children in bright clothing are cavorting and squealing. Norma Jean wads up the cake
wrapper and squeezes it tightly in her hand. Without looking at Leroy, she says, "I
want to leave you."

Leroy takes a bottle of Coke out of the cooler and flips off the cap. He holds the
bottle poised near his mouth but cannot remember to take a drink. Finally he says,
"No, you don't."

"Yes, I do."

"I won't let you."   140

"You can't stop me."

"Don't do me that way."

Leroy knows Norma Jean will have her own way. "Didn't I promise to be home from now on?" he says.

"In some ways, a woman prefers a man who wanders," says Norma Jean. "That sounds crazy, I know."

"You're not crazy."   145

Leroy remembers to drink from his Coke. Then he says, "Yes, you *are* crazy. You and me could start all over again. Right back at the beginning."

"We *have* started all over again," says Norma Jean. "And this is how it turned out."

"What did I do wrong?"

"Nothing."

"Is this one of those women's lib things?" Leroy asks.   150

"Don't be funny."

The cemetery, a green slope dotted with white markers, looks like a subdivision site. Leroy is trying to comprehend that his marriage is breaking up, but for some reason he is wondering about white slabs in a graveyard.

"Everything was fine till Mama caught me smoking," says Norma Jean, standing up. "That set something off."

"What are you talking about?"

"She won't leave me alone—*you* won't leave me alone." Norma Jean seems to be   155
crying, but she is looking away from him. "I feel eighteen again. I can't face that all over again." She starts walking away. "No, it *wasn't* fine. I don't know what I'm saying. Forget it."

Leroy takes a lungful of smoke and closes his eyes as Norma Jean's words sink in. He tries to focus on the fact that thirty-five hundred soldiers died on the grounds around him. He can only think of that war as a board game with plastic soldiers. Leroy almost smiles, as he compares the Confederates' daring attack on the Union camps and Virgil Mathis's raid on the bowling alley. General Grant, drunk and furious, shoved the Southerners back to Corinth, where Mabel and Jet Beasley were married years later, when Mabel was still thin and good-looking. The next day, Mabel and Jet visited the battleground, and then Norma Jean was born, and then she married Leroy and they had a baby, which they lost, and now Leroy and Norma Jean are here at the same battleground. Leroy knows he is leaving out a lot. He is leaving out the insides of history. History was always just names and dates to him. It occurs to him that building a house of logs is similarly empty—too simple. And the real inner workings of a marriage, like most of history, have escaped him. Now he sees that building a log house is the dumbest idea he could have had. It was clumsy of him to think Norma Jean would want a log house. It was a crazy idea. He'll have to think of something else, quickly. He will wad the blueprints into tight balls and fling them into the lake. Then he'll get moving again. He opens his eyes. Norma Jean has moved away and is walking through the cemetery, following a serpentine brick path.

Leroy gets up to follow his wife, but his good leg is asleep and his bad leg still hurts him. Norma Jean is far away, walking rapidly toward the bluff by the river, and he tries to hobble toward her. Some children run past him, screaming noisily. Norma Jean has reached the bluff, and she is looking out over the Tennessee River. Now she turns toward Leroy and waves her arms. Is she beckoning to him? She seems to be doing an exercise for her chest muscles. The sky is unusually pale—the color of the dust ruffle Mabel made for their bed.

Lorrie Moore

How to Become a Writer 1985

Marie Lorena Moore was born in 1957 in Glens Falls, New York. Her father was an insurance company executive who wrote short stories and composed music for the church choir, and her mother was a school nurse. Moore graduated summa cum laude from St. Lawrence University in 1978 and spent two years in New York City as a paralegal. She did graduate work in creative writing at Cornell University, submitting a thesis that became her first collection of short stories, Self-Help (1985). Many of the pieces in this volume are what Moore has described as "second person, mock-imperative narratives [which] were written as stylistic experiments: Let's see what happens when one eliminates the subject, leaves the verb shivering at the start of a clause; what happens when one

Lorrie Moore

appropriates the 'how-to' form for a fiction, for an irony, for a 'how-not-to.' . . . The self-help proffered here, then, is perhaps only that of art itself, which, if you agree with Oscar Wilde, is quite useless." After her novel Anagrams was published in 1986, Moore began teaching at the University of Wisconsin at Madison, where she is now a professor of English. Her second novel, Who Will Run the Frog Hospital? (1994), recalls her adolescence in Glens Falls in the early 1970s. She has also published a novel for children, The Forgotten Helper (1987), and two further collections of short fiction, Like Life (1990) and Birds of America (1998), which spent several weeks on the best-seller lists, an unusual accomplishment for a book of stories. Her Collected Stories was published in Britain in 2008.

First, try to be something, anything, else. A movie star/astronaut. A movie star/missionary. A movie star/kindergarten teacher. President of the World. Fail miserably. It is best if you fail at an early age—say, fourteen. Early, critical disillusionment is necessary so that at fifteen you can write long haiku sequences about thwarted desire. It is a pond, a cherry blossom, a wind brushing against sparrow wing leaving for mountain. Count the syllables. Show it to your mom. She is tough and practical. She has a son in Vietnam and a husband who may be having an affair. She believes in wearing brown because it hides spots. She'll look briefly at your writing, then back up at you with a face blank as a donut. She'll say: "How about emptying the dishwasher?" Look away. Shove the forks in the fork drawer. Accidentally break one of the freebie gas station glasses. This is the required pain and suffering. This is only for starters.

In your high school English class look only at Mr. Killian's face. Decide faces are important. Write a villanelle about pores. Struggle. Write a sonnet. Count the syllables: nine, ten, eleven, thirteen. Decide to experiment with fiction. Here you don't have to count syllables. Write a short story about an elderly man and woman who accidentally shoot each other in the head, the result of an inexplicable malfunction of a shotgun which appears mysteriously in their living room one night. Give it to Mr. Killian as your final project. When you get it back, he has written on it: "Some of your images are quite nice, but you have no sense of plot." When you are home, in the privacy of your own room, faintly scrawl in pencil beneath his black-inked comments: "Plots are for dead people, pore-face."

Take all the babysitting jobs you can get. You are great with kids. They love you. You tell them stories about old people who die idiot deaths. You sing them songs like "Blue Bells of Scotland," which is their favorite. And when they are in their pajamas and have finally stopped pinching each other, when they are fast asleep, you read every sex manual in the house, and wonder how on earth anyone could ever do those things with someone they truly loved. Fall asleep in a chair reading Mr. McMurphy's *Playboy*. When the McMurphys come home, they will tap you on the shoulder, look at the magazine on your lap, and grin. You will want to die. They will ask you if Tracey took her medicine all right. Explain, yes, she did, that you promised her a story if she would take it like a big girl and that seemed to work out just fine. "Oh, marvelous," they will exclaim.

Try to smile proudly.

Apply to college as a child psychology major.   5

As a child psychology major, you have some electives. You've always liked birds. Sign up for something called "The Ornithological Field Trip." It meets Tuesdays and Thursdays at two. When you arrive at Room 134 on the first day of class, everyone is sitting around a seminar table talking about metaphors. You've heard of these. After a short, excruciating while, raise your hand and say diffidently, "Excuse me, isn't this Birdwatching One-oh-one?" The class stops and turns to look at you. They seem to all have one face—giant and blank as a vandalized clock. Someone with a beard booms out, "No, this is Creative Writing." Say: "Oh—right", as if perhaps you knew all along. Look down at your schedule. Wonder how the hell you ended up here. The computer, apparently, has made an error. You start to get up to leave and then don't. The lines at the registrar this week are huge. Perhaps you should stick with this mistake. Perhaps your creative writing isn't all that bad. Perhaps it is fate. Perhaps this is what your dad meant when he said, "It's the age of computers, Francie, it's the age of computers."

Decide that you like college life. In your dorm you meet many nice people. Some are smarter than you. And some, you notice, are dumber than you. You will continue, unfortunately, to view the world in exactly these terms for the rest of your life.

The assignment this week in creative writing is to narrate a violent happening. Turn in a story about driving with your Uncle Gordon and another one about two old people who are accidentally electrocuted when they go to turn on a badly wired desk lamp. The teacher will hand them back to you with comments: "Much of your writing is smooth and energetic. You have, however, a ludicrous notion of plot." Write another story about a man and a woman who, in the very first paragraph, have their lower torsos accidentally blitzed away by dynamite. In the second paragraph, with the insurance money, they buy a frozen yogurt stand together. There are six more paragraphs. You read the whole thing out loud in class. No one likes it. They say your sense of plot is outrageous and incompetent. After class someone asks you if you are crazy.

Decide that perhaps you should stick to comedies. Start dating someone who is funny, someone who has what in high school you called "a really great sense of humor" and what now your creative writing class calls "self-contempt giving rise to comic form." Write down all of his jokes, but don't tell him you are doing this. Make up anagrams of his old girlfriend's name and name all of your socially handicapped characters with them. Tell him his old girlfriend is in all your stories and then watch how funny he can be, see what a really great sense of humor he can have.

Your child psychology advisor tells you you are neglecting courses in your major.   10
What you spend the most time on should be what you're majoring in. Say yes, you understand.

In creative writing seminars over the next two years, everyone continues to smoke cigarettes and ask the same things: "But does it work?" "Why should we care about this character?" "Have you earned this cliché?" These seem like important questions.

On days when it is your turn, you look at the class hopefully as they scour your mimeographs for a plot. They look back up at you, drag deeply, and then smile in a sweet sort of way.

You spend too much time slouched and demoralized. Your boyfriend suggests bicycling. Your roommate suggests a new boyfriend. You are said to be self-mutilating and losing weight, but you continue writing. The only happiness you have is writing something new, in the middle of the night, armpits damp, heart pounding, something no one has yet seen. You have only those brief, fragile, untested moments of exhilaration when you know: you are a genius. Understand what you must do. Switch majors. The kids in your nursery project will be disappointed, but you have a calling, an urge, a delusion, an unfortunate habit. You have, as your mother would say, fallen in with a bad crowd.

Why write? Where does writing come from? These are questions to ask yourself. They are like: Where does dust come from? Or: Why is there war? Or: If there's a God, then why is my brother now a cripple?

These are questions that you keep in your wallet, like calling cards. These are   15
questions, your creative writing teacher says, that are good to address in your journals but rarely in your fiction.

The writing professor this fall is stressing the Power of the Imagination. Which means he doesn't want long descriptive stories about your camping trip last July. He wants you to start in a realistic context but then to alter it. Like recombinant DNA. He wants you to let your imagination sail, to let it grow big-bellied in the wind. This is a quote from Shakespeare.

Tell your roommate your great idea, your great exercise of imaginative power: a transformation of Melville to contemporary life. It will be about monomania and the fish-eat-fish world of life insurance in Rochester, New York. The first line will be "Call me Fishmeal," and it will feature a menopausal suburban husband named Richard, who because he is so depressed all the time is called "Mopey Dick" by his witty wife Elaine. Say to your roommate: "Mopey Dick, get it?" Your roommate looks at you, her face blank as a large Kleenex. She comes up to you, like a buddy, and puts an arm around your burdened shoulders. "Listen, Francie," she says, slow as speech therapy. "Let's go out and get a big beer."

*

The seminar doesn't like this one either. You suspect they are beginning to feel sorry for you. They say: "You have to think about what is happening. Where is the story here?"

The next semester the writing professor is obsessed with writing from personal experience. You must write from what you know, from what has happened to you. He wants deaths, he wants camping trips. Think about what has happened to you. In three years there have been three things: you lost your virginity; your parents got divorced; and your brother came home from a forest ten miles from the Cambodian border with only half a thigh, a permanent smirk nestled into one corner of his mouth.

About the first you write: "It created a new space, which hurt and cried in a   20
voice that wasn't mine, 'I'm not the same anymore, but I'll be okay.'"

About the second you write an elaborate story of an old married couple who stumble upon an unknown land mine in their kitchen and accidentally blow themselves up. You call it: "For Better or for Liverwurst."

About the last thing you write nothing. There are no words for this. Your typewriter hums. You can find no words.

At undergraduate cocktail parties, people say, "Oh, you write? What do you write about?" Your roommate, who has consumed too much wine, too little cheese, and no crackers at all, blurts: "Oh, my god, she always writes about her dumb boyfriend."

Later on in life you will learn that writers are merely open, helpless texts with no real understanding of what they have written and therefore must half-believe anything and everything that is said of them. You, however, have not yet reached this stage of literary criticism. You stiffen and say, "I do not," the same way you said it when someone in the fourth grade accused you of really liking oboe lessons and your parents really weren't just making you take them.

Insist you are not very interested in any one subject at all, that you are interested   25
in the music of language, that you are interested in—in—syllables, because they are the atoms of poetry, the cells of the mind, the breath of the soul. Begin to feel woozy. Stare into your plastic wine cup.

"Syllables?" you will hear someone ask, voice trailing off, as they glide slowly toward the reassuring white of the dip.

Begin to wonder what you do write about. Or if you have anything to say. Or if there even is such a thing as a thing to say. Limit these thoughts to no more than ten minutes a day; like sit-ups, they can make you thin.

You will read somewhere that all writing has to do with one's genitals. Don't dwell on this. It will make you nervous.

Your mother will come visit you. She will look at the circles under your eyes and hand you a brown book with a brown briefcase on the cover. It is entitled: *How to Become a Business Executive*. She has also brought the *Names for Baby* encyclopedia you asked for; one of your characters, the aging clown-schoolteacher, needs a new name. Your mother will shake her head and say: "Francie, Francie, remember when you were going to be a child psychology major?"

Say: "Mom, I like to write."   30
She'll say: "Sure you like to write. Of course. Sure you like to write."

Write a story about a confused music student and title it: "Schubert Was the One with the Glasses, Right?" It's not a big hit, although your roommate likes the part where the two violinists accidentally blow themselves up in a recital room. "I went out with a violinist once," she says, snapping her gum.

Thank god you are taking other courses. You can find sanctuary in nineteenth-century ontological snags and invertebrate courting rituals. Certain globulur mollusks have what is called "Sex by the Arm." The male octopus, for instance, loses the end of one arm when placing it inside the female body during intercourse. Marine biologists call it "Seven Heaven." Be glad you know these things. Be glad you are not just a writer. Apply to law school.

From here on in, many things can happen. But the main one will be this: you decide not to go to law school after all, and, instead, you spend a good, big chunk of your adult life telling people how you decided not to go to law school after all. Somehow you end up writing again. Perhaps you go to graduate school. Perhaps you work odd jobs and take writing courses at night. Perhaps you are working on a novel and writing down all the clever remarks and intimate personal confessions you hear during the day. Perhaps you are losing your pals, your acquaintances, your balance.

You have broken up with your boyfriend. You now go out with men who,   35
instead of whispering "I love you," shout: "Do it to me, baby." This is good for your writing.

Sooner or later you have a finished manuscript more or less. People look at it in a vaguely troubled sort of way and say, "I'll bet becoming a writer was always a fantasy of yours, wasn't it?" Your lips dry to salt. Say that of all the fantasies possible in the world, you can't imagine being a writer even making the top twenty. Tell them you were going to be a child psychology major. "I bet," they always sigh, "you'd be great with kids." Scowl fiercely. Tell them you're a walking blade.

Quit classes. Quit jobs. Cash in old savings bonds. Now you have time like warts on your hands. Slowly copy all of your friends' addresses into a new address book.

Vacuum. Chew cough drops. Keep a folder full of fragments.

> *An eyelid darkening sideways.*
> *World as conspiracy.*
> *Possible plot? A woman gets on a bus.*
> *Suppose you threw a love affair and nobody came?*

At home drink a lot of coffee. At Howard Johnson's order the cole slaw. Consider how it looks like the soggy confetti of a map: where you've been, where you're going—"You Are Here," says the red star on the back of the menu.

Occasionally a date with a face blank as a sheet of paper asks you whether writers   40
often become discouraged. Say that sometimes they do and sometimes they do. Say it's a lot like having polio.

"Interesting," smiles your date, and then he looks down at his arm hairs and starts to smooth them, all, always, in the same direction.

Joyce Carol Oates

Where Are You Going, Where Have You Been?   1970

Joyce Carol Oates
© Jill Krementz, Inc.

Joyce Carol Oates was born in 1938 into a blue collar, Catholic family in Lockport, New York. As an undergraduate at Syracuse University, she won a Mademoiselle *magazine award for fiction. After graduating with top honors, she took a master's degree in English at the University of Wisconsin and went on to teach at several universities: Detroit, Windsor, and Princeton. A remarkably prolific writer, Oates has produced more than twenty-five collections of stories, including* High Lonesome: Stories 1966–2006, *and forty novels, including* them, *winner of a National Book Award in 1970,* Because It Is Bitter, and Because It Is My Heart *(1990), and more recently,* Black Girl/White Girl *(2006),* The Gravedigger's Daughter *(2007), and* My Sister, My Love *(2008). She also writes poetry, plays, and literary criticism.* On Boxing *(1987) is her nonfiction memoir and study of fighters and fighting.* Foxfire *(1993), her twenty-second novel, is the story of a girl gang in upstate New York. Her 1996 Gothic novella,* First Love, *is a bizarre tale of terror and torture. Violence and the macabre may inhabit her best stories, but Oates has insisted that these elements in her work are never gratuitous. The 1985 film* Smooth Talk, *directed by Joyce Chopra, was based on "Where Are You Going, Where Have You Been?"*

For Bob Dylan

Her name was Connie. She was fifteen and she had a quick nervous giggling habit of craning her neck to glance into mirrors, or checking other people's faces to make sure her own was all right. Her mother, who noticed everything and knew everything and who hadn't much reason any longer to look at her own face, always scolded Connie about it. "Stop gawking at yourself, who are you? You think you're so pretty?" she would say. Connie would raise her eyebrows at these familiar complaints and look right through her mother, into a shadowy vision of herself as she was right at that moment: she knew she was pretty and that was everything. Her mother had been pretty once too, if you could believe those old snapshots in the album, but now her looks were gone and that was why she was always after Connie.

"Why don't you keep your room clean like your sister? How've you got your hair fixed—what the hell stinks? Hair spray? You don't see your sister using that junk."

Her sister June was twenty-four and still lived at home. She was a secretary in the high school Connie attended, and if that wasn't bad enough—with her in the same building—she was so plain and chunky and steady that Connie had to hear her praised all the time by her mother and her mother's sisters. June did this, June did that, she saved money and helped clean the house and cooked and Connie couldn't do a thing, her mind was all filled with trashy daydreams. Their father was away at work most of the time and when he came home he wanted supper and he read the newspaper at supper and after supper he went to bed. He didn't bother talking much to them, but around his bent head Connie's mother kept picking at her until Connie wished her mother was dead and she herself was dead and it was all over. "She makes me want to throw up sometimes," she complained to her friends. She had a high, breathless, amused voice which made everything she said sound a little forced, whether it was sincere or not.

There was one good thing: June went places with girl friends of hers, girls who were just as plain and steady as she, and so when Connie wanted to do that her mother had no objections. The father of Connie's best girl friend drove the girls the three miles to town and left them off at a shopping plaza, so that they could walk through the stores or go to a movie, and when he came to pick them up again at eleven he never bothered to ask what they had done.

They must have been familiar sights, walking around that shopping plaza in their   5
shorts and flat ballerina slippers that always scuffed the sidewalk, with charm bracelets jingling on their thin wrists; they would lean together to whisper and laugh secretly if someone passed by who amused or interested them. Connie had long dark blond hair that drew anyone's eye to it, and she wore part of it pulled up on her head and puffed out and the rest of it she let fall down her back. She wore a pull-over jersey blouse that looked one way when she was at home and another way when she was away from home. Everything about her had two sides to it, one for home and one for anywhere that was not home: her walk that could be childlike and bobbing, or languid enough to make anyone think she was hearing music in her head, her mouth which was pale and smirking most of the time, but bright and pink on these evenings out, her laugh which was cynical and drawling at home—"Ha, ha, very funny"—but high-pitched and nervous anywhere else, like the jingling of the charms on her bracelet.

Sometimes they did go shopping or to a movie, but sometimes they went across the highway, ducking fast across the busy road, to a drive-in restaurant where older kids hung out. The restaurant was shaped like a big bottle, though squatter than a real bottle, and on its cap was a revolving figure of a grinning boy who held a hamburger aloft. One night in mid-summer they ran across, breathless with daring, and right away someone leaned out a car window and invited them over, but it was just a boy from high school they didn't like. It made them feel good to be able to ignore him. They went up through the maze of parked and cruising cars to the bright-lit, fly-infested restaurant, their faces pleased and expectant as if they were entering a sacred building that loomed out of the night to give them what haven and what blessing they yearned for. They sat at the counter and crossed their legs at the ankles, their thin shoulders rigid with excitement, and listened to the music that made everything so good: the music was always in the background like music at a church service, it was something to depend upon.

A boy named Eddie came in to talk with them. He sat backwards on his stool, turning himself jerkily around in semi-circles and then stopping and turning again, and after a while he asked Connie if she would like something to eat. She said she did and so she tapped her friend's arm on her way out—her friend pulled her face up into a brave droll look—and Connie said she would meet her at eleven, across the way. "I just hate to leave her like that," Connie said earnestly, but the boy said that she wouldn't be alone for long. So they went out to his car and on the way Connie couldn't help but let her eyes wander over the windshields and faces all around her, her face gleaming with a joy that had nothing to do with Eddie or even this place; it might have been the music. She drew her shoulders up and sucked in her breath with the pure pleasure of being alive, and just at that moment she happened to glance at a face just a few feet from hers. It was a boy with shaggy black hair, in a convertible jalopy painted gold. He stared at her and then his lips widened into a grin. Connie slit her eyes at him and turned away, but she couldn't help glancing back and there he was still watching her. He wagged a finger and laughed and said, "Gonna get you, baby," and Connie turned away again without Eddie noticing anything.

She spent three hours with him, at the restaurant where they ate hamburgers and drank Cokes in wax cups that were always sweating, and then down an alley a mile or so away, and when he left her off at five to eleven only the movie house was still open at the plaza. Her girl friend was there, talking with a boy. When Connie came up the two girls smiled at each other and Connie said, "How was the movie?" and the girl said, "*You* should know." They rode off with the girl's father, sleepy and pleased, and Connie couldn't help but look at the darkened shopping plaza with its big empty parking lot and its signs that were faded and ghostly now, and over at the drive-in restaurant where cars were still circling tirelessly. She couldn't hear the music at this distance.

Next morning June asked her how the movie was and Connie said, "So-so."

She and that girl and occasionally another girl went out several times a week   10
that way, and the rest of the time Connie spent around the house—it was summer vacation—getting in her mother's way and thinking, dreaming, about the boys she met. But all the boys fell back and dissolved into a single face that was not even a face, but an idea, a feeling, mixed up with the urgent insistent pounding of the music and the humid night air of July. Connie's mother kept dragging her back to the daylight by finding things for her to do or saying, suddenly, "What's this about the Pettinger girl?"

And Connie would say nervously, "Oh, her. That dope." She always drew thick clear lines between herself and such girls, and her mother was simple and kindly enough to believe her. Her mother was so simple, Connie thought, that it was maybe cruel to fool her so much. Her mother went scuffling around the house in old bedroom slippers and complained over the telephone to one sister about the other, then the other called up and the two of them complained about the third one. If June's name was mentioned her mother's tone was approving, and if Connie's name was mentioned it was disapproving. This did not really mean she disliked Connie and actually Connie thought that her mother preferred her to June because she was prettier, but the two of them kept up a pretense of exasperation, a sense that they were tugging and struggling over something of little value to either of them. Sometimes, over coffee, they were almost friends, but something would come up—some vexation that was like a fly buzzing suddenly around their heads—and their faces went hard with contempt.

One Sunday Connie got up at eleven—none of them bothered with church—and washed her hair so that it could dry all day long, in the sun. Her parents and sister were going to a barbecue at an aunt's house and Connie said no, she wasn't interested, rolling her eyes to let her mother know just what she thought of it. "Stay home alone then," her mother said sharply. Connie sat out back in a lawn chair and watched them drive away, her father quiet and bald, hunched around so that he could back the car out, her mother with a look that was still angry and not at all softened through the windshield, and in the back seat poor old June all dressed up as if she didn't know what a barbecue was, with all the running yelling kids and the flies. Connie sat with her eyes closed in the sun, dreaming and dazed with the warmth about her as if this were a kind of love, the caresses of love, and her mind slipped over onto thoughts of the boy she had been with the night before and how nice he had been, how sweet it always was, not the way someone like June would suppose but sweet, gentle, the way it was in movies and promised in songs; and when she opened her eyes she hardly knew where she was, the back yard ran off into weeds and a fence-line of trees and behind it the sky was perfectly blue and still. The asbestos "ranch house" that was now three years old startled her—it looked small. She shook her head as if to get awake.

It was too hot. She went inside the house and turned on the radio to drown out the quiet. She sat on the edge of her bed, barefoot, and listened for an hour and a half to a program called XYZ Sunday Jamboree, record after record of hard, fast, shrieking songs she sang along with, interspersed by exclamations from "Bobby King": "An' look here you girls at Napoleon's—Son and Charley want you to pay real close attention to this song coming up!"

And Connie paid close attention herself, bathed in a glow of slow-pulsed joy that seemed to rise mysteriously out of the music itself and lay languidly about the airless little room, breathed in and breathed out with each gentle rise and fall of her chest.

After a while she heard a car coming up the drive. She sat up at once, startled,   15 because it couldn't be her father so soon. The gravel kept crunching all the way in from the road—the driveway was long—and Connie ran to the window. It was a car she didn't know. It was an open jalopy, painted a bright gold that caught the sunlight opaquely. Her heart began to pound and her fingers snatched at her hair, checking it, and she whispered "Christ, Christ," wondering how bad she looked. The car came to a stop at the side door and the horn sounded four short taps as if this were a signal Connie knew.

She went into the kitchen and approached the door slowly, then hung out the screen door, her bare toes curling down off the step. There were two boys in the car and now she recognized the driver: he had shaggy, shabby black hair that looked crazy as a wig and he was grinning at her.

"I ain't late, am I?" he said.

"Who the hell do you think you are?" Connie said.

"Toldja I'd be out, didn't I?"

"I don't even know who you are."   20

She spoke sullenly, careful to show no interest or pleasure, and he spoke in a fast bright monotone. Connie looked past him to the other boy, taking her time. He had fair brown hair, with a lock that fell onto his forehead. His sideburns gave him a fierce, embarrassed look, but so far he hadn't even bothered to glance at her. Both boys wore sunglasses. The driver's glasses were metallic and mirrored everything in miniature.

"You wanta come for a ride?" he said.

Connie smirked and let her hair fall loose over one shoulder.

"Don'tcha like my car? New paint job," he said. "Hey."

"What?"   25

"You're cute."

She pretended to fidget, chasing flies away from the door.

"Don'tcha believe me, or what?" he said.

"Look, I don't even know who you are," Connie said in disgust.

"Hey, Ellie's got a radio, see. Mine's broke down." He lifted his friend's arm and   30 showed her the little transistor the boy was holding, and now Connie began to hear the music. It was the same program that was playing inside the house.

"Bobby King?" she said.

"I listen to him all the time. I think he's great."

"He's kind of great," Connie said reluctantly.

"Listen, that guy's *great*. He knows where the action is."

Connie blushed a little, because the glasses made it impossible for her to see just   35
what this boy was looking at. She couldn't decide if she liked him or if he was just a
jerk, and so she dawdled in the doorway and wouldn't come down or go back inside.
She said, "What's all that stuff painted on your car?"

"Can'tcha read it?" He opened the door very carefully, as if he was afraid it
might fall off. He slid out just as carefully, planting his feet firmly on the ground,
the tiny metallic world in his glasses slowing down like gelatine hardening and in
the midst of it Connie's bright green blouse. "This here is my name, to begin with,"
he said. ARNOLD FRIEND was written in tarlike black letters on the side, with a drawing of a round grinning face that reminded Connie of a pumpkin, except it wore
sunglasses. "I wanta introduce myself, I'm Arnold Friend and that's my real name
and I'm gonna be your friend, honey, and inside the car's Ellie Oscar, he's kinda
shy." Ellie brought his transistor radio up to his shoulder and balanced it there.
"Now these numbers are a secret code, honey," Arnold Friend explained. He read
off the numbers 33, 19, 17 and raised his eyebrows at her to see what she thought of
that, but she didn't think much of it. The left rear fender had been smashed and
around it was written, on the gleaming gold background: DONE BY CRAZY WOMAN
DRIVER. Connie had to laugh at that. Arnold Friend was pleased at her laughter and
looked up at her. "Around the other side's a lot more—you wanta come and see
them?"

"No."

"Why not?"

"Why should I?"

"Don'tcha wanta see what's on the car? Don'tcha wanta go for a ride?"   40

"I don't know."

"Why not?"

"I got things to do."

"Like what?"

"Things."   45

He laughed as if she had said something funny. He slapped his thighs. He was
standing in a strange way, leaning back against the car as if he were balancing himself. He wasn't tall, only an inch or so taller than she would be if she came down to
him. Connie liked the way he was dressed, which was the way all of them dressed:
tight faded jeans stuffed into black, scuffed boots, a belt that pulled his waist in and
showed how lean he was, and a white pull-over shirt that was a little soiled and
showed the hard small muscles of his arms and shoulders. He looked as if he probably
did hard work, lifting and carrying things. Even his neck looked muscular. And his
face was a familiar face, somehow: the jaw and chin and cheeks slightly darkened, because he hadn't shaved for a day or two, and the nose long and hawk-like, sniffing as
if she were a treat he was going to gobble up and it was all a joke.

"Connie, you ain't telling the truth. This is your day set aside for a ride with me
and you know it," he said, still laughing. The way he straightened and recovered from
his fit of laughing showed that it had been all fake.

"How do you know what my name is?" she said suspiciously.

"It's Connie."

"Maybe and maybe not."

"I know my Connie," he said, wagging his finger. Now she remembered him even better, back at the restaurant, and her cheeks warmed at the thought of how she sucked in her breath just at the moment she passed him—how she must have looked to him. And he had remembered her. "Ellie and I come out here especially for you," he said. "Ellie can sit in back. How about it?"

"Where?"

"Where what?"

"Where're we going?"

He looked at her. He took off the sunglasses and she saw how pale the skin around his eyes was, like holes that were not in shadow but instead in light. His eyes were chips of broken glass that catch the light in an amiable way. He smiled. It was as if the idea of going for a ride somewhere, to some place, was a new idea to him.

"Just for a ride, Connie sweetheart."

"I never said my name was Connie," she said.

"But I know what it is. I know your name and all about you, lots of things," Arnold Friend said. He had not moved yet but stood still leaning back against the side of his jalopy. "I took a special interest in you, such a pretty girl, and found out all about you like I know your parents and sister are gone somewheres and I know where and how long they're going to be gone, and I know who you were with last night, and your best girl friend's name is Betty. Right?"

He spoke in a simple lilting voice, exactly as if he were reciting the words to a song. His smile assured her that everything was fine. In the car Ellie turned up the volume on his radio and did not bother to look around at them.

"Ellie can sit in the back seat," Arnold Friend said. He indicated his friend with a casual jerk of his chin, as if Ellie did not count and she should not bother with him.

"How'd you find out all that stuff?" Connie said.

"Listen: Betty Schultz and Tony Fitch and Jimmy Pettinger and Nancy Pettinger," he said, in a chant. "Raymond Stanley and Bob Hutter—"

"Do you know all those kids?"

"I know everybody."

"Look, you're kidding. You're not from around here."

"Sure."

"But—how come we never saw you before?"

"Sure you saw me before," he said. He looked down at his boots, as if he were a little offended. "You just don't remember."

"I guess I'd remember you," Connie said.

"Yeah?" He looked up at this, beaming. He was pleased. He began to mark time with the music from Ellie's radio, tapping his fists lightly together. Connie looked away from his smile to the car, which was painted so bright it almost hurt her eyes to look at it. She looked at that name, ARNOLD FRIEND. And up at the front fender was an expression that was familiar—MAN THE FLYING SAUCERS. It was an expression kids had used the year before, but didn't use this year. She looked at it for a while as if the words meant something to her that she did not yet know.

"What're you thinking about? Huh?" Arnold Friend demanded. "Not worried about your hair blowing around in the car, are you?"

"No."

"Think I maybe can't drive good?"

"How do I know?"

"You're a hard girl to handle. How come?" he said. "Don't you know I'm your   75
friend? Didn't you see me put my sign in the air when you walked by?"

"What sign?"

"My sign." And he drew an X in the air, leaning out toward her. They were
maybe ten feet apart. After his hand fell back to his side the X was still in the air,
almost visible. Connie let the screen door close and stood perfectly still inside it, listening to the music from her radio and the boy's blend together. She stared at Arnold
Friend. He stood there so stiffly relaxed, pretending to be relaxed, with one hand idly
on the door handle as if he were keeping himself up that way and had no intention of
ever moving again. She recognized most things about him, the tight jeans that
showed his thighs and buttocks and the greasy leather boots and the tight shirt,
and even that slippery friendly smile of his, that sleepy dreamy smile that all the
boys used to get across ideas they didn't want to put into words. She recognized all
this and also the singsong way he talked, slightly mocking, kidding, but serious
and a little melancholy, and she recognized the way he tapped one fist against the
other in homage to the perpetual music behind him. But all these things did not
come together.

She said suddenly, "Hey, how old are you?"

His smile faded. She could see then that he wasn't a kid, he was much older—
thirty, maybe more. At this knowledge her heart began to pound faster.

"That's a crazy thing to ask. Can'tcha see I'm your own age?"   80

"Like hell you are."

"Or maybe a coupla years older, I'm eighteen."

"Eighteen?" she said doubtfully.

He grinned to reassure her and lines appeared at the corners of his mouth. His
teeth were big and white. He grinned so broadly his eyes became slits and she saw
how thick the lashes were, thick and black as if painted with a black tarlike material.
Then he seemed to become embarrassed, abruptly, and looked over his shoulder at
Ellie. "*Him*, he's crazy," he said. "Ain't he a riot, he's a nut, a real character." Ellie
was still listening to the music. His sunglasses told nothing about what he was thinking. He wore a bright orange shirt unbuttoned halfway to show his chest, which was a
pale, bluish chest and not muscular like Arnold Friend's. His shirt collar was turned
up all around and the very tips of the collar pointed out past his chin as if they were
protecting him. He was pressing the transistor radio up against his ear and sat there
in a kind of daze, right in the sun.

"He's kinda strange," Connie said.   85

"Hey, she says you're kinda strange! Kinda strange!" Arnold Friend cried. He
pounded on the car to get Ellie's attention. Ellie turned for the first time and Connie
saw with shock that he wasn't a kid either—he had a fair, hairless face, cheeks reddened slightly as if the veins grew too close to the surface of his skin, the face of a
forty-year-old baby. Connie felt a wave of dizziness rise in her at this sight and she
stared at him as if waiting for something to change the shock of the moment, make it
all right again. Ellie's lips kept shaping words, mumbling along with the words blasting in his ear.

"Maybe you two better go away," Connie said faintly.

"What? How come?" Arnold Friend cried. "We come out here to take you for a
ride. It's Sunday." He had the voice of the man on the radio now. It was the same
voice, Connie thought. "Don'tcha know it's Sunday all day and honey, no matter
who you were with last night today you're with Arnold Friend and don't you forget

it!—Maybe you better step out here," he said, and this last was in a different voice. It was a little flatter, as if the heat was finally getting to him.

"No. I got things to do."

"Hey."   90

"You two better leave."

"We ain't leaving until you come with us."

"Like hell I am—"

"Connie, don't fool around with me. I mean, I mean, don't fool *around*," he said, shaking his head. He laughed incredulously. He placed his sunglasses on top of his head, carefully, as if he were indeed wearing a wig, and brought the stems down behind his ears. Connie stared at him, another wave of dizziness and fear rising in her so that for a moment he wasn't even in focus but was just a blur, standing there against his gold car, and she had the idea that he had driven up the driveway all right but had come from nowhere before that and belonged nowhere and that everything about him and even about the music that was so familiar to her was only half real.

"If my father comes and sees you—"   95

"He ain't coming. He's at a barbecue."

"How do you know that?"

"Aunt Tillie's. Right now they're—uh—they're drinking. Sitting around," he said vaguely, squinting as if he were staring all the way to town and over to Aunt Tillie's backyard. Then the vision seemed to get clear and he nodded energetically. "Yeah. Sitting around. There's your sister in a blue dress, huh? And high heels, the poor sad bitch—nothing like you, sweetheart! And your mother's helping some fat woman with the corn, they're cleaning the corn—husking the corn—"

"What fat woman?" Connie cried.

"How do I know what fat woman. I don't know every goddam fat woman in the   100
world!" Arnold Friend laughed.

"Oh, that's Mrs. Hornby. . . . Who invited her?" Connie said. She felt a little light-headed. Her breath was coming quickly.

"She's too fat. I don't like them fat. I like them the way you are, honey," he said, smiling sleepily at her. They stared at each other for a while, through the screen door. He said softly, "Now what you're going to do is this: you're going to come out that door. You're going to sit up front with me and Ellie's going to sit in the back, the hell with Ellie, right? This isn't Ellie's date. You're my date. I'm your lover, honey."

"What? You're crazy—"

"Yes, I'm your lover. You don't know what that is but you will," he said. "I know that too. I know all about you. But look: it's real nice and you couldn't ask for nobody better than me, or more polite. I always keep my word. I'll tell you how it is, I'm always nice at first, the first time. I'll hold you so tight you won't think you have to try to get away or pretend anything because you'll know you can't. And I'll come inside you where it's all secret and you'll give in to me and you'll love me—"

"Shut up! You're crazy!" Connie said. She backed away from the door. She put   105
her hands against her ears as if she'd heard something terrible, something not meant for her. "People don't talk like that, you're crazy," she muttered. Her heart was almost too big now for her chest and its pumping made sweat break out all over her. She looked out to see Arnold Friend pause and then take a step toward the porch lurching. He almost fell. But, like a clever drunken man, he managed to catch his balance. He wobbled in his high boots and grabbed hold of one of the porch posts.

"Honey?" he said. "You still listening?"

"Get the hell out of here!"

"Be nice, honey. Listen."

"I'm going to call the police—"

He wobbled again and out of the side of his mouth came a fast spat curse, an   110
aside not meant for her to hear. But even this "Christ!" sounded forced. Then he began to smile again. She watched this smile come, awkward as if he were smiling from
inside a mask. His whole face was a mask, she thought wildly, tanned down onto his
throat but then running out as if he had plastered makeup on his face but had forgotten about his throat.

"Honey—? Listen, here's how it is. I always tell the truth and I promise you this:
I ain't coming in that house after you."

"You better not! I'm going to call the police if you—if you don't—"

"Honey," he said, talking right through her voice, "honey, I'm not coming in
there but you are coming out here. You know why?"

She was panting. The kitchen looked like a place she had never seen before,
some room she had run inside but which wasn't good enough, wasn't going to help
her. The kitchen window had never had a curtain, after three years, and there were
dishes in the sink for her to do—probably—and if you ran your hand across the table
you'd probably feel something sticky there.

"You listening, honey? Hey?"   115

"—going to call the police—"

"Soon as you touch the phone I don't need to keep my promise and can come
inside. You won't want that."

She rushed forward and tried to lock the door. Her fingers were shaking. "But
why lock it," Arnold Friend said gently, talking right into her face. "It's just a screen
door. It's just nothing." One of his boots was at a strange angle, as if his foot wasn't in
it. It pointed out to the left, bent at the ankle. "I mean, anybody can break through a
screen door and glass and wood and iron or anything else if he needs to, anybody at
all and specially Arnold Friend. If the place got lit up with a fire honey you'd come
running out into my arms, right into my arms and safe at home—like you knew I was
your lover and'd stopped fooling around. I don't mind a nice shy girl but I don't like
no fooling around." Part of those words were spoken with a slight rhythmic lilt, and
Connie somehow recognized them—the echo of a song from last year, about a girl
rushing into her boyfriend's arms and coming home again—

Connie stood barefoot on the linoleum floor, staring at him. "What do you
want?" she whispered.

"I want you," he said.   120

"What?"

"Seen you that night and thought, that's the one, yes sir. I never needed to look
any more."

"But my father's coming back. He's coming to get me. I had to wash my hair
first—" She spoke in a dry, rapid voice, hardly raising it for him to hear.

"No, your daddy is not coming and yes, you had to wash your hair and you
washed it for me. It's nice and shining and all for me, I thank you, sweetheart," he
said, with a mock bow, but again he almost lost his balance. He had to bend and adjust his boots. Evidently his feet did not go all the way down; the boots must have
been stuffed with something so that he would seem taller. Connie stared out at him
and behind him Ellie in the car, who seemed to be looking off toward Connie's right,
into nothing. This Ellie said, pulling the words out of the air one after another as if
he were just discovering them, "You want me to pull out the phone?"

"Shut your mouth and keep it shut," Arnold Friend said, his face red from bend- 125
ing over or maybe from embarrassment because Connie had seen his boots. "This
ain't none of your business."

"What—what are you doing? What do you want?" Connie said. "If I call the police they'll get you, they'll arrest you—"

"Promise was not to come in unless you touch that phone, and I'll keep that
promise," he said. He resumed his erect position and tried to force his shoulders back.
He sounded like a hero in a movie, declaring something important. He spoke too
loudly and it was as if he were speaking to someone behind Connie. "I ain't made
plans for coming in that house where I don't belong but just for you to come out to
me, the way you should. Don't you know who I am?"

"You're crazy," she whispered. She backed away from the door but did not want
to go into another part of the house, as if this would give him permission to come
through the door. "What do you . . . You're crazy, you . . ."

"Huh? What're you saying, honey?"

Her eyes darted everywhere in the kitchen. She could not remember what it was, 130
this room.

"This is how it is, honey: you come out and we'll drive away, have a nice ride.
But if you don't come out we're gonna wait till your people come home and then
they're all going to get it."

"You want that telephone pulled out?" Ellie said. He held the radio away from
his ear and grimaced, as if without the radio the air was too much for him.

"I toldja shut up, Ellie," Arnold Friend said, "you're deaf, get a hearing aid, right?
Fix yourself up. This little girl's no trouble and's gonna be nice to me, so Ellie keep to
yourself, this ain't your date—right? Don't hem in on me. Don't hog. Don't crush.
Don't bird dog. Don't trail me," he said in a rapid meaningless voice, as if he were running through all the expressions he'd learned but was no longer sure which one of them
was in style, then rushing on to new ones, making them up with his eyes closed, "Don't
crawl under my fence, don't squeeze in my chipmunk hole, don't sniff my glue, suck my
popsicle, keep your own greasy fingers on yourself!" He shaded his eyes and peered in at
Connie, who was backed against the kitchen table. "Don't mind him honey he's just a
creep. He's a dope. Right? I'm the boy for you and like I said you come out here nice
like a lady and give me your hand, and nobody else gets hurt, I mean, your nice old
bald-headed daddy and your mummy and your sister in her high heels. Because listen:
why bring them in this?"

"Leave me alone," Connie whispered.

"Hey, you know that old woman down the road, the one with the chickens and 135
stuff—you know her?"

"She's dead!"

"Dead? What? You know her?" Arnold Friend said.

"She's dead—"

"Don't you like her?"

"She's dead—she's—she isn't here any more—" 140

"But don't you like her, I mean, you got something against her? Some grudge or
something?" Then his voice dipped as if he were conscious of a rudeness. He touched
the sunglasses perched on top of his head as if to make sure they were still there.
"Now you be a good girl."

"What are you going to do?"

"Just two things, or maybe three," Arnold Friend said. "But I promise it won't
last long and you'll like me that way you get to like people you're close to. You will.

It's all over for you here, so come on out. You don't want your people in any trouble, do you?"

She turned and bumped against a chair or something, hurting her leg, but she ran into the back room and picked up the telephone. Something roared in her ear, a tiny roaring, and she was so sick with fear that she could do nothing but listen to it—the telephone was clammy and very heavy and her fingers groped down to the dial but were too weak to touch it. She began to scream into the phone, into the roaring. She cried out, she cried for her mother, she felt her breath start jerking back and forth in her lungs as if it were something Arnold Friend were stabbing her with again and again with no tenderness. A noisy sorrowful wailing rose all about her and she was locked inside it the way she was locked inside the house.

After a while she could hear again. She was sitting on the floor with her wet back against the wall. 145

Arnold Friend was saying from the door, "That's a good girl. Put the phone back."

She kicked the phone away from her.

"No, honey. Pick it up. Put it back right."

She picked it up and put it back. The dial tone stopped.

"That's a good girl. Now come outside." 150

She was hollow with what had been fear, but what was now just an emptiness. All that screaming had blasted it out of her. She sat, one leg cramped under her, and deep inside her brain was something like a pinpoint of light that kept going and would not let her relax. She thought, I'm not going to see my mother again. She thought, I'm not going to sleep in my bed again. Her bright green blouse was all wet.

Arnold Friend said, in a gentle-loud voice that was like a stage voice, "The place where you came from ain't there any more, and where you had in mind to go is cancelled out. This place you are now—inside your daddy's house—is nothing but a cardboard box I can knock down any time. You know that and always did know it. You hear me?"

She thought, I have got to think. I have to know what to do.

"We'll go out to a nice field, out in the country here where it smells so nice and it's sunny," Arnold Friend said. "I'll have my arms around you so you won't need to try to get away and I'll show you what love is like, what it does. The hell with this house! It looks solid all right," he said. He ran a fingernail down the screen and the noise did not make Connie shiver, as it would have the day before. "Now put your hand on your heart, honey. Feel that? That feels solid too but we know better, be nice to me, be sweet like you can because what else is there for a girl like you but to be sweet and pretty and give in?—and get away before her people come back?"

She felt her pounding heart. Her hand seemed to enclose it. She thought for 155 the first time in her life that it was nothing that was hers, that belonged to her, but just a pounding, living thing inside this body that wasn't really hers either.

"You don't want them to get hurt," Arnold Friend went on. "Now get up, honey. Get up all by yourself."

She stood up.

"Now turn this way. That's right. Come over here to me—Ellie, put that away, didn't I tell you? You dope. You miserable creepy dope," Arnold Friend said. His words were not angry but only part of an incantation. The incantation was kindly. "Now come out through the kitchen to me honey and let's see a smile, try it, you're a brave sweet little girl and now they're eating corn and hotdogs cooked to bursting over an outdoor fire, and they don't know one thing about you and never did and honey you're better than them because not a one of them would have done this for you."

Connie felt the linoleum under her feet; it was cool. She brushed her hair back out of her eyes. Arnold Friend let go of the post tentatively and opened his arms for her, his elbows pointing in toward each other and his wrists limp, to show that this was an embarrassed embrace and a little mocking, he didn't want to make her self-conscious.

She put out her hand against the screen. She watched herself push the door   160 slowly open as if she were safe back somewhere in the other doorway, watching this body and this head of long hair moving out into the sunlight where Arnold Friend waited.

"My sweet little blue-eyed girl," he said, in a half-sung sigh that had nothing to do with her brown eyes but was taken up just the same by the vast sunlit reaches of the land behind him and on all sides of him, so much land that Connie had never seen before and did not recognize except to know that she was going to it.

Tim O'Brien

The Things They Carried   1990

Tim O'Brien was born in 1946 in Austin, Minnesota. Immediately after graduating summa cum laude from Macalester College in 1968, he was drafted into the U.S. Army. Serving as an infantryman in Vietnam, O'Brien attained the rank of sergeant and won a Purple Heart after being wounded by shrapnel. Upon his discharge in 1970, he began graduate work at Harvard. In 1973 he published If I Die in a Combat Zone, Box Me Up and Ship Me Home, *a mixture of memoir and fiction about his wartime experiences. His 1978 novel* Going After Cacciato *won the National Book Award, and is considered by some critics to be the best book of American fiction about the Vietnam War. "The Things They Carried" was first pub-*

Tim O'Brien

lished in Esquire *in 1986, and later became the title piece in a book of interlocking short stories published in 1990. His other novels include* The Nuclear Age *(1985),* In the Lake of the Woods *(1994),* Tomcat in Love *(1998) and* July, July *(2002). O'Brien currently teaches at Texas State University–San Marcos.*

First Lieutenant Jimmy Cross carried letters from a girl named Martha, a junior at Mount Sebastian College in New Jersey. They were not love letters, but Lieutenant Cross was hoping, so he kept them folded in plastic at the bottom of his rucksack. In the late afternoon, after a day's march, he would dig his foxhole, wash his hands under a canteen, unwrap the letters, hold them with the tips of his fingers, and spend the last hour of light pretending. He would imagine romantic camping trips into the White Mountains in New Hampshire. He would sometimes taste the envelope flaps, knowing her tongue had been there. More than anything, he wanted Martha to love him as he loved her, but the letters were mostly chatty, elusive on the matter of love. She was a virgin, he was almost sure. She was an English major at Mount Sebastian, and she wrote beautifully about her professors and roommates and midterm exams, about her respect for Chaucer and her great affection for Virginia Woolf. She often quoted lines of poetry; she never mentioned the war, except to say, Jimmy, take care of yourself. The letters weighed 10 ounces. They were signed Love, Martha, but Lieutenant Cross understood that Love was only a way of signing and did not mean what he sometimes pretended it meant. At dusk, he would carefully return the letters to his rucksack. Slowly, a bit distracted, he would get up and move among his men, checking the perimeter; then at full dark he would return to his hole and watch the night and wonder if Martha was a virgin.

The things they carried were largely determined by necessity. Among the necessities or near-necessities were P-38 can openers, pocket knives, heat tabs, wristwatches, dog tags, mosquito repellent, chewing gum, candy, cigarettes, salt tablets, packets of Kool-Aid, lighters, matches, sewing kits, Military Payment Certificates, C rations, and two or three canteens of water. Together, these items weighed between 15 and 20 pounds, depending upon a man's habits or rate of metabolism. Henry Dobbins, who was a big man, carried extra rations; he was especially fond of canned peaches in heavy syrup over pound cake. Dave Jensen, who practiced field hygiene, carried a toothbrush, dental floss, and several hotel-sized bars of soap he'd stolen on R&R° in Sydney, Australia. Ted Lavender, who was scared, carried tranquilizers until he was shot in the head outside the village of Than Khe in mid-April. By necessity, and because it was SOP,° they all carried steel helmets that weighed 5 pounds including the liner and camouflage cover. They carried the standard fatigue jackets and trousers. Very few carried underwear. On their feet they carried jungle boots—2.1 pounds—and Dave Jensen carried three pairs of socks and a can of Dr. Scholl's foot powder as a precaution against trench foot. Until he was shot, Ted Lavender carried six or seven ounces of premium dope, which for him was a necessity. Mitchell Sanders, the RTO,° carried condoms. Norman Bowker carried a diary. Rat Kiley carried comic books. Kiowa, a devout Baptist, carried an illustrated New Testament that had been presented to him by his father, who taught Sunday school in Oklahoma City, Oklahoma. As a hedge against bad times, however, Kiowa also carried his grandmother's distrust of the white man, his grandfather's old hunting hatchet. Necessity dictated. Because the land was mined and booby-trapped, it was SOP for each man to carry a steel-centered, nylon-covered flak jacket, which weighed 6.7 pounds, but which on hot days seemed much heavier. Because you could die so quickly, each man carried at least one large compress bandage, usually in the helmet band for easy access. Because the nights were cold, and because the monsoons were wet, each carried a green plastic poncho that could be used as a raincoat or groundsheet or makeshift tent. With its quilted liner, the poncho weighed almost two pounds, but it was worth every ounce. In April, for instance, when Ted Lavender was shot, they used his poncho to wrap him up, then to carry him across the paddy, then to lift him into the chopper that took him away.

R&R: the military abbreviation for "rest and rehabilitation," a brief vacation from active service. SOP: standard operating procedure.   RTO: radio and telephone operator.

*

They were called legs or grunts.

To carry something was to hump it, as when Lieutenant Jimmy Cross humped his love for Martha up the hills and through the swamps. In its intransitive form, to hump meant to walk, or to march, but it implied burdens far beyond the intransitive.

Almost everyone humped photographs. In his wallet, Lieutenant Cross carried two photographs of Martha. The first was a Kodacolor snapshot signed Love, though he knew better. She stood against a brick wall. Her eyes were gray and neutral, her lips slightly open as she stared straight-on at the camera. At night, sometimes, Lieutenant Cross wondered who had taken the picture, because he knew she had boyfriends, because he loved her so much, and because he could see the shadow of the picture-taker spreading out against the brick wall. The second photograph had been clipped from the 1968 Mount Sebastian yearbook. It was an action shot—women's volleyball—and Martha was bent horizontal to the floor, reaching, the palms of her hands in sharp focus, the tongue taut, the expression frank and competitive. There was no visible sweat. She wore white gym shorts. Her legs, he thought, were almost certainly the legs of a virgin, dry and without hair, the left knee cocked and carrying her entire weight, which was just over one hundred pounds. Lieutenant Cross remembered touching that left knee. A dark theater, he remembered, and the movie was *Bonnie and Clyde*, and Martha wore a tweed skirt, and during the final scene, when he touched her knee, she turned and looked at him in a sad, sober way that made him pull his hand back, but he would always remember the feel of the tweed skirt and the knee beneath it and the sound of the gunfire that killed Bonnie and Clyde, how embarrassing it was, how slow and oppressive. He remembered kissing her good night at the dorm door. Right then, he thought, he should've done something brave. He should've carried her up the stairs to her room and tied her to the bed and touched that left knee all night long. He should've risked it. Whenever he looked at the photographs, he thought of new things he should've done.

What they carried was partly a function of rank, partly of field specialty.

As a first lieutenant and platoon leader, Jimmy Cross carried a compass, maps, code books, binoculars, and a .45-caliber pistol that weighed 2.9 pounds fully loaded. He carried a strobe light and the responsibility for the lives of his men.

As an RTO, Mitchell Sanders carried the PRC-25 radio, a killer, 26 pounds with its battery.

As a medic, Rat Kiley carried a canvas satchel filled with morphine and plasma and malaria tablets and surgical tape and comic books and all the things a medic must carry, including M&M's° for especially bad wounds, for a total weight of nearly 20 pounds.

As a big man, therefore a machine gunner, Henry Dobbins carried the M-60, which weighed 23 pounds unloaded, but which was almost always loaded. In addition, Dobbins carried between 10 and 15 pounds of ammunition draped in belts across his chest and shoulders.

As PFCs or Spec 4s, most of them were common grunts and carried the standard M-16 gas-operated assault rifle. The weapon weighed 7.5 pounds unloaded, 8.2 pounds with its full 20-round magazine. Depending on numerous factors, such as topography and psychology, the riflemen carried anywhere from 12 to 20 magazines,

M&M's: comic slang for medical supplies.

usually in cloth bandoliers, adding on another 8.4 pounds at minimum, 14 pounds at maximum. When it was available, they also carried M-16 maintenance gear—rods and steel brushes and swabs and tubes of LSA oil—all of which weighed about a pound. Among the grunts, some carried the M-79 grenade launcher, 5.9 pounds unloaded, a reasonably light weapon except for the ammunition, which was heavy. A single round weighed 10 ounces. The typical load was 25 rounds. But Ted Lavender, who was scared, carried 34 rounds when he was shot and killed outside Than Khe, and he went down under an exceptional burden, more than 20 pounds of ammunition, plus the flak jacket and helmet and rations and water and toilet paper and tranquilizers and all the rest, plus the unweighed fear. He was dead weight. There was no twitching or flopping. Kiowa, who saw it happen, said it was like watching a rock fall, or a big sandbag or something—just boom, then down—not like the movies where the dead guy rolls around and does fancy spins and goes ass over teakettle—not like that, Kiowa said, the poor bastard just flat-fuck fell. Boom. Down. Nothing else. It was a bright morning in mid-April. Lieutenant Cross felt the pain. He blamed himself. They stripped off Lavender's canteens and ammo, all the heavy things, and Rat Kiley said the obvious, the guy's dead, and Mitchell Sanders used his radio to report one U.S. KIA° and to request a chopper. Then they wrapped Lavender in his poncho. They carried him out to a dry paddy, established security, and sat smoking the dead man's dope until the chopper came. Lieutenant Cross kept to himself. He pictured Martha's smooth young face, thinking he loved her more than anything, more than his men, and now Ted Lavender was dead because he loved her so much and could not stop thinking about her. When the dustoff arrived, they carried Lavender aboard. Afterward they burned Than Khe. They marched until dusk, then dug their holes, and that night Kiowa kept explaining how you had to be there, how fast it was, how the poor guy just dropped like so much concrete. Boom-down, he said. Like cement.

In addition to the three standard weapons—the M-60, M-16, and M-79—they carried whatever presented itself, or whatever seemed appropriate as a means of killing or staying alive. They carried catch-as-catch-can. At various times, in various situations, they carried M-14s and CAR-15s and Swedish Ks and grease guns and captured AK-47s and Chi-Coms and RPGs and Simonov carbines and black market Uzis and .38-caliber Smith & Wesson handguns and 66 mm LAWs and shotguns and silencers and blackjacks and bayonets and C-4 plastic explosives. Lee Strunk carried a slingshot; a weapon of last resort, he called it. Mitchell Sanders carried brass knuckles. Kiowa carried his grandfather's feathered hatchet. Every third or fourth man carried a Claymore antipersonnel mine—3.5 pounds with its firing device. They all carried fragmentation grenades—14 ounces each. They all carried at least one M-18 colored smoke grenade—24 ounces. Some carried CS or tear gas grenades. Some carried white phosphorus grenades. They carried all they could bear, and then some, including a silent awe for the terrible power of the things they carried.

In the first week of April, before Lavender died, Lieutenant Jimmy Cross received a good-luck charm from Martha. It was a simple pebble, an ounce at most. Smooth to the touch, it was a milky white color with flecks of orange and violet, oval-shaped, like a miniature egg. In the accompanying letter, Martha wrote that she had found the

KIA: killed in action.

pebble on the Jersey shoreline, precisely where the land touched water at high tide, where things came together but also separated. It was this separate-but-together quality, she wrote, that had inspired her to pick up the pebble and to carry it in her breast pocket for several days, where it seemed weightless, and then to send it through the mail, by air, as a token of her truest feelings for him. Lieutenant Cross found this romantic. But he wondered what her truest feelings were, exactly, and what she meant by separate-but-together. He wondered how the tides and waves had come into play on that afternoon along the Jersey shoreline when Martha saw the pebble and bent down to rescue it from geology. He imagined bare feet. Martha was a poet, with the poet's sensibilities, and her feet would be brown and bare, the toenails unpainted, the eyes chilly and somber like the ocean in March, and though it was painful, he wondered who had been with her that afternoon. He imagined a pair of shadows moving along the strip of sand where things came together but also separated. It was phantom jealousy, he knew, but he couldn't help himself. He loved her so much. On the march, through the hot days of early April, he carried the pebble in his mouth, turning it with his tongue, tasting sea salt and moisture. His mind wandered. He had difficulty keeping his attention on the war. On occasion he would yell at his men to spread out the column, to keep their eyes open, but then he would slip away into daydreams, just pretending, walking barefoot along the Jersey shore, with Martha, carrying nothing. He would feel himself rising. Sun and waves and gentle winds, all love and lightness.

What they carried varied by mission.

When a mission took them to the mountains, they carried mosquito netting, 15 machetes, canvas tarps, and extra bug juice.

If a mission seemed especially hazardous, or if it involved a place they knew to be bad, they carried everything they could. In certain heavily mined AOs,° where the land was dense with Toe Poppers and Bouncing Betties, they took turns humping a 28-pound mine detector. With its headphones and big sensing plate, the equipment was a stress on the lower back and shoulders, awkward to handle, often useless because of the shrapnel in the earth, but they carried it anyway, partly for safety, partly for the illusion of safety.

On ambush, or other night missions, they carried peculiar little odds and ends. Kiowa always took along his New Testament and a pair of moccasins for silence. Dave Jensen carried night-sight vitamins high in carotene. Lee Strunk carried his slingshot; ammo, he claimed, would never be a problem. Rat Kiley carried brandy and M&M's candy. Until he was shot, Ted Lavender carried the starlight scope, which weighed 6.3 pounds with its aluminum carrying case. Henry Dobbins carried his girlfriend's pantyhose wrapped around his neck as a comforter. They all carried ghosts. When dark came, they would move out single file across the meadows and paddies to their ambush coordinates, where they would quietly set up the Claymores and lie down and spend the night waiting.

Other missions were more complicated and required special equipment. In mid-April, it was their mission to search out and destroy the elaborate tunnel complexes in the Than Khe area south of Chu Lai. To blow the tunnels, they carried one-pound blocks of pentrite high explosives, four blocks to a man, 68 pounds in all. They carried wiring, detonators, and battery-powered clackers. Dave Jensen carried earplugs. Most

AOs: areas of operation.

often, before blowing the tunnels, they were ordered by higher command to search them, which was considered bad news, but by and large they just shrugged and carried out orders. Because he was a big man, Henry Dobbins was excused from tunnel duty. The others would draw numbers. Before Lavender died there were 17 men in the platoon, and whoever drew the number 17 would strip off his gear and crawl in headfirst with a flashlight and Lieutenant Cross's .45-caliber pistol. The rest of them would fan out as security. They would sit down or kneel, not facing the hole, listening to the ground beneath them, imagining cobwebs and ghosts, whatever was down there— the tunnel walls squeezing in—how the flashlight seemed impossibly heavy in the hand and how it was tunnel vision in the very strictest sense, compression in all ways, even time, and how you had to wiggle in—ass and elbows—a swallowed-up feeling— and how you found yourself worrying about odd things: Will your flashlight go dead? Do rats carry rabies? If you screamed, how far would the sound carry? Would your buddies hear it? Would they have the courage to drag you out? In some respects, though not many, the waiting was worse than the tunnel itself. Imagination was a killer.

On April 16, when Lee Strunk drew the number 17, he laughed and muttered something and went down quickly. The morning was hot and very still. Not good, Kiowa said. He looked at the tunnel opening, then out across a dry paddy toward the village of Than Khe. Nothing moved. No clouds or birds or people. As they waited, the men smoked and drank Kool-Aid, not talking much, feeling sympathy for Lee Strunk but also feeling the luck of the draw. You win some, you lose some, said Mitchell Sanders, and sometimes you settle for a rain check. It was a tired line and no one laughed.

Henry Dobbins ate a tropical chocolate bar. Ted Lavender popped a tranquilizer   20 and went off to pee.

After five minutes, Lieutenant Jimmy Cross moved to the tunnel, leaned down, and examined the darkness. Trouble, he thought—a cave-in maybe. And then suddenly, without willing it, he was thinking about Martha. The stresses and fractures, the quick collapse, the two of them buried alive under all that weight. Dense, crushing love. Kneeling, watching the hole, he tried to concentrate on Lee Strunk and the war, all the dangers, but his love was too much for him, he felt paralyzed, he wanted to sleep inside her lungs and breathe her blood and be smothered. He wanted her to be a virgin and not a virgin, all at once. He wanted to know her. Intimate secrets: Why poetry? Why so sad? Why that grayness in her eyes? Why so alone? Not lonely, just alone—riding her bike across campus or sitting off by herself in the cafeteria—even dancing, she danced alone—and it was the aloneness that filled him with love. He remembered telling her that one evening. How she nodded and looked away. And how, later, when he kissed her, she received the kiss without returning it, her eyes wide open, not afraid, not a virgin's eyes, just flat and uninvolved.

Lieutenant Cross gazed at the tunnel. But he was not there. He was buried with Martha under the white sand at the Jersey shore. They were pressed together, and the pebble in his mouth was her tongue. He was smiling. Vaguely, he was aware of how quiet the day was, the sullen paddies, yet he could not bring himself to worry about matters of security. He was beyond that. He was just a kid at war, in love. He was twenty-four years old. He couldn't help it.

A few moments later Lee Strunk crawled out of the tunnel. He came up grinning, filthy but alive. Lieutenant Cross nodded and closed his eyes while the others clapped Strunk on the back and made jokes about rising from the dead.

Worms, Rat Kiley said. Right out of the grave. Fuckin' zombie.

The men laughed. They all felt great relief.   25

Spook city, said Mitchell Sanders.

Lee Strunk made a funny ghost sound, a kind of moaning, yet very happy, and right then, when Strunk made that high happy moaning sound, when he went *Ahhooooo*, right then Ted Lavender was shot in the head on his way back from peeing. He lay with his mouth open. The teeth were broken. There was a swollen black bruise under his left eye. The cheekbone was gone. Oh shit, Rat Kiley said, the guy's dead. The guy's dead, he kept saying, which seemed profound—the guy's dead. I mean really.

The things they carried were determined to some extent by superstition. Lieutenant Cross carried his good-luck pebble. Dave Jensen carried a rabbit's foot. Norman Bowker, otherwise a very gentle person, carried a thumb that had been presented to him as a gift by Mitchell Sanders. The thumb was dark brown, rubbery to the touch, and weighed four ounces at most. It had been cut from a VC corpse, a boy of fifteen or sixteen. They'd found him at the bottom of an irrigation ditch, badly burned, flies in his mouth and eyes. The boy wore black shorts and sandals. At the time of his death he had been carrying a pouch of rice, a rifle, and three magazines of ammunition.

You want my opinion, Mitchell Sanders said, there's a definite moral here.

He put his hand on the dead boy's wrist. He was quiet for a time, as if counting a   30 pulse, then he patted the stomach, almost affectionately, and used Kiowa's hunting hatchet to remove the thumb.

Henry Dobbins asked what the moral was.

Moral?

You know. *Moral.*

Sanders wrapped the thumb in toilet paper and handed it across to Norman Bowker. There was no blood. Smiling, he kicked the boy's head, watched the flies scatter, and said, It's like with that old TV show—Paladin. Have gun, will travel.

Henry Dobbins thought about it.   35

Yeah, well, he finally said. I don't see no moral.

There it *is*, man.

Fuck off.

They carried USO stationery and pencils and pens. They carried Sterno, safety pins, trip flares, signal flares, spools of wire, razor blades, chewing tobacco, liberated joss sticks and statuettes of the smiling Buddha, candles, grease pencils, *The Stars and Stripes*, fingernail clippers, Psy Ops leaflets, bush hats, bolos, and much more. Twice a week, when the resupply choppers came in, they carried hot chow in green mermite cans and large canvas bags filled with iced beer and soda pop. They carried plastic water containers, each with a two-gallon capacity. Mitchell Sanders carried a set of starched tiger fatigues for special occasions. Henry Dobbins carried Black Flag insecticide. Dave Jensen carried empty sandbags that could be filled at night for added protection. Lee Strunk carried tanning lotion. Some things they carried in common. Taking turns, they carried the big PRC-77 scrambler radio, which weighed 30 pounds with its battery. They shared the weight of memory. They took up what others could no longer bear. Often, they carried each other, the wounded or weak. They carried infections. They carried chess sets, basketballs, Vietnamese-English dictionaries, insignia of rank, Bronze Stars and Purple Hearts, plastic cards imprinted with the Code of Conduct. They carried diseases, among them malaria and dysentery. They carried lice and ringworm and leeches and paddy algae and various rots and molds. They carried the land itself—Vietnam, the place, the soil—a powdery orange-red dust that covered their boots and fatigues and faces. They carried the sky. The whole atmosphere, they carried it, the humidity, the monsoons, the stink of fungus and decay, all of it, they carried gravity. They moved like mules. By daylight they took sniper fire, at night they were mortared, but it was not battle, it was just the endless march, village to village, without purpose, nothing won or lost. They marched for the sake of the march. They plodded along slowly, dumbly, leaning forward against the heat, unthinking, all blood and bone, simple grunts, soldiering with their legs, toiling up the hills and down into the paddies and across the rivers and up again and down, just humping, one step and then the next and then another, but no volition, no will, because it was automatic, it was anatomy, and the war was entirely a matter of posture and carriage, the hump was everything, a kind of inertia, a kind of emptiness, a dullness of desire and intellect and conscience and hope and human sensibility. Their principles were in their feet. Their calculations were biological. They had no sense of strategy or mission. They searched the villages without knowing what to look for, not caring, kicking over jars of rice, frisking children and old men, blowing tunnels, sometimes setting fires and sometimes not, then forming up and moving on to the next village, then other villages, where it would always be the same. They carried their own lives. The pressures were enormous. In the heat of early afternoon, they would remove their helmets and flak jackets, walking bare, which was dangerous but which helped ease the strain. They would often discard things along the route of march. Purely for comfort, they would throw away rations, blow their Claymores and grenades, no matter, because by nightfall the resupply choppers would arrive with more of the same, then a day or two later still more, fresh watermelons and crates of ammunition and sunglasses and woolen sweaters—the resources were stunning—sparklers for the Fourth of July, colored eggs for Easter—it was the great American war chest—the fruits of science, the smokestacks, the canneries, the arsenals at Hartford, the Minnesota forests, the machine shops, the vast fields of corn and wheat—they carried like freight trains; they carried it on their backs and shoulders—and for all the ambiguities of Vietnam, all the mysteries and unknowns, there was at least the single abiding certainty that they would never be at a loss for things to carry.

After the chopper took Lavender away, Lieutenant Jimmy Cross led his men   40
into the village of Than Khe. They burned everything. They shot chickens and dogs, they trashed the village well, they called in artillery and watched the wreckage, then they marched for several hours through the hot afternoon, and then at dusk, while Kiowa explained how Lavender died, Lieutenant Cross found himself trembling.

He tried not to cry. With his entrenching tool, which weighed five pounds, he began digging a hole in the earth.

He felt shame. He hated himself. He had loved Martha more than his men, and as a consequence Lavender was now dead, and this was something he would have to carry like a stone in his stomach for the rest of the war.

All he could do was dig. He used his entrenching tool like an ax, slashing, feeling both love and hate, and then later, when it was full dark, he sat at the bottom of his foxhole and wept. It went on for a long while. In part, he was grieving for Ted

Lavender, but mostly it was for Martha, and for himself, because she belonged to another world, which was not quite real, and because she was a junior at Mount Sebastian College in New Jersey, a poet and a virgin and uninvolved, and because he realized she did not love him and never would.

Like cement, Kiowa whispered in the dark. I swear to God—boom, down. Not a word.

I've heard this, said Norman Bowker.   45

A pisser, you know? Still zipping himself up. Zapped while zipping.

All right, fine. That's enough.

Yeah, but you had to see it, the guy just—

I *heard*, man. Cement. So why not shut the fuck *up*?

Kiowa shook his head sadly and glanced over at the hole where Lieutenant   50
Jimmy Cross sat watching the night. The air was thick and wet. A warm dense fog had settled over the paddies and there was the stillness that precedes rain.

After a time Kiowa sighed.

One thing for sure, he said. The lieutenant's in some deep hurt. I mean that crying jag—the way he was carrying on—it wasn't fake or anything, it was real heavy-duty hurt. The man cares.

Sure, Norman Bowker said.

Say what you want, the man does care.

We all got problems.   55

Not Lavender.

No, I guess not, Bowker said. Do me a favor, though.

Shut up?

That's a smart Indian. Shut up.

Shrugging, Kiowa pulled off his boots. He wanted to say more, just to lighten up   60
his sleep, but instead he opened his New Testament and arranged it beneath his head as a pillow. The fog made things seem hollow and unattached. He tried not to think about Ted Lavender, but then he was thinking how fast it was, no drama, down and dead, and how it was hard to feel anything except surprise. It seemed unchristian. He wished he could find some great sadness, or even anger, but the emotion wasn't there and he couldn't make it happen. Mostly he felt pleased to be alive. He liked the smell of the New Testament under his cheek, the leather and ink and paper and glue, whatever the chemicals were. He liked hearing the sounds of night. Even his fatigue, it felt fine, the stiff muscles and the prickly awareness of his own body, a floating feeling. He enjoyed not being dead. Lying there, Kiowa admired Lieutenant Jimmy Cross's capacity for grief. He wanted to share the man's pain, he wanted to care as Jimmy Cross cared. And yet when he closed his eyes, all he could think was Boom-down, and all he could feel was the pleasure of having his boots off and the fog curling in around him and the damp soil and the Bible smells and the plush comfort of night.

After a moment Norman Bowker sat up in the dark.

What the hell, he said. You want to talk, *talk*. Tell it to me.

Forget it.

No, man, go on. One thing I hate, it's a silent Indian.

For the most part they carried themselves with poise, a kind of dignity. Now   65
and then, however, there were times of panic, when they squealed or wanted to squeal

but couldn't, when they twitched and made moaning sounds and covered their heads and said Dear Jesus and flopped around on the earth and fired their weapons blindly and cringed and sobbed and begged for the noise to stop and went wild and made stupid promises to themselves and to God and to their mothers and fathers, hoping not to die. In different ways, it happened to all of them. Afterward, when the firing ended, they would blink and peek up. They would touch their bodies, feeling shame, then quickly hiding it. They would force themselves to stand. As if in slow motion, frame by frame, the world would take on the old logic—absolute silence, then the wind, then sunlight, then voices. It was the burden of being alive. Awkwardly, the men would reassemble themselves, first in private, then in groups, becoming soldiers again. They would repair the leaks in their eyes. They would check for casualties, call in dustoffs, light cigarettes, try to smile, clear their throats and spit and begin cleaning their weapons. After a time someone would shake his head and say, No lie, I almost shit my pants, and someone else would laugh, which meant it was bad, yes, but the guy had obviously not shit his pants, it wasn't that bad, and in any case nobody would ever do such a thing and then go ahead and talk about it. They would squint into the dense, oppressive sunlight. For a few moments, perhaps, they would fall silent, lighting a joint and tracking its passage from man to man, inhaling, holding in the humiliation. Scary stuff, one of them might say. But then someone else would grin or flick his eyebrows and say, Roger-dodger, almost cut me a new asshole, *almost.*

There were numerous such poses. Some carried themselves with a sort of wistful resignation, others with pride or stiff soldierly discipline or good humor or macho zeal. They were afraid of dying but they were even more afraid to show it.

They found jokes to tell.

They used a hard vocabulary to contain the terrible softness. *Greased,* they'd say. *Offed, lit up, zapped while zipping.* It wasn't cruelty, just stage presence. They were actors. When someone died, it wasn't quite dying, because in a curious way it seemed scripted, and because they had their lines mostly memorized, irony mixed with tragedy, and because they called it by other names, as if to encyst and destroy the reality of death itself. They kicked corpses. They cut off thumbs. They talked grunt lingo. They told stories about Ted Lavender's supply of tranquilizers, how the poor guy didn't feel a thing, how incredibly tranquil he was.

There's a moral here, said Mitchell Sanders.

They were waiting for Lavender's chopper, smoking the dead man's dope.   70

The moral's pretty obvious, Sanders said, and winked. Stay away from drugs. No joke, they'll ruin your day every time.

Cute, said Henry Dobbins.

Mind blower, get it? Talk about wiggy. Nothing left, just blood and brains.

They made themselves laugh.

There it is, they'd say. Over and over—there it is, my friend, there it is—as if the   75 repetition itself were an act of poise, a balance between crazy and almost crazy, knowing without going, there it is, which meant be cool, let it ride, because Oh yeah, man, you can't change what can't be changed, there it is, there it absolutely and positively and fucking well *is.*

They were tough.

They carried all the emotional baggage of men who might die. Grief, terror, love, longing—these were intangibles, but the intangibles had their own mass and specific gravity, they had tangible weight. They carried shameful memories. They carried the common secret of cowardice barely restrained, the instinct to run or freeze or hide, and in many respects this was the heaviest burden of all, for it could never be put down, it required perfect balance and perfect posture. They carried their reputations. They carried the soldier's greatest fear, which was the fear of blushing. Men killed, and died, because they were embarrassed not to. It was what had brought them to the war in the first place, nothing positive, no dreams of glory or honor, just to avoid the blush of dishonor. They died so as not to die of embarrassment. They crawled into tunnels and walked point and advanced under fire. Each morning, despite the unknowns, they made their legs move. They endured. They kept humping. They did not submit to the obvious alternative, which was simply to close the eyes and fall. So easy, really. Go limp and tumble to the ground and let the muscles unwind and not speak and not budge until your buddies picked you up and lifted you into the chopper that would roar and dip its nose and carry you off to the world. A mere matter of falling, yet no one ever fell. It was not courage, exactly; the object was not valor. Rather, they were too frightened to be cowards.

By and large they carried these things inside, maintaining the masks of composure. They sneered at sick call. They spoke bitterly about guys who had found release by shooting off their own toes or fingers. Pussies, they'd say. Candy-asses. It was fierce, mocking talk, with only a trace of envy or awe, but even so the image played itself out behind their eyes.

They imagined the muzzle against flesh. So easy: squeeze the trigger and blow away a toe. They imagined it. They imagined the quick, sweet pain, then the evacuation to Japan, then a hospital with warm beds and cute geisha nurses.

And they dreamed of freedom birds.

At night, on guard, staring into the dark, they were carried away by jumbo jets. They felt the rush of takeoff. *Gone!* they yelled. And then velocity—wings and engines—a smiling stewardess—but it was more than a plane, it was a real bird, a big sleek silver bird with feathers and talons and high screeching. They were flying. The weights fell off; there was nothing to bear. They laughed and held on tight, feeling the cold slap of wind and altitude, soaring, thinking *It's over, I'm gone!*—they were naked, they were light and free—it was all lightness, bright and fast and buoyant, light as light, a helium buzz in the brain, a giddy bubbling in the lungs as they were taken up over the clouds and the war, beyond duty, beyond gravity and mortification and global entanglements—*Sin loi!* ° they yelled. *I'm sorry, mother-fuckers, but I'm out of it, I'm goofed, I'm on a space cruise, I'm gone!*—and it was a restful, unencumbered sensation, just riding the light waves, sailing that big silver freedom bird over the mountains and oceans, over America, over the farms and great sleeping cities and cemeteries and highways and the golden arches of McDonald's, it was flight, a kind of fleeing, a kind of falling, falling higher and higher, spinning off the edge of the earth and beyond the sun and through the vast, silent vacuum where there were no burdens and where everything weighed exactly nothing—*Gone!* they screamed. *I'm sorry but I'm gone!*—and so at night, not quite dreaming, they gave themselves over to lightness, they were carried, they were purely borne.

On the morning after Ted Lavender died, First Lieutenant Jimmy Cross crouched at the bottom of his foxhole and burned Martha's letters. Then he burned the two photographs. There was a steady rain falling, which made it difficult, but he used heat tabs

80

Sin loi: Vietnamese for sorry.

and Sterno to build a small fire, screening it with his body, holding the photographs over the tight blue flame with the tips of his fingers.

He realized it was only a gesture. Stupid, he thought. Sentimental, too, but mostly just stupid.

Lavender was dead. You couldn't burn the blame.

Besides, the letters were in his head. And even now, without photographs, 85 Lieutenant Cross could see Martha playing volleyball in her white gym shorts and yellow T-shirt. He could see her moving in the rain.

When the fire died out, Lieutenant Cross pulled his poncho over his shoulders and ate breakfast from a can.

There was no great mystery, he decided.

In those burned letters Martha had never mentioned the war, except to say, Jimmy, take care of yourself. She wasn't involved. She signed the letters Love, but it wasn't love, and all the fine lines and technicalities did not matter. Virginity was no longer an issue. He hated her. Yes, he did. He hated her. Love, too, but it was a hard, hating kind of love.

The morning came up wet and blurry. Everything seemed part of everything else, the fog and Martha and the deepening rain.

He was a soldier, after all. 90

Half smiling, Lieutenant Jimmy Cross took out his maps. He shook his head hard, as if to clear it, then bent forward and began planning the day's march. In ten minutes, or maybe twenty, he would rouse the men and they would pack up and head west, where the maps showed the country to be green and inviting. They would do what they had always done. The rain might add some weight, but otherwise it would be one more day layered upon all the other days.

He was realistic about it. There was that new hardness in his stomach. He loved her but he hated her.

No more fantasies, he told himself.

Henceforth, when he thought about Martha, it would be only to think that she belonged elsewhere. He would shut down the daydreams. This was not Mount Sebastian, it was another world, where there were no pretty poems or midterm exams, a place where men died because of carelessness and gross stupidity. Kiowa was right. Boom-down, and you were dead, never partly dead.

Briefly, in the rain, Lieutenant Cross saw Martha's gray eyes gazing back at him. 95

He understood.

It was very sad, he thought. The things men carried inside. The things men did or felt they had to do.

He almost nodded at her, but didn't.

Instead he went back to his maps. He was now determined to perform his duties firmly and without negligence. It wouldn't help Lavender, he knew that, but from this point on he would comport himself as an officer. He would dispose of his good-luck pebble. Swallow it, maybe, or use Lee Strunk's slingshot, or just drop it along the trail. On the march he would impose strict field discipline. He would be careful to send out flank security, to prevent straggling or bunching up, to keep his troops moving at the proper pace and at the proper interval. He would insist on clean weapons. He would confiscate the remainder of Lavender's dope. Later in the day, perhaps, he would call the men together and speak to them plainly. He would accept the blame for what had happened to Ted Lavender. He would be a man about it. He would look them in the eyes, keeping his chin level, and he would issue the new SOPs in a calm, impersonal tone of voice, a lieutenant's voice, leaving no room for argument or discussion. Commencing immediately, he'd tell them, they would no longer abandon equipment along the route of march. They would police up their acts. They would get their shit together, and keep it together, and maintain it neatly and in good working order.

He would not tolerate laxity. He would show strength, distancing himself.   100

Among the men there would be grumbling, of course, and maybe worse, because their days would seem longer and their loads heavier, but Lieutenant Jimmy Cross reminded himself that his obligation was not to be loved but to lead. He would dispense with love; it was not now a factor. And if anyone quarreled or complained, he would simply tighten his lips and arrange his shoulders in the correct command posture. He might give a curt little nod. Or he might not. He might just shrug and say, Carry on, then they would saddle up and form into a column and move out toward the villages west of Than Khe.

Tillie Olsen

I Stand Here Ironing   1961

Tillie Olsen (1912–2007) was born in Omaha, into a family of blue-collar workers who had fled Czarist Russia to escape persecution. Olsen grew up in poverty and quit school in eleventh grade to work. She later declared, "Public libraries were my college." As a member of the Young Communist League, she strove to organize Kansas City meat-packers, and was once thrown into jail. After her first husband deserted her, leaving her with one child, she married a printer and labor activist, Jack Olsen, and had three more children. Although in the 1930s she published fiction in a distinguished little magazine, Partisan Review, *the demands of motherhood, political activity, and factory and office jobs left her scant time to write until 1955. Then her youngest daughter began school and Olsen was awarded a creative writing fellowship at Stanford University. A lifelong crusader for causes, she was active in the feminist movement. "I Stand Here Ironing," from her first book,* Tell Me a Riddle *(1961), reads like autobiography. Olsen subsequently published* Yonnondio *(1974), an unfinished novel begun at age nineteen, and* Silences *(1978), a study of why writers—especially women writers—stop writing. She was the recipient of several honorary degrees, and in 1981 the city of San Francisco designated a Tillie Olsen day.*

Tillie Olsen

I stand here ironing, and what you asked me moves tormented back and forth with the iron.

"I wish you would manage the time to come in and talk with me about your daughter. I'm sure you can help me understand her. She's a youngster who needs help and whom I'm deeply interested in helping."

"Who needs help." . . . Even if I came, what good would it do? You think because I am her mother I have a key, or that in some way you could use me as a key? She has lived for nineteen years. There is all that life that has happened outside of me, beyond me.

And when is there time to remember, to sift, to weigh, to estimate, to total? I will start and there will be an interruption and I will have to gather it all together again. Or I will become engulfed with all I did or did not do, with what should have been and what cannot be helped.

She was a beautiful baby. The first and only one of our five that was beautiful at   5
birth. You do not guess how new and uneasy her tenancy in her now-loveliness. You did not know her all those years she was thought homely, or see her poring over her baby pictures, making me tell her over and over how beautiful she had been—and would be, I would tell her—and was now, to the seeing eye. But the seeing eyes were few or non-existent. Including mine.

I nursed her. They feel that's important nowadays. I nursed all the children, but with her, with all the fierce rigidity of first motherhood, I did like the books then said. Though her cries battered me to trembling and my breasts ached with swollen-ness, I waited till the clock decreed.

Why do I put that first? I do not even know if it matters, or if it explains anything.

She was a beautiful baby. She blew shining bubbles of sound. She loved motion, loved light, loved color and music and textures. She would lie on the floor in her blue overalls patting the surface so hard in ecstasy her hands and feet would blur. She was a miracle to me, but when she was eight months old I had to leave her daytimes with the woman downstairs to whom she was no miracle at all, for I worked or looked for work and for Emily's father, who "could no longer endure" (he wrote in his good-bye note) "sharing want with us."

I was nineteen. It was the pre-relief, pre-WPA world of the depression. I would start running as soon as I got off the streetcar, running up the stairs, the place smelling sour, and awake or asleep to startle awake, when she saw me she would break into a clogged weeping that could not be comforted, a weeping I can hear yet.

After a while I found a job hashing at night so I could be with her days, and it   10
was better. But it came to where I had to bring her to his family and leave her.

It took a long time to raise the money for her fare back. Then she got chicken pox and I had to wait longer. When she finally came, I hardly knew her, walking quick and nervous like her father, looking like her father, thin, and dressed in a shoddy red that yellowed her skin and glared at the pockmarks. All the baby loveliness gone.

She was two. Old enough for nursery school they said, and I did not know then what I know now—the fatigue of the long day, and the lacerations of group life in the kinds of nurseries that are only parking places for children.

Except that it would have made no difference if I had known. It was the only place there was. It was the only way we could be together, the only way I could hold a job.

And even without knowing, I knew. I knew the teacher that was evil because all these years it has curdled into my memory, the little boy hunched in the corner, her rasp, "why aren't you outside, because Alvin hits you? that's no reason, go out, scaredy." I knew Emily hated it even if she did not clutch and implore "don't go Mommy" like the other children, mornings.

She always had a reason why we should stay home. Momma, you look sick,   15
Momma, I feel sick. Momma, the teachers aren't there today, they're sick. Momma,

we can't go, there was a fire there last night. Momma, it's a holiday today, no school, they told me.

But never a direct protest, never rebellion. I think of our others in their three-, four-year-oldness—the explosions, the tempers, the denunciations, the demands— and I feel suddenly ill. I put the iron down. What in me demanded that goodness in her? And what was the cost, the cost to her of such goodness?

The old man living in the back once said in his gentle way: "You should smile at Emily more when you look at her." What *was* in my face when I looked at her? I loved her. There were all the acts of love.

It was only with the others I remembered what he said, and it was the face of joy, and not of care or tightness or worry I turned to them—too late for Emily. She does not smile easily, let alone almost always as her brothers and sisters do. Her face is closed and somber, but when she wants, how fluid. You must have seen it in her pantomimes, you spoke of her rare gift for comedy on the stage that rouses a laughter out of the audience so dear they applaud and applaud and do not want to let her go.

Where does it come from, that comedy? There was none of it in her when she came back to me that second time, after I had had to send her away again. She had a new daddy now to learn to love, and I think perhaps it was a better time.

Except when we left her alone nights, telling ourselves she was old enough.   20

"Can't you go some other time, Mommy, like tomorrow?" she would ask. "Will it be just a little while you'll be gone? Do you promise?"

The time we came back, the front door open, the clock on the floor in the hall. She rigid awake. "It wasn't just a little while. I didn't cry. Three times I called you, just three times, and then I ran downstairs to open the door so you could come faster. The clock talked loud. I threw it away, it scared me what it talked."

She said the clock talked loud again that night I went to the hospital to have Susan. She was delirious with the fever that comes before red measles, but she was fully conscious all the week I was gone and the week after we were home when she could not come near the new baby or me.

She did not get well. She stayed skeleton thin, not wanting to eat, and night after night she had nightmares. She would call for me, and I would rouse from exhaustion to sleepily call back: "You're all right, darling, go to sleep, it's just a dream," and if she still called, in a sterner voice, "now go to sleep, Emily, there's nothing to hurt you." Twice, only twice, when I had to get up for Susan anyhow, I went in to sit with her.

Now when it is too late (as if she would let me hold and comfort her like I do the   25
others) I get up and go to her at once at her moan or restless stirring. "Are you awake, Emily? Can I get you something?" And the answer is always the same: "No, I'm all right, go back to sleep, Mother."

They persuaded me at the clinic to send her away to a convalescent home in the country where "she can have the kind of food and care you can't manage for her, and you'll be free to concentrate on the new baby." They still send children to that place. I see pictures on the society page of sleek young women planning affairs to raise money for it, or dancing at the affairs, or decorating Easter eggs or filling Christmas stockings for the children.

They never have a picture of the children so I do not know if the girls still wear those gigantic red bows and the ravaged looks on the every other Sunday when parents can come to visit "unless otherwise notified"—as we were notified the first six weeks.

Oh it is a handsome place, green lawns and tall trees and fluted flower beds. High up on the balconies of each cottage the children stand, the girls in their red bows and white dresses, the boys in white suits and giant red ties. The parents stand below shrieking up to be heard and the children shriek down to be heard, and between them the invisible wall: "Not To Be Contaminated by Parental Germs or Physical Affection."

There was a tiny girl who always stood hand in hand with Emily. Her parents never came. One visit she was gone. "They moved her to Rose Cottage" Emily shouted in explanation. "They don't like you to love anybody here."

She wrote once a week, the labored writing of a seven-year-old. "I am fine. How is the baby. If I write my leter nicly I will have a star. Love." There never was a star. We wrote every other day, letters she could never hold or keep but only hear read—once. "We simply do not have room for children to keep any personal possessions," they patiently explained when we pieced one Sunday's shrieking together to plead how much it would mean to Emily, who loved so to keep things, to be allowed to keep her letters and cards.

Each visit she looked frailer. "She isn't eating," they told us.

(They had runny eggs for breakfast or mush with lumps, Emily said later, I'd hold it in my mouth and not swallow. Nothing ever tasted good, just when they had chicken.)

It took us eight months to get her released home, and only the fact that she gained back so little of her seven lost pounds convinced the social worker.

I used to try to hold and love her after she came back, but her body would stay stiff, and after a while she'd push away. She ate little. Food sickened her, and I think much of life too. Oh she had physical lightness and brightness, twinkling by on skates, bouncing like a ball up and down up and down over the jump rope, skimming over the hill; but these were momentary.

She fretted about her appearance, thin and dark and foreign-looking at a time when every little girl was supposed to look or thought she should look a chubby blonde replica of Shirley Temple. The doorbell sometimes rang for her, but no one seemed to come and play in the house or be a best friend. Maybe because we moved so much.

There was a boy she loved painfully through two school semesters. Months later she told me how she had taken pennies from my purse to buy him candy. "Licorice was his favorite and I brought him some every day, but he still liked Jennifer bet-ter'n me. Why, Mommy?" The kind of question for which there is no answer.

School was a worry to her. She was not glib or quick in a world where glibness and quickness were easily confused with ability to learn. To her overworked and ex-asperated teachers she was an overconscientious "slow learner" who kept trying to catch up and was absent entirely too often.

I let her be absent, though sometimes the illness was imaginary. How different from my now-strictness about attendance with the others. I wasn't working. We had a new baby, I was home anyhow. Sometimes, after Susan grew old enough, I would keep her home from school, too, to have them all together.

Mostly Emily had asthma, and her breathing, harsh and labored, would fill the house with a curiously tranquil sound. I would bring the two old dresser mirrors and her boxes of collections to her bed. She would select beads and single earrings, bottle tops and shells, dried flowers and pebbles, old postcards and scraps, all sorts of odd-ments; then she and Susan would play Kingdom, setting up landscapes and furniture, peopling them with action.

Those were the only times of peaceful companionship between her and Susan. I have edged away from it, that poisonous feeling between them, that terrible

30

35

40

balancing of hurts and needs I had to do between the two, and did so badly, those earlier years.

Oh there are conflicts between the others too, each one human, needing, demanding, hurting, taking—but only between Emily and Susan, no, Emily toward Susan that corroding resentment. It seems so obvious on the surface, yet it is not obvious. Susan, the second child, Susan, golden- and curly-haired and chubby, quick and articulate and assured, everything in appearance and manner Emily was not; Susan, not able to resist Emily's precious things, losing or sometimes clumsily breaking them; Susan telling jokes and riddles to company for applause while Emily sat silent (to say to me later: that was *my* riddle, Mother, I told it to Susan); Susan, who for all the five years' difference in age was just a year behind Emily in developing physically.

I am glad for that slow physical development that widened the difference between her and her contemporaries, though she suffered over it. She was too vulnerable for that terrible world of youthful competition, of preening and parading, of constant measuring of yourself against every other, of envy, "If I had that copper hair," "If I had that skin. . . ." She tormented herself enough about not looking like the others, there was enough of the unsureness, the having to be conscious of words before you speak, the constant caring—what are they thinking of me? without having it all magnified by the merciless physical drives.

Ronnie is calling. He is wet and I change him. It is rare there is such a cry now. That time of motherhood is almost behind me when the ear is not one's own but must always be racked and listening for the child cry, the child call. We sit for a while and I hold him, looking out over the city spread in charcoal with its soft aisles of light. "*Shoogily,*" he breathes and curls closer. I carry him back to bed, asleep. *Shoogily.* A funny word, a family word, inherited from Emily, invented by her to say: *comfort.*

In this and other ways she leaves her seal, I say aloud. And startle at my saying it. What do I mean? What did I start to gather together, to try and make coherent? I was at the terrible, growing years. War years. I do not remember them well. I was working, there were four smaller ones now, there was not time for her. She had to help be a mother, and housekeeper, and shopper. She had to set her seal. Mornings of crisis and near hysteria trying to get lunches packed, hair combed, coats and shoes found, everyone to school or Child Care on time, the baby ready for transportation. And always the paper scribbled on by a smaller one, the book looked at by Susan then mislaid, the homework not done. Running out to that huge school where she was one, she was lost, she was a drop; suffering over the unpreparedness, stammering and unsure in her classes.

There was so little time left at night after the kids were bedded down. She would struggle over books, always eating (it was in those years she developed her enormous appetite that is legendary in our family) and I would be ironing, or preparing food for the next day, or writing V-mail° to Bill, or tending the baby. Sometimes, to make me laugh, or out of her despair, she would imitate happenings or types at school.   45

I think I said once: "Why don't you do something like this in the school amateur show?" One morning she phoned me at work, hardly understandable through the weeping: "Mother, I did it. I won, I won; they gave me first prize; they clapped and clapped and wouldn't let me go."

V-mail: short for Victory mail, a system, involving microfilming and air delivery, for quick and efficient correspondence with family members serving overseas during World War II.

Now suddenly she was Somebody, and as imprisoned in her difference as she had been in anonymity.

She began to be asked to perform at other high schools, even in colleges, then at city and statewide affairs. The first one we went to, I only recognized her that first moment when thin, shy, she almost drowned herself into the curtains. Then: Was this Emily? The control, the command, the convulsing and deadly clowning, the spell, then the roaring, stamping audience, unwilling to let this rare and precious laughter out of their lives.

Afterwards: You ought to do something about her with a gift like that—but without money or knowing how, what does one do? We have left it all to her, and the gift has as often eddied inside, clogged and clotted, as been used and growing.

She is coming. She runs up the stairs two at a time with her light graceful step, and I know she is happy tonight. Whatever it was that occasioned your call did not happen today.   50

"Aren't you ever going to finish the ironing, Mother? Whistler painted his mother in a rocker. I'd have to paint mine standing over an ironing board." This is one of her communicative nights and she tells me everything and nothing as she fixes herself a plate of food out of the icebox.

She is so lovely. Why did you want me to come in at all? Why were you concerned? She will find her way.

She starts up the stairs to bed. "Don't get me up with the rest in the morning." "But I thought you were having midterms." "Oh, those," she comes back in, kisses me, and says quite lightly, "in a couple of years when we'll all be atom-dead° they won't matter a bit."

She has said it before. She *believes* it. But because I have been dredging the past, and all that compounds a human being is so heavy and meaningful in me, I cannot endure it tonight.

I will never total it all. I will never come in to say: She was a child seldom smiled   55
at. Her father left me before she was a year old. I had to work her first six years when there was work, or I sent her home and to his relatives. There were years she had care she hated. She was dark and thin and foreign-looking in a world where the prestige went to blondeness and curly hair and dimples, she was slow where glibness was prized. She was a child of anxious, not proud, love. We were poor and could not afford for her the soil of easy growth. I was a young mother, I was a distracted mother. There were other children pushing up, demanding. Her younger sister seemed all that she was not. There were years she did not want me to touch her. She kept too much in herself, her life was such she had to keep too much in herself. My wisdom came too late. She has much to her and probably little will come of it. She is a child of her age, of depression, of war, of fear.

Let her be. So all that is in her will not bloom—but in how many does it? There is still enough left to live by. Only help her to know—help make it so there is cause for her to know—that she is more than this dress on the ironing board, helpless before the iron.

---

atom-dead: killed by an exchange of atomic bombs between the United States and the Soviet Union.

Tobias Wolff

The Rich Brother   1985

*Tobias Wolff was born in Birmingham,
Alabama, in 1945, the son of an aerospace
engineer and a waitress and secretary. Following
his parents' divorce, Tobias moved with his
mother to Washington State while his older
brother, Geoffrey, remained with their father (a
pathological liar who was the subject of Geoffrey
Wolff's acclaimed memoir* The Duke of Deception*). Tobias Wolff's own memoir,* This Boy's
Life *(1989), describes, among other things, his
tense relationship with his abusive stepfather; it
was the basis for the 1993 film starring Robert
De Niro and Leonardo DiCaprio. In 1964
Wolff joined the Army, where he spent four
years, including a year in Vietnam as a Special
Forces language expert. This experience is*

Tobias Wolff

recounted in a second memoir, In Pharaoh's Army: Memories of the Lost War *(1994).
After his military service, he earned a bachelor's degree at Oxford University and a master's
at Stanford University, where he currently teaches in the creative writing program. Wolff is
the author of five volumes of fiction, the novella* The Barracks Thief *(1984, PEN/Faulkner
Award), the novel* Old School *(2003), and four volumes of short stories, most recently* Our
Story Begins: New and Selected Stories *(2008).*

*Acknowledging Raymond Carver (his onetime faculty colleague at Syracuse University)
and Flannery O'Connor as influences, Wolff writes stories that, in the words of one critic,
create a "sometimes comic, always compassionate world of ordinary people who suffer
twentieth-century martyrdoms of growing up, growing old, loving and lacking love, living with
parents and lovers and wives and their own weaknesses." Wolff lives in Northern California.*

There were two brothers, Pete and Donald.

Pete, the older brother, was in real estate. He and his wife had a Century 21 fran-
chise in Santa Cruz. Pete worked hard and made a lot of money, but not any more
than he thought he deserved. He had two daughters, a sailboat, a house from which
he could see a thin slice of the ocean, and friends doing well enough in their own
lives not to wish bad luck on him. Donald, the younger brother, was still single. He
lived alone, painted houses when he found the work, and got deeper in debt to Pete
when he didn't.

No one would have taken them for brothers. Where Pete was stout and hearty
and at home in the world, Donald was bony, grave, and obsessed with the fate of his
soul. Over the years Donald had worn the images of two different Perfect Masters°
around his neck. Out of devotion to the second of these he entered an ashram° in
Berkeley, where he nearly died of undiagnosed hepatitis. By the time Pete finished
paying the medical bills Donald had become a Christian. He drifted from church to

---

Perfect Masters: in Hindu mysticism, God-realized souls who work to help others toward the
realization of God. *ashram:* secluded place where a community of Hindus lead lives of simplicity and meditation.

church, then joined a pentecostal community that met somewhere in the Mission District° to sing in tongues and swap prophecies.

Pete couldn't make sense of it. Their parents were both dead, but while they were alive neither of them had found it necessary to believe in anything. They managed to be decent people without making fools of themselves, and Pete had the same ambition. He thought that the whole thing was an excuse for Donald to take himself seriously.

The trouble was that Donald couldn't content himself with worrying about his own soul. He had to worry about everyone else's, and especially Pete's. He handed down his judgments in ways that he seemed to consider subtle: through significant silence, innuendo, looks of mild despair that said, *Brother, what have you come to?* What Pete had come to, as far as he could tell, was prosperity. That was the real issue between them. Pete prospered and Donald did not prosper.

At the age of forty Pete took up sky diving. He made his first jump with two friends who'd started only a few months earlier and were already doing stunts. He never would have used the word *mystical*, but that was how Pete felt about the experience. Later he made the mistake of trying to describe it to Donald, who kept asking how much it cost and then acted appalled when Pete told him.

"At least I'm trying something new," Pete said. "At least I'm breaking the pattern."

Not long after that conversation Donald also broke the pattern, by going to live on a farm outside Paso Robles. The farm was owned by several members of Donald's community, who had bought it and moved there with the idea of forming a family of faith. That was how Donald explained it in the first letter he sent. Every week Pete heard how happy Donald was, how "in the Lord." He told Pete that he was praying for him, he and the rest of Pete's brothers and sisters on the farm.

"I only have one brother," Pete wanted to answer, "and that's enough." But he kept this thought to himself.

In November the letters stopped. Pete didn't worry about this at first, but when he called Donald at Thanksgiving Donald was grim. He tried to sound upbeat but he didn't try hard enough to make it convincing. "Now listen," Pete said, "you don't have to stay in that place if you don't want to."

"I'll be all right," Donald answered.

"That's not the point. Being all right is not the point. If you don't like what's going on up there, then get out."

"I'm all right," Donald said again, more firmly. "I'm doing fine."

But he called Pete a week later and said that he was quitting the farm. When Pete asked him where he intended to go, Donald admitted that he had no plan. His car had been repossessed just before he left the city, and he was flat broke.

"I guess you'll have to stay with us," Pete said.

Donald put up a show of resistance. Then he gave in. "Just until I get my feet on the ground," he said.

"Right," Pete said. "Check out your options." He told Donald he'd send him money for a bus ticket, but as they were about to hang up Pete changed his mind. He knew that Donald would try hitchhiking to save the fare. Pete didn't want him out on the road all alone where some head case would pick him up, where anything could happen to him.

Mission District: run-down and, at one time, dangerous section of San Francisco.

"Better yet," he said, "I'll come and get you."

"You don't have to do that. I didn't expect you to do that," Donald said. He added, "It's a pretty long drive."

"Just tell me how to get there."   20

But Donald wouldn't give him directions. He said that the farm was too depressing, that Pete wouldn't like it. Instead, he insisted on meeting Pete at a service station called Jonathan's Mechanical Emporium.

"You must be kidding," Pete said.

"It's close to the highway," Donald said. "I didn't name it."

"That's one for the collection," Pete said.

The day before he left to bring Donald home, Pete received a letter from a man   25
who described himself as "head of household" at the farm where Donald had been living. From this letter Pete learned that Donald had not quit the farm, but had been
asked to leave. The letter was written on the back of a mimeographed survey form asking people to record their response to a ceremony of some kind. The last question said:

What did you feel during the liturgy?

　　a) Being
　　b) Becoming
　　c) Being and Becoming
　　d) None of the Above
　　e) All of the Above

Pete tried to forget the letter. But of course he couldn't. Each time he thought of
it he felt crowded and breathless, a feeling that came over him again when he drove
into the service station and saw Donald sitting against a wall with his head on his
knees. It was late afternoon. A paper cup tumbled slowly past Donald's feet, pushed
by the damp wind.

Pete honked and Donald raised his head. He smiled at Pete, then stood and
stretched. His arms were long and thin and white. He wore a red bandanna across his
forehead, a T-shirt with a couple of words on the front. Pete couldn't read them because the letters were inverted.

"Grow up," Pete yelled. "Get a Mercedes."

Donald came up to the window. He bent down and said, "Thanks for coming.
You must be totally whipped."

"I'll make it." Pete pointed at Donald's T-shirt. "What's that supposed to say?"   30

Donald looked down at his shirt front. "Try God. I guess I put it on backwards.
Pete, could I borrow a couple of dollars? I owe these people for coffee and sandwiches."

Pete took five twenties from his wallet and held them out the window.

Donald stepped back as if horrified. "I don't need that much."

"I can't keep track of all these nickels and dimes," Pete said. "Just pay me back
when your ship comes in." He waved the bills impatiently. "Go on—take it."

"Only for now." Donald took the money and went into the service station office.   35
He came out carrying two orange sodas, one of which he gave to Pete as he got into
the car. "My treat," he said.

"No bags?"

"Wow, thanks for reminding me." Donald balanced his drink on the dashboard, but the slight rocking of the car as he got out tipped it onto the passenger's

seat, where half its contents foamed over before Pete could snatch it up again. Donald looked on while Pete held the bottle out the window, soda running down his fingers.

"Wipe it up," Pete told him. "Quick!"

"With what?"

Pete stared at Donald. "That shirt. Use the shirt." 40

Donald pulled a long face but did as he was told, his pale skin puckering against the wind.

"Great, just great," Pete said. "We haven't even left the gas station yet."

Afterwards, on the highway, Donald said, "This is a new car, isn't it?"

"Yes. This is a new car."

"Is that why you're so upset about the seat?" 45

"Forget it, okay? Let's just forget about it."

"I said I was sorry."

Pete said, "I just wish you'd be more careful. These seats are made of leather. That stain won't come out, not to mention the smell. I don't see why I can't have leather seats that smell like leather instead of orange pop."

"What was wrong with the other car?"

Pete glanced over at Donald. Donald had raised the hood of the blue sweatshirt 50 he'd put on. The peaked hood above his gaunt, watchful face gave him the look of an inquisitor.

"There wasn't anything wrong with it," Pete said. "I just happened to like this one better."

Donald nodded.

There was a long silence between them as Pete drove on and the day darkened toward evening. On either side of the road lay stubble-covered fields. A line of low hills ran along the horizon, topped here and there with trees black against the grey sky. In the approaching line of cars a driver turned on his headlights. Pete did the same.

"So what happened?" he asked. "Farm life not your bag?"

Donald took some time to answer, and at last he said, simply, "It was my fault." 55

"What was your fault?"

"The whole thing. Don't play dumb, Pete. I know they wrote to you." Donald looked at Pete, then stared out the windshield again.

"I'm not playing dumb."

Donald shrugged.

"All I really know is they asked you to leave," Pete went on. "I don't know any of 60 the particulars."

"I blew it," Donald said. "Believe me, you don't want to hear the gory details."

"Sure I do," Pete said. He added, "Everybody likes the gory details."

"You mean everybody likes to hear how someone messed up."

"Right," Pete said. "That's the way it is here on Spaceship Earth."

Donald bent one knee onto the front seat and leaned against the door so that he 65 was facing Pete instead of the windshield. Pete was aware of Donald's scrutiny. He waited. Night was coming on in a rush now, filling the hollows of the land. Donald's long cheeks and deep-set eyes were dark with shadow. His brow was white. "Do you ever dream about me?" Donald asked.

"Do I ever dream about you? What kind of a question is that? Of course I don't dream about you," Pete said, untruthfully.

"What do you dream about?"

"Sex and money. Mostly money. A nightmare is when I dream I don't have any."

"You're just making that up," Donald said.

Pete smiled.

"Sometimes I wake up at night," Donald went on, "and I can tell you're dreaming about me."

"We were talking about the farm," Pete said. "Let's finish that conversation and then we can talk about our various out-of-body experiences and the interesting things we did during previous incarnations."

For a moment Donald looked like a grinning skull; then he turned serious again. "There's not much to tell," he said. "I just didn't do anything right."

"That's a little vague," Pete said.

"Well, like the groceries. Whenever it was my turn to get the groceries I'd blow it somehow. I'd bring the groceries home and half of them would be missing, or I'd have all the wrong things, the wrong kind of flour or the wrong kind of chocolate or whatever. One time I gave them away. It's not funny, Pete."

Pete said, "Who did you give the groceries to?"

"Just some people I picked up on the way home. Some fieldworkers. They had about eight kids with them and they didn't even speak English—just nodded their heads. Still, I shouldn't have given away the groceries. Not all of them, anyway. I really learned my lesson about that. You have to be practical. You have to be fair to yourself." Donald leaned forward, and Pete could sense his excitement. "There's nothing actually wrong with being in business," he said. "As long as you're fair to other people you can still be fair to yourself. I'm thinking of going into business, Pete."

"We'll talk about it," Pete said. "So, that's the story? There isn't any more to it than that?"

"What did they tell you?" Donald asked.

"Nothing."

"They must have told you something."

Pete shook his head.

"They didn't tell you about the fire?" When Pete shook his head again Donald regarded him for a time, then folded his arms across his chest and slumped back into the corner. "Everybody had to take turns cooking dinner. I usually did tuna casserole or spaghetti with garlic bread. But this one night I thought I'd do something different, something really interesting." Donald looked sharply at Pete. "It's all a big laugh to you, isn't it?"

"I'm sorry," Pete said.

"You don't know when to quit. You just keep hitting away."

"Tell me about the fire, Donald."

Donald kept watching him. "You have this compulsion to make me look foolish."

"Come off it, Donald. Don't make a big thing out of this."

"I know why you do it. It's because you don't have any purpose in life. You're afraid to relate to people who do, so you make fun of them."

"Relate," Pete said.

"You're basically a very frightened individual," Donald said. "Very threatened. You've always been like that. Do you remember when you used to try to kill me?"

"I don't have any compulsion to make you look foolish, Donald—you do it yourself. You're doing it right now."

"You can't tell me you don't remember," Donald said. "It was after my operation. You remember that."

"Sort of." Pete shrugged. "Not really."

"Oh yes," Donald said. "Do you want to see the scar?" 95

"I remember you had an operation. I don't remember the specifics, that's all. And I sure as hell don't remember trying to kill you."

"Oh yes," Donald repeated, maddeningly. "You bet your life you did. All the time. The thing was, I couldn't have anything happen to me where they sewed me up because then my intestines would come apart again and poison me. That was a big issue, Pete. Mom was always in a state about me climbing trees and so on. And you used to hit me there every chance you got."

"Mom was in a state every time you burped," Pete said. "I don't know. Maybe I bumped into you accidentally once or twice. I never did it deliberately."

"Every chance you got," Donald said. "Like when the folks went out at night and left you to baby-sit. I'd hear them say good night, and then I'd hear the car start up, and when they were gone I'd lie there and listen. After a while I would hear you coming down the hall, and I would close my eyes and pretend to be asleep. There were nights when you would stand outside the door, just stand there, and then go away again. But most nights you'd open the door and I would hear you in the room with me, breathing. You'd come over and sit next to me on the bed—you remember, Pete, you have to— you'd sit next to me on the bed and pull the sheets back. If I was on my stomach you'd roll me over. Then you would lift up my pajama shirt and start hitting me on my stitches. You'd hit me as hard as you could, over and over. I was afraid that you'd get mad if you knew I was awake. Is that strange or what? I was afraid that you'd get mad if you found out that I knew you were trying to kill me." Donald laughed. "Come on, you can't tell me you don't remember that."

"It might have happened once or twice. Kids do those things. I can't get all 100 excited about something I maybe did twenty-five years ago."

"No maybe about it. You did it."

Pete said, "You're wearing me out with this stuff. We've got a long drive ahead of us and if you don't back off pretty soon we aren't going to make it. You aren't, anyway."

Donald turned away.

"I'm doing my best," Pete said. The self-pity in his own voice made the words sound like a lie. But they weren't a lie! He was doing his best.

The car topped a rise. In the distance Pete saw a cluster of lights that blinked out 105 when he started downhill. There was no moon. The sky was low and black.

"Come to think of it," Pete said, "I did have a dream about you the other night." Then he added, impatiently, as if Donald were badgering him, "A couple of other nights, too. I'm getting hungry," he said.

"The same dream?"

"Different dreams. I only remember one of them. There was something wrong with me, and you were helping out. Taking care of me. Just the two of us. I don't know where everyone else was supposed to be."

Pete left it at that. He didn't tell Donald that in this dream he was blind.

"I wonder if that was when I woke up," Donald said. He added, "I'm sorry I got into 110 that thing about my scar. I keep trying to forget it but I guess I never will. Not really. It was pretty strange, having someone around all the time who wanted to get rid of me."

"Kid stuff," Pete said. "Ancient history."

They ate dinner at a Denny's on the other side of King City. As Pete was paying the check he heard a man behind him say, "Excuse me, but I wonder if I might ask which way you're going?" and Donald answer, "Santa Cruz."

"Perfect," the man said.

Pete could see him in the fish-eye mirror above the cash register: a red blazer with some kind of crest on the pocket, little black moustache, glossy black hair combed down on his forehead like a Roman emperor's. A rug, Pete thought. Definitely a rug.

Pete got his change and turned. "Why is that perfect?" he asked.   115

The man looked at Pete. He had a soft, ruddy face that was doing its best to express pleasant surprise, as if this new wrinkle were all he could have wished for, but the eyes behind the aviator glasses showed signs of regret. His lips were moist and shiny. "I take it you're together," he said.

"You got it," Pete told him.

"All the better, then," the man went on. "It so happens I'm going to Santa Cruz myself. Had a spot of car trouble down the road. The old Caddy let me down."

"What kind of trouble?" Pete asked.

"Engine trouble," the man said. "I'm afraid it's a bit urgent. My daughter is sick.   120
Urgently sick. I've got a telegram here." He patted the breast pocket of his blazer.

Before Pete could say anything Donald got into the act again. "No problem," Donald said. "We've got tons of room."

"Not that much room," Pete said.

Donald nodded. "I'll put my things in the trunk."

"The trunk's full," Pete told him.

"It so happens I'm traveling light," the man said. "This leg of the trip anyway. In   125
fact, I don't have any luggage at this particular time."

Pete said, "Left it in the old Caddy, did you?"

"Exactly," the man said.

"No problem," Donald repeated. He walked outside and the man went with him. Together they strolled across the parking lot, Pete following at a distance. When they reached Pete's car Donald raised his face to the sky, and the man did the same. They stood there looking up. "Dark night," Donald said.

"Stygian," the man said.

Pete still had it in his mind to brush him off, but he didn't do that. Instead he   130
unlocked the door for him. He wanted to see what would happen. It was an adventure, but not a dangerous adventure. The man might steal Pete's ashtrays but he wouldn't kill him. If Pete got killed on the road it would be by some spiritual person in a sweatsuit, someone with his eyes on the far horizon and a wet Try God T-shirt in his duffel bag.

As soon as they left the parking lot the man lit a cigar. He blew a cloud of smoke over Pete's shoulder and sighed with pleasure. "Put it out," Pete told him.

"Of course," the man said. Pete looked in the rearview mirror and saw the man take another long puff before dropping the cigar out the window. "Forgive me," he said. "I should have asked. Name's Webster, by the way."

Donald turned and looked back at him. "First name or last?"

The man hesitated. "Last," he said finally.

"I know a Webster," Donald said. "Mick Webster."   135

"There are many of us," Webster said.

"Big fellow, wooden leg," Pete said.

Donald gave Pete a look.

Webster shook his head. "Doesn't ring a bell. Still, I wouldn't deny the connection. Might be one of the cousinry."

"What's your daughter got?" Pete asked.   140

"That isn't clear," Webster answered. "It appears to be a female complaint of some nature. Then again it may be tropical." He was quiet for a moment, and added: "If indeed it *is* tropical, I will have to assume some of the blame myself. It was my own vaulting ambition that first led us to the tropics and kept us in the tropics all those many years, exposed to every evil. Truly I have much to answer for. I left my wife there."

Donald said quietly, "You mean she died?"

"I buried her with these hands. The earth will be repaid, gold for gold."

"Which tropics?" Pete asked.

"The tropics of Peru." 145

"What part of Peru are they in?"

"The lowlands," Webster said.

"What's it like down there? In the lowlands."

"Another world," Webster said. His tone was sepulchral. "A world better imagined than described."

"Far out," Pete said. 150

The three men rode in silence for a time. A line of trucks went past in the other direction, trailers festooned with running lights, engines roaring.

"Yes," Webster said at last, "I have much to answer for."

Pete smiled at Donald, but Donald had turned in his seat again and was gazing at Webster. "I'm sorry about your wife," Donald said.

"What did she die of?" Pete asked.

"A wasting illness," Webster said. "The doctors have no name for it, but I do." 155 He leaned forward and said, fiercely, "*Greed.* My greed, not hers. She wanted no part of it."

Pete bit his lip. Webster was a find and Pete didn't want to scare him off by hooting at him. In a voice low and innocent of knowingness, he asked, "What took you there?"

"It's difficult for me to talk about."

"Try," Pete told him.

"A cigar would make it easier."

Donald turned to Pete and said, "It's okay with me." 160

"All right," Pete said. "Go ahead. Just keep the window rolled down."

"Much obliged." A match flared. There were eager sucking sounds.

"Let's hear it," Pete said.

"I am by training an engineer," Webster began. "My work has exposed me to all but one of the continents, to desert and alp and forest, to every terrain and season of the earth. Some years ago I was hired by the Peruvian government to search for tungsten in the tropics. My wife and daughter accompanied me. We were the only white people for a thousand miles in any direction, and we had no choice but to live as the Indians lived—to share their food and drink and even their culture."

Pete said, "You knew the lingo, did you?" 165

"We picked it up." The ember of the cigar bobbed up and down. "We were used to learning as necessity decreed. At any rate, it became evident after a couple of years that there was no tungsten to be found. My wife had fallen ill and was pleading to be taken home. But I was deaf to her pleas, because by then I was on the trail of another metal—a metal far more valuable than tungsten."

"Let me guess," Pete said. "Gold?"

Donald looked at Pete, then back at Webster.

"Gold," Webster said. "A vein of gold greater than the Mother Lode itself. After I found the first traces of it nothing could tear me away from my search—not the sickness of my wife or anything else. I was determined to uncover the vein, and so I did—but not before I laid my wife to rest. As I say, the earth will be repaid."

Webster was quiet. Then he said, "But life must go on. In the years since my wife's death I have been making the arrangements necessary to open the mine. I could have done it immediately, of course, enriching myself beyond measure, but I knew what that would mean—the exploitation of our beloved Indians, the brutal destruction of their environment. I felt I had too much to atone for already." Webster paused, and when he spoke again his voice was dull and rushed, as if he had used up all the interest he had in his own words. "Instead I drew up a program for returning the bulk of the wealth to the Indians themselves. A kind of trust fund. The interest alone will allow them to secure their ancient lands and rights in perpetuity. At the same time, our investors will be rewarded a thousandfold. Two-thousandfold. Everyone will prosper together."

"That's great," said Donald. "That's the way it ought to be."

Pete said, "I'm willing to bet that you just happen to have a few shares left. Am I right?"

Webster made no reply.

"Well?" Pete knew that Webster was on to him now, but he didn't care. The story had bored him. He'd expected something different, something original, and Webster had let him down. He hadn't even tried. Pete felt sour and stale. His eyes burned from cigar smoke and the high beams of road-hogging truckers. "Douse the stogie," he said to Webster. "I told you to keep the window down."

"Got a little nippy back here."

Donald said, "Hey, Pete. Lighten up."

"Douse it!"

Webster sighed. He got rid of the cigar.

"I'm a wreck," Pete said to Donald. "You want to drive for a while?"

Donald nodded.

Pete pulled over and they changed places.

Webster kept his counsel in the back seat. Donald hummed while he drove, until Pete told him to stop. Then everything was quiet.

Donald was humming again when Pete woke up. Pete stared sullenly at the road, at the white lines sliding past the car. After a few moments of this he turned and said, "How long have I been out?"

Donald glanced at him. "Twenty, twenty-five minutes."

Pete looked behind him and saw that Webster was gone. "Where's our friend?"

"You just missed him. He got out in Soledad.° He told me to say thanks and good-bye."

"Soledad? What about his sick daughter? How did he explain her away?"

"He has a brother living there. He's going to borrow a car from him and drive the rest of the way in the morning."

"I'll bet his brother's living there," Pete said. "Doing fifty concurrent life sentences. His brother and his sister and his mom and his dad."

"I kind of liked him," Donald said.

Soledad: city in central California, site of a state prison.

"I'm sure you did," Pete said wearily.

"He was interesting. He's been places."

"His cigars had been places, I'll give you that."

"Come on, Pete."

"Come on yourself. What a phony." 195

"You don't know that."

"Sure I do."

"How? How do you know?"

Pete stretched. "Brother, there are some things you're just born knowing. What's the gas situation?"

"We're a little low." 200

"Then why didn't you get some more?"

"I wish you wouldn't snap at me like that," Donald said.

"Then why don't you use your head? What if we run out?"

"We'll make it," Donald said. "I'm pretty sure we've got enough to make it. You didn't have to be so rude to him," Donald added.

Pete took a deep breath. "I don't feel like running out of gas tonight, okay?" 205

Donald pulled in at the next station they came to and filled the tank while Pete went to the men's room. When Pete came back, Donald was sitting in the passenger's seat. The attendant came up to the driver's window as Pete got in behind the wheel. He bent down and said, "Twelve fifty-five."

"You heard the man," Pete said to Donald.

Donald looked straight ahead. He didn't move.

"Cough up," Pete said. "This trip's on you."

"I can't." 210

"Sure you can. Break out that wad."

Donald glanced up at the attendant, then at Pete. "Please," he said. "Pete, I don't have it anymore."

Pete took this in. He nodded, and paid the attendant.

Donald began to speak when they left the station but Pete cut him off. He said, "I don't want to hear from you right now. You just keep quiet or I swear to God I won't be responsible."

They left the fields and entered a tunnel of tall trees. The trees went on and on. 215 "Let me get this straight," Pete said at last. "You don't have the money I gave you."

"You treated him like a bug or something," Donald said.

"You don't have the money," Pete said again.

Donald shook his head.

"Since I bought dinner, and since we didn't stop anywhere in between, I assume you gave it to Webster. Is that right? Is that what you did with it?"

"Yes." 220

Pete looked at Donald. His face was dark under the hood but he still managed to convey a sense of remove, as if none of this had anything to do with him.

"Why?" Pete asked. "Why did you give it to him?" When Donald didn't answer, Pete said, "A hundred dollars. Gone. Just like that. I *worked* for that money, Donald."

"I know, I know," Donald said.

"You don't know! How could you? You get money by holding out your hand."

"I work too," Donald said. 225

"You work too. Don't kid yourself, brother."

Donald leaned toward Pete, about to say something, but Pete cut him off again.

"You're not the only one on the payroll, Donald. I don't think you understand that. I have a family."

"Pete, I'll pay you back."

"Like hell you will. A hundred dollars!" Pete hit the steering wheel with the 230 palm of his hand. "Just because you think I hurt some goofball's feelings. Jesus, Donald."

"That's not the reason," Donald said. "And I didn't just *give* him the money."

"What do you call it, then? What do you call what you did?"

"I *invested* it. I wanted a share, Pete." When Pete looked over at him Donald nodded and said again, "I wanted a share."

Pete said, "I take it you're referring to the gold mine in Peru."

"Yes," Donald said. 235

"You believe that such a gold mine exists?"

Donald looked at Pete, and Pete could see him just beginning to catch on. "You'll believe anything," Pete said. "Won't you? You really will believe anything at all."

"I'm sorry," Donald said, and turned away.

Pete drove on between the trees and considered the truth of what he had just said—that Donald would believe anything at all. And it came to him that it would be just like this unfair life for Donald to come out ahead in the end, by believing in some outrageous promise that would turn out to be true and that he, Pete, would reject out of hand because he was too wised up to listen to anybody's pitch anymore except for laughs. What a joke. What a joke if there really was a blessing to be had, and the blessing didn't come to the one who deserved it, the one who did all the work, but to the other.

And as if this had already happened Pete felt a shadow move upon him, darken- 240 ing his thoughts. After a time he said, "I can see where all this is going, Donald."

"I'll pay you back," Donald said.

"No," Pete said. "You won't pay me back. You can't. You don't know how. All you've ever done is take. All your life."

Donald shook his head.

"I see exactly where this is going," Pete went on. "You can't work, you can't take care of yourself, you believe anything anyone tells you. I'm stuck with you, aren't I?" He looked over at Donald. "I've got you on my hands for good."

Donald pressed his fingers against the dashboard as if to brace himself. "I'll get 245 out," he said.

Pete kept driving.

"Let me out," Donald said. "I mean it, Pete."

"Do you?"

Donald hesitated. "Yes," he said.

"Be sure," Pete told him. "This is it. This is for keeps." 250

"I mean it."

"All right. You made the choice." Pete braked the car sharply and swung it to the shoulder of the road. He turned off the engine and got out. Trees loomed on both sides, shutting out the sky. The air was cold and musty. Pete took Donald's duffel bag from the back seat and set it down behind the car. He stood there, facing Donald in the red glow of the taillights. "It's better this way," Pete said.

Donald just looked at him.

"Better for you," Pete said.

Donald hugged himself. He was shaking. "You don't have to say all that," he told 255
Pete. "I don't blame you."

"Blame me? What the hell are you talking about? Blame me for what?"

"For anything," Donald said.

"I want to know what you mean by blame me."

"Nothing. Nothing, Pete. You'd better get going. God bless you."

"That's it," Pete said. He dropped to one knee, searching the packed dirt with his 260
hands. He didn't know what he was looking for, his hands would know when they
found it.

Donald touched Pete's shoulder. "You'd better go," he said.

Somewhere in the trees Pete heard a branch snap. He stood up. He looked at Donald, then went back to the car and drove away. He drove fast, hunched over the wheel,
conscious of the way he was hunched and the shallowness of his breathing, refusing to
look in the mirror above his head until there was nothing behind him but darkness.

Then he said, "A hundred dollars," as if there were someone to hear.

The trees gave way to fields. Metal fences ran beside the road, plastered with
windblown scraps of paper. Tule fog hung above the ditches, spilling into the road,
dimming the ghostly halogen lights that burned in the yards of the farms Pete passed.
The fog left beads of water rolling up the windshield.

Pete rummaged among his cassettes. He found Pachelbel's Canon° and pushed it 265
into the tape deck. When the violins began to play he leaned back and assumed an attentive expression as if he were really listening to them. He smiled to himself like a
man at liberty to enjoy music, a man who has finished his work and settled his debts,
done all things meet and due.

And in this way, smiling, nodding to the music, he went another mile or so and
pretended that he was not already slowing down, that he was not going to turn back,
that he would be able to drive on like this, alone, and have the right answer when his
wife stood before him in the doorway of his home and asked, Where is he? Where is
your brother?

Pachelbel's Canon: musical composition by Johann Pachelbel (1653–1706); it became widely known
through its use in the film _Ordinary People_ (1980).

Susan Glaspell at work, around 1913.

WRITING

13

WRITING ABOUT
A STORY

Don't write merely to be understood.
Write so that you cannot possibly be misunderstood.

—ROBERT LOUIS STEVENSON

Assigned to write an essay on William Faulkner's "A Rose for Emily," a student might well wonder, "What can I say that hasn't been said a thousand times before?" Often the most difficult aspect of writing about a story, poem, or play is the feeling that we have nothing of interest to contribute to the ongoing conversation about some celebrated literary work. There's always room, though, for a reader's fresh take on an old standby.

Remember that in the study of literature common sense is never out of place. For most of a class hour, a professor once rhapsodized about the arrangement of the contents of W. H. Auden's *Collected Poems*. Auden, he claimed, was a master of thematic continuity, who had brilliantly placed the poems in the order that they ingeniously complemented each other. Near the end of the hour, his theories were punctured—with a great inaudible pop—when a student, timidly raising a hand, pointed out that Auden had arranged the poems in the book not by theme but in alphabetical order according to the first word of each poem. The professor's jaw dropped: "Why didn't you say that sooner?" The student was apologetic: "I—I was afraid I'd sound too *ordinary*."

Don't be afraid to state a conviction, though it seems obvious. Does it matter that you may be repeating something that, once upon a time or even just the other day, has been said before? What matters more is that you are actively engaged in thinking about literature. There are excellent old ideas as well as new ones. You have something to say.

In this chapter many of the discussions and examples refer to Edgar Allan Poe's short story "The Tell-Tale Heart" (page 36). If you haven't already read it, you can do so in only a few minutes, so that the rest of this chapter will make more sense to you.

READ ACTIVELY

Unlike a brief poem or a painting that you can take in with one long glance, a work of fiction—even a short story—may be too complicated to hold all at once in the mind's eye. Before you can write about it, you may need to give it two or more careful readings, and even then, as you begin to think further about it, you will probably have to thumb through it to reread passages. The first time through, it is best just to read attentively, open to whatever pleasure and wisdom the story may afford. The second time, you will find it useful to read with pencil in hand, either to mark your text or to take notes to jog your memory. To work out the design and meaning of a story need not be a boring chore, any more than it is to land a fighting fish and to study it with admiration. Here are some steps to get you started:

- **Preview the text.** To get acquainted with a work of literature before you settle in for a closer reading, skim it for an overview of its content and organization. Take a quick look at all parts of the work. Even a book's cover, preface, introduction, footnotes, and biographical notes about the author can provide you with some context for reading the work itself.

- **Take notes. Annotate the text.** Read with a highlighter and pencil at hand, making appropriate annotations to the text. Later, you'll easily be able to review these highlights, and, when you write your paper, quickly refer to supporting evidence.

  - Underline words, phrases, or sentences that seem interesting or important, or that raise questions.
  - Jot down brief notes in the margin (*"key symbol—this foreshadows the ending,"* for example, or *"dramatic irony"*).
  - Use lines or arrows to indicate passages that seem to speak to each other— for instance, all the places in which you find the same theme or related symbols.

- **Read closely.** Once you have begun reading in earnest, don't skim or skip over words you don't recognize; sometimes, looking up those very words will unlock a piece's meaning.

- **Reread as needed.** If a piece is short, read it several times. Often, knowing the ending of a short story will allow you to extract new meaning from its beginning and middle. If the piece is longer, reread the passages you thought important enough to highlight.

On the next page is a sample of an annotated passage from paragraph 3 of Edgar Allan Poe's "The Tell-Tale Heart."

who is his listener?

Is this true?

Now this is the point. You fancy me mad. (Madmen know nothing).
But you should have seen *me*. You should have seen how wisely I proceeded—with what caution—with what foresight—with what dissimulation I went to work! I was never kinder to the old man than during the

He's not so mad he doesn't know what he's doing

whole week before I killed him. And every night, about midnight, I
turned the latch of his door and opened it—oh, so gently! And then,
when I had made an opening sufficient for my head, I put in a dark
lantern, all closed, closed, so that no light shone out, and then I thrust in

He's strangely happy! excited

my head. Oh, you would have laughed to see how cunningly I thrust it
in! I moved it slowly—very, very slowly, so that I might not disturb the
old man's sleep. It took me an hour to place my whole head within the
opening so far that I could see him as he lay upon his bed. Ha!—would a

Careful planning

madman have been so wise as this? And then, when my head was well in
the room, I undid the lantern cautiously—oh, so cautiously—cautiously
(for the hinges creaked)—I undid it just so much that a single thin ray

Creepy image. Who is the vulture here?

What did he expect?!

fell upon the vulture eye. And this I did for seven long nights—every
night just at midnight—but I found the eye always closed; and so it was
impossible to do the work; for it was not the old man who vexed me, but

Peculiar obsession

his Evil Eye.

THINK ABOUT THE STORY

Once you have reread the story, you can begin to process your ideas about it. To get
started, try the following steps:

- **Identify the protagonist and the conflict.** Whose story is being told? What
  does that character desire more than anything else? What stands in the way of
  that character's achievement of his or her goal? The answers to these questions
  can give you a better handle on the story's plot.
- **Consider the story's point of view.** What does it contribute to the story?
  How might the tale change if told from another point of view?

- **Think about the setting.** Does it play a significant role in the plot? How does setting affect the story's tone?

- **Notice key symbols.** If any symbols catch your attention as you go, be sure to highlight each place in which they appear in the text. What do these symbols contribute to the story's meaning? (Remember, not every image is a symbol— only those important recurrent persons, places, or things that seem to suggest more than their literal meaning.)

- **Look for the theme.** Is the story's central meaning stated directly? If not, how does it reveal itself?

- **Think about tone and style.** How would you characterize the style in which the story is written? Consider elements such as diction, sentence structure, tone, and organization. How does the story's style contribute to its tone?

PREWRITING: DISCOVER YOUR IDEAS

Once you have given the story some preliminary thought, it is time to write as a means of discovering what it is you have to say. Brainstorming, clustering, listing, freewriting, keeping a journal, and outlining all can help you clarify your thoughts about the story and, in doing so, generate ideas for your paper. While you don't need to use *all* these techniques, try them to find the one or two that work best for you.

- **Brainstorm.** If you aren't sure what, exactly, to say about a story, try jotting down everything you can think of about it. Work quickly, without pausing to judge what you have written. Set yourself a time limit of ten or fifteen minutes and keep writing even if you think you have said it all. A list that results from brainstorming on "The Tell-Tale Heart" might look something like this:

> madness? seems crazy
> unreliable narrator
> Could story be a dream?
> Could heartbeat be supernatural?
> heartbeat = speaker's paranoia
> tone: dramatic, intense, quick mood changes
> glee/terror
> lots of exclamation points
> telling his story to listener
> old man = father? boss? friend?
> old man's gold/treasures
> old man's eye = motive
> vulture eye = symbolic
> Calls plotting murder "work"
> careful/patient
> Chops up body
> perfect crime
> Policemen don't hear heartbeat
> Guilt makes him confess

- **Cluster.** Clustering involves generating ideas by diagramming the relationship among your many ideas. First, write your subject at the center of a sheet of paper and circle it. Then, jot down ideas as they occur to you, drawing lines to link each idea to related ones. Here is an example of how you might cluster your ideas about "The Tell-Tale Heart."

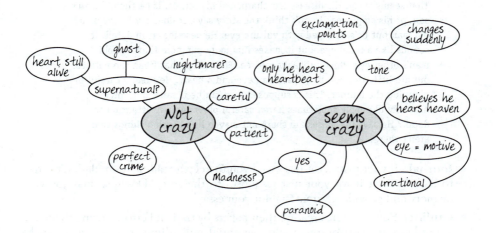

- **List.** Using your notes and annotations as a guide, list information that seems useful, adding any notes that help you to keep track of your thought process. Use different headings to organize related concepts. Your lists might look something like this:

Unreliable Narrator	Other Possibilities
mood swings	nightmare
insists too much on being sane	supernatural
confusion	heart still alive?
disease	ghost's heartbeat?
sharpened senses	
loved old man	
murder	
patience	
guilt	
hearing things	

- **Freewrite.** Before you try to write a coherent first draft of your essay, take time to write freely, exploring your ideas as they occur to you. Writing quickly, without thinking too hard about grammar or spelling, can call forth surprising new ideas that wouldn't arrive if you were composing in a more reflective, cautious manner. To freewrite, give yourself a set amount of time—fifteen or twenty minutes. Put your pen to paper (or your fingers to the keys) and write without pausing to think. Keep going even if you run out of things to say. A freewrite on "The Tell-Tale Heart" might look like this:

The guy seems crazy. He keeps insisting he's sane, so maybe others have accused him of being insane. He's speaking to someone—a judge? a fellow inmate? The story feels spoken out loud, like a dramatic monologue. His mood changes really quickly. One minute he's gleeful, and then impatient, then terrified. The story is full of dashes and exclamation points. He says he can hear everything in heaven and earth and even some things in hell. That seems crazy. His disease has sharpened his senses. Is he the old man's son, or his employee? I don't think the story says. It does say he loves the old man but he's obsessed with vulture eye. He describes it in detail. It sounds like a blind eye, but it makes him more paranoid than the old man's other eye which probably can see. The things that freak the narrator out are little things—body parts, an eye and a heart. He's really careful in planning the murder. This is supposed to mean he is sane, but don't mentally ill people sometimes hatch careful plots and pay attention to detail? He says his senses are sharp but maybe he's hearing things that aren't there?

- **Journal.** If your instructor has asked you to keep a reading journal, don't forget to look back at it for your first responses to the story. Doing so may jog your memory and provide raw material for your essay.

- **Outline.** Some writers organize their papers by trial and error, writing them and going back in, cutting out useless material and filling in what seems to be missing. For a more efficient approach to organization, though, try making an outline—a simple list of points arranged in an order that makes logical sense. Such an outline might look like this:

    1. Point of view is ironic (speaker is mad/unreliable)
            hears things in heaven/hell
            excited tone
            focus on strange detail
    2. Can we trust story really happened?
            nightmare?
            more interesting if actual
    3. Supernatural elements?
            ghost heartbeat?
            heart still alive?
    4. More interesting/believable if speaker is mad

WRITE A ROUGH DRAFT

Once your prewriting exercises have sparked an idea or two, you will be ready to begin shaping your thoughts into a rough draft. You can still keep your approach loose and informal; don't worry yet about phrasing things perfectly or pinning down the ideal word. For now, your goal is to begin finding a shape for your argument.

- **Remember your purpose.** Before you begin work on your first draft, be sure to check the assignment you have been given. There is no sense in writing even the most elegant *analysis* (in which you focus on one particular element of a story) if you have been told to write an *explication* (a detailed, line-by-line interpretation of a passage).

- **Consider your audience.** Though your professor and classmates will likely be your paper's actual audience, the assignment might specify hypothetical readers. Whoever your audience may be, keep their needs in mind as you write.

- **Define your topic narrowly.** Worried about having enough to say, students sometimes frame their topic so broadly that they can't do justice to it in the allotted number of pages. Your paper will be stronger if you go more deeply into your subject than if you choose a gigantic subject and touch on most aspects of it only superficially. A thorough explication of a short story is hardly possible in a 250-word paper, but an explication of a paragraph or two could work in that space. A profound topic ("The Character of Hamlet") might overflow a book, but a more focused one ("Hamlet's View of Acting" or "Hamlet's Puns") could result in a manageable paper.

- **Formulate your thesis.** Before you get going on your rough draft, you will need a thesis sentence summing up your paper's main idea. Begin with a provisional thesis to give your argument direction. As you write, be sure to keep your provisional thesis in mind; doing so will help you stay on track. Here is a working thesis for a paper on "The Tell-Tale Heart":

WORKING THESIS

The story contains many hints that the narrator of "The Tell-Tale Heart" is crazy.

While this thesis gives its author something to work toward, it isn't yet as sharp as it could be. Most readers would agree that the story's narrator shows obvious signs of insanity. A more compelling thesis would go into the specifics of what, exactly, gives away the narrator's madness, or it might spell out the implications of this madness for the story. The following reworked version of this thesis sentence does both:

REVISED THESIS

The narrator's tenuous hold on reality and his wild shifts in mood indicate that he is insane and, therefore, that his point of view is untrustworthy.

Like this statement, your thesis should be decisive and specific. As you write a rough draft, your task is to persuade readers of the wisdom of your thesis.

- **Back up your thesis with evidence.** The bulk of your essay should be spent providing evidence that proves your thesis. Because the most persuasive evidence tends to be that which comes from the story itself, be sure to quote as needed. As you flesh out your argument, check back frequently to make sure your thesis continues to hold up to the evidence. If you find that the facts of the story don't bear out your thesis, the problem may be with the evidence or with the thesis itself. Could your point be better proved by presenting different evidence? If so, exchange what you have for more convincing information. If not, go back in and refine your thesis sentence. Then make sure that the rest of the evidence bears out your new and improved thesis.

■ **Organize your argument.** Choose the points you need to prove your thesis and present them, along with supporting evidence, in whatever order best makes your case. A rough outline is often a useful tool.

CHECKLIST: Writing a Rough Draft

☐ What is your essay's purpose?
☐ Who is your audience? What do they need to know?
☐ What is your thesis? Is it debatable?
☐ Does everything in your essay support your thesis?
☐ Is your argument sensibly organized?

REVISE YOUR DRAFT

A writer rarely—if ever—achieves perfection on the first try. For most of us, good writing is largely a matter of revision. Once your first draft is done, you can—and should—turn on your analytical mind. Painstaking revision is more than just tidying up grammar and spelling. It might mean expanding your ideas or sharpening the focus by cutting out any unnecessary thoughts. To achieve effective writing, you must have the courage to be merciless. Tear your rough drafts apart and reassemble their pieces into a stronger order.

First, though, it is an excellent idea to get feedback on your draft from a trusted reader—a classmate, a roommate, a tutor in your school's writing center, or, even your instructor—who can tell you which ideas are, and are not, coming across clearly, or where your argument is persuasive and where it could be more convincing. For writers at all levels of expertise, there simply is no substitute for constructive criticism from a thoughtful reader. If, however, you find readers are in short supply, put your rough draft away for at least an hour or two, and reread it with fresh eyes before you begin revising.

The following is an example of how one student used his instructor's comments to improve his paper's opening paragraph. (The final paper is printed later in the chapter on page 640.)

DRAFT OF OPENING PARAGRAPH

The narrator of Edgar Allan Poe's "The Tell-Tale Heart" is a very mysterious and murderous character. The reader doesn't know much about him, except for how he speaks and what he has to say for himself. There is one important fact revealed by evidence in the story. The story contains many hints that the narrator of "The Tell-Tale Heart" is crazy.

Provide specifics.

Tell me more!

Why is this important?

What are some of these?

REVISED OPENING PARAGRAPH

    Although there are many things we do not know about the narrator of Edgar Allan Poe's story "The Tell-Tale Heart"—is he a son? a servant? a companion?—there is one thing we are sure of from the start. He is mad. In the opening paragraph, Poe makes the narrator's condition unmistakable, not only from his excited and worked-up speech (full of dashes and exclamation points), but also from his wild claims. He says it is merely some disease which has sharpened his senses that has made people call him crazy. Who but a madman, however, would say, "I heard all things in the heaven and in the earth," and brag how his ear is a kind of radio, listening in on hell? The narrator's tenuous hold on reality and his wild shifts in mood indicate that he is mad and, therefore, that his point of view is untrustworthy.

    Remember that revision means more than just cleaning up typos and doing away with stray semicolons. Revision might mean fleshing out your ideas with new paragraphs, rearranging material, or paring away passages that detract from your focus. As you rewrite, make sure every paragraph has a topic sentence that announces its main idea. Feel free to link your ideas with transitional words and phrases such as "moreover," "in addition," or "in contrast," to help your reader understand how each new idea relates to the one that precedes it.

CHECKLIST: Revising Your Draft

- ☐ Is your thesis clear? Does it say something significant but not entirely obvious about the story?
- ☐ Does all your evidence serve to advance the argument put forth in your thesis?
- ☐ Is your argument clear and logical?
- ☐ Do transitional words and phrases help signal movement from one idea to the next?
- ☐ Does your introduction draw the reader in? Does it prepare the reader for what follows?
- ☐ Does your conclusion tie up the paper's loose ends? Does it avoid merely restating what has come before?
- ☐ Does each paragraph contain a topic sentence?
- ☐ Does the paper have an interesting and compelling title?

WHAT'S YOUR PURPOSE? COMMON APPROACHES TO WRITING ABOUT FICTION

It is crucial to keep your paper's purpose in mind. When you write an academic paper, you are likely to have been given a specific set of marching orders. Maybe you have been asked to write for a particular audience besides the obvious one (your professor, that is). Perhaps you have been asked to describe your personal reaction to a literary work. Maybe your purpose is to interpret a work, analyzing how one or more of its elements contribute to its meaning. You may have been instructed to write an evaluation in which you judge a work's merits. Let the assignment dictate your paper's tone and content. Below are several commonly used approaches to writing about fiction.

Explication

Explication is the patient unfolding of meanings in a work of literature. An explication proceeds carefully through a story, usually interpreting it line by line—perhaps even word by word, dwelling on details a casual reader might miss and illustrating how a story's smaller parts contribute to the whole. Alert and willing to take pains, the writer of such an essay notices anything meaningful that isn't obvious, whether it is a colossal theme suggested by a symbol or a little hint contained in a single word.

To write an honest explication of an entire story takes time and space, and is a better assignment for a long term paper, an honors thesis, or a dissertation than a short essay. A thorough explication of Nathaniel Hawthorne's "Young Goodman Brown," for example, would likely run much longer than the rich and intriguing short story itself. Ordinarily, explication is best suited to a short passage or section of a story: a key scene, a critical conversation, a statement of theme, or an opening or closing paragraph. In a long critical essay that doesn't adhere to one method all the way through, the method of explication may appear from time to time, as when the critic, in discussing a story, stops to unravel a particularly knotty passage. Here are some tips for writing a successful explication of your own:

- **Focus on the details that strike you as most meaningful.** Do not try to cover everything.

- **Try working through the original passage sentence by sentence.** If you choose this method, be sure to vary your transitions from one point to the next, to avoid the danger of falling into a boring singsong: "In the first sentence I noticed . . . ," "In the next sentence . . . ," "Now in the third sentence . . . ," and "Finally, in the last sentence. . . . "

- **Consider working from a simple outline.** In writing the explication that follows of a passage from "The Tell-Tale Heart," the student began with a list of points she wanted to express:

  1. Speaker's extreme care and exactness—typical of some mental illnesses.
  2. Speaker doesn't act by usual logic but by a crazy logic.
  3. Dreamlike connection between latch and lantern and old man's eye.

Storytellers who are especially fond of language invite closer attention to their words than others might. Edgar Allan Poe, for one, is a poet sensitive to the rhythms of his sentences and a symbolist whose stories abound in potent suggestions. Here is a student's explication of a short but essential passage in "The Tell-Tale Heart." The passage occurs in the third paragraph of the story, and to help us follow the explication, the student quotes the passage in full at the paper's beginning.

Kim 1

Susan Kim
Professor A. M. Lundy
English 100
20 May 2009

By Lantern Light: An Explication
of a Passage in Poe's "The Tell-Tale Heart"

And every night, about midnight, I turned the latch of his door
and opened it—oh, so gently! And then, when I had made an
opening sufficient for my head, I put in a dark lantern, all closed,
closed, so that no light shone out, and then I thrust in my head.
Oh, you would have laughed to see how cunningly I thrust it in!
I moved it slowly—very, very slowly, so that I might not disturb
the old man's sleep. It took me an hour to place my whole head
within the opening so far that I could see him as he lay upon
his bed. Ha!—would a madman have been so wise as this? And then,
when my head was well in the room, I undid the lantern
cautiously—oh, so cautiously—cautiously (for the hinges
creaked)—I undid it just so much that a single thin ray fell upon
the vulture eye. And this I did for seven long nights—every night
just at midnight—but I found the eye always closed; and so it was
impossible to do the work; for it was not the old man who vexed
me, but his Evil Eye. (par. 3)

Quotes passage to be explicated

Although Edgar Allan Poe has suggested in the first lines of his story "The
Tell-Tale Heart" that the person who addresses us is insane, it is only when we
come to the speaker's account of his preparations for murdering the old man that
we find his madness fully revealed. Even more convincingly than his earlier words
(for we might possibly think that someone who claims to hear things in heaven and
hell is a religious mystic), these preparations reveal him to be mad. What strikes us
is that they are so elaborate and meticulous. A significant detail is the exactness of
his schedule for spying: "every night just at midnight." The words with which he
describes his motions also convey the most extreme care (and I will indicate them
by italics): "how wisely I proceeded—with *what caution*," "I turned the latch of his
door and opened it—oh, so *gently!*" "how *cunningly* I thrust it [my head] in! I
moved it slowly—*very, very slowly*," "I undid the lantern *cautiously*—oh, *so
cautiously*—*cautiously*." Taking a whole hour to intrude his head into the room, he
asks, "Ha!—would a madman have been so wise as this?" But of course the word

Thesis sentence

Textual evidence supports thesis

wise is unconsciously ironic, for clearly it is not wisdom the speaker displays, but an absurd degree of care, an almost fiendish ingenuity. Such behavior, I understand, is typical of certain mental illnesses. All his careful preparations that he thinks prove him sane only convince us instead that he is mad.

Topic sentence on narrator's mad logic

Obviously his behavior is self-defeating. He wants to catch the "vulture eye" open, and yet he takes all these pains not to disturb the old man's sleep. If he behaved logically, he might go barging into the bedroom with his lantern ablaze, shouting at the top of his voice. And yet, if we can see things his way, there *is* a strange logic to his reasoning. He regards the eye as a creature in itself, quite apart from its possessor. "It was not," he says, "the old man who vexed me, but his Evil Eye." Apparently, to be inspired to do his deed, the madman needs to behold the eye—at least, this is my understanding of his remark, "I found the eye always closed; and so it was impossible to do the work." Poe's choice of the word *work*, by the way, is also revealing. Murder is made to seem a duty or a job; and anyone who so regards murder is either extremely cold-blooded, like a hired killer for a gangland assassination, or else deranged. Besides, the word suggests again the curious sense of detachment that the speaker feels toward the owner of the eye.

Conclusion pushes thesis further, making it more specific.

In still another of his assumptions, the speaker shows that he is madly logical, or operating on the logic of a dream. There seems a dreamlike relationship between his dark lantern "all closed, closed, so that no light shone out," and the sleeping victim. When the madman opens his lantern so that it emits a single ray, he is hoping that the eye in the old man's head will be open too, letting out its corresponding gleam. The latch that he turns so gently, too, seems like the eye, whose lid needs to be opened in order for the murderer to go ahead. It is as though the speaker is *trying* to get the eyelid to lift. By taking such great pains and by going through all this nightly ritual, he is practicing some kind of magic, whose rules are laid down not by our logic, but by the logic of dreams.

Kim 3

Work Cited

Poe, Edgar Allan. "The Tell-Tale Heart." *An Introduction to Fiction.* Ed. X. J.
Kennedy and Dana Gioia. 11th ed. New York: Longman, 2010. 36–40.
Print.

An unusually well-written essay, "By Lantern Light" cost its author two or three careful revisions. Rather than attempting to say something about *everything* in the passage from Poe, she selects only the details that strike her as most meaningful. In her very first sentence, she briefly shows us how the passage functions in the context of Poe's story: how it clinches our suspicions that the narrator is mad. Notice too that the student who wrote the essay doesn't inch through the passage sentence by sentence, but freely takes up its details in an order that seems appropriate to her argument.

Analysis

Examining a single component of a story can afford us a better understanding of the entire work. This is perhaps why in most literature classes students are asked to write at least one **analysis** (from the Greek: "breaking up"), an essay that breaks a story or novel into its elements and, usually, studies one part closely. One likely topic for an analysis might be "The Character of James Baldwin's Sonny," in which the writer would concentrate on showing us Sonny's highly individual features and traits of personality. Other topics for an analysis might be "Irony in Ha Jin's 'Saboteur,'" or "Setting in Kate Chopin's 'The Storm,'" or "The Unidentified Narrator in 'A Rose for Emily.'"

To be sure, no element of a story dwells in isolation from the story's other elements. In "The Tell-Tale Heart," the madness of the leading character apparently makes it necessary to tell the story from a special point of view and probably helps determine the author's choice of theme, setting, symbolism, tone, style, and ironies. But it would be mind-boggling to try to study all those elements simultaneously. For this reason, when we write an analysis, we generally study just one element, though we may suggest—probably at the start of the essay—its relation to the whole story. Here are two points to keep in mind when writing an analysis:

- **Decide upon a thesis, and include only relevant insights.** As tempting as it might be to include your every idea, stick to those that will help to prove your point.

- **Support your contentions with specific references to the story you are analyzing.** Quotations can be particularly convincing.

The following paper is an example of a solid, brief analysis. Written by a student, it focuses on just one element of "The Tell-Tale Heart"—the story's point of view.

Frederick 1

Mike Frederick

Professor Stone

English 110

18 January 2009

The Hearer of the Tell-Tale Heart

States author and work

Although there are many things we do not know about the narrator of Edgar Allan Poe's story "The Tell-Tale Heart"—is he a son? a servant? a companion?—there is one thing we are sure of from the start. He is mad. In the opening paragraph, Poe makes the narrator's condition unmistakable, not only from his excited and worked-up speech (full of dashes and exclamation points), but also from his wild claims. He says it is merely some disease which has sharpened his senses that has made people call him crazy. Who but a madman, however, would say, "I heard all things in the heaven and in the earth," and brag how his ear is a kind of radio, listening in on hell? The narrator's tenuous hold on reality and his wild shifts in mood indicate that he is insane and, therefore, that his point of view is untrustworthy.

Thesis statement

Topic sentence— how point of view determines emphasis

Because the participating narrator is telling his story in the first person, some details in the story stand out more than others. When the narrator goes on to tell how he watches the old man sleeping, he rivets his attention on the old man's "vulture eye." When a ray from his lantern finds the Evil Eye open, he says, "I could see nothing else of the old man's face or person" (par. 9). Actually, the reader can see almost nothing else about the old man anywhere in the rest of the story. All we are told is that the old man treated the younger man well, and we gather that the old man was rich, because his house is full of treasures. We do not have a clear idea of what the old man looks like, though, nor do we know how he talks, for we are not given any of his words. Our knowledge of him is mainly confined to his eye and its effect on the narrator. This confinement gives that symbolic eye a lot of importance in the story. The narrator tells us all we know and directs our attention to parts of it.

Raises question, then explores answer

This point of view raises an interesting question. Since we are dependent on the narrator for all our information, how do we know the whole story isn't just a nightmare in his demented mind? We have really no way to be sure it isn't, as far as I can see. I assume, however, that there really is a dark shuttered house and an old man and real policemen who start snooping around when screams are heard in the neighborhood, because it is a more memorable story if

Frederick 2

it is a crazy man's view of reality than if it is all just a terrible dream. But we
can't take stock in the madman's interpretation of what happens. Poe keeps
putting distances between what the narrator says and what we are
apparently supposed to think. For instance: the narrator has boasted that he
is calm and clear in the head, but as soon as he starts trying to explain why
he killed the old man, we gather that he is confused, to say the least. "I
think it was his eye!" the narrator exclaims, as if not quite sure (par. 2). As
he goes on to explain how he conducted the murder, we realize that he is a
man with a fixed idea working with a patience that is certainly mad, almost
diabolical.

Topic sentence on how narrator's madness is revealed

Some readers might wonder if "The Tell-Tale Heart" is a story of the
supernatural. Is the heartbeat that the narrator hears a ghost come back to
haunt him? Here, I think, the point of view is our best guide to what to
believe. The simple explanation for the heartbeat is this: it is all in the
madman's mind. Perhaps he feels such guilt that he starts hearing things.
Another explanation is possible, one suggested by Daniel Hoffman, a critic who
has discussed the story: the killer hears the sound of his *own* heart (227).
Hoffman's explanation (which I don't like as well as mine) also is a natural
one, and it fits the story as a whole. Back when the narrator first entered the
old man's bedroom to kill him, the heartbeat sounded so loud to him that he
was afraid the neighbors would hear it too. Evidently they didn't, and so
Hoffman may be right in thinking that the sound was only that of his own
heart pounding in his ears. Whichever explanation you take, it is a more down-
to-earth and reasonable explanation than (as the narrator believes) that the
heart is still alive, even though its owner has been cut to pieces. Then, too,
the police keep chatting. If they heard the heartbeat, wouldn't they leap to
their feet, draw their guns, and look all around the room? As the author keeps
showing us in the rest of the story, the narrator's view of things is
untrustworthy. You don't kill someone just because you dislike the look in his
eye. You don't think that such a murder is funny. For all its Gothic atmosphere
of the old dark house with a secret hidden inside, "The Tell-Tale Heart" is not a
ghost story. We have only to see its point of view to know it is a study in
abnormal psychology.

Raises question, then explores answer

Secondary source paraphrase

Restatement of thesis

Frederick 3

Works Cited

Hoffman, Daniel. *Poe Poe Poe Poe Poe Poe Poe*. New York: Anchor, 1973. Print.

Poe, Edgar Allan. "The Tell-Tale Heart." *An Introduction to Fiction*. Ed. X. J. Kennedy and Dana Gioia. 11th ed. New York: Longman, 2010. 36–40. Print.

The temptation in writing an analysis is to include all sorts of insights that the writer proudly wishes to display, even though they aren't related to the main idea. In the preceding essay, the student resists this temptation admirably. In fairly plump and ample paragraphs, he works out his ideas and supports his contentions with specific references to Poe's story. Although his paper is not brilliantly written and contains no insight so fresh as the suggestion (by the writer of the first paper) that the madman's lantern is like the old man's head, still, it is a good brief analysis. By sticking faithfully to his purpose and by confronting the problems he raises ("How do we know the whole story isn't just a nightmare?"), the writer persuades us that he understands not only the story's point of view but also the story in its entirety.

The Card Report

Another form of analysis, a **card report** breaks down a story into its various elements. Though card reports tend to include only as much information as can fit on both sides of a single 5- by 8-inch index card, they are at least as challenging to write as full-fledged essays. The author of a successful card report can dissect a story into its elements and describe them succinctly and accurately. A typical card report on "The Tell-Tale Heart" follows. In this assignment, the student was asked to include the following:

1. The story's title and the date of its original publication.
2. The author's name and dates of birth and death.
3. The name (if any) of the main character, along with a description of that character's dominant traits or features.
4. Similar information for other characters.
5. A short description of the setting.
6. The point of view from which the story is told.
7. A terse summary of the story's main events in chronological order.
8. A description of the general tone, or, in other words, the author's feelings toward the central character or the main event.
9. Some comments on the style in which the story is written. Brief illustrative quotations are helpful if space allows.
10. Whatever kinds of irony the story contains and what they contribute to the story.

11. The story's main theme, in a sentence.
12. Key symbols (if the story has any), with an educated guess at what each symbol suggests.
13. Finally, an evaluation of the story as a whole, concisely setting forth the student's opinion of it. (Some instructors consider this the most important part of the report, and most students find that, by the time they have so painstakingly separated the ingredients of the story, they have arrived at a definite opinion of its merits.)

As you might expect, fitting so much information on one card is like trying to engrave the Declaration of Independence on the head of a pin. The student who wrote this report had to spoil a few trial cards before he was able to complete the assignment. The card report is an extreme exercise in making every word count, a worthwhile discipline in almost any kind of writing. Some students enjoy the challenge, and most are surprised at how thoroughly they come to understand the story. A longer story, even a novel, may be analyzed in the same way, but insist on taking a second card if you are asked to analyze an especially hefty and complicated novel.

Front of Card

Carly Grace   English 101

Story: "The Tell-Tale Heart," 1850

Author: Edgar Allan Poe (1809-1849)

Central character: An unnamed younger man whom people call mad, who claims that a nervous disease has greatly sharpened his sense perceptions. He is proud of his own cleverness.

Other characters: The old man, whose leading feature is one pale blue, filmed eye; said to be rich, kind, and lovable. Also three policemen, not individually described.

Setting: A shuttered house full of wind, mice, and treasures; pitch dark even in the afternoon.

Narrator: The madman himself.

Events in summary: (1) Dreading one vulture-like eye of the old man he shares a house with, a madman determines to kill its owner. (2) Each night he spies on the sleeping old man, but finding the eye shut, he stays his hand. (3) On the eighth night, finding the eye open, he suffocates its owner beneath the mattress and conceals the dismembered body under the floor of the bedchamber. (4) Entertaining some inquiring police officers in the very room where the body lies hidden, the killer again hears (or thinks he hears) the beat of the victim's heart. (5) Terrified, convinced that the police also hear the heartbeat growing louder, the killer confesses.

Tone: Horror at the events described, skepticism toward the narrator's claims to be sane, detachment from his gaiety and laughter.

Back of Card

Style: Written as if told aloud by a deranged man eager to be believed, the story is punctuated by laughter, interjections ("Hearken!"), nervous halts, and fresh beginnings—indicated by dashes that grow more frequent as the story goes on and the narrator becomes more excited. Poe often relies on general adjectives ("mournful," "hideous," "hellish,") to convey atmosphere; also on exact details (the lantern that emits "a single dim ray, like the thread of a spider").

Irony: The whole story is ironic in its point of view. Presumably the author is not mad, nor does he share the madman's self-admiration. Many of the narrator's statements therefore seem verbal ironies: his account of taking an hour to move his head through the bedroom door.

Theme: Possibly "Murder will out," but I really don't find any theme either stated or clearly implied.

Symbols: The vulture eye, called an Evil Eye (in superstition, one that can implant a curse), perhaps suggesting too the all-seeing eye of God the Father, from whom no guilt can be concealed. The ghostly heartbeat, sound of the victim's coming back to be avenged (or the God who cannot be slain?). Death watches: beetles said to be death omens, whose ticking sound foreshadows the sound of the tell-tale heart *as a watch makes when enveloped in cotton.*

Evaluation: Despite the overwrought style (to me slightly comic-bookish), a powerful story, admirable for its conclusion and for its memorable portrait of a deranged killer. Poe knows how it is to be mad.

Comparison and Contrast

If you were to write on "The Humor of Alice Walker's 'Everyday Use' and John Updike's 'A & P,'" you would probably employ one or two methods. You might use **comparison,** placing the two stories side by side and pointing out their similarities, or **contrast,** pointing out their differences. Most of the time, in dealing with a pair of stories, you will find them similar in some ways and different in others, and you'll use both methods. Keep the following points in mind when writing a comparison-contrast paper:

- **Choose stories with something significant in common.** This will simplify your task, and also help ensure that your paper hangs together. Before you start writing, ask yourself if the two stories you've selected throw some light on each other. If the answer is no, rethink your story selection.

▪ **Choose a focus.** Simply ticking off every similarity and difference between two stories would make for a slack and rambling essay. More compelling writing would result from better-focused topics such as "The Experience of Coming of Age in James Joyce's 'Araby' and William Faulkner's 'Barn Burning'" or "Mother-Daughter Relationships in Alice Walker's 'Everyday Use' and Tillie Olsen's 'I Stand Here Ironing.'"

▪ **Don't feel you need to spend equal amounts of time on comparing and contrasting.** If your chosen stories are more similar than different, you naturally will spend more space on comparison, and vice versa.

▪ **Don't devote the first half of your paper to one story and the second half to the other.** Such a paper wouldn't be a comparison or contrast so much as a pair of analyses yoked together. To reap the full benefits of the assignment, let the two stories mingle.

▪ **Before you start writing, draw up a brief list of points you would like to touch on.** Then address each point, first in one story and then in the other. A sample outline follows for a paper on William Faulkner's "A Rose for Emily" and Katherine Mansfield's "Miss Brill." The essay's topic is "Adapting to Change: The Characters of Emily Grierson and Miss Brill."

1. Adapting to change (both women)
   Miss Brill more successful
2. Portrait of women
   Miss Emily—unflattering
   Miss Brill—empathetic
3. Imagery
   Miss Emily—morbid
   Miss Brill—cheerful
4. Plot
   Miss Emily
   - loses sanity
   - refuses to adapt
   Miss Brill
   - finds place in society
   - adapts
5. Summary: Miss Brill is more successful

▪ **Emphasize the points that interest you the most.** This strategy will help keep you from following your outline in a plodding fashion ("Well, now it's time to whip over to Miss Brill again . . .").

▪ **If the assignment allows, consider applying comparison and contrast in an essay on a single story.** You might, for example, analyze the attitudes of the younger and older waiters in Hemingway's "A Clean, Well-Lighted Place." Or you might contrast Mrs. Turpin's smug view of herself with the young Mary Grace's merciless view of her in Flannery O'Connor's "Revelation."

The following student-written paper compares and contrasts the main characters in "A Rose for Emily" and "Miss Brill." Notice how the author focuses the discussion on a single aspect of each woman's personality—the ability to adapt to change and the passage of time. By looking through the lens of three different elements of the short story—diction, imagery, and plot—this clear and systematic essay convincingly argues its thesis.

Ortiz 1

Michelle Ortiz

Professor Gregg

English 200

25 May 2009

Successful Adaptation in

"A Rose for Emily" and "Miss Brill"

In William Faulkner's "A Rose for Emily" and Katherine Mansfield's "Miss Brill," the reader is given a glimpse into the lives of two old women living in different worlds but sharing many similar characteristics. Both Miss Emily and Miss Brill attempt to adapt to a changing environment as they grow older. Through the authors' use of language, imagery, and plot, it becomes clear to the reader that Miss Brill is more successful at adapting to the world around her and finding happiness.

> Clear statement of thesis

In "A Rose for Emily," Faulkner's use of language paints an unflattering picture of Miss Emily. His tone evokes pity and disgust rather than sympathy. The reader identifies with the narrator of the story and shares the townspeople's opinion that Miss Emily is somehow "perverse." In "Miss Brill," however, the reader can identify with the title character. Mansfield's attitude toward the young couple at the end makes the reader hate them for ruining the happiness that Miss Brill has found, however small it may be.

> Textual evidence on language supports thesis.

The imagery in "A Rose for Emily" keeps the reader from further identifying with Miss Emily by creating several morbid images of her. For example, there are several images of decay throughout the story. The house she lived in is falling apart and described as "filled with dust and shades . . . an eyesore among eyesores." Emily herself is described as being "bloated like a body long submerged in motionless water." Faulkner also uses words like "skeleton," "dank," "decay," and "cold" to reinforce these morbid, deathly images.

> Imagery in Faulkner's story supports argument.

Ortiz 2

Contrasting imagery in Mansfield's story supports argument.

In "Miss Brill," however, Mansfield uses more cheerful imagery. The music and the lively action in the park make Miss Brill feel alive inside. She notices the other old people that are in the park are "still as statues," "odd," and "silent." She says they "looked like they'd just come from dark little rooms or even—even cupboards." Her own room is later described as a "cupboard," but during the action of the story she does not include herself among those other old people. She still feels alive.

Characters contrasted with examples drawn from plots.

Through the plots of both stories the reader can also see that Miss Brill is more successful in adapting to her environment. Miss Emily loses her sanity and ends up committing a crime in order to control her environment. Throughout the story, she refuses to adapt to any of the changes going on in the town, such as the taxes or the mailboxes. Miss Brill is able to find her own special place in society where she can be happy and remain sane.

The final conclusion is stated and the thesis is restated.

In "A Rose for Emily" and "Miss Brill" the authors' use of language and the plots of the stories illustrate that Miss Brill is more successful in her story. Instead of hiding herself away she emerges from the "cupboard" to participate in life. She adapts to the world that is changing as she grows older, without losing her sanity or committing crimes, as Miss Emily does. The language of "Miss Brill" allows the reader to sympathize with the main character. The imagery in the story is lighter and less morbid than in "A Rose for Emily." The resulting portrait is of an aging woman who has found creative ways to adjust to her lonely life.

Response Paper

One popular form of writing assignment is the **response paper,** a short essay that expresses your personal reaction to a work of literature. Both instructors and students often find the response paper an ideal introductory writing assignment. It provides you with an opportunity to craft a focused essay about a literary work, but it does not usually require any outside research. What it does require is careful reading, clear thinking, and honest writing.

The purpose of a response paper is to convey your thoughts and feelings about an aspect of a particular literary work. It isn't a book report (summarizing the work's content) or a book review (evaluating the quality of a work). A response paper expresses what you experienced in reading and thinking about the assigned text. Your reaction should reflect your background, values, and attitudes in response to the work, not what the instructor thinks about it. You might even consider your response paper a conversation with the work you have just read. What questions does it seem to ask you? What reactions does it elicit? You might also regard your paper as a personal message to your instructor telling him or her what you really think about one of the reading assignments.

Of course, you can't say everything you thought and felt about your reading in a short paper. Focus on an important aspect (such as a main character, setting, or theme) and discuss your reaction to it. Don't gush or meander. Personal writing doesn't mean disorganized writing. Identify your main ideas and present your point of view in a clear and organized way. Once you get started you might surprise yourself by discovering that it's fun to explore your own responses. Stranger things have happened.

Here are some tips for writing a successful response paper of your own:

- **Make quick notes as you read or reread the work.** Don't worry about writing anything organized at this point. Just write a word or two in the margin noting your reactions as you read (e.g., "how unpleasant!" or "very interesting"). These little notes will jog your memory when you go back to write your paper.

- **Consider which aspect of the work affected you the most.** That aspect will probably be a good starting point for your response.

- **Be candid in your writing.** Remember that the literary work is only half of the subject matter of your paper. The other half is your reaction.

- **Try to understand and explain why you have reacted the way you did.** It's not enough just to state your responses. You also want to justify or explain them.

- **Refer to the text in your paper.** Demonstrate to the reader that your response is based on the text. Provide specific textual details and quotations wherever relevant.

The following paper is one student's response to Tim O'Brien's story "The Things They Carried" (page 595).

Martin 1

Ethan Martin

English 99

Professor Merrill

31 March 2009

Response to "The Things They Carried"

Reading Tim O'Brien's short story "The Things They Carried" became a very personal experience. It reminded me of my father, who is a Vietnam veteran, and the stories he used to tell me. Growing up, I regularly asked my dad to share stories from his past—especially about his service in the United States Marine Corps. He would rarely talk about his tour during the Vietnam War for more than a few minutes, and what he shared was usually the same: the monsoon rain could chill to the bone, the mosquitoes would never stop biting, and the M-16 rifles often jammed in a moment of crisis. He dug a new foxhole where he slept every night, he traded the cigarettes from his C-rations for food, and—since he was the radio man of his platoon—the combination of his backpack and radio was very heavy during the long, daily walks through rice paddies and jungles. For these reasons, "The Things They Carried" powerfully affected me.

While reading the story, I felt as if I was "humping" (597) through Vietnam with Lieutenant Jimmy Cross, Rat Kiley, Ted Lavender, and especially Mitchell Sanders—who carries the 26-pound radio and battery. Every day, we carry our backpacks to school. Inside are some objects that we need to use in class: books, paper, and pens. But most of us probably include "unnecessary" items that reveal something about who we are or what we value—photographs, perfume, or good-luck charms. O'Brien uses this device to tell his story. At times he lists the things that the soldiers literally carried, such as weapons, medicine, and flak jackets. These military items weigh between 30 and 70 pounds, depending on one's rank or function in the platoon. The narrator says, "They carried all they could bear, and then some, including a silent awe for the terrible power of the things they carried" (598).

Some of this "terrible power" comes from the sentimental objects the men keep. Although these are relatively light, they weigh down the hearts of the soldiers. Lt. Jimmy Cross carries 10-ounce letters and a pebble from Martha, a girl in his hometown who doesn't love him back. Rat Kiley carries comic books, and Norman Bowker carried a diary. I now own the small, water-logged Bible that my father carried through his tour in Vietnam, which was a gift from his mother. When I open its pages, I can almost hear his voice praying to survive the war.

The price of such survival is costly. O'Brien's platoon carries ghosts, memories, and "the land itself" (602). Their intangible burdens are heavier than what they carry in their backpacks. My father has always said that, while he was in Vietnam, an inexpressible feeling of death hung heavy in the air, which he could not escape. O'Brien notes that an emotional weight of fear and cowardice "could never be put down, it required perfect balance and perfect posture" (605), and I wonder if this may be part of what my father meant.

Both Tim O'Brien and my father were wounded by shrapnel, and now they both carry a Purple Heart. They carry the weight of survival. They carry memories that I will never know. "The Things They Carried" is not a war story about glory and honor. It is a portrait of the psychological damage that war can bring. It is a story about storytelling and how hard it can be to find the truth. And it is a beautiful account of what the human heart can endure.

Martin 3

Work Cited

O'Brien, Tim. "The Things They Carried." *An Introduction to Fiction.* Ed. X. J.
Kennedy and Dana Gioia. 11th ed. New York: Longman, 2010. 595–607.
Print.

THE FORM OF YOUR FINISHED PAPER

If your instructor has not specified the form of your finished paper, follow the guidelines in the current edition of the *MLA Handbook for Writers of Research Papers*, which you will find more fully described in the chapter "Writing a Research Paper." In brief:

- Choose standard letter-size (8 1/2 × 11) white paper.
- Use standard, easy-to-read type fonts, such as Times New Roman. Be sure the italic type style contrasts with the regular style.
- Give your name, your instructor's name, the course number, and the date at the top left-hand corner of your first page, starting one inch from the top.
- On all pages, give your last name and the page number in the upper right-hand corner, one-half inch from the top.
- Remember to give your paper a title that reflects your thesis.
- Leave an inch or two of margin on all four sides of each page and a few inches of blank paper or an additional sheet after your conclusion, so that your instructor can offer comments.
- If you include a works-cited section, begin it on a new page.
- Double-space your text, including quotations and notes. Don't forget to double-space the works-cited page also.
- Italicize the titles of longer works—books, full-length plays, periodicals, and book-length poems such as *The Odyssey*. The titles of shorter works—poems, articles, or short stories—should appear in quotation marks.

TOPICS FOR WRITING

What kinds of topics are likely to result in papers that will reveal something about works of fiction? Here is a list of typical topics, suitable for papers of various lengths, offered in the hope of stimulating your own ideas. For additional ideas, see "More Topics for Writing" at the end of most chapters in this book.

TOPICS FOR WRITING BRIEF PAPERS (250–500 WORDS)

1. Explicate the opening paragraph or first few lines of a story. Show how the opening prepares the reader for what will follow. In an essay of this length, you will need to limit your discussion to the most important elements of the

passage you explicate; there won't be room to deal with everything. Or, as thoroughly as the word count allows, explicate the final paragraph of a story. What does the ending imply about the fates of the story's characters, and about the story's take on its central theme?

2. Select a story that features a first-person narrator. Write a concise yet thorough analysis of how that character's point of view colors the story.

3. Following the directions on page 642, write a card report on any short story in this book.

4. Consider a short story in which the central character has to make a decision or must take some decisive step that will alter the rest of his or her life. Faulkner's "Barn Burning" is one such story; another is Updike's "A & P." As concisely and as thoroughly as you can, explain the nature of the character's decision, the reasons for it, and its probable consequences (as suggested by what the author tells us).

5. Choose two stories that might be interesting to compare and contrast. Write a brief defense of your choice. How might these two stories illuminate each other?

6. Choose a key passage from a story you admire. As closely as the word count allows, explicate that passage and explain why it strikes you as an important moment in the story. Concentrate on the aspects of the passage that seem most essential.

7. Write a new ending to a story of your choice. Try to imitate the author's writing style. Add a paragraph explaining how this exercise illuminates the author's choices in the original.

8. Drawing on your own experience, make the case that a character in any short story behaves (or doesn't behave) as people do in real life. Your audience for this assignment is your classmates; tailor your tone and argument accordingly.

TOPICS FOR WRITING MORE EXTENDED PAPERS (600–1,000 WORDS)

1. Write an analysis of a short story, focusing on a single element, such as point of view, theme, symbolism, character, or the author's voice (tone, style, irony). For a sample paper in response to this assignment, see "The Hearer of the Tell-Tale Heart" (page 640).

2. Compare and contrast two stories with protagonists who share an important personality trait. Make character the focus of your essay.

3. Write a thorough explication of a short passage (preferably not more than four sentences) in a story you admire. Pick a crucial moment in the plot, or a passage that reveals the story's theme. You might look to the paper "By Lantern Light" (page 637) as a model.

4. Write an analysis of a story in which the protagonist experiences an epiphany or revelation of some sort. Describe the nature of this change of heart. How is the reader prepared for it? What are its repercussions in the character's life? Some possible story choices are Alice Walker's "Everyday Use," William Faulkner's "Barn Burning," Raymond Carver's "Cathedral," James Baldwin's "Sonny's Blues," and, not surprisingly, Flannery O'Connor's "Revelation."

5. Imagine you are given the task of teaching a story to your class. Write an explanation of how you would address this challenge.

6. Imagine a reluctant reader, one who would rather play video games than crack a book. Which story in this book would you recommend to him or her? Write an essay to that imagined reader, describing the story's merits.

TOPICS FOR WRITING LONG PAPERS (1,500 WORDS OR MORE)

1. Write an analysis of a longer work of fiction. Concentrate on a single element of the story, quoting as necessary to make your point.
2. Read three or four short stories by an author whose work you admire. Concentrating on a single element treated similarly in all of the stories, write an analysis of the author's work as exemplified by your chosen stories.
3. Adapt a short story in this book into a one-act play. This may prove harder than it sounds; be sure to choose a story in which most of the action takes place in the physical world and not in the protagonist's mind. Don't forget to include stage directions.
4. Describe the process of reading a story for the first time and gradually learning to understand and appreciate it. First, choose a story you haven't yet read. As you read it for the first time, take notes on aspects of the story you find difficult or puzzling. Read the story a second time. Now write about the experience. What uncertainties were resolved when you read the story the second time? What, if any, uncertainties remain? What has this experience taught you about reading fiction?
5. Choose two stories that treat a similar theme. Compare and contrast the stance each story takes toward that theme, marshalling quotations and specifics as necessary to back up your argument.
6. Browse through newspapers and magazines for a story with the elements of good fiction. Now rewrite the story *as* fiction. Then write a one-page accompanying essay explaining the challenges of the task. What did it teach you about the relative natures of journalism and fiction?

14 WRITING A RESEARCH PAPER

A writer is a person for whom writing is more difficult than it is for other people.

—THOMAS MANN

Oh no! You have been assigned a research paper, and every time you even think about starting it, your spirits sink and your blood pressure rises. You really liked the story by Ernest Hemingway, but when you entered his name in the college library catalogue it listed 135 books about him. Time to switch authors, you decide. How about Emily Dickinson? She was fun to talk about in class, but when you Google her name, the computer states that there are over 8.4 million entries. What should you do? The paper is due in two weeks, not twenty years. Why would an otherwise very nice instructor put you through this mental trauma?

Why is it worthwhile to write a research paper? (Apart from the fact that you want a passing grade in the class, that is.) While you can learn much by exploring your own responses to a literary work, there is no substitute for entering into a conversation with others who have studied and thought about your topic. Literary criticism is that conversation. Your reading will expose you to the ideas of others who can shed light on a story, poem, or play. It will introduce you to the wide range of informed opinions that exist about literature, as about almost any subject. Sometimes, too, your research will uncover information about an author's life that leads you to new insights into a literary work. Undertaking a research paper gives you a chance to test your ideas against those of others, and in doing so to clarify your own opinions.

BROWSE THE RESEARCH

The most daunting aspect of the research paper may well be the mountains of information available on almost any literary subject. It can be hard to know where to begin. Sifting through books and articles is part of the research process. Unfortunately, the first material uncovered in the library or on the Internet is rarely the evidence you need to develop or support your thesis. Keep looking until you uncover helpful sources.

Another common pitfall in the process is the creeping feeling that your idea has already been examined a dozen times over. But take heart: like Odysseus, tie yourself to the mast so that when you hear the siren voices of published professors, you can listen without abandoning your own point of view. Your idea may have been treated, but not yet by you. Your particular take on a topic is bound to be different from someone else's. After all, thousands of books have been written on Shakespeare's plays, but even so there are still new things to say.

CHOOSE A TOPIC

- **Find a topic that interests you.** A crucial first step in writing a research paper is coming up with a topic that interests you. Start with a topic that bores you, and the process will be a chore, and will yield dull results. But if you come up with an intriguing research question, seeking the answer will be a more engaging process. The paper that results will inevitably be stronger and more interesting.

- **Find a way to get started.** Browsing through books of literary criticism in the library, or glancing at online journal articles, can help to spark an idea or two. Prewriting techniques such as brainstorming, freewriting, listing, and clustering can also help you to generate ideas on a specific work of literature. If you take notes and jot down ideas as they occur to you, when you start the formal writing process you will discover you have already begun. For a closer discussion of preparing to write, see page 630.

- **Keep your purpose and audience in mind.** Refer often to the assignment, and approach your essay accordingly. Think of your audience as well. Is it your professor, your classmates, or some other hypothetical reader? As you plan your essay, keep your audience's expectations and needs in mind.

- **Develop a general thesis that you hope to support with research, and look for material that will help you demonstrate its plausibility.** Remember: the ideal research paper is based on your own observations and interpretations of a literary text.

BEGIN YOUR RESEARCH

Print Resources

Writing a research paper on literature calls for two kinds of sources: primary sources, or the literary works that are your subject, and secondary sources, or the books, articles, and Web resources that discuss your primary sources. When you are hunting down secondary sources, the best place to begin is your campus library. Plan to spend some time thumbing through scholarly books and journals, looking for passages that you find particularly interesting or that pertain to your topic. Begin your search with the online catalog to get a sense of where you might find the books and journals you need.

To choose from the many books available on your library's shelves and through interlibrary loan, you might turn to book reviews for a sense of which volumes would best suit your purpose. *Book Review Digest* contains the full texts of many book reviews, and excerpts of others. The *Digest* may be found in printed form in the reference section of your campus library, which may also provide access to the online version. Whether you are using the online or print version, you will need the author's name, title, and date of first publication of any book for which you hope to find a review.

Scholarly journals are another excellent resource for articles on your topic. Indexes to magazines and journals may be found in your library's reference section. You may also find an index to print periodicals on your library's Web site.

Online Databases

Most college libraries subscribe to specialized online or CD-ROM database services covering all academic subjects—treasure troves of reliable sources. If you find yourself unsure how to use your library's database system, ask the reference librarian to help you get started. The following databases are particularly useful for literary research:

- The *MLA International Bibliography,* the Modern Language Association's database, is an excellent way to search for books and full-text articles on literary topics.

- *JSTOR,* a not-for-profit organization, indexes articles or abstracts from an archive of journals on language, literature, and African American studies.

- *Literature Resource Center* (Thomson Gale) provides biographies, bibliographies, and critical analyses of more than 120,000 authors and their work. This information is culled from journal articles and reference works.

- *Literature Online (LION)* provides a vast searchable database of critical articles and reference works as well as full texts of more than 300,000 works of prose, poetry, and drama.

- *Project MUSE,* a collaboration between publishers and libraries, offers access to more than 400 journals in the humanities, arts, and social sciences.

- EBSCO, a multisubject resource, covers literature and the humanities, as well as the social sciences, medical sciences, linguistics, and other fields.

Your library may provide access to some or all of these databases, or it may offer other useful ones. Many college library home pages provide students with access to subscription databases, which means that if you really can't bear to leave your comfy desk at home, you can still pay a virtual visit.

Reliable Web Sources

While online databases are a handy and reliable source for high-quality information, you may find yourself looking to supplement journal articles with information and quotations from the Internet. If so, proceed with care. While the journal articles in online databases have been reviewed for quality by specialists and librarians, Web sites may be written and published by anybody for any purpose, with no oversight. Even the online reference site *Wikipedia,* for example, is an amalgamation of voluntary contributors, and is rife with small factual errors and contributor biases. Carefully analyze the materials you gather online or you may find yourself tangled in the spidery threads of a dubious Web site. To garner the best sources possible, take these steps:

- **Learn to use Internet search engines effectively.** If you enter general terms such as the author's name and story title into an Internet search engine, you may well find yourself bombarded with thousands of hits. For a more efficient approach to navigating the Internet, try using an "advanced" search option, entering keywords to get results that contain those words (LITERARY CRITICISM A DOLL'S HOUSE or SYMBOLISM THE LOTTERY).

- **Begin your search at a reliable Web site.** Helpful as an advanced search may be, it won't separate valuable sources from useless ones. To weed out sloppy and inaccurate sites, begin your search with one of the following excellent guides through cyberspace:

- *Library of Congress.* Fortunately, you don't have to trek to Washington to visit this venerable institution's annotated collection of Web sites in the Humanities and Social Sciences Division. For your purpose—writing a literary research paper—access the Subject Index <http://www.loc.gov/rr/main/alcove9>, click on "Literatures in English" and then on "Literary Criticism." This will take you to a list of metapages and Web sites with collections of reliable critical and biographical materials on authors and their works. (A metapage provides links to other Web sites.)
- *Internet Public Library.* Created and maintained by the University of Michigan School of Information and Library Studies, this site <http://www.ipl.org> lets you search for literary criticism by author, work, country of origin, or literary period.
- *Library Spot.* Visit <http://www.libraryspot.com> for a portal to over 5,000 libraries around the world, and to periodicals, online texts, reference works, and links to metapages and Web sites on any topic including literary criticism. This carefully maintained site is published by Start Spot Mediaworks, Inc., in the Northwestern University/Evanston Research Park in Evanston, Illinois.
- *Voice of the Shuttle.* Research links in over 25 categories in the humanities and social sciences, including online texts, libraries, academic Web sites, and metapages may be found at this site. Located at <http://vos.ucsb.edu> it was developed and is maintained by Dr. Alan Liu in the English Department of the University of California.

CHECKLIST: Finding Reliable Sources

☐ Begin at your campus library. Ask the reference librarian for advice.
☐ Check the library catalog for books and journals on your topic.
☐ Look into the online databases subscribed to by your library.
☐ Locate reputable Web sites by starting at a reputable Web site designed for that purpose.

Visual Images

The Web is an excellent source of visual images. If a picture, chart, or graph will enhance your argument, you may find the perfect one via an image search on *Google, Ditto,* or other search engines. The Library of Congress offers a wealth of images documenting American political, social, and cultural history—including portraits, letters, and original manuscripts—at <http://memory.loc.gov>. Remember, though, that not all images are available for use by the general public. Check for a copyright notice to see if its originator allows that image to be reproduced. If so, you may include the photograph, provided you credit your source as you would if you were quoting text.

One note on images: use them carefully. Choose visuals that provide supporting evidence for the point you are trying to make or enhance your reader's understanding of the work. Label your images with captions. Your goal should be to make your argument more convincing. In the example below, a reproduction of Brueghel's painting helps to advance the author's argument and provide insight into Auden's poem.

Fig. 1. *Landscape with the Fall of Icarus* by Pieter Brueghel the Elder (c. 1558, Musées royaux des Beaux-Arts de Belgique, Brussels).

W. H. Auden's poem "Musée des Beaux Arts" refers to a specific painting to prove its point that the most honest depictions of death take into account the way life simply goes on even after the most tragic of events. In line 14, Auden turns specifically to Pieter Brueghel the Elder's masterwork *The Fall of Icarus* (see Fig. 1), pointing to the painting's understated depiction of tragedy. In this painting, the death of Icarus does not take place on center stage. A plowman and his horse take up the painting's foreground, while the leg of Icarus falling into the sea takes up a tiny portion of the painting's lower-right corner. A viewer who fails to take the painting's title into account might not even notice Icarus at all.

CHECKLIST: Using Visual Images

- ☐ Use images as evidence to support your argument.
- ☐ Use images to enhance communication and understanding.
- ☐ Refer to the images in your text.
- ☐ Label image as "Fig. 1" and provide title or caption.
- ☐ Check copyrights.
- ☐ Include source in works-cited list.

EVALUATE YOUR SOURCES

Print Resources

It's an old saying, but a useful one: don't believe everything you read. The fact that a book or article is printed and published doesn't necessarily mean it is accurate or unbiased. Be discriminating about printed resources.

Begin your search in a place that has taken some of the work out of quality control—your school library. Books and articles you find there are regarded by librarians as having some obvious merit. If your search takes you beyond the library, though, you will need to be discerning when choosing print resources. As you weigh the value of printed matter, take the following into account:

- **Look closely at information provided about the author.** Is he or she known for expertise in the field? What are the author's academic or association credentials? Is there any reason to believe that the author is biased in any way? For example, a biography of an author written by that author's child might not be as unbiased as one written by a scholar with no personal connections.

- **Determine the publisher's reliability.** Books or articles published by an advocacy group might be expected to take a particular—possibly biased—slant on an issue. Be aware also that some books are published by vanity presses, companies that are paid by an author to publish his or her books. As a result, vanity press-published books generally aren't subject to the same rigorous quality control as those put out by more reputable publishing houses.

- **Always check for a publication date.** If a document lists an edition number, check to see whether you are using the latest edition of the material.

- **For periodicals, decide whether a publication is an academic journal or a popular magazine.** What type of reputation does it have? Obviously, you do not want to use a magazine that periodically reports on Elvis sightings and alien births. And even articles on writers in magazines such as *Time* and *People* are likely to be too brief and superficial for purposes of serious research. Instead, choose scholarly journals designed to enhance the study of literature.

Web Resources

As handy and informative as the Internet is, it sometimes serves up some pretty iffy information. A Web site, after all, can be created by anyone with a computer and access to the Internet—no matter how poorly qualified that person might be. Be discerning when it comes to the Internet. Here are some tips on choosing your sources wisely:

- **Check a site's authorship or sponsorship.** Is the site's creator or sponsor known to you or reputable by association? Look closely at information provided about the author. Is he or she known for expertise in the field? What are the author's academic or association credentials? Is the Web entry unsigned and anonymous? If the Web site is sponsored by an organization, is it a reputable one? While government or university-sponsored sites may be considered reliable, think carefully about possible biases in sites sponsored by advocacy or special interest groups.

  A word of warning: individual student pages posted on university sites have not necessarily been reviewed by that university and are not reliable sources of information. Also, postings on the popular encyclopedia Web site

Wikipedia are not subject to a scholarly review process and have been noted to contain a number of inaccuracies. It's safer to use a published encyclopedia.

- **Look at the site's date of publication.** When was it last updated? In some cases you may want to base your essay on the most current information or theories, so you will want to steer toward the most recently published material.
- **Is this an online version of a print publication?** If so, what type of reputation does it have?
- **Make your own assessment of the site.** Does the content seem consistent with demonstrated scholarship? Does it appear balanced in its point of view?
- **Consult experts.** Cornell University has two good documents with guidance for analyzing sources, posted at <http://www.library.cornell.edu/services/guides.html>. The titles are "Critically Analyzing Information Sources" and "Distinguishing Scholarly from Non-Scholarly Periodicals." The UCLA College Library also provides useful information: "Thinking Critically About World Wide Web Resources" (<http://www2.library.ucla.edu/libraries>).

CHECKLIST: Evaluating Your Sources

Print

- ☐ Who wrote it? What are the author's credentials?
- ☐ Is he or she an expert in the field?
- ☐ Does he or she appear to be unbiased toward the subject matter?
- ☐ Is the publisher reputable? Is it an advocacy group or a vanity press?
- ☐ When was it published? Do later editions exist? If so, would a later edition be more useful?

Web

- ☐ Who wrote it? What are the author's credentials?
- ☐ Is he or she an expert in the field?
- ☐ Who sponsors the Web site? Is the sponsor reputable?
- ☐ When was the Web site published? When was it last updated?
- ☐ Is the Web site an online journal or magazine? Is it scholarly or popular?
- ☐ Does content seem consistent with demonstrated scholarship?
- ☐ Can you detect obvious bias?

ORGANIZE YOUR RESEARCH

- **Get your thoughts down on notecards or the equivalent on your laptop.** Once you have amassed your secondary sources, it will be time to begin reading in earnest. As you do so, be sure to take notes on any passages that pertain to your topic. A convenient way to organize your many thoughts is to write them down on index cards, which are easy to shuffle and rearrange. You'll need 3- × 5-inch cards for brief notes and titles and 5- × 8-inch cards for more in-depth notes. Confine your jottings to one side of the card; notes on the back can easily be overlooked. Write a single fact or opinion on each card. This will make it easier for you to shuffle the deck and reenvision the order in which you deliver information to your reader.

■ **Keep careful track of the sources of quotations and paraphrases.** As you take notes, make it crystal clear which thoughts and phrases are yours and which derive from others. (Remember, *quotation* means using the exact words of your source and placing the entire passage in quotation marks and citing the author. *Paraphrase* means expressing the ideas of your source in your own words, again citing the author.) Bear in mind the cautionary tale of well-known historian Doris Kearns Goodwin. She was charged with plagiarizing sections of two of her famous books when her words were found to be jarringly similar to those published in other books. Because she had not clearly indicated on her notecards which ideas and passages were hers and which came from other sources, Goodwin was forced to admit to plagiarism. Her enormous reputation suffered from these charges, but you can learn from her mistakes and save your own reputation—and your grades.

■ **Keep track of the sources of ideas and concepts.** When an idea is inspired by or directly taken from someone else's writing, be sure to jot down the source on that same card or your computer file. Your deck of cards or computer list will function as a working bibliography, which later will help you put together a works-cited list. To save yourself work, keep a separate list of the sources you're using. Then, as you make the note, you need write only the material's author or title and page reference on the card in order to identify your source. It's also useful to classify the note in a way that will help you to organize your material, making it easy, for example, to separate cards that deal with a story's theme from cards that deal with point of view or symbolism.

■ **Make notes of your own thoughts and reactions to your research.** When a critical article sparks your own original idea, be sure to capture that thought in your notes and mark it as your own. As you plan your paper, these notes may form the outline for your arguments.

Some useful note cards taken on the critical essay on page 691 about Joyce Carol Oates's short story "Where Are You Going, Where Have You Been?" might look something like this:

Direct quotation from critic

THEME

Schulz and Rockwood, p. 692

"There is a terrible irony here, for although the story is full of fairy tales, Connie, its protagonist, is not. Connie represents an entire generation of young people who have grown up—or tried to—without the help of those bedtime stories which not only entertain the child, but also enable him vicariously to experience and work through problems which he will encounter in adolescence."

Paraphrase of critic

THEME
Schulz and Rockwood, p. 692
Ironic that while story steeped in fairy tales, Connie is not. Connie stands for her whole generation that grew up without fairy tales.
Missed benefits of fairy tales for child: working through life's problems.

Critic's idea

THEME
Schulz and Rockwood, p. 692

Many fairy tales underlie "Where Are You Going ?" e.g.
    Snow White
    Cinderella
    Sleeping Beauty
    Little Red Riding Hood

Your own idea

THEME or CHARACTER?
My Idea
Is Arnold the big bad wolf?   Can I find clues in story?

■ **Make photocopies or printouts to simplify the process and ensure accuracy.**
Scholars once had to spend long hours copying out prose passages by hand. Luckily, for a small investment you can simply photocopy your sources to ensure accuracy in quoting and citing your sources. In fact, some instructors will require you to hand in photocopies of your original sources with the final paper, along with

printouts of articles downloaded from an Internet database. Even if this is not the case, photocopying your sources and holding onto your printouts can help you to reproduce quotations accurately in your essay—and accuracy is crucial.

REFINE YOUR THESIS

As you read secondary sources and take notes, you should begin to refine your essay's thesis. This, in turn, will help you to winnow your stacks of source material down to the secondary sources that will best help you to make your point. Even your revised thesis doesn't have to be etched in stone. It should simply give you a sense of direction as you start to plan your essay.

- **Be willing to fine-tune your thesis or even rework it completely.** Your research may reveal that you have misinterpreted an idea, or that others have already argued your thesis. Of course, it is annoying to find that you may be wrong about something, or that someone else has taken off with what you thought was your original argument, but don't let these discoveries put you off. If you run across arguments similar to your own, use them to refine your thoughts. (These sources also may well be useful to bolster your own thesis.)
- **Let your initial idea be the jumping-off point to other, better ideas.** Say, for example, that you plan to write about the peculiar physical description of Arnold Friend in Joyce Carol Oates's story "Where Are You Going, Where Have You Been?" You may have noticed he has trouble standing in his shoes, and you want to explore that odd detail. If you research this character, you may find Arnold Friend likened to the devil (whose cloven hooves might give him similar problems with standard-issue cowboy boots), or to the wolf in "Little Red Riding Hood" (also a character who would have a hard time managing human clothes). At that point, you may think, "Okay, my idea is shot. Everyone has written about this aspect of the Oates character." Well, just use your new knowledge to sharpen your focus. Can you think of other stories that deal with potentially supernatural, possibly even evil, characters? What about Nathaniel Hawthorne's "Young Goodman Brown"? Or Flannery O'Connor's "A Good Man Is Hard to Find"? How might you compare Arnold Friend with Hawthorne's devil or O'Connor's Misfit?

ORGANIZE YOUR PAPER

With your thesis in mind and your notes spread before you, draw up an outline—a rough map of how best to argue your thesis and present your material. Determine what main points you need to make, and look for quotations that support those points. Even if you generally prefer to navigate the paper-writing process without a map, you will find that an outline makes the research-paper writing process considerably smoother. When organizing information from many different sources, it pays to plan ahead.

WRITE AND REVISE

As with any other kind of essay, a research paper rarely, if ever, reaches its full potential in a single draft. Leave yourself time to rewrite. The knowledge that your first draft isn't your final one can free you up to take chances and to jot down your ideas as quickly as they occur to you. If your phrasing is less than elegant, it hardly matters in a first draft; the main point is to work out your ideas on paper. Rough out the paper, working as quickly as you can. Later you can rearrange paragraphs and smooth out any rough patches.

Once you've got the first draft down, it's an excellent idea to run it by a friend, a writing center tutor, or even your instructor. A writer can't know how clear or persuasive his or her argument is without a trusted reader to give feedback.

When you finally do revise, be open to making both large and small changes. Sometimes revising means adding needed paragraphs, or even refining the thesis a bit further. Be willing to start from scratch if you need to, but even as you take the whole picture into account, remember that details are important too. Before you hand in that final draft, be sure to proofread for small errors that could detract from the finished product.

MAINTAIN ACADEMIC INTEGRITY

Papers for Sale Are Papers that "F"ail

Do not be seduced by the apparent ease of cheating by computer. Your Internet searches may turn up several sites that offer term papers to download (just as you can find pornography, political propaganda, and questionable get-rich-quick schemes!). Most of these sites charge money for what they offer, but a few do not, happy to strike a blow against the "oppressive" insistence of English teachers that students learn to think and write.

Plagiarized term papers are an old game: the fraternity file and the "research assistance" service have been around far longer than the computer. It may seem easy enough to download a paper, put your name at the head of it, and turn it in for an easy grade. As any writing instructor can tell you, though, such papers usually stick out like a sore thumb. The style will be wrong, the work will not be consistent with other work by the same student in any number of ways, and the teacher will sometimes even have seen the same phony paper before. The ease with which electronic texts are reproduced makes this last possibility increasingly likely.

The odds of being caught and facing the unpleasant consequences are reasonably high. It is far better to take the grade you have earned for your own effort, no matter how mediocre, than to try to pass off someone else's work as your own. Even if, somehow, your instructor does not recognize your submission as a plagiarized paper, you have diminished your character through dishonesty and lost an opportunity to learn something on your own.

A Warning Against Internet Plagiarism

Plagiarism detection services are a professor's newest ally in the battle against academic dishonesty. Questionable research papers can be sent to these services (such as Turnitin.com and EVE2), which perform complex searches of the Internet and of a growing database of purchased term papers. The research paper will be returned to the professor with plagiarized sections annotated and the sources documented. The end result may be a failing grade on the essay, possibly a failing grade for the course, and, depending on the policies of your university, the very real possibility of expulsion.

ACKNOWLEDGE ALL SOURCES

The brand of straight-out dishonesty described above is one type of plagiarism. There is, however, another, subtler kind: when students incorporate somebody else's words *or* ideas into their papers without giving proper credit. To avoid this second—sometimes quite accidental—variety of plagiarism, familiarize yourself with the conventions for acknowledging sources. First and foremost, remember to give credit to any writer who supplies you with ideas, information, or specific words and phrases.

Quotations

■ **Acknowledge your source when you quote a writer's words or phrases.** When you use someone else's words or phrases, you should reproduce his or her exact words in quotation marks, and be sure to properly credit the source.

> Already, Frost has hinted that Nature may be, as Radcliffe Squires
>
> suggests, "Nothing but an ash-white plain without love or faith or hope,
>
> where ignorant appetites cross by chance" (87).

■ **If you quote more than four lines, set your quotation off from the body of the paper.** Start a new line; indent one inch (or ten spaces), and type the quotation, double-spaced. (You do not need to use quotation marks, as the format already tells the reader the passage is a quotation.)

> Samuel Maio made an astute observation about the nature of Weldon Kees's
>
> distinctive tone:
>
> > Kees has therefore combined a personal subject matter with an
> >
> > impersonal voice—that is, one that is consistent in its tone
> >
> > evenly recording the speaker's thoughts without showing any
> >
> > emotional intensity which might lie behind those thoughts. (136)

Citing Ideas

■ **Acknowledge your source when you mention a critic's ideas.** Even if you are not quoting exact words or phrases, be sure to acknowledge the source of any original ideas or concepts you have used.

> Another explanation is suggested by Daniel Hoffman, a critic who has
>
> discussed the story: the killer hears the sound of his *own* heart (227).

■ **Acknowledge your source when you paraphrase a writer's words.** To paraphrase a critic, you should do more than just rearrange his or her words: you should translate them into your own original sentences—again, always being sure to credit the original source. As an example, suppose you wish to refer to an insight of Randall Jarrell, who commented as follows on the images of spider, flower, and moth in Robert Frost's poem "Design":

> RANDALL JARRELL'S ORIGINAL TEXT
>
> Notice how the *heal-all*, because of its name, is the one flower in all the world picked to be the altar for this Devil's Mass; notice how *holding up* the moth brings something ritual and hieratic, a ghostly, ghastly formality, to this priest and its sacrificial victim.[1]

---

[1]*Poetry and the Age* (New York: Knopf, 1953) 42.

It would be too close to the original to write, without quotation marks, these sentences:

PLAGIARISTIC REWORDING

Frost picks the *heal-all* as the one flower in all the world to be the altar for this Devil's Mass. There is a ghostly, ghastly formality to the spider *holding up* the moth, like a priest holding a sacrificial victim.

This rewording, although not exactly in Jarrell's language, manages to steal his memorable phrases without giving him credit. Nor is it sufficient just to include Jarrell's essay in the works-cited list at the end of your paper. If you do, you are still a crook; you merely point to the scene of the crime. Instead, think through Jarrell's words to the point he is making, so that it can be restated in your own original way. If you want to keep any of his striking phrases (and why not?), put them exactly as he wrote them in quotations marks:

APPROPRIATE PARAPHRASE, ACKNOWLEDGES SOURCE

As Randall Jarrell points out, Frost portrays the spider as a kind of priest in a Mass, or Black Mass, elevating the moth like an object for sacrifice, with "a ghostly, ghastly formality" (42).

Note also that this improved passage gives Jarrell the credit not just for his words but for his insight into the poem. Both the idea and the words in which it was originally expressed are the properties of their originator. Finally, notice the page reference that follows the quotation (this system of documenting your sources is detailed in the next section).

DOCUMENT SOURCES USING MLA STYLE

You must document everything you take from another source. When you quote from other writers, when you borrow their information, when you summarize or paraphrase their ideas, make sure you give them proper credit. Identify the writer by name and cite the book, magazine, newspaper, pamphlet, Web site, or other source you have used.

The conventions that govern the proper way to document sources are available in the *MLA Handbook for Writers of Research Papers*, 7th ed. (New York: MLA, 2009). The following brief list of pointers is not meant to take the place of the *MLA Handbook* itself, but to give you a quick sense of the rules for documentation.

List of Sources

Keep a working list of your research sources—all the references from which you might quote, summarize, paraphrase, or take information. When your paper is in finished form, it will end with a neat copy of the works you actually used (once called a "Bibliography," now entitled "Works Cited").

Parenthetical References

In the body of your paper, every time you refer to a source, you need only to provide information to help a reader locate it in your works-cited list. You can usually give just the author's name and a page citation in parentheses. For example, if you are writing a paper on Weldon Kees's sonnet "For My Daughter" and want to include an observation you found on page 136 of Samuel Maio's book *Creating Another Self*, write:

> One critic has observed that the distinctive tone of "For My Daughter"
> depends on Kees's combination of personal subject matter with an
> impersonal voice (Maio 136).

If you mention the author's name in your sentence, you need give only the page number in your reference:

> As Samuel Maio has observed, Kees creates a distinctive tone in this sonnet
> by combining a personal subject with an impersonal voice (136).

If you have two books or magazine articles by Samuel Maio in your works-cited list, how will the reader tell them apart? In your text, refer to the title of each book or article by condensing it into a word or two. Condensed book titles are italicized, and condensed article titles are still placed within quotation marks.

> One critic has observed that the distinctive tone of "For My Daughter"
> depends on Kees's combination of personal subject matter with an
> impersonal voice (Maio, *Creating* 136).

Works-Cited List

Provide a full citation for each source on your works-cited page.   At the end of your paper, in your list of works cited, your reader will find a full description of your source—in the above examples, a critical book:

> Maio, Samuel. *Creating Another Self: Voices in Modern American Personal*
> *Poetry*. 2nd ed. Kirksville, MO: Thomas Jefferson UP, 2005. Print.

Put your works-cited list in proper form.   The *MLA Handbook* provides detailed instructions for citing a myriad of different types of sources, from books to online databases. Here is a partial checklist of the *Handbook*'s recommendations for presenting your works-cited list.

1. Start a new page for the works-cited list, and continue the page numbering from the body of your paper.
2. Center the title, "Works Cited," one inch from the top of the page.
3. Double-space between all lines (including after title and between entries).
4. Type each entry beginning at the left-hand margin. If an entry runs longer than a single line, indent the following lines one-half inch (or five full spaces) from the left-hand margin.
5. Alphabetize each entry according to the author's last name.
6. Include three sections in each entry: author, title, publication or access information. (You will, however, give slightly different information for a book, journal article, online source, or other reference.)

Citing Print Sources in MLA Style

For a book citation

    a. **Author's full name** as it appears on the title page, last name first, followed by a period.

    b. **Book's full title** (and subtitle, if it has one, separated by a colon) followed by a period. Remember to italicize the title. Also provide edition and volume information, if applicable, followed by a period.

    c. **Publication information:** City of publication followed by a colon; name of publisher followed by a comma; year of publication followed by a period; and publication medium—*Print*—followed by a period.

        (1) **Make your citation of the city of publication brief, but clear.** If the title page lists more than one city, cite only the first. For U.S. cities, you need not provide the state unless the name of the city alone may be confusing or is unfamiliar. For cities outside the United States, add a country abbreviation if the city is unfamiliar. For Canadian cities, use the province abbreviation. (Examples: Rome, GA; Leeds, Eng.; Victoria, BC)

        (2) **Shorten the publisher's name.** Eliminate articles (*A, An, The*), business abbreviations (*Co., Corp., Inc., Ltd.*), and descriptive words (*Books, House, Press, Publishers*). The exception is a university press, for which you should use the letters *U* (for University) and *P* (for Press). Use only the first listed *surname* of the publisher.

Publisher's Name	Proper Citation
Harvard University Press	Harvard UP
University of Chicago Press	U of Chicago P
Farrar, Straus and Giroux, Inc.	Farrar
Alfred A. Knopf, Inc.	Knopf

    d. **Optional additional information:** Any additional information that may be helpful for your reader can be provided at the end of a citation. For example, if the book is part of an established series or part of a multivolume set, put the name of the series or the complete work here.

The final citation for a book should read:

    Author's Last name, First name. *Book Title.* Ed. or vol. Publication city:

        Publisher, Year. Print.

For a journal or periodical article citation

    a. **Author's name,** last name first, followed by a period.

    b. **Title of article** followed by a period, all within quotation marks.

    c. **Journal publication information:** journal title (italicized); volume number followed by period, issue number; year of publication in parentheses followed by a colon; inclusive page numbers of the entire article followed by a period; and publication medium—*Print*—followed by a period.

or

> **Periodical publication information:** periodical title (italicized); day month year followed by a colon; page numbers of article (for continuous articles use inclusive pages, such as 31–33; for newspapers use starting page, such as C1+) followed by a period; and publication medium—*Print*—followed by a period.

The final citation for a journal article should read:

> Author's Last name, First name. "Article Title." *Journal* Volume.Issue
>
> (Year): Pages. Print.

The final citation for a periodical article should read:

> Author's Last name, First name. "Article Title." *Periodical* Day Month Year:
>
> Pages. Print.

Citing Web Sources in MLA Style

Like print sources, Internet sources should be documented with care. Before you begin your Internet search, be aware of the types of information you will want for your works-cited list. You can then record the information as you go. Keep track of the following information:

- Author's name
- Title of document
- Full information about publication in print form, when available
- Title of scholarly project, database, periodical, or professional or personal site
- Editor's name of project or database
- Date of electronic publication or last update
- Institution or organization sponsoring the Web site
- Date *you* accessed the source
- Web site address or URL

Although many Web sites provide much of this information at the beginning or ending of an article or at the bottom of the home page, you will find that it is not always available. Also note that as Web pages and even sites may sometimes disappear or change, you are well-advised to print out important pages for future reference.

For a Web resource citation

> a. **Author or editor's name,** last name first, followed by a period.
> b. **Title of work,** within quotation marks or italicized as appropriate, followed by a period.
> c. **Title of Web site,** in italics, followed by a period.
> d. **Sponsor or publisher of Web site** followed by a comma. If not available, use *N.p.*
> e. **Publication date** followed by a period. If data is not available, use *n.d.*
> f. **Publication medium—*Web*—**followed by a period.

    g. **Date *you* accessed information:** day month year that you viewed document online.

    h. **Optional URL:** if there is some reason your reader may not be able to access your Web page with the information provided, you may include the full URL, enclosed in angle brackets <>.

The final citation for a Web source should read:

> Author's Last name, First name. "Document Title." *Web site.* Web site
> Sponsor, Publication date. Web. Access Day Month Year.

For a print journal accessed on the Web

    a. **Provide information for standard print citation**

        (1) **Author's name,** last name first, followed by a period.

        (2) **Title of work,** within quotation marks or italicized as appropriate, followed by a period.

        (3) **Print publication information:** journal title in italics; volume and issue number; year; page references, as available. If no pages are available, use *n. pag.*

    b. **Provide Web access information**

        (1) **Title of Web site or database,** italicized.

        (2) **Publication medium—*Web*—**followed by period.

        (3) **Date *you* accessed information:** day month year that you viewed document online.

The final citation for a scholarly journal article obtained on the Web should read:

> Author's Last name, First name. "Article Title." *Journal* Volume.Issue (Year):
> Pages. *Web site or Online Database.* Web. Access Day Month Year.

Sample List of Works Cited

For a paper on Weldon Kees's "For My Daughter," a student's works-cited list might look as follows:

Works Cited

Grosholz, Emily. "The Poetry of Memory." *Weldon Kees: A Critical
    Introduction.* Ed. Jim Elledge. Metuchen, NJ: Scarecrow, 1985. 46–47.
    Print.

Kees, Weldon. *The Collected Poems of Weldon Kees.* Ed. Donald Justice.
    Lincoln: U of Nebraska P, 1975. Print.

Lane, Anthony. "The Disappearing Poet: What Ever Happened to Weldon
    Kees?" *New Yorker.* CondéNet, 4 July 2005. Web. 22 Aug. 2009.

Maio, Samuel. *Creating Another Self: Voice in Modern American Personal
    Poetry.* 2nd ed. Kirksville, MO: Thomas Jefferson UP, 2005. Print.

Nelson, Raymond. "The Fitful Life of Weldon Kees." *American Literary History* 1 (1989): 816–52. Print.

Reidel, James. *Vanished Act: The Life and Art of Weldon Kees.* Lincoln: U of Nebraska P, 2003. Print.

---, ed. *Weldon Kees.* Nebraska Center for Writers, Creighton U, n.d. Web. 26 Aug. 2009.

Ross, William T. *Weldon Kees.* Boston: Twayne, 1985. Print. Twayne's US Authors Ser. 484.

"Weldon Kees." *Poetry Out Loud.* National Endowment for the Arts and the Poetry Foundation, n.d. Web. 20 Sept. 2009.

See the Reference Guide for Citations at the end of this chapter for additional examples of the types of citations that you are likely to need for your essays, or check the seventh edition of the *MLA Handbook.*

As you put together your works-cited list, keep in mind that the little things—page numbers, quotation marks—count. Documentation may seem tedious, but it has an important purpose: it's for the reader of your paper who wants to pursue a topic you have researched. Luckily, you don't have to know the rules by heart. You can refer as necessary to the *MLA Handbook* or to the examples in this book.

SAMPLE STUDENT RESEARCH PAPER—PAGE 334

Professor Michael Cass of Mercer University asked his class to select the fiction writer on their reading list whose work had seemed most impressive and write a research paper defending that author's claim to literary greatness. See page 334 to read the research essay Stephanie Crowe wrote to fulfill the assignment.

CONCLUDING THOUGHTS

A well-crafted research essay is a wondrous thing—as delightful, in its own way, as a well-crafted poem or short story or play. Good essays prompt thought and add to knowledge. Writing a research paper sharpens your own mind and exposes you to the honed insights of other thinkers. Think of anything you write as a piece that could be published for the benefit of other people interested in your topic. After all, such a goal is not as far-fetched as it seems: this textbook, for example, features a number of papers written by students. Why shouldn't yours number among them? Aim high.

REFERENCE GUIDE FOR CITATIONS

Here is a comprehensive summary of the types of citations you are likely to need for most student papers. The format follows the current MLA standards for works-cited lists.

Print Publications
Books

No Author Listed

The Chicago Manual of Style, 15th ed. Chicago: U of Chicago P, 2003. Print.

One Author

Middlebrook, Diane Wood. *Anne Sexton: A Biography*. Boston: Houghton, 1991. Print.

Two or Three Authors

Jarman, Mark, and Robert McDowell. *The Reaper: Essays*. Brownsville, OR: Story Line, 1996. Print.

Four or More Authors

Phillips, Rodney, et al. *The Hand of the Poet*. New York: Rizzoli, 1997. Print.

or

Phillips, Rodney, Susan Benesch, Kenneth Benson, and Barbara Bergeron. *The Hand of the Poet*. New York: Rizzoli, 1997. Print.

Two Books by Same Author

Bawer, Bruce. *The Aspect of Eternity*. St. Paul: Graywolf, 1993. Print.

---. *Diminishing Fictions: Essays on the Modern American Novel and Its Critics*. St. Paul: Graywolf, 1988. Print.

Corporate Author

Poets and Writers. *A Writer's Guide to Copyright*. New York: Poets and Writers, 1979. Print.

Author and Editor

Shakespeare, William. *The Sonnets*. Ed. G. Blakemore Evans. Cambridge, Eng.:
Cambridge UP, 1996. Print.

One Editor

Monteiro, George, ed. Conversations with Elizabeth Bishop. Jackson: UP of
Mississippi, 1996. Print.

Two Editors

Craig, David, and Janet McCann, eds. *Odd Angles of Heaven: Contemporary Poetry by
People of Faith*. Wheaton, IL: Shaw, 1994. Print.

Translation

Dante Alighieri. *Inferno: A New Verse Translation*. Trans. Michael Palma. New York:
Norton, 2002. Print.

Introduction, Preface, Foreword, or Afterword

Thwaite, Anthony, Preface. *Contemporary Poets*. Ed. Thomas Riggs. 6th ed. New
York: St. James, 1996. vii–viii. Print.

Lapham, Lewis. Introduction. *Understanding Media: The Extensions of Man*. By
Marshall McLuhan. Cambridge: MIT P, 1994. vi–x. Print.

Work in an Anthology

Rodriguez, Richard. "Aria: A Memoir of a Bilingual Childhood." *The Best American
Essays of the Century*. Ed. Robert Atwan and Joyce Carol Oates. Boston:
Houghton, 2001. 447–66. Print. Best American Ser.

Translation in an Anthology

Neruda, Pablo. "We Are Many." Trans. Alastair Reid. *Literature: An Introduction to
Fiction, Poetry, Drama, and Writing*. Ed. X. J. Kennedy and Dana Gioia. 11th
ed. New York: Longman, 2010. 922. Print.

Multivolume Work

Wellek, René. *A History of Modern Criticism, 1750–1950*. 8 vols. New Haven: Yale UP,
    1955–92. Print.

One Volume of a Multivolume Work

Wellek, René. *A History of Modern Criticism, 1750–1950*. Vol. 7. New Haven: Yale UP,
    1991. Print.

Book in a Series

Ross, William T. *Weldon Kees*. Boston: Twayne, 1985. Print. Twayne's US Authors
    Ser. 484.

Republished Book

Ellison, Ralph. *Invisible Man*. 1952. New York: Vintage, 1995. Print.

Revised or Subsequent Editions

Janouch, Gustav. *Conversations with Kafka*. Trans. Goronwy Rees. Rev. ed. New
    York: New Directions, 1971. Print.

Reference Books

Signed Article in Reference Book

Cavoto, Janice E. "Harper Lee's *To Kill a Mockingbird*." *The Oxford Encyclopedia of
    American Literature*. Ed. Jay Parini. Vol. 2. New York: Oxford UP, 2004.
    418–21. Print.

Unsigned Encyclopedia Article—Standard Reference Book

"James Dickey." *The New Encyclopaedia Britannica: Micropaedia*. 15th ed. 1987.
    Print.

Dictionary Entry

"Design." *Merriam-Webster's Collegiate Dictionary*. 11th ed. 2003. Print.

Periodicals

Journal

Salter, Mary Jo. "The Heart Is Slow to Learn." *New Criterion* 10.8 (1992): 23–29. Print.

Signed Magazine Article

Gioia, Dana. "Studying with Miss Bishop." *New Yorker* 5 Sept. 1986: 90–101. Print.

Unsigned Magazine Article

"The Real Test." *New Republic* 5 Feb. 2001: 7. Print.

Newspaper Article

Lyall, Sarah. "In Poetry, Ted Hughes Breaks His Silence on Sylvia Plath." *New York Times* 19 Jan. 1998, natl. ed.: A1+. Print.

Signed Book Review

Fugard, Lisa. "Divided We Love." Rev. of *Unaccustomed Earth,* by Jhumpa Lahiri. *Los Angeles Times* 30 Mar. 2008: R1. Print.

Unsigned, Untitled Book Review

Rev. of *Otherwise: New and Selected Poems*, by Jane Kenyon. *Virginia Quarterly Review* 72 (1996): 136. Print.

Web Publications

Web Site

Liu, Alan, ed. Home Page. *Voice of the Shuttle.* Dept. of English, U of California, Santa Barbara, n.d. Web. 17 Oct. 2008.

Document on a Web Site

"A Hughes Timeline." *PBS Online.* Public Broadcasting Service, 2001. Web. 20 Sept. 2008.

"Wallace Stevens." *Poets.org.* Academy of American Poets, n.d. Web. 20 Sept. 2009.

Online Reference Database

"Brooks, Gwendolyn." *Encyclopaedia Britannica Online.* Encyclopaedia Britannica, 2007. Web. 15 Feb. 2007.

Entire Online Book, Previously Appeared in Print

Jewett, Sarah Orne. *The Country of the Pointed Firs*. Boston: Houghton, 1910.
    Bartleby.com. Web. 10 Oct. 2009.

Article in Online Newspaper

Atwood, Margaret. "The Writer: A New Canadian Life-Form." *New York Times*. New
    York Times, 18 May 1997. Web. 20 Aug. 2008.

Article in Online Magazine

Garner, Dwight. "Jamaica Kincaid: The Salon Interview." *Salon*. Salon Media Group,
    13 Jan. 1996. Web. 15 Feb. 2006.

Article in Online Scholarly Journal

Carter, Sarah. "From the Ridiculous to the Sublime: Ovidian and Neoplatonic
    Registers in *A Midsummer Night's Dream*." *Early Modern Literary Studies* 12.1
    (2006): 1–31. Web. 18 Jan. 2009.

Article from a Scholarly Journal, Part of an Archival Online Database

Finch, Annie, "My Father Dickinson: On Poetic Influence." *Emily Dickinson Journal*
    17.2 (2008): 24–38. *Project Muse*. Web. 18 Jan. 2009.

Article Accessed via a Library Subscription Service

Seitler, Dana. "Unnatural Selection: Mothers, Eugenic Feminism, and Charlotte
    Perkins Gilman's Regeneration Narratives." *American Quarterly* 55.1 (2003):
    61–87. *ProQuest*. Web. 7 July 2008.

Painting or Photograph Accessed Online

Bruegel, Pieter, *Landscape with the Fall of Icarus*. 1558. Musées royaux des Beaux-
    Arts de Belgique, Brussels. *ibiblio.org*. Center for the Public Domain and
    UNC-CH. Web. 21 Nov. 2008.

CD-ROM Reference Works

CD-ROM Publication

"Appall." *The Oxford English Dictionary*. 2nd ed. Oxford: Oxford UP, 1992. CD-ROM.

Periodically Published Information, Collected on CD-ROM

Kakutani, Michiko. "Slogging Surreally in the Vietnamese Jungle." Rev. of *The Things They Carried*, by Tim O'Brien. *New York Times* 6 Mar. 1990: C6. CD-ROM. *New York Times Ondisc*. UMI-ProQuest. Oct. 1993.

Miscellaneous Sources

Compact Disc (CD)

Shakespeare, William. *The Complete Arkangel Shakespeare: 38 Fully-Dramatized Plays*. Narr. Eileen Atkins and John Gielgud. Read by Imogen Stubbs, Joseph Fiennes, et al. Audio Partners, 2003. CD.

Audiocassette

Roethke, Theodore. *Theodore Roethke Reads His Poetry*. Caedmon, 1972. Audiocassette.

Videocassette

Henry V. By William Shakespeare. Dir. Laurence Olivier. Perf. Laurence Olivier. Two Cities Films. 1944. Paramount, 1988. Videocassette.

DVD

Hamlet. By William Shakespeare. Perf. Laurence Olivier, Eileen Herlie, and Basil Sydney. Two Cities Films. 1948. Criterion, 2000. DVD.

Film

Hamlet. By William Shakespeare. Dir. Franco Zeffirelli. Perf. Mel Gibson, Glenn Close, Helena Bonham Carter, Alan Bates, and Paul Scofield. Warner, 1991. Film.

Television or Radio Program

Moby Dick. By Herman Melville. Dir. Franc Roddam. Perf. Patrick Stewart and Gregory Peck. 2 episodes. USA Network. 16–17 Mar. 1998. Television.

15 CRITICAL APPROACHES TO LITERATURE

Literary criticism should arise out of a debt of love.

—GEORGE STEINER

Literary criticism is not an abstract, intellectual exercise; it is a natural human response to literature. If a friend informs you she is reading a book you have just finished, it would be odd indeed if you did not begin swapping opinions. Literary criticism is nothing more than discourse—spoken or written—about literature. A student who sits quietly in a morning English class, intimidated by the notion of literary criticism, will spend an hour that evening talking animatedly about the meaning of rock lyrics or comparing the relative merits of the *Star Wars* trilogies. It is inevitable that people will ponder, discuss, and analyze the works of art that interest them.

The informal criticism of friends talking about literature tends to be casual, unorganized, and subjective. Since Aristotle, however, philosophers, scholars, and writers have tried to create more precise and disciplined ways of discussing literature. Literary critics have borrowed concepts from other disciplines, such as philosophy, history, linguistics, psychology, and anthropology, to analyze imaginative literature more perceptively. Some critics have found it useful to work in the abstract area of **literary theory**, criticism that tries to formulate general principles rather than discuss specific texts. Mass media critics, such as newspaper reviewers, usually spend their time evaluating works—telling us which books are worth reading, which plays not to bother seeing. But most serious literary criticism is not primarily evaluative; it assumes we know that *Othello* or *The Metamorphosis* is worth reading. Instead, such criticism is analytic; it tries to help us better understand a literary work.

In the following pages you will find overviews of ten critical approaches to literature. While these ten methods do not exhaust the total possibilities of literary criticism, they represent the most widely used contemporary approaches. Although presented separately, the approaches are not necessarily mutually exclusive; many critics mix methods to suit their needs and interests. For example, a historical critic may use formalist techniques to analyze a poem; a biographical critic will frequently use psychological theories to analyze an author. The summaries try neither to provide a history of each approach nor to present the latest trends in each school. Their purpose is to give you a practical introduction to each critical method and then provide representative examples of it. If one of these critical methods interests you, why not try to write a class paper using the approach?

FORMALIST CRITICISM

Formalist criticism regards literature as a unique form of human knowledge that needs to be examined on its own terms. "The natural and sensible starting point for work in literary scholarship," René Wellek and Austin Warren wrote in their influential *Theory of Literature*, "is the interpretation and analysis of the works of literature themselves." To a formalist, a story is not primarily a social, historical, or biographical document; it is a literary work that can be understood only by reference to its intrinsic literary features—that is, those elements found in the text itself. To analyze a story, therefore, the formalist critic focuses on the words of the text rather than facts about the author's life or the historical milieu in which the text was written. The critic pays special attention to the formal features of the text—the style, structure, imagery, tone, and genre. These features, however, are usually not examined in isolation, because formalist critics believe that what gives a literary text its special status as art is how all its elements work together to create the reader's total experience.

A key method that formalists use to explore the intense relationships within a story is **close reading**, a careful step-by-step analysis and explication of a text. The purpose of close reading is to understand how various elements in a literary text work together to shape its effects on the reader. Since formalists believe that the various stylistic and thematic elements of a literary work influence each other, these critics insist that form and content cannot be meaningfully separated. The complete interdependence of form and content is what makes a text literary. When we extract a work's theme or paraphrase its meaning, we destroy the aesthetic experience of the work.

Cleanth Brooks (1906–1994)

The Formalist Critic   1951

Here are some articles of faith I could subscribe to:

> *That literary criticism is a description and an evaluation of its object.*
>
> *That the primary concern of criticism is with the problem of unity—the kind of whole which the literary work forms or fails to form, and the relation of the various parts to each other in building up this whole.*
>
> *That the formal relations in a work of literature may include, but certainly exceed, those of logic.*
>
> *That in a successful work, form and content cannot be separated.*
>
> *That form is meaning.*
>
> *That literature is ultimately metaphorical and symbolic.*
>
> *That the general and the universal are not seized upon by abstraction, but got at through the concrete and the particular.*
>
> *That literature is not a surrogate for religion.*
>
> *That, as Allen Tate says, "specific moral problems" are the subject matter of literature, but that the purpose of literature is not to point a moral.*
>
> *That the principles of criticism define the area relevant to literary criticism; they do not constitute a method for carrying out the criticism.*

• • •

The formalist critic knows as well as anyone that poems and plays and novels are written by men—that they do not somehow happen—and that they are written as expressions of particular personalities and are written from all sorts of motives—for money, from a desire to express oneself, for the sake of a cause, etc. Moreover, the formalist critic knows as well as anyone that literary works are merely potential until they are read—that is, that they are recreated in the minds of actual readers, who vary enormously in their capabilities, their interests, their prejudices, their ideas. But the formalist critic is concerned primarily with the work itself. Speculation on the mental processes of the author takes the critic away from the work into biography and psychology. There is no reason, of course, why he should not turn away into biography and psychology. Such explorations are very much worth making. But they should not be confused with an account of the work. Such studies describe the process of composition, not the structure of the thing composed, and they may be performed quite as validly for the poor work as for the good one. They may be validly performed for any kind of expression—non-literary as well as literary.

From "The Formalist Critic"

Michael Clark (b. 1946)

Light and Darkness in "Sonny's Blues"   1985

"Sonny's Blues" by James Baldwin is a sensitive story about the reconciliation of two brothers, but it is much more than that. It is, in addition, an examination of the importance of the black heritage and of the central importance of music in that heritage. Finally, the story probes the central role that art must play in human existence. To examine all of these facets of human existence is a rather formidable undertaking in a short story, even in a longish short story such as this one. Baldwin not only undertakes this task, but he does it superbly. One of the central ways that Baldwin fuses all of these complex elements is by using a metaphor of childhood, which is supported by ancillary images of light and darkness. He does the job so well that the story is a *tour de force*, a penetrating study of American culture.

• • •

Sonny's quest is best described by himself when he writes to the narrator: "I feel like a man who's been trying to climb up out of some deep, real deep and funky hole and just saw the sun up there, outside. I got to get outside." Sonny is a person who finds his life a living hell, but he knows enough to strive for the "light." As it is chronicled in this story, his quest is for regaining something from the past—from his own childhood and from the pasts of all who have come before him. The means for doing this is his music, which is consistently portrayed in terms of light imagery. When Sonny has a discussion with the narrator about the future, the narrator describes Sonny's face as a mixture of concern and hope: "[T]he worry, the thoughtfulness, played on it still, the way shadows play on a face which is staring into the fire." This fire image is reinforced shortly afterward when the narrator describes Sonny's aspirations once more in terms of light: "[I]t was as though he were all wrapped up in some cloud, some fire, some vision all his own." To the narrator and to Isabel's family, the music that Sonny plays is simply "weird and disordered," but to Sonny, the music is seen in starkly positive terms: his failure to master the music will mean "death," while success will mean "life."

The light and dark imagery culminates in the final scene, where the narrator, apparently for the first time, listens to Sonny play the piano. The location is a Greenwich Village club. Appropriately enough, the narrator is seated "in a dark corner." In contrast, the stage is dominated by light, which Baldwin reiterates with a succession of images: "light . . . circle of light . . . light . . . flame . . . light." Although Sonny has a false start, he gradually settles into his playing and ends the first set with some intensity: "Everything had been burned out of [Sonny's face], and at the same time, things usually hidden were being burned in, by the fire and fury of the battle which was occurring in him up there."

The culmination of the set occurs when Creole, the leader of the players, begins to play "Am I Blue?" At this point, "something began to happen." Apparently, the narrator at this time realizes that this music *is* important. The music is central to the experience of the black experience, and it is described in terms of light imagery:

> Creole began to tell us what the blues were all about. They were not about anything very new. He and his boys up there were keeping it new, at the risk of ruin, destruction, madness, and death, in order to find new ways to make us listen. For, while the tale of how we suffer, and how we are delighted, and how we may triumph is never new, it always must be heard. There isn't any other tale to tell, it's the only light we've got in all this darkness.

From "James Baldwin's 'Sonny's Blues': Childhood, Light, and Art"

BIOGRAPHICAL CRITICISM

Biographical criticism begins with the simple but central insight that literature is written by actual people and that understanding an author's life can help readers more thoroughly comprehend the work. Anyone who reads the biography of a writer quickly sees how much an author's experience shapes—both directly and indirectly— what he or she creates. Reading that biography will also change (and usually deepen) our response to the work. Sometimes even knowing a single important fact illuminates our reading of a poem or story. Learning, for example, that poet Josephine Miles was confined to a wheelchair or that Weldon Kees committed suicide at forty-one will certainly make us pay attention to certain aspects of their poems we might otherwise have missed or considered unimportant. A formalist critic might complain that we would also have noticed those things through careful textual analysis, but biographical information provides the practical assistance of underscoring subtle but important meanings in the poems. Though many literary theorists have assailed biographical criticism on philosophical grounds, the biographical approach to literature has never disappeared because of its obvious practical advantage in illuminating literary texts.

It may be helpful here to make a distinction between biography and biographical criticism. **Biography** is, strictly speaking, a branch of history; it provides a written account of a person's life. To establish and interpret the facts of a poet's life, for instance, a biographer would use all the available information—not just personal documents such as letters and diaries but also the poems—for the possible light they might shed on the subject's life. A biographical *critic*, however, is not concerned with re-creating the record of an author's life. Biographical criticism focuses on explicating the literary work by using the insight provided by knowledge of the author's life.

Quite often, biographical critics will examine the drafts of a story to see both how the work came into being and how it might have been changed from its autobiographical origins.

A reader, however, must use biographical interpretations cautiously. Writers are notorious for revising the facts of their own lives; they often delete embarrassments and invent accomplishments while changing the details of real episodes to improve their literary impact. John Cheever, for example, frequently told reporters about his sunny, privileged youth; after the author's death, his biographer Scott Donaldson discovered a childhood scarred by a distant mother; a failed, alcoholic father; and nagging economic uncertainty. Likewise, Cheever's outwardly successful adulthood was plagued by alcoholism, sexual promiscuity, and family tension. The unsettling facts of Cheever's life significantly changed the way critics read his stories. The danger in the case of a famous writer (Sylvia Plath and F. Scott Fitzgerald are two modern examples) is that the life story can overwhelm and eventually distort the work. A shrewd biographical critic always remembers to base an interpretation on what is in the text itself; biographical data should amplify the meaning of the text, not drown it out with irrelevant material.

Virginia Llewellyn Smith

Chekhov's Attitude to Romantic Love   1973

It has been shown that the theme of love being destroyed by a cruel fate did not always have for Chekhov the appeal of the tragic: that it could also serve him as a good framework on which to build farce. Nor could one claim that the theme of illicit passion found its source in Chekhov's own imagination, let alone experience: Tolstoy's *Anna Karenina°* had been published in the later 1870s, before any of Chekhov's work. Nonetheless the coincidence of plot and emotion found in "About Love" and "The Lady with the Dog," together with the fact that the theme occupied Chekhov chiefly in the 1890s, has given rise to some speculation as to whether in fact Chekhov's own love-life during those years suffered as one critic puts it from the interference of a *force majeure.°* Since in this period Chekhov's private life is no longer a closed book (although many pages are indecipherable) the search for the romantic heroine becomes more complex. It becomes feasible to try to connect with her image certain women whose relations with Chekhov are at least partially illuminated and illuminating. Of Chekhov's female friends three in particular must now claim our attention.

No other single work of Chekhov's fiction constitutes a more meaningful comment on Chekhov's attitude to women and to love than does "The Lady with the Dog." So many threads of Chekhov's thought and experience appear to have been woven together into this succinct story that it may be regarded as something in the nature of a summary of the entire topic.

Gurov, the hero of the story, may at first appear no more closely identifiable with Chekhov himself than are many other sympathetic male characters in Chekhov's fiction: he has a post in a bank and is a married man with three children. It is because he has this wife and family that his love-affair with Anna Sergeevna leads him into an *impasse*. And the affair itself, involving Gurov's desperate trip to Anna's home

---

Anna Karenina: Leo Tolstoy's novel (1875–1877) dealt explicitly with an adulterous affair.   *force majeure:* French for an "irresistible force."

town, has no obvious feature in common with anything we know of Chekhov's amorous liaisons.

And yet Chekhov's own attitudes and experience have clearly shaped Gurov's character and fate. The reader is told that Gurov "was not yet forty": Chekhov was thirty-nine when he wrote "The Lady with the Dog." Gurov "was married young" (*ego zhenili rano*): there is a faint implication in the phrase that an element of coercion played some part in his taking this step—a step which Chekhov, when he was young, managed to avoid. As in general with early marriages in Chekhov's fiction, Gurov's has not proved a success. His wife seems "much older than he" and imagines herself to be an intellectual: familiar danger-signals. She is summed-up in three words: "stiff, pompous, dignified" (*pryamaya, vazhnaya, solidnaya*) which epitomize a type of woman (and man) that Chekhov heartily disliked.

• • •

Gurov has had, however, liaisons that were, for him, enjoyable—and these we note, were brief: as was Chekhov's liaison with Yavorskaya and indeed, so far as we know, all the sexual relationships that he had before he met Olga Knipper.

"Frequent experience and indeed bitter experience had long since taught [Gurov] that every liaison which to begin with makes such a pleasant change . . . inevitably evolves into a real and extremely complex problem, and the situation eventually becomes a burden." That his friendships with, for instance, Lika and Avilova should evolve into a situation of this kind seems to have been exactly what Chekhov himself feared: he backed out of these friendships as soon as there appeared to be a danger of close involvement.

Gurov cannot do without the company of women, and yet he describes them as an "inferior breed": his experience of intimacy with women is limited to casual affairs and an unsatisfactory marriage. Chekhov also enjoyed the company of women and had many female friends and admirers: but he failed, or was unwilling, to involve himself deeply or lastingly with them. That in his work he should suggest that women are an inferior breed can be to some extent explained by the limited knowledge of women his self-contained attitude brought him—and perhaps, to some extent, by a sense of guilt concerning his inability to feel involved.

Gurov's behaviour to Anna Sergeevna at the beginning of their love-affair is characterized by an absence of emotional involvement, just such as appears in Chekhov's attitude towards certain women. There is a scene in "The Lady with the Dog" where, after they have been to bed together, Gurov eats a watermelon while Anna Sergeevna weeps over her corruption. It is not difficult to imagine Chekhov doing something similarly prosaic—weeding his garden, perhaps—while Lika poured out her emotional troubles to him.

Gurov's egocentricity is dispelled, however, by the potent influence of love, because Anna Sergeevna turns out to be the ideal type of woman: pitiable, defenseless, childlike, capable of offering Gurov an unquestioning love. Love is seen to operate as a force for good: under its influence Gurov feels revulsion for the philistinism of his normal life and associates.

• • •

Chekhov wrote "The Lady with the Dog" in Yalta in the autumn of 1899, not long after he and Olga were there together (although they were not, as yet, lovers) and had made the trip back to Moscow together. In the Kokkoz valley, it will be remembered, they apparently agreed to marry: and so by then, we may presume, Chekhov knew what it was to love.

From *Anton Chekhov and the Lady with the Dog*

Emily Toth (b. 1944)

The Source for Alcée Laballière in "The Storm" 1990

In January 1898, right after Kate Chopin had finished writing her controversial novel *The Awakening*, about one woman's quest for love (and sexual fulfillment) outside of marriage, a St. Louis newspaper asked her to answer the question, "Is Love Divine?"

Chopin's response was telling. She wrote, "I am inclined to think that love springs from animal instinct, and therefore is, in a measure, divine. One can never resolve to love this man, this woman or child, and then carry out the resolution unless one feels irresistibly drawn by an indefinable current of magnetism."

In that case, it was no doubt magnetism that led Kate Chopin to the handsome, wealthy Creole planter Albert Sampité (pronounced "Al-bear Sam-pi-TAY") after the death of her husband Oscar. This may also be why Kate Chopin's widowhood stories emphasize hope, not bereavement; spring, not winter; possibility, not loss. After Oscar died, Kate—who had grown up in a house full of widows who managed their own lives and their own money—decided to run Oscar's businesses herself.

She became an accomplished entrepreneur, a brisk businesswoman during the day who nevertheless kept the dark night as her own, with its prospects for silence and mystery and sin. Men flocked to aid the handsome widow in 1883, but when villagers gossiped generations later about who was "sweet on Kate," one name kept recurring. It was no secret to anyone—including his wife—that Albert Sampité was pursuing Kate Chopin. An examination of Chopin's stories show that the male characters who kindle desire and who devote themselves to sexual pleasure are named Alcée, an abbreviated form of Albert Sampité. Al. S——é and Alcée are both pronounced "Al-say."

It was not unseemly, or even odd, for Monsieur Sampite (his family dropped the accent mark, though they continued to use French pronunciation) to meet with Madame Chopin at the point where their lands intersected. When merchandise arrived for Kate's store, by boat from New Orleans, she had to go down to the landing to get her goods. It was not uncommon for a local planter like Albert Sampite to be at the landing at the same time. Somehow, too, Albert Sampite became involved in Kate Chopin's money matters. Papers that he saved show that Albert was apparently helping Kate to collect money owed her—and he also valued her financial records enough to keep them with his own personal papers.

There were still other ways in which a willing couple could make connections. And in a sudden storm, it was not impossible for two people to take refuge alone together in a house—a sensual scenario Kate Chopin sketched out, years later, in her most explicit short story, "The Storm."

Kate and Albert were discreet about their romance, by the standards of a century later. If anyone wrote down dates and places and eyewitness descriptions, none of those survive—although Cloutierville residents would certainly have been able to recognize him in her writings. But an affair in the 1880s was not simply a matter of physical consummation. Much less than that could be called "making love": flirting, significant glances, stolen kisses, secret silences.

Kate Chopin, in her diary eleven years after the first spring of her widowhood, suggested that more than flirting had gone on in her life: "I had loved—lovers who were not divine," she wrote, and "And then, there are so many ways of saying good night!" And even in her published writings, Kate left proof that her relationship with

Albert Sampite was much more than a casual friendship. It shaped what she wrote
about women and men, and love and lust and forbidden desires.

Adapted from Kate Chopin

HISTORICAL CRITICISM

Historical criticism seeks to understand a literary work by investigating the social,
cultural, and intellectual context that produced it—a context that necessarily includes the artist's biography and milieu. Historical critics are less concerned with
explaining a work's literary significance for today's readers than with helping us
understand the work by re-creating, as nearly as possible, the exact meaning and
impact it had on its original audience. A historical reading of a literary work begins
by exploring the possible ways in which the meaning of the text has changed over
time. An analysis of Nathaniel Hawthorne's "Young Goodman Brown," for
instance, might carefully examine how certain words had different connotations for
the story's original readers than they do today. It might also explore the probable
associations a nineteenth-century New England reader would have made with
certain images and events, especially in regard to the religious and sacrilegious
elements of Hawthorne's theological horror story.

Reading ancient literature, no one doubts the value of historical criticism.
There have been so many social, cultural, and linguistic changes that some older
texts are incomprehensible without scholarly assistance. But historical criticism can
even help one better understand modern texts. In studying Chinua Achebe's story
"Civil Peace," for example, one learns a great deal by considering two rudimentary
historical facts—the year in which the work was first published (1972) and the
nationality of its author (Nigerian)—and then asking how this information has
shaped the meaning of the story. From 1963 to 1970 a bloody civil war was fought in
West Africa when the predominantly Ibo region seceded from Nigeria to proclaim
itself the independent nation of Biafra. Achebe's story, therefore, depicts the time
immediately after the war's end, and its narrator is a member of the defeated Biafran
faction. Even these two basic historical observations help explain a great deal about
the social, political, and psychological context of Achebe's story. That fact that one
million Ibos died in the war from either violence or starvation also clarifies why the
narrator counts himself "happy" and "lucky" for the "blessing" that only one of his
children died. (An American story of 1972 would almost certainly consider the
death of one child a terrible tragedy.) In writing a paper on a story, you might
explore how the time and place of its creation affect its meaning. For a splendid
example of how to re-create the historical context of a literary work's genesis, read
the account by John King on the Argentine factors that helped shape Jorge Luis
Borges's use of fantasy in his short stories.

John King

The Argentine Context of Borges's Fantastic Fiction   1987

Borges traveled with his family to Europe in 1914, when he was fifteen, and did not
return to Buenos Aires until 1921. He lived in Switzerland and Spain, he learned
Latin, French and German, became acquainted with the modernist movements in
Europe and began to write. He was thus well equipped to become an active member

of the literary avant-garde which emerged in Buenos Aires and in other capital cities of Latin America in the 1920s.

• • •

Argentina was living a period of prosperity, one of the richest nations in the world as a result of having entered into the world division of labor as an important part of the informal British Empire. In the cultural sphere, there was a strong press, a community of writers, a consolidated reading public and an expanding university. One can also see in Argentina the beginnings of export-led industrialization and consumerism (the mirage of the American way of life and the new technologies of the second industrial revolution that so obsessed the modernists), although once again it would take until the 1960s for the marketplace to develop fully. Finally, there was the imaginative proximity of social revolution with the Mexican Revolution, student reforms in the Argentine University of Córdoba, and the attraction of Bolshevism. In 1921, a youthful Borges could be found writing poems in praise of revolution: "Bolshevik Epic" and "Russia."

The vanguard movement in Buenos Aires was full of youthful iconoclasm and pastiche but it did not generate many literary works of lasting value, nor did it threaten the solid structures of Argentine society, with its climate of sexual and moral repression, its apoliticism and its powerful State. Perhaps most importantly it helped to legitimate the idea of the professional writer, not in an economic sense (it was impossible to live from writing: Borges's father paid for the publication of his early works and Borges did not even consider trying to sell any copies), but in the writer's perception of himself as a writer and of literature as a craft with its own separate rules rather than the divertissement of statesmen and politicians. The vanguard also provided Borges with opportunities to begin his life-long attack on the dogmas of the literary Academy. He began to question simple, social readings of literature, mocking the earnest pious radicals of the time (the so-called Boedo group, named after a working-class district in Buenos Aires) who proclaimed an easy correspondence between literature and social text.

• • •

The optimism of the 1920s came to an end in Argentina with the Great Slump, a military coup and the beginnings of what has been termed the "Infamous Decade" of Argentine history, when elections were rigged and power was maintained in a direct and brutal form. In terms of fiction, the 1930s is a somewhat barren decade throughout Spanish America, with very little relief from a dull, realistic, regionalist aesthetic. Throughout this time Borges worked quietly towards his magisterial short stories of the late 1930s and early 1940s. He wrote book reviews and short essays, for the literary magazine *Sur*—the major journal of the twentieth century in Latin America—and for a time edited his own literary pages in a popular magazine *El Hogar*. It was at the end of the decade, however, that he moved quietly onto the offensive, publishing in quick succession a series of significant essays, prologues and short stories. In an Argentina influenced by clericalism, nationalism and military might, in a world held in the grip of totalitarian orders and in a literary establishment dominated by dull realist writers such as Manuel Gálvez, Borges began to undermine the foundations of such systems. In a mainly complimentary review of Luis Saslavsky's film La Fuga ("The Flight"), he wrote in 1937, "To idolize a ridiculous scarecrow because it is autochthonous, to fall asleep for the fatherland, to take pleasure in tedium because it is a national product all seem absurd to me." In repeated articles he warned against the dangers of nationalist autarchy.

Borges also equated nationalism with the realist text. In the preface to a work by his close friend Adolfo Bioy Casares, *The Invention of Morel (La invención de Morel)*, 1940, a beautifully wrought short novel about a man on a desert island who falls in love with a woman who is later revealed as a holographic image, Borges lambasts novelists and critics who uphold the tenets of the "psychological" novel. Such a form, he states, "would have us forget that it is a verbal artifice . . . The adventure story, on the other hand, does not propose to be a transcription of reality: it is an artificial object, no part of which lacks justification." At the same time Borges published two short stories, "Pierre Menard, Author of the Quixote" and "Tlön, Uqbar, Orbis Tertius," and edited with Bioy Casares and his wife Silvina Ocampo an anthology of fantastic literature. In a prologue to this anthology Bioy helps us to locate his friend's work. Borges, he argues, has created "a new literary genre which is both essay and fiction; they are exercises of unceasing intelligence and fortunate imagination, lacking all languor, all human elements, pathetic or sentimental . . . aimed at intellectual readers, interested in philosophy and almost specialists in literature." Deliberately polemical in tone, Bioy offers the fantastic as an antidote to the realist text and sees in Borges's work a twentieth-century form of the fantastic, one in which horror and fear have been replaced by literary and metaphysical speculation. All fantastic texts question and subvert the real, the monological vision of the realist text and single or unitary ways of perceiving the world. In the nineteenth century, a gradual displacement of residual supernaturalism and magic and increasingly secularized thought produced very different interpretations of fantasy: demonology was replaced by psychology to explain "otherness." By the twentieth century, fantastic texts had become increasingly nonreferential, concerned not so much with the relationship between language and the real world "outside" the text, as with a quest for fictional autonomy. Bioy sees Borges as in the vanguard of such a movement, which "creates and satisfies a desire for a literature that talks about literature and abstract thought."

A form of literature particularly appropriate for an attack on the realist text is detective fiction. The detective story is a form in which the relevance or the necessity of the content should not be in doubt. Its construction is such that every presence in the book, animate or inanimate, is a clue and not an intrusion for the purposes of atmosphere or naturalism. The reader, like the detective himself, has to interpret everything as evidence, and as the amount of evidence grows, so the hypotheses accounting for it must constantly be renewed. In attacking the psychological novel, Borges reminded novelists that they had forgotten how to tell a story. He has often remarked that if one reads detective stories and then takes up novels afterwards, the later appear shapeless.

"Jorge Luis Borges: A View from the Periphery"

Kathryn Lee Seidel

The Economics of Zora Neale Hurston's "Sweat"   1991

"Sweat" functions at one level as a documentary of the economic situation of Eatonville in the early decades of the twentieth century. Hurston uses a naturalistic narrator to comment on the roles of Delia and Sykes Jones as workers as well as marriage partners, but ultimately the story veers away from naturalistic fiction and becomes a modernist rumination on Delia as an artist figure. The story's coherence of theme and structure makes it one of Hurston's most powerful pieces of fiction.

Preserved not only as a place but as an idea of a place, Eatonville, Florida, retains the atmosphere of which Hurston wrote. As putatively the oldest town in the United States incorporated by blacks, Eatonville possesses understandable pride in its unique history. When Hurston writes of Eatonville in "How It Feels To Be Colored Me," she implies that her childhood place was idyllic because "it is exclusively a colored town," one in which the young Zora was happily unaware of the restrictions that race conferred elsewhere. However, this gloss of nostalgia can be read simultaneously with "Sweat," published only two years earlier . . . [where] Hurston reveals the somber and multifaced variations of life in Eatonville in the first part of this century.

Economically Eatonville in "Sweat" exists as a twin, a double with its neighbor, the town of Winter Park. Far from being identical, the twin towns are configured like Siamese twins, joined as they are by economic necessity. Winter Park is an all-white, wealthy town that caters to rich northerners from New England who journey south each fall to "winter" in Florida—"snowbirds," as the natives call them. Winter Park then as now boasts brick streets, huge oaks, landscaped lakes, and large, spacious houses. To clean these houses, tend these gardens, cook the meals, and watch the children of Winter Park, residents of Eatonville made a daily exodus across the railroad tracks on which Amtrak now runs to work as domestics. . . . What is unique about Eatonville and Winter Park is that they are not one town divided in two but two towns. Eatonville's self-governance, its pride in its historic traditions, and its social mores were thus able to develop far more autonomously than those in the many towns . . . where the black community had to struggle to develop a sense of independent identity.

In "Sweat" we see the results of this economic situation. On Saturdays the men of the town congregate on the porch of the general store chewing sugarcane and discussing the lamentable marriage of Delia and Sykes Jones. Although these men may be employed during the week, Sykes is not. Some working people mentioned besides Joe Clarke, the store owner, are the woman who runs a rooming house where Bertha, Sykes's mistress, stays, the minister of the church Delia attends, and the people who organize dances that Sykes frequents. Work as farm laborers on land owned by whites is probably available, but it pays very little and is seasonal. Jacqueline Jones points out that in 1900, not long before the time of the story, 50 to 70 percent of adult black women were employed full time as compared to only 20 percent of men.[1] A black man might be unemployed 50 percent of the time. One reason that unemployed men congregated at the local general store was not merely out of idleness, as whites alleged, nor out of a desire to create oral narratives, as we Hurston critics would like to imagine, but there they could be "visible to potential employers," as Jones asserts.

There is not enough work for the men as it is, but the townspeople discuss Sykes's particular aversion to what work is available. Old man Anderson reports that Sykes was always "ovahbearin' . . . but since dat white w'oman from up north done teached 'im how to run a automobile, he done got too beggety to live—an' we oughter kill 'im." The identity of this woman and her exact role in Sykes's life is not referred to again, but if she was a Winter Park woman, then perhaps Sykes worked for a time as a driver for residents there. All the more ironic, then, his comment to Delia in which he berates her for doing white people's laundry: "ah done

---

[1]Jacqueline Jones, *Labor of Love, Labor of Sorrow: Black Women, Work, and the Family from Slavery to the Present* (New York: Basic Books, 1985) 113.

tole you time and again to keep them white folks' clothes outa this house." The comment suggests that Sykes does not work out of protest against the economic system of Eatonville in which blacks are dependent on whites for their livelihood. Has he chosen to be unemployed to resist the system? Within the story, this reading is fragile at best. The townspeople point out that Sykes has used and abused Delia; he has "squeezed" her dry, like a piece of sugarcane. They report that she was in her youth a pert, lively, and pretty girl, but that marriage to a man like Sykes has worn her out.

In fact, Delia's work is their only source of income. In the early days of their marriage Sykes was employed, but he "took his wages to Orlando," the large city about ten miles from Eatonville, where he spent every penny. At some point Sykes stopped working and began to rely entirely on Delia for income. As she says, "Mah tub of suds is filled yo' belly with vittles more times than yo' hands is filled it. Mah sweat is done paid for this house." Delia's sense of ownership is that of the traditional work ethic; if one works hard, one can buy a house and support a family. That Delia is the breadwinner, however, is a role reversal but not ostensibly a liberation; her sweat has brought her some meager material rewards but has enraged her husband.

Although she may at one time have considered stopping work so that Sykes might be impelled to "feel like man again" and become a worker once more, at the time of the story that possibility is long past. Sykes wants her to stop working so she can be dainty, not sweaty, fat, not thin. Moreover, he wants to oust her from the house so that he and his girlfriend can live there. . . . Sykes's brutality is a chosen compensation because he does not participate in the work of the community. He chooses instead to become the town's womanizer and bully who spends his earnings when he has them; he lives for the moment and for himself.

. . . With her house she possesses not only a piece of property, but she also gains the right to declare herself as a person, not a piece of property. Because Sykes has not shared in the labor that results in the purchase of this property, he remains in a dependent state. He is rebellious against Delia who he feels controls him by denying him the house he feels ought to be his; his only reason for this assertion is that he is a man and Delia is his wife.

Thus, the economics of slavery in "Sweat" becomes a meditation on marriage as an institution that perpetuates the possession of women for profit. Indeed, Sykes is the slaveholder here; he does not work, he is sustained by the harsh physical labor of a black woman, he relies on the work of another person to obtain his own pleasure (in this case buying presents for his mistress Bertha). He regards Delia's property and her body as his possessions to be disposed of as he pleases. Sykes's brutal beatings of Delia and his insulting remarks about her appearance are the tools with which he perpetuates her subordination to him for the sixteen years of their marriage.

From "The Artist in the Kitchen: The Economics of
Creativity in Hurston's 'Sweat'"

PSYCHOLOGICAL CRITICISM

Modern psychology has had an immense effect on both literature and literary criticism. The psychoanalytic theories of the Austrian neurologist Sigmund Freud changed our notions of human behavior by exploring new or controversial areas such as wish fulfillment, sexuality, the unconscious, and repression. Perhaps Freud's greatest contribution to literary study was his elaborate demonstration of how much human mental process was unconscious. He analyzed language, often in the form of jokes and conversational slips of the tongue (now often called "Freudian slips"), to show how it reflected the speaker's unconscious fears and desires. He also examined symbols, not only in art and literature but also in dreams, to study how the unconscious mind expressed itself in coded form to avoid the censorship of the conscious mind. His theory of human cognition asserted that much of what we apparently forget is actually stored deep in the unconscious mind, including painful traumatic memories from childhood that have been repressed.

Freud admitted that he himself had learned a great deal about psychology from studying literature. Sophocles, Shakespeare, Goethe, and Dostoyevsky were as important to the development of his ideas as were his clinical studies. Some of Freud's most influential writing was, in a broad sense, literary criticism, such as his psychoanalytic examination of Sophocles' Oedipus in *The Interpretation of Dreams* (1900). In analyzing Sophocles' tragedy *Oedipus the King,* Freud paid the classical Greek dramatist the considerable compliment that the playwright had such profound insight into human nature that his characters display the depth and complexity of real people. In focusing on literature, Freud and his disciples such as Carl Jung, Ernest Jones, Marie Bonaparte, and Bruno Bettelheim endorsed the belief that great literature truthfully reflects life.

Psychological criticism is a diverse category, but it often employs three approaches. First, it investigates the creative process of the arts: what is the nature of literary genius, and how does it relate to normal mental functions? Such analysis may also focus on literature's effects on the reader. How does a particular work register its impact on the reader's mental and sensory faculties? The second approach involves the psychological study of a particular artist. Most modern literary biographers employ psychology to understand their subject's motivations and behavior. One book, Diane Middlebrook's controversial *Anne Sexton: A Biography* (1991), actually used tapes of the poet's sessions with her psychiatrist as material for the study. The third common approach is the analysis of fictional characters. Freud's study of Oedipus is the prototype for this approach, which tries to bring modern insights about human behavior into the study of how fictional people act. While psychological criticism carefully examines the surface of the literary work, it customarily speculates on what lies underneath the text—the unspoken or perhaps even unspeakable memories, motives, and fears that covertly shape the work, especially in fictional characterizations.

Sigmund Freud (1856–1939)

The Destiny of Oedipus   1900

Translated by James Strachey

If *Oedipus the King* moves a modern audience no less than it did the contemporary Greek one, the explanation can only be that its effect does not lie in the contrast between destiny and human will, but is to be looked for in the particular nature of the material on which that contrast is exemplified. There must be something which makes a voice within us ready to recognize the compelling force of destiny in the *Oedipus,* while we can dismiss as merely arbitrary such dispositions as are laid down in *Die Ahnfrau*° or other modern tragedies of destiny. And a factor of this kind is in fact involved in the story of King Oedipus. His destiny moves us only because it might have been ours—because the oracle laid the same curse upon us before our birth as upon him. It is the fate of all of us, perhaps, to direct our first sexual impulse towards our mother and our first hatred and our first murderous wish against our father. Our dreams convince us that that is so. King Oedipus, who slew his father Laius and married his mother Jocasta, merely shows us the fulfillment of our own childhood wishes. But, more fortunate than he, we have meanwhile succeeded, insofar as we have not become psychoneurotics, in detaching our sexual impulses from our mothers and in forgetting our jealousy of our fathers. Here is one in whom these primeval wishes of our childhood have been fulfilled, and we shrink back from him with the whole force of the repression by which those wishes have since that time been held down within us. While the poet, as he unravels the past, brings to light the guilt of Oedipus, he is at the same time compelling us to recognize our own inner minds, in which those same impulses, though suppressed, are still to be found. The contrast with which the closing Chorus leaves us confronted—

> look upon Oedipus.
> This is the king who solved the famous riddle
> And towered up, most powerful of men.
> No mortal eyes but looked on him with envy,
> Yet in the end ruin swept over him.

—strikes as a warning at ourselves and our pride, at us who since our childhood have grown so wise and so mighty in our own eyes. Like Oedipus, we live in ignorance of these wishes, repugnant to morality, which have been forced upon us by Nature, and after their revelation we may all of us well seek to close our eyes to the scenes of our childhood.

From *The Interpretation of Dreams*

Gretchen Schulz (b. 1943) and R. J. R. Rockwood

Fairy Tale Motifs in "Where Are You Going, Where Have You Been?"   1980

In her fiction both short and long Miss Oates makes frequent use of fairy tale material. Again and again she presents characters and situations which parallel corresponding motifs from the world of folk fantasy. And never is this more true than in the present story ["Where Are You Going, Where Have You Been?"]—never in all the novels and collections of short stories which she has written at last count. Woven into the complex texture of "Where Are You Going, Where Have You Been?" are motifs from such tales as "The Spirit in the Bottle," "Snow White," "Cinderella," "Sleeping Beauty," "Rapunzel," "Little Red Riding Hood," and "The Three Little Pigs." *The Pied Piper of Hamelin*, which ends tragically and so according to [Bruno] Bettelheim does not qualify as a proper fairy tale, serves as the "frame device" that contains all the other tales.

Die Ahnfrau: The Foremother, a verse play by Franz Grillparzer (1791–1872), Austrian dramatist and poet.

There is a terrible irony here, for although the story is full of fairy tales, Connie, its protagonist, is not. Connie represents an entire generation of young people who have grown up—or tried to—without the help of those bedtime stories which not only entertain the child, but also enable him vicariously to experience and work through problems which he will encounter in adolescence. The only "stories" Connie knows are those of the sexually provocative but superficial lyrics of the popular songs she loves or of the equally insubstantial movies she attends. Such songs and movies provide either no models of behavior for her to imitate, or dangerously inappropriate ones. Connie has thus been led to believe that life and, in particular, love will be "sweet, gentle, the way it was in the movies and promised in songs." She has no idea that life actually can be just as grim as in folk fairy tales. The society that is depicted in "Where Are You Going, Where Have You Been?" has failed to make available to children like Connie maps of the unconscious such as fairy tales provide, because it has failed to recognize that in the unconscious past and future coalesce, and that, psychologically, where the child is going is where he has already been. Since Connie has been left—in the words of yet another of the popular songs—to "wander through that wonderland alone"—it is small wonder, considering her lack of spiritual preparation, that Connie's journey there soon becomes a terrifying schizophrenic separation from reality, with prognosis for recovery extremely poor.

• • •

Bettelheim points out that a fairy tale like "Spirit in the Bottle" deals with two problems that confront the child as he struggles to establish a sense of identity: parental belittlement, and integration of a divided personality. In Connie's case, her mother's belittling remarks that "Connie couldn't do a thing, her mind was all filled with trashy daydreams," certainly have contributed to Connie's two-sidedness, with her one personality "for home" and another for "anywhere that was not home," a division also apparent in the relationship between Connie and the "girl friend" who accompanies her to the bottle-shaped restaurant—the two are so poorly differentiated as to suggest a mere *doubling* of Connie, rather than two separate individuals. While such personality division may at first glance seem pathological, it is not, according to Bettelheim, necessarily abnormal, since the "manner in which the child can bring some order into his world view is by dividing everything into opposites," and that "in the late-oedipal and post-oedipal ages, this splitting extends to the child himself."

• • •

To be assured of safe passage through what Bettelheim terms "that thorniest of thickets, the oedipal period," a child like Connie would need to have absorbed the wisdom of the other fairy tales to which Miss Oates alludes, tales such as "Snow White," "Cinderella," "Rapunzel," and "Little Red Riding Hood." By their applicability to Connie's situation, these tales reveal that at its deepest level Connie's most compelling psychological problem is *unresolved oedipal conflict, aggravated by sibling rivalry.*

Suggestive of "Snow White" is Connie's "habit of craning her neck to glance into mirrors, or checking other people's faces to make sure her own was all right" (as though other people's faces were mirrors, too); and we are told also that her mother, "who noticed everything and knew everything"—as though with the wicked queen's magic power—"hadn't much reason any longer to look at her own face," and so was jealous of her daughter's beauty and "always after Connie." Arnold Friend's sunglasses also mirror everything, which means that, in this instance, he personifies the Magic Mirror and, of course, he finds Connie the fairest one of all. In his words, "Seen you that night and thought, that's the one, yes sir, I never needed to look anymore." Though he thus serves as Prince, there is a hint of the dwarf motif in Arnold's short stature and obvious phallicism; and most particularly is this true of his friend, Ellie Oscar, a case of arrested development, whose face is that of a "forty-year-old baby." Connie's "Someday My Prince Will Come" daydreams, plus the many references to how dazed and sleepy she always is, especially the day Arnold comes for her, when she "lay languidly about the airless little room" and "breathed in and breathed out with each gentle rise and fall of her chest"—these too, suggest "Snow White" and, for that matter, "Sleeping Beauty," whose heroine in the Brothers Grimm is, like Connie, fifteen.

The oedipal implications of "Snow White" are evident in the fact that, as Bettelheim points out, the queen's Magic Mirror speaks not with the mother's but the daughter's voice, revealing the jealous child's own sense of inferiority and frustration projected onto her mother. The father's romantic feelings for the daughter are never at issue in such a fairy tale and he is generally depicted as weak, ineffectual, and oblivious to the struggle that issues between mother and daughter—exactly as in Miss Oates's story.

> From "In Fairyland Without a Map: Connie's Exploration Inward
> in Joyce Carol Oates's 'Where Are You Going, Where Have You Been?'"

MYTHOLOGICAL CRITICISM

Mythological critics look for the recurrent universal patterns underlying most literary works. **Mythological criticism** is an interdisciplinary approach that combines the insights of anthropology, psychology, history, and comparative religion. If psychological criticism examines the artist as an individual, mythological criticism explores the artist's common humanity by tracing how the individual imagination uses symbols and situations—consciously or unconsciously—in ways that transcend its own historical milieu and resemble the mythology of other cultures or epochs.

A central concept in mythological criticism is the **archetype**, a symbol, character, situation, or image that evokes a deep universal response. The idea of the archetype came into literary criticism from the Swiss psychologist Carl Jung, a lifetime student of myth and religion. Jung believed that all individuals share a "collective unconscious," a set of primal memories common to the human race, existing below each person's conscious mind. Archetypal images (which often relate to experiencing primordial phenomena like the sun, moon, fire, night, and blood), Jung believed, trigger the collective unconscious. We do not need to accept the literal truth of the collective unconscious, however, to endorse the archetype as a helpful critical concept. Northrop Frye defined the archetype in considerably less occult terms as "a symbol, usually an image, which recurs often enough in literature to be recognizable as an element of one's literary experience as a whole."

Identifying archetypal symbols and situations in literary works, mythological critics almost inevitably link the individual text under discussion to a broader context of works that share an underlying pattern. In discussing Shakespeare's *Hamlet*, for instance, a mythological critic might relate Shakespeare's Danish prince to other mythic sons avenging the deaths of their fathers, like Orestes from Greek myth or Sigmund of Norse legend; or, in discussing *Othello*, relate the sinister figure of Iago to the devil in traditional Christian belief. Critic Joseph Campbell took such comparisons even further; his compendious study *The Hero with a Thousand Faces* demonstrates how similar mythic characters appear in virtually every culture on every continent.

Carl Jung (1875–1961)

The Collective Unconscious and Archetypes   1931

Translated by R. F. C. Hull

A more or less superficial layer of the unconscious is undoubtedly personal. I call it the *personal unconscious*. But this personal unconscious rests upon a deeper layer, which does not derive from personal experience and is not a personal acquisition but is inborn. This deeper layer I call the *collective unconscious*. I have chosen the term "collective" because this part of the unconscious is not individual but universal; in contrast to the personal psyche, it has contents and modes of behavior that are more or less the same everywhere and in all individuals. It is, in other words, identical in all men and thus constitutes a common psyche substrate of a suprapersonal nature which is present in every one of us.

Psychic existence can be recognized only by the presence of contents that are *capable of consciousness*. We can therefore speak of an unconscious only in so far as we are able to demonstrate its contents. The contents of the personal unconscious are chiefly the *feeling-toned complexes*, as they are called; they constitute the personal and private side of psychic life. The contents of the collective unconscious, on the other hand, are known as *archetypes*. . . .

For our purposes this term is apposite and helpful, because it tells us that so far as the collective unconscious contents are concerned we are dealing with archaic or—I would say—primordial types, that is, with universal images that have existed since the remotest times. The term "representations collectives," used by Lévy-Bruhl to denote the symbolic figures in the primitive view of the world, could easily be applied to unconscious contents as well, since it means practically the same thing. Primitive tribal lore is concerned with archetypes that have been modified in a special way. They are no longer contents of the unconscious, but have already been changed into conscious formulae taught according to tradition, generally in the form of esoteric teaching. This last is a typical means of expression for the transmission of collective contents originally derived from the unconscious.

Another well-known expression of the archetypes is myth and fairy tale. But here too we are dealing with forms that have received a specific stamp and have been handed down through long periods of time. The term "archetype" thus applies only indirectly to the "representations collectives," since it designates only those psychic contents which have not yet been submitted to conscious elaboration and are therefore an immediate datum of psychic experience. In this sense there is a considerable difference between the archetype and the historical formula that has evolved. Especially on the higher levels of esoteric teaching the archetypes appear in a form that reveals quite unmistakably the critical and evaluating influence of conscious elaboration. Their immediate manifestation, as we encounter it in dreams and visions, is much more individual, less understandable, and more naïve than in myths, for example. The archetype is essentially an unconscious content that is altered by becoming conscious and by being perceived, and it takes its color from the individual consciousness in which it happens to appear.

From The Collected Works of C. G. Jung

Edmond Volpe (b. 1922)

Myth in Faulkner's "Barn Burning" 1964

"Barn Burning" however is not really concerned with class conflict. The story is centered upon Sarty's emotional dilemma. His conflict would not have been altered in
any way if the person whose barn Ab burns had been a simple poor farmer, rather
than an aristocratic plantation owner. The child's tension, in fact, begins to surface
during the hearing in which a simple farmer accuses Ab of burning his barn. The
moral antagonists mirrored in Sarty's conflict are not sharecropper and aristocrat.
They are the father, Ab Snopes, versus the rest of mankind. Major De Spain is not
developed as a character; his house is important to Sarty because it represents a
totally new and totally different social and moral entity. Within the context of the
society Faulkner is dealing with, the gap between the rich aristocrat and the poor
sharecropper provides a viable metaphor for dramatizing the crisis Sarty is undergoing. Ab Snopes is by no means a social crusader. The De Spain manor is Sarty's
first contact with a rich man's house, though he can recall, in the short span of his
life, at least a dozen times the family had to move because Ab burned barns. Ab does
not discriminate between rich and poor. For him there are only two categories: blood
kin and "they," into which he lumps all the rest of mankind. Ab's division relates to
Sarty's crisis and only by defining precisely the nature of the conflict the boy is
undergoing can we determine the moral significance Faulkner sees in it. The clue to
Sarty's conflict rests in its resolution.

• • •

   The boy's anxiety is created by his awakening sense of his own individuality.
Torn between strong emotional attachment to the parent and his growing need to
assert his own identity, Sarty's crisis is psychological and his battle is being waged far
below the level of his intellectual and moral awareness.

   Faulkner makes this clear in the opening scene with imagery that might be
described as synesthesia. The real smell of cheese is linked with the smell of the hermetic meat in the tin cans with the scarlet devils on the label that his "intestines
believed he smelled coming in intermittent gusts momentary and brief between the
other constant one, the smell and sense just a little of fear because mostly of despair
and grief, the old fierce pull of blood." The smells below the level of the olfactory
sense link the devil image and the blood image to identify the anxiety the father creates in the child's psyche. Tension is created by the blood demanding identification
with his father against "*our enemy* he thought in that despair; *ourn! mine and hisn
both! He's my father!*" Sarty's conflict is played out in terms of identification, not in
moral terms. He does not think of his father as bad, his father's enemies as good.

   Ab unjustly accuses Sarty of intending to betray him at the hearing, but he
correctly recognizes that his son is moving out of childhood, developing a mind
and will of his own and is no longer blindly loyal. In instructing the boy that everyone is the enemy and his loyalty belongs to his blood, Ab's phrasing is revealing:
" 'Don't you know all they wanted was a chance to get at me because they knew I
had them beat?' " Ab does not use the plural "us." It is "I" and "they." Blood loyalty
means total identification with Ab, and in the ensuing scenes, Snopes attempts to
make his son an extension of himself by taking him to the De Spain house, rise up
before dawn to be with him when he returns the rug, accompany him to the hearing against De Spain and finally make him an accomplice in the burning of De
Spain's barn.

The moral import of Ab's insistence on blood loyalty is fully developed by the satanic imagery Faulkner introduces in the scene at the mansion. As they go up the drive, Sarty follows his father, seeing the stiff black form against the white plantation house. Traditionally the devil casts no shadow, and Ab's figure appears to the child as having "that impervious quality of something cut ruthlessly from tin, depthless, as though sidewise to the sun it would cast no shadow." The cloven hoof of the devil is suggested by Ab's limp upon which the boy's eyes are fixed as the foot unwaveringly comes down into the manure. Sarty's increasing tension resounds in the magnified echo of the limping foot on the porch boards, "a sound out of all proportion to the displacement of the body it bore, as though it had attained to a sort of vicious and ravening minimum not to be dwarfed by anything." At first Sarty thought the house was impervious to his father, but his burgeoning fear of the threat the father poses is reflected in his vision of Ab becoming magnified and monstrous as the black arm reaches up the white door and Sarty sees "the lifted hand like a curled claw."

The satanic images are projected out of the son's nightmarish vision of his father, but they are reinforced by the comments of the adult narrator. Sarty believes Snopes fought bravely in the Civil War, but Ab, we are told, wore no uniform, gave his fealty to no cause, admitted the authority of no man. He went to war for booty. Ab's ego is so great it creates a centripetal force into which everything must flow or be destroyed. The will-less, abject creature who is his wife symbolizes the power of his will. What Ab had done to his wife, he sets out to do to the emerging will of his son. Ab cannot tolerate any entity that challenges the dominance of his will. By allowing his hog to forage in the farmer's corn and by dirtying and ruining De Spain's rug, he deliberately creates a conflict that requires the assertion of primacy. Fire, the element of the devil, is the weapon for the preservation of his dominance. Ab's rage is not fired by social injustice. It is fired by a pride, like Lucifer's, so absolute it can accept no order beyond its own. In the satanic myth, Lucifer asserts his will against the divine order and is cast out of heaven. The angels who fall with Lucifer become extensions of his will. In the same way, Ab is an outcast and pariah among men. He accepts no order that is not of his blood.

From "'Barn Burning': A Definition of Evil"

SOCIOLOGICAL CRITICISM

Sociological criticism examines literature in the cultural, economic, and political context in which it is written or received. "Art is not created in a vacuum," critic Wilbur Scott observed, "it is the work not simply of a person, but of an author fixed in time and space, answering a community of which he is an important, because articulate part." Sociological criticism explores the relationships between the artist and society. Sometimes it looks at the sociological status of the author to evaluate how the profession of the writer in a particular milieu affected what was written. Sociological criticism also analyzes the social content of literary works—what cultural, economic, or political values a particular text implicitly or explicitly promotes. Finally, sociological criticism examines the role the audience has in shaping literature. A sociological view of Shakespeare, for example, might look at the economic position of Elizabethan playwrights and actors; it might also study the political ideas expressed in the plays or discuss how the nature of an Elizabethan theatrical audience (which was usually all male unless the play was produced at court) helped determine the subject, tone, and language of the plays.

An influential type of sociological criticism has been Marxist criticism, which focuses on the economic and political elements of art. Marxist criticism, as in the work of the Hungarian philosopher Georg Lukacs, often explores the ideological content of literature. Whereas a formalist critic would maintain that form and content are inextricably blended, Lukacs believed that content determines form and that, therefore, all art is political. Even if a work of art ignores political issues, it makes a political statement, Marxist critics believe, because it endorses the economic and political status quo. Consequently, Marxist criticism is frequently evaluative and judges some literary work better than others on an ideological basis; this tendency can lead to reductive judgment, as when Soviet critics rated Jack London a novelist superior to William Faulkner, Ernest Hemingway, Edith Wharton, and Henry James, because he illustrated the principles of class struggle more clearly. London was America's first major working-class writer. To examine the political ideas and observations found in his fiction can be illuminating, but to fault other authors for lacking his instincts and ideas is not necessarily helpful in understanding their particular qualities. There is always a danger in sociological criticism—Marxist or otherwise—of imposing the critic's personal politics on the work in question and then evaluating it according to how closely it endorses that ideology. As an analytical tool, however, Marxist criticism and sociological methods can illuminate political and economic dimensions of literature that other approaches overlook.

Georg Lukacs (1885–1971)

Content Determines Form   1962

What determines the style of a given work of art? How does the intention determine the form? (We are concerned here, of course, with the intention realized in the work; it need not coincide with the writer's conscious intention.) The distinctions that concern us are not those between stylistic "techniques" in the formalistic sense. It is the view of the world, the ideology or *Weltanschauung*° underlying a writer's work, that counts. And it is the writer's attempt to reproduce this view of the world which constitutes his "intention" and is the formative principle underlying the style of a given piece of writing. Looked at in this way, style ceases to be a formalistic category. Rather, it is rooted in content; it is the specific form of a specific content.

Content determines form. But there is no content of which Man himself is not the focal point. However various the *données*° of literature (a particular experience, a didactic purpose), the basic question is, and will remain: what is Man?

Here is a point of division: if we put the question in abstract, philosophical terms, leaving aside all formal considerations, we arrive—for the realist school— at the traditional Aristotelian dictum (which was also reached by other than purely aesthetic considerations): Man is *zoon politikon*,° a social animal. The Aristotelian dictum is applicable to all great realistic literature. Achilles and Werther, Oedipus and Tom Jones, Antigone and Anna Karenina: their individual existence—their *Sein an sich*,° in the Hegelian terminology; their "ontological being," as a more fashionable

---

Weltanschauung: German for "world view," an outlook on life.   *données* French for "given"; it means the materials a writer uses to create his or her work or the subject or purpose of a literary work. *zoon politikon*: Greek for "political animal."   *Sein an sich*: the German philosopher G. W. F. Hegel's term for "pure existence."

terminology has it—cannot be distinguished from their social and historical environment. Their human significance, their specific individuality cannot be separated from the context in which they were created.

From Realism in Our Time

Daniel P. Watkins (b. 1952)

Money and Labor in "The Rocking-Horse Winner" 1987

It is a commonplace that D. H. Lawrence's "The Rocking-Horse Winner" is a story about the devastating effect that money can have on a family, and, further, that Lawrence's specific objections in the story are not to money abstractly conceived but to money as it is understood and valued by capitalist culture. This is one of Lawrence's most savage and compact critiques of what he elsewhere calls "the god-damn bourgeoisie" and of individuals who, despite their natural or potential goodness, "swallow the culture bait" and hence become victims to the world they (wrongly) believe holds the key to human happiness.

• • •

The class nature of labor under capital is presented symbolically in the story in terms of the adult and non-adult worlds. That is, social reality is controlled by parents whose primary concern is to bring in money sufficient to "the social position which they (have) to keep up." While they have a small income, and while "The father went in to town to some office," they never are really seen to work actively and productively. Rather, they set a tone of need in their world that generates intense and pervasive anxiety, which then is passed down to their children, who interiorize the values and attitudes of the adult world and set about (as best they can) to satisfy the demands of that world. Even when money is produced, however, the demands of the adult world are never fully met, but, quite the reverse, intensify further, so that more labor is necessary. In this context, work is not a means of meeting basic human needs, but rather only a way of producing greater sums of money, and thus it is clearly socially unproductive. Seen from this perspective, it is not important that the parents are not capitalists in the crudest sense (that is, they are not drawn as investors of money); what is important is that they both set the tone (economic scarcity) and determine the values (consumerism) of the world they inhabit, and in addition expropriate the wealth that others produce for their own private consumption.

Young Paul exemplifies vividly the sort of work that arises under capital. Simply put, he is a laborer for his mother, to whom he gives all of his money, only to find that the more he gives the more she needs. It is true, of course, that as a handicapper he invests money, betting on a profitable return on his investment, and that in this sense he is a sort of capitalist; indeed, it is his betting that is the literal sign of the economic relations controlling the world of the story. But at the same time his character is made to carry a much larger symbolic significance, for what he is investing, in real terms, is himself, selling his skills to generate wealth that he is not free to possess, but that is necessary to the maintenance of existing social relations. As his mother touches the money he earns, she uses it not to satisfy family needs—it has little or no *use* value—but to extend her social position and social power, and the process of extension of course is never-ending, requiring ever greater sums of money: "There were certain new furnishings, and Paul had a tutor. He was *really* going to Eton, his father's school, in the following autumn. There were flowers in the winter, and a blossoming of the luxury Paul's mother had been used to. And yet the voices in the house, behind the sprays of mimosa and almond-blossom, and from under the piles of iridescent cushions, simply trilled and screamed in a sort of ecstasy: 'There *must* be more money!'" This passage clearly focuses the priority of money over commodity and the relentlessness with which the power associated with money controls even the most personal dimension of life.

The work itself that Paul performs cannot, under such conditions, be personally satisfying, and this is shown powerfully by the sort of work he does. The rocking horse is a brilliant symbol of non-productive labor, for even while it moves it remains stationary: even while Paul is magically (humanly) creative, producing untold wealth for his mother, he does not advance in the least, and in fact becomes increasingly isolated and fearful that even the abilities he now possesses will be taken from him. The labor, which drives him to "a sort of madness," that consumes him to an ever greater degree, leaves him nothing for himself, driving him down a terrible path to emotional and then physical distress. He is never satisfied with what he produces because it in no way relieves the pressure that his world places on him, and thus his anxiety and alienation grow to the point of destroying any sense of real personal worth and removing him literally from all meaningful social exchange, as when he takes his rocking horse to his bedroom and rides alone late into the night trying to find the key to wealth.

From "Labor and Religion in D. H. Lawrence's
'The Rocking-Horse Winner'"

GENDER CRITICISM

Gender criticism examines how sexual identity influences the creation and reception of literary works. Gender studies began with the feminist movement and was influenced by such works as Simone de Beauvoir's *The Second Sex* (1949) and Kate Millett's *Sexual Politics* (1970) as well as sociology, psychology, and anthropology. Feminist critics believe that culture has been so completely dominated by men that literature is full of unexamined "male-produced" assumptions. They see their criticism correcting this imbalance by analyzing and combating patriarchal attitudes. Feminist criticism has explored how an author's gender influences—consciously or unconsciously—his or her writing. While a formalist critic such as Allen Tate emphasized the universality of Emily Dickinson's poetry by demonstrating how powerfully the language, imagery, and mythmaking of her poems combine to affect a generalized reader, Sandra M. Gilbert, a leading feminist critic, has identified attitudes and assumptions in Dickinson's poetry that she believes are essentially female. Another important theme in feminist criticism is analyzing how sexual identity influences the reader of a text. If Tate's hypothetical reader was deliberately sexless, Gilbert's reader sees a text through the eyes of his or her sex. Finally, feminist critics carefully examine how the images of men and women in imaginative literature reflect or reject the social forces that have historically kept the sexes from achieving total equality.

Recently, gender criticism has expanded beyond its original feminist perspective. In the last twenty years or so, critics in the field of gay and lesbian studies—some of whom describe their discipline as "queer theory"—have explored the impact of different sexual orientations on literary creation and reception. Seeking to establish a canon of classic gay and lesbian authors, these critics argue that sexual orientation is so central a component of human personality (especially when it necessarily puts one at odds with established social and moral norms) that to ignore it in connection with such writers amounts to a fundamental misreading and misunderstanding of their work. A men's movement has also emerged in response to feminism, seeking not to reject feminism but to rediscover masculine identity in an authentic, contemporary way. Led by poet Robert Bly, the men's movement has paid special attention to interpreting poetry and fables as myths of psychic growth and sexual identity.

Elaine Showalter (b. 1941)

Toward a Feminist Criticism   1979

Feminist criticism can be divided into two distinct varieties. The first type is concerned with *woman as reader*—with woman as the consumer of male-produced literature, and with the way in which the hypothesis of a female reader changes our apprehension of a given text, awakening us to the significance of its sexual codes. I shall call this kind of analysis the *feminist critique*, and like other kinds of critique it is a historically grounded inquiry which probes the ideological assumptions of literary phenomena. Its subjects include the images and stereotypes of women in literature, the omissions of and misconceptions about women in criticism, and the fissures in male-constructed literary history. It is also concerned with the exploitation and manipulation of the female audience, especially in popular culture and film; and with the analysis of woman-as-sign in semiotic systems. The second type of feminist criticism is concerned with *woman as writer*—with woman as the producer of textual meaning, with the history, themes, genres, and structures of literature by women. Its subjects include the psychodynamics of female creativity; linguistics and the problem of a female language; the trajectory of the individual or collective female literary career; literary history; and, of course, studies of particular writers and works. No term exists in English for such a specialized discourse, and so I have adapted the French term *la gynocritique*: "gynocritics" (although the significance of the male pseudonym in the history of women's writing also suggested the term "georgics").

The feminist critique is essentially political and polemical, with theoretical affiliations to Marxist sociology and aesthetics; gynocritics is more self-contained and experimental, with connections to other modes of new feminist research. In a dialogue between these two positions, Carolyn Heilbrun, the writer, and Catharine Stimpson, editor of the journal *Signs: Women in Culture and Society*, compare the feminist critique to the Old Testament, "looking for the sins and errors of the past," and gynocritics to the New Testament, seeking "the grace of imagination." Both kinds are necessary, they explain, for only the Jeremiahs of the feminist critique can lead us out of the "Egypt of female servitude" to the promised land of the feminist vision. That the discussion makes use of these Biblical metaphors points to the connections between feminist consciousness and conversion narratives which often appear in women's literature; Carolyn Heilbrun comments on her own text, "When I talk about feminist criticism, I am amazed at how high a moral tone I take."

From "Toward a Feminist Poetics"

Nina Pelikan Straus

Transformations in *The Metamorphosis* 1989

Traditionally, critics of *Metamorphosis* have underplayed the fact that the story is about not only Gregor's but also his family's and, especially, Grete's metamorphosis. Yet it is mainly Grete, woman, daughter, sister, on whom the social and psychoanalytic resonances of the text depend. It is she who will ironically "blossom" as her brother deteriorates; it is she whose mirror reflects women's present situations as we attempt to critique patriarchal dominance in order to create new lives that avoid the replication of invalidation. . . .

If Grete is a symbol of anything, it is the irony of self-liberation in relation to the indeterminacy of gender roles. Grete's role as a woman unfolds as Gregor's life as a man collapses. It is no accident that this gender scrolling takes place in the literature of a writer who had curious experiences in his life with women—experiences of his own weakness and of women's strengths. Traditionally, the text has been read not as revealing brother-sister or gender-based relationships, however, but as revealing a father-son conflict or Oedipus complex.

• • •

The word "shame" is central to both Grete and Gregor's experiences. It is a shame that Gregor cannot get out of bed, that he cannot get up to go to work, that his voice fails him, that he cannot open the door of his room with his insect pincers, that he must be fed, that he stinks and must hide his body that is a shame to others. Shame comes from seeing oneself through another's eyes, from Gregor's seeing himself through Grete's eyes, and from the reader's seeing Grete through the narrator's eyes. The text graphically mirrors how we see each other in various shameful (and comic) conditions. Through Gregor's condition, ultimately shameful because he is reduced to the dependency of an ugly baby, Kafka imagines what it is like to be dependent on the care of women. And Kafka is impressed with women's efforts to keep their households and bodies clean and alive. This impression is enlarged with every detail that humiliates and weakens Gregor while simultaneously empowering Grete, who cares for Gregor, ironically, at his own—and perhaps at Kafka's—expense.

The change or metamorphosis is in this sense a literary experiment that plays with problems the story's title barely suggests. For Kafka there can be no change without an exchange, no flourishing of Grete without Gregor's withering; nor can the meaning of transformation entail a final closure that prevents further transformations. The metamorphosis occurs both in the first sentence of the text—"When Gregor Samsa awoke one morning from unsettling dreams, he found himself changed in his bed into a monstrous vermin"—and in the last paragraph of the story, which describes Grete's transformation into a woman "blossoming" and "stretching" toward the family's "new dreams" once Gregor has been transformed into garbage. Grete's final transformation, rendered in concrete bodily terms, is foreshadowed in Gregor's initial transformation from human into vermin. This deliberately reflective textual pattern implies that only when the distorting mirrors of the sexist fun house are dismantled can the sons of the patriarchs recognize themselves as dehumanized and dehumanizing. Only when Grete blooms into an eligible young woman, ripe for the job and marriage markets, can we recognize that her empowerment is also an ironic reification. She has been transformed at another's expense, and she will carry within her the marketplace value that has ultimately destroyed Gregor.

From "Transforming Franz Kafka's *Metamorphosis*"

READER-RESPONSE CRITICISM

Reader-response criticism attempts to describe what happens in the reader's mind while interpreting a text. If traditional criticism assumes that imaginative writing is a creative act, reader-response theory recognizes that reading is also a creative process. Reader-response critics believe that no text provides self-contained meaning; literary texts do not exist independently of readers' interpretations. A text, according to this critical school, is not finished until it is read and interpreted. As Oscar Wilde remarked in the preface to his novel *The Picture of Dorian Gray* (1891), "It is the spectator, and not life, that art really mirrors." The practical problem then arises, however, that no two individuals necessarily read a text in exactly the same way. Rather than declare one interpretation correct and the other mistaken, reader-response criticism recognizes the inevitable plurality of readings. Instead of trying to ignore or reconcile the contradictions inherent in this situation, it explores them.

The easiest way to explain reader-response criticism is to relate it to the common experience of rereading a favorite book after many years. Rereading a novel as an adult, for example, that "changed your life" as an adolescent, is often a shocking experience. The book may seem substantially different. The character you remembered liking most now seems less admirable, and another character you disliked now seems more sympathetic. Has the book changed? Very unlikely, but *you* certainly have in the intervening years. Reader-response criticism explores how different individuals (or classes of individuals) see the same text differently. It emphasizes how religious, cultural, and social values affect readings; it also overlaps with gender criticism in exploring how men and women read the same text with different assumptions.

While reader-response criticism rejects the notion that there can be a single correct reading for a literary text, it doesn't consider all readings permissible. Each text creates limits to its possible interpretations. As Stanley Fish admits in the following critical selection, we cannot arbitrarily place an Eskimo in William Faulkner's story "A Rose for Emily" (though Professor Fish does ingeniously imagine a hypothetical situation where this bizarre interpretation might actually be possible).

Stanley Fish (b. 1938)

An Eskimo "A Rose for Emily"   1980

The fact that it remains easy to think of a reading that most of us would dismiss out of hand does not mean that the text excludes it but that there is as yet no elaborated interpretive procedure for producing that text. . . . Norman Holland's analysis of Faulkner's "A Rose for Emily" is a case in point. Holland is arguing for a kind of psychoanalytic pluralism. The text, he declares, is "at most a matrix of psychological possibilities for its readers," but, he insists, "only some possibilities . . . truly fit the matrix": "One would not say, for example, that a reader of . . . 'A Rose for Emily' who thought the 'tableau' [of Emily and her father in the doorway] described an Eskimo was really responding to the story at all—only pursuing some mysterious inner exploration."

Holland is making two arguments: first, that anyone who proposes an Eskimo reading of "A Rose for Emily" will not find a hearing in the literary community. And that, I think, is right. ("We are right to rule out at least some readings.") His second argument is that the unacceptability of the Eskimo reading is a function of the text, of what he calls its "sharable promptuary," the public "store of structured language" that sets limits to the interpretations the words can accommodate. And that, I think, is wrong. The Eskimo reading is unacceptable because there is at present no interpretive strategy for producing it, no way of "looking" or reading (and remember, all acts of looking or reading are "ways") that would result in the emergence of obviously Eskimo meanings. This does not mean, however, that no such strategy could ever come into play, and it is not difficult to imagine the circumstances under which it would establish itself. One such circumstance would be the discovery of a letter in which Faulkner confides that he has always believed himself to be an Eskimo changeling. (The example is absurd only if one forgets Yeats's *Vision* or Blake's Swedenborgianism° or James Miller's recent elaboration of a homosexual reading of *The Waste Land*.) Immediately the workers in the Faulkner industry would begin to reinterpret the canon in the light of this newly revealed "belief" and the work of reinterpretation would involve the elaboration of a symbolic or allusive system (not unlike mythological or typological criticism) whose application would immediately transform the text into one informed everywhere by Eskimo meanings. It might seem that I am admitting that there is a text to be transformed, but the object of transformation would be the text (or texts) given by whatever interpretive strategies the Eskimo strategy was in the process of dislodging or expanding. The result would be that whereas we now have a Freudian "A Rose for Emily," a mythological "A Rose for Emily," a Christological "A Rose for Emily," a regional "A Rose for Emily," a sociological "A Rose for Emily," a linguistic "A Rose for Emily," we would in addition have an Eskimo "A Rose for Emily," existing in some relation of compatibility or incompatibility with the others.

Again the point is that while there are always mechanisms for ruling out readings, their source is not the text but the presently recognized interpretive strategies for producing the text. It follows, then, that no reading, however outlandish it might appear, is inherently an impossible one.

From *Is There a Text in This Class?*

Michael J. Colacurcio (b. 1936)

The End of Young Goodman Brown   1995

Having begun by assuming that all visible sanctity was real sanctity and by presuming his own final perseverance in faith, having next despaired of *all* virtue, he [Goodman Brown] ends by doubting the existence of any unblighted goodness but his own. There is simply no other way to account for the way Goodman Brown spends the rest of his life. Evidently he clings to the precious knowledge that he, at least, resisted the wicked one's final invitation to diabolical communion; accordingly, the lurid satisfactions of Satan's anti-covenant are not available to him. But neither are the sweet delights of the Communion of the Saints. He knows he resisted the "last, last crime" of witchcraft, but his deepest suspicion seems to be that Faith did not resist. Or if that seems too strong a formulation for tender-minded readers, he cannot make his faith in Faith prevail. Without such a prevailing faith, he is left outside the bounds of all communion: his own unbartered soul is the only certain locus of goodness in a world otherwise altogether blasted.

Yeats's Vision *or Blake's Swedenborgianism:* Irish poet William Butler Yeats and Swedish mystical writer Emanuel Swedenborg both claimed to have received revelations from the spirit world; some of Swedenborg's ideas are embodied in the long poems of William Blake.

It would be easy enough to praise Young Goodman Brown for his recovery from the blasphemous nihilism of his mid-forest rage against the universe; for his refusal to translate his cosmic paranoia into an Ahabian plan of counterattack. Or, from another point of view, it would even be possible to suggest that if the Devil's proffered community of evil is the only community possible, perhaps he should have accepted membership instead of protecting the insular sacredness of his own separate and too precious soul. Perhaps salvation is not worth having—perhaps it is meaningless—in a universe where depravity has undone so many. But both of these moral prescriptions miss Hawthorne's principal emphasis, which, as I read the tale, is on the problem of faith and evidence; on that peculiar kind of "doubt" (in epistemological essence, really a kind of negative faith) which follows from a discrediting of evidences formerly trusted. Brown is damned to stony moral isolation because his "evidential" Puritan biases have led him all unprepared into a terrifying betrayal of Faith. He believes the Devil's spectral suggestions not merely because he is naive, though he is that; and not merely because he is incapable of the sort of evidential subtlety by which John Cotton instructed the very first members of those newly purified New England churches in the art of separating sheep and goats, or by which the Mathers sermonized the court of Oyer and Terminer on the occult art of the distinguishing of spirits. Brown believes the Devil because, at one level, the projected guilt of a man in bad faith *is* specter evidence and because, even more fundamentally, absolute moral quality is related to outward appearance as a real person is to his specter.

In short, Hawthorne suggests, one had better not raise such ultimate questions at all: to do so is to risk the appearance-and-reality question in its most pernicious, even "paranoic" form. At best one would be accepting the deceptive appearances of sanctity, as Goodman Brown evidently continued to be accepted at the communion table of a community which never suspected his presumption, despair, blasphemy, and his near approach to witchcraft. . . . And at worst, if one is already in bad faith, his penetrating glimpses into the "reality" behind the appearances will be no more than spectral projections of his own guilty wishes. . . . The truly naive will simply accept the smiling light of daytime, church-day appearances; the already compromised will "see" in others (as irrevocable commitment) what already pre-exists in themselves (as fantasy, wish, desire, or momentary intention). The only alternative would seem to be the acceptance of some ultimate and fundamental equality in a common moral struggle; a healthy skepticism about all moral appearances, firmly wedded to the faith that, whatever men may fantasize, or however they may fall, they generally love the good and hate the evil.

From *The Province of Piety: Moral History in Hawthorne's Early Tales*

DECONSTRUCTIONIST CRITICISM

Deconstructionist criticism rejects the traditional assumption that language can accurately represent reality. Language, according to deconstructionists, is a fundamentally unstable medium; consequently, literary texts, which are made up of words, have no fixed, single meaning. Deconstructionists insist, according to critic Paul de Man, on "the impossibility of making the actual expression coincide with what has to be expressed, of making the actual signs coincide with what is signified." Since they believe that literature cannot definitively express its subject matter, deconstructionists tend to shift their attention away from *what* is being said to *how* language is being used in a text.

Paradoxically, deconstructionist criticism often resembles formalist criticism; both methods usually involve close reading. But while a formalist usually tries to demonstrate how the diverse elements of a text cohere into meaning, the deconstructionist approach attempts to show how the text "deconstructs," that is, how it can be broken down—by a skeptical critic—into mutually irreconcilable positions. A biographical or historical critic might seek to establish the author's intention as a means to interpreting a literary work, but deconstructionists reject the notion that the critic should endorse the myth of authorial control over language. Deconstructionist critics like Roland Barthes and Michel Foucault have therefore called for "the death of the author," that is, the rejection of the assumption that the author, no matter how ingenious, can fully control the meaning of a text. They have also announced the death of literature as a special category of writing. In their view, poems and novels are merely words on a page that deserve no privileged status as art; all texts are created equal—equally untrustworthy, that is.

Deconstructionists focus on how language is used to achieve power. Since they believe, in the words of critic David Lehman, that "there are no truths, only rival interpretations," deconstructionists try to understand how some "interpretations" come to be regarded as truth. A major goal of deconstruction is to demonstrate how those supposed truths are at best provisional and at worst contradictory.

Deconstruction, as you may have inferred, calls for intellectual subtlety and skill. If you pursue your literary studies beyond the introductory stage, you will want to become more familiar with its assumptions. Deconstruction may strike you as a negative, even destructive, critical approach, and yet its best practitioners are adept at exposing the inadequacy of much conventional criticism. By patient analysis, they can sometimes open up the most familiar text and find unexpected significance.

Roland Barthes (1915–1980)

The Death of the Author 1968

Translated by Stephen Heath

Succeeding the Author, the scriptor no longer bears within him passions, humours, feelings, impressions, but rather this immense dictionary from which he draws a writing that can know no halt: life never does more than imitate the book, and the book itself is only a tissue of signs, an imitation that is lost, infinitely deferred.

Once the Author is removed, the claim to decipher a text becomes quite futile. To give a text an Author is to impose a limit on that text, to furnish it with a final signified, to close the writing. Such a conception suits criticism very well, the latter then allotting itself the important task of discovering the Author (or its hypostases: society, history, psyché, liberty) beneath the work: when the Author has been found, the text is "explained"—victory to the critic. Hence there is no surprise in the fact that, historically, the reign of the Author has also been that of the Critic, nor again in the fact that criticism (be it new) is today undermined along with the Author. In the multiplicity of writing, everything is to be *disentangled*, nothing *deciphered*; the structure can be followed, "run" (like the thread of a stocking) at every point and at every level, but there is nothing beneath: the space of writing is to be ranged over, not pierced; writing ceaselessly posits meaning ceaselessly to evaporate it, carrying out a systematic exemption of meaning. In precisely this way literature (it would be better from now on to say *writing*), by refusing to assign a "secret," an ultimate meaning, to the text (and to the world as text), liberates what may be called an anti-theological activity, an activity that is truly revolutionary since to refuse to fix meaning is, in the end, to refuse God and his hypostases—reason, science, law.

From "The Death of the Author"

Barbara Johnson (b. 1947)

Rigorous Unreliability 1987

As a critique of a certain Western conception of the nature of signification, deconstruction focuses on the functioning of claim-making and claim-subverting structures within texts. A deconstructive reading is an attempt to show how the conspicuously foregrounded statements in a text are systematically related to discordant signifying elements that the text has thrown into its shadows or margins, an attempt both to recover what is lost and to analyze what happens when a text is read solely in function of intentionality, meaningfulness, and representativity. Deconstruction thus confers a new kind of readability on those elements in a text that readers have traditionally been trained to disregard, overcome, explain away, or edit out—contradictions, obscurities, ambiguities, incoherences, discontinuities, ellipses, interruptions, repetitions, and plays of the signifier. In this sense it involves a reversal of values, a revaluation of the signifying function of everything that, in a signified-based theory of meaning, would constitute "noise." Derrida° has chosen to speak of the values involved in this reversal in terms of "speech" and "writing," in which "speech" stands for the privilege accorded to meaning as immediacy, unity, identity, truth, and presence, while "writing" stands for the devalued functions of distance, difference, dissimulation, and deferment.

This transvaluation has a number of consequences for the appreciation of literature. By shifting the attention from intentional meaning to writing as such, deconstruction has enabled readers to become sensitive to a number of recurrent literary topoi° in a new way.

• • •

In addition, by seeing interpretation itself as a fiction-making activity, deconstruction has both reversed and displaced the narrative categories of "showing" and "telling," mimesis and diegesis.° Instead of according moments of textual self-interpretation an authoritative metalinguistic status, deconstruction considers anything the text says about itself to be another fiction, an allegory of the reading process. Hence, the privilege traditionally granted to showing over telling is reversed: "telling" becomes a more sophisticated form of "showing," in which what is "shown" is the breakdown of the show/tell distinction. Far from doing the reader's work for her, the text's self-commentary only gives the reader more to do. Indeed, it is the way in which a text subverts the possibility of any authoritative reading by inscribing the reader's strategies into its own structures that often, for de Man, ends up being constitutive of literature as such.

Deconstructors, therefore, tend to privilege texts that are self-reflexive in interestingly and rigorously unreliable ways. Since self-reflexive texts often explicitly posit themselves as belated or revolutionary with respect to a tradition on which they comment, deconstruction can both reinstate the self-consciously outmoded or overwritten (such as Melville's *Pierre*°) and canonize the experimental or avant-garde. But because deconstruction has focused on the ways in which the Western white male philosophico-literary tradition subverts itself *from within*, it has often tended to remain within the confines of the established literary and philosophical canon. . . . If

---

Derrida: Jacques Derrida (1930–2004), French philosopher active in the development of deconstructionism.   *topoi:* the plural of the Greek *topos,* for "place"; it means a commonly used literary device.   *diegesis:* the main events of a story, the basic plot, as distinct from the narration. *Pierre: Pierre, or the Ambiguities* (1852), a complex novel by Herman Melville, was a failure during the author's lifetime; it was not widely read until the mid-twentieth century.

it has questioned the boundary lines of literature, it has done so not with respect to the noncanonical but with respect to the line between literature and philosophy or between literature and criticism. It is as a rethinking of those distinctions that deconstruction most radically displaces certain traditional evaluative assumptions.

From A *World of Difference*

CULTURAL STUDIES

Unlike the other critical approaches discussed in this chapter, cultural criticism (or **cultural studies**) does not offer a single way of analyzing literature. No central methodology is associated with cultural studies. Nor is cultural criticism solely, or even mainly, concerned with literary texts in the conventional sense. Instead, the term *cultural studies* refers to a relatively recent interdisciplinary field of academic inquiry. This field borrows methodologies from other approaches to analyze a wide range of cultural products and practices.

To understand cultural studies, it helps to know a bit about its origins. In the English-speaking world, the field was first defined at the Centre for Contemporary Cultural Studies of Birmingham University in Britain. Founded in 1964, this graduate program tried to expand the range of literary study beyond traditional approaches to canonic literature in order to explore a broader spectrum of historical, cultural, and political issues. The most influential teacher at the Birmingham Centre was Raymond Williams (1921–1983), a Welsh socialist with wide intellectual interests. Williams argued that scholars should not study culture as a canon of great works by individual artists but rather examine it as an evolutionary process that involves the entire society. "We cannot separate literature and art," Williams said, "from other kinds of social practice." The cultural critic, therefore, does not study fixed aesthetic objects so much as dynamic social processes. The critic's challenge is to identify and understand the complex forms and effects of the process of culture.

A Marxist intellectual, Williams called his approach cultural materialism (a reference to the Marxist doctrine of dialectical materialism), but later scholars soon discarded that name for two broader and more neutral terms, cultural criticism and cultural studies. From the start, this interdisciplinary field relied heavily on literary theory, especially Marxist and feminist criticism. It also employed the documentary techniques of historical criticism combined with political analysis focused on issues of social class, race, and gender. (This approach flourished in the United States, where it is called New Historicism.) Cultural studies is also deeply antiformalist, since the field concerns itself with investigating the complex relationships among history, politics, and literature. Cultural studies rejects the notion that literature exists in an aesthetic realm separate from ethical and political categories.

A chief goal of cultural studies is to understand the nature of social power as reflected in "texts." For example, if the object of analysis were a sonnet by Shakespeare, the cultural studies adherent might investigate the moral, psychological, and political assumptions reflected in the poem and then deconstruct them to see what individuals, social classes, or gender might benefit from having those assumptions perceived as true. The relevant mission of cultural studies is to identify both the overt and covert values reflected in a cultural practice. The cultural studies critic also tries to trace out and understand the structures of meaning that hold those assumptions in place and give them the appearance of objective representation. Any analytical technique that helps illuminate these issues is employed.

In theory, a cultural studies critic might employ any methodology. In practice, however, he or she will most often borrow concepts from deconstruction, Marxist analysis, gender criticism, race theory, and psychology. Each of these earlier methodologies provides particular analytical tools that cultural critics find useful. What cultural studies borrows from deconstructionism is its emphasis on uncovering conflict, dissent, and contradiction in the works under analysis. Whereas traditional critical approaches often sought to demonstrate the unity of a literary work, cultural studies often seeks to portray social, political, and psychological conflicts that the work masks. What cultural studies borrows from Marxist analysis is an attention to the ongoing struggle between social classes, each seeking economic (and therefore political) advantage. Cultural studies often asks questions about what social class created a work of art and what class (or classes) served as its audience. Among the many things that cultural studies borrowed from gender criticism and race theory is a concern with social inequality between the sexes and races. It seeks to investigate how these inequities have been reflected in the texts of a historical period or a society. Cultural studies is, above all, a political enterprise that views literary analysis as a means of furthering social justice.

Since cultural studies does not adhere to any single methodology (or even a consistent set of methodologies), it is impossible to characterize the field briefly, because there are exceptions to every generalization offered. What one sees most clearly are characteristic tendencies, especially the commitment to examining issues of class, race, and gender. There is also the insistence on expanding the focus of critical inquiry beyond traditional high literary culture. British cultural studies guru Anthony Easthope can, for example, analyze with equal aplomb Gerard Manley Hopkins's "The Windhover," Edgar Rice Burroughs' *Tarzan of the Apes*, a Benson and Hedges cigarette advertisement, and Sean Connery's eyebrows. Cultural studies is infamous—even among its practitioners—for its habitual use of literary jargon. It is also notorious for its complex intellectual analysis of mundane materials, such as Easthope's analysis of a cigarette ad, which may be interesting in its own right but remote from most readers' literary experience. Some scholars, however, use the principles of cultural studies to provide new social, political, and historical insights into canonic texts. Omnivorous, iconoclastic, and relentlessly analytic, cultural criticism has become a major presence in contemporary literary studies.

Vincent B. Leitch (b. 1944)

Poststructuralist Cultural Critique   1992

Whereas a major goal of New Criticism and much other modern formalistic criticism is aesthetic evaluation of freestanding texts, a primary objective of cultural criticism is cultural critique, which entails investigation and assessment of ruling and oppositional beliefs, categories, practices, and representations, inquiring into the causes, constitutions, and consequences as well as the modes of circulation and consumption of linguistic, social, economic, political, historical, ethical, religious, legal, scientific, philosophical, educational, familial, and aesthetic discourses and institutions. In rendering a judgment on an aesthetic artifact, a New Critic privileges such key things as textual coherence and unity, intricacy and complexity, ambiguity and irony, tension and balance, economy and autonomy, literariness and spatial form. In mounting a critique of a cultural "text," an advocate of poststructuralist cultural criticism evaluates such things as degrees of exclusion and inclusion, of complicity and resistance, of domination and letting-be, of abstraction and situatedness, of violence and tolerance, of monologue and polylogue, of quietism and activism, of sameness and otherness, of oppression and emancipation, of centralization and decentralization. Just as the aforementioned system of evaluative criteria underlies the exegetical and judgmental labor of New Criticism, so too does the above named set of commitments undergird the work of poststructuralist cultural critique.

Given its commitments, poststructuralist cultural criticism is, as I have suggested, suspicious of literary formalism. Specifically, the trouble with New Criticism is its inclination to advocate a combination of quietism and asceticism, connoisseurship and exclusiveness, aestheticism and apoliticism. . . . The monotonous practical effect of New Critical reading is to illustrate the subservience of each textual element to a higher, overarching, economical poetic structure without remainders. What should be evident here is that the project of poststructuralist cultural criticism possesses a set of commitments and criteria that enable it to engage in the enterprise of cultural critique. It should also be evident that the cultural ethicopolitics of this enterprise is best characterized, using current terminology, as "liberal" or "leftist," meaning congruent with certain socialist, anarchist, and libertarian ideals, none of which, incidentally, are necessarily Marxian. Such congruence, derived from extrapolating a generalized stance for poststructuralism, constitutes neither a party platform nor an observable course of practical action; avowed tendencies often account for little in the unfolding of practical engagements.

From *Cultural Criticism, Literary Theory, Poststructuralism*

Mark Bauerlein (b. 1959)

What Is Cultural Studies? 1997

Traditionally, disciplines naturally fell into acknowledged subdivisions, for example, as literary criticism broke up into formalist literary criticism, philological criticism, narratological analysis, and other methodologically distinguished pursuits, all of which remained comfortably within the category "literary criticism." But cultural studies eschews such institutional disjunctions and will not let any straitening adjective precede the "cultural studies" heading. There is no distinct formalist cultural studies or historicist cultural studies, but only cultural studies. (Feminist cultural studies may be one exception.) Cultural studies is a field that will not be parceled out to the available disciplines. It spans culture at large, not this or that institutionally separated element of culture. To guarantee this transcendence of disciplinary institutions, cultural studies must select a name for itself that has no specificity, that has too great an extension to mark off any expedient boundaries for itself. "Cultural studies" serves well because, apart from distinguishing between "physical science" and "cultural analysis," the term provides no indication of where any other boundaries lie.

This is exactly the point. To blur disciplinary boundaries and frustrate the intellectual investments that go along with them is a fundamental motive for cultural studies practice, one that justifies the vagueness of the titular term. This explains why the related label "cultural criticism," so much in vogue in 1988, has declined. The term "criticism" has a narrower extension than does "studies," ruling out some empirical forms of inquiry (like field work) that "studies" admits. "Studies" preserves a methodological openness that "criticism" closes. Since such closures have suspect political intentions behind them, cultural studies maintains its institutional purity by disdaining disciplinary identity and methodological uniformity.

• • •

A single approach will miss too much, will overlook important aspects of culture not perceptible to that particular angle of vision. A multitude of approaches will pick up an insight here and a piece of knowledge there and more of culture will enter into the inquiry. A diversity of methods will match the diversity of culture, thereby sheltering the true nature of culture from the reductive appropriations of formal disciplines.

But how do cultural critics bring all these methods together into a coherent inquiry? Are there any established rules of incorporating "important insights and knowledge" coming out of different methods into a coherent scholarly project of cultural studies? How might a scholar use both phonemic analysis and deconstruction in a single inquiry when deconstructionist arguments call into question the basic premises of phonetics? What scholar has the competence to handle materials from so many disciplines in a rigorous and knowing manner? Does cultural criticism as a "studies" practice offer any transdisciplinary evaluative standards to apply to individual pieces of cultural criticism? If not, if there are no clear methodological procedures or evaluative principles in cultural studies, it is hard to see how one might popularize it, teach it, make it into a recognized scholarly activity. In practical terms, one does not know how to communicate it to others or show students how to do it when it assumes so many different methodological forms. How does one create an academic department out of an outspokenly antidisciplinary practice? What criteria can faculty members jointly invoke when they are trying to make curricular and personnel decisions?

Once again, this is precisely the point. One reason for the generality of the term is to render such institutional questions unanswerable. Cultural studies practice mingles methods from a variety of fields, jumps from one cultural subject matter to another, simultaneously proclaims superiority to other institutionalized inquiries (on a correspondence to culture basis) and renounces its own institutionalization—gestures that strategically forestall disciplinary standards being applied to it. By studying culture in heterogenous ways, by clumping texts, events, persons, objects, and ideologies into a cultural whole (which, cultural critics say, is reality) and bringing a melange of logical argument, speculative propositions, empirical data, and political outlooks to bear upon it, cultural critics invent a new kind of investigation immune to methodological attack.

From *Literary Criticism: An Autopsy*

▶ TERMS FOR *review*

Formalist criticism ▶ A school of criticism that focuses on the *form* of a literary work. A key method that formalists use is close reading, a step-by-step analysis of the elements in a text.

Biographical criticism ▶ The practice of analyzing a literary work by using knowledge of the author's life to gain insight. Although the work is understood as an independent creation, the *biography* of the author provides the practical assistance of underscoring subtle but important meanings.

Historical criticism ▶ The practice of analyzing a literary work by investigating the social, cultural, and intellectual context that produced it, including the author's biography and milieu.

Psychological criticism ▶ The application of the analytical tools of psychology and psychoanalysis to authors and/or fictional characters in order to understand the underlying motivations and meanings of a literary work.

Mythological criticism ▶ The practice of analyzing a literary work by looking for recurrent universal patterns. It explores the ways in which an individual imagination uses myths and symbols shared by different cultures and epochs.

Sociological criticism ▶ The practice of analyzing a literary work by examining the cultural, economic, and political context in which it was written or received. It primarily explores the relationship between the artist and society.

Gender criticism ▶ The examination of the ways in which sexual identity influences the creation, interpretation, and evaluation of literary works. Feminism, gay culture, and the men's movement all play key roles in gender criticism.

Reader-response criticism ▶ The practice of analyzing a literary work by describing what happens in the reader's mind while interpreting the text, on the assumption that no literary text exists independently of readers' interpretations and that there is no single fixed interpretation of any literary work.

Deconstructionist criticism ▶ A school of criticism that rejects the traditional assumption that language can accurately represent reality. Deconstructionists believe that literary texts can have no single meaning; therefore, they concentrate their attention on *how* language is being used in a text, rather than what is being said.

Cultural studies ▶ A contemporary interdisciplinary field of academic study that focuses on understanding the social power encoded in "texts"—which may include any analyzable phenomenon from a traditional poem to an advertising image or actor's face.

GLOSSARY OF LITERARY TERMS

Allegory A narrative in verse or prose in which the literal events (persons, places, and things) consistently point to a parallel sequence of symbolic ideas. This narrative strategy is often used to dramatize abstract ideas, historical events, religious systems, or political issues. An allegory has two levels of meaning: a literal level that tells a surface story and a symbolic level in which the abstract ideas unfold. The names of allegorical characters often hint at their symbolic roles. For example, in Nathaniel Hawthorne's "Young Goodman Brown," Faith is not only the name of the protagonist's wife but also a symbol of the protagonist's religious faith.

All-knowing narrator *See* **Omniscient narrator**.

Allusion A brief (and sometimes indirect) reference in a text to a person, place, or thing—fictitious or actual. An allusion may appear in a literary work as an initial quotation, a passing mention of a name, or a phrase borrowed from another writer—often carrying the meanings and implications of the original. Allusions imply a common set of knowledge between reader and writer and operate as a literary shorthand to enrich the meaning of a text.

Analysis The examination of a piece of literature as a means of understanding its subject or structure. An effective analysis often clarifies a work by focusing on a single element such as tone, irony, symbolism, imagery, or rhythm in a way that enhances the reader's understanding of the whole. *Analysis* comes from the Greek word meaning to "undo," to "loosen."

Anecdote A short narrative usually consisting of a single incident or episode. Often humorous, anecdotes can be real or fictional. When they appear within a larger narrative as a brief story told by one character to another, the author usually employs them to reveal something significant to the larger narrative.

Antagonist The most significant character or force that opposes the protagonist in a narrative or drama. The antagonist may be another character, society itself, a force of nature, or even—in modern literature—conflicting impulses within the protagonist.

Anticlimax An unsatisfying and trivial turn of events in a literary work that occurs in place of a genuine climax. An anticlimax often involves a surprising shift in tone from the lofty or serious into the petty or ridiculous. The term is often used negatively to denote a feeble moment in a plot in which an author fails to create an intended effect. Anticlimax, however, can also be a strong dramatic device when a writer uses it for humorous or ironic effect.

Antihero A protagonist who is lacking in one or more of the conventional qualities attributed to a hero. Instead of being dignified, brave, idealistic, or purposeful, for instance, the antihero may be buffoonish, cowardly, self-interested, or weak. The antihero is often considered an essentially modern form of characterization, a satiric or frankly realistic commentary on traditional portrayals of idealized heroes or heroines. Modern examples range from Kafka's many protagonists to Beckett's tramps in *Waiting for Godot*.

Apprenticeship novel *See* ***Bildungsroman.***

Archetype A recurring symbol, character, landscape, or event found in myth and literature across different cultures and eras. The idea of the archetype came into literary criticism from the Swiss psychologist Carl Jung who believed that all individuals share a "collective unconscious," a set of primal memories common to the human race that exists in our subconscious. An example of an archetypal character is the devil who may appear in pure mythic form (as in John Milton's *Paradise Lost*) but occurs more often in a disguised form like Fagin in Charles Dickens's *Oliver Twist* or Abner Snopes in William Faulkner's "Barn Burning."

Atmosphere The dominant mood or feeling that pervades all or part of a literary work. Atmosphere is the total effect conveyed by the author's use of language, images, and physical setting. Atmosphere is often used to foreshadow the ultimate climax in a narrative.

Authorial intrusion *See* **Editorial point of view**.

Bildungsroman German for "novel of growth and development." Sometimes called an **apprenticeship novel**, this genre depicts a youth who struggles toward maturity, forming a worldview or philosophy of life. Dickens's *David Copperfield* and Joyce's *Portrait of the Artist as a Young Man* are classic examples of the genre.

Biographical criticism The practice of analyzing a literary work by using knowledge of the author's life to gain insight.

Biography A factual account of a person's life, examining all available information or texts relevant to the subject.

Central intelligence The character through whose sensibility and mind a story is told. Henry James developed this term to describe a narrator—not the author—whose perceptions shape the way a story is presented. (*See also* **Narrator.**)

Character An imagined figure inhabiting a narrative or drama. By convention, the reader or spectator endows the fictional character with moral, dispositional, and emotional qualities expressed in what the character says—the dialogue—and by what he or she does—the action. What a character says and does in any particular situation is motivated by his or her desires, temperament, and moral nature. (*See also* **Dynamic character** and **Flat character**.)

Character development The process in which a character is introduced, advanced, and possibly transformed in a story. This development can prove to be either static (the character's personality is unchanging throughout the narrative) or dynamic (the character's personality undergoes some meaningful change during the course of the narrative). (*See also* **Dynamic character**.)

Characterization The techniques a writer uses to create, reveal, or develop the characters in a narrative. (*See also* **Character**.)

Climax The moment of greatest intensity in a story, which almost inevitably occurs toward the end of the work. The climax often takes the form of a decisive confrontation between the protagonist and antagonist. In a conventional story, the climax is followed by the **resolution** or **dénouement** in which the effects and results of the climactic action are presented. (*See also* **Falling action, Rising action**.)

Closed dénouement One of two types of conventional dénouement or resolution in a narrative. In closed dénouement, the author ties everything up at the end of the story so that little is left unresolved. (*See also* **Open dénouement**.)

Close reading A method of analysis involving careful step-by-step explication of a poem in order to understand how various elements work together. Close reading is a common practice of formalist critics in the study of a text.

Colloquial English The casual or informal but correct language of ordinary native speakers, which may include contractions, slang, and shifts in grammar, vocabulary, and diction. Conversational in tone, *colloquial* is derived from the Latin *colloquium*, "speaking together." (*See also* **Diction**, **Levels of diction**.)

Coming-of-age story *See* **Initiation story**.

Comparison In the analysis or criticism of literature, one may place two works side-by-side to point out their similarities. The product of this, a comparison, may be more meaningful when paired with its counterpart, a **contrast**.

Complication The introduction of a significant development in the central conflict in a drama or narrative between characters (or between a character and his or her situation). Traditionally, a complication begins the rising action of a story's plot. Dramatic conflict (motivation versus obstacle) during the complication is the force that drives a literary work from action to action. Complications may be *external* or *internal* or a combination of the two. A fateful blow such as an illness or an accident that affects a character is a typical example of an *external* complication—a problem the characters cannot turn away from. An *internal* complication, in contrast, might not be immediately apparent, such as the result of some important aspect of a character's values or personality.

Conclusion In plotting, the logical end or outcome of a unified plot, shortly following the climax. Also called **resolution** or **dénouement** ("the untying of the knot"), as in resolving or untying the knots created by plot complications during the rising action. The action or intrigue ends in success or failure for the protagonist, the mystery is solved, or misunderstandings are dispelled. Sometimes a conclusion is ambiguous; at the climax of the story the characters are changed, but the conclusion suggests different possibilities for what that change is or means.

Concrete diction *See* **Diction**.

Conflict In Greek, *agon,* or contest. The central struggle between two or more forces in a story. Conflict generally occurs when some person or thing prevents the protagonist from achieving his or her intended goal. Opposition can arise from another character, external events, preexisting situations, fate, or even some aspect of the main character's own personality. Conflict is the basic material out of which most plots are made. (*See also* **Antagonist**, **Character**, **Complication**, **Rising action**.)

Connotation An association or additional meaning that a word, image, or phrase may carry, apart from its literal denotation or dictionary definition. A word picks up connotations from all the uses to which it has been put in the past. For example, an owl in literature is not merely the literal bird. It also carries the many associations (connotations, that is) attached to it.

Contrast A contrast of two works of literature is developed by placing them side-by-side to point out their differences. This method of analysis works well with its opposite, a **comparison**, which focuses on likenesses.

Convention Any established feature or technique in literature that is commonly understood by both authors and readers. A convention is something generally agreed on to be appropriate for its customary uses, such as the sonnet form for a love poem or the opening "Once upon a time" for a fairy tale.

Conventional symbols Literary symbols that have a conventional or customary effect on most readers. We would respond similarly to a black cat crossing our path or a young bride in a white dress. These are conventional symbols because they carry recognizable connotations and suggestions.

Cosmic irony Also called **irony of fate**, it is the irony that exists between a character's aspiration and the treatment he or she receives at the hands of fate. Oedipus's ill-destined relationship with his parents is an example of cosmic irony.

Cultural studies A contemporary interdisciplinary field of academic study that focuses on understanding the social power encoded in "texts." Cultural studies defines "texts" more broadly than literary works; they include any analyzable phenomenon from a traditional poem to an advertising image or an actor's face. Cultural studies has no central critical methodology but uses whatever intellectual tools are appropriate to the analysis at hand.

Deconstructionist criticism A school of criticism that rejects the traditional assumption that language can accurately represent reality. Deconstructionists believe that literary texts can have no single meaning; therefore, they concentrate their attentions on *how* language is being used in a text, rather than on *what* is being said.

Denotation The literal, dictionary meaning of a word. (*See also* **Connotation**.)

Dénouement The resolution or conclusion of a literary work as plot complications are unraveled after the climax. In French, *dénouement* means "unknotting" or "untying." (*See also* **Closed dénouement, Conclusion, Open dénouement**.)

Deus ex machina Latin for "a god from a machine." The phrase refers to the Greek playwrights' frequent use of a god, mechanically lowered to the stage from the skene roof, to resolve human conflict with judgments and commands. Conventionally, the phrase now refers to any forced or improbable device in plot resolution.

Dialect A particular variety of language spoken by an identifiable regional group or social class of persons. Dialects are often used in literature in an attempt to present a character more realistically and to express significant differences in class or background.

Dialogue The direct representation of the conversation between two or more characters. (*See also* **Monologue.**)

Diction Word choice or vocabulary. Diction refers to the class of words that an author decides is appropriate to use in a particular work. Literary history is the story of diction being challenged, upheld, and reinvented. **Concrete diction** involves a highly specific word choice in the naming of something or someone. **Abstract diction** contains words that express more general ideas or concepts. More concrete diction would offer *boxer puppy* rather than *young canine*, *Lake Ontario* rather than *body of fresh water*. Concrete words refer to what we can immediately perceive with our senses. (*See also* **Levels of diction**.)

Didactic fiction A narrative that intends to teach a specific moral lesson or provide a model for proper behavior. This term is now often used pejoratively to describe a story in which the events seem manipulated in order to convey an uplifting idea, but much classic fiction has been written in the didactic mode—Aesop's *Fables*, John Bunyan's *The Pilgrim's Progress*, and Harriet Beecher Stowe's *Uncle Tom's Cabin*.

Dramatic point of view A point of view in which the narrator merely reports dialogue and action with minimal interpretation or access to the characters' minds. The dramatic point of view, as the name implies, uses prose fiction to approximate the method of plays (where readers are provided only with set descriptions, stage directions, and dialogue, and thus must supply motivations based solely on this external evidence).

Dynamic character A character who, during the course of the narrative, grows or changes in some significant way. (*See also* **Character development**.)

Editing The act of rereading a draft in order to correct mistakes, cut excess words, and make improvements.

Editorial omniscience When an omniscient narrator goes beyond reporting the thoughts of his or her characters to make a critical judgment or commentary, making explicit the narrator's own thoughts or philosophies.

Editorial point of view Also called **Authorial intrusion**. The effect that occurs when a third-person narrator adds his or her own comments (which presumably represent the ideas and opinions of the author) into the narrative.

Endnote An additional piece of information that the author includes in a note at the end of a paper. Endnotes usually contain information that the author feels is important to convey but not appropriate to fit into the main body of text. (*See also* **Footnote**.)

Epigraph A brief quotation preceding a story or other literary work. An epigraph usually suggests the subject, theme, or atmosphere the story will explore.

Epiphany A moment of insight, discovery, or revelation by which a character's life is greatly altered. An epiphany generally occurs near the end of a story. The term, which means "showing forth" in Greek, was first used in Christian theology to signify the manifestation of God's presence in the world. This theological idea was first borrowed by James Joyce to refer to a heightened moment of secular revelation.

Episode An incident in a large narrative that has unity in itself. An episode may bear close relation to the central narrative, but it can also be a digression.

Episodic plot, episodic structure A form of plotting where the individual scenes and events are presented chronologically without any profound sense of cause-and-effect relationship. In an episodic narrative the placement of many scenes could be changed without greatly altering the overall effect of the work.

Epistolary novel Novel in which the story is told by way of letters written by one or more of the characters. This form often lends an authenticity to the story, a sense that the author may have discovered these letters; but in fact they are a product of the author's invention.

Explication Literally, an "unfolding." In an explication an entire poem is explained in detail, addressing every element and unraveling any complexities as a means of analysis.

Exposition The opening portion of a narrative or drama. In the exposition, the scene is set, the protagonist is introduced, and the author discloses any other background information necessary to allow the reader to understand and relate to the events that are to follow.

Fable A brief, often humorous narrative told to illustrate a moral. The characters in fables are traditionally animals whose personality traits symbolize human traits. Particular animals have conventionally come to represent specific human qualities or values. For example, the ant represents industry, the fox craftiness, and the lion nobility. A fable often concludes by summarizing its moral message in abstract terms. For example, Aesop's fable "The North Wind and the Sun" concludes with the moral "Persuasion is better than force." (*See also* **Allegory**.)

Fairy tale A traditional form of short narrative folklore, originally transmitted orally, that features supernatural characters such as witches, giants, fairies, or animals with human personality traits. Fairy tales often feature a hero or heroine who seems destined to achieve some desirable fate—such as marrying a prince or princess, becoming wealthy, or destroying an enemy.

Falling action The events in a narrative that follow the climax and bring the story to its conclusion, or dénouement.

Fantasy A narrative that depicts events, characters, or places that could not exist in the real world. Fantasy has limited interest in portraying experience realistically. Instead, it freely pursues the possibilities of the imagination. Fantasy usually includes elements of magic or the supernatural. Sometimes it is used to illustrate a moral message as in fables. Fantasy is a type of romance that emphasizes wish fulfillment (or nightmare fulfillment) instead of verisimilitude.

Feminist criticism *See* **Gender criticism**.

Fiction From the Latin *ficio*, "act of fashioning, a shaping, a making." Fiction refers to any literary work that—although it might contain factual information—is not bound by factual accuracy, but creates a narrative shaped or made up by the author's imagination. Drama and poetry (especially narrative poetry) can be considered works of fiction, but the term now usually refers more specifically to prose stories and novels. Historical and other factual writing also requires shaping and making, but it is distinct from fiction because it is not free to invent people, places, and events; forays from documented fact must identify themselves as conjecture or hypothesis. Nonfiction, as the name suggests, is a category conventionally separate from fiction. Certainly an essay or work of literary journalism is "a made thing," and writers of nonfiction routinely employ the techniques used by fiction writers (moving forward and backward in time, reporting the inner thoughts of characters, etc.), but works of nonfiction must be not only true but factual. The truth of a work of fiction depends not on facts, but on how convincingly the writer creates the world of the story.

First-person narrator A story in which the narrator is a participant in the action. Such a narrator refers to himself or herself as "I" and may be a major or minor character in the story. His or her attitude and understanding of characters and events shapes the reader's perception of the story being told.

Flashback A scene relived in a character's memory. Flashbacks can be related by the narrator in a summary or they can be experienced by the characters themselves. Flashbacks allow the author to include events that occurred before the opening of the story, which may show the reader something significant that happened in the character's past or give an indication of what kind of person the character used to be.

Flat character A term coined by English novelist E. M. Forster to describe a character with only one outstanding trait. Flat characters are rarely the central characters in a narrative and are often based on **stock characters**. Flat characters stay the same throughout a story. (*See also* **Dynamic character**.)

Folklore The body of traditional wisdom and customs—including songs, stories, myths, and proverbs—of a people as collected and continued through oral tradition.

Folktale A short narrative drawn from folklore that has been passed down through an oral tradition. (*See also* **Fairy tale**, **Legend**.)

Footnote An additional piece of information that the author includes at the bottom of a page, usually noted by a small reference number in the main text. A footnote might supply the reader with brief facts about a related historical figure or event, the definition of a foreign word or phrase, or any other relevant information that may help in understanding the text. (*See also* **Endnote**.)

Foreshadowing In plot construction, the technique of arranging events and information in such a way that later events are prepared for, or shadowed, beforehand. The author may introduce specific words, images, or actions in order to suggest significant later events. The effective use of foreshadowing by an author may prevent a story's outcome from seeming haphazard or contrived.

Formal English The heightened, impersonal language of educated persons, usually only written, although possibly spoken on dignified occasions. (*See also* **Levels of diction**.)

Formalist criticism A school of criticism which argues that literature may only be discussed on its own terms; that is, without outside influences or information. A key method that formalists use is close reading, a step-by-step analysis of the elements in a text.

Gender criticism Gender criticism examines how sexual identity influences the creation, interpretation, and evaluation of literary works. This critical approach began with feminist criticism in the 1960s and 1970s which stated that literary study had been so dominated by men that it contained many unexamined "male-produced" assumptions. Feminist criticism sought to address this imbalance in two ways: first in insisting that sexless interpretation was impossible, and second by articulating responses to the texts that were explicitly male or female. More recently, gender criticism has focused on gay and lesbian literary identity as interpretive strategies.

General English The ordinary speech of educated native speakers. Most literate speech and writing is general English. Its diction is more educated than **colloquial English**, yet not as elevated as **formal English**. (*See also* **Levels of diction**.)

Genre A conventional combination of literary form and subject matter, usually aimed at creating certain effects. A genre implies a preexisting understanding between the artist and the reader about the purpose and rules of the work. A horror story, for example, combines the form of the short story with certain conventional subjects, style, and theme with the expectation of frightening the reader. Major short story genres include science fiction, gothic, horror, and detective tales.

Gothic fiction A genre that creates terror and suspense, usually set in an isolated castle, mansion, or monastery populated by mysterious or threatening individuals. The Gothic form, invented by Horace Walpole in *The Castle of Otranto* (1764), has flourished in one form or another ever since. The term *Gothic* is also applied to medieval architecture, and Gothic fiction almost inevitably exploits claustrophobic interior architecture in its plotting—often featuring dungeons, crypts, torture chambers, locked rooms, and secret passageways. In the nineteenth century, writers such as Nathaniel Hawthorne, Edgar Allan Poe, and Charlotte Perkins Gilman brought the genre into the mainstream of American fiction.

Hero The central character in a narrative. The term is derived from the Greek epic tradition, in which *heroes* were the leading warriors among the princes. By extension, *hero* and *heroine* have come to mean the principal male and female figures in a narrative or dramatic literary work, although many today call protagonists of either sex *heroes*. When a critic terms the protagonist a *hero*, the choice of words often implies a positive moral assessment of the character. (*See also* **Antihero**.)

Historical criticism The practice of analyzing a literary work by investigating the social, cultural, and intellectual context that produced it—a context that necessarily includes the artist's biography and milieu. Historical critics strive to recreate the exact meaning and impact a work had on its original audience.

Historical fiction A type of fiction in which the narrative is set in another time or place. In historical fiction, the author usually attempts to recreate a faithful picture of daily life during the period. For example, Robert Graves's *I, Claudius* depicts the lives of the ancient Roman ruling class in the early Imperial age. Historical fiction sometimes introduces well-known figures from the past. More often it places imaginary characters in a carefully reconstructed version of a particular historical era.

Impartial omniscience Refers to an omniscient narrator who, although he or she presents the thoughts and actions of the characters, does not judge them or comment on them. (Contrasts with **Editorial omniscience**.)

Impressionism In fiction, a style of writing that emphasizes external events less than the impression those events make on the narrator or protagonist. Impressionist short stories, like Katherine Mansfield's "Miss Brill," usually center the narrative on the chief characters' mental lives rather than the reality around them.

Initiation story Also called **Coming-of-age story**. A narrative in which the main character, usually a child or adolescent, undergoes an important experience or rite of passage—often a difficult or disillusioning one—that prepares him or her for adulthood. James Joyce's "Araby" is a classic example of an initiation story.

In medias res A Latin phrase meaning "in the midst of things" that refers to a narrative device of beginning a story midway in the events it depicts (usually at an exciting or significant moment) before explaining the context or preceding actions. Epic poems such as Virgil's *Aeneid* or John Milton's *Paradise Lost* commonly begin *in medias res*, but the technique is also found in modern fiction.

Innocent narrator Also called **naive narrator**. A character who fails to understand all the implications of the story he or she tells. Of course, virtually any narrator has some degree of innocence or naiveté, but the innocent narrator—often a child or childlike adult—is used by an author trying to generate irony, sympathy, or pity by creating a gap between what the narrator knows and what the reader knows. Mark Twain's Huckleberry Finn—despite his mischievous nature—is an example of an innocent narrator.

Interior monologue An extended presentation of a character's thoughts in a narrative. Usually written in the present tense and printed without quotation marks, an interior monologue reads as if the character were speaking aloud to himself or herself, for the reader to overhear. A famous example of interior monologue comes at the end of *Ulysses* when Joyce gives us the rambling memories and reflections of Molly Bloom.

Ironic point of view The perspective of a character or narrator whose voice or position is rich in ironic contradictions. (*See also* **Irony**.)

Irony A literary device in which a discrepancy of meaning is masked beneath the surface of the language. Irony is present when a writer says one thing but means something quite the opposite. There are many kinds of irony, but the two major varieties are **verbal irony** (in which the discrepancy is contained in words) and **situational irony** (in which the discrepancy exists when something is about to happen to a character or characters who expect the opposite outcome). (*See also* **Cosmic irony, Irony of fate, Sarcasm, Verbal irony**.)

Irony of fate A type of situational irony that can be used for either tragic or comic purposes. Irony of fate is the discrepancy between actions and their results, between what characters deserve and what they get, between appearance and reality. In

Sophocles' tragedy, for instance, Oedipus unwittingly fulfills the prophecy even as he takes the actions a morally good man would take to avoid it. (*See also* **Cosmic irony**.)

Legend A traditional narrative handed down through popular oral tradition to illustrate and celebrate a remarkable character, an important event, or to explain the unexplainable. Legends, unlike other folktales, claim to be true and usually take place in real locations, often with genuine historical figures.

Levels of diction In English, there are conventionally four basic levels of formality in word choice, or four levels of diction. From the least formal to the most elevated they are **vulgate, colloquial English, general English**, and **formal English**. (*See also* **Diction**.)

Limited omniscience Also called third-person limited point of view. A type of point of view in which the narrator sees into the minds of some but not all of the characters. Most typically, limited omniscience sees through the eyes of one major or minor character. In limited omniscience, the author can compromise between the immediacy of first-person narration and the mobility of third person.

Literary genre *See* **Genre**.

Literary theory Literary criticism that tries to formulate general principles rather than discuss specific texts. Theory operates at a high level of abstraction and often focuses on understanding basic issues of language, communication, art, interpretation, culture, and ideological content.

Local color The use of specific regional material—unique customs, dress, habits, and speech patterns of ordinary people—to create atmosphere or realism in a literary work.

Locale The location where a story takes place.

Magic realism Also called **magical realism**. A type of contemporary narrative in which the magical and the mundane are mixed in an overall context of realistic storytelling. The term was coined by Cuban novelist Alejo Carpentier in 1949 to describe the matter-of-fact combination of the fantastic and everyday in Latin American fiction. Magic realism has become the standard name for an international trend in contemporary fiction such as Gabriel García Márquez's *One Hundred Years of Solitude*.

Metafiction Fiction that consciously explores its own nature as a literary creation. The Greek word *meta* means "upon"; metafiction consequently is a mode of narrative that does not try to create the illusion of verisimilitude but delights in its own fictional nature, often by speculating on the story it is telling. The term is usually associated with late-twentieth-century writers like John Barth, Italo Calvino, and Jorge Luis Borges.

Microcosm The small world as created by a poem, play, or story that reflects the tensions of the larger world beyond. In some sense, most successful literary works offer a microcosm that illuminates the greater world around it.

Minimalist fiction Contemporary fiction written in a deliberately flat, unemotional tone and an appropriately unadorned style. Minimalist fiction often relies more on dramatic action, scene, and dialogue than complex narration or authorial summary. Examples of minimalist fiction can be found in the short stories of Raymond Carver and Bobbie Ann Mason.

Monologue An extended speech by a single character. The term originated in drama, where it describes a solo speech that has listeners (as opposed to a **soliloquy**, where the character speaks only to himself or herself). A short story or even a novel can be written in monologue form if it is an unbroken speech by one character to another silent character or characters.

Moral A paraphrasable message or lesson implied or directly stated in a literary work. Commonly, a moral is stated at the end of a fable.

Motif An element that recurs significantly throughout a narrative. A motif can be an image, idea, theme, situation, or action (and was first commonly used as a musical term for a recurring melody or melodic fragment). A motif can also refer to an element that recurs across many literary works like a beautiful lady in medieval romances who turns out to be an evil fairy or three questions that are asked a protagonist to test his or her wisdom.

Motivation What a character in a story or drama wants. The reasons an author provides for a character's actions. Motivation can be either *explicit* (in which reasons are specifically stated in a story) or *implicit* (in which the reasons are only hinted at or partially revealed).

Myth A traditional narrative of anonymous authorship that arises out of a culture's oral tradition. The characters in traditional myths are usually gods or heroic figures. Myths characteristically explain the origins of things—gods, people, places, plants, animals, and natural events—usually from a cosmic view. A culture's values and belief systems are traditionally passed from generation to generation in myth. In literature, myth may also refer to boldly imagined narratives that embody primal truths about life. Myth is usually differentiated from legend, which has a specific historical base.

Mythological criticism The practice of analyzing a literary work by looking for recurrent universal patterns. Mythological criticism explores the artist's common humanity by tracing how the individual imagination uses myths and symbols that are shared by different cultures and epochs.

Naive narrator *See* **Innocent narrator**.

Narrator A voice or character that provides the reader with information and insight about the characters and incidents in a narrative. A narrator's perspective and personality can greatly affect how a story is told. (*See also* **Omniscient narrator, Point of view**.)

Naturalism A type of fiction or drama in which the characters are presented as products or victims of environment and heredity. Naturalism, considered an extreme form of realism, customarily depicts the social, psychological, and economic milieu of the primary characters. Naturalism was first formally developed by French novelist Émile Zola in the 1870s. In promoting naturalism as a theory of animal behavior, Zola urged the modeling of naturalist literature and drama on the scientific case study. The writer, like the scientist, was to record objective reality with detachment; events onstage should be reproduced with sufficient exactness to demonstrate the strict laws of material causality. Important American Naturalists include Jack London, Theodore Dreiser, and Stephen Crane. (*See also* **Realism**.)

Nonfiction novel A genre in which actual events are presented as a novel-length story, using the techniques of fiction (flashback, interior monologues, etc.). Truman Capote's *In Cold Blood* (1966), which depicts a multiple murder and subsequent trial in Kansas, is a classic example of this modern genre.

Nonparticipant narrator A narrator who does not appear in the story as a character but is capable of revealing the thoughts and motives of one or more characters. A nonparticipant narrator is also capable of moving from place to place in order to describe action and report dialogue. (*See also* **Omniscient narrator**.)

Nouvelle The French term for the short prose tale (called **novella** by Italian Renaissance writers) that usually depicted in relatively realistic terms illicit love, ingenious trickery, and sensational adventure, often with an underlying moral. Marguerite de Navarre's *Heptameron* is a classic collection of *nouvelle*.

Novel An extended work of fictional prose narrative. The term *novel* usually implies a book-length narrative (as compared to more compact forms of prose fiction such as the short story). Because of its extended length, a novel usually has more characters, more varied scenes, and a broader coverage of time than a short story.

Novella In modern terms, a prose narrative longer than a short story but shorter than a novel (approximately 30,000 to 50,000 words). Unlike a short story, a novella is long enough to be published independently as a brief book. Classic modern novellas include Franz Kafka's *The Metamorphosis*, Joseph Conrad's *Heart of Darkness*, and Thomas Mann's *Death in Venice*. During the Renaissance, however, the term *novella* originally referred to short prose narratives such as those found in Giovanni Boccaccio's *Decameron*.

Objective point of view *See* **Dramatic point of view**.

Observer A type of first-person narrator who is relatively detached from or plays only a minor role in the events described.

O. Henry ending *See* **Trick ending**.

Omniscient narrator Also called **all-knowing narrator**. A narrator who has the ability to move freely through the consciousness of any character. The omniscient narrator also has complete knowledge of all of the external events in a story. (*See also* **Nonparticipant narrator**.)

Open dénouement One of the two conventional types of dénouement or resolution. In open dénouement, the author ends a narrative with a few loose ends, or unresolved matters, on which the reader is left to speculate. (*See also* **Closed dénouement**.)

Oral tradition The tradition within a culture that transmits narratives by word of mouth from one generation to another. Fables, folktales, ballads, and songs are examples of some types of narratives found originally in an oral tradition.

Parable A brief, usually allegorical narrative that teaches a moral. The parables found in Christian literature, such as "The Parable of the Prodigal Son" (Luke 15:11–32), are classic examples of the form. In parables, unlike fables (where the moral is explicitly stated within the narrative), the moral themes are implicit and can often be interpreted in several ways. Modern parables can be found in the works of Franz Kafka and Jorge Luis Borges.

Paradox A statement that at first strikes one as self-contradictory, but that on reflection reveals some deeper sense. Paradox is often achieved by a play on words.

Parallelism An arrangement of words, phrases, clauses, or sentences side-by-side in a similar grammatical or structural way. Parallelism organizes ideas in a way that demonstrates their coordination to the reader.

Paraphrase The restatement in one's own words of what we understand a literary work to say. A paraphrase is similar to a summary, although not as brief or simple.

Parody A mocking imitation of a literary work or individual author's style, usually for comic effect. A parody typically exaggerates distinctive features of the original for humorous purposes.

Participant narrator A narrator that participates as a character within a story. (*See also* **First-person narrator**.)

Persona Latin for "mask." A fictitious character created by an author to be the speaker of a poem, story, or novel. A persona is always the narrator of the work and not merely a character in it.

Picaresque A type of narrative, usually a novel, that presents the life of a likable scoundrel who is at odds with respectable society. The narrator of a picaresque was originally a *picaro* (Spanish for "rascal" or "rogue") who recounts his adventures tricking the rich and gullible. This type of narrative rarely has a tight plot, and the episodes or adventures follow in a loose chronological order.

Plot The particular arrangement of actions, events, and situations that unfold in a narrative. A plot is not merely the general story of a narrative but the author's artistic pattern made from the parts of the narrative, including the exposition, complications, climax, and dénouement. How an author chooses to construct the plot determines the way the reader experiences the story. Manipulating a plot, therefore, can be the author's most important expressive device when writing a story. More than just a story made up of episodes or a bare synopsis of the temporal order of events, the plotting is the particular embodiment of an action that allows the audience to see the causal relationship between the parts of the action. (*See also* **Climax, Falling action, Rising action**.)

Point of view The perspective from which a story is told. There are many types of point of view, including first-person narrator (a story in which the narrator is a participant in the action) and third-person narrator (a type of narration in which the narrator is a nonparticipant).

Print culture A culture that depends primarily on the printed word—in books, magazines, and newspapers—to distribute and preserve information. In recent decades the electronic media have taken over much of this role from print.

Protagonist The central character in a literary work. The protagonist usually initiates the main action of the story, often in conflict with the antagonist. (*See also* **Antagonist**.)

Psychological criticism The practice of analyzing a literary work through investigating three major areas: the nature of literary genius, the psychological study of a particular artist, and the analysis of fictional characters. This methodology uses the analytical tools of psychology and psychoanalysis to understand the underlying motivations and meanings of a literary work.

Pulp fiction A type of formulaic and quickly written fiction originally produced for cheap mass circulation magazines. The term *pulp* refers to the inexpensive woodpulp paper developed in the mid-nineteenth century on which these magazines were printed. Most pulp fiction journals printed only melodramatic genre work—westerns, science fiction, romance, horror, adventure tales, or crime stories.

Reader-response criticism The practice of analyzing a literary work by describing what happens in the reader's mind while interpreting the text. Reader-response critics believe that no literary text exists independently of readers' interpretations and that there is no single fixed interpretation of any literary work.

Realism An attempt to reproduce faithfully the surface appearance of life, especially that of ordinary people in everyday situations. As a literary term, *realism* has two meanings—one general, the other historical. In a general sense, realism refers to the representation of characters, events, and settings in ways that the spectator will consider plausible, based on consistency and likeness to type. This sort of realism does not necessarily depend on elaborate factual description or documentation but more on the author's ability to draft plots and characters within a conventional framework of social, economic, and psychological reality. In a historical sense, Realism (usually capitalized) refers to a movement in nineteenth-century European literature and theater that rejected the idealism, elitism, and romanticism of earlier verse dramas and prose fiction in an attempt to represent life truthfully. Realist literature customarily focused on the middle class (and occasionally the working class) rather than the aristocracy, and it used social and economic detail to create an accurate account of human behavior. Realism began in France with Honoré de Balzac, Gustave Flaubert, and Guy de Maupassant and then moved internationally. Other major Realists include Leo Tolstoy, Henry James, Anton Chekhov, and Edith Wharton.

Regionalism The literary representation of a specific locale that consciously uses the particulars of geography, custom, history, folklore, or speech. In regional narratives, the locale plays a crucial role in the presentation and progression of a story that could not be moved to another setting without artistic loss. Usually, regional narratives take place at some distance from the literary capital of a culture, often in small towns or rural areas. Examples of American regionalism can be found in the writing of Willa Cather, Kate Chopin, William Faulkner, and Eudora Welty.

Resolution The final part of a narrative, the concluding action or actions that follow the climax. (*See also* **Conclusion, Dénouement.**)

Retrospect *See* **Flashback**.

Rising action That part of the play or narrative, including the exposition, in which events start moving toward a climax. In the rising action the protagonist usually faces the complications of the plot to reach his or her goal.

Romance In general terms, romance is a narrative mode that employs exotic adventure and idealized emotion rather than realistic depiction of character and action. In the romantic mode—out of which most popular genre fictions develop—people, actions, and events are depicted more as we wish them to be (heroes are very brave, villains are very bad) rather than the complex ways they usually are. Medieval romances (in both prose and verse) presented chivalric tales of kings, knights, and aristocratic ladies. Modern romances, emerging in the nineteenth century, were represented by adventure novels like Sir Walter Scott's *Ivanhoe* or Nathaniel Hawthorne's *The House of the Seven Gables*, which embodied the symbolic quests and idealized characters of earlier, chivalric tales in slightly more realistic terms, a tradition carried on in contemporary popular works like the *Star Wars* and James Bond films.

Round character A term coined by English novelist E. M. Forster to describe a complex character who is presented in depth and detail in a narrative. Round characters are those who change significantly during the course of a narrative. Most often, round characters are the central characters in a narrative. (*See also* **Flat character**.)

Sarcasm A conspicuously bitter form of irony in which the ironic statement is designed to hurt or mock its target. (*See also* **Irony**.)

Satiric comedy A genre using derisive humor to ridicule human weakness and folly or attack political injustices and incompetence. Satiric comedy often focuses on ridiculing characters or killjoys, who resist the festive mood of comedy. Such characters, called humors, are often characterized by one dominant personality trait or ruling obsession.

Scene In drama, the scene is a division of the action in an act of the play. There is no universal convention as to what constitutes a scene, and the practice differs by playwright and period. Usually, a scene represents a single dramatic action that builds to a climax (often ending in the entrance or exit of a major character). In this last sense of a vivid and unified action, the term can be applied to fiction.

Selective omniscience The point of view that sees the events of a narrative through the eyes of a single character. The selectively omniscient narrator is usually a nonparticipant narrator.

Sentimentality A usually pejorative description of the quality of a literary work that tries to convey great emotion but fails to give the reader sufficient grounds for sharing it.

Setting The time and place of a literary work. The setting may also include the climate and even the social, psychological, or spiritual state of the participants.

Short Story A prose narrative too brief to be published in a separate volume—as novellas and novels frequently are. The short story is usually a focused narrative that presents one or two main characters involved in a single compelling action.

Situational Irony *See* **Irony.**

Sketch A short, static, descriptive composition. Literary sketches can be either fiction or nonfiction. A sketch usually focuses on describing a person or place without providing a narrative.

Sociological criticism The practice of analyzing a literary work by examining the cultural, economic, and political context in which it was written or received. Sociological criticism primarily explores the relationship between the artist and society.

Static character *See* **Flat character.**

Stock character A common or stereotypical character that occurs frequently in literature. Examples of stock characters are the mad scientist, the battle-scarred veteran, or the strong-but-silent cowboy. (*See also* **Archetype.**)

Stream of consciousness Not a specific technique, but a type of modern narration that uses various literary devices, especially interior monologue, in an attempt to duplicate the subjective and associative nature of human consciousness. Stream of consciousness often focuses on imagistic perception in order to capture the preverbal level of consciousness.

Style All the distinctive ways in which an author, genre, movement, or historical period uses language to create a literary work. An author's style depends on his or her characteristic use of diction, imagery, tone, syntax, and figurative language. Even sentence structure and punctuation can play a role in an author's style.

Subject The main topic of a poem, story, or play.

Summary A brief condensation of the main idea or story of a literary work. A summary is similar to a paraphrase, but less detailed.

Suspense Enjoyable anxiety created in the reader by the author's handling of plot. When the outcome of events is unclear, the author's suspension of resolution intensifies the reader's interest—particularly if the plot involves characters to whom the reader or audience is sympathetic. Suspense is also created when the fate of a character is clear to the audience, but not to the character. The suspense results from the audience's anticipation of how and when the character will meet his or her inevitable fate.

Symbol A person, place, or thing in a narrative that suggests meanings beyond its literal sense. Symbol is related to allegory, but it works more complexly. In an allegory an object has a single additional significance. By contrast, a symbol usually contains multiple meanings and associations. In Herman Melville's *Moby-Dick*, for example, the great white whale does not have just a single significance but accrues powerful associations as the narrative progresses.

Symbolic act An action whose significance goes well beyond its literal meaning. In literature, symbolic acts usually involve some conscious or unconscious ritual element like rebirth, purification, forgiveness, vengeance, or initiation.

Synopsis A brief summary or outline of a story or dramatic work.

Tale A short narrative without a complex plot, the word originating from the Old English *talu*, or "speech." Tales are an ancient form of narrative found in folklore, and traditional tales often contain supernatural elements. A tale differs from a short story by its tendency toward less developed characters and linear plotting. British writer A. E. Coppard characterized the underlying difference by claiming that a story is something that is written and a tale is something that is told. The ambition of a tale is usually similar to that of a yarn: revelation of the marvelous rather than illumination of the everyday world.

Tall tale A humorous short narrative that provides a wildly exaggerated version of events. Originally an oral form, the tall tale assumes that its audience knows the narrator is distorting the events. The form is often associated with the American frontier.

Theme A generally recurring subject or idea conspicuously evident in a literary work. A short didactic work like a fable may have a single obvious theme, but longer works can contain multiple themes. Not all subjects in a work can be considered themes, only the central subject or subjects.

Thesis sentence A summing-up of the one main idea or argument that an essay or critical paper will embody.

Third-person narrator A type of narration in which the narrator is a nonparticipant. In a third-person narrative the characters are referred to as "he," "she," or "they." Third-person narrators are most commonly omniscient, but the level of their knowledge may vary from total omniscience (the narrator knows everything about the characters and their lives) to limited omniscience (the narrator is limited to the perceptions of a single character).

Tone The attitude toward a subject conveyed in a literary work. No single stylistic device creates tone; it is the net result of the various elements an author brings to creating the work's feeling and manner. Tone may be playful, sarcastic, ironic, sad, solemn, or any other possible attitude. A writer's tone plays an important role in establishing the reader's relationship to the characters or ideas presented in a literary work.

Total omniscience A type of point of view in which the narrator knows everything about all of the characters and events in a story. A narrator with total omniscience can also move freely from one character to another. Generally, a totally omniscient narrative is written in the third person.

Trick ending A surprising climax that depends on a quick reversal of the situation from an unexpected source. The success of a trick ending is relative to the degree in which the reader is surprised but not left incredulous when it occurs. The American writer O. Henry popularized this type of ending.

Understatement An ironic figure of speech that deliberately describes something in a way that is less than the true case.

Unreliable narrator A narrator who—intentionally or unintentionally—relates events in a subjective or distorted manner. The author usually provides some indication early on in such stories that the narrator is not to be completely trusted.

Verbal irony A statement in which the speaker or writer says the opposite of what is really meant. For example, a friend might comment, "How graceful you are!" after you trip clumsily on a stair.

Verisimilitude The quality in a literary work of appearing true to life. In fiction, verisimilitude is usually achieved by careful use of realistic detail in description, characterization, and dialogue. (*See also* **Realism**.)

Vulgate From the Latin word *vulgus*, "mob" or "common people." The lowest level of formality in language, vulgate is the diction of the common people with no pretensions at refinement or elevation. The vulgate is not necessarily vulgar in the sense of containing foul or inappropriate language; it refers simply to unschooled, everyday language.

CREDITS

Literary Credits: Fiction

Chinua Achebe: "Dead Men's Path," copyright © 1972, 1973 by Chinua Achebe, from *Girls at War and Other Stories* by Chinua Achebe. Used by permission of Doubleday, a division of Random House, Inc.

Sherman Alexie: "This Is What It Means to Say Phoenix, Arizona" from *The Lone Ranger and Tonto Fistfight in Heaven* by Sherman Alexie. Copyright © 1993, 2005 by Sherman Alexie. Used by permission of Grove/Atlantic, Inc.

Elizabeth Ammons: "Biographical Echoes in 'The Yellow Wallpaper'" excerpted from *Conflicting Stories: American Women Writers at the Turn of The Century*, copyright © 1991. Reprinted by permission of Oxford University Press.

Inés Arredondo: "The Shunammite" by Inés Arredondo as translated by Alberto Manguel. © Alberto Manguel. Reprinted by permission of Guillermo Schavelzon & Asociados, Agencia Literaria.

Margaret Atwood: "Happy Endings" from *Good Bones and Simple Murders* by Margaret Atwood, copyright © 1983, 1992, 1994, by O.W. Toad Ltd. A Nan A. Talese Book. Used by permission of Doubleday, a division of Random House, Inc.

Houston A. Baker and Charlotte Pierce-Baker: Excerpt from "Patches: Quilts and Community in Alice Walker's 'Everyday Use'" by Houston A. Baker and Charlotte Pierce-Baker from *The Southern Review 21* (Summer 1985). Reprinted by permission of the authors.

James Baldwin: "Sonny's Blues" © 1957 by James Baldwin was originally published in *Partisan Review*. Copyright renewed. Collected in *Going to Meet the Man*, published by Vintage Books. Reprinted by arrangement with the James Baldwin Estate.

James Baldwin: From *Notes of a Native Son* by James Baldwin. Copyright © 1955, renewed 1983, by James Baldwin. Reprinted by permission of Beacon Press, Boston.

Jorge Luis Borges: "The Gospel According to Mark" from *Collected Fictions* by Jorge Luis Borges, translated by Andrew Hurley, copyright © 1998 by Maria Kodama; translation copyright © 1998 by Penguin Putnam Inc. Used by permission of Viking Penguin, a division of Penguin Group (USA) Inc.

T. Coraghessan Boyle: "Greasy Lake" from *Greasy Lake and Other Stories* by T. Coraghessan Boyle, © 1979, 1981, 1982, 1983, 1984, 1985 by T. Coraghessan Boyle. Used by permission of Viking Penguin, a division of Penguin Group (USA) Inc.

Nancy Bunge: From *Studies in Short Fiction Series-Nathaniel Hawthorne* © 1993 Gale, a part of Cengage Learning, Inc. Reproduced by permission. www.cengage.com/permissions.

Raymond Carver: "Cathedral" from *Cathedral* by Raymond Carver, copyright © 1981, 1982, 1983 by Raymond Carver. Used by permission of Alfred A. Knopf, a division of Random House, Inc.

Raymond Carver: Excerpts from "On Writing" from *Fires: Essays, Poems, Stories* by Raymond Carver. Copyright © 1983, 1984 by the Estate of Raymond Carver, reprinted with permission of The Wylie Agency LLC.

John Cheever: "The Swimmer" from *The Stories of John Cheever* by John Cheever, copyright © 1978 by John Cheever. Used by permission of Alfred A. Knopf, a division of Random House, Inc.

Anton Chekhov: "The Lady with the Pet Dog" translated by Avrahm Yarmolinsky, from *The Portable Chekhov* by Anton Chekhov, edited by Avrahm Yarmolinsky, copyright 1947, © 1968 by Viking Penguin, Inc., renewed © 1975 by Avrahm Yarmolinsky. Used by permission of Viking Penguin, a division of Penguin Group (USA) Inc.

Barbara Christian: Excerpt from the Introduction to *Everyday Use* by Alice Walker, edited by Barbara T. Christian, from *The Women Writers: Text and Context Series*. Copyright © 1994 by Rutgers, the State University. Reprinted by permission of Rutgers University Press.

Sandra Cisneros: "The House on Mango Street" from *The House on Mango Street*. Copyright © 1984 by Sandra Cisneros. Published by Vintage Books, a division of Random House, Inc., and in hardcover by Alfred A. Knopf in 1994. By permission of Susan Bergholz Literary Services, New York, NY and Lamy, NM. All rights reserved.

Louise S. Cowan: From "Passing by the Dragon" by Louise S. Cowan in "Revelation" by Flannery O'Connor, *The Trinity Forum Reading 40* (Summer 2005) (McLean, VA: The Trinity Forum, Inc., 2005). Used by permission.

Ralph Ellison: "Battle Royal," copyright 1948 by Ralph Ellison, from *Invisible Man* by Ralph Ellison. Used by permission of Random House, Inc.

William Faulkner: "A Rose for Emily," copyright 1930 and renewed 1958 by William Faulkner, "Barn Burning," copyright 1950 by Random House, Inc. Copyright renewed 1977 by Jill Faulkner Summers, from *Collected Stories of William Faulkner* by William Faulkner. Used by permission of Monacelli Press, a division of Random House, Inc.

Kathleen Feeley: Excerpt from *Flannery O'Connor: Voice of The Peacock*, 1972, by permission of Fordham University Press.

Literary Credits: Writing

Michael Colacurcio: Excerpts from "Visible Sanctity and Spectar Evidence: The Tryal of G.B.," in *The Province of Piety*, pp. 302–303. Copyright 1995, Duke University Press. All rights reserved. Used by permission of the publisher.

Stanley Fish: Reprinted by permission of the publisher from *Is There a Text in This Class?: The Authority of Interpretive Communities* by Stanley Fish, pp. 345–347, Cambridge, Mass.: Harvard University Press, Copyright © 1980 by the President and Fellows of Harvard College.

Barbara Johnson: "Rigorous Unreliability" from *A World of Difference*. pp. 17–19. © 1987. Reprinted with permission of The Johns Hopkins University Press.

Carl Jung: "The Collective Unconscious and Archetypes" translated by R. F. C. Hull from *The Collected Works of C. G. Jung*, 1931.

John King: "Excerpts from "The Early Writing" and "Towards a Theory of Fantastic Literature." From "Jorge Luis Borges: A View of the Periphery." From *On Modern Latin American Fiction*. Edited by John King. © 1987 by John King. Reprinted by permission of the author.

Vincent Leitch: Excerpt from *Cultural Criticism, Literary Theory, Poststructuralism* by Vincent B. Leitch. Copyright © 1992 Columbia University Press. Reprinted with permission of the publisher.

Georg Lukacs: "Content Determines Form" from *Realism in Our Time*, translated by John and Necke Mander, 1962.

Gretchen Schulz and R. J. R. Rockwood: "In Fairyland Without a Map: Connie's Exploration Inward in Joyce Carol Oates' 'Where Are You Going, Where Have You Been?'" by Gretchen and R. J. R. Rockwood. Copyright © 1980 by Gretchen E. Schulz and R. J. R. Rockwood. Reprinted by permission.

Kathryn L. Seidel: Excerpts from pp. 169–173 from "The Artist in the Kitchen: The Economics of Creativity in Huston's 'Sweat'" from *Sweat*, ed by Cheryl Wall. Reprinted with permission of the University Press of Florida.

Elaine Showalter: "Towards a Feminist Poetics" from *New Feminist Criticism: Essays on Women, Literature, and Theory*. Reprinted by permission of the author.

Virginia Llewellyn Smith: "Chekhov's Attitude to Romantic Love" from *Anton Chekhov and the Lady with the Dog* by Virginia Llewellyn Smith. Reprinted by permission of Oxford University Press.

Nina Pelikan Straus: "Transformations in *The Metamorphosis*" from *Signs: Journal of Women in Culture and Society*, 14.3 (1989) pp. 651–67. Reprinted by permission of the author.

Emily Toth: "The Source for Alcée LaBallière in 'The Storm'" adapted from *Kate Chopin: A Life of the Author of The Awakening* by Emily Toth. Reprinted by permission of the author.

Edmond Volpe: "'Barn Burning': a Definition of Evil" from *Faulkner, the Unappeased Imagination: A Collection of Critical Essays*, edited by Glen O. Carey. Reprinted with permission.

Daniel P. Watkins: Excerpt from "Labor and Religion in D. H. Lawrence's 'The Rocking-Horse Winner'" from *Studies in Short Fiction*, Volume 24, No. 3, Summer, 1987. Reprinted by permission of the author.

Photo Credits

INDEX OF MAJOR THEMES

If you prefer to study by theme or want to research possible subjects for an essay, here is a listing of stories arranged into fourteen major themes.

Individual Versus Society

Loneliness and Alienation

Love and Desire

Men and Women/Marriage

Nature

Race, Class, and Culture

War, Murder, and Violence

Woman's Identity

INDEX OF AUTHORS AND TITLES

Each page number immediately following a writer's name indicates a quotation from or reference to that writer. A number in **bold** refers you to the page on which you will find the author's biography.

INDEX OF LITERARY TERMS

Page numbers indicate discussion of terms in anthology. A page number in **bold** indicates entry in the **Glossary of Literary Terms.**